Come and Explore
Your National Parks

Your Guide to the
National Parks

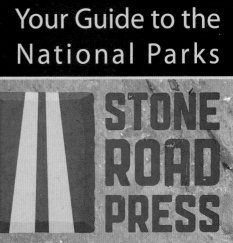
STONE
ROAD
PRESS

Your Guide to the National Parks, First Edition

ISBN 978-1-62128-000-2
Library of Congress Control Number (LCCN): 2012934277

Printed in the United States of America
Published by: Stone Road Press
Author/Cartographer/Photographer/Designer: Michael Joseph Oswald
Editor: Derek Pankratz

Corrections/Contact

This guide book has been researched and written with the greatest attention to detail in order to provide you with the most accurate and pertinent information. Unfortunately, travel information—especially pricing—is subject to change and inadvertent errors and omissions do occur. Should you encounter a change, error, or omission while using this guide book, we'd like to hear about it. (If you found a wonderful place, trail, or activity not mentioned, we'd love to hear about that too.) Please contact us by sending an e-mail to corrections@stoneroadpress.com. Your contributions will help make future editions better than the last.

You can contact us online at www.StoneRoadPress.com or follow us on

Facebook: www.facebook.com/thestoneroadpress
Twitter: www.twitter.com/stoneroadpress (@stoneroadpress)
Flickr: www.flickr.com/photos/stoneroadpress

Disclaimer

Your safety is important to us. If any activity is beyond your ability or threatened by forces outside your control, do not attempt it. The maps in this book, although accurate and to scale, are not intended for hiking. Serious hikers should purchase a detailed, waterproof, topographical map. It is also suggested that you write or call in advance to confirm information when it matters most.

The primary purpose of this guide book is to enhance our readers' national park experiences, but the author, editor, and publisher cannot be held responsible for any experiences while traveling.

Cover and Full Page Photo Credits

Front cover: Zion Narrows, Zion National Park (Adam Belles)
Intro Pages: Half Dome, Yosemite National Park (Shutterstock); Lake Francis Falls, Glacier National Park (NPS)
Previous Page and Back Cover Background: Brooks Falls, Katmai National Park (Dmitry Azovtsev, www.daphoto.info)
Opposite "About the Author:" Toroweap, Grand Canyon National Park (Shutterstock)
Opposite "Contents:" Desolation Peak, North Cascades National Park (Basil Tsimoyianis/NPS)
Page 27: Fort Jefferson Archways, Dry Tortugas National Park (John Engler/NPS)
After the Index: Redwood National Park (Shutterstock); El Capitán, Yosemite National Park (Michael Joseph Oswald)
Back cover inset (top to bottom): Mule train, Grand Canyon National Park (Michael Joseph Oswald); Yellowstone Map (NPS); Yosemite Valley, Yosemite National Park (Bala Sivakumar, www.wanderingmonkphoto.com)

Big Meadows - Shenandoah National Park

Acknowledgements

I am incredibly thankful for the assistance of my immensely talented editor, Derek Pankratz, whose general thoughtfulness, incomparable comprehension, and willingness to question everything from commas to content has greatly improved the final shape of this guide book.

Many thanks to the creative guru, Luke Holschbach (www.jukes.us), whose sharp wit and playful humor made working together a complete joy; he also created an engaging and imaginative website for Stone Road Press.

Special thanks to all of the photo contributors. Your work helped capture the true beauty and grandeur of the national parks that I once thought could only be recognized in person.

Morning basketball guys. Manitowoc Public Library Book Club ladies. Thank you. You provided an escape from countless hours spent writing, designing, and staring at a wall lost in thought. Guys, I'll continue to see you on the court Monday, Wednesday, and Friday mornings. Ladies, I'll be at the library proudly representing the male population every third Thursday of the month.

Matt, Karen, Kate, and the kids, thank you so much for paging through my work, hunting down errors and providing valuable input. Ben, Curt, Mikell, Duke, and Josh, we've been through a lot together and this project was no different. Thank you for your time, criticism, input, compliments, and most importantly your friendship. It's not just these few that deserve a bit of gratitude. I am indebted to all friends, family, and those of you I met while wandering my way across the country and through the parks.

Which brings me to the men and women of the National Park Service. You are as precious as the parks you protect, deserving of the most heartfelt thanks for the dedication and passion you exude as stewards of these treasured landscapes.

Most of all, I would like to thank my parents, who raised their children selflessly with unconditional love, compassion, and kindness. You taught us to live and allowed us to dream. Thank you for allowing this particular dream to come true at your wonderful writer's retreat out on the farm. Most feelings are left unsaid in our family, but it's not too late for them to be written. I have an immense amount of love and gratitude for the two of you and *everything* you have given to me. And now it's time that I start giving back—selflessly, just like you.

Most reference material regarding the national parks was obtained directly from the parks while visiting or from the National Park Service and its website (www.nps.gov), but one work proved to be an invaluable resource. Dayton Duncan's *The National Parks: America's Best Idea* (2009) is a must-read for all park enthusiasts. It provided a wealth of historical context, allowing me to better understand and appreciate the park system as a whole.

About the Author

You might be wondering "why in the world should I listen to this guy standing on a rock at the Grand Canyon?" Allow me to tell you…during my exploration of the parks I quickly realized most visitors only explore areas accessible by car. Families zip through, stop at the occasional pull-out or parking lot for a quick photo-op, then continue along their merry way. While most parks cater to motorists, one cannot experience their essence from the comfort of your driver's seat. You must walk among the trees and the mountains. Listen to wildlife all around you. Sit back, close your eyes and immerse yourself in nature. America's 58 national parks are irreplaceable treasures, yet they are *our* parks, preserved for our enjoyment, and if you want to experience them to their fullest you're going to need a good guide.

That's where I come in. I admit my first trip to a national park was your typical affair. A group of friends drove to the South Rim of the Grand Canyon. We peered in, snapped a few photos, shrugged and returned to our rental car. Did we know that adventurous hikers were resting their tired legs at Phantom Ranch nearly 5,000 feet below at the canyon's floor? No. Did we know how to reach the North Rim? Probably not. The point is, we didn't know much about the Grand Canyon. In all we spent no more than three hours in the park. We were your typical park visitors, and each year millions follow in our footsteps.

I've come a long way since those first steps atop the South Rim. While researching this book I spent two full years exploring and photographing the parks, living almost exclusively in my tent. As I passed from park-to-park I learned that this was much more than an assignment; it became an awakening. It was a communion with life and land as I learned to immerse myself in nature. (I also learned how to get to the North Rim, and even hiked down to Phantom Ranch to prove to myself that people were making regular trips to the canyon floor.) Did I hike all the trails and participate in all of the activities listed in this book? No. But I did log thousands of miles hiking, paddling, and pedalling my way across America and through its parks. More importantly, I've exhaustively researched every site in this book, integrating those findings with my unique perspective and with the opinions of hundreds of park patrons and National Park Service employees.

These are the footsteps you should follow, and holding this book is the first step to an unforgettable adventure.

MJ Oswald

ABOUT THE AUTHOR

Sunrise from Hillman Peak - Crater Lake National Park

Contents

CONTENTS

Zabriskie Point Sunrise - Death Valley National Park

Plan Your Trip

Park Passes

Most United States National Parks require guests to pay an entrance fee. Entrance fees vary from park to park, and rates may be per individual, per vehicle, and a few rates are even charged per day. If you plan on visiting several national parks in a calendar year or visiting the same (fee required) national park several times the America the Beautiful Passes can minimize the damage to your wallet. A pass is not only your ticket to the national parks, it provides access to more than 2,000 federal recreation sites including national monuments (e.g., Devil's Tower), national memorials, national recreation areas, and all other lands managed by the Bureau of Land Management and Bureau of Reclamation.

Annual Pass • $80: This pass is valid for one year, beginning from the date of sale. It is available to the general public and provides access to, and use of, federal recreation sites that charge an entrance fee or standard amenity fee. It does not provide discounted camping or program/tour rates. The pass can be purchased by calling (888) 275-8747

Ext. 1, in person, or online at www. store.usgs.gov/pass.

Don't automatically purchase an annual pass if you're planning a multi-park vacation. No entrance fee is charged at the following national parks: Cuyahoga Valley, Mammoth Cave, Great Smoky Mountains, Congaree, Biscayne, U.S. Virgin Islands, American Samoa, Voyageurs, Wind Cave, Hot Springs, Great Basin, Channel Islands, Redwood, North Cascades, Glacier Bay, Wrangell–St. Elias, Kenai Fjords, Lake Clark, Katmai, Gates of the Arctic, and Kobuk Valley.

Senior Pass • $10: This is a lifetime pass for U.S. citizens or permanent residents age 62 or over. The pass provides lifetime access to, and use of, federal recreation sites that charge an entrance fee. The senior pass also provides a 50% discount on camping fees and certain park programs/tours. The pass must be purchased in person.

Access Pass • Free: This is a lifetime pass for U.S. citizens or permanent residents with permanent disabilities (documentation required).

The pass provides lifetime access to, and use of, federal recreation sites that charge an entrance or standard amenity fee. It also provides a 50% discount on camping fees and some park programs/tours. It must be obtained in person.

Volunteer Pass • Free: This pass is given to volunteers who accumulate 500 service hours on a cumulative basis. The pass provides access to, and use of, federal recreation sites that charge an entrance fee for a year, beginning from the date of award. The volunteer pass does not provide discounted camping or tour/program rates.

If you plan on visiting one national park several times in a calendar year you may be better off purchasing an individual park annual pass. They range from $15–50 and are typically good for one vehicle for one year from the date of purchase. Even if you think you might return just one more time within a year it is almost always worthwhile to purchase the park annual pass.

Another way to save a few dollars is to visit during National Park Service Free Entrance Days (page 5).

What to Pack

If you're like me you probably wait until the night before your vacation to begin packing. You grab everything you might need and throw it in a suitcase or backpack. Anything left behind won't be noticed until you need it on your trip. Avoid these situations by compiling packing lists (for each family member) and packing a few days in advance. Everyone knows to pack the essentials like cell phone charger, money, hygiene products, and clothes, so here are a few suggestions that you may not think of.

For Any Trip

Garbage and Small Resealable Bags: Not only are bags incredibly useful storage devices, you can use them to waterproof your gadgets. I still use a small resealable bag as my wallet. Its combination of transparency, durability, waterproofness, and low-cost-to-volume ratio cannot be beat.

Duct Tape: I always have a roll of duct tape in my car. It's also a good practice to wrap the base of a water bottle or hiking pole with duct tape for when you venture away from your car.

Headlamp: Whether reading in your tent or searching under a car seat for the National Park Pass you just dropped, a headlamp is sure to be a handy device. Plus, kids love them.

For the National Parks

Binoculars, clothes that layer (temperature and winds change dramatically based on elevation, location, and time), insect repellent, sunscreen, snacks and water, first-aid kit, journal or sketchpad, a good book, and camera (plus extra batteries).

For Hiking

Backpack, hydration system or water bottle, compass and map (know how to use them), GPS (know how to use it), hiking stick/poles, pocket knife, whistle, and water filter.

For Camping

Camp stove with fuel, rope, clothes pins, flashlight(s), folding chairs, hammock, water jug, tarp, ear plugs, and a deck of cards.

For Biking

Water, spare tube, patch-kit, pump, tire irons, multi-tool, and bike shorts.

For Paddling

Bilge pump, rescue bag, knife, booties, gloves, helmet, and whistle.

Leave No Trace

Remember that the National Parks are for everyone to enjoy. Whether you're an avid outdoorsman or just passing through, all visitors of the parks should practice these simple Leave No Trace principles.

1. Plan Ahead and Prepare
2. Travel/Camp on Durable Surfaces
3. Dispose of Waste Properly
4. Leave What You Find
5. Minimize Campfire Impacts
6. Respect Wildlife
7. Be Considerate of Other Visitors

Proper waste disposal is commonly referred to as "Pack it In, Pack it Out" or "Leave Only Footprints, Take Only Photographs." Practice these simple and sensible principles and our most remarkable and irreplaceable treasures will remain for the enjoyment of future generations.

Economical Travel

Vacations can be expensive. A trip to a national park is often seen as an affordable adventure, but the costs of lodging, dining, tours, entrance fees, and gas can add up quickly. Some costs are unavoidable; others can be minimized using these practical tips.

Lodging: Park lodges are beautiful but expensive. Discounts are rarely available during peak-season and many lodges book months in advance. Travel during off-season for the best deals on in-park lodging.

More economical lodging is often found beyond park boundaries. Most gateway cities offer everything from chain hotels to B&Bs. A few of the best lodging choices and their standard rates are included in the "What's Nearby" sections of this book. Before making reservations price check your options using online tools like Orbitz or Priceline. It's usually best to make reservations a few weeks in advance. Book too early and you'll pay the standard rate. Book too late and you might pay standard or more depending on availability. If you're making an unplanned stop at a hotel and unable to check pricing with the aforementioned online tools, the best way to receive a discount is to ask for one. Occasionally a hotel will have a room that is not up to their typical standards (e.g., no air conditioning) that they'll offer at a deep discount. If

you don't mind the room's defect, the hotel will not mind checking you in.

Another option is to use the money you would have spent on a hotel room on a tent, sleeping bag, and mat instead. Camping isn't for everyone, but it's definitely worth giving a try. You can avoid campground fees (and truly explore the park) by camping in the parks' wilderness areas. Most parks allow backcountry camping with a free permit (see park sections for details). By no means do you have to be a seasoned backpacker to enjoy the park's backcountry. However, you may want to consult with a park ranger to help plan an itinerary suitable for your experience, as well as get a brief overview of backcountry regulations. Most parks require that you set up camp a certain distance from all roads, trails, and water sources and practice Leave No Trace principles.

Walmart provides unexpected savings for travelers with a camper, RV, trailer, or truck. Most stores allow free overnight parking. To take advantage of this courtesy, they ask that you park in the back of the lot and notify a manager that you plan on spending the night (especially if you're the first to stop in for the night). Walmart's intent is to provide a safe location for weary travelers and truck drivers so they don't endanger other motorists. Do not take advantage of this benefit by getting comfortable and camping

out in the parking lot for an extended period of time.

Dining: The best way to avoid dining at expensive restaurants is to pack a cooler. Bringing a loaf of bread, jam, and peanut butter can prevent a few trips to the nearest town for a snack or meal. A list of grocery stores is conveniently located in the "What's Nearby" sections.

Activities: Discounts are more difficult to come by for activities. Asking is a good place to start, especially if you're part of a decent sized group. Outfitters would rather get your business then see you walk out their door. Many outfitters offer "early-bird" discounts or "online only" specials. It's also a good idea to navigate your way around their website looking for coupons or simply search for the "outfitter's name" plus the word "coupon" and see what's returned.

Entrance Fees: These are non-negotiable, but the National Parks Service offers free entrance days. The list of fee free dates is available at www.nps.gov/findapark/feefreeparks.htm.

If you plan on visiting several federal fee areas in the same year consider buying an annual pass (page 2).

Gas: Most national parks are vast regions located in extremely remote sections of the U.S. It will take a lot of gas simple to get to the park much less around it. Remember to top off your gas tank before entering. A few parks have gas stations (see park sections), but you can expect to pay a modest premium.

Acadia, Glacier, Rocky Mountain, Bryce Canyon, Zion, Grand Canyon, Sequoia, and Yosemite offer free shuttle services during peak tourism season. Take advantage of these shuttles. Not only are they free, they allow you to enjoy the magnificent vistas rather than stare at the road.

Camping Regulations

Camping is one of the national parks' main attractions. Children and adults alike love the freedom of spending a night under the stars. To do so, campers must adhere to a few basic regulations that help protect park resources and ensure an enjoyable stay for all of the campground's patrons and your fellow park visitors.

1. Camp only in designated sites.
2. Leave something of little value to indicate occupancy (important for vans and RVs).
3. Store all food and cooking equipment in an enclosed vehicle or hard-sided food locker (particularly in parks with healthy bear or raccoon populations).
4. Do not leave fires unattended.
5. Observe campground specific quiet hours and generator hours.
6. Check out on time.
7. Lock valuables in your vehicle and out of sight.

Regulations regarding maximum length of stay, speed limits, gathering wood, and pets change from campground to campground. Specific regulations should be posted at self-check-in stations or handed out when you register for your campsite upon arrival, or they can be found prior to arrival at each park's website.

Road Construction

All of the most popular parks have been adapted to suit the modern motorist. Paved roadways venture across regions once declared impassable by foot. Ingenuity, perseverance, hard work and millions of tons of concrete now allow automobiles to twist and turn along rugged mountain slopes and craggy coastlines through some of the most beautiful scenery you'll find anywhere in the world. Roads were built to increase tourism and accessibility, but they were also carefully designed to retain aesthetic beauty. You won't find a bridge across the Grand Canyon or a parking lot next to Half Dome, but roads lead to stunning viewpoints of these iconic settings.

Park roads require regular maintenance. Repairing roads in these remote and rugged regions can be a difficult task—a task made more challenging since construction and tourism seasons coincide with one another. To get the most of your vacation try to plan around road construction. Current and upcoming construction plans are typically listed on a park's website. If you can't find construction information there, a friendly park ranger is just a phone call away.

Safety

It is important that park visitors follow safety precautions and park regulations to enjoy a safe visit and prevent injuries. In the unlikely event someone is injured, know where to go to receive proper medical treatment. A few parks have medical facilities on-site, but most do not. Carry a cell phone, but do not rely on it; cell coverage is spotty in most parks.

Accidents can still happen, even to the park's most cautious guests. Occasionally an accident results in death. The number one cause of fatalities in the parks might surprise you: it's car accidents. Sure, other drivers are beyond your control, but that doesn't mean that you and I should refrain from wearing our seat belts, obeying the rules of the road, and driving attentively and cautiously. Far less dangerous are the hazards most often associated with a trip to the national parks:

Drowning: Visitors should use extreme caution near water. River crossings can be challenging due to uneven footing, moss covered rocks, and slippery logs. One misstep could lead to being swept down river or over a waterfall.

Hypothermia: Rivers and lakes. High elevations. Alaska. These places have one thing in common: they're cold. Extended exposure to any cold environment can lead to hypothermia, the progressive degradation, both physically and mentally, caused by the chilling of the inner core of the human body. To help prevent hypothermia, wear water-resistant clothing or clothing that wicks away moisture. It's also a good idea to pack a sweater, warm hat, and rain gear for any hike.

Dehydration: It's important to stay hydrated. Remember to carry a day pack with ample water and snacks.

Giardia: Giardia is caused by a parasite found in lakes and streams. If consumed it causes persistent, severe diarrhea, abdominal cramps, and nausea. To prevent giardia use an approved filter, boil water, or drink from sources clearly labeled

Staged rock accident - Rocky Mountain National Park

Grizzly Bear - Denali National Park © Frank Kovalchek (flickr/Alaskan Dude)

"potable" (e.g., water fountains). Filters should be capable of removing particles as small as one micron.

Falling Trees/Rocks: Parks do their best to proactively close trails that pose a significant threat due to falling rocks or trees, but hikers must always be aware of their surroundings. Also, don't kick or throw rocks off cliffs or ledges. There may be hikers below you.

Wildlife/Bears: Do not approach wildlife. This is particularly true of bears. Know the differences between grizzly and black bears. Grizzlies are blond to nearly black and sometimes have silver-tipped guard hairs. They have a dished-in face and a large hump of heavy muscle above the shoulders. There claws are around 4 inches. Black bears also range from blond to black. They are typically smaller with a straighter face from tip of the nose to ears. They do not have a prominent hump above their shoulders and their claws are about 1.5 inches long. Most bear–human encounters occur when hikers startle or provoke the animal. Visitors often wear bells to scare away bears. I've heard conflicting reports about the bells' effectiveness, but if they make you feel safer you should wear them. The best way to avoid an encounter is to hike with a group and talk as you go. Many hikers carry bear spray, non-lethal deterrent similar to pepper spray.

Firearms: As of February 22, 2010, federal law allows people who can legally possess firearms under applicable federal, state, and local laws, to carry firearms in the national parks.

Where to See Wildlife
Wildlife is transient. The best way to pinpoint your desired animal is to ask a park ranger about current activity and feeding areas. Dawn and dusk are typically prime viewing times for large mammal species.

Respect Wildlife
When you do spot wildlife remember that these are not tame animals, and should not be approached. Visitors are often injured when they get too close. Stay at least 100 yards away from bears and wolves and 25 yards away from all other animals (like bison, elk, bighorn sheep, moose, deer, and coyotes). Absolutely do not feed wildlife. It harms them and is illegal.

Photography Tips
Modern cameras eliminate most of the difficulty in taking photographs, but a few helpful tips can lead to outstanding results. The best photography is done at dusk and dawn. During these hours light is not too dim and not too bright. Image stabilization has come a long way, but a tripod is useful (especially in low-light).

Know the Rule of Thirds: an image should be imagined as divided into nine equal parts by two equally-spaced horizontal and vertical lines. Place your primary subject along the vertical lines or at any of the four intersections (see below) rather than centering your subject. Use this rule for interesting and well-balanced shots, but don't be afraid to break it from time to time.

My Mom at Bryce Canyon

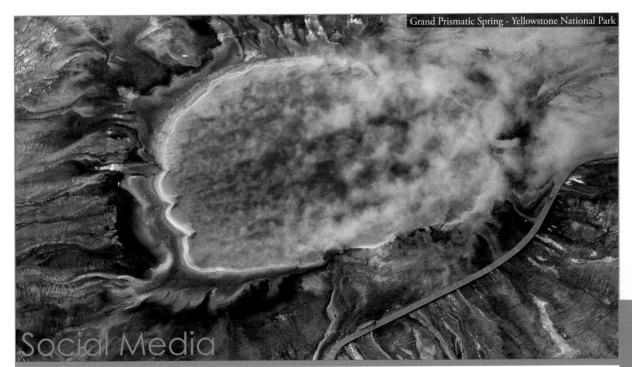

Grand Prismatic Spring - Yellowstone National Park

Social Media

Stone Road Press
facebook.com/TheStoneRoadPress
Twitter: @StoneRoadPress

National Park Service
@NatlParkService

National Park Foundation
@GoParks

American Samoa
Official Facebook Page
@amer_samoanps

Arches
facebook.com/ArchesNationalPark
@ArchesNPS

Biscayne
@BiscayneNPS

Bryce Canyon
facebook.com/BryceCanyonnps
@BryceCanyonNPS

Canyonlands
facebook.com/CanyonlandsNationalPark
@CanyonlandsNPS

Crater Lake
@CraterLakeNPS

Denali
facebook.com/DenaliNPS
@DenaliNPS

Dry Tortugas
facebook.com/DryTortugasNationalPark
@DryTortugasNPS

Everglades
facebook.com/EvergladesNationalPark
@EvergladesNPS

Gates of the Arctic
Official Facebook Page
@GatesArcticNPS

Glacier
facebook.com/GlacierNationalPark
@GlacierNPS

Glacier Bay
facebook.com/GlacierBayNationalPark
@GlacierBayNPS

Grand Canyon
@GrandCanyonNPS

Grand Teton
facebook.com/GrandTetonNPS
@GrandTetonNPS

Great Basin
facebook.com/GreatBasinNPS
@GreatBasinNPS

Great Sand Dunes
facebook.com/greatsanddunesnpp
@greatsanddunes

Great Smoky Mtns
@SmokiesRoadsNPS

Guadalupe Mountains
facebook.com/guadalupe.mountains

Haleakalā
Official Facebook Page
@HaleakalaNPS

Joshua Tree
facebook.com/joshuatreenp
@JoshuaTreeNP

Katmai
@KatmaiNPS

Lassen Volcanic
facebook.com/LassenNPS
@LassenNPS

Mount Rainier
@MountRainierNPS

North Cascades
facebook.com/NorthCas-
cadesNationalPark
@NCascadesNPS

Olympic
@HRWinterAccess

Petrified Forest
@PetrifiedNPS

Redwood
facebook.com/RedwoodNPS
@RedwoodNPS

Rocky Mountain
Official Facebook Page
@RMNPOfficial

Saguaro
facebook.com/saguaronationalpark

Sequoia & Kings Canyon
Official Facebook Page
@SequoiaKingsNPS

Shenandoah
@ShenandoahNPS

Theodore Roosevelt
facebook.com/TheodoreRoos-
eveltNationalPark
@TRooseveltNPS

Wrangell–St. Elias
facebook.com/WrangellSt.EliasNPP
@WrangellStENPS

Yellowstone
@YellowstoneNPS

Yosemite
facebook.com/YosemiteNPS
@YosemiteNPS

Zion
@ZionNPS

In addition, many U.S. National Parks have flickr photostreams and youtube channels. Look them up to find some of the latest high quality park photos and informational videos.

Highline Trail - Glacier National Park © Sam & Katie Johnsrud

Best of the Best

Top 10 Parks

Having trouble deciding which national park to visit? Close your eyes and pick from this short list of the best.

Glacier (page 246): If heaven is here on earth, it's probably Glacier National Park. John Muir called it "the best care-killing scenery in the continent." I agree.

Yosemite (page 498): Yosemite Valley is one of those places you have to see to believe. Throw in sequoia trees, thunderous waterfalls, and some of the best backcountry hiking and you've got an incomparable wonderland.

Acadia (page 30): What once was the premier vacation destination for the wealthy is now a scenic retreat for everyone. Acadia offers some of the most diverse activities and geography of all the national parks.

Crater Lake (page 538): The water of Crater Lake is the deepest, purest blue you'll ever see. The lake is extraordinary all year round, but access is limited in winter.

Zion (page 404): Locals called Zion "Yosemite National Park in color." These colorful sandstone walls are easily accessed thanks to Zion Tunnel (which leads directly into the canyon) and a convenient and easy-to-use shuttle system.

Mount Rainier (page 550): Such stunning scenery so close to the Seattle metropolitan area makes including Mount Rainier National Park in this list an easy decision.

Grand Teton (page 204): The skyline of the Teton Range is as iconic as that of New York City, but 100% more natural.

Grand Canyon (page 416): The park is hot and busy during the summer, but few guests forget their first sight of this magnificent canyon. Try the North Rim for a less crowded experience.

Death Valley (page 476): The largest national park in the contiguous U.S. holds a collection of oddities worthy of Ripley's Believe It or Not, but you better believe all these attractions are real.

Yellowstone (page 218): Yellowstone has it all. Gushing geysers, brilliant canyons, alpine lakes, abundant wildlife, and magnificent mountains make a trip here feel like you're visiting several parks at once.

Top 20 Attractions

These are the most beautiful individual landmarks you'll find in the 58 parks.

Crater Lake • Crater Lake (page 538): This is the one place I'd choose above all others to take a lawn chair, grill, cooler, and a few of my closest friends to sit and enjoy the view.

Yosemite Valley • Yosemite (page 498): Perhaps the most beautiful valley in the world. Half Dome, El Capitán, and Yosemite Falls (all located in the valley) are worthy of inclusion in this list as separate entries.

Bryce Amphitheater • Bryce Canyon (page 396): This is the sort of scenery that has a direct connection to your inner-soul. The colorful and eerie rock formations are no doubt unforgettable.

Mount McKinley • Denali (page 600): It's the tallest mountain in North America, and more prominent than Mount Everest. Of course it's on this list.

Grand Canyon of the Yellowstone • Yellowstone (page 218): Golden yellow canyon walls frame Upper and Lower Falls of the Yellowstone River.

Toroweap Overlook • Grand Canyon (page 438): Seclusion adds to the scenic views afforded at this overlook towering high above treacherous Lava Falls. It's only accessible via an unpaved road.

Grand Prismatic Spring • Yellowstone (page 218): Uninspiring up close, the concentric circles of oranges, yellows, greens, and blues are mesmerizing from afar (Fairy Falls Trail).

Big Room • Carlsbad Caverns (page 298): Caves are cool and Carlsbad's Big Room is one of the coolest.

Mather Point • Grand Canyon (page 434): The best vista to soak in the size of the canyon carved by the Colorado River.

Zion Canyon • Zion (page 404): Zion Narrows, Angel's Landing, and Court of the Patriarchs are a few of the notable landmarks within this beautiful canyon formed by the Virgin River.

General Sherman • Sequoia (page 493): I never thought a tree would make this list, but stand next to General Sherman and you'll quickly understand why.

Haleakalā Summit • Haleakalā (page 654): The summit is more like visiting a distant planet than a park.

Delicate Arch • Arches (page 368): Delicate Arch joins Crater Lake in the vehicle license plate club. That doesn't mean that the site has to be amazing, but this one is.

Inspiration Point - Bryce Canyon National Park

The Racetrack • Death Valley (page 483): The Racetrack is the quirkiest entry. Here rocks slowly slide their way across a bone dry playa.

Brown Bears of Brooks Falls • Katmai (page 622): The scenery here is nice, but its residents are better. Brown bears fish at the falls in July and September.

Garden Wall • Glacier (page 246): A steep arête that separates the Many Glacier area from Lake McDonald valley.

Johns Hopkins Inlet • Glacier Bay (page 586): Calving glaciers and abundant sea life make this a hot spot for cruise ships and kayakers.

The Wall • Badlands (page 176): Outside of the Grand Canyon, the Badlands Wall is the most magnificent marvel of eroded rock in the United States.

The Maze • Canyonlands (page 381): The Maze isn't the jaw-dropping, awe-inspiring masterpiece that most of these attractions are, but what it lacks in scenic beauty it makes up for with mystery and intrigue.

Old Faithful • Yellowstone (page 234): Somewhat of a novelty, this regularly spouting 100-ft tall geyser is a must-see for all of Yellowstone's first-time visitors.

Best Scenic Drives

The parks have become motorists' favorite travel destinations. This book would not be complete without a list of the very best drives they have to offer.

Going-to-the-Sun Road • Glacier (page 261): The best drive in the country is only open from mid-June through mid-September (most years) and cyclists are not permitted during periods of peak motorist traffic.

Denali Park Road • Denali (page 602): Only accessible via shuttle/tour bus from late May through mid-September (most years) with a "Road Lottery" held for individuals in late September.

Rim Drive • Crater Lake (page 541): I absolutely love everything about this lake. In summer you can drive around the caldera filled with the bluest water you'll ever see. In winter the road is closed, but that doesn't stop cross-country skiers and snowshoers from completing the circuit.

Wawona Road • Yosemite (page 503): Wawona Road makes the list thanks to one of the most memorable views in the world: Tunnel View. It provides the first glimpse of Yosemite Valley. Don't forget to set aside extra time to hike to Inspiration Point.

John D. Rockefeller Jr., Memorial Pkwy • Grand Teton (page 214): This roadway connects two of the American West's greatest treasures: Yellowstone and Grand Teton.

Trail Ridge Road • Rocky Mountain (page 329): This scenic thoroughfare penetrates the Rockies and travels above 11,000 feet elevation for 8 miles. Pullouts along the way provide some of the best mountain vistas and access to trails.

Park Loop Road • Acadia (page 45): 27-miles of pure bliss as it loops around the eastern half of Mount Desert Island with a spur road to Cadillac Mountain, the tallest peak in the park.

US-101 • Redwood (page 530): For my gallons of gas there are more scenic stretches of the Pacific Coastline along CA-1 and US-101, but the park's towering redwoods add contrast to California's rocky and rugged coastline.

Badlands Loop Road • Badlands (page 179): Easily the best scenic detour while traveling across South Dakota on I-90.

Skyline Drive • Shenandoah (page 73): The 105-mile highway is Shenandoah's main attraction, providing access to campgrounds, trailheads, and visitor facilities.

Delicate Arch - Arches National Park

Best Lodges

Most lodges in the parks were built not just to serve a purpose, but to compliment the environment. These lodging facilities are works of architecture truly worthy of the landscapes they accent.

El Tovar • Grand Canyon (page 430)
Ahwahnee • Yosemite (page 509)
Jenny Lake Lodge • Grand Teton (page 208)
Old Faithful Inn • Yellowstone (page 226)
Crater Lake Lodge • Crater Lake (page 542)
Paradise Inn • Mount Rainier (page 554)
Zion Lodge • Zion (page 408)
Many Glacier Lodge • Glacier (page 252)
Glacier Park Lodge • Glacier (page 252)
Rock Harbor Lodge • Isle Royale (page 156)
Le Conte • Great Smoky Mtns (page 95)

The 16 Best Trails

It's nice to see the parks from the comfort of your vehicle or lodge, but to really get out there and explore nature you need to strap on a pair of hiking boots and hit the trails. Provided below are my personal favorites.

Highline • Glacier (page 254): The Garden Wall section from Logan Pass to Granite Park Lodge is outstanding. It's a popular hike, but what it lacks in solitude it makes up for in wildlife and expansive mountain views.

The Narrows • Zion (page 411): There may be better slot canyon hikes in Utah (nearby Buckskin Gulch comes to mind), but there isn't a single slot canyon more famous than Zion's Narrows. The stretch between its mouth and Orderville Canyon is best.

Delicate Arch • Arches (page 372): Delicate Arch is magnificent, but what really makes it "pop" is its presentation. The trail leading to this colorful sandstone arch is one of the best designed hikes in the park system.

Half Dome • Yosemite (page 510): The climb to the top of Half Dome (aided by cables) is nearly as inspiring as the view from its summit.

Wilderness Waterway • Everglades (page 132): This 99-mile paddling trail is the best way to explore the "River of Grass."

The Precipice • Acadia (page 37): Steel ladders and rungs aid hikers aiming to reach the summit of Champlain Mountain for classic Acadian views.

South Kaibab • Grand Canyon (page 432): One of two routes into the Grand Canyon from its South Rim. The views are superb, but there's no water and very little shade.

Bright Angel • Grand Canyon (page 432): The other route into the canyon. Shade and water are available along the way.

Angel's Landing • Zion (page 410): Hiking to the Landing isn't for everyone. Following the knife-edge ridgeline may stir up a fear of heights you never knew you had.

Sliding Sands • Haleakalā (page 659): This trail transports hikers to an otherworldly landscape inside Haleakalā Crater.

Iceberg Lake • Glacier (page 254): On a hot summer day you might catch hikers swimming with icebergs, but its scenery and wildlife is the real draw.

Grinnell Glacier • Glacier (page 254): Mountains, lakes, and slowly receding glaciers highlight this moderate trek.

Cascade Canyon • Grand Teton (page 210): One of the most rewarding loop hikes around. It's long, but ambitious hikers can complete the hike to Lake Solitude in a day.

Mount Washburn • Yellowstone (page 228): Two separate trails lead to the mountain's summit and a lookout tower.

Alum Cave • Great Smoky Mtns (page 100): Scenic views of the Smoky Mountains are provided along this steep and strenuous trail leading to Le Conte Lodge.

Old Rag • Shenandoah (page 70): Most hikes through Shenandoah begin along Skyline Drive, but not Old Rag. You begin at the park boundary and gradually hike/scramble to the top of Old Rag Mountain.

Best for Hiking

Try one of these parks if you're looking to put a few miles on your favorite pair of hiking boots.

Yosemite (page 510)
Glacier (page 254)
Denali (page 605)
Sequoia & Kings Canyon (page 494)
North Cascades (page 576)
Rocky Mountain (page 331)
Yellowstone (page 227)
Mount Rainier (page 557)
Acadia (page 37)
Great Smoky Mountains (page 100)

Best for Backpacking

The best way to commune with these wonderful natural abodes is to strap a pack on your back and enjoy a few days of perfect solitude in the backcountry.

Intro to Backpacking

Uncertain about hiking with 40+ pounds of gear on your back? Nervous about camping in the untamed wilderness? Try one of these parks. They're like training wheels for beginning backpackers.

Best for Paddling

Gain a new perspective of these watery wonderlands by floating or boating miles of wide open waterways at the following parks.

Best for Whitewater

Very few activities get your blood pumping quite like whitewater rafting does. These parks offer commercial trips on some of the most turbulent rivers.

Grizzly bear and cubs - Katmai National Park

Best for Biking

Don't forget to bring your bicycle to these national parks.

Death Valley (page 483)
Acadia (page 40)
Denali (page 607)
Everglades (page 134)
Olympic (page 564)
Shenandoah (page 70)
Theodore Roosevelt (page 198)
Glacier (page 260)
Great Smoky Mountains (page 102)
Grand Teton (page 213)
Cuyahoga Valley (page 57)
Saguaro (page 316)
Yellowstone (page 234)

Best for Horse Rides

Visitors can still wander through these parks on horseback much like early American explorers did. Each one is horse/rider-friendly with miles of trails designated for stock, corrals, and commercial outfitters that offer guided trail rides or multi-day pack trips.

Yellowstone (page 233)
Rocky Mountain (page 334)
Bryce Canyon (page 402)
Theodore Roosevelt (page 197)
Joshua Tree (page 462)

Shenandoah (page 72)
Glacier (page 260)
Great Smoky Mountains (page 103)
Sequoia & Kings Canyon (page 493)
Zion (page 413)
Haleakalā (page 659)
Yosemite (page 513)
Acadia (page 40)

Best for Fishing

Anglers will find plenty of fish in these parks.

Yellowstone (page 236)
Alaska Nat'l Parks (pages 586–633)
Everglades (page 134)
North Cascades (page 578)
Biscayne (page 122)
Great Smoky Mountains (page 103)
Dry Tortugas (page 143)
Grand Teton (page 214)
Isle Royale (page 160)
Rocky Mountain (page 334)
Shenandoah (page 72)

Best for Rock Climbing

Rock climbing seems to increase in popularity each year, and many of the best locations in the United States are found among the mountains and cliffs at these national parks.

Yosemite (page 514)

Grand Teton (page 213)
Joshua Tree (page 460)
Black Canyon (page 352)
Acadia (page 42)
Rocky Mountain (page 335)
Sequoia & Kings Canyon (page 493)
Zion (page 413)
Arches (page 374)
Canyonlands (page 386)
Capitol Reef (page 394)

Best for Mtn Climbing

There are mountains and then there are MOUNTAINS. Denali's Mount McKinley—the tallest peak in North America—is the latter. The following parks have some of the best mountain scenery and climbs range from multi-day treks that require specialized equipment to day-hikes to summits with spectacular vistas.

Denali (page 606)
Mount Rainier (page 555)
Wrangell–St. Elias (page 598)
North Cascades (page 578)
Lake Clark (page 617)
Rocky Mountain (page 331)
Glacier (page 254)
Sequoia & Kings Canyon (page 494)
Yellowstone (page 227)
Olympic (page 566)

Trunk Bay Beach - U.S. Virgin Islands National Park © Fred Hsu

Best for Stargazing

One of the national parks' most underrated activities is stargazing. Many city dwellers aren't able to see the night sky in its natural state, but in the parks, when the sky is clear, the stars twinkle and dance.

Haleakalā (page 660)
Gates of the Arctic (page 660)
Utah National Parks (pages 374–415)
Grand Canyon (page 416)
Great Basin (page 446)
Joshua Tree (page 462)
Big Bend (page 282)
Carlsbad Caverns (page 300)

Best Off-Road Driving

With a high-clearance 4WD vehicle you can "unlock" seldom visited sites thanks to miles of unpaved (and sometimes impassable) roads at these parks.

Death Valley (page 483)
Canyonlands (page 385)
Capitol Reef (page 394)
Grand Canyon (page 438)
Great Basin (page 448)
Arches (page 374)

Best for SCUBA

The national parks aren't limited to land activities. At these locations you can explore the life, wrecks, and terrain that exist under the sea.

Virgin Islands (page 649)
Isle Royale (page 160)
American Samoa (page 683)
Dry Tortugas (page 142)
Biscayne (page 123)
Channel Islands (page 470)
Crater Lake (page 544)

Best for Beaches

Seldom do you need to pack your swimsuit for a trip to a national park; these are the exceptions.

Virgin Islands (page 649)
American Samoa (page 683)
Olympic (page 569)
Haleakalā (page 660)
Acadia (page 42)
Redwood (page 530)
Biscayne (page 123)
Dry Tortugas (page 142)
Great Sand Dunes (page 342)

Channel Islands (page 470)

Best for Waterfalls

For the soothing sight and sounds of plummeting water pay a visit to one of these parks.

Yosemite (page 510)
Haleakalā (page 660)
Great Smoky Mountains (page 100)
Shenandoah (page 70)
Cuyahoga Valley (page 56)
Olympic (page 566)
Glacier (page 254)
Mount Rainier (page 557)
North Cascades (page 576)

Best for Caves

Children love the dark mysterious passages and ornate rock formations found at these national parks.

Carlsbad Caverns (page 298)
Mammoth Cave (page 84)
Wind Cave (page 188)
Great Basin (page 444)
Sequoia & Kings Canyon (page 493)
Hawai'i Volcanoes (page 671)
Channel Islands (page 469)

Best for Culture

While most parks show signs of human occupation spanning the last 10,000 years, only a few have substantial archeological sites.

Mesa Verde (page 354)
Channel Islands (page 464)
Kobuk Valley (page 630)
Shenandoah (page 64)
Great Smoky Mountains (page 92)
Hawai'i Volcanoes (page 664)
Everglades (page 128)
Theodore Roosevelt (page 192)

Best for Winter

Most visitors flock to the parks in summer when children are out of school and the temperature has warmed, but many are equally inviting during the winter. Some attract visitors thanks to uncommonly warm winters, others offer unique activities like snowmobiling, cross-country skiing, snowboarding, and downhill skiing.

Warm Winters

Death Valley (page 476)
Haleakalā (page 654)
Everglades (page 126)
Hawai'i Volcanoes (page 664)
Joshua Tree (page 456)
Big Bend (page 278)
American Samoa (page 680)
Virgin Islands (page 644)
Saguaro (page 310)

Cold Winters

Crater Lake (page 59)
Mount Rainier (page 557)
Yellowstone (page 236)
Sequoia & Kings Canyon (page 494)
Voyageurs (page 164)
Cuyahoga Valley (page 59)

Best for Bird Watching

Birds seem to be everywhere, but these parks are well-known for the diversity and abundance of their flying friends.

Everglades (page 135)
Acadia (page 43)
Dry Tortugas (page 143)
Congaree (page 114)
Haleakalā (page 660)
Big Bend (page 284)
Great Sand Dunes (page 344)

Best for Wildlife

Fishing bears. Migrating caribou. Grazing bison. Feeding whales. This is just a sampling of the wildlife on display at these parks.

Katmai (page 622)
Kobuk Valley (page 630)
Yellowstone (page 237)
Everglades (page 135)
Denali (page 608)
Isle Royale (page 161)
Great Smoky Mountains (page 103)

Lake Clark (page 616)
Glacier Bay (page 592)

Best for Photography

If you want to return from your vacation with a postcard-perfect photograph, visit these parks to snap a few pictures.

Yellowstone (page 236)
Yosemite (page 515)
Arches (page 374)
Bryce Canyon (page 396)
Grand Canyon (page 416)
Denali (page 600)
Zion (page 404)
Grand Teton (page 204)
Glacier Bay (page 586)
Canyonlands (page 376)

Best Sunrise Spots

Whether you're in search of that perfect sunrise photograph or a romantic morning with a loved one, you won't regret the early wake-up call to visit these sites.

Haleakalā Summit • Haleakalā (page 657)
Zabriskie Point • Death Valley (page 479)
Cadillac Mountain • Acadia (page 34)
Sunrise • Bryce Canyon (page 398)
Mesa Arch • Canyonlands (page 379)
Delicate Arch • Arches (page 370)
Signal Mountain • Grand Teton (page 206)
Landscape Arch • Arches (page 370)
Watchman Overlook • Crater Lake (page 541)

Carriage Ride - Acadia National Park

Best Sunset Spots

Brilliant sunsets are often captured from these picturesque locations.

Cape Royal • Grand Canyon (page 421)
Snake River Overlook • Grand Teton (page 207)
Shi Shi and Rialto Beaches • Olympic (page 562)
Delicate Arch • Arches (page 370)
Glacier Point • Yosemite (page 512)
The Window • Big Bend (page 283)
Dante's View • Death Valley (page 479)
Bass Harbor Head Lighthouse • Acadia (page 44)
Hot Springs • Big Bend (page 281)

Best for Couples

Couples will find these parks exciting, adventurous, and romantic.

Virgin Islands (page 644)
Grand Teton (page 204)
Acadia (page 30)
Hawai'i Volcanoes (page 664)
Haleakalā (page 654)
Mount Rainier (page 550)
Rocky Mountain (page 326)
Glacier (page 246)
Yellowstone (page 218)
Great Smoky Mountains (page 92)

Best for Families

Some parks are more family friendly than others thanks to easy accessibility, short trails, and guaranteed sights and sounds that are sure to spark your child's imagination.

Carlsbad Caverns (page 294)
Hawai'i Volcanoes (page 664)
Everglades (page 126)
Great Sand Dunes (page 338)
Yellowstone (page 218)
Sequoia & Kings Canyon (page 486)
Wind Cave (page 184)
Arches (page 368)
Acadia (page 30)
Mammoth Cave (page 80)

Best for Day Trips

A few parks are conveniently located near major metropolitan areas allowing a quick day-trip to hike or sit and relax in these natural wonderlands.

Mount Rainier • Seattle (page 550)
Olympic • Seattle (page 560)
Rocky Mountain • Denver (page 326)
Joshua Tree • Los Angeles (page 456)
Everglades • Miami (page 126)

Shenandoah • Washington D.C. (page 64)
Congaree • Columbia (page 110)
Saguaro • Tucson (page 310)
Cuyahoga Valley • Cleveland/Akron (page 52)

Best for Train Travel

Railroads played an important role in the establishment of the early national parks, and it is still king at these destinations.

Glacier (page 247)
Grand Canyon (page 431)
Denali (page 601)
Cuyahoga Valley (page 58)

Best Ranger Programs

I highly recommend all ranger programs, but these are a few personal favorites. The price is almost always right, too, as most are free of charge.

Wild Cave Tours (fee) • Mammoth Cave (page 84), Wind Cave (page 188), and Carlsbad Caverns (page 298)
Bat Flight Program • Carlsbad Caverns (page 299)
Sled Dog Demonstration • Denali (page 608)
Slough Slog • Everglades (page 135)
Adventure Hikes • Yellowstone (page 239)
Ranger III (fee) • Isle Royale (page 156)
Cliff Palace (fee) • Mesa Verde (page 358)

Balcony House (fee) • Mesa Verde (page 358)
Guided Canoe Tour • Congaree (page 116)
Discovery Hikes (fee) • Denali (page 608)
North Canoe Voyage • Voyageurs (page 171)

Best Concessioner Tours

Concessioner tours tend to be a bit pricey, but they are an effective and efficient means of touring a national park. These are the best of the concessioner offerings.

Red Bus Tours • Glacier (page 260)
Canyon Raft Trip • Grand Canyon (page 424)
Mule Ride • Grand Canyon (page 427)
Dive-In Theater • Acadia (page 44)
Carriage Rides • Acadia (page 40)
Captain's Cruise • Isle Royale (page 161)
Snowcoach Tours • Yellowstone (page 236)
Crater Lake Boat Tour (page 542)

Most Underrated

Great Smoky Mountains, the most visited park, receives more than 9 million annual visitors. Others are so lightly trafficked people aren't even aware of their existence. These are a few of the seldom visited and underappreciated national parks.

North Cascades (page 572)
Black Canyon of the Gunnison (page 346)
Great Sand Dunes (page 338)
Capitol Reef (page 388)
Isle Royale (page 152)

Worst for Traffic

A trip to a national park is supposed to be a relaxing and rejuvenating experience, allowing you to escape from the daily grind. The ideal vacation doesn't include sitting in bumper-to-bumper traffic, but that's the reality at these parks during peak tourism season.

Acadia: July–August (page 32)
Great Smoky Mountains: mid-June–mid-August & October (page 94)
Yosemite: Summer (page 500)
Yellowstone: July–August (page 219)
Rocky Mtn: June–August (page 327)
Grand Canyon: Summer (page 429)
Zion: Summer (page 405)
Glacier: July–August (page 247)
Mount Rainier: July–August & Winter Weekends (page 551)

Do Not Detour For...

Whenever I'm within 100 miles of a park you can expect an immediate detour for a quick hike, photo-op, or to spend a night in the wilderness, but there are a few exceptions to this rule.

Hot Springs (page 270)
Biscayne (page 118)
Cuyahoga Valley (page 52)
Voyageurs (page 164)
Saguaro (page 310)
Channel Islands (page 464)
Lassen Volcanic (page 522)

Worst for Bugs

An unusually wet winter or spring can result in bumper crops of black flies and mosquitoes in just about any area, but there are a few parks that are notorious for their pesky insects. Try to avoid these sites during the specified time frame.

Everglades: Summer (page 126)
Alaska National Parks: mid-June–mid-July (pages 586–633)
Yosemite: early Summer (page 498)
Sequoia & Kings Canyon: early Summer (page 486)
Acadia: mid-May–mid-June (page 30)
Isle Royale: late June–late July (page 152)

Backcountry Cabins

Looking to get away from it all without sleeping in a tent? Several parks have backcountry lodges that are only accessible by foot. Most lack electricity and other luxuries.

Sperry and Granite Park Chalets • Glacier (page 253)
Phantom Ranch • Grand Canyon (page 430)
High Sierra Camps • Yosemite (page 509)
Mauna Loa, Pu'u'ula'ula, & Red Hill • Hawai'i Volcanoes (page 671)
Hōlua, Kapalaua, and Palikū Cabins • Haleakalā (page 658)
Le Conte Lodge • Great Smoky Mountains (page 95)
Wrangell–St. Elias (page 596)
Kenai Fjords (page 612)
Lake Clark (page 616)
Katmai (page 620)
Gates of the Arctic (page 626)
Drakesbad Ranch • Lassen Volcanic (page 522)

Best Campgrounds

Many of the parks' campgrounds are nondescript accommodations lacking scenic views and privacy. Others are exceptional with stunning vistas, access to great hiking trails, and well-equipped facilities. These are the best of the best.

Squaw Flats • Canyonlands (page 382)
Wonder Lake • Denali (page 604)
Devil's Garden • Arches (page 372)
Isle au Haut • Acadia (page 36)
Voyageurs (page 168)
Jenny Lake • Grand Teton (page 209)
Cottonwood • Theodore Roosevelt (page 195)
Cinnamon Bay • Virgin Islands (page 648)
Many Glacier • Glacier (page 253)
Pine Springs • Guadalupe Mtns (page 290)
Isle Royale (page 156)

Best Oddities

There are weird and unexplainable oddities and events across the country; many exist within the parks.

The Racetrack • Death Valley (page 483)
Ubehebe Crater • Death Valley (page 476)
Waterpocket Fold • Capitol Reef (page 388)
Upheaval Dome • Canyonlands (page 376)
Synchronous Fireflies • GRSM (page 104)
Triple Divide • Glacier (page 254)
Badwater Basin • Death Valley (page 476)

Best Superlatives

The national parks are brimming with superlatives. These are the most impressive.

Mount McKinley • Denali (page 600): Highest mountain peak in North America with a summit elevation of 20,320-ft.

Badwater Basin • Death Valley (page 476): Lowest point in North America with an elevation of 282 feet below sea level.

Mount Whitney • Sequoia (page 486): Highest mountain peak in the contiguous United States with an elevation of 14,505-ft.

Mount Rainier (page 550): Rising to 14,410-ft, Mount Rainier is the tallest volcano in the contiguous United States.

Crater Lake (page 538): Deepest lake in the United States with a 1,943-ft maximum depth and average depth of 1,148-ft. It's also the purest lake in North America.

The Wave - Coyote Buttes North, Vermilion Cliffs National Monument

Mammoth Cave (page 80): By far the world's longest known cave system with more than 367 miles of passageways.

Yosemite Falls • Yosemite (page 511): The tallest waterfall in North America. Sentinel Falls, the second tallest waterfall, is also located in Yosemite National Park.

Kolob Arch • Zion (page 410): It's the largest free-standing arch in the park system.

Yellowstone (page 234): The largest concentration of geysers in the world.

Wrangell–St. Elias (page 594): The largest unit in the national park system and the continent's largest quantity of glaciers.

Harding Icefield • Kenai Fjords (page 610): The largest icefield contained entirely in the United States.

General Sherman • Sequoia (page 486): The largest known tree by volume at 52,600 ft^3 (roughly the size of 16 blue whales).

Hyperion • Redwood (page 530): The world's tallest known living tree at 379.3 ft.

Best Beyond the Parks

Great natural sights and scenes of the United States don't begin and end with the national parks. Here are just a few of the non-park wonders mentioned in this guide book. (NM = National Monument, NME = National Memorial, NRA = National Recreation Area, NVM = National Volcanic Monument, NCA = National Conservation Area)

Washington Mall (Lincoln Mem., Washington Mon., Jefferson Mem., etc. • page 79)
Mt Rushmore NME (page 203)
Custer State Park (page 203)
Jewel Cave NM (page 203)
Devils Tower NM (page 203)
Craters of the Moon NM (page 245)
Lake Ouachita State Park (page 277)
White Sands NM (page 322)
Lost Dutchman State Park (page 322)
Garden of the Gods (page 366)
Dinosaur NM (page 367)
Hovenweep NM (page 366)
Dead Horse Point State Park (page 451)

Kodachrome Basin State Park (page 452)
Buckskin Gulch (page 452)
The Wave (page 452)
Paria Canyon (page 452)
Grand Staircase–Escalante NM (page 452)
Cedar Breaks NM (page 452)
Glen Canyon NRA (page 453)
Havasu Falls (page 434)
Lake Mead NRA/Hoover Dam (page 453)
Red Rock Canyon NCA (page 453)
Pinnacles NM (page 521)
Devil's Postpile NM (page 521)
Golden Gate NRA (page 521)
Muir Woods NM (page 521)
Lava Beds NM (page 548)
Oregon Caves NM (page 549)
John Day Fossil Beds NM (page 582)
Mount St. Helens NVM (page 582)
Buck Island Reef NM (page 653)
Molokini (page 663)
Mauna Kea (page 679)
'Akaka Falls State Park (page 678)

Sunset from Snake River Overlook - Grand Teton National Park

Suggested Trips

I've put together a few suggested trips to help plan your national parks vacation. Trip mileage and duration was estimated based on departure from the nearest major city. Choosing where to spend the night, what to pack, when and where to eat, and whether you obey the speed limit are completely up to you. I've also included a few suggested pit-stops to help break up particularly long stretches spent behind the windshield.

Rocky Mountain High

Parks Visited: Grand Teton (2 nights, page 204), Yellowstone (3 nights, page 218), and Glacier (4 nights, page 246)

Begins/Ends: Jackson, WY
Estimated Driving Distance: 1,200 miles
Estimated Trip Length: 10 days

Road Trip Breakdown
Jackson, WY to Grand Teton: 41 miles, ~1 hour via US-191
Grand Teton to Yellowstone: 55 miles, ~1.5 hours via US-191/ John D. Rockefeller, Jr. Memorial Pkwy
Yellowstone to Glacier: 460 miles, ~9 hours via US-89, I-90, US-287, and US-89.
Glacier to Jackson: 514 miles, ~9 hours via several Montana State Highways, I-90, and I-15

Potential Pit-Stops: Bar T 5 Covered Wagon Cookout (800.772.5386, www.bart5.com) • Jackson, WY; Museum of the Rockies (406.994.2251, www.museumoftherockies.org) • Bozeman, MT; Montana State Capitol • Helena, MT; The Montana Historical Society (406.444.2511, www.montanahistoricalsociety.org) • Helena, MT; Last Chance Train Tours (406.442.1023, www.lctours.com) • Helena, MT; Holter Museum of Art (406.442.6400, www.holtermuseum.org) • Helena, MT; Conrad Mansion Museum (406.755.2166, www.conradmansion.com) • Kalispell, MT; Butte Trolley Tour (800.735.6814) • Butte, MT; Craters of the Moon National Monument (208.527.1300, www.nps.gov/crmo) • Arco, ID

Notes: The parks are open year-round but Teton Park Road, Yellowstone Park Roads, and Going-to-the-Sun Road are all closed seasonally.

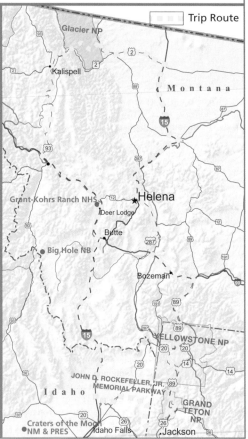

Cascades and Coastland

Parks Visited: North Cascades (2 nights, page 572), Mount Rainier (3 nights, page 550), and Olympic (3 nights, page 560)

Begins/Ends: Seattle, WA
Estimated Driving Distance: 600 miles
Estimated Trip Length: 1 week

Potential Pit-Stops: River Belle Dinner Theater (360.336.3012, www.riverbelledinnertheatre.com) • Mount Vernon, WA; Mt St. Helens Nat'l Mon. • Amboy, WA; Harbinger Winery (360.452.4262, www.harbinger-winery.com) • Port Angeles, WA; Twilight in Forks Tours (360.374.8687, www.twilight.inforks.com) • Forks, WA

Canyons and Culture

Parks Visited: Great Sand Dunes (2 nights, page 338), Black Canyon of the Gunnison (2 nights, page 346), Mesa Verde (2 nights, page 354), Canyonlands (2 nights, page 376), and Arches (2 nights, page 368)

Begins/Ends: Denver, CO
Estimated Driving Distance: 1,300 miles
Estimated Trip Length: 10 days

Potential Pit-Stops: Florissant Fossil Beds (719.748.3253, www.nps.gov/flfo) • Florissant, CO; Garden of the Gods (719.634.6666, www.gardenof-gods.com) • Colorado Springs, CO; Curecanti NRA (970.641.3127, www.nps.gov/cure) • Gunnison, CO; Museum of the Mountain West (970.249.4162, www.mountainwestmuseum.com) • Montrose, CO; Durango & Silverton Narrow Gauge Railroad & Museum (888.872.4607, www.durangotrain.com) • Durango, CO; Soaring Tree Top Adventures (970.769.2357, www.soaringcolorado.com) • Durango, CO; Yucca House NM (970.529.4465, www.nps.gov/yuho) • Mesa Verde, CO; Hovenweep NM (970.562.4282, www.nps.gov/hove) • Cortez, CO; Dead Horse Point State Park (435.259.2614, www.stateparks.utah.gov/parks/dead-horse) • Moab, UT.

Best of the Midwest

Parks Visited: Isle Royale (3 nights, page 152), and Voyageurs (3 nights, page 164)

Begins/Ends: Minneapolis, MN
Estimated Driving Distance: 850 miles
Estimated Trip Length: 1 week

Potential Pit-Stops: Apostle Islands NL (715.779.3397, www.nps.gov/apis) • Bayfield, WI; Devil's Kettle Waterfall • Judge Magney State Park • Grand Marais, MN; Grand Portage NM (218.475.0123, www.nps.gov/grpo) • Grand Marais, MN; NA Bear Center (877.365.7879, www.bear.org); Boundary Waters Canoe Area (www.canoecountry.com); Dorothy Molter Museum (218.365.4451, www.rootbeerlady.com); and Int'l Wolf Center (218.365.4695, www.wolf.org) all in Ely, MN.

Notes: Isle Royale is reached by ferry (fee) from Grand Portage, MN (www.isleroyaleboats.com); Houghton, MI; or Copper Harbor, MI (www.isleroyale.com). Ferries typically run from June through September. Touring cyclists can take their bikes aboard, providing transportation from Houghton to Grand Portage via Isle Royale or vice versa.

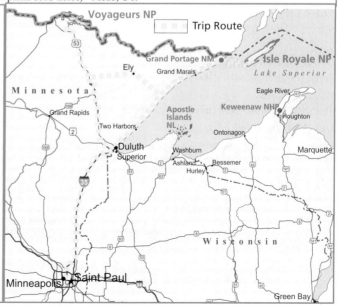

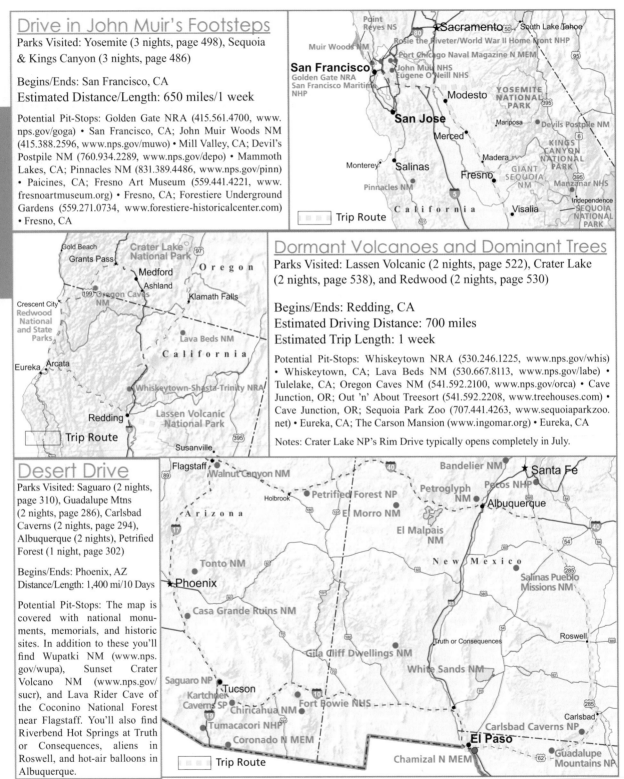

Drive in John Muir's Footsteps

Parks Visited: Yosemite (3 nights, page 498), Sequoia & Kings Canyon (3 nights, page 486)

Begins/Ends: San Francisco, CA
Estimated Distance/Length: 650 miles/1 week

Potential Pit-Stops: Golden Gate NRA (415.561.4700, www.nps.gov/goga) • San Francisco, CA; John Muir Woods NM (415.388.2596, www.nps.gov/muwo) • Mill Valley, CA; Devil's Postpile NM (760.934.2289, www.nps.gov/depo) • Mammoth Lakes, CA; Pinnacles NM (831.389.4486, www.nps.gov/pinn) • Paicines, CA; Fresno Art Museum (559.441.4221, www.fresnoartmuseum.org) • Fresno, CA; Forestiere Underground Gardens (559.271.0734, www.forestiere-historicalcenter.com) • Fresno, CA

Trip Route

Dormant Volcanoes and Dominant Trees

Parks Visited: Lassen Volcanic (2 nights, page 522), Crater Lake (2 nights, page 538), and Redwood (2 nights, page 530)

Begins/Ends: Redding, CA
Estimated Driving Distance: 700 miles
Estimated Trip Length: 1 week

Potential Pit-Stops: Whiskeytown NRA (530.246.1225, www.nps.gov/whis) • Whiskeytown, CA; Lava Beds NM (530.667.8113, www.nps.gov/labe) • Tulelake, CA; Oregon Caves NM (541.592.2100, www.nps.gov/orca) • Cave Junction, OR; Out 'n' About Treesort (541.592.2208, www.treehouses.com) • Cave Junction, OR; Sequoia Park Zoo (707.441.4263, www.sequoiaparkzoo.net) • Eureka, CA; The Carson Mansion (www.ingomar.org) • Eureka, CA

Notes: Crater Lake NP's Rim Drive typically opens completely in July.

Trip Route

Desert Drive

Parks Visited: Saguaro (2 nights, page 310), Guadalupe Mtns (2 nights, page 286), Carlsbad Caverns (2 nights, page 294), Albuquerque (2 nights), Petrified Forest (1 night, page 302)

Begins/Ends: Phoenix, AZ
Distance/Length: 1,400 mi/10 Days

Potential Pit-Stops: The map is covered with national monuments, memorials, and historic sites. In addition to these you'll find Wupatki NM (www.nps.gov/wupa), Sunset Crater Volcano NM (www.nps.gov/sucr), and Lava Rider Cave of the Coconino National Forest near Flagstaff. You'll also find Riverbend Hot Springs at Truth or Consequences, aliens in Roswell, and hot-air balloons in Albuquerque.

Trip Route

Panorama from Rambler Mine - Wrangell–St. Elias National Park

Exploring the Last Frontier

Parks Visited: Kenai Fjords (2 nights, page 610), Wrangell–St. Elias (3 nights, page 594), and Denali (4 nights, page 600)

Begins/Ends: Anchorage, AK
Estimated Driving Distance: 1,200 miles
Estimated Trip Length: 10 days

Potential Pit-Stops: Anchorage Museum (907.929.9200, www.anchoragemuseum.org); Alaska Native Heritage Center (800.315.6608, www.alaskanative.net); Horse Trekkin' Alaska (907.868.3728, www.horsetrekkinalaska.com) • Anchorage, AK; Bardy's Trail Rides (907.224.7863, www.sewardhorses.com) • Seward, AK

Notes: All park roads are seasonal. Kenai Fjords offers one road that leads to Exit Glacier, two hiking trails, a campground, and visitor center. Wrangell–St. Elias has two access roads, but most of the park is undeveloped wilderness with limited accessibility. Denali Park Road is only open to tour and shuttle buses (fee).

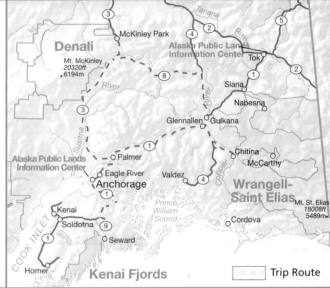

Cruising Canyon Country

Parks Visited: Grand Canyon (3 nights, page 416), Bryce Canyon (2 nights, page 396), Capitol Reef (1 night, page 388), and Zion (3 nights, page 404)

Begins/Ends: Las Vegas, NV
Estimated Driving Distance: 1,100 miles
Estimated Trip Length: 10 days

Potential Pit-Stops: Hoover Dam (702.494.2517); Lake Mead NRA (702.293.8906, www.nps.gov/lake) • Boulder City, NV; Route 66 Museum (928.753.9889, www.kingmantourism.org) • Kingman, AZ; Glen Canyon NRA (928.608.6200, www.nps.gov/glca) • Page, AZ; Coral Pink Sand Dunes State Park (435.648.2800, www.stateparks.utah.gov/parks/coral-pink) • Kanab, UT; Best Friends Animal Sanctuary (435.644.2001, www.bestfriends.org) • Kanab, UT; Vermillion Cliffs National Monument w/ The Wave and Buckskin Gulch (435.688.3200, www.blm.gov/az) • Kanab, UT; Grand Staircase Escalante-National Monument (435.644.4300, www.blm.gov/ut) • Kanab, UT; Cedar Breaks NM (435.586.9451, www.nps.gov/cebr) • Cedar City, UT; Frontier Homestead State Park Museum • Cedar City, UT

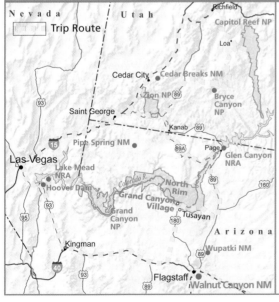

An anhinga - Everglades National Park

Badlands are Good Lands

Parks Visited: Wind Cave (2 nights, page 184), Badlands (2 nights, page 176), and Theodore Roosevelt (2 nights, page 192)

Begins/Ends: Rapid City, SD
Estimated Driving Distance: 850 miles
Estimated Trip Length: 1 week

Road Trip Breakdown

Rapid City to Wind Cave: 60 miles, ~1 hour via US-16, US-385, and SD-87
Wind Cave to Badlands: 125 miles, ~2.5 hours via Rapid City and I-90
Badlands to Theodore Roosevelt: 300 miles, ~5.5 hours via Rapid City, US-85, and I-94
Theodore Roosevelt to Rapid City: 240 miles, ~4 hours

Potential Pit-Stops: Mount Rushmore National Memorial (605.574.2523, www.nps.gov/moru) • Keystone, SD; Jewel Cave National Monument (www.nps.gov/jeca, 605.673.8300) • Custer, SD; The Mammoth Site (605.745.6017, www.mammothsite.com) • Hot Springs, SD; Motorcycle Hall of Fame (614.856.2222, www.motorcyclemuseum.org) • Sturgis, SD; Reptile Gardens (605.342.5873, www.reptilegardens.com) • Rapid City, SD; Storybook Island (605.342.6357, www.storybookisland.org) • Rapid City, SD; Circle B Chuckwagon (605.348.7358, www.circle-b-ranch.com) • Rapid City, SD; Cosmos Mystery Area (605.343.9802, www.cosmosmysteryarea.com) • Rapid City, SD; Museum of Geology (605.394.2467, www.museum.sdsmt.edu) • Rapid City, SD

The Scenic Side of South Florida

Parks Visited: Biscayne (1 night, page 118), Everglades (3 nights, page 126), and Dry Tortugas (2 nights, page 138)

Begins/Ends: Miami, FL
Estimated Driving Distance: 450 miles
Estimated Trip Length: 1 week

Potential Pit-Stops: John Pennekamp, Bahia Honda, Curry Hammock, and Long Key State Parks (850. 245.2157, www.floridastateparks.org) • Florida Keys, FL

Notes: Dry Tortugas can only be reached by boat or floatplane and the only overnight accommodations consist of 8 primitive campsites.

Using this Guide

View from above the clouds at Haleakalā Summit - Haleakalā National Park © Ted Bobosh

About the Guide

The United States has 58 national parks. Each one is uniquely beautiful, brimming with life, adventure, and fun. Activities and attractions differ from park to park and season to season, and the possibilities are nearly limitless. But most visitors only have a few days to explore these vast expanses of unspoiled wilderness. To make those few days count plan your trip wisely with the help of a guide who has tested the park's trails and learned its history.

Let this book be *Your Guide to the National Parks of the United States*. The 58 national parks are broken into seven regions: East, North, South, Southwest, West, Alaska, and Remote Islands (see below).

Within these sections the parks are included in geographical order (not alphabetical), allowing parks that are commonly visited on the same trip to be found adjacent to one another. Each park section includes an introduction, basic logistical information, maps, popular activities, the basics (accessibility, pets, and weather), and a brief vacation planner. You'll also find a collection of popular restaurants, grocery stores, lodging facilities, festivals, and attractions (including commercial outfitters) that are located nearby. All information has been researched and assembled with the greatest attention to detail so that the parks' most interesting facts and exciting activities are right here at your fingertips.

Introductions

"There is nothing more practical than the preservation of beauty, than the preservation of anything that appeals to the higher emotions of mankind."

– Theodore Roosevelt

President Theodore Roosevelt was a practical man who liked big things, so it comes as no surprise that he was one of the most influential individuals in the history of the national parks. Each introduction tells stories about men and women like President Roosevelt and events, both natural and historic, that helped shape the parks as we know them today.

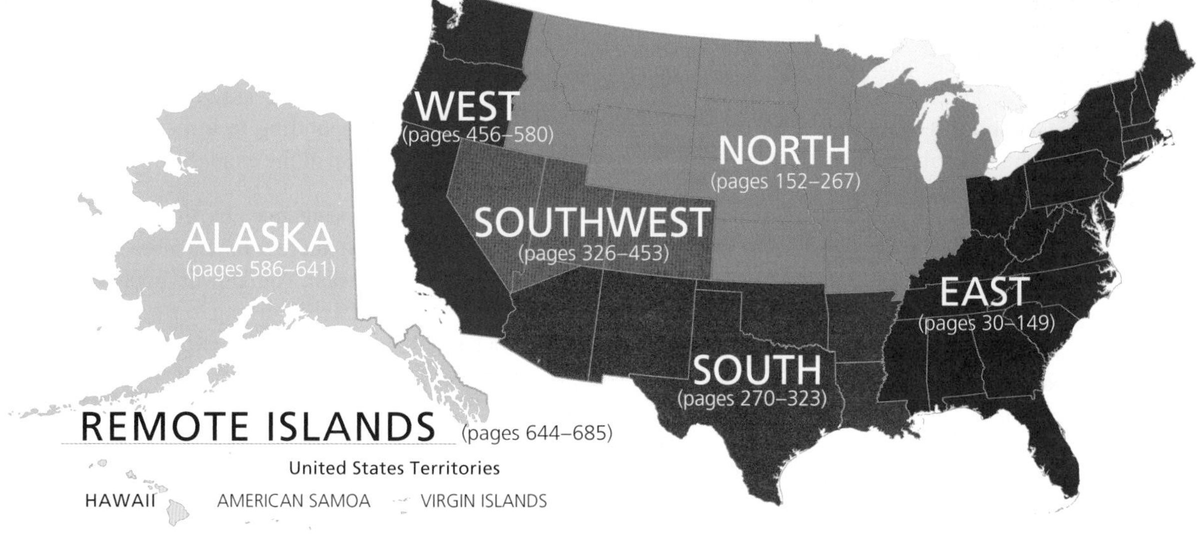

WEST
(pages 456–580)

NORTH
(pages 152–267)

ALASKA
(pages 586–641)

SOUTHWEST
(pages 326–453)

EAST
(pages 30–149)

SOUTH
(pages 270–323)

REMOTE ISLANDS (pages 644–685)

United States Territories

HAWAII   AMERICAN SAMOA   VIRGIN ISLANDS

Dream Lake - Rocky Mountain National Park

Logistics

Logistical data like contact information, accommodations, operating hours, and entrance fees are listed right up front alongside the introduction. Close by you'll find a "When to Go" section. It includes practical information about peak seasons and closures. Hours of operation for primary visitor facilities may also be detailed here. A "Transportation & Airports" section covers all pertinent information about how to reach and get around the park. Everything you need to know about park shuttles, airports, and Amtrak is found here. Driving directions are typically provided to the park's most popular entrance(s) and are often accompanied with a regional map displaying major highways and interstates. If a park has multiple units or popular developed regions you can expect to find a "Regions"

section describing each one. Names, locations, dates, and rates of campgrounds and lodges found within the park are usually listed in an easy to read table. Accommodations beyond park boundaries are discussed in the "What's Nearby" sections of this Guide.

Maps

Large legible maps are included to aid in planning your trip. Markers help pinpoint trailheads and popular attractions.

The maps in this book are not intended for hiking. You can purchase a high-quality topographical park map at most visitor centers. The maps used for the Suggested Trips (pages 18–22) and What's Nearby sections only show federal highways and interstates. Always use a road map or GPS when traveling.

Activities

The activity most often associated with a trip to one of the national parks is hiking. (Don't forget to pack your hiking boots.) This guide book chronicles hiking in great detail. Most park sections include a hiking table with essential trail information like trailhead location, distance, and difficulty. More often than not trailheads are assigned a number corresponding to a marker on the park map at the exact trailhead location.

Hiking may be the main attraction but there's much more to do at the parks. You can do everything from SCUBA diving to flightseeing, mule rides to train excursions, biking to snowmobiling. All the most popular activities are discussed in detail and outfitter information (including pricing) is included whenever applicable. These sections are concluded by a

Mountain climbers forging ahead - Denali National Park

quick discussion about the park's best adult- and child-oriented activities: The Ranger and Junior Ranger Programs.

Ranger Programs

Ranger Programs vary from park to park, but wherever your vacation takes you you can expect a variety of walks, talks, and evening programs to be offered, especially if you're traveling during peak tourism season. Park rangers are, literally, at home in the parks and they happen to be extremely gracious hosts. Take a tour with a ranger to get a taste of their enthusiasm, knowledge, and humor. To top it off, most of the programs are free. Ranger program schedules change from week to week and year to year. To get a current schedule of events check the park's website, free newspaper, or bulletin boards conveniently located at campgrounds, visitor centers, and sometimes along roadways.

For Families

In my opinion, the most underrated park activity is the Junior Ranger Program. It features activities prepared especially for school-aged children, but visitors of all ages are welcome to participate at most parks. Activity booklets are typically free. These hard copies allow families to complete the Junior Ranger activities on their own terms. Activities may direct children to places especially interesting to younger visitors, or to other ranger guided programs. After completing a specified number of activities for the child's age, participants return the booklet to a park ranger and he or she is awarded a patch, badge, and/or certificate unique to the park. While these activities are designed specifically for kids the entire family may discover the importance of the park and gain a more intimate connection with these special places.

The Basics

Following the activities you'll find a few more park basics, including a quick description of the region's flora and fauna. Information ranges from plants and animals you're likely to encounter to invasive, endangered, and reintroduced species found throughout the park.

The next animals discussed in the book are those that we bring with us, our pets. In general pets are not allowed on trails, in buildings, or in the

An Eastern Cottonmouth - Congaree National Park

backcountry. Bringing your pet with you will greatly limit what you can do during the course of your visit. If you still wish to bring your pet, it must be kept on a leash no more than six feet in length at all times.

You'll also find information regarding accessibility for individuals with disabilities. The parks are continually working to increase the accessibility of trails, attractions, and facilities, but many still fail to meet ADA guidelines. If you or someone you are traveling with has any special needs it is best to discuss them with a park employee at least a week before you arrive.

Climate and weather is discussed in the most general terms. A small graph of average temperatures and precipitation provides a quick glimpse of what you can expect weather-wise throughout the year. Weather is difficult to predict, so these averages only provide a

baseline for planning your trip. It's always best to pack for all reasonable weather possibilities. Whether you're departing on a 2-hour hike or a multi-day trek, make a habit of checking the local weather forecast before you depart.

Vacation Planner

The vacation planner supplies a rough itinerary for first time visitors, quickly hitting the park's most popular attractions in an efficient manner. With that said, you're doing a disservice to yourself and your family if you only allow a few hours for a national park excursion. The first and best advice you can receive when embarking on a national park vacation is to slow down, take your time, get out of your car and enjoy these magnificent landscapes. Don't be afraid to explore on your own. Venture away from the crowds, off the beaten path. If what they say about "misery loving company" is

true, then just maybe "happiness loves solitude." In my mind, there's no better place to find solitude than the National Parks, and it usually only takes a couple miles of hiking to find a little slice of it for yourself.

What's Nearby

For the most part, the national parks are situated far from major interstates and large metropolitan areas. Most visitors cover an awful lot of ground before arriving at their final destination, passing by dozens of interesting attractions along the way. This section details only the most exciting of these road-trip pit-stops (many are worth an extended stay) as well as a fairly comprehensive list of restaurants, grocery stores, lodging facilities, and festivals outside park boundaries.

Welcome to Your
National Parks

Acadia • Pages 30–51

© Jack Rigby

Cuyahoga Valley • Pages 52–63

Shenandoah • Pages 64–79

THE EAST

Mammoth Cave • Pages 80–91

THE EAST

Frenchman Bay, the Porcupine Islands, and Bar Harbor as seen from Cadillac Mountain © guillenperez 2009

PO Box 177
Bar Harbor, ME 04609
Phone: (207) 288-3338
Website: www.nps.gov/acad

Established: February 26, 1919
July 8, 1916 (National Monument)
Size: 47,390 Acres
Annual Visitors: 2.5 Million
Peak Season: July – August

Hiking Trails: 140 Miles
Carriage Trails: 45 Miles

Activities: Hiking, Biking, Rock
Climbing, Whale Watching, Fishing, Paddling, and Bird Watching

Campgrounds: Blackwoods and
Seawall on Mount Desert Island
($20/night), Duck Harbor on Isle au
Haut ($25/permit, 3-night max)
Backcountry Camping: Not Allowed

Park Hours: All day, every day
Entrance Fee: $20 (late June–early
October), $10 (May–late June,
October), Free (Winter)

Acadia - Maine

The coast of Maine and **Mount Desert Island (MDI)** has an allure, a gravity that inexplicably draws people away from their big city life and frantic lifestyles. Here time slows down; visitors are given the chance to enjoy the little things that often go unnoticed. Nature is heard. Waves cracking against granite cliffs. A bullfrog's guttural croak. The rat-a-tat-tat of a woodpecker. A choir of singing sparrows. While it can feel like your first time truly experiencing nature, today's tourists are far from the first to enjoy the beauty of Maine's Atlantic Coast. The deep blue lakes, bald granite mountaintops, and surf splashed cliffs of Acadia National Park have been treasured for more than a century.

About 25,000 years ago MDI wasn't even an island. It was continental mainland, occupied by a massive sheet of ice. The ice receded, but not without leaving a number of visible marks. Somes Sound, the only fjord along the U.S. Atlantic Coast, was carved by slow moving glacial ice, then submerged when it melted. **Bubble Rock**, a 14-ton glacial erratic, was carried 19 miles from its original resting place to be deposited precariously at the top of **South Bubble**. As the ice melted, water poured down the slopes of the recently shaved mountaintops; lakebeds were filled, the seas rose, and as the coast drowned in melt water an island was formed.

Long after glaciers covered the coast, the **Abenaki** people used the island as their seasonal home. A home they called "Pemetic" or "the sloping land." Food was abundant. Fishing and hunting were relatively simple. Shellfish, plants, and berries were easily gathered. For the Abenaki people, life was good along the coast of Maine. It also was an appropriate home for the Abenaki or "People of the Dawn": **Cadillac Mountain** on MDI, the tallest peak along the U.S. Atlantic Coast, is the first place in the continental U.S. to experience dawn.

In 1604, **Samuel de Champlain** spotted the barren peak of **Cadillac Mountain** from his ship. Not noticing the forested hills around it, he declared the island "l'Isle des Monts Déserts" or "the island of the bare mountains." The island may as well have been barren for the next 150 years as nations quarreled over the region. It passed hands several times between Natives, French, English, and Americans, but was never permanently occupied and seldom visited.

Thomas Cole and **Frederic Church**, painters from the Hudson River School, helped rediscover MDI in the mid-19th century. Their work of the region helped bring the island into the public eye. At first, artists, professors, and other intellectuals known as "rusticators" made the multi-day journey here. These travellers required little in terms of accommodations as they hiked from place to place enjoying the area's simple lifestyle and sublime beauty.

Not long after the rusticators exposed MDI's beauty, developers were clamoring to increase access to the island. Direct steamboat service from Boston was offered in the 1860s. A rail line was completed in the 1880s. By this time MDI was the place to be for the East Coast's elite. Some of the wealthiest visitors, known locally as "cottagers," purchased large tracts of land where they built lavish summer homes they ironically referred to as "cottages." A stretch of mansions near Bar Harbor commonly called "**Millionaires' Row**" burned to the ground during the great fire of 1947. The inferno razed more than 17,000 acres, including 10,000 acres of park land, before blowing into the Atlantic.

Still, development was MDI's main threat, not nature. Residents felt that its scenic beauty needed to be protected. **John D. Rockefeller, Jr.** and **George B. Dorr**, both "cottagers" turned conservationists, were two of the park's greatest advocates. Rockefeller built 57 miles of carriage roads, donated thousands of acres of land, and spent $3.5 million on the potential park. Dorr blazed trails, donated land, and became the park's first superintendent. Acadia National Park was eventually created, cobbled together entirely from private donations. It successfully protected some of the area's most rugged shorelines and beautiful landscapes for the enjoyment of the people.

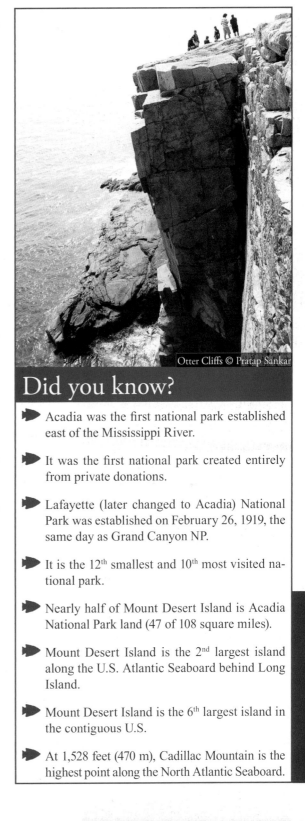

Otter Cliffs © Pratap Sankar

Did you know?

- Acadia was the first national park established east of the Mississippi River.

- It was the first national park created entirely from private donations.

- Lafayette (later changed to Acadia) National Park was established on February 26, 1919, the same day as Grand Canyon NP.

- It is the 12th smallest and 10th most visited national park.

- Nearly half of Mount Desert Island is Acadia National Park land (47 of 108 square miles).

- Mount Desert Island is the 2nd largest island along the U.S. Atlantic Seaboard behind Long Island.

- Mount Desert Island is the 6th largest island in the contiguous U.S.

- At 1,528 feet (470 m), Cadillac Mountain is the highest point along the North Atlantic Seaboard.

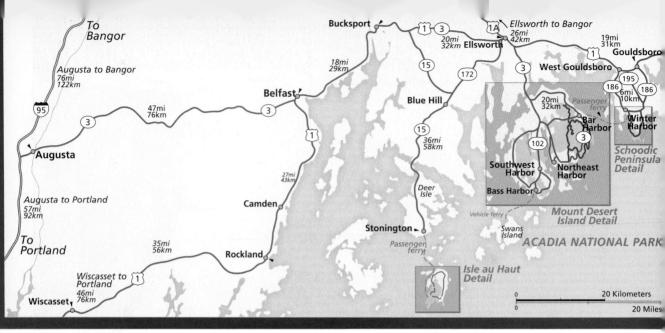

When to Go

Acadia is open all year. The park experiences heavy traffic during July and August. Fall foliage attracts large crowds from September to early October. **Hulls Cove Visitor Center** is closed from November through mid-April. Most of Park Loop Road is closed from December through mid-April.

Blackwoods Campground is open all year. The campground entrance road is closed from December through March; at this time campers must hike in from the entrance on Route 3.

Transportation & Airports

Help reduce traffic congestion, parking, and air pollution by riding the free **Island Explorer Shuttle**. The shuttle runs from late June through early October. Seven regularly scheduled routes link hotels, inns, campgrounds, and Bar Harbor Airport with popular park destinations (but not **Cadillac Mountain**). Maps and timetables are available at the visitor center and on the **Island Explorer** website (www.exploreacadia.com).

Bar Harbor Airport (BHB) is 10 miles from **Hulls Cove Visitor Center**. Bangor International (BGR) is 49 miles away. Portland International (PWM) is about 3 hours away. Logan International (BOS) in Boston is 5–6 hours away.

Regions of Acadia

Acadia National Park is made up of three distinct regions: Mount Desert Island (MDI), Schoodic Peninsula, and Isle au Haut. MDI is the park's centerpiece, where most attractions, lodging, and restaurants are found. The island is broken into eastern (extremely busy) and western (quiet) halves by Somes Sound. Schoodic Peninsula is the only section of the park on the mainland. It's located just east of MDI, across Frenchman Bay. You'll find views similar to those at MDI, but with much smaller crowds. Both MDI and Schoodic Peninsula are accessible by car and have scenic park loop roadways for motorists. Seven smaller islands, including Isle au Haut, are also preserved by the park. None of the smaller islands are accessible by car.

Directions

To arrive at Mount Desert Island from the south take I-95 north to Augusta, Maine, then Route 3 east through Ellsworth and on to Mount Desert Island.

To arrive at Schoodic Peninsula from Ellsworth take Route 3 south and turn left onto US Hwy 1. Continue east to West Gouldsboro. Go south on Route 186 to Winter Harbor, then follow signs to the park entrance.

Isle au Haut is inaccessible to automobiles. People may access the island by the **Mail Boat** from Stonington. To arrive at Stonington from Ellsworth take Route 172 south to Route 15 and on to Stonington.

ACADIA

Schoodic Peninsula

About one in ten visitors of Acadia National Park make the trip to Schoodic Peninsula. Here you'll find a much more secluded and intimate experience than the park's more popular areas. But fewer visitors mean fewer facilities. There are only two restrooms and one picnic area. Camping is not permitted on the peninsula's park land, but you can find private camping and other lodging options nearby. In summer, **Downeast Windjammer Cruises** (207.288.2984, www.downeast-twindjammer.com) operates a passenger ferry that makes the one hour trip between Bar Harbor and Winter Harbor. **Island Explorer Shuttle** provides transportation to and from the ferry terminals. Should you choose to travel by car, it's a 45 mile drive around Frenchman Bay from Bar Harbor. Once you've arrived at the peninsula, a six-mile, one-way loop road offers stunning views of the dramatic Maine coastline. A narrow gravel road weaves its way up to the highest point on the peninsula, Schoodic Head.

Isle au Haut

Named by **Samuel de Champlain** in 1604, Isle au Haut or "High Island" is a rugged and relatively remote island five miles south of Stonington, Maine. Today, a few thousand day-trippers and some 500 campers travel aboard the **Mail Boat** (207.367.5193, www.isleauhaut.com) from Stonington each year. About half the island is park land; the rest is owned and occupied by summer residents and a year-round fishing community. Over the years the relationship between residents and visitors has become contentious and a visitor capacity limit has been adopted. Isle au Haut visitors should exit the **Mail Boat** at Duck Harbor Landing, stay within park boundaries, and camp at one of the five designated sites (each with its own lean-to). Camping costs $25/site with a 3 night maximum stay.

Schoodic Peninsula

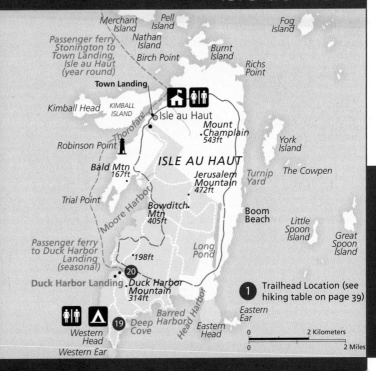

Isle au Haut

Mount Desert Island (MDI)

To many visitors, Mount Desert Island and Acadia National Park are synonymous. Almost two thirds of the park is on MDI and it is the only destination of most of the 2.5 million people who flock to Acadia each year. About half of the island is protected under park ownership. The boundary raggedly weaves its way around private property and the Atlantic seashore. The park and island are nearly split in half by a natural, glacially-carved barrier, Somes Sound. It is the only fjord on the U.S. Atlantic Coast.

Within park boundaries lies an enchanting place where granite cliffs and angry seas, mountaintops and clear blue skies, people and wildlife come together. Eight mountains exceed 1,000 feet. Diminutive in stature compared to their western counterparts, they still find a way to take your breath away. Hiking from sea level to summit is enough to leave even the avid hiker gasping for air. And if that fails to do the trick, the panoramic views afforded from these barren mountaintops definitely will. Should you only go to one mountaintop, make it the **Cadillac**. Its summit can be reached by car, bike, or foot. Many visitors drive to the summit before the sun rises in order to bask in the first rays of sun as they rise up over the Atlantic Ocean. Don't worry if you aren't a morning person; the views overlooking Bar Harbor, Frenchman Bay, and the Porcupine Islands are spectacular rain or shine, sun or fog, morning until evening. On a clear day you can see **Mount Katahdin**, Maine's tallest mountain, which stands some 100 miles away. Thrill-seekers unafraid of heights and searching for adventure should scale **Champlain Mountain** via **Precipice Trail**. Steel rungs, ladders, and railings aid hikers along the harrowing journey. The Trail is closed during winter, and it closes once more from late spring until early summer when peregrine falcons nest on the precipitous mountain's face.

Twenty-six freshwater lakes and ponds are found on MDI, providing a wide variety of activities. You can swim in the Atlantic at **Sand Beach** or the much warmer, fresher water of **Echo Lake**. **Long Pond** is a great place for a quiet paddle. **Jordan Pond** offers stunning views of the **Bubble Mountains** (South and North Bubble). View the bubbles from **Jordan Pond House** while enjoying one of their famous pastries, a popover.

A trip to Acadia is not complete without touring the 27-mile **Park Loop Road**, but if you'd like to escape the hum of automobiles go out and explore the carriage roads. These crushed stone paths are enjoyed by bikers, hikers, and horse riders. Be sure to pick up a map at **Hulls Cove Visitor Center**, just north of Bar Harbor on Route 3, before heading out on the carriage roads.

You'll find the majority of park facilities on MDI, but you won't find any lodging within park boundaries. Bar Harbor, the island's largest city, is the most popular destination for dining, lodging, and shopping. Additional accommodations are available in Northeast Harbor and Southwest Harbor. For a list of the area's popular dining and lodging facilities, please refer to pages 48–49.

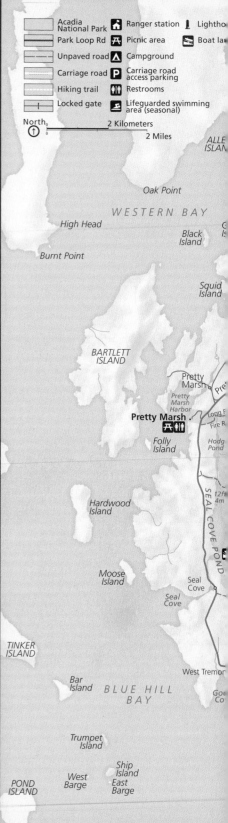

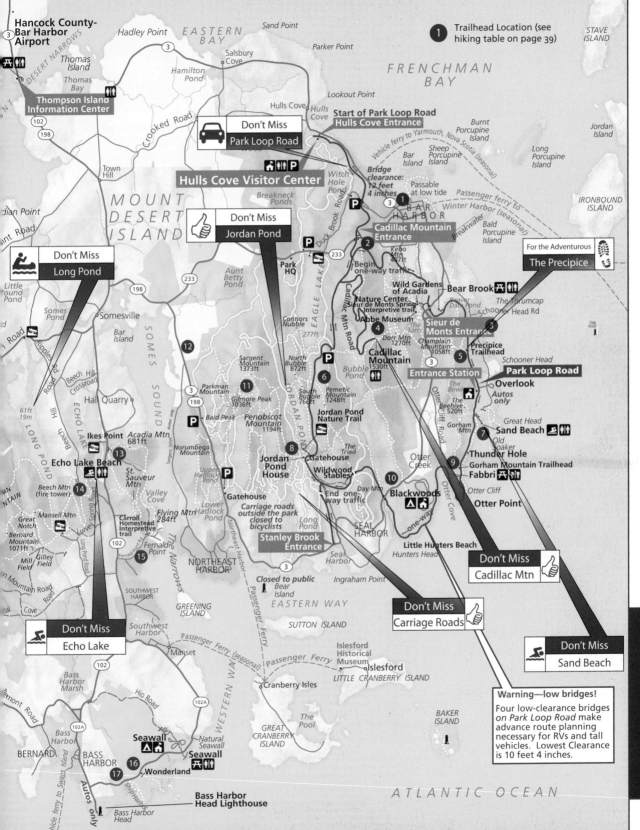

Hancock County-
Bar Harbor
Airport

EASTERN
BAY

Sand Point

Parker Point

FRENCHMAN
BAY

STAVE
ISLAND

1 Trailhead Location (see hiking table on page 39)

Hadley Point

Thomas
Island

Thomas
Bay

Salsbury
Cove

Hamilton
Pond

Lookout Point

Burnt
Porcupine
Island

Jordan
Island

Thompson Island
Information Center

Hulls Cove

Hulls
Cove

Start of Park Loop Road
Hulls Cove Entrance

Vehicle ferry to Yarmouth, Nova Scotia (seasonal)

Bar
Island

Sheep
Porcupine
Island

Long
Porcupine
Island

Crooked Road

Town
Hill

Don't Miss
Park Loop Road

Witch
Hole
Pond

Bridge
clearance:
12 feet
4 inches

Passable
at low tide

Passenger ferry to
Winter Harbor (seasonal)

IRONBOUND
ISLAND

MOUNT
DESERT
ISLAND

Breakneck
Ponds

Hulls Cove Visitor Center

BAR
HARBOR

Bald
Porcupine
Island

Breakwater

For the Adventurous
The Precipice

Don't Miss
Jordan Pond

Cadillac Mountain
Entrance

Kebo
Mtn
407ft

Don't Miss
Long Pond

Aunt
Betty
Pond

Park
HQ

Begin
one-way traffic

Wild Gardens
of Acadia

Bear Brook

The Thrumcap

Nature Center
Sieur de Monts Spring
Interpretive trail

Dorr Mtn
1270ft

Sieur de
Monts Entrance

**Precipice
Trailhead**

Egg
Rock

Somesville

Connors
Nubble

Abbe Museum

Champlain
Mountain
1058ft

Somes
Pond

Bar
Island

277ft

Cadillac
Mountain

Schooner Head Rd

Schooner Head

Bass
Harbor

Sargent
Mountain
1373ft

North
Bubble
872ft

1530ft

Entrance Station

Park Loop Road

Overlook

Autos
only

SOMES

Parkman
Mountain

Gilmore Peak
1036ft

South
Bubble
766ft

Pemetic
Mountain
1248ft

Bubble
Pond

The
Bowl

The
Beehive
520ft

Great Head

Beech Hill
Crossroad

Hall Quarry

Bald Peak

Penobscot
Mountain
1194ft

Jordan Pond
Nature Trail

Gorham
Mtn

Sand Beach

Echo Lake Beach

Acadia Mtn
681ft

Ikes Point

Norumbega
Mountain

The
Triad

Gatehouse

Wildwood
Stables

Otter
Creek

Thunder Hole

Gorham Mountain Trailhead

Fabbri

Beech Mtn
(fire tower)

Jordan
Pond
House

Day Mtn

Blackwoods

Otter Cliff

Otter Point

Great
Notch

St.
Sauveur
Mtn

Valley
Cove

Upper
Hadlock
Pond

Gatehouse

End one-
way traffic

Bernard
Mountain
1071ft

Flying Mtn
284ft

Carriage roads
outside the park
closed to
bicyclists

Long
Pond

SEAL
HARBOR

Little Hunters Beach

Don't Miss
Cadillac Mtn

Mill
Field

Gilley
Field

Carroll
Homestead
Interpretive
trail

Fernald
Point

Lower
Hadlock
Pond

**Stanley Brook
Entrance**

Seal
Harbor

Hunters Head

NORTHEAST
HARBOR

SOUTHWEST
HARBOR

Closed to public

Bear
Island

Ingraham Point

EASTERN WAY

Don't Miss
Carriage Roads

Don't Miss
Echo Lake

Southwest
Harbor

GREENING
ISLAND

SUTTON ISLAND

Manset

Don't Miss
Sand Beach

Bass
Harbor
Marsh

Passenger Ferry (seasonal)

Passenger Ferry

Islesford
Historical
Museum

Islesford

LITTLE CRANBERRY ISLAND

Warning—low bridges!
Four low-clearance bridges
on Park Loop Road make
advance route planning
necessary for RVs and tall
vehicles. Lowest Clearance
is 10 feet 4 inches.

BERNARD

BASS
HARBOR

Seawall

Seawall

Wonderland

Cranberry Isles

GREAT
CRANBERRY
ISLAND

The
Pool

BAKER
ISLAND

ACADIA

Hio Road

Bass Harbor
Head Lighthouse

Bass
Harbor
Head

Autos
only

ATLANTIC OCEAN

Acadia Camping

	Open	Fees	Sites	Notes
Blackwoods (located on Route 3, 5 miles south of Bar Harbor)*	May–October	$20/night	306	No hook-ups Showers 0.5-mile away 35-ft max RV Reservations suggested from May–October
	April & November	$10/night	6 people, 2 tents, 1 car limit per site	
	December–March	Free		
Seawall (located on Route 102A, 4 miles south of Southwest Harbor)*	late May–early Sept	$20/night for drive-in	218	No hook-ups Showers 0.5-mile away 35-ft max RV Half the sites are sold on a first-come, first-served basis
		$14/night for walk-in	6 people, 2 tents, 1 car limit per site	
Duck Harbor (located on Isle au Haut, accessible by mail boat from Stonington, ME)**	mid-May–mid-October	$25/site with a maximum stay of 3 nights	5 Each site has a lean-to shelter 6 people/site	Primitive Camping Reservation required
Backcountry Camping	Backcountry camping is prohibited at Acadia National Park			
*Reservations can be made up to six months in advance by calling 877-444-6777 or clicking www.recreation.gov				
**Reservation requests can be made after April 1. Call (207) 288-3338 for a reservation form or visit www.nps.gov/acad/planyourvisit/upload/iahreserve.pdf				

Acadia Lodging

None Available in Park	See pages 48–49 for accommodations outside the park

The Acadia Coastline

Hiking

Acadia National Park has some of the best maintained trails of all the national parks. It's a true day hiker's paradise with more than 140 miles of short, one-way trails. In fact, all of the trails are intended to be day-hikes as backcountry camping is not permitted within park boundaries.

In 1999, **Friends of Acadia** and the park committed $13 million for trail restoration. That same year Acadia became the first national park whose trails are maintained by a private endowment, **Acadia Trails Forever**. Their work allows visitors to enjoy the great outdoors without having to worry about getting lost. Trails—many of which were trod by Native Americans or the park's first superintendent, **George Dorr**—are well marked with cairns (small, pyramid-like rock piles) and blue blazes painted onto trees and rocks.

At least 6,000 years ago—long before cairns were carefully built atop the barren mountaintops and blue blazes were painted on tree trunks—Native Americans forged their own trails across MDI in search of coastal waters where they found nourishment through fishing and gathering shellfish. All that remains of their existence are huge piles of shells and a vast network of well-worn trails. Rumors of a fantastical city of gold drew European sailors to Maine in the mid-1500s. Rusticators arrived in the mid-to-late 1800s to explore the island on foot, taking delight in its earthly wonders. At the turn of the century, the same trails trod by Native Americans, gold-seekers, and rusticators were blazed once more by George B. Dorr, a summer resident and member of the Hancock County Trustees of Public Reservations who worked tirelessly to protect the natural beauty of the area. He set on these paths and many of his own with a newfound purpose: the pursuit of land and monetary donations from wealthy island residents. Today, Dorr is affectionately referred to as the "Father of Acadia National Park." Thanks to the efforts of Dorr and many others, these trails are now yours to explore.

While you won't find commemoration to Dorr anywhere along his favorite hiking trails, he is remembered by a mountaintop; **Dorr Mountain** is the third tallest peak in the park. Four trails lead to its summit, including the short and steep **Ladder Trail**. The ascent is aided by three sets of steel ladders and numerous granite steps that were carved and placed in 1893 and restored by the **Civilian Conservation Corps (CCC)** in the 1930s. The trailhead is found at **Sieur de Monts Spring** directly behind the Spring House. To complete the 3.3-mile journey to Dorr Mountain summit take Ladder Trail

Marker at the summit of Dorr Mountain © Justin D. Henry

Did you know?

➤ George Dorr was the first Superintendent of Acadia National Park, a position he held for 25 years at an initial salary of $1.00/month.

➤ George Dorr built the Spring House at **Sieur de Monts** in 1909 and carved "The Sweet Waters of Acadia" on a nearby rock.

➤ Beavers were once exterminated on the island due to excessive trapping. Dorr helped reintroduce them in 1920.

➤ Upon Dorr's death his ashes were scattered from a plane above a part of the island he especially loved.

➤ Acadia has more than 104 miles of hiking trails on MDI, 18 miles on Isle au Haut, and 3 miles on the Schoodic Peninsula.

➤ Native Americans were living on Mount Desert Island at least 6,000 years ago.

View of Frenchman Bay from Precipice Trail

Best of Acadia

Adventure Hike: **Precipice**
Runner-up: Beehive
2nd Runner-up: Penobscot Mountain

Mountain Hike: **Acadia Mountain**
Runner-up: Cadillac South Ridge
2nd Runner-up: Beech Mountain

Coastal Hike: **Great Head**
Runner-up: Schoodic Head
2nd Runner-up: Ocean Path

Family Hike: **Ship Harbor**
Runner-up: Bubble Rock
2nd Runner-up: Bar Island

Did you know?

➤ In 1947 a fire burned nearly half of Mount Desert Island (17,000 acres).

➤ The fire helped diversify plant and animal life on the island. Deciduous trees now grow on land that was once dominated by red spruce.

to Schiff Path (East Face Dorr Trail) and return via South Ridge Dorr Trail and Canon Brook Trail.

There are five more ladder trails in Acadia. Of these, **Precipice Trail** is the most notorious. The trailhead is 7.3 miles from Hulls Cove Visitor Center on Park Loop Road. It quickly climbs the steep east face of Champlain Mountain. It's recommended that you ascend 0.9 mile along Precipice Trail and return via Champlain Mountain North Ridge Trail and Orange & Black Path, making a 2.5-mile loop. The trail may close from mid-March to mid-August in order to protect nesting peregrine falcons. During this time you'll often find a park ranger with a telescope conducting Peregrine Watch (page 43) in the Precipice Trail Parking Area. Continuing along Park Loop Road you will arrive at another popular ladder trail, the **Beehive**. It begins across the road from Sand Beach Parking Area. Follow Beehive Trail 0.8 miles to its summit, then follow Bowl Trail back to Park Loop Road completing a 1.6-mile loop. **Jordan Cliff Trailhead** is found behind Jordan Pond Gift Shop at Carriage Road junction #15. This hike begins with excellent views of Jordan Pond as you start the 2.2-mile (one-way) ascent to the top of Penobscot Mountain. Take in the 360° panoramic views at the summit before heading back down **Penobscot Mountain Trail**, which loops back to Jordan Pond Gift Shop. The 2.2-mile **Perpendicular Trail** (Mansell Mountain) begins at the south end of Long Pond near Southwest Harbor. The sixth and final ladder trail, 0.5-mile **Beech Cliff Trail**, begins behind the ranger house at Echo Lake Parking Area. Be aware that these are some of the most challenging trails in the park and should not be attempted by small children, anyone afraid of heights, and pets.

Acadia has plenty of trails that appeal to families and people of all ages. **Bar Island** can be reached at low tide by crossing a sand bar right from downtown Bar Harbor. Have your kids try to push a 14-ton boulder over a cliff at the steep but short, 1.0-mile **Bubble Rock Trail**. During a storm or rising tide you may want to head down **Ocean Path** to listen to the waves explode at **Thunder Hole**. (See the hiking table on page 39 for the location and difficulty of these and many other Acadian hiking trails.) Another great destination for casual hiking is the 45 miles of **carriage roads** (page 40), which are concentrated around the Jordan Pond Area but extend as far north as Hulls Cove Visitor Center and south to Route 3 near the Stanley Brook Entrance.

The dense network of short trails and the Island Explorer Shuttle allow Acadia's hikers to be creative with their itineraries. It's easy to avoid out-and-back hikes by combining several trails and utilizing the park shuttle (page 32), which stops at many of the park trailheads.

Acadia Hiking Trails

	Trail Name	Trailhead (# on map)	Length	Notes (Roundtrip distances unless noted otherwise)
Easy	Bar Island - 👍	Bar Harbor located at the end of Bridge Street (1)	~1.4 miles	A sandbar to Bar Island appears at low tide, be sure to check the tide tables
	Great Meadow	Bar Harbor located off Cromwell Harbor Road (1)	2.0 miles	A loop trail across private land that connects Bar Harbor to Acadia
	Summit Path	Cadillac Mtn Summit Parking Lot (4)	0.4 mile	A paved path around the summit
	Ocean Path - 👍	Sand Beach Upper parking lot (7)	4.4 miles	Passes Thunder Hole and Otter Cliffs
	Wonderland	Seawall Campground, off Route 102A, 0.9 miles from Seawall (16)	1.4 miles	Rocky shoreline, cobble beach, and spruce forests
Moderate	Great Head	East end of Sand Beach (7)	1.5 miles	Loop trail with sea cliff and beach views
	Cadillac North Ridge	Park Loop Road, 3.2 miles from the start of Park Loop Road (2)	4.4 miles	Views of Bar Harbor • Shorter and steeper than South Ridge Trail
	Tarn Trail	Sieur de Monts Spring, Tarn Parking Lot off Route 3 (3)	2.4 miles	Hike through woods along Otter Creek and by beaver ponds
	Bubble Rock - 👍	Bubble Rock Parking Lot, off Park Loop Road (6)	1.0 mile	Steep but short hike up South Bubble to a peculiarly placed glacial erratic (big rock)
	Jordan Pond - 👍	Jordan Pond Boat Ramp (8)	3.2 miles	Loop along the edge of Jordan Pond
	Gorham Mtn	Gorham Mtn Parking Area, 1 mile past Sand Beach on Park Loop Road (9)	1.8 miles	Wide open views of the ocean • Connects to The Bowl, Beehive, and Cadillac Cliffs
	Beech Mtn - 👍	Beech Mtn Parking Lot, off Beech Mountain Road (14)	1.1 miles	Alternate from end of Long Pond Rd, Ascend West Ridge Tr and return via Valley Tr (~3 miles)
	Flying Mtn	Fernald Cove Parking Area, Fernald Point Rd (15)	1.2 miles	Explore tide pools at Valley Cove
	Ship Harbor	Off Rte 102A, 2 miles from Seawall (17)	1.2 miles	A good spot for blueberries and birds
	Schoodic Head - 👍	Schoodic Peninsula, Blueberry Hill Parking Lot (18)	2.5 miles	Combine Alder, Schoodic Head and Anvil Trails for a loop to Schoodic Head
	Goat Trail	Isle au Haut, via Western Head Road and Duck Harbor Mountain trail (19)	2.1 miles (one-way)	Rugged and rocky hike with spectacular coastal vistas
Strenuous	Precipice - 👍	1.75 miles beyond Sieur de Monts Spring entrance on Park Loop Road (5)	1.8 miles	Iron rungs and ladders • Can make a 2.5 mile loop by combining (in order) Precipice, Champlain North Ridge, and Orange & Black Trails • Not for children or those afraid of heights
	Beehive - 👍	Sand Beach Area, across Park Loop Road from Sand Beach parking lot (7)	1.6 miles	Iron rungs and ladders • Not for children or those afraid of heights
	Penobscot Mountain	Behind Jordan Pond Gift Shop (8)	~3.7 miles	Ascend Jordan Cliff (ladder) Trail or Jordan Pond/Deer Brook Trails and descend Penobscot Mtn Trail
	Cadillac South Ridge	Route 3 about 100 feet south of Blackwoods Campground (10)	7.0 miles	Hike to Cadillac from Blackwoods Campground on one of the park's longer trails
	Grandgent	Trailhead at Sargent Mtn Summit (11)	1.0 mile	Leads to Sargent Mtn's summit
	Giant Slide	1.1 mile from the junction of Route 198 and 233 (12)	2.8 miles	Fairly challenging trail along Sargent Brook to the summit of Sargent Mtn
	Acadia Mtn - 👍	Acadia Mountain Parking Lot, west side of Route 102 (13)	2.5 miles	Best views of Somes Sound in the park, return via fire road
	Duck Harbor Mountain	Isle au Haut, accessible from Western Head Road (20)	2.4 miles	Panoramic views of Isle au Haut • Most strenuous hike on the isle

ACADIA

Fall leaves on a Carriage Road © Liza Daly

Carriage Roads

Acadia National Park's 45 miles of carriage roads provide a great place to get away from the hum of the internal combustion engine. These crushed stone paths offer an extremely unique and scenic venue for visitors to hike, bike, ride horses, or take a carriage ride courtesy of **Carriages of Acadia (Wildwoods Stables)**.

Carriages of Acadia • (877) 276-3622
Park Loop Road, half mile south of Jordan Pond
Open: mid-June–early October
Rates: $18–24.50 (see website for more details)
www.carriagesofacadia.com

Did you know?

➤ To keep some of the islands most beautiful land from being overrun by motorists **John D. Rockefeller, Jr.** oversaw and commissioned the construction of carriage roads on Mount Desert Island.

➤ Rockefeller built 57 miles of carriage roads and spent more than $3.5 million developing MDI before donating thousands of acres to the park for everyone to enjoy.

Biking

Eastern MDI's **carriage roads** are your best bet for a relaxing bike ride at Acadia National Park. The 45-mile network of broken-stone roads extends all the way from Hulls Cove Visitor Center to Seal Harbor and includes 17 carefully crafted stone-faced bridges. Some of the most scenic stretches skirt **Jordan Pond** and **Eagle Lake**. The 8-mile roundtrip ride to **Day Mountain** is one of the circuits you can begin from **Jordan Pond Gatehouse** and is the only summit that can be reached via carriage path. No matter where you go be sure to carry a map of the carriage roads (available at Hulls Cove Visitor Center or the park's website), because you'll encounter several junctions even on the shortest of rides. Also note that the 12 miles of carriage roads south of Jordan Pond are on private property and off-limits to cyclists. However, horses and walkers are allowed to wander along these roadways.

The quieter western side of Mount Desert Island has two gravel roads for biking. **Seal Cove Road** (4 miles) connects Southwest Harbor and Seal Cove. **Hio Road** (2.5 miles) connects Seawall Campground with Highway 102 at Bass Harbor Marsh.

The 27-mile **Park Loop Road** offers scenic and hilly terrain for road cyclists. If you feel like challenging yourself, take the 3.5 mile **Mountain Loop Road** to the summit of **Cadillac Mountain**. It's seriously tough pedalling going up, but the return trip downhill is a breeze (make sure your brakes work well). Due to Park Loop Road's steep grades, tight turns, and abundance of tourist traffic during the summer months, it's best to pedal here in the off-season. For less congested biking try the loop around Schoodic Peninsula's scenic coastline or Route 102/102A on the western side of MDI.

Biking at Isle au Haut is not encouraged. You are not allowed to bike on any hiking trails and there is no single-track within the park.

Bike rental is available at:

Bar Harbor Bicycle • (207) 288-3998 • www.barharborbike.com
141 Cottage Street; Bar Harbor, ME 04609 • Open: March–December

Acadia Bike & Canoe • (207) 288-5000 • www.acadiabike.com
48 Cottage Street; Bar Harbor, ME 04609 • Open: All Year

Southwest Cycle • (207) 244-5856 • www.southwestcycle.com
370 Main Street; Southwest Harbor, ME 04679 • Open: April–January

ACADIA

A couple paddle their canoe at Jordan Pond © guillenperez 2009

Paddling

Acadia National Park has paddling in spades for people of all experience levels. Inexperienced paddlers are sure to enjoy the glacially-carved lakes and ponds or perhaps a guided tour with a local outfitter (see right). **Eagle Lake**, **Long Pond**, **Jordan Pond**, and **Echo Lake** are a few of the most popular freshwater paddle-spots, with at least one boat launch available at each.

More experienced paddlers can take to the open waters of the Atlantic Ocean where you are free to explore Acadia's islands, inlets, and coves. You can also avoid a ride aboard the **Mail Boat** (207.367.5193, www.isleauhaut.com) to Isle au Haut by paddling the five miles of water separating it from Stonington, ME.

Paddling allows visitors to see the park from a different perspective and gain a new appreciation for this scenic land. It's also an excellent way to view the park's wildlife. Enjoy the tranquility of these majestic waters but remember to use caution, especially when paddling alone. Cold water, swift currents, erratic weather, and dense fog can make paddling at Acadia challenging. Check the weather and tide tables before heading out on the water. If you plan on exploring any of Acadia's remote smaller islands be sure to discuss your itinerary with a local park ranger because birds may be nesting on the shorelines.

National Park Canoe & Kayak Rental • (207) 244-5854
Pretty Marsh Road, Rte 102; Mount Desert, ME 04660
Open: May–October
www.nationalparkcanoerental.com

Maine State Kayak • (877) 481-9500
254 Main Street; Southwest Harbor, ME 04679
Open: May–September
www.mainestatekayak.com

National Park Sea Kayak Tours • (800) 347-0940
39 Cottage Street; Bar Harbor, ME 04609
Open: Memorial Day–October
www.acadiakayak.com

Acadia Outfitters • (207) 288-8118
106 Cottage Street; Bar Harbor, ME 04609
Open: May–October
www.acadiaoutfitters.com

Aquaterra Adventures (no rentals) • (877) 386-4124
1 West Street; Bar Harbor, ME 04609
Open: May–September
www.aquaterra-adventures.com

Coastal Kayaking Tours • (800) 526-8615
48 Cottage Street; Bar Harbor, ME 04609
Open: All Year
www.acadiafun.com

ACADIA

Rock Climbing at Otter Cliffs © Nadya Peek

 # Swimming

On hot summer days many of Acadia's guests migrate to the beaches. **Sand Beach** and **Echo Lake Beach** are staffed with a lifeguard during the summer. The 55°F water found at Sand Beach might be refreshing to some, but it's downright frigid to others. The freshwater of **Echo Lake** is considerably warmer, especially near the end of summer. For more secluded swimming head to the park's western side where you can paddle yourself to swimming holes in **Seal Cove**, **Round**, and **Hodgdon Ponds**. **Lake Wood**, on the north end of the island, has a small beach with automobile access.

Swimming is prohibited at all lakes used for drinking water. These include Upper and Lower Hadlock Ponds, Bubble and Jordan Ponds, Eagle Lake, and the southern half of Long Pond.

Fishing

To fish any of the freshwater lakes in Acadia you'll need a freshwater fishing license. Maine residents 16 and older and non-residents 12 and older require a license. Licenses are available at Walmart in Ellsworth and Paradis True Value in Bar Harbor. Freshwater fishing season is generally from April until September. Trout, salmon, perch, and bass are commonly caught in freshwater lakes and ponds.

A license is not required for salt water fishing. **Sargent Drive** (Somes Sound) and **Frazer Point** (Schoodic Peninsula) are two salt water fishing areas within the park. Mackerel typically run from mid-July to September at these locations.

Be sure to respect private property and follow all boating and fishing regulations.

Rock Climbing

Acadia's mountains may not be big, but they are precipitous. The sheer granite walls offer some of the most unique rock climbing opportunities in the United States. **Otter Cliffs** is the most famous and popular climbing spot. The **South Wall of Champlain Mountain**, **Central Slabs**, **South Bubble**, and **Great Head** are also great climbing areas. Climbers at **Otter Cliffs**, **Canada Cliffs**, and **South Wall** should sign in at **daily use logs**, which are available at the climbing areas, park headquarters, visitor center, and campgrounds. With a wide variety of climbing routes Acadia is a wonderful destination for beginners to learn how to rock climb. If you'd like to give it a try consider contacting one of the following experienced outfitters:

Atlantic Climbing School • (207) 288-2521 • Open: Seasonal
67 Main Street; Bar Harbor, ME 04609
www.climbacadia.com • Half-Day: $95/Person (2 People)

Acadia Mountain Guides • (207) 288-8186 • Open: Seasonal
228 Main Street; Bar Harbor, ME 04609
www.acadiamountainguides.com • Half-Day: $90/Person (2 People)

Winter Activities

Winter activities at Acadia are hit or miss. The park averages about five feet of snow each year, but rain is just as likely during the winter months. January and February are the most reliable months for winter weather. When there is snow, Acadia becomes a winter wonderland with plenty to do.

Two short sections of **Park Loop Road** remain open during the winter for motorists. **Blackwoods Campground** remains open, but campers must walk from the campground entrance road on Route 3 to the campsites. **Snowmobiles** are allowed on Park Loop Road and most fire roads. However, the maximum speed is 35 mph on Park Loop Road, and 25 mph on all unpaved roads. Snowmobilers must follow all state snowmobile laws. **Dog sleds** may be pulled by no more than four dogs. **Ice fishing** is popular on the many lakes and ponds. **Snowshoe, cross-country ski, and ice skate rentals** are available in Bar Harbor.

Cadillac Mountain Sports • (207) 288-2521 • Open: All Year
67 Main Street; Bar Harbor, ME 04609
www.cadillacsports.com

 # Bird Watching

Acadia is one of the premier bird-watching areas in the United States. **More than 300 bird species** have been identified on MDI and the surrounding waters.

After being reintroduced in the 1980s, **peregrine falcons** have become one of the park's main flying attractions. These raptors have been nesting on the cliffs of **Champlain Mountain** since 1991. If you'd like to observe these magnificent birds, join a park ranger or volunteer for **Peregrine Watch**. The program takes place at Precipice Trail Parking Area and is offered most days from mid-May through mid-August, weather permitting. Another popular nesting location is **Beech Cliffs** above Echo Lake.

Birds are everywhere, but a few locations are better than others. **Sieur de Monts Springs** is an excellent choice if you're looking to spot cedar waxwings, pileated woodpeckers, and the minuscule ruby-throated hummingbird. **Beaver Brook** and **Beaver Dam Pond** are popular habitats for herons, ducks, and bald eagles.

Birdwatchers will definitely want to walk around the **Otter Cliffs** area. Here you might find any number of seabirds, including double breasted cormorant, black guillemot, and northern gannet. **Schoodic Peninsula**, **Wonderland**, **Ship Harbor**, and **Seawall** provide bird enthusiasts with promising chances of seeing a wide variety of seabirds. Songbirds serenade cyclists, carriage riders, and hikers along the many miles of carriage roads.

Cadillac Mountain's wide open summit provides an excellent vantage point to see bald eagles and peregrine falcons as they patrol the sky high above the park's granite peaks. In fact, bird watching is so good here that the park has a **Hawk Watch** station at Cadillac's summit from mid-August until mid-October. Park rangers aid visitors in spotting raptors as they make their winter migration from Maine and Canada to warmer locales further south.

Birdwatchers on a trip to Acadia will not want to forget their binoculars and bird book. Also, be sure to stop at Hulls Cove Visitor Center to get the latest information on migratory birds, peregrine falcons, and ranger-led bird watch programs. You can also find information on ranger-led bird watching programs in the park's newspaper, *The Beaver Log*.

A park ranger handles a baby peregrine falcon

Did you know?

▶ Bar Harbor's shoreline was nicknamed "Millionaire's Row" due to lavish "cottages" built by families with names like Rockefeller, Morgan, Ford, Vanderbilt, Carnegie, and Astor.

▶ Fog common to Acadia is largely due to the Labrador Current, a cold water current from the Arctic Ocean, which meets the warm Gulf Stream near the park. The 48°F (9°C) Labrador Current helps cool the Gulf of Maine.

▶ Peregrine falcons were completely absent east of the Mississippi by the 1960s, but a gradual recovery has occurred since banning DDT in the 1970s. Birds were reintroduced to the park by researchers in 1984. Today, you may spot peregrine falcons along the Precipice and Valley Cove cliffs in late spring and early summer.

▶ Peregrine falcons can dive at speeds up to 202 mph (325 km/h), making it the fastest member of the animal kingdom.

ACADIA

Bass Harbor Head Lighthouse © guillenperez 2009

Did you know?

▶ Many believe that Leif Ericson and the Vikings landed on MDI around 1000 AD.

▶ Bass Harbor Head Lighthouse is one of the East Coast's most photographed lighthouses.

▶ The light from Bass Harbor Head Lighthouse can be seen up to 13 miles away.

▶ Cadillac Mountain was originally named Green Mountain.

▶ Cadillac Mountain sees the first rays of sun in the U.S. from October 7 to March 7.

▶ During the late 1800s a hotel was built on Cadillac Mountain's summit. Visitors reached the summit by taking a steamer across Eagle Lake, then passenger cars pushed them up the mountainside by a 10-ton locomotive. In the first year 3,000 visitors made the half-hour trip to the summit for $2.50/passenger.

▶ More than 1,100 plant species, 40 mammal species, and 300 bird species inhabit Acadia National Park.

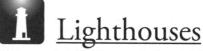 # Lighthouses

There are four lighthouses in the vicinity of MDI. Of these, **Bass Harbor Head Lighthouse** is the easiest to access. It marks the entrance into Blur Hill Bay and is located at the end of Route 102A on the western half of MDI near Bass Harbor. **Egg Rock Lighthouse** is located at the mouth of Frenchman Bay. It can be seen from Park Loop Road. **Baker Island** is the oldest lighthouse in the area. It's located seven miles from MDI, and can be accessed by kayak or boat. **Bear Island Lighthouse** is closed to the public, but it can be viewed on boat cruises departing from Northeast Harbor.

 # Boat Tours

Baker Island Cruise explores the island's unique natural and cultural history with the help of a park ranger. Call (207) 288-2386 for reservations and info.

Dive-In Theater Boat Cruise sets out in search of underwater life. Passengers scour the surface of Frenchman Bay for seals, porpoises, and seabirds, while a diver hunts for marine life on the ocean floor. Occasionally the diver returns to the boat with live specimens for a real hands-on experience. For more information call (207) 288-3483 or click www.divered.com. For tickets call (800) 979-3370.

Frenchman Bay Cruise takes you aboard a 151-foot, four-mast schooner where you'll search for wildlife as a ranger tells tales of the Maine Coast. For more information call (207) 288-4585 or click www.downeastwindjammer.com.

Discover Acadia's past aboard the **Islesford Historical Cruise** by visiting **Little Cranberry Island's Islesford Historical Museum**. For more information call (207) 276-5352 or click www.barharborcruises.com.

Bass Harbor Cruises (207.244.5785, www.bassharbor-cruises.com) offers a variety of wildlife and historical cruises. Or sail aboard the oldest working friendship sloop with **Downeast Friendship Sloop Charters** (207.266.5210, www.sailacadia.com). You can also go on a whale or puffin watch with **Bar Harbor Whale Watching** (207.288.2386, www.barharborwhales.com).

Reservations are recommended for all cruises. Schedules and fees vary. All tours are seasonal.

A tired fox yawns while sitting on the side Park Loop Road © Pat Hawks (www.pathawks.com)

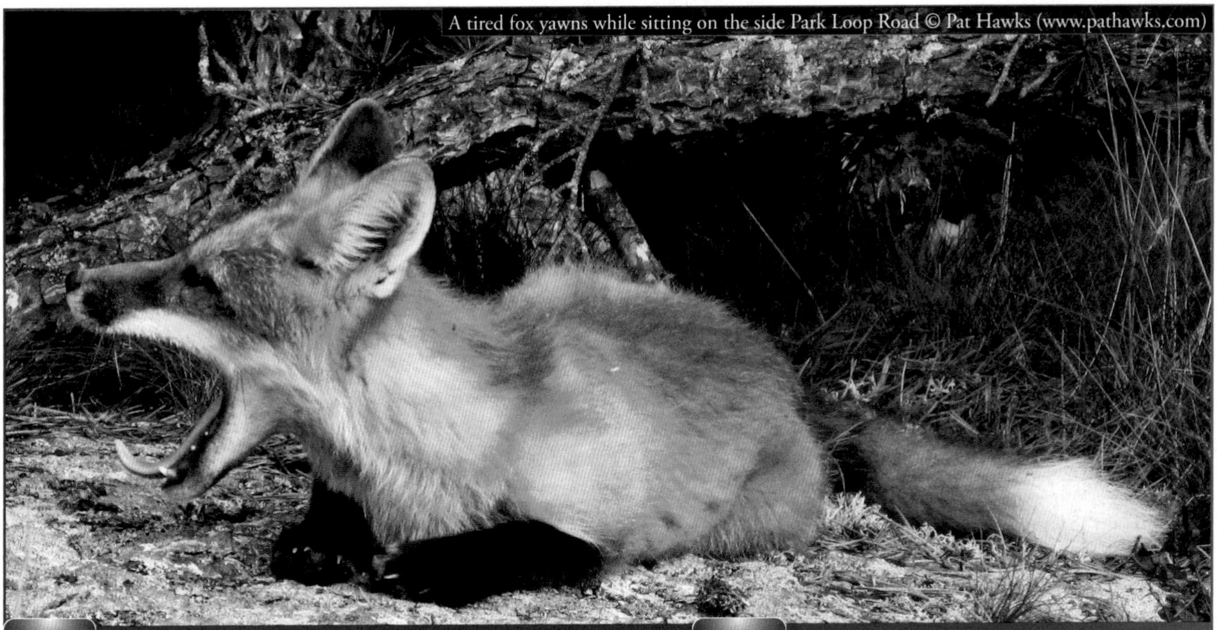

Driving

The 27-mile **Park Loop Road** is a must-see for first-time visitors. There are a number of turnouts and parking and picnic areas where you can stop and enjoy the scenery. Parking is also allowed along the road's right-hand side wherever it's one-way. Watch for evidence of the great fire of 1947 as you drive. Thick evergreen forests give way to sun-loving deciduous trees that replaced thousands of acres of pine that perished in flames. One of the most serene Park Loop Road experiences is to drive to **Cadillac Mountain's summit** early in the morning to see the sunrise. Grab a blanket, coffee, and a loved one, and then wait atop the barren peak for the first rays of light. If you can resist the temptation to return to your hotel for a nap, the early start allows you to visit popular destinations like Jordan Pond and Otter Cliffs before the afternoon crowds roll in—always a good idea during the summer months. Traffic peaks between 10am and 3pm.

Be sure to plan ahead if you will be arriving in an RV or tall vehicle as there are four low-clearance bridges (the lowest is 10' 4"). If you'd like to escape Park Loop Road gridlock, drive on over to the **Schoodic Peninsula**. Here you'll find a 6-mile, one-way loop that takes you along seas that are just as angry and cliffs just as dramatic as those back on MDI.

Small islands, including Isle au Haut, are inaccessible to cars.

Flora & Fauna

Many of Acadia's picturesque attractions are named for their occupants: Seal Harbor, Beaver Pond, Eagle Lake, and Otter Cliffs. All of these creatures reside in the park (although "otter" areas were named for the river dwelling variety, not the playful sea otters). Fortunate visitors might spot moose, black bear, red fox, porcupine, deer, whale, sea urchin, starfish, or lobster while exploring the park. **Black flies** and **mosquitoes** are two pests that you'd rather not encounter on vacation, but if you plan on traveling between May and June, chances are you'll be greeted by these winged nuisances, so pack your bug repellent.

Over 1,100 plant species live in Acadia, and 25 of these are state-listed rare plants. Walking about the park you're sure to notice a wide variety of trees, wildflowers, ferns, shrubs, mosses, lichens, and freshwater plants. The favorite plant of many visitors is the wild blueberry bush. Maine is the country's number one producer of wild blueberries, and these delectable snacks can be found all over MDI. They are typically ripe for the picking in late summer.

Visitor Centers:

Hulls Cove Visitor Center • (207) 288-3338
On Route 3 just south of Hulls Cove
Open: mid-April–October
Hours: 8am–4:30pm (July–August, 8am–6pm)
A long staircase leads up to the Visitor Center, but there is an alternate parking area for people with disabilities if you follow a short road at the south end of the main parking area.

Thompson Island Information Center
On Route 3 at the head of MDI
Open: mid-May–mid-September

Park Headquarters*
On Route 233 near Eagle Lake
Open: All Year, M–F (except federal holidays)
Closed weekends from mid-April–October
*Serves as the park's visitor center during winter

For Kids: Kids of all ages can take part in the **Junior Ranger Program** from mid-May through mid-October. Acadia also offers numerous children's programs that explore the park's ecology, geography, and history. Check the park's newspaper, *The Beaver Log*, for a current schedule of events. Families also enjoy playing at **Sand Beach** (page 42), **picking blueberries**, **hiking** (page 37), or taking a **boat tour** (page 44).

Ranger Programs: Be sure to pick up the park's publication, *The Beaver Log*, to see a current schedule of ranger-led programs. You'll find a wide variety of regularly scheduled educational walks, bike rides, and even a photography tour. Most of the programs are free of charge. The knowledge and enthusiasm exhibited by the park rangers makes activities, from hiking to stargazing, more exciting and interesting. If you have an extra hour or two and aren't exactly sure what to do, you cannot go wrong by joining a ranger program.

Pets are permitted in the park, but must be kept on a leash no more than six feet in length at all times, and are not allowed on swimming beaches, in public buildings, on the ladder trails, and at Isle au Haut.

Accessibility: The Visitor Center, some restrooms, the carriage paths, and the Island Explorer Shuttle are wheelchair accessible. The Wild Gardens of Acadia paths, Wonderland Trail, Ship Harbor Trail, and Jordan Pond Trails are accessible to wheelchair users, but may require some assistance. Carriages of Acadia (page 40) operates two wheelchair accessible carriages. If you have accessibility questions, please call the park information center at (207) 288-3338, ext. 0.

Weather: Acadia's weather is extremely unpredictable and can change without warning any day of the year, so come prepared for all conditions. Rainfall is common in every month. MDI is often shrouded in fog during the summer months. Daytime summer highs can range from 45°F to 90°F. Below is a graph of the area's average temperatures and precipitation.

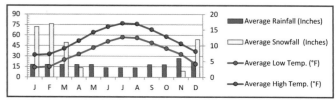

Vacation Planner

The average visitor spends three-and-a-half days at Acadia. So, here's a 3-day itinerary to help get you started. Dining, grocery stores, lodging, festivals, and attractions outside the park are listed on pages 48–51.

You'll want to begin your Acadian adventure at **Hulls Cove Visitor Center**. It's the best place to introduce yourself to the park and rangers will be on duty ready and willing to answer your questions. Before you leave, grab a park newspaper, watch the 15-minute video, and browse the exhibits until your curiosities have been satisfied. Next, begin driving **Park Loop Road**. Be sure to stop at **Sand Beach Parking Area**. Adventurous souls in your group should head across Park Loop Road to hike up **Beehive Ladder Trail**. The rest can play at the beach or hike **Great Head Trail**. When everyone has returned, it's time to get back in your car to continue along Park Loop Road to **Jordan Pond House**, which has been serving tourists for more than a century. This is a great place to enjoy lunch or a snack, like one of their **famous popovers**. At the very least take in the views of Jordan Pond where the two bubbles stand guard at the pond's far end. These bubbles are your next destination. As you're driving to the **Bubble**

Sand Beach with the Beehive in the background © Lee Coursey

Rock Parking Area look up at the east face of **South Bubble**. You'll notice a large boulder (Bubble Rock) precariously positioned as if it could roll down the mountain slope with the slightest nudge. Check it out by hiking up the 1-mile trail to the top of South Bubble. You don't have to race up the trail, Bubble Rock isn't going anywhere. To prove it, give it a push and see if it will budge. After you've had your fun, return to the car and complete the circuit around Park Loop Road. You may want to end your first day in Acadia with an evening boat tour of Frenchman Bay (page 44).

While eating breakfast, page through *The Beaver Log* you picked up the previous day. You might be able to catch a morning photography or bird watching tour. Be sure to note the time and location of any interesting ranger programs. In the meantime, drive over to MDI's quiet western side. If the weather cooperates, rent a kayak from **National Park Canoe & Kayak** (page 41, reservations may be required). The outfitter is conveniently located on **Long Pond**, so there's no need to transport heavy gear in order to enjoy a casual paddle in a pristine wilderness area. Return your kayak(s) and once you've lost your sea legs, hike to the top of nearby **Acadia Mountain**. It's one of the best hikes in the park, and the views are sublime. Relaxing at **Echo Lake Beach** is a nice alternative for anyone not interested in a somewhat strenuous hike. Whenever you feel like eating you can find plenty of good restaurants in Southwest Harbor. It's also a quality place to pit-stop before continuing south on Route 102 to the end of Route 102A, where you'll find **Bass Harbor Head Lighthouse**. This is one of the best locations to watch the sun set on another glorious day in Acadia.

Say "goodbye" to MDI by waking up early enough to see the sunrise from **Cadillac Mountain**. Bring a thermos of hot chocolate or coffee and a blanket along, because early Acadian mornings can be chilly and the barren mountaintop is unprotected from the wind. Dragging yourself out of bed will be completely justified as the first rays of light peek out from beyond the Atlantic Ocean. An early morning also means you'll have more time to enjoy your final day of vacation. Perhaps you have some unfinished shopping to complete in downtown Bar Harbor or you'd like to hike **Precipice Trail**. If you have the time, you might even want to leave MDI in favor of Acadia's **Schoodic Peninsula**. Should you choose to make the 45-minute drive back to Maine's mainland, you'll find the effort worthwhile. The same majestic coastlines are here, but without the crowds. **Frazer Head** is a great place to picnic and you can drive up to **Schoodic Head**, the peninsula's highest point.

Dining

Bar Harbor

Jordan Pond House • (207) 276-3316
In the park on Park Loop Rd • Entrée: $11–21
www.thejordanpondhouse.com

Lompoc Café & Brew Pub
36 Rodick St • (207) 288-9392 • Entrée: $9–17
www.lompoccafe.com
Notes: Bocce Ball & Live Entertainment

Jordan's Restaurant • (207) 288-3586
80 Cottage St • Entrée: $6–12

McKay's Public House • (207) 288-2002
231 Main St • Entrée: $16–27
www.mckayspublichouse.com

The Thirsty Whale • (207) 288-9335
40 Cottage St • Entrée: $7–15
www.thirstywhaletavern.com

Havana • (207) 288-2822
318 Main St • Entrée: $19–29
www.havanamaine.com

2 Cats • (207) 288-2808
130 Cottage St • Best Breakfast in town!
www.2catsbarharbor.com

Rupununi American Bar and Grill
119 Main St • (207) 288-2886 • Entrée: $16–29
www.rupununi.com

Maggie's Restaurant • (207) 288-9007
6 Summer St • Entrée: $16–24
www.maggiesbarharbor.com

Jeannie's Breakfast House
15 Cottage St • (207) 288-4166 • Entrée: ~$10
www.jeanniesbreakfast.com

Town Hill Bistro • (207) 288-1011
1317 ME-102 • Entrée: $17–20
www.townhillbistro.com

Galyn's • (207) 288-9706
17 Main St • Dinner: $7–22
www.galynsbarharbor.com

Rosalie's Pizza • (207) 288-5666
46 Cottage St • Pizza: $8–22
www.rosaliespizza.com

West Street Café • (207) 288-5242
76 West St • Entrée: $12–29
www.weststreetcafe.com

Mache Bistro • (207) 288-0447
135 Cottage St • Entrée: $16–26
www.machebistro.com

Geddy's Pub • (207) 288-5077
19 Main St • Entrée: $12–26
www.geddys.com

Poor Boy's Gourmet • (207) 288-4148
300 Main St • Entrée: $12–26
www.poorboysgourmet.com

Café This Way • (207) 288-4483
14 Mount Desert St • Entrée: $15–24
www.cafethisway.com

Side Street Café • (207) 801-2591
49 Rodick St • Entrée: $6–16
www.sidestreetbarharbor.com

Portside Grill • (207) 288-4086
38 Cottage St • Entrée: $14–25
www.portsidegrill.com

Leary's Landing Irish Pub • (207) 841-1586
2 Mount Desert St • Entrée: $8–17
www.learyslanding.com

Mama Di Matteo's • (207) 288-3666
34 Kennebec Place • Entrée: $15–20
www.mamadimatteos.com

Michelle's Fine Dining • (207) 288-0038
194 Main St • Entrée: $24–54
www.ivymanor.com

China Joy • (207) 288-8668
195 Main St • Entrée: $7–12

Bar Harbor Blues Café • (207) 288-2600
16 Mount Desert St • Entrée: ~$9
www.barharborbluescafe.com

Randonnee Café • (207) 288-9592
37 Cottage St • Entrée: $5–7
www.randonneecafe.com

Jack Russell's Steak House & Brewery
102 Eden St • (207) 288-5214 • Entrée: $13–34
www.bhmaine.com

The Reading Room • (207) 288-3351
7 Newport Dr • Entrée: $24–37
www.barharborinn.com

MDI's Quiet Side

Redbird Provisions Restaurant
11 Sea St; Northeast Harbor
(207) 276-3006 • Entrée: $22–30
www.redbirdprovisions.com

Red Sky • (207) 244-0476 • Entrée: $19–30
14 Clark Point Rd; Southwest Harbor
www.redskyrestaurant.com

Fiddlers' Green • (207) 244-9416
411 Main St; Southwest Harbor • Entrée: $17–38
www.fiddlersgreenrestaurant.com

Little Notch Pizzeria • (207) 244-3357
340 Main St; Southwest Harbor • Entrée: $6–10

Eat-A-Pita & Café 2 • (207) 244-4344
326 Main St; Southwest Harbor

Sips • (207) 244-4550
4 Clark Point Rd; Southwest Harbor

Quietside Café & Ice Cream Shop
360 Main St; Southwest Harbor • (207) 244-9444

Demuros Top of the Hill Restaurant
1 Main St; Southwest Harbor • (207) 244-0033

Beal's Lobster Pier
182 Clark Point Rd; Southwest Harbor
(207) 244-3202 • Lobster: Market Price
www.bealslobster.com

Chow Maine Ciao Maine • (207) 669-4142
19 Clark Point Rd; Southwest Harbor
www.chow-maine.com • Entrée: $8–28

Breakfast At Grumpy's • (207) 244-1082
11 Apple Ln; Southwest Harbor • Entrée: ~$10
www.breakfastatgrumpys.com

XYZ Restaurant • (207) 244-5221
80 Seawall Rd; Southwest Harbor
www.xyzmaine.com • Entrée: $24

Xanthus Restaurant • (207) 244-5036
22 Claremont Rd; Southwest Harbor
www.theclaremonthotel.com • Entrée: ~$24

Thurston's Lobster Pound
Steamboat Wharf Rd; Bernard
(207) 244-7600 • Lobster: Market Price
www.thurstonslobster.com

Schoodic Peninsula

Chase's Restaurant • (207) 963-7171
193 Main St; Winter Harbor

Fisherman's Inn • (207) 963-5585
7 Newman St; Winter Harbor
www.fishermansinnmaine.com

Downeast Deli • (207) 963-2700
ME-186; Prospect Harbor, ME 04693

Grocery Stores

Hannaford Supermarkets • (207) 288-3621
86 Cottage St; Bar Harbor
www.hannaford.com

Sawyer's Market • (207) 244-3315
344 Main St; Southwest Harbor

Pine Tree Market • (207) 276-3335
121 Main St; Northeast Harbor

Walmart Supercenter • (207) 667-6780
17 Myrick St; Ellsworth

Lodging

Bar Harbor

Bar Harbor Inn • (207) 288-3351
7 Newport Dr • Rates: $199–379/night
www.barharborinn.com

Harborside Hotel, Spa & Marina
55 West St • (207) 288-5033 • Rates: $229–869
www.theharborsidehotel.com

Bar Harbor Hotel-Bluenose Inn
90 Eden St • (207) 288-3348 • Rates: $190–430
www.barharborhotel.com

Castlemaine Inn • (207) 288-4563
39 Holland Ave • Rates: $119–269
www.castlemaineinn.com

Bar Harbor Manor • (207) 288-3829
47 Holland Ave • Rates: $99–189
www.barharbormanor.com

Mira Monte Inn • (207) 288-426369
Mount Desert St • Rates: $188-256
www.miramonte.com

Highbrook Motel • (207) 288-3591
94 Eden St • Rates: $93–113
www.highbrookmotel.com

Bar Harbor Grand Hotel • (207) 288-5226
269 Main St • Rates: $235
www.barharborgrand.com

Balance Rock Inn • (207) 288-2610
21 Albert Meadow • Rates: $225–395
www.balancerockinn.com

Acadia Inn • (207) 288-3500
98 Eden St • Rates: $185
www.acadiainn.com

Acadia Hotel • (207) 288-5721
20 Mt Desert St • Rates: $139–159
www.acadiahotel.com

Primrose Inn B&B • (207) 288-4031
73 Mt Desert St • Rates: $159–284
www.primroseinn.com

Bar Harbor Motel • (207) 288-3453
100 Eden St • Rates: $144–154
www.barharbormotel.com

Edenbrook Motel • (207) 288-4975
96 Eden St • Rates: $90–120
www.edenbrookmotelbh.com

Quimby House Inn • (207) 288-5811
109 Cottage St • Rates: $105–150
www.quimbyhouse.com

Black Friar Inn • (207) 288-5091
10 Summer St • Rates: $135–175
www.blackfriarinn.com

Moseley Cottage • (207) 288-5548
12 Atlantic Ave • Rates: $105–275
www.moseleycottage.net

Cleftstone Manor • (207) 288-8086
92 Eden St • Rates: $130–195
www.cleftstone.com

Maples Inn • (207) 288-3443
16 Roberts Ave • Rates: $160–215
www.maplesinn.com

Anne's White Columns Inn • (207) 288-5357
57 Mt Desert St • Rates: $110–165
www.anneswhitecolumns.com

Aysgarth Station • (207) 288-9655
20 Roberts Ave • Rates: $125–155
www.aysgarth.com

Canterbury Cottage • (207) 288-2112
12 Roberts Ave • Rates: $145–155
www.canterburycottage.com

Bar Harbor Regency • (207) 288-9723
123 Eden St • Rates: $142–190
www.barharborregency.com

Aurora Inn • (207) 288-3771
68 Mount Desert St • Rates: $169
www.aurorainn.com

The Bayview • (207) 288-5861
111 Eden St • Rates: $240–400
www.thebayviewbarharbor.com

Seacroft Inn • (207) 288-4669
18 Albert Meadows • Rates: $99–139
www.seacroftinn.com

Anchorage Motel • (207) 288-3959
51 Mount Desert St • Rates: $89–139
www.anchoragebarharbor.com

Holbrook House • (207) 288-4970
74 Mount Desert St • Rates: $89–179
www.holbrookhouse.com

High Seas Motel • (207) 288-5836
339 ME-3 • Rates: $75–145
www.highseasmotel.com

Inn At Bay Ledge • (207) 288-4204
150 Sand Point Rd • Rates: $150–475
www.innatbayledge.info

Emery's On the Shore • (207) 288-3432
181 Sand Point Rd • Weekly Rates: $590–1,100
www.emeryscottages.com

Bass Cottage Inn • (207) 288-1234
14 The Field • Rates: $230–370
www.basscottage.com

Hearthside Inn • (207) 288-4533
7 High St • Rates: $130–175
www.hearthsideinn.com

Ullikana In the Field • (207) 288-9552
16 The Field • Rates: $195–345
www.ullikana.com

Atlantean Cottage B&B • (207) 288-5703
11 Atlantic Ave • Rates: $180–250
www.atlanteaninn.com

Chiltern Inn • (207) 288-3371
11 Cromwell Harbor Rd • Rates: $189–399
www.chilterninnbarharbor.com

MDI's Quiet Side

Asticou Inn • (207) 276-3344
15 Peabody Dr; Northeast Harbor
www.asticou.com • Rates: $155–380

Colonels Suites • (207) 288-4775
143 Main St; Northeast Harbor
www.colonelssuites.com • Rates: $219

Harborside Inn • (207) 276-3272
48 Harborside Rd; Northeast Harbor
www.harboursideinn.com • Rates: $125–195

Clark Point Inn B&B • (207) 244-9828
109 Clark Point Rd; Southwest Harbor
www.clarkpointinn.com • Rates: $125–295

The Kingsleigh B&B • (207) 244-5302
373 Main St; Southwest Harbor
www.kingsleighinn.com • Rates: $160–315

Café Dry Dock & Inn • (207) 244-5842
357 Main St; Southwest Harbor
www.cafedrydockinn.com • Rates: $110–185

Lindenwood Inn • (207) 244-5335
118 Clark Point Rd; Southwest Harbor
www.lindenwoodinn.com • Rates: $155–295

The Inn at Southwest • (207) 244-3835
371 Main St; Southwest Harbor
www.innatsouthwest.com • Rates: $140–190

Cranberry Hill Inn • (207) 244-5007
60 Clark Point Rd; Southwest Harbor
www.cranberryhillinn.com • Rates: $110–155

The Claremont Hotel • (207) 244-5036
22 Claremont Rd; Southwest Harbor
www.theclaremonthotel.com • Rates: $225–335

Harbor Ridge • (207) 244-7000
39 Freeman Ridge Rd; Southwest Harbor
www.harborridge.com • Rates: $160–245

Schoodic Peninsula

Acadia's Oceanside Meadows Inn
202 Corea Rd; Prospect Harbor • (207) 963-5557
www.oceaninn.com • Rates: $149–209

Black Duck Inn • (207) 963-2689
36 Crowley Island Rd; Corea
www.blackduck.com • Rates: $140–200

Bluff House • (207) 963-7805
57 Bluff House Rd; Gouldsboro
www.bluffinn.com • Rates: $85–120

Not all dining and lodging facilities are listed. Most chain hotels can be found nearby in Ellsworth, ME (~22 miles/40 minutes northwest of Acadia NP).

Festivals

Bar Harbor

Birding Festival • June
www.acadiabirdingfestival.com

Fourth of July • pancake breakfast, parade, lobster bake, lobster races, and fireworks

Strawberry Festival • July

Bar Harbor Music Festival • July
www.barharbormusicfestival.org

Native American Festival • July

Acadia Outdoor Concert • July

Bike Bonanza & Ice Cream Social • August

Bar Harbor Jazz Festival • August

Bar Harbor Fine Arts Festival • August

Acadia Night Sky Festival • September
www.nightskyfestival.org

Garlic Festival • September • www.nostrano.com

Early Bird PJ Sale and Bed Races • November

MDI's Quiet Side

Open Garden Day • July
Northeast Harbor • www.gcmdgardenday.com

MDI Marathon • October
Northeast Harbor • www.mdimarathon.org

Harbor House Westside Bike Ride • May
Southwest Harbor • www.harborhousemdi.org

Flamingo Festival • July • Southwest Harbor

Oktoberfest • October
Southwest Harbor • www.acadiaoktoberfest.com

Beyond MDI

Windjammer Days Festival • June
Boothbay Harbor • www.boothbayharbor.com

Old Port Festival • June
Portland • www.portlandmaine.com

Blistered Fingers Bluegrass Festival • June
Litchfield • www.blisteredfingers.com

Legacy of the Arts Festival • June
Trenton • www.legacyartsfestival.com

Yarmouth Clam Festival • July
Yarmouth • www.clamfestival.com

Bates Dance Festival • July
Lewiston, ME • www.batesdancefestival.org

Bowdoin Int'l Music Festival • July
Brunswick • www.bowdoinfestival.org

North Atlantic Blues Festival • July
Rockland • www.northatlanticbluesfestival.com

Northeast Historic Film Festival • July
Bucksport • www.oldfilm.org

Maine International Film Festival • July
Waterville (between Augusta and Bangor) • www.miff.org

Maine Lobster Festival • August
Rockland • www.mainelobsterfestival.com

Machias Blueberry Festival • August
Machias • www.machiasblueberry.com

Great Falls Balloon Festival • August
Lewiston • www.greatfallsballoonfestival.com

American Folk Festival • August
Bangor, ME • www.americanfolkfestival.com

Camden Int'l Film Festival • September
Camden • www.camdenfilmfest.org

Attractions

In the Park

Isleford Historical Museum • Cranberry Island
Open: Seasonal • Admission: Free (fee to reach island)

Abbe Museum
Sieur de Monts Spring • www.abbemuseum.org
Open: Seasonal • Admission: $3

Wild Gardens of Acadia • Sieur de Monts Spring
Open: All Year • Admission: Free

Near the Park

Acadia Nat'l Park Tours • (207) 288-0300
Bus tour of the park and Bar Harbor
53 Main St; Bar Harbor
www.acadiatours.com
Open: Seasonal • Rates: $27.50/Adult

Oli's Trolley • (207) 288-9899
Trolley tour of the park and MDI
1 Harbor Ln; Bar Harbor
www.acadiaislandtours.com
Open: Seasonal • Rates: $15–29/Adult

Scenic Flights of Acadia • (207) 667-6527
Bar Harbor Rd; Trenton
www.scenicflightsofacadia.com
Open: All Year • Rates: $46–188

Acadia Air Tours • (207) 288-0703
1 West St; Bar Harbor
www.acadiaairtours.com
Open: All Year • Rates: $155–355

Ben&Bill's Chocolate Emporium
Chocolate and ice cream shop
66 Main St; Bar Harbor • (207) 288-3281
www.benandbills.com • Seasonal

Criterion Theatre • (207) 288-3441
Movie/Performing Arts Theater
35 Cottage St; Bar Harbor
www.criteriontheatre.com
Open: Seasonal • Tickets: $8/Adult

Real Pizza Cinerama • (207) 288-3811
Movie Theater
33 Kennebec Place; Bar Harbor
www.reelpizza.net
Open: Seasonal • Tickets: $6/Seat

Lulu Lobster Boat • (207) 963-2341
Lobster boat tour
55 West St; Bar Harbor
www.lululobsterboat.com
Open: Seasonal • Rates: $30/Adult

ImprovAcadia • (207) 288-2503
Improvisational comedy show
15 Cottage St, 2nd Floor; Bar Harbor
www.improvacadia.com
Open: Seasonal • Tickets: $15/Adult

Pirate's Cove Miniature Golf • (207) 288-2133
368 ME-3; Bar Harbor
www.piratescove.net/location/7
Open: Seasonal • Rates: $8.50/Adult

Abbe Downtown Museum • (207) 288-3519
Explores Maine's Native American Heritage
24 Mount Desert St; Bar Harbor
www.abbemuseum.org
Open: All Year • Admission: $6

Bar Harbor Oceanarium • (207) 288-5005
1351 ME-3; Bar Harbor
www.theoceanarium.com
Open: Seasonal

Bar Harbor Historical Society • (207) 288-0000
33 Ledgelawn Ave; Bar Harbor
www.barharborhistorical.org
Open: Seasonal • Admission: Free

Kebo Valley Golf Club • (207) 288-3000
136 Eagle Lake Rd; Bar Harbor
www.kebovalleyclub.com

Atlantic Brewing Co • (207) 288-2337
15 Knox Rd; Town Hill, ME
www.atlanticbrewing.com
Open: Seasonal • Admission: Free

Seal Cove Auto Museum • (207) 244-9242
1414 Tremont Rd; Seal Cove
Open: Seasonal • Admission: $5/Adult

Acadia Repertory Theater
1154 Main St; Mount Desert
www.acadiarep.com
Open: Seasonal • Tickets: $23/Adult

Wendell Gilley Museum • (207) 244-7555
4 Herrick Rd; Southwest Harbor
www.wendellgilleymuseum.org
Open: Seasonal • Admission: $5/Adult

Big Chicken Barn • (207) 667-7308
Antiques and paper collectibles
1768 Bucksport Rd; Ellsworth
www.bigchickenbarn.com

Beyond the Park

Burnham Tavern Museum · Site of the
American Revolution's first naval battle
Main St; Machias · Seasonal
www.burnhamtavern.com

Seashore Trolley Museum · (207) 967-2712
World's largest electric rail museum
195 Log Cabin Rd; Kennebunkport
www.trolleymuseum.org
Open: Seasonal · Admission: $8/Adult

Desert of Maine · (207) 865-6962
96 Desert Rd; Freeport, ME 04032
www.desertofmaine.com
Open: Seasonal · Admission: $10.50/Adult

L.L. Bean Flagship Store · (877) 755-2326
95 Maine St; Freeport, ME 04033

Musical Wonder House · (207) 882-7163
16-18 High St; Wiscasset, ME 04578
www.musicalwonderhouse.com
Open: Seasonal · Admission: $10-45/Adult

Camden Hills State Park · (207) 263-3109
280 Belfast Rd; Camden, ME 04843

Maine Coastal Islands NWR · (207) 546-2124
PO Box 279; Milbridge, ME 04658

Baxter State Park · (207) 723-5140
Mt Katahdin is this park's centerpiece
64 Balsam Dr; Millinocket
www.baxterstateparkauthority.com

Maine Rafting · (207) 991-8448
14 Carriage Ln; Hampden
www.mainerafting.com
Open: Seasonal · Rates: $79+/Paddler

Northern Outdoors Adventure Resort
Old Canada Rd National Scenic Byway,
1771 US Route 201; The Forks, ME 04985
www.northernoutdoors.com
Seasonal · Rates: $74+/Paddler · (207) 663-4466

North Country Rivers · (207) 672-4814
36 Main St; Bingham, ME 04920
www.northcountryrivers.com
Open: Seasonal · Rates: $59+/Paddler

Victoria Mansion · (207) 772-4841
109 Danforth St; Portland
www.victoriamansion.org
Open: All Year · Admission: $15/Adult

Portland Museum of Art · (207) 775-6148
Seven Congress Square; Portland
www.portlandmuseum.org
Open: All Year · Admission: $10/Adult

Allagash Brewing · (207) 878-5385
50 Industrial Way; Portland
www.allagash.com
Open: All Year · Admission: Free

Children's Museum & Theatre of Maine
142 Free St; Portland · (207) 828-1234
www.kitetails.org
Open: All Year · Admission: $9/Person

Portland Observatory · (207) 774-5561
138 Congress St; Portland
www.portlandlandmarks.org
Open: All Year · Admission: Tour Dependent

Pineapple Ketch · (207) 468-7262
Sailing excursions
95 Ocean Ave; Kennebunkport
www.pineappleketch.com
Open: Seasonal · Rates: $40/Person

Franciscan Monastery · (207) 967-2011
28 Beach Ave; Kennebunk
www.framon.net
Open: All Year · Admission: Free

Salem Witchhouse · (978) 744-8815
Home of Judge Corwin's witch trials
310½ Essex St; Salem, MA 01970
www.salemweb.com/witchhouse
Open: Seasonal · Admission: $10.25/Adult

Hammond's Castle · (970) 283-2080
An eccentric inventor's castle
80 Hesperus Ave; Gloucester, MA 09130
www.hammondcastle.org
Open: Seasonal · Admission: $10/Adult

Paper House · (972) 546-2629
House built in 1922 out of newspapers
52 Pigeon Hill St; Rockport, MA 01966
www.paperhouserockport.com
Open: Seasonal · Admission: $2/Adult

Boston Science Museum · (617) 723-2500
1 Museum Of Science Driveway; Boston
www.mos.org
Open: All Year · Admission: $21/Adult

Fenway Park · (617) 226-6666
4 Yawkey Way; Boston
www.redsox.com
Open: All Year · Tour: $12/Adult

Samuel Adams Brewery · (617) 368-5080
30 Germania St; Boston
www.samueladams.com
Open: All Year · Tour: Donation Suggested

USS Constitution Museum · (617) 426-1812
Building 22, Charlestown Navy Yard; Boston
www.ussconstitutionmuseum.org
Open: All Year · Tour: Donation Suggested

Harpoon Brewery · (617) 574-9551
306 Northern Ave; Boston
www.harpoonbrewery.com
Open: All Year · Tour: Free

JFK Presidential Library and Museum
Columbia Point; Boston · (866) 535-1960
www.jfklibrary.org
Open: All Year · Admission: $12/Adult

Skinny House (Boston)
*A 4-story narrow (10.4 feet wide) house built
out of spite*
44 Hull St; Boston, MA 02113

Great Boston Molasses Flood Plaque
*In 1919, 2-million gallons of molasses flooded these
streets · The molasses was clocked at ~35 mph*
529 Commercial St; Boston, MA 02109

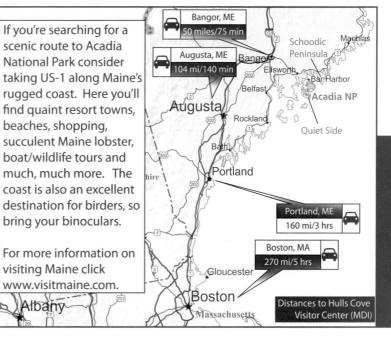

If you're searching for a scenic route to Acadia National Park consider taking US-1 along Maine's rugged coast. Here you'll find quaint resort towns, beaches, shopping, succulent Maine lobster, boat/wildlife tours and much, much more. The coast is also an excellent destination for birders, so bring your binoculars.

For more information on visiting Maine click www.visitmaine.com.

Bangor, ME 50 miles/75 min
Augusta, ME 104 mi/140 min
Portland, ME 160 mi/3 hrs
Boston, MA 270 mi/5 hrs

Distances to Hulls Cove Visitor Center (MDI)

WHAT'S NEARBY

51

A great blue heron prepares for take-off

15610 Vaughn Road
Brecksville, Ohio 44141
(216) 524-1497 or (800) 445-9667
Website: www.nps.gov/cuva

Established: October 11, 2000
Size: 33,000 Acres
Annual Visitors: 2.5 Million
Peak Season: Summer

Hiking Trails: 186 Miles

Activities: Hiking, Biking, Train
Rides, Picnicking, Golf, Horseback
Riding, Fishing, Paddling, Bird
Watching, Cross-Country Skiing,
Snowshoeing, Downhill Skiing,
Sledding, Concerts, Theater, Art
Exhibits, Museums, and Festivals

Campgrounds: No Car Camping
5 Primitive Sites are available at
Stanford House for long distance
bikers/hikers on the Towpath Trail

Park Hours: All day, every day
(some areas close at dusk)
Entrance Fee: None

Cuyahoga Valley - Ohio

Northeastern Ohio might not be a place you expect to find a national park. Towering mountains and gaping gorges are nowhere to be found. But the national parks are all about surprises, and considering its location deep in the middle of the rust belt, Cuyahoga Valley might be the greatest surprise of them all. Miles of undeveloped land are nestled between the sprawling cities of Akron and Cleveland. The valley's geographic beauty may not be as grand or majestic as the natural wonders of the West, but it's an area rich in history and culture. Now a recreational respite, this area has endured decades of development, trade, industry, and pollution before a few thoughtful conservationists began to push for a new era of preservation and protection. The Cuyahoga Valley's history is far from typical of most national parks, but its present is the same: the area has been restored and protected for the enjoyment of the people.

As the Cuyahoga River twists and turns for 22 miles through the center of the park it lives up to its name, meaning "crooked" in the Iroquois language. The same Native Americans who named the river used it as a trade route for thousands of years. By 1795, the river formed the northern boundary between Indian Territory and the United States.

Imaginary boundaries were drawn and erased. Treaties written then ignored. It wasn't long until Ohio became the hub of American industrialization. In 1827, the **Ohio & Erie Canal** was completed. It connected the Great Lakes region with the Gulf of Mexico via the Mississippi, Ohio, and Cuyahoga Rivers. The route dramatically improved shipping of goods and people to the Great Plains States. Companies like BF Goodrich and Standard Oil prospered, while the Cuyahoga River perished.

The region's rapid development, booming industry, alarming population growth, and inadequate infrastructure spawned a river filled with sewage and industrial waste. So saturated with oils, gases, and chemicals, it was infamously referred to as "the river that burned," catching fire at least thirteen times between 1868 and 1969. A fire in 1969 was short in duration, lasting only 24 minutes, but huge in environmental impact, prompting Time Magazine to write that the water "oozes rather than flows" and that a person "does not drown but decays." The pointed article helped galvanize an environmental movement, which spurred the passing of water quality legislation. State and federal environmental agencies and Earth Day were established thanks to the "river that burned" and the activism it inspired. President Gerald Ford signed a bill creating **Cuyahoga Valley National Recreation Area** in 1974 and in 2000, Congress changed its designation to a national park. Decades of treatment and restoration efforts have improved water quality. Wildlife has returned. But it's far from the pristine waterway it once was. Boating and swimming are still not recommended and fish caught in these waters are not to be eaten.

The Cuyahoga Valley has been used for recreational purposes since the late 19th century. Recreation began with modest boat trips and carriage rides. Eventually, railroads led to obsolescence of the **Ohio & Erie Canal**, but the path used by horses and mules to tow seafaring vessels is still used today by hikers and bikers. Twenty miles of the 101-mile **Towpath Trail** passes through Cuyahoga Valley and it is one of the park's most popular destinations. The railway also serves as a tourist attraction. **Cuyahoga Valley Scenic Railroad** travels from Canton to Akron and on to Cleveland, making seven stops within the park. Themed excursions, including everything from beer tasting to book reading, are offered throughout the year. The park's urban location lends itself to some atypical attractions like golf courses, a music center and theater, and a ski resort. You can also explore several original and re-created heritage sites where employees in time-period wardrobe serve as your guides.

Cuyahoga Valley's unique combination of nature, history, development, destruction, and restoration has formed a park that is as much a walk through history as it is a walk in the wild. If you take the time to experience some of the park's time period presentations and ranger-led excursions you are sure to have an entertaining, educational, and memorable experience.

Best of Cuyahoga Valley

Waterfall Hike: Brandywine Falls
Runner-up: Blue Hen Falls
2nd Runner-up: Buttermilk Falls

Leaf-Peeping Hike: The Ledges
Runner-up: Tinkers Creek Gorge

Family Fun: Ride the Railroad
Runner-up: Bike Ohio & Erie Towpath
2nd Runner-up: Hike to Ice Box Cave

Did you know?

▶ Established in 2000, Cuyahoga Valley is one of the newest national parks.

▶ From the 1830s to the 1860s, Ohio became the third most prosperous state, largely due to success of the Ohio & Erie Canal.

▶ The cities of Boston and Peninsula were centers for ship-building and canal commerce during the booming canal days.

Directions

Canal Visitor Center is approximately 11 miles from downtown Cleveland. Traveling by car, from the north, take I-77 south to exit 157 for OH-21/Granger Road/Brecksville Road toward OH-17. Merge onto OH-21/Brecksville Rd. Turn left at Rockside Road. Turn right at Canal Road. The visitor center will be on your right.

Canal Visitor Center
7104 Canal Road, intersection of Canal and Hillside Roads; Valley View, OH 44125 (81° 36.805' W) (41° 22.355' N).

Boston Store Visitor Center is approximately 18 miles from downtown Akron. Traveling by car, from the south, take OH-8 north. Turn left at E Hines Road and continue on to Boston Mills Road. The visitor center will be on your left.

Boston Store Visitor Center
1548 Boston Mills Road, east of Riverview Road; Peninsula, OH 44264 (81° 33.512' W) (41° 15.803' N).

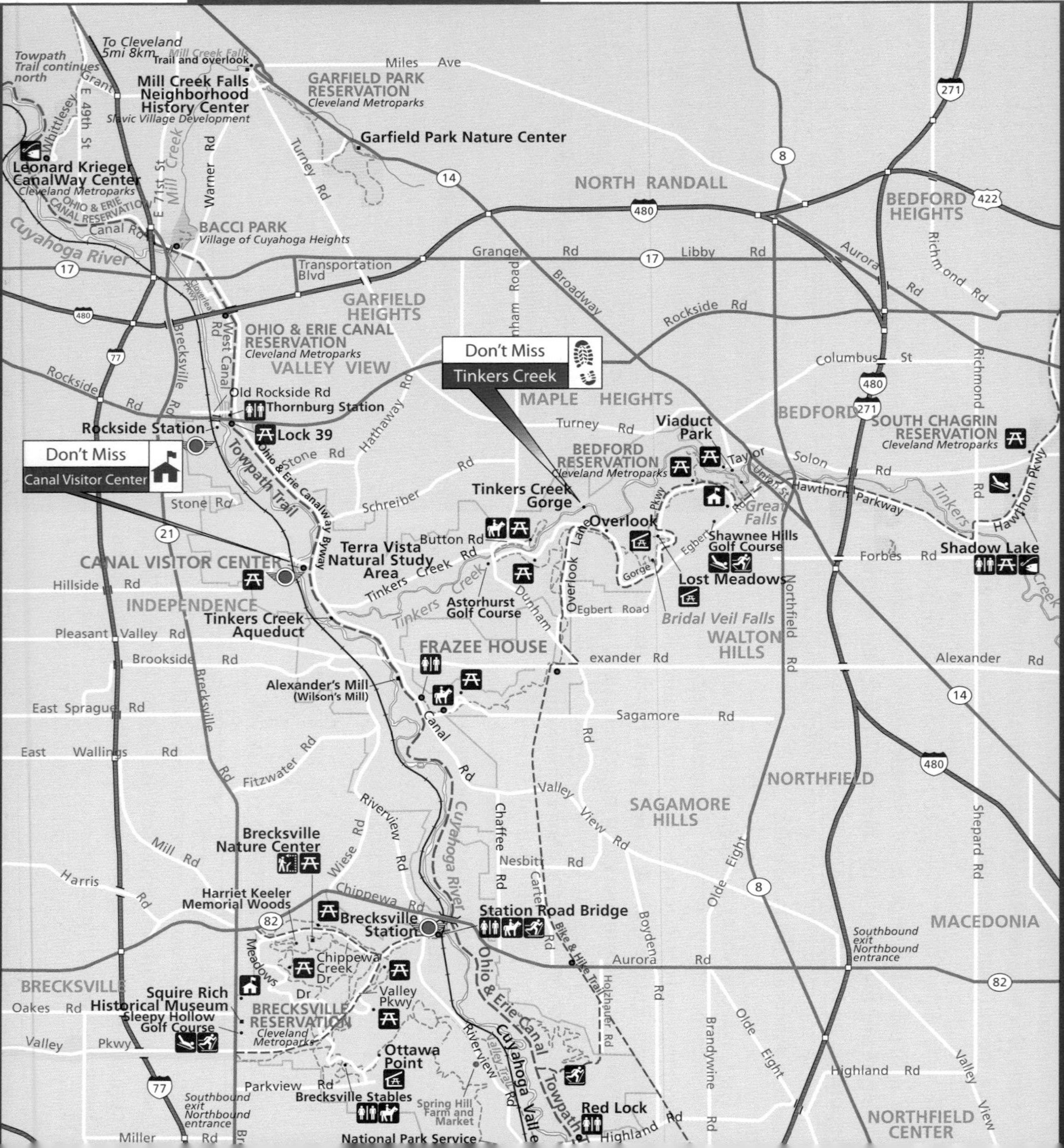

When to Go

Cuyahoga Valley is open all year. Weekends are busy, especially during the summer. Spring wildflowers and fall foliage tend to attract crowds that are larger than usual. Winter visitation is moderate.

Boston Store Visitor Center is open all year, daily from 10am–4pm.

Canal Visitor Center is open daily from 10am–4pm in the summer and from 10am–4pm, Wed–Sun from fall to spring.

Frazee House, located at 7733 Canal Road in Valley View about 3 miles south of Rockside Road, was closed for stabilization at the time of publication. Check the park's website for info.

Hunt Farm Visitor Information Center has the following hours:

• Spring: Sat and Sun, 10am–4pm

• Summer: Daily, 10am–4pm

• Fall: Sat & Sun, 10am–4pm

• Winter: Closed

NPS Park Headquarters is open all year, Mon–Fri, 8am–4:30pm

Peninsula Depot Visitor Center has the following hours:

• Spring: Sat and Sun, 10am–5pm

- Summer: Mon and Tue, 10am–4pm; Wed–Sun, 9am–7pm

- Fall: Wed–Sun in September and October, 9am–7pm, Sat and Sun in November, 10am–4pm

- Winter: Sat and Sun, 10am–4pm

Winter Sports Center at Kendall Lake is open Saturdays and Sundays, January through February, Martin Luther King Day and Presidents' Day, 10am–4pm

Stanford Campsites (thru-hikers and bikers only • reservation required) Open late May–Oct • $18/day (330) 657-2900, ext. 119 6093 Stanford Road; Peninsula, OH 44264 (81° 33.414' W) (41° 16.233' N)

Transportation & Airports

Cuyahoga Valley National Park is located in an urban area. Many roads provide access to the park. Greyhound (800.231.2222, www.greyhound.com) has a bus station in downtown Cleveland and Akron. Amtrak (800.872.7245 or www.amtrak.com) serves Cleveland.

Cuyahoga Valley Scenic Railroad (800.468.4070, www.cvsr.com) travels from Canton–Akron–Cleveland, making seven stops within park boundaries.

The closest airports are Cleveland Hopkins International Airport (CLE) and Akron–Canton Regional Airport (CAK).

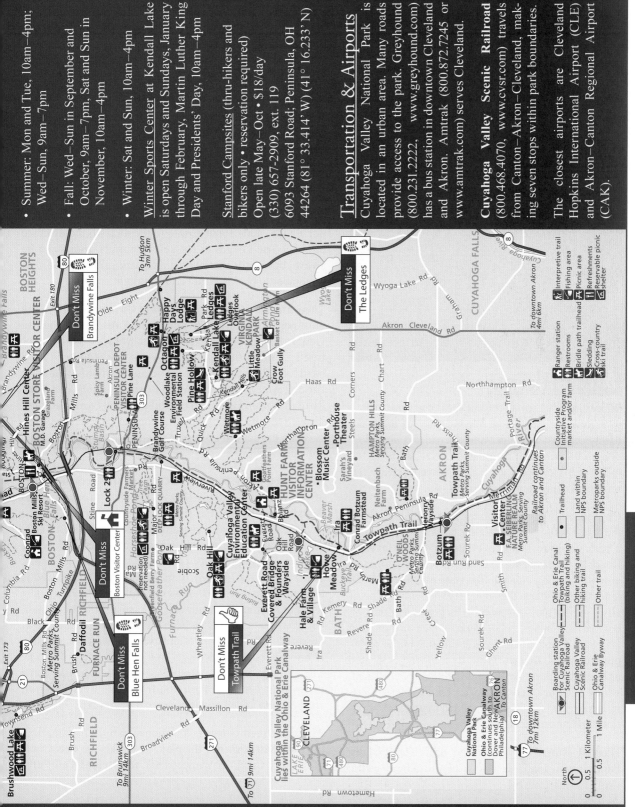

Brandywine Falls in the summer ©Tom Jones

Hiking

Many city dwellers search out sites of natural beauty to escape the stress and frenetic pace of an urban lifestyle. The Cuyahoga Valley provides such a location for the people of Akron and Cleveland. With 186 miles of hiking trails it's a great place to clear your mind and enjoy some fresh air.

Cuyahoga Valley was used for recreation as early as the late 1800s, but the region wasn't developed as a park until the 1910s to 1920s. In 1929, Hayward Kendall, a Cleveland coal baron, willed 430 acres around Ritchie Ledges to the state of Ohio with the lone stipulation that the "property should be perpetually used for park purposes." His generous donation created Virginia Kendall Park, named in honor of Hayward's mother. Here you'll find one of the park's premier hikes, **Ledges Trail**. Its trailhead is located at Ledges Parking Area just off Kendall Park Road, which becomes Truxell Road. This moderate 2.2-mile hike leads to dramatic eroded sandstone formations known as The Ledges.

Haskell Run Trail is located near The Ledges. Parking is available at Happy Days Lodge Parking Area on the north side of Route 303. The trailhead for this easy 0.5-mile hike is in the southeast corner of the parking lot directly adjacent to the lodge.

Haskell Run and Ledges Trail intersect the trail to **Ice Box Cave**. It's not exactly a cave, but kids still enjoy the trek to a cool, moist, 50-foot deep slit in solid rock. To pick up the trail from Haskell Run, simply take a short connector trail up a hill and to the left after crossing the first wooden bridge. Wooden steps make the climb easier, and the connector trail intersects Ledges Trail. Turn left along the base of Ritchie Ledges and continue about 0.4-mile to the cave. An excursion to **Ice Box Cave** (closed at time of publication to slow the spread of a disease to the park's bat population) adds about 1 mile to the total hiking distance of either The Ledges or Haskell Run trails. It may not be a cave, but it still can be cold and dark in the Ice Box, so remember to pack a jacket and flashlight.

There are more than 70 waterfalls in Cuyahoga Valley. The most popular is 60-foot **Brandywine Falls**, which you can view from an overlook near Inn at Brandywine Falls, or trek 1.25 miles through Brandywine Gorge to get a first-hand look. This moderate hike begins at Brandywine Falls Parking Area on Stanford Mills Road, west of Brandywine Road in Boston Heights. The trail to Brandywine Falls and its overlook are two of the most popular park destinations. You can expect a bit of company, but the views and hike are well worth it.

Blue Hen is the next waterfall on the pecking order of Cuyahoga Valley's Most Popular. Compared to Brandywine Falls, Blue Hen is merely a trickle, but the small amount of water cascading over rock has considerable appeal. Three narrow ribbons of water fall over a wide, rocky face before cascading into a shallow pool. The 1.2-mile trail is easy to moderate, and its trailhead is located on Boston Mills Road one mile west of Riverview Road in Boston. The trailhead parking area is quite small, but overflow parking has been added on the south side of the road. A viewing area offers excellent views of the falls. A bit of scrambling will get you to the waterfall's base. The slightly more impressive 20-foot **Buttermilk Falls** is less than 1-mile downstream from Blue Hen. This trail was recently added and is a more rugged trek.

Tinkers Creek Gorge is a National Natural Landmark in the northeast corner of the park, and holds the Great Falls of Tinkers Creek in Viaduct Park and **Bridal Veil Falls**.

Bridal Veil Falls Trailhead is located on Gorge Parkway, 1.4 miles northwest of Egbert Road and about 1 mile east of Overlook Lane in Bedford Reservation. It's an easy 0.25-mile hike to the falls.

Chippewa Creek Trail begins at Brecksville Nature Center parking lot on Chippewa Creek Drive, about 0.5-mile south of State Route 82. This scenic 2.5-mile loop follows both sides of Chippewa Creek. Note that the creek may be impassable during periods of high water. For a moderate to difficult hike, try the Old Carriage Trail between Jaite and Boston. This 5.25 mile trip starts at Red Lock Trailhead located on Highland Road, one half mile east of Riverview and Vaughn Roads.

The 1,300 mile **Buckeye Trail** circles the state of Ohio and runs for 30 miles through Cuyahoga Valley, briefly joining Towpath Trail in the park's southern half. It is well maintained by the Buckeye Trail Association and can be accessed from eight locations within the park. Stretches vary from easy to difficult and anywhere from 1.5 to 7 miles between access points. **Towpath Trail** is another great hiking choice. The segment north of Ira Road Trailhead (see map on page 55) is particularly nice.

Ice Box Cave

Rays of sunlight shining through the Ledges

 # Biking

There are four major bicycle trails in the Cuyahoga Valley. Most renowned of these is the **Ohio & Erie Towpath Trail**. This 101-mile crushed stone path follows the historic Ohio & Erie Canal Route, and 20 of its most scenic miles span the length of the park. Along the way you'll find picnic areas, restrooms, and train depots. Thanks to the **Cuyahoga Valley Scenic Valley Railroad** (page 58) you can have an incredibly unique biking experience. Bike from depot to depot and then take the train back to where you started. With the railroad's **Bike Aboard!** Program cyclists and their bikes ride the train for the reasonable price of $2/person.

You'll also find more than 70 miles of paved bike paths in the park. **Summit County Bike & Hike Trail** follows the park's border for nearly 17 miles. Just between Brecksville and Bedford Metroparks you'll find over 60 miles of paved trails.

If you need to rent a bike or pick up last minute parts there are a few shops in the area. Each of the following businesses offers bike rental:

Century Cycles • (330) 657-2209 (rentals only)
1621 Main Street; Peninsula, OH 44264
Mon–Thu: 10am–8pm, Fri–Sat: 10am–6pm, Sun: noon–5pm
www.centurycycles.com

Bike: $8/hour; Trailer: $8/hour; Tag-a-long: $4/hour

Blimp City Bike & Hike • (330) 836-6600
1720 Merriman Road; Akron, OH 44313
Tues–Thurs: 10am–8pm, Fri & Sat: 10am–6pm,
Sun: Noon–5pm, Mon: Closed
www.blimpcitybikeandhike.com

Bike: $8/hour

Ernie's Bicycle Shop • (330) 832-5111
135 Lake Ave NW; Massillon, OH 44647
Mon–Fri: 10am–8pm, Sat: 8am–6pm, Sun: 10am–5pm
November 1–March 31, Sun 10am–5pm
www.erniesbikeshop.com

Bike: $5–10/hour

The following bicycle shops do not offer bike rental.

Brecksville Velo Sport • (440) 740-0154
7740 Chippewa Road; Brecksville, OH 44141
Mon–Fri: 10am–6pm, Sat: 10am–5pm, Sun: Closed
www.breckvelosport.com

Falls Wheel & Wrench Bike Shop • (330) 928-0533
2445 State Road; Cuyahoga Falls, OH 44223
Mon–Fri: 10am–8pm, Sat: 10am–6pm, Sun: noon–4pm
www.fallswheelandwrench.com

The Cuyahoga Valley Scenic Railroad © Jack Rigby

Scenic Railroad

One of the most unique and entertaining experiences in the valley is taking a ride aboard the **Cuyahoga Valley Scenic Railroad (CVSR)**. Owned by the National Parks Service (NPS), it's one of the oldest, longest, and most scenic tourist excursions the NPS offers. The hard part isn't deciding whether or not to ride the CVSR; it's choosing which excursion to take.

Akron Explorer lets visitors combine a train ride through the Cuyahoga Valley with a trip to one of Akron's main attractions: **Akron Art Museum**, **Akron Zoo**, **Hale Farm & Village**, or you can have lunch at the **Spaghetti Warehouse**.

Peninsula Explorer Tour stops at **Peninsula** where passengers can enjoy unique shops, galleries, and restaurants during a 1.5 hour layover.

National Park Scenic Excursion ($10–25) gives visitors a relaxing, enjoyable trip to see the wildlife and scenery of Cuyahoga Valley.

Young at Heart Program ($12 for 55+, $17/adult, $12/child) gives adults ages 55 and older an opportunity to explore the natural and cultural history of the park. Seasonal wine and beer-tasting trains are also offered ($45–55 coach/club, $65–75 first class, and $80–92 executive class/dome seats).

In winter, **The Polar Express** is offered, where children are encouraged to wear pajamas aboard the train while *The Polar Express* is read out loud. **A Christmas Tree Adventure** brings families to

Heritage Farms where they can pick out a Christmas tree to buy and take home.

Be sure to call CVSR or click on their website to view all seasonal excursions. It's common for National Park rangers to narrate train rides. Passengers will find their knowledge and spirit to be both enlightening and entertaining. The depth and variety of excursions offered by the CVSR make it an attraction that appeals to just about everyone.

Cuyahoga Valley Railroad • (800) 468-4070
2325 Stine Road; Peninsula, OH 44264
www.cvsr.com
Adult: $8–26, Senior: $8–20, Child: $8–12

Horseback Riding

Exploring the park on horseback provides an interesting perspective of the park's landscapes and wildlife, and there are 86 miles of signed and designated horse trails at Cuyahoga Valley. However, there are no horse rental or guide services within the park, so visitors keen on riding must trailer their own horses in. Station Road parking lot, close to Brecksville Reservation, has large pull-through parking spots allowing easy parking and access. Here you'll find several miles of trails around **Brecksville Stables Area**. If you're unfamiliar with the area, be sure to inquire about trail closures, difficulty, and access before heading out for a ride.

Water Activities

Current restoration efforts are improving water quality of the Cuyahoga River, but high pollutant levels are frequently recorded, especially after heavy rainfalls. While the **Cuyahoga River** can be **paddled**, it is not recommended and there are no paddle-sport outfitters in the area. Swimming is prohibited.

Fishing, however, is permitted. More than 65 species of fish are found in the park. Catch-and-release fishing is encouraged, and eating fish from the river is not recommended. Motorboats are prohibited within the park, and lakes are occasionally closed for resource management. A fishing license is required in accordance with Ohio regulations. Kendall Lake, Indigo Lake, Brushwood Lake, Conrad Farm Pond, Goosefeather Pond, and Arrington Pond are recommended fishing locations.

Winter Activities

There are nearly as many ways to enjoy Cuyahoga Valley National Park in winter as there are in summer. **Winter Sports Center at Kendall Lake Shelter** (located at 1000 Truxell Road, two miles west of Akron Cleveland Road, in Peninsula) offers **cross-country skiing** and **snowshoeing**. The Winter Sports Center is open daily (when snow depth is greater than four inches), Dec 26–31; Sat & Sun, Jan 2–Feb 28; Martin Luther King Day, and President's Day, 10am–4pm. Call (330) 657-2752 to confirm.

Snowshoe rental is available at **Boston Store Visitor Center** (open daily from 10am–4pm except Christmas and New Year's Day) when snow depth is four inches or greater. Snowshoes cost $5 per pair per day. A popular winter hike is **The Ledges** where you may be able to see spectacular icicle formations.

Cross-country ski rental is available at the **Winter Sports Center** ($15/day, $7.50/half-day) when snow depth is six inches or greater. Ski instruction is also available with advanced registration (330.657.2752). **Towpath Trail** is straight, flat, and popular among cross-country skiers.

Ice fishing is permitted on the park's lakes and ponds. **Sledding** is available at **Kendall Hills** on Quick Road. Parking is available at Pine Hallow (5465 Quick Road, Peninsula) or Little Meadow (5249 Quick Road, Peninsula) Parking Areas.

Brandywine Ski Resort offers downhill skiing and snowboarding. Tubing is available Friday through Sunday next door at **Polar Blast Tubing Park**.

Boston Mills & Brandywine Ski Resort • (800) 875-4241
1146 W Highland Road; Northfield, OH 44067
www.bmbw.com
Lift Ticket: $28–41 (Adult), $28–36 Junior, Free (Child & Senior)
Rental: $28 (Adult & Senior), $23 (Junior & Child)
Helmet: $10
Lessons: $20 (Group), $45 (Private)
Boston Mills: Mon–Thurs 10am–9:30pm, Fri 10am–10pm, Sat 9am–10pm, Sun 9am–9pm

Brandywine: Mon–Thurs: 3:30pm–9:30pm, Fri: 3:30pm–10pm, Sat: 9am–10pm, Sun: 10am–9pm

Polar Blast: Fri: 5pm–10pm, Sat: 10am–10pm, Sun: 10am–9pm

A turtle hiding out in the Cuyahoga Valley

Golf

There are four privately owned and operated golf courses within the park.

Astorhurst Country Club • (440) 439-3636
7000 Dunham Road; Cleveland, OH 44146
www.golfastorhurst.com
Rates: $15.50–16.50/9-holes, $27–29/18-holes

Brandywine Golf Course • (330) 657-2525
5555 Akron Peninsula Road; Peninsula, OH 44264
www.golfbrandywine.com
Rates: $15–19/9-holes, $21–31/18-holes

Shawnee Hills Golf Course • (440) 232-7184
18753 Egbert Road; Bedford, OH 44146
www.clemetparks.com
Rates: $9.50–23

Sleepy Hollow Golf Course • (440) 526-4285
9445 Brecksville Road; Cleveland, OH 44141
www.clemetparks.com
Rates: $16–27

For Kids

Kids (ages 7–12) can take part in the park's **Junior Ranger Program** and children (ages 4–6) can participate in the **Junior Ranger, Jr. Program**. These programs are typically offered during the summer. The park also offers multi-day camps and ranger-led hikes throughout the summer. Check seasonal park schedules online or at a visitor center for an up-to-date listing of all the great programs geared towards children. Hiking to **Blue Hen Falls** or **Ice Box Cave** (page 56), or riding the rails (page 58) are excellent family activities.

A white-tailed deer and its reflection

Flora & Fauna

More than 900 plant species thrive in Cuyahoga Valley. Spring, when wildflowers are in bloom, and fall, when deciduous trees are shedding their leaves, are the most popular seasons to view the valley's plantlife. Wildflowers are most abundant in moist areas near creeks and streams far from trees whose leaves block the sun's light. You may encounter these flowers: spring beauty, yellow trout lily, toothwort, hepatica, bloodroot, dwarf ginseng, Virginia bluebells, spring cress, purple cress, rue anemone, foam flower, twin leaf, bishop's cap, squirrel corn, violets, jack-in-the-pulpit, and many species of trillium. The grasses, trees, and wildflowers play an important role in making this a special place, so appreciate them, or at the very least, don't step on or pick any flowers.

Just as the park serves as a retreat for weary city-dwellers, it is a refuge for a variety of wildlife. For the most part mammals consist of small critters like squirrels, chipmunks, and mice. But you'll also find white-tailed deer, raccoons, and woodchucks scurrying about. You may not see beavers, but you will see their handiwork in the form of felled trees and dammed streams. If you're lucky you may catch a glimpse of a coyote or river otter. These species naturally returned to the park in recent years. Also residing here are dozens of species of reptiles, amphibians, insects, and birds.

Bird Watching

Cuyahoga Valley is an ideal location for **bird watching**. The park's varied landscapes provide habitat for **more than 248 species**. After an extended absence due to excessive pollution, blue herons and bald eagles are once again nesting here. Herons are often seen in February as they scavenge for materials to build or repair their nests. Hundreds of nests have been found perched high above the Cuyahoga River at sites north of Route 82 and just south of Bath Road. From February until July you can see herons at either **Bath Road heronry** (from a pullout along Bath Road) or **Pinery Narrows heronry** (from Towpath Trail, 0.5-mile north of Station Road Bridge). Nesting bald eagles can also be found in this area. They returned in 2006 after an absence of more than 70 years.

Beaver Marsh is a great place to spot wood ducks and other waterfowl during their migrations in March and November. Solitary vireos, winter wrens, hermit thrushes, and black-throated warblers frequent the moist hemlocks near Ritchie Ledges in late spring. Red-breasted nuthatches and golden-crowned kinglets call **Horseshoe Pond** their home from late October through early March. The grassland near the **former coliseum site** (near the intersection of I-80 and I-271 on W. Streetsboro Rd/OH-303) is now habitat for eastern meadowlark, bobolink, savannah sparrow, grasshopper sparrow, and Henslow's sparrow. These species can be seen during their summer breeding season, and it is asked that you stay on the edge of the grassland from April to August because many of these birds nest on the ground.

Basics

Ranger Programs: If the land is the park's body, then the rangers are its soul. Joining a ranger-led excursion is one of the best ways to enhance your visit. You have a myriad of choices, ranging from bird watching to monarch butterfly monitoring, alien invasions (invasive plant and animal species) to surveying a cemetery, and star gazing to bat watching. Check the park's schedule online or at a visitor center, and then let the rangers make your visit a little more memorable.

Pets: Pets must be kept on a leash no more than six feet in length at all times. Only service animals are allowed in park buildings and on the train.

Accessibility: Canal and Boston Store Visitor Centers, as well as Hunt Farm Visitor Information Center, Frazee House, Happy Days Lodge, and Towpath Trail are accessible to wheelchair users. Contact the park or CVSR (page 58) with specific questions, comments, and concerns.

Weather: Weather in the Cuyahoga Valley is typical of the Midwest. Winters are cold and often snowy. The Cleveland area averages 61 inches of snowfall, but annual accumulation varies greatly from year to year. Average annual precipitation is 35 inches, with 20 inches accumulating between the months of April and September. Summers are typically hot and humid with unpredictable thunderstorms. Most guests travel to the park in summer, but fall might be the ideal time to visit, when cool, crisp, clear days and colorful foliage make the valley particularly inviting.

Blue Hen Falls © Eduard Toerek

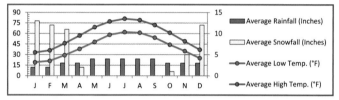

Vacation Planner

Most visitors travel to the park on a summer weekend when many ranger programs are offered and the majority of park attractions are open for business. The following two day itinerary will help you plan your Cuyahoga Valley vacation. Please note that camping is not available in the park and **Inn at Brandywine Falls** (page 62) provides the only lodging. Dining, grocery stores, lodging, festivals, and attractions outside the park are listed on pages 62–63.

Day 1

Begin your trip at **Canal Visitor Center**. It's a renovated 1820s Canal House where you can watch a short video on the park, view exhibits, and have your questions answered. Exhibits explore the history of the **Ohio & Erie Canal**. You can even witness a demonstration of how a lock works at **Lock 38**, the last operational lock in the park. Remember to browse the list of ranger-led activities, and plan around any excursions you want to take part in. From here it's a short drive to **Tinker's Creek Gorge** (page 56). Decide for yourself whether you walk the trails or take in the beautiful vistas from overlooks along Tinkers Creek Road, then return to **Ohio & Erie Canal Scenic Byway** and head south along the length of the park. Along the way you'll pass **Frazee House** (stop if you're interested in early 19th century architecture). Continue south to Boston Mills Road, where you'll want to head west to **Blue Hen Falls**

parking area (page 56). Stretch your legs on this short but rewarding hike. Before calling it a day in the Cuyahoga Valley, stop at **Brandywine Falls** (page 56), the crown jewel of the park. It's an excellent place to picnic or watch the sunset.

Day 2

Start your day by driving to Kendall Park Road. Stop at **Ledges** for a late morning hike. Then return to Riverview Road, continuing south to **Ira**. Here you'll explore **Towpath Trail** on foot (or bike). As you walk through **Beaver Marsh**, imagine horses and mules pulling boats through the canal. Nearby is a reconstructed version of the 1870s **Everett Road Covered Bridge**. Ohio led the nation in covered bridge construction when they were in fashion. Everett Road Covered Bridge is one of more than 2,000 covered bridges in the state, but it is important enough to the community and the park that it was rebuilt after a flood destroyed it in 1975. **Hale Farm and Village** is located nearby. You could easily spend an entire day at this site where you are transported to the 1860s. Watch spinning, weaving, pottery-making, blacksmithing, candle-making, glass-blowing, basket-making, and other aspects of 19th century farm-life in Cuyahoga Valley.

When you consider everything the Cuyahoga Valley has to offer, two days isn't nearly enough time to experience it all. Be sure to come back and ride the **Cuyahoga Valley Scenic Railroad** (page 58), take in a concert at **Blossom Music Center** (summer home of the **Cleveland Orchestra**) or a play at **Porthouse Theater** (page 63).

CUYAHOGA VALLEY

Dining

Winking Lizard • (330) 467-1002
1615 Main St; Peninsula, OH 44264
www.winkinglizard.com • Entrée: $7–11

Fisher's Café & Pub • (330) 657-2651
1607 Main St; Peninsula, OH 44264
www.fisherscafeandpub.com • Entrée: $8–17

Fisher's Café & Pub • (330) 657-2651
1391 Boston Mills Rd W; Peninsula, OH 44264

Babushka's Kitchen • (330) 468-0402
9199 Olde 8 Rd; Northfield Center, OH 44067
www.babushkafoods.com

Angie's Pizza • (216) 524-8100
6932 Hillside Rd; Independence, OH 44131

Aladdin's Eatery • (216) 642-7550
6901 Rockside Rd; Independence, OH 44131
www.aladdinseatery.com

Lockkeepers • (216) 524-9404
8001 Rockside Rd; Valley View, OH 44125
www.lockkeepers.com • Entrée: $17–33

Austin's Wood Fire Grille • (440) 546-1003
8121 Chippewa Rd; Cleveland, OH 44141
www.austinsrestaurants.com • Entrée: $13–28

Vaccaro's Trattoria • (330) 666-6158
1000 Ghent Rd; Akron, OH 44333
www.vactrat.com • Entrée: $14–29

Ken Stewart's Lodge • (330) 666-8881
1911 N Clevleand-Massillon Rd; Bath, OH 44333
www.kenstewartsonline.com • Entrée: $15–40

Downtown 140 • (330) 655-2940
140 N Main St; Hudson, OH 44236
www.downtown140.com • Entrée: $18–30

Hudsons On the Green • (330) 650-1955
80 N Main St; Hudson, OH 44236
www.3foodies.com • Entrée: $8–20

Yours Truly Restaurant • (330) 656-2900
36 S Main St; Hudson, OH 44236
www.ytr.com • Entrée: $9–13

Carrie Cerino's Ristorante • (440) 237-3434
8922 Ridge Rd; North Royalton, OH 44133
www.carriecerinos.com • Entrée: $14–28

Creekside Restaurant and Bar • (440) 546-0555
8803 Brecksville Rd; Brecksville, OH 44141
www.creeksiderestaurant.com • Entrée: $14–22

2182 Brecksville • (440) 717-9463
8918 Brecksville Rd; Brecksville, OH 44141
www.2182brecksville.com • Entrée: $15–27

Courtyard Café • (440) 526-9292
7600 Chippewa Rd; Brecksville, OH 44141
www.courtyardbrecksville.com • Entrée: $9–21

Shoeless Joe's BBQ • (330) 467-2271
9377 Olde 8 Rd; Northfield, OH 44067
www.sjbbq.com • Entrée: $4–17

Tinkers Creek Road Tavern • (216) 642-3900
14000 Tinkers Creek Rd; Walton Hills, OH 44146

Fat Casual BBQ • (330) 748-4690
223 East Highland Rd; Macedonia, OH 44056

Long-Yun Restaurant • (330) 908-3988
307 Highland Rd E; Macedonia, OH 44056

Pulp Juice & Smoothie Bar • (330) 467-0022
746 E Aurora Rd # 11; Macedonia, OH 44056

Grocery Stores

Heinen's Fine Foods • (440) 740-0535
8383 Chippewa Rd, Brecksville, OH 44141
www.heinens.com

Sam's Club • (440) 232-2582
23300 Broadway Ave; Oakwood Village, OH 44146

Walmart Supercenter • (216) 587-0110
22209 Rockside Rd; Bedford, OH 44146

Lodging

Inn At Brandywine Falls • (330) 467-1812
8230 Brandywine Rd; Northfield, OH 44067
www.innatbrandywinefalls.com
Rates: $139–325/night

Shady Oaks Farm B&B • (330) 468-2909
241 West Highland Road; Northfield, OH 44067
www.shadyoaksfarmbnb.com
Rates: $150–250/night

Jeremiah B King Guest House • (330) 650-0199
272 N Main St, Hudson, OH 44236
www.kingguesthouse.com
Rates: $155–175/night

Hudson's Historic Inn • (330) 342-0340
34 Aurora St; Hudson, OH 44236
www.hudsonshistoricinn.com
Rates: $150–170/night

The Cobbler Shop B&B • (800) 287-1547
121 E Second St; Zoar, OH 44697
www.cobblershop.com
Rates: $125–150/night

Hilton Garden Inn • (330) 405-4488
8971 Wilcox Dr; Twinsburg, OH 44087
www.clevelandtwinsburg.stayhgi.com
Rates: $159–193/night

Most restaurant and hotel chains can be found nearby in Macedonia and Richfield. Rates are subject to change.

Festivals

Chalk Art Festival • May
Public Square; Medina, OH

Northeast Ohio Polka Fest • June
Old Firehouse Winery; 5499 Lake Rd; Geneva-on-the-Lake, OH
www.oldfirehousewinery.com

Riverfront Irish Festival • June
Riverfront Centre, Riverfront Parkway
Cuyahoga Falls, OH
www.riverfrontirishfest.com

Avon Heritage Duct Tape Festival • June
Veteran's Mem. Park; 37001 Detroit Rd; Avon, OH
www.ducttapefestival.com

Pioneer Festival • (330) 666-3711 • June
Hale Farm & Village; 2686 Oak Hill Rd; Bath, OH 44210 • www.wrhs.org

Italian American Festival • July
Riverfront Centre, Riverfront Parkway
Cuyahoga Falls, OH • (330) 699-9911
www.festaitalianacf.com/festa

Pro Football Hall of Fame Festival • July
2121 George Halas Dr NW; Canton, OH
www.profootballhoffestival.com
(330) 456-8207

Akron Arts Expo • July
Hardesty Park; Wallhaven Dr; Akron, OH
www.akronartsexpo.org • (330) 375-2835

National Hamburger Festival • August
Lock 3 Park, 200 S Main St; Akron, OH
www.hamburgerfestival.com • (716) 565-4141

Twins Day Festival • August
World's largest gathering of twins • Twinsburg, OH

Yankee Peddler Festival • September
Clay's Park Resort • (412) 831-2526
OH-93 and OH-21; Canal Fulton, OH
www.yankeepeddlerfestival.com

Loyal Oak Cider Festival • September
Crawford-Knecht Cider Mill; Akron-Wadsworth and Cleveland Massillon Rds; Norton, OH • (330) 825-8866

IngenuityFest • September
Detroit Superior Bridge; Cleveland, OH
www.ingenuitycleveland.com

Oktoberfest • September
Riverfront Centre, Riverfront Parkway; Cuyahoga Falls, OH • (330) 699-9911
www.oktoberfestcfo.com

Barberton Mum Fest • September
Lake Anna Park & Gazebo, Barberton
www.cityofbarberton.com/govt/MumFest

Hale Farm Harvest Festival • October
Hale Farm and Village • (877) 425-3327
2686 Oak Hill Rd; Bath, OH

Covered Bridge Festival • October
Covered Bridge Capital of the World: Ashtabula, OH
www.coveredbridgefestival.org

Attractions

In the Park

Blossom Music Center • (330) 920-8040
1145 W Steels Corners Rd; Cuyahoga Falls, OH 44223

Hale Farm & Village • (330) 666-3711
2686 Oak Hill Rd; Bath, OH 44210
www.wrhs.org • Tickets: Depends on Program

Cuyahoga Valley Historical Msm
1775 Main St; Peninsula; OH 44264 • (330) 657-2892
www.peninsulalibrary.org

Brecksville Nature Center • (440) 526-1012
9305 Brecksville Rd; Cleveland, OH 44141
www.brecksville.oh.us

Porthouse Theatre Co • (330) 672-3884
1145 W Steels Corners Rd; Cuyahoga Falls, OH 44223

Near the Park

Geauga Lake's Wildwater Kingdom
1100 Squires Rd; Aurora, OH 44202 • (330) 562-8303
www.geaugalake.com • Admission: $30/Adult

Regal Cinemas Hudson Cinema 10
5339 Darrow Rd; Hudson, OH 44236 • (330) 655-3584
www.regmovies.com • Tickets: ~$10/Adult

Cinemark At Macedonia • (330) 908-1005
8161 Macedonia Commons Blvd; Macedonia, OH 44056
www.cinemark.com • Tickets: ~$9/Adult

Fun 'n' Stuff • (330) 467-0820
661 Highland Rd E; Macedonia, OH 44056
www.fun-n-stuff.com

North Woods Bowling Lanes • (330) 467-7925
10435 Valley View Rd; Macedonia, OH 44056
www.northwoodslanes.com

Dittrick Museum of Med History • (216) 368-3648
Located at Case Western Reserve University
11000 Euclid Ave; Cleveland, OH 44106
www.case.edu • Admission: Free

Cleveland Museum of Art • (216) 421-7340
11150 E Blvd; Cleveland, OH 44106
www.clevelandart.org • Admission: Free

USS Cod • (216) 566-8770
1034 N Marginal Rd; Cleveland, OH 44114
www.usscod.org • Admission: $7/Adult

A Christmas Story House • (216) 298-4919
Original house from the movie: A Christmas Story
3159 W 11th St; Cleveland, OH 44109
www.achristmasstoryhouse.com • Admission: $8/Adult

West Side Market • (216) 664-3386
Ste C9, 1979 W 25th St; Cleveland, OH 44113
www.westsidemarket.org

Cleveland Browns Stadium • (440) 891-5001
1085 W 3rd St, Cleveland, OH 44114
www.clevelandbrowns.com • Tours: $5/Person

Progressive Field • (216) 420-4487
Home of the Cleveland Indians
2401 Ontario St; Cleveland, OH 44115
www.cleveland.indians.mlb.com • Tours: $7.50/Adult

Quicken Loans Arena • (216) 420-2000
Home of the Cleveland Cavaliers
1 Center Court, Cleveland, OH 44115-4001
www.nba.com/cavaliers

Lake View Cemetery • (216) 421-2665
12316 Euclid Ave, Cleveland, OH 44106
www.lakeviewcemetery.com

Great Lakes Science Center • (216) 574-6262
601 Erieside Ave; Cleveland, OH 44114
www.glsc.org • Admission: $10/Adult

Cleveland Metroparks Zoo • (216) 661-6500
3900 Wildlife Way; Cleveland, OH 44109
www.clemetzoo.com • Admission: $11/Adult

Rock and Roll Hall of Fame and Museum
1100 Rock and Roll Blvd; Cleveland, OH 44114
www.rockhall.com • (216) 781-7625 • Admission: $22/Adult

Old Arcade • (216) 696-1408
401 Euclid Ave # 155; Cleveland, OH 44114
www.theclevelandarcade.com

Akron Zoological Park • (330) 375-2525
500 Edgewood Ave; Akron, OH 44307
www.akronzoo.org • Admission: $10/Adult

McKinley Presidential Library & Museum
800 McKinley Monument Drive NW; Canton,
OH 44708 • (330) 455-7043
www.mckinleymuseum.org • Admission: $8/Adult

Canton Classic Car Museum • (330) 455-3603
123 6th St SW; Canton, OH 44702
www.cantonclassiccar.org • Admission: $7.50/Adult

Canton Palace Theatre • (330) 454-8172
Performing Arts/Movie Theater
605 Market Ave N; Canton, OH 44702
www.cantonpalacetheatre.org

Pro Football Hall of Fame • (330) 456-8207
2121 George Halas Dr NW; Canton, OH 44708
www.profootballhof.com • Admission: $21/Adult

Beyond the Park

Kelleys Island Ferry • (419) 798-9763
See Kelly's Island's Glacial Grooves
510 W Main St; Lakeside Marblehead, OH 43440
www.kelleysislandferry.com

Warther Museum • (330) 343-7513
See incredible wood carvings
331 Karl Ave; Dover, OH 44622
www.warthers.com • Admission: $13/Adult

Henry Ford Museum • (313) 982-6001
Home of Edison's Last Breath
20900 Oakwood Blvd; Dearborn, MI 48124
www.thehenryford.org • Admission: $15/Adult

Cedar Point/Soak City Amusent Parks
1 Cedar Point Dr, Sandusky; OH 44870 • (419) 627-2350
www.cedarpoint.com • Admission: $47/Adult

Kalahari Waterpark Resort • (419) 433-7200
7000 Kalahari Dr; Sandusky, OH 44870
www.kalahariresorts.com • Admission: $39/Adult

The Merry-Go-Round Museum • (419) 626-6111
301 Jackson St; Sandusky, OH 44870
www.merrygoroundmuseum.org • Admission: $6/Adult

Ghostly Manor Thrill Center • (419) 626-4467
Ghostly Manor ($11), 4D Theater ($7), Skateworld
3319 Milan Rd; Sandusky, OH 44870
www.ghostlymanor.com

Detroit

Ann Arbor

Detroit, MI
170 mi/3 hrs

Cleveland, OH
11 mi/20 min

Toledo

Perry's Victory

Sandusky

Cleveland

Bowling Green

Cuyahoga Valley NP

Akron

Canton

For more information on visiting Ohio click www.discoverohio.com.

Pittsburgh

Columbus, OH
135 mi/2.5 hrs

Ohio

Distances to Canal Visitor Center

Pittsburgh, PA
120 mi/2 hrs

Columbus

The sun rising up over the Virginia Piedmont © Owen Byrne (www.flickr.com/photos/ojbyrne)

3655 US Highway 211 East
Luray, VA 22835
Phone: (540) 999-3500
Website: www.nps.gov/shen

Established: December 26, 1935
Size: 199,000 Acres
Annual Visitors: 1.2 Million
Peak Season: October

Hiking Trails: 511 Miles
Horse Trails: 180 Miles
Driving: 105-Mile Skyline Drive

Activities: Hiking, Biking, Rock
Climbing, Horseback Riding, Bird
Watching, and Fishing

Campgrounds ($15–17/night): Big
Meadows, Mathews Arm, Loft
Mountain, Lewis Mountain
Lodging ($87–285/night): Big
Meadows Lodge, Skyland Resort,
Lewis Mountain

Park Hours: All day, every day
Entrance Fee: $10 (Dec–Feb), $15
(March–Nov) • Vehicle

Shenandoah - Virginia

Shenandoah National Park is centered on a long narrow stretch of the **Blue Ridge Mountains**. Forested mountaintops give way to the Shenandoah River Valley to the west and the gentle hills of the Virginia Piedmont to the east. The 105-mile **Skyline Drive** bisects the park as it follows the mountains' crest. Located just 75 miles from the nation's capital, it may come as no surprise that the formation of Shenandoah had as much to do with politics and personalities as with natural forces.

Long before it received federal government protection, the Shenandoah region served many purposes to many different people. Native Americans hunted and gathered for survival. Loggers and miners tapped the land for its resources. Union and Confederate soldiers shed blood deep in the Shenandoah Valley.

Eventually resorts began to crop up high atop the mountains, and for the past century **Skyland Resort** has served as recreational hub of Shenandoah. Ironically, Skyland never intended to be a company specializing in tourism. Between 1854 and 1866, a large tract of land within present park boundaries exchanged hands between numerous mining companies on speculation of substantial copper and iron deposits. Miners Lode Copper Company found the land to be commercially unsuccessful. However, **George Freeman Pollock**, son of one of the primary shareholders, convinced his father that the land had value as a resort. On October 1, 1889, Pollock's father and Stephen M. Allen formed the **Blue Ridge Stonyman Park Preserve**. Guests paid $9.50 per week to sleep in tents outfitted with cots, chairs, washstands, and pitchers. An idea far more prosperous than mines ever were, but not enough to cover debt owed on the land's initial purchase. Stonyman Preserve had to be put up for sale at public auction to satisfy the mortgage. George Freeman Pollock, jobless and unsure of his future, was allowed to buy the Blue Ridge land on credit. He renamed it Skyland Resort, but his attempts at business fared much like his father's. He found himself in continuous debt, never actually gaining title to the land. Pollock may not have been much of a businessman, but he was a successful marketer. He threw elaborate balls, costume parties, jousts, musicals, pageants, and bonfires. His other skill was pandering to Washington's politicians. He became one of the most influential local advocates for the construction of **Skyline Drive** and the formation of a national park, but at the time of the park's establishment in 1935, Pollock had $67,107 in outstanding liens against a property appraised at less than $30,000.

Growth and success of national parks in the west sparked Congress to commission the Southern Appalachian Committee to perform a thorough and wide-ranging survey of prospective locations in the east. The committee's survey proposed that land of present day **Mammoth Cave**, **Shenandoah**, and the **Great Smoky Mountains** met the ideals of a U.S. National Park, and on February 25, 1924, Congress authorized establishment of Shenandoah National Park. Authorization was easy, but procuring land for the park proved challenging. More than 1,000 privately owned tracts had to be turned over to federal ownership, a drastic change compared to western parks where most land was already federally owned. The state of Virginia responded by acquiring 1,088 tracts of land through condemnation and eminent domain, then donating all of it to the federal government. Some 465 mountain residents moved or were forced to move, but a handful were allowed to live out their lives within the park. The last life-long resident, Annie Bradley Shenk, passed away in 1979 at the age of 92.

By the time the park was established, development was well underway thanks to the effort of George Freeman Pollock and President Roosevelt's New Deal. Forty miles of **Skyline Drive** were already completed. Ten **CCC** camps, housing as many as 1,000 workers, were set-up. The CCC built trails and facilities around Skyland and Skyline Drive, which would become the primary attractions of a successful park that presently receives more than one million annual visitors.

The first car to pay at the North Entrance

A visitor enjoys the view from Skyline Drive

Directions

The park has four entrances: Front Royal, via I-66 and Route 340; Thornton Gap, via Route 211; Swift Run Gap, via Route 33; and Rockfish Gap, via I-64 and Route 250.

Pittsburgh, PA to North Entrance (~190 miles): Travel east on I-76 to exit 161. Take I-70 East to US-522 South. Continue on US-522 to Route 37 South to I-81. Take I-81 South to I-66 East. Follow I-66 to Front Royal, VA and follow park signs to the entrance.

Washington, D.C. to North Entrance (~70 miles): Travel west on I-66 to Front Royal, Virginia. Exit onto Route 34. From here, signs will direct you to the park's entrance.

Washington, D.C. to Thornton Gap Entrance (~81 miles): Travel west on I-66 to exit 43A. Take US-29 South to Warrenton, VA. Take US-211 West into the park.

Richmond, VA to South Entrance (~90 miles): Travel west on I-64 to exit 99. From here, signs will direct you to the park's entrance.

Richmond, VA to Swift Run Gap Entrance (~95 miles): Travel west on I-64 to Charlottesville, VA. Take the exit to US-29 North. Turn left onto US-33 West into the park.

SHENANDOAH

When to Go

Shenandoah National Park is open all year, but the majority of visitors arrive in October for colorful displays of fall foliage. If you plan on visiting during this time, it is advised that you arrive early, preferably on a weekday. Skyline Drive, the only public road through the park, closes occasionally for inclement weather. Several park facilities operate seasonally.

It's a good idea to begin your trip at one of its **visitor centers:** Dickey Ridge or Harry F. Byrd, Sr. Both locations offer exhibits, an information desk, a bookstore, and an orientation film. You can also find restrooms, first aid, and backcountry permits here. The best resource the visitor centers offer is their staff of friendly park rangers who lead guests on ranger programs and are available to answer questions.

Dickey Ridge Visitor Center
Mile 4.6 on Skyline Drive
Open: Thurs–Mon, April–mid-May; Daily, early May–early Nov; TBD, rest of November; Closed from late November–late March

Harry F. Byrd, Sr. Visitor Center
Milepost 51 on Skyline Drive
Open: Daily, late March–late Nov

Loft Mountain Information Center
Mile 79.5 on Skyline Drive
Open: Weekends & Holidays, mid-May–October

There are a couple waysides where you'll find gas, food, gifts, and camping supplies.

Elkwallow Wayside
Milepost 24 on Skyline Drive
Open: mid-April–early November

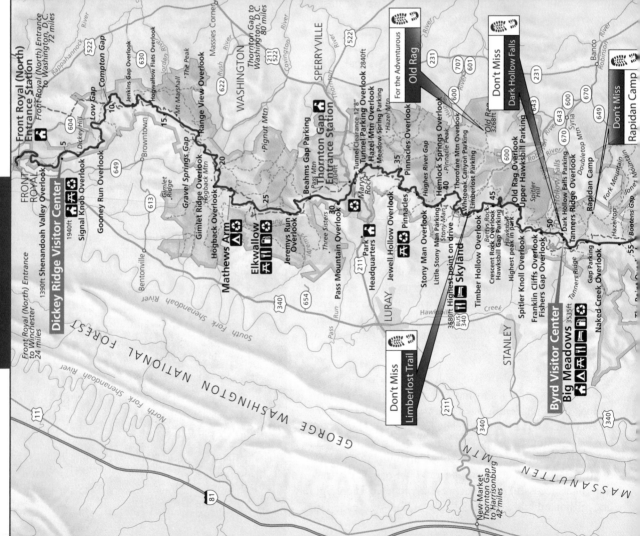

Big Meadows Wayside
Milepost 51 on Skyline Drive
Open: mid-March–late November

Loft Mountain Wayside
Mile 79.5 on Skyline Drive
Open: late April–early November

Most picnic grounds are open all year, but those listed below are seasonal.

Dickey Ridge Picnic Grounds
Mile 4.6 on Skyline Drive
Open: April–late November

Big Meadows Picnic Grounds
Milepost 51 on Skyline Drive
Open: late March–late November

Lewis Mountain Picnic Grounds
Mile 57.6 on Skyline Drive
Open: early April–early November

Transportation & Airports

Shenandoah National Park was designed with motorists in mind. Four entrances provide access to 105-mile scenic Skyline Drive. See page 65 for directions to the park.

The closest airports are Washington Dulles International (IAD) (56 miles east of Front Royal) and Reagan International (DCA) (70 miles east of Front Royal). Closer to the park you'll find two smaller airports: Shenandoah Valley Regional Airport (SHD) (27 west of Swift Run Gap), and Charlottesville–Albemarle (CHO) (31 miles east of Rockfish Gap).

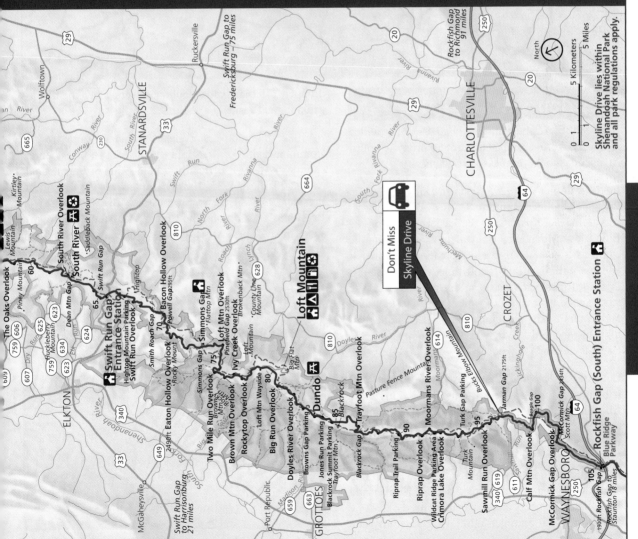

Skyline Drive lies within Shenandoah National Park and all park regulations apply.

SHENANDOAH

67

President Franklin Delano Roosevelt visits a CCC camp in Shenandoah National Park

Presidents in the Park

Before the region became a national park, it provided recreation, refuge, and a backdrop to promote political agendas for several U.S. Presidents.

In the summer of 1929, **Herbert Hoover**, the 31st President, bought **Rapidan Camp**. At the time, it was a 164 acre parcel on the eastern slope of the Blue Ridge Mountains. Hoover envisioned using the camp as a place of rest and recreation for himself and his wife during difficult times. Unfortunately, difficult times were the norm during his term. The stock market crashed in October of 1929, less than eight months after inauguration. The remainder of his first and only term was spent combatting the Great Depression that ensued.

But life at Rapidan Camp wasn't all trials and tribulations. Friends, family, and politicians were frequently entertained there during Hoover's presidency. Charles Lindbergh, Mrs. Thomas A. Edison, the Edsel Fords, and British Prime Minister Ramsay MacDonald all show up on the cabin's guest registry. Being just a 3 hour drive from Washington, Rapidan Camp was used as a meeting place for Hoover and his cabinet members and department heads. It was a fully functional Summer White House; an airplane dropped off mail and telephones were conveniently located in the President's Cabin.

In 1932, the Hoovers donated Rapidan Camp to the Commonwealth of Virginia for use as a Presidential summer retreat. It officially became part of Shenandoah National Park in 1935. **Jimmy Carter** was the last sitting President to visit the camp, but the **"Brown House"** or **President's Cabin** and the **Prime Minister's Cabin** still stand today. These structures have been restored to their original appearance and are open to the public only during ranger-led tours.

Franklin D. Roosevelt, the 32nd President, used the region as part of a highly visible public relations effort to buoy the negative psychological impact of the Great Depression. He visited a CCC camp in 1933, and three years later he returned to officially dedicate the park.

The "Brown House"

Big Meadows Lodge

Shenandoah Camping

	Open	Fees	Sites	Notes
Mathews Arm (Mile 22.2)*	mid-May–October	$15/night	179	No Showers No Laundry
Big Meadows (Milepost 51)*	late March–Nov	$17/night	217	Showers, Laundry, and Campstore Available
Lewis Mountain (Mile 57.6)	mid-April–October	$15/night	16 Tent/16 RV	Showers, Laundry, and Campstore Available
Loft Mountain (Mile 79.5)*	mid-May–October	$15/night	45 Tent/167 RV	Showers, Laundry, and Campstore Available
Dundo Group (Mile 83.7)*	mid-April–mid-July	$35/night	7 Group Sites	Reservations Required
Backcountry Camping	A free permit is required. Backcountry planning information and application form are available at www.nps.gov/shen/planyourvisit/campbc.htm or call (540) 999-3500			

*Reservations can be made up to six months in advance by calling (877) 444-6777 or clicking www.recreation.gov

Each campground is near a section of the Appalachian Trail, and has at least one accessible site. No campgrounds have hook-ups for water, electricity, or sewage. Mathews Arm, Big Meadows, and Loft Mountain have dump stations and sites that will accommodate large RVs. About 80% of the sites at Mathews Arm and Loft Mountain are first-come, first-served.

Shenandoah Lodging

Big Meadows Lodge (Milepost 51)	mid-May–November	Rooms $109–187	25 rooms in the main lodge as well as 72 additional rooms in rustic cabins
Skyland Resort (Mile 41.7)	April–November	Rooms $87–285 Cabins $262	179 guest rooms, rustic cabins, and modern suites
Lewis Mtn Cabins (Mile 57.6)	April–November	Rooms $109 Tent Cabin $30	Several furnished cabins with private baths and grills

Call (800) 999-4714 or (540) 843-2100 or click www.visitshenandoah.com for additional information on park lodging

Best of Shenandoah

Mountain Hike: Old Rag
  Runner-up: Bearfence Mountain

Waterfall Hike: Cedar Run/Whiteoak
  Runner-up: Rose River Falls
  2nd Runner-up: Dark Hollow Falls

Family Hike: Fox Hollow Nature Trail
  Runner-up: Stony Man Nature Trail

Historic Hike: Mill Prong (Rapidan Camp)
  Runner-up: Hickerson Hollow

Picnic Locations: Big Meadows
  Runner-up: Pinnacles
  2nd Runner-up: South River

Activities: Drive Skyline Drive
  Runner-up: Horseback Riding

Biking

The twists, turns, and hills of **Skyline Drive** are a welcome challenge to road cyclists visiting Shenandoah National Park. Bikes are permitted on all paved surfaces within the park, but Skyline Drive, in particular, experiences heavy motorist traffic during the summer and October. Most park rangers won't recommend biking along Skyline Drive because it's fairly narrow and busy, but if you start your ride early enough (before 10am) traffic shouldn't be much of a problem. At this time cyclists should be prepared for poor visibility. Early morning fog is common, and you'll encounter darkness any time of year at the 600-foot long Mary's Rock Tunnel (Mile 32). Bikes are prohibited on unpaved roads, grass, and trails. There are no mountain bike trails within the park. If you'd like to join a group on a multi-day bicycle adventure, two outfitters offer guided bicycle trips.

Carolina Tailwinds, Inc. • (888) 251-3206
PO Box 24716; Winston-Salem, NC 27114
www.carolinatailwinds.com • Rates: $1350–1575

Women Tours, Inc. • (800) 247-1444
792 Ebony Street; Pocatello, ID 83201
www.womantours.com • Rates: $1990

Hiking/Backpacking

Leave Skyline Drive in favor of Shenandoah's wilder side. Yes, some of the views from the road are postcard-perfect, especially in October, but you won't see a single waterfall and wildlife sightings are limited to deer, squirrels, and birds. To witness the depth of history and nature Shenandoah has to offer one must strap on a pair of hiking shoes and ramble a few miles beyond the road.

There are 511 miles of trails here, ranging from short strolls through open meadows to steep, rocky scrambles atop exposed mountains. All trails are marked with colored blazes. White is for the **Appalachian Trail**; roughly 101 miles of the 2,184 mile trail run parallel to Skyline Drive through the park. Blue indicates park hiking trails and yellow marks trails designated for horse use, which are also open to hikers. Most of the trailheads are located at parking areas along Skyline Drive. A few, like that of the immensely popular **Old Rag Trail**, are located near the park boundary. Old Rag is a long (5.4 miles roundtrip) and challenging hike to the summit of Old Rag Mountain (3,268 feet). The shortest route begins near Nethers on Route 600 which terminates at the park's eastern boundary. Old Rag can also be reached from the park's interior via Old Rag Fire Road, but it's longer (15+ miles roundtrip) and less scenic.

Old Rag isn't for everyone, but there are trails to satisfy hikers of all interests and abilities along Skyline Drive. The shortest and most popular waterfall hike is **Dark Hollow Falls Trail**. Thomas Jefferson once admired this 70-ft falls. **Limberlost Trail** is fully accessible to wheelchair users and is an excellent hike in June when mountain laurel is in bloom. Hiking on **Fox and Hickerson Hollow Trails** allow hikers with an active imagination to travel to the times of early mountain residents who lived in the hollows for more than 100 years before being moved off their land for the creation of the park. Remnants of their presence still stand to this day. Simple mountain folk weren't the only occupants of these hills. **Rapidan Camp** served as the Summer White House for **President Herbert Hoover** while in office. **Mill Prong Trail** leads to the historic structure (only open and accessible during ranger programs).

Backpackers have more than 500 miles of trails and 190,000 acres of wilderness at their disposal. A free permit is required for all overnight stays in the backcountry. Permits are available by mail, phone (540.999.3500 - fill out online permit application before calling), or in person.

Shenandoah Hiking Trails

	Trail Name	Trailhead	Length	Notes (Roundtrip distances)
Easy	Fox Hollow Nature	Skyline Drive Mile 4.6	2.0 miles	Leads to Fox Home Site • Cemetery and old farm fence remnants are visible (can be shortened to 1.2 miles)
	Dickey Ridge	Mile 4.6	2.7 miles	Hike along a small stream through overgrown fields
	Snead Farm	Mile 4.6	1.4 miles	Gravel fire road leads hikers to an old farm and orchard
	Hickerson Hollow	Mile 9.2	2.2 miles	A horse trail leads into an old mountain resident's hollow
	Traces Nature	Mile 22.2	1.7 miles	Trail through a mature oak forest and old homesteads
	Little Stony Man Cliffs	Mile 39.1	0.9 mile	Excellent views along this extremely short hike
	Stony Man Nature - 👍	Mile 41.7	1.6 miles	Easy climb to the park's second highest point (4,011 ft)
	Limberlost	Mile 43	1.3 miles	Winding trail through hemlock forests, old homesteads, wetlands, and over Whiteoak Canyon Run
	Crescent Rock	Mile 45.6	3.3 miles	Leads hikers to a grove of Limberlost hemlock
	Deadening Nature	Mile 79.4	1.3 miles	Leads to a spectacular overlook atop Loft Mountain
	Blackrock Summit	Mile 84.8	0.8 mile	Short hike to rock outcroppings and beautiful views
Moderate	Compton Peak	Mile 10.4	2.4 miles	Fairly steep and rocky hike to scenic views
	Mary's Rock (Panorama)	Mile 31.6	3.7 miles	Longer and more difficult than the hike from Meadow Spring Parking Area, but the same excellent views
	Mary's Rock (Meadow Spring)	Mile 32.7	2.8 miles	Outstanding views of the Panorama area
	Hawksbill Mtn Summit - 👍	Mile 46.7	2.1 miles	Rocky trail to the park's tallest peak (4,051 ft) • You can also find a 1.7 mile (roundtrip) and 2.9 mile circuit to Hawksbill at Mile 45.6
	Rose River Falls	Mile 49.4	4.0 miles	See as many as four cascades after a heavy rain
	Dark Hollow Falls	Mile 50.7	1.4 miles	The shortest waterfall hike in the park
	Lewis Falls	Mile 51.4	2.0 miles/ 3.3 miles	Out-and-back from Skyline Drive to the 81-ft falls • 3.3-mile circuit begins from Big Meadows Amphitheater
	Mill Prong - 👍	Mile 52.8	4.0 miles	Roundtrip hike to Hoover's Rapidan Camp
	Bearfence Mountain - 👍	Mile 56.4	0.8 mile	Short scramble over rocks to broad panoramic views
	South River Falls	Mile 62.8	2.6 miles	Third tallest waterfall in the park (83-ft tall)
	Jones Run Falls	Mile 84.1	3.4 miles	A nice casual hike to 42-foot cascade
Strenuous	Little Devil Stairs	Mile 19.4	7.7 miles	Follow Keyser Run Fire Road to Little Devil Stairs
	Overall Run Falls	Mile 21.1	6.5 miles	Hike to the tallest waterfall in the park (93-ft tall)
	Cedar Run/ Whiteoak Circuit - 👍	Mile 42.6	8.2 miles	One of the most strenuous hikes in the park • From Hawksbill Gap, take Cedar Run–Link–Whiteoak–Whiteoak Fire Road–Horse Trail • You'll see multiple waterfalls and cascades along the way
	Doyles River Falls	Mile 81.1	3.2 miles	Fairly rigorous hike to the 28-ft upper falls and 63-ft lower falls
	Old Rag - 👍	Near Nethers on Route 600	5.4 miles (out-and-back)	Challenging and popular hike/scramble • Parking area is at the park's eastern boundary, not Skyline Drive • Start on Ridge Tr and return via Saddle Tr (7.1 miles)

SHENANDOAH

Rock Climbing

You won't find any of Shenandoah's rock climbing routes on the wish lists of serious climbers, but **Little Stony Man Cliffs** is a great place for beginners to learn the basics of climbing and rappelling. From mid-May to mid-September visitors can take part in an introductory rock climbing course offered by Aramark. The course is available on Mondays, Wednesdays, and Fridays, departing from **Skyland Resort**. Three day advance reservation is required. Cost includes guide, one night lodging, and a bag lunch.

ARAMARK • (800) 778-2871 (for reservations)
PO Box 727; Luray, VA 22835
www.visitshenandoah.com
Rates: $133 (double room), $174 (single room)

Horseback Riding

Horses are allowed on more than 180 miles of trails. To help visitors with their own horse(s) the park provides a Trail Ride Planning Guide:

www.nps.gov/shen/planyourvisit/horseback-trail-rides.htm

You'll also find a list of parking areas suitable for horse trailers with an estimate of available parking based on the season. Be aware that the park's lodges and campgrounds do not accommodate horses and they are not allowed to sleep in their trailer. Bringing your own horse gives riders the freedom to explore deeper into Shenandoah's wilderness. However, these freedoms require more responsibility. You should travel with a map, ride trails that are suitable to your ability, and check the extended weather forecast before heading out.

Aramark provides horse rides free of those responsibilities. One or two-and-a-half hour guided trail rides are available from early April until late November. The horse stable is located near **Skyland Resort** (Mile 41.7). All riders must be at least 4'10" and weigh less than 250 pounds.

ARAMARK • (540) 999-2210 (for same day reservations)
PO Box 727; Luray, VA 22835 • www.visitshenandoah.com
Rates: $40 (1 hour), $75 (2.5 hours), $6–12 (Pony Rides)

Fishing

Some 70 streams begin in the Blue Ridge Mountains and flow into the valleys surrounding Shenandoah National Park. These streams are inhabited by a variety of species, with eastern brook trout among the most popular game fish. When fishing in the park anglers must adhere to Virginia fishing regulations. All Virginia residents 16 years and older and non-residents 12 years and older are required to have a Virginia state fishing license. A 5-day non-resident license can be purchased at **Big Meadows Wayside** (page 67) or from local sporting goods stores outside park boundaries. If you're looking for sound fishing advice or to hire a guide, try one of the following **local outfitters**:

Murray Enterprises/Murray's Fly Shop • (540) 984-4212
PO Box 156; Edinburg, VA 22824
www.murraysflyshop.com
Full-Day Rates: 1–2 People $375, 3 People $425, 4 People $475

Page Valley Fly Fishing • (540) 743-7952
Luray, VA 22835
www.pagevalleyflyfishing.com
Rates: 1 Person $150 (half-day)/$200 (full-day)
2 People $200 (half-day)/$300 (full-day)

Bird Watching

About 95% of Shenandoah National Park is forested and 40% of the total area is designated wilderness, providing an excellent habitat for birds. **More than 200 species of resident and transient birds use the park**. Nearly half of the species breed here, but only thirty make the park their year-round home. Local species include tufted titmice, red-tailed hawk, Carolina chickadee, wild turkey, barred owl, and downy woodpecker.

Exotic species also call the park home. In the summer of 2000 the park resumed its **Peregrine Falcon Restoration Program**. It has been a success and today visitors may spot these beautiful raptors soaring high above the Blue Ridge Mountains. **Cerulean warbler** and **scarlet tanager** also reside in the park, but are seldom seen. The Cerulean warbler, once common in the lower Mississippi valley, has declined in numbers due to loss of habitat. The park hosts a healthy population of scarlet tanagers, but most bird watchers wouldn't know it. These feathered friends spend most of their time high above the ground in the upper canopy of trees.

Skyline Drive

Skyline Drive is a National Scenic Byway that runs 105-miles from north to south spanning the entire length of the park. Milepost markers, located on the west side of the road, make locating the park's facilities and services on Skyline Drive a snap. They're also an important tool for using this guide book as the location of park trailheads, campgrounds, and lodgings are all defined by their milepost. When travelling this scenic drive be sure to follow the 35 mph speed limit. Typical to mountain driving, you'll find steep hills, sharp turns, and frequent stops (75 overlooks). Be aware of **Mary's Rock Tunnel** (Mile 32)—RVs, horse trailers, and other vehicles taller than 12' 8" will have to detour around.

In 1931, crews broke ground on Skyline Drive. Political posturing and the Great Depression slowed the pace of the project. The stretch from Rockfish Gap to Front Royal wasn't completed until 1939 at a total cost near $5 million or $50,000 per mile. Contractors built the highway, but it would not have been completed without the CCC's help. They graded the slope on either side of the roadway, and built many of the guardrails and guard walls. Other sections of the road were built simply to see if it was possible. Legend holds that the 670-foot Mary's Rock Tunnel was designed to settle a challenge between the Bureau of Public Roads and National Park Landscape Architects. After completion, facilities were needed to accommodate guests. In western parks infrastructure was developed independently by powerful railways. Shenandoah didn't have the luxury of a railroad's deep pockets. In 1937, with no plan and few ideas, Congress turned to a concessioner, Virginia Sky-Line Company (now Aramark). Sky-Line dictated much of the park's direction and development from 1937 to 1942.

Winter Activities

Shenandoah is more or less neglected during the winter months. All campgrounds, lodging, and waysides are closed. Skyline Drive occasionally closes during inclement weather. Big Meadows averages more than thirty inches of snow each year. Still, many hardy **hikers** enter the park to view a completely different environment. Ground covered in snow. Trees without leaves. Waterfalls turned to ice. Bears holed up for winter. Facilities may be closed, but there's still 196,000 acres of land open for **backcountry camping**.

Whiteoak Canyon

Did you know?

▶ Established in December of 1935, Shenandoah became the first national park created from a large, populated expanse of private land. In 2011 Shenandoah celebrated its 75th anniversary.

▶ Skyline Drive, a 105 mile scenic byway, is the park's main attractions. Its path follows the mountain's ridge and trails trod by Indians and early settlers.

▶ The Appalachian Trail follows a course similar to Skyline Drive, spanning the park's length in roughly 101 miles. In its entirety, the Appalachian Trail is approximately 2,184 miles long, extending all the way from Singer Mountain in Georgia to Mount Katahdin in Maine.

▶ At 4,051 feet, Hawksbill Mountain is the highest peak in the park. It's more than 10,000 feet lower than the summit of Mount Whitney, the highest peak in the contiguous United States located in Sequoia–Kings Canyon National Park in California.

Old Rag Mountain in the background

The Appalachian Trail

For Kids

Children (ages 7–12) have the opportunity to become a **Shenandoah National Park Junior Ranger**. Kids (ages 13 and older) will enjoy the entire set of **Ranger Explorer Guides**. Activity booklets can be picked up in the park or are available for print at:

www.nps.gov/shen/forkids/jr-ranger-explorer.htm

Ranger-led tours and talks are another family favorite. In fact, attending a ranger program may be the spark your child needs to ignite interest in the Junior Ranger Program. The personalities of the rangers are so infectious they may even inspire your child to one say don the iconic "Smoky the Bear" hat that has become the symbol of the illustrious park rangers. If they like the hats, but don't want the job that comes with it, you can also pick one up at a nearby visitor center.

Ranger Programs: The best way to truly see the park is under the thoughtful guidance of a park ranger. They are happy to share with you knowledge of bears, raptors, and other wildlife and plantlife on a series of walks, talks, and evening programs. You can learn about the **history of Skyland Resort** on a tour of **Historic Massanutten Lodge**, hike the **Appalachian Trail**, or stroll through CCC-era structures as Shenandoah rangers shower you with entertaining and educational anecdotes that have been passed down through generations of rangers. For a current schedule of all of the programs and events visit the park website or pick up a free copy of the park publication, **_Shenandoah Overlook_** (available at entrance stations and visitor centers).

Flora & Fauna: Shenandoah's forests are classified as "oak-hickory" but many other trees take root within the park. Pine, maple, birch, basswood, blackgum, tulip poplar, chestnut, and a few stands of hemlock can all be found here. Mountain laurel, which blooms in June, can be found along Skyline Drive. It is a native species, but these shrubs were planted by the CCC in the 1930s. Variation in latitude and elevation help create astounding diversity. **More than 1,000 species of ferns, grasses, lichens, mosses, fungi and wildflowers exist in the park**.

The creation of Shenandoah National Park helped re-establish the area as a refuge for wildlife. In the 1700s, early European settlers noted the region's abundance and diversity of animals. By the late 1800s, American bison, elk, beaver, and river otter were extirpated. Many over-hunted species have now returned or been reintroduced. Shenandoah is home to one of the densest populations of black bears in the United States. **Somewhere between 300 and 500 bears reside here**. In all there are **more than 50 species of mammals** in the park. White-tail deer and gray squirrels are often seen along the roadway, while bobcats, black bears, moles, and shrews are more elusive. Ten species of toads and frogs and fourteen species of salamanders or newts live here. Twenty-five species of reptiles have found refuge in Shenandoah including eighteen snakes, five turtles, three skinks, and one lizard. Viewing and photographing wildlife is a popular activity, but please help keep wildlife wild. Be sure to stay a safe distance from animals and never feed or provoke them.

Pets: Pets are allowed in the park, but must be kept on a leash no more than six feet in length at all times. They are allowed on the following trails: Limberlost, Old Rag, and Dark Hollow Falls. Only service animals are permitted in park buildings.

Accessibility: Sites accessible to wheelchair users are available at all picnic areas and campgrounds. Most facilities and restrooms are accessible with assistance. Lewis Mountain, Skyland Resort, and Big Meadows Lodge offer wheelchair accessible lodging. Many ranger programs are accessible, including the van tour to Rapidan Camp. Limberlost Trail is fully accessible.

Weather: Come prepared for all kinds of weather. Storms are common throughout the year, but peak in September. Snow can fall any day from October to April, but is most common in January and February. Roads are often slippery with ice in winter and foggy in spring. The mountains in Shenandoah are usually 10°F cooler than the valley.

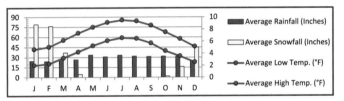

Vacation Planner

Shenandoah is a popular weekend getaway for citizens of nearby communities and Washington, D.C. The park can become excessively busy along **Skyline Drive**, but peace and quiet is only a few miles along a tranquil hiking trail away. Most trails and overlooks feature similar views and scenery, but a few are better than others. This two-day vacation planner is provided to help you choose what to do on your Shenandoah National Park vacation. The hike to **Old Rag** (page 70) is highly recommended, but not included in the planner because its trailhead is not located along Skyline Drive. Joining a **ranger program** (check the current issue of the *Shenandoah Overlook*) is also encouraged. First-time visitors should stop at one of the park's two visitor centers. **Dickey Ridge Visitor Center** (Mile 4.7) is conveniently located near the park's north entrance. If entering the park from the south it won't be until Mile 51 that you reach **Harry F. Byrd Visitor Center**. Regardless which one you stop at, a short orientation video, exhibits, a bookstore, information desk, backcountry permits, and park rangers will be at your disposal to help introduce

Big Meadows © woodleywonderworks

yourself to the park. This template assumes that you are entering from the north entrance (Front Royal). **Camping** and **lodging** are available within the park (page 69). Dining, grocery stores, lodging, festivals, and attractions outside the park are listed on pages 76–79.

Day 1 After stopping at **Dickey Ridge Visitor Center**, catch a glimpse of what Virginia mountain life was like by hiking the short **Fox Hollow Trail**. The trailhead is located just across the road from the visitor center. After the hike return to Skyline Drive and head south about 30 miles to **Mary's Rock Tunnel** (Mile 32). Here you'll hike to the top of Mary's Rock, which provides outstanding views of the Virginia piedmont and Thornton Gap Entrance Station. Two trails lead to the top of Mary's Rock. The trail north of the tunnel is shorter and easier than the one on the south side. This is a good place to settle in for the night. There are plenty of lodging accommodations outside the park in Luray and Sperryville, or continue along Skyline Drive a few miles further south to Skyland or Big Meadows (stop at **Stony Man Overlook** along the way).

Day 2 On your second day in the park, sign up for a **guided trail ride** (page 72) or spend the day on a **rock climbing adventure** (page 72, 3-day advance reservation required). If not, take one of the park's longer and more scenic hikes, like **Cedar Run/Whiteoak Circuit** (page 71). **Bearfence Mountain** (page 71) is a short yet challenging climb, providing breathtaking views that should not be missed before exiting the park.

Dining

In the Park

Skyline Resort • (888) 896-3833
Mile 41.7 Skyline Drive • Entrée: $13–24

Big Meadows Lodge • (888) 896-3833
Mile 51.0 Skyline Drive • Entrée: $13–23
www.visitshenandoah.com (for both)

Near the Park

Spelunker's • (540) 631-0300
116 South St; Front Royal, VA 22630
www.spelunkerscustard.com • Entrée: $4–6

The Wine and Duck Restaurant • (540) 636-1000
117 E Main St; Front Royal, VA 22630

Soul Mountain Restaurant • (540) 636-0070
300 E Main St; Front Royal, VA 22630

Main Street Mill Restaurant • (540) 636-3123
500 E Main St; Front Royal, VA 22630

Victorias Restaurant • (540) 636-0008
231 Chester St; Front Royal, VA 22630

Royal Oak Tavern • (540) 551-9953
101 W 14th St; Front Royal, VA 22630
www.royaloaktavern.net • Entrée: $10–19

Melting Pot Pizza • (540) 636-6146
138 W 14th St; Front Royal, VA 22630
www.meltingpotpizza.com • Entrée: $6–20

Golden China Restaurant • (540) 635-3688
1423 N Shenandoah Ave; Front Royal, VA 22630

Jalisco Mexican Restaurant • (540) 635-7348
1303 N Royal Ave; Front Royal, VA 22630

L'Dees Pancake House • (540) 635-3791
522 E Main St; Front Royal, VA 22630
www.ldeespancakehouse.com

Lucky Star Lounge • (540) 635-5297
205 A E Main St; Front Royal, VA 22630
www.zen2go.net • Entrée: $12

Apartment 2g • (540) 636-9293
206 S Royal Ave; Front Royal, VA 22630
www.jsgourmet.com • Entrée: $50 (5-course)

Mamma Mia Pizza Pasta & Subs • (540) 652-6062
701 S 3rd St; Shenandoah, VA 22849
www.mammamiarestaurant.net • Entrée: $13–19

Farmhouse Restaurant • (540) 778-2285
326 Hawksbill Park Rd; Stanley, VA 22851

Ciro's Pizza • (540) 778-1112
558 W Main St; Stanley, VA 22851

Brick Oven Pizzeria • (540) 778-5555
323 E Main St; Stanley, VA 22851

China Shop • (540) 778-2900
558 W Main St, # B; Stanley, VA 22851

Main Street Café • (540) 778-1555
208 W Main St; Stanley, VA 22851

Prince Michel Vineyard and Winery
154 Winery Ln; Leon, VA 22725
www.princemichel.com • (540) 547-9720

Artisans Grill • (540) 743-7030
2 E Main St; Luray, VA 22835
www.artisansgrill.com • Entrée: $18–24

Uncle Bucks Restaurant • (540) 743-2323
42 E Main St; Luray, VA 22835

Dan's Steak House • (540) 743-6285
8512 US-211 W; Luray, VA 22835

Mindi's Mexican Restaurant • (540) 743-7550
1033 US-211 W; Luray, VA 22835

Tastee Freez • (540) 743-6196
402 W Main St; Luray, VA 22835

Thunderbird Café • (540) 289-5094
42 Island Ford Rd; McGaheysville, VA 22840
www.thethunderbirdcafe.com • Entrée: $7–10

Hank's Smokehouse • (540) 289-7667
49 Bloomer Springs Rd; McGaheysville, VA 22840
www.hankssmokehouse.com • Entrée: $13–19

Log Cabin Barbecue • (540) 289-9400
11672 Spotswood Tr; Elkton, VA 22812
www.logcabinbarbecue.com • Entrée: $7–20

Pig-N Steak • (540) 948-3130
313 Washington St; Madison, VA 22727
www.pigandsteak.com • Entrée: $10–13

Giovanna's Italian Eatery • (540) 948-5454
2679 S Seminole Tr; Madison, VA 22727

Thornton River Grille • (540) 987-8790
3710 Sperryville Pike; Sperryville, VA 22740
www.thorntonrivergrille.com • Entrée: $17–19

Rudy's Pizza • (540) 987-9494
3710 Sperryville Pike; Sperryville, VA 22740

Griffin Tavern • (540) 675-3227
659 Zachary Taylor Hwy; Flint Hill, VA 22627
www.griffintavern.com • Entrée: $13–34

Scotto's Italian Restaurant & Pizzeria
1412 W Broad St; Waynesboro, VA 22980
www.scottos.net • (540) 942-8715 • Entrée: $10–18

Gavid's Steak House • (540) 949-6353
1501 W Broad St; Waynesboro, VA 22980

Massaki Japanese Steakhouse • (540) 946-9191
109 Lew Dewitt Blvd # B; Waynesboro, VA 22980
www.massakisteakhouse.com • Entrée: $12–24

Chickpeas • (540) 942-9711
415 W Main St; Waynesboro, VA 22980

Mi Rancho Restaurant • (540) 941-5980
408 E Main St; Waynesboro, VA 22980

Weasie's Kitchen • (540) 943-0500
130 E Broad St; Waynesboro, VA 22980

Tailgate Grill • (540) 941-8451
1106 W Broad St; Waynesboro, VA 22980

Blue Mountain Brewery • (540) 456-8020
9519 Critzers Shop Rd; Afton, VA 22920
www.bluemountainbrewery.com • Entrée: ~$10

La Cocina Del Sol • (434) 823-5469
1200 Crozet Ave; Crozet, VA 22932

Da Luca Café & Wine Bar • (434) 205-4251
Old Trail Dr; Crozet, VA 22932
www.dalucacafe.com • Entrée: $14–17

Crozet Pizza • (434) 823-2132
5794 3 Notch'd Rd; Crozet, VA 22932
www.crozetpizza.net • Entrée: $12–24

Tea House • (434) 823-2868
325 Four Leaf Ln, # 6; Charlottesville, VA 22903

Pesto Mediterranean Grill • (434) 823-7080
375 Four Leaf Ln, # 101; Charlottesville, VA 22903
www.pestomedgrill.com • Entrée: $11–19

Grocery Stores

Whole Foods Market • (434) 973-4900
300 Shoppers World Court; Charlottesville, VA 22901

Walmart • (434) 973-1412
975 Hilton Heights Rd; Charlottesville, VA 22901

Food Lion • (540) 942-2992
990 Hopeman Parkway; Waynesboro, VA 22980

Food Lion • (540) 298-9455
14811 Spotswood Tr; Elkton, VA 22827

Food Lion • (540) 249-0665
83 Augusta Ave; Grottoes, VA 24441

Food Lion • (540) 778-2081
558 W Main St # A; Stanley, VA 22851

Walmart Supercenter • (540) 743-4111
1036 US-211 West; Luray, VA 22835

Food Lion • (540) 743-4502
1400 US-211 West; Luray, VA 22835

Food Lion • (540) 622-2704
260 Remount Rd; Front Royal, VA 22630

Lodging

In the Park

Skyline Resort • (888) 896-3833
Mile 41.7 Skyline Drive
www.visitshenandoah.com • Rates: See page 69

Big Meadows Lodge • (888) 896-3833
Mile 51.0 Skyline Drive
www.visitshenandoah.com • Rates: See page 69

Lewis Mountain Cabins • (888) 896-3833
Mile 57.5 Skyline Drive
www.visitshenandoah.com • Rates: See page 69

Near the Park

<u>Woodward House</u> • (800) 635-7011
413 S Royal Ave; Front Royal, VA 22630
www.acountryhome.com • Rates: $110–225

<u>Killahevlin B&B</u> • (540) 636-7335
1401 N Royal Dr; Front Royal, VA 22630
www.vairish.com • Rates: $155–285

<u>Cool Harbor Motel</u> • (540) 635-2191
141 W 15th St; Front Royal, VA 22630
www.coolharbormotel.com • Rates: $65–75

<u>Lackawanna B&B</u> • (540) 636-7945
236 Riverside Dr; Front Royal, VA 22630
www.lackawannabb.com • Rates: $144–174

<u>Middleton Inn</u> • (540) 675-2020
176 Main St; Washington, VA 22747
www.middletoninn.com • Rates: $275–625

<u>Gay Street Inn</u> • (540) 316-9220
160 Gay St; Washington, VA 22747
www.gaystreetinn.com • Rates: $169–249

<u>Heritage House B&B</u> • (540) 675-3207
291 Main St; Washington, VA 22747
www.heritagehousebb.com • Rates: $175–275

<u>Inn At Little Washington</u> • (540) 675-3800
309 Middle St; Washington, VA 22747
www.theinnatlittlewashington.com • Rates: $425–2,400

<u>Blue Rock Inn</u> • (540) 987-3388
12567 Lee Highway; Washington, VA 22747
www.thebluerockinn.com • Rates: $195–245

<u>Foster Harris House B&B</u> • (540) 675-3757
189 Main St; Washington, VA 22747
www.fosterharris.com • Rates: $199–339

<u>Fairlea Farm B&B</u> • (540) 675-3679
636 Mount Salem Ave; Washington, VA 22747
www.fairleafarm.com • Rates: $155–205

<u>Bear Bluff</u> • (503) 383-9336
551 River Valley Rd; Rileyville, VA 22650
www.shenandoahcabinrentals.com • Rates: $195–225

<u>Hopkins Ordinary B&B</u> • (540) 987-3382
47 Main St; Sperryville, VA 22740
www.hopkinsordinary.com • Rates: $169–239

<u>Cave Hill Farm B&B</u> • (540) 289-7441
9875 Cave Hill Rd; McGaheysville, VA 22840
www.cavehillfarmbandb.com • Rates: $159–199

<u>Massanutten</u> • (540) 289-9441
1822 Resort Dr; Elkton, VA 22827
www.massresort.com • Rates: $150

<u>Shenandoah Valley Farm & Inn</u> (540) 289-5402
882 Bloomer Springs Rd; McGaheysville, VA 22840
www.shenvalfarm.com • Rates: $75–85

<u>William Cox Inn</u> • (434) 985-8139
455 Touchstone Ln; Stanardsville, VA 22973
www.williamcoxinn.com • Rates: $170–189

<u>Once Upon A Mountain</u> • (540) 743-1724
974 Cross Mountain Rd; Luray, VA 22835

<u>Old Massanutten Lodge B&B</u> • (540) 269-8800
3448 Caverns Dr; Keezletown, VA 22832
www.oldmassanuttenlodge.com • Rates: $140–170

<u>Shadow Mountain Escape</u> • (540) 843-0584
1132 Jewell Hollow Rd; Luray, VA 22835
www.shadowmountainescape.com • Rates: $185–210

<u>South Court Inn B&B</u> • (888) 749-8055
160 S Court St; Luray, VA 22825
www.southcourtinn.com • Rates: $150–225

<u>Yogi Bear's Jellystone Camp</u> • (540) 743-4002
2250 US-211 E; Luray, VA 22835
www.campluray.com • Rates: $48–69

<u>Graves Mountain Lodge</u> • (540) 923-4231
205 Graves Mountain Ln; Syria, VA 22743
www.gravesmountain.com • Rates: $78–135

<u>Sharp Rock Vineyards and B&B</u> • (540) 987-8020
5 Sharp Rock Rd; Sperryville, VA 22740
www.sharprockvineyards.com • Rates: $200–225

<u>Piney Hill B&B</u> • (540) 778-5261
1048 Piney Hill Rd; Luray, VA 22835
www.pineyhillbandb.com • Rates: $160–195

<u>Mimslyn Inn</u> • (540) 743-5105
401 W Main St; Luray, VA 22835
www.mimslyninn.com • Rates: $115–325

<u>Victorian Inn</u> • (540) 860-4229
138 E Main St; Luray, VA 22835
www.victorianinnluray.com

<u>Mayne View B&B</u> • (540) 743-7921
439 Mechanic St; Luray, VA 22835
www.mayneview.com • Rates: $99–129

<u>Woodruff House B&B</u> • (540) 743-1494
330 Mechanic St; Luray, VA 22835
www.woodruffinns.com • Rates: $95

<u>White Fence B&B</u> • (540) 778-2115
275 Chapel Rd; Stanley, VA 22851
www.whitefencebb.com • Rates: $175

<u>Milton House B&B</u> • (540) 778-2495
113 W Main St; Stanley, VA 22851
www.miltonhouseinn.com • Rates: $115–195

<u>Daughter of the Stars B&B</u> • (540) 244-8197
188 E Main St; Stanley, VA 22851
www.daughterofthestars.net • Rates: $95–104

<u>Dulaney Hollow Old Rag Mountain</u>
VA-231; Madison, VA 22727 • (540) 923-4470

<u>Shenandoah Hill KOA</u> • (540) 948-4186
110 Campground Ln; Madison, VA
www.shenandoahhills.com

<u>Inn at Sugar Hollow Farm</u> • (434) 823-7086
6051 Sugar Hollow Rd; Crozet, VA 22932
www.sugarhollow.com • Rates: $150–330

<u>Montfair Resort Farm</u> • (434) 823-5202
2500 Bezaleel Dr; Crozet, Va., VA 22932
www.montfairresortfarm.com • Rates: $138–176

<u>Iris Inn B&B</u> • (540) 943-1991
191 Chinquapin Dr; Waynesboro, VA 22980
www.irisinn.com • Rates: $179–299

<u>Residence Inn</u> • (540) 943-7426
44 Windigrove Dr; Waynesboro, VA 22980
www.marriott.com • Rates: $129

<u>Tree Streets Inn</u> • (540) 949-4484
421 Walnut Ave; Waynesboro, VA 22980
www.treestreetsinn.com • Rates: $100–130

<u>Belle Hearth B&B</u> • (540) 943-1910
320 S Wayne Ave; Waynesboro, VA 22980
www.bellehearth.com • Rates: $99–135

Not all dining and lodging facilities are listed. Many chain hotels and restaurants can be found nearby in Harrisonburg, Luray, Waynesboro, and Front Royal.

Festivals
Near the Park

<u>Virginia Wine Showcase</u> • February
300+ locally-grown award-winning wines
www.vawineshowcase.org • Chantilly, VA

<u>Chocolate Lovers Festival</u> • February
A variety of chocolate-related activities
www.chocolatefestival.net • Fairfax, VA

<u>Highland Maple Festival</u> • March
50+ year tradition explores maple syrup-making
www.highlandcounty.org/maple • Monterey, VA

<u>Virginia Festival of the Book</u> • March
www.vabook.org • Charlottesville, VA

<u>Historic Garden Week</u> • April
Dubbed "America's Largest Open House"
www.vagardenweek.org • Statewide, VA

<u>Virginia Wine & Craft Festival</u> • May
Wine, food, crafts, and live entertainment
www.wineandcraftfestival.com • Front Royal, VA

<u>Pony Swim and Auction</u> • July
Assateague Island and Chincoteague Island, VA
www.assateagueisland.com/ponyswim/ponyswim

<u>Hot Air Balloon Rally</u> • 4th of July
Music, balloon rides, classic car show, and more
www.sunriserotarylexva.org • Lexington, VA

<u>Old Fiddlers Convention</u> • August
World's oldest and largest fiddlers' convention
www.oldfiddlersconvention.com • Galax, VA

<u>Smith Mtn Lake Wine Festival</u> • September
www.visitsmithmountainlake.com • Moneta, VA

<u>Apple Butter Festival</u> • September
www.visitshenandoah.com • Skyland Resort

<u>Rappahannock County Farm Tour</u> • September
Link Community Center, Sperryville, VA
www.farmtour.visitrappahannockva.com

Richmond Folk Festival • October
www.richmondfolkfestival.org • Richmond, VA

International Gold Cup • October
Horse steeplechase races
www.vagoldcup.com • The Plains, VA

Fall Foliage Art Show • October
www.SVACart.com • Waynesboro, VA

Apple Harvest Festival • October
www.gravesmountain.com • Syria, VA

Taste of Culpeper • October
www.culpeperdowntown.com • Culpeper, VA

Harvest & Leaf Peep Festival • October
www.ducardvineyards.com • Madison, VA

Virginia Film Festival • November
www.virginiafilmfestival.org • Charlottesville, VA

Washington DC

Int'l Wine & Food Festival • February
Ronald Reagan Building and International
Trade Center; Washington, DC
www.wineandfooddc.com • (617) 385-5021

National Cherry Blossom Festival • March/April
One of the best times to visit Washington DC
www.nationalcherryblossomfestival.org

Filmfest DC • April
www.filmfestdc.org • (202) 628-FILM

Fiesta Asia! • May
Pennsylvania Ave NW; Washington, DC
www.asiaheritagefoundation.org • (703) 920-0620

National Capitol Barbecue Battle • June
Pennsylvania Ave NW; Washington, DC
www.bbqdc.com • (202) 828-3099

Capitol Jazz Fest • June
10475 Little Patuxent Parkway; Columbia, MD
www.capitaljazz.com • (301) 780-9300

Capitol Pride • June
23rd St & P St NW; Washington, DC
www.capitalpride.org • (202) 797-3510

Festa Italiana • June
www.festaitalianadc.com • (202) 923-7845

DC Jazz Festival • June
www.dcjazzfest.org

Smithsonian Folklife Festival • June/July
www.festival.si.edu • (202) 633-1000

Adams Morgan Days Festival • September
DC's longest running street festival
www.adamsmorgandayfestival.com

National Book Festival • September
www.loc.gov/bookfest • (888) 714-4696

Turkish Festival • October
2011 Readers Choice Best Festival
Pennsylvania Ave NW; Washington, DC
www.turkishfestival.org • (888) 282-3236

Attractions

Appalachian Outdoors Adventure • (540) 743-7400
*Gear and apparel store • Great place to get
outdoor activity & event information*
18 E Main St; Luray, VA 22835
www.appalachianoutdoorsadventures.com

Shenandoah Caverns • (540) 477-3115
261 Caverns Rd; Quicksburg, Virginia 22847
www.shenandoahcaverns.com • Admission: $23/Adult

Luray Caverns • (540) 743-3821
101 Cave Hill Rd; Luray, VA 22835
www.luraycaverns.com • Admission: $23/Adult

Caverns Country Club • (540) 743-7111
910 TC Northcott Blvd; Luray, VA 22835
www.luraycaverns.com • Rates: $30–40

Shenandoah River Outfitters • (800) 622-6632
6502 S Page Valley Rd; Luray, VA 22835
www.shenandoahriver.com • Rates: $36–90

Page Twin Theatre • (540) 743-4444
33 E Main St; Luray, VA 22835

Luray Valley Farm Museum • (540) 743-1297
629 W Main St; Luray, VA 22835

Luray Lanes • (540) 743-3535
52 W Main St; Luray, VA 22835

George Washington NF • Luray, VA

Luray Zoo • (540) 743-4113
1087 US-211; West Luray, VA 22835
www.lurayzoo.com • Admission: $10/Adult

Virginia Quilt Museum • (540) 433-3818
301 S Main St; Harrisonburg, VA 22801
www.vaquiltmuseum.org • Admission: $5/Adult

Harrisonburg Children's Museum • (540) 442-8900
30 N Main St; Harrisonburg, VA 22802
www.hcmuseum.org • Admission: $5/Person

Regal Cinemas Stadium 14 • (540) 434-7661
381 University Blvd; Harrisonburg, VA 22801
www.regmovies.com

New Market Walking Tours • (540) 740-3747
9317 N Congress St; New Market, VA 22844
www.appleblossominn.net

Civil War Museum • (540) 832-2944
400 S Main St; Gordonsville, VA 22942
www.hgiexchange.org • Admission: $6/Adult

Edith J. Carrier Arboretum and Botanical Gardens
MSC 3705, 780 University Blvd; Harrisonburg, VA 22807 • (540) 568-3194

Lakeview Golf Course • (540) 434-8937
4101 Shen Lake Dr; Harrisonburg, VA 22801
www.lakeviewgolf.net • Rates: $27-32 (18 Holes)

Page County Heritage Museums • (540) 743-6698
223 Hamburg Rd; Luray, VA 22835

Woodstone Meadows Golf Course • (540) 289-9441
1822 Resort Dr; McGaheysville, VA 22840

Massanutten Ski Resort • (540) 289-9441
Waterpark, golf, snow sports, and spa
1822 Resort Dr; McGaheysville, VA 22840
www.massresort.com

Bryce Resort • (540) 856-2124
Golf, Zip Line, Bungee, and Snow Sports
1982 Fairway Dr; Basye, VA 22810
www.bryceresort.com

Packsaddle Ridge Golf Club • (540) 269-8188
3067 Pack Saddle Tr; Keezletown, VA 22832
www.packsaddle.net • Rates: $30–40 (18 Holes)

Hull's Drive In • (540) 463-2621
2367 N Lee Hwy; Lexington, VA 24450
www.hullsdrivein.com

Cows-N-Corn • (540) 439-4806
Fall • Corn Maze, Haunted Hayride • Seriously cool stuff, check it out
5225 Catlett Road; Midland, VA 22728
www.cows-n-corn.com

Jefferson National Forest • (540) 291-2188
27 Ranger Ln; Natural Bridge, VA 24578

Foamhenge • (540) 464-2253
A to-scale foam version of the UK's Stonehenge
Hwy 11 South; Natural Bridge, VA

Hunt Bigfoot with a Redneck • (540) 464-2253
Hwy 130; Natural Bridge, VA

Virginia Safari Park • (540) 291-3205
229 Safari Ln; Natural Bridge, VA 24578
www.virginiasafaripark.com

Washington DC

Library of Congress • (202) 707-5000
www.loc.gov • Tours Available

The Pentagon • (703) 697-1776
*Tour reservations are required (available
8–90 days in advance)*
1400 Defense Pentagon
www.pentagon.afis.osd.mil/index.html

Arlington National Cemetery • (703) 607-8000
Arlington, VA 22211
www.arlingtoncemetery.org

City Segway Tours • (877) 734-8687
624 9th St Northwest
www.citysegwaytours.com • Rates: $60–70

Bike and Roll • (202) 842-2453
Rear Plaza • On 12th St between Penn and
Constitution Ave & 1100 Pennsylvania Ave NW
www.bikethesites.com • Rates: $35–53

DC by Foot • (202) 370-1830
1740 18th St Northwest Suite 304
www.dcbyfoot.com • Free (Private Tours for fee)

The Reflecting Pool and Washington Monument

DC Metro Food Tours • (202) 683-8847
305 S St Asaph St Suite 4; Alexandria, VA 22314
www.dcmetrofoodtours.com • Rates: $55

Lincoln Memorial • (202) 426-6895
900 Ohio Dr Southwest

National Shrine of the Immaculate Conception
400 Michigan Ave NE • (202) 526-1287
www.nationalshrine.com • Free Tours

Newseum • (202) 292-6100
555 Pennsylvania Ave
www.newseum.org • Admission: $22/Adult

Washington Monument • (202) 426-6841
www.nps.gov/wamo • Free Admission (ticket Req'd)

Washington National Cathedral • (202) 537-6243
Massachusetts Ave NW & Wisconsin Ave NW
www.cathedral.org

Walk of the Town • (240) 672-6306
Washington DC, Northwest, DC 20560
www.walkofthetowndc.com • Free

Old Town Trolley Tours • (202) 832-9800
50 Massachusetts Ave, NE
www.trolleytours.com • Tour: $32/Adult

Nat'l Gallery of Art Sculpture Garden • (202) 737-4215
4th St Northwest
www.nga.gov/feature/sculpturegarden/general • Free

Korean War Veterans Memorial • (202) 619-7222
10 Daniel French Dr Southwest

National Air and Space Museum • (202) 633-1000
Two Locations: 900 Jefferson St Northwest
& Independence Ave Southwest
www.nasm.si.edu • Free (Tickets required for
many lectures and events)

U.S. Holocaust Memorial Museum • (202) 488-0400
100 Raoul Wallenberg Place SW
www.ushmm.org • Free

Smithsonian National Museum of Natural History • (202) 633-1000
1000 Constitution Ave Northwest
www.mnh.si.edu • Free

Smithsonian American Art Museum • (202) 633-7970
F Street Northwest
www.americanart.si.edu • Free

Smithsonian National Zoo • (202) 633-4800
3001 Connecticut Ave
www.nationalzoo.si.edu • Free

National Portrait Gallery • (202) 633-8300
801 F St Northwest
www.npg.si.edu • Free

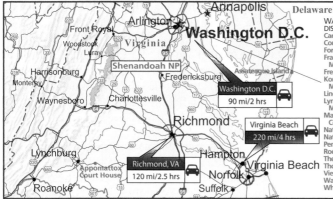

WASHINGTON, D.C. AREA
DISTRICT OF COLUMBIA
Carter G. Woodson Home
Constitution Gardens
Ford's Theatre
Franklin Delano Roosevelt
  Memorial
Frederick Douglass
Korean War Veterans
  Memorial
Lincoln Memorial
Lyndon Baines Johnson
  Memorial Grove
Mary McLeod Bethune
  Council House
National Capital Parks
National Mall
Pennsylvania Avenue
Rock Creek
Theodore Roosevelt Island
Thomas Jefferson Memorial
Vietnam Veterans Memorial
Washington Monument
White House

World War II Memorial
MARYLAND
Antietam
Catoctin Mountain
Chesapeake and Ohio Canal
  (also D.C., W.Va.)
Clara Barton
Fort Washington
Greenbelt
Monocacy
Piscataway
Potomac Heritage Trail
  (also Pa., Va., D.C.)
Thomas Stone
VIRGINIA
Arlington House,
  The Robert E. Lee Memorial
George Washington Birthplace
George Washington Memorial
  Parkway (also Md.)
Manassas
Prince William Forest
Wolf Trap

WASHINGTON, D.C. AREA
PROFESSIONAL SPORTS TEAMS:

DC United (MLS)
Washington Redskins (NFL)
Washington Nationals (MLB)
Washington Wizards (NBA)
Washington Mystics (WNBA)
Washington Capitals (NHL)

For more information on visiting Virginia click www.virginia.org

Driving Distances to Byrd Visitor Center

A ranger leads a tour of Mammoth Cave

MAMMOTH CAVE

1 Mammoth Cave Parkway
PO Box 7
Mammoth Cave, KY 42259
Phone: (270) 758-2180
Website: www.nps.gov/maca

Established: July 1, 1941
Size: 52,830 Acres
Annual Visitors: 500,000
Peak Season: Summer & Weekends

Total Cave Length: 367+ Miles
Public Cave Trails: ~14 Miles
Hiking Trails: 80 Miles

Activities: Cave Tours ($4–48),
Backpacking/Hiking, Paddling,
Biking, Horseback Riding, Fishing

Campgrounds ($12–20/night):
Mammoth Cave, Houchin's Ferry
and Maple Grove Campgrounds
Lodging: Mammoth Cave Hotel

Park Hours: All day, every day
(Cave Tours available during Visitor
Center Hours • see page 81)
Entrance Fee: None

Mammoth Cave - Kentucky

At more than 367 miles in length, **Mammoth Cave** is the longest cave system in the world, and the competition isn't close. Mammoth earns its name by being more than twice as long as its next closest rival, **Jewel Cave** in South Dakota. And several new miles of passages are discovered each year, leaving geologists to believe there could be as many as 600 additional miles of cave yet to be discovered.

The first known cave exploration took place some 4,000 years ago. Native Americans mined the cave's upper levels for more than two millennia. They sought gypsum, selenite, and mirabilite, among other minerals. Proof of their presence was left in the form of ancient artifacts: cane torches, gourd bowls, cloth, a handful of petroglyphs, and even their remains. Constant temperature, humidity, and salty soil make a cave a particularly good environment for preserving human remains. Several "mummies" were buried in an organized fashion. Others, like the remains of a primitive man pinned beneath a rock, tell stories about the lives and times of these ancient people. Decades of exploration have uncovered thousands of artifacts but few answers about the purpose of minerals sought by these early residents. Perhaps a greater mystery is why—after 2,000 years—they left Mammoth Cave and never returned.

Mammoth Cave was rediscovered by **John Houchins** near the turn of the 19th century. Legend has it that Houchins shot and wounded a black bear near the cave's entrance. The injured animal led its hunter to the cave, and the rest, as they say, is history.

In 1812, after 2,000 years of anonymity, the cave's underground passageways were once again being mined. The **War of 1812** was brewing, and British strategy successfully cut-off America's gunpowder supplies in the east. Fortunately for the American Army, Mammoth Cave had large deposits of calcium nitrate, which through a simple process could be converted into gunpowder. This cave and its minerals ended up playing a pivotal role in a war hundreds of miles away.

As a result Mammoth Cave received considerable publicity, and by 1816 visitors were showing up to tour the mysterious labyrinth. But local citizens had other uses in mind. An enthusiastic clergyman used the cave as a church, and a doctor from Louisville purchased it for use as a tuberculosis treatment center. These ventures failed, but **cave tours** were an undeniable success—so successful that they have been conducted without interruption, through the Civil War to the present day. Slaves led many of the tours. **Stephen Bishop**, a slave with quick wit, good humor, and a curious spirit, was one of the best and most passionate guides. He became the first to map the cave system and cross **Bottomless Pit**. Along the way, he discovered and named many of the cave's features, including **Gorin's Dome** and 192-ft tall **Mammoth Dome**. Work continued by **Max Kämper**, a German geologist and mapmaker who set out to create a comprehensive map of the cave in 1908. Guided by **Ed Bishop**, great-nephew of Stephen, Kämper discovered **Kämper Hall**, **Elizabeth's Dome**, and **Violet City**. Together, they mapped and surveyed all of the passages known at the time.

By 1920, tens of thousands of tourists visited Mammoth Cave each year, causing locals to seek out their piece of the tourism pie. **George Morrison**, a wealthy oilman, found what he called the "New Entrance to Mammoth Cave." He "found" it with the help of drills and explosives. **Floyd Collins**, pioneer and explorer, was determined to find a lucrative new cave. While exploring **Sand Cave**, a rock wedged his ankle leaving him trapped near the cave's entrance. After 17 days of failed rescue attempts Collins died of exposure. The event created a "carnival atmosphere" rife with dozens of journalists and sensational stories, which sparked the movement to make Mammoth Cave a national park. When this idea came to fruition in 1941 only 40 miles of passageways had been surveyed. Since then, several cave networks have been connected, creating the largest such area in the world, of which about fourteen miles of passages are available for tours.

When to Go

Mammoth Cave National Park is open all year. The weather underground is nearly a constant 54°F. The park is busiest in summer and on holiday weekends. During this time reservations are recommended for cave tours (especially for Wild Cave, River Styx, and Intro to Caving Tours). Tours are given daily throughout the year, except on Christmas Day. Fewer tours are offered during the park's off-season.

Mammoth Cave Visitor Center • (270) 758-2328
1 Mammoth Cave Pkwy; Mammoth Cave, KY 42259
Open: Daily from 8am–5pm (extended hours during summer and holidays)
Closed: December 25

Transportation & Airports

Mammoth Cave Railroad Bike and Hike Trail connects Mammoth Cave Hotel to Park City. There is a Greyhound Bus Station (800.231.2222, www.greyhound.com) in Cave City and taxi service is available to the park. There are no bridges across Green River within the park, but it can be crossed with the aid of a free ferry. Green River Ferry operates year-round from 6am–9:55pm. Houchin's Ferry operates March–November from 10:15am–9:55pm.

The nearest large commercial airports are Louisville International (SDF) and Nashville International (BNA). Both are approximately 90 miles from the park. Bowling Green-Warren County Regional (BWG) is a smaller airport located 35 miles southwest of the park.

Directions

Arriving from the North: Take I-65 South to Exit 53 (Cave City Exit). Turn Right onto KY-70. Follow KY-70/255 as it becomes Mammoth Cave Parkway. Mammoth Cave Parkway leads directly to the Visitor Center.

Arriving from the South: Take I-65 North to Exit 48 (Park City Exit). Turn left onto KY-255. Follow KY-255 until it becomes Park City Road, which leads into the park. Turn left where Park City Road joins Mammoth Cave Parkway and follow it to the Visitor Center.

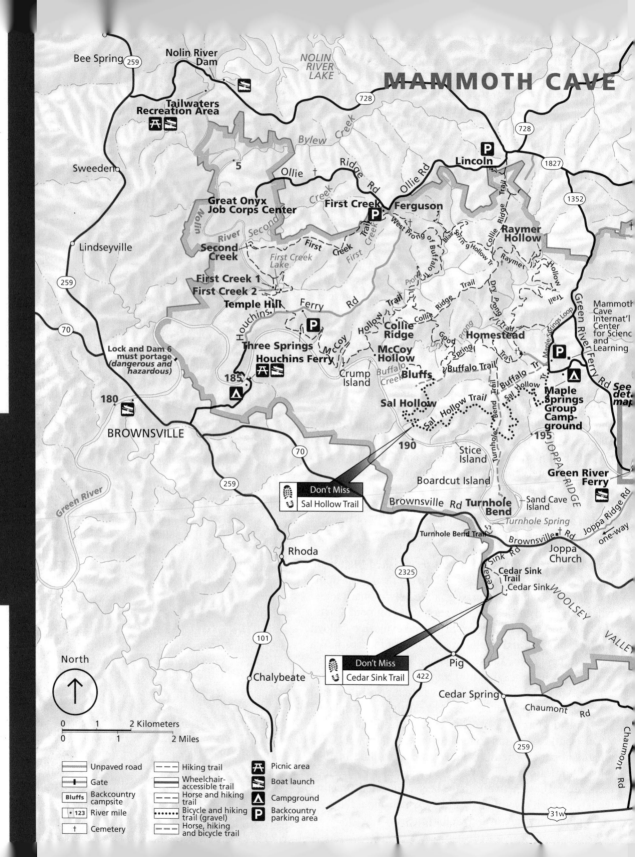

MAMMOTH CAVE

Bee Spring (259)
Nolin River Dam

NOLIN RIVER LAKE

Tailwaters Recreation Area

(728)

Sweeden

(728)

Bylew Creek

Ollie

Ridge Rd

Lincoln

(1827)

Great Onyx Job Corps Center

First Creek

Ferguson

Ollie Rd

(1352)

West Prong of Buffalo

Raymer Hollow

Blair Spring Hollow Tr

Collie Ridge Trail

Raymer Hollow Trail

Lindseyville

Second Creek

First Creek Lake

First Creek Trail

First Creek

Second Creek

First Creek 1
First Creek 2

Temple Hill

Ferry

Rd

Houchins

Hollow Trail

Collie Ridge

Collie Ridge Trail

Dry Prong Trail

Good Spring

Maple Springs Loop

Green River Ferry Trail

Mammoth Cave Internat'l Center for Science and Learning

(259)

(70)

Lock and Dam 6 must portage (dangerous and hazardous)

Three Springs
Houchins Ferry

McCoy Hollow Trail

Collie Ridge

McCoy Hollow

Homestead

Buffalo Trail

Good Spring Trail

Sal Hollow Tr

Buffalo Tr

Maple Springs Group Campground

See detail map

180

Crump Island

Crump Creek

Bluffs

Buffalo Trail

Sal Hollow Trail

185

BROWNSVILLE

Sal Hollow

Sal Hollow Trail

190

195

JOPPA RIDGE

Green River Ferry

Green River

(70)

(259)

Stice Island

Boardcut Island

Turnhole Bend

Sand Cave Island

Joppa Ridge Rd

Don't Miss
Sal Hollow Trail

Brownsville Rd

Turnhole Bend

Rhoda

Turnhole Spring

Turnhole Bend Trail

Brownsville Rd

Joppa Church

WOOLSEY VALLEY

one-way

(2325)

Cedar Sink Trail

Cedar Sink

(101)

Cedar Sink Rd

Chalybeate

Don't Miss
Cedar Sink Trail

Pig

(422)

Cedar Spring

Chaumont Rd

(259)

(31W)

North

↑

| 0 | 1 | 2 Kilometers |
| 0 | 1 | 2 Miles |

	Unpaved road	‑ ‑ ‑	Hiking trail	🏕	Picnic area
	Gate		Wheelchair-accessible trail	⛵	Boat launch
Bluffs	Backcountry campsite		Horse and hiking trail	⛺	Campground
• 123	River mile	•••••	Bicycle and hiking trail (gravel)	🅿	Backcountry parking area
†	Cemetery		Horse, hiking and bicycle trail		

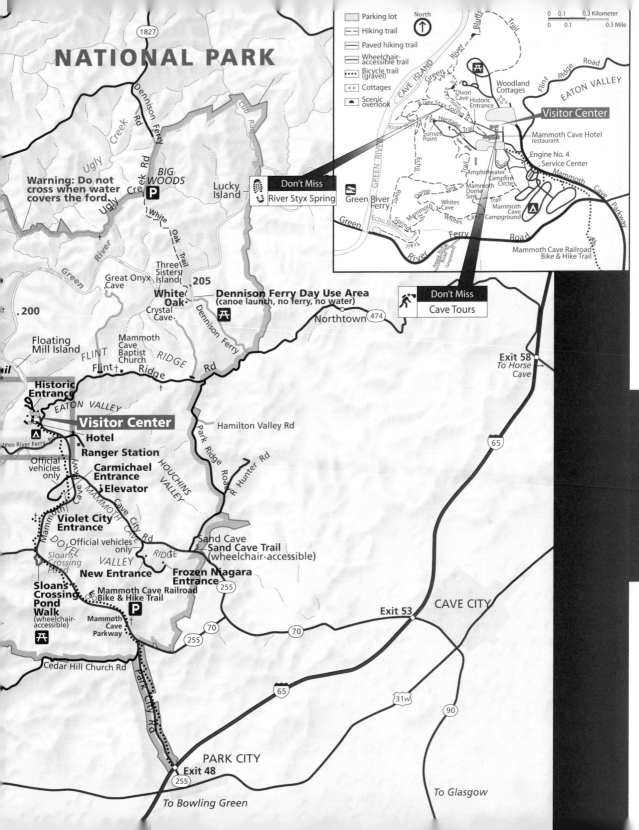

NATIONAL PARK

MAMMOTH CAVE

Warning: Do not cross when water covers the ford.

1827

BIG WOODS

Ugly Creek Rd

Dennison Ferry Rd

Lucky Island

Cub Run

Don't Miss
River Styx Spring

White Oak Trail

Three Sisters Island

Great Onyx Cave

White Oak

205

Crystal Cave

Dennison Ferry Day Use Area
(canoe launch, no ferry, no water)

Dennison Ferry

Green River

200

Floating Mill Island

FLINT RIDGE Rd

Flint †

Mammoth Cave Baptist Church

Northtown 474

Don't Miss
Cave Tours

Exit 58
To Horse Cave

Historic Entrance

EATON VALLEY

Visitor Center

Green River Ferry Rd

Hotel

Ranger Station

Official vehicles only

Carmichael Entrance
Elevator

Hamilton Valley Rd

Park Ridge Road

R Hunter Rd

65

HOUCHINS VALLEY

MAMMOTH CAVE Rd

Violet City Entrance

DOYEL VALLEY

Official vehicles only

Cave City Rd

RIDGE

Sloans Crossing Pond

New Entrance

Sand Cave
Sand Cave Trail
(wheelchair-accessible)

Frozen Niagara Entrance

255

Sloans Crossing Pond Walk
(wheelchair-accessible)

Mammoth Cave Railroad Bike & Hike Trail

Mammoth Cave Parkway

P

70

255

70

Exit 53

CAVE CITY

65

31w

90

Cedar Hill Church Rd

Park City Rd

PARK CITY

Exit 48

255

To Bowling Green

To Glasgow

Map legend (inset)

Parking lot
Hiking trail
Paved hiking trail
Wheelchair-accessible trail
Bicycle trail (gravel)
Cottages
Scenic overlook

North

0   0.1   0.3 Kilometer
0   0.1   0.3 Mile

CAVE ISLAND

Green River

Bluffs Trail

Flint Ridge Road

EATON VALLEY

Woodland Cottages

Dixon Cave

Historic Entrance

Visitor Center

River Styx

River Styx Spring Tr

Heritage Trail

Sunset Point

Mammoth Cave Hotel restaurant

Engine No. 4
Service Center

Green River Ferry

Echo River

Mammoth Dome Sink

Amphitheater
Campfire Circle

Mammoth Cave Campground

Dome Sink

Whites Cave

Whites Cave Trail

Mammoth Cave Parkway

Mammoth Spring

Echo River Trail

Jogpa Ridge Trail (unpaved)

Green River Ferry Road

Mammoth Cave Railroad Bike & Hike Trail

A ranger lighting the cave with a torch

Cave Tours

Tours began in 1816 and have continued to the present day without interruption. All of the original tours entered the cave's **Historic Entrance**. Native Americans from some 4,000 years ago, wealthy easterners under the guidance of a slave named Stephen Bishop, and patients hoping an extended stay underground at Dr. Croghan's Tuberculosis Hospital would cure what ailed them, all have at least one thing in common. They passed walked through the Historic Entrance and into the mystery and darkness of Mammoth Cave. Today, it is reserved for tourists. Tours such as **Mammoth Passage, Historic, Making of Mammoth, Discovery, Violet City Lantern, River Styx, and Trog** all begin here. Park rangers guide visitors through the passages, slowly satisfying guests' curiosities while regaling them with stories of the cave's incredible history and geology. More than two-thirds of the park's guests take a cave tour.

Images of caves usually begin with dripping stalactites hanging from the ceiling; stubby, rounded stalagmites protruding from the floor; and a collection of otherworldly rock formations. But most of Mammoth Cave is drab and undecorated. Its plainness is caused by a hard, thick layer of sandstone just above the passageways. This cap prevents water, the key component of cave feature formation, from seeping in. However, there are a few locations, like **Frozen Niagara**, where the sandstone cap rock has dissolved, allowing water to seep through the cave's limestone strata. In these sections, formations were slowly created by water combined with carbon dioxide, which is able to dissolve limestone. These solutes precipitate and over time—tens of thousands of years—accumulation of precipitates leads to cave formations. The most noteworthy of which can be seen on these tours: **Frozen Niagara, New Entrance, Grand Avenue, and Snowball**.

Kentucky Cave Shrimp are the park's most notable occupants. These eyeless, albino shrimp were discovered by Stephen Bishop, and it was later determined that they live exclusively in the water of the cave's lower levels. While no tours explore these regions, you can walk the banks of River Styx, the Dead Sea, and Lake Lethe on the **River Styx Tour**.

While exploring the cave take note of the names of each room. Many names come from their shape or appearance, but others are derived from the cave's unique history. Names of owners, explorers, and visitors are all found among the passages and rooms. **Booth's Amphitheater** is named for **Edwin Booth**, who recited Hamlet's famous soliloquy in that room. Edwin is overshadowed by his infamous brother, John Wilkes Booth, who assassinated President Lincoln. **Ole Bule Concert Hall** is named for the famous violinist. Conservationist, writer, and national park advocate John Muir visited in September of 1867, but he was just an "unknown nobody" walking to Florida at the time.

Tours come in all lengths and difficulties. **Frozen Niagara** is the easiest, and it is suitable for visitors who require the aid of a cane or walker. **Wild Cave** is the most strenuous. It's a real spelunking adventure. Participants spend much of the six hour tour crawling on hands and knees as they squeeze through tight spaces. All Wild Cave participants must be at least 16 years old, meet certain size requirements (to fit through openings), and wear high-top, lace-up hiking boots. An adult must accompany visitors under age 18. Cameras are not allowed, because there isn't any opportunity to use them. It is recommended that you wear gym shorts and a t-shirt under coveralls (provided). You will get dirty. Coin-operated showers are available at the service center on Mammoth Cave Parkway.

Mammoth Passage, Frozen Niagara, and Mammoth Cave Discovery Tours are not available by reservation. Tickets for these tours must be purchased on the same day at the Visitor Center. All other tours can be reserved in advance by calling (877) 444-6777 or clicking www.recreation.gov.

Mammoth Cave Camping

	Open	Fees	Sites	Notes
Mammoth Cave (0.25 mile from the Visitor Center)*	All Year	$17/night $20/night	105 4 Group	Showers at Service Center (March–Nov)
Houchin's Ferry (15 miles from the Visitor Center)	All Year	$12/night	12	Water and Pit Toilets No RVs, No Showers
Maple Springs Group (6 miles from Visitor Center)*	All Year	$22/night $30/night	4 Equestrian 3 Group	Water and Pit Toilets No RVs, No Showers
Backcountry Camping	A free permit is required to camp at any of the twelve backcountry campsites in the park. Obtain a backcountry permit in person at the Visitor Center.			

Mammoth Cave Lodging

	Open	Fees		Notes
Mammoth Cave Hotel (Next to the Visitor Center)	All Year	Rooms $59–104		A variety of rooms and cottages are available near the visitor center

Mammoth Cave Tours

Tour (Capacity)	Rate	Length	Notes
Mammoth Passage (40)	$5 (Adults)/$3.50 (Youth)	1.25 hours	Short and easy tour that delves into the cave's cultural and natural history
Frozen Niagara (36)	$10/$8	1.25 hours	A very short trek suitable for small children and elderly family members
Discovery -👍	$4/$2.50	0.5 hour	Self-guiding tour of the Rotunda
Historic* (120)	$12/$8	2 hours	Learn about the cave's visitors during the 19th and early 20th centuries
New Entrance* (114)	$12/$8	2 hours	Domes, pits, and dripstone formations
Grand Avenue* (78)	$24/$18	4.5 hours	Strenuous tour that follows Snowball and Frozen Niagara Tours' routes
Snowball* (38)	$14/$9	3 hours	See various gypsum formations and stop for lunch in the Snowball Room
Violet City Lantern* (38) -👍	$15/$11	3 hours	Strenuous trip lit only by lanterns
River Styx* (40) -👍	$13/$9	2.5 hours	View a few underground waterways
Star Chamber* (40)	$12/$8	2.5 hours	Visit site of the Tuberculosis Hospital
Frozen Niagara Photo* (30)	$10/$8	1.5 hours	Photo friendly tour of cave formations
Trog* (12)	Not Available/$14	2.5 hours	Kids-only trip of rarely used passages
Intro to Caving* (20)	$23/$18	3.5 hours	Hiking boots required, chest or hip measurement must be less than 42"
Wild Cave (14)* -👍	$48/Not Available	6–6.5 hours	Requirements: hiking boots , less than 42" chest/hip, and 16+ years old

Youth is 6–12 years of age. Golden Age, Golden Access, and America the Beautiful Senior and Access Passes receive a 50% discount from the listed adult tour prices. River Styx, Niagara Photo, and Trog are only offered in the summer.

*Campground and tour reservations can be made in advance by calling (877) 444-6777 or clicking www.recreation.gov

MAMMOTH CAVE

Best of Mammoth Cave

Adventure Cave Tours: Wild Cave
Runner-up: Intro to Caving

Family Cave Tour: Violet City Lantern
Runner-up: River Styx
2nd Runner-up: Discovery

Family Hike: Cedar Sink Trail
Runner-up: Green River Bluffs Trail

Did you know?

➤ Mammoth Cave earned its name from the size of its chambers and avenues, not from the prehistoric woolly mammoth.

➤ Stalactites grow downward, hanging "tight" to the ceiling, while stalagmites grow upward, they "might" reach the ceiling someday.

➤ In 1839, Dr. Croghan purchased Mammoth Cave. He believed its preservative qualities would aid in the recovery of his patients suffering from tuberculosis, which had no known cure at the time.

Horseback Riding

The entire network of trails north of Green River is open to horse use. Overnight accommodations are available for horseback riders at **Maple Springs Group Campground**; sites 1–4 are designed specifically to accommodate horses. Day-use riders can park trailers at Lincoln Trailhead, across the road from Maple Springs Campground bulletin board at Maple Springs Trailhead, and 0.25 mile north of Maple Springs Campground at Good Springs Church. Be sure to follow all rules specific to visitors with horses. There are two outfitters outside park boundaries; **Double J Stables** is the only outfitter that offers horse rental.

Double J Stables & Campgrounds • (270) 286-8167
542 Lincoln School Road; Mammoth Cave, KY 42259
www.doublejstables.com ($15/hr, $25/2hr, $85/5hr)

D Bar K Horse Camp • (270) 286-0217
510 Ollie Road; Mammoth Cave, KY 42259
www.dbarkhorsecamp.com

Hiking/Backpacking

Even if you'd like to you can't spend all day inside the cave. Above the dark caverns lies a world of trees, water, and light that is best enjoyed on foot. On a busy day several thousand visitors explore the park's underground world, but few of them experience what's right out in the open, just waiting to be hiked. Above ground are signs of the caves beneath your feet. Trails skirt alongside rivers that disappear into the earth and sinkholes that lead to the dark unknown.

There are 23 miles of hiking trails south of the Green River. Most of these begin at or near the visitor center or Mammoth Cave Campground. If you don't plan on taking a cave tour that enters through the Historic Entrance be sure to hike **River Styx Spring Trail**. This 0.6-mile trail leads past the Historic Entrance, which is worth a quick look. The trail continues on to the site where River Styx exits Mammoth Cave. Eventually it leads to the banks of the Green River before looping back to the visitor center. If you care to extend River Styx Spring Trail, continue north along the 1.1-mile **Green River Bluffs Trail**. From this stretch you'll see Cave Island protruding from the Green River. Continue past the island to a scenic overlook. The trail concludes at the visitor center picnic area. Just south of the visitor center is **Heritage Trail**. This 0.3-mile trek loops around "Old Guides Cemetery" where tour guides like Stephen Bishop are buried. It terminates at sunset point, and then loops back to the visitor center. The 2.2-mile **Echo River Trail** and 2.0-mile Mammoth Dome Sink Trail connect to Heritage Trail Loop. **Cedar Sink Trail** is another good hiking opportunity. Its trailhead is located on Cedar Sink Road just south of Brownsville Road.

More than 55 miles of backcountry trails are found north of the Green River. To reach them you must cross the river—using Green River Ferry—to Maple Springs Group Campground, which serves as a hub for many hiking trails. This is the best area of the park to escape overcrowding that may occur near the visitor center. Even during peak season you may feel like you're the only person around (which might be true). The 8.1-mile **Sal Hollow Trail** and 2.8-mile **Buffalo Trail** are two of the most beautiful and secluded hikes. This region also provides excellent backpacking opportunities thanks to 12 campsites sprinkled throughout the backcountry.

 # Biking

Mammoth Cave Railroad Bike and Hike Trail is popular among pedalers. It follows the route used by early visitors arriving at Mammoth Cave from Park City by rail and stagecoach. You can also bike on 101 miles of roadway found in the park. During the off-season, the 10-mile circuit leaving the visitor center via **Flint Ridge Road** to **Park Ridge Road** to **Cave City Road** is a pleasant pedal with easy to moderate climbs. Bicycles are prohibited on hiking trails south of Green River and around the visitor center. Mountain biking is allowed on some trails north of the Green River including **Sal Hollow Trail** (recommended). Stop in at the visitor center for mountain bike trail information and maps.

 # Paddling

Paddling is another great way to enjoy Mammoth Cave's above ground attractions. At normal water levels **Green and Nolin Rivers** provide a casual float for paddlers of any experience level. Green River meanders through the park for 25 miles, with boat landings at Dennison Ferry, Green River Ferry, and Houchin's Ferry. Be aware that there is an unmarked lock and dam past Houchin's Ferry just a short distance beyond the park boundary. For a nice paddle launch your canoe or kayak on Nolin River just below Nolin River Dam at Tailwaters Recreation Area. Paddle downstream to the confluence of Nolin and Green Rivers. When you reach Green River paddle upstream a short distance to the take-out at Houchin's Ferry. For help planning a multi-day paddle or to hire a guide, contact one of the following outfitters:

Big Buffalo Crossing • (270) 524-7883
1 River Road; Munfordville, KY 42765
www.bigbuffalocrossing.com
Rates: $40 (half-day), $60 (full-day), $80−90/canoe (overnight)

Green River Canoeing • (270) 773-5712
3061 Mammoth Cave Road; Cave City, KY 42127
www.mammothcavecanoe.com
Rates: $50 (half-day), $65 (full-day), $65−95/canoe (overnight)

Kentucky River Runners • (270)776-2876 or (270)792-6127
www.kyriverrunners.com
Rates: $75−85 (full-day)

Mammoth Cave Canoes & Kayak • (270) 773-3366
1240 Old Mammoth Cave Road; Cave City, KY 42127
www.mammothcavecanoe-k.com
Rates: $50 (half-day), $65 (full-day), $85/canoe (overnight)

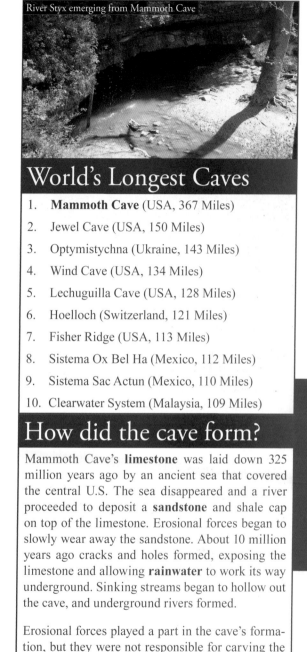

River Styx emerging from Mammoth Cave

World's Longest Caves

1. **Mammoth Cave** (USA, 367 Miles)
2. Jewel Cave (USA, 150 Miles)
3. Optymistychna (Ukraine, 143 Miles)
4. Wind Cave (USA, 134 Miles)
5. Lechuguilla Cave (USA, 128 Miles)
6. Hoelloch (Switzerland, 121 Miles)
7. Fisher Ridge (USA, 113 Miles)
8. Sistema Ox Bel Ha (Mexico, 112 Miles)
9. Sistema Sac Actun (Mexico, 110 Miles)
10. Clearwater System (Malaysia, 109 Miles)

How did the cave form?

Mammoth Cave's **limestone** was laid down 325 million years ago by an ancient sea that covered the central U.S. The sea disappeared and a river proceeded to deposit a **sandstone** and shale cap on top of the limestone. Erosional forces began to slowly wear away the sandstone. About 10 million years ago cracks and holes formed, exposing the limestone and allowing **rainwater** to work its way underground. Sinking streams began to hollow out the cave, and underground rivers formed.

Erosional forces played a part in the cave's formation, but they were not responsible for carving the passageways. The cave was created and continues to grow because **limestone is soluble in groundwater** under the right conditions. Water combined with carbon dioxide forms a weak carbonic acid able to dissolve limestone. Limestone that previously inhabited Mammoth's subterranean passages was dissolved and carried away in solution by rainwater.

Saltpeter leaching vats

Fishing

A state fishing license is not required for fishing in **Green and Nolin Rivers** as long as you are within park boundaries. Bass, crappie, bluegill, muskellunge, and catfish are commonly caught in these waters.

Live bait other than worms is prohibited at Sloan's Crossing Pond and First Creek Lake. Minnows and worms are allowed for river fishing. Fish size and quantity restrictions follow Kentucky Department of Fish & Wildlife regulations.

For Kids: Mammoth Cave offers a few kid-centric tours and programs. **Trog** (page 84) is a kid-only (ages 8–12) cave tour. **Introduction to Caving** is open to children 10 and up, as well as their parents. The park also provides a seasonal **Nature Track** for kids. Refer to the activity schedules for all ranger-led programs (available online or at the visitor center).

Kids can also participate in the park's **Junior Ranger Program**. Grab a free Junior Ranger booklet at the Visitor Center Information Desk, then complete enough activities to receive a Junior Ranger badge and certificate.

Ranger Programs: In addition to all of the ranger-led cave tours, Mammoth Cave offers ranger-led walks, campfires, evening programs, and auditorium programs. If you have some time to burn during your visit, look no further than the ranger programs. All of the activities (outside of the cave tours) are free of charge and exceptionally entertaining. A schedule of these events is available at the visitor center or park website.

Flora & Fauna: **More than 1,300 species of flowering plants** grow within park boundaries. This extreme biodiversity is due to the general geography being situated in a transitional zone between cooler climates to the north and sub-tropical climates to the south. In spring, meadows erupt in a colorful display of wildflowers. Between February and March, more than 60 species of herbaceous wildflowers bloom to the delight of hikers. During this time the park hosts an annual wildflower day, with programs focusing on flowers, ecology, and conservation held throughout the day by park rangers and volunteers. Please refer to the park's website for event details.

The park also protects a few swaths of grassland similar to what once covered 3 to 5 million acres of neighboring land before it was settled and developed. You'll find several species of grasses including the western dwarf dandelion, which is common in western prairie states, but can only be found in Kentucky at Mammoth Cave National Park.

There are **45 species of mammals** that inhabit Mammoth Cave National Park. You'll probably see white-tailed deer and squirrels, while bobcats, coyotes, foxes, raccoons, skunks, beaver, and mink are seldom spotted. Wild turkeys, bald eagles, and blue herons are just a few bird species that provide some pretty decent **bird watching**. Several species of bat reside in the cave. It also supports a wide variety of creepy-crawly insects, crustaceans, and fish. About 130 animal species are regular inhabitants of the cave system.

Pets: Pets must be kept on a leash no more than six feet in length at all times. All pets, except service animals, are prohibited in the cave. Mammoth Cave Hotel allows them in Woodland Cottages, but they are not allowed in any other facilities. The hotel also operates a kennel for visitors with pets.

Accessibility: While the park offers wheelchair accessible camping, picnicking, lodging, trails, dining, and visitor center facilities, its main attraction—the cave—is not accessible to individuals in wheelchairs.

Weather: The weather above ground is moderate. Wet springs, hot summers, dry falls, and cold winters are the norm. While the weather above ground is difficult to predict, weather in the cave is easily anticipated. Subterranean temperatures only fluctuate a degree or two from the 54°F average. Cave temperature doesn't stabilize until you're a fair distance from its entrance.

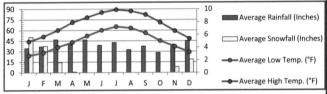

Vacation Planner

Vacations are almost always too short, and for that reason, most visitors race into the park, take a quick tour, and head on to their next destination. A lot can be missed in these whirlwind visits. This simple 2-day itinerary helps maximize your valuable time. First, a few basics on cave tours and park facilities need to be covered. When considering which cave tour to take, be honest about your size, fitness level, and any phobias that you might have. Park rangers will measure guests to make sure you will fit through tight spaces encountered on **Wild Cave** and **Introduction to Caving Tours**. Don't be afraid to split up if your group can't settle on a "one-size-fits-all" tour. Most tours can be reserved in advance. Making **reservations** is always a good idea, but it's imperative for **Wild Cave**, **Intro to Caving**, **River Styx**, and **Violet City Lantern Tours**. If the tour you want is full, you can check for cancellations 30 minutes prior to departure; you might get lucky. The park offers several **campgrounds** (page 85) for overnight visitors, but only one **hotel** (page 85). Dining, grocery stores, lodging, festivals, and attractions outside the park are listed on pages 90–91.

Every trip to Mammoth Cave should begin at the **visitor center**. This is where you can grab brochures, receive answers to all the questions you conjured while cooped up in the car, and view a current schedule of cave tours and ranger programs. It's basically the main hub for all park activities, and more importantly the location where cave tour tickets are purchased (if you haven't made advance

192-foot tall Mammoth Dome

reservations) and tour groups meet before heading beneath the surface. Do not forget to check the schedule of above-ground ranger-led activities, and take note of any that interest you. For example, a campfire program is a fantastic way to spend the evening. For a proper introduction to Mammoth Cave hike **River Styx Spring Trail** (page 86) and take the **Discovery Tour** (page 85). Try to catch a **Campfire Talk**; if not, get some rest because a big day of spelunking awaits you tomorrow.

If you like crawling through tight passages in complete darkness sign up for the **Wild Cave Tour** (page 84, reservations recommended). To me, every knee-bruising, pants-ripping, belly-crawling, head bumping (you wear a helmet) minute is worth the trouble. However, it's definitely not for everyone. You spend six hours in cramped, damp darkness, but what makes this and the rest of the Mammoth Cave tours so memorable is the park rangers' spellbinding stories. Non-Wild Cavers in your group should consider taking **Frozen Niagara**, **Violet City Lantern**, or **River Styx Tour** (page 85). If they'd rather stay above ground, **Sal Hollow Trail** (page 86) is the place to be.

Dining

In the Park
Mammoth Cave Hotel • (270) 758-2225
792 Beaver Dam Chapel Rd; Smiths Grove, KY 42171
www.mammothcavehotel.com

Near the Park
Porky Pig Diner • (270) 597-2422
125 Park Boundary Rd; Smiths Grove, KY 42171

Watermill Restaurant • (270) 773-3186
803 Mammoth Cave Rd, Cave City, KY 42127

El Mazatlan • (270) 773-7448
105 Gardner Ln; Cave City, KY 42127
www.el-mazatlan.com • Entrée: $7–14

Michaels Restaurant • (270) 773-2551
210 Broadway St; Cave City, KY 42127

Cream & Sugar Café • (270) 773-2822
105 Broadway St; Cave City, KY 42127

Sahara Steak House • (270) 773-345
413 E Happy Valley St; Cave City, KY 42127

Briar Creek Restaurant • (270) 286-9775
7020 Nolin Dam Rd; Mammoth Cave, KY 42259

Linda's Restaurant • (270) 286-0222
KY-259 N; Bee Spring, KY 42207

Laura's Hilltop Restaurant • (270) 597-9945
1409 KY-259 N; Brownsville, KY 42210

Mis Amigos Mexican Grill • (270) 597-9105
600 KY-259; Brownsville, KY 42210

Pizza Paradise • (270) 597-2224
1457 KY-259 N, Brownsville, KY 42210

Old School Bar B Q • (270) 597-2087
210 S Main St, Brownsville, KY 42210

Red Roof BBQ • (270) 286-0121
898 Moutardier Rd; Leitchfield, KY 42754

Dem' Bones BBQ • (270) 242-3510
124 W Main St; Clarkson, KY 42726

Big Bubba Bucks Belly Bustin • (270) 524-3333
1802 Main St; Munfordville, KY 42765

Snappy's Pizza & Pasta • (270) 786-8686
103 S Dixie St; Horse Cave, KY 42749
www.snappyspizzaandpasta.com • Pizza: $5–17

Big Moose's BBQ Smokehouse • (270) 651-1913
525 W Main St; Glasgow, KY 42141

Los Mariachis • (270) 651-3229
802 Happy Valley Rd, Glasgow, KY 42141

Gale 'n' Dale's • (270) 651-2489
405 Happy Valley Rd; Glasgow, KY 42141

Grocery Stores
Save-A-Lot • (270) 773-2402
9584 Happy Valley Rd; Cave City, KY 42127

Walmart Supercenter • (270) 678-1003
2345 Happy Valley Rd; Glasgow, KY 42141

Save-A-Lot • (270) 597-2171
1445 Ky Hwy 259 N; Brownsville, KY 42210

Food Lion • (270) 651-1718
214 South L Rogers Wells Blvd; Glasgow, KY 42141

Lodging

In the Park
Mammoth Cave Hotel • (270) 758-2225
792 Beaver Dam Chapel Rd; Smiths Grove, KY 42171
www.mammothcavehotel.com • Rates: $59–104

Near the Park
Victorian House B&B • (270) 563-9403
110 N Main St; Smiths Grove, KY 42171

Bryce Inn • (270) 563-5141
592 S Main St; Smiths Grove, KY 42171
www.bryceinn.com

Wayfarer • (270) 773-3366
1240 Old Mammoth Cave Rd; Cave City, KY 42127

Oakes Motel & Camp Ground • (270) 773-4740
5091 Mammoth Cave Rd; Cave City, KY 42127
www.mammothcave.com/oaks.htm

Wigwam Village • (270) 773-3381
601 N Dixie Hwy; Cave City, KY 42127
www.wigwamvillage.com • Rates: $40–70

Cave Country RV Campground • (270) 773-4678
216 Gaunce Dr; Cave City, KY 42127
www.cavecountryrv.com • Rates: $35–37

Diamond Caverns Resort • (270) 749-2891
660 Doyle Rd; Cave City, Kentucky 42127

Jellystone Park Camp Resort • (270) 773-3840
1002 Mammoth Cave Rd; Cave City, KY 42127
www.jellystonemammothcave • Rates: $20–246

Park View Motel • (270) 773-3463
3906 Mammoth Cave Rd; Cave City, KY 42127
www.parkviewmotel.com

Park Mammoth Resort • (270) 749-4101
22850 Louisville Rd; Park City, KY 42160
www.parkmammothresort.us

Horse Cave KOA • (270) 786-2819
489 Flint Ridge Rd; Horse Cave, KY 42749

Country Hearth Inn Horse Cave • (270) 786-2165
425 Flint Ridge Rd; Horse Cave, KY 42749

Serenity Hill B&B • (270) 597-9647
3600 Mammoth Cave Rd; Brownsville, KY 42210
www.serenityhillbedandbreakfast.com • Rates: $90–100

Four Seasons Country Inn B&B • (270) 678-1000
4107 Scottsville Rd; Glasgow, KY 42141
www.fourseasonscountryinn.com • Rates: $79–130

Hall Place • (270) 651-3176
313 S Green St; Glasgow, KY 42141

Not all dining and lodging facilities are listed. Many chain hotels and restaurants can be found nearby in Cave City, Park City, Glasgow, and Bowling Green.

Festivals
Hillbilly Days • April
www.hillbillydays.com • Pikeville, KY

Kentucky Derby Festival • May
www.kdf.org • Louisville, KY

International Bar-B-Q Festival • May
www.bbqfest.com • Owensboro, KY

Great American Brass Band Festival • June
www.gabbf.com • Danville, KY

CMA Music Festival • June
Largest country music party in the world.
www.cmafest.com • Nashville, TN

Old Time Fiddlers Contest • July
Rough River Dam State Park; Falls of Rough, KY

Jane Austen Festival • July
www.jasnalouisville.com • Louisville, KY

Int'l Newgrass Festival • August
www.newgrassfestival.com • Oakland, KY

Horse Cave Heritage Festival • September
www.horsecaveky.com • Horse Cave, KY

International Festival • September
www.BGInternationalFest.com • Bowling Green

National Jug Band Jubilee • September
www.jugbandjubilee.com • Louisville, KY

Kentucky Bourbon Festival • September
www.kybourbonfestival.com • Bardstown, KY

World Chicken Festival • September
Dedicated to the first KFC and its history.
www.chickenfestival.com • London, KY

Jerusalem Ridge Festival • September/October
Real bluegrass from its birthplace.
www.jerusalemridgefestival.org • Rosine, KY

St James Court Art Show • September/October
www.stjamescourtartshow.com • Louisville, KY

Festival of Trains • December
www.historicrailpark.com • Bowling Green, KY

Attractions

Near the Park
Mammoth Cave Wax Museum • (270) 773-3010
901 Mammoth Cave Rd; Cave City, KY 42127

Onyx Cave • (270) 773-3530
101 Huckleberry Knob Rd; Cave City, KY 42127
www.onyxcave.com

Jesse James Riding Stables • (270) 773-2560
3057 Mammoth Cave Rd; Cave City, KY 42127

Mammoth Cave Wildlife Museum • (270) 773-2255
409 E Happy Valley St; Cave City, KY 42127
Admission: $8/Adult
www.mammothcavewildlifemuseum.com

Dinosaur World • (270) 773-4345
711 Mammoth Cave Rd; Cave City, KY 42127
www.dinoworld.net • Admission: $13/Adult

Historic Diamond Caverns • (270) 749-2233
1900 Mammoth Cave Parkway; Park City, KY 42160
www.diamondcaverns.com • Tour: $16/Adult

Kentucky Down Under • (270) 786-2635
Kangeroos to didgeridoos, a little Australia in KY.
3700 L and N Turnpike Rd; Horse Cave, KY 42749
www.kdu.com • Admission: $22/Adult

Hidden River Cave • (270) 786-1466
119 E Main St; Horse Cave, KY 42749
www.cavern.org • Admission: $15/Adult

Highlander Bowl • (270) 651-9020
110 Park Ave; Glasgow, KY 42141

Beyond the Park

Skyline Drive-in Theatre • (270) 932-2800
5600 Hodgenville Rd; Greensburg, KY 42743
www.skylinedrivein.com • Tickets: $6/Adult

Great Escape Theaters • (270) 782-3112
2625 Scottsville Rd; Bowling Green, KY 42104
www.greatescapetheatres.com

Tri City Drive In • (270) 274-3168
US-231 S; Beaver Dam, KY 42320

National Corvette Museum • (270) 781-7973
350 Corvette Dr; Bowling Green, KY 42101
www.corvettemuseum.com • Admission: $10/Adult

Lost River Cave • (270) 393-0077
2818 Nashville Rd; Bowling Green, KY 42101
www.lostrivercave.com • Admission: $15/Adult

Shaker Village of Pleasant Hill • (800) 734-5611
3501 Lexington Rd; Harrodsburg, KY 40383
www.shakervillageky.org • Admission: $15/Adult

Heaven Hill Bourbon • (502) 337-1000
1311 Gilkey Run Rd; Bardstown, KY 40004
www.bourbonheritagecenter.com • Free

Abraham Lincoln Birthplace • (502) 549-3741
7120 Bardstown Rd; Hodgenville, KY 42748
www.nps.gov/abli • Admission: Free

Louisville Slugger Museum • (502) 588-7228
800 W Main St; Louisville, KY 40202
www.sluggermuseum.org • Admission: $10/Adult

Louisville Historic Tours • (502) 637-2922
1340 S 4th St; Louisville, KY 4020
www.louisvillehistorictours.com • Tours: $15–25

Muhammad Ali Center • (502) 584-9254
144 N 6th St; Louisville, KY 40202
www.alicenter.org • Admission: $9/Adult

Frazier Int'l History Museum • (502) 753-5663
829 W Main St; Louisville, KY 40202
www.fraziermuseum.org • Admission: $19/Adult

Speed Art Museum • (502) 634-2700
2035 S 3rd St; Louisville, KY 40208
www.speedmuseum.org • Admission: $10/Adult

Thomas Edison House/Farmington • (502) 585-5247
729 E Washington St; Louisville, KY 40202
www.edisonhouse.org • Admission: $5/Adult

Kentucky Derby Museum • (502) 637-1111
704 Central Ave; Louisville, KY 40208
www.derbymuseum.org • Admission: $13/Adult

Churchill Downs • (502) 636-4400
700 Central Ave; Louisville, KY 40208
www.churchilldowns.com

Louisville Zoo • (502) 238-5348
1100 Trevilian Way; Louisville, KY 40213
www.louisvillezoo.org • Admission: $13/Adult

KentuckyShow! • (502) 562-7800
501 W Main St; Louisville, KY 40202
www.kentuckyshow.com • Tickets: $7

City Taste Tours • (502) 589-1628
332 W Broadway; Louisville, KY 40202
www.citytastetours.com • Tours: $39–65

Louisville Equestrian Center • (502) 267-0881
2612 S English Station Rd; Louisville, KY 40299
www.louisvilleequestriancenter.com

Waverly Hills Sanatorium • (502) 933-2142
Paralee Ln; Louisville, Kentucky 40272
www.therealwaverlyhills.com • Tours: $22–100

NashTrash Tours • (615) 226-7300
772 Harrison St; Nashville, TN 37219
www.nashtrash.com • $32/Adult

Ryman Auditorium • (615) 889-3060
116 5th Ave N; Nashville, TN 37210
www.ryman.com • Tours: $13–17

Tennessee State Museum • (615) 741-2692
505 Deaderick St; Nashville, TN 37243
www.tnmuseum.org • Admission: Free

Chaffin's Barn Dinner Theatre • (615) 646-9977
8204 TN-100; Nashville, TN 37221
www.dinnertheatre.com • Tickets: $35–50

Hatch Showprint • (615) 256-2805
Oldest letterpress poster print shop in the U.S.
316 Broadway; Nashville, TN 37201

Buffalo Trace Distillery • (502) 696-5926
113 Great Buffalo Tr; Frankfort, KY 40601
www.buffalotrace.com • Tour: Free

Mary Todd Lincoln House • (859) 233-9999
578 West Main St; Lexington, KY 40507
www.mtlhouse.org • Admission: $9/Adult

Kentucky Horse Park • (859) 233-4303
1579 Astaire Dr; Lexington, KY 40511
www.kyhorsepark.com • Admission: $9–16/Adult

Alltech's Lexington Brewing • (859) 887-3406
401 Cross St; Lexington, KY 40508
www.kentuckyale.com • Tour: Free

Keeneland • (859) 254-3412
4201 Versailles Rd; Lexington, KY 40510
www.keeneland.com • Horse races & Tours Available

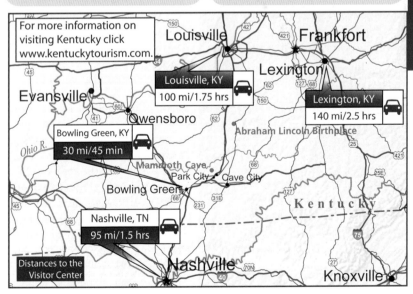

For more information on visiting Kentucky click www.kentuckytourism.com.

Louisville, KY — 100 mi/1.75 hrs

Lexington, KY — 140 mi/2.5 hrs

Bowling Green, KY — 30 mi/45 min

Nashville, TN — 95 mi/1.5 hrs

Distances to the Visitor Center

Deer grazing in Cades Cove as fog rises like smoke from the mountains

107 Park Headquarters Road
Gatlinburg, TN 37738
Phone: (865) 436-1200
Website: www.nps.gov/grsm

Established: June 15, 1934
Size: 521,621 Acres
Annual Visitors: 9.5 Million
Peak Season: Summer & October

Hiking Trails: 850 Miles
Horse Trails: 550 Miles

Activities: Driving, Hiking,
Backpacking, Paddling, Biking,
Horseback Riding, and Fishing

Campgrounds ($14–23/night):
Abrams Creek, Balsam Mountain,
Big Creek, Cades Cove (All Year),
Cataloochee, Cosby, Deep Creek,
Elkmont, Look Rock, Smokemont
Backcountry Camping: Permitted
Lodging ($116/night per person):
Le Conte Lodge (Hike-in only)

Park Hours: All day, every day
Entrance Fee: None

Great Smoky Mountains - TN/NC

The location and geography of Great Smoky Mountains National Park (GRSM) have led to two incredible phenomena: mass tourism and unparalleled biodiversity. The park straddles the **Smoky Mountains** on the Tennessee–North Carolina border, less than a day's drive from one-third of the entire U.S. population—and on a busy day it might feel like they are all visiting at the same time. It's not true, but the park's 9.5 million annual visitors is still impressive. That's more than double the next closest national park's annual total. Another 11 million people pass through each year for non-recreational purposes. These staggering numbers lead to frequent bouts of bumper-to-bumper traffic and occasional gridlock, making the park feel constrictive and small even though it is one of the largest protected areas in the country.

This region sought protection under the formation of a national park to spare trees covering the mountains' slopes from logging and paper companies bent on stripping the land bare. Both sides got what they wanted. Many trees were clear-cut, but others were saved by a park, and eventually the region was designated an **International Biosphere Reserve** and a **UNESCO World Heritage Site** due to its biodiversity. GRSM is home to the greatest diversity of plant, animal, and insect life of any region in a temperate climate zone. A fact largely due to abundant annual precipitation (as much as 85 inches in some locations) and varied elevation (ranging from 876 feet at the mouth of Abrams Creek to 6,643 feet at the summit of Clingman's Dome). A hiker travelling from these two extremes experiences the same flora and fauna diversity as hiking all 2,184 miles of the Appalachian Trail from Georgia to Maine. That same hiker passes one of the largest blocks of deciduous old-growth forest in North America, home to 100 species of trees, more than any other U.S. National Park.

For centuries **Cherokee Indians** have lived among these trees, hunting and gathering what they needed to survive. Claims of gold and the Indian Removal Act forced them to Oklahoma on what came to be known as the "Trail of Tears." A few small American settlements sprang up, but substantial amounts of gold were never found. As the East continued to develop, industry's eye focused on the area's most abundant natural resource, its trees. By the mid-1920s, 300,000 acres had been clear-cut by logging and paper companies. Dramatic changes caused by reckless logging inspired **Horace Kephart**, author and park supporter, to ask the question "Shall the Smoky Mountains be made a national park or a desert?"

A question demanding an immediate answer. In 1926, **President Calvin Coolidge** signed a bill authorizing the formation of Great Smoky Mountains National Park, with the provision that no federal funds would be used to procure land. It was a serious hurdle to overcome. Parks in the West were formed mostly from land already owned by the federal government. Here on the East Coast, some 6,600 tracts of land needed to be purchased from more than 1,000 private landowners and a handful of logging and paper companies for a total price of $10 million. People from all walks of life banded together, donating every penny they could spare. Overwhelming public support prompted Tennessee and North Carolina to promise $3 million for the potential park, bringing the total to $5 million—still only half the required sum.

Thankfully, a philanthropist with deep pockets came to the aid of the park. **John D. Rockefeller, Jr.**, son of the wealthiest man in America, ultimately donated the entire $5 million balance. He made just one request. That a plaque honoring his mother be placed within the park (**Rockefeller Memorial** at **Newfound Gap**).

Despite this promising turn, the stock market crash in 1929 resulted in North Carolina and Tennessee being unable to honor their pledges to the new park. During these troubling times, **Franklin D. Roosevelt** intervened, allocating $1.5 million of federal funds to complete the land purchase. This marked the first time the U.S. government spent its own money to buy land for a national park. Effort, time, and money from small communities to wealthy philanthropists and governments helped create what is now the most popular national park in the United States.

Abrams Falls

Best of The Smokies

Adventure Hike: **Alum Cave Trail**
  Runners-up: Rocky Top
  2nd Runner-up: Mt Cammerer

Waterfall Hike: **Ramsay Cascades**
  Runner-up: Rainbow Falls

Family Hike: **Clingman's Dome**
  Runner-up: Cades Cove Nature Trail
  2nd Runner-up: Laurel Falls

Scenic Drive: **Cades Cove**
  Runner-up: Roaring Fork Motor Trail

Did you know?

- Receiving about 9 million annual visitors, Great Smoky Mountains (GRSM) is the most visited U.S. National Park.

- GRSM is the first national park in which federal funds were used to buy land.

- GRSM has the greatest biodiversity of any region in a temperate climate zone.

- At 6,643 feet, Clingman's Dome is the third highest peak east of the Mississippi.

- GRSM is the most polluted national park, with about 30 days of poor air quality per year.

- GRSM receives more rainfall then any place in the continental U.S. other than the Pacific Northwest and parts of Alaska.

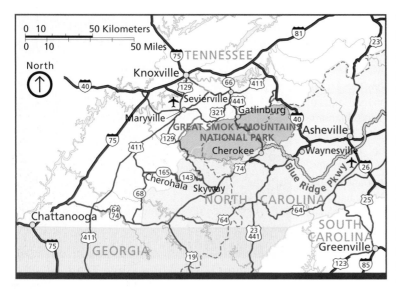

Directions

There are three main entrances.

Gatlinburg, TN Entrance: From I-40, take Exit 407 (Sevierville) to TN-66 S. Continue straight onto US-441 S at the Sevierville intersection. US-441 leads directly into the park.

Townsend, TN Entrance: From the north via I-40 in Knoxville take Exit 386B to US-129 S to Alcoa/Maryville. At Maryville proceed on US-321/TN-73 E through Townsend. Continue on TN-73 into the park.

From the south via I-75 take Exit 376 to I-140 E towards Oak Ridge/Maryville. Merge onto I-140 E via Exit 376B toward Maryville. Turn onto US-129 S (Alcoa Highway) at Exit 11A and head toward Alcoa. Turn onto TN-35 and follow it to US-321 N. Follow US-321 N/TN-73 E through Townsend and continue on TN-73 into the park.

Cherokee, NC Entrance: From the north via I-40, take Exit 27 to US-74 W toward Waynesville. Turn onto US-19 to Cherokee. Turn onto US-441 N at Cherokee and follow it into the park.

From the south follow US-441/US-23 N. At Dillsboro merge onto US-74 W/US-441 N. Merge onto US-441 at Exit 74. Continue on US-441 into the park.

These are the main entrances to the park, but there are several ancillary entrances that lead to sites and facilities that are more remote and less crowded. Balsam Mountain, Abrams Creek, Big Creek, and Cataloochee are great first-come, first-served campgrounds where visitors can enjoy a more relaxed and quaint experience at Great Smoky Mountains National Park.

When to Go

The park is almost perfect in summer and fall. "Almost" is the operative word. The problem is that this perfection is nobody's secret. A typical weekend summer day draws more than 60,000 visitors. Unless bumper-to-bumper traffic is your idea of a good time, you may want to schedule your vacation around the two peak seasons: mid-June to mid-August, and the month of October. During these times, visitation is so heavy that even park officials advise that you try to visit during the "off-season." Should you choose to ignore the park's advice, you can still enjoy its attractions. Start touring early (before 10am), as most visitors explore the park between 10am to 6pm. When the masses are out-and-about you'll want to avoid popular destinations like **Cades Cove Loop** and **Newfound Gap**. But the best way to escape the crowds is to park your car and hike some of the park's 850 miles of trails. Relatively speaking, very few visitors explore the park on foot.

The park is open all year. **Sugarlands**, **Cades Cove**, **Oconaluftee** and **Sevierville Visitor Centers** are open every day except Christmas. **Townsend Visitor Center** and **Gatlinburg Welcome Center** are open every day except Thanksgiving and Christmas. The only year-round campground is Cades Cove, but a few of Cades Cove Loop's historic structures are seasonal.

Transportation & Airports

Public transportation does not provide service to the park from any major city in the area. Gatlinburg offers a trolley service (Tan Route, $2 fare) to the park between June and October.

Asheville Regional Airport (AVL) is 55 miles east of the park's Cherokee Entrance. McGhee Tyson Airport (TYS), just south of Knoxville in Alcoa, TN is 50 miles west of the Gatlinburg Entrance.

Great Smoky Mountains Camping

	Open	Fees	Sites	Location
Abrams Creek	mid-March–October	$14	16	Very west side of park, NE of Chilhowee
Balsam Mountain	mid-May–mid-October	$14	46	On Heintooga Ridge Road, SE corner
Big Creek (Tent-only)	mid-March–October	$14	12	NE corner, take Exit 451 from I-40
Cades Cove*	All Year	$17–20	159	Near entrance of Cades Cove Loop
Cataloochee	mid-March–October	$17	27	Very east side off Cove Creek Road
Cosby*	mid-March–October	$14	165	NE corner, just south of TN-73
Deep Creek	April–October	$17	92	Follow the signs north from Bryson City
Elkmont*	mid-March–November	$17–23	220	Near Sugarlands Visitor Center
Look Rock	mid-May–October	$14	68	West side off Foothills Parkway
Smokemont*	All Year	$17–20	142	Just past Oconaluftee Visitor Center
Backcountry Camping	A free permit is required for all backcountry camping in the park. Permits must be picked up in person at one of the Visitor Centers, Ranger Stations, or Campground Offices. You must stay at a designated campsite or shelter. All shelters and many campsites require advance reservation. To make reservations and receive more info call (865) 436-1231.			

*Reservations for mid-May through October can be made in advance by calling 877-444-6777 or clicking www.recreation.gov

There are no showers or electrical or water hook-ups in the park. Shower facilities are available in nearby communities. Inquire about the nearest facilities upon check-in at the campground. Group sites are available at Big Creek, Cades Cove, Cataloochee, Cosby, Deep Creek, Elkmont, and Smokemont (15–30 people/site, $26–65/night, reservations required)

Great Smoky Mountains Lodging

	Open	Fees	Location
Le Conte Lodge (Hike-in only)	March–November	$121/Adult $85/Child	The shortest hike to this high altitude lodge is 5.5 miles up Alum Cave Trail • Meals are included in rates • 2 and 3 bedroom cabins are available

Call (865) 429-5704 or click www.leconte-lodge.com for reservations and additional information.

Grotto Falls © Exothermic Photography

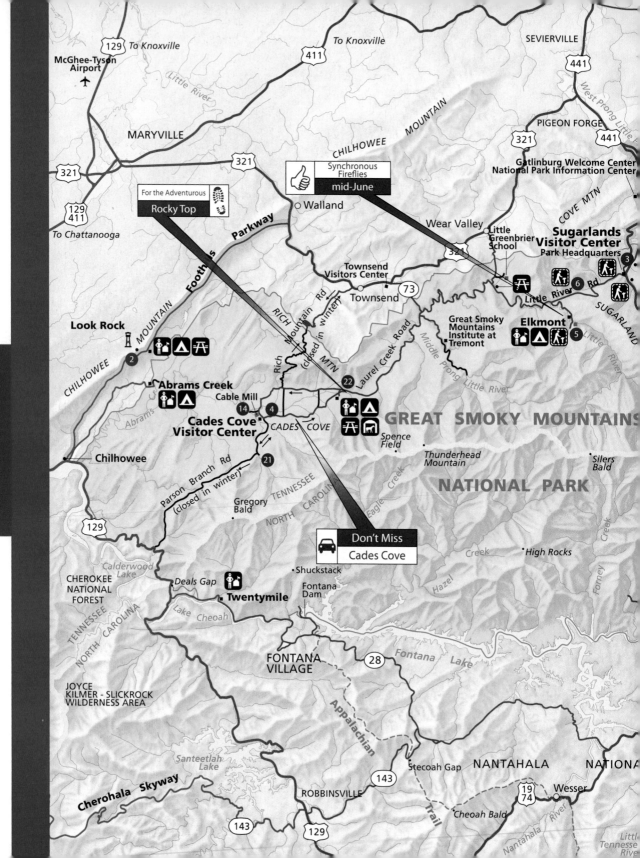

129 To Knoxville

McGhee-Tyson Airport

411 To Knoxville

SEVIERVILLE

441

MARYVILLE

321

321

129 411

To Chattanooga

CHILHOWEE MOUNTAIN

Look Rock

2

CHILHOWEE

Walland

Foothills Parkway

Synchronous Fireflies
mid-June

For the Adventurous
Rocky Top

CHILHOWEE MOUNTAIN

Wear Valley

321

Little Greenbrier School

Townsend Visitors Center

73 Townsend

RICH Mountain Rd (closed in winter)

Rich Mountain Rd

Laurel Creek Road

22

PIGEON FORGE

321 441

Gatlinburg Welcome Center
National Park Information Center

COVE MTN

Sugarlands Visitor Center
Park Headquarters

3

Little River

6

Elkmont

5

SUGARLAND

Great Smoky Mountains Institute at Tremont

Abrams Creek

Cable Mill

Cades Cove Visitor Center

14

CADES COVE

4

21

Abrams

Chilhowee

Parson Branch Rd (closed in winter)

TENNESSEE

NORTH CAROLINA

Gregory Bald

129

GREAT SMOKY MOUNTAINS

Spence Field

Thunderhead Mountain

Silers Bald

NATIONAL PARK

Middle Prong Little River

Eagle Creek

High Rocks

Creek

Hazel

Forney

Creek

CHEROKEE NATIONAL FOREST

Calderwood Lake

Deals Gap

Twentymile

Lake Cheoah

Don't Miss
Cades Cove

Shuckstack

Fontana Dam

FONTANA VILLAGE

28

Fontana Lake

JOYCE KILMER - SLICKROCK WILDERNESS AREA

TENNESSEE

NORTH CAROLINA

Appalachian

Santeetlah Lake

Cherohala Skyway

143

ROBBINSVILLE

129

Stecoah Gap

NANTAHALA

NATIONA

19 74

Wesser

143

Cheoah Bald

Trail

Nantahala River

Little Tennessee River

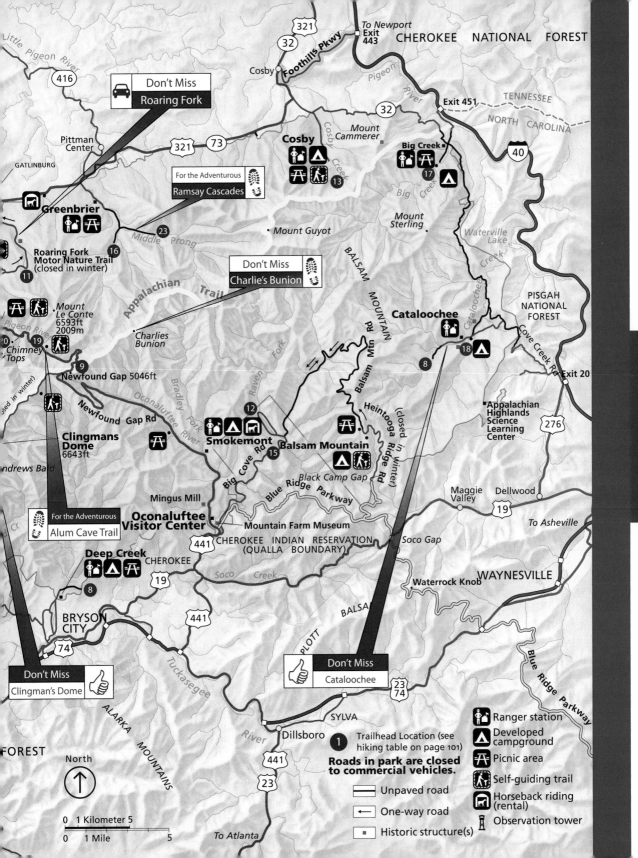

Little Pigeon River

416

Don't Miss
Roaring Fork

321 73

Pittman
Center

GATLINBURG

Greenbrier

Roaring Fork
Motor Nature Trail
(closed in winter)

11

Pigeon River

Mount
Le Conte
6593ft
2009m

19

0

Chimney
Tops

closed in winter

9

Newfound Gap 5046ft

Newfound Gap Rd

Clingmans
Dome
6643ft

Andrews Bald

For the Adventurous
Alum Cave Trail

Deep Creek

8

BRYSON
CITY

74

Don't Miss
Clingman's Dome

FOREST

ALARKA MOUNTAINS

North

0 1 Kilometer 5
0 1 Mile 5

To Atlanta

321

To Newport
Exit
443

CHEROKEE NATIONAL FOREST

32

Cosby

Foothills Pkwy

Pigeon River

32

Exit 451

TENNESSEE

NORTH CAROLINA

Mount
Cammerer

Cosby

13

For the Adventurous
Ramsay Cascades

23

Middle Prong

Appalachian Trail

Mount Guyot

Don't Miss
Charlie's Bunion

Charlies
Bunion

16

Cosby Creek

Big Creek

Big Creek

17

40

Mount
Sterling

Waterville
Lake

BALSAM MOUNTAIN

Balsam Mtn Rd

Cataloochee Creek

Cove Creek Rd

PISGAH
NATIONAL
FOREST

Cataloochee

18

8

Exit 20

276

Bradley Fork

Oconaluftee River

Raven Fork

12

Smokemont

15

Big Cove Rd

Balsam Mountain

Heintooga
Ridge Rd
(closed in winter)

Black Camp Gap

Blue Ridge Parkway

Appalachian
Highlands
Science
Learning
Center

Maggie
Valley

Dellwood

19

To Asheville

Mingus Mill

Oconaluftee
Visitor Center

441

Mountain Farm Museum

CHEROKEE INDIAN RESERVATION
(QUALLA BOUNDARY)

CHEROKEE

19

Soco Creek

Soco Gap

Waterrock Knob

WAYNESVILLE

441

PLOTT BALSA

Don't Miss
Cataloochee

23
74

Tuckasegee

River

Dillsboro

SYLVA

441

23

Blue Ridge Parkway

1 Trailhead Location (see
hiking table on page 101)

Roads in park are closed
to commercial vehicles.

Unpaved road

One-way road

Historic structure(s)

Ranger station

Developed
campground

Picnic area

Self-guiding trail

Horseback riding
(rental)

Observation tower

Original Settlers

Uncertainty exists as to when **Cherokee Indians** settled in the Smokies, but **Hernando de Soto** passed through numerous Cherokee villages during his exploration of the southern Appalachian Mountains in 1540. Cherokee people called this region "Tsiyahi" or "place of the river otter," and they referred to the mountains as being "shaconage" or "blue, like smoke." Life in the mountains may have been simple, but their culture was advanced. They established permanent villages, cultivated crops, had a sophisticated political system, and women were given an equal voice among tribal members. Marriage was only allowed between different clans and children took the clan of their mother. Each village had a seven-sided council house where tribal meetings took place, one side for each of the seven Cherokee Clans: Bird, Paint, Deer, Wolf, Blue, Long Hair, and Wild Potato. Each tribe selected a Peace Chief who ruled during peaceful times, and a War Chief who ruled during times of war—an ancient system of checks and balances.

Unfortunately, no balance was found between Native American and American interests. By 1820 many Cherokee had adopted an American way of life, purchasing store-bought goods and running plantations. But even with their refined lifestyle, the prospect of gold and **President Andrew Jackson's** political leanings doomed their chances of retaining land they inhabited for centuries. The **Indian Removal Act**, signed into law by President Jackson in 1830, and **Treaty of New Echota** led to the forced removal of Cherokee people. More than 14,000 Cherokee were escorted by the U.S. Army out of Southern Appalachia in 1838. Battling despair, disease, and bitter cold, only 10,000 survived the six-month journey to Oklahoma. The National Park Service protects a physical **Trail of Tears** today, but the actual "Trail" is far more figurative in nature. It refers to the forcible relocation and movement of Native Americans, which opened up more land for settlement and commercialization. About 400 Cherokee, known as the **Oconaluftee**, were allowed to continue living on land in the Great Smoky Mountains owned by a sympathetic white man, **William Holland Thomas.** Thomas, who was adopted by Cherokee Indians as a boy, repaid their kindness by serving as their attorney and advisor. Other Cherokee, without their own defender, were left to fend for themselves as refugees in the mountains. **Tsali**, one of the refugees, became a Cherokee hero when he surrendered to the Americans. He was executed, but his ultimate sacrifice allowed the remaining Cherokee to live among the Oconaluftee. Today, some 11,000 Cherokee Indians still reside here within the **Qualla Boundary**.

By 1850, 685 American settlers populated **Cades Cove**. For the most part they lived self-sufficiently, farming the fertile land once used by the Cherokee. Families lived in simple log homes about 18'-by-20' (360 square feet) where an entire family consisting of grandparents, parents, and five to twelve children would sleep under one roof. Children attended school for three to five years, with each "year" lasting about three months and costing $1 a month for each child.

Much like the fate of the Cherokee Indians, sadness and turmoil would find the American settlers of the Smoky Mountains. When the **Civil War** began in 1861, settlements, even families, were torn apart by conflicting loyalties. No slaves had ever worked the land of Cades Cove, yet young men fought for both the Union and the Confederacy. In one particularly sad story, **Russell Gregory**, a father and Union sympathizer, who was murdered by Confederate rebels after his son pointed out their home. Today, Russell is remembered by a tombstone, which reads "Russell Gregory murdered by North Carolina rebels." His son was eventually buried next to him in Cades Cove's Primitive Baptist Church Cemetery.

Once again, families were forced to leave the Smoky Mountains in the 1930s. Many residents had become dependent of logging companies who were clear-cutting the area's trees at a frantic rate. About half of the 1,000 families living in the mountains opposed creation of a national park to protect their jobs and homes. The park won out. Families were forced to move, but not without a fight. They took their battle all the way to the Supreme Court where they won and were awarded a life-time lease on their land. One family remains in the park to this day, and 78 historic structures preserve Southern Appalachian heritage.

The inspiring landscapes of GRSM—once home to Indians and settlers alike, including significant historic and cultural landmarks as well as the Cherokee Indian Reservation (Qualla Boundary)—are now visited by millions of tourists.

Driving

Great Smoky Mountains is a motorists' park. Indeed, the idea of a park in the Smoky Mountains drew much of its support from peoples' demands for a highway between Knoxville, TN and Asheville, NC. Today, more than 384 miles of drivable roads, most of them paved, provide unprecedented access to the Smokies' interior. **Cades Cove Loop Road** is the park's most popular destination, and **Roaring Fork Motor Nature Trail** isn't far behind. Both of these routes allow visitors to see wildlife and nature from the comfort of a motor vehicle.

The perimeter of **Cades Cove** is traced by an 11-mile, one-way loop road, beginning and ending at the eastern terminus of **Laurel Creek Road**. If you'd like to conclude your driving tour of Cades Cove prematurely (maybe because of excessive traffic) you can exit the loop via two seasonal, steep, winding, unpaved roads: **Rich Mountain Road** and **Parson Branch Road**. If traffic is manageable you'll want to stick around, because the loop provides some of the best opportunities to spot white-tailed deer and black bear. You'll also find the largest open-air museum in the Smoky Mountains where pioneer homesteads, barns, churches, and mills have been restored to their 19th century appearances. While many of these structures are removed from the road, all of them are well-marked and easily accessible.

The loop starts where Smoky Mountain settlement began. First stop is also the first cabin built in the Smokies, **John Oliver Place**. Next you'll find **Primitive Baptist Church**, which was established in 1827, but the congregation worshipped in a small log structure until 1887 when the larger white frame church (seen at this stop) was erected. A small cemetery where many of the early settlers are buried is located nearby. Religion was the cause of many disagreements in the Cove. In 1839 expelled members of Primitive Baptist Church formed **Missionary Baptist Church** (site 7). (Once the Civil War began, the church was forced to close its doors because the congregation was mostly Union sympathizers, but Confederate support also ran deep among the cove's 700 citizens.) Continuing along the loop is a short spur road to **Abrams Falls Trailhead** and **Elijah Oliver Place**. A 0.5-mile hike leads to the homestead of another Oliver family. It's 5 miles (roundtrip) to 20-foot Abrams Falls. **John Cable Mill** and **Cades Cove Visitor Center** are located near the loop's midway point. Rangers, gifts, and restrooms make this one of the more popular

An old wagon in Cades Cove © James Jordan

stops, but you shouldn't leave without browsing the time-period exhibits on display. The only original building left behind is the mill where early settlers ground corn. All others were brought here by the National Park Service to aid in their demonstrations of early farm life (schedules are available at the visitor center). Energy and attitudes permitting, there are a few more sites to see on the second half of the loop. You'll pass **Henry Whitehead Place**, **Cades Cove Nature Trail**, **Dan Lawson Place**, and **Carter Shields Cabin** before you've come full circle.

Roaring Fork Nature Trail is a 6-mile one-way road that begins and ends in Gatlinburg. The road's 10 mph speed limit is testament to the amount of twists, turns, and traffic you'll encounter. Along the way you'll pass several restored homes and buildings and **Rainbow Falls Trailhead**. Rainbow Falls is best seen on a sunny day after a heavy rain, when the trail lives up to its name and the **Place of a Thousand Drips** will be dripping. Rain or shine, the hike is pleasant any time of year.

Newfound Gap and **Clingman's Dome Roads** are must-sees. **Balsam Mountain** and **Heintooga Ridge Roads** around **Balsam Mountain**, and **Cove Creek Road** to the **Cataloochee Valley** are great places to avoid summer and fall crowds while enjoying similar majestic views of the Smoky Mountains.

The lookout at Clingman's Dome

Hiking/Backpacking

There are 850 miles of hiking trails, including 70 miles of the **Appalachian Trail**, at GRSM. Many of which either start at or lead to 10 front country campgrounds, dozens of backcountry campsites, or 15 backcountry shelters. Whether it's a multi-day trek along the Appalachian Trail, a short jaunt through historic settlements; a knee-jarring, mountain-climbing work-out to a 6,000 foot summit; or a casual creek-side stroll to a cascading waterfall, the Smokies have it all. Here are a few of the park's best trails to help you choose where to hike.

Spring brings about some of the most colorful wild-flower displays on the East Coast. Creekside trails are ideal locations to see wildflowers due to cool moist air and wet ground. **Oconaluftee River Trail** (begins at Oconaluftee Visitor Center), **Deep Creek Trail** (begins at the end of Deep Creek Road), **Kanati Fork Trail** (begins just north of Kephart Prong foot-bridge on Newfound Gap Road), **Little River Trail** (begins just before Elkmont Campground Entrance), **Middle Prong Trail** (begins at the end of Tremont

Road), and **Porters Creek Trail** (begins at Greenbrier Entrance) are all excellent spring wildflower hikes.

The park's waterfalls are popular hiking destinations all year round. Spring snowmelt causes streams and waterfalls to swell, but trails are often muddy and busy. Crowds subside from late fall to early spring, and trees have shed their leaves opening up new views. **Cataract Falls** is a short hike departing from Sugarlands Visitor Center. The paved path to **Laurel Falls** is one of the easiest and most popular waterfall hikes in the park. The route to **Grotto and Abrams Falls** are a little more challenging, but nothing the average hiker should be intimidated by. Then there's **Ramsay Cascades**, the tallest waterfall in the park, and quite possibly its most strenuous day-hike. There's plenty of beautiful scenery along the way, and most of the hike is a gradual climb, before things get steep and rocky near the cascades.

Summer is a great time to hike to one of the park's sun-soaked, wind-swept balds or 6,000 foot summits. To reach a summit you must inevitably head uphill, but not all of these trails are difficult. **Clingman's Dome Trail** (0.5 mile) leads to the park's highest point, but it's also one of its easiest summit hikes. One of the most difficult trails is the 14.4-mile **Bullhead Trail** to Mount Le Conte. It's sure to make you sweat as you gain 3,993 feet in elevation along the way. **Rocky Top** is another strenuous trail, but it rewards hardy hikers with the best views in the park. With a pinch of planning you can take one of four trails to the top of Mount Le Conte (the park's third highest peak) and spend a relaxing night at Le Conte Lodge (www.leconte-lodge.com). **Alum Cave Trail** is short, steep, and strenuous, but it provides some of the most majestic scenery anywhere in the park. **Trillium Gap and Boulevard Trails** are longer, more gradual hikes to the summit. **Bullhead Trail** is both long and difficult. No matter which route you choose it's going to be a challenge, but your effort will be rewarded with a night at Le Conte Lodge, a Smoky Mountain paradise.

For easy hikes look no further than the old homesteaders' villages. **Woody Place**, **Cades Cove Nature**, **Porter's Creek**, and **Little Cataloochee Trails** are relatively flat hikes that allow visitors to reimagine life in the Smokies during the 1800s.

Backpackers are required to obtain a free permit and stay at designated campsites and shelters while camping in the backcountry. To plan your backpacking trip visit the park's website or call the Backcountry Reservation Office (865.436.1231).

Great Smoky Mountains Hiking Trails

	Name	Trailhead (# on map)	Length	Notes (Roundtrip distances)
Easy	Clingman's Dome - 👍	Clingman's Dome Parking Area (1)	0.5 mile	Short but steep hike to an observation tower atop the highest peak in the Smoky Mountains
	Look Rock	Near Look Rock Campground (2)	0.5 mile	Views similar to Clingman's Dome, but fewer visitors
	Sugarlands Valley Nature Trail	Sugarlands Visitor Center (3)	0.5 mile	Self-guiding nature trail that is accessible to individuals in wheelchairs
	Cades Cove Nature Trail	About 1 mile past Cades Cove Visitor Center (5)	2.0 miles	Great family hike • Brochures explain the area's cultural and historical significance
	Cucumber Gap	Elkmont/ Little River Parking Area (5)	5.6 miles	Wildflowers in spring and a 20-foot waterfall
	Laurel Falls	Laurel Falls Parking Area (6)	2.6 miles	One of the park's most popular destinations
	Indian Creek	End of Deep Creek Road (7)	1.6 miles	Toms Branch Falls and Indian Creek Falls
	Woody Place	End of Cataloochee Road (8)	2 miles	Follow the Rough Fork Trail to an 1880s home
Moderate	Andrews Bald	Clingman's Dome Parking Area (1)	3.5 miles	Highly rewarding, relatively short hike
	Charlie's Bunion	Newfound Gap Parking Area (9)	8.1 miles	Follows the Appalachian Trail to a rock outcropping named for Charlie Conner's bunion
	Rainbow Falls	Rainbow Falls Parking Area (10)	5.4 miles	80-foot falls produces rainbows when sunny
	Grotto Falls	Roaring Fork Motor Nature Trail Stop #5 (11)	2.6 miles	Pass old growth hemlock forest to a 25-foot high falls that you hike above and below
	Smokemont Loop	Smokemont Campground (12)	6.5 miles	The journey begins on the Bradley Fork Trail
	Hen Wallow Falls	Cosby Picnic Area (13)	4.4 miles	Hike to a narrow 90-foot high waterfall
	Abram's Falls	Cades Cove Loop, past Stop #10 (14)	5.0 miles	Flat, popular, well-maintained trail leading to a 20-foot waterfall
	Mingo Falls - 👍	Qualla Boundary (15)	0.4 mile	Spectacular 120-foot waterfall
	Porter's Creek	Greenbrier Entrance (16)	4.0 miles	Spring wildflowers, old-growth forest and waterfalls • Spur trail (1 mile) to cantilevered barn
	Mouse Creek Falls - 👍	Big Creek Trail, Waterville Road via Exit 451 from I-40 (17)	4.0 miles	Follows an old railroad grade, there's a great swimming hole (Midnight Hole) at 1.4 miles
	Boogerman Loop	Cataloochee Campground (18)	7.4 miles	Great hike in a less popular portion of the park
	Little Cataloochee - 👍	Just west of Cataloochee Campground (18)	6.0 miles	Hike through remnants of Little Cataloochee Cove where 1,200 people used to live
Strenuous	Bullhead	Just off Cherokee Orchard Loop Rd (10)	14.4 miles	Least traveled route to Mount Le Conte
	Mt Cammerer	Cosby, Lower Gap Trailhead (13)	12.0 miles	Great hike to panoramic views and a fire tower built by the CCC in the 1930s
	Alum Cave - 👍	Alum Cave Bluffs Parking Area (19)	4.4 miles	Views to the west from Cliff Top and to the east from Myrtle Point • 11 miles to Mount Le Conte
	Chimney Tops - 👍	Just off Newfound Gap Road (20)	10.0 miles	The most popular hike in the park
	Gregory Bald	Cades Cove, Parson Branch Rd (21)	11.3 miles	Bald named for Russell Gregory who was murdered by Confederate troops
	Rich Mountain	Cades Cove just before loop begins (22)	8.5 miles	Excellent views of Cades Cove and wildlife
	Rocky Top - 👍	Cades Cove Campground, Anthony Creek Trailhead (22)	13.9 miles	Hike to Spence Field then continue along the Appalachian Trail to Rocky Top (inspiration for the University of Tennessee's fight song)
	Ramsay Cascades - 👍	Greenbrier Entrance, follow Signs (23)	8.0 miles	Tallest waterfall in the park at 100-feet

Stopping to watch the sun rise over Cades Cove during an early morning bike ride

Biking

Bicycles are allowed on most of the roads within the park, but that doesn't mean you should bike them. **Cades Cove Loop Road**—the one recommended location—is narrow, bumpy, and packed with motorists, but it gets better during scheduled motor-free periods. During these times cyclists are free to enjoy the sights and sounds of the Cove, without having to navigate through throngs of traffic stopping and starting whenever they like. If you miss out on these designated times, try to pedal the loop early in the day (before 10am). Bicycles can be rented ($6/hour) from Cades Cove Campground Store (865.448.9034, www.explorecadescove.com) near Cades Cove Campground, open from summer through fall.

Clingman's Dome Road is a good challenge for cyclists, but this climb should also be reserved for an early morning or during the brief window when the steep road is closed to motorists but free of snow in early spring.

Bikes are prohibited on all park trails except Gatlinburg, Oconaluftee River, and Lower Deep Creek Trails.

Paddling

Mountain lakes and streams provide water activities ranging from leisurely flatwater paddling to adrenaline-pumping whitewater runs. Paddling offers an unobtrusive, peaceful, and less stressful way to view wildlife and fall colors. **Fontana and Calderwood Lakes** are the most popular locations for flatwater. Both of these lakes skirt the park's southeastern boundary. Fontana Lake has a handful of marinas between Bryson City and Fontana Dam where you can launch your boat. At Calderwood Lake, a 5-mile dammed section of the Little Tennessee River, you'll find a boat ramp near Cheoah Dam. It's an ideal location for an out-and-back paddle.

Steep mountain slopes and an abundance of rain and snow make for some of the East Coast's best whitewater paddling. Several outfitters offer whitewater raft, kayak, and innertube float trips in TN and NC. Turn to page 109 for a complete list of outfitters.

Smoky Mountain Kayaking • (865) 705-8678
3002 Shadowbrook Drive; Maryville, TN 37803
www.smokymountainkayaking.com
Rates: 4 hours, $40/person (Guided Flatwater)

River Rat Tubing & Kayak • (865) 448-8888
205 Wears Valley Road; Townsend, TN 37882
www.smokymtnriverrat.com
Rates: Tubing, $13/person; Kayaking, $15/person

Fishing

Fishing is allowed in all of the park's 2,115 miles of streams, except Bear Creek at its junction with Forney Creek in North Carolina and Lynn Camp Prong upstream of its confluence with Thunderhead Prong in Tennessee. These two areas are closed to help repopulate brook trout. Depending on which state you are in, a valid Tennessee or North Carolina fishing license is required. Trout (brook, brown, and rainbow) and smallmouth bass have a seven inch minimum and possession limit of five. Fishing is permitted year-round and there are several outfitters that can help you catch your limit.

Smoky Mountain Gillies LLC • 865-577-4289
4524 Martin Mill Pike; Knoxville, TN 37920
www.smokymountaingillies.com
Rates: 1 Person $200 (half-day)/$275 (full-day)

The Smoky Mountain Angler • (865)436-8746
466 Brookside Village Way Suite 8; Gatlinburg, TN 37738
www.smokymountainangler.com
Rates: 1 Person $175 (half-day)/$250 (full-day)

Smoky Mountain Fly Guide • (423) 586-6198
1695 Lake Park Circle; Morristown, TN 37814
www.smokymountainflyguide.com
Rates: 1 Person $175 (half-day)/$225 (full-day)

Smoky Mountain Fly Fishing • (828) 497-1555
PO Box 1169, 626 Tsali Blvd; Cherokee, NC 28719
www.smokymountainflyfishing.net
Rates: 1 Person $150 (half-day)/$225 (full-day)

Smoky Mountains on the Fly • (828) 586-4787
www.smokyonthefly.com
Rates: 1 Person $150 (half-day)/$225 (full-day)

Horseback Riding

Nearly 550 of the park's 850 miles of hiking trails are open to horses. Five drive-in horse campgrounds are open from April until mid-November: Anthony Creek (near Cades Cove Campground), Big Creek, Cataloochee, Round Bottom (near Oconaluftee Visitor Center), and Tow String (near Oconaluftee Visitor Center). Guests without their own horses can take a ride with one of the following outfitters:

Cades Cove Riding Stables • (865) 448-9009
10018 Campground Drive; Townsend, TN 37882
www.cadescovestables.com
Open: April–early January (9am–4:30pm) • Rates: $25/hr
Ranger-led hayrides and carriage rides are available

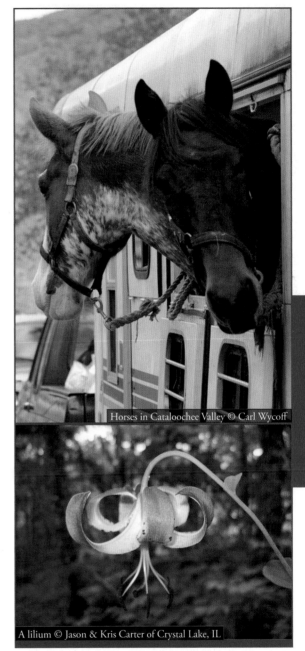
Horses in Cataloochee Valley © Carl Wycoff

A lilium © Jason & Kris Carter of Crystal Lake, IL

Smokemont Riding Stable • (828) 497-2373
135 Smokemont Riding Stable Road; Cherokee, NC 28719
www.smokemontridingstable.com
Open: late March–October (9am–5pm) • Rates: $25/hour

Smoky Mountain Riding Stables • (865) 436-5634
Highway 321, East Parkway; Gatlinburg, TN 37738
www.sugarlandridingstables.com
Open: mid-March–November • Rates: $25/hour

Balsam Wildflower © Jim R. Rogers

For Kids: The park offers ranger-led programs for children from spring to fall (check online or in person at a visitor center for a current schedule of events). Children between the ages of 5 and 12 have the opportunity to become a **junior ranger**. Junior Ranger Activity Booklets can be purchased for $2.50 at any visitor centers or at Elkmont and Cades Cove Campgrounds. Complete the booklet, and then return to a visitor center to receive a junior ranger badge. The junior ranger program runs all year long.

Ranger Programs: Attending a ranger program should be a mandatory requirement at all national parks. Make sure you grab a park newspaper from one of the visitor centers to browse a current schedule of ranger-led activities and pick out which program(s) you'll attend. GRSM offers **Cable Mill Demonstrations** and hayrides in Cades Cove, but there are many other hikes, lunches, talks, and camp-fires held throughout the park where rangers impart their wisdom and humor on those willing to listen. One ranger program even invites visitors to learn to play the hog fiddle. Seasonal programs like **Autumn Arrives** and **The Smokies Synchronous Fireflies** are so unique and enjoyable you may want to specifi-cally plan your trip around them.

Flora & Fauna: Incomparable biodiversity resulted in the park's designation as a **UNESCO World Heritage Site** and **International Biosphere Reserve**. GRSM is home to **more than 1,600 species of flow-ering plants**, which helped inspire its billing as "the Wildflower National Park." Wildflowers bloom year-round, but spring is the ultimate time to view an abundance of colorful blossoms. The week-long **Spring Wildflower Pilgrimage Festival** celebrates these living decorations and features programs and guided walks that explore the park's amazing biodi-versity. You can help save the wildflowers by staying on hiking trails when exploring the backcountry,

and it is illegal to pick wildflowers. Beyond flowers, you'll find more than 100 native tree species and over 100 native shrub species. **There are more tree species here than any other U.S. National Park, and more species than in all of Northern Europe.**

More than 200 species of birds, 50 native species of fish, 80 types of reptiles and amphibians, and 66 spe-cies of mammals are protected in GRSM. Spotting wild-life is often easiest in winter after trees have shed their leaves. During the remainder of the year open areas like **Chataloochee** and **Cades Cove** are great spots for wildlife viewing. White-tailed deer, wild turkey, squirrels, and bats are your most probable sightings, but don't count out seeing the symbol of the park, the black bear. GRSM provides the **largest protected bear habitat in the East**, and it's home to approximately 1,500 bears. The park's 30 species of salamander are enough to earn the title of "**Salamander Capital of the World**." However, the most unique wildlife display comes from one of its smallest occupants, the **Smoky Mountain Synchronous Fireflies**. The name sounds like a circus act—a description not far from reality—but these tiny insects aren't performing for you; their flashing light patterns are part of a mating dis-play. It's special because the individual fireflies are able to synchronize their light patterns. Such a spectacle is only known to occur in one other place in the world (Southeast Asia). These phosphorescent flies perform nightly for a two week period around the middle of June (dates change from year to year). To see the show you must camp at Elkmont or take a $1 round-trip trolley ride from Sugarlands Visitor Center. (Personal vehicles are not permitted.) Visitors should follow a few simple rules so you do not disrupt the fireflies or other guests. Cover your flashlight with red or blue cellophane. Only use your flashlight (pointed toward the ground) when walking to your viewing spot. Stay on the trail at all times, do not catch fireflies, and pack out your garbage.

Pets: Pets are allowed in the park, but must be kept on a leash no more than six feet in length at all times. They are not allowed on hiking trails with the exception of Gatlinburg Trail and Oconaluftee River Trail.

Accessibility: Temporary Parking Permits are available at Sugarlands and Oconaluftee Visitor Centers for visitors with disabilities. Elkmont, Smokemont, and Cades Cove have campsites accessible to wheelchair users. Much of the park is accessible by car, but almost all trails are rugged and inaccessible. Cades Cove Complex and Amphitheater,

Oconaluftee Mountain Farm Museum, and Sugarlands Valley Nature Trail are fully accessible.

Weather: Visitors can receive current park weather forecasts by calling (865) 436-1200 ext. 630. The area's temperate climate makes the park a pleasant place to visit just about any time of year. However, high elevation areas receive considerable precipitation (85" annually). Lower elevations average 55" of precipitation each year. September and October are the driest months.

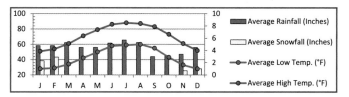

Vacation Planner

The park is big. The roads are busy. There's a lot to see and visitors typically have a limited amount of time. This is the predicament faced by GRSM visitors. Here's a full 3-day itinerary to use as a blueprint for planning your Smoky Mountains vacation. Try to fit at least one **ranger program** into your schedule. If you plan on traveling in June, check the park's website to see if **fireflies** are lighting the night sky at Elkmont (page 104). Camping and lodging (hike-in only) are available within the park (page 95). Gatlinburg, Sevierville, and Pigeon Forge are three of the largest tourist traps you'll ever find. Pick one, and plan a full day just to have a look around. Where to stay and eat is up to you, but a fairly thorough list including some of the area's finer dining, grocery stores, lodging, festivals, and attractions outside the park can be found on pages 106–109.

Enter via Gatlinburg, TN and continue directly to **Sugarlands Visitor Center**. Browse the exhibits, watch a short film, and ask rangers any questions you've come up with. Once you've introduced yourselves to the park, head back to your car and backtrack to Gatlinburg. Catch **Roaring Fork Motor Nature Trail** (page 99). Follow the 10 mph speed limit, and if you've already had too much windshield time for the day, get out and hike to **Rainbow Falls** (5.4 miles, page 101). Time permitting continue east on TN-73 to Greenbrier Entrance. Work up a hunger by completing the strenuous 8-mile trek to **Ramsay Cascades**. If you don't have the time or energy for a difficult hike, no problem, continue driving east around the park's perimeter to Cosby and/or Cataloochee. Both regions offer excellent scenery.

Staying on the TN side, return to Sugarlands, but this time follow Little River Road west to Laurel Creek Road all the way to **Cades Cove** (page 99).
Try to arrive early, because this is the most visited destination in the park, and traffic begins to pile up around 10 am. Cades Cove is popular because there's a little something for everyone here. History buffs will be intrigued by old settlement homesteads, mills, and churches. Nature lovers can hike to **Abrams Falls** (page 101) or take the 13.9-mile trek to **Rocky Top** (page 101). Activity lovers can **ride horses** (page 103), **rent bicycles** (page 102), enjoy a **carriage ride**, or even sit on a bale of hay while a park ranger tells stories about early settler life in the Cove. It's conceivable to spend the entire day here. If you plan on camping in summer, hopefully you have reservations at Cades Cove or Elkmont Campgrounds (page 95), otherwise you may want to exit the park via Parson Branch Road (unpaved) and check out Abrams Creek and Look Rock campgrounds (page 95) for availability.

There's no better way of spending a night in the Smokies than hiking to **Le Conte Lodge** (page 95). Once again pass Sugarlands Visitor Center, but continue on **Newfound Gap Road**. Take note of **Alum Cave Trail Parking Area;** you'll be returning here later. Drive to **Clingman's Dome Road** and follow it to its end where you will hike the short trail to a scenic overlook. This is the highest peak in the Smokies. Next you'll hike to the third tallest peak. Return to **Alum Cave Trail** (page 100) Parking Area and hike 5.5 miles (one-way) to spend the night at **Le Conte Lodge** (reservations required), where you'll be served a hearty dinner with wine. Afterward you're free to spend the evening without electricity in one of their rustic cabins. A perfect spot to enjoy all the grandeur the Smokies have to offer. Breakfast will be served in the morning before you have to hike back down to the parking area. Once you've returned to your car, continue along Newfound Gap Road and stop at **Newfound Gap** to read the plaque placed here in memory of **Laura Rockefeller** (page 92) before exiting the park.

Dining

West Side

Dolce Uva Wine Bar Café • (865) 277-7585
463 Parkway; Gatlinburg, TN 37738
www.uvawinebarcafe.com • Entrée: $14–18

Smoky Mtn Brewery & Restaurant • (865) 436-4200
1004 Parkway, # 501; Gatlinburg, TN 37738
www.coppercellar.com • Entrée: $7–11

Park Grill • (865) 436-2300
1110 Parkway; Gatlinburg, TN 37738
www.parkgrillsteakhouse.com • Entrée: $19–38

Best Italian Café & Pizzeria • (865) 430-4090
968 Parkway, # 9; Gatlinburg, TN 37738
www.bestitalian.com • Entrée: $13–22

Pancake Pantry • (865) 436-4724
628 Parkway; Gatlinburg, TN 37738
www.pancakepantry.com

Bennett's Pitt Bar B Que • (865) 436-2400
714 River Rd; Gatlinburg, TN 37738
www.bennetts-bbq.com

Cherokee Grill • (865) 436-4287
1002 Parkway; Gatlinburg, TN 37738
www.coppercellar.com • Entrée: $13–23

Wild Plum • (865) 436-3808
555 Buckhorn Rd; Gatlinburg, TN 37738

Mountain Lodge Restaurant • (865) 436-2547
913 E Parkway; Gatlinburg, TN 37738

Log Cabin Pancake House • (865) 436-7894
327 Historic Nature Tr; Gatlinburg, TN 37738
www.logcabinpancakehouse.com

Donut Friar • (865) 436-7306
634 Parkway, # 15; Gatlinburg, TN 37738

The Peddler Steakhouse • (865) 436-5794
820 River Rd; Gatlinburg, TN 37738
www.peddlergatlinburg.com • Entrée: $19–38

Calhoun's Restaurant • (865) 436-4100
1004 Parkway, # 101; Gatlinburg, TN 37738
www.coppercellar.com • Entrée: $8–22

Brass Lantern Restaurant • (865) 436-4168
402 River Rd; Gatlinburg, TN 37738
www.brasslanterngatlinburg.com • Entrée: $9–17

No Way Jose's Mexican Cantina • (865) 430-5673
555 Parkway; Gatlinburg, TN 37738
www.nowayjosescantina.com • Entrée: $8–15

Cheese Cupboard & Hofbrauhaus • (865) 436-9511
634 Parkway, # 14; Gatlinburg, TN 37738

Coffee & Company • (865) 430-3650
490 E Parkway; Gatlinburg, TN 37738

Mountain Edge Grill • (865) 436-0013
631 Parkway, # B4; Gatlinburg, TN 37738
www.mtnedge.com • Entrée: $14–18

Del's Pizza • (865) 933-0900
2946 Winfield Dunn Pkwy; Kodak, TN 37764

Gondolier Italian Restaurant • (865) 428-8050
964 Dolly Parton Pkwy; Sevierville, TN 37862
www.gondolierpizza.com

Applewood Farmhouse Restaurant • (865) 429-8644
220 Apple Valley Rd; Sevierville, TN 37862
www.applewoodrestaurant.com

Bear Camp Grill • (865) 453-0181
3275 Wears Valley Rd; Sevierville, TN 37862

El Mesquite • (865) 428-4168
815 Parkway; Sevierville, TN 37862

Little Italian Kitchen • (865) 453-3001
2467 Boyds Creek Hwy # 3; Sevierville, TN 37876

Red Rooster Pancake House • (865) 428-3322
3215 Parkway; Pigeon Forge, TN 37863

Kinkaku Japanese Steakhouse • (865) 774-7698
3152 Parkway, # 1; Pigeon Forge, TN 37863
www.pigeonforgejapanese.com • All-U-Can-Eat: $15

Little Tokyo Japanese Restaurant • (865) 908-055
2430 Teaster Ln, # 212; Pigeon Forge, TN 37863

Huck Finn's Catfish • (865) 429-3353
3334 Parkway; Pigeon Forge, TN 37863
www.huckfinnsrestaurant.com

Old Mill Restaurant • (865) 429-3463
175 Old Mill Ave; Pigeon Forge, TN 37863
www.oldmillsquare.com

East Side

Jimmy Mac's Restaurant • (828) 488-4700
121 Main St; Bryson City, NC 28713

Cork & Bean • (828) 488-1934
16 New Fontana Rd; Bryson City, NC 28713
www.brysoncitycorkandbean.com

Filling Station Deli Sub Shop • (828) 488-1919
145 Everett St; Bryson City, NC 28713
www.thefillingstationdeli.com • Entrée: $4–7

Mtn Perks Espresso Bar • (828) 488-9561
9 Depot St; Bryson City, NC 28713
www.mtnperks.com

Guayabitos Mexican Restaurant • (828) 488-133
236 US-19 S; Bryson City, NC 28713

Nabers Drive In • (828) 488-2877
1245 Main St; Bryson City, NC 28713

Blue Ridge Grill • (828) 488-888
80 Songbird Forest Rd; Bryson City, NC 28713

Bar-B-Que Wagon • (828) 488-9521
610 Main St; Bryson City, NC 28713

Sweet Onion • (828) 456-5559
39 Miller St; Waynesville, NC 28786
www.sweetonionrestaurant.com • Entrée: $12–22

Mountain Perks Espresso Bar • (828) 488-9561
9 Depot St; Bryson City, NC 28713

Everett Street Diner • (828) 488-0123
126 Everett St; Bryson City, NC 28713

Bogart's Restaurant • (828) 452-1313
303 S Main St; Waynesville, NC 28786
www.bogartswaynesville.com • Entrée: $11–23

Clyde's Restaurant • (828) 456-9135
2107 South Main St; Waynesville, NC 28786

Bocelli's Italian Eatery • (828) 456-4900
319 N Haywood St; Waynesville, NC 28786
www.bocellisitalianeatery.com • Entrée: $11–18

Big Mountain Barbeque • (828) 454-0720
79 Elysinia Ave; Waynesville, NC 28786
www.bigmountainbbq.com

Tap Room • (828) 456-5988
176 Country Club Dr; Waynesville, NC 28786
www.thewaynesvilleinn.com • Entrée: $13–20

Fat Buddies Ribs & BBQ • (828) 456-6368
193 Waynesville Plz; Waynesville, NC 28786
www.fatbuddiesribsandbbq.com • Entrée: $11–17

Sagebrush Steakhouse • (828) 452-5822
895 Russ Ave; Waynesville, NC 28786
www.sagebrushsteakhouse.com • Entrée: $9–22

Hurley's Creekside Dining • (828) 926-1566
4352 Soco Rd; Maggie Valley, NC 28751
www.hurleysmaggievalley.com • Entrée: $14–18

Nick & Nate's Pizza • (828) 586-3000
38 The Villages Overlook; Sylva, NC
www.nickandnatespizza.com

Guadalupe Café • (828) 586-9877
606 W Main St; Sylva, NC 28779
www.guadalupecafe.com • Entrée: $3–9

Country Vittles Restaurant • (828) 926-1820
3589 Soco Rd; Maggie Valley, NC 28751

Snappy's Italian Pizzeria • (828) 926-6126
2769 Soco Rd; Maggie Valley, NC 28751
www.snappysitalian.net • Entrée: $12–18

Joey's Pancake House • (828) 926-0212
4309 Soco Rd; Maggie Valley, NC 28751
www.joeyspancake.com

Cataloochee Ranch • (828) 926-1401
119 Ranch Dr; Maggie Valley, NC 28751
www.cataloocheeranch.com

Legends Sports Grill • (828) 926-9464
3865 Soco Rd; Maggie Valley, NC 28751
www.legendsofmaggievalley.com

Kostas Family Restaurant • (828) 631-0777
489 Haywood Rd; Moncure, NC 27559
www.kostasdillsboro.com

Grocery Stores

Food City • (865) 430-3116
1219 E Parkway; Gatlinburg, TN 37738

Kroger • (865) 429-0874
220 Wears Valley Rd; Pigeon Forge, TN 37863

Walmart Supercenter • (865) 429-0029
1414 Parkway; Sevierville, TN 37862

Food Lion • (865) 428-0558
320 W Main St; Sevierville, TN 37862

Townsend IGA • (865) 448-3010
7945 E Lamar Alexander Pkwy; Townsend, TN 37882

Walmart Supercenter • (828) 456-4828
135 Town Center Loop; Waynesville, NC 28786

Lodging

In the Park

Le Conte Lodge • (865) 429-5704
On top of Mount Le Conte, hike-in only, no electricity, shared bathroom
Reservation Office: 250 Apple Valley Rd; Sevierville, TN 37862
www.leconte-lodge.com • Rates: $116/Adult

West Side

Lodge At Buckberry Creek • (865) 430-8030
961 Campbell Lead Rd; Gatlinburg, TN 37738
www.buckberrylodge.com • Rates: $180–460

Jack Huff's Hotel • (800) 322-1817
204 Cherokee Orchard Rd; Gatlinburg, TN 37738
www.jackhuffs.com • Rates: $51–150

Mountain Laurel Chalets • (865) 436-5277
440 Ski Mountain Rd; Gatlinburg, TN 37738
www.mtnlaurelchalets.com • Rates: $120+

Riverhouse Motor Lodge • (865) 436-7821
610 River Rd; Gatlinburg, TN 37738
www.riverhousemotels.com • Rates: $43–174

Riverhouse at the Park • (865) 436-2070
205 Ski Mountain Rd; Gatlinburg, TN 37738
www.riverhousegatlinburg.com • Rates: $47–174

Deer Ridge Resort • (865) 436-2325
3710 Weber Rd; Gatlinburg, TN 37738
www.deerridge.com • Rates: $99–460

Brookside Resort • (865) 436-5611
463 E Parkway; Gatlinburg, TN 37738
www.brooksideresort.com • Rates: $80–125

Laurel Springs Lodge B&B • (888) 430-9211
204 Hill St; Gatlinburg, TN 37738
www.laurelspringslodge.com • Rates: $129–159

The Foxtrot B&B • (888) 436-3033
1520 Garrett Ln; Gatlinburg, TN 37738
www.thefoxtrot.com • Rates: $165–205

Buckhorn Inn • (865) 436-4668
2140 Tudor Mtn Rd; Gatlinburg, TN 37738
www.buckhorninn.com • Rates: $115–320

Four Sisters Inn • (865) 430-8411
425 Stuart Ln; Gatlinburg, TN 37738
www.4sistersinn.com • Rates: $180–460

Cabins For You • (865) 436-2109
436 East Parkway; Gatlinburg, TN 37738
www.cabinsforyou.com • Rates: $115+

Hippensteal's Mtn View Inn • (865) 436-5761
4201 Tatem Marr Way; Sevierville, TN 37876
www.hippensteal.com • Rates: $194

Mountain Aire Inn • (865) 453-5576
1008 Parkway; Sevierville, TN 37862

Berry Springs Lodge • (865) 908-7935
2149 Seaton Springs Rd; Sevierville, TN 37862
www.berrysprings.com • Rates: $105–225

Braeside Inn B&B • (865) 429-5859
115 Ruth Ln; Sevierville, TN 37862
www.braesideinnbb.com • Rates: $95–189

Blue Mountain Mist Country Inn • (865) 428-2335
1811 Pullen Rd; Sevierville, TN 37862
www.bluemountainmist.com • Rates: $180–460

Calico Inn B&B • (865) 428-3833
757 Ranch Way; Sevierville, TN 37862
www.calico-inn.com • Rates: $109–125

Persephone's Farm Retreat • (865) 428-3904
2279 Hodges Ferry Rd; Sevierville, TN 37876
www.bedandbreakfast.cc • Rates: $139

Timber Tops • (865) 429-0831
1440 Upper Middle Creek Rd; Sevierville, TN 37876
www.yourcabin.com • Rates: $155+

Little Valley Mountain Resort • (800) 581-7225
2229 Little Valley Rd; Sevierville, TN 37862
www.littlevalleymountainresort.com • Rates: $129+

Quail Ridge Inn B&B • (865) 436-8287
2765 King Hollow Rd; Sevierville, TN 37876
www.quailridgebandb.com • Rates: $130–140

Inn At Christmas Place • (865) 868-0525
119 Christmas Tree Ln; Pigeon Forge, TN 37868
www.innatchristmasplace.com • Rates: $119–329

Park Tower Inn • (865) 453-8605
201 Sharon Dr; Pigeon Forge, TN 37863
www.parktowerinn.com • Rates: $40–90

Music Road Inn • (800) 429-7700
314 Henderson Chapel Rd; Pigeon Forge, TN 37863
www.musicroadinn.com • Rates: $149–199

Riverstone Resort • (866) 908-0990
212 Dollywood Ln; Pigeon Forge, TN 37868
www.riverstoneresort.com • Rates: $140–240

Bunkhouse Inn • (865) 448-6377
7249 E Lamar Alexander Pkwy; Townsend, TN 37882

Dancing Bear Lodge • (865) 448-6000
133 Apple Valley Way; Townsend, TN 37882
www.dancingbearlodge.com • Rates: $190–260

Pioneer Cabins • (865) 448-6100
288 Boat Gunnel Rd; Townsend, TN 37882
www.pioneercabins.com • Rates: Call

Riverstone Lodge • (865) 448-6677
8511 TN-73; Townsend, TN 37882
www.riverstonelodge.com • Rates: $180–460

Highland Manor Inn • (800) 213-9462
7766 E Larmar Alexander Pkwy; Townsend, TN 37882
www.highlandmanor.com • Rates: $90

Creekwalk Inn • (423) 487-4000
164 Midddle Creek Rd; Cosby, TN 37722
www.whisperwoodretreat.com • Rates: $139–229

East Side

Lake View Lodge • (800) 742-6492
171 Lakeview Lodge Dr; Bryson City, NC 28713

Windover Inn B&B • (866) 452-4411
117 Old Hickory St; Waynesville, NC 28786
www.windoverinn.com • Rates: $103–180

Folkestone Inn B&B • (828) 488-2730
101 Folkestone Rd; Bryson City, NC 28713
www.folkestoneinn.com • Rates: $101–170

Inn at Iris Meadows • (828) 456-3877
304 Love Ln; Waynesville, NC 28786
www.irismeadows.com • Rates: $225–300

Oak Hill B&B • (828) 456-7037
224 Love Ln; Waynesville, NC 28786
www.oakhillonlovelane.com • Rates: $150–235

Brookside Mtn Mist B&B • (828) 452-6880
142 Country Club Dr; Waynesville, NC 28786
www.brooksidemountainmistbb.com • Rates: $139–179

Yellow House • (828) 452-0991
89 Oakview Dr; Waynesville, NC 28786
www.theyellowhouse.com • Rates: $149–265

Andon-Reid Inn B&B • (828) 452-3089
92 Daisy Ave; Waynesville, NC 28786
www.andonreidinn.com • Rates: $129–209

Alamo Motel • (828) 926-8750
1485 Soco Rd; Maggie Valley, NC 28751
www.alamomotel.com • Rates: $39–139

Abbey Inn • (828) 926-1188
6375 Soco Rd; Maggie Valley, NC 28751
www.abbeyinn.com • Rates: $44–89

Not all dining and lodging facilities are listed. Many chain hotels and restaurants can be found nearby in Sevierville, Gatlinburg, Pigeon Forge, Waynesville, and Asheville.

Festivals

Mountain Quiltfest • March
www.mountainquiltfest.com • Pigeon Forge, TN

Winter Carnival of Magic • March
www.wintercarnivalofmagic.com • Pigeon Forge, TN

Blue Ridge Food & Wine Festival • April
www.blueridgewinefestival.com • Blowing Rock, NC

Spring Wildflower Pilgrimage • April/May
www.springwildflowerpilgrimage.org • GRSM

The Biltmore Festival of Flowers • April/May
www.biltmore.com • Asheville, NC

TroutFest • May
www.troutfest.org • Townsend, TN

Scottish Festival & Games • May
www.gsfg.org • Gatlinburg, TN

Bloomin' BBQ and Bluegrass Festival • May
www.bloominbbq.com • Sevierville, TN

Riverbend Festival • June
www.riverbendfestival.com • Chattanooga, TN

Bonnaroo Music & Arts Festival • June
One of the permier music festivals in the U.S.
www.bonnaroo.com • Manchester, TN

Secret City Festival • June
www.secretcityfestival.com • Oak Ridge, TN

Smoky Mountain Pottery Festival • June
www.smokymountains.org

KidsFest • June/August
www.dollywood.com • Dollywood (Pigeon Forge, TN)

Midnight 4th of July Parade • July
www.eventsgatlinburg.com • Gatlinburg, TN

Tomato Festival • July • Rutledge, TN
www.graingercountytomatofestival.com

Grandfather Mtn Scottish Highland Games • July
www.gmhg.org • Linville, NC

Folkmoot USA • July • www.folkmootusa.org
Waynesville and Maggie Valley, NC

Cherokee Bluegrass Festival • August
www.cherokeebluegrass.com • Cherokee, NC

Smoky Mountain Folk Festival
Lake Junaluska, NC • August
www.smokymountainfolkfestival.com

Moonlight Race • August • Maggie Valley, NC
www.maggievalleymoonlightrun.com

Time Warner Cable BBQ & Blues • September
www.charlottebbqandblues.com • Charlotte, NC

Boomsday • September
www.boomsday.org • Knoxville, TN

Smoky Mtn Harvest Festival • September
www.smokymountainharvestfestival.com • Pigeon Forge

Dumplin Valley Bluegrass Festival • September
www.dumplinvalleybluegrass.com • Kodak, TN

Davy Crockett Days • October
www.townofrutherford.org • Rutherford, TN

Lake Eden Arts Festival • October
www.theleaf.com • Black Mountain, NC

Woolly Worm Festival • October
www.woollyworm.com • Banner Elk, NC

National Storytelling Festival • October
www.storytellingcenter.net • Jonesborough, TN

Winterfest • November–February
Gatlinburg • Pigeon Forge • Sevierville
www.smokymountainwinterfest.com

Attractions

Near the Park

CLIMB Works Canopy • (865) 325-8116
155 Branam Hollow Rd; Gatlinburg, TN 37738
www.climbworkscanopy.com • Rates: $89/Adult

A Walk In the Woods • (865) 436-8283
4413 E Scenic Dr; Gatlinburg, TN 37738
www.awalkinthewoods.com • Rates: $30+

Ripley's Aquarium • (865) 430-8808
88 River Rd; Gatlinburg, TN 37738
www.gatlinburg.ripleyaquariums.com • $23/Adult

Rafting In the Smokies • (866) 853-6020
813 E Parkway; Gatlinburg, TN 37738
www.raftinginthesmokies.com

Sweet Fanny Adams Theatre • (865) 436-4039
461 Parkway; Gatlinburg, TN 37738
www.sweetfannyadams.com • Rates: $35–39

Ole Smoky Distillery • (865) 277-7741
903 Parkway, # 129; Gatlinburg, TN 37738

Space Needle • (865) 436-4629
115 Historic Nature Tr; Gatlinburg, TN 37738
www.gatlinburgspaceneedle.com • Rates: $7.50/Adult

Fannie Farkle's Amusement • (865) 436-4057
656 Parkway; Gatlinburg, TN 37738
www.fanniefarklesgatlinburg.com

Rocky Top Playhouse • (865) 365-1060
1811 Parkway, # 103; Sevierville, TN 37862
www.rockytopplayhouse.com

Smoky Mtn Outdoors • (800) 771-7238
3299 Hartford Rd; Hartford, TN 37753
www.smokymountainrafting.com • Rafting: $39

Foxfire Mtn Adventures • (865) 453-1998
3757 Thomas Lane; Sevierville, TN 37876
www.foxfiremountain.com

Rocky Top Playhouse • (865) 365-1060
1811 Parkway, # 103; Sevierville, TN 37862
www.rockytopplayhouse.com • Tickets: $25/Adult

Five Oaks Riding Stables • (865) 453-8644
1628 Parkway; Sevierville, TN 37862
www.fiveoaksridingstables.com

Hillside Winery • (865) 908-8482
229 Collier Dr; Sevierville, TN 37862
www.hillsidewine.com

Rainforest Adventures • (865) 428-4091
109 Nascar Dr; Sevierville, TN 37862
www.rfadventures.com • Admission: $12/Adult

Ripley's Old Macdonald's Mini Golf
1639 Parkway; Sevierville, TN 37862
www.ripleys.com • (865) 428-9128

Walden Creek Stables • (865) 429-0411
2709 Waldens Creek Rd; Sevierville, TN 37862
www.waldencreekstables.com • Rates: $25–90

Wahoo Zip Lines • (865) 453-7301
1200 Matthews Hollow Rd; Sevierville, TN 37876
www.wahoozip.com • Rates: $89

Cirque de Chine • (800) 826-2933
179 Collier Dr; Sevierville, TN 37862
www.smokymountainpalace.com • Tickets: $30/Adult

Adventure Park at Five Oaks • (865) 453-8644
1628 Parkway; Sevierville, TN 37862
www.adventureparkatfiveoaks.com • Zipline: $60

Forbidden Caverns • (865) 453-5972
455 Blowing Cave Rd; Sevierville, TN 37876
www.forbiddencavern.com • Tours: $14+

Parrot Mtn and Gardens • (865) 774-1749
1471 McCarter Hollow Rd; Sevierville, TN 37862
www.parrotmountainandgardens.com • $15/Adult

Smoky Mtn Llama Treks • (865) 428-6042
1839 Creek Hollow Way; Sevierville, TN 37876
www.smokymountainllamatreks.com • $45+

Scenic Helicopter Tours • (865) 453-5867
1227 Airport Rd; Sevierville, TN 37862
www.flyscenic.com • Tours: $30–300

Wonder Works • (865) 868-1800
100 Music Rd; Pigeon Forge, TN 37863
www.wonderworksonline.com • Admission: $13/Adult

Dixie Stampede Dinner & Show • (865) 453-4400
3849 Parkway; Pigeon Forge, TN 37863
www.dixiestampede.com • Tickets: $45/Adult

Miracle Theater • (865) 428-7469
2046 Parkway; Pigeon Forge, TN 37863
www.miracletheater.com • Tickets: $40/Adult

Tennessee Shindig • (888) 908-3327
2391 Parkway; Pigeon Forge, TN 37863
www.tnshindig.com • Tickets: $40/Adult

Comedy Barn Theater • (865) 428-5222
2775 Parkway; Pigeon Forge, TN 37863
www.comedybarn.com • Tickets: $25/Adult

Dollywood • (865) 428-9488
2700 Dollywood Parks Blvd; Pigeon Forge, TN 37863
www.dollywood.com • Admission: $57/Adult

Smith Family Theater • (865) 429-8100
2330 Parkway; Pigeon Forge, TN 37863
www.smithfamilytheater.com • Tickets: $40/Adult

Adventure Raceway • (865) 428-2971
2945 Parkway; Pigeon Forge, TN 37863
www.adventuregolfandraceway.com • ~$6

The Forge Cinemas • (877) 698-5576
2530 Parkway, #7; Pigeon Forge, TN 37863
www.theforgecinemas.com

Blackwood B'fast Variety Show • (865) 908-7469
119 Music Rd; Pigeon Forge, TN 37863
www.blackwoodsshow.com • Tickets: $29/Adult

Grand Majestic Theater • (865) 774-1587
125 Music Mtn Dr; Pigeon Forge, TN 37863
www.thegrandmajestic.com

Smoky Mtn Zipline • (865) 429-9004
509 Mill Creek Rd; Pigeon Forge, TN 37863
www.smokymountainziplines.com • $40+

Bluff Mtn Adventures • (865) 428-7711
2186 Parkway; Pigeon Forge, TN 37863
www.bluffmountainadventures.com • $48+

ZORB® Smoky Mtns • (865) 428-2422
203 Sugar Hollow Rd; Pigeon Forge, TN 37863
www.zorb.com • Rates: $33+/Trip

Parkway Drive-In Theatre • (865) 379-7884
2909 E Lamar Alexander Pkwy; Maryville, TN 37804
www.bluemoontheatres.com • Tickets: $8/Adult

Nantahala Outdoor Center • (800) 232-7238
13077 US-19 W; Bryson City, NC 28713
www.noc.com • Rafting: $34+/Adult

Nantahala Gorge Canopy Tours • (800) 451-9972
10345 US-19 W; Bryson City, NC 28713
www.adventureamericaziplinecanopytours.com • $79 per

Smoky Mtn Jet boats • (828) 488-0522
22 Needmore Rd; Bryson City, NC 28713
www.needmore.com • Rates: $31/Adult

Deep Creek Tube Center • (828) 488-6055
1090 West Deep Creek Rd; Bryson City, NC 28713
www.deepcreekcamping.com • Rental: $4/Tube

Great Smoky Mtns Railroad • (828) 586-8811
226 Everett St; Bryson City, NC 28713
www.gsmr.com • Tickets: $49–92/Adult

Endless River Adventures • (828) 488-6199
14157 US-19 W; Bryson City, NC 28713
www.endlessriveradventures.com • $39+

Adventurous Fast Rivers Rafting • (828) 488-2386
14690 US-19 W; Bryson City, NC 28713
www.white-water.com • Rates: $27+

Wildwater Cheoah River • (800) 451-9972
8364 Tapoco Rd; Robbinsville, NC 28771
www.wildwaterrafting.com • Rates: $46+

Pisgah National Forest • (828) 257-4200
NC-80 and Blue Ridge Pkwy; Burnsville, NC 28714

Nantahala National Forest • (828) 524-6441
90 Sloan Rd; Franklin, NC 28734

Tweetsie Railroad • (828) 264-9061
300 Tweetsie Railroad Ln; Blowing Rock, NC 28605
www.tweetsie.com • Admission: $34/Adult

Docs Rocks Gem Mine • (828) 264-4499
129 Mystery Hill Ln; Blowing Rock, NC 28605
www.docsrocks.net • Tours: $25/Person

Beyond the Park

Tennessee Theatre • (865) 684-1200
604 South Gay St; Knoxville, TN 37902
www.tennesseetheatre.com • Tickets: Vary

Regal Cinemas Riviera Stadium 8 • (865) 522-6801
510 South Gay St; Knoxville, TN 37902
www.regmovies.com

Ijams Nature Center • (865) 577-4717
2915 Island Home Ave; Knoxville, TN 37920
www.ijams.org • Admission: Free

Minister's Treehouse • The World's Biggest
Treehouse • Beehive Lane; Crossville, TN 38571

Tennessee Aquarium • (423) 265-0695
201 Chestnut St; Chattanooga, TN 37402
www.tnaqua.org • Admission: $25/Adult

Raccoon Mtn Caverns • (423) 821-9403
319 West Hills Dr; Chattanooga, TN 37419
www.raccoonmountain.com • Tours: $14+

Lake Winnepesaukah Amusement Park
1730 Lakeview Dr; Rossville, GA 30741
www.lakewinnie.com • (706) 866-5681 • $5

Blue Ridge Parkway • (828) 271-4779
199 Hemphill Knob Rd; Asheville, NC 28803
www.nps.gov/blri

Ghost Hunters of Asheville • (828) 779-4868
1 Battery Park Ave; Asheville, NC 28806
www.ghosthuntersofasheville.com • Tours: $17/Adult

Biltmore Estate • (828) 225-1333
1 Lodge St; Asheville, NC 28803
www.biltmore.com • Tickets: $59/Adult

Thomas Wolfe Memorial • (828) 253-8304
52 N Market St; Asheville, NC 28801
www.wolfememorial.com • Admission: $1/Adult

Billy Graham Library • (704) 401-3200
4330 Westmont Dr; Charlotte, NC 28217
www.billygrahamlibrary.org • Admission: Free

U.S. National Whitewater Center
5000 Whitewater Center PKWY; Charlotte, NC 28214
www.usnwc.org • Multiple Activities

NASCAR Hall of Fame • (704) 654-4400
400 E MLK Blvd; Charlotte, NC 28202
www.nascarhall.com • Admission: $20/Adult

Hendrick Motorsports • (704) 455-3400
4400 Papa Joe Hendrick Blvd; Charlotte, NC 28262
www.hendrickmotorsports.com

WHAT'S NEARBY

Nashville, TN
220 mi/3.75 hrs

Knoxville, TN
40 mi/40 mins

Asheville, NC
90 mi/1.75 hrs

For more information on visiting Tennessee and North Carolina click www.tnvacation.com & www.visitnc.com.

Chattanooga, TN
150 mi/2.75 hrs

Charlotte, NC
200 mi/3.75 hrs

Driving Distances to Sugarlands Visitor Center

100 National Park Road
Hopkins, SC 29061
Phone: (803) 776-4396
Website: www.nps.gov/cong

Established: November 10, 2003
Size: 24,000 Acres
Annual Visitors: 120,000
Peak Season: Spring & Fall

Activities: Hiking, Paddling, Bird Watching, Fishing, Ranger Tours

Campgrounds: Backcountry, group, and after-hours camping are available

Park Hours: All day, every day
Entrance Fee: None

Did you know?

▶ This region was called Congaree Swamp National Monument until 2003 (when Congress made it a national park), but it is actually a floodplain. A floodplain is a flat or nearly flat land that experiences periodic flooding. A swamp is a wetland with shallow bodies of water and a number of hammocks, or dry-land protrusions.

Spanish moss hanging from trees at Weston Lake

Congaree - South Carolina

Congaree is akin to a rarely visited, scaled down combination of Redwood and Everglades National Parks. It protects the largest contiguous expanse of old growth bottomland hardwood forest left in the United States. You'll never confuse the towering bald cypress and loblolly pine for their West Coast rivals, the redwood and giant sequoia, but they are massive by East Coast standards. Several national and state champion trees reside within the park's boundary. Congaree's canopy averages an impressive 130-feet, making it as tall as any temperate deciduous forest in the world. When navigable, Cedar Creek provides a narrow, maze-like waterway reminiscent of the Everglade's "River of Grass" (minus

the grass and throw in some moss). Trees and waterways provide habitat for a multitude of plants and animals. In fact, the park was recognized as an **International Biosphere Reserve** in 1983, and was designated a **Globally Important Bird Area** in 2001. A floodplain forest draped with Spanish moss, and the natural tranquility and wildness, give the illusion of traveling back in time to a primeval forest. These waterways and trees have helped shape the history of not only a park, but the entire region. Water protected and nourished trees. Trees attracted conservationists. And now this unique environment is protected and preserved for future generations to enjoy.

Hernando de Soto was first to detail an encounter with **Congaree Indians** in 1540. His exploration continued north through Appalachia, but natives stayed, living along what is now named the Congaree River. Around the turn of the 18th century, Congaree Indians were decimated by smallpox brought by European explorers. By 1715, the tribe consisted of 22 men and 70 women and children. Today they are gone but not forgotten; a river and park bear the name of the area's original inhabitants.

Frequent flooding rapidly renewed the soil's nutrients, enabling trees to thrive and reach record heights. Surprisingly, floods weren't beneficial to area farmers. Decades were spent trying to coax crops from the nutrient-rich land, but standing water stifled most agricultural activities. Farmers moved out of the floodplain, and **Santee River Cypress Logging Company** moved in. They purchased an exceptional tract of hardwood along the Congaree River in 1905, but regular flooding proved to be as troublesome to loggers as it was to farmers. Heavy logging equipment couldn't be moved across the wet and muddy earth. They could only access trees along the waterways where another problem arose—actually they sank, many of these trees were too green to float. Some remain to this day in the places they fell along the riverbank. After ten years of logging, the floodplain was left relatively unscathed. In 1969, high timber prices and advancements in logging equipment brought attention back to the uncut lumber of the Congaree River. This time floodwaters wouldn't be enough to save the trees. Thankfully, the **Sierra Club** stepped in. Their grassroots campaign to save the trees culminated in establishment of Congaree Swamp National Monument in 1976. Incorrectly labeled a swamp, the area does not contain standing water throughout most of the year, so it's actually a floodplain. Regardless, new legislation protected this land, its trees, and its waterways from future human exploitation.

Nothing could protect the monument from **Hurricane Hugo**. In 1989 winds whipped through the forests, toppling many champion trees and permanently changing the park's landscape. But with tragedy came new life and diversity. Sunlight could once again penetrate the canopy. Nature ran its course, and new growth sprang up across the floodplain. Downed trees became habitat for plants and animals. Land unsuitable for farming and logging proved to be suitable for life. A flourishing ecosystem for bobcat, white-tailed deer, river otter, snakes and insects, fungi and ferns, is on display at Congaree National Park.

When to Go

Congaree National Park is open all year. Harry Hampton Visitor Center is open from 8:30am to 5pm every day except Christmas. During daylight savings time the visitor center is open until 7pm on Fridays, Saturdays, and Sundays.

Congaree rarely receives larger crowds than it can accommodate, but if you intend on joining a park ranger on a free Owl Prowl, canoe trip, or hike, it's a good idea to call the park at (803) 776-4396 to make a reservation. Part of the reason why the park's visitation rate is so low is the fact that its least hospitable time is summer when most families go on vacation. Summers are hot, humid, and buggy. The best time to visit is between fall and spring when there are fewer bugs and temperatures are moderate. Congaree is a floodplain, not a swamp, and flooding is most common in late winter/early spring. Cedar Creek can be impossible to navigate during periods of high and low water. If you plan on paddling, it's a good idea to call the park for current water conditions before you depart.

Directions

Congaree National Park is located 20 miles southeast of Columbia, SC.

From Columbia/Spartanburg (~20 miles): Take I-26 E (toward Charleston) to Exit 116. Turn onto I-77 N toward Charlotte (left exit). After about five miles take Exit 5. Turn off onto SC-48 E (Bluff Road), following the brown and white Congaree National Park signs. Continue southeast toward Gadsden for approximately 14 miles before turning right onto Mt. View Road. Turn right onto Old Bluff Road. Turn left at the large park entrance sign and proceed to Harry Hampton Visitor Center for parking.

From Charleston (~115 miles): Take I-26 W (toward Spartanburg) to Exit 116. Turn onto I-77 N toward Charlotte, taking exit 5. Follow the directions from above for Columbia/Spartanburg (from Exit 5) to reach the park.

From Charlotte (~110 miles): Take I-77 S to Exit 5. Follow the directions above for Columbia/Spartanburg (from Exit 5) to reach the park.

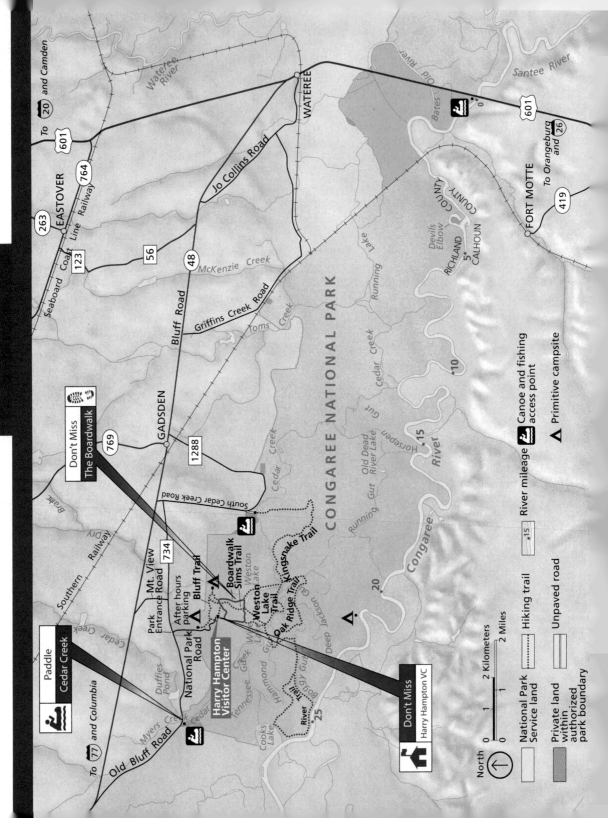

 Hiking

The park is small and wet allowing just 20 miles of hiking trails. An ambitious hiker with an early start can easily hike Congaree's entire trail network in a single day. All of the trails except the Boardwalk are well-marked with colored blazes leading you through primeval forests and wetland.

The **Boardwalk** is the only trail most visitors hike. It's an elevated, wheelchair accessible walkway. Self-guided brochures for this 2.4-mile circuit through old-growth forest to Weston Lake and back are available at the visitor center. The forest drips with Spanish moss and cypress knees protrude from the earth, creating a setting worthy of a mystical fairy tale. (Knees are part of the bald cypress root system and they have been measured up to six feet tall.) The Boardwalk is elevated, but sections can become inaccessible during periods of flooding.

Bluff Trail is a 0.7-mile hike, marked by blue blazes, providing access to The Boardwalk and campground. Along the way you'll pass through a young plantation of loblolly pines.

The 4.6-mile **Weston Lake Loop Trail** is marked by yellow blazes. This trail continues from Weston Lake to the northern shore of Cedar Creek. It skirts the creek for a short distance through old growth forest before returning to the visitor center.

Oak Ridge Trail is a 7.5-mile hike, marked by red blazes, that loops around the southern shoreline of Cedar Creek before joining River Trail and returning to the visitor center.

River Trail is 10.4 miles long and marked by white blazes. As the name suggests, this trail reaches the shores of the Congaree River. Along the way you'll be able to see successional stages of forest life, since much of the forest along the river was logged prior to the park's establishment.

The 11.1-mile **Kingsnake Trail** is marked by orange blazes and connects South Cedar Creek Road Canoe Landing to the visitor center. It's an excellent choice for bird watching or spotting wildlife as you pass through a large cypress–tupelo slough.

A luna moth

Transportation & Airports

Public transportation does not provide service to or around Congaree National Park. The closest airports are Columbia Metropolitan (CAE), Charlotte Douglas International (CLT), and Charleston International (CHS), 24, 96, and 100 miles away, respectively.

Camping

Campers must obtain a free camping permit and regulations at the **Harry Hampton Visitor Center**. The park has three camping options: Longleaf Campground, Bluff Campsite, and backcountry camping. **Longleaf Campground** is located on the east side of National Park Road, near the park gate. All eight sites are walk-in, but are no more than 50 yards from the parking area. Chemical toilets are nearby, and drinking water is available from a spigot outside the visitor center when it's open. **Bluff Campsite** has three designated sites about one mile from the visitor center parking area. Restrooms and water are not available. **Backcountry camping** is allowed as long as you are at least 200 feet from trails and 500 feet from buildings and The Boardwalk.

Best of Congaree

Hikes: The Boardwalk
> Runner-up: Weston Lake Loop
> 2nd Runner-up: River Trail

Ranger Programs: Owl Prowl
> Runner-up: Guided Canoe Tour
> 2nd Runner-up: Big Tree Hike

An American kestrel

Bird Watching

Remember to pack your binoculars. Congaree is a park for birds and bird watchers, with **more than 170 species** spotted here. This includes eight species of woodpeckers: red-bellied, red-cockaded, red-headed, pileated, downy, hairy, yellow-bellied sapsucker, and yellow shafted flicker. Even the **legendary ivory-billed woodpecker** is believed to reside among the old growth forest.

Owls are one of the most popular residents. More than 20 years ago a park ranger decided to lead a night-time "**Owl Prowl.**" It was a hit then, and still is today. If you'd like to go on the prowl for owls, make sure you plan ahead, because reservations are required (call 803.776.4396 for reservations).

Fishing

Fishing is permitted anywhere in the park except Weston Lake. A valid South Carolina State Fishing License is required, and all state laws and limits apply. To help prevent introduction of non-native species, live bait, such as minnows, amphibians, and fish eggs, are prohibited. When trying to reach your desired fishing location please use access roads rather than The Boardwalk.

Congaree's fish are almost as varied as the species of trees that line the shores. Largemouth bass, striped bass, perch, and crappie are a few of the commonly caught game fish. Prehistoric fish like garfish, mudfish, and shortnose sturgeon can also be found lurking beneath the surface of the murky water. Congaree River has a healthy population of white perch, white bass, catfish, carp, and suckers.

Paddling

Paddling is an excellent way to explore the park and to view its record holding trees. You are welcome to bring your own canoe or kayak to explore **Cedar Creek** or the **Congaree River**, but a better alternative is to join a park ranger on one of the free canoe trips that depart every Saturday and Sunday. The park provides everything you need: canoes, life jackets, and paddles. Children must be at least five years old to attend. Reservations are required, and can be made by calling the park at (803) 776-4396 (not accepted via voice mail). Always check the weather before leaving, because trips are cancelled if it's 45°F or below, the water level on Cedar Creek is 10 feet or above, or wind speed is 30 mph or greater.

Two landings on Cedar Creek within the park, and another landing on the Congaree River outside the park, allow paddlers to create a variety of trips. Cedar Creek slowly meanders through Congaree's old growth forest, making it perfect for an **out-and-back paddle**. Start at **Cedar Creek Landing**, just east of the park entrance at the end of South Cedar Creek Road. Pick your pleasure, upstream or downstream, and then paddle until your heart's content (or, rather, half content) before turning around. Even though the current is slow, remember that paddling upstream will be more difficult and take more time than paddling downstream. Plan appropriately.

By putting in at **Bannister's Bridge**, west of the park entrance on Old Bluff Road, paddlers can float along Cedar Creek as it winds through swaths of bald cypress. The trail is fairly well marked, but there's always a chance you paddle into a dead end or two, especially when the water level is high. Near the half-way point you can take a narrow channel to **Wise Lake**, which was a channel of the Congaree River some 10,000 years ago before the river altered course to its current location nearly 2.5 miles away. The channel may be inaccessible at low water levels. It is located on the right-hand side of Cedar Creek, shortly after you pass beneath a small hiking bridge. The entire trip is roughly 7 miles (4–6 hours) to the take-out at **Cedar Creek Landing**. You will need to arrange transportation between put-in and take-out.

A 20-mile trip from **Cedar Creek Landing to the 601 Bridge** is perfect for tireless or overnight paddlers. (If you plan on spending the night, be sure to stop at the visitor center for a camping permit.) Cedar Creek eventually joins the **Congaree River**, but the paddle trail takes a safer detour following **Mazyck's Cut** to the Congaree. Beyond the junction with Mazyck's Cut, Cedar Creek is unmarked and uncleared, so it is highly recommended that paddlers follow the trail. Three trail markers and a wooden sign point paddlers in the appropriate direction. Once you've reached the Congaree, you've got another 13 miles to the 601 Bridge take-out. Once again, you'll have to arrange transport.

If that isn't enough, paddlers can take on the **Congaree River Blue Trail**. It's a 50-mile adventure beginning in Columbia, the capital of South Carolina, and continuing downstream to Congaree National Park.

 ## Biking

Bicycles are allowed in the park but all trails, including The Boardwalk, are closed to cyclists. That leaves the 1.5-mile **National Park Road** as the lone stretch of pavement for bikers. A few roads surrounding the park offer decent, flat pedalling, but it's not really worth the effort of bringing a bike to Congaree.

 ## Flora & Fauna

The park's skyline is dominated by many of the eastern United States' tallest trees. About 20 trees hold state or national records for size. The largest is a 169-foot tall, 17-foot diameter loblolly pine. More than 98% of park land is designated wilderness covered with **75 species of trees**, including: cherrybark oak, paw, water oak, bald cypress, tupelo, American holly, laurel oak, and ironwood. The Congaree River flows through the park for 23 miles, with a miniscule elevation change of 20 feet. The elevation difference, no matter how slight, affects vegetation growth. You'll find that loblolly pines grow on higher ground, while bald cypress and tupelo thrive in low areas of standing water. And the park isn't all about trees. There are 22 distinct plant communities filled with fungi, ferns, flowers, and shrubs that flourish beneath the park's dense canopy.

Most animals found in the park are commonly described with words like creepy, crawly, or nocturnal. For the most part insects aren't bothersome until the middle of summer, when mosquitoes rule the wetlands. **Four poisonous snake species** inhabit the park. These include coral snake,

A great horned owl

An eastern cottonmouth

copperhead, canebrake rattler, and cottonmouth. Snakes are fairly common, so use caution when near rocks, holes, downed trees, or other spots where a snake might be hiding. Bobcats, raccoons, opossums, and owls are most active at night. In the morning and evening you may see white-tailed deer, squirrels, or river otter. You might be tempted to stare at the ground searching for poisonous snakes, but look up from time to time. The park is loaded with interesting moths, butterflies, and birds. A good spotting can be the fondest memory of a trip to Congaree.

A green anole © Linda Tanner

For Kids: Congaree's **Junior Ranger Program** gives kids ages 12 and under the opportunity to receive a certificate and prize for completing a free activity booklet (available at the visitor center). The booklet takes approximately three hours to complete. These activities help engage children in their surroundings while they explore the park. It's also filled with facts that both children and adults will find fun and exciting. If workbooks aren't your kid's style, there's a short introductory film that plays regularly at the visitor center.

Ranger Programs: A little bit of planning is required for a few of the park's ranger programs: **Big Tree Hike**, **Guided Canoe Tour**, and **Owl Prowl** require **reservations** which can be made by calling (803) 776-4396. If you miss out on one of these programs, don't worry, there are additional regularly scheduled, ranger-led hikes, chats, lectures, and campfires that are all free of charge and do not require a reservation. A current schedule of events can be found at the park's website or in the free newspaper (available at the visitor center).

Pets: Pets are allowed in the park, but must be kept on a leash no more than six feet in length at all times. Pets, except service animals, are not permitted in park buildings.

Accessibility: The parks two most popular attractions, Harry Hampton Visitor Center and The Boardwalk, are completely accessible to individuals in wheelchairs. Some Ranger Programs like the Congaree Campfire Chronicles are accessible.

Weather: Summers are hot and humid. Memorial Day and Thanksgiving are the two busiest days due to comfortable weather during spring and fall. Winters are mild. On average the park floods ten times each year. Most flooding occurs in winter.

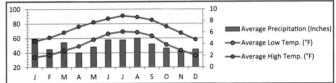

Vacation Planner

For all intents and purposes Congaree is for day-trippers. It only has ten designated campsites and there are no lodging facilities in or around the park. Day-trips are often spontaneous, but you should do a bit of advance planning for a trip to Congaree. Joining an **Owl Prowl** (page 114) or **Canoe Tour** (page 114) requires advance reservations. These tours are highly recommended and popular, so check them out. You may want to attend both. If so, it's likely you become infected with the ranger's enthusiasm and passion for the area. **Paddlers** should anticipate the stretch of water from **Bannister's Bridge to Cedar Creek Landing** to take at least a half-day, and **Cedar Creek to the Congaree** is a very full day. If you're looking for a place to sleep or eat, your best bet is Columbia (20 miles to the north). Dining, grocery stores, lodging, festivals, and attractions outside the park are listed on page 117.

Begin your trip at **Harry Hampton Visitor Center**. Here you'll find an exhibit area, a small gift shop, and a short introductory film. Park rangers are available to answer your questions. Remember to pick up a park newspaper, *Boardwalk Talk*, before leaving. If you failed to reserve a spot for a **Canoe Tour**, **Big Tree Hike**, or **Owl Prowl**, you should definitely browse the day's schedule of events found in the newspaper. If you can't find anything that meets your interests or schedule, head outdoors and walk **The Boardwalk** (self-guiding brochures are available at the visitor center). Notice the bald cypress knees that have pierced the ground. They are actually part of the tree's root system, making them exceedingly difficult to topple even though they're planted in wet soil. If you have time and energy, continue along **Weston Lake Trail** (page 113) or **Kingsnake Trail** (page 113). Be sure to arrive back at the visitor center in time for any ranger programs you may have selected.

CONGAREE

Dining

Big T Bar-B-Q • (803) 353-0488
2520 Congaree Rd; Hopkins, SC 29052

Eric's San Jose Mexican Rest. • (803) 783-6650
6118 Garners Ferry Rd; Columbia, SC 29209
www.ericssanjose.com • Entrée: $7–11

Blue Marlin • (803) 799-3838
1200 Lincoln St; Columbia, SC 29201
www.bluemarlincolumbia.com • Entrée: $16–23

Motor Supply Co Bistro • (803) 256-6687
920 Gervais St; Columbia, SC 29201
www.motorsupplycobistro.com • Entrée: $20+

Julia's German Stammtisch • (803) 738-0630
4341 Fort Jackson Blvd; Columbia, SC 29205
www.julias.vpweb.com • Entrée: $14–17

Za's Brick Oven Pizza • (803) 771-7334
2930 Devine St, # E; Columbia, SC 29205
www.zasbrickovenpizza.com • Entrée: $7–13

Mo Mo's Bistro • (803) 252-2700
2930 Devine Street; Columbia, SC 29205
www.momos-bistro.com • Entrée: $18–27

Blue Cactus Café • (803) 929-0782
2002 Greene St, # H; Columbia, SC 29205
www.bluecactuscafe.com • Entrée: $7–10

Garibaldi's of Columbia • (803) 771-8888
2013 Greene St; Columbia, SC 29205
www.garibaldicolumbia.com • Entrée: $9–30

Dianne's on Devine • (803) 254-3535
2400 Devine St; Columbia, SC 29205
www.diannesondevine.com • Entrée: $15–34

Saluda's Restaurant • (803) 799-9500
751 Saluda Ave; Columbia, SC 29205
www.saludas.com • Entrée: $19–31

Grocery Stores

Piggly Wiggly • (803) 655-6186
305 Harry C Raysor Dr; St Matthews, SC 29135

Food Lion • (803) 695-9757
9013 Garners Ferry Rd; Hopkins, SC 29061

Walmart Supercenter • (803) 783-1277
7520 Garners Ferry Rd; Columbia, SC 29209

Publix • (803) 806-8839
2800 Rosewood Drive; Columbia, SC 29205

Lodging

Sheraton • (803) 988-1400 • ~$175
1400 Main Street; Columbia, SC 29201

The Inn at USC • (803) 779-7779
1619 Pendleton Street; Columbia, SC 29201
www.innatusc.com • Rates: $100

The Inn At Claussen's • (803) 765-0440
2003 Greene St; Columbia, SC 29205
www.theinnatclaussens.com • Rates: $100

TownePlace Suites • (803) 695-0062
250 East Exchange Blvd; Columbia, SC 29209

Candlewood Suites • (803) 727-1299 • ~$75
921 Atlas Road; Columbia, SC 29209

Holiday Inn • (803) 695-1111 • ~$100
7329 Garners Ferry Rd; Columbia, SC 29209

Hilton • (803) 744-7800 • ~$150
924 Senate Street; Columbia, SC 29201

Hampton Inn • (803) 231-2000 • ~$140
822 Gervais Street; Columbia, SC 29201

Staybridge Suites • (803) 451-5900 • ~$100
1913 Huger St; Columbia, SC 29201

Chestnut Cottage B&B • (803) 256-1718
1718 Hampton St; Columbia, SC 29201
www.chesnutcottage.com • Rates: $159–229

Sleep Inn • (803) 531-7200 • ~$90
3689 St Matthews Rd; Orangeburg, SC 29118

Southern Lodge • (803) 531-7333 • ~$60
3616 Saint Matthews Rd; Orangeburg, SC 29118

Not all dining and lodging facilities are listed. Many chain hotels and restaurants can be found nearby in Columbia and Orangeburg.

Festivals

Spoleto USA • May/June
www.spoletousa.org • Charleston, SC

Greek Festival • September
www.columbiasgreekfestival.com • Columbia, SC

South Carolina State Fair • October
www.scstatefair.org • Columbia, SC

Chitlin Strut • November
www.chitlinstrut.com • Salley, SC

Nearby Attractions

Kensington Mansion • (803) 353-0456
4001 Mccords Ferry Rd; Eastover, SC 29044
www.kensingtonmansion.org • Admission: $5/Adult

Edventure Children's Museum • (803) 779-3100
211 Gervais St; Columbia, SC 29201
www.edventure.org • Admission: $9.50

Columbia Museum of Art • (803) 799-2810
1515 Main St; Columbia, SC 29201
www.columbiamuseum.org • Admission: $10/Adult

House Museum Tours • (803) 252-1770
1616 Blanding St; Columbia, SC 29201
www.historiccolumbia.org • Admission: $6/Adult

Nickelodeon Movie Theater • (803) 254-3433
937 Main Street; Columbia, SC 29201
www.nickelodeon.org • Tickets: ~$7

The Comedy House • (803) 798-9898
2768 Decker Blvd; Columbia, SC 29206
www.comedyhouse.com

Marionette Theatre • (803) 252-7366
401 Laurel St; Columbia, SC 29201
www.cmtpuppet.org • Tickets: ~$6

EdVenture • (803) 779-3100
211 Gervais St; Columbia, SC 29201
www.edventure.org • Admission: $9.50

Riverbanks Zoo • (803) 779-8717
500 Wildlife Parkway; Columbia, SC 29210
www.riverbanks.org • Admission: $12/Adult

AMC Theatres - Dutch Square 14 • (888) 262-4386
421-80 Bush River Rd; Columbia, SC 29210

SC State Museum • (803) 898-4921
301 Gervais Street; Columbia, SC 29201
www.southcarolinastatemuseum.org • Admission: $7

Poinsett State Park • (803) 494-8177
6660 Poinsett Park Rd; Wedgefield, SC 29168

Morris Museum of Art • 706-724-7501
1 Tenth St; Augusta, GA 30901
www.themorris.org • Admission: $5/Adult

Museum of History • (706) 722-8454
560 Reynolds Street; Augusta, GA 30901
www.augustamuseum.org • Admission: $4/Adult

Country Club • (706) 364-1862
Suite F, 2834 Washington Rd; Augusta, GA 30909
www.augustacountry.com • Dance Lessons & Shows

Classic Carriage Works • (843) 853-3747
10 Guignard Street; Charleston, SC 29401
www.classiccarriage.com • Rates: $17–22

Spiritline Harbor Tours • (843) 722-2628
360 Concord St, # 201; Charleston, SC 29401
www.spiritlinecruises.com • Tour: $17+

SC Aquarium • (843) 577-3474
100 Aquarium Wharf; Charleston, SC 29401
www.scaquarium.org • Admission: $25/Adult

Original Charleston Walks • (843) 408-0010
www.charlestonwalks.com • Tours: Call for rates

Culinary Tours • (843) 727-1100
40 North Market St; Charleston, SC 29401
www.culinarytoursofcharleston.com • $42

Charleston Museum • (843) 722-2996
360 Meeting Street; Charleston, SC 29403
www.charlestonmuseum.org • Admission: $10+

Dante Fascell Visitor Center
9700 SW 328 Street
Homestead, FL 33033
Phone: (305) 230-7275
Website: www.nps.gov/bisc

Established: June 28, 1980
Size: 172,971 Acres
Annual Visitors: 470,000
Peak Season: Winter and Spring

<u>Hiking Trails (8.25 total miles)</u>
Convoy Point • 0.25 mile
Elliott Key • 0.75 mile, self-guided
Elliott Key • 7 miles, self-guided
Adams Key • 0.25 mile, self guided

Activities: SCUBA, Snorkeling,
Boat Tours, Sailing, Kiteboarding,
Paddling, and Bird Watching

Campgrounds: Boca Chita Key and
Elliott Key (primitive camping)
Camping Fee: $15/night*
Backcountry Camping: Prohibited
Lodging: None within Park

Park Hours: All day, every day (water) • Day-use only (Adams Key)
Entrance Fee: None

*Additional $5/night fee for campers
docking a boat overnight

A snorkeler dives beneath the water near Elkhorn Reef

BISCAYNE

<u>Biscayne - Florida</u>

In the 1960s, Biscayne Bay's mangrove forests were declared "a form of wasteland" by well-to-do businessmen, who saw roads, bridges, buildings, and an oil refinery as the only way to revitalize an otherwise useless wilderness. Thankfully, a swell of opposition rose up from the public. Politicians, actors, writers, and environmentalists banded together to help preserve the longest undeveloped shoreline on Florida's east coast. Today, 40 small emerald isles and their mangrove shorelines remain untethered to civilization by roads thanks to the creation of Biscayne National Park. But there's more here than unaltered islands and forests. More than 95% of the park is water, and beneath its surface lies an underwater wilderness completely unique among United States National Parks. A vast array of wildlife—along with thousands of weary urban dwellers—seek refuge and respite here. Not a single one of these visitors would consider this priceless landscape a "form of wasteland."

Israel Jones was among the first to enjoy the seclusion and wilderness of Biscayne. He moved to Florida in 1892, searching for work. After nine years as caretaker to the Walter S. Davies Grant, handyman at the Peacock Inn, and foreman of a pineapple farm, he chose to work for himself. With his savings, he purchased two islands on the southern edge of Caesar Creek. Two years later he moved his family to **Old Rhodes Key**, where he started a business, raised a family, and left a legacy. Israel cleared gumbo-limbo, palmetto, and mahogany trees to reveal a coral limestone base suitable for farming key limes and pineapples. Weathering several years of indebtedness, he eventually became one of the largest producers of pineapples and limes on the east coast of Florida. Reinvesting his profits into real estate, he purchased **Totten Key** for $1 an acre. The property, all 212 acres, later sold for $250,000. Good, lucky, or both, Israel had proven himself to be a keen businessman who understood the value of an education. He hired a live-in teacher for his sons, and helped create the Negro Industrial School in Jacksonville. His children used their education to follow in their father's footsteps. **Arthur and Lancelot Jones** continued to farm limes after the death of their parents. They also began guiding visitors on fishing excursions. Lancelot's fishing expertise was well known in the area and he was often hired to guide wealthy visitors of the Cocolobo Club on Adams Key. During the 1940s and 50s Lancelot served as fishing guide to the likes of **Herbert Hoover**, **Lyndon B. Johnson**, **Richard Nixon**, and other well-known politicians.

Other prominent people wanted to use the region for more than its fish. **Daniel Ludwig**, a billionaire developer, announced plans for an industrial seaport called **Seadade** in 1962. Development included an oil refinery and dredging a 40-foot wide channel through Biscayne Bay. Fill from the dredging project would be used to form new islands, which would eventually connect North Key Largo to Key Biscayne by a series of roads and bridges. The project drew considerable support thanks to the prospect of new jobs and increased property value. But it also had opponents. **Herbert W. Hoover**, vacuum cleaner magnate and childhood visitor to the area, led legislators on dramatic blimp rides over the proposed development. As the park movement gained momentum, Seadade supporters razed a 6-lane "spite highway" the entire 7-mile length of **Elliott Key**. Today, **Elliott Key Boulevard** follows Spite Highway, and it is the only significant hiking trail in the park. In 1968 Congress, led by Representative **Dante Fascell** (the visitor center's namesake), passed a bill to protect "a rare combination of terrestrial, marine, and amphibious life in a tropical setting of great natural beauty." On October 18, 1968, President Lyndon Johnson, who decades earlier had gone fishing with Lancelot Jones, signed a bill creating Biscayne National Monument. Lancelot Jones sold his property to the National Parks Service in 1970 and was granted the right to live out his life in his family home.

When to Go

The 95% of the park that is water is open 24 hours a day. Adams Key (accessible by boat) is a day-use area only. Winter is the most pleasant time to visit. During the summer, visitors must brave mosquitoes, high temperatures and humidity, frequent thunderstorms, and the occasional hurricane.

Convoy Point, where you'll find the park's headquarters and visitor center, is open daily from 7am–5:30pm. **Dante Fascell Visitor Center** is open daily from 9am–5pm.

The park's concessioner, **Biscayne National Underwater Parks**, runs a gift shop with food, drinks, and souvenirs which is open from 9am–5pm. They also offer kayak and canoe rentals and boat, snorkel, and SCUBA tours. The visitor center and concessioner are located at the same address.

Biscayne National Underwater Parks, Inc.
9700 SW 328 Street; Homestead, FL 33033
(305) 230-1100 • www.biscayneunderwater.com
Rates: Please see specific activities sections

Directions

Most visitors enter the park by private boat, but Convoy Point serves as hub for all land activities and concessioner services.

From Miami to Convoy Point (37 miles): Take FL-821 South (Partial Toll Road) to Exit 6 for SW 137th Ave toward Speedway Blvd (Toll Road). Keep left at the fork following signs to Air Reserve Station/Job Cargs Canter. Turn left at SW 137th Ave . Turn left at SW 328th St/N Canal Drive. The visitor center will be on your left.

You can also take US-1 South to SW 137th Ave. Turn left onto 137th Ave. Turn right onto SW 328th St/N Canal Drive.

From Everglades National Park/Flamingo Area (56 miles): Follow the Main Park Rd east to Ingraham Hwy. Continue on Ingraham Hwy until Tower Rd. Turn left on Tower Rd. After about 2 miles, turn right onto SW 344th St. Continue onto W Palm Dr, which will turn into SW 138th Ct and then Speedway Blvd and finally SW 137th Ave. Turn right at SW 328th St/N Canal Dr.

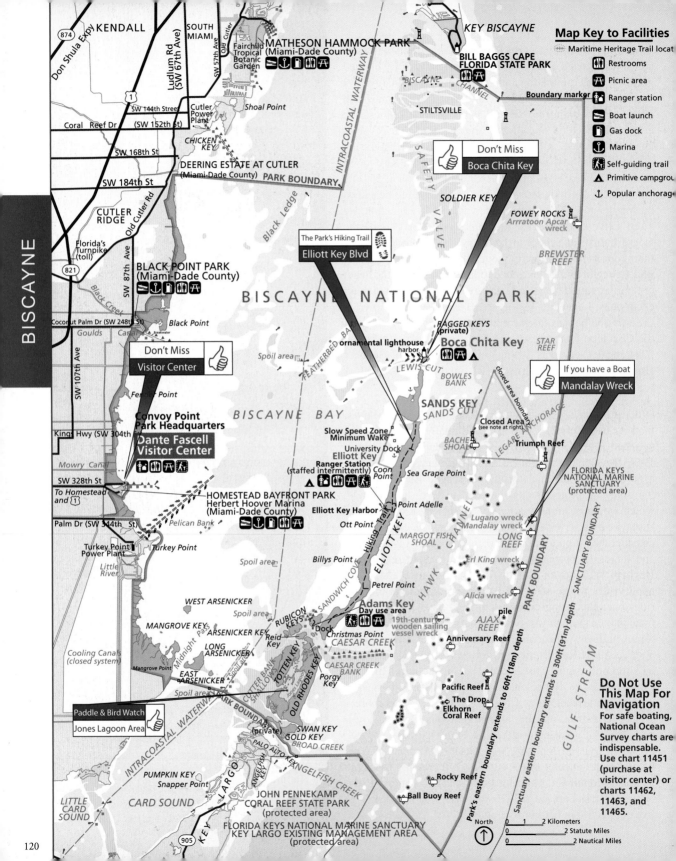

Map Key to Facilities

- ⬡ Maritime Heritage Trail locat
- 🚻 Restrooms
- ⛱ Picnic area
- 🏠 Ranger station
- ⛵ Boat launch
- ⛽ Gas dock
- ⚓ Marina
- 🥾 Self-guiding trail
- ⛺ Primitive campgrou
- ⚓ Popular anchorag

KENDALL
874 | SOUTH MIAMI

Don Shula Expy
Ludlum Rd (SW 67th Ave)
SW 57th Ave
SW 40th Cutler

Fairchild Tropical Botanic Garden

MATHESON HAMMOCK PARK
(Miami-Dade County)
🚻⛵⛽⛱⛱

KEY BISCAYNE

BILL BAGGS CAPE FLORIDA STATE PARK
🚻⛱

1 | SW 144th Street
Coral Reef Dr (SW 152nd St)
Cutler Power Plant

Shoal Point

STILTSVILLE

BISCAYNE CHANNEL

Boundary marker

SW 168th St

CHICKEN KEY

SW 184th St

DEERING ESTATE AT CUTLER
(Miami-Dade County)

PARK BOUNDARY

Black Ledge

SAFETY VALVE

SOLDIER KEY

FOWEY ROCKS
Arrratoon Apcar wreck

Don't Miss 👍
Boca Chita Key

CUTLER RIDGE

Florida's Turnpike (toll)
821

Old Cutler Rd
SW 87th Ave

BLACK POINT PARK
(Miami-Dade County)
⛵⚓🚻⛱

BREWSTER REEF

The Park's Hiking Trail 👣
Elliott Key Blvd

Black Creek

Coconut Palm Dr (SW 248th St)
Black Point
Breakwater

Goulds Canal

B I S C A Y N E   N A T I O N A L   P A R K

SW 107th Ave

Fen̄ _ Point

Don't Miss 👍
Visitor Center

RAGGED KEYS (private)

ornamental lighthouse
harbor

Boca Chita Key
🚻⛱⛺

STAR REEF

FEATHERBED BANK
Spoil area

LEWIS CUT
BOWLES BANK

If you have a Boat 👍
Mandalay Wreck

Kings Hwy (SW 304th)

Convoy Point Park Headquarters

Dante Fascell Visitor Center
🚻⛱🥾⛱

BISCAYNE BAY

SANDS CUT

SANDS KEY

closed area boundary

Mowry Canal

Slow Speed Zone Minimum Wake

University Dock

Elliott Key
Ranger Station
(staffed intermittently)
⛺🚻⛱🥾

Coon Point

Sea Grape Point

Closed Area
(see note at right)

BACHE SHOAL

Triumph Reef

LEGARE ANCHORAGE

FLORIDA KEYS NATIONAL MARINE SANCTUARY
(protected area)

SW 328th St
To Homestead and 1
⛱⛺

HOMESTEAD BAYFRONT PARK
Herbert Hoover Marina
(Miami-Dade County)
⛵⚓🚻⛱⛱

Pelican Bank

Elliott Key Harbor

Point Adelle

Ott Point

MARGOT FISH SHOAL

Lugano wreck
Mandalay wreck

LONG REEF

Erl King wreck

HAWK CHANNEL

Palm Dr (SW 344th St)

Turkey Point Power Plant
Turkey Point

Little River

Billys Point

Alicia wreck

PARK BOUNDARY

SANCTUARY BOUNDARY

Spoil area

WEST ARSENICKER

Spoil area

MANGROVE KEY

ARSENICKER KEY

Petrel Point

Adams Key
Day use area
🚻⛱

19th-century wooden sailing vessel wreck

pile

AJAX REEF

Anniversary Reef

Cooling Canals (closed system)

LONG ARSENICKER

RUBICON KEYS

Dock

Christmas Point
CAESAR CREEK

Reid Key

Mangrove Point

EAST ARSENICKER

Spoil area

CUTTER BANK SHALLOWS

TOTTEN KEY

OLD RHODES KEY

CAESAR CREEK BANK

Porgy Key

Pacific Reef

The Drop
Elkhorn Coral Reef

Paddle & Bird Watch 👍
Jones Lagoon Area

INTRACOASTAL WATERWAY

PARK BOUNDARY

KEY LARGO

PUMPKIN KEY
Snapper Point

ANGELFISH CREEK

SWAN KEY
GOLD KEY
BROAD CREEK

PALO ALTO KEY

Rocky Reef

Ball Buoy Reef

LITTLE CARD SOUND

CARD SOUND

905

JOHN PENNEKAMP CORAL REEF STATE PARK
(protected area)

**FLORIDA KEYS NATIONAL MARINE SANCTUARY
KEY LARGO EXISTING MANAGEMENT AREA**
(protected area)

Park's eastern boundary extends to 60ft (18m) depth

Sanctuary eastern boundary extends to 300ft (91m) depth

GULF STREAM

Do Not Use This Map For Navigation
For safe boating, National Ocean Survey charts are indispensable. Use chart 11451 (purchase at visitor center) or charts 11462, 11463, and 11465.

North
0   1   2 Kilometers
0   2 Statute Miles
0   2 Nautical Miles

Indians and Pirates

Long before developers envisioned the Florida Keys connected from Miami to Key West and the Joneses were living on Old Rhodes Island, the area was inhabited by the **Tequesta Indians**. Little evidence of their existence remains, but scientists believe many archeological sites are hidden beneath the floor of Biscayne Bay. It is also presumed the bay was a vast savannah prior to the last Ice Age, where Indians hunted mastodons and woolly mammoths.

In the more recent past, Native Americans fished and hunted sea turtles, sharks, sailfish, stingrays, and other sea mammals like manatee and porpoise. By the time **Ponce de León** sailed across Biscayne Bay in 1513, the Tequesta were using hollowed-out canoes, making pottery, and hunting with bows and arrows. The tribe prospered. Sea life was abundant. Not having to tend crops of corn for sustenance allowed considerable free time to focus on religion and art. As elsewhere, the arrival of Europeans marked the beginning of their end. By 1763, smallpox and measles, coupled with raids by other Indian tribes and the Spanish, had wiped out the entire Tequesta tribe.

Spanish explorers left the Americas with boatloads of riches, riches that would spark an era of violence and greed. Nations of the world began patrolling the seas waiting to loot Spanish ships, and pirate activity was common near what is now Biscayne National Park. One of the most famous pirates was Black Caesar, whom Caesar Creek is now named for. **Black Caesar** was an 18th century African pirate who had evaded numerous slave traders before a hurricane left him shipwrecked along the Florida reefs. Eventually he was able to recruit a crew, and together they attacked ships on the open sea. They frequently avoided capture by running into Caesar Creek and other narrow inlets between Elliott and Old Rhodes Key. Legend claims they would hide their boat by sinking it in shallow water. Once the patrol boat passed, they would pump out the water, raising the boat. Another legend states Black Caesar buried 26 bars of solid gold on Elliott Key a treasure that remains hidden to this day. His work led to a pirate promotion when he left the waters of Biscayne Bay to join Blackbeard in raiding American ships sailing across the mid-Atlantic.

Biscayne's underwater wilderness

Transportation & Airports
Miami–Dade Public Transit offers transportation to Homestead and Florida City, but not directly to the park headquarters. Call 3-1-1 or click www.miamidade.gov for more information. Most visitors reach the park's islands by private boat, but Biscayne National Underwater Parks, Inc. provides regularly scheduled service to Boca Chita Key.

Miami International (MIA) is the closest large commercial airport (about 35 miles away).

Camping
Boca Chita and Elliott Campgrounds are open all year. Sites fill early on a first-come, first-served basis, especially between December and April. Camping costs $15/night with an additional $5/night charge if you are docking a boat. Group sites are available for $30/night. Payment should be made upon arrival at the kiosks available near the harbor. You must bring your own food and water to the islands. RV camping is not available, and the islands can only be reached by boat. A concessioner provides transport for a fee during the winter and spring.

Boca Chita Key is the most popular island in the park. Here you'll find 39 designated waterfront sites. Toilets are available but drinking water, showers, and sinks are not.

Elliott Key, the park's largest island, has 40 waterfront and forested campsites. Restrooms with sinks and cold water showers are available. Drinking water is also available on the island, but the system occasionally goes down.

Boca Chita Key and the Miami skyline

Stiltsville

In 1933, at the tail end of prohibition, **"Crawfish" Eddie Walker** decided to build a shack on stilts above the shallow waters of Biscayne Bay just south of Cape Florida. He was the first to build a home in this strategic location, one mile off shore where gambling was legal. Eddie's idea caught on. In 1940, the Quarterback Club was built near Crawfish Eddie's, and it became the place to be in Miami. Illicit activities were common, forcing police to make regular raids. During Stiltsville's heyday, as many as 27 structures rose out of the waters of Biscayne Bay. Hurricanes made for relatively short-lived establishments, and in 1992 Hurricane Andrew wiped out all but seven buildings.

Today, access to these buildings is by permission only. Those wishing to tour Stiltsville should call the Stiltsville Trust Group's chair, Gail Baldwin at (305) 443-2266. If you aren't curious enough to take a tour, the history and sheer existence of these precariously perched domiciles is at least worth a photograph.

Fishing

Biscayne Bay's fishing is nearly as good today as it was when Lancelot Jones guided future presidents to local hotspots. For the most part, fishing and harvesting is regulated by state law. All anglers 16 and older require a Florida State Saltwater Fishing License to fish in Biscayne National Park, and they must follow regulations pertaining to size, season, limit, and method. Outfitters offer fishing excursions in Biscayne Bay where you can expect to catch bonefish, tarpon, and permit.

Kestrel Outfitters • (954) 923-8990 (Home) or (561) 271-6006 (Cell)
www.flatsfishingmiami.com
Rates: 1–2 People $400 (half-day)/$500 (full-day)

Biscayne Fishing Guide • (786) 412-4859
www.biscaynefishingguide.com
Rates: 1–2 People $375 (half-day)/$450 (full-day)

Caught Lookin' Charters
(305) 362 6460 (Home) or (305)333-8149 (Cell)
www.caughtlookincharters.com
Rates: 1–2 People $400 (half-day)/$500 (full-day)

Shallow Tails Guide Service • (786) 390-9069
www.biscaynebayfishing.com
Rates: 1–2 People $400 (half-day)/$550 (full-day)

Boat Tours

Biscayne National Underwater Park, Inc. (305.230.1100, www.biscayneunderwater.com) offers boat tours. The ranger guided boat tour to **Boca Chita Key** is the most interesting. On this three hour journey you'll learn about the island's wildlife, plantlife, and history. Guests are also invited to tour the island's lighthouse. **Glass bottom boat tours** appeal to many visitors, but they're not always exciting as the water can be murky and lifeless at times.

Biscayne National Underwater Parks, Inc. • (305) 230-1100
www.biscayneunderwater.com
Boca Chita Tour: $35 (Adults), $20 (Children ages 2–12)
Elliot Key Island Adventure: Pricing to be determined
Glass Bottom Tour: $45 (Adults), $35 (Children ages 2–12)
Private Boat Rentals: Start at $345

SCUBA & Snorkel

More than 50 shipwrecks and a significant portion of the **third largest barrier reef in the world** make Biscayne National Park one of the best SCUBA and snorkel destinations in the United States.

Wreck-diving was first made popular by treasure hunters who inhabited Elliott Key. Today, a **Maritime Heritage Trail** connects six of the park's wrecks. Mooring buoys, maps, and site cards aid divers and snorkelers on their exploration of each site. All sites except the **Mandalay** are best suited for SCUBA divers. **Ranger-guided snorkel trips** to selected sites on the trail are offered (additional details available at the park's website and visitor center). For those interested in snorkeling, SCUBA diving, or learning to SCUBA, **Biscayne National Underwater Park, Inc.** (305.230.1100, www.biscayneunderwater.com) can help. They offer two snorkel trips, one to the reef and another to the bay. The reef is the preferred destination, but rough water can cancel the trip or redirect it to the bay. In the event that your reef snorkel trip is moved, you should cancel and hold off until the seas calm enough that the reef is accessible (if you have the time).

Biscayne National Underwater Parks, Inc. • (305) 230-1100
www.biscayneunderwater.com
Ranger Guided Maritime Heritage Snorkel Adventure: $45/person
Bay Snorkel Tour: $40/person
Reef Snorkel Tour: $45/person
Reef SCUBA Diving: $99/person
Learn to Dive: $350/person

Stiltsville © miamism.com

Paddling

Paddling is a great way to explore the mangrove shorelines and shallow flats surrounding **Jones Lagoon**, where you might see sharks, rays, upside-down jellies, and wading birds. **Kayak and canoe rentals** are available from the park concessioner, **Biscayne National Underwater Parks, Inc.** (305.230.1100, www.biscayneunderwater.com). The only problem with renting is that all rental canoes and kayaks must stay in the immediate vicinity of **Dante Fascell Visitor Center**. Visitors with their own boats can launch for free from the visitor center. **Overnight parking** is available for anyone planning on camping at either of the park's primitive campgrounds (page 121), but you must obtain a **free permit** (available at the visitor center) prior to departure. **Elliott Key** is approximately seven miles from shore. Do not attempt to cross the bay during periods of inclement weather or adverse water conditions. In winter and spring the park concessioner provides boat service to Elliott Key and they can provide transport for canoes, kayaks, and paddlers. The park generally offers **guided canoe and kayak trips** from January to April. Check the park's website or visitor center for a current schedule of events.

Snorkelers at the Florida reef

Bird Watching

More than 170 species of birds have been recorded within the park. **Convoy Point** and **Black Point** are two of the better mainland birding locations, but to really experience the multitude of sea birds visitors must hit the water. **Jones Lagoon**, just south of Caesar Creek, is the park's premier birding location. Here you're sure to spot cormorants, brown pelicans, and anhinga.

For Kids: Kids will enjoy **boat tours**, **snorkel trips**, and **paddling** (all found on page 123) through mangrove forests found at Biscayne, but there are also several attractions geared especially for children. On the second Sunday of each month, from December to April, the park holds a **Family Fun Fest**. It's a free program at Dante Fascell Visitor Center that highlights the region's diverse resources using five hands-on activity booths. Participants receive a "passport" that is punched each time they complete a station. Anyone who completes all five stations receives a special prize.

Children can also participate in the park's **Junior Ranger Program**. An activity booklet can be downloaded from the park website or hard copies are available free of charge at Dante Fascell Visitor Center. The program is jointly administered between **Big Cypress National Preserve**, **Biscayne National Park**, and **Everglades National Park**. Complete the activities for Biscayne National Park to earn a badge. If you complete the entire book you will earn a South Florida National Parks Junior Ranger Patch.

Ranger Programs: Ranger-led activities are available at several locations within the park, with most programs offered during the park's busy season (Christmas Day–April). **Boat tours** are administered daily, but they do not offer daily ranger-led hikes or lectures. Visit the park's website to check out a current schedule of events before arriving at the park. You can also find a schedule of events in the park newspaper (available for free at Dante Fascell Visitor Center).

Flora & Fauna: Hundreds of species of plants can be found here. Most obvious are the mangrove forests that line the shores and are a cornerstone of the entire ecosystem. Birds, manatees, and crocodiles visit these masses of twisted roots and branches with great frequency. Smaller fish seek protection from larger predators among the half-sunken mangrove roots where trapped leaves provide nourishment for a variety of sea-life. If you go on a SCUBA, snorkel, or boat tour, it's likely that you see beds of sea grass. These underwater pastures are all-you-can-eat, self-service buffets for sea turtles and manatees, and a nursery for small fishes and invertebrates. The park's islands and mainland contain numerous cacti, ferns, trees, shrubs, and wildflowers. Many appear on lists of threatened and endangered species while others are non-native, exotic plants introduced by humans. Non-native species pose a serious threat to native plants as they compete for the same limited supply of water and nutrients.

The majority of wildlife at Biscayne National Park is hidden beneath the sea. Underwater inhabitants include **512 species of fish**, a handful of crustaceans like crabs and lobsters, dolphins, manatees, a few species of whale, and several mollusks like squid, snails, and oysters. Lucky snorkelers or SCUBA divers may spot a graceful sea turtle. **Green**, **loggerhead**, **leatherback**, and **hawksbill turtles**, all endangered species, can be found here. The **American crocodile** is another endangered species that finds refuge among the park's mangrove islands. Harvest, harassment, harm, or any other interference with these species is strictly prohibited.

Rare creatures also live above the water. **Schaus' swallowtail butterfly**, for example, are estimated at fewer than 70 adults remaining in the world, and they are only found on North Key Largo and a few small Keys in Biscayne National Park. That said, most animals living above sea level fall under the category of pests. **Mosquitoes** are common year-round, but are particularly pesky during the summer. **Raccoons** inhabit the islands and are frequently found rummaging through visitors' coolers and picnic baskets. Travel with animal-proof coolers and do not sleep with food in your tent.

Pets: Pets are only allowed in the developed areas of Elliott Key and Convoy Point. They must be kept on a leash no more than six feet in length at all times. Pets, except service animals, are prohibited from all other areas of the park.

Accessibility: More than 95% of the park is covered by water, so accessibility is directly dependent on your transportation (usually a boat). Concessioner-operated boat trips offer limited accessibility (with assistance) to individuals who require the use of a wheelchair. Always make arrangements ahead of time by contacting Biscayne National Underwater, Inc. (305.230.1100, www.biscayneunderwater.com). Dante Fascell Visitor Center and Jetty Trail are fully accessible to wheelchair users. Boca Chita Key is the only island within the park that has sidewalks.

Weather: When visiting Biscayne National Park be especially observant of the weather. A subtropical climate provides abundant sunshine all year long, but thunderstorms with massive amounts of lightning are common, and hurricanes batter the land occasionally. Winters are generally dry and mild, with an average high temperature of 68°F in January. Summers are often hot and humid with an average high temperature of 82°F in July. Scattered thunderstorms are most common in summer. Hurricane season lasts from June to November. Biscayne Bay is relatively well protected, but if skies grow dark or the wind begins to pick up, boaters should head for shore rather than get caught in a thunderstorm.

An endangered green sea turtle

An endangered American Crocodile

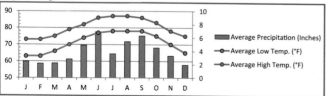
Average Precipitation (Inches)
Average Low Temp. (°F)
Average High Temp. (°F)

Vacation Planner

To get the most out of a trip to Biscayne National Park you need to be prepared. Whether it's booking a **boat tour** (page 123) or just checking the park's website for a current schedule of events, every little bit you do beforehand will increase your chances of an enjoyable experience. **Renting canoes or kayaks** (page 123) is a fun way to spend a few hours. Bringing your own watercraft is even better, because it allows you to paddle across the bay to the northern Florida Keys. Most visitors arrive via private boat, but it's not a requirement. **Biscayne National Underwater Parks, Inc.** (305.230.1100, www.biscayneunderwater.com) offers transportation to Boca Chita Key and personal private charters. Dining, grocery stores, lodging, festivals, and attractions outside the park are listed on pages 145–149.

Day 1 For a day in the park, begin at **Dante Fascell Visitor Center**. Ask questions. Watch a short film. Browse exhibits. As for activities, you're at the mercy of the park's concessioner. Recommended activities include: **reef snorkel**, **ranger-guided Maritime Heritage Trail snorkel**, **paddling Jones Lagoon**, and **Boca Chita Boat Tour** (page 123).

An alligator hatchling

40001 State Road 9336
Homestead, Florida 33034
Phone: (305) 242-7700
Website: www.nps.gov/ever

Established: December 6, 1947
Size: 1,509,000 Acres
Annual Visitors: 1 Million
Peak Season: December–April

Hiking Trails: 50+ Miles
Wilderness Waterway: 99 Miles

Activities: Paddling, Hiking, Biking, Fishing, Bird Watching, Ranger Programs, Boat Tours

Campgrounds: Long Pine Key (first-come, first-served) and Flamingo (reservations accepted)
Camping Fee: $16/night
Backcountry Camping: Permitted at Designated Sites with a Backcountry Permit ($10 plus $2/night)
Lodging: None

Park Hours: All day, every day
Entrance Fee: $10 • Vehicle

Everglades - Florida

Wherever you look the circle of life is on display in the Everglades. From alligator holes to mangrove coasts, lofty pine to dwarf cypress forests, grassy waterways to man-made canals, life flourishes and flounders, thrives and perishes, dies and is reborn. When Americans began to develop South Florida in the late 19th century, humans threw this circle of life into a tailspin. It's not to late to recover, but our actions will ultimately destroy or preserve this irreplaceable wilderness.

Whether you're looking at the Everglades from above, atop the 45-foot high observation deck at Shark Valley, or from the seat of a kayak in a maze of waterways, one thing you're sure to notice is its size. At 1,509,000 acres, it's the largest wilderness area east of the Mississippi River. Hidden among its immensity are small pockets of life that are even more incredible.

Alligators reside at the top of the food chain for good reason. Their vise-like jaws and razor sharp teeth make a fearsome predator, but they aren't all predatory. Alligators burrow in mud creating small pools of water. When the dry season sets in, water levels decrease so much that alligator holes are often the only available source of freshwater, providing an important habitat for fish and amphibians trying to survive from one year to the next. Mammals congregate at these gator holes, drinking water and feeding on smaller prey. Meanwhile, alligators lay motionless, waiting to attack as they feed. Eventually, the region floods again, and fish and amphibians, survivors of life in a gator hole, are free to repopulate the fresh water prairies.

Quantity, quality, and type of water shape the plant and animal life of the Everglades' ecosystems. **Cypress** trees adapted to survive in areas frequently covered with standing fresh water. These hearty conifers are surrounded by woody, conical protrusions called "knees" that provide oxygen to the roots below. Dwarf cypresses reside in areas with less water and poorer soil. Spanish moss, orchids, and ferns grow from the trees' branches and trunks. Along the salt water coast you'll find jungle-like **mangrove forests**. The park protects the largest continuous system of mangroves in the world. These plants have also acclimated to extreme conditions. They acquired a high tolerance for salt water, winds, tides, temperatures, and muddy soils. Mangroves also serve as the first line of defense against hurricanes. Sturdy roots and dense branches are capable of absorbing and deflecting flood water, helping prevent coastal erosion. They also act as a nursery and food depot for marine and bird species.

Sadly, human actions are altering many of the area's natural life cycles. Nearly all of the park land's pine forests were logged. Dade County was once covered with more than 186,000 acres of pine rockland forest. Today, only 20,000 acres remain. **Florida panthers** have been ravaged by loss of habitat, poor water quality, and hunting. Now, perhaps ten exist in the park. In the early 1900s, alligators, birds, frogs, and fish were hunted on a massive scale. Since the 1930s, the number of nesting wading birds in the southern Everglades has declined by 93% from 265,000 to 18,500. Most were killed for their plumes, commonly used to decorate women's hats. Today, the greatest threat the Everglades faces is **depletion and diversion of water**. Man-made dikes, levees, and canals have been constructed to bring water to South Florida's urban areas, cutting off the region's water supply. A park brochure offers a sad and honest description of the state of the Everglades' water: "Freshwater flowing into the park is engineered. With the help of pumps, floodgates, and retention ponds along the park's boundary, Everglades is presently on life support, alive but diminished." Come to the Everglades. Witness the abundance of life still struggling to survive. See for yourself if condos, strip malls, and roadways are worth destroying one of the world's most magnificent natural wonders. It's not too late to save the Everglades. Changing its course is up to us. All we need to do is act now, before it really is too late.

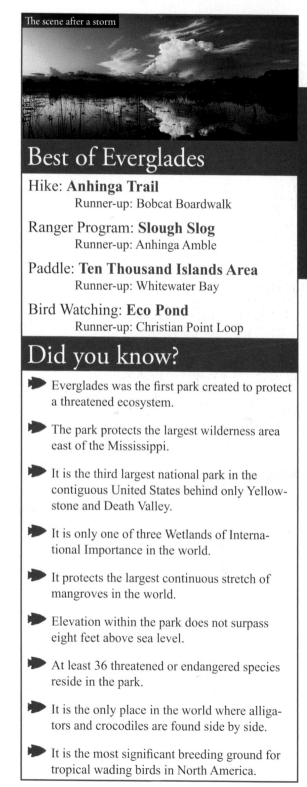

The scene after a storm

Best of Everglades

Hike: **Anhinga Trail**
Runner-up: Bobcat Boardwalk

Ranger Program: **Slough Slog**
Runner-up: Anhinga Amble

Paddle: **Ten Thousand Islands Area**
Runner-up: Whitewater Bay

Bird Watching: **Eco Pond**
Runner-up: Christian Point Loop

Did you know?

- Everglades was the first park created to protect a threatened ecosystem.

- The park protects the largest wilderness area east of the Mississippi.

- It is the third largest national park in the contiguous United States behind only Yellowstone and Death Valley.

- It is only one of three Wetlands of International Importance in the world.

- It protects the largest continuous stretch of mangroves in the world.

- Elevation within the park does not surpass eight feet above sea level.

- At least 36 threatened or endangered species reside in the park.

- It is the only place in the world where alligators and crocodiles are found side by side.

- It is the most significant breeding ground for tropical wading birds in North America.

When to Go

Everglades National Park is open all year, but some tours, attractions, and hours of operation are seasonal. Southern Florida experiences two seasons. Most guests visit the Everglades during the dry season (December–April). It's typically comfortable with fewer bugs, thunderstorms, and hurricanes. The wet season (March–November) is hot and humid, with thick swarms of mosquitoes. Thunderstorms are common and hurricanes may pass through the area. Hurricane season spans from June to November. Needless to say, you do not want to be camping when hurricane force winds rip through the Everglades. Very few visitors come to the park during the wet season. All three of South Florida's National Parks are best visited during the winter.

A few entrances to the park are not always open. Ernest F. Coe Visitor Center Entrance and Gulf Coast Entrance are open 24 hours per day. Chekika Entrance is closed due to flooding from May through November; it is open from dawn until dusk for the remainder of the year. Shark Valley Entrance is open daily from 8:30am–6pm.

Ernest F. Coe Visitor Center (305.242.7700) is open daily from 9am–5pm.

Shark Valley Visitor Center (305.221.8776) is open daily from 9:15am–5:15pm.

Royal Palm (305.242.7700), Flamingo (239.695.2945), and Gulf Coast (239.695.3311) Visitor Centers are open daily, but hours vary depending on staffing and season. If you are not visiting the park during peak season it is a good idea to call for hours and information.

Airports

Miami International Airport (MIA) is about 40 miles northeast of Ernest F. Coe Visitor Center. On the Gulf Coast, Southwest Florida International Airport (RSW), located in Fort Myers, is about 80 miles northwest of Everglades City. The smaller Naples Municipal Airport (APF) is just 35 miles northwest of Everglades City.

People

"There are no other Everglades in the world. They are, they have always been, one of the unique regions of the earth; remote, never wholly known. Nothing anywhere else is like them." – Marjory Stoneman Douglas

In 1904, **Napoleon Bonaparte Broward** ran his campaign for governor of Florida on a platform of draining South Florida, to create "The Empire of the Everglades." Broward won, ordered drainage to commence, and faced staunch opposition. **Frank Stoneman**, publisher of the Miami Herald, was one of his most stalwart opponents. The governor took note and turned to childish pranks, refusing to validate an election for Circuit Court Judge won by Stoneman. In 1915, Frank's daughter, **Marjory**, moved to Florida, joining the Herald as a society columnist. By 1923 she had become a freelance writer and joined the **Everglades Tropical National Park Committee**. Later she would become the most powerful public voice supporting the Everglades.

Ernest F. Coe, a land developer turned conservationist, moved to South Florida in 1925 when he was 60 years old. He spent his next 25 years leading the Everglades Tropical National Park Committee, earning him the title of "father of the Everglades." He drew up plans for a park that included more than two million acres, including Key Largo and Big Cypress. Driven by Coe's passion and Senator Spessard Holland's politicking, a smaller park was finally authorized in 1934, with the stipulation that no federal funds be allocated for at least five years.

Thanks to Coe's tireless work procuring funds and the Florida legislature's commitment to raise $2 million to purchase private land, the park was formally established in December 1947. That same year, **Marjory Stoneman Douglas** published *The Everglades: River of Grass* after spending five years studying the land and water. Her work helped convince public opinion of the Everglades' value as a treasured river rather than a worthless swamp. Douglas lived to be 108 years old and worked to restore the Everglades until the end. Today, many of the regions originally in Ernest F. Coe's vision of Everglades National Park have been protected. They include Big Cypress National Preserve, Biscayne National Park, John Pennekamp Coral Reef State Park, Ten Thousand Islands National Wildlife Reserve, and Florida Keys National Marine Sanctuary. Parks exist, but they still face many of the threats Douglas and Coe fought against.

An egret wading in shallow water

Restoration

More than 50% of the original Everglades have already been destroyed by development and changes in water flow. Everglades National Park protects half of what remains, but without immediate intervention the entire area will soon dry up and become devoid of life. The region used to be one of the most uniquely balanced ecosystems in the world, where all forms of life adapted to the rise and fall of water flowing into the 'Glades from **Lake Okeechobee** and the **Kissimmee River**. The same year the park was established, Congress authorized creation of the **Central and South Florida Flood Control Project**. More than 1,000 miles of canals and flood control structures were built to divert excess water to the Gulf, the Atlantic, and Florida Bay. Once completed, the Everglades was completely cut-off from its natural water supplies. By the 1960s, the park was visibly suffering.

In response, the federal government (which had effectively starved the region of water for more than a decade) approved legislation set to improve the health of the Everglades. In 1989, **President H.W. Bush** signed the **Everglades National Park Protection and Expansion Act**. It closed the park to air boats, directed the Department of the Army to restore water to the area, and put an additional 100,000 acres of land under park control. The **Comprehensive Everglades Restoration Plan** was passed in 2000. It promised $10.5 billion to restore, preserve, and protect the Everglades, but as of September 2008 none of the assigned projects have been completed. Clearly, there's more to be done. Please, donate your time and/or money to help restore the park, or write a letter to your representatives. We must act now, before it's too late and there's nothing left to save.

Transportation

Transportation is not available to or around Everglades National Park.

Directions

Everglades has five visitor centers and four park entrances that are frequented by motorists.

<u>Main Entrance/Ernest F. Coe Visitor Center/Royal Palm Visitor Center/Flamingo Visitor Center (from Miami):</u> Take Florida Turnpike/Route 821 (Toll Road) south until it ends and merges with US-1 at Florida City. Turn right at the first traffic light. Follow the signs to the park.

If arriving from the Florida Keys turn left on Palm Drive in Florida City, and follow the signs to the park.

The Ernest F. Coe Visitor Center is on your right just before the park entrance station. Royal Palm is a smaller information center three miles beyond the park entrance. Flamingo is another 38 miles southwest of the entrance station. Visitors should allow an hour to drive from the Main Entrance Station to Flamingo.

<u>Chekika Entrance (from Highway 41/Tamiami Trail):</u> Located near the eastern edge of the park, take Krome Avenue (SW 177th Avenue) south. Turn right at Richmond Drive (SW 168th Street) and follow it into the park.

<u>Shark Valley Visitor Center (from US-41/Tamiami Trail):</u> US-41 crosses the Florida peninsula from east to west, providing access to Shark Valley and its visitor center. Follow US-41 (~40 miles from downtown Miami and 75 miles from Naples). Shark Valley Loop Road is south of US-41. The visitor center and Tram Tour departure point are a short distance from the highway.

<u>Gulf Coast Visitor Center (from I-75):</u> Gulf Coast Visitor Center is located on the very western edge of the park, 5 miles south of US-41 (Tamiami Trail). From I-75 (Toll Road) take exit 80 to merge onto FL-29 S. Follow FL-29 for 20 miles to Everglades City and follow the signs to the park.

Regions of The Everglades

Everglades is an expansive wilderness, much of which is completely inaccessible to automobiles. There are four entrances dispersed along the park's perimeter. The Main Entrance, located along the eastern boundary, and Shark Valley Entrance are the most popular entry points due to a variety of attractions and proximity to Miami. A short description of each region is provided below.

Main Entrance/Ernest F. Coe/Flamingo: The main entrance is your number one choice for hiking, biking, and paddling trails. Flamingo is situated at the end of Main Park Road, 38 miles southwest of the entrance. Flamingo marks the terminus of the 99-mile wilderness waterway. It's also a spot where boat tours and canoe and kayak rentals are offered. Both of the park's campgrounds, numerous hiking/biking/paddling trails, and three picnic areas are found between the Main Park Entrance and Flamingo.

Shark Valley: Shark Valley is popular for its 15-mile paved loop road. Visitors are no longer allowed to drive the loop, but you are encouraged to bike or walk as much as time and attitudes allow. The only vehicles permitted on the loop are open-sided trams (fee) that transport visitors to and from an observation tower at the loop's half-way point. This is arguably the best location to see vast sawgrass prairies that have become synonymous with the Everglades. Shark Valley also provides excellent opportunities for alligator viewing and bird watching. Nearby you'll find several non-park affiliated attractions, including air-boat tours and alligator farms (page 148).

Chekika: Here you'll find a picnic area and a short self-guided hiking trail.

Gulf Coast: Gulf Coast Entrance is the gateway to Ten Thousand Islands. Boat tours and kayak rentals are available for those wishing to explore the maze of mangrove islands. It also marks the northwestern end of the 99-mile Wilderness Waterway. No hiking trails are available. A visitor center provides backcountry permits, brochures, exhibits, and an introductory film.

Camping

Long Pine Key Campground ($16/night) is located seven miles from the main entrance. The camp has 108 sites for tents and RVs and one group site. Restrooms, water, grills, picnic tables, and a dump station are available. You'll also find a small pond for fishing, an amphitheater, and several hiking trails in the area. Hook-ups and showers are not available. All sites (except the group site) are available on a first-come, first-served basis.

Flamingo Campground ($16/night, $30/night with electrical hook-ups) is located at the end of Main Park Road. It has 234 drive-in sites (55 with a view of the water, 41 with electric hook-ups). Restrooms, cold water showers, grills, picnic tables, dump stations, and an amphitheater are available. Hook-ups are not. Hiking, paddling, and salt water fishing are popular activities. Reservations are accepted at www.recreation.gov or (239) 695-0124.

Backcountry camping is available at several designated sites throughout the park. A permit is required ($10/permit and $2/night) and must be obtained in person at the main entrance station (for Ernest Coe and Old Ingraham sites) and Flamingo or Gulf Coast Visitor Centers (for all other sites).

EVERGLADES

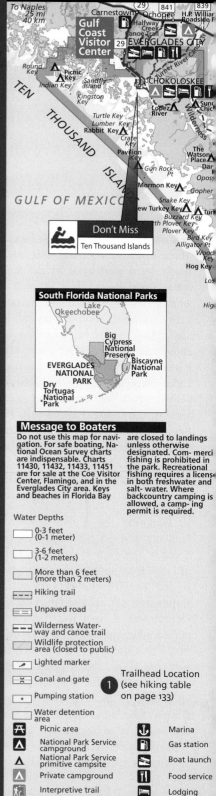

Mapping Everglades Ecosystems

South Florida National Parks

Message to Boaters

Do not use this map for navigation. For safe boating, National Ocean Survey charts are indispensable. Charts 11430, 11432, 11433, 11451 are for sale at the Coe Visitor Center, Flamingo, and in the Everglades City area. Keys and beaches in Florida Bay are closed to landings unless otherwise designated. Com- merci fishing is prohibited in the park. Recreational fishing requires a license in both freshwater and salt- water. Where backcountry camping is allowed, a camp- ing permit is required.

Water Depths

0-3 feet (0-1 meter)

3-6 feet (1-2 meters)

More than 6 feet (more than 2 meters)

Hiking trail

Unpaved road

Wilderness Waterway and canoe trail

Wildlife protection area (closed to public)

Lighted marker

Canal and gate

Pumping station

Water detention area

Picnic area

National Park Service campground

National Park Service primitive campsite

Private campground

Interpretive trail

Trailhead Location (see hiking table on page 133)

Marina

Gas station

Boat launch

Food service

Lodging

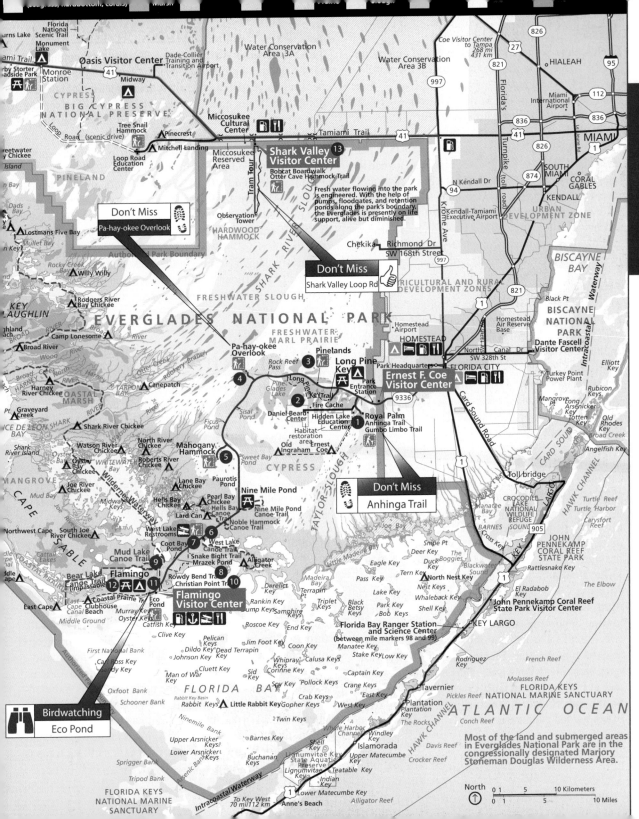

Coe Visitor Center
to Tampa
268 mi
431 km

Don't Miss
Pa-hay-okee Overlook

Don't Miss
Shark Valley Loop Rd

Fresh water flowing into the park
is engineered. With the help of
pumps, floodgates, and retention
ponds along the park's boundary,
the Everglades is presently on life
support, alive but diminished.

Shark Valley Visitor Center 13

Bobcat Boardwalk
Otter Cave Hammock Trail

Observation
Tower

HARDWOOD
HAMMOCK

Authorized Park Boundary

FRESHWATER SLOUGH

FRESHWATER
MARL PRAIRIE

EVERGLADES NATIONAL PARK

Pa-hay-okee
Overlook

Rock Reef
Pass

Pinelands

Long Pine
Key

Park
Entrance
Station

Park Headquarters

Ernest F. Coe Visitor Center

9336

Long Pine Key Trail

Fire Cache

Daniel Beard
Center

Hidden Lake
Education Center

Habitat
restoration
area

Old Ingraham

Ernest
Coe

Royal Palm 1
Anhinga Trail
Gumbo Limbo Trail

Mahogany
Hammock 5

CYPRESS

Don't Miss
Anhinga Trail

Lane Bay
Chickee

Paurotis
Pond

Nine Mile Pond

Pearl Bay
Chickee

Hells Bay
Chickee

Nine Mile Pond
Canoe Trail

Noble Hammock
Canoe Trail

Hells Bay
Canoe

Lard Can

West Lake
Restrooms 6

West Lake
Canoe Trail 7

Coot Bay
Pond

Snake Bight Trail

Mrazek Pond

Alligator
Creek

Mud Lake
Canoe Trail 9

Bear Lake
Canoe Trail
(Impassable)

Flamingo 12 11

Rowdy Bend Tr
Christian Point Tr 10 8

Coastal Prairie Tr

Eco
Pond

**Flamingo
Visitor Center**

TAYLOR SLOUGH

Birdwatching
Eco Pond

BISCAYNE
BAY

AGRICULTURAL AND RURAL
DEVELOPMENT ZONES

URBAN
DEVELOPMENT
ZONE

HIALEAH

Miami
International
Airport

MIAMI

SOUTH
MIAMI

CORAL
GABLES

KENDALL

Coe Visitor Center
to Tampa

N Kendall Dr

Kendall-Tamiami
Executive Airport

Chekika

Richmond Dr
SW 168th Street

Homestead
Air Reserve
Base

North Canal Dr
SW 328th St

HOMESTEAD

FLORIDA CITY

Dante Fascell
Visitor Center

BISCAYNE
NATIONAL
PARK

Black Pt

Turkey Point
Power Plant

Elliott
Key

Card Sound Road

Mangrove
Pt

Long
Arsenicker
Key

Old
Rhodes
Key

Rubicon
Keys

Broad Creek

Angelfish Key

Toll bridge

CROCODILE
LAKE
NATIONAL
WILDLIFE
REFUGE

BARNES
SOUND

CARD SOUND

Manatee
Bay

CROSS KEY

905

JOHN
PENNEKAMP
CORAL REEF
STATE PARK

Rattlesnake Key

Turtle Reef

Turtle Harbor

Carysfort
Reef

El Radabob
Key

The Elbow

KEY LARGO

John Pennekamp Coral Reef
State Park Visitor Center

Joe Bay

Snipe Pt

Deer Key

Duck Key

The
Boggies

Eagle Key

Tern Key

North Nest Key

Blackwater
Sound

Rodriguez
Key

French Reef

Molasses Reef

Tavernier

Plantation
Key

Plantation
Key

Pickles Reef

FLORIDA KEYS
NATIONAL MARINE SANCTUARY

Davis Reef

Conch Reef

Crocker Reef

Hawk Channel

Little Madeira Bay

Madeira
Bay

Terrapin
Pt

Pass Key

Lake Key

Nest Keys

Whaleback Key

Shell Key

Florida Bay Ranger Station
and Science Center
(between mile markers 98 and 99)

Rankin Key

Jump Key

Pelican
Keys

Samphire
Keys

Derelict
Key

Triplet
Keys

Black
Betsy
Keys

Park Key

Bob Key

Low Key

Stake Key

Manatee Key

Roscoe Key

End Key

Coon Key

Calusa Keys

Captain Key

Crane Keys

East Key

West Key

Gopher Keys

Clive Key

Dildo Key

Dead Terrapin
Key

Johnson Key

Man of War
Key

Cluett Key

Sid
Key

Whipray Keys

Corinne Key

Sky Key

Pollock Keys

FLORIDA BAY

Rabbit Key Basin

Rabbit Keys

Little Rabbit Key

Crab Keys

Twin Keys

Islamorada

Windley
Key

Shell
Key

Upper Matecumbe
Key

Teatable Key

Lignumvitae
State Aquatic
Preserve
Lignumvitae
Key

Indian
Key

Lower Matecumbe Key

Anne's Beach

Alligator Reef

To Key West
70 mi/112 km

FLORIDA KEYS
NATIONAL MARINE
SANCTUARY

Schooner Bank

Oxfoot Bank

First National Bank

Carl Ross Key

Sandy Key

East Cape

Murray Key

Oyster Keys

Catfish Key

Middle Ground

Ninemile Bank

Buchanan Keys

Upper Arsnicker
Keys

Lower Arsnicker
Keys

Sprigger Bank

Barnes Key

Tripod Bank

Whale Harbor
Channel

ATLANTIC OCEAN

Most of the land and submerged areas
in Everglades National Park are in the
congressionally designated Marjory
Stoneman Douglas Wilderness Area.

North

| 0 1 | 5 | 10 Kilometers |
| 0 1 | 5 | 10 Miles |

 Paddling

The essence of the Everglades is found among its grassy waterways. To get there you must paddle. Day-trips or multi-day adventures? You'll find some of the best in the world. Whitewater? Look somewhere else. There's little to no current; it's all paddling here. These creeks and rivers flow into Florida Bay at the blistering speed of 0.25-mile per day. At that rate, it would take more than a year to float the 99-mile Wilderness Waterway. Low water levels can impede your paddling goals. If you plan on departing between late February and March, discuss your itinerary with a park ranger to assure that the desired route is completely navigable. Also be prepared for strong winds and tides.

Flamingo has the most paddling variety. **Nine Mile Pond** is a great place to spot birds and alligators. Access to the 5-mile trail is just off Main Park Road at Nine Mile Pond Picnic/Parking Area. A little further south is **Noble Hammock Canoe Trail**. This 1.9-mile loop requires good maneuvering skills (or a small kayak) to navigate a maze of mangrove-lined creeks and ponds. Opposite this launch site is **Hells Bay Canoe Trail**, another extremely narrow trail (5.5 miles, one-way) through dense mangroves. **Hells Bay** is an excellent location to test yourself for the Wilderness Waterway. One campsite and two chickees (permit required • page 132) are found along the way. Anyone looking down on this trail from above would wonder how this maze of mangroves is navigated. It's actually quite easy thanks to more than 160 poles marking the way. Continuing along Main Park Road is **West Lake Trail** (8.1 miles, one-way), which leads to Alligator Creek backcountry campsite. Next up is **Mud Lake Loop**, a 7.5-mile trail with excellent birding opportunities (requires a short portage between Bear Lake and Buttonwood Canal). You can also venture out into **Florida Bay** for more wide open paddling. **Kayak and canoe rentals** are available at **Flamingo and Gulf Coast Visitor Centers**. **Shurr Adventure Kayaking** in Everglades City offers guided paddle trips.

Shurr Adventures Kayaking • (239) 695-2576
PO Box 642; Everglades City, FL 34139 • www.shurradventures.net
Rates: $80–150 (day), $350+ (multi-day)

 Wilderness Waterway

The Wilderness Waterway is a 99-mile trail connecting Flamingo and Everglades City. The best time to paddle is between December and April. It takes at least eight days to complete. Do not consider this to be the sort of adventure that you can complete on a whim. You must plan ahead. There are many routes and dozens of campsites along the way. The park's website provides a trip planning guide to make sure you are properly prepared. Park rangers at Flamingo and Gulf Coast Visitor Centers are also happy to help plan your trip. Backcountry permits are required and must be obtained in person at Flamingo or Gulf Coast Visitor Centers. Permits cost $10 plus $2 per night per person. They are only available up to one day prior to your departure date. You'll be in the backcountry, but solitude can still be difficult to find. Remember that motorboats are allowed in most wilderness areas, and some campsites have capacity for as many as 60 campers.

Hiking

The best way to explore the park may be by boat, but that doesn't mean that great hiking trails don't exist in the Everglades. Most trailheads are found along Main Park Road between Ernest Coe Visitor Center and Flamingo. **Anhinga Trail** is an absolute must hike. It's a short and easy stroll that begins at Royal Palm Visitor Center and immediately immerses hikers into the park's amazingly unique biodiversity. It's highly likely you'll see alligators along this half-mile loop.

If toothy, prehistoric-looking creatures aren't your cup of tea, try **Mahogany Hammock Trail**. It's a 0.5-mile boardwalk located 20 miles from the Main Park Entrance. Trees are the main attraction here, including the largest living mahogany tree in the United States. **West Lake Trail** (31 miles from the Main Park Entrance) is a short boardwalk through mangroves. Visitors will also find good hiking opportunities at Long Pine Key and Flamingo Campgrounds. There's a short, self-guided hiking trail at Chekika Picnic Area on the eastern edge of the park. Hiking is more enjoyable if you see a little wildlife (at a safe distance), so always discuss your intentions with a park ranger to learn the best hiking locations to see animals at the time of your visit. A more complete listing of the park's hiking trails is provided on the following page.

Everglades Hiking Trails

	Trail Name	Trailhead Location (# on map)	Length	Notes (Roundtrip distances unless noted otherwise)
Long Pine Key Area	Anhinga - 👍	Royal Palm Visitor Center (1)	0.8 mile	If you only hike one trail in the park this is the one • Great opportunities to spot wildlife • Ranger-led hikes available per schedule
	Gumbo-Limbo - 👍	Royal Palm Visitor Center (1)	0.4 mile	Self-guiding trail that leads to a hardwood hammock in the middle of a sea of sawgrass
	Old Ingraham Highway	Royal Palm Visitor Center (1)	11.0 miles (one-way)	Provides access to two backcountry campsites • Bikes allowed
	Long Pine Key	Begins just west of Long Pine Key Campground/Ends at Pine Glades Lake along Main Park Road (2)	7.0 miles (one-way)	Running parallel to Main Park Road you travel from the campground to Pine Glades Lake • Bikes allowed
	Pineland	About 7 miles from the Main Park Entrance (3)	0.5 mile	A short loop through a forest of pines, palmettos, and wildflowers
	Pa-hay-okee Overlook - 👍	About 13 miles from the Main Park Entrance (4)	0.25 mile	A great hike to a bird's eye view of the vast "river of grass"
	Mahogany Hammock - 👍	About 20 miles from the Main Park Entrance (5)	0.5 mile	A short self-guiding trail that leads to Mahogany Hammock where the largest living mahogany tree in the U.S. resides
Flamingo Area	West Lake - 👍	About 7 miles north of Flamingo on Main Park Road (6)	0.5 mile	Self-guiding boardwalk trail that passes through mangroves to the edge of West Lake
	Snake Bight	About 4 miles north of Flamingo on Main Park Road (7)	1.8 miles (one-way)	This tropical hardwood hammock is another excellent birding location • Bikes allowed
	Rowdy Bend	About 3 miles north of Flamingo on Main Park Road (8)	2.6 miles (one-way)	Connects to Snake Bight Trail • Bikes allowed
	Bear Lake	About 2 miles north of Flamingo on Main Park Road (9)	1.6 miles (one-way)	Trail ends at Bear Lake after meandering through a hardwood hammock mixed with a variety of mangroves
	Christian Point	About 1 mile north of Flamingo on Main Park Road (10)	1.6 miles (one-way)	Excellent location for bird watching
	Eco Pond	At Flamingo (11)	0.5 mile	A small fresh water pond often frequented by wading birds, song birds, and alligators
	Guy Bradley	At Flamingo (11)	1.0 mile (one-way)	Connects the visitor center and the amphitheater along the shore of Florida Bay
	Bayshore Loop	At Flamingo (11)	2.0 miles	Trail along Florida Bay that provides good opportunities for spotting butterflies and birds
	Coastal Prairie	At the back of Flamingo Campground's Loop C (12)	6.0 miles (one-way)	An old settlement road that leads to Clubhouse Beach and a backcountry campsite
Shark Valley	Bobcat Boardwalk	Behind Shark Valley Visitor Center (13)	0.3 mile	A short, self-guiding trail that passes through a sawgrass slough and hardwood forest
	Otter Cave Hammock	Behind Shark Valley Visitor Center (13)	1.0 mile	Limestone trail that passes through a tropical hardwood forest • Often flooded in summer
	Tram Road - 👍	Shark Loop Road (13)	15.0 miles	Paved road leads to a 45-foot tall observation tower • May spot alligators, egrets, and snail kites • Bikes allowed

 # Biking

If you're looking for grueling mountain climbs, this isn't the place for you. The park's maximum elevation is 8 feet above sea level, and no, that is not a typo. What you will find are flat paved roads and a handful of dirt hiking trails that allow bicycles. The 15-mile **Shark Valley Loop** is the most popular biking destination. Taking a bike to the 45-foot observation tower is a great alternative to the tram tour. Bike rental is available at **Shark Valley Tram Tours, Inc.** (350.221.8455, www.sharkvalleytramtours.com) for $7.50/hour.

Snake Bight, Rowdy Bend, Bear Lake, and Guy Bradley Trails, near Flamingo, permit bicycles. **Long Pine Key** and **Old Ingraham Highway** are two trails near Long Pine Key Campground where bikes are permitted. Use caution when biking on trails to avoid hikers who share these paths.

Main Park Road is a longer option for early-risers. During peak-season, traffic begins to pick up around 10am and die down around 5pm.

 # Boat Tours

Boat tours are available courtesy of concessioners located at Flamingo and Gulf Coast Visitor Centers. **Flamingo's tour** leads guests through the **Buttonwood Canal** where they explore **Whitewater Bay backcountry**. Stop in at Flamingo Marina to purchase tickets or make reservations. On the opposite end of the park visitors can enjoy a tour of **Ten Thousand Islands**. While sailing the seas, you may see all sorts of wildlife, including bottle-nosed dolphins, manatees, ospreys, and pelicans. As you pass the sea of islands (far fewer than 10,000) imagine a time when Calusa Indians paddled from island to island and fished these waterways. It has been hundreds of years since they inhabited the area, but archaeological evidence remains to this day, including mountains of shells left on small tree islands.

Air boats are not allowed within the park, but you will find several **air boat operators** (page 148) outside the park along Tamiami Trail (US-41).

 # Fishing

More than one third of the park is covered by navigable water creating ample fishing opportunities. Whether it's fresh or salt water you're fishing in, a Florida State Fishing License is required for anyone 16 and older. A few of the fish that are frequently caught within the park include: snapper, sea trout, bass, and bluegill. It is possible to fish from the shoreline, but good locations are extremely limited. There are countless fishing spots for those with a boat. Before heading out on the water, be sure to know the state fishing regulations and catch limits. No boat? No problem. A number of fishing guides provide service from Everglades City for guests looking to spend a few hours out on the water.

Everglades City Go Fish Guide Service • (239) 695-0687
400 Buckner Square; Everglades City, FL 34139
www.gofishguides.com
Rates: 1 Person $350 (half-day)/$550 (full-day)

Captain Derrick Daffin • (239) 695-3513 • (Call for rates)
41 E. Flamingo Drive; Everglades City, FL 34139
www.fishingintheeverglades.com

Hook N Line Charters • (239) 253-9926
201 West Broadway; Everglades City, FL 34139
www.hooknlinecharters.com
Rates: 1–3 People $350 (half-day)/$550 (full-day)

Everglades Absolute Fishing Charters • (239) 695-2608
406 South Storter Avenue; Everglades City, FL 34139
www.evergladesabsolutefishing.com
Rates: 1–2 People $375 (half-day)/$550 (full-day)

Captain Dan Fishing • (239) 695-4566
305 Collier Avenue; Chokoloskee, FL 34139
www.captdanny.com
Rates: 1–2 People $350 (half-day)/$550 (full-day)

Capt Becky Campbell Fishing Charters • (239) 695-2029
Everglades City, FL 34139
www.evergladesfishingcharters.com
Rates: 1–2 People $375 (half-day)/$575 (full-day)

Steve Cox Guide Service • (561) 371-2087 • (239) 695-8497
33 Plantation Drive; Everglades City, FL 34139
www.fish-everglades.com
Rates: 1–2 People $350 (half-day)/$550 (full-day)

Everglades City Fishing Charters • (239) 253-9926
200 Hibiscus Street W; Everglades City, FL 34139
www.evergladescityfishingcharters.com
Rates: 1–3 People $350 (half-day)/$550 (full-day)

Everglades Coastline Fishing Charters • (239) 695-2429
PO Box 34; Everglades City, FL 34139
www.evergladescoastlinecharters.com
Rates: 1–2 People $350 (half-day)/$550 (full-day)

For Kids

Kids get a kick out of seeing **alligators**. The best chance to see these reptilian friends is at **Shark Valley Loop Road, Anhinga Trail**, or outside the park along **Tamiami Trail (US-41)**. Children ages 12 and older will love the ranger-led **Slough Slog**. Slough sloggers must bring water, sturdy close-toed, lace up shoes, and long pants. The program is limited to 15 participants. To sign up or receive additional information, visit Ernest F. Coe Visitor Center or call (305) 242-7700.

Children are encouraged to participate in the **Junior Ranger Program**. Junior Ranger booklets are available at the park website or visitor centers. Complete the activities for Everglades National Park to earn a park badge. The program is jointly administered by **Big Cypress National Preserve, Biscayne National Park**, and **Everglades National Park**. Completing the entire book will earn you a South Florida National Parks Junior Ranger Patch.

Ranger Programs

Everglades' ranger programs include walks, talks, slogs, and tours. Most programs begin at one of the park's visitor centers. Guests are able to enjoy an **Early Bird Walk, Canoe Trip, Shoreline Stroll, West Lake Walk, Bayside Talk, Mahogany Hammock Walk, Naturalist Knapsack**, and evening programs at Flamingo Visitor Center. Gulf Coast Visitor Center offers an **Eye on the Everglades** program where a park ranger discusses ecology, history, and other important issues currently impacting the park. Guests are invited to join an "**Anhinga Amble**" or "**Glades Glimpses**," which depart from Royal Palm Visitor Center. **Shark Bites Program** offers hands on learning at Shark Valley. A current schedule of ranger programs can be found at the park website or its newspaper (available at most entrance stations and visitor centers).

Fauna

The Everglades is the most important breeding ground for tropical wading birds in North America. Sixteen species inhabit the park. Most common is the white ibis, but you may also encounter wood storks, great blue herons, green-backed herons, and roseate spoonbills. Birds of prey, such as ospreys, short-tailed hawks, bald eagles, red-tailed hawks and snail kites also soar high above the "river of

One of a handful of Florida panthers living in the park

grass." In all **more than 350 species of birds** have been identified within the park, making it a favorite destination among the **bird watching** community.

For others, it's the **alligators** that steal the show. Alligators only reside in the park's fresh water. **Anhinga Trail** and **Shark Valley** are two of the best locations to spot a gator. The lower the water level, the farther north you have to go to find these freshwater reptiles.

There are **more than 50 other species of reptiles** inhabiting the park, including the endangered or threatened **American crocodile, green sea turtle**, and **eastern indigo**. With so many flying and swimming attractions, the park's **40 species of mammals** often go unnoticed. The **Florida panther** is rarely seen because of its stealthy travel and diminished numbers (maybe 10 left in the park) due to habitat loss. Other popular mammals include white-tailed deer, river otter, cottontail, and manatee.

A world of life exists beneath the water's surface. **Nearly 300 species of fresh and salt water fish** swim in the park's waters. You won't find any sweeping mountain panoramas here, but you'll definitely find some of the world's most diverse and interesting wildlife.

A great blue heron

Flora

Visitors constantly pass from one ecosystem to the next while exploring the Everglades. Each has its own unique plant and animal life. (See the map on page 130 for a pictorial view of the park's ecosystems.) A multitude of trees, lichens, ferns, fungi, and wildflowers combine to total **more than 1,000 species of documented plants**.

Sawgrass marshes cover the heart of the park. These marshes are the largest of their kind in the world and the reason it is known as "the river of grass." The region is uncommonly flat, yet "high" ground plays an important role in its biodiversity. Slash pines and palmetto trees occupy the elevated regions, while other trees have adapted to grow in the marshy areas. Hardwood hammocks of mahogany, gumbo-limbo, and cocoa palm trees are able to grow within the marsh in places where limestone is situated slightly above sea level. Trees that can survive in standing water are also found here. Cypress trees manage to live in fresh water, while mangroves have become resilient to the extreme and salty conditions along the coast.

Pets

Pets must be kept on a leash no more than six feet in length at all times and are only permitted on public roadways, roadside campgrounds and picnic areas, maintained grounds surrounding public facilities and residential areas, and aboard boats.

Accessibility

All five visitor centers are accessible to individuals in wheelchairs. Several hiking trails have a paved or boardwalk surface that allows wheelchair accessibility. They include: Anhinga Trail, Gumbo Limbo Trail, Pineland Trail, Pa-hay-okee Overlook, Mahogany Hammock Trail, West Lake Trail, and Bobcat Hammock. Long Pine Key and Flamingo Campgrounds have accessible campsites, restrooms, and parking. Only one backcountry campsite is accessible to individuals with mobility impairments, Pearl Bay Chickees, located about four hours (by canoe) from Main Park Road. The site features handrails, a canoe dock, and an accessible chemical toilet. Many of the ranger-led programs (page 135) are fully accessible. Check the park website or newspaper for details. Boat (page 134) and Shark Valley Tram Tours (350.221.8455, www.sharkvalleytramtours.com) are accessible.

 # Weather

The Everglades enjoy the same subtropical climate as the rest of southern Florida. Summers are hot and humid with frequent thunderstorms. Hurricane season stretches from June to November. Thunderstorms and hurricanes are bad news, but mosquitoes are a constant nuisance in summer when they reign over the park. If you plan on traveling to the Everglades between May and November pack plenty of bug spray. Most visitors choose to visit between December and April when temperatures are comfortable and regular winds help keep the bugs at bay. This time frame also features the widest variety of attractions and longest hours of operation.

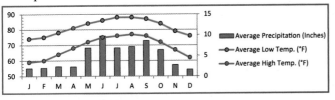

Vacation Planner

Everglades National Park has three main regions (page 130): Main Entrance to Flamingo, Shark Valley, and Gulf Coast. It's conceivable that you could visit all three in a single day, but to do so would require an awful lot of driving (300+ miles beginning and ending in Miami). It's better to take your time, enjoy the sites, and enjoy a region one day at a time. Feel free to treat each day as an individual trip, since none of the regions are connected by roadways. Lodging and dining facilities are not available inside the park. Dining, grocery stores, lodging, festivals, and attractions outside the park are listed on pages 145–149.

 A trip to the Everglades should begin at **Ernest Coe Visitor Center**. Quickly introduce yourself to the park by browsing exhibits and watching a short film. Don't forget to check the schedule of ranger-led activities (page 135). You may even want to make advance reservations (305.242.7700) for a **Slough Slog**, which is exceptional. If not, don't worry, as all the ranger programs are enjoyable. Note the time and location of any programs that interest you, and head into the park. Immediately stop at **Royal Palm** to hike **Anhinga Trail**. It's the best hiking trail. Take your time searching for wildlife before returning to your car and Main Park Road. If you plan on camping at **Long Pine Key** now is the time to secure a site. You don't have to set up camp right away, but at least register and

leave something of little value in your site. If you packed a cooler and are planning an extended hike/bike/paddle, you may want to set up camp right away since there's a good chance you won't return until evening. Continue southwest on the park road. **Pahay-okee** is worth a stop, especially if you don't plan on visiting Shark Valley (Day 2). Next is **Mahogany Hammock**. If you like trees, pull over and have a look. Return to your car and drive to **Flamingo**. This stretch of road (and Flamingo) is home to some of the park's best **hiking** (page 133), **biking** (page 134), and **paddling** (page 132). You won't have time to do them all, but **West Lake Trail** is recommended for hiking, **Hell's Bay Trail** for paddling, and **Snake Bight/Rowdy Bend Trail** for biking. You'll also find a nice campground at **Flamingo** (page 130).

 If you spent the night in Flamingo, wake up early to watch for wildlife. **Eco and Mrazek Ponds** are good locations to watch for birds. If you camped at Long Pine Key you've got another opportunity to catch one of the rangers' **Glades Glimpses**, **Anhinga Ambles**, or **Slough Slogs**. You have plenty of time to spare, because today you're just heading to **Shark Valley**. While driving, decide whether you want to take bicycles (available for rent at Shark Valley) or the **Tram Tour** along 15-mile Shark Valley Loop Road to an observation deck. The Tram Tour takes 2 hours. Biking at a casual pace requires a similar amount of time. You may want to allow even more time, because you'll be mesmerized by the amount of wildlife you'll see along the way. Exploring Shark Valley is at the top of the list when it comes to "must-do" activities at Everglades.

Shark Valley Tram Tours • (305) 221-8455
Shark Valley Loop Road; Miami, FL 33194 • Bike Rental: $7/hr
www.sharkvalleytramtours.com • Tram Tour: $18.25/Adult

 Complete your adventure by traveling to **Gulf Coast Visitor Center** at the park's western edge. This area is popular as a terminus for the 99-mile **Wilderness Waterway** (page 132), **boat tours** (page 134), and **paddling** (page 132). If you aren't interested in any of these things, you may want to skip this region altogether, or head further up the coast to **Marco Island** to sit on the beach.

Fort Jefferson dominates Garden Key and Dry Tortugas National Park

Dry Tortugas - Florida

Dry Tortugas Park Headquarters is at Everglades National Park
40001 State Road 9336
Homestead, Florida 33034
Phone: (305) 242-7700

Write the Park at:
PO Box 6208; Key West, FL 33041
Website: www.nps.gov/drto

Established: October 26, 1992
January 4, 1935 (Nat'l Monument)
Size: 64,700 Acres
Annual Visitors: 54,000
Peak Season: April–May

Activities: Snorkeling, SCUBA, Bird Watching, Paddling, Fishing

Campgrounds: There are 8 primitive campsites on Garden Key
Camping Fee: $3 per person/night
Overflow camping and one group site are also available.
Lodging: None

Park Hours: All Year
Entrance Fee: $5/Person (17 & older)

The collection of United States national parks is best defined by its awe-inspiring vistas, gaping canyons, rugged mountains, and spouting geysers. Natural wonders whose images proved America was as beautiful as it was prosperous. Among this collection hides an aberration of sorts. Just 70 miles southwest of Key West is a park centered around a military fort. **Fort Jefferson** is a man-made military relic, whose massive brick structure serves as centerpiece of the Dry Tortugas. Many visitors are attracted to the area's military past, but there's also a unique world of natural wonders to be enjoyed above and below the sea. Seven low-lying keys and their surrounding waters provide sanctuary for an array of bird and marine life. Beneath the water is a snorkeler's playground filled with colorful corals, corroding shipwrecks, and casual sea turtles.

Now endangered, the region's once dense population of sea turtles provided inspiration for the archipelago's name. In 1513, **Juan Ponce de León** claimed to have caught some 160 turtles in the waters surrounding the islands, declaring them "las Tortugas (The Turtles)." Years later the word "Dry" was added to warn mariners of the island's lack of fresh water. As American prosperity increased, the 75-mile wide strait between the Gulf of Mexico and Atlantic Ocean became a busy shipping route as massive amounts of cotton, meat, livestock, coffee, tobacco, and other merchandise were shipped from the Gulf Coast. Something was needed to suppress piracy and protect the trade route.

Peering through a window to Fort Jefferson's moat

Fort Jefferson was the solution. Construction began in 1847, and after 16 million bricks and 30 years of intermittent work, the fortress remained unfinished. Even in its incomplete state it was the most sophisticated coastal fortress from Maine to California and the largest masonry structure in the western hemisphere. Its design called for 420 heavy-guns and 2,000 soldiers. The fort served as a prison for deserters of the Union Army during the Civil War. In 1888, the Army turned the fortress over to the Marine Hospital Service to be used as a quarantine station. In 1908, **President Theodore Roosevelt** observed the area's importance as a refuge for birds and created the Tortugas Keys Reservation.

Nearly a quarter of a century later, the area's recreational usefulness was recognized when **President Franklin D. Roosevelt** established Fort Jefferson National Monument in 1935, and in 1992 it was designated as a national park. Fort Jefferson, although in need of maintenance, is still standing guard over the gulf. Life is teeming beneath the sea. Thousands of migratory birds flock to the islands, including about 80,000 sooty terns that nest on the keys between February and September. In fact, more sooty terns visit the park each year than tourists, making Dry Tortugas an excellent choice for a relaxing vacation in a tropical paradise with a military past.

When to Go

The park is open all year. April and May are considered the best months to visit due to calm seas, few thunderstorms, and comfortable temperatures. Fort Jefferson is open daily from dawn until dusk. Middle and East Keys close from April to mid-October for turtle nesting.

Directions & Transportation

The park is 70 miles southwest of Key West, FL. It can only be reached by sea plane or boat. Three boat and sea plane operators provide service to and from the park:

<u>Dry Tortugas National Park Ferry</u> • (305) 294-7009
240 Margaret Street; Key West, FL 33040
www.yankeefreedom.com
Rates: $165 (adult)/$120 (child 4–16) (Includes Park Entrance)

<u>Sunny Days Catamarans</u> • (305) 296-5556
201 Elizabeth Street; Key West, FL 33040
www.sunnydayskeywest.com
Rates: $145 (adult)/$100 (child 3-16) plus Entrance Fee

<u>Key West Seaplane Adventures</u> • (305) 293-9300
3471 South Roosevelt Blvd; Key West, FL 33040
www.keywestseaplanecharters.com
Rates: Adult $249(half)/$435(full), Child (3–12) $199/$349

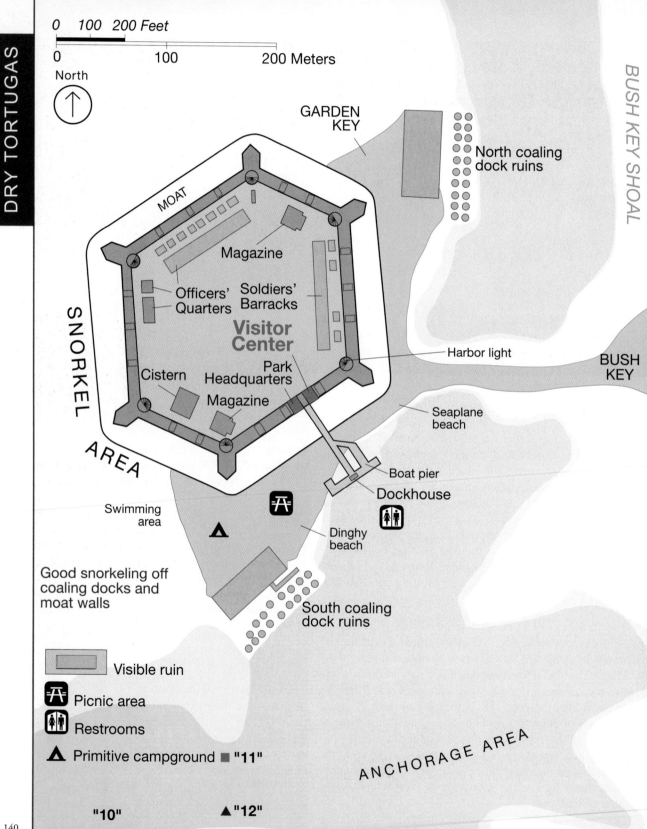

DRY TORTUGAS

0   100   200 Feet

0   100   200 Meters

North

GARDEN
KEY

North coaling
dock ruins

BUSH KEY SHOAL

MOAT

Magazine

SNORKEL

Officers'
Quarters

Soldiers'
Barracks

Visitor
Center

Harbor light

BUSH
KEY

Cistern

Park
Headquarters

AREA

Magazine

Seaplane
beach

Swimming
area

Boat pier

Dockhouse

Good snorkeling off
coaling docks and
moat walls

Dinghy
beach

South coaling
dock ruins

Visible ruin

Picnic area

Restrooms

Primitive campground   ■ "11"

ANCHORAGE AREA

"10"   ▲ "12"

140

Fort Jefferson

In the early 19th century, the U.S. was in search of an ideal location for a fort to protect the profitable Gulf Coast–Atlantic Ocean trade route. Dry Tortugas was just the place, but when U.S. Navy Commodore David Porter visited these remote keys in 1825 he declared them completely unsuitable. He called the islands specks of land without a trace of fresh water among a sea of blue, and probably not even stable enough to build the fort they desired.

Four years later, Commodore John Rodgers revisited the Dry Tortugas. He believed it to be the perfect location. In 1847, after 17 years of engineering studies and bureaucratic delays construction of Fort Jefferson began. The fort, named for the third president, was to be the scourge of the seas, equipped with 420 heavy-guns and a fleet of warships capable of running down ships wise enough to remain beyond firing range. It took a huge workforce to build such an immense structure, including blacksmiths, machinists, carpenters, and masons. Even the resident prisoners and slaves helped build the behemoth. By 1860, more than $250,000 (~$10 million today) had been spent on a fort that wasn't half completed. During the Civil War an influx of prisoners, mostly Union deserters, caused the fort's population to peak at more than 1,500, and new prisoners were immediately put to work.

In 1865, the fort welcomed its most famous prisoner, **Dr. Samuel Mudd,** who was convicted of conspiracy in the assassination of **President Abraham Lincoln**. It is believed that he set, splinted, and bandaged **John Wilkes Booth's** broken leg shortly after Booth shot the President at Ford's Theater. Not long after his arrival, the prison's doctor died during an outbreak of yellow fever. Mudd temporarily took over the position. Soldiers, feeling indebted to Mudd, petitioned the president on his behalf, and four years after he arrived Mudd was pardoned by President Andrew Johnson.

By 1888, the usefulness of Fort Jefferson was waning and damage caused by the corrosive tropical environment and frequent hurricanes created high maintenance costs. The Army decided to turn the fort over to the Marine Hospital Service. They used it as a quarantine station up until the 1930s when it was officially handed over to the National Park Service, which possesses it today.

Small fish hiding in brain coral

Fort Jefferson and its moat

 Camping

There are 8 primitive campsites on **Garden Key** near Fort Jefferson. These sites are available on a first-come, first-served basis for $3 per person per night, payable at a self-service pay station. If the primitive sites are full, an overflow camping area is available. One group site is available for groups of 10–20 campers by reservation (call 305.242.7700). Campers must bring all food and water required for the duration of their stay. Composting toilets are available in the campground. Wood fires are prohibited.

Hiking

Besides underwater, the only real place to explore Dry Tortugas is **Fort Jefferson** itself. Here you'll find a self-guided tour that takes visitors through the history of the 50-foot tall, three-story, heavily armored fort. Visitors can also walk along the park's 0.6-mile long seawall and moat where you may be able to spot various sea creatures.

Brain coral

Paddling

Paddling allows observant visitors to keep an eye on what's happening above and below the water. Crystal clear waters provide a window to life beneath the sea. When you aren't watching the creatures stirring below your boat, look along the horizon for migratory birds. **Bush and Long Keys** are the closest islands to Fort Jefferson and where you are most likely to find nesting birds. **Loggerhead**, the largest key of the Dry Tortugas, is three miles away. It's perfect for swimming and snorkeling and never busy, since visitation is limited to 24 visitors per day. To get to Loggerhead Key you must pass deep open water with a swift current. (Inexperienced paddlers should not head out into open water.) No matter where you paddle, a **boating permit** is required. If you plan on paddling to Loggerhead Key, it must be listed on your permit. Permits are free and may be obtained on arrival from a park staff member. **Shark and Coral Special Protection Zones** are closed to paddling. You should ask where these areas are in order to avoid them. Ferries will transport your kayak(s) to Dry Tortugas, but they have limited space. It is a good idea to confirm space requirements prior to arrival.

SCUBA

Dry Tortugas National Park is located at the far western end of the Florida Keys. These islands are not tethered to the mainland by roads and bridges, so SCUBA divers must arrive by private boat or charter.

Beneath the water divers will find the **Caribbean's largest and healthiest reef system**. One of the highlights is **Sherwood Forest**, featuring a canopy of mushroom-shaped formations. **More than 400 species of fish** reside here; of them, hammerhead sharks, barracuda, and Goliath grouper are frequently seen. Dolphins and turtles are also common to the area. The following charters are allowed to conduct dives in the park.

Sea Clusive • (305) 744-9928
17195 Kingfish Ln W; Sugarloaf Shores, FL 33042
www.seaclusive.com
Charter Rates: $2,600/day (8 Guest minimum)

Research Vessel Tiburon, Inc • (305) 849-0352
1107 Key Plaza 299; Key West, FL
www.researchvesseltiburon.com

Seawillow Sailing LLC • (504) 460-1346
www.schoonerjollyrover.com

Spree Expeditions • (281) 970-0534
www.spreeexpeditions.com

Snorkeling

More than 99% of the park is water, so you really have to get in or under the water to experience it. Dry Tortugas just might be the best snorkeling the Florida Keys has to offer. The water is clean, clear, and warm. A boat or sea plane trip is required to reach them, but once you're there, the reef is yours to explore whenever you want. A designated snorkel area is available on **Garden Key**, southwest of Fort Jefferson along its outer wall. You can walk right into the water from the designated swimming area. The area features chest-deep water, turtle grass, and coral. Coral reefs make up a very small fraction of the underwater environment, but they provide habitat for more than 25% of the area's fish population. If you traveled to the island by one of the boat operators, they usually carry a few sets of snorkel gear for their passengers to use. You can also take a private charter service for a more intimate snorkel adventure:

Calypso Watersports Charter • (305) 451-1988
257 Atlantic Blvd; Key Largo, FL 33037
www.calypsosailing.com
Rates: Call for rates (Groups of 6 to 36 are required)

Fishing

Due to excessive commercial fishing new regulations prohibit fishing in about half of the park's waters. The ban was required to help repopulate a once thriving fish community. Good fishing is still possible in and around Dry Tortugas, and the scenery and climate is a serious bonus. Calm water makes spring and summer the preferred seasons for fishing. Grouper and snapper are commonly caught. Dry Tortugas National Park fishing excursions are available from several Key West area charters. A wide variety of multi-day, multi-angler trips are available ranging anywhere from $600–3,300 (call for exact rates).

Dream Catcher Charters
5555 College Road; Key West, FL 33040
(888) 362-3474 • (305) 292-7212 • (305) 304-5808 (Mobile)
www.dreamcatchercharters.com

Lethal Weapon • (305) 296-6999
1418 Angela Street; Key West, FL 33040
www.lethalweaponcharters.com

Andy Griffiths Charters • (305) 296-2639
40 Key Haven Road; Key West, FL 33040
www.fishandy.com

Eddie Griffiths Charters • (305) 587-3437
Key West, Marquesas Keys/Dry Tortugas
www.fishcapteddie.com

Compass Rose Charters • (305) 294-3399
1801 N Roosevelt Blvd; Key West, FL 33040
www.fishnkw.com

Charter Boat Triple Time • (305) 296-8210
2419 Patterson Ave; Key West, FL 33040
www.fishtripletime.com

For Kids

Dry Tortugas is a great park for kids. Children of all ages love the water, the beach, the wildlife, and they might even love Fort Jefferson. If the fort's history isn't holding their attention, they will at least have fun climbing the spiral staircases, gazing into the moat, and pretending to fire 19th century cannons.

Children can also become **Junior Rangers**. A free workbook is available online or at the visitor center. Complete it to earn a park badge. The program is recommended for children ages 8–13.

Bird Watching

Nearly 300 bird species have been identified within park boundaries. Most notable are tropical and migratory species that delight bird watchers as they pit-stop in the Dry Tortugas. Only 7 species nest here regularly; most commonly seen are brown and black noddies, magnificent frigatebirds, and masked and brown boobies. Spring is prime time for bird watching. The **Audubon Society** sponsors guided birding tours in April and May. Between May and September **80,000 sooty terns** nest on Bush Key. Bush Key is visible from Garden Key and Fort Jefferson, but don't leave your binoculars at home.

Boat Tours

Sunny Days and **Yankee Freedom** provide boat service to Dry Tortugas National Park from Key West, FL (see page 139 for contact information and rates). The trip takes approximately two hours each way. Breakfast and lunch are served aboard the boat. They have limited space available to transport personal kayaks. A few sets of snorkel gear are usually available for you to use. Knowledgeable guides provide tours of Fort Jefferson. Snorkelers and swimmers will be able to rinse off with freshwater on board the boat. Complimentary soft drinks, water, and tea are available throughout the day.

Ranger Programs

When you arrive at Dry Tortugas check the announcement board near the dock to see what ranger-led activities are taking place that day. Several rangers live on the island, and they provide intermittent tours.

Guests who reach the island via one of the two boat operators (page 139) typically receive a 45-minute guided tour of the fort.

During April and early May, the **Audubon Society** sponsors guided bird watching trips.

An aerial view of Loggerhead Key

Vacation Planner

The length of your Dry Tortugas Vacation depends on how you arrive and if you're going to camp. **Tour boats** (page 143) afford guests right around 4 hours of free time on **Garden Key**, and schedules are somewhat predetermined. While you can do your own thing, most guests take a tour of **Fort Jefferson** with the boat operator. Then you have lunch aboard the boat, and are left with a small amount of free time to **swim** or **snorkel**. If you arrive by seaplane you can choose whether you want to spend 4 or 8 hours basking in the tropical setting. For most visitors four hours is more than enough to tour Fort Jefferson, swim, paddle (if you brought along your kayak), and relax in the South Florida sun. If you'd like more time, bring your tent with you and camp (page 141) at one of 8 primitive sites on the island. South Florida's best restaurants, grocery stores, lodging, festivals, and attractions are listed on pages 145–149.

 Immediately check the dockside announcement board for a listing of daily **ranger-led activities** when you reach **Garden Key**. It's recommended you attend any tours offered while you're on the island. There isn't a whole lot of room to roam, so your free-time activities are limited to the basics: **bird watching** (page 143), **snorkeling** (page 142), and **paddling** (page 142).

Flora & Fauna

The park's vegetation is fairly limited. You'll find a variety of palms and succulents, but several islands are nothing more than sand, almost completely devoid of life. Sea grasses and other marine plant life can be found underwater.

Nearly 300 species of birds have been identified in the park, but only 7 species nest here regularly. The park protects the most active turtle nesting site in the Florida Keys. **Hawksbill, loggerhead, and green sea turtles** are commonly seen swimming in the park's waters. Each year female sea turtles climb onto sandy beaches of Middle and East Keys to lay their eggs before retreating back to the sea. You'll also find an amazing variety of coral, fish, and other marine life underwater. Sea fans, anemones, lobster, and sponges are often found on the sea floor. Coral reef inhabitants may include numerous colorful reef fish and their predators: amberjacks, groupers, wahoos, tarpon, sharks, and barracudas.

Basics

Pets: Pets are permitted on Garden Key but are not allowed inside Fort Jefferson. They must be kept on a leash no more than six feet in length.

Accessibility: The dock, campground, visitor center, bottom level of Fort Jefferson, and tour boats are accessible to individuals in wheelchairs.

Weather: Dry Tortugas National Park experiences three seasons. December to March is the winter season when you can expect windy weather and angry seas. The tropical storm season spans from June to November. It is marked by hot and humid days with occasional thunderstorms. Hurricane activity is not unheard of during this time. Finally, there's tourist season, which includes April and May. This period provides nearly perfect weather for a tropical vacation. Due to the highly erratic nature of the area's weather, visitors should check an extended weather forecast the day before you intend to leave for vacation.

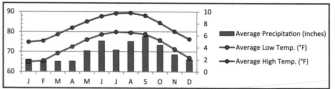

Dining

East of the Everglades

Casita Tejas • (305) 248-8224
27 N Krome Ave.; Homestead, FL 33030
www.casitatejas.com • Entrée: $10–12

Mario's Latin Café • (305) 247-2470
1090 N Homestead Blvd; Homestead, FL 33030

La Quebradita Taqueria • (305) 245-4586
702 N Krome Ave; Homestead, FL 33030

Sams Kitchen • (305) 246-2990
1320 N Krome Ave; Homestead, FL 33030

Mamma Mia • (305) 248-3133
538 Washington Ave; Homestead, FL 33030

Royal Palm Grill & Deli • (305) 246-5701
806 N Krome Ave; Homestead, FL 33030

Nikko Japanese Restaurant • (305) 242-8772
827 N Homestead Blvd; Homestead, FL 33030

China Yan • (305) 245-8822
2846 NE 8th St; Homestead, FL 33033

Shiver's BBQ • (305) 248-2272
28001 S Dixie Hwy; Homestead, FL 33033
www.shiversbbq.com

Portofino Coal Fired Pizza • (786) 243-4000
Ste 112, 650 NE 22 Ter; Homestead, FL 33033
www.portofinocoalfiredpizza.com • Pizza: $16+

Bangkok Cuisine • (305) 248-6611
27319 S Dixie Hwy; Homestead, FL 33032
www.bangkokcuisinemiami.com • Entrée: $11–17

Miyagi Sushi Bar & Grill • (305) 248-3333
Ste 102, 650 NE 22nd Ter; Homestead, FL 33033
www.miyagisushibar.com • Entrée: $10–25

Black Point Ocean Grill • (305) 258-3918
24775 SW 87th Ave; Homestead, FL 33032

Captain's Restaurant & Seafood
404 SE 1st Ave; Homestead, FL 33034

Sonny's Real Pit Bar-B-Q • (305) 245-8585
33505 S Dixie Hwy; Homestead, FL 33034
www.sonnysbbq.com

Rosita's Restaurant • (305) 246-3114
199 W Palm Dr; Florida City, FL 33034

West of the Everglades

Joanie's Blue Crab Café • (239) 695-2682
39395 Tamiami Tr E; Ochopee, FL 34141
www.joaniesbluecrabcafe.com • Entrée: $7–16

City Seafood • (239) 695-4700
609 Begonia Str; Everglades, FL 34139
www.cityseafood1.com • Entrée: $8–11

Camellia Street Grill • (239) 695-2003
208 Camellia St; Everglades, FL 34139

Little Bar Restaurant • (239) 394-5663
205 Harbor Pl; Goodland, FL 34140
www.littlebarrestaurant.com

House of Mozart • (239) 642-5220
151 S Barfield Dr; Marco Island, FL 34145
www.houseofmozart.com • Entrée: $19–30

Da Vinci Ristorante Italiano • (239) 389-1888
599 S Collier Blvd, # 113; Marco Island, FL 34145
www.ristorantedavinci.com • Entrée: $15–34

Cocomo's Grill • (239) 394-3600
945 N Collier Blvd; Marco Island, FL 34145
www.cocomosgrill.com • Entrée: $11–25

Vic's Island Pizza • (239) 642-5662
910 N Collier Blvd; Marco Island, FL 34145
www.vicsislandpizza.com

Dolphin Tiki Bar & Café • (239) 394-4048
1001 N Barfield Dr; Marco Island, FL 34145

Hoot's Breakfast & Lunch • (239) 394-4644
563 E Elkcam Circle; Marco Island, FL 34145
www.hootsbreakfastandlunch.com • $4–8

Chefs' Express • (239) 393-2433
176 Royal Palm Dr; Marco Island, FL 34145
www.thechefsexpress.com • Breakfast: $6–19

Island Café • (239) 394-7578
918 N Collier Blvd; Marco Island, FL 34145
www.theislandcafe.com • Entrée: $19–29

Café de Marco • (239) 394-6262
244 Palm St; Marco Island, FL 34145
www.cafedemarco.com

Davide Italian Café & Deli • (239) 393-2233
688 Bald Eagle Dr; Marco Island, FL 34145
www.davideitaliancafe.com • Pizza: $13+

Italian Deli • (239) 394-9493
247 N Collier Blvd # 104; Marco Island, FL 34145

The Florida Keys

Sundowner • (305) 451-5566
103900 Overseas Hwy; Key Largo, FL 33037
www.sundownerskeylargo.com • Entrée: $15–31

The Buzzards Roost • (305) 453-3746
21 Garden Cove Dr; Key Largo, FL 33037
www.buzzroost.com • Entrée: $18–30

Mrs. Mac's Kitchen • (305) 451-3722
99336 Overseas Hwy; Key Largo, FL 33037
www.mrsmacskitchen.com • Entrée: $10–17

Snappers Restaurant • (305) 852-5956
139 Seaside Ave; Key Largo, FL 33037
www.snapperskeylargo.com • Entrée: $13–26

New York Style Pizza • (305) 451-1461
100600 Overseas Hwy; Key Largo, FL 33037

Marlin's Restaurant • (305) 451-2454
102770 Overseas Hwy; Key Largo, FL 33037

Num-Thai & Sushi Bar • (305) 451-5955
103200 Overseas Hwy, # 3; Key Largo, FL 33037

Eco Eats • (305) 451-3902
99607 Overseas Hwy; Key Largo, FL 33037

Harriette's Restaurant • (305) 852-8689
95700 Overseas Hwy; Key Largo, FL 33037

Vallarta Mexican Seafood • (305) 451-4083
105045 Overseas Hwy; Key Largo, FL 33037

Rib Daddy's • (305) 451-0900
102570 Overseas Hwy; Key Largo, FL 33037
www.ribdaddysrestaurant.com • Entrée: $10–30

Tasters Grille & Market • (305) 853-1177
91252 Overseas Hwy; Tavernier, FL 33036
tastersgrille.com • Entrée: $12–27

Old Tavernier • (305) 852-6012
90311 Old Highway; Tavernier, FL 33070
www.oldtavernier.com • Entrée: $14–32

Morada Bay • (305) 664-0604
81590 Overseas Hwy; Islamorada, FL 33036
www.moradabay-restaurant.com • Entrée: $21–29

Pierre's • (305) 664-3225
81600 Overseas Hwy; Islamorada, FL 33036
www.pierres-restaurant.com • Entrée: $18–42

Village Gourmet • (305) 664-4030
82751 Overseas Hwy; Islamorada, FL 33036

Braza Lena • (305) 664-4940
83413 Overseas Hwy; Islamorada, FL 33036
www.brazalena.com

Marker 88 Restaurant • (305) 852-9315
87900 Overseas Hwy; Islamorada, FL 33036
www.marker88.info

Midway Café • (305) 664-2622
80499 Overseas Hwy; Islamorada, FL 33036

Made 2 Order Café • (305) 852-3251
90691 Old Highway; Tavernier, FL 33070
www.made2orderonline.com • Entrée: $10–15

Sparky's Landing • (305) 289-7445
Key Colony Beach; FL 33051
sparkyslanding.com • Entrée: $24–38

Barracuda Grill • (305) 743-3314
4290 Overseas Hwy; Marathon, FL 33050

The Hurricane • (305) 743-2220
4650 Overseas Hwy; Marathon, FL 33050
www.hurricaneblues.com • Entrée: $12–18

Fish Tales Market & Eatery • (305) 743-9196
11711 Overseas Hwy; Marathon, FL 33050
www.floridalobster.com • Sandwich: $4–8

Butterfly Café • (305) 289-7177
2600 Overseas Hwy; Marathon, FL 33050

Stuffed Pig • (305) 743-4059
3520 Overseas Hwy; Marathon, FL 33050
www.thestuffedpig.com

Frank's Grill • (305) 289-7772
11400 Overseas Hwy; Marathon, FL 33050
www.franksgrillmarathon.com

Stout's Restaurant • (305) 743-6437
8349 Overseas Hwy; Marathon, FL 33050

Herbie's Restaurant • (305) 743-6373
6350 Overseas Hwy; Marathon, FL 33050

Keys Fisheries Market • (305) 743-4353
3390 Gulfview Ave; Marathon, FL 33050
www.keysfisheries.com • Entrée: $10–22

Lencho's Restaurant • (305) 743-4500
1622 Overseas Hwy; Marathon, FL 33050

Boondock's Grille & Drafthouse • (305) 872-4094
27205 Overseas Hwy; Summerland Key, FL 33042

Square Grouper • (305) 745-8880
22658 Overseas Hwy; Summerland Key, FL 33042
www.squaregrouperbarandgrill.com • Entrée: $16–32

Wharf Bar & Grill • (305) 745-3322
25163 Overseas Hwy; Summerland Key, FL 33042
www.wharfbarandgrill.com • Entrée: $10–20

2 For 20 Pizza • (305) 872-7444
30348 Overseas Hwy; Big Pine Key, FL 33043

Coco's Kitchen • (305) 872-4495
283 Key Deer Blvd; Big Pine Key, FL 33043
www.cocoskitchen.com • Breakfast: $4–8

Little Palm's Dining • (305) 872-2551
28500 Overseas Hwy, Lower Keys, FL 33042

Blue Heaven • (305) 296-8666
729 Thomas St; Key West, FL 33040
www.blueheavenkw.com

Hurricane Hole • (305) 294-0200
5130 US-1; Key West, FL 33040
www.hurricaneholekeywest.com • Entrée: $13–24

HogFish Bar & Grille • (305) 293-4041
6810 Front St; Stock Island, FL 33040
www.hogfishbar.com • Entrée: $17–24

Camille's Restaurant • (305) 296-4811
1202 Simonton St; Key West, FL 33040
www.camilleskeywest.com • Entrée: $17–26

Thai Life Floating • (305) 296-9907
1801 N Roosevelt Blvd; Key West, FL 33040
www.thailifekeywest.com

El Siboney Restaurant • (305) 296-4184
900 Catherine St; Key West, FL 33040
www.elsiboneyrestaurant.com • Sandwich: $10–16

Matthessen 4th of July • (305) 294-8089
1110 White St; Key West, FL 33040
www.mattheessens.com

Better Than Sex • (305) 296-8102
411 Petronia St; Key West, FL 33040

La Trattoria • (305) 296-1075
524 Duval St; Key West, FL 33040
www.latrattoria.us • Entrée: $14–40

Shanna Key Irish Pub & Grill • (305) 295-8880
1900 Flagler Ave; Key West, FL 33040
www.shannakeyirishpub.com • Entrée: $9–18

Azur Restaurant • (305) 292-2987
425 Grinnell St; Key West, FL 33040
www.azurkeywest.com • Entrée: $11–28

Sarabeth's Kitchen • (305) 293-8181
530 Simonton St; Key West, FL 33040
www.sarabeth.com

Santiago's Bodega • (305) 296-7691
207 Petronia St; Key West, FL 33040
www.santiagosbodega.com • Tapas: $7–12

B O's Fish Wagon • (305) 294-9272
801 Caroline St; Key West, Florida 33040
www.bosfishwagon.com • Entrée: $14–24

Lobo's Grill • (305) 296-5303
5 Key Lime Square; Key West, FL 33040
www.loboskw.com • Sandwich: $7–10

Help Yourself Organic • (305) 296-7766
829 Fleming St; Key West, FL 33040
www.helpyourselfcafe.com • Sandwich: ~$10

Sandy's Café • (305) 295-0159
1026 White St; Key West, FL 33040

Kennedy Café • (305) 809-9000
924 Kennedy Dr, # A; Key West, FL 33040

Flaming Buoy Filet • (305) 295-7970
1100 Packer St; Key West, FL 33040

Pepe's Café • (305) 294-7192
806 Caroline St; Key West, Florida 33040
www.pepescafe.net • Entrée: $10–30

Thai Island • (305) 296-9198
711 Eisenhower Dr; Key West, FL 33040
www.thaiislandrestaurant.com • Entrée: $15–21

Bonnie & Clyde Restaurant • (305) 293-9500
3800 N Roosevelt Blvd; Key West, FL 33040

Café Des Artistes Pisces • (305) 294-7100
1007 Simonton St; Key West, FL 33040
www.pisceskeywest.com • Entrée: $27–44

Origami Japanese • (305) 294-0092
1075 Duval St, # C3; Key West, FL 33040

The Café • (305) 296-5515
509 Southard St; Key West, FL 33040
www.thecafekw.com

Caroline's • (305) 294-7511
310 Duval St; Key West, FL 33040

Grocery Stores
East of the Everglades
Whole Foods Market • (305) 971-0900
11701 South Dixie Hwy; Pinecrest, FL 33156

Costco • (305) 964-4227
13450 SW 120th St; Kendall, FL 33186

Publix Super Market • (305) 242-5530
3060 NE 41st Ter; Homestead, FL 33033

Winn-Dixie • (305) 246-3998
30346 Old Dixie Hwy; Homestead, FL 33033

Walmart Supercenter • (305) 242-4447
33501 S Dixie Hwy; Florida City, FL 33034

West of the Everglades
Whole Foods Market • (239) 552-5100
9101 Strada Pl; Naples, FL 34108

Publix Super Market • (239) 775-8800
4860 Davis Blvd; Naples, FL 34104

Walmart Supercenter • (239) 254-8310
5420 Juliet Blvd; Naples, FL 34109

Costco • (239) 596-6404
6275 Naples Blvd; Naples, FL 34109

Winn-Dixie • (239) 352-6159
4849 Golden Gate Pkwy; Naples, FL 34116

The Florida Keys
Winn-Dixie • (305) 451-0328
105300 Overseas Hwy; Key Largo, FL 33037

Publix Super Market • (305) 451-0808
101437 Overseas Hwy; Key Largo, FL 33037

Winn-Dixie • (305) 852-5904
91200 Overseas Hwy, # 14; Tavernier, FL 33070

Winn-Dixie • (305) 743-3636
5585 Overseas Hwy; Marathon, FL 33050

Publix Super Market • (305) 289-2920
5407 Overseas Hwy; Marathon, FL 33050

Winn-Dixie • (305) 872-4124
251 Key Deer Blvd; Big Pine Key, FL 33043

Publix Super Market • (305) 296-2225
3316 N Roosevelt Blvd; Key West, FL 33040

Winn-Dixie • (305) 294-3664
2760 N Roosevelt Blvd; Key West, FL 33040

Albertsons • (305) 292-2013
1112 Key Plz; Key West, FL 33040

Lodging
East of the Everglades
Floridian Inn • (305) 247-7020
990 N Homestead Blvd; Homestead, FL 33030
www.floridianhotel.com • Rates: $59–69/night

Everglades Int'l Hostel • (305) 248-1122
20 SW 2nd Ave; Florida City, FL 33034
www.evergladeshostel.com • Rates: $28–100

Florida City RV Park • (305) 248-7889
601 NW 3rd Ave; Florida City, FL 33034

Everglades Motel • (305) 247-4117
605 S Krome Ave; Homestead, FL 33030

The Inn of Homestead • (305) 248-2121
1020 N Homestead Blvd; Homestead, FL 33030
www.theinn.ofhomestead.com

West of the Everglades

Ivey House B&B • (239) 695-3299
107 Camelia St; Everglades, FL 34139
www.iveyhouse.com • Rates: $74–179

Everglades City Motel • (239) 695-4224
310 Collier Ave; Everglades, FL 34139
www.evergladescitymotel.com • Call for rates

River Wilderness Waterfront Villas • (239) 695-4499
210 Collier Ave; Everglades, FL 34139
www.river-wilderness.com • Call for rates

The Captain's Table Lodge & Villas • (239) 695-4211
102 E Broadway St; Everglades, FL 34139
www.captainstablehotel.com • Rates: $65–170

Everglades Rod and Gun Club Hotel • (239) 695-2101
200 Riverside Dr; Everglades, FL 34139
www.evergladesrodandgun.com • Rates: $95–140

Marco Beach Ocean Resort • (239) 393-1400
480 S Collier Blvd; Marco Island, FL 34145
www.marcoresort.com • Rates: $149+

Olde Marco Island Inn & Suites • (239) 394-3131
100 Palm St; Marco Island, FL 34145
www.oldemarcoinn.com • Rates: $126+

The Boat House Motel • (239) 642-2400
1180 Edington Pl; Marco Island, FL 34145
www.theboathousemotel.com • Rates: $96–192

Beach Club of Marco • (239) 394-9951
901 S Collier Blvd; Marco Island, FL 34145
www.beachclubvacationrentals.com • Rates: $100+

Surf Club • (239) 642-5800
540 S Collier Blvd; Marco Island, FL 34145
www.surfclub.hgvc.com

Lakeside Inn • (239) 394-1161
155 1st Ave; Marco Island, FL 34145
www.marcoislandlakeside.com • Rates: $94+

Port of the Islands • (239) 394-7700
12323 Union Rd; Naples, FL 34114
www.poihotels.com • Rates: $49–89

The Florida Keys

Rock Reef Resort • (305) 852-2401
97850 Overseas Hwy; Key Largo, FL 33037
www.rockreefresort.com • Rates: $77–260

Dove Creek Lodge • (305) 852-6200
147 Seaside Ave; Key Largo, FL 33037
www.ascendcollection.com • Rates: $229+

Kona Kai Resort • (305) 852-7200
97802 Overseas Hwy; Key Largo, FL 33037
www.konakairesort.com • Rates: $199–369

Azul Del Mar • (305) 451-0337
104300 Overseas Hwy; Key Largo, FL 33037
www.azulkeylargo.com • Rates: $139+

Largo Lodge Motel • (305) 451-0424
101740 Overseas Hwy; Key Largo, FL 33037
www.largolodge.com • Rates: $115–195

Island Bay Resort • (305) 852-4087
92530 Overseas Hwy; Tavernier, FL 33070
www.islandbayresort.com • Rates: $129–219

Coconut Palm Inn • (305) 852-3017
198 Harborview Dr; Tavernier, FL 33070
www.coconutpalminn.com • Rates: $129–239

The Moorings Village • (305) 664-4708
123 Beach Rd; Islamorada, FL 33036
www.themooringsvillage.com

Coral Bay Resort • (305) 664-5568
75690 Overseas Hwy; Islamorada, FL 33036
www.coralbayresort.com • Rates: $119–305

Pines and Palms Resort • (305) 664-4343
80401 Old Hwy; Islamorada, FL 33036
www.pinesandpalms.com • Rates: $89–239

Tranquility Bay • (305) 289-0888
2600 Overseas Hwy; Marathon, FL 33050
www.tranquilitybay.com • Rates: $300+

Cocoplum Beach and Tennis Club • (305) 743-0240
109 Coco Plum Dr; Marathon, FL 33050
www.cocoplum.com • Rates: $100–360

Bay View Inn • (305) 289-1525
3 North Conch Ave; Marathon, FL 33050
www.bayviewinn.com • Rates: $119–179

Valhalla Beach Resort • (305) 289-0616
56243 Ocean Dr; Marathon, FL 33050
www.valhallabeach.com • Rates: $89–150

Coral Lagoon • (305) 289-1323
12399 Overseas Hwy, # 1; Marathon, FL 33050
www.corallagoonresort.com • Rates: $279+

Sea Scape Resort • (305) 743-6212
1075 75th St Ocean E; Marathon, FL 33050
www.seascapemotelandmarina.com • Rates: $125+

Anchor Inn Motel • (305) 743-2213
7931 Overseas Hwy; Marathon, FL 33050
www.anchorinnkeys.com

Deer Run B&B • (305) 872-2015
1997 Long Beach Dr; Big Pine Key, FL 33043
www.deerrunfloridabb.com • Rates: $225–355

Parmer's Resort • (305) 872-2157
565 Barry Ave; Summerland Key, FL 33042
www.parmersresort.com • Rates: $99–324

Royal Palm RV Park • (305) 872-9856
163 Cunningham Ln; Big Pine Key, FL 33043
www.royalpalmrvpark.homestead.com • Rates: $51

White Ibis Inn • (954) 302-2822
125 Colson Dr; Cudjoe Key, FL 33042
www.whiteibisinn.com • Rates: $320–720

Pier House Resort and Spa • (305) 296-4600
1 Duval St; Key West, FL 33040
www.pierhouse.com • Rates: $200+

Southernmost Hotel • (305) 296-6577
1319 Duval St; Key West, FL 33040
www.southernmostresorts.com • Rates: $185+

The Southernmost House • (877) 552-9821
1400 Duval St; Key West, FL 33040
www.southernmosthouse.com • Rates: $180+

Ocean Key Resort & Spa • (305) 296-7701
0 Duval St; Key West, FL 33040
www.oceankey.com • Rates: $349+

Key West Harbor Inn • (305) 296-0898
219 Elizabeth St; Key West, FL 33040
www.keywestharborinn.com • Rates: $165–405

Almond Tree Inn • (305) 296-5415
512 Truman Ave; Key West, FL 33040
www.almondtreeinn.com

Marrero's Guest Mansion • (305) 294-6977
410 Fleming St; Key West, FL 33040
www.marreros.com • Rates: $100–230

Duval Inn • (877) 418-6900
511 Angela St; Key West, FL 33040
www.duvalinn.com • Rates: $99–229

Mermaid & The Alligator B&B • (800) 773-1894
729 Truman Ave; Key West, FL 33040
www.kwmermaid.com • Rates: $149–318

Eden House • (305) 296-6868
1015 Fleming St; Key West, FL 33040
www.edenhouse.com • Rates: $115–300

Orchid Key Inn • (305) 296-9915
1004 Duval St; Key West, FL 33040
www.orchidkey.com

Paradise Inn • (305) 293-8007
819 Simonton St; Key West, FL 33040
www.theparadiseinn.com • Rates: $169–599

Tropical Inn • (305) 294-9977
812 Duval St; Key West, FL 33040
www.tropicalinn.com • Rates: $158–398

The Gardens Hotel • (305) 294-2661
526 Angela St; Key West, FL 33040
www.gardenshotel.com • Rates: $165–695

Seascape, An Inn • (305) 296-7776
420 Olivia St; Key West, FL 33040
www.seascapetropicalinn.com • Rates: $129–234

Santa Maria Suites Resort • (305) 296-5678
1401 Simonton St; Key West, FL 33040
www.santamariasuites.com • Rates: $300+

Coco Plum Inn • (305) 295-2955
615 Whitehead St; Key West, FL 33040
www.cocopluminn.com • Rates: $229–269

The Grand B&B • (888) 947-2630
1116 Grinnell St; Key West, FL 33040
www.thegrandguesthouse.com • Rates: $98–248

Alexander Palms Court • (305) 296-6413
715 South St; Key West, FL 33040
www.alexanderpalms.com • Rates: $110–320

Café Marquesa • (305) 292-1244
600 Fleming St; Key West, FL 33040
www.marquesa.com • Rates: $150–395

Speakeasy Inn Guesthouse • (305) 296-2680
1117 Duval St; Key West, FL 33040
www.speakeasyinn.com • Rates: $129+

Parrot Key Resort • (305) 809-2200
2801 N Roosevelt Blvd; Key West, FL 33040
www.parrotkeyresort.com • Rates: $169+

Knowles House B&B • (305) 296-8132
1004 Eaton St; Key West, FL 33040
www.knowleshouse.com • Rates: $119–249

Casa 325 Guest House • (305) 292-0011
325 Duval St; Key West, FL 33040
www.casa325.com • Rates: $115–395

Key West B&B • (305) 296-7274
415 William St; Key West, FL 33040
www.keywestbandb.com • Rates: $79–285

Not all dining and lodging facilities are listed. Many chain hotels and restaurants can be found nearby in Miami, Homestead, Naples, Key Largo, Islamorada, and Key West.

Festivals

Art Deco Weekend Festival • January
Miami Beach, FL • www.miamiandbeaches.com

Florida Renaissance Festival • January
www.ren-fest.com • Miami

South Beach Wine&Food Festival • February
www.sobewineandfoodfest.com • South Beach

Big "O" Birding Festival • March
www.bigobirdingfestival.com • Moore Haven

Sunfest • April/May
www.sunfest.com • West Palm Beach, FL

Underwater Music Festival • July
31020 Overseas Hwy; Big Pine Key, FL

Hemingway Days • July
www.sloppyjoes.com/lookalikes.htm • Key West

Bon Festival • August
www.morikami.org • Delray Beach, FL

Pioneer Days • September
www.pioneerfloridamuseum.org • Dade City

International Film Festival • October
www.fliff.com/events/asp • Fort Lauderdale

Biketoberfest • October
www.biketoberfest.org • Daytona Beach, FL

American Sandsculpting Festival • November
www.sandsculptingfestival.com/event.php • Fort Myers

Winterfest • December • Fort Lauderdale, FL
www.winterfestparade.com

Attractions
Miami/South Beach
Miami Culinary Tours • (786) 942-8856
1000 5th St, Ste 200; Miami Beach, FL 33139
www.miamiculinarytours.com • Tours: $59

Miami Food Tours • (786) 228-7651
429 Lenox Ave, Ste P-606; Miami Beach, FL 33139
www.miamifoodtours.com • Tours: $53–60

Miami Tour Company • (305) 260-6855
429 Lenox Ave; Miami Beach, FL 33139
www.miamitourcompany.com • Boat/Bus Tours

Miami Jet Ski Rental • (305) 457-1619
401 Biscayne Blvd, #31; Miami, FL 33132
www.miamijetskirental.com

Santa's Enchanted Forest • (305) 893-0090
7900 Bird Rd; Miami, FL 33155
www.santasenchantedforest.com

Oleta River State Park • (305) 919-1844
3400 NE 163rd St; Miami, FL 33160
www.floridastateparks.org • Fee: $6/Vehicle

Holocaust Memorial • (305) 538-1663
1933 Meridian Ave; Miami, FL 33139
www.holocaustmmb.org • Admission: Free

Vizcaya Museum & Gardens • (305) 250-9133
3251 S Miami Ave; Miami, FL 33129
www.vizcayamuseum.org • Admission: $15/Adult

Zoo Miami • (305) 251-0400
12400 SW 152nd St; Miami, FL 33177
www.miamimetrozoo.com • Admission: $16/Adult

East of the Everglades
Miami Gliders • (786) 243-7640
Bldg 10, 28790 SW 217th Ave; Homestead, FL 33030
www.miamigliders.com • Glider Rides: $99+

Gator Park • Airboat Tours • (305) 559-2255
24050 SW 8th St; Miami, FL 33194
www.gatorpark.com • Rates: $22/Adult

Everglades Safari Park • (305) 226-6923
26700 SW 8th St, PO Box 961465; Miami, FL 33194
www.evergladessafaripark.com • Rates: $23/Adult

Everglades Alligator Farm • (305) 247-2628
40351 SW 192nd Ave; Florida City, FL 33034
www.everglades.com • Rates: $23/Adult

Shark Valley Tram Tours • (305) 221-8455
Shark Valley Loop Rd; Miami, FL 33194
www.sharkvalleytramtours.com • Rates: $18/Adult

Everglades Hummer Adventures • (786) 210-6158
www.evergladeshummeradventures.com • $249+

Coral Castle • (305) 248-6345
28655 S Dixie Hwy; Homestead, FL 33033
www.coralcastle.com • Admission: $12/Adult

R F Orchids • (305) 245-4570
28100 SW 182nd Ave; Homestead, FL 33030
www.rforchids.com

Flagship Cinemas • (305) 248-7400
2250 NE 8th St; Homestead, FL 33033
www.flagshipcinemas.com • Tickets: $9

West of the Everglades
Everglades Rentals & Eco Adventures
107 Camelia St; Everglades, FL 34139
www.evergladesadventures.com • (239) 695-4666

Corkscrew Swamp Audubon • (239) 348-9151
375 Sanctuary Rd; Naples, FL 34120

Big Cypress National Preserve • (239) 695-2000
33100 Tamiami Trl E; Ochopee, FL 34141

Skunk Ape Research HQ • (239) 695-2275
40904 Tamiami Tr East; Ochopee, FL 34141
www.skunkape.info

Island Hoppers • (239) 207-4100
2005 Mainsail Dr; Naples, FL 34114
www.ravenair.net • Tours: $59+

Naples Pier
878 5th Ave S; Naples, Florida 34102

Delnor-Wiggins Pass State Park • (239) 597-6196
11135 Gulfshore Dr; Naples, FL 34108
www.floridastateparks.org • Fee: $6/Vehicle

Marco Movies • (239) 642-1111
599 S Collier Blvd, #103; Marco Island, FL 34145
www.marcomovies.com

The Florida Keys
Sterling Capt Everglades Tours • (305) 853-5161
100 Buttonwood Ave; Key Largo, FL 33037

Scuba Shack • (305) 735-4312
97684 Overseas Hwy; Key Largo, FL 33037
www.keylargoscubashack.com • Trips: $40+

Sea Dwellers Dive Center • (800) 451-3640
99850 Overseas Hwy; Key Largo, FL 33037
www.seadwellers.com • Charters: $80+

Caribbean Watersports • (305) 852-4707
97000 Overseas Hwy; Key Largo, FL 33037
www.caribbeanwatersports.com

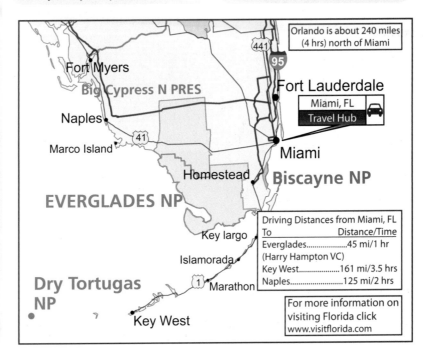

John Pennekamp Coral Reef State Park
Popular snorkel/SCUBA destination with Christ of the Abyss (an 8.5-ft tall statue of Jesus in about 25-ft of water)
102601 US-1; Key Largo, Florida 33037
www.pennekamppark.com • (305) 451-1202

Key Largo Parasail • (305) 453-0440
103900 Overseas Hwy; Key Largo, FL 33037
www.keylargoparasail.com • Rates: $39+

Skydive Key West • (305) 745-4386
MM 17 Overseas Hwy; Sugarloaf Key, FL 33042
www.skydivekeywest.com • Rates: $265

Wild Bird Center • (305) 852-4486
93600 Overseas Hwy; Tavernier, FL 33070
www.wildbird.com

Dolphin Cove Research & Ed Center • (305) 451-4060
101900 Overseas Hwy; Key Largo, FL 33037
www.dolphinscove.com • Rates: $135+

Dolphins Plus • (305) 451-1993
31 Corrine Pl; Key Largo, FL 33037
www.dolphinsplus.com • Rates: $135+

Sea Horse Charters • (305) 664-5020
83413 Overseas Hwy; Islamorada, FL 33036
www.floridakeysfishing-charters.com • $600+

Robbie's • (305) 664-9814
77522 B Overseas Hwy; Islamorada, FL 33036
www.robbies.com • *Party Boat Fishing & More*

Bud N' Mary's Marina • (800) 742-7945
79851 Overseas Hwy; Islamorada, FL 33036
www.budnmarys.com • Fishing: $375 (half-day)

Skins and Fins Charters • (305) 393-0363
79786 Overseas Hwy; Islamorada, FL 33036
www.skinsandfinscharters.com • Call for Rates

Catch Em' All Florida Keys Charter Fishing
1410 Overseas Hwy; Marathon, FL 33050
www.catch-em-all.com • (888) 882-7766

History of Diving Museum • (305) 664-9737
82990 Overseas Hwy; Islamorada, FL 33036
www.divingmuseum.org • Admission: $12/Adult

Theater of the Sea • (305) 664-2431
84721 Overseas Hwy; Islamorada, FL 33036
www.theaterofthesea.com • Rates: $75+

Paradise Yoga • (305) 517-9642
81927 Overseas Hwy; Islamorada, FL 33036
www.paradiseyoga.com

Curry Hammock State Park
Marathon, Florida 33050 • (305) 289-2690
www.floridastateparks.org • Fee: $5/Vehicle

Turtle Hospital • (305) 743-2552
2396 Overseas Hwy; Marathon, FL 33050
www.turtlehospital.org

Captain Hook's Marina & Dive Center
11833 Overseas Hwy; Marathon, FL 33050
www.captainhooks.com • (305) 743-2444

Marathon Cinema • (305) 743-0288
5101 Overseas Hwy; Marathon, FL 33050

Long Key State Park • (305) 664-4815
67400 Overseas Hwy; Long Key, FL 33001
www.floridastateparks.org • Fee: $5/Vehicle

Bahia Honda State Park • (305) 872-3210
36850 Overseas Hwy; Big Pine Key, FL 33043
www.bahiahondapark.com • Fee: $8/Vehicle

Captain Conch Charter • (305) 293-7993
1801 N Roosevelt Blvd; Key West, FL 33040
www.keywestcaptconch.com • Call for Rates

Key West Butterfly and Nature Conservatory
1316 Duval St; Key West, FL 33040
www.keywestbutterfly.com • (305) 293-9258

Harry S Truman Little White House • (305) 294-9911
111 Front St; Key West, FL 33040
www.trumanlittlewhitehouse.com • $15/Adult

Key West Toy Factory • (305) 296-0003
291 Front St; Key West, FL 33040
www.keywesttoyfactory.com

Fort Zachary Taylor Historic State Park
Key West, FL 33040 • (305) 292-6713

Mel Fisher Maritime Heritage Museum
200 Greene St, Key West • (305) 294-2633
www.melfisher.org • Admission: $12.50/Adult

E. Hemingway Home&Museum • (305) 294-1575
907 Whitehead St; Key West, Florida 33040
www.hemingwayhome.com • $12.50/Adult

Key West Shipwreck Historeum Museum
1 Whitehead St; Key West, FL • (305) 292-8990
www.shipwreckhistoreum.com • $14/Adult

Key West Aquarium • (305) 296-2051
1 Whitehead St; Key West, FL 33040
www.keywestaquarium.com • $14/Adult

Wild about Dolphins • (305) 294-5026
6000 Peninsular Ave; Key West, FL 33040
www.wildaboutdolphins.com

Eco-Discovery Center • (305) 809-4750
33 E Quay Rd; Key West, FL 33040
www.floridakeys.noaa.gov • Admission: Free

Yoga on the Beach • (305) 296-7352
100 Southard St; Key West, FL 33040

All About You Salon • (305) 292-0818
1712 N Roosevelt Blvd; Key West, FL 33040
www.allaboutyoukw.com • $55 (30-min massage)

Tropic Cinema • (305) 295-9493
416 Eaton St; Key West, FL 33040-6512

Regal Cinemas • (305) 296-7211
3338 N Roosevelt Blvd; Key West, FL 33040

Orlando is about 240 miles (4 hrs) north of Miami

Miami, FL
Travel Hub

Driving Distances from Miami, FL

To	Distance/Time
Everglades	45 mi/1 hr
(Harry Hampton VC)	
Key West	161 mi/3.5 hrs
Naples	125 mi/2 hrs

For more information on visiting Florida click www.visitflorida.com

Theodore Roosevelt • Pages 192–203

Grand Teton • Pages 204–217

© Frank Kovalchek (flickr/Alaskan Dude)

Yellowstone • Pages 218–245

Glacier • Pages 246–267

THE NORTH

Looking out over the Canada–US border from the top of Mount Franklin

800 East Lakeshore Drive
Houghton, Michigan 4993
Phone: (906) 482-0984
Website: www.nps.gov/isro

Established: April 3, 1940
Size: 571,790 Acres
Annual Visitors: 16,000
Peak Season: July–August
Hiking Trails: 165 Miles

Activities: Hiking, Camping,
Backpacking, Paddling, Fishing,
Boat Tours, and SCUBA Diving

Campgrounds: 36 Campgrounds
accessible by boat and trail*
Camping Fee: Free
Reservations: None
Lodging: Rock Harbor Lodge
(Rooms and Cottages available)
Rates: $229–254/night

Open: mid-April–October
Entrance Fee: $4/Person per day

*A permit is required for all over-
night stays in the park.

Isle Royale - Michigan

Isle Royale, born of fire, sculpted by glaciers, nearly drowned in water, is a wilderness wonderland left mostly unaltered by man's creations. Millions of years ago this archipelago of about 400 islands was formed by what scientists believe to have been the world's largest lava flow. An amount of lava so immense that the earth's surface sunk under its weight, forming the Superior basin. As the basin formed, Isle Royale began to rise and tilt. Today, effects of this ancient geologic activity can still be seen in Isle Royale's ridgelines. The northwest ridges are generally steep and rugged, because the lagging edge ripped away from the crust. The leading edge (southeast slope) is more gradual, as it faces the point of compression.

About 10,000 years ago the last glacier to reach Lake Superior receded. As it scraped the island's ridgelines, pulverizing rock, a thin layer of soil was left behind. As the glacier melted, Isle Royale appeared and water poured into Lake Superior. Wind and water brought plant life to the island. Birds and insects arrived. Moose and caribou swam 15 miles from Canada's shoreline. An unseasonably cold winter allowed wolves to reach the island by crossing a frozen sheet of ice.

The trip to these remote islands, while not nearly as difficult as it was for plants and animals, is still challenging for humans. Isle Royale remains untethered to the mainland, completely inaccessible to motorists. The only way to reach the park is by boat or seaplane. Diehard backpackers and paddlers make the trip across Lake Superior to immerse themselves in something increasingly scarce: undeveloped wilderness.

Best of Isle Royale

Transportation Service: *Ranger III* (out of Houghton, MI; operated by the NPS)

Campsite (near Rock Harbor): Lane Cove
Runner-up: McCargoe Cove
2nd Runner-up: Moskey Basin
3rd Runner-up: Chippewa Harbor

Campsite (near Windigo): Huginnin Cove
Runner-up: Little Todd
2nd Runner-up: Siskiwit Bay

Hike (near Rock Harbor): Stoll Trail
Runner-up: Suzy's Cave

Hike (near Windigo): Feldtmann Lake
Runner-up: Windigo Nature Walk

Paddle Destination: McCargoe Cove
Runner-up: Five Finger Bay

Long before tourists stepped foot on the island, Indians were exploring its ridges and shorelines. Thousands of shallow pits indicate they were mining copper here more than 4,000 years ago. They continued to mine for some 1,500 years, but no one knows why. **Benjamin Franklin** was well aware of the mineral's value. Some historians believe Franklin insisted the Treaty of Paris draw the border between a newly formed United States and England's Canada north of Isle Royale because of its copper. By the 1920s, lumber and mining companies—having exhausted nearly all the dollarable resources of Michigan's mainland—eyed the island's trees and minerals. **Albert Stoll**, a journalist for the Detroit News, wanted to preserve what commercial interests sought to exploit. Inspired by Stoll's passion and enthusiasm, the Detroit News backed his interest and launched a decade-long campaign to protect the region as a national park. In 1931 the federal government acted upon their pleas. President Herbert Hoover signed into law a bill creating Isle Royale National Park, provided no federal funds were used to acquire land. Timing couldn't have been worse as the economy was reeling during the Great Depression and money was hard to come by. **President Franklin D. Roosevelt** ignored the federal mandate and steered funds from the New Deal to buy land for the park, preserving one of the most majestic and undeveloped regions of the contiguous United States.

When to Go

Isle Royale National Park is one of the few parks in the contiguous United States that closes during the winter (November until mid-April). August is the best time of the year to make a trip to the island. Weather is typically warm, pests like black flies and mosquitoes are beginning to diminish, and blueberries are often ripe for the picking. The park's facilities hold regular operating hours during peak season (July–August).

Rock Harbor Visitor Center
July–August, Daily, 8am–6pm

Windigo Visitor Center
July–August, Daily, 8am–4:30pm

Hours are reduced in May, June, and September. Please call (906) 482-0984 for a current schedule.

Houghton Visitor Center • Park Headquarters
June–July, Mon–Fri, 8am–6pm; Sat, 11am–6pm
Aug–Sept, Mon–Fri, 8am–4:30pm; Sat, 2pm–4pm
mid-September–May, Mon–Fri, 8am–4:30pm
Closed during fall and winter holidays

Transportation

Most visitors reach Isle Royale by ferry from one of three locations: Houghton, Michigan; Copper Harbor, Michigan; or Grand Portage, Minnesota. If you have a choice, take the **Ranger III** out of Houghton. It's the longest trip (6 hours, one-way), but also the least expensive and most enjoyable. During the voyage a park ranger will regale you with stories (and possibly a song). As an added convenience, you'll be able to obtain a backcountry permit while aboard the *Ranger III*, rather than having to stop at the visitor center when you arrive. Additional information is provided in the table on page 156.

Airports

The closest airport to Grand Portage, MN is Thunder Bay International (YQT) in Ontario, Canada. It is approximately 40 miles northeast of Grand Portage. Houghton County Memorial (CMX) is located in Houghton, MI, about 40 miles southwest of Copper Harbor.

Directions

Vehicles are not allowed on Isle Royale, but parking is available at all departure locations (for a nominal fee).

To Grand Portage, MN (145 miles from Duluth): From the south follow MN-61 northeast along the coast of Lake Superior. Turn right onto Stevens Road to enter Grand

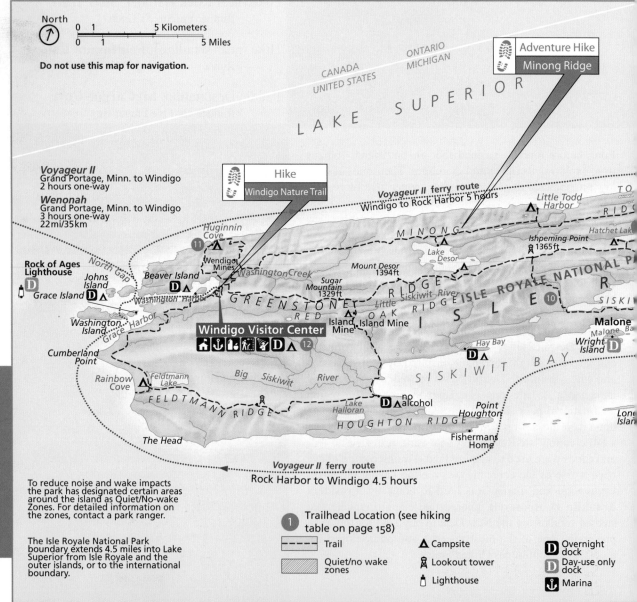

North

0   1   5 Kilometers
0   1   5 Miles

Do not use this map for navigation.

Adventure Hike
Minong Ridge

CANADA / UNITED STATES — ONTARIO / MICHIGAN

L A K E   S U P E R I O R

Voyageur II
Grand Portage, Minn. to Windigo
2 hours one-way

Wenonah
Grand Portage, Minn. to Windigo
3 hours one-way
22mi/35km

Hike
Windigo Nature Trail

Voyageur II ferry route
Windigo to Rock Harbor 5 hours

Little Todd Harbor

TO
RIDG

Hatchet Lak

M I N O N G

Huginnin Cove

Lake Desor

Ishpeming Point
1365ft

Rock of Ages Lighthouse
Johns Island
Grace Island

North Gap

Beaver Island

Wendigo Mines

Washington Creek

Mount Desor
1394ft

R I D G E

ISLE ROYALE NATIONAL PA

Washington Harbor

Sugar Mountain
1329ft

Little Siskiwit River

OAK RIDGE

I S L E

R

SISKI

Washington Island

Grace Harbor

G R E E N S T O N E
R E D

Windigo Visitor Center

Island Mine · Island Mine

Malone
Malone Ba
Wright Island

Cumberland Point

Rainbow Cove

Feldtmann Lake

Big Siskiwit River

S I S K I W I T   B A Y

Hay Bay

Point Houghton

Long Islan

F E L D T M A N N   R I D G E

Lake Halloran

no alcohol

H O U G H T O N   R I D G E

Fishermans Home

The Head

Voyageur II ferry route
Rock Harbor to Windigo 4.5 hours

To reduce noise and wake impacts the park has designated certain areas around the island as Quiet/No-wake Zones. For detailed information on the zones, contact a park ranger.

The Isle Royale National Park boundary extends 4.5 miles into Lake Superior from Isle Royale and the outer islands, or to the international boundary.

1 Trailhead Location (see hiking table on page 158)

- - - - - Trail
▨ Quiet/no wake zones

▲ Campsite
♜ Lookout tower
⚲ Lighthouse

🅓 Overnight dock
🅓 Day-use only dock
⚓ Marina

Portage. Follow County Road 73/Store Road to the right. Turn left on Mile Creek Road. Turn right onto Bay Road. After a little more than one mile, turn right onto Upper Road which leads to the ferry terminal.

From Thunder Bay, travel southwest on MN-61. Turn left onto County Rd 73/Store Road to head into Grand Portage which leads to Mile Creek Road. Follow the previous directions from this point.

To Houghton/Copper Harbor (215/261 miles from Green Bay, WI): US-41 passes Isle Royale Visitor Center in Houghton. To arrive at the visitor center, turn right onto Franklin Street just after US-41 becomes one-way.

Continue onto Lakeshore Drive and the visitor center. US-41 continues north to Copper Harbor. In Copper Harbor take the first left onto 5th St to reach the ferry terminal.

Ferry Terminal Information:

Grand Portage Transportation Line • (218) 475-0024
402 Upper Road; Grand Portage, MN 55605
www.isleroyaleboats.com

Isle Royale Ferry Services Inc • (906) 289-4437
60 5th Street; Copper Harbor, MI 49918
www.isleroyale.com

Isle Royale National Park • (906) 482-0984
800 East Lakeshore Drive; Houghton, MI 49931
Reservations: www.pasty.com/isro/nps3.php

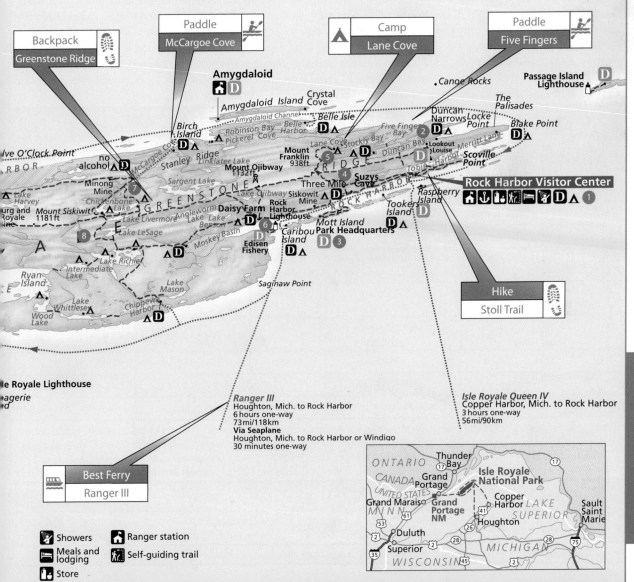

Copper Harbor's *Isle Royale Queen IV*

Lodging and Camping

Rock Harbor Lodge provides the park's only (non-camping) overnight accommodations. It is located on Rock Harbor, near the northeast tip of Isle Royale. The location is hard to beat, but the accommodations are basic and it's fairly expensive. For the nightly rate ($229) a visitor could purchase a tent, sleeping bag, and mat to be used exploring the **36 backcountry campsites** littered across the 45-mile long, 9-mile wide Isle Royale and a few smaller islands. Camping is free and sites are assigned on a first-come, first-served basis. Visitation is relatively modest and sites are almost always available, but those closest to the docks are almost always the first to fill. A free permit is required for all overnight stays. Permits are obtained at a visitor center or aboard the ***Ranger III***.

Isle Royale Transportation Services

		Ranger III	*Isle Royale Queen IV*	*Voyageur II*	*Sea Hunter*	Seaplane
	Operator	National Park	Private	Private	Private	Private
	Departs	Houghton, MI	Copper Harbor, MI	Grand Portage, MN		Houghton, MI
	Duration	5 hours	3 hours	2 hours	1.5 hours	< 1 hour
	Open	June–Sept	May–Sept	May–Sept	June–Sept	May–Sept
	Schedule	9am*	8am (Copper Harbor) 2:45pm (Rock Harbor)	7:30am	8:30am (Grand Portage) 2pm (Windigo)	Every 2 hours starting at 8am
Rates (one-way)	Adults	$50 (low)/ $60 (high)	$57 (low)/ $65 (high)	$64	$64	$290 (round-trip)
	Children	$20	$28.50 (low)/ $32.50 (high)	$44	$44	Free (under 2 years old)
	Kayak	$20	$25	$33	$33	N/A
	Phone	(906) 482-0984	(906) 289-4437	(888) 746-2305		(218) 721-0405
	Website	www.nps.gov/isro	www.isleroyale.com	www.isleroyaleboats.com		www.royaleairservice.com

Trips to Isle Royale are not made every day of the week. Be sure to check the operator's website or call to confirm their departure schedule. Fares and duration are for one-way trips except where stated otherwise. Operators consider children to be 11 years old and younger. The *Ranger III* offers free rides to kids (age 6 and under). All reservations require full payment.
Ranger III departs from Houghton on Tuesdays and Fridays at 9am. It departs from Rock Harbor at 9am on Wednesdays and Saturdays.

Isle Royale Lodging

Rock Harbor Lodge	Open: May– September	$229–254 (Room)/ $222–246 (Cottage)	The lower rate is for non-peak season (May–July 4). Dining and kayak/canoe rental is available on-site.

Call (906) 337-4993 in summer or (866) 644-2003 in winter or click www.foreverlodging.com to make reservations.

Isle Royale Camping

← Northeast

Location on Isle Royale from the Southwest →

Campground	Max Nights	Tent Sites	Shelters	Group Sites	Fire Pit	Boat Access
Blake Point	3	1	1	0	No	Yes
Duncan Narrows	3	1	2	0	Yes	Yes
Rock Harbor	1	11	9	3	No	Yes
Tookers Island	3	0	2	0	No	Yes
Duncan Bay	3	1	0	0	Yes	Yes
Lane Cove - 👍	3	5	0	0	No	Yes
Belle Isle	5	1	6	0	Yes	Yes
Three Mile	1	4	8	3	No	Yes
Caribou Island	3	1	2	0	No	Yes
Daisy Farm - 👍	3	6	16	3	No	Yes
Pickerel Cove	2	1	0	0	No	Yes
Birch Island	3	1	1	0	No	Yes
Moskey Basin - 👍	3	2	6	2	No	Yes
Chippewa Harbor - 👍	3	2	4	1	Yes	Yes
McCargoe Cove - 👍	3	3	6	3	Yes	Yes
Chickenbone East	2	3	0	1	No	Yes
Chickenbone West	2	6	0	3	No	Yes
Lake Richie Canoe	2	3	0	0	No	Yes
Lake Whittlesey	2	3	0	0	No	Yes
Lake Richie	2	4	0	2	No	Yes
Intermediate Lake	2	3	0	0	No	Yes
Wood Lake	2	3	0	0	No	Yes
Todd Harbor	3	5	1	3	Yes	Yes
Malone Bay - 👍	3	0	5	2	Yes	Yes
Hatchet Lake	2	5	0	3	No	No
Little Todd	2	3	0	0	Yes	Yes
Desor North	2	3	0	0	No	No
Desor South	2	7	0	0	No	No
Hay Bay	3	1	0	0	No	Yes
Siskiwit Bay - 👍	3	4	2	3	Yes	Yes
Island Mine	3	4	0	2	No	No
Huginnin Cove	3	5	0	0	No	No
Washington Creek (Windigo)	3	5	10	4	No	Yes
Beaver Island	3	0	3	0	No	Yes
Feldtmann Lake	2	5	0	2	No	No
Grace Island	3	0	2	0	No	Yes

Isle Royale Hiking Trails

	Trail Name	Trail Location (# on map)	Length	Notes (One-way distances unless loop)
Easy	Tobin Harbor	Near Rock Harbor Seaplane Dock (1)	3.0 miles	Alternative to Rock Harbor Trail
	Stoll - 👍	Northeast corner of Rock Harbor (1)	4.2 miles	Two loops cross back and forth from the shorelines of Lake Superior and Tobin Harbor to Scoville Point
	Suzy's Cave	Southwest of Rock Harbor's Dock (1)	3.8 miles	Take Rock Harbor Trail to the spur trail to Suzy's Cave • Loop back to Rock Harbor via Tobin Harbor Trail
	Mott Island Circuit	Mott Island Seaplane Dock (3)	2.6 miles	Short, seldom-hiked loop trail accessible by boat
	East Chickenbone	0.5 miles from McCargoe Cove (7)	1.6 miles	Connects McCargoe Cove and Greenstone Ridge Trail
	Windigo Nature Walk	Up the hill past Windigo Visitor Center (12)	1.2 miles	Self-guided nature trail through hardwood forest
Moderate	Rock Harbor and Lake Ritchie	Southwest of Rock Harbor's Dock (1)	12.9 miles	Combine Rock Harbor and Lake Ritchie Trails to hike past busy camps at Three Mile and Daisy Farm to more remote locations near the center of the island
	Greenstone Ridge - 👍	Spans from Windigo to Lookout Louise (2, 5)	42.2 miles	Best known trail on Isle Royale
	Mount Franklin	0.2 miles west of Three Mile Camp (4)	2.0 miles	Hike between Rock Harbor and Greenstone Ridge to a dramatic view of the Island's north side
	Daisy Farm and Mount Ojibway	Daisy Farm Campground (6)	5.1 miles	Loop trail starting and ending at Daisy Farm • Passes Mount Ojibway Tower on Greenstone Ridge
	Indian Portage and Lake Mason	Spans the island's width from McCargoe Cove to Chippewa Harbor (8)	10.6 miles	Isolated trail accessible by The Greenstone and Rock Harbor Trails or by boat at McCargoe Cove and Chippewa Harbor • South section is lightly traveled
	Hatchet Lake	Greenstone and Minong Connector (9)	2.6 miles	Short connecting trail between ridgelines
	Huginnin Cove	Near Washington Creek Campground (11)	9.4 miles	Loop trail that passes ridges, wetlands, and a mine
	Feldtmann Lake/ Ridge and Island Mine	Near the main dock at Windigo (12)	23.5 miles	A loop that leads to Grace Creek Overlook, Feldtmann Lake, Siskiwit Bay, Island Mine, and 3 campgrounds, before returning on Greenstone Ridge
Strenuous	Lookout Louise - 👍	Northeast terminus of Greenstone Ridge (2)	1.0 mile	Perhaps the most spectacular view in the park, but the hike is straight uphill to reach it
	Lane Cove	Continues north from Mount Franklin (5)	2.4 miles	Great first destination for hikers leaving Rock Harbor
	Minong Ridge - 👍	Spans from Windigo to McCargoe Cove (7, 11)	26 miles	Wilder, less maintained and less traveled alternative to The Greenstone • Excellent chances of seeing moose
	Ishpeming	Malone Bay Camp to Ishpeming Point (10)	7.0 miles	Steady climb to the park's second highest point

Hiking

More than 99% of the park is designated wilderness, making Isle Royale and its 165-mile network of trails one of the best hiking regions in the Midwest. Most trails are hidden in the backcountry, far from landing docks, only trafficked by backpackers and overnight paddlers. But there are some extremely rewarding short hikes around Windigo and Rock Harbor where most visitors arrive. **Windigo Nature Walk** is a great first hike and introduction to the island. Trail guides for the 1.2-mile walk are available at the visitor center. Another pleasant hike near Windigo is the 3.6-mile (roundtrip) trek along **Feldtmann Lake Trail** to Grace Creek Overlook. The rest of the Feldtmann Lake/Island Mine Trail is seldom hiked, but the first 1.8 miles are a popular destination for day-hikers seeking views of Grace Harbor from this majestic overlook. Adventurous day-hikers may want to try taking **Minong Ridge Trail** to Minong Ridge Overlook. After hiking up and down over rocky and rugged terrain for 3 miles (one-way) you'll be rewarded with spectacular vistas of Canada's shoreline.

Rock Harbor is precariously positioned on a thin slice of land between Tobin Harbor and Lake Superior. There's more water than land, but you can still find several good hiking trails in the area. **Stoll Memorial Trail** is just northeast of the dock. It recognizes the time and energy Albert Stoll, a Detroit News journalist, spent in his effort to protect the region. About 2 miles of it are self-guided. In all, it's nearly 5 miles to the trail's terminus at Scoville Point and back. You'll pass craggy cliffs, harbor views, and remnants of ancient mines along the way. Heading southwest from Rock Harbor are **Tobin Harbor and Rock Harbor Trails**. They run parallel to one another, weaving from shoreline to thick forests as they follow alongside the bodies of water that share their names. Regardless of which trail you choose, you'll have the opportunity to take a short spur trail to **Suzy's Cave**. It's more of an eroded arch than a cave, but still worth a quick peek. Both of these trails are among the park's busiest. Rock Harbor is usually the busier of the two because it serves as a direct route to Three Mile and Daisy Farm Campgrounds. Hikers like to beeline to these locations in order to secure a shelter for the night. Raspberry Island, only accessible by boat, has a short interpretive trail to Rock Harbor Lighthouse near Edisen Fishery.

Backpacking

Isle Royale is one of the premier backpacking parks in the United States. For starters, it's nearly impossible to get seriously lost. The island is roughly 45 miles long and 9 miles wide; unless you're walking in circles, you can only go so far.

Greenstone Ridge, commonly referred to as "The Greenstone," follows the spine of the island and is the most notable long-distance hiking trail at Isle Royale. There aren't any campsites located directly on its 42-mile length, but several short spur trails lead to more secluded camping locations. It is reasonable to cover the entire length of the trail from Lookout Louise to Windigo in 3 days, camping at Chickenbone Lake and Lake Desor. However, plan a longer trip allowing more time to explore the many bays and lakes and to wait out bad weather (if needed).

Running parallel to The Greenstone is **Minong Ridge Trail**. It covers 26 miles of wild and rugged terrain, and is much more difficult to traverse than its well-maintained counterpart. The challenge, abundance of wildlife, and lack of hikers attract backpackers to Minong, but these adventurous souls are few and far between. You have a better chance of spotting moose than another hiker. Just don't get lost while looking for wildlife; pay close attention to the cairns lining the barren ridgelines. Also, watch where you step because the terrain is rugged and the trail is undeveloped, lacking bridges and walkways that are integrated into most of Isle Royale's other trails. Minong Trail is best hiked from east to west (McCargoe Cove to Windigo). *Voyageur II* makes scheduled stops at McCargoe Cove. You can also hike in or take a water-taxi.

You must stay at established campsites (page 157) unless off-trail arrangements are made when you obtain your backcountry permit. Permits are required for all overnight stays at campgrounds, off-trail (only recommended for experienced backpackers) sites, docks, or at anchor, and can be obtained aboard the *Ranger III* (page 156) or upon arrival at Rock Harbor or Windigo Visitor Centers.

SCUBA Diving

Isle Royale's rugged landscape is enough to include it with the United States' great natural landmarks, but there's a completely different world to be explored beneath the frigid waters of Lake Superior. Park's boundaries extends 4.5 miles from the islands' shorelines. **More than 25 ships have run aground or wrecked** on the surrounding reefs, and most are relatively well-maintained due to the cool, clean, fresh water. Mooring buoys are available at nine wrecks, including the 183-foot *SS America*, the park's most popular wreck. This passenger and package steamer ran aground in the North Gap of Washington Harbor, and its bow is visible from above water (its bow sits just two feet below the surface, while its stern is some 80 feet deep). Visitors arriving at Windigo aboard the ferry from Grand Portage, MN will stop to view the massive steamer without having to jump into Lake Superior's water, which ranges from 34–55°F.

Even though it's some of the best wreck diving anywhere, only a few hundred visitors experience this underwater world each year. Divers must be experienced and prepared for the lake's cold water and potentially tight confines of its many shipwrecks. No facilities are available to fill air tanks within the park. All divers must register at one of the visitor centers before diving. Charter services are available back on the mainland to take you on an ultimate Isle Royale adventure.

Superior Trips LLC • (763) 785-9516
7348 Symphony St NE; Fridley, MN 55432
www.superiortrips.com

Scuba Center • www.scubacenter.com
5015 Penn Ave South; Minneapolis, MN 55419
1571 Century Point; Eagan, MN 55121
(612) 925-4818 (Minneapolis) • (651) 681-8434 (Eagan)
Rates: $895 (4-nights, meals and lodging aboard boat)

Isle Royale Charters • (269) 270-8334
Boat is docked at the Grand Portage Marina
E-mail: info@isleroyalecharters.com
www.isleroyalecharters.com

MN-Blackdog Diving, LLC • (507) 878-3247
E-mail: anderson@bevcomm.net
www.mn-blackdogdiving.com

Paddling

Experienced paddlers will find some amazing open water paddling opportunities at Isle Royale. Bringing your kayak or canoe with you unlocks a multitude of campsites, coves, and bays that cannot be reached on foot. You can explore the island's inland lakes, but you better have sturdy shoulders or a kayak cart. Portages can be as long as two miles, covering steep and rugged terrain. However, the rewards are always worth the effort. After putting a mile or two of dirt path behind you, you'll be left to enjoy the tranquil side of the island from the seat of watercraft. One of the more rigorous routes beginning at **Rock Harbor** takes paddlers southwest past **Rock Harbor Lighthouse** into **Moskey Basin**. From Moskey Basin dock it's a two mile (mostly flat) portage to **Lake Ritchie** (a popular paddle-site). Four more portages take you from **Lake LeSage** to **Lake Livermore** to **Chickenbone Lake** and finally to **McCargoe Cove**, crossing the width of the island to its northern shoreline. **Five Fingers** is another great destination for paddlers departing Rock Harbor. Remember that weather and waves can change in an instant. *Voyageur II* offers paddler and boat transportation (fee) to several locations.

Canoe & Kayak Rental & Tours

Rock Harbor Marina has canoes and kayaks for rent.
15' & 17' Canoe: $23 (half-day), $39 (full-day)
Kayak: $32.50 (half-day), $57.50 (full-day)

Rock Harbor Lodge also offers a Kayak Ecotour that departs from Houghton aboard the *Ranger III*. The price includes all meals, 4 nights lodging at Rock Harbor Lodge, sea kayak gear, and guide.
Rates: $1,506 Single/$2,690 Double Occupancy

Fishing

Isle Royale's lake trout populations are the most productive and genetically diverse in all of Lake Superior. Waters within park boundaries provide excellent opportunities for catching both trout and salmon. Interior lakes offer habitat for a healthy population of walleye and northern pike. Anglers (17 and older) must have a Michigan State Fishing License if you plan to fish inland lakes or streams. A license is not required to fish Lake Superior. Rock Harbor Lodge provides fishing charter services for island visitors.

Isle Royale Fishing Charters • (906) 337-4993
www.foreverlodging.com
Rates: $388 (4 hours for 4 anglers), $718 (8 hours for 4 anglers)

Boat Tours

A unique and easy way to explore the park's coastline and harder to reach sections is to hop aboard the **M.V. Sandy** on a sightseeing tour. All tours depart from Rock Harbor dock. A list of available tours with a short description and rates is provided below. Children are considered to be 11 years of age and younger.

Passage Island • ($38/Adult, $19/Child)
This tour stops at Passage Island Lighthouse, which was built in 1881. You'll be required to hike about 2 miles and traverse several steep inclines on this 4.5 hour journey.

Hidden Lake/Lookout Louise • ($38/Adult, $19/Child)
If your goal is to hike the entire Greenstone Ridge Trail you may want to take this shuttle/tour to Lookout Louise, the trail's northeast endpoint. The section of Greenstone Ridge between Lookout Louise and Mount Franklin is one of the most scenic stretches, but its location beyond Rock Harbor causes it to be skipped by most visitors. Roundtrip takes 3.5 hours.

Captain's Cruise • ($38/Adult, $19/Child)
You'll pass Rock Harbor Lighthouse as the Captain of the *M.V. Sandy* guides passengers to scenic locations like Middle Island Passage and Lorelei Lane during this 3.5 hour scenic cruise.

Northside Cruise/Minong Mine • ($45.50/Adult, $22.75/Child)
This tour heads to the opposite side of the island, stopping at McCargoe Cove where passengers tour a late 19th century copper mine. From here you'll have the option to climb back aboard the *M.V. Sandy* for the return trip or hike 15 miles back to Rock Harbor. It's a 6.5 hour adventure, so remember to pack a lunch and plenty of water.

Edisen Fishery/Rock Harbor Lighthouse • ($38/Adult, $19/Child)
Tour a lighthouse and historic commercial fishery on this 4 hour trip.

Raspberry Island/Sunset Cruise • ($38/Adult, $19/Child)
Passengers walk about Raspberry Island before cruising around Scoville and Blake Points as the sun sets.

The *M.V. Sandy* is also available for use as a one-way water bus to Hidden Lake ($15.50/passenger, no child discount), McCargoe Cove ($26), or Daisy Farm ($17.50). They'll drop you off or pick you up from any spot on the island (weather permitting). You can make reservations for water taxi service at Rock Harbor Marina. Rates are based on number of passengers and mileage. There is a maximum of six people with backpacks or four people and two canoes per trip.

1–5 miles: $62 for 1–2 People ($4/additional person)
6–10 miles: $122 for 1–2 People ($6/additional person)
11–15 miles: $172 for 1–2 People ($8/additional person)
16–20 miles: $239 for 1–2 People ($10/additional person)
21–15 miles: $335 for 1–2 People ($12/additional person)

Boats can be rented from Rock Harbor Marina (motor costs extra).
14' & 16' Aluminum Boat: $23 (half-day), $39 (full-day)
9.9hp Engine: $23 (half-day), $39 (full-day)
15hp Engine: $34 (half-day), $57 (full-day)

View from Mount Ojibway Lookout Tower

Flora & Fauna

Compared to the rest of the contiguous U.S., Isle Royale is extremely isolated. It's so isolated that only a few mammal species reside here. You'll find more than 40 mammals on the surrounding mainland, but only 18 inhabit the park. Species like caribou and coyote have disappeared. Others, like **moose and wolves**, have found a way to reach the island within the last century. It's widely believed that moose, excellent swimmers among the animal kingdom, swam to the island, motivated by the scent of abundant vegetation. Wolves arrived a few decades later when an exceptionally cold winter left the passage between Ontario, Canada and Isle Royale frozen solid. The presence of moose and their natural predator, wolves, in a closed environment such as Isle Royale creates an ideal setting to study predator-prey relationship. Scientists have studied the park's wolves and moose since 1958. You can even lend a hand by joining a research expedition ($450 for 9 days). Find out more at www.isleroyalewolf.org. In addition to these larger mammals, snowshoe hare, beaver, red fox, red squirrel, at least 40 species of fish, and a handful of amphibians and reptiles reside in the park. Pests are also abundant. **Mosquitoes, black flies, and gnats are worst in June and July.**

The island is primarily forested with a mixture of boreal and northern hardwoods. Spruce, fir, pine, birch, aspen, maple, and ash are commonly found. Blueberries and thimbleberries grow wild on open ridge tops. They typically ripen between late July and August, providing a tasty snack while hiking about the island.

Placid water from the southern shore of Isle Royale © Derek and Heidi Pankratz

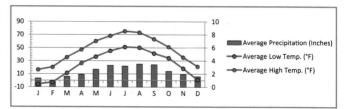

For Kids: Most children will like the boat ride across Lake Superior (unless the water is rough). You'll also find activities specifically designed for children once you arrive at Rock Harbor or Windigo. Children between the ages of 6 and 12 can participate in the park's **Junior Ranger Program**. Complete the free activity booklet (takes 1–2 days) with the help of parents and the park rangers to receive a unique certificate and badge. Rangers also provide engaging interactive programs. Guests of all ages will find the ranger programs enjoyable.

Ranger Programs: In addition to the *M.V. Sandy* **Boat Tours** (page 161) from Rock Harbor Marina and the ranger narrated boat ride to Isle Royale aboard the *Ranger III* (page 156), there are many ranger-led programs offered at the park's Windigo and Rock Harbor locations.

It's amazing how much more enjoyable a park ranger can make a simple walk along the shorelines. If you have the chance to join one of these activities, do it! The program schedule is subject to change, so check online, at the visitor center, or in the park's newspaper, *The Greenstone*, for a current listing.

Pets: Pets are not allowed within the park. However, special conditions do apply to guide dogs. Please contact the park (906.482.0984) for additional information.

Accessibility: All transportation services and Rock Harbor Lodge are accessible with assistance to individuals in wheelchairs. Trails are narrow and rugged with limited access.

Weather: The park's weather is moderated by Lake Superior. Its massive body of water has an average temperature of 45°F, cooling summer highs and warming winter lows. Ambient temperature seldom reaches 80°F on the islands. Dense fog and thunder storms are common during spring and summer. Paddlers should be prepared to head to shore if the wind changes abruptly. Lake Superior's rough waters have received notoriety, thanks largely to the *Edmund Fitzgerald* and Gordon Lightfoot, but it's a rare occasion that inclement weather delays or postpones a departure to or from the island.

Vacation Planners

Remote location and a contingent of moderately-obsessed regulars help give Isle Royale an average stay of 3.5 days. A day-trip is conceivable from Grand Portage or Copper Harbor, but you'll spend more than $100 to ride a ferry for 4–6 hours, which leaves you with just a few hours to enjoy the scenery. For the real Isle Royale experience, the wild side is where you need to go. To get there you'll need at least three days. It's possible to hike from Rock Harbor to Windigo in 3 days, but for this exercise it's more prudent to create a separate 3-day itinerary for visitors of Rock Harbor and visitors of Windigo. Dining, grocery stores, lodging, festivals, and attractions on the mainland are listed on pages 173–175.

Vacation Planner (Rock Harbor)

A sample 3-day itinerary for guests arriving at **Rock Harbor** is provided below. **This is a backpacking trip.** A tent is required for camping at Lane Cove. Shelters are available at Daisy Farm.

Day 1 If you didn't arrive aboard *Ranger III* (page 156), pop in the visitor center to get a back-country permit (let the ranger know that you would like to camp at Lane Cove and Daisy Farm). Today, you'll hike 7.4 miles to **Lane Cove**. Begin by heading west on either **Rock Harbor or Tobin Harbor Trail**. Taking the detour to **Suzy's Cave** is

ISLE ROYALE

up to you. Tobin Harbor Trail takes you directly past it, while Rock Harbor Trail requires roughly a 1 mile detour. What you're really looking for is **Mount Franklin Trail**. Take it north to Greenstone Ridge where the trail intersects **Greenstone and Lane Cove Trails**. **Mount Franklin**, a short distance west along The Greenstone is a nice place to pause for a snack, drink, or photo. Otherwise, **Lane Cove**, where you'll spend the night, is just 2.4 miles from the intersection.

Day 2

There's no need to rush today, you're only going to hike seven miles. The route backtracks along **Lane Cove Trail**, to **Mount Franklin** and **Mount Ojibway Overlook** via **The Greenstone**. From **Mount Ojibway Overlook** it's 5.1 miles along **Daisy Farm Trail** to camp.

Day 3

Return to **Rock Harbor** (either to camp for the night, to catch the *Ranger III* back to Houghton, or to catch the *Royale Queen IV* back to Copper Harbor). The last leg is 7.2 miles along **Rock Harbor Trail**. You should have plenty of time to catch a **ranger program**, hike **Stoll Trail** (page 159), or take a **shower** (coin operated).

Vacation Planner (Windigo)

A sample 3–4-day itinerary beginning at **Windigo** is provided below. A tent is required for Feldtmann Lake and Island Mine Camps. Siskiwit Bay has two shelters.

Day 1

First stop in at the **visitor center** to get a backcountry permit (let the ranger know that you would like to camp at Feldtmann Lake and Siskiwit Bay). You'll probably want to start hiking right away, because it's 8.8 miles along **Feldtmann Lake/Ridge Trail** to the camp.

Day 2

Today, hike 10.5 miles from Feldtmann Lake Camp to **Siskiwit Bay Camp** via **Feldtmann Ridge Trail**. Along the way you'll skirt the shores of Siskiwit Bay. If you want to continue hiking, it's another 4.4 miles to Island Mine Camp, but this site is one of the least desirable camping destinations on the island.

Day 3

To return to Windigo (11.0 miles from Siskiwit Bay) you'll take **Indian Mine Trail** to **The Greenstone**, which leads back to Windigo where you can catch your ferry or spend another night close to the docks. You'll probably want to take advantage of the coin-operated showers too.

Camping at Lane Cove

Did you know?

▶ Lake Superior is the largest of the Great Lakes in surface area (31,820 sq mi) and volume (2,900 cu mi). It is the largest freshwater lake in the world (by surface area), and the third largest in volume (exceeded only by Lake Baikal in Siberia and Lake Tanganyika in Africa).

▶ Lake Superior accounts for roughly 10% of the world's surface freshwater. Water from all other Great Lakes could fit inside Lake Superior.

▶ Lake Superior holds enough water to cover the 48 contiguous states at a uniform depth of 5 ft.

▶ It is the cleanest Great Lake. Average underwater visibility is 27 feet.

▶ A paddler who stops at Siskiwit Lake's Ryan Island is on the largest island on the largest lake (Siskiwit) on the largest island (Isle Royale) on the largest freshwater lake in the world (Lake Superior).

▶ If you were to walk the entire shoreline of Lake Superior, you would cover 2,726 miles (including islands).

▶ Isle Royale is the largest of Michigan's 14 wilderness areas.

Cold weather opens new areas to motorists by way of Rainy Lake Ice Road

3131 US Highway 53
International Falls, Minnesota 56649
Phone: (218) 283-6600
Website: www.nps.gov/voya

Established: April 8, 1975
Size: 218,054 Acres
Annual Visitors: 254,000
Peak Season: Summer

Activities: Paddling, Boating,
Fishing, Hiking, Camping, and
Winter Activities

Drive-in Campgrounds: None
Backcountry Campsites*: 200+
Access: Boat Only
Camping Fee: Free
Lodging: Kettle Falls Hotel
Access: Boat or Seaplane
Rates: $60–80/night (room)
$180–340/night (villa • 3 day min)

Park Hours: All day, every day
Entrance Fee: None

*A permit is required for all over-
night stays in the park.

Voyageurs - Minnesota

It is appropriate that Minnesota, the land of 10,000 lakes, is home to a national park made mostly of islands and lakes. It's a park where travel is by boat, not car. Visitors carry a paddle in their hands rather than a walking stick. After a long day's journey adventurers rest their tired arms and blistered hands by a campfire, rather than their sore feet.

One other thing about this place that feels like Minnesota: the winters are numbingly cold. Freezing temperatures can make the region feel downright unbearable, but it's far from uninhabitable. In fact, people have lived here since glacial waters of Lake Agassiz receded some 10,000 years ago. **Cree, Monsoni, and Assiniboin tribes** were living here in the late 17th century. In 1688, these tribes were the first Native American contacts of French–Canadian explorer **Jacques de Noyon**. He and his band of voyageurs, known for their strength and endurance, were in search of beaver pelts. Fur trade was the leading industry in the New World, and animal populations in the east were approaching extinction due to overhunting. Trappers like de Noyon were continually pushing west seeking new animal populations to harvest. By the mid-18th century, Ojibwa Indians took up residence in the Rainy Lake area, supplying fur traders with food, furs, and canoes in exchange for manufactured goods.

Over the course of the next century rapid development stressed the United States' resources. By the 1880s, a **logging** frenzy had reached Minnesota's U.S.–Canada border and the present-day site of Voyageurs

National Park. Forests were clear-cut as quickly as humanly possible, with logs rafted down the rivers to increase efficiency. Hoist Bay was named for the act of hoisting floating logs from the waters of Namakan Lake where they were loaded onto a train.

While loggers were clear-cutting trees, miners were blasting through rock hoping for gold. Several gold mines, most notable being **Little American Mine**, were constructed beginning in the 1880s. Rainy Lake City, a town bustling with miners and their families, sprang up overnight. By 1898 gold mines went bust and in 1901 Rainy Lake City was a ghost town.

The next enterprise to take the region by storm was **commercial fishing**, especially for caviar, eggs of lake sturgeon. Without refrigeration there was no way to transport their catch. Fishing fizzled and gave way to **bootlegging** during the era of Prohibition. The maze of waterways along the United States–Canada border proved to be a perfect location for boaters to smuggle alcohol.

Today's industry is **tourism**. As early as 1891, legislation had been written to protect the area now known as Voyageurs National Park, but the request fell on deaf ears. Trees were harvested. Minerals were mined. Dams were constructed at International Falls, Kettle Falls, and Squirrel Falls. Commercial interests scarred the scenic landscapes, and **Ernest Oberholtzer** stood in opposition. He championed the park idea and was one of eight founding members of the **Wilderness Society**. He used his position to lobby Washington to create a national park of this region he explored as a child by canoe. It took decades, but in 1975—when Oberholtzer was 90 years old—the park was finally established.

Voyageurs is a place changed by human enterprises. But nature itself is a powerful agent of change. In summer boats glide across the water as loons float on its surface. Bald eagles soar above the lakes and trees. Quietly, leaves turn yellow, brown, and orange. Rain turns to snow. Water becomes ice. Year to year, day to day, the park is in a constant state of flux. But one thing remains the same: visitors find peace and solace out on the water. They are at home in the wilderness, much like the voyageurs and Ernest Oberholtzer were before them.

When to Go

The park is open all year, but its weather and landscapes are dramatically different from summer to winter. In summer most visitors explore the region by houseboat, canoe, or kayak. In winter, snowmobilers race across the frozen lakes while cross-country skiers and snowshoers make use of snow-covered hiking trails. Rainy Lake is the only year-round visitor center. It's typically open daily from 10am–4pm, but it closes on Monday and Tuesday from late September through December. Kabetogama and Ash River Visitor Centers close in late September and re-open in late May.

Transportation & Airports

Most of the park, including all campsites and Kettle Falls Hotel, is only accessible by boat or seaplane. Public transportation does not reach this remote location. The closest airport is Falls International (INL) in International Falls, MN, located about 25 miles northwest of Kabetogama. Taxis and rental cars are available at the airport.

Directions

The park is best explored by boat, but all three of the park's visitor centers can be reached by car.

To Rainy Lake Visitor Center: (13 miles from International Falls): Take MN-11 east out of International Falls. The visitor center is located along MN-11.

Ash River and Kabetogama Lake Visitor Centers are accessed via US-53.

To Ash River Visitor Center (145 miles from Duluth): Take US-53 North about 131 miles. Turn right at Ash River Trail/Ness Road. Continue for 8 miles before turning left onto Mead Wood Road, which leads directly to the visitor center.

To Kabetogama Lake Visitor Center (140 miles from Duluth): Take US-53 North about 134 miles. Turn right onto Gamma Road/Salmi Road. After 1.3 miles turn right onto Gappa Road. Keep left at the fork, and then turn right into the visitor center parking lot.

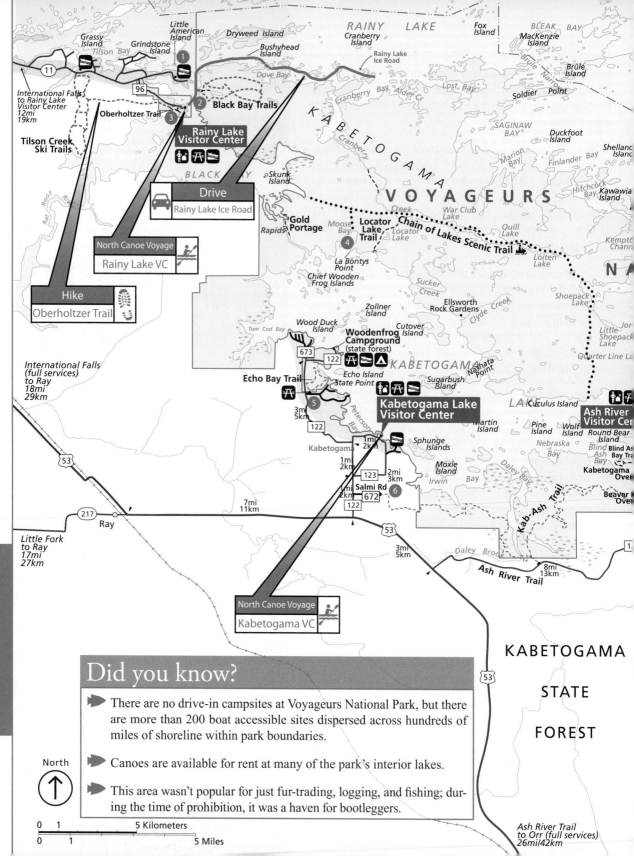

VOYAGEURS

RAINY LAKE
Fox Island
BLEAK BAY
MacKenzie Island
Brûlé Island

Grassy Island
Tilson Bay
Grindstone Island
Little American Island
Dryweed Island
Bushyhead Island
Cranberry Island
Rainy Lake Ice Road
Brûlé Narrows
Soldier Point

(11)
96
International Falls to Rainy Lake Visitor Center
12mi
19km

Oberholtzer Trail
Black Bay Trails

Tilson Creek Ski Trails

Rainy Lake Visitor Center

Drive
Rainy Lake Ice Road

North Canoe Voyage
Rainy Lake VC

Hike
Oberholtzer Trail

BLACK BAY
Skunk Island

KABETOGAMA

Cranberry Bay
Alder Cr
Lost Bay
SAGINAW BAY
Duckfoot Island
Shelland Island
Finlander Bay
Marion Bay
Hitchcock Bay
Kawawia Island

VOYAGEURS

Gold Portage
Rapids
Moose Bay
Locator Lake Trail
Locator Lake
Chain of Lakes Scenic Trail
War Club Lake
Creek
Quill Lake
Loiten Lake
Kempto Chann
N A

La Bontys Point
Chief Wooden Frog Islands
Sucker Creek
Ellsworth Rock Gardens
Clyde Creek
Shoepack Lake
Little Shoepack
Quarter Line La

International Falls (full services) to Ray
18mi
29km

Tom Cod Bay
Wood Duck Island
Zollner Island
Cutover Island
Woodenfrog Campground (state forest)
673
122
KABETOGAMA
Nashata Point
Sugarbush Island

Echo Bay Trail
Echo Island State Point

LAKE
Cuculus Island
Ash River Visitor Cen

3mi
5km
122
Kabetogama
1mi
2km
Petersor Bay
Kabetogama Lake Visitor Center
Sphunge Islands
Martin Island
Pine Island
Wolf Island
Nebraska Bay
Round Bear Island
Daley Bay
Blind Ash Bay Tra
Kabetogama Ove

(53)
217
Ray
Little Fork to Ray
17mi
27km

7mi
11km
1mi
2km
123
1mi
2km
Salmi Rd
672
122
2mi
3km
Moxie Island
Irwin Bay
6
Kab-Ash Trail
Beaver Ove

(53)
3mi
5km
Daley Brook
Ash River Trail
8mi
13km

North Canoe Voyage
Kabetogama VC

KABETOGAMA

STATE

FOREST

(53)

Did you know?

➤ There are no drive-in campsites at Voyageurs National Park, but there are more than 200 boat accessible sites dispersed across hundreds of miles of shoreline within park boundaries.

➤ Canoes are available for rent at many of the park's interior lakes.

➤ This area wasn't popular for just fur-trading, logging, and fishing; during the time of prohibition, it was a haven for bootleggers.

North
↑

0   1   5 Kilometers
0   1   5 Miles

Ash River Trail to Orr (full services)
26mil 42km

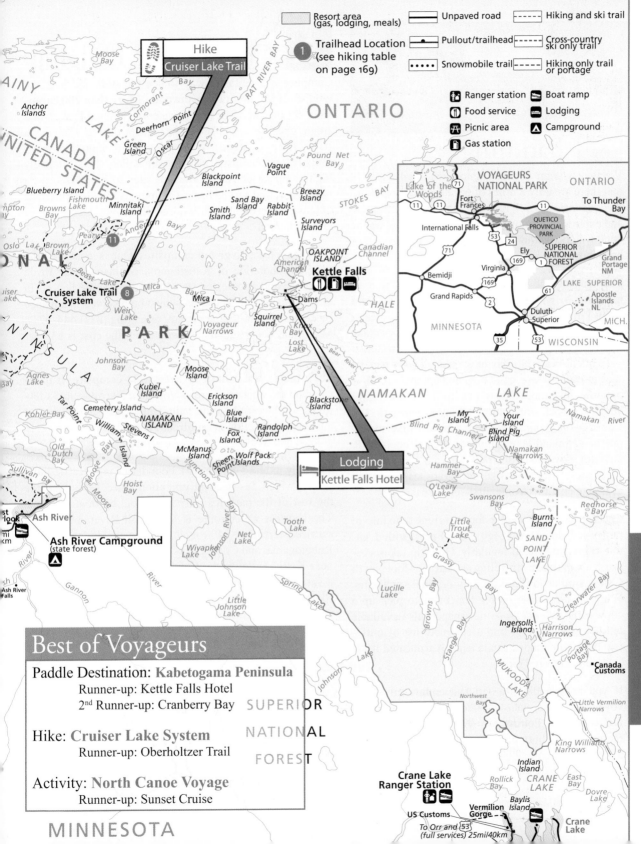

Legend

Resort area (gas, lodging, meals)

1 Trailhead Location (see hiking table on page 169)

Unpaved road

Pullout/trailhead

Snowmobile trail

Hiking and ski trail

Cross-country ski only trail

Hiking only trail or portage

Ranger station
Food service
Picnic area
Gas station

Boat ramp
Lodging
Campground

Hike
Cruiser Lake Trail

Lodging
Kettle Falls Hotel

Kettle Falls

Best of Voyageurs

Paddle Destination: **Kabetogama Peninsula**
  Runner-up: Kettle Falls Hotel
  2nd Runner-up: Cranberry Bay

Hike: **Cruiser Lake System**
  Runner-up: Oberholtzer Trail

Activity: **North Canoe Voyage**
  Runner-up: Sunset Cruise

No paved roadways beyond this point

Paddling

Voyageurs is an anomaly among national parks in that there are only 8 miles of paved roadways within its boundaries. If you're going to really get out there and explore the region, you'll have to head out on the open water, whether by canoe, kayak, motorboat, or houseboat.

The majority of water exploration occurs in four main lakes: **Kabetogama, Namakan, Rainy, and Sand Point**. More than 500 islands, 84,000 acres of water, and infinitely many boating possibilities make it easy to get lost in a maze of forests and water. If your intent is a multi-day or even a half-day trip, be sure to travel with a good map and compass (GPS is optional, just know how to use it). If you don't have your own boat, think about taking a **water taxi** to Kabetogama Peninsula where you can hike to any one of 17 inland lake campsites. Rental boats ($10/day) are provided by the park for your enjoyment at 11 of these sites. Just like the campsites, boats are available on a first-come, first-served basis.

Check at a visitor center for a current schedule of ranger-led activities (page 171). **Free guided canoe trips** are offered regularly. One trip takes visitors back in time by traveling aboard a 26-foot **North Canoe** similar to those used by original voyageurs. While at the visitor center remember to pick up a copy of *The Rendezvous* newspaper (also available online), where you'll find a complete list of outfitters providing guided canoe trips. A truncated list is available on page 175.

If you believe the strength and endurance of the voyageurs is in you, consider navigating around **Kabetogama Peninsula**. This 75-mile voyage requires two short portages, one at Gold Portage, a rapid between Kabetogama and Rainy Lake, and another at Kettle Falls Dam. Other than that, it's all wide open flat water as you trace the jagged shoreline for seven days (on average).

Camping & Lodging

Camping is a fantastic way to see the stars and hear the wildlife of Minnesota's northwoods. **More than 200 campsites** dot the shorelines of Voyageurs National Park. Not a single one is accessible by car (except during winter, via Rainy Lake Ice Road). With 655 miles of shoreline, that's roughly one campsite every three miles. This relatively high campsite density allows all sites to be offered on a first-come, first served basis. Camping is free, but you must obtain an overnight permit (also free) at any visitor center or boat launch.

Voyageurs has two **group campsites**. One is located on the northern shoreline of Kabetogama peninsula near Brule Narrows, and another on its southern shoreline just north of Cuculus Island. These sites must be reserved in advance by clicking www.recreation.gov or calling (877) 444-6777. Maximum occupancy is 30 people and the cost is $35 per night.

There's also one **handicap accessible campsite**. It is located on the western shore of Voyageur Narrows, just a few miles southwest of Kettle Falls Hotel. The site is free but advance reservation is required. Please call (218) 875-2111 at least one week ahead to make arrangements.

The only lodging within park boundaries is at **Kettle Falls Hotel**, which has been in operation since 1918. Just like the rest of the park it's only accessible by boat or plane. The shortest water route is from Ash River, but shuttle service (starting at $40 roundtrip) is available from Rainy, Kabetogama, and Crane Lakes as well. The hotel is situated near Kettle Falls on the Canada–U.S. border. They have a variety of lodging accommodations, ranging from basic rooms to villa suites. The hotel closes in winter, and there is a three night minimum stay for all villas and suites.

Kettle Falls Hotel • (218) 875-2070 • www.kettlefallshotel.com
10502 Gamma Road; Kabetogama, MN 56669
Rates: $80/night (Room), $180/night (Villa), $340/night (Suite)

Drive-in camping is available near the park's southern boundary at **Wooden Frog State Forest Campground** (59-sites, 218.365.7229, CR-22; Kabetogama State Forest, MN) on Kabetogama Lake and **Ash River Campground** (8-sites, 218.365.7229, CR-126; Orr, MN) in Ash River. Camping at either location costs $12 per night. Please refer to page 173 for additional accommodations.

Hiking

Voyageurs is dominated by water, making its hiking trails more afterthought than main attraction. Even so, you'll find some great opportunities within the park and a boat isn't needed to reach all of them. **Oberholtzer Trail** begins near Rainy Lake Visitor Center before passing through forests and wetlands. The first 0.25-mile is wheelchair accessible and you'll find two overlooks along its 1.7-mile length.

Not surprisingly, most trailheads are only accessible by boat. **Cruiser Lake Trail System**, a 9.5-mile network, is the best way to explore Kabetogama Peninsula by foot. It leads to several inland lakes as the path crosses from Kabetogama Lake to Rainy Lake. It's also a great trail for backpackers. Campsites are available at Little Shoepack, Jorgens, Quarter Line, Elk, Agnes, Cruiser, Beast, Brown, and Oslo Lakes—many of which have boats available for rent ($10/day • first-come, first-served). **Black Bay Beaver Pond**, near the northwest point of Kabetogama Peninsula, provides a fairly short hike through pine forest to an active beaver pond.

	Trail Name	Trailhead (# on map)	Access	Length	Notes (Roundtrip distances unless noted otherwise)
Easy	Little American Island	Rainy Lake (1)	Boat	0.25 mile	Self-guided loop trail that explores Minnesota's late 19th century gold rush
	Black Bay Beaver Pond	Across Black Bay north of Rainy Lake Visitor Center (2)	Boat	1.2 miles	Takes hikers to an active beaver pond
	Oberholtzer	Outside Rainy Lake Visitor Center (3)	Land/Car	1.7 miles	Hikes to two scenic overlooks
	Echo Bay	Off County Road 122, 3 miles from Kabetogama Lake Visitor Center (5)	Land/Car	2.5 miles	Excellent bird watching trail • Good location for cross-country skiing in winter
	Sullivan Bay	Ash River Visitor Center (10)	Land/Car	1.5 miles	Tracked snowshoe trail in winter
Moderate	Beast Lake	Namakan Lake (8)	Boat	2.5 mile	Steep climbs at the beginning and end to reach ridgeline (one-way)
	Blind Ash	Kabetogama Lake Overlook (9)	Land/Car	2.5 miles	A pleasant wooded loop
	Anderson Bay	East end of Rainy Lake just past Kempton Channel (11)	Boat	1.75 miles	This short loop rewards hikers with a cliff top view of Rainy Lake
Strenuous	Locator Lake	Across Kabetogama Lake North of the Visitor Center (4)	Boat	4.0 miles	A hilly out-and-back that passes through forests and wetlands
	Kab-Ash	Connects Kabetogama Lake and Ash River Visitor Centers (6)	Land/Car	27.9 miles	Four separate trailheads are located along the trail (one-way & loops)
	Cruiser Lake - 👍	Rainy or Kabetogama Lake (7)	Boat	9.5 miles	Crosses Kabetogama Peninsula (one-way)

Snowshoe prints on Black Bay Beaver Pond

Bald Eagles are commonly seen

A lone gray wolf

Fishing

Voyageurs is home to some of the **best fishing in the Midwest**. Walleye, northern pike, muskellunge, pan-fish, yellow perch, and bass are commonly caught. Visitors with their own boat can launch at any of ten boat ramps lining the southern shorelines of the park's lakes. If you don't have your own boat or would like access to a knowledgeable guide there are several outfitters (page 175) that provide guided fishing expeditions.

Ice fishing is also popular recreation at Voyageurs. Winter anglers must come prepared for northern Minnesota's brand of cold. Temperatures are frequently below zero, snow drifts and the wind whips, leaving even the hardiest of fishermen dreading the thought of exiting their warm fishing shanties. A handful of vendors provide ice fishing guides and/or shelters (page 175). For a complete list of fishing guides pick-up the park's newspaper, *The Rendezvous*, at one of the visitor centers or download it from the park's website.

Boat Tours

More than a third of the park is water, and much of its beauty and mystique cannot be grasped without heading out onto the open water. Boat tours are the perfect way to explore Voyageurs if you don't have your own watercraft, but they can get expensive (especially for large families).

Up-to-date information about these tours can also be found in the current issue of *The Rendezvous*.

Departing Rainy Lake Visitor Center (aboard *The Voyageur*):

Kettle Falls Cruise • ($50 Adult/$25 Child)
This tour takes passengers to historic Kettle Falls Hotel.
Gold Mine Tour • ($20 Adult/$15 Child)
The gold rush also hit Minnesota. This trip leads to Little American Island to view an abandoned gold mine.
Discovery Cruise • ($25 Adult/$15 Child)
Search for gold mines and wildlife on this 2-hour journey.
Grand Tour • ($30 Adult/$15 Child)
Gold Mine and Discovery Tours rolled into one.
Bald Eagle Watch • ($20 Adult/$15 Child)
Starwatch Tour • ($20 Adult/$15 Child)
Sunset Cruise • ($25 Adult/$15 Child)

Departing Kabetogama Lake Visitor Center (aboard *The Otter*):

Kettle Falls Cruise • ($40 Adult/$25 Child)
Ellsworth Rock Gardens • ($25 Adult/$15 Child)
More than 100 rock sculptures made by Jack Ellsworth.
Hoist Bay Tour • ($30 Adult/$15 Child)

Reservations can be made in person at each respective visitor center or until midnight the night before the tour by contacting the park's national call center (877.444.6777, www.recreation.gov).

At the time of publication tours were no longer available at Ash River Visitor Center.

Winter Activities

In winter, canoes and hiking boots are retired in favor of **cross-country skis** and **snowshoes**. **Black Bay and Echo Bay Trails** are two popular destinations for cross-country skiing. **Tilson Connector Trail**, accessible from Rainy Lake Visitor Center, is a 10-mile network of well-groomed trails. **Kab-Ash Trail** from Kabetogama Lake to Ash River is a long ungroomed trail for experienced skiers. Trail maps and conditions are available at the park website. Park personnel maintain three tracked snowshoe trails: **Blind Ash Bay, Sullivan Bay, and Oberholtzer.** **Rainy Lake Visitor Center** has snowshoes that they'll lend out on a first-come, first-served basis for free, and cross-country skis are available for rent ($5/day). You may want to call the visitor center at (218) 286-5258 or (888) 381-2873 for sizing and availability.

One of the more controversial winter activities is **snow-mobiling.** Critics contend their noise and air pollution are ruining the pristine environment, but snowmobilers are still allowed on **frozen lake surfaces** and **Chain of Lakes Scenic Trail.** In all, there are 110 miles of staked and groomed trails to explore the vast expanses of snow, ice, and forests.

Snowmobilers aren't the only motorized vehicles driving on ice, as the magic of wintertime turns a paddler's paradise into a motorist's retreat. Any automobile can drive straight down the boat ramp near Rainy Lake Visitor Center and keep going for seven miles to the mouth of Cranberry Bay. **Rainy Lake Ice Road** is open to cars and trucks weighing less than 7,000 pounds. Islands usually only accessible by boat can be viewed from the warmth of your car. Winter also provides the only opportunity for drive-up camping. You are allowed to park and camp along the ice road if you can endure the cold. A free overnight permit (available at the visitor center) is required for winter camping. Even without spending the night, driving an ice road is a unique national park experience. A trip that becomes even more memorable if you're lucky enough to spot a lone gray wolf crossing the ice surface, or more likely, a pack of fishing shanties where ice fishermen escape the harsh Minnesotan winter.

 ## For Kids

Voyageurs has more activities geared to children than the average park. For starters, children of all ages can dress up in traditional voyageurs' clothing at any of the park's visitor centers. To feel like a modern day voyageur, sign up for the free ranger-led **North Canoe Voyage** (page 171). **Children's tables** are available at each visitor center, filled with kid-friendly activities like coloring and stamping. Children also have the opportunity to become **Junior Rangers** by completing a free activity booklet (available at any of the visitor centers). Upon comple-tion, children are rewarded with a certificate, badge, and

patch. Six **Discovery Packs** are also available at the visitor centers. They help families explore the park's geology, wildlife, and history through an as-sortment of educational materials. Packs are loaned out, free of charge, for an hour or an entire day. They must be checked out by an adult with a valid driver's license.

A **Voyageurs Adventure for Kids** meets at Kabetogama Lake Visitor Center, where a park naturalist leads children on a unique adventure. They are invited to dress as a voyageur, trying on their leggings, sashes, and colorful chamois, before beginning exploring the park with a ranger.

Call or visit the park's website to find a current schedule of events.

 ## Ranger Programs

In addition to boat tours (page 170), the park of-fers numerous free ranger-led activities. Visitors can explore the history of the voyageurs, for whom the park is named, on the **free North Canoe Voyage** that departs from both Rainy Lake (218.286.5258) and Kabetogama Lake (218.875.2111) Visitor Centers. Advance reservations are available beginning in late May by calling the respective visitor center.

Campfire programs are held frequently and special speakers occasionally make an appearance to dis-cuss topics suitable to their expertise. Check a cur-rent issue of *The Rendezvous* or the park website to view a schedule of events.

Flora & Fauna

Wildlife has attracted visitors to Voyageurs since the first European explorers arrived in 1688. In summer, bear, deer, Canadian lynx, and moose are roaming about. But, you're more likely to see some of the **240 species of birds.** Two of the most frequently spotted and popular species are the common loon and bald eagle. In winter you may see tracks of snowshoe hare or gray wolf.

The park is dominated by water, but you can find forests, marshes, and peatlands. Spruce, fir, pine, aspen, and birch are common trees.

 # Basics

Pets: Pets are not allowed on trails or in the backcountry. They are allowed in developed areas like visitor centers, picnic areas, and boat ramps, but must be on a leash no longer than six feet in length at all times.

Accessibility: The park's visitor centers, Kettle Falls Hotel, the first 0.25-mile of Oberholtzer Trail, and most boat tours are wheelchair accessible. Most of the park is reached by boat, making accessibility dependent on your individual method of transport (private or commercial). If you plan on hiring the services of an outfitter, discuss any potential accessibility requirements with them prior to arrival.

Weather: International Falls, the closest city to Voyageurs National Park, holds the title for coldest city in the lower 48 states. This standard should give you a pretty good idea what the climate is going to be like. Summers are short and comfortable with average highs reaching the upper 70s°F in July and August. Winters tend to be long and cold. Temperatures below 0°F are common and average January highs are in the teens.

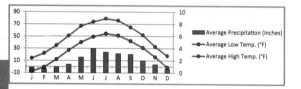

Vacation Planner

Not sure what to do? Where to paddle? Whether or not you should even visit Voyageurs? Here's a 3-day itinerary to jump-start your Voyageurs vacation planning. It assumes you have your own kayak(s) or canoe(s). Dining, grocery stores, lodging, festivals, and attractions inside and outside of the park are listed on pages 173–175.

Day 1 **Ash River Visitor Center** is a great place to introduce yourself to the region. You can ask park rangers questions, watch a short film, browse updated exhibits, and find information on upcoming **ranger programs** and **Boat Tours (available in**

the current issue of *The Rendezvous*). If your schedule allows, the **North Canoe Voyage** (page 171) is highly recommended. Make advance reservations in person at Kabetogama Lake Visitor Center or by calling (218) 875-2111. The North Canoe Voyage Program is also offered at Rainy Lake Visitor Center (call 218.286.5258 for reservations).

Don't worry if you can't fit it into your schedule, because you're going to be spending two nights in the wilderness camping on Kabetogama Peninsula. It also means that you're going to need a free **overnight camping permit**; get one while you're at Ash River Visitor Center. Let the ranger know you plan on camping at sites B6 on Elk Lake and K34 on Sugarbush Island. You'll want to make sure you have enough time to paddle 4 miles and set up camp (1–2 hours). If time permits, hike the short **Blind Ash Bay Trail** (page 169). It begins near the visitor center at Kabetogama Lake Overlook. From here you'll be able to see Sugarbush Island, where you'll camp the following night. With your permit secured and second night's camping location scouted, prep your gear for launch at Ash River boat ramp. Begin paddling north to **Round Bear Island**. You can paddle around either side of the island, but heading to the east requires a short but easy portage. After passing the island head to your right into **Lost Bay**. Near the back of the bay you'll find a short portage leading to **Elk Lake** and your campsite.

 Day 2 Today all you have to get done is an 8-mile paddle to **Sugarbush Island**, so you'll have some free time. Fortunately, the nearby **Cruiser Lake Trail System** (page 169) is one of the best places to burn a little time. Once you're finished hiking, make the portage back into **Lost Bay** and follow the northern shore of Kabetogama Lake all the way to **Nashata Point**. Paddle around to the island's southern shore where you'll camp for the night.

 Day 3 Back to **Ash River Visitor Center** you go. It's about an 8 mile paddle (depending on what path you take). If you're lucky, you may return in time to catch a ranger program and the ranger might suggest a new paddle route for your next visit to Voyageurs.

As your map-reading and navigational skills progress, think about venturing farther from the visitor centers into Rainy Lake and even Canadian waters.

VOYAGEURS

Dining

Michigan's Upper Peninsula

Harbor Haus Restaurant • (906) 289-4502
Dining with a German/Austrian flavor
77 Brockway Ave; Copper Harbor, MI 49918
www.harborhaus.com

Slim's Café • (906) 337-3212
Well-known for their Sunday turkey dinner
8 Mohawk St; Mohawk, MI 49950

Michigan House Café & Brew Pub
300 6th St; Calumet, MI 49913
(906) 337-1910 • Entrée: $10–24
www.michiganhousecafe.com

Lindell's Chocolate Shoppe • (906) 296-8083
300 Calumet St; Lake Linden, MI 49945

Kaleva Café • (906) 482-6001
234 Quincy St; Hancock, MI 49930
www.mykaleva.com • Breakfast: $5–9

Ambassador Restaurant • (906) 482-5054
126 Shelden Ave; Houghton, MI 49931
www.theambassadorhoughton.com • Entrée: $8–12

Ming's Asian Bistro • (906) 482-9888
901 W Sharon Ave, # 6; Houghton, MI 49931

Mine Shaft • (906) 482-1230
Bowling, go-carts, arcade, and food
915 Razorback Dr; Houghton, MI 49931
www.mineshaftfun.com • Entrée: $10–20

Library Restaurant Bar Brew • (906) 487-5882
62 Isle Royale St; Houghton, MI 49931

Suomi Home Bakery & Restaurant • (906) 482-3220
54 Huron St; Houghton, MI 49931

Joey's Seafood & Grill • (906) 483-0500
304 Shelden Ave; Houghton, MI 49931
www.joeys-grill.com • Entrée: $11–24

Four Seasons Tea Room • (906) 482-3233
606 Shelden Ave; Houghton, MI 49931
www.fourseasonstearoom.com

Pilgrim River Steakhouse • (906) 482-8595
47409 US-41; Houghton, MI 49931
www.pilgrimriver.com

J J's Wok N Grill • (906) 483-4868
200 Pearl St, # 6; Houghton, MI 49931

Northern Minnesota

Sven & Ole's • (218) 387-1713
9 W Wisconsin St; Grand Marais, MN 55604
www.svenandoles.com • Specialty Pizza: $15–21

Crooked Spoon Café • (218) 387-2779
17 W Wisconsin St; Grand Marais, MN 55604
www.crookedspooncafe.com • Entrée: $19–25

Angry Trout Café • (218) 387-1265
408 W MN-61; Grand Marais, MN 55604
www.angrytroutcafe.com

My Sister's Place • (218) 387-1915
410 E MN-61; Grand Marais, MN 55604
www.mysistersplacerestaurant.com

Gun Flint Tavern • (218) 387-1563
111 W Wisconsin St; Grand Marais, MN 55604
www.gunflinttavern.com

The Pie Place • (218) 387-1513
207 W Wisconsin St; Grand Marais, MN 55604
www.northshorepieplace.com • Entrée: $14–25

Chez Jude Rest. & Wine Café • (218) 387-9113
411 W MN-61; Grand Marais, MN 55604
www.chezjude.com • Entrée: $12–30

Blue Water Café • (218) 387-1597
20 Wisconsin St; Callaway, MN 56521
www.bluewatercafe.com • Dinner: $10–13

World's Best Donuts • (218) 387-1345
Title is not much of an exaggeration
10 E Wisconsin St; Grand Marais, MN 55604
www.worldsbestdonutsmn.com

Sydney's Frozen Custard • (218) 387-2693
14 S Broadway; Grand Marais, MN 55604

Fitger's Brewhouse Brewery and Grille
Elk burgers, custom brews, and live music
600 E Superior St; Duluth, MN 55802
www.brewhouse.net • (218) 279-2739

Pickwick Restaurant • (218) 623-7425
508 E Superior St; Duluth, MN 55802
www.pickwickduluth.com • Entrée: $17–30

Pizza Luce • (218) 727-7400
11 E Superior St; Duluth, MN 55802
www.pizzaluce.com • Specialty Pizza: $14–22

Hanabi • (218) 464-4412
110 N 1st Ave W; Duluth, MN 55802
www.hanabimn.com • Entrée: $9–24

Sir Benedict's Tavern On The Lake • (218) 728-1192
805 E Superior St; Duluth, MN 55802
www.sirbens.com • Sandwiches: ~$9

Sammy's Pizza & Restaurant • (218) 727-8551
103 W 1st St; Duluth, MN 55802
www.mysammys.com

Bait N' Bite • (218) 875-2281
9634 Gamma Rd; Kabetogama, MN 56669

Lure Me In • (218) 875-2100
9602 Gamma Rd; Kabetogama, MN 56669

Almost Lindys Swill & Grill • (218) 286-3364
3003 County Road 20; International Falls, MN 56649
www.almostlindys.com • Entrée: $14–25

Coffee Landing Café • (218) 283-8316
444 3rd St; International Falls, MN 56649

Chocolate Moose Restaurant • (218) 283-8888
2501 2nd Ave. W; International Falls, MN 56649
www.chocolatemooserestaurant.com • Entrée: $11–19

Giovanni's • (218) 283-2600
301 3rd Ave; International Falls, MN 56649
www.giosifalls.com • Pasta: $9–13

Many chain restaurants can be found in Houghton, International Falls, and Duluth.

Grocery Stores

Michigan's Upper Peninsula

Gas Lite General Store • (906) 289-4652
39 Gratiot St; Copper Harbor, MI 49918

Mohawk Superette • (906) 337-2102
158 Stanton Ave; Mohawk, MI 49950

Louie's Super Foods • (906) 337-2311
340 4th St; Calumet, MI 49913

SuperValu • (906) 296-3221
5400 Bridge St; Lake Linden, MI 49945

Econofoods • (906) 487-9675
1000 W Sharon Ave; Houghton, MI 49931

Walmart Supercenter • (906) 482-0639
995 Razorback Dr; Houghton, MI 49931

Festival Foods • (906) 482-7500
47401 M-26; Houghton, MI 49931

Northern Minnesota

Super One • (218) 283-8440
1313 3rd St; International Falls, MN 56649

SuperValu • (218) 283-4475
1907 Valley Pine Circle; International Falls, MN 56649

Lodging

Michigan's Upper Peninsula

Mariner North • (906) 289-4637
255 Gratiot St; Copper Harbor, MI 49918
www.manorth.com • Rates: $83+

Minnetonka Resort • (906) 289-4449
560 Gratiot St; Copper Harbor, MI 49918
www.minnetonkaresort.com • Rates: $70+

Bella Vista Motel • (906) 289-4213
180 6th St; Copper Harbor, MI 49918
www.bellavistamotel.com • Rates: $62–95

Lake Fanny Hooe Resort & Camp
Motel/cottage/chalet ($90–120), campsites ($28–40)
505 2nd St; Copper Harbor, MI 49918
www.fannyhooe.com • (906) 289-4451

Shoreline Resort • (906) 289-4441
122 Front St; Eagle Harbor, MI 49950
www.shorelineresort.com • Rates: $75+

Eagle Lodge • (906) 289-4294
13051 M-26 Lakeshore Dr; Eagle Harbor, MI 49950
www.eaglelodge-lakeside.com • Rates: $85–150

Laurium Manor Inn • (906) 337-2549
320 Tamarack St; Laurium, MI 49913
www.laurium.info • Rates: $79–179

Eagle River Inn • (906) 337-0666
5033 Front St; Eagle River, MI 49950
www.eagleriverinn.com • Rates: $65+

Keweenaw Mountain Lodge • (906) 289-4403
14252 US-41; Grant Township, MI 49918
www.atthelodge.com • Rates: $99–189

Sunset Bay Resort & Campground
Cabins ($135), RV ($30–35) and Tent ($25) sites
2701 Sunset Bay Beach Rd; Allouez, MI 49805
www.sunset-bay.com • (906) 337-2494

White House Motel • (906) 337-3010
3606 US-41; Mohawk, MI 49950
www.whitehousemotel.com • Rates: $50–66

Mt Bohemia • (906) 289-4105
100 Lac La Belle Rd; Mohawk, MI 49950
www.mtbohemia.com • Rates: $65–80

Big Bay Point Lighthouse B&B • (906) 345-9957
You actually sleep inside the lighthouse
4674 County Road KCB; Big Bay, MI 49808
www.bigbaylighthouse.com • Rates: $137+

Vic's Cabins • (906) 337-8427
58696 US-41; Calumet, MI 49913
www.vicscabins.com • Rates: $49–59

Magnuson Hotel Franklin Square Inn • (888) 487-1700
820 Shelden Ave; Houghton, MI 49931
www.houghtonlodging.com • Rates: $90+

Sheridan on the Lake B&B • (906) 482-7079
47026 Sheridan Place; Houghton, MI 49931
www.sheridanonthelake.com • Rates: $109–139

City of Houghton RV Park • (906) 482-8745
1100 W Lakeshore Dr; Houghton, MI 49931

Northern Minnesota

Grand Portage Lodge • (218) 475-0156
70 Casino Dr; Grand Portage, MN 55605
www.grandportage.com • Rates: $95+

Ryden's • (218) 475-2330 • www.rydensstore.net
9301 Ryden Rd; Grand Portage, MN 55605

Sweetgrass Cove Guesthouse • (218) 475-2421
6880 E MN-61; Grand Portage, MN 55605
www.sweetgrasscove.com • Rates: $150

Best Western Plus • (218) 387-2240
104 1st Ave E; Grand Marais, MN 55604

MacArthur House B&B • (218) 387-1840
520 W 2nd St; Grand Marais, MN 55604
www.macarthurhouse.net • Rates: $94+

Gunflint Motel • (218) 387-1454
101 5th Ave W; Grand Marais, MN 55604
www.gunflintmotel.com • Rates: $59–99

Golden Eagle Lodge & Nordic Ski Center
468 Clearwater Rd; Grand Marais, MN 55604
www.golden-eagle.com • (218) 388-2203

East Bay Suites • (800) 414-2807
21 Wisconsin St; Grand Marais, MN 55604
www.eastbaysuites.com • Rates: $154+

Naniboujou Lodge & Restaurant • (218) 387-2688
20 Naniboujou Tr; Grand Marais, MN 55604
www.naniboujou.com • Rates: $79+

The Inn on Lake Superior • (218) 726-1111
350 Canal Park Dr; Duluth, MN 55802
www.innonlakesuperior.com • Rates: $87+

Fitger's Inn • (888) 348-4377
600 E Superior St; Duluth, MN 55802
www.fitgers.com • Rates: $130+

A G Thomson House B&B • (218) 724-3464
2617 E 3rd St; Duluth, MN 55812
www.thomsonhouse.biz • Rates: $169+

Kettle Falls Hotel • (218) 875-2070
Only in-park (Voyageurs) lodging, boat/plane access
10502 Gamma Rd; Kabetogama, MN 56669
www.kettlefallshotel.com • Rates: $80–290

Harmony Beach Resort • (218) 875-2811
10002 County Rd 123; Kabetogama, MN 56669
www.harmonybeachresort.com • Rates: $115+

Northern Lights Resort • (218) 875-2591
12723 County Rd 332; Kabetogama, MN 56669
www.nlro.com • Rates: $135+

Voyageur Park Lodge • (218) 875-2131
10436 Waltz Rd; Kabetogama, MN 56669
www.voyageurparklodge.com • Rates: $145+

Arrowhead Lodge • (218) 875-2141
10473 Waltz Rd; Kabetogama, MN 56669
www.arrowheadlodgeresort.com • Rates: $35/person

Trails End Resort • (218) 993-2257
Cabins ($125+), rooms ($80), and campsites ($30–40)
6310 Crane Lake Rd; MN 55771
www.trails-end-resort.com

Ash-Ka-Nam Resort • (218) 374-3181
10209 Ash River Tr; Orr, MN 55771
www.ashkanamresortandlodge.com • Rates: $100+

Voyageurs Landing Resort • (218) 993-2401
7510 Gold Coast Rd; Crane Lake, MN 55725
www.voyageurslanding.com • Rates: $75+

Scott's Peaceful Valley Resort • (218) 993-2330
7559 Gold Coast Rd; Crane Lake, MN 55725
www.scottspeacefulvalley.com • Rates: $95+

Voyageur Motel • (218) 283-9424
1210 3rd Ave; International Falls, MN 56649
www.voyageurmotel.net • Rates: $49+

Tee Pee Motel • (218) 283-8494
1501 2nd Ave W; International Falls, MN 56649

Sha Sha Resort • (218) 286-3241
1664 MN-11 E; International Falls, MN 56649
www.shashaonrainylake.com • Cabins: $200+

Thunderbird Lodge • (218) 286-3151
2170 County Rd 139; International Falls, MN 56649
www.thunderbirdrainylake.com • Rates: $89+

Home Town Café Motel & RV Park • (218) 278-4788
112 Main St; Littlefork, MN 56653

Arnold's Campground & RV Park • (218) 285-9100
2031 2nd Ave; International Falls, MN 56649
www.arnoldsfishing.com • Camping: $15–24

Many chain hotels can be found in Houghton, International Falls, and Duluth.

Festivals

Michigan's Upper Peninsula
Winter Carnival • February
Houghton • www.mtu.edu/carnival

Great Bear Chase • March
Cross-Country ski marathon
Calumet • www.bearchase.org

Porcupine Mtns Music Fest • August
Ontonagon • www.porkiesfestival.org

Marquette Blues Festival • September
Marquette • www.marquetteareabluessociety.com

Northern Minnesota
Icebox Days • January
International Falls • www.internationalfallsmn.us

Voyageurs Classic Sled Dog Race • January
Northome • www.whiteoakclassicsleddograce.com

Doheny Curling Bonspiel • January
Eveleth • (218) 744-1302

Homegrown Music Festival • April
Duluth • www.duluthhomegrown.com

Dylan Days • May
Hibbing • www.dylandays.com

Pulling for Peace "International Tug-of-War" • July
International Falls • www.internationaltugofwar.com

Moondance Jam • July
Walker • www.moondancejam.com

Bayfront Blues • August
Duluth • www.bayfrontblues.com

Attractions

Michigan's Upper Peninsula

Keweenaw Adventure • (906) 289-4303
Sea kayaking, bike tours, and canoe rentals
155 Gratiot St; Copper Harbor, MI 49918
www.keweenawadventure.com

Copper Harbor Lighthouse • (906) 337-2310
Provides a short (1.5 hours) Lighthouse Boat Tour
14447 M-26; Copper Harbor Marina, MI
www.copperharborlighthouse.com • Rates: $16/Adult

Delaware Copper Mine Tours • (906) 289-4688
7804 Delaware Mine Rd; Mohawk, MI 49950
www.delawarecopperminetours.com

McLain State Park • (906) 482-0278
Really nice park with Lake Superior views
18350 M-203; Hancock, MI 49931
www.michigan.gov/dnr • Camping: $26

Hancock Rec. Area • (906) 482-7413
Fishing, swimming, volleyball, and horseshoes
2000 Jasberg St (M-203); Hancock, MI 49930
www.cityofhancock.com • Camping: $14–22

Quincy Mine Tours • (906) 482-3101
49750 US-41; Hancock, MI 49930
www.quincymine.com • Admission: $18/Adult

Mt Bohemia • (906) 289-4105
Possibly the best ski resort east of the Mississippi
100 Lac Labelle Rd; Mohawk, MI 49950
www.mtbohemia.com • Lift Ticket: $50

Mont Ripley Ski Area • (906) 487-2340
49051 N Ski Hill; Hancock, MI 49930
www.sportsrec.mtu.edu • Lift Ticket: $30+

Michigan Tech Nordic Ski Trails and Forest
22 miles of trails for biking, hiking, skiing
Sharon Ave; Houghton, Michigan 49931
www.sportsrec.mtu.edu • Pass: $6–10

Keweenaw Brewing Co • (906) 482-5596
408 Shelden Ave; Houghton, MI 49931
www.keweenawbrewing.com

Rogers Cinema 5 • (906) 482-0781
47420 Highway Rd; Houghton, MI 49931

Pic Theater • (906) 482-3470
426 Quincy St; Hancock, MI 49930

Pictured Rocks National Lakeshore
PO Box 40; Munising, MI 49862 • (906) 387-3700
www.nps.gov/piro • Boat Tour: $35/Adult

Island Resort & Casino • (906) 466-2941
US 399 Hwy 2; Harris, MI 49845
www.islandresortandcasino.com

Northern Minnesota

Grand Portage National Monument
170 Mile Creek Rd; Grand Portage, MN 55605
www.nps.gov/grpo • (218) 475-0123

Grand Portage Casino • (218) 475-2401
72 Casino Dr; Grand Portage, MN 55605

Great Lakes Aquarium • (218) 740-3474
353 Harbor Dr; Duluth, MN 55802
www.glaquarium.org • Admission: $15.50/Adult

Lake Superior Railroad Museum • (218) 733-7590
506 W Michigan St; Duluth, MN 55802
www.lsrm.org • Admission: $12/Adult

Vista Fleet • (218) 722-6218
323 Harbor Dr; Duluth, MN 55802
www.vistafleet.com • Rates: $16+

Lake Superior Maritime Center • (218) 727-2497
600 S Lake Ave; Duluth, MN 55802
www.lsmma.com • Admission: Free

Glensheen Historic Estate • (218) 726-8910
3300 London Rd; Duluth, MN 55804
www.d.umn.edu/glen • Admission: $5–26/Adult

Edgewater Resort & Waterpark • (800) 777-7925
2400 London Rd; Duluth, MN 55812
www.duluthwaterpark.com

Spirit Mountain Recreation • (218) 628-2891
9500 Spirit Mountain Pl; Duluth, MN 55810
www.spiritmt.com • Lift Tickets: $25+

Lake Superior Zoo • (218) 723-3748
7210 Fremont St; Duluth, MN 55807
www.lszoo.org • Admission: $10/Adult

Marcus Duluth Cinema • (218) 729-0335
300 Harbor Dr; Duluth, MN 55802

Ebels Voyageur Houseboats • (218) 374-3571
10326 Ash River Tr; Orr, MN 55771
www.ebels.com • Rates: $299+/day

Northernaire Houseboats • (218) 286-5221
2690 County Rd 94; International Falls, MN 56649
www.northernairehouseboats.com • Rates: $265+/day

Comet Theater • (218) 666-5814
102 S River St; Cook, MN 55723
www.comettheater.com • Tickets: $7/Adult

Cine 1 & 2 • (218) 283-2342
1319 3rd Street; International Falls, MN 56649
www.cine5theatre.com

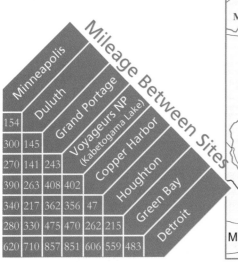

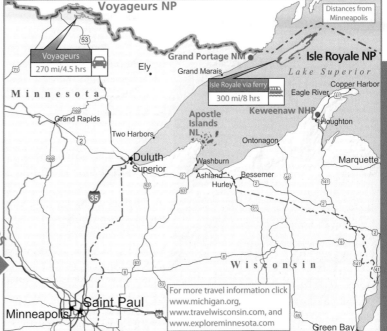

Admiring a masterpiece of erosional forces: Badlands Wall

25216 Ben Reifel Road
Interior, SD 57750
Phone: (605) 433-5361
Website: www.nps.gov/badl

Established: November 10, 1978
Size: 244,000 Acres
Annual Visitors: 1 Million
Peak Season: Summer

Activities: Hiking, Camping, Driving, Biking, Stargazing, Fossil Hunting, and Horseback Riding

Campgrounds: Cedar Pass ($15–28/night), Sage Creek (primitive • free)

Backcountry Camping: Permitted (free, no permit required)

Lodging: Cedar Pass Lodge
Open: mid-April–mid-October
Rates: $85–115/night

Park Hours: All day, every day
Entrance Fee: $15 • Vehicle
$10 • Motorcycle
$7 • Individual (foot, bike, etc.)

Badlands - South Dakota

The Badlands is a swath of semi-arid land bisected by a 60-mile rock wall with steep pinnacles and spires that used to be a daunting site to Indians, fur trappers, and homesteaders. Lack of water, scorching sun, arctic winters, and bone-chilling north winds make the mixed-grass prairies and colorful rock formations of western South Dakota uncommonly hostile. Lakota Sioux and French fur trappers felt the same way. Lakota called it "mako sica." To trappers, it was "les mauvaises terres à traverser." Two words, one translation: "bad lands." Spanish explorers were even less complimentary. They referred to the rugged buttes, dusty siltstones, and gaping gullies as "tierra baldía" or "waste land." But as they say, one man's trash is another man's treasure.

For more than 150 years, the Badlands have been treasured by **archaeologists** and **paleontologists**. Buried in layers of shale, sandstone, volcanic ash, and siltstone are millions of years of history. **Ancient fossils**, some 35 million years old, retell the story of a shallow sea that once covered the region. Geologic forces caused the sea to drain. Subtropical forests began to grow and rivers and streams deposited layers of debris. Ash from volcanic eruptions in the West was carried by the wind, adding to the geologic stratification. Within it you'll find fossils of small saber-toothed cats, hornless rhinos, three-toed horses, ancient camels, squid, and turtles. As water and wind wear away the earth's surface new fossils are exposed. Each discovery is another page turned in the history of the Badlands, a story scientists are eager to read. Today, the park's **White River area** is widely regarded as one of the **richest mammal fossil beds in the world**.

Erosion and deposition have also played a part in this extreme topography. Intense rains and piercing winds have worn away layers of loose, fine-grained rock. Steep slopes funnel water and sediment to the valley floor rapidly and efficiently. Vegetation capable of slowing these erosional forces is unable to grow in the semi-arid climate and jagged rock formations. It's the perfect storm of climatic and geologic conditions, resulting in **an inch of rock eroding each year**. It will continue for centuries until the "Badlands Wall" is nothing at all.

A perfectly flat plain may have been all **homesteaders** were expecting. Drawn to the Badlands by promises of free land and prospect of gold in the Black Hills, easterners began gobbling up lots of land, 160 acres at a time. An abundance of land didn't make up for the harsh conditions. Much like the lives of Lakota Indians and French fur trappers before them, it was a struggle to survive and nearly impossible to coax enough crops out of the ground to support a family. But they tried; cattle replaced bison and wheat fields displaced grasslands. They tended to the land as best they could, but the land never gave back, and only the hardiest homesteaders hung on to life in the Badlands.

Homesteaders and other 19th century developments left their mark on South Dakota's prairies. Today only **one in every 50 prairie areas remain**, and Badlands protects the largest prairie in the National Park System. Inexplicably, the prairie is teeming with life. Bison and pronghorn graze. Prairie dogs scurry about their burrows. Sure-footed bighorn sheep traverse the rocky slopes. Swift fox and black-footed ferret (once thought to be extinct) have been reintroduced by biologists. Where humans failed to survive a healthy prairie ecosystem has flourished, showing the land might not be so bad after all.

Did you know?

▶ The park was originally named Teton National Park.

▶ Badlands possesses one of the world's richest fossil beds. A 35 million year old tortoise fossil is one of many big finds.

▶ Original inhabitants hunted mammoth and bison (North America's largest land mammal) across the Badlands.

When to Go

The park is open all year, but extreme weather conditions can cause uncomfortable or difficult touring. Summer high temperatures can exceed 110°F. Winter lows may dip below -40°F. Ben Reifel Visitor Center, located on Badlands Loop Road (Hwy 240), is open every day except Thanksgiving, Christmas, and New Year's. It is typically open from 8am to 5pm, but hours are extended in summer and shortened in winter. Cedar Pass Lodge, near the visitor center, is the only in-park lodging and is open in summer. On South Dakota Hwy 27, about 20 miles south of the town of Scenic, you'll find White River Visitor Center. It's open seasonally (June to mid-September) from 10am to 4pm.

Transportation & Airports

Public transportation does not serve the park. The closest airport is Rapid City Regional (RAP), located 67 miles west of the park on Hwy 44. Car rental is available at the airport.

Directions

Badlands National Park is located in southwestern South Dakota just south of Interstate 90.

Arriving on I-90 from the east, take Exit 131 (Interior) and follow park signs to the Northeast Entrance. From the west take Exit 110 (Wall) and follow signs leading to the park's Pinnacles Entrance. Highway 44 (from Rapid City) provides a more scenic alternate route. Take Hwy 44 east to Interior. Continue on Hwy 377, which leads directly to the park's Interior Entrance.

BADLANDS

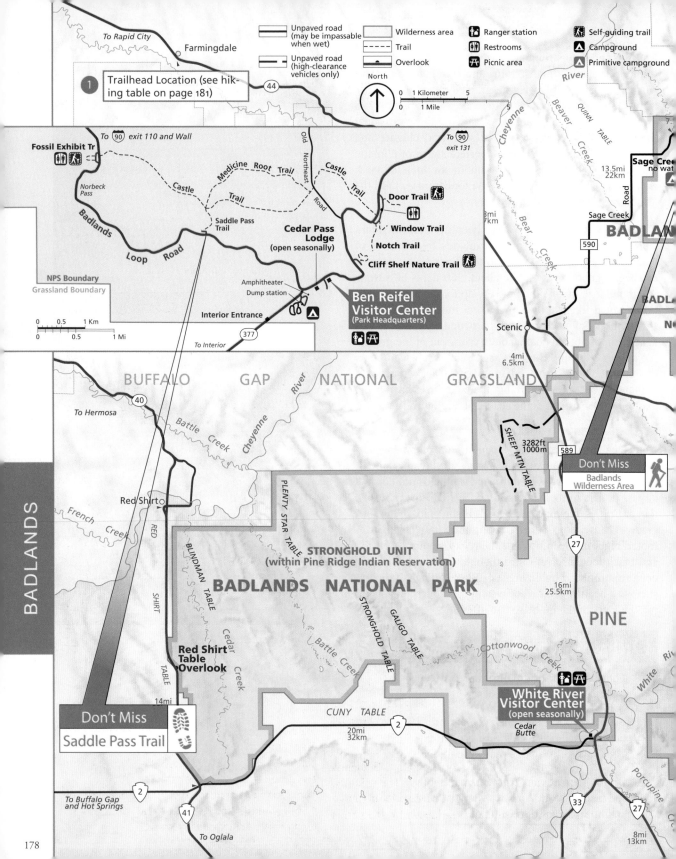

Legend

- Unpaved road (may be impassable when wet)
- Unpaved road (high-clearance vehicles only)
- Wilderness area
- Trail
- Overlook
- Ranger station
- Restrooms
- Picnic area
- Self-guiding trail
- Campground
- Primitive campground

North

| 0 | 1 Kilometer | 5 |
| 0 | 1 Mile | 5 |

1 Trailhead Location (see hiking table on page 181)

To Rapid City

Farmingdale

To **90** exit 110 and Wall

To **90** exit 131

Fossil Exhibit Tr

Norbeck Pass

Castle Trail

Medicine Root Trail

Castle Trail

Castle Trail

Door Trail

Window Trail

Notch Trail

Saddle Pass Trail

Cedar Pass Lodge (open seasonally)

Cliff Shelf Nature Trail

Badlands Loop Road

Northeast Road

Old

NPS Boundary

Grassland Boundary

| 0 | 0.5 | 1 Km |
| 0 | 0.5 | 1 Mi |

Amphitheater

Dump station

Interior Entrance

377

To Interior

Ben Reifel Visitor Center (Park Headquarters)

Scenic

River

Cheyenne

Beaver Creek

QUINN TABLE

13.5mi 22km

Sage Cree no wat

590

BADLAN

Sage Creek Road

Bear Creek

8mi 7km

4mi 6.5km

BUFFALO   GAP   NATIONAL   GRASSLAND

To Hermosa

40

Battle Creek

Cheyenne River

SHEEP MTN TABLE

3282ft 1000m

589

Don't Miss
Badlands Wilderness Area

Red Shirt

French Creek

RED SHIRT TABLE

BLINDMAN TABLE

Cedar Creek

PLENTY STAR TABLE

STRONGHOLD UNIT
(within Pine Ridge Indian Reservation)

BADLANDS   NATIONAL   PARK

Battle Creek

STRONGHOLD TABLE

GALIGO TABLE

Cottonwood Creek

27

16mi 25.5km

PINE

Red Shirt Table Overlook

14mi

Don't Miss

Saddle Pass Trail

CUNY TABLE

2

20mi 32km

Cedar Butte

White River Visitor Center (open seasonally)

White Ri

To Buffalo Gap and Hot Springs

2

41

To Oglala

33

27

Porcupine

8mi 13km

BADLANDS

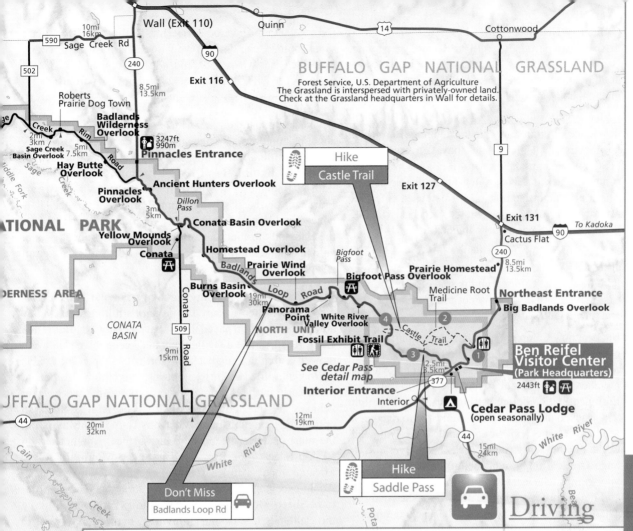

Driving

A park was authorized here in 1929 with the stipulation that South Dakota had to construct a road through its most significant rock formations. **Badlands Loop Road** was built and Badlands National Monument was established in 1939. For your gallon of gas, Badlands is one of the best scenic detours you'll find in the country. While driving along I-90, you can take Hwy 240 for a 42-mile scenic detour through the Badlands between Exits 110 and 131. From the interstate it's not obvious that one of the most amazing natural wonders in the world is a few miles to the south. Once you reach the Pinnacles or Northeast Entrance, eroded stone formations appear out of nowhere and Hwy 240 becomes Badlands Loop Road. It provides access to **11 overlooks**, **Ben Reifel Visitor Center**, **Cedar Pass Lodge and Campground**, and trailheads for the park's

most popular hikes. **Door, Window, Notch, Cliff Shelf Nature, and Fossil Exhibit Trails** are pleasant short hikes found along Badlands Loop Road. Visitors should allow at least 60 minutes to drive the 42-mile loop, but it wouldn't be difficult to spend an entire day hiking trails and poking around the visitor center.

Visitors searching for a more primitive experience should drive **Sage Creek Rim Road**. This unpaved and washboard road intersects Badlands Loop Road just south of Pinnacles Entrance. It features a bunch of overlooks, **Robert's Prairie Dog Town**, and this rugged road is your best bet for seeing wildlife like bison, deer, bighorn sheep, and fox. Shortly before the road exits the park, there is a spur road leading to **Sage Creek Campground**. The Road closes at times in winter and after heavy rains in spring.

Badlands National Park has two maintained drive-in campgrounds, both are open year-round. Backcountry camping is also allowed. The park does not have showers. Open campfires are not permitted due to the flammable nature of prairie grass.

Cedar Pass Campground: Cedar Pass is the only developed campground. It is located near Ben Reifel Visitor Center. All 96 sites have covered picnic tables and exceptional views of Badlands Wall. Cold running water and flush toilets are available nearby. There is a dump station ($1.00 per use). Sites are available on a first-come, first-served basis for $15 per night or $28 per night with hook-ups.

Sage Creek Primitive Campground: Sage Creek is accessed via the unpaved, deep-rutted Sage Creek Rim Road. The campground is free on a first-come, first-served basis. Water is not available. Pit toilets and picnic tables are located nearby.

Backcountry Camping: Camping in the park's backcountry is allowed and does not require an overnight permit. However, backpackers should contact a staff member at Ben Reifel Visitor Center or Pinnacles Entrance Station before setting out on an overnight trip. Backcountry users are also advised to register at Medicine/Castle Trail Loop, Saddle Pass Trailhead, Conata Picnic Area, Sage Creek Basin Overlook, or Sage Creek Campground before departing. Set up your campsite at least 0.5-mile from roads and trails and make sure it cannot be seen from the roadway. There is little to no water in the backcountry, so carry in enough for the duration of your trip.

Cedar Pass Lodge (605.433.5460 • 1 Cedar St. (Box 5); Interior, SD 57750 • www.cedarpasslodge.com • $85–115/night): Cedar Pass Lodge provides the only lodging, gift store, and restaurant in the park. It is located near Ben Reifel Visitor Center on Badlands Loop Road. Before its first incarnation burned down in the 1930s, Cedar Pass Lodge was a dance hall where bands like "Hotsy Totsy Boys" and "Honolulu Fruit Gum Orchestra" were conducted by a bandleader named Lawrence Welk.

Fossils: Multi-colored layers of fragile sedimentary rock made more than spectacular scenery, they made spectacular fossils. Prehistoric fossils are extremely rare around the world, but in Badlands they are common. So common, a visitor occasionally stumbles upon one. In summer of 2010, a seven-year old girl from Atlanta discovered a museum-quality skull of a small saber-toothed cat. Should you unearth the next amazing fossil, leave it where it is and notify a ranger. It is illegal to collect fossils, flowers, rocks, and animals from federal property.

If you don't spark the next big dig, you can still learn all about paleontology, fossils, and the park's ancient history by viewing exhibits and replicas at **Ben Reifel Visitor Center** and **Fossil Exhibit Trail**. Fossil Exhibit is the last hiking trail on Badlands Loop Road if you entered via Northeast Entrance, or the first trail from Pinnacles Entrance. It is educational in nature, but expect your kids to be playing on the Badlands formations rather than learning about extinct animals found within the rock's layers. Regardless, this trail is a great stop for families.

Biking is not a very common activity. For starters, bicycles are not permitted on any of the park's hiking trails. They are only allowed on paved and unpaved roadways. **Badlands Loop Road** can be a challenging and scenic bike ride when motorists aren't racing back and forth at 45 mph. The road is narrow and filled with twists, turns, and climbs. It's best to pedal early in the morning or closer to evening when fewer vehicles are out and about. **Sage Creek Rim Road** is an option for mountain bikers, but this rutted roadway is not the most posterior-friendly biking surface. Another reason to skip Sage Creek Rim Road is **Sheep Mountain Road**. Located about 4 miles south of the tiny town of Scenic, it's an excellent mountain biking destination. The road follows Sheep Mountain Table for 7 miles (one-way). Biking the Badlands may sound uninviting, but you may want to seriously consider toting your two-wheelers for other trails located nearby. **George S. Mickelson Trail** in Deadwood and **Centennial Trail** in Sturgis are excellent pedalling alternatives for the adrenaline junky.

Stargazing is one of the most underrated activities in any location far from big city lights that tend to drown out nightscapes. At Badlands you can admire otherworldly rock formations by day, and gaze into another world at night. Enjoy an evening stargazing program with a park ranger or simply sit outside your tent, staring up at the stars.

Horseback Riding is allowed anywhere in the park except on marked trails, roads, highways, and developed areas. You must trailer in your own horses, as guided rides are not offered presently. A portion of Sage Creek Campground is designated for horse use, and there is a watering hole 0.5-mile southwest of camp.

Hiking

If the temperature is 110°F or you've arrived in the middle of a "gully washers," not leaving your car is understandable. If not, get out and meet the Badlands face-to-face. Hiking through passes in the wall along deep canyons and towering pinnacles is a perfect way to commune with this unique landscape. On a comfortable day you may be tempted to take a long, casual hike on **Castle Trail**. A few miles south of Northeast Entrance is Door/Window Trail Parking Area where three excellent trails (**Door, Window, and Notch**) begin. Each one is less than a mile roundtrip, supplying its own perspective of Badlands Wall and the erosional forces responsible for it. Short on time, sure-footed guests in search of fantastic views should drive no further than **Saddle Pass Trailhead**. It's a 0.25-mile climb up and into the Badlands. Please refer to the hiking table below for a complete list of trails. You are allowed to explore beyond designated trails, but be aware of hidden canyons and cracks in the floor. Off-trail hikers must have exceptional map reading skills, as similar looking landscapes make route finding difficult.

Badlands Hiking Trails

	Trail Name	Trailhead (# on map)	Length	Notes
Easy	Door - 👍	Badlands Loop Road, more than one mile north of Ben Reifel Visitor Center (1)	0.75 mile	This self-guided trail gives visitors access to the other side of Badlands Wall
	Window	Badlands Loop Road, more than one mile north of Ben Reifel Visitor Center (1)	0.25 mile	The "window" has eroded away while harder rock above forms its frame
	Fossil Exhibit	Badlands Loop Road, more than 4 miles west of Ben Reifel Visitor Center (4)	0.25 mile	Fossil enthusiasts can view replicas of fossils that were unearthed here
Moderate	Notch - 👍	Badlands Loop Road, more than one mile north of Ben Reifel Visitor Center (1)	1.5 miles	Hikers climb a wooden ladder for dramatic views of White River Valley
	Cliff Shelf	Badlands Loop Road, less than one mile north of Ben Reifel Visitor Center (1)	0.5 mile	Short loop that follows a boardwalk and climbs stairs along Badlands Wall
	Castle - 👍	Connects Fossil Exhibit Trail and Door/Window Trail Parking Areas (1, 4)	10.0 miles	The longest trail in the park passes mostly level terrain and Badlands formations
	Medicine Root	Spur from Castle Trail (2)	4.0 miles	Detour through a mixed-grass prairie
	Saddle Pass - 👍	Badlands Loop Road, about 3 miles west of Ben Reifel Visitor Center (3)	0.25 mile	Short, steep climb straight up the Badlands Wall

Brule formations

A bison at Cedar Pass Campground © Theodore Scott

For Kids: **Fossils** (page 180) and kids are almost always a winning combination, so **Fossil Exhibit Trail** and **Ben Reifel Visitor Center** are two good destinations for families. Everyone's favorite fossils, dinosaurs, have yet to be unearthed here, but many other prehistoric beasts have been found fossilized in Badlands' soft rock layers. The elephant-sized titanothere and the ancient scavenger archaeotherium (nicknamed the "big pig" even though it's not genetically related to pigs) lived in the area millions of years ago. A three toed horse, an ancient camel, a small sabre-tooth cat, and several other mammals and sea creatures have also been found. As the ground continues to erode, new fossils are exposed and discovered by paleontologists and visitors. The White River Area is one of the world's most productive fossil beds.

If your children are more interested in animals that are still scurrying about, stop at **Robert's Prairie Dog Town** on **Sage Creek Rim Road**. These little critters are sure to draw a few giggles as they pop in and out of their burrows, barking among their friends.

Kids also have the opportunity to become a **Junior Ranger**. Your child can join this exclusive club one of two ways: by completing the free junior ranger activity book (available at either visitor center) or by attending an official Junior Ranger Program during the summer. Check online or at a visitor center for an up-to-date schedule of events. When completed, return it to one of the visitor centers, where your child will be awarded an official Badlands National Park Junior Ranger badge.

Ranger Programs: From June to mid-September Badlands' rangers give walks, talks, and presentations. You can find a weekly listing of **ranger-led activities** on white bulletin boards along Badlands Loop Road, at visitor centers (call or stop-in), or at the park's website. If you're enchanted by the spires and buttes of Badlands Wall, you may want to join a ranger on "**Geology Walk**." Confused about why fossils of ancient sea creatures were found in the middle of this prairie land? "**Fossil Talk**" is the ranger program for you. Curious about more recent life on the prairie, including today's wildlife? Hop aboard a "**Prairie Walk**." In addition to these activities the park offers a **Night Sky Program**, a Junior Ranger Program, and a "ranger's choice" Evening Program. Most programs take place at Cedar Pass Campground's Amphitheater.

Flora & Fauna: There was a time when prairie sprawled across more than a third of North America. These areas were too wet to be deserts and too dry to support trees. Today, most are gone, but the largest remaining prairie protected by the National Park System is located at Badlands. Nearly 50% of the park is mixed-grass prairie, a combination of short and tall grass. The other half of is Badlands rock formations with small areas of woodlands, wetlands, and shrublands mixed in. **More than 400 species of plants** survive in this dry and rocky environment. Of these, nearly 60 are grasses.

Semi-arid land also provides habitat for a surprising diversity of wildlife: **55 mammal species, 120 bird species, and 19 species of reptiles and amphibians**. Park biologists have determined these prairies can sustain nearly 800 bison, far fewer than the original herds that numbered more than one million but a healthy population by today's standards. Bighorn sheep, swift fox, pronghorn, mule deer, coyotes, and prairie dogs also reside here. Among Badlands' animals, **black-footed ferrets** have the most remarkable story. These nocturnal critters—once thought to be extinct—were accidentally rediscovered in Wyoming. About 12 ferrets were taken into captivity, and search for suitable habitats began. Badlands was selected because its prairie dog population (black-footed ferrets' primary food source) was healthy and free of diseases. Today park biologists monitor the ferret population. They are reproducing naturally and in an apparent state of self-sustainability.

The seldom-visited **Badlands Wilderness Area**, accessed via Sage Rim Road (unpaved), is by far the best location to view wildlife.

Pets: Pets are permitted in the park, but must be kept on a leash no more than six feet in length at all times. They are allowed in developed areas like campgrounds. Pets, with the exception of service animals, are not allowed on hiking trails, in public buildings, or in the backcountry.

Accessibility: Ben Reifel and White River Visitor Centers are accessible to wheelchair users. Cedar Pass Campground has two fully-accessible sites. Cedar Pass Lodge is fully accessible. Fossil Exhibit and Windows Trails as well as the first section of Door and Cliff Shelf Trails have accessible boardwalks. Ranger programs held at Cedar Pass Campground Amphitheater are accessible, but ranger-led walks and hikes generally are not due to rugged terrain.

Weather: The Badlands received its name due to relatively inhospitable living conditions. Lack of water and extreme weather have made even the hardiest homesteaders pack up and move elsewhere. Things haven't changed much. The region is semiarid, receiving an average of 16 inches of rain each year, but it's known for brief, intense rainfalls, commonly called "gully-washers." The driest months are from November to January, when it can be bitterly cold. The wettest months are May and June, at which time trails are often muddy and unhikeable. Average high temperatures in July and August reach the low 90s°F but it's not uncommon to crack 100°F. January is the coldest month with average highs around freezing.

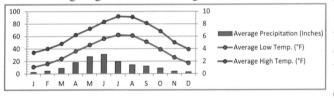

Vacation Planner

The average trip here lasts a little more than 5 hours. This is just enough to drive **Badlands Loop Road**, hike **Door, Window, and Notch Trails**, and making a quick stop at the visitor center. Try to spend at least one night, allowing time to join a **ranger program** (page 182) and **see the stars** (page 180). **Lodging** is available at Cedar Pass Lodge and there are two **campgrounds** within the park (page 180). Nearby dining, grocery stores, lodging, festivals, and attractions are listed on pages 201–203.

Day 1 Arrive at **Northeast Entrance**, stopping at **Door/Window Trail Parking Area** to get a closer look at Badlands Wall. Hike any or all three of the trails that begin here (Door, Window, and Notch • page 181). Together

Shadows on the Brule formation

Best of Badlands

Hike: **Notch Trail**
Runner-up: Saddle Pass Trail

they shouldn't take more than 2–3 hours. Next stop, **Ben Reifel Visitor Center**, where you can watch a short film and browse exhibits. If you haven't already checked the program schedule online or on the white bulletin boards lining Badlands Loop Road, take a look at the visitor center. **Ranger programs** are always a recommended activity. The visitor center also has a nice picnic area, making it a good spot to stop and have lunch. A few hours before sunset return to Door/Window Parking Area. This time head to the west side of the road and hike **Castle Trail** (page 181) to **Saddle Pass** then return to the parking area via **Medicine Root Trail**. Notice as the sun gets closer to the horizon the rock's colors become more vibrant and distinct.

Castle Trail is also a good destination for a day hike. It connects to **Fossil Exhibit Trail** where any individuals and children uninterested in a long hike can be waiting to pick up one-way hikers. It's roughly 10 miles from Door/Window Parking Area to Fossil Exhibit Trail.

Day 2 Complete the rest of **Badlands Loop Road**. If anyone missed the view from Saddle Pass, stop to hike the 0.25-mile **Saddle Pass Trail** (page 181). Although short, it is definitely not for the timid. Continue west, stopping at overlooks whenever the scenery strikes you, and drive down **Sage Creek Rim Road**. This is where most of the Badlands' wildlife hangs out. Here you'll have an excellent chance of seeing bison, prairie dogs, and pronghorn before you leave.

A park ranger at Windy City Lake

26611 US Highway 385
Hot Springs, South Dakota 57747
Phone: (605) 745-4600
Website: www.nps.gov/wica

Established: January 9, 1903
Size: 28,295 Acres
Annual Visitors: 580,000
Peak Season: Summer

Activities: Hiking, Scenic Driving,
Biking, and Horseback Riding

Cave Tours
Open: All Year
Fee: $7–23 (1–4 hours)

Campgrounds: Elk Mountain
Fee: $12/night ($6/night in winter)
Backcountry Camping: Permitted*
Lodging: None

Park Hours: All day, every day
Entrance Fee: None

*Backcountry camping is restricted
to the northwest corner of the park
and requires a free permit

Wind Cave - South Dakota

Long before European fur traders and eastern miners arrived, Lakota Sioux considered the area now known as Wind Cave National Park sacred. They spoke of a "hole that breathes cool air" and left tipi rings near the cave's only natural entrance. Indian legend describes this opening as the site where bison first emerged to roam the prairies. While evidence that bison originated from the cave is scant, scientists know, with some certainty, why the cave is so "windy." It's all about air pressure. Air flows into the abyss when pressure outside the cave is greater than pressure inside. However, when pressure is greater inside the cave, gusts of air blow out of its natural opening.

One summer day, a strong wind blowing out of this opening knocked a hat from the top of **Tom Bingham's** head. Tom and his brother, Jesse, **rediscovered the cave in 1881**. And so the story goes. While displaying their find to a few locals, Tom leaned over the small chasm only to have a gust of wind blow off his hat, ultimately falling into the cavern below. Tom and Jesse were first to rediscover the cave, but they weren't willing to be first to enter the unknown world below. That honor was left for Charlie Crary, a local miner, who entered Wind Cave with a small lantern and a ball of twine to trace his path. Shortly after this discovery, **South Dakota Mining Company** took an interest in the cave. The company hired **J.D. McDonald** to lay claim to a homestead directly above the cave and begin examining its passages for gold. His 16-year-old son, **Alvin**, did most of the exploring. Much to the mining company's dismay he wasn't seeking gold. Alvin charted new passages

Boxwork

for the simple pleasure of witnessing and exploring a place never seen before by human eyes.

Things turned contentious in 1899. J.D. McDonald and a partner entered a dispute over land ownership with South Dakota Mining Company. The Department of Interior ruled that no one was entitled to the land as it was not being used properly for mining nor did it comply with the terms of the Homestead Act. Two years later, 1,000 acres surrounding the cave became federal property and **tours** were given for free by **Elmer McDonald** (another son of J.D.). On January 9, 1903 legislation passed creating Wind Cave, the eighth national park of the United States and first created to protect a cave, ensuring visitors could satisfy their own curiosities exploring the mysteries of the unknown just like Alvin McDonald did.

Very few visitors explore the rolling grasslands and ponderosa pine forests above this subterranean labyrinth. These landscapes and the wildlife that live there are worthy of federal protection by themselves. Lakota called this region "Pahá Sápa" or "**Black Hills**," a name earned by the cover of trees that look black compared to a sea of grass surrounding them. By the time the park was established in 1903, bison, elk, and pronghorn were no longer found here. Park employees attempted reintroduction programs to restore the habitat to its original state. Today, Wind Cave National Park is home to one of four free-roaming, genetically pure **bison herds** on publicly owned lands. **Pronghorn** are seen in the prairies and **elk** can be heard bugling in the backcountry.

Whether your curiosities take you to the backcountry or underground passages, you'll begin to realize why Lakota Sioux considered this area sacred. It's the same indescribable gravitational force that drew Alvin McDonald deeper and deeper into the cave.

Flowstone

Frostwork and Popcorn Cave Formations

Did you know?

- ▶ Wind Cave was established in 1903 by President Theodore Roosevelt, one of the leading advocates of the National Park Idea.

- ▶ It was the 8th national park established in the U.S. and today it's the 7th oldest.

- ▶ It was the first park established to protect a cave.

- ▶ With more than 130 miles of explored passages, it is the 4th longest cave in the world. Estimates predict that only 5% of the cave has been discovered.

- ▶ It is considered to be the densest cave in the world based on volume of passages per area.

- ▶ Wind Cave is most notable for its calcite formations known as boxwork. It contains 95% of the world's discovered boxwork cave formations, but very few stalactites and stalagmites.

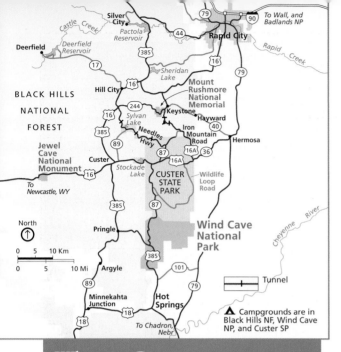

When to Go

The park is open all year. Wind Cave Visitor Center is open daily from 8am to 4:30pm, with extended hours in summer. It closes on Thanksgiving, Christmas, and New Year's Day. Cave tours are offered daily at the visitor center.

Transportation & Airports

Public transportation does not serve the park. The closest airport is Rapid City Regional (RAP), located about 60 miles to the northeast.

Directions

Wind Cave is located at the southern tip of South Dakota's Black Hills. It is 6 miles north of Hot Springs, SD and 1.5 hours drive from Rapid City, SD. Several routes are available if traveling from the north (two are listed below).

Via US-385/US-16 (60 miles): The longest and fastest route provides opportunity for a short detour to **Mount Rushmore**. Follow US-16 W for 40 miles. Turn right at Custer St/Mt. Rushmore Rd. Continue for a 0.5-mile before turning left at US-385 S, which leads into the park.

Via SD-79/SD-87 (55 miles): Take SD-79 S from Rapid City. Turn right at SD-36W and continue onto US-16 Alt W. Turn left to follow SD-87 S, which leads into the park.

Camping

For the reasonable price of $12 per night visitors can camp at **Elk Mountain Campground**, located near the park's western boundary, one mile north of the visitor center. All sites are available on a first-come, first-served basis, but the camp rarely fills to capacity. Pull-through sites are available for RVs. Hook-ups, dump stations, and showers are not available. Restrooms with cold water are located nearby. Water is turned off from late fall through early spring. During this time vault toilets are available and the camping fee is reduced to $6/night. Campfire wood is available near the camp's entrance. No cost is associated with wood, but donations are accepted. Group camping is available by reservation only. Reservations can be made by calling (605) 745-4600.

Hiking/Backpacking

Hiking is one of the most underrated and underutilized attractions at Wind Cave. These badlands are a transitional region, highlighted by the convergence of western ponderosa pine forests and eastern mixed-grass prairies. Three self-guided nature trails (featuring interpretive signs along the way or brochures at the trailhead) help you learn about the park's ecology. **Rankin Ridge Nature Trail** is located on SD-87 near the North Entrance. It's a short loop that leads to the highest point in the park and extraordinary views. **Elk Mountain Nature Trail** begins at the campground. It provides the perfect example of overlapping pine and prairie ecosystems. **Prairie Vista Nature Trail** begins near the visitor center, then loops around a quiet prairie grassland. All three of these trails are about one mile long.

The remaining trails are longer out-and-back treks, but a nice scenic loop (< 5 miles) can be formed by connecting a few trails together. Begin on **Lookout Point Trail**, and follow a short stretch of **Highland Creek Trail to Centennial Trail**. From the intersection, take Centennial Trail west, along Beaver Creek, back to Lookout Point/Centennial Trailhead where you started. The park's northwest corner is open to backcountry camping.

Backpackers can extend this smaller loop by making a figure 8. Hike in on **Lookout Point Trail**, but continue east on **Highland Creek Trail**. Return via **Centennial Trail**, but this time use **Sanctuary Trail** as the connector.

Wind Cave Hiking Trails

	Trail Name	Length	Location (# on map)/Notes (Roundtrip distances)
Easy	Wind Cave Canyon	3.6 miles	Begins just east of the visitor center on the east side of US-385 (3) • Great trail for bird watching
	Cold Brook Canyon	2.8 miles	Located on the west side of US-385 near the south entrance (2) • Passes a prairie dog town
	East Bison Flats	7.4 miles	Gobbler Pass near the south entrance (1) • Traverses rolling prairies then joins Wind Cave Canyon
	Lookout Point	4.4 miles	Centennial Trailhead (4) • Views of 1999 wildfire and vast prairies before ending at Beaver Creek
Strenuous	Sanctuary	7.2 miles	Near the north entrance (5) • Intersects Centennial Trail and terminates at Highland Creek Trail
	Centennial	12.0 miles	Trailhead is on the east side of SD-87, just north of the SD-87/US-385 intersection (4) • This is actually a 6-mile sampling of the 111-mile Centennial Trail that extends north to Bear Butte
	Boland Ridge	5.2 miles	Begins in the eastern corner on the east side of NPS 6 (7) • Guaranteed excellent views • May see elk
	Highland Creek - 👍	17.2 miles	Begins off Wind Cave Canyon Trail and continues north to NPS 5 near the northern boundary (6)

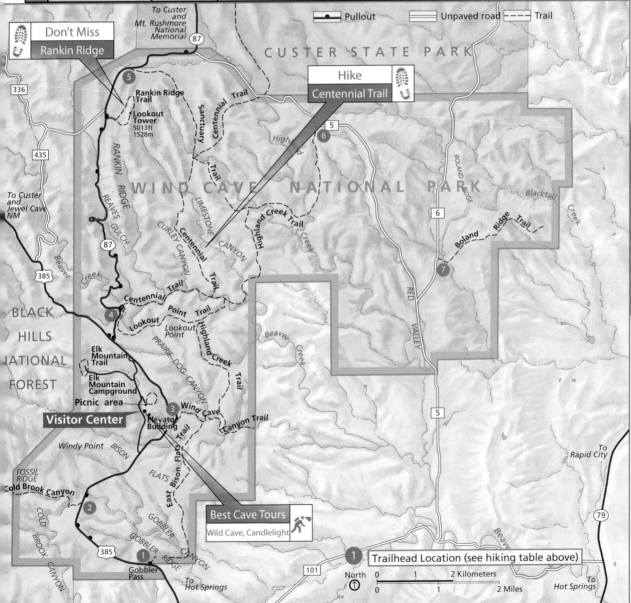

187

WIND CAVE

Cave Tours

In 1891, **Alvin McDonald** (pictured on the opposite page), self-proclaimed "permanent guide" of Wind Cave, began a systematic exploration of the cave's passageways. The young man first entered the cave when he was 16 years old with a candle and a ball of twine to trace his path back to the surface. For the next three years he spent several hours per day mapping passages, inspecting chasms, and exploring the unknown. In March of 1891 alone he registered 134 hours in the cave over the course of 34 trips. By the end of that year he had surveyed several miles of passages and had written in his diary…"**have given up the idea of finding the end of Wind Cave**." Sadly, Alvin died at the age of 20 while in Chicago with his father showing cave specimens. His body was returned to the place he loved so much, buried near the cave's natural entrance where a bronze plaque marks his grave. His diary is on display at the visitor center. In all, Alvin McDonald explored 8 to 10 miles of the cave, naming many of its rooms and passages. Alvin gave up on finding the cave's end, but modern explorers have not. Today, it measures 132 miles in length, the **fourth longest cave in the world**, and experts believe that only 5 percent of the entire network has been discovered. Each year, about four new miles are mapped out, with no end in sight.

The only way for guests to explore the cave is on a **guided tour**, many of which follow routes Alvin McDonald and Katie Stable (guide for 11 years until 1902) pioneered more than a century ago. If you'd like to share a similar experience, take the **Candlelight Tour**. A park ranger leads groups of no more than 10 through an unlit section of the cave. The candle bucket you hold in your hand provides the only light. It's an excellent tour and one of two that allow reservations (strongly recommended). The other, the **Wild Cave Tour**, requires reservations. It's a blast for adventurous individuals who have a little spelunker inside of them (and not the least bit claustrophobic or afraid of getting dirty). The trip lasts four hours. Much of the time will be spent on your hands and knees or in other precarious positions as you traverse sections of the cave few visitors get the chance to see. You may encounter long waits for non-reservation tours during the summer. Tour schedules are subject to change. Please call (605) 745-4600 to confirm tour times.

WIND CAVE

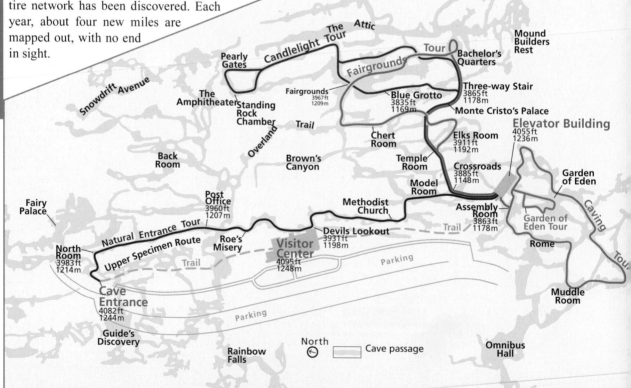

Wind Cave Tours

Tour (Group Size)	Rates (Adult/Youth)	Duration	Notes
Garden of Eden	$7/$3.50	1 hour	Least strenuous tour that visits small samples of boxwork, popcorn, and flowstone (page 185) • Enter and exit by elevator
Natural Entrance	$9/$4.50	1.25 hours	A quick hike to the natural entrance before entering via a man-made entrance • Exit by elevator • 300 stairs
Fairgrounds 👍	$9/$4.50	1.5 hours	Explore boxwork, popcorn, and frostwork in two levels of the cave • Enter and exit by elevator • 450 stairs
Candlelight (10)* 👍	$9/$4.50	2 hours	Harken back to the original cave tours by Alvin McDonald • Each visitor carries a candle bucket • Minimum age of 8
Wild Cave (10)* 👍	$23/Not Permitted	4 hours	Cavers get dirty as you crawl, squeeze, and climb through sections of the cave very few visit • Minimum age of 16

Youth is 6–16 years of age. Golden Age, Golden Access, and America the Beautiful Senior and Access Pass holders pay youth rates.

*Tour reservations can be made up to one month in advance by calling the park at (605) 745-4600 (required for Wild Cave Tour). Wild Cave and Candlelight Tours are only available from mid-June to early September. Long pants, long-sleeved shirts, and sturdy, lace-up boots are required apparel for the Wild Cave Tour. Gloves are recommended.

Tickets are sold at the visitor center. All tours except Wild Cave and Candlelight Tours are sold on a first-come, first-served basis. The cave is a constant 53°F all year, so dress accordingly. Sandals are not recommended footwear.

Alvin McDonald

A bison barricade

Black-footed ferrets

Currently no outfitters provide guided horse rides within the park, but there are a couple of outfitters offering services beyond park boundaries (page 202).

<u>Driving:</u> You don't have to hit the trails to get a good view of prairie dog towns, bison, and undulating hills. The park is extremely accessible to motorists. Pullouts along **US-385** and **SD-87** provide outstanding views of under-appreciated scenery. Obey the speed limits and watch for wildlife. In the past 20 years more than 80 bison have been hit by motorists, and you don't want an ornery bison on your hands, do you?

<u>For Kids:</u> Wind Cave is one of the best national parks for children. Below the surface lies the 4th longest cave network in the world. Children can poke around these dimly lit passageways on any one of the park's **guided cave tours** (page 188). If confined dark spaces aren't for you, there's just as much to do back on the surface. A relatively small area and healthy animal populations make Wind Cave a great place to view animals. Sometimes you see wildlife up-close and personal without even trying. Bison can be found lumbering alongside (or on) the paved roadways. Children up to age 12 may participate in the **Junior Ranger Program**. Free activity booklets are available at the visitor center. Once completed, return to the visitor center to receive a certificate and badge.

<u>Ranger Programs:</u> The park's most notable tours are those that occur in the cave's passageways, but you'll also find quality ranger programs above the surface. **Prairie hikes** (2 hours long) are offered daily during the summer beginning at 9am and departing from the visitor center. Occasionally, the park offers evening hikes to a nearby prairie dog town. You arrive at dusk, because the goal is to spot the endangered (and nocturnal) black-footed ferret. Remember to bring a flashlight. Evening hikes depart from Elk Mountain Campground Amphitheater. Interested visitors should call or stop by the visitor center (605.745.4600) for more details. Additionally, campfire programs and Ranger Talks are offered throughout the summer. For a complete schedule, check the latest issue of the park's free publication, *Passages*.

<u>Flora & Fauna:</u> Today, **Wind Cave is one of the best national parks for animal watching** and its small size

Other Activities

<u>Biking:</u> All paved roadways are open to cyclists. If there's heavy traffic moving about the park you may want to stick to pedalling **US-385**, because it has wider shoulders. **SD-87** is winding and narrow, but it can be fun (and challenging) to bike up to **Rankin Ridge**, the highest point in the park at 5,013 feet. The other two roads, **NPS-5** and **NPS-6**, pass through rolling grasslands. As a whole, Wind Cave is small and very manageable by way of bicycle. Bikes are not permitted on hiking trails or in the backcountry.

<u>Horseback Riding:</u> An alternative method of transportation is to travel by horse. The entire park, except for hiking trails, near water sources, on roadways, and in campground and picnic areas, is open to horseback riding. All visitors must obtain a free permit from the visitor center prior to riding.

makes wildlife viewing easy and fairly predictable. This wasn't the case in 1903 when it was established. At the time bison, pronghorn, bear, and elk were all extirpated from the region. In 1913, 14 bison were donated to the park by the New York Zoological Society. **Black-footed ferret**, a predator of prairie dogs, was reintroduced in 2007. The reintroduction program has been successful and now you can attend evening programs (page 190) where visitors—armed with a flashlight—try to spot these mink-like critters. Sometimes a brigade of **bison** form a road-block holding up traffic. Even though they are the largest terrestrial animal in North America, a motivated bison can reach speeds up to 40 mph. On the other end of the size spectrum, prairie dogs scurry from burrow to burrow squawking all the while.

Ponderosa pine forests, common to North America's western regions, occur in great abundance. Prairies, covering more than half the park, erupt in a sea of color from late spring to summer when wildflowers are in bloom.

<u>Pets</u>: When in the park, pets must be kept on a leash no more than six feet in length. They are prohibited from public buildings, the backcountry, and all hiking trails (except Elk Mountain and Prairie Vista Nature Trails). Pets are allowed at Elk Mountain Campground.

<u>Accessibility</u>: The cave and visitor center are accessible to individuals in wheelchairs, and a special cave tour ($5/adult, $2.50 with Senior or Access Pass) is offered for visitors with special needs. For more information or to make arrangements please contact the park. Elk Mountain Campground has two wheelchair accessible campsites.

<u>Weather</u>: Situated at the southern tip of South Dakota's Badlands, Wind Cave enjoys a much warmer and drier climate than the northern hills. January is the coldest month, with average high temperatures around 37°F. Average annual snowfall is 30 inches, fairly evenly distributed between December and March. May and June are the wettest months of the year, receiving roughly 3 inches of rain per month. The hottest month of the year is August when highs average 88°F. However, warm afternoons can quickly turn into brisk evenings with strong winds blowing from the north.

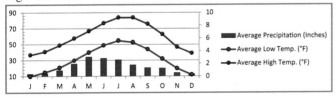

Best of Wind Cave

Family Cave Tour: **Candlelight**
　　Runner-up: Fairgrounds

Adventure Cave Tour: **Wild Cave**
　　Note: Minimum age of 16

Family Hike: **Wind Cave Canyon**
　　Runner-up: Cold Brook Canyon

Adventure Hike: **Highland Creek**
　　Runner-up: Sanctuary

Nearby Attractions: **Mount Rushmore***
　　Runner-up: Custer State Park*
　　2nd Runner-up: Jewel Cave NM*
　　3rd Runner-up: Devil's Tower NM*

*See page 203 for contact information, details, and other nearby attractions.

Vacation Planner

Wind Cave's primary attractions can all be seen in an action-packed, fun-filled day, but a longer visit gives you the opportunity to take another cave tour or explore the backcountry. Try to visit the park during summer so you can enjoy its two best cave tours: **Wild Cave and Candlelight Tours** (reservations can be made up to one month in advance and are required for Wild Cave). Nearby dining, grocery stores, lodging, festivals, and attractions are listed on pages 201–203.

Note that your day is going to be scheduled around a cave tour. If you did not make reservations for the **Candlelight or Wild Cave Tour**, head directly to the visitor center to check availability. If they're booked, the **Fairgrounds Tour** (page 189) is a more than passable substitute. Before, after, and in between cave tours take the time to hike **Prairie Vista Nature Trail**, which begins near the visitor center, and **Rankin Ridge Nature Trail** (page 186), which begins near the North Entrance. Stopping at a **prairie dog town** is another good idea.

The Little Missouri River as seen from South Unit's Wind Canyon Overlook

PO Box 7; Medora, ND 58645
North Unit: (701) 842-2333
South Unit: (701) 623-4730 ext. 3417
Website: www.nps.gov/thro

Established: November 10, 1978
Size: 70,447 Acres
Annual Visitors: 620,000
Peak Season: Summer

Activities: Hiking, Paddling, Camping, Scenic Driving, Horseback Riding, Biking, Fishing, Cross-Country Skiing, and Snowshoeing

Campgrounds: Cottonwood (South Unit) and Juniper (North Unit)
First-come, first-served
Fee: $10/night
$5/night during the off-season
Backcountry Camping: Permitted*
Lodging: None

Park Hours: All day, every day
Entrance Fee: $10 • Vehicle
$5 • Individual (foot, bike, etc.)

*A free permit is required for backcountry camping in the park

Theodore Roosevelt - North Dakota

Cliffs, gullies, and badlands formations of Theodore Roosevelt National Park are as rugged and relentless as its namesake. September of 1883, **Theodore Roosevelt** arrived in the town of Little Missouri a bespectacled, affluent New York City kid. Time spent in the Dakota badlands influenced him so deeply that he later wrote, "**I would not have been President if it had not been for my experiences in North Dakota.**" Roosevelt came to "**bag a buffalo,**" but he would do much more than hunt. Romanced by the West's lawless lifestyle and potential for economic success, Roosevelt bought into the booming cattle industry, purchasing **Maltese Cross Ranch** for $14,000. The one-and-a-half story cabin with wooden floors and separate rooms was, to locals, a "mansion". Today, it is preserved at the park's South Unit.

Roosevelt returned to New York, where **tragedy struck** on February 14, 1884. Just hours apart, Theodore's mother and wife passed away. Stricken by grief, all Roosevelt could write in his diary was a large "X" and one sentence: "The light has gone out in my life." Searching for solace, he returned to Maltese Cross Ranch. However, the ranch's location on a busy carriage road near the train station lacked the sort of solitude he desired for thought and reflection, prompting him to establish **Elkhorn Ranch**.

Roosevelt's days as a ranchman were short-lived. Nearly 60 percent of his cattle froze or starved to death during the winter of 1886–87. (His livestock's fate was better than most; nearly 80 percent of the area's cattle

Maltese Cross Ranch cabin

Best of Theodore Roosevelt

Hike (South Unit): **Painted Canyon**
> Runner-up: Wind Canyon
> 2nd Runner-up: Talkington

Hike (North Unit): **Sperati**
> Runner-up: Caprock Coulee
> 2nd Runner-up: Achenbach Loop

Activity (South Unit): **Horseback Riding**
Activity (North Unit): **Paddling**

Did you know?

➤ Theodore Roosevelt conserved an estimated 230 million acres of land by establishing 51 Federal Bird Reservations, 4 National Game Reserves, 150 National Forests, 5 National Parks, and 18 National Monuments.

➤ He inspired the creation of the "Teddy" Bear by refusing to shoot a bear tied and beaten by his attendants because it would be unsportsmanlike.

➤ He became the 26th President of the United States after the assassination of President William McKinley.

➤ He remains the youngest person to assume the office of President of the United States.

died that year.) Within two years, the small meat-packing town of Medora turned into a ghost town. Roosevelt closed Elkhorn Ranch, and in 1898 sold his remaining cattle interests. Today, Elkhorn Ranch is a part of the park. The structures' materials have been scavenged, leaving nothing more than sections of foundation. Interpretive panels provide insight into Roosevelt's domain that once stood proudly above the banks of the Little Missouri.

Roosevelt may have left Elkhorn Ranch as a failure in cattle business, but he returned to New York a hardened ranchman with newfound appreciation of wilderness and the strenuous life of a frontiersman. He is often referred to as America's **"Conservationist President,"** earning this title by preserving and protecting an estimated 230 million acres of land of ecological and scenic value.

Through efforts of the National Park Service visitors can experience North Dakota's badlands just as Theodore Roosevelt did (except while driving in cars rather than riding on horseback). Bison (or buffalo), pronghorn, and elk have been reintroduced after being overhunted. Artifacts from Roosevelt's time are on display, including rifles and ranch clothing. Period pieces and several of Roosevelt's personal effects, including a traveling trunk, remain in Maltese Cross Cabin, which can be toured with a park ranger. For all he has done for future generations of America and the welfare of the nation's irreplaceable resources, it is fitting that the land that helped mold such an extraordinary man now bears his name.

When to Go

The park is open all year. Occasionally in winter portions of the South Unit's Scenic Loop Drive and the North Unit's Scenic Road close due to snow and ice. South Unit Visitor Center is open daily from 8am–4:30pm (closed on Thanksgiving, Christmas Day, and New Year's Day). Painted Canyon Visitor Center is open from April to mid-November from 8:30am–4:30pm. North Unit Visitor Center is open daily from April to mid-November and from Friday to Sunday for the rest of the year from 9am–5:30pm. Cottonwood and Juniper Campgrounds are open all year, but with limited services from October to mid-May. May and June are typically the best months to see wildflowers and to paddle the Little Missouri River.

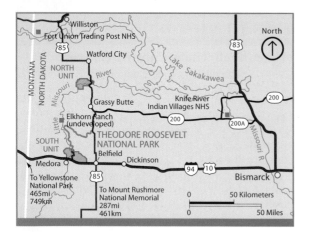

Transportation & Airports

Public transportation does not serve the park. There are small regional airports at Williston and Dickinson. Bismarck Municipal Airport (BIS) is 136 miles east of the South Unit on I-94.

Directions

The park consists of three separate units, all of which are in western North Dakota, north of I-94.

To the South Unit: South Unit's entrance is in the old meat-packing town of Medora, ND. Medora can be reached by taking Exits 24 or 27 from I-94. South Unit Visitor Center and Maltese Cross Cabin are located on the west side of East River Road near the entrance. The Montana–North Dakota State Line is 26 miles west of Medora and Bismarck, ND is 134 miles to the east.

Painted Canyon Visitor Center is located just off I-94 at Exit 32, 7 miles east of Medora, ND.

To the North Unit: North Unit's entrance is just off US-85, 69 miles north of the South Unit. Head east on I-94 to Exit 43. Take US-85 North to the park's entrance and North Unit Visitor Center.

To the Elkhorn Ranch Unit: A gravel road, 35 miles north of Medora, passes through Little Missouri National Grassland to Theodore Roosevelt's Elkhorn Ranch site. The gravel road stretches from the northernmost point of the South Unit's Scenic Loop Drive to US-85. It can be impassable at times. Before leaving, you should stop at (or call) a visitor center to receive current road conditions.

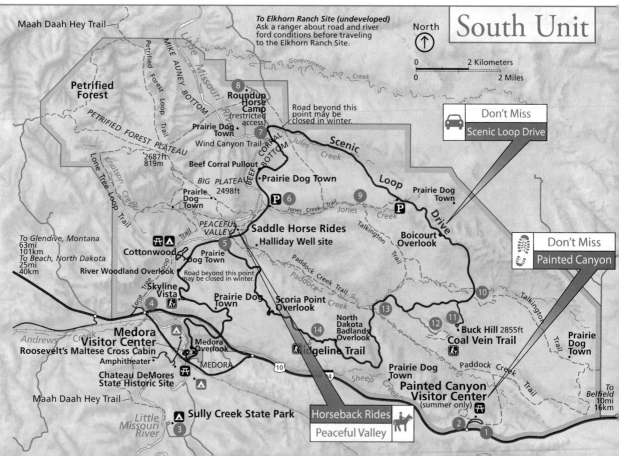

Camping

Cottonwood (76 sites) and **Juniper** (50 sites) are the primary campgrounds in the South and North Units, respectively. All sites are available on a first-come, first-served basis. Both campgrounds have pull-through sites for RVs, but hook-ups are not available. Restrooms, water, grills, and picnic tables are located nearby. The camping fee is $10/night. It is reduced to $5/night during the off-season (October–mid-May). Each campground has a group campsite that accommodates a minimum of 7 campers. Group sites must be reserved by calling (701.623.4730 ext. 3426 for Cottonwood and 701.842.2333 for Juniper).

Roundup Group Horse Campground is intended for horseback riders. It may also be used by groups of 7–20 campers. Fees for a group site are $2 per person per night and $1 per horse per night, with a $20 minimum each night. These sites must be reserved (mail or fax only).

Backcountry camping is allowed, but campers must obtain a free permit from North or South Unit Visitor Center.

Driving

Driving is the most popular activity. South Unit visitors circle the park via 36-mile **Scenic Loop Drive**, stopping at pullouts to read interpretive signs and soak in the views. It begins just beyond East River Road and provides access to many of the South Unit's hiking trails and **Peaceful Valley Ranch**. Drive slowly to spot bison, pronghorn, elk, and wild horses. The residents you can't miss are the playful prairie dogs who scurry about their little prairie dog towns.

The North Unit offers a 14-mile (one-way) **Scenic Drive** that ends at **Oxbow Overlook** where you'll find outstanding panoramic views. As you make your way, watch for wildlife. Mule deer are frequently seen crossing the upper grasslands. Witness the power of erosion at **Cannonball Concretions Pullout**. Eye the main agent of erosion, the Little Missouri River, from **River Bend and Oxbow Overlooks**.

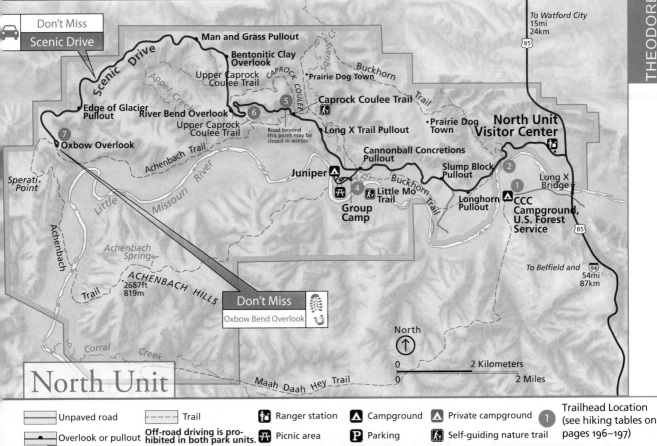

A multitude of hiking opportunities exist at both the North and South Unit of Theodore Roosevelt National Park. Whether by horse or foot, all visitors should leave the roadways and explore a few miles of trails that provide a closer look at eroded badlands, bustling prairie dog towns, steep canyons, colorful rock layers, and lush bottomlands. These are the landscapes that helped transform Theodore Roosevelt into the United States' "Conservationist President".

Most of the **South Unit's hiking trails** are accessed via **Scenic Loop Drive**. **Jones Creek, Lower Talkington, and Paddock Creek Trails** bisect the loop drive as they follow (usually) dry creek beds. If you arrive after a heavy thunderstorm or recent snow melt check trail conditions prior to hiking, as the creeks occasionally run causing trails to be muddy or impassable. At times you may have to cross running water.

Paddock and Talkington Trails continue east past Scenic Loop Drive all the way to the park's eastern boundary. The boundary is difficult to miss because you'll encounter a 7-foot fence meant to keep bison and wild horses in and grazing cattle out.

You'll find the **3rd largest Petrified Forest in the U.S.** in the northwest corner of the South Unit. To have a look, take the 16-mile **Petrified Loop Trail**, accessed via an unpaved road through National Grassland just a few miles west of the park entrance. Travel about 6 miles on the gravel road to a parking area where you'll pass through an opening in the park fence to begin your hike.

North Unit's Buckhorn Trail is great for seeing bison, prairie dogs, and deer. It's fairly long (11.0 miles) but can be completed in a day. If you really want to push day-hiking to the limits, try **Achenbach Trail**. Check with park rangers about Little Missouri River crossing conditions (2 crossings required) before you begin. Hiking the trail after a heavy rain is not advised.

Wear sturdy shoes when hiking, because the park's clay surfaces become slippery when wet.

Theodore Roosevelt • South Unit Hiking Trails

	Trail Name	Length	Location (# on map)/Notes (One-way distances unless loop)
Easy	Coal Vein Loop	0.8 mile	Located off a short unpaved spur road from the easternmost section of Scenic Loop Drive (12) • Visible after-effects of a fire that burned here from 1951 to 1977 when a coal seam caught fire
	Buck Hill	0.1 mile	Accessed via a paved spur road off the eastern section of Scenic Loop Drive (11) • Note the differences in vegetation between the drier, hotter south-facing slopes and the wetter, cooler north-facing slopes
	Wind Canyon Loop	0.3 mile	Accessed from Scenic Loop Drive just south of the access road to Roundup Horse Camp (7) • Short climb to an overlook of the Little Missouri River and a wind sculpted canyon • Popular loop trail
	Painted Canyon - 👍	0.9 mile	Trailhead is located at Painted Canyon Visitor Center (2) • Short loop that descends into the canyon
	Ridgeline Nature Loop	0.6 mile	Accessed from southern portion of Scenic Loop Drive (14) • Steep climb to a self-guided loop
	Jones Creek	3.7 miles	Bisects Scenic Loop Drive following Jones Creek and crossing it twice (6) • The creek is usually dry, but can be muddy and wet (especially in spring) • Parking is available at each end of the trail
	Lower Paddock Creek	4.4 miles	Bisects Scenic Loop Drive (5) • Passes a prairie dog town and crosses the creek numerous times • Paddock Creek is typically dry, but can be wet and muddy (especially in spring)
	Upper Paddock Creek	7.7 miles	Paddock Creek Trail continues to the east from the lower section's intersection with Scenic Loop Drive (13) • Intersects Painted Canyon and Upper Talkington Trails before reaching the park's eastern border
	Painted Canyon	2.0 miles	Trailhead is at Painted Canyon Visitor Center (1) • Extremely steep descent into the canyon • Continues through the canyon until it ends at Upper Paddock Creek Trail
	Upper Talkington	4.0 miles	Trail continues east from Lower Talkington Trail's intersection with Scenic Loop Drive (10) • It crosses the creek a few more times before reaching Upper Paddock Creek Trail and the park's eastern border
	Lower Talkington	4.1 miles	The trail is accessed from either Jones Creek Trail, the east end of Lower Paddock Creek Trail, or the easternmost portion of Scenic Loop Drive (9) • Also follows a creek that is usually dry
	Lone Tree Loop	11.7 miles	Joins Maah Daah Hey Trail from Medora into the park before it diverges for a 6.3-mile loop section (4)
	Petrified Forest Loop - 👍	16.0 miles	Accessed from Roundup Horse Camp by crossing the Little Missouri River (8) • Also accessible from the western boundary • Provides access to the park's greatest collection of petrified wood
Strenuous	Maah Daah Hey	96.0 miles	Hikers and horses can take this trail that connects South and North Units (3) • Badlands and grasslands

Horseback Riding

You can explore North Dakota's badlands by horse, just like Theodore Roosevelt did more than 100 years ago. All hiking trails, except developed nature trails, are open to stock. The South Unit is better suited for horse riders thanks to a larger network of trails, Roundup Group Horse Campground, and **Peaceful Valley Ranch**. Peaceful Valley is one of the United States' first "dude" ranches. Unless you're using Roundup Horse Camp (page 195), multi-day trips require horse riders to camp in the backcountry. Another option is to board your horse(s) and camp at Cottonwood or Juniper Campgrounds (page 195). Boarding stables are available at Peaceful Valley Ranch and outside the park (page 202). The CCC Campground near the North Unit's entrance also allows horses.

Peaceful Valley Ranch, located near the beginning of South Unit's Scenic Loop Drive, is open 7 days a week between Memorial Day and Labor Day. All rides longer than 1.5 hours require reservations and experienced riders. Shadow Country Outfitters is currently contracted to operate the ranch.

Shadow Country Outfitters • (701) 623-4568
PO Box 308; Medora, ND 58645
www.ctctel.com/peacefulvalley/
Open: May–September (5–7 rides per day)
Rates: $30 (1.5 hours), $50 (2.5 hours)

Wild horses

Theodore Roosevelt • North Unit Hiking Trails

	Trail Name	Length	Location (# on map)/Notes (One-way distances unless loop)
Easy ← → **Strenuous**	Little Mo Nature	1.1 miles	This loop is a self-guided nature trail beginning at Juniper Campground (4)
	Sperati - 🦶	1.5 miles	Short portion of Achenbach Trail departing from Oxbow Overlook at the end of Scenic Drive (7)
	Caprock Coulee	0.8 mile	On Scenic Drive, about 1.5 miles west of Juniper Campground (5) • This is the trail's self-guided portion
	Upper Caprock Coulee	5.7 miles	A continuation of Caprock Coulee's self-guided portion that loops back to the trailhead (5)
	Buckhorn Loop	11.0 miles	Accessed at several locations, this trail loops around the park's northeastern section (3, 4)
	Achenbach Loop - 🦶	16.0 miles	Accessed from Juniper Campground, and Oxbow and River Bend Overlooks (5) • Crosses the river twice
	Maah Daah Hey	96.0 miles	Hikers and horses can take this trail that connects South and North Units (1) • Badlands and grasslands

Theodore Roosevelt dressed as a Badlands hunter

Did you know?

- Theodore Roosevelt survived an attempted assassination while campaigning in Milwaukee, WI as the Bull Moose Party's presidential candidate. The assassin's bullet passed through a 50-page speech and the eyeglasses case he had in his pocket before becoming lodged in his chest. He completed the 90-minute speech before going to the hospital.

- He won the Nobel Peace Prize for helping negotiate the end of the Russo–Japanese War.

- He served as New York City Police Commissioner, creating drastic reform in one of America's most corrupt police departments.

- He was colonel of the "Rough Riders" during the Spanish–American War.

- He wrote 18 books and hundreds of articles.

- In 1905, he demanded football change their rules to become safer after 18 deaths in the sport that year. From his meeting the forward pass was installed, a neutral zone where six men needed to be lined up was established, the first down was changed from 5 to 10 yards, and gang tackling and mass formations were banned.

 # Paddling

Just as Maah Daah Hey Trail connects South and North Units for hikers, the **Little Missouri River** connects the two for paddlers. A trip from Medora (South Unit) to **Long X Bridge** (North Unit) on US-85 is 110 miles. The journey takes a week and requires considerable planning, as you are traversing relatively uncivilized terrain where cell phones rarely work and drinkable water is not readily available (without treatment). The river is not navigable all year round. Water levels must be raised by heavy rains or snowmelt. **May and June are the best months** to paddle, as temperatures are comfortable and the water is usually navigable after spring thaw. It's a trip that you won't soon forget. The route is filled with spectacular scenery and wildlife viewing opportunities abound. There are no designated campsites along the way, but camping is allowed on National Forest land. Camping is prohibited on adjacent private property. You will have to portage around the wildlife fence that crosses the river at the park boundaries.

 # Other Activities

Biking: All park roads are open to bicycles. Biking is a really nice alternative to driving, due to small crowds, abundant wildlife, and varied terrain. **Both park units' Scenic Drives** are hilly, but the North Unit is a bit more strenuous. Bicycles are not allowed off-road in the park. However, bikers can take **Maah Daah Hey Trail** through Little Missouri National Grasslands between North and South Units. Check out **Dakota Cyclery** (888.321.1218, www.dakotacyclery. com) for guided tours and bike rentals. They can hook you up with a lockable trailer. They'll even move it from stop to stop so you don't have to carry heavy gear. Altogether this is some of the best pedaling you'll find in the Dakotas.

Fishing: It's not a very popular activity, but blue gills and catfish can be caught in the Little Missouri River.

Winter Activities: What the Little Missouri River is good for is **cross-country skiing**. Frozen water creates a flat, well-defined surface to explore on skis during the winter time (which can extend from October to April). **Park Roads** are also used for skiing. With 30 inches of annual snowfall, snowshoeing is possible, but snow tends to blow and drift.

For Kids: Theodore Roosevelt National Park is a wonderful place for children to see wildlife and appreciate nature. The park offers **Family Fun Packs**, which help explore these amazing surroundings. The packs contain field guides, binoculars, hand lenses, and suggested activities. Check one out for a day at either North or South Unit Visitor Center. Children (ages 6 and up) are invited to become **Junior Rangers**. Pick up a free Junior Ranger Activity Booklet from either visitor center, complete the activities, and return to a visitor center to receive a certificate and an official Junior Ranger Badge. During the summer, **Junior Ranger Family Fun Days** are offered about once a month. For more information or to inquire about registering your Junior Ranger call South Unit Visitor Center at (701) 623-4466.

Ranger Programs: Park rangers provide guided walks, talks, and campfire programs from mid-June to early September. A current schedule of activities is available online or at either visitor center. A typical talk or walk provides visitors with a ranger's perspective regarding the life and land you are about to explore. South Unit visitors have the opportunity to **tour Roosevelt's Maltese Cross Cabin** (available daily in summer).

 # Flora & Fauna

Badlands are known for their inhospitable conditions, but a visit to Theodore Roosevelt National Park reveals a world of great plant and animal diversity. **More than 400 species of plants** are found in the park. Prairies burst with life when wildflowers bloom in spring. They also help sustain healthy populations of large grazing mammals.

Bison, wild horses, elk, pronghorn, mule deer, and white-tailed deer all reside in the wide-open prairies. The North Unit keeps a small herd of longhorn steers as a living history exhibit. Stop at a prairie dog town and you'll hear the occupants barking from the stoop of their burrows. This region wasn't always as rich in wildlife as it is today. Westward expansion led to severe overhunting. Several species were eliminated from North Dakota only to be reintroduced by the National Park Service. Bison were restored at the South Unit in 1956 and the North Unit in 1962. Elk were next to return to the South Unit in 1985 and bighorn sheep eventually followed at the North Unit. Through the park's conservation efforts the land and wildlife are much like they were when a wealthy easterner named Theodore Roosevelt arrived in September of 1883.

Mule deer near Riverbend Overlook

The view from Oxbow Bend

 Pets

Pets are permitted in the park, but must be kept on a leash no more than six feet in length at all times. They are not allowed in park buildings, on trails, or in the backcountry.

Accessibility

The park's visitor centers and Maltese Cross Cabin are wheelchair accessible. Accessible sites and restrooms are available at Cottonwood and Juniper Campgrounds. A few shorter trails like Skyline Vista Overlook and Boicourt Overlook in the South Unit and Little Mo Nature Trail in the North Unit are wheelchair accessible.

A bison calf

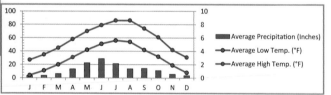

Weather

The three park units share fairly similar climates. Summers are hot with average highs in the 70s and 80s°F. Winters are cold with average lows in the single digits. It's fairly dry, receiving only about 15 inches of precipitation each year, but thunderstorms in summer and blizzards in winter can occur with little to no warning.

Average Precipitation (Inches)
Average Low Temp. (°F)
Average High Temp. (°F)

Vacation Planner

Each park unit has its own distinct features and attractions. The road to **Elkhorn Ranch** is rough (and sometimes impassable) and its structures are gone, but the scenery is nice and interpretive signs with Roosevelt's words describe the land as he saw it. **Painted Canyon Visitor Center/Overlook** is well worth a stop (especially during early morning/late evening); take Exit 32 off I-94 to have a look at Painted Canyon's colorful broken hills. While these areas are nice, this vacation planner will spend one day each at the park's South and North Units. Nearby dining, grocery stores, lodging, festivals, and attractions are listed on pages 201–203.

Day 1

A full day at the **South Unit** should begin at the **visitor center** (even if you've already stopped at Painted Canyon Visitor Center). You'll find relics from Roosevelt's time, a short video, and information on ranger programs. If you'd like to see

what an 1880's North Dakotan mansion looked like, check out **Roosevelt's Maltese Cross Cabin** just behind the visitor center. You must be accompanied by a park ranger, but tours are given regularly and often upon request. First (and often the only) thing visitors do upon arriving at the South Unit is drive the 36-mile **Scenic Loop Drive**. You should too. Driving clock-wise, make the following stops: **Wind Canyon Trail, Boicourt Overlook, Buck Hill, and Scoria Point Overlook**. **Wind Canyon Overlook** provides a bird's eye view of Little Missouri River as it ambles northward. **Boicourt Overlook** provides fantastic views of badlands formations. It's fairly common to spot a number of the park's 100-plus wild horses between this stop and **Buck Hill**, so keep your eyes open. Squeeze in a stop or two at prairie dog towns; they're hilariously chatty. The loop ends near **Peaceful Valley Ranch**. This is where you break into groups of cowboys/cowgirls and hikers. Horseback riders are left in the very capable hands of **Shadow Country Outfitters** (page 197). Hikers take a 1.5-hour, out-and-back trek on **Lower Paddock Creek Trail** (page 196).

Day 1

North Unit Visitor Center is conveniently located at the park's entrance. Stop in, look around, inquire about ranger programs, watch the park's short introductory film, and head back to the 14-mile **Scenic Drive**. **Cannonball Concretions Pullout** is an easy stop to witness stone oddities created by erosional forces. Continuing along stop at **River Bend Overlook**. Here you'll find a shelter built by the CCC in the 1930s where outstanding views of a gentle bend in the Little Missouri are available. Continue northwest on Scenic Drive. You'll pass through a perfect example of grassland that once covered nearly a third of the United States. The drive ends at **Oxbow Overlook** where you can hike 1.5-miles (roundtrip) to **Sperati Point**. If you want more, return to Juniper Campground to hike the 11-mile (4–7 hours) **Buckhorn Trail** (page 197). It provides a tour of the park's finest prairie dog towns and passes through sagebrush flats and badlands. Opt for **Little Mo** (short for Missouri) **Trail** if you're short on time.

Dining

Near Badlands & Wind Cave

Red Rock Restaurant • (605) 279-2388
506 Glenn St; Wall, SD 57790

Mocha Moose • (605) 279-2023
511 Main St; Wall, SD 57790 • *Ice Cream*

Elkton House Restaurant • (605) 279-2152
203 South Blvd; Wall, SD 57790

Firehouse Brewing Co • (605) 348-1915
610 Main St; Rapid City, SD 57701
www.firehousebrewing.com • Entrée: $16–25

Corn Exchange • (605) 343-5070
727 Main St; Rapid City, SD 57701
www.cornexchange.com • Entrée: $18–26

Delmonico Grill • (605) 791-1664
609 Main St; Rapid City, SD 57701
www.delmonicogrill.biz • Entrée: $19–44

Golden Phoenix • (605) 348-4195
2421 W Main St; Rapid City, SD 57702

Philly Ted's Cheesesteak & Subs • (605) 348-6113
1415 N Lacrosse St; Rapid City, SD 57701

Colonial House Restaurant • (605) 342-4640
2501 Mt Rushmore Rd; Rapid City, SD 57701
www.colonialhousernb.com • Entrée: $10–20

Tally's Silver Spoon • (605) 342-7621
530 6th St; Rapid City, SD 57701
www.tallyssilverspoon.com • Entrée: $22–39

Minervas Restaurant & Bar • (605) 394-9505
2211 N Lacrosse St; Rapid City, SD 57701
www.minervas.net • Entrée: $14–30

Piesano's Pacchia • (605) 341-6941
3618 Canyon Lake Dr, # 121; Rapid City, SD 57702
www.piesanospacchia.com • Pizza: $17–24

Sanford's Grub & Pub • (605) 721-1463
306 7th St; Rapid City, SD 57701

B & L Bagels • (605) 399-1777
512 Main St # 120; Rapid City, SD 57701

Hitchrail Restaurant & Saloon • (605) 673-2697
421 Northern St; Pringle, SD 57773

Dale's Family Restaurant • (605) 745-3028
745 Battle Mountain Ave; Hot Springs, SD 57747

Springs Steakhouse • (605) 745-6208
902 N River St; Hot Springs, SD 57747

All Star Sports Grill • (605) 745-7827
310 S Chicago St; Hot Springs, SD 57747

China Buffet • (605) 745-4126
333 N River St; Hot Springs, SD 57747

Stone Soup & Mud Pies • (605) 891-9632
407 N River St; Hot Springs, SD 57747

Blue Vervain Restaurant • (605) 745-6005
603 N River St; Hot Springs, SD 57747
www.bluevervain.com • Entrée: $18–42

Dakota Cowboy Restaurant • (605) 673-4613
216 W Mt Rushmore Rd; Custer, SD 57730

Sage Creek Grille • (605) 673-2424
611 Mt Rushmore Rd; Custer, SD 57730

Baker's Bakery & Café • (605) 673-2253
541 Mt Rushmore Rd; Custer, SD 57730
www.bakersbakery.biz • Breakfast: $5–8

Pizza Works • (605) 673-2020
429 Mt Rushmore Rd; Custer, SD 57730
www.custerpizzaworks.com • Pizza: $6–28

Purple Pie Place • (605) 673-4070
19 Mt Rushmore Rd; Custer, SD 57730
www.purplepieplace.com

Near Theodore Roosevelt

Cowboy Café • (701) 623-4343
215 4th St; Medora, ND 58645

Pizza Palace • (701) 628-4481
285 3rd Ave; Medora, ND 58645

Bully Café • (701) 623-5854
316 Pacific Ave; Medora, ND 58645

Elkhorn Café • (701) 623-2239
314 Pacific Ave; Medora, ND 58645

Boots Bar & Grill • (701) 623-2668
PO Box 435; Medora, ND 58645

Trapper's Pizzeria • (701) 575-8585
803 US-85 N; Belfield, ND 58622
www.trapperskettle.com

J D's BBQ • (701) 483-2277
789 State Ave; Dickinson, ND 58601

Brickhouse Grille • (701) 483-9900
2 W Villard St; Dickinson, ND 58601
www.brickhousegrilleonline.com

Six Shooters Showhall & Café • (701) 842-6683
130 N Main St; Watford City, ND 58854

Twist Drive-In • (701) 842-3595
404 2nd Ave SW; Watford City, ND 58854

Outlaws Bar Grill • (701) 842-6859
120 S Main St; Watford City, ND 58854
www.outlawsbarngrill.com • Entrée: $13–26

Ginny's Restaurant • (701) 444-6315
601 2nd Ave SW; Watford City, ND 58854

Dakotan Restaurant • (701) 842-2595
608 2nd Ave SW; Watford City, ND 58854

Many chain restaurants can be found along I-90 in South Dakota (particularly in Rapid City) and I-94 in North Dakota.

Grocery Stores

Near Badlands & Wind Cave

Badland's Grocery • (605) 433-5445
10 Main St; Interior, SD 57750

Wall Food Center • (605) 279-2331
103 W South Blvd; Wall, SD 57790

Safeway • (605) 342-8455
730 Mtn View Rd; Rapid City, SD 57701

Safeway • (605) 348-5125
2120 Mt Rushmore Rd; Rapid City, SD 57701

Walmart Supercenter • (605) 342-9444
1200 N Lacrosse St; Rapid City, SD 57701

Lynn's Dakotamart • (605) 745-3203
505 S 6th St; Hot Springs, SD 57747

Sonny's Super Foods • (605) 745-5979
801 Jensen Hwy; Hot Springs, SD 57747

Robb's Inc Grocery • (605) 745-4557
144 S Chicago St; Hot Springs, SD 57747

Custer County Market • (605) 673-2247
444 Mt Rushmore Rd; Custer, SD 57730

Near Theodore Roosevelt

Ferris Store • (701) 623-4447
251 Main St; Medora, ND 58645

Beach Food Center • (701) 872-4364
181 Central Ave N; Beach, ND 58621

Walmart Supercenter • (701) 225-8504
2456 3rd Ave W; Dickinson, ND 58601

Walmart Supercenter • (701) 572-8550
4001 2nd Ave W; Williston, ND 58801

Lodging

Near Badlands & Wind Cave

Cedar Pass Lodge • (605) 433-5460
Only lodging in Badlands National Park
1 Cedar St (Box 5); Interior, SD 57750
www.cedarpasslodge.com • Rates: $85–115/night

Circle View Guest Ranch • (605) 433-5582
20055 E SD-44; Scenic; SD 57780
www.circleviewranch.com • Rates: $95–150

Frontier Cabins • (605) 279-2619
1101 S Glenn St; Wall, SD 57790
www.frontiercabins.net • Rates: $65–190

Dakota Memories B&B • (605) 279-2948
608 Glenn St; Wall, SD 57790
www.dakotamemorieswallsd.com • Rates: $110

Sunshine Inn • (605) 279-2178
608 Main St; Wall, SD 57790
www.sunshineinnatwallsd.com • Rates: $65–190

Sleepy Hollow Campground • (605) 279-2100
118 4th Ave W; Wall, SD 57790
www.sleepyhollowsd.com • Rates: $19–27

Triangle Ranch B&B • (605) 859-2122
Lodge, motel, RV sites, cabins, trail rides,
archery, volleyball, and fishing available
23950 Recluse Rd; Philip, SD 57567
www.triangleranchbb.com

Badlands Ranch and Resort • (605) 433-5599
20910 Craven Rd; Interior, SD 57750
www.badlandsranchandresort.com • Rates: $65–190

Badlands/White River KOA • (605) 433-5337
20720 SD-44; Interior, SD 57750

Historic Log Cabin Motel • (605) 745-5166
1246 Sherman St; Hot Springs, SD 57747
www.historiclogcabins.com • Rates: $49+

Lake Park Campground • (800) 644-2267
Lodge, cottage, RV, and camping available
2850 Chapel Ln; Rapid City, SD 57702
www.lakeparkcampground.com

Rapid City KOA • (605) 348-2111
3010 E SD-44; Rapid City, SD 57703

Mystery Mtn Resort • (605) 342-5368
13752 S US-16; Rapid City, SD 57702
www.mysterymountain.us • Rates: $74–279

Peregrine Pointe B&B • (605) 348-3987
23451 Peregrine Pt; Rapid City, SD 57702
www.peregrinebb.com • Rates: $100–160

Red Rock River Resort • (605) 745-4400
603 N River St; Hot Springs, SD 57747
www.redrockriverresort.com • Rates: $85+

FlatIron Hist. Sandstone Inn • (605) 745-5301
745 N River St; Hot Springs, SD 57747
www.flatiron.bz • Rates: $49–179

A Dakota Dream B&B • (605) 745-4633
801 Almond St; Hot Springs, SD 57747

Custer Mansion B&B • (605) 673-3333
35 Centennial Dr; Custer, SD 57730
www.custermansionbb.com • Rates: $80+

Bavarian Inn Motel • (605) 673-2802
855 N 5th St; Custer, SD 57730
www.bavarianinnsd.com • Rates: $79+

White House Resort • (605) 666-4917
115 Swanzey St; Keystone, SD 57751

President's View Mt Rushmore • (605) 666-4212
106 US-16A; Keystone, SD 57751

Powder House Lodge • (605) 666-4646
24125 US-16A; Keystone, SD 57751
www.powderhouselodge.com

Alpine Inn • (605) 574-2749
133 Main St; Hill City, SD 57745
www.alpineinnhillcity.com • Rates: $70+

Mount Rushmore KOA • (605) 574-2525
12620 SD-244; Hill City, SD 57745
www.palmergulch.com • *Lodge/Cabins/Camp*

Rafter J Bar Ranch • (605) 574-2527
12325 Rafter J-Bar Rd; Hill City, SD 57745
www.rafterj.com • Rates: $59+

Horse Thief Campground & Resort • (605) 574-2668
24391 SD-87 S; Hill City, SD 57745
www.horsethief.com • Rates: $21+

Heartland Campground • (605) 255-5460
24743 S SD-79; Hermosa, SD 57744
www.heartlandcampground.com • Rates: $20+

Near Theodore Roosevelt

Rough Riders Hotel • (701) 623-4444
301 3rd Ave; Medora, ND 58645
www.medora.com • Rates: $150

Diamond Bar B&B • (701) 623-4913
14996 27th St SW; Medora, ND 58645

Eagle Ridge Lodge • (701) 623-2216
14937 Dutchmans Rd SW; Medora, ND 58645
www.eagleridgelodge.com

McKenzie Inn • (701) 444-3980
132 3rd St SW; Watford City, ND 58854
www.mckenzieinn.com

Four Eyes Motel • (701) 444-4126
124 S Main St; Watford City, ND 58854

Roosevelt Inn & Suites • (701) 842-3686
600 2nd Ave SW; Watford City, ND 58854
www.rooseveltinn.com • Rates: $90+

El Rancho Motor Hotel • (701) 572-6321
1623 2nd Ave West; Williston, ND 58801
www.elranchomotel.net

Tobacco Gardens Resort • (701) 842-4199
4781 Hwy 1806 W; Watford City, ND 58854
www.tobaccogardens.com • Camping: $15+

Coyote Charlie's RV Park • (701) 842-3498
1612 11th Ave SE; Watford City, ND 58854

Cherry Creek RV Park • (701) 570-0147
1008 4 Ave; Watford City, ND 58854

Many chain hotels can be found along I-90
in South Dakota and I-94 in North Dakota.

Festivals
Near Badlands & Wind Cave

Black Hills Stock Show & Rodeo
January • Rapid City • www.centralstatesfair.com

Mt Rushmore Independence Day • July
Mount Rushmore • www.mtrushmore.net

Sturgis Motorcycle Rally • August
Sturgis • www.sturgismotorcyclerally.com

Rock 'N Rev Festival • August
Sturgis • www.rocknrevfestival.com

Buffalo Roundup & Arts Festival
September • Custer State Park

Mickelson Trail Trek • September
Black Hills • www.mickelsontrail.com

Black Hills Pow Wow • October
Rapid City • www.blackhillspowwow.com

Near Theodore Roosevelt

Antique Classic Car Show • June
Medora • www.medora.com

Roughrider Days • June
Dickinson • www.roughriderdaysfair.com

Mountain Roundup Rodeo • July
Killdeer • www.killdeer.com

Roughrider 4WD Rendezvous • July
Watford City • (701) 852-2787

Ukrainian Festival • July
Dickinson • (701) 483-1486

Northern Plains Ethnic Festival • August
Dickinson • www.visitdickinson.com

Attractions
Near Badlands & Wind Cave

Wall Drug Store • (605) 279-2175
510 Main St; Wall, SD 57790 • www.walldrug.com

Minute Man Missile NHP • (605) 433-5552
21280 SD-240; Philip, SD 57567
www.nps.gov/mima • Tours: $5/Adult

Pirates Cove Adventure Golf • (605) 343-8540
1500 N Lacrosse St; Rapid City, SD 57701

Gray Line Tours • (605) 342-4461
1600 E St Patrick St; Rapid City, SD 57703
www.blackhillsgrayline.com • Tours: $56+

Circle B Ranch • (605) 348-7358
Gun fights, trail rides, and chuckwagon jamboree
22735 US-385; Rapid City, SD 57702
www.circle-b-ranch.com

Museum of Geology • (605) 394-2467
501 E Saint Joseph St; Rapid City, SD 57701
www.museum.sdsmt.edu • Free

Flags & Wheels Indoor Racing • (605) 341-7585
405 12th St; Rapid City, SD 57701
www.flagsandwheels.com • Rates: $5+

Chapel In the Hills • (605) 343-9426
3788 Chapel Ln; Rapid City, SD 57702
www.chapel-in-the-hills.org • Free

Bear Country USA • (605) 343-2290
13820 S US-16; Rapid City, SD 57702
www.bearcountryusa.com • Rates: $16/Adult

Storybook Island • (605) 342-6357
1301 Sheridan Lake Rd; Rapid City, SD 57702
www.storybookisland.org • Admission: $2

Cosmos Mystery Area • (605) 343-9802
24040 Cosmos Rd; Rapid City, SD 57702
www.cosmosmysteryarea.com • Tour: $9.50/Adult

The Journey Museum • (605) 394-6923
222 New York St; Rapid City, SD 57701
www.journeymuseum.org • Tours: $6/Adult

Black Hills Maze • (605) 343-5439
6400 S US-16; Rapid City, SD 57701
www.blackhillsmaze.com • Maze: $9

Old Mac Donald's Farm • (605) 737-4815
23691 Busted 5 Court; Rapid City, SD 57702
www.oldmacsfarm.blackhills.com • Admission: $10.50

Reptile Gardens • (605) 342-5873
8955 S US-16; Rapid City, SD 57702
www.reptilegardens.com • Admission: $11–15/Adult

Rushmore Waterslide Park • (605) 348-8962
1715 Catron Blvd; Rapid City, SD 57701
www.rushmorewaterslide.com • Admission: $15/Adult

Watiki Indoor Water Park • (605) 718-2474
1314 N Elk Vale Rd; Rapid City, SD 57703
www.watikiwaterpark.com • Admission: $12/Adult

Mostly Chocolates • (605) 341-2264
1919 Mt Rushmore Rd, # 1; Rapid City, SD 57701
www.bhchocolates.com

Carmike Cinema 10 • (605) 341-5888
230 Knollwood Dr; Rapid City, SD 57701

Elks Theatre • (605) 341-4149
512 6th St; Rapid City, SD 57701

Mt Rushmore Nat'l Mem. • (605) 574-2523
13000 SD-244, #81; Keystone, SD 57751
www.nps.gov/moru • Parking: $11/vehicle

Crazy Horse Memorial • (605) 673-4681
12151 Ave of the Chiefs; Crazy Horse, SD 57730
www.crazyhorsememorial.org • Admission: $27/car

Paradise Valley Trail Rides • (605) 578-1249
12702 Box Elder Forks Rd; Nemo, SD 57759
www.paradisevalleyadventures.com

Rockin R Rides • (605) 673-2999
24853 Village Ave; Custer, SD 57730
www.rockingrtrailrides.com • Rates: $28 (1 hr)

Spirit Horse Escape • (605) 673-6005
11596 US-16; Custer, SD
www.spirithorseescape.com • Rates: $30 (1 hr)

Custer State Park • (605) 255-4515
13329 US-16A; Custer, SD 57730
www.custerstatepark.info

L&J Golden Circle Tours • (605) 673-4349
695 W Mt Rushmore Rd; Custer, SD 57730
www.goldencircletours.com • Tours: $91+

Jewel Cave NM • (605) 673-8300
11149 US-16; Custer, SD 57730
www.nps.gov/jeca • Cave Tours: $4–27/Adult

Black Hills Playhouse • (605) 255-4141
24834 S Playhouse Rd; Custer, SD 57730
www.blackhillsplayhouse.com • Tickets: $28–35/Adult

Black Hills Balloons • (605) 673-2520
PO Box 210; Custer, SD 57730
www.blackhillsballoons.com • Rates: $295/Adult

The Mammoth Site • (605) 745-6017
1800 US-18 Bypass; Hot Springs, SD 57747
www.mammothsite.org • Admission: $8/Adult

Pioneer Museum • (605) 745-5147
300 N Chicago St; Hot Springs, SD 57747
www.pioneer-museum.com • Admission: $5/Adult

Black Hills Putt 4 Fun • (605) 745-7888
640 S 6th St; Hot Springs, SD 57747
www.putt4fun.us • Rates: $7/Adult

Hot Springs Theatre • (605) 745-4169
241 N River St; Hot Springs, SD 57747

Black Hills Wild Horse Sanctuary • (605) 745-5955
SD-71 S; Hot Springs, SD
www.gwtc.net/~iram/ • Tours: $50+/Adult

1880 Train • (605) 574-2222
222 Railroad Ave; Hill City, SD 57745
www.1880train.com • Rates: $24/Adult

Sylvan Rocks Climbing School & Guide Service
Discover Climbing Adventure: $28/person
301 Main St; Hill City, SD 57745
www.sylvanrocks.com • (605) 574-2425

Devil's Tower NM • (307) 467-5283
US Highway 14; Devils Tower, WY 82714
www.nps.gov/deto • Entrance Fee: $10/car

Near Theodore Roosevelt

Cowboy Hall of Fame • (701) 623-2000
250 Main St; Medora, ND 58645
www.northdakotacowboy.com

Medora Musical • (800) 663-6721
Burning Hills Amphitheater; Medora, ND
www.medora.com • Tickets: $34/Adult

Doll House Museum • (701) 623-4444
485 Broadway; Medora, ND 58645

Cedar Canyon Spa • (701) 623-1772
350 3rd Ave; Medora, ND 58645
www.cedarcanyonspa.com • Massage: $40 (30 min.)

Putt N Stuff Miniature Golf • (701) 290-2388
930 Sims St; Dickinson, ND 58601

Dakota Dinosaur Museum • (701) 225-3466
200 Museum Dr East; Dickinson, ND 58601
www.dakotadino.com • Admission: $7/Adult

Lewis & Clark Trail Museum • (701) 828-3595
102 Indiana Ave E; Alexander, ND 58831

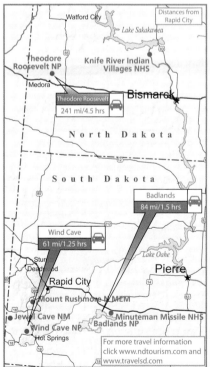

For more travel information click www.ndtourism.com and www.travelsd.com

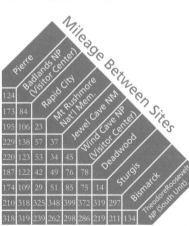

Mileage Between Sites

	Pierre	Badlands NP (Visitor Center)	Rapid City	Mt Rushmore Nat'l Mem.	Jewel Cave NM	Wind Cave NP (Visitor Center)	Deadwood	Sturgis	Bismarck	Theodore Roosevelt NP (South Unit)
	124									
	173	84								
	195	106	23							
	229	138	57	37						
	220	123	53	34	45					
	187	122	42	49	76	78				
	174	109	29	51	85	75	14			
	210	318	325	348	399	372	319	297		
	318	319	239	262	298	286	219	211	134	

View from Snake River Overlook as the sun sets behind the Teton Range

PO Drawer 170; Moose, WY 83012
Phone: (307) 739-3300
Website: www.nps.gov/grte

Established: February 26, 1929
Size: 309,995 Acres
Annual Visitors: 2.7 Million
Peak Season: July–August
Hiking Trails: ~230 Miles

Activities: Hiking, Backpacking,
Biking, Horseback Riding, Paddling,
Rock Climbing, Fishing, and Winter
Activities

Campgrounds: Colter Bay, Head-
waters, Gros Ventre, Jenny Lake,
Lizard Creek, and Signal Mountain
Camping Fee: $20–64/night
Backcountry Camping: Permitted*

Park Hours: All day, every day
Entrance Fee: $25 • Vehicle
$20 • Motorcycle
$12 • Individual (foot, bike, etc.)

*Must obtain a free permit and use
an approved, portable bear canister

Grand Teton - Wyoming

"If you have ever stood at Jenny Lake and looked across to Cascade Canyon weaving its sinuous way toward the summit of the Tetons, you will know the joy of being in a sacred place, designed by God to be protected forever." – Horace Albright

Thanks to the tireless efforts of **Horace Albright** and deep pockets of **John D. Rockefeller, Jr.**, Grand Teton National Park now preserves one of America's iconic landmarks, allowing future generations to stand at Jenny Lake, looking across to Cascade Canyon and Grand Teton. But creating the park was no easy task. The Teton's remarkable, if not sacred, appearance was indisputable, but not all inhabitants believed it should be protected.

Native Americans camped along Jackson Lake while hunting game more than 11,000 years ago. In the 17th century, **French fur trappers** named the range's three tallest peaks "Les Trois Tetons" or "The Three Nipples." Would you expect anything less from rugged frontiersmen removed from society (and women) for long periods? By the 18th and 19th centuries trappers had thoroughly explored the Three Tetons, and the valley below had become fur trapper **David Jackson's** favorite place to "hole-up." Today this valley is known as Jackson Hole, named after David in 1829. In the late 19th century, homesteaders began trickling into the Hole. Only the hardiest—or most stubborn—were able to en-dure unforgiving winters, living off crops grown during the brief sum-mer. That very same Jackson Hole brand of stubbornness would greet

Horace Albright head on in the 1920s, when he made it his mission to preserve the Tetons under protection of the recently created National Park Service.

Albright's pet project took shape while serving as Superintendent of Yellowstone. Here he had the opportunity to escort congressmen, dignitaries, and two Presidents to the southern expanses of Yellowstone where the Tetons could be seen looming in the background. It wasn't until 1926 that Albright met a man with the resources and ambition to make his dream a reality. **John D. Rockefeller, Jr.** and his wife toured the Tetons with Albright and then invited him to New York to discuss his project. Rockefeller, convinced of the park idea, formed Snake River Land Company of Salt Lake City and began buying up properties surrounding the Tetons under the guise of a cattle ranch. Subterfuge was required because a vast majority of ranchers were anti-park. Bull-headed and stubborn, they refused to cede rights to the land.

In 1929, Congress redesignated national forest land consisting of the Teton Range and six glacial lakes at its base to form a small Grand Teton National Park. Rockefeller tried to donate his properties, only to have it refused. Undeterred, he continued to purchase land, acquiring an additional 35,000 acres for $1.4 million. In 1943, more than a decade later, he became increasingly frustrated that donating his land was more difficult than acquiring it. He wrote a letter to **President Franklin D. Roosevelt** suggesting he would sell the land if the government would not accept it. That same year President Roosevelt invoked the **Antiquities Act** to create Jackson Hole National Monument. It placed 221,610 acres of land east of Grand Teton National Park under Park Service control, but once again failed to include Rockefeller's holdings.

Many locals were outraged by use of executive order, and in protest they drove 500 cattle across the monument. The dispute wasn't settled until 1950. After WWII the economy in Jackson Hole improved largely due to tourism to the new National Monument. Anti-park sentiment began to wane and finally the monument, park, and Rockefeller's properties were merged to form today's Grand Teton National Park. To this day the Rockefellers' conservation efforts have continued. In 2001, **Laurance Rockefeller**, son of John D. Rockefeller, Jr., donated the family's **JY Ranch**, which is now open to the public as Laurance S. Rockefeller Preserve (just as his father would have wanted it).

When to Go

Grand Teton National Park is open all year. Craig Thomas Discovery & Visitor Center is open every day except Christmas. All established campgrounds close in winter, but camping is still available at Colter Bay Visitor Center Parking Lot. The park is incredibly crowded during July and August. At this time campgrounds fill up before lunch-time, parking lots are often full, and hiking trails and roads become congested. You can still find isolation and solitude by hiking into the backcountry, or travel during September and October when the park is less crowded and weather remains pleasant.

Transportation

Grand Teton Lodge Company (800.628.9988, www.gtlc.com) provides transportation around Jackson Hole, and narrated bus tours. **Alltrans** (800.443.6133, www.alltransparkshuttle.com) offers daily service between Jackson and the park for $12 (per day for an unlimited number of rides) from late May until late September.

Airports

Jackson Hole Airport (JAC) is located inside the park. A Hertz Rent-A-Car is available on-site. The nearest large airport is Salt Lake City International (SLC), more than 300 miles to the south.

Directions

The Teton Range forms an impassable wall to the west, making the park accessible to motorists from the north, south, and east.

From the North: Most visitors arrive by car from Yellowstone National Park's South Entrance (~6 miles away) via John D. Rockefeller, Jr. Memorial Parkway. It's one of the most scenic highways in the United States.

From the South: From Jackson, WY (~4 miles) take US-26/US-89/US-191 north, which leads directly to the south entrance station and Craig Thomas Discovery & Visitor Center.

From the East: US-26/287 enters from the east at Moran where it intersects US-26/89/191, at Moran Entrance Station.

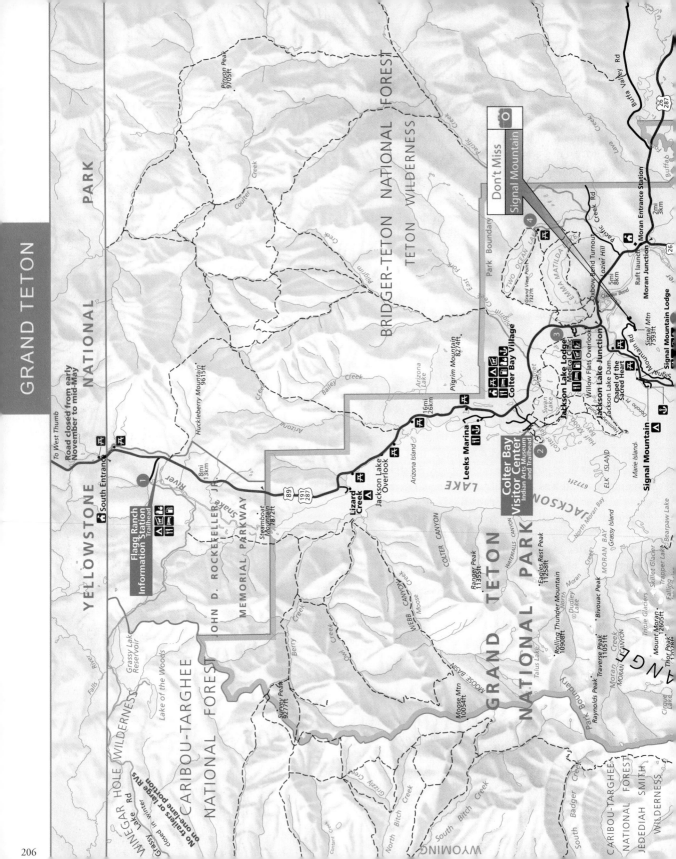

GRAND TETON NATIONAL PARK

YELLOWSTONE NATIONAL PARK

BRIDGER-TETON NATIONAL FOREST

TETON WILDERNESS

WYOMING

CARIBOU-TARGHEE NATIONAL FOREST

JEDEDIAH SMITH WILDERNESS

JEDEDIAH SMITH WILDERNESS

WINEGAR HOLE WILDERNESS

JOHN D. ROCKEFELLER JR MEMORIAL PARKWAY

Don't Miss
Signal Mountain

Pinyon Peak
9705ft

Huckleberry Mountain
9615ft

Steamboat Mountain
7872ft

Pilgrim Mountain
8274ft

Arizona Lake

Arizona Island

Ranger Peak
11355ft

Eagles Rest Peak
11258ft

Rolling Thunder Mountain
10908ft

Bivouac Peak
10825ft

Traverse Peak
11051ft

Reynolds Peak

Mount Moran
12605ft

Thor Peak
12028ft

Moran Canyon

Moran Bay
North Moran Bay

Bearpaw Lake
Trapper Lake
Leigh Lake

ELK ISLAND

Marie Island

Signal Mountain

Signal Mtn
7593ft

Signal Mountain Lodge

Jackson Lake Junction

Jackson Lake Dam

Jackson Lake Lodge
Medical Clinic

Willow Flats Overlook

Chapel of the Sacred Heart

Colter Bay Village

Colter Bay Visitor Center
Indian Arts Museum and Trailhead

Leeks Marina

Jackson Lake Overlook

Lizard Creek

Flagg Ranch Information Station
Trailhead

South Entrance
To West Thumb

Road closed from early November to mid-May

No trailers or large RVs

Winter closed in winter
Grassy Lake Rd

Lake of the Woods

Grassy Lake Reservoir

Falls River

Snake River

Moose Mtn
10054ft

Moose Basin

Survey Peak
9277ft

Talus Lake

Dudley Lake

Cirque Lake

Skillet Glacier
Triple Glaciers

Two Ocean Lake

Emma Matilda

Oxbow Bend Turnout
Grand View Point
1932ft

Cozzie Hill

Pacific Creek Rd

Moran Junction
Moran Entrance Station

Buffalo Valley Rd

Raft launch

Oxbow Bend

WEBB CANYON

COLTER CANYON

WATERFALLS CANYON

GRASSY CANYON

JACKSON LAKE

Coulter Creek

Pilgrim Creek

Pacific Creek

Lava Creek

Swan Lake

Half Moon Bay

Grassy Island

Moran Creek

Badger Creek

North Bitch Creek

South Bitch Creek

Grizzly Creek

Owl Creek

Berry Creek

8mi 13km

16mi 26km

2mi 3km

5mi 8km

89 191 287

26 287

26

1

2

3

4

206

Lodging

Paddling the Snake River © woodleywonderworks

The unique, and often contentious, history of Grand Teton's creation has allowed a variety of commercial interests to be tucked away within park boundaries. From **Dornan's Spur Ranch** at the park's southern reaches to **Headwaters Lodge & Resort (at Flagg Ranch)** near the northern boundary, you can find lodging accommodations that suit your itinerary, if not your budget. **Jenny Lake Lodge** has earned the title of "most expensive lodging in the National Park System." Warranted or not, rates aren't steep enough to prevent guests, drawn to the lodge's incomparable combination of fine dining and majestic scenery, from returning annually. **American Alpine Club Climber's Ranch** caters to rock climbers. Not only is it affordable, it's extremely accessible, merely three miles south of Jenny Lake and four miles north of Park Headquarters. Everything in between is listed below.

Grand Teton Lodging

	Open	Rates	Notes
Dornan's Spur Ranch (307.733.2415 ext 300, www.dornans.com)	All Year	$150–205/night (1 BR) $250/night (2BR)	Dining, grocery, deli, gasoline, and equipment rental available
AAC Climber's Ranch (307.733.7271, www.americanalpineclub.org)	mid-June–mid-Sept	$14–22/night	Lower rate is for AAC members
Jenny Lake Lodge (800.628.9988, www.gtlc.com)	late May–mid-Oct	$225–620/night	Dinner and breakfast included in rate
Signal Mountain Lodge (307.543.2831, www.signalmountainlodge.com)	mid-May–mid-Oct	$132–170/night (1 BR) $185–197/night (2 BR)	Dining, float trips, guided fishing excursions available
Jackson Lake Lodge (800.628.9988, www.gtlc.com)	late May–early Oct	$229–775/night	Restaurants, adventure outfitters, and park tours available
Triangle X Ranch (307.733.2183, www.trianglex.com)	late May–late Sept late Dec–mid-March	$1,600+ per person per week	Lodging, meals, horseback riding, and activities included
Colter Bay Cabins (800.628.9988, www.gtlc.com)	late May–late Sept	$65/night (shared bath) $119–165/night (1BR) $179–219/night (2BR)	Semi-private (shared bathroom) and private cabins are available
Headwaters Lodge & Resort (800.443.2311, www.gtlc.com)	mid-May–late Sept	$179–189/night	Adventure outfitter and national park tour services available

Camping

Don't let prohibitive lodging rates keep you from spending the night. There are several reasonably priced, well-maintained, and extremely popular campgrounds. Most campsites are available on a first-come, first-served basis. **Jenny Lake and Signal Mountain Campgrounds** are the most popular; both typically fill to capacity before noon in summer. You should plan on arriving before 9am on a weekend. Reservations are available at **Colter Bay RV Park and Tent Village** (800.628.9988) and **Headwaters** (800.443.2311). The only in-park, public showers and laundry are available at Colter Bay. Numerous free primitive campgrounds are dispersed throughout the park. A few are located along unpaved Grassy Lake Road near Flagg Ranch Information Station.

Grand Teton Camping

	Open	Fees	Sites	Notes
Colter Bay	late May–late Sept	$20.50	350	Walk-in sites available ($8/night)
Colter Bay Tent Village	early June–early Sept	$50	66	Tent Cabins, call for info (800.628.9988)
Colter Bay RV Park	late May–late Sept	$56	112	RV Sites with hook-ups
Headwaters at Flagg Ranch	mid-May–mid-Sept	$35–64	175	Hook-ups available
Gros Ventre	early May–early Oct	$20.50	350	Sites along Gros Ventre River rarely fill
Jenny Lake	late May–early Oct	$20.50	49	Tents only, 10 walk-in sites available
Lizard Creek	mid-June–early Sept	$20.50	60	$5/night for hikers or bikers w/o a car
Signal Mountain	early May–mid-Oct	$20/49(RV)	86	One RV hook-up site available
Backcountry Camping	Permitted at designated sites and regions of the park with a free permit obtained from the Craig Thomas Discovery & Visitor Center, Jenny Lake Ranger Station, or Colter Bay Visitor Center. An approved bear canister must be used for food storage in the backcountry.			
Winter Camping	In winter, guests may camp in the parking lot near Colter Bay Visitor Center ($5/night)			

Hiking

Lake Solitude

No matter where you are in the park, you're sure to be close to spectacular views of the Teton Range and amazing hiking trails. More than 230 miles of trails cross the flats of Jackson Hole, wind through picturesque canyons into the Teton Range, and weave their way to majestic mountaintops. Jenny Lake's postcard-perfect backdrops set the stage for a few of the park's most popular hiking trails. A few of which should not be skipped: **Jenny Lake Loop**, **Hidden Falls Trail**, and **Cascade Canyon Trail**. (Their extreme beauty also makes them three of the most heavily trafficked trails.) If you'd like to enjoy all of these sites while limiting the wear and tear on your favorite set of hiking boots, shorten these trails by taking a shuttle boat across Jenny Lake to the mouth of Cascade Canyon. The shuttle departs near Jenny Lake Visitor Center from mid-May through September. This shortcut—sparing your feet four miles of hiking—costs $10 roundtrip per adult and $5 for children. It's a good idea to use the shuttle if you plan on hiking beyond Hidden Falls to Inspiration Point or Lake Solitude. The distance for all Jenny Lake Area hikes listed in the hiking table on the following page consider the entire hiking distance, subtract four miles if you ride Jenny Lake Boat Shuttle.

Many of the park's features have been named accurately. For example, there's no finer place to search your mind and soul for encouragement than **Inspiration Point**. Others are not so accurate; there's little solitude to be found en route to **Lake Solitude**, and the trails through **Paintbrush and Cascade Canyons** continue to increase in popularity.

If it's solitude you crave, you'll have to get away from the tourism hubs centered on Jenny and Jackson Lakes. Hiking up to **Signal Mountain** is an option for more peaceful environs, as most visitors choose to drive their vehicles to the top for its splendid views of Jackson Hole and the Teton Range. **Emma Matilda Lake** and **Two Ocean Lake Trails** can be combined to make a large 13.2-mile loop around the lakes. To see what the area looked like in the early 20th century when hardy homesteaders were moving in, hike around **Menors Ferry Historic District** or take the **Cunningham Cabin Loop**.

Grand Teton Hiking Trails

	Trail Name	Trailhead (# on map)	Length	Notes (Roundtrip distances)
Easy	Polecat Creek Loop	Flagg Ranch (1)	2.5 miles	Short, flat hike above a marsh
	Flagg Canyon	Flagg Ranch (1)	4.0 miles	Out-and-back along Snake River
	Lakeshore	Colter Bay (2)	2.0 miles	Views of Teton Range across Jackson Lake
	Heron Pond & Swan Lake	Colter Bay (2)	3.0 miles	Hike to two ponds through bird habitat
	Lunch Tree Hill	Jackson Lake Lodge (3)	0.5 mile	Self-guiding trail overlooking Willow Flats
	Christian Pond Loop	Jackson Lake Lodge (3)	3.3 miles	Nice loop to Teton views and pond
	Leigh Lake - 👆	Leigh Lake (6)	1.8 miles	Hike along String and Leigh Lake's shores
	String Lake	String Lake (7)	3.7 miles	Trail loops around the lake
	Jenny Lake Loop - 👆	Jenny Lake (8)	7.1 miles	Trail follows the park's second largest lake
	Taggart Lake	Taggart Lake (10)	3.0 miles	Hike across sagebrush flats
	Menors Ferry Hist. District - 👆	Menors Ferry (11)	0.3 mile	Homesteaders lived here in 1894
	Lake Creek–Woodland Loop	L.S. Rockefeller Preserve (13)	3.1 miles	Leads to north shore of Phelps Lake
	Cabin Loop	Cunningham Cabin (17)	0.8 mile	Preserved historic homestead
Moderate	Hermitage Point	Colter Bay (2)	9.7 miles	Long but easy hike to Jackson Lake shore
	Two Ocean Lake	Two Ocean Lake (4)	6.4 miles	Trail loops around Two Ocean Lake
	Emma Matilda Lake	Two Ocean Lake (4)	10.7 miles	Trail loops around Emma Matilda Lake
	Signal Mountain	Signal Mountain (5)	6.8 miles	Hike to one of the best views in the park
	Bearpaw Lake - 👆	Leigh Lake (6)	8.0 miles	Views of Mount Moran and alpine lakes
	Hidden Falls - 👆	Jenny Lake (8)	5.2 miles	Hike around Jenny Lake to 200-ft cascade
	Taggart Lake–Beaver Creek	Taggart Lake (10)	3.9 miles	To Taggart Lake • Returns via Beaver Cr
	Taggart Lake–Bradley Lake	Taggart Lake (10)	5.9 miles	Very nice loop to two glacial lakes
	Phelps Lake Overlook	Death Canyon (12)	2.0 miles	Climbs to an overlook of Phelps Lake
	Aspen–Boulder Ridge Loop	L.S. Rockefeller Preserve (13)	5.8 miles	Reaches the shore of Phelps Lake
	Phelps Lake Loop	L.S. Rockefeller Preserve (13)	6.6 miles	Travels around Phelps Lake
	Granite Canyon	Top of the Tram (15)	12.3 miles	Downhill from mountaintop to village
Strenuous	Holly Lake	Leigh Lake (6)	13.0 miles	Through Paintbrush Canyon to lake
	Paintbrush–Cascade Loop - 👆	String Lake (7)	19.0 miles	Phenomenal but difficult circuit
	Inspiration Point - 👆	Jenny Lake (8)	6.0 miles	Past Hidden Falls overlooks Jenny Lake
	Forks of Cascade Canyon	Jenny Lake (8)	13.6 miles	Excellent mountain views (popular)
	Lake Solitude - 👆	Jenny Lake (8)	19.0 miles	Long day hike but worth every minute
	South Fork Cascade Canyon	Jenny Lake (8)	24.8 miles	Leads to Schoolroom Glacier
	Amphitheater Lake - 👆	Lupine Meadows (9)	10.1 miles	Difficult but incredible hike to glacial lakes
	Garnet Canyon	Lupine Meadows (9)	8.4 miles	Hike through a Teton Range Canyon
	Phelps Lake	Death Canyon (12)	4.2 miles	Proceeds past overlook to Phelps Lake
	Death Canyon–Static Peak	Death Canyon (12)	7.9 miles	To Phelps Lake and back to Death Canyon
	Static Peak Divide	Death Canyon (12)	16.3 miles	A series of switchbacks leads to high ridge
	Marion Lake	Top of the Tram (15)	11.8 miles	Follows Granite Creek to a pristine lake
	Table Mountain	Teton Canyon (16)	12.0 miles	Great views of Grand Teton

Best of Grand Teton

Activity: Floating Snake River

Runner-up: Biking Multi-Use Pathway

2nd Runner-up: Trail Ride/Dude Ranch

Backpacking

Many hikes listed on page 211 can be combined into multi-day backpacking loops, which are ideal treks. Loops eliminate repeating scenery, arranging a shuttle service, or using multiple cars. From **String Lake Trailhead** (Trailhead # 7 on page 206) backpackers can combine **Cascade Canyon and Paintbrush Canyon Trails** to make a 19.2-mile loop to Lake Solitude. If you're a little wary of being in the backcountry alone this is a good option as it's quite busy in summer. The loop passes **Hidden Falls**, **Inspiration Point**, **Lake Solitude**, and **Holly Lake**. Alternatively, from **Granite Canyon Parking Area** (Trailhead # 14 on page 207) backpackers can hike a 19.3-mile loop, the **Granite Canyon and Open Canyon Circuit** via Valley Trail. Hikers looking to add a few more miles should continue past the junction on **Open Canyon Trail** to **Marion Lake**.

There are more than 230 miles of hiking trails here and many more extend beyond park boundaries. The wilderness is to be explored, but it must also be respected. **Free permits** are required for all overnight stays in the backcountry (available at Jenny Lake Ranger Station and Craig Thomas Discovery & Visitor Center). Backpackers should always travel with a good **topographical map**. When planning a trip try to be as realistic as possible about how many miles you can cover in a day. Be sure to take into consideration the ability of every member of your group and the weight of your pack. Snow cover can persist in the high country well into summer; prospective hikers must carry (and know how to use) an **ice axe** if they wish to pass these regions. It's also bear country. Food must be stored in approved, portable **bear-proof canisters**. Canisters are available for use at ranger stations and visitor centers.

Reservations are accepted for the park's designated backcountry sites. Make reservations online at nps.gov/grte/planyourvisit/bcres.htm for a one-time $25 reservation fee (if successful).

Boating

Grand Teton National Park provides an incredible array of water adventures. **Float trips** down the winding **Snake River** are a peaceful way to enjoy mountain vistas and view wildlife. They are offered by many of the park's lodging facilities: **Headwaters Lodge & Resort** (800.443.2311, $60 Adult/$40 Child), **Grand Teton Lodge Company** (307.543.2811, $55/$35), **Signal Mountain Lodge** (307.543.2831, $59/$37), **Triangle X Ranch** (307.733.5500, $60/$42), and **Lost Creek Ranch** (included in lodging rate). **Barker–Ewing Float Trips** (800.365.1800, $60/$40) and **Solitude Float Trips** (888.704.2800, $60/$40) are also authorized to administer float trips here. These trips cover 10 of the most picturesque miles of water you'll ever see in your life. Grand Teton looms in the background for the entire three hour journey. Trips are generally available from mid-May until late September. **O.A.R.S.** (www.oars.com) provides an alternative to the float trip with their 1–3 day kayak adventures ($273–659).

If you have your own kayak, canoe, or raft, you can take the same route float trips take. All you have to do is launch at Deadman's Bar Road and land near Moose Junction/Menor's Ferry. The route is not especially technical or treacherous and current is generally gentle as you wind your way across Jackson Hole. You may encounter bars, eddies, and the occasional downed tree, but it's rarely splashy. In order to float the river you must obtain a non-motorized **boat permit** ($20/season, $10/7-day) and an Aquatic Invasive Species decal ($5 WY residents, $15 non-residents). Motorized boats require comparable permits ($40/season, $20/7-day).

If you don't have your own boat or you'd rather leave it at home, **canoe or kayak rental** is available from **Jenny Lake Boating**, **Grand Teton Lodge Company**, and **Signal Mountain Lodge**. Rentals are available for use at Jenny or Jackson Lake on a first-come, first-served basis for $14–17 per hour. **Jackson Lake Marina** also provides **fishing boats** ($36/hour), **pontoon boats** ($80/hour), and **deck cruisers** ($99/hour) for **rent**.

Barker–Ewing River Trips • (800) 365-1800 • (307) 733-1000
945 W Broadway; Jackson, WY 83001 • www.barker-ewing.com

Solitude Float Trips • (307) 733-2871
110 East Karns Ave; Jackson, WY 83001 • www.solitudefloattrips.com

Jenny Lake Boating • (307) 734-9227
PO Box 111; Moose, WY 83012 • www.jennylakeboating.com

Biking

Biking is permitted on all park roadways. Pedalling is relatively easy because most roads cross the flat expanse of Jackson Hole rather than working their way into the mountains, rewarding cyclists with beautiful mountain landscapes without all the heavy cranking associated with arduous climbs. Roads are often crowded (especially in summer), but early morning or late evening and off-season rides can be splendid. In 2009, a **Multi-Use Pathway** (non-motorized transport only) was completed between Dornan's Spur Ranch and South Jenny Lake. **Teton Park Road** is recommended for road cyclists, and the 52-mile unpaved **Grassy Lake Road** is a hot-spot for mountain bikers (but it's not singletrack). Adventure Sports at Dornan's Spur Ranch provides bike rental.

Adventure Sports • (307) 733-3307
5 Dornans Road; Moose, WY 83012
www.dornans.com
Bike Rental: $12 (hour), $28 (half-day), $36 (24 hours)

Horseback Riding

Dude ranches are alive and well at Grand Teton. In fact, business is so good that ranches are often booked to capacity months in advance. These ranches are hardly inexpensive, but horse enthusiasts seeking "all-you-can-ride" accommodations will not find a better destination in the National Park System. **Triangle X Ranch** offers an all-inclusive modern western adventure for $1,600 per person per week. **Lost Creek Ranch & Spa**, located near Triangle X Ranch but just outside the park boundary, offers an all-inclusive package for $13,200 for as many as 4 people per week. Each additional person costs another $700 per week. Alcohol, babysitting, fishing trips, skeet shooting, and other activities cost extra. A more affordable alternative for the horse enthusiast is to take a **guided trail ride** provided by **Headwaters Lodge & Resort** (800.443.2311) or Grand Teton Lodge Company (307.543.2811). Both outfitters have regularly scheduled 1-hour rides for $36 (longer rides are available). Horseback riding is also available at **Jenny Lake Lodge**, but only to the lodge's guests.

Lost Creek Ranch & Spa • Jackson Hole • (307) 733-3435
95 Old Ranch Road; Moose, WY 83012
www.lostcreek.com

Triangle X Guest Ranch • (307) 733-2183
2 Triangle X Ranch Road; Moose, WY 83012
www.trianglex.com

Snake River Float Trip

Menors Ferry General Store

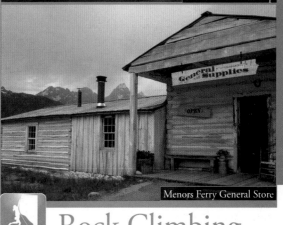

Rock Climbing

With plenty of granite to go around, Grand Teton is one of the premier rock climbing parks. It attracts climbers from all around the world, and everyone from beginners to experts will find routes suitable to their ability level. Check the park's climbing and backcountry website at www.tetonclimbing.blogspot.com for additional information, routes, and conditions. Information can also be obtained at Jenny Lake Ranger Station in person or on the phone by calling (307) 739-3343 in summer and (307) 739-3309 in winter. If you'd like to join a commercial climbing guide, you can find those too:

Exum Mountain Guides • (307) 733-2297
PO Box 56, Moose; WY 83012-0056
www.exumguides.com
Open: June–September
Rates: $140 (Level I), $160 (Level II), $160 (Snow School)

Jackson Hole Mountain Guides • (307) 733-4979
165 N Glenwood St # 2; Jackson, WY 83001
www.jhmg.com
Open: June–September
Rates: $140 (Basic), $155 (Intermediate), $200 (Advanced), $160 (Ice Climb) • courses last from 8:30am–4:30pm

The Tetons and Snake River (Ansel Adams photo)

 # Winter Activities

A few park lodges remain open during winter and visitors can also **camp on Colter Bay Visitor Center's parking area**. It's quite the contrast from summer when lodges are filled to capacity and parking spots are hard to come by. Cars and visitors may be few and far between but activities are everywhere. The best way to explore the park in winter is with the aid of a set of **cross-country skis** or **snowshoes**. Moose–Wilson Road, Signal Mountain Road, and Teton Park Road close in winter, providing a proper surface for skiers and snowshoers. **Phelps Lake Overlook, Jenny Lake Trail, Taggart Lake/ Beaver Creek Loop, Swan Lake–Heron Pond Loop, and Polecat Creek Loop** listed in the hiking table on page 211 are popular ski/snowshoe trails. If you don't want to explore the Tetons on your own, you can join a park ranger for a **guided snowshoe trek**. Trips usually take place from late December to mid-March and they depart from Craig Thomas Discovery & Visitor Center. Reservations can be made starting December 1st of each year by calling (307) 739-3399. These excursions are free, but a donation of $5 per adult and $2 per child is suggested.

Some areas of the park allow **snowmobiling**. It is a highly controversial activity due to the associated noise and air pollution. Interested parties should contact a visitor center for current information. **Backcountry skiing and snowboarding** are allowed within the park, and many of the park's lakes are open for **ice fishing**.

 # Driving

There are miles upon miles of roadways with strategically placed pullouts and picnic areas allowing motorists to enjoy the park's magnificence through their windshield. Beginning at the north end you'll encounter **John D. Rockefeller, Jr. Memorial Parkway** joining Grand Teton and Yellowstone, an entirely separate entity operated by the NPS. Once you enter the park, you'll skirt around Jackson Lake until **Teton Park Road** veers to the west of the Snake River and **US-89/US-191/US-287** continues along its eastern shore. Teton Park Road continues along the base of the Teton Range to Moose Junction. In between are the "don't miss" side-trips up **Signal Mountain Road** (if you don't hike to the viewpoint) and one-way **Jenny Lake Scenic Drive**. As you approach Moose Junction you'll come across **Moose–Wilson Road**, which leads to fantastic hiking trails and **Laurence S. Rockefeller Preserve**. Views from **US-26/US-89/US-191** on the east side of Snake River are equally amazing. If you have time, watch the sunset from **Snake River Overlook** where Ansel Adams took the historic photograph pictured to the left.

 # Fishing

Grand Teton's 50 miles of the 1,056-mile long Snake River and more than 100 alpine lakes provide ample opportunity for anglers searching for the catch of the day. Fishermen must follow Wyoming regulations and licensing requirements. Most park lodges sell fishing licenses. Grand Teton Lodge Company (Jackson Lake, $80/hour • Snake River, $475 full-day), Headwaters Lodge & Resort (Snake River, $450 full-day, $375 half-day), Triangle X Ranch (Snake River, $450 full-day, $375 half-day), and Signal Mountain Lodge (Jackson Lake, $80/hour, $280 half-day) all offer guided fishing tours. There are two additional outfitters who specialize in fishing trips.

Snake River Angler • (307) 733-3699
12170 Dornan Road; Moose, WY 83012
www.snakeriverangler.com
Rates: Snake River, $475 (full-day)

Jack Dennis Fly Fishing Trips • (307) 734-8103
70 South King Street; Jackson, WY 83001
www.jackdennis.com
Rates: Snake River, $475 (full-day)

For Kids: Children like the Tetons. They'll enjoy just about everything: **floating Snake River**, **paddling Jenny Lake**, **watching wildlife**, **joining a park ranger on a guided tour**, and much more. In addition to child-oriented ranger activities, the park offers a **Junior Ranger Program**. Children ages 8–12, may participate in this unique program that explores the wonders of Grand Teton and its environs. Group size is limited to 12. Reservations are required and can be made at any of the visitor centers. Upon completion of the Junior Ranger Activity Booklet, return to a visitor center so your child can be christened as the park's newest Junior Naturalist and receive a badge.

Ranger Programs: It may appear that it costs a fortune to experience the Tetons. But the best way to discover them is free: with a park ranger on one of their guided programs that are equally enjoyable for children and adults. From June until early September you'll find a wide variety of programs offered in and around the park's Visitor Centers and Laurance S. Rockefeller Preserve.

Activities range from a 30 minute talk about the park's biology to a 3 hour ramble on a trail. There are also campfire programs, a boat cruise, museum tour, and all sorts of walks and talks. The hike to **Hidden Falls** from Jenny Lake can be enhanced by joining a ranger on a first-come, first-served basis for the first 25 hikers. They take **Jenny Lake Boat Shuttle** to shorten the hike, so show up prepared with your shuttle token ($10 round-trip/$7 one-way for Adults • $5/$5 for Children ages 2–11). At Colter Bay you can take the **Fire & Ice Cruise** of Jackson Lake, which is narrated by a park ranger. This tour is only available with advance ticket purchase ($26/Adult • $13/Child age 3–11). Reservations can be made by calling Colter Bay Marina at (307) 543-2811. These are the only programs that charge a fee. There are dozens of additional programs listed in the park's newspaper, ***The Grand Teton Guide*** (available online or at any visitor center). So, for your trip to the Tetons think about skipping the expensive commercial experiences and join a ranger on your exploration of this natural wonderland.

Flora & Fauna: **More than 1,000 species of vascular plants** inhabit Grand Teton National Park, including 900 flowering species. The park's forests are mostly coniferous, with whitebark pine, limber pine, subalpine fir, and

Did you know?

➤ Grand Teton National Park is home to the largest wintering elk herd in North America.

➤ No one had settled along the west bank of Snake River until the 1890s when Bill Menor built a ferry at Moose to transport patrons across the river.

➤ The Teton Range forms one of the most postcard-perfect scenes in America because its mountains rise from a large fault straight up from the floor of Jackson Hole without any foothills cluttering the vista.

Englemann spruce capable of surviving at elevations up to 10,000 feet. Lodgepole pine, Douglas fir, and blue spruce are found closer to the valley floor where the soil is deep enough to support tree growth. A smaller sampling of deciduous trees reside along rivers and lakeshores.

Seeing the park's wildlife in its natural environment is just as enthralling as a brilliant Teton sunset. Moose, bear, and elk are the most popular residents, but there are **61 mammals** inhabiting the park. Bison, pronghorn, and mule deer are often seen grazing along the road side. Motorists should pass with caution as these animals have become indifferent to traffic. Car accidents kill more than 100 large mammals each year at Grand Teton.

Pets: Pets are permitted in the park, but must be kept on a leash no more than six feet in length at all times. They are prohibited from all hiking trails, visitor centers, other public buildings, and the backcountry. Pets are allowed at campgrounds, picnic areas, and parking lots.

Accessibility: All visitor centers are accessible to individuals who require the use of a wheelchair. All in-park lodging facilities have accessible rooms. The Multi-use Pathway, which runs parallel to Teton Park Road, and South Jenny Lake Trail are easily accessible paved trails. Colter Bay, Jackson Lake Dam, Laurance S. Rockefeller Preserve, Menor's Ferry Historic District, and String Lake are other areas of the park suggested for wheelchairs users.

John Moulton Barn on Mormon Row and Grand Teton

Grand Teton Visitor and Information Centers

Facility (Phone)	Location	Open	Notes
Craig Thomas Discovery & Visitor Center • (307.739.3399)	In Moose, 0.5-mile west of Moose Junction on Teton Park Road	All Year, except Christmas Daily from 9am–5pm Extended hours in summer	Primary Visitor Center, boat and backcountry permits available
Jenny Lake Visitor Center • (307.739.3392)	On Teton Park Road, 8 miles north of Moose Junction	mid-May–September Daily from 8am–5pm Extended hours in summer	Boat permits available
Jenny Lake Ranger Station • (307.739.3343)	On Teton Park Road, 8 miles north of Moose Junction	mid-May–mid-September Daily from 8am–5pm	Rock climbing info and backcountry permits available
Colter Bay Visitor Center & Indian Arts Museum • (307.739.3594)	On Highway 89/191/287, 0.5-mile west of Colter Bay Junction	May–mid-October Daily from 8am–5pm Extended hours in summer	Boat and backcountry permits available
Flagg Ranch Information Station • (307.543.2372)	On Highway 89/191/287, 16 miles north of Colter Bay	early June–early Sept Daily from 9am–3:30pm	Info on John D. Rockefeller, Jr. Memorial Parkway
Laurence S. Rockefeller Preserve Center • (307.739.3654)	On Moose-Wilson Road, 4 miles south of Moose	late May–late September Daily from 9am–6pm Extended hours in summer	Interactive exhibits; sales and permits are not available

Weather

Most visitors arrive between May and September. Long intimidating winters keep tourists away during winter. Snowfall averages more than 170 inches per year, most of which falls between November and March, but snow and frost are possible during any month. Jackson Hole has a semi-arid climate, receiving about 20 inches of precipitation annually, fairly evenly distributed throughout the year. Even the warmest months are cool at night near the Tetons. July and August have an average low temperature right around 40°F. That's a stark contrast to average highs, which are about 80°F. No matter what time of year, it's best to wear multiple layers of clothing while exploring the park. Temperatures change with wind, elevation, and time of day, and afternoon thunderstorms are common.

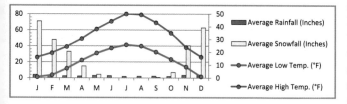

Vacation Planner

Grand Teton is an excellent alternative to its busy neighbor to the north, Yellowstone National Park (page 218). If you're headed to Yellowstone and only planning a day at Grand Teton, you may want to recalibrate your schedule, allowing more time with the Three Tetons. Three days is barely enough to experience its main attractions. A little more time and you can head into the **backcountry** (page 212), take a **fishing excursion** (page 214), or attend a slew of **ranger programs** (page 215). Nearby dining, grocery stores, lodging, festivals, and attractions are listed on pages 242–245.

Day 1

First stop: **Craig Thomas Discovery & Visitor Center**. The recently renovated facility has excellent exhibits and it's the perfect place to receive a proper introduction to the park. Don't forget to pick up a newspaper, *The Grand Teton Guide*. It will tell you when and where to go for **ranger programs** (plus loads of other useful information). Once you've had a thorough look around, return to **Moose Junction** and turn left onto US-26/US-89/US-191. Drive the entire length through Moran Junction all the way to **Colter Bay Village**. Grand Teton looms to the west

all the while. Pull over whenever it strikes your fancy. **Glacier View Turnout** and **Snake River Overlook** are two of the best pit-stops. Spend the night in (or near) **Colter Bay**. If you have an hour to spare, walk along **Lakeshore Path** (page 211). It's an excellent trail to wander about at dusk as the sun is ducking behind the Teton Range. If you don't feel like hiking, check the newspaper to see if you can catch an evening program at the campground. Better yet, do both.

Day 2

Wake-up before the sun and backtrack to **Jackson Lake Junction** where you'll turn right onto **Teton Park Road**. After a few miles, take a left onto **Signal Mountain Road**. Drive to the summit (page 214, large vehicles and trailers should not attempt) to watch the sunrise. Sitting atop Signal Mountain while the first rays of sunlight illuminate the Tetons is well worth the effort of packing up on a crisp and cool morning. The early morning yields another bonus. You'll have a decent shot at securing a site at **Jenny Lake Campground** (page 209). (No guarantees though, it's extremely difficult to predict day-to-day camping volume.) You'll also have enough time to reach **Hidden Falls** (page 210) and **Inspiration Point** (continue to **Lake Solitude** if you feel up to it and don't mind spending the entire day on foot). These Jenny Lake Area trails are often busy by 10am. To avoid the masses, consider taking the 10.2-mile hike to **Amphitheater Lake** (page 211) instead, which departs from Lupine Meadows Trailhead. If you have a suspicion a stunning sunset is on the horizon, drive back to **Snake River Overlook** on US 26/US-89/US-191. For sunsets, this spot cannot be beat.

Day 3

End your vacation in style by exploring the park by horse on a **trail ride** (page 213) or by raft on a **float trip of Snake River** (page 212). If you've already exceeded your budget or are just not interested in horses or boats, check the newspaper once more to see what ranger programs are offered that day. If all else fails take **Moose-Wilson Road** (near Moose Junction) to **Laurance S. Rockefeller Preserve**. Browse the exhibits and then hike 6.6 miles around **Phelps Lake Loop** (page 211).

Midway Geyser Basin's Grand Prismatic Spring as seen from Fairy Falls Trail © Frank Kovalchek (flickr/Alaskan Dude)

Yellowstone - Wyoming

Long after Americans reached the Pacific Ocean, explorers, fur trappers, and frontiersmen began filling in blank spots left between the East and West Coasts. In the 1850s—before Wyoming became a territory— one of these unmapped regions was reported as a rugged wilderness of boiling mud, steaming rivers, and petrified birds. Such reports were promptly disregarded as myth in the East, colorful yarns spun by colorful men, and publishers curtly responded "We do not print fiction." Still, these landscapes captured the curiosity of several expedition parties. In 1871 the U.S. government deployed the **Hayden Geological Survey** to uncover the truth. **Ferdinand V. Hayden**, painter **Thomas Moran**, and photographer **William Henry Jackson** were sent to assess what really existed. Less than one year later, **President Ulysses S. Grant** signed the **Act of Dedication**, effectively making Yellowstone the world's first National Park. This large tract of land in northwestern Wyoming Territory, barely extending into Montana and Idaho Territories, was set aside, preserved for the enjoyment of the people. Much like the area's first explorers, today's visitors come across steaming rivers, towering waterfalls dropping into deep canyons, bubbling mud-pots, hot spring terraces, and boiling water gushing from the earth. Sights so amazing that they inspire the same disbelief of 19th century publishers and politicians. Yet it is real. Guests can see it. Touch it. Smell it. It is Yellowstone.

The first people known to have explored the land known today as Yellowstone were **Native Americans**. Discovery of obsidian arrowheads dating back 11,000 years suggests they used this land as a hunting

PO Box 168
Yellowstone Nat'l Park, WY 82190
Phone: (307) 344-7381
Website: www.nps.gov/yell

Established: March 1, 1872
Size: 2,221,766 Acres
Annual Visitors: 3.6 Million
Peak Season: July–August
Hiking Trails: 1,000+ Miles

Activities: Hiking, Biking, Fishing, Photography, Horseback Riding, Boating, Wildlife Viewing, Scenic Driving, and Winter Activities

Facilities: 12 Campgrounds, 6 Lodges, 10 Visitor Centers
Camping Fee: $12–45/night
Backcountry Camping: Permitted*

Park Hours: All day, every day
Entrance Fee: $25 • Vehicle
$20 • Motorcycle
$12 • Individual (foot, bike, etc.)

*Must obtain a free permit no more than 48 hours prior to departure

ground shortly after glaciers from the last great ice age receded. By the **Lewis and Clark Expedition of 1805**, trappers had already named the river "Roche Jaune" or "Rock Yellow River" referring to yellow sandstones found along its banks. (It is a common misconception that the river was named for yellow coloring caused by rhyolite lava seen at the Grand Canyon of the Yellowstone.) In 1806, **John Colter** left Lewis and Clark's Expedition to work for Missouri Fur Trading Company, exploring the regions comprising present-day Yellowstone and Grand Teton National Parks. He is believed to be the first white man to see Yellowstone Lake, at least one geyser, and the Teton Range. While Lewis and Clark would have believed Colter's accounts, many jokingly referred to the land of boiling mudpots and steaming rivers as "Colter's Hell."

Few explorers ventured into Colter's Hell until 1871, when **Hayden's Geological Survey** explored the region. During the expedition, a party member suggested the area should be set aside as a national park. Hayden agreed and became the most enthusiastic and devoted advocate of this newly conceived park idea. His report declared the land unsuitable for farming because of its high elevation. Mining was impossible because of its volcanic origins. These findings combined with images and paintings collected

When to Go

Yellowstone is open all year, but more than half of the park's three million annual visitors arrive between July and August. Visiting in September or October is a nice alternative. It's less crowded, wildlife is still active, and the weather is comfortable. About 80,000 people visit the park each winter to see an enchanting wonderland created by the combination of snow and geothermal features. Mammoth Campground is open all year. Year-round lodging is available at Old Faithful and Mammoth Hot Springs. North and Northeast Entrance provide the only year-round access to wheeled vehicles. All other entrances close, allowing roads to be groomed for the winter season. The road between North and Northeast Entrances and the road from Mammoth Hot Springs to the parking area at Upper Terraces are the only roads plowed for wheeled vehicles during winter. All interior roads can only be accessed by over-snow vehicles in winter. The open close date for over-snow vehicle roads is subject to change based on the amount of snowfall. Park entrances are closed once again in late March or early April to clear the roads for the upcoming summer season.

Best of Yellowstone

Attraction: Grand Canyon of the Yellowstone
  Runner-up: Grand Prismatic Spring
  2nd Runner-up: Norris Geyser Basin
  3rd Runner-up: Boiling River
  4th Runner-up: Yellowstone Lake

Activity: Yellowstone Institute Programs
  Runner-up: Western Cookout & Trail Ride
  2nd Runner-up: Snowcoach Tours

Wildlife Viewing: Lamar Valley
  Runner-up: Hayden Valley

Short Hike: Mount Washburn Trail
  Runner-up: Uncle Tom's Trail

Backpack: Black Canyon of the Yellowstone
  Runner-up: Sky Rim Loop

Transportation & Airports

Public transportation is available to several gateway cities near Yellowstone. Visitors can reach West Yellowstone aboard a bus/shuttle from Salt Lake City (208.656.8824, www.saltlakeexpress.com) and airports at Bozeman, MT; Idaho Falls, ID; and Jackson Hole, WY. Commercial transportation to the park is also available from Cody and Jackson, WY (406.640.0631, www.yellowstoneroadrunner.com). At this time, the park does not provide a public shuttle to explore its 142-mile Grand Loop Road.

Yellowstone Regional (COD) in Cody, WY is close to the East (27 miles) and Northeast Entrances (76 miles). Jackson Hole Airport (JAC), located in Grand Teton National Park is about 50 miles from the Southern Entrance. Gallatin Field (BZN) just outside Bozeman, MT, is about 90 miles from the North Entrance. Billings' Logan International (BIL) is 67 miles from the Northeast Entrance. Idaho Falls Regional (IDA) is about 110 miles from the West Entrance. Between June and early September, Yellowstone Airport, (WYS) located in West Yellowstone, MT, is serviced from Salt Lake City International Airport (SCL) in Utah.

during the expedition were enough to convince Congress to withdraw this region from public auction. On March 1, 1872, **President Grant** signed a law creating Yellowstone National Park, the first of its kind anywhere in the world.

N.P. Langford became the park's first superintendent (allowing him to sign his name "National Park Langford"). It was not a glamorous position. He was denied salary, funding, and staff. Without resources to protect the park, it was vulnerable to poachers, vandals, and others seeking to raid its resources. **Philetus Norris** was appointed as Yellowstone's second superintendent, and first to receive a salary. Although meager, he received enough funding to begin construction on a system of roads and to hire **Henry Yount** as gamekeeper. Yount is widely regarded as the first park ranger, but he resigned when it was obvious the job of preventing poaching and vandalism was far too great a task for one man.

Protecting the park would only become more difficult as **tourism** increased. Completion of the **Northern Pacific Railroad** line to Livingston, MT and the park's northern entrance had dramatic results. Visitation increased from 300 in 1872 to more than 5,000 in 1883. The railroad sought to develop the area's prime locations with help from an amiable superintendent named **Rufus Hatch**. Under Hatch's leadership, trash was discarded in streams and fumaroles, tourists were charged exorbitant amounts, animals were killed for food, trees were chopped for construction, and coal was mined from park land. America's first and only national park was being exploited by everyone, developers, poachers, and its stewards. Many sympathetic Americans believed Hatch was destroying the park. To prove this point, Civil War hero **General Phillip Sheridan** invited **President Chester A. Arthur** to join him on a Yellowstone camping trip. The first Presidential visit led to legislation appropriating $40,000 for the park, regulating Hatch's development, and allowing the Secretary of the Interior to summon troops to prevent vandalism and hunting.

To protect the country's last free-roaming bison herd, **General Sheridan and Troop M of the 1st United States Cavalry,** summoned by order of the Secretary of the Interior, rode to the rescue. Their temporary residence lasted 32 years, during which they built structures, enforced regulations, oversaw construction of **Roosevelt Arch**, and created many of the management principles adopted by the National Park Service when it assumed control in 1918.

More than half a century after its establishment, the park idea was beginning to take shape. It was a long and arduous journey to form a park that is truly "for the Benefit and Enjoyment of the People," as Roosevelt Arch states. But this too has become as real as the yarn-spinners' tales of bubbling mud, towering geysers, and golden canyons.

Did you know?

▶ Yellowstone is the world's first national park.

▶ The park (over 2.2 million acres) is larger than Rhode Island and Delaware combined. Roughly 96% of the land is in Wyoming, another 3% in Montana, and 1% in Idaho. About 80% of the park land is forested.

▶ Yellowstone Lake (131.7 square miles) is one of the largest high-altitude lakes in North America.

▶ There are approximately 290 year-round waterfalls higher than15-feet, including Lower Falls of the Yellowstone River (308 ft), tallest in the park.

▶ It is home to the world's largest collection of plants and animals, including 67 species of mammals, approximately 406 species of thermophiles, 186 species of lichens, 1,150 species of native vascular plants, and 200 species of non-native plants.

▶ Half of the world's geothermal features, including 300 geysers, are found at Yellowstone.

▶ Steamboat Geyser (Norris Geyser Basin) at more than 400-ft is the tallest geyser in the world, erupting with no noticeable pattern and sometimes years between eruptions.

▶ Old Faithful spouts 3,700 to 8,400 gallons of 204°F water about 100-ft in the air every 60–110 minutes.

▶ Mammoth Hot Springs deposits an estimated two tons of calcium carbonate each day.

▶ Geyser basins are full of interesting color combinations. The blues of Norris are due to silica in suspension in the water. Red-orange colors are often caused by cyanobacteria or iron-oxides and arsenic compounds. Some springs are emerald green in color; this is due to blue refracted light in combination with yellow sulfur lining the pool.

Directions

Yellowstone is huge. It's larger than the states of Delaware and Rhode Island combined. Five roads lead into the park: one from each side, and another from the northeast corner. Remember that the only park roads open all year to wheeled vehicles are those connecting North and Northeast Entrances and a 0.5-mile section of road from Mammoth Hot Springs to Upper Terrace Parking Area. Current road conditions are available by calling 511 and selecting "Yellowstone National Park Tourist Information." Below you'll find short descriptions of traveling directions to each entrance from the nearest major city.

North Entrance (40 miles from Livingston, MT): From I-90 take Exit 333 near Livingston, MT for US-89 S toward City Center/Yellowstone National Park. Turn onto US-89 S. Drive about 52 miles through Gardiner, MT, under Roosevelt Arch, and into the park's North Entrance.

West Entrance (108 miles from Idaho Falls, ID): From Idaho Falls, ID (I-15) take US-20 E more than 100 miles to West Yellowstone, MT. Turn left at US-191 S/US-20 E/US-287 S/Yellowstone Ave, which leads across the Montana–Wyoming border and into the park.

South Entrance (57 miles from Jackson, WY): You'll take one of the most scenic highways in the United States, US-191 N/US-287 N/US-89 N/ John D. Rockefeller, Jr. Parkway, about 38 miles north through Grand Teton National Park to South Entrance.

East Entrance (52 miles from Cody, WY): Take US-14 W/US-16 W/US-20 W/Sheridan Avenue (following signs to Yellowstone) about 25 miles west to the park entrance.

Northeast Entrance (81 miles from Cody, WY): Take WY-120/Depot Road north about 16 miles. Turn left at Chief Joseph Hwy/State WY-296, which turns into Crandall Road then Dead Indian Hill Road, and finally Sunlight Basin Road before it intersects with US-212 W/Beartooth Hwy (closed seasonally). Turn left onto Beartooth Hwy to Cooke City, MT and Northeast Entrance.

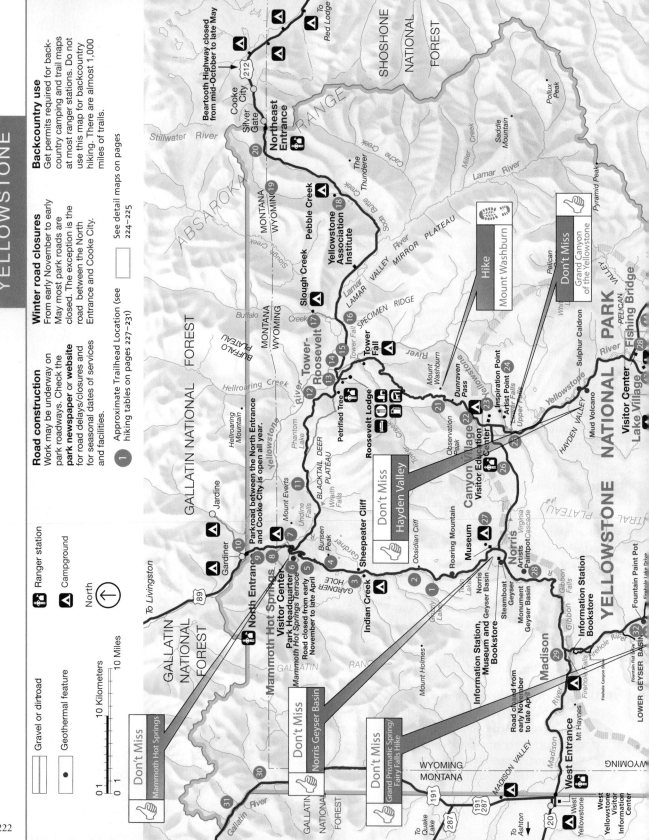

Backcountry use

Get permits required for back-country camping and trail maps at most ranger stations. Do not use this map for backcountry hiking. There are almost 1,000 miles of trails.

Winter road closures

From early November to early May most park roads are closed. The exception is the road between the North Entrance and Cooke City.

See detail maps on pages 224–225

Road construction

Work may be underway on park roadways. Check the **park newspaper** or **website** for road delays/closures and for seasonal dates of services and facilities.

Approximate Trailhead Location (see hiking tables on pages 227–231)

Gravel or dirt road

Geothermal feature

Ranger station

Campground

North

Don't Miss
Mammoth Hot Springs

Don't Miss
Norris Geyser Basin

Don't Miss
Grand Prismatic Spring/
Fairy Falls Hike

Don't Miss
Hayden Valley

Hike
Mount Washburn

Don't Miss
Grand Canyon
of the Yellowstone

GALLATIN NATIONAL FOREST

SHOSHONE NATIONAL FOREST

ABSAROKA RANGE

YELLOWSTONE NATIONAL PARK

Beartooth Highway closed from mid-October to late May

212

Cooke City

Silver Gate

Northeast Entrance

Pebble Creek

Yellowstone Association Institute

Slough Creek

Tower-Roosevelt

Tower Fall

Petrified Tree

Roosevelt Lodge

Mount Washburn

Dunraven Pass

Inspiration Point

Artist Point

Observation Peak

Canyon Village
Visitor Education Center

Gardiner

Jardine

North Entrance

Mammoth Hot Springs
Visitor Center
Park Headquarters

Road closed from early November to late April

Indian Creek

Sheepeater Cliff

Obsidian Cliff

Roaring Mountain

Norris
Museum
Information Station
and Geyser Basin
Bookstore

Steamboat Geyser

Norris
Artists Paintpot

Madison
Information Station
Bookstore

Road closed from early November to late April

Fountain Paint Pot

LOWER GEYSER BASIN

West Entrance

West Yellowstone
West Yellowstone
Visitor Information
Center

89

WYOMING
MONTANA

191
287

To Livingston

To Ashton

To Quake Lake

89

To Red Lodge

Stillwater River

Buffalo Creek

BUFFALO PLATEAU

BLACKTAIL DEER PLATEAU

Hellroaring Creek

Yellowstone River

MIRROR PLATEAU

SPECIMEN RIDGE

LAMAR VALLEY

Lamar River

Soda Butte Creek

Cache Creek

Miller Creek

Saddle Mountain

Pollux Peak

Pyramid Peak

The Thunderer

PELICAN VALLEY

Pelican Creek

HAYDEN VALLEY

Mud Volcano

Sulphur Caldron

Fishing Bridge

Visitor Center
Lake Village

CENTRAL PLATEAU

Virginia Cascade

Gibbon Falls

Gibbon River

Firehole River

Firehole Falls

Firehole Canyon Drive

Fountain Flat Drive

Mt Haynes

MADISON VALLEY

Madison River

Mount Holmes

GALLATIN RANGE

Grizzly Lake

Mount Everts

Bunsen Peak

GARDNER'S HOLE

Gardner River

Undine Falls

Wraith Falls

Phantom Lake

Hellroaring Mountain

Tower Creek

Tower Fall

Upper Falls

Lower Falls

Yellowstone River

Gallatin River

20

30

31

10

9

8

6

5

4

3

2

1

7

11

12

13

14

15

16

17

18

19

20

21

22

23

24

26

27

28

29

32

Mammoth Hot Springs Terrace

0   10 Kilometers
0   10 Miles

222

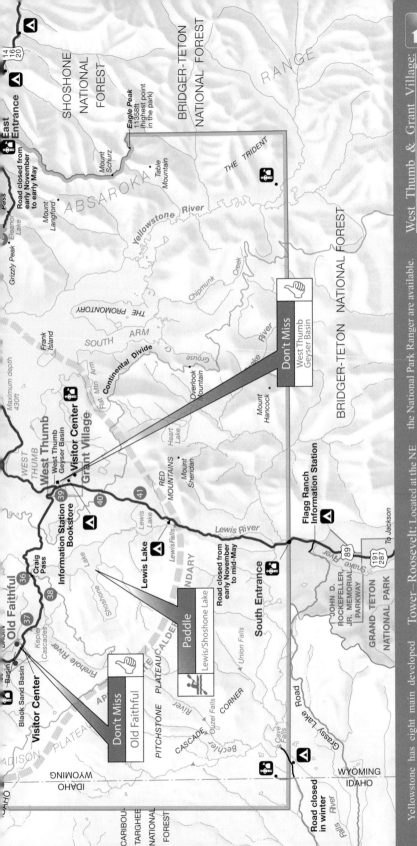

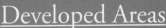

Developed Areas

West Thumb & Grant Village: Located at the southern end of GLR, West Thumb of Yellowstone Lake offers a geyser basin near the shoreline. Campground, store, lodging, showers, gas, and visitor center are available.

Fishing Bridge & Lake Village: Located at the north end of Yellowstone Lake, Fishing Bridge is a popular place to watch cutthroat trout, but fishing is banned. An RV park, gas, store, and dining are available at fishing bridge. You will find lodging, dining, camping, medical station, store, and a ranger station at Old Lake Village.

the National Park Ranger are available.

Madison: Located southwest of Norris, where Madison and Firehole Rivers converge. Thermal features, a popular 75–80°F swimming hole just below Firehole Falls, campground, and information station are available nearby.

Old Faithful: Old Faithful—the most iconic feature of the park—is located at the southwest corner of GLR. Nearby you'll find Midway Geyser Basin, home to the most colorful feature, Grand Prismatic Spring. Just about everything you can imaging is available at Old Faithful Village (except a campground).

Yellowstone has eight main developed areas centered on the park's most breathtaking natural attractions. Each area is located on or near Grand Loop Road (GLR). GLR forms a giant figure-8 connecting all five entrances. See pages 224–225 for detailed maps of most developed areas.

Mammoth Hot Springs: Located just 5 miles from the North Entrance, you'll find spectacular terraces formed of travertine (calcium carbonate—the main ingredient in heartburn relief tablets). Lodging, dining, gas, campground, post office, shopping, visitor center, and medical station are available.

Tower–Roosevelt: Located at the NE corner of GLR, you'll find Petrified Tree, Specimen Ridge, Tower Fall, and some of the best hiking trails. Lodging, camping, a store, and gas are available.

Canyon Village: Located near GLR's center, this is one of the most popular regions, including Grand Canyon of the Yellowstone. Gas, lodging, dining, a store, visitor center, and showers are available.

Norris: Situated opposite Canyon Village at the center of GLR is Norris, the oldest and hottest thermal area, and home to Steamboat, the world's tallest geyser. A campground and Museum of

Yellowstone has 12 established campgrounds providing more than 2,000 campsites. That's a lot of campsites, but as many as 50,000 visitors can enter the park on a single day in July or August. This influx of guests causes congested roads, shoulder-to-shoulder hiking, and full campgrounds. Yellowstone does not offer overflow camping areas, but there are a fair amount of campgrounds and RV parks outside the park.

Campgrounds fill up from time to time, but try not to feel pressured into making reservations before you arrive. In fact, the best way to visit Yellowstone is to have a bit of flexibility in your travel arrangements. With all the amazing scenery, wildlife, and tourists, it's inevitable that you end up deviating from your pre-planned itinerary. When these instances occur, it's nice to have flexible overnight arrangements, allowing you to sleep nearby rather than forcing a potentially long drive (possibly at night) to the next destination or reserved accommodations. And large campgrounds usually do not fill up until the late afternoon, if at all.

Pebble Creek, Slough Creek, and Tower Fall are primitive campgrounds with vault toilets. Their small size and stunning environment cause them to fill early.

A camper who secures a site at one of these locations is also more likely to spend a few extra nights, exacerbating the shortage problem.

Most campgrounds have a couple pull-through campsites, but very few can accommodate RVs longer than 30 feet. It is recommended that visitors with large RVs make reservations at **Fishing Bridge RV Park**. This campground is for hard-sided vehicles only. Tents and tent-trailers are prohibited.

Backcountry camping is also popular. A **free backcountry user permit** is required for any overnight stay in the backcountry and must be obtained in person at one of the locations listed in the camping table on page 225. Try to obtain a permit at the location closest to where your trip begins so you can receive up-to-date information regarding trail conditions and wildlife activity. Most backcountry campsites have a maximum stay of three days.

All campers should be aware that Yellowstone is bear country. Do not keep food in your tent, keep a clean camp, and store food in air-tight containers (bear canisters for backpackers).

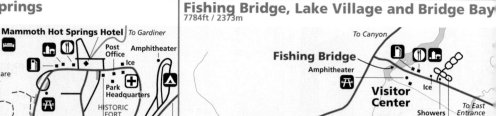

Services and Facilities

Winter road closures From early November to early May most park roads are closed. The exception is the road between the North Entrance and Cooke City. It is open all year.

From mid-December to early March, oversnow vehicles may be used only on the unplowed, groomed park roads. Call park headquarters for regulations or check the park website, **www.nps.gov/yell**.

Emergencies For medical or other emergencies contact a ranger or call **307-344-7381** or **911**. Check the park newspaper or website for seasonal dates of services and facilities.

🐎 Horse rental   ⛽ Gas station (some have auto repair)
➕ Medical clinic   🚤 Boat launch   🥾 Self-guiding trail _ _ _ _.
🧍 Ranger station   🛏 Lodging   🅿 Picnic area
🔺 Campground   🍴 Food service   🏪 Store

Mammoth Hot Springs
6239ft / 1902m

Fishing Bridge, Lake Village and Bridge Bay
7784ft / 2373m

Yellowstone Camping

	Open	Fee	Sites	Notes
Bridge Bay*	late May–mid-Aug	$20.50	431	Near the Bridge Bay Marina • Dump station
Canyon*	early June–early Aug	$25	272	Coin operated shower and laundry
Fishing Bridge RV*	mid-May–late Aug	$45	346	Hook-ups, sewer, coin operated shower and laundry
Grant Village*	mid-June–mid-Sept	$25	420	Dump station, coin operated shower and laundry
Madison*	early May–late Oct	$20.50	272	Dump station, but no hook-ups
Indian Creek	mid-June–mid-Sept	$12	75	No generators or hook-ups, vault toilets
Lewis Lake 👍	mid-June–early Nov	$12	85	Small campsites • Very few pull-through sites
Mammoth	All Year	$14	85	Only year-round campground
Norris	late May–late Sept	$14	>100	Walk-in and tent sites with a few RV-friendly sites
Pebble Creek 👍	mid-June–late Sept	$12	>27	Small primitive camping area with a few RV spaces
Slough Creek 👍	late May–late Oct	$12	23	Access via 2.5-mile dirt road (popular • arrive early)
Tower Fall	mid-May–late Sept	$12	32	Best suited for tents or small RVs

*Run by Xanterra Parks & Resorts and available for reservation (866.439.7375, www.yellowstonenationalparklodges.com) All other campgrounds are operated by the National Park Service and available on a first-come, first-served basis

Backcountry	Yellowstone has more than 300 designated backcountry campsites, many of which are available for advance reservation ($20/trip fee for reservations only accepted in person or by mail) by completing the reservation form (available online) and mailing it to: Backcountry Office; PO Box 168; Yellowstone National Park, WY 82190 All backcountry campers require a free backcountry permit that must be obtained in person not more than 48 hours in advance. Permits are available from Canyon, Grant Village, and Mammoth Visitor Centers; Bechler, Bridge Bay, Old Faithful, South Entrance, and Tower Ranger Stations; and West Yellowstone Information Center between June and August.
Group Camping	Available at Madison, Grant, and Bridge Bay Campgrounds for large organized groups with a group leader ($51–81/night). Reservations are required • Call (307) 344-7311 or (866) 439-7375.
Winter Camping	Mammoth Campground is open and backcountry camping is available with a permit

Old Faithful
7365ft / 2254m

To Madison · Grand Geyser · Firehole River · Geyser Hill · Castle Geyser · Old Faithful Inn · Old Faithful Geyser · Old Faithful Lodge · Post Office · Visitor Center · Snow Lodge · No camping or overnight recreational vehicle parking · To West Thumb and Grant Village

0 0.1 0.4 Km
0 0.1 0.4 Mi

West Thumb and Grant Village
7733ft / 2357m

To Lake Village · Duck Lake · West Thumb · West Thumb Geyser Basin · To Old Faithful · Information Station Bookstore · YELLOWSTONE LAKE · Grant Village · Amphitheater · Visitor Center · Showers Laundry Ice · Post Office · To South Entrance · Lodge Registration

0 0.5 Km
0 0.5 Mi

Canyon Village
7734ft / 2357m

To Tower-Roosevelt · Amphitheater · To Norris · Visitor Education Center · Showers-Laundry · Canyon Lodge · North Rim Drive · Lower Falls 308ft 94m · Lookout Point · Upper Falls View · one-way · Grand View · Inspiration Point · Yellowstone River · Artist Point · Uncle Tom's Trail · South Rim Drive · Clear Lake · Upper Falls 109ft 33m

0 0.5 Km
0 0.5 Mi

Wolves bedding down

Lodging

Yellowstone's lodging facilities are attractions themselves, worthy of standing side-by-side with the most wonderful natural architecture the United States has to offer. Many visitors find **Old Faithful Inn** more impressive than the eponymous geyser visible from many of the rooms. It's a bit pricey, with rooms starting at $96/night, but you stopping in to admire the architecture is free of charge. Other lodgings are equally rustic and more secluded. If it's a true wild West experience you seek, **Roosevelt Lodge** is where you'll find it. The **Lodge's Roughrider Cabins**—the park's most economical lodging—are suitable for 1–6 adults and cost just $65/night. Inspired by President Theodore Roosevelt, who frequented the park, they provide no-frills lodging with few furnishings, no bathroom, and heat supplied by a wood burning stove. All accommodations are non-smoking, and televisions, radios, air conditioning, and internet are not available at most facilities.

Yellowstone Lodging

	Open	Rates	Notes
Canyon Lodge 👍	early June–late Sept	$96/night (Motel Style) $179/night (Lodge)	Canyon's Dunraven Lodge is widely regarded as the best lodging in the park
Grant Village	late May–early Oct	$152/night	Overlooks Yellowstone Lake
Lake Lodge Cabins	early June–early Oct	$69–179/night	Cozy cabins with cafeteria style dining
Lake Yellowstone	mid-May–late Sept	$130–549/night	Basic rooms to a Presidential Suite
Mammoth Hot Springs	mid-May–mid-Oct mid-Dec–mid-March	$81–449/night	Motel-style rooms with shared restrooms to suites with cable TV
Old Faithful Lodge	mid-May–late Sept	$67–110/night	Simple accommodations
Old Faithful Inn	early May–early Oct	$96–499/night	Most requested lodging in the park
Old Faithful Snow Lodge 👍	late April–late Oct mid-Dec–mid-March	$96–206/night	The newest lodging facility, but managed to stay true to park-style design
Roosevelt Lodge	mid-June–early Sept	$65*–110/night	*Based on 1–6 people (primitive lodge)

For reservations call Xanterra Parks and Resorts at (866) 439-7375 or click www.yellowstonenationalparklodges.com
Rates are per night, for up to 2 adults and do not include tax and utility fee

Liberty Cap - Mammoth Hot Springs

Hiking

More than 1,000 miles of trails makes selecting the right one challenging. To begin whittling down your hiking options, consider which regions you plan on visiting. Trails have been broken down into six areas and sorted by difficulty. Many trails close seasonally due to poor conditions or an increase in bear activity. Call (307) 344-2160 for closures. Boardwalks connect the most interesting geothermal features (page 234). Dirt-packed, tree-covered, gloriously natural hiking trails lead far away from traffic filled roads and bustling facilities.

Mammoth Area Hiking Trails

	Trail Name	Trailhead (# on map)	Length	Notes (Roundtrip distances unless noted otherwise)
Easy		Fort Yellowstone and Mammoth Hot Springs are two popular self-guiding trails accessed at Mammoth Hot Springs		
	Grizzly Lake	1 mile south of Beaver Lake Picnic Area on Mammoth–Norris Road (1)	4.0 miles	Hike into a valley and to Grizzly Lake • Trail continues, joining Mt Holmes Trail
	Boiling River - 👍	Parking Area near 45th parallel sign north of Mammoth Hot Springs (8)	1.0 mile	Short hike to a swimming area where hot spring water and Gardner River meet
Moderate	Bunsen Peak	Across from Glen Creek Trailhead on Mammoth–Norris Road (4, 6 alt.)	4.2 miles	Fairly easy summit to panoramic views
	Osprey Falls		8.0 miles	Alt. through Sheepeater Canyon to 150-ft falls
	Beaver Ponds Loop	Just north of Liberty Cap (6)	5.0 miles	Nice loop through meadows and aspen
	Lava Creek - 👍	Across from Lava Creek Picnic Area on Mammoth–Tower Rd (7, 11)	3.5 miles (one-way)	Pass 60-ft Undine Falls, follow Gardner River, cross a bridge to Mammoth Camp
	Rescue Creek	7 miles east of Mammoth on Mammoth-Tower Road (9, 11)	8.0 miles (one-way)	Ends 1 mile south of NE Entrance
	Black Canyon of the Yellowstone - 👍	Hellroaring Trailhead 3.5 miles west of Tower Junction (10, 11, 12)	18.5 miles (one-way)	Long day or 2-day hike from Hellroaring Trailhead to Gardiner, MT
	Blacktail Creek/Yellowstone River	7 miles east of Mammoth on Mammoth–Tower Road (11, 12)	12.0 miles (one-way)	Crosses a river, joins Yellowstone River Trail, and ends in Gardiner, MT
Strenuous	Mount Holmes	3 miles south of Indian Creek Camp (2)	20.0 miles	Hike to 10,336-ft summit of Mount Holmes
	Bighorn Pass	Indian Creek Campground (3)	16.0 miles	Through grizzly country to 9,022 ft pass
	Electric Peak	4 miles south of Mammoth on Mammoth–Norris Road (5)	18.0 miles	Take Snow Pass/Sportsman Lake Trail to a 3.1 mile spur trail that leads to the summit
	Sepulcher Mountain	Between Liberty Cap and the stone house next to Mammoth Terraces (6)	11.0 miles	Follows Beaver Ponds Trail to Sepulcher Mt Trail junction and to the 9,652 ft summit

Tower Falls © Frank Kovalchek (flickr/Alaskan Dude)

Don't pass on some of the longer hikes because of their length. The first few miles of long trails can be just as rewarding as their entirety. For instance, **Specimen Ridge Trail** climbs to a fantastic overlook of Grand Canyon of the Yellowstone after little more than a mile. **Forces of the Northern Range** (not listed below) is a popular self-guiding trail that explains how volcanoes, glaciers, and fire shaped the land. Its trailhead is located 8 miles east of Mammoth Hot Springs on Mammoth–Tower Road.

Tower Area Hiking Trails

	Trail Name	Trailhead (# on map)	Length	Notes (Roundtrip distances unless noted otherwise)
Moderate	Lost Lake	Behind Roosevelt Lodge (13)	4.0 miles	Loop trail skirts Lost Lake, reaches Petrified Tree before returning to the lodge
	Yellowstone River Picnic Area	1.25 miles northeast of Tower Junction on Northeast Entrance Road (13)	3.7 miles	Follows the rim of Yellowstone Canyon • Great location to spot peregrine falcons and osprey
	Garnet Hill	50 yards north of Tower Junction on Northeast Entrance Road (14)	7.5 miles	Follows an old dirt coach road, then Elk Cr to an intersection of Hellroaring Trail and Garnet Hill
	Fossil Forest	4 miles east of Tower Junction on Northeast Entrance Road (16)	3–4 miles	Lightly traveled, unmaintained, unmarked trail that leads to several petrified samples
	Slough Creek	On dirt road toward Slough Creek Camp where the road bears left (17)	2.0/4.5 mi. (one-way)	Follows an old wagon trail • Distances are to the first two meadows • Trail continues beyond
	Pebble Creek	Near Pebble Creek Bridge on Northeast Entrance Road (18)	12.0 miles (one-way)	Do a portion of this trail that leads to Warm Creek Picnic Area
Strenuous	Hellroaring - 👍	3.5 miles west of Tower Junction (12)	4.0 miles	Definitely one of the best hikes
	Specimen Ridge - 👍	2.5 miles east of Tower Junction on Northeast Entrance Road (16)	17.5 miles (one-way)	Follow the ridgeline and rock cairns past Grand Canyon of the Yellowstone
	Petrified Trees	5.3 miles east of Roosevelt Junction (16)	3.0 miles	Climbs 1,200 feet rapidly to nice petrified trees
	Bliss Pass	Pebble Creek Trail intersects Bliss Pass at mile 6.6 (19)	20.6 miles (one-way)	Connects Slough Creek and Pebble Creek Trails over Bliss Pass
	Mt Washburn - 👍	Chittenden or Dunraven Pass Parking Areas south of Tower Junction (21)	2.5/3.1 mi. (one-way)	Out-and-back or arrange a shuttle between the two parking areas • Bicycles are permitted

Canyon, one of the busiest areas, is often filled with motorists. You can avoid the commotion by taking one of the trails listed below. All short trails around Upper and Lower Falls have been omitted from the table; you can't miss them as you drive along the north and south sides of the canyon. One of them, **Uncle Tom's Cabin**, is a must-hike. It descends 500 feet via a series of paved inclines and more than 300 steps to an up close look at Lower Falls. **Brink of Lower Falls** and **Brink of Upper Falls** are also worth a visit.

Lower Falls of Grand Canyon of the Yellowstone

Canyon Area Hiking Trails

	Trail Name	Trailhead (# on map)	Length	Notes (Roundtrip distances unless noted otherwise)
Easy	Howard Eaton	0.25 mile west of Canyon Junction on Norris–Canyon Road (25, 27, 28)	2.5–12 miles	Section of an old 150-mile trail • Leads to Cascade, Grebe, Wold, and Ice Lakes as well as Norris Camp
	Cascade Lake	0.3 mile south of Cascade Lake Picnic Area (22)	5.0 miles	There are two trails that lead to Cascade Lake • This is the prettier route of the two
	Point Sublime	Artist Point Overlook (24)	2.5 miles	Follow South Rim Trail to this point
	Grebe Lake	3.5 miles west of Canyon Junction on Norris–Canyon Road (26)	6.0 miles	Follows an old fire road • Shorter alternative to Howard Eaton Trail
	Observation Peak	Cascade Lake Trailhead (22)	11.0 miles	Climbs 1,400 feet in 3 miles
Strenuous	Seven Mile Hole	Glacial Boulder Pullout near Inspiration Point (23)	11.0 miles	Follow Glacial Boulder Trail to the only trail that leads into Grand Canyon of the Yellowstone

Grand Prismatic Spring - Midway Geyser Basin

This table combines three distinct areas: **Norris**, **Madison**, and **Old Faithful**. Their major attractions are **Lower, Middle, and Upper Geyser Basins** (page 234). Hiking can provide better views of geothermal features, while other trails lead deep into the mountains. Don't miss **Fairy Falls Trail**, it's the best.

Old Faithful–Norris Hiking Trails

	Trail Name	Trailhead (# on map)	Length	Notes (Roundtrip distances unless noted otherwise)
Easy	Artists' Paint Pot	4.5 miles south of Norris Junction (28)	1.0 mile	Peculiar geothermal features
Moderate	Fairy Falls - 🥾	End of Fountain Flat Drive, 10 miles north of Old Faithful (32)	7.0 miles	Access views of Grand Prismatic Spring
	Sentinel Meadows		3.0 miles	Skirts along Firehole River
	Solfatara Creek	Norris Campground (27)	6.5 miles	One-way trail along creek
	Monument Valley	5 miles south of Norris Junction (28)	2.0 miles	Tough climb to views of Gibbon Canyon
	Purple Mountain	0.25-mile north of Madison Junction, near Madison Camp (29)	6.0 miles	Not the most picturesque mountain, but it is convenient for campers
	Mystic Falls	Back of Biscuit Basin Boardwalk (35)	2.5 miles	70-ft falls of the Firehole River
	Observation Point - 🥾	Behind Old Faithful (36)	1.0 mile	Better spot to view Old Faithful than the bleachers
	Mallard Lake - 🥾	South of Old Faithful Lodge Cabins (36)	6.8 miles	Can return via Mallard Cr for 12-mi loop
	Howard Eaton	Across Grand Loop Road from Old Faithful Ranger Station (36)	5.8 miles	Out-and-back that traverses spruce forests down to Lone Star Geyser
	Lone Star Geyser - 🥾	Near Kepler Cascades Parking Area (37)	4.8 miles	Partially paved trail follows Firehole River
	Divide	6.8 miles south of Old Faithful Junction (38)	3.4 miles	Views of Shoshone Lake and forests en route to the Continental Divide
Strenuous	High Lake Loop	Access via Specimen Creek Trail at Milepost 26 of US-191 (30)	23.0 miles	Multi-day hike to two alpine loops through mountain country
	Sky Rim Loop - 🥾	Access via Dailey Creek Trail at Milepost 31 of US-191 (31)	18.0 miles	Steep, rocky, exposed trail with beautiful mountain scenery and wildlife
	Mallard Creek	3.8 miles north of Old Faithful Junction toward Madison (34)	9.2 miles	Alternate route to Mallard Lake across hilly terrain and burned forest

Yellowstone Lake

It's hard to appreciate the size of Yellowstone Lake from its shores. View this massive alpine lake from shore to shore by driving to **Lake Butte** (East Entrance Road) or hiking to **Lake Overlook**, where on a clear day you can see clear across Yellowstone Lake to the Teton Range. You'll also have a bird's eye view of West Thumb, a smaller caldera created by volcanic eruption some 100,000 years ago that has since filled with water. A nice hike beginning at West Thumb is **Heart Lake Loop**, a popular destination for both hikers and anglers.

Fishing Bridge/Lake Village Hiking Trails

	Trail Name	Trailhead (# on map)	Length	Notes (Roundtrip distances unless noted otherwise)
Easy	Howard Eaton	East side of Fishing Bridge (28)	7.0 miles	Ends at LeHardy's Rapids
	Natural Bridge	Bridge Bay Marina Parking Lot (42)	3.0 miles	Convenient for campers at Bridge Bay
	Elephant Back Mountain	South of Fishing Bridge Junction (43)	3.6 miles	Views of massive Yellowstone Lake
	Pelican Creek	West end of Pelican Cr Bridge (44)	1.3 miles	Traverses several of Yellowstone's habitats
	Storm Point - ✋	Indian Pond Pullout (44)	2.3 miles	Views of Indian Pond & Yellowstone Lake
	Pelican Valley	End of a gravel road across from Indian Pond (44)	6.8 miles	Prime grizzly habitat above Pelican Valley and into the park's backcountry
Strenuous	Avalanche Peak	Pullout at west end of Eleanor Lake toward East Entrance (45)	4.0 miles	2,100 ft climb in just 2 miles to views of some of the park's tallest peaks

West Thumb/Grant Village Hiking Trails

	Trail Name	Trailhead (# on map)	Length	Notes (Roundtrip distances unless noted otherwise)
Easy	Shoshone Lake	8.8 miles W of West Thumb Junction (37)	6.0 miles	Hike to the park's largest backcountry lake
	Lake Overlook	West Thumb Geyser Parking Lot (39)	2.0 miles	High view of Yellowstone's West Thumb
	Duck Lake		1.0 mile	Views of Duck and Yellowstone Lake
	Riddle Lake	3 miles south of Grant Village intersection (40)	4.8 miles	Trail crosses the Continental Divide to a pretty little lake
	Lewis River Channel/ Dogshead Loop	5 miles south of Grant Village intersection (41)	7/11 miles	7-mile out-and-back through rugged terrain with a 4-mile loop option at the end
Strenuous	Heart Lake - ✋	5.4 miles south of Grant Village (41)	15.0 miles	Most people day-hike to the lake and return
	Mt Sheridan Lookout	Intersects Heart Lake Trail (41)	6.0 miles	Leads to a fire lookout station

Truman C. Everts

In 1870, **Truman C. Everts** joined an expedition exploring present-day Yellowstone. At Yellowstone Lake, Everts wandered away from the group. After being lost for two days his horse ran away. Left with little more than the clothes on his back, Everts began walking aimlessly. A month passed without success from the expedition's search attempts; they decided to complete their work and return East to confirm the existence of "Colter's Hell" and spread word of the unfortunate predicament of their companion.

Everts's situation worsened when he broke through brittle ground while crossing a geyser basin, scalding his hip. Next, he managed to start a fire with an opera glass, only to severely burn his hands in its flames. Consuming only elk thistle, he withered away to skin and bones. A full 37 days after his separation, a man, no more than 50 pounds, was spotted crawling along a hillside. Incoherent but alive, Everts was able to make a full recovery and later pen the book *Thirty-Seven Days in Peril*. His adventure created considerable publicity for Yellowstone and helped create the world's first national park. He was even given the opportunity to be its first superintendent. (Not surprisingly, he declined.) Today, the legend lives on. Elk thistle is called **Everts' Thistle** and a 7,831-ft peak in northwestern Wyoming is named **Mount Everts**.

Don't expect to be rewarded for getting lost. It's a huge inconvenience, not only to you, but to park staff. Be prepared. Carry a compass and quality map. GPS users should know how to use it and carry extra batteries. Plan your route, stay on marked trails, and keep track of your group at all times.

Backpacking

There are more than 1,000 miles of trails and 300 designated backcountry campsites at Yellowstone. Backpackers planning on spending the night in the backcountry require a **free permit** (page 225). You may not camp beyond designated sites. Advance reservations are accepted in person or by mail for a one-time $20/permit fee (if successful). Fires are only allowed in established fire rings, and dead and down wood may be used as firewood. Trailheads have a trail registration box, so record your itinerary on the registration sheet before departing for your trek. This information aids rangers if you or your party becomes lost and a search is required. Posts, orange blazes on trees, and cairns mark established trails. Very few of Yellowstone's rivers and streams have bridges. Seal important items in plastic bags, and use a long sturdy stick when attempting to ford a river. If a waterway looks impassable, you probably shouldn't attempt to cross it. Water is cold and swift (especially after it rains). Much of the park's backcountry is unprotected and experiences severe winds. Carry a tent suitable for windy conditions. Finally, Yellowstone is grizzly bear country. Keep your camp clean, and sleep at least 100 yards up wind from where you cook. For additional information and backcountry permit reservation form check out the **Backcountry Trip Planner** available at www.nps.gov/yell.

First-time backpackers should start with one of the shorter trails listed in the hiking tables (pages 227–231; maps with the location of all backcountry campsites are available in the Backcountry Trip Planner). A good place for your first backcountry trip is **Yellowstone River/ Hellroaring Creek Area**. Multiple trailheads access the area and designated campsites are frequent, rarely more than 0.5-mile apart.

The **Thorofare Area** is a fantastic spot for backpackers. Try starting at **Nine Mile Trailhead**, located nine miles east of Fishing Bridge on East Entrance Road. From here, the trail leads 34 miles to Bridger Lake, just past Thorofare Ranger Station. A ranger station that presently holds the distinction of "most remote location in the lower 48 states" by being 20 miles from the nearest road of any kind. **Shoshone Lake Area** is another popular backpacking destination. Sites along the lake's shoreline are occupied almost every night in summer. Several land trails lead to the lake, but it's also accessible to paddlers via Lewis Lake and Lewis River Channel.

 # Boating

Whether you plan on exploring Yellowstone's waters in a motorized boat, kayak, canoe, or even a float tube you must obtain a **permit** before hitting the water. They are available in person at South Entrance, Lewis Lake Campground, Grant Village Backcountry Office, and Bridge Bay Ranger Station. In addition to these locations, permits for non-motorized watercraft are also available at West Entrance, Northeast Entrance, Mammoth Backcountry Office, Old Faithful Backcountry Office, Canyon Backcountry Office, Bechler Ranger Station, West Contact Station, and West Yellowstone Chamber of Commerce. Permits are $20/$10 (annual/7-day) for motorized boats and $10/$5 for non-motorized watercrafts. Grand Teton boating permits are honored at Yellowstone, but owners still need to register their watercraft in Yellowstone and obtain a validation sticker. To help protect wildlife all types of watercraft are prohibited from streams and rivers with the exception of the channel between **Lewis and Shoshone Lakes** where non-motorized boats are allowed.

Motorized boats are permitted on most of **Yellowstone Lake** and **Lewis Lake**. Boat launches are located at Lewis Lake and Bridge Bay Marina.

Xanterra Parks & Resorts has **motorized boats** ($47/hour) and **rowboats** ($10/hour) for **rent** at **Bridge Bay Marina**. Boat rentals are available from mid-June to early September on a first-come, first-served basis. The rental office opens at 8am.

 # Guided Bus/Van Tours

Xanterra Parks & Resorts offers bus/van tours like "**Firehole Basin Adventure**" ($48/Adult), a tour of the lower half of Grand Loop Road; "**Evening Wildlife Encounters**" ($63), a great opportunity to spot bear and bison; "**Geyser Gazers**" ($26), 1.5 hours in the Fire Hole where steam billows from the earth; "**Wake up to Wildlife**" ($78.50); and the extremely popular 10.5 hour "**Yellowstone in a Day**" ($71). Tours are half price for children ages 3–11, and children 2 years and under are free. Don't see anything you like? Xanterra can help you plan a custom guided bus/van tour ($356+/passenger for 5 hours). To make reservations call (866) 439-7375 or click www.yellowstonenationalparklodges.com.

 # Driving

Driving Yellowstone is all about 142-mile **Grand Loop Road** that makes a giant "figure-eight" in the center of the park. Much of this loop was planned during the park's early days when it was still under U.S. military administration. All five park entrances lead to the loop. The **top half** takes visitors to locations such as **Mammoth Hot Springs**, **Petrified Tree**, **Tower Fall**, **Norris Geyser Basin**, and **Sheepeater Cliff**. **Lamar Valley** is located along **Northeast Entrance Road**, which is an immensely popular hiking and wildlife viewing area. The **lower half** passes **Grand Canyon of the Yellowstone**, **Hayden Valley**, **Fishing Bridge**, **West Thumb Geyser Basin**, **Upper Geyser Basin (Old Faithful)**, **Midway Geyser Basin (Grand Prismatic Spring)**, and **Lower Geyser Basin**. Motorists cross the Continental Divide twice between West Thumb and Old Faithful. **South Entrance Road** leads to **John D. Rockefeller, Jr. Memorial Parkway** and passes **Lewis Lake** (popular for paddling). One of the biggest mistakes Yellowstone visitors can make is to believe they can drive Grand Loop Road in one day. Plan on spending a minimum of three days. In summer, the roadway can be extremely busy. Start touring early, and don't forget to pull completely off the road when you stop to view wildlife. Finally, drive safely and have fun.

 # Horseback Riding

Xanterra Parks & Resorts offers 1-hour ($38) and 2-hour ($58) **trail rides** that depart from Mammoth Hot Springs Hotel, Roosevelt Lodge and Cabins, and Canyon Lodge and Cabins. A favorite activity from Roosevelt Lodge is the 1–2 hour ($66–80) trail ride to a **western style cookout**. Both are interpretive rides featuring knowledgeable guides who educate riders on the park's history and geography. Minimum age is 8 years old. Riders ages 8–11 must be accompanied by an adult. Minimum height is 4-ft. Maximum weight is 240 pounds. Helmets are available upon request. You can also join an **outfitter** (page 244) on a multi-day backcountry llama, mule, or horse excursion.

Biking

Bicycles are allowed on all park roads and a few trails, but strictly prohibited from backcountry trails and boardwalks. Two gravel roads are ideal for **mountain bikes**: **Old Gardiner Road**, which connects Mammoth Hot Springs and Gardiner, and **Blacktail Plateau Drive**, which runs parallel to a short section of Grand Loop Road (GLR) between Tower and Mammoth. These roads are one-way for motorists, but cyclists may travel in either direction. These roads are also a good alternative to the busy GLR.

To explore some of the park's **300 miles of paved roadways** you'll want to pedal early or late in the day or between mid-May and mid-April when the winter snowmobiling season has ended and roads remain closed to motorized vehicles in order to prepare for the upcoming tourist season. During this time, cyclists are free to pedal between West Entrance (West Yellowstone) and Mammoth Hot Springs (weather permitting). If you're thinking about it, make sure you come prepared. It will be cold, and all of the park's services and facilities will be closed. Dress in layers and stock up on supplies in Gardiner or West Yellowstone before you arrive. To pedal when the weather is more pleasant, try going early in the morning or later in the evening during the busy tourist season. Occasionally, bicycle clubs hold evening **full moon rides**. The moon may be bright, but not bright enough. You'll need front and rear lights. Still, pedalling GLR at night is not the best idea. If it interests you search the web or ask around for more details.

The simplest pedalling excursions are found at **bicycle approved trails**. **Bunsen Peak Road** (6 miles) near Mammoth, **Riverside Trail** (1.4 miles) near the West Entrance, **Fountain Freight Road** (5.5 miles) and **Lone Star Geyser Road** (2 miles) near Old Faithful, and **Mount Washburn** (3 miles) from Chittenden Road to its summit near Tower are open to bicycles. **Xanterra** has bikes for **rent** ($8/hour, $25/4-hour, $35/24-hour) at **Old Faithful Snow Lodge**.

Touring cyclists receive discounted rates ($5/night) at campgrounds with biker/hiker campsites.

Geysers & Hot Springs

The park is centered on top **Yellowstone Caldera**, the largest supervolcano on the continent, measuring 45 by 30 miles. It is considered an active volcano, but there have only been three eruptions in the last 2 million years. The last one, 640,000 years ago, was 1,000 times larger than Mt St. Helens' eruption in 1980. Although few and far between, volcanic activity helped shape the region and its caldera. The Yellowstone hotspot, consisting of the heat source (earth's core), plume, and magma chamber, have endowed the region with **more than 10,000 geothermal features, including 300 geysers**. Thermal features and one to three thousand tiny annual earthquakes (all virtually undetectable by people) are proof of present-day volcano activity.

Now that you're scared silly, remember, scientists are constantly monitoring these activities, and it is very unlikely an eruption will occur in the next thousand or even 10,000 years. So, scratch "witness a cataclysmic volcanic eruption" off your "Yellowstone To-Do List." It's just not going to happen. However, you'll definitely want to visit the ever-changing geyser basins.

Mammoth Hot Springs is located in the northwest corner just beyond the caldera boundary. A road leads through the upper terrace, but there's also a self-guiding boardwalk that winds its way through the terraced pools and travertine formations.

Traveling south on Grand Loop Road from Mammoth you'll encounter **Norris Geyser Basin**. Its unique acidic (opposed to alkaline) waters allow different classes of bacterial thermophiles to live here. Thermophiles create the different color patterns you see in and around the basin's water. Norris is home to several geysers. Among them is **Steamboat**, the world's tallest active geyser. Its eruptions hurl super-heated water more than 300 feet into the air, but they occur irregularly, often separated by more than a year. **Echinus Geyser** is also on the unpredictable side, but it may erupt multiple times per day. There's no guarantee that you'll see a geyser erupt like at Old Faithful, but Norris Geyser Basin and its self-guiding boardwalk is a "must-do" activity. There's just something about Norris that feels more unique and ethereal than other basins. Its baby blue pools surrounded by white rocks are inviting and comforting, even as steam ominously billows out of vents lining the boardwalk.

Continuing on Grand Loop Road between Norris and Madison, is **Monument Geyser Basin**. Contrary to the name there are no active geysers here. Its monuments are rocky spires containing silica (glass) that have also been discovered on the floor of Yellowstone Lake. Scientists believe that these spires formed thousands of years ago when the area was submerged by a glacially dammed lake. Reach this basin by taking a steep 1-mile trail that begins just south of **Artists' Paint Pots**. The Paint Pots are two bubbling mudpots.

Between Madison and Old Faithful you'll find, in order, **Lower, Midway, and Upper Geyser Basins**. Lower Geyser Basin has a much lower concentration of geothermal features and it's highlight is **Fountain Paint Pots**. They are mud pots, hot springs containing boiling mud rather than water. You'll find a self-guiding trail explaining the four types of geothermal features; geysers, hot springs, fumaroles, and mud pots. **Midway Geyser Basin** is small in size, but its geothermal features are large and colorful. Midway is home to **Grand Prismatic Spring**, the largest hot spring in Yellowstone (370-ft wide, 121-ft deep). From up-close its beauty is obscured by its size. The best vantage point is from a nearby hill situated along **Fairy Falls Trail** (page 230). Of all the geothermal features to see, the sight of Grand Prismatic Spring from Fairy Falls Trail is the most likely to leave you breathless. **Excelsior Geyser**, which pours hot water into the **Firehole River**, is another noteworthy site.

Upper Geyser Basin boasts **Old Faithful** and the highest concentration of geothermal features in the park. If you want to see a geyser erupt, this is the spot. **Old Faithful** pumps 200+°F water 100–185 feet in the air once every 60–110 minutes. Prediction times are posted at most buildings in the area or you can call (307) 344-2751. **Observation Point** (accessed by a short but steep 1-mile trail) is a more peaceful position to watch the eruption. Nearby **Castle Geyser** also erupts regularly, approximately once every 13 hours.

East of Old Faithful is **West Thumb Geyser Basin**. Thermal features extend from the shoreline to beneath the surface of Yellowstone Lake, providing some outstanding views along the lakeshore.

All major geothermal areas are listed above, but many others are scattered throughout the park. **Mud Volcano** and **Sulfur Cauldron** are located near Hayden Valley. **Gibbon, Heart Lake, Lone Star, and Shoshone Geyser Basins** are all found in the backcountry.

Upper Terrace - Mammoth Hot Springs

Norris Geyser Basin

Old Faithful - Upper Geyser Basin

Swimming

There are two popular swimming holes. One spot is located on **Gardner River**, two miles north of Mammoth on North Entrance Road at a spot known as **Boiling River**. The other is a pool below **Firehole Falls** near Madison Junction. Swimming in Yellowstone Lake is not advised because water temperature rarely exceeds 60°F.

Winter Activities

Yellowstone is more incredible in winter even though you lose the unbridled freedom to cruise its open roads in your car. **North Entrance Road**, **Northeast Entrance Road** and **Mammoth–Tower Road** of the **Grand Loop** are the only roads open to wheeled vehicles during winter. Cars are left behind in favor of **snowmobiles** and **snowcoaches**. All snowmobile parties must be accompanied by a **professional guide** employed by a licensed **concessioner** (page 244).

Xanterra offers an array of **snowcoach tours** from Mammoth and Old Faithful between late December and early March. Rates listed below are for adults. Children (ages 3–11) cost about half the adult rate. West Yellowstone to Old Faithful ($62), Old Faithful to Mammoth ($76), and Tour of the Grand Canyon ($135) are a few of the basic trips. From Mammoth you can take tours of Norris Geyser Basin ($62), Wake Up to Wildlife ($41), and Lamar Valley Wildlife ($32). The following tours depart from Old Faithful: Firehole Basin Adventure ($35); Steam, Stars, and Soundscapes ($38); and Winter Photo Safari ($162).

Xanterra also offers a selection of **ski, snowshoe, snowmobile,** and **custom guided tours**. For a complete listing click www.yellowstonenational-parklodges.com. **Mammoth Hot Springs** and **Old Faithful Snow Lodge** are equipped to **rent snowshoes** and **cross-country skis**. Many of the parks most popular hiking trails are groomed for skiers during the winter. Ski instruction and ski repair services are also available.

Fishing

Fishing has been a popular activity since the park was established. Before you dip your line in the water in hope of catching the renowned **Yellowstone cutthroat**, you'll have to obtain a **permit for all anglers 16 and older**. A 3-day ($15), 7-day ($20), and season ($35) permit are available. Children under 15 may fish without one if they are under direct supervision of an adult with a permit or they may obtain a free permit that must be signed by a responsible adult. Permits are available at all ranger stations, visitor centers, and Yellowstone Park General Stores. Yellowstone fishing regulations, seasons, and recommendations are lengthy and complicated. Anglers should visit the park website or discuss their plans with a park ranger prior to fishing. Popular locations for watching trout like **LeHardy's Rapids** (June only) and **Fishing Bridge** prohibit fishing. A list of **guides and outfitters** along with rates is provided on page 244. **Xanterra** provides **charter fishing on Yellowstone Lake** for $152–196 for two hours. They also provide full-day **guided fly fishing excursions** ($390 1-person, $418 (2), $468 (3), and $520 (4)). **Fishing gear** (rod, reel, waders) can be **rented** for $26.50. It is the guest's responsibility to obtain a valid fishing permit before the excursion.

Photography

What better way to remember Yellowstone than a collection of your very own professional-quality photographs. Whether you're taking images with a point-and-shoot or high-end DSLR, a **Yellowstone photo tour** is sure to send you home with jaw-dropping images you can't wait to decorate your home with. While the scenery does most of the work, an experienced photo tour guide can teach subtle tips and techniques that will make your vacation shots pop. **Xanterra** offers a **5-hour Picture Perfect Photo Safari** aboard a historic yellow bus (page 233). Tours depart from Old Faithful Inn and Yellowstone Hotel, and require a minimum of two paying customers. They are generally available from late May until late September. They meet at the hotel between 5:45am and 6:45am to take advantage of the soft morning light. Rates are $81 per adult and $40.50 per child. Several outfitters are permitted to conduct photography tours and classes within the park. Refer to page 244 for a list of outfitters, complete with contact information and rates.

Buffalo in Hayden Valley

For Kids

Yellowstone provides several online and in-park activities designed specifically for kids. Online activities (www.nps. gov/yell/forkids) include things like an **Animal Alphabet Book** or an **Antler/Horn Match Game**. It's educational fun for all ages that can help build excitement for that Yellowstone vacation you're planning.

Once you've arrived, children (ages 5–12) have the opportunity to become a **Yellowstone National Park Junior Ranger**. The program introduces kids to the wonders of Yellowstone and their role in preserving these treasures for future generations. Children must complete a 12-page activity booklet to become a Junior Ranger. The booklet is available at any visitor center for the reasonable price of $3. Once your child completes the activities, attends a **ranger-led program** (page 239), and **hikes a park trail** (page 227), he/she will receive a Junior Ranger Badge marking admission into the Yellowstone Junior Ranger Club. You may need to check out one of the **Junior Ranger Snowpacks** to become a Junior Ranger during the winter. Snowshoes (page 236) may also be required. Packs and snowshoes are available at Mammoth and Old Faithful Visitor Centers.

Flora & Fauna

Yellowstone is more zoo than park. There are **over 1,350 plant species and 67 species of mammals**. It is home to the **highest density of mammals in the contiguous United States**, making Yellowstone one of the absolute best locations to view wildlife.

Bison and **grizzly bears** are the stars. You may see Yellowstone cutthroat trout, elk, moose, gray wolf, coyote, and bighorn sheep. Lynx, mountain lion, and bobcat also reside here, but it's highly unlikely you'll cross their paths. There are two easily accessible areas for wildlife viewing: **Hayden Valley**, located between Canyon and Lake Villages, and **Lamar Valley**, located along Northeast Entrance Road just east of Tower. Be careful when viewing wildlife. You should stay at least 25 yards away from all mammals, and 100 yards away from predatory species like bears and wolves.

The landscape is covered with forests (80% of area), grasslands (15%), and water (5%). Forests are dominated by lodgepole pines, but much of the plant life is still recovering from a forest fire that burned more than a third of the park in 1988.

Bumblebee and wildflower in Lamar Valley - Specimen Trail

Yellowstone Visitor and Information Centers

Facility	Phone	Open	Notes
Albright Visitor Center (Mammoth)	(307) 344-2263	Daily, All Year, 9am–5pm extended hours in summer	Museum of people in the park from Native Americans to NPS Rangers, Gallery of Thomas Moran, and Theater
West Yellowstone Info Center	(307) 344-2876	late April–early November, mid-December–mid-March	Information for those using the West Entrance, located at West Yellowstone Chamber of Commerce
Old Faithful Visitor Center	(307) 344-2751	mid-April–early November, mid-December–mid-March	The newest Visitor Center at Yellowstone features exhibits on hydrothermal features and other geologic phenomena
Canyon Visitor Education Center	(307) 344-2550	May–mid-October	Explores the geology of Yellowstone, including its volcanoes, geysers, hot springs, and geologic history
Fishing Bridge Visitor Center	(307) 344-2450	late May–September	Explores the park's wildlife • Backcountry office and bookstore are available
Grant Visitor Center	(307) 344-2650	late May–September	Named for President Ulysses S. Grant, the Visitor Center explores the role of fire at Yellowstone
Madison Information Station	(307) 344-2876	late May–late September	Information and Yellowstone Association bookstore
Museum of Park Rangers (Norris)	(307) 344-735	May–late September Dates and hours of operation are subject to change	Short movie and exhibits about Park Rangers
Norris Geyser Basin Museum	(307) 344-281		Explores the park's unique geothermal geology
West Thumb Info Station	(307) 344-2650	May–late September	Information and Yellowstone Association bookstore

YELLOWSTONE

Ranger Programs

Yellowstone is brash and exuberant. Water drops hundreds of feet then passes through a beautiful yellow canyon. Water and mud boil vigorously. Bison and bear lumber along roadways. Geysers send columns of water shooting into the air. And then there's the smell. Many of the geothermal features are accompanied with a sulfuric smell, similar to rotten eggs. Yellowstone gets in your face and your nose. It's screaming for attention. And the best way to immerse all of your senses is on a ranger-led activity.

Rangers entertain guests with talks, walks, adventure hikes, and evening programs all year long. Programs take place in all areas. To find out exactly what, when, and where they are, pick up a park newspaper, *The Yellowstone Today*, from a visitor center or entrance station. It is also available for download at the park website.

Almost all programs are free of charge. One exception is **Yellowstone Lake Scenic Cruise**, which requires a fee and advance reservation. Xanterra Parks & Resorts operates the tour, while a park ranger narrates. It costs $15 for adults and $9 for children (ages 2–11). For reservations call (307) 344-7311 or stop by the Bridge Bay Marina.

Talks, walks, and evening programs are all great, but the **Adventure Hikes** are where it's at. If your schedule permits, join a ranger on at least one of the following: **Hayden Valley Venture**, **Gem of the Rockies**, or **Fairy Falls Frolic**. You will not regret it. Tours are limited to 15 people. You must sign up in person, in advance, at a specific visitor center. Refer to the park newspaper for details. Most Adventure Hikes are available from mid-June through August. The selection is reduced for fall, but programs are still available at all major areas. In winter only evening programs, afternoon talks, and snowshoe walks are available.

Since there are dozens of programs, all of which are incredibly rewarding, it's a good practice to take your favorite (or what you think will be your favorite) Yellowstone attraction and join a ranger-led activity for that feature. Ultimately you can't go wrong. You can close your eyes and point to the list of activities in the newspaper if you'd like.

Park rangers can even help plan your vacation before you arrive through a series of free videos and podcasts available at the park website and iTunes, respectively.

Grand Prismatic Spring

Basics

Pets: Pets are allowed in the park, but must be kept on a leash no more than six feet in length at all times. They are prohibited from trails, the backcountry, and all hydrothermal basins. They can go where your car can go and they may be walked no more than 100 feet from a road or parking area. Visitors with pets must be careful. There's a possibility pets could become prey for bear, coyote, wolf, owl, or other predators commonly found in the park.

Accessibility: For a complete listing of the park's facilities deemed accessible to wheelchair users, pick up a free copy of *Accessibility in Yellowstone* from any entrance or visitor center. Wheelchair accessible lodging is available in all areas of the park. Most campgrounds have at least one wheelchair accessible campsite. Old Faithful, Canyon, Grant, and Albright (Mammoth) Visitor Centers are fully accessible. A wheelchair accessible fishing ramp and platform are available on Madison River at Mt Haynes Overlook (3.5 miles west of Madison Junction). Many of the walkways and self-guiding trails have at least one wheelchair accessible walkway. Wheelchairs are available for rent at medical clinics.

Weather: Yellowstone has a typical mountain climate: cold long winters and short hot summers. Average highs in summer max out around 80°F, and winter average lows hover around 10°F. Snow is common from fall to spring, with an annual average accumulation of 72 inches. It's not a secret that the best months to visit (weather-wise) are July and August. The weather is great, but crowds can be unbearable. June and September are nice alternatives.

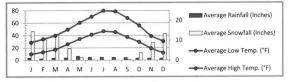

West Thumb Geyser Basin (page 234). It provides a sampling of geothermal features and it's also a great location to appreciate the sheer size of Yellowstone Lake. Its most notable features are Fishing Cone, a small geyser where a fisherman famously caught and boiled a fish when it fell off his hook into the roiling water (fishing is prohibited), and Abyss Pool. Walk the basin's boardwalk (1–2 hours). If you're still looking for a hike, the 2-mile Lake Overlook Trail (page 231), which departs from West Thumb Geyser Basin Parking Area is a great choice. Return to Grand Loop Road following the shoreline of Yellowstone Lake to the northeast. If it's June when trout are running, stop at Fishing Bridge. Your next stop is Hayden Valley. Watch for bison grazing the grasslands and search for grizzlies along the shores of Yellowstone River. Allow at least an hour in the Valley before continuing on to Canyon (a good place to spend your first night). Spend the evening exploring Grand Canyon of the Yellowstone (page 229) and its surroundings. Take South Rim Drive to Artist Point and North Rim Drive to Grand View and Inspiration Point. Uncle Tom's Trail is a bit of a challenge but well worth the effort. Allow a minimum of 2–3 hours at Canyon Village. Visit Grand Canyon of the Yellowstone in late evening or early morning for the best photos.

Day 2

If yesterday's stop at Hayden Valley didn't produce the kind of wildlife viewing you were imagining, join the 2-hour long "Wildlife Watching in Hayden Valley" program that usually meets at 7am (confirm time in your park newspaper) or backtrack and have another look around on your own. If your photographs of Grand Canyon of the Yellowstone failed to meet your expectations, catch the early rays of sun as they illuminate yellow rock and plummeting waters of Upper and Lower Falls. Once you're ready to return to Grand Loop Road take the middle of the figure-eight from Canyon to Norris. Do not skip Norris Geyser Basin (page 234). Pressed for time, make a quick stop at Norris to hike around Porcelain Basin, located just north of the museum. If there's no rush spend 1–2 hours wandering about the extensive boardwalk. Next, drive north to Mammoth Hot Springs (page 234). Roaring Mountain and Sheepeater Cliff are excellent stops in between. The travertine terraces of Mammoth Hot Springs are nice and Albright Visitor Center is fantastic, but this is the one destination you should consider skipping if you're running behind schedule. Upper Terrace is slightly better than Lower Terrace. Now drive east to Tower–Roosevelt (page 228). With enough time, money, and love of horses, take a 1- or

Petrified Tree - Tower–Roosevelt Area

Planning a Yellowstone vacation is a daunting task. Camping or lodging? What regions to visit? Are Xanterra's activities worth the money? What's the best section of Grand Loop Road? The first three questions are personal preferences. The last one, well, that's easy too. Drive all 142-miles. To drive the loop and see its main attractions, plan on spending at least three FULL days at Yellowstone. Browse the park's newspaper for a current listing of ranger programs (page 239). Find time to attend at least one ranger-led tour during your visit. A rough outline for three perfect days in the park is provided below. The planner assumes you will arrive at South Entrance via John D. Rockefeller Jr., Memorial Parkway and Grand Teton National Park (page 204). Nearby dining, grocery stores, lodging, festivals, and attractions are listed on pages 242–244.

Day 1

Entering South Entrance, you'll pass Lewis and Shoshone Lakes, the park's best destination for paddling (page 233). Paddlers should stop and enjoy the morning from the seat of your kayak; everyone else continue north to Grant Village. Stop at

2-hour horseback ride to a delicious steak dinner. The Western Dinner Cookout/Trail Ride (page 233) is wonderful. Regular trail rides are offered for those not wanting a hearty meal. The last cookout checks-in at Roosevelt Lodge at 1:45pm. Work off the extra weight you just put on by hiking **Specimen Ridge Trail** (page 228), located in **Lamar Valley**. This fantastic wildlife viewing area is situated along Northeast Entrance Road, where you're all but guaranteed to see free-roaming buffalo. Specimen Ridge is an excellent hike that leads into the mountains. After just one mile the trail rewards its hikers with outstanding views of **Grand Canyon of the Yellowstone**. You'll also come across ancient petrified trees. Speaking of petrified trees, as you're driving Grand Loop, you'll see signs for "**Petrified Tree**" (pictured on the opposite page). If it looks interesting to you, by all means stop, but skipping it in favor of **Tower Falls** or taking another hike is a recommended alternative.

Day 3

Start your morning out right with a waterfall and a hike. To reach **Tower Fall** return to **Grand Loop Road** and turn left at Tower–Roosevelt Junction toward Canyon Village. You can't miss the parking area. Check out the falls then drive south to **Mount Washburn** (page 228). Two trails lead to its 10,243-ft summit, and on clear days you can see all the way to the Teton Range. From **Dunraven Pass** the trail is 3.1 miles with an elevation gain near 1,400 feet. The route from **Chittenden Parking Area** is shorter but steeper, gaining about 1,500 feet in 2.5 miles. Driving south on Grand Loop Road Chittenden Parking Area is before Dunraven Pass Parking Area. Regardless which route you hike, it's beautiful and the trek will take roughly 3–4 hours to complete. This is one of the most popular trails, so expect it to be busy, particularly during summer. Once you've completed the hike return to your car to complete Grand Loop Road. Travel past Canyon Village, Norris, and Madison, stopping at **Midway Geyser Basin**. Monument Geyser Basin, Gibbon Falls, and Madison are decent areas to stop, but hardly essential. Stop if you have time, but allot at least 4 hours to explore **Lower** (the least impressive of these three, if you need to scratch one), **Midway, and Upper Geyser Basins** (page 234). Hike **Fairy Falls Trail** (page 230) at **Midway** for a stunning view of **Grand Prismatic Spring**. It's nice from the boardwalk, but its color and beauty is often obscured by the size of this somewhat psychedelic hot spring. Finish your trip by stopping at **Upper Geyser Basin** to see the park's most iconic feature, **Old Faithful**. Hike to **Observation Point** (page 230) where the geyser will salute you with one of its reliable eruptions.

Chromatic Spring - Upper Geyser Basin

Bison and Yellowstone River

Mileage Between Sites

	North Entrance	Mammoth Hot Springs	Tower-Roosevelt	Northeast Entrance	Canyon Village	Norris	Madison	West Entrance	Fishing Bridge	East Entrance	Old Faithful	West Thumb
	5											
	23	18										
	52	47	29									
	42	37	19	48								
	26	21	31	60	12							
	40	35	45	74	26	14						
	54	49	59	88	40	28	14					
	58	53	35	64	16	28	42	56				
	85	80	62	91	43	55	69	83	27			
	56	51	61	90	42	30	16	30	38	65		
	73	68	66	85	37	47	33	47	21	48	17	
	95	90	78	107	59	69	55	69	43	70	39	22

South Entrance

Dining

West Yellowstone Area

Ernie's Bakery & Deli • (406) 646-9467
406 US-20; West Yellowstone
www.erniesbakery.com • Sandwiches: $7–15

Pete's Rocky Mtn Pizza Co • (406) 646-7820
112 N Canyon St; West Yellowstone

Beartooth Barbecue • (406) 646-0227
111 N Canyon St; West Yellowstone

Buckaroo Bills Ice Cream • (406) 646-7901
24 N Canyon St; West Yellowstone

Bar N Ranch • (406) 646-0300
890 Buttermilk Creek Rd; West Yellowstone
www.bar-n-ranch.com • Entrée: $24–45

Arrowleaf Ice Cream • (406) 646-9776
27 N Canyon St; West Yellowstone

Madison Crossing Lounge • (406) 646-7621
121 Madison Ave; West Yellowstone
www.madisoncrossinglounge.com • Entrée: $9–19

Running Bear Pancake House • (406) 646-7703
538 Madison Ave; West Yellowstone

Wild West Pizzeria • (406) 646-4400
14 Madison Ave; West Yellowstone
www.wildwestpizza.com

Woodside Bakery • (406) 646-7779
17 Madison Ave; West Yellowstone

North Entrance/Gardiner

Sawtooth Deli • (406) 848-7600
220 Park St; Gardiner, MT 59030

K Bar & Café • (406) 848-9995
202 W Main St; Gardiner, MT 59030

Rosie's • (406) 848-7434
206 W Park St; Gardiner, MT 59030
www.redsbluegoosesaloon.com • Entrée: $15–26

Outlaws Pizza • (406) 848-7733
906 Scott St; Gardiner, MT 59030

East of the Parks

Miners Saloon • (406) 838-2214
208 Main St; Cooke City, MT 59020

Beartooth Café • (406) 838-2475
14 Main St; Cooke City, MT 59020
www.beartoothcafe.com • Entrée: $13–30

Montana Jacks Bar and Grill • (406) 328-4110
1383 Nye Rd; Dean, MT 59028 • www.mtjacks.com

Red Lodge Café & Lounge • (406) 446-1619
16 S Broadway Ave; Red Lodge, MT 59068

Adriano's Italian Restaurant • (307) 527-7320
1244 Sheridan Ave; Cody, WY 82414

Wyoming's Rib & Chop House • (307) 527-7731
1367 Sheridan Ave; Cody, WY 82414
www.ribandchophouse.com • Entrée: $12–35

Proud Cut Saloon • (307) 527-6905
1227 Sheridan Ave; Cody, WY 82414

Peter's Café & Bakery • (307) 527-5040
1219 Sheridan Ave; Cody, WY 82414
www.peters-cafe.com • Sandwiches: $5–8

Sunset House Restaurant • (307) 587-2257
1651 8th St; Cody, WY 82414
www.sunsethousecody.com

Jackson/Grand Teton Area

Rendezvous Bistro • (307) 739-1100
380 S US-89; Jackson, WY 83001
www.rendezvousbistro.net • Entrée: $16–29

Pearl Street Bagels • (307) 739-1218
145 West Pearl Ave; Jackson, WY 83001

Moo's Gourmet Ice Cream • (307) 733-1998
110 Center St; Jackson, WY 83001
www.moosjacksonhole.com

Blue Lion Restaurant • (307) 733-3912
160 N Millward St; Jackson, WY 83001
www.bluelionrestaurant.com • Entrée: $16–43

Wild Sage Restaurant • (307) 733-2000
175 N Jackson St, #2; Jackson, WY 83001
www.rustyparrot.com • Entrée: $33–45

The Bird in Jackson • (307) 732-2473
4125 S Pub Pl; Jackson, WY 83001
www.thebirdinjackson.com • Burgers: $7–17

Bar T Five • (307) 733-5386
812 Cache Creek Dr; Jackson, WY 83001
www.bart5.com • Covered Wagon Cookout: $43

Stiegler's Restaurant • (307) 733-1071
3535 Moose Wilson Rd; Wilson, WY 83014
www.stieglersrestaurant.com • Entrée: $18–46

Million Dollar Cowboy Steakhouse • (307) 733-4790
25 N Cache Dr; Jackson, WY 83001
www.cowboysteakhouse.net • Entrée: $20–52

Snake River Grill • (307) 733-0557
84 E Broadway; Jackson, WY 83001
www.snakerivergrill.com • Entrée: $20–49

The Bunnery Bakery • (307) 734-0075
130 N Cache Dr; Jackson, WY 83001
www.bunnery.com • Breakfast: $5–10

Sweetwater Restaurant • (307) 733-3553
85 King St; Jackson, WY 83001
www.sweetwaterjackson.com • Entrée: $22–28

Teton Thai • (307) 733-0022
135 N Cache Dr; Jackson, WY 83001
www.tetonthai.com • Curry/Rice Dishes: $14–18

Trio An American Bistro • (307) 734-8038
45 S Glenwood St; Jackson, WY 83001
www.bistrotrio.com • Entrée: $15–28

Burke's Chop House • (307) 733-8575
72 South Glenwood St; Jackson, WY 83001
www.burkeschophousejacksonhole.com • Entrée: $14–29

Merry Piglets Mexican Café • (307) 733-2966
160 N Cache Dr; Jackson, WY 83001
www.merrypiglets.com • Tex-Mex: $12–21

The Kitchen • (307) 734-1633
155 N Glenwood St; Jackson, WY 83001
www.kitchenjacksonhole.com • Entrée: $20–52

Koshu • (307) 733-5283
200 W Broadway; Jackson, WY 83001
www.koshuwinebar.com • Entrée: $14–28

Backcountry Provisions • (307) 734-9420
Provides box lunches for outdoor adventures
85 W Deloney Ave; Jackson, WY 83001
www.backcountryprovisions.com

Billy's Giant Hamburgers • (307) 733-3279
55 N Cache St; Jackson, WY 83001

Mountain High Pizza Pie • (307) 733-3646
120 W Broadway; Jackson, WY 83001

e.leaven Food Co • (307) 733-5600
175 Center St; Jackson, WY 83001
www.eleavenfood.com • Breakfast: $5–9

Snake River Brew Co. • (307) 739-2337
265 S Millward St; Jackson, WY 83001
www.snakeriverbrewing.com

Many chain restaurants can be found in Livingston, MT; Cody, WY; and Jackson, WY.

Grocery Stores

West Yellowstone Area

Food Roundup Supermarket • (406) 646-7501
107 Dunraven St; West Yellowstone

North Entrance/Gardiner

North Entrance Shopping Center • (406) 848-7524
701 Scott St; Gardiner, MT 59030

Emigrant General Store • (406) 333-4434
3 Murphy Ln; Emigrant, MT 59027

Albertsons-Sav-on • (406) 222-1177
2120 Park St S; Livingston, MT 59047

East of the Parks

Albertsons-Osco • (307) 527-7007
1825 17th St; Cody, WY 82414

Walmart Supercenter • (307) 527-4673
321 Yellowstone Ave; Cody, WY 82414

Jackson/Grand Teton Area

Albertsons-Sav-on • (307) 733-5950
105 Buffalo Way; Jackson, WY 83001

Lodging

West Yellowstone Area

Firehole Ranch • (406) 646-7294
11500 Hebgen Lake Rd; West Yellowstone
www.fireholeranch.com • Rates: $515+/person/night

Yellowstone Inn • (406) 646-7633
601 US-20; West Yellowstone
www.yellowstoneinn.net

One Horse Motel • (406) 646-7677
216 N Dunraven St; West Yellowstone
www.onehorsemotel.com • Rates: $79+

Brandin' Iron Inn • (406) 646-9411
201 Canyon St; West Yellowstone
www.vacationyellowstone.com • Rates: $139+

Alpine Motel • (406) 646-7544
120 Madison Ave; West Yellowstone
www.alpinemotelwestyellowstone.com • Rates: $80+

Lazy G Motel • (406) 646-7586
123 N Hayden St; West Yellowstone
www.lazygmotel.com • Rates: $68+

Three Bear Lodge • (800) 646-7353
217 Yellowstone Ave; West Yellowstone
www.threebearlodge.com

Madison Arm Resort • (406) 646-9328
Tent and RV sites, cottages, cabins, and boat rentals
5475 Madison Arm Rd; Hebgen Lake, MT 59758
www.madisonarmresort.com

North Entrance/Gardiner

Travelodge • (406) 848-7520
109 Hellroaring; Gardiner, MT 59030
www.travelodge.com • Rates: $165–210/night

Yellowstone River Motel • (406) 848-7303
14 E Park St; Gardiner, MT 59030
www.yellowstonerivermotel.com • Rates: $89+

Hillcrest Cottages • (406) 848-7353
200 Scott St; Gardiner, MT 59030
www.hillcrestcottages.com • Rates: $60–80

Gardiner Guest House B&B • (406) 848-9414
112 Main St; Gardiner, MT 59030
www.gardinerguesthouse.com • Rates: $90–145

Headwaters of the Yellowstone B&B • (406) 848-7073
9 Olson Ln; Gardiner, MT 59030
www.headwatersyellowstone.com • Rates: $125+

Yellowstone Basin Inn • (406) 848-7080
4 Maiden Basin Dr; Gardiner, Mt 59030
www.yellowstonebasininn.com • Rates: $75–395

Mtn Sky Guest Ranch • (406) 333-4911
480 Big Creek Rd; Pray, MT 59065
www.mtnsky.com • Rates: $3,365+/week

Hawley Mtn Guest Ranch • (406) 932-5791
4188 Main Boulder Rd; McLeod, MT 59052
www.hawleymountain.com • Rates: $1,008+/person/week

Lone Mountain Guest Ranch • (406) 995-4644
750 Lone Mtn Ranch Rd; Big Sky, MT 59716
www.lmranch.com • various packages available

Elkhorn Ranch • (406) 995-4291
33133 Gallatin Rd; Gallatin Gateway, MT 59730
www.elkhornranchmt.com • Rates: $2,465/rider/week

Covered Wagon Ranch • (406) 995-4237
34035 Gallatin Rd; Gallatin Gateway, MT 59730
www.coveredwagonranch.com • Rates: $910+/3 nights

East of the Parks

Log Cabin Café & B&B • (800) 863-0807
106 US-212 W; Silver Gate, MT 59081
www.thelogcabincafe.com • Rates: $99+

Elk Horn Lodge • (406) 838-2332
103 Main St; Cooke City, MT 59020
www.elkhornlodgemt.com

Seven D Ranch • (307) 587-9885
907 Spruce Dr; Cody, WY 82414
www.7dranch.com • Rates: $1,680+/person/week

Mayor's Inn • (307) 587-0887
1413 Rumsey Ave; Cody, WY 82414
www.mayorsinn.com • Rates: $125+

Crossed Sabres Ranch • (307) 587-3750
829 N Fork Hwy; Cody, WY 82414
www.crossedsabresranch.com • Rates: $125+

Pahaska Tepee Resort • (307) 527-7701
183 N Fork Hwy, # 1; Cody, WY 82414
www.pahaska.com • Rates: $130+

Jackson/Grand Teton Area

Pony Express Motel • (307) 733-3835
1075 W Broadway; Jackson, WY 83001
www.ponyexpressmotel.com • Rates: $60+

Flat Creek Ranch • (307) 733-0603
Upper Flat Creek Rd; Jackson, WY 83001
www.flatcreekranch.com • Rates: $760+/cabin/night

The Wort Hotel • (307) 733-2190
50 N Glenwood St; Jackson, WY 83001
www.preferredboutique.com • Rates: $359+

Jackson Hole Lodge • (307) 733-2992
420 W Broadway; Jackson, WY 83001
www.jacksonholelodge.com • Rates: $169+

Amangani Resort • (307) 734-7333
1535 N E Butte Rd; Jackson, WY 83001
www.amanresorts.com • Rates: $975+

Rusty Parrot Lodge • (307) 733-2000
175 N Jackson St; Jackson, WY 83001
www.rustyparrot.com • Rates: $195+

Homewood Suites • (307) 739-0808
260 Millward St; Jackson, WY 83001
www.jacksonwy.homewoodsuites.com • Rates: $100+

Miller Park Lodge • (307) 733-4858
155 N Jackson; Jackson, WY 83001
www.millerparklodge.net • Rates: $139+

Anglers Inn • (307) 733-3682
265 N Millward; Jackson, WY 83001
www.anglersinn.net • Rates: $135+

Cowboy Village Resort • (307) 733-3121
120 Flat Creek Dr; Jackson, WY 83001

Elk Country Inn • (307) 733-2364
480 W Pearl St; Jackson, WY 83001

Rustic Inn/Creekside Resort & Spa • (307) 733-2357
475 N Cache; Jackson, WY 83001
www.rusticinnatjh.com • Rates: $99+

Four Seasons • (307) 732-5000
7680 Granite Loop Rd; Teton Village, WY 83025
www.fourseasons.com • Rates: $650+

Heart Six Ranch • (307) 543-2477
16985 Buffalo Valley Rd; Moran, WY 83013
www.heartsix.com • Rates: $89+, packages available

Festivals

Buffalo Bill Birthday Ball • February
Cody, WY • www.codykc.org/bbbb.html

Snowmobile Expo • March
West Yellowstone • www.snowmobileexpo.com

Elkfest/Antler Sale • May
Jackson, WY • www.jacksonholechamber.com

Custer's Last Stand/Little Bighorn Days
June • Hardin, MT • www.custerlaststand.org

Grand Teton Music Festival • June
Grand Teton National Park • www.nps.gov/grte

Red Ants Pants Festival • July
www.redantspantsmusicfestival.com

Montana Folk Festival • July
Butte, MT • www.montanafolkfestival.com

Yellowstone Jass Festival • July
Cody, WY • www.yellowstonejazz.com

Cody Stampede • July
Cody, WY • www.codystampederodeo.com

An Ri Ra Montana Irish Festival
August • Missoula, MT • www.mtgaelic.org

Sweet Pea Festival • August
Bozeman • www.sweetpeafestival.org

Crow Fair and Rodeo • August
Crow Agency, MT • www.crow-fair.com

Running of the Sheep 'Sheep Drive'
September • Reed Point, MT • (406) 326-2315

Yellowstone Ski Festival • November
West Yellowstone • www.yellowstoneskifestival.com

Attractions

West Yellowstone Area

Pinecone Playhouse • (406) 646-4107
121 Madison Ave; West Yellowstone, MT
www.pineconeplayhouse.com

Yellowstone IMAX Theatre • (406) 646-4100
101 S Canyon St; West Yellowstone
www.yellowstoneimax.com • Ticket: $9/Adult

Bears Den Cinema • (406) 646-7777
15 N Electric St; West Yellowstone

Grizzly & Wolf Discovery Center • (800) 257-2570
201 South Canyon; West Yellowstone
www.grizzlydiscoveryctr.org • Admission: $10.50/Adult

Yellowstone Vacations • (800) 426-7669
One-stop shop for year-round Yellowstone vacationing
415 Yellowstone Ave: West Yellowstone
www.yellowstonevacations.com

Buffalo Bus Tours • (800) 426-7669
415 Yellowstone Ave; West Yellowstone
www.winterinyellowstone.com • Rates: $109+

Trout Hunter • (208) 558-9900
3327 N US-20; Island Park, ID 83429
www.trouthunt.com • Rates: $425+ (full-day)

Henry's Fork Anglers • (208) 558-7525
3340 US-20; Island Park, ID 83429
www.henrysforkanglers.com • Rates: $490+ (full-day)

Madison River Outfitters • (406) 646-9644
117 Canyon St; West Yellowstone
www.madisonriveroutfitters.com • Rates: $450 (full-day)

Yellowstone Mtn Guides • (406) 646-7230
892 McClellan; West Yellowstone
www.yellowstone-guides.com

Yellowstone Expeditions • (406) 646-9333
Snowcoach, cross-country ski, & snowshoe tours
536 Firehole Ave; West Yellowstone
www.yellowstoneexpeditions.com

Yellowstone Alpen Guides • (406) 646-9591
555 Yellowstone Ave; West Yellowstone
www.yellowstoneguides.com

Diamond P Ranch • (406) 646-7246
2856 Targhee Pass Hwy; West Yellowstone
www.yellowstonehorses.com • Trail Ride: $68 (half-day)

Back Country Adventures • (406) 646-9317
Snowmobile rental & tours ($174+)
224 S Electric St; West Yellowstone
www.backcountry-adventures.com

Yellowstone Arctic Yamaha • (406) 646-9636
Snowmobile rental & tours ($174+)
208 N Electric St; West Yellowstone
www.yellowstonesnowmobiles.com

Yellowstone Adventures • (406) 646-7735
Snowmobile rental & tours ($184+)
131 Dunraven St; West Yellowstone
www.yellowstoneadventures.com

Sun Valley Trekking • (208) 788-1966
Hiking, climbing, mtn biking, snowshoe, and ski tours
703 1st Ave N; Hailey, ID 83333 • www.svtrek.com

North Entrance/Gardiner

Wild West Rafting • (406) 848-2252
Whitewater, float trips, trail rides, and kayaking
906 Scott St; Gardiner, MT 59030
www.wildwestrafting.com • Rates: $39 (half-day)

Flying Pig Rafting • (406) 848-7510
Whitewater, trail rides, and Yellowstone Tours
511 Scott St; Gardiner, MT 59030
www.flyingpigrafting.com • Rates: $43 (half-day)

Montana Whitewater Rafting • (406) 763-4465
Whitewater, kayak, trail rides, fly fishing, and ziplining
603 Scott St; Gardiner, MT 59030
www.montanawhitewater.com • Rates: $40 (half-day)

Yellowstone Association • (406) 848-2400
Tours, seminars, and field courses available
318 W Park St; Gardiner, MT 59030
www.yellowstoneassociation.org

Yellowstone Rough Riders • (406) 223-3924
*Horse rides ($95+), pack trips ($350/day/
person), and fishing trips ($180+/person)*
PO Box 447; Gardiner, MT 59030
www.yellowstoneroughriders.com

Hell's A Roarin' Outfitters • (406) 848-7578
164 Crevice Rd; Gardiner, MT 59030
www.hellsaroarinoutfitters.com

Big Wild Adventures • (406) 848-7000
Backpacking & Canoe Trips ($1,500–2,100)
222 Tom Miner Creek Rd; Emigrant, MT 59027
www.bigwildadventures.com

Slough Creek Outfitters • (406) 222-7455
PO Box 117; Emigrant, MT 59027
www.sloughcreekoutfitters.com • Rates: $400 (full-day)

Black Mountain Outfitters • (406) 222-7455
PO Box 117; Emigrant, MT 59027
www.blackmountainoutfitters.com • Rates: $300/person/day

Black Otter Guide Services • (406) 333-4362
131 Pray Rd; Livingston, MT 59047
www.blackotterguideservice.com • Rates: $200+/person/day

Safari Yellowstone • (406) 222-8557
Livingston, MT • *Available winter & summer*
www.safariyellowstone.com • Rates: $125+

Rockin' HK Outfitters • (406) 333-4505
116 Chicory Rd; Livingston, MT 59047
www.rockinhk.com • *3–10 day trips available*

Anderson's Yellowstone Angler • (406) 222-7130
5256 US-89 S; Livingston, MT 59047
www.yellowstoneangler.com • Rates: $475 (full-day)

Hatch Finders Flyshop • (406) 222-0989
113 W Park St, # 3; Livingston, MT 59047
www.hatchfinders.com • Rates: $450 (full-day)

Wilderness Photo Expeditions • (406) 222-2302
402 S 5th St; Livingston, MT 59047
www.tmurphywild.com

Empire Twin Theatre • (406) 222-0111
106 N 2nd St; Livingston, MT 59047

Headwaters Guide Services • (406) 763-4761
611 Garnet Mtn Way; Gallatin Gateway, MT 59730
www.headwatersguideservice.com • Rates: $390 (full-day)

Sunrise Pack Station • (406) 388-2236
202 Custer Ave; Belgrade, MT 59714
www.sunrisepackstation.com

Yellowstone Safari Company • (406) 586-1155
All sorts of safaris, available winter and summer
PO Box 42; Bozeman, MT 59771
www.yellowstonesafari.com

Medicine Lake Outfitters • (406) 388-4938
Pack trips, trail rides, and fishing available
3246 Linney Rd; Bozeman, MT 59718
www.packtrips.com

Off the Beaten Path • (800) 445-2995
7 E Beall St, # C; Bozeman, MT 59715
www.offthebeatenpath.com • Rates: $2,595+ (6 days)

Llama Trips in Yellowstone • (406) 587-2661
Bozeman, MT • www.yellowstonellamatrips.com

Custer National Forest • (406) 657-6200
1310 Main St; Billings, MT 59105

The Club at Spanish Peaks • (406) 993-5400
Skiing, horseback rides, mountain biking, and more
181 Clubhouse Fork; Big Sky, MT 59716
www.spanish-peaks.com

Jake's Horses • (406) 995-4630
47430 Gallatin Rd; Big Sky, MT 59716
www.jakeshorses.com • Rates: $250+/person/day

Big Sky Resort • (406) 995-5750
Skiing, sleigh rides, Yellowstone tours, and more
1 Lone Mountain Trail; Big Sky, MT 59716
www.bigskyresort.com

East of the Parks

Beartooth Plateau Outfitters • (406) 445-2293
819 Clear Creek Rd; Roberts, MT 59070
www.beartoothoutfitters.com • Rates: $290+/person/day

Skyline Guide Services • (406) 838-2380
Fishing, trail rides, hunting, and snowmobiling
31 Kersey Lake Rd; Cooke City, MT 59020
www.flyfishyellowstone.com

Stillwater Outfitters • (406) 838-2267
714 US-212; Cooke City, MT 59020
www.stillwateroutfitters.com • Rates: $300/person/day

John Henry Lee Outfitters • (307) 455-3200
617 Horse Creek Rd; Dubois, WY 82513
www.johnhenrylee.com

Ron Dube's Wilderness Adventures • (307) 527-7815
191 Whit Creek Rd; Wapiti, WY 82450

Sheep Mesa Outfitters • (307) 587-4305
11 Road 2Abw; Cody, WY 82414
www.sheepmesaoutfitters.com • Rates: $300/person/day

K Bar Z Ranch & Outfitter • (307) 587-4410
3477 Crandall Rd; Cody, WY 82414
www.agonline.com/KBarZ/activities.htm

Grub Steak Expeditions • (307) 527-6316
3513 Sheridan Ave; Cody, WY 82414
www.grubsteaktours.com • Rates: $490 (full-day)

Boulder Basin Outfitters • (307) 587-3404
3348 N Fork Hwy; Cody, WY 82414
www.boulderbasinoutfitters.com

Cody Rodeo Company • (307) 587-5913
1291 Sheridan Ave; Cody, WY 82414
www.codystampederodeo.com

The Cody Cattle Co. • (307) 587-9410
1910 Demaris Dr; Cody, WY 82414
www.thecodycattlecompany.com • Tickets: $24/Adult

Buffalo Bill Hist. Center • (307) 587-4771
720 Sheridan Ave; Cody, WY 82414
www.bbhc.org • Admission: $18/Adult

Jackson/Grand Teton Area

Teton Mtn Bike Tours • (307) 733-0712
545 N Cache St; Jackson, WY 83002
www.tetonmtbike.com • Tour: $60 (half-day)

Snake River Kayak & Canoe • (307) 733-9999
Rafting, kayak, sea kayak, and canoe trips
260 N Cache St; Jackson, WY 83001
www.snakeriverkayak.com • Rentals available

World Cast Anglers • (307) 733-6934
485 W Broadway; Jackson, WY 83001
www.worldcastanglers.com • Rates: $485 (full-day)

Jackson Hole Kayak School • (307) 733-2471
Lessons, tours, and rentals available
945 W Broadway; Jackson, WY 83001
www.jacksonholekayak.com

Wilderness Trails • (307) 733-5171
Hoback Junction; Jackson, WY 83001
www.wildernesstrailsinc.com

Granite Hot Springs • (307) 734-7400
Granite Creek Rd; Jackson, Wyoming 83001

Snow King Resort • (307) 733-5200
400 E Snow King Ave; Jackson, WY 83001
www.snowking.com • Lift Ticket: $42/Adult

Profile Massage | ENSO Spa • (307) 413-8949
235 E Broadway; Jackson, WY 83001
www.profilemassage.com • Massage: $55 (30 min.)

Jackson Hole Historical Society & Museum
105 N Glenwood St; Jackson, WY 83001
www.jacksonholehistory.org • (307) 733-2414 • Free

National Elk Refuge • (307) 733-9212
675 E Broadway; Jackson, WY 83001
www.nationalelkrefuge.fws.gov

Mill Iron Ranch Hunting • (307) 733-6390
5 US-89; Jackson • www.millironranch.net

Jackson Hole Llamas
PO Box 12500; Jackson, WY 83002
www.jhllamas.com • Rates: $625+

BrushBuck Guide Services • (888) 282-5868
Jackson • www.brushbuckphototours.com

Grand Teton Tours • (307) 413-5488
Jackson, WY • www.grandtetontours.com

Jackson Hole Wildlife Safaris • (307) 690-6402
650 W Broadway; Jackson, WY 83001
www.jacksonholewildlifesafaris.com

Jackson Hole Snowmobile Tours • (307) 733-6850
515 N Cache Dr; Jackson, WY
www.jacksonholesnowmobile.com

Ripley's Believe It Or Not • (307) 734-0000
140 N Cache St; Jackson, WY

Lewis & Clark River Expeditions • (307) 733-4022
Whitewater & float trips available
335 N Cache; Jackson, WY
www.lewisandclarkriverrafting.com

Teton Theatre • (307) 733-4939
120 N Cache; Jackson, WY

Jackson Hole Playhouse • (307) 733-6994
145 W Deloney Ave; Jackson
www.jhplayhouse.com

Jackson Hole Cinema • (307) 733-4939
295 W Pearl St; Jackson, WY
www.jacksonholecinemas.com • Tickets: $9/Adult

Jackson Hole Rafting & Whitewater
650 W Broadway; Jackson
www.jhww.com • (307) 733-1007

Wilderness Ventures •
(307) 733-2122
Multi-day hiking expeditions
4030 Lake Creek Dr; Wilson
www.wildernessventures.com

AJ De Rosa's Wooden Boat
Tours • (307) 733-3061
5455 W WY-22; Wilson
www.woodboattours.com • Rates: $690

Teton Troutfitters • (307) 733-5362
PO Box 536; Wilson, WY
www.tetontroutfitters.com •
Rates: $550 (full-day)

Westbank Anglers •
(307) 733-6483
3670 Moose Wilson Rd; Wilson
www.westbank.com • Rates:
$475 (full-day)

Yellowstone Outfitters •
(307) 543-2418
Trail and wagon rides, and hunting
23590 Buffalo Valley Rd;
Moran, WY 83013
www.yellowstoneoutfitters.com

Dry Ridge Outfitters • (208) 354-2284
160 N 4th St E.; Driggs, ID 83422
www.dryridge.com • Rates: $235/person/day

Craters of the Moon Nat'l Monument
US-26; Arco, ID 83213 • (208) 527-1300
www.nps.gov/crmo • Entrance Fee: $8/vehicle

Transportation Services

Yellowstone Snowcoach Tours • (800) 426-7669
415 Yellowstone Ave; West Yellowstone
www.winterinyellowstone.com

Yellowstone Tour & Travel • (406) 646-9310
211 Yellowstone Ave; West Yellowstone
www.yellowstone-travel.com

Karst Stage • (406) 586-8567
511 N Wallace Ave; Bozeman, MT 59715
www.karststage.com • tours & shuttle

Alltrans • (307) 733-3135
Summer and winter shuttle services
1680 W Martin Ln; Jackson, WY 83001
www.jacksonholealltrans.com

Yellowstone Explorers • (307) 739-8687
310 E Broadway; Jackson, WY 83001

RV Repair

Repairs By Ob • (406) 646-9084
512 Gibbon Ave; West Yellowstone

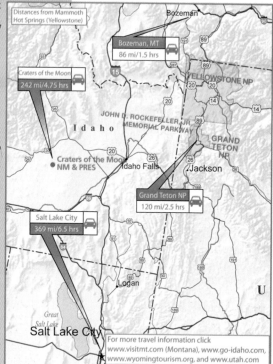

A ranger-led tour to Grinnell Glacier

PO Box 128
West Glacier, Montana 59936
Phone: (406) 888-7800
Website: www.nps.gov/glac

Established: May 11, 1910
Size: 1,013,594 Acres
Annual Visitors: 2.2 Million
Peak Season: July–August
Hiking Trails: 745 Miles

Activities: Hiking, Biking, Fishing,
Horseback Riding, Boating, Bus
and Boat Tours, Photography,
Skiing and Snowshoeing

13 Established Campgrounds
Camping Fee: $10–23/night
Backcountry Camping: Permitted*
6 Park Lodges and Hotels
Rates: $70–229/night

Park Hours: All day, every day
Entrance Fee: $25 • Vehicle
$12 • Individual (foot, bike, etc.)

*A $5/2.50 (Adult/Child) Back-
country Permit is required

Glacier - Montana

George Bird Grinnell came to northwestern Montana on a hunting expedition; he found a land so beautiful and majestic that he named it "the
Crown of the Continent." More than 100 glaciers capped the mountains' rugged peaks. Turquoise lakes dotted the high country. Green
forests spread out as far as his eye could see. It was a land completely
unspoiled by human hands. Grinnell returned again and again. He was
drawn by the prominence of the mountains, purity of the lakes, and
peacefulness of his surroundings. These Rocky Mountain landscapes
inspired him to spend the better part of two decades working to protect
this special area as a national park.

Grinnell found an unlikely ally in the **Great Northern Railway**.
Following the blueprint created by Southern Pacific Railroad at
Yosemite National Park, the Great Northern hoped to stimulate passenger service by promoting scenic wonders like Glacier. In 1891, rail
crossed the Continental Divide at Marias Pass, just south of the present-
day park boundary. That same year, George Bird Grinnell wrote in his
journal that the land surrounding St. Mary Lake should be a national
park. The Great Northern couldn't agree more. They knew it would be
much easier to deal with the federal government rather than negotiating
with hundreds of private land owners.

In 1897 land was set aside as the **Lewis and Clark Forest Preserve**,
largely due to lobbying by Grinnell and the railway. Grinnell continued
to pursue the idea of a national park, and his efforts proved successful

on May 11, 1910 when **President William Howard Taft** signed legislation establishing Glacier, the nation's tenth National Park.

The **Great Northern Railway** had gotten their wish too, receiving sole rights to develop the area. Glacier Park Lodge and Many Glacier Hotel were erected. Chalets were built in the backcountry at Sperry, Granite Park, Cut Bank, and Gunsight Lake. **Blackfeet Indians**, who once hunted the Rockies' western slopes and performed ceremonies on the shores of St. Mary Lake, sold more than 800,000 acres of their land to the U.S. government for $1.5 million. Not long after tribal members were camped in tipis atop McAlpin Hotel in New York City as a publicity stunt for the railroad. They rode the subway and visited the Brooklyn Bridge. They danced at the annual Travel and Vacation Show. Everywhere they went, people referred to them as "the Indians of Glacier National Park." Blackfeet were at the park too, standing in traditional clothing, waiting to greet visitors. This advertising campaign was yet another attempt by the Great Northern Railway to get Americans to "**See America First**."

The campaign worked. Upper-middle class Americans were flocking to these wonders of the western frontier. Tourists arrived by train and were catered to by the railway's subsidiary companies. George Bird Grinnell believed tourism ruined Yellowstone and Glacier. **Stephen Mather**, the first director of the National Park Service, understood that tourism was the only thing that could save them. The parks needed to be made dollarable or the government would give in to constant pressures of commercial interests like mining, logging, and oil. Mather envisioned park roads as spectacular feats of engineering, an attraction in and of themselves. At Glacier, the goal was to build a road through the center of the park, across the Continental Divide, and Mather approved construction of a much more expensive route carved into the face of Garden Wall.

Dedicated on July 15, 1933, **Going-to-the-Sun Road** still serves as the park's main attraction. It crosses the crown of the continent, providing access for millions of guests to the awe-inspiring alpine lakes, knife-edge ridgelines, and craggy mountaintops that George Bird Grinnell so admired. It connects lodges originally established by the Great Northern Railway, the very same places where today's visitors spend a night or two after exploring Glacier National Park and taking the time to "See America First."

Best of Glacier

Attraction: Going-to-the-Sun Road
Runner-up: Logan Pass
2nd Runner-up: Many Glacier
3rd Runner-up: St. Mary Lake

Activity: Red Bus Tours
Runner-up: Flathead River Rafting

Short Hike: Avalanche Lake
Runner-up: Hidden Lake/Overlook

Moderate Hike: Highline Trail
Runner-up: Grinnell Glacier
2nd Runner-up: Iceberg Lake
3rd Runner-up: Sperry Chalet

Area to Backpack: Goat Haunt
Runner-up: Cut Bank

When to Go

Glacier is open all year, but long winters cause road and facility closures from fall through spring. Most roads and facilities are open from late May to early September, but Going-to-the-Sun Road (GTSR) first opens for public use around mid-June until mid-September, but these dates vary from year to year. For example, in 2011 GTSR didn't open fully until July 12. Most park visitors arrive between July and August when the weather is best and GTSR is open. Cross-country skiers and snowshoers frequent the park from December to April.

Airports & Amtrak

The nearest airport is Glacier Park International (GPI), located near Kalispell, 30 miles from the West Entrance. Great Falls International (GTF) is the closest airport to the eastern boundary (about 140 miles from East Glacier Village). Car rental is available at each airport.

Amtrak (800.872.7245 or www.amtrak.com) serves West Glacier and East Glacier. One-way fare from Chicago, IL costs about $200. Glacier Park Inc., operates shuttle service to and from the train stations ($6–10 one-way).

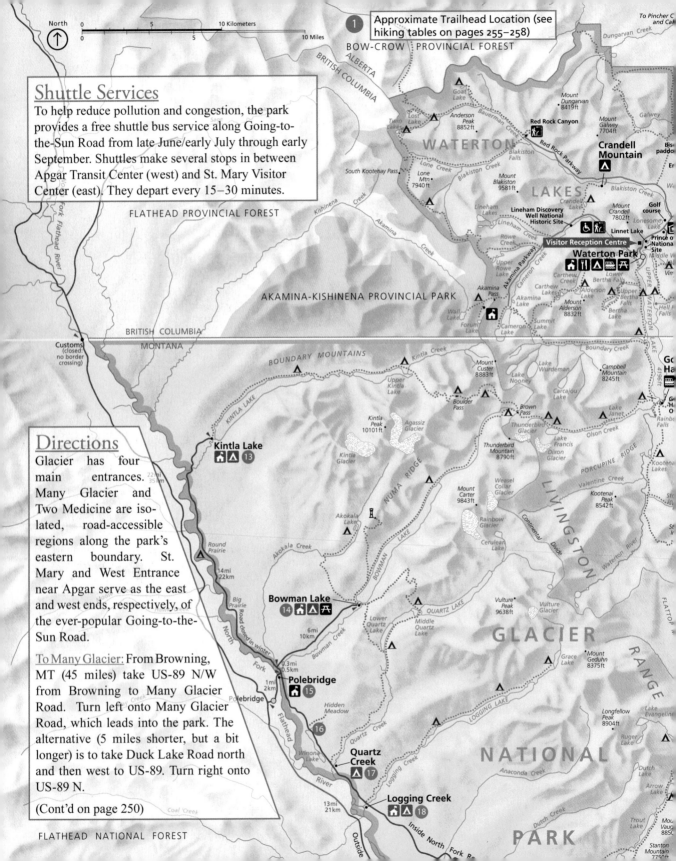

North

0   5   10 Kilometers
0   5   10 Miles

1 Approximate Trailhead Location (see hiking tables on pages 255–258)

Shuttle Services

To help reduce pollution and congestion, the park provides a free shuttle bus service along Going-to-the-Sun Road from late June/early July through early September. Shuttles make several stops in between Apgar Transit Center (west) and St. Mary Visitor Center (east). They depart every 15–30 minutes.

Directions

Glacier has four main entrances. Many Glacier and Two Medicine are isolated, road-accessible regions along the park's eastern boundary. St. Mary and West Entrance near Apgar serve as the east and west ends, respectively, of the ever-popular Going-to-the-Sun Road.

To Many Glacier: From Browning, MT (45 miles) take US-89 N/W from Browning to Many Glacier Road. Turn left onto Many Glacier Road, which leads into the park. The alternative (5 miles shorter, but a bit longer) is to take Duck Lake Road north and then west to US-89. Turn right onto US-89 N.

(Cont'd on page 250)

Waterton–Glacier International Peace Park

On June 18, 1932, **Waterton Lakes National Park** in Canada united with Glacier National Park to form the world's first **International Peace Park**. The parks retain well-defined borders and independent staffs, but they cooperate in wildlife management, scientific research, and some visitor services (like the ranger-led **International Peace Park Hike** • page 262). Waterton Lakes' activities are not covered in this guide, but the hike to **Crypt Lake** is worth a quick mention. It is one of the best hikes in the world, but not one to be attempted by individuals scared of heights or confined spaces. A short boat ride ($18/Adult, $9/Child) leads to the trailhead where you'll hike past running streams and sparkling waterfalls before a steel ladder climbs to a short tunnel. Next, you traverse a narrow, completely exposed cliff-edge with the aid of a cable. Continuing, you end at a perfect cirque nestled on the Canada–U.S. border. Remember to leave Crypt Lake with enough time to catch the ferry back to the dock (hikers have been left behind). Also remember to **bring your passport**. You'll need it to pass through the customs station where you drive in and out of Canada.

Regions

Many Glacier: Widely revered as the most beautiful area of Glacier National Park, Many Glacier is as close to the park's backcountry as you can get in a car. (But please leave your car behind for a while, the hiking here is first-rate.)

Goat Haunt: Goat Haunt is in the park's backcountry. You can hike in, or arrive by boat from Waterton Lakes National Park in Canada (ID required if arriving by boat and hiking south into Glacier National Park).

Inside North Fork Road from South to North: Logging Creek, Quartz Creek, Polebridge, Bowman Lake, and Kintla Lake are relatively uncrowded thanks to access via unpaved North Fork Road.

Map labels:

Waterton Lakes — Crypt Lake Trail

Don't Miss — Iceberg Lake Trail

Don't Miss — Grinnell Glacier Trail

Paddle — St. Mary Lake

To Calgary / To Lethbridge — Cardston, Alberta–Remington Carriage Centre

BLOOD INDIAN RESERVE — Belly River

Customs (summer only)

CANADA / UNITED STATES — Customs

ALBERTA / MONTANA

Chief Mountain International Highway

NATIONAL PARK

Sofa Mountain 8252ft

Maskinonge Lake

Kaina Mountain 9489ft

Belly River

Chief Mountain 9080ft / 2767m

Gable Pass

Gable Mountain 9262ft

Slide Lake

Cosley Lake

Glenns Lake

Elizabeth Lake

Mokowanis Lake

Old Sun Glacier

Margaret Lake

Ipasha Lake

Redgap Pass

Pola Lake

Ahern Glacier

Ptarmigan Tunnel

Apikuni Mountain 9068ft

Swiftcurrent Ridge Lake

Helen Lake

Kennedy Lake

Many Glacier Entrance

Ptarmigan Falls

Many Glacier Information

Iceberg Lake

Redrock Falls

Swiftcurrent Nature Trail

Swiftcurrent Lake

Bullhead Lake

Granite Park Chalet

Swiftcurrent Pass

Lake Josephine

Grinnell Lake

Grinnell Glacier

Cataract Creek

Mt Gould 9553ft

Mount Siyeh 10014ft

The Loop

Packers Roost

GARDEN WALL

Weeping Wall

Triple Arches

Cracker Lake

Mount Siyeh

Piegan Pass

Logan Pass Visitor Center 6646ft

Mt Oberlin 8180ft

Clements Mtn 8760ft

Hidden Lake Nature Trail

Siyeh Bend

Going-to-the-Sun Mtn 9642ft

Sunrift Gorge

Baring Falls

Jackson Glacier Overlook

Reynolds Mtn

Hidden Lake

Trail of the Cedars Nature Trail

Otokomi Lake

Goat Lake

Rose Creek

Sun Point Nature Trail

SAINT MARY LAKE

Rising Sun

St. Mary

Going-to-the-Sun Road

Saint Mary Entrance

Saint Mary Visitor Center

Saint Mary

Napi Point

Babb

Duck Lake

DUCK LAKE

Hudson Bay Divide

LOWER SAINT MARY LAKE

Saint Mary River

Otatso Creek

Kennedy Creek

Swiftcurrent

LAKE SHERBURNE

EAST FLATTOP MOUNTAIN

BLACKFEET INDIAN RESERVATION

To Browning

North Fork Belly River

Crooked Creek

Belly River

30mi 47km

10mi 16km

4mi 6km

12mi 19km

9mi 14km

18mi 29km

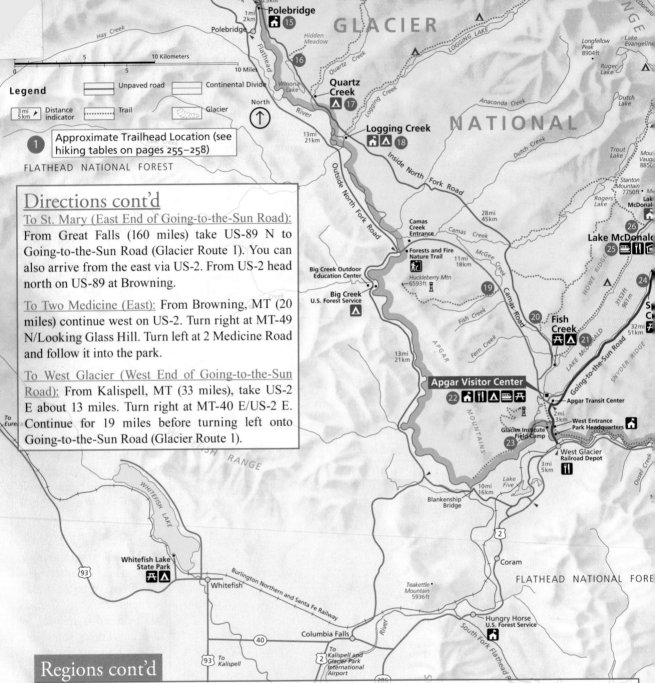

Legend

| | Unpaved road | | Continental Divide |
| | Trail | | Glacier |

Distance indicator — 3 mi / 5 km

1 Approximate Trailhead Location (see hiking tables on pages 255–258)

North ↑

FLATHEAD NATIONAL FOREST

Directions cont'd

To St. Mary (East End of Going-to-the-Sun Road): From Great Falls (160 miles) take US-89 N to Going-to-the-Sun Road (Glacier Route 1). You can also arrive from the east via US-2. From US-2 head north on US-89 at Browning.

To Two Medicine (East): From Browning, MT (20 miles) continue west on US-2. Turn right at MT-49 N/Looking Glass Hill. Turn left at 2 Medicine Road and follow it into the park.

To West Glacier (West End of Going-to-the-Sun Road): From Kalispell, MT (33 miles), take US-2 E about 13 miles. Turn right at MT-40 E/US-2 E. Continue for 19 miles before turning left onto Going-to-the-Sun Road (Glacier Route 1).

Regions cont'd

Two Medicine: Original train depot before Going-to-the-Sun Road (GTSR) was constructed. Today, it's a somewhat off-the-beaten-path destination with outstanding hiking and camping.

Cut Bank: More remote region as access is via an unpaved road. **Cut Bank Creek Trail** is outstanding.

Along GTSR (from East to West) St. Mary: The park's eastern gateway is heavily trafficked and for good reason: vistas along St. Mary Lake are some of the most spectacular, not only in the park, but in the world.

Logan Pass: Extremely popular, but Logan Pass is THE one must-stop destination along GTSR.

Lake McDonald: This area, boasting the largest lake in the park, bustles with activity all summer long. Lodging, dining, boat and horse tours are all available here.

Apgar: The park's western gateway is Apgar. Here you'll find lodging, dining, camping, boat tours, and a visitor center.

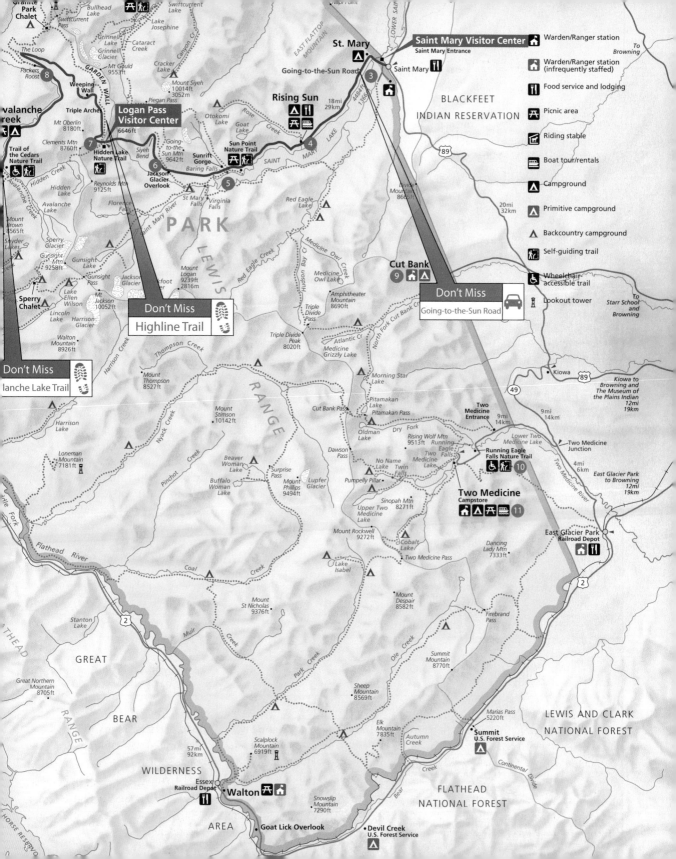

Granite Park
Chalet
Bullhead
Lake
Swiftcurrent
Lake
Swiftcurrent
Pass
The Loop
Grinnell
Lake
Lake Josephine
Cataract Creek
Grinnell
Glacier
Packers
Roost
8
GARDEN
WALL
Mt Gould
9553ft
Piegan Pass
Weeping
Wall
Cracker Lake
Mount Siyeh
10014ft
3052ft
East Flattop Mountain
Napi Point
St. Mary

Saint Mary Visitor Center
Saint Mary Entrance

Avalanche
Creek
Triple Arches
Logan Pass
Visitor Center
6646ft
Mt Oberlin
8180ft
Hidden Lake
Nature Trail
7
Clements Mtn
8760ft
Going-to-the-
Sun Road
Siyeh
Bend
6
Jackson
Glacier
Overlook
Reynolds Mtn
9125ft
Otokomi
Lake
Goat
Lake
Sun Point
Nature Trail
Sunrift
Gorge
Baring Falls
5
Rising Sun

Going-to-the-Sun Road
Saint Mary

BLACKFEET
INDIAN RESERVATION

89

Don't Miss
Going-to-the-Sun Road

Trail of
the Cedars
Nature Trail
Hidden
Lake
Avalanche
Lake
Mount
Brown
8565ft
Florence
Falls
St Mary
Falls
Virginia
Falls
Red Eagle
Lake
Divide
Mountain
8665ft

PARK
LEWIS

Sperry
Glacier
Snyder
Lakes
Gunsight
Mtn
9258ft
Gunsight
Lake
Jackson
Glacier
Sperry
Chalet
Mt
Jackson
10052ft
Lake
Ellen Wilson
Gunsight
Pass
Lincoln
Lake
Harrison
Glacier
Mount
Logan
9239ft
2816m
Red Eagle Creek
Medicine Owl Creek
Medicine
Owl Lake
Cut Bank
9

Don't Miss
Highline Trail

Walton
Mountain
8926ft
Harrison
Lake
Thompson Creek
Harrison Creek
Mount
Thompson
8527ft
Amphitheater
Mountain
8690ft
Triple
Divide
Pass
Triple Divide
Peak
8020ft
Atlantic Cr
Medicine
Grizzly Lake

Kiowa
89
Kiowa to
Browning and
The Museum of
the Plains Indian
12mi
19km

Don't Miss
lanche Lake Trail

Harrison
Lake
Loneman
Mountain
7181ft
RANGE
Nyack Creek
Mount
Stimson
10142ft
Cut Bank Pass
Morning Star
Lake
Pitamakan
Lake
Pitamakan Pass
Two
Medicine
Entrance
49
9mi
14km
9mi
14km

Flathead
River
Pinchot
Creek
Beaver
Woman
Lake
Surprise
Pass
Buffalo
Woman
Lake
Mount
Phillips
9494ft
Lupfer
Glacier
Oldman
Lake
Dry Fork
Dawson
Pass
No Name
Lake
Twin
Falls
Rising Wolf Mtn
9513ft
Running
Eagle
Falls
Two
Medicine
Lake
Running Eagle
Falls Nature Trail
Lower Two
Medicine Lake
Two Medicine
Junction
4mi
6km
East Glacier Park
to Browning
12mi
19km

Harrison
Lake
Coal
Creek
Mulr
Creek
Lake
Isabel
Pumpelly Pillar
Sinopah Mtn
8271ft
Upper Two
Medicine
Lake
Mount Rockwell
9272ft
Cobalt
Lake
Two Medicine Pass
Dancing
Lady Mtn
7333ft
Two Medicine
Campstore
11
East Glacier Park
Railroad Depot

GREAT
Stanton
Lake
2
Mount
St Nicholas
9376ft
Park Creek
Mount
Despair
8582ft
Firebrand
Pass

BEAR
57mi
92km
Scalplock
Mountain
6919ft
Sheep
Mountain
8569ft
Summit
Mountain
8770ft
Ole Creek
LEWIS AND CLARK
NATIONAL FOREST

WILDERNESS
AREA
Essex
Railroad Depot
Walton
Snowslip
Mountain
7290ft
Elk
Mountain
7835ft
Autumn
Creek
Bear Creek
Marias Pass
5220ft
Summit
U.S. Forest Service
Continental Divide
FLATHEAD
NATIONAL FOREST
2
Goat Lick Overlook
Devil Creek
U.S. Forest Service

Warden/Ranger station
To
Browning

Warden/Ranger station
(infrequently staffed)

Food service and lodging

Picnic area

Riding stable

Boat tour/rentals

Campground

Primitive campground

Backcountry campground

Self-guiding trail

Wheelchair-
accessible trail

Lookout tower
To
Starr School
and
Browning

20mi
32km

Lodging

Bearhat and Hidden Lake

Glacier has several in-park accommodations available for summer visitors. All properties are operated by **Glacier Park Inc**, (406.892.2525 or 403.236.3400 from Canada, www.glacierparkinc.com). **Glacier Park Lodge** and **Many Glacier Hotel** are original structures built by the Great Northern Railway in the early 1900s, a few years after the park was established. John Lewis established Lewis Glacier Hotel in 1913-1914. He envisioned Glacier as "America's Switzerland," and used traditional Swiss chalet-style architecture. In 1930 it was bought by Great Northern Railway and renamed **Lake McDonald Lodge**. Today, the park's lodges are as popular as ever. Reservations are recommended. Most fill to capacity during their brief tourist season. It is expensive to spend a night in America's Switzerland. You're paying for location, and there's no better way to visit the park than sleeping within its boundaries. The best bargains are rooms priced for quad occupancy at **Glacier Park Lodge** ($224/night), **Many Glacier Hotel** ($228), and **Village Inn at Apgar** ($194 & $236).

Glacier Lodging

	Open	Rates	Notes
Glacier Park Lodge (East Glacier)	mid-June–late Sept	$145–449/night	Golf, spa, and dining are available
Lake McDonald Lodge (In SW region of park on Going-to-the-Sun Road)	late May–late Sept	$128–182/night	Cabins available, dining on-site • Swiss chalet-style design
Many Glacier Hotel	mid-June–mid-Sept	$155–294/night	Dining and boat tours on-site
Rising Sun Motor Inn (Going-to-the-Sun Road, 5.5 miles from St. Mary)	mid-June–mid-Sept	$124–141/night	Centralized location with Two Dog Flats Grill
Swiftcurrent Motor Inn (Many Glacier Area)	early June–late Sept	$73–141/night	Rooms are in three separate buildings, some rooms have a shared bathroom
Village Inn at Apgar	late May–mid-Sept	$136–236/night	Only in-park lodging on the west side

For reservations or additional information call Glacier Park Inc., at (406) 892-2525 or click www.glacierparkinc.com

Glacier Camping

	Open	Fee	Sites	Notes
Apgar 👍	early May –mid-Oct	$20	192	25 sites with 40-foot parking space • F, DS, PC, HB
Avalanche	mid-June–early Sept	$20	86	Maximum parking space of 26-feet • F, HB
Bowman Lake	late May–mid-Sept	$15	48	Dirt access road, large units not recommended • PC
Cut Bank	late May–mid-Sept	$10	14	Dirt access road, primitive camping, no potable H_2O
Fish Creek* 👍	early June–mid-Sept	$23	178	18 sites with 35-foot parking space • F, DS, PC, HB
Kintla Lake 👍	late May–mid-Sept	$15	13	Dirt access road, large units not recommended • PC
Logging Creek	early July–late Sept	$10	7	Dirt access road, primitive camping, no potable H_2O
Many Glacier	late May–late Sept	$20	109	13 sites with 35-foot parking space • F, DS, PC, HB
Quartz Creek	early July–late Nov	$10	7	Dirt access road, primitive camping, no potable H_2O
Rising Sun	late May–mid-Sept	$20	83	10 sites with 25-foot parking space • F, DS, PC, HB
Sprague Creek	mid-May–mid-Sept	$20	25	No towed units allowed, max space is 21-feet • F, HB
St. Mary* 👍	mid-May–mid-Sept	$23	148	25 sites have 35-foot parking space • F, DS, PC, HB
Two Medicine	mid-May–mid-Sept	$20	99	13 sites with 32-foot parking space • F, DS, PC, HB

*Campsites can be reserved, June through Labor Day, by calling (877) 444-6777 or clicking www.recreation.gov
F = Flush Toilets, DS = Dump Station, PC = Primitive Camping (after the open dates), HB = Hike/Bike Sites ($5–8/night)

Backcountry	A Backcountry User Permit is required for all overnight camping in the backcountry. Trips between June 15 and September 30 may be reserved for a $30 reservation fee. Advance reservations are only accepted via mail or fax (406.888.5819). The reservation form is available online at www.nps.gov/glac. Between June 1 and September 30 permits cost $5 (age 16+), $2.50 (8–15), and free (7 and under) per person per night. Permits may be obtained from the following locations: Apgar Backcountry Permit Center, St. Mary Visitor Center, Many Glacier Ranger Station, Two Medicine Ranger Station, Polebridge Ranger Station, and Waterton Lakes National Park Visitor Reception Center.
Group Camping	Group sites are available at Apgar*, Many Glacier, St. Mary, and Two Medicine ($53 plus $5 per person after first 9 campers)
Winter Camping	Available at St. Mary and Apgar from December 1–March 31

Drive-in **campgrounds** are located along Going-to-the-Sun Road and the park's east and west boundaries. **Many Glacier** is a popular campground in a spectacular setting on the eastern side. It's a highly recommended camping destination, but if you're hoping to secure a site you'll want to arrive early. **St. Mary and Fish Creek** are the only campgrounds that allow reservations (up to five months in advance). All other campgrounds are listed in the table above.

Two **hike-in chalets** located in the backcountry allow visitors to access the heart of the park, miles from roads and automobiles, without sacrificing a bed and warm meal. **Granite Park Chalet** (www.graniteparkchalet.com, $90/night) is located just west of the Continental Divide, a few miles north of Going-to-the-Sun Road. It can be accessed via Highline, Loop, Swiftcurrent, and Fifty Mountain/Waterton Lake Trails. A kitchen with stove is available for guests to cook their own meals (carried in or chosen from the chalet's menu of freeze-dried foods). **Sperry Chalet** (www.sperrychalet.com, $185/night per person) sits on a ledge overlooking Lake McDonald. Guests are served dinner and breakfast at specified times, and are given a trail lunch. Sperry Trail starts at Lake McDonald Lodge's parking lot and heads southeast to the chalet. Horse trips from the park's concessioner (page 260) are also available from Lake McDonald Horse Barn to Sperry Chalet. An alternative hiking route is Gunsight Pass Trail (more scenic, but longer). All visitors must pack out what is packed in. If you only intend on staying at a chalet a Backcountry User Permit is not required. These chalets provide a unique opportunity to explore hiking trails that few guests take the time to enjoy. The alternative for exploring the park's backcountry is to stay at one of the designated **backcountry campsites** located along more than 700 miles of trails.

Hiking

Wildflowers along Highline Trail © Sam and Katie Johnsrud

Glacier is the ultimate hiking destination. More than 700 miles of trails crisscross one million acres of mountainous terrain, providing access to an unparalleled collection of blue-green alpine lakes, knife-edge arêtes, rugged and prominent mountains, and textbook examples of glacial geology. A hiker could spend a month here and still be left in awe of the rocky pinnacles reaching toward the sky.

Every area has its gems, but one region stands out. **Many Glacier** is without a doubt the best of the best. The second you pass through the entrance you feel like you've driven into a postcard and it only gets better from here. The prominence and jagged nature of these mountains is overwhelming. Here you'll find two of the best treks: **Grinnell Glacier and Iceberg Lake Trails**. Each can be completed in 3–5 hours, but pack a lunch and make a day of it. **Grinnell Glacier Trail** allows hikers to view (and step foot on) one of the park's endangered species: glaciers. The trek begins near Many Glacier Hotel and once you reach the shores of Lake Josephine, you are showered with spectacular mountain views as the snowmelt pours from their steep slopes. Just beyond the lake is a viewpoint/picnic area, where you can continue on to the glacier and Upper Grinnell Lake.

Iceberg Lake Trail begins at Iceberg Ptarmigan Trailhead, then passes Ptarmigan Falls before passing through a field of beargrass, along a babbling creek, and up into the high-country. Left in the shadows of Mount Wilbur and the Continental Divide, Iceberg Lake receives little sunlight. The result is massive icebergs floating about the perfect glacial cirque (sometimes into August).

Highline Trail (Trailhead at Logan Pass • Going-to-the-Sun Road) follows **Garden Wall** along the Continental Divide. This hike should be written at the very top of your list of "don't miss" activities.

Even though Grinnell Glacier, Iceberg Lake, and Highline Trails are fairly long day hikes, don't anticipate much solitude. These are three of the park's most beautiful and popular treks.

The following pages provide additional hiking information broken down by region. **All trail mileages are for one-way hiking**. Trails at Glacier are more difficult than those found at most parks. Expect a strenuous trail to traverse several steep climbs with the potential for switchbacks; even moderate trails may encounter more than 1,000 feet in elevation change. Remember that you're in grizzly country. Hike in groups, and know what to do should you encounter an aggressive bear. Any trailhead that is followed by a (Shuttle Stop) means that it is on or near the park's shuttle route that follows Going-to-the-Sun Road (page 248).

Logan Pass, St. Mary, and Many Glacier Hiking Trails

	Trail Name	Trailhead (# on map)	Length	Notes (One-way distances)
Easy	Appekunny Falls	1.1 miles east of Many Glacier Hotel (1)	1.0 mile	Viewpoint of water falling from a hanging valley
	Grinnell Lake - 👍	Grinnell Glacier Trailhead or Many Glacier Hotel (2)	3.4 miles	Hike in and out, or take shortcut via boat trip
		Using concession boat from Many Glacier Hotel	0.9 mile	
	Redrock Falls	Swiftcurrent Trailhead (2)	1.8 miles	Short leisurely hike
	Ptarmigan Falls	Iceberg Ptarmigan Trailhead (2)	2.6 miles	Falls on Iceberg Lake route
	Swiftcurrent Nature Tr	Grinnell Glacier Trailhead or Many Glacier Hotel (2)	2.5 miles	Short and flat path
	St. Mary Falls - 👍	St. Mary Falls Trailhead (Shuttle Stop) (3)	1.1 miles	Very popular trail with multiple access options
		Using concession operated boat from Rising Sun	1.5 miles	
	Virginia Falls - 👍	St. Mary Falls Trailhead (Shuttle Stop) (3)	1.5 miles	Switchbacks from St. Mary Falls lead to Virginia Falls
		Using concession operated boat from Rising Sun	2.2 miles	
	Beaver Pond Loop	1913 Ranger Station Parking Area (3)	3.0 miles	Popular short, flat loop trail
	Red Eagle Lake	1913 Ranger Station Parking Area (3)	7.6 miles	Easy hike, but long
	Baring Falls	Sunrift Gorge Pullout (Shuttle Stop) (5)	1.0 mile	Short descent to falls
	Sun Point Nature Trail	Sun Point Parking Area (Shuttle Stop) (5)	0.8 mile	Skirts along St. Mary Lake
	Sunrift Gorge	Sunrift Gorge Pullout (Shuttle Stop) (5)	200 feet	Very short, easily accessible
Moderate	Cracker Lake	South end of Many Glacier Hotel Parking Area (2)	6.1 miles	Follows horse trail ride route
	Grinnell Glacier Viewpoint - 👍	Grinnell Glacier Trailhead or Many Glacier Hotel (2)	5.5 miles	Definitely one of the best hikes in the park
		Using concession boat from Many Glacier Hotel	3.8 miles	
	Iceberg Lake - 👍	Iceberg Ptarmigan Trailhead (2)	4.8 miles	Another day hiker's favorite
	Ptarmigan Lake - 👍	Iceberg Ptarmigan Trailhead (2)	4.3 miles	Veers from Iceberg Lake Trail to Ptarmigan Lake
	Piegan Pass	Piegan Pass Trailhead (Siyeh Bend Shuttle Stop) (6)	4.5 miles	Less popular east side of the Garden Wall
		South end of Many Glacier Hotel Parking Area (2)	8.3 miles	
	Granite Park Chalet	Continental Divide sign at Logan Pass (Shuttle Stop) (7)	7.6 miles	The AMAZING Highline Trail
		Swiftcurrent Trailhead at Many Glacier (2)	7.5 miles	Tedious Swiftcurrent Pass
		Loop Trailhead on Going-to-the-Sun Road (8)	4.0 miles	Shortest route via the Loop
	Otokomi Lake	Next to Rising Sun Campstore (4)	5.2 miles	Meadows lead to scenic lake
	Hidden Lake/Overlook - 👍	Logan Pass Visitor Center (Shuttle Stop) (7)	1.5/3.5 mi	Distances to overlook/lake
Strenuous	Ptarmigan Tunnel - 👍	Iceberg Ptarmigan Trailhead (2)	5.2 miles	Connects Many Glacier and Belly River Areas
	Swiftcurrent Pass	Swiftcurrent Trailhead (2)	6.6 miles	Across the pass you'll find Granite Park Chalet
	Siyeh Pass Area - 👍	Piegan Pass Trailhead (Siyeh Bend Shuttle Stop) (6)	4.7 miles	High elevation hike through varied ecosystems
		Sunrift Gorge Pullout, 10 miles west of St. Mary	5.6 miles	
	Gunsight Pass - 👍	Gunsight Pass Trailhead (Shuttle Stop) (6)	9.2 miles	More difficult, but also more beautiful alternative route ending at Sperry Chalet
	Highline Trail - 👍	Continental Divide sign at Logan Pass (Shuttle Stop) (7)	20+ miles	Follows Continental Divide to U.S.–Canada Border

Hiker on Medicine Grizzly Lake Trail © Derek and Heidi Pankratz

If you are looking for seclusion and solitude, these are the regions of the park for you. Cut Bank, located in the southeast corner, is seldom visited (relatively speaking). It doesn't attract the swarms of tourists that race across Going-to-the-Sun Road, without sacrificing the majestic mountain scenery. **Triple Divide Pass** is one of the more unique hiking destinations. Depending on where a drop of water lands within a one-square-foot area of **Triple Divide Peak**, that droplet could end up in Hudson Bay, the Gulf of Mexico, or the Pacific Ocean. The views along the way to the peak are equally amazing.

Two Medicine and Cut Bank Hiking Trails

	Trail Name	Trailhead (# on map)	Length	Notes (One-way distances)
Easy	Atlantic Falls	Cut Bank Trailhead (9)	4.0 miles	Waterfall seen en route to Pitamakan Pass
	Running Eagle Falls - 👍	Running Eagle Falls Trailhead (10)	0.3 mile	A short wheelchair accessible trail
	Apistoki Falls	0.25 mile east of 2 Med. Ranger Station (11)	0.6 mile	Short and easy waterfall hike
	Aster Park - 👍	South Shore Trailhead (11)	1.9 miles	Views of Two Medicine Lake
	Twin Falls	North Shore Trailhead (11)	3.8 miles	A short spur trail from Upper Two Medicine Lake Trail leads to Twin Falls
		Using concession boat	0.9 mile	
	Upper Two Medicine Lake	North Shore Trailhead (11)	5.0 miles	After Twin Falls the trail continues to Upper Two Medicine Lake
		Using concession boat	2.2 miles	
Moderate	Medicine Grizzly Lake	Cut Bank Trailhead (9)	6.0 miles	Spur trail from Triple Divide Trail
	Rockwell Falls	South Shore Trailhead (11)	3.4 miles	Follow South Shore Trail to Cobalt Lake
	Cobalt Lake - 👍	South Shore Trailhead (11)	5.7 miles	Last two miles to the lake are steep
	No Name Lake	North Shore Trailhead (11)	5.0 miles	Pretty lake north of Upper Two Medicine
Strenuous	Triple Divide Pass	Cut Bank Trailhead (9)	7.2 miles	From here water flows west, south, and north
	Scenic Point	0.25 mile east of 2 Med. Ranger Station (11)	3.1 miles	Short climb to a wonderful viewpoint
	Dawson Pass - 👍	North Shore Trailhead (11)	6.7 miles	Combine with Pitamakan Pass for an 18.8-mi loop
	Pitamakan Pass	North Shore Trailhead (11)	6.9 miles	Follows Cut Bank Creek to two lakes
	Oldman Lake	North Shore Trailhead (11)	5.7 miles	Follows Dry Fork to lake near Pitamakan Pass

North Fork is located along the park's western boundary, north of Going-to-the-Sun Road. It's a nice, relatively secluded area with a variety of easy and mostly flat hikes that explore the western foothills. **Goat Haunt** is located in the backcountry at the south end of Upper Waterton Lake near the U.S.–Canada Border. It's a popular stop for backpackers, but can also be reached as a day hike from **Canada's Waterton Lakes National Park**. Here, an out-and-back trek to Goat Haunt is possible thanks to **Waterton Shoreline Cruise's** (403.859.2362, www.watertoncruise.com) boat rides back to Waterton. One-way fare is $24/adults, $12/youth (ages 13–17), and $9/child (ages 4–12). Boats typically run from June until September.

Lake Francis Falls

Goat Haunt and North Fork Hiking Trails

	Trail Name	Trailhead (# on map)	Length	Notes (One-way distances)
Easy	Rainbow Falls	Goat Haunt Backcountry Ranger Station (12)	1.0 mile	Short hike to falls on Waterton River
	Waterton Townsite	Goat Haunt Backcountry Ranger Station (12)	7.0 miles	Crosses U.S.–Canada Border to Waterton
	Goat Haunt Overlook	Goat Haunt Backcountry Ranger Station (12)	1.0 mile	Climb to overlook of Upper Waterton Lake
	Kootenai Lakes	Goat Haunt Backcountry Ranger Station (12)	2.5 miles	Backcountry hike to a small lake
	Lake Janet	Goat Haunt Backcountry Ranger Station (12)	3.3 miles	Backcountry hike to alpine lake
	Covey Meadow	Polebridge Ranger Station (15)	1.5 miles	Short and easy loop trail through meadow
	Hidden Meadow	3 miles south of Polebridge Ranger Station (16)	1.2 miles	Short and flat hike through a very nice meadow
	Logging Lake	Near Logging Creek Ranger Station (18)	4.5 miles	This trail is popular among fishermen
Moderate	Lake Francis	Goat Haunt Backcountry Ranger Station (12)	6.2 miles	Another lake beyond Lake Janet
	Kintla Lake Head	0.25 miles west of Kintla Lake Camp (13)	6.6 miles	Easy, but long hike along lakeshore
	Bowman Lake Head - 👍	Bowman Lake Ranger Station (14)	7.1 miles	Flat & easy but long hike to lake and camp
	Akokala Lake	Bowman Lake Ranger Station (14)	5.8 miles	Crosses Akokala Creek to small lake
	Numa Lookout	Bowman Lake Ranger Station (14)	7.2 miles	Views across Bowman Lake
	Quartz Lake - 👍	Bowman Lake Picnic Area (14)	6.0 miles	These trails offer a nice opportunity for a little more than a 12-mile loop hike to the shores of Quartz Lake and back around Middle and Lower Quartz Lakes
	Lower Quartz Lake	Bowman Lake Picnic Area (14)	3.0 miles	
		Just north of Quartz Creek Camp (17)	6.9 miles	

The **Lake McDonald Area** has a fairly dense collection of easy to moderate hiking trails. **Apgar Lookout Trail** provides expansive panoramas. And **Sperry Trailhead**, located on Going-to-the-Sun Road, serves as an access point to the region's most beautiful hikes. That includes the 6.4-mile (one-way) trail to **Sperry Chalet** (page 253) where you can spend a night in the wilderness and enjoy a warm dinner and breakfast before returning to civilization.

Wild Goose Island Overlook, St. Mary Lake

Lake McDonald Hiking Trails

	Trail Name	Trailhead (# on map)	Length	Notes (One-way distances)
Easy	Howe Lake	Howe Lake Trailhead on Inside North Fork Road (20)	2.0 miles	Continues past lake to ridge
	Rocky Point	0.2 miles north of Fish Creek Campground (21)	1.1 miles	Overlook of Lake McDonald
	Fish Creek to Apgar Hiking Path	Near McDonald Creek Bridge (Shuttle Stop) (21, 22)	1.2 miles	Short and flat connecting path between Fish Creek and Apgar
	Lake McDonald West Shore	Lakeshore at Fish Creek Campground (21) 2.8 miles west on North Lake McDonald Road (26)	7.0 miles	A mostly level and easily accessible trail around the lake
	McDonald Creek Bike Path	Asphalt path 50 yards south of Apgar Visitor Center (Shuttle Stop) (22)	1.5 miles	Connects Apgar and West Glacier
	Johns Lake Loop	Johns Lake Trailhead (27)	3.0 miles	Short loop off GTSR
	Trail of Cedars	Avalanche Picnic Area (Shuttle Stop) (28)	0.7 mile	Wheelchair accessible loop
	Avalanche Lake - 👍	Avalanche Gorge Bridge on Trail of the Cedars (28)	2.0 miles	Extremely popular hike
Moderate	Apgar Lookout - 👍	At the end of Glacier Institute Road, about 2.0 miles from Going-to-the-Sun Road (23)	3.3 miles	Hike up switchbacks to a view of several 10,000-ft peaks
	Fish Lake	Sperry Trailhead (Shuttle Stop) (24)	2.9 miles	Just south of Sperry Trail
	Lincoln Lake - 👍	Lincoln Lake (24)	8.0 miles	Secluded/Beaver Chief Falls
	Trout Lake	Trout Lake Trailhead (26)	4.2 miles	Popular horse trail
Strenuous	Huckleberry Lookout	Huckleberry Mt Trailhead on Camas Road (19)	6.0 miles	Look for a huckleberry snack
	Mt Brown Lookout	Sperry Trailhead (Shuttle Stop) (25)	5.3 miles	Steep, but spectacular
	Sperry Chalet - 👍	Sperry Trailhead (Shuttle Stop) (25)	6.4 miles	Shortest route to the chalet
	Snyder Lake	Sperry Trailhead (Shuttle Stop) (25)	4.4 miles	Breaks north of Sperry Trail

Backpacking

The one sure-fire way to escape the sea of summer tourists is to strap a pack to your back, and head into the wilderness (more than 95% of the park's area).

From the beginning of May until the end of October all backpackers must camp in designated sites with an overnight **backcountry use permit** (page 253). Permits cost $5 per night per person for adults and $2.50 for children (ages 8–15). Children under 7 are free. They may be reserved in advance from June 15 to September 15 for an additional $30 nonrefundable fee. **Reservations** are highly recommended for sites within a day's hike of the primary trailhead. To reserve your sites/permit, you must fill out an **application form** (available at the park website). Permits must be obtained in person no sooner than one day before your trip's departure. You cannot request a backcountry permit without planning your route. Along the park's trails there are more than 60 backcountry campgrounds and 200+ campsites. Choose a route with every member of the group in mind. If it's your first time camping in the backcountry think about staying near Going-to-the-Sun Road or one of the park's developed areas.

All **campgrounds** have tent sites, pit toilets, food hanging or storage devices, and food preparation areas. Set up camp and prepare and store food where you're supposed to. Fires are only allowed in designated fire pits, and are not available at all camps. For the most part, all that is expected of you is simple courtesy toward your surroundings and fellow backpackers.

Very few incidents occur, but backpackers must be well aware of the inherent dangers. To some, the danger is part of the allure; to others, it's a reason to stay away. Weather, wildlife, and accidents are all unpredictable forces of nature that can cause serious problems in the backcountry. **Check the extended weather forecast** before your trip. **Travel with a group** and carry a **first-aid kit**, a **good topographic map,** and a **compass** (most importantly, know how to use them). **Treat your water** (boil or filter). Know how to react should you encounter a bear or mountain lion. In reality these dangers are nothing to be afraid of. While there are no guarantees, with a little bit of knowledge and ample preparation you can nearly assure yourself a safe once-in-a-lifetime experience in a one-of-a-kind environment. Without exception, all first-time, multi-day expeditions should be planned carefully, well in advance.

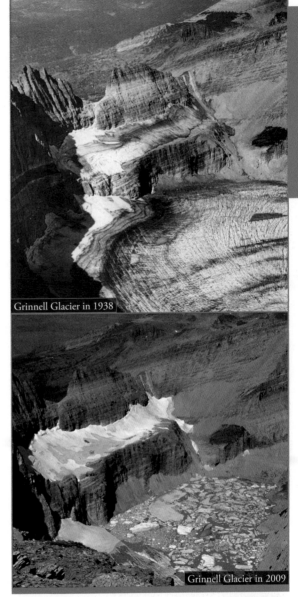

Grinnell Glacier in 1938

Grinnell Glacier in 2009

Glacier's Glaciers

In 1850 there were 150 glaciers in the park. Today, there are 25, all of which are shrinking in size. **Grinnell Glacier** is pictured above in 1938 and again in 2009. Proof is in the photos. The climate is changing, and the glaciers are receding. If current climate patterns persist, scientists predict no glaciers will remain by the year 2030.

View along Going-to-the-Sun Road

Biking

Biking **Going-to-the-Sun Road (GTSR)** is becoming more popular each year. Cross-country pedalers often choose Logan Pass as their destination to cross the Continental Divide because of its breathtaking scenery. However, it typically first opens in mid-June, depending on the amount of spring snow. But have an alternate route in mind, because in 2011 GTSR did not open completely until July 12.

Once it opens, it is almost immediately flooded with motorists. Traffic is heaviest between 10am and 3pm, and **GTSR is closed to bike use from 11am to 4pm (mid-June until Labor Day)**. This closure affects the road from Apgar turn-off to Sprague Creek Campground and eastbound from Logan Creek to Logan Pass. This means you'll have to squeeze in your heart-pumping, leg-burning ride in the morning or evening.

Winds can be extremely strong, especially on the park's eastern side. Portions of GTSR can be under construction, and often unpaved, so use extreme caution when approaching blind corners and steep downhill stretches. The road is narrow, and cyclists must pull to the shoulder if four or more vehicles stack behind you. Several campgrounds (page 253) along GTSR have reduced fee campsites for cyclists traveling without a vehicle. Bike rental is not available in the park.

Fishing

Fishing is allowed, but strict regulations are enforced to preserve the park's native fish populations. A few areas experience fishing closures to aid in repopulating certain species. River and stream fishing season is from the third Saturday in May through November 30. Lake fishing is open all year. Bull trout and cutthroat trout are subject to catch and release, except at a few designated areas. A fishing license is not required, but park regulations must be followed. Stop at a visitor center to obtain a copy of current regulations and to be briefed on fishing closures. **Glacier Park Inc.**, offers full-day ($450 based on two anglers) and half-day ($350) fishing excursions. For more information call (406) 892-2525 or click their website at www.glacierparkinc.com.

Horseback Riding

Guided trail rides are available at **Many Glacier**, **Lake McDonald**, and **Apgar**. Swan Mountain Outfitters (877.888.5557, www.swanmountainoutfitters.com/glacier/) is the park's trail ride concessioner. Stables are typically open from mid-May until mid-September. Rides come in a variety of lengths for reasonable prices: 1-hour ($40), 2-hour ($60), half-day ($107), and full-day ($160).

Red Bus & Boat Tours

Red Bus Tours: Red buses are 17-passenger convertible touring sedans. They form the oldest fleet of passenger carrying vehicles anywhere in the world. Operating since the late 1930s, these antique autos have earned the name **"red jammers,"** because of the gear jamming that occurred while scaling the steep grades of Going-to-the-Sun Road. Do not let their antique status deter you from the tour. The entire fleet was rebuilt in 2001 to run on propane, and they've been going strong ever since.

If you only have a day, a red bus tour is the most relaxing, informative, and comprehensive way to experience the park. A variety of tours are offered departing from various lodgings. The most inclusive is **Big Sky Circle Tour**. It departs from Glacier Park Lodge ($80/Adult, $40/Child), Glacier Meadows RV Park ($85/$42.50), and Izzak Walton Inn ($90/$45). In 8.5 hours you'll loop around the southern boundary following US-2, crossing the Continental Divide at Marias Pass, and then you'll return through the heart of the park via all 50 miles of Going-to-the-Sun Road, crossing the divide once more at Logan Pass. Individual tours of **Going-to-the-Sun Road**, **Waterton Lakes National Park (Canada)**, and the park's other entrances are also available. **Eastern Alpine Tour** is the least expensive offering. This 2.5 hour long tour departs Rising Sun Motor Inn, and costs $30/Adult and $15/Child. It's also available from St. Mary Lodge, St. Mary KOA, Many Glacier Hotel, and Swiftcurrent Motor Inn, but is longer and more expensive from these locations. All tours typically run from mid-June until mid-September. For a complete listing of departure locations, rates, and dates call (406) 892-2525 or click www.glacierparkinc.com.

Sun Tours (800.786.9220, www.glaciersuntours.com) offers tours of the park aboard their 25-passenger, large windowed, air-conditioned coaches. Trips departing East Glacier or Browning are 7.5 hours long and cost $75/Adult, $25/Child (5–12 years old), and children under 5 are free. A four hour tour costs $40/Adult and $20/Child.

Boat Tours: Not to be outdone by the "**Red Jammers**," many of the wooden tour boats have been in operation since before the Great Depression. From these historic boats you can sit back and enjoy some of the most majestic alpine scenery found anywhere in the world (without having to trudge up a steep mountain trail). Boat tours are available at **Lake McDonald Lodge** (Lake McDonald), **Many Glacier Hotel** (Swiftcurrent Lake), **Rising Sun Motor Inn** (St. Mary Lake), and **Two Medicine** (Two Medicine Lake). Cruises range from 45 minutes to 1.5 hours, and cost between $16 to $24 per adult and $8 to $12 per child. Tours typically operate from mid-June until Labor Day. For a complete listing of tour descriptions, rates, and dates call (406) 257-2426 or click www.glacierparkboats.com.

Driving

Going-to-the-Sun Road (GTSR) exists because of the foresight of **Stephen Mather**, the National Park Service's first Director, who chose to construct a more expensive, less obtrusive route across the divide. This route unlocks many of the most spectacular landscapes to motorists. Whether it's in your own car, a Red Jammer, or the park's free shuttle (page 248), do not skip touring GTSR. A word of warning about taking your own car: parking areas (Logan Pass in particular) do fill up. You should really consider taking the free shuttle.

Red Jammers © Bruce Tuten (Savannah, Georgia)

Mountain Goat

Boating/Rafting

Hundreds of streams originate and flow from these mountains. Triple Divide Peak, just west of Cut Bank, is essentially the apex of the continent. Within one square-foot, water from the peak can become part of the Columbia, Mississippi, and Saskatchewan River systems. Respectively, these rivers flow into the Pacific Ocean, Gulf of Mexico, and Hudson Bay. Altogether there are more than 700 lakes here, but only 131 are named. Lake McDonald is the largest at 9.4 miles long and 1.5 miles wide. It's also the deepest at 464 feet. The lakes are popular spots for boating and paddling. **Motorized watercraft** (except jet-skis) are permitted on Lake McDonald, Waterton, Sherburne, St. Mary, Bowman, and Two Medicine Lakes. Bowman and Two Medicine Lakes are limited to boats with motors not exceeding ten horsepower. **Motorboats, rowboats, canoes, and kayaks are available for rent at Many Glacier, Lake McDonald, St. Mary Lake, and Two Medicine Lake**. Rentals are provided by **Glacier Boat Co.** (406.257.2426, www.glacierparkboats.com).

Several **rafting companies** (page 266) offer inflatable kayak trips on the Middle and North Forks of Flathead River. North Fork forms the park's western boundary while Middle Fork is just outside the park.

Glacial melt lake as seen from Highline Trail © Sam and Katie Johnsrud

Winter Activities

In winter, Going-to-the-Sun Road is buried beneath several feet of snow, but trails remain open to intrepid **snowshoers** and **cross-country skiers**. If you plan on visiting in winter, it's a good idea to check with a park ranger about weather and snow conditions before heading out. Information is available at Apgar Information Center on weekends, and Park headquarters (near West Glacier) and Hudson Bay District Office (near St. Mary) on weekdays. Ranger stations are open intermittently depending on staffing. **Ski trails** are available at Apgar (West Glacier), Lake McDonald, North Fork, St. Mary, Two Medicine, and Marias Pass Areas. Most routes are unmarked, so plan ahead and carry a map. Be sure to sign the trail registry before heading out. **Backcountry camping** is allowed (with a permit) during winter, but it should only be attempted by experienced, well-equipped parties. **Ice fishing** is allowed within park boundaries.

<u>Visitor Centers:</u> Glacier has three visitor centers. All three are situated along Going-to-the-Sun Road: one on each end, and another in the middle. **St. Mary Visitor Center** is located at the scenic byway's eastern end. It's open daily, mid-May through mid-October, from 8am to 5pm. Hours are extended to 7am–9pm from late June to Labor Day. **Logan Pass Visitor Center** is located on the Continental Divide. It's opening date depends on the amount of spring snow, but it usually opens by mid-June. Hours are typically 9:30am–4:30pm, but extend to 7am–9pm from late June through Labor Day. **Apgar Visitor Center** is located on the western end of GTSR. It's open between May and June daily from 9am–5pm. **Ranger stations** at **Many Glacier** and **Two Medicine** are open between late May and mid-September from 7am–5pm.

<u>Glacier Institute</u> (406.755.1211, www.glacierinstitute.org) provides educational adventures for children and adults.

<u>For Kids:</u> For children, whether it's the rugged magnificence of the Rocky Mountains, coming face-to-face with a mountain goat, or catching a glimpse of a grizzly bear as it runs away, Glacier National Park is often a spell-binding place. To help introduce children to these experiences and other natural wonders, a **Junior Ranger Program** is offered for children at least 5 years old. To become a Junior Ranger, children are asked to complete five activities from the free Junior Ranger booklet (available at any visitor center), and to attend a Ranger-led Program. Children receive an official Junior Ranger badge and certificate upon completion.

<u>Ranger Programs:</u> Intimidated by the vast network of trails? Unsure what activities are worth the money? Scared of bears? Join a Ranger Program. They're structured, free (unless a boat trip is required), and safe. Grab a copy of the park's newspaper, ***The Waterton–Glacier Guide***, for a complete listing of ranger-led activities.

Thanks to the park's partnership with Canada's Waterton Lakes National Park, you can take part in the unique **International Peace Park Hike** with rangers from both parks. The journey begins at Waterton (Canada) and from there you hike across the U.S.–Canada border to Goat Haunt. The trip back to Waterton is an easy one. All you have to do is hop aboard a boat (page 249, fee) and enjoy the ride as you travel the length of Waterton

Lake. Remember your passport. You won't need it to cross the backcountry border, but it is required at all roadway customs stations found along the U.S.–Canada border. Each hike is limited to 25 people. Registration is required. Reservations are only accepted for the next scheduled hike in person or over the phone at Waterton (403.859.5133) or St. Mary Visitor Center (604.732.7750).

Many Glacier is a great area for ranger programs. The best hikes are made even better by joining a ranger to **Grinnell Glacier** or **Iceberg Lake** (page 254). The trip to Grinnell Glacier includes a short boat trip for a moderate fee ($23, one-way).

Two Medicine area offers programs less frequently than sites like Many Glacier or Logan Pass, but they are no less spectacular. Full-day hikes to **Cobalt Lake**, **Dawson Pass**, and **Fireband Pass** are a few of the highlighted programs. At St. Mary, the **"History in the Making"** program is great for families. In just three hours you'll explore the park's past, present, and future. You'll even get to write a letter that will be placed in a time capsule. At Logan Pass you can join a ranger on a **Highline Trail Hike** (page 254) to Granite Park Chalet or skirt Garden Wall to Haystack Butte. An assortment of walks, talks, and evening programs are available at Lake McDonald Valley. In short, you can't go wrong wherever you go. In summer you'll find engaging ranger programs in any developed area.

Flora & Fauna: First thought to come to the minds of many visitors is **grizzly bears**. They might be afraid of them. Intrigued by them. Maybe, want to cuddle with them. Or they just know that a healthy population of some 700 grizzlies roam the northern continental divide area. For the most part bears are shy and skittish, just like the rest of the animal kingdom (only bigger and furrier). But some can be extremely dangerous, especially if you startle one or find yourself between a mother and her cub. Still, bears have only been responsible for a handful of deaths, nowhere near the quantity of the park's number one killer (drowning).

You may see a bear on your visit to Glacier, but it's more likely that you return home having seen mountain goats, bighorn sheep, and deer. Glacier protects a remarkably intact ecosystem. Nearly all of its known plant and animal species still exist. Woodland caribou and bison are the only missing mammals. Gray wolf naturally returned to the area in the 1980s. Canadian lynx, wolverine, moose, elk, coyote, and mountain lion also call glacier home. **More than 270 species of birds** visit or reside here as well.

Moose and calf

About 1,000 species of plants exist at Glacier. Wildflowers can be seen during every season except winter. Beargrass is commonly found between June and July. Trees are dominated by conifers, but deciduous cottonwoods and aspens can be found in the lower elevations.

Pets: Pets are allowed in the park, but must be kept on a leash no more than six feet in length at all times. They are only allowed in drive-in campgrounds, along park roads open to motor vehicles, and in picnic areas. Pets are prohibited from all hiking trails and the backcountry.

Accessibility: Apgar and St. Mary Visitor Centers are wheelchair accessible. A few of the park's interpretive programs are accessible; these programs are highlighted in the park's newspaper, *The Waterton–Glacier Guide*, available at visitor centers and entrance stations. Trail of the Cedars and Running Eagle Falls Nature Trail are fully accessible.

Weather: Visitors should come prepared for all weather conditions. The temperature difference from low altitude to high altitude is usually about 15°F. Most rain falls in the park's western valleys. The eastern slopes are normally sunny and windy. Summer highs can reach 90°F, but overnight lows can drop into the 20s°F. Snow is possible any month of the year. In August of 2005, eight inches of snow fell in a single night, forcing hundreds of backpackers out of the backcountry. Winter snowpack averages 16 feet. It closes Going-to-the-Sun Road for most of the year. The scenic byway is usually completely open by mid-June, but occasionally, like in 2011, it does not open completely until mid-July.

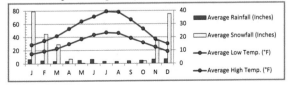

Vacation Planner

To hikers, backpackers, and admirers of natural beauty, Glacier invokes feelings of pure bliss. Enter this majestic land and you'll want to stay forever. Sadly, visitors come and go, taking with them only memories and photographs. It's incredibly difficult to get enough of Glacier. There are dozens of sites where you'd like to pull out a lawn chair, kick-up your feet and enjoy the views. But, this is unrealistic. Busy work schedules and busier lifestyles limit most guests' time to no more than a few days. If you only have a day, drive **Going-to-the-Sun Road** (page 261), stopping at **Logan Pass** to hike **Highline Trail** (page 254). Three days allows enough time to visit the most beautiful developed areas, but it's hardly enough time to get into the **backcountry** (page 259) or explore **Waterton Lakes National Park** (page 249). Below is a sample three day itinerary. It visits the most popular areas and attractions. This isn't to say that **Cut Bank** and **Two Medicine**, along the park's eastern boundary, aren't worth a visit. Nor that hiking to **Goat Haunt** isn't a good idea. It covers the most popular and arguably the most beautiful destinations. As is the case with any national park vacation, squeeze in the **ranger programs** (page 262) whenever you can. Nearby dining, grocery stores, lodging, festivals, and attractions are listed on pages 265–267.

Begin your trip at **Many Glacier** and plan on arriving early. You'll have to if you want to secure a campsite, but an early arrival allows sufficient time to hike a couple of this area's wonderful trails (a must for all hiking enthusiasts). Two in particular should be at the top of your wish list. **Iceberg Lake and Grinnell Glacier Trails** (page 254) are essential hikes. An ambitious hiker can complete both trails in a day (more than 20 miles of hiking). **Grinnell Glacier Trail** can be shortened by 3.4 miles (roundtrip) by boarding a boat operated by **Glacier Parks Boat Co.** (406.257.2426, www.glacierparkboats.com). A one-way ticket costs $23.75/Adult and $12/Child. Those of you who enjoy hiking at a more leisurely pace or sitting and enjoying a picnic should choose one or the other. It's extremely easy to fill free time at Many Glacier. You can complete the short hike from Many Glacier Hotel to **Appekunny Falls** or rest your feet in the waters of **Swiftcurrent Lake**. Schedule permitting, spend the evening with a park ranger at the campground or Many Glacier Hotel.

Tired of hiking? If you answered "yes" spend today on a **Red Bus Tour** (page 260). **International Peace Park Tour** (valid passport required) departs from Many Glacier Hotel, but other locations are available on the park's east side.

Red Bus Tours aren't for everyone. Although unique, educational and altogether enjoyable, they are expensive and can take all day. An alternative to the Red Bus Tour, is to head over to St. Mary Lake Visitor Center. Take the **shuttle** to **Logan Pass** (drive yourself if you plan on **camping** • page 253). Here you'll find **Highline Trail** (page 254). An absolute must and the best trail in the park. Underline it. Circle it. Star it. Highlight it. Do whatever you have to do to remind yourself to hike this trail. It's more than 20 miles long, but you don't have to hike far to appreciate its stunning beauty. However, the farther you go, the greater the rewards. It follows the **Continental Divide** and **Garden Wall** for much of its length. The cliffs are precipitous and the scenery is mesmerizing. Hike as far as you care to, no matter what the distance you will not be disappointed. To experience the backcountry without sleeping in a tent consider reserving a night at **Granite Park Chalet** (page 253), which can be accessed via Highline Trail (among others). **Hidden Lake Self-Guiding Nature Trail**, also at Logan Pass, is a nice little hike.

If you went with the **Red Jammer** yesterday, hike **Highline Trail** today. Otherwise, get an early start and take the shuttle (or car, if you must) to **Avalanche Lake** (page 258) for a 4-mile hike to waterfalls and an alpine lake. It's a popular destination, so the earlier the better. If, through some sort of Glacier Park miracle your legs are fresh and ready for a 12+ mile hike, climb back aboard the **shuttle** and exit at **Sperry Trailhead** (page 258). Hike to **Sperry Chalet** for an incredible view of **Lake McDonald**. If you were interested in spending the night at Granite Park Chalet but it was booked, give Sperry a try. There'd be no better way to end a trip in this magical place. Those hiking out-and-back to Sperry Chalet should make sure you return in time to catch the last shuttle).

Non-hikers, skip Sperry Trail and exit the shuttle at **Lake McDonald Lodge**, where you can wander the shores, reflecting upon your vacation as the mountains reflect in the shimmering water.

Dining

East of Glacier National Park

Park Café • (406) 732-5566
3147 US-89; Browning, MT 59417
www.parkcafe.us • Breakfast: $5–13

Serranos Mexican Rest. • (406) 226-9392
29 Dawson Ave; East Glacier Pk, MT 59434

Luna's Restaurant • (406) 226-4433
1112 US-49; East Glacier Pk, MT 59434

Firebrand Food & Ale • (406) 226-9374
20629 US-2; East Glacier Pk, MT 59434

Two Medicine Grill • (406) 226-9227
314 US-2; East Glacier Pk, MT 59434

Whistlestop Restaurant • (406) 226-9292
1024 MT-49; East Glacier Park, MT 59434

Backpackers Inn • (406) 226-9392
29 Dawson Ave; East Glacier Park, MT 59434

Junction Café • (406) 338-2386
US-2 & US-89; Browning, MT 59417

Cattle Baron • (406) 732-4033
3 Babb St; Babb, MT 59411

Two Sisters Café • (406) 732-5535
Babb, Blackfeet, MT 59411
www.twosistersofmontana.com

Leaning Tree Café • (406) 338-5322
MT-464; Blackfeet, MT 59411

West of Glacier National Park

Eddie's Café & Ice Cream • (406) 888-5361
1 Fish Creek Campground; Apgar, MT 59936
www.eddiescafegifts.com

Northern Lights Saloon & Café • (406) 888-9963
255 Polebridge Loop; Polebridge, MT 59928

Glacier Grill & Pizza • (406) 387-4223
10126 E US-2; Coram, MT 59913

Elkhorn Grill • (406) 387-4030
105 Hungry Horse Blvd; Hungry Horse, MT 59919

The Huckleberry Patch • (800) 527-7340
8868 US-2 E; Hungry Horse, MT 59919
www.huckleberrypatch.com • pie, fudge, & gifts

Montana Coffee Traders • (406) 892-7696
30 9th St W; Columbia Falls, MT 59912
www.coffeetraders.com • coffee, tea, & gifts

Nite Owl Restaurant • (406) 892-3131
522 9th St W; Columbia Falls, MT 59912
www.niteowlbackroom.com

Three Forks Grille • (406) 892-2023
729 Nucleus Ave; Columbia Falls, MT 59912
www.threeforksgrille.com • Entrée: $15–23

Buffalo Café • (406) 862-2833
514 3rd St; Whitefish, MT 59937

Café Kandahar • (406) 862-6247
3824 Big Mtn Rd; Whitefish, MT 59937
www.cafekandahar.com

Tupelo Grille • (406) 862-6136
17 Central Ave; Whitefish, MT 59937
www.tupelogrille.com • Entrée: $18–29

Wasabi Sushi Bar • (406) 863-9283
419 2nd St E; Whitefish, MT 59937
www.wasabimt.com

Ciao Mambo • (406) 863-9600
234 2nd St E; Whitefish, MT 59937
www.ciaomambo.com

Great Northern Bar & Grill • (406) 862-2816
27 Central Ave; Whitefish, MT 59937
www.greatnorthernbar.com • Sandwiches: $5–8

Sweet Peaks Ice Cream • (406) 863-9973
419 3rd St; Whitefish, MT 59937
www.sweetpeaksicecream.com

MacKenzie River Pizza • (406) 862-6601
9 Central Ave; Whitefish, MT 59937
www.mackenzieriverpizza.com

McGarry's Roadhouse • (406) 862-6223
510 Wisconsin Ave; Whitefish, MT 59937
www.mcgarrysroadhouse.com • Entrée: $17–30

Rising Sun Bistro • (406) 862-1236
549 Wisconsin Ave; Whitefish, MT 59937
www.risingsunbistro.com • Entrée: $14–29

Ed & Mully's Restaurant • (406) 862-1980
3905 Big Mtn Rd; Whitefish, MT 59937
www.skiwhitefish.com

Pescado Blanco • (406) 862-3290
235 1st St; Whitefish, MT 59937
www.pescadoblanco.com • Dinners: $12–21

Bulldog Saloon • (406) 862-5636
144 Central Ave; Whitefish, MT 59937

Piggyback Barbeque • (406) 863-9895
102 Wisconsin Ave; Whitefish, MT 59937
www.piggybackbbq.com • Sandwiches: $7–10

Quickee Sandwich Shop • (406) 862-9866
28 Lupfer Ave; Whitefish, MT 59937
www.thequickee.com • Entrée: $10–14

Whitefish Lake Restaurant • (406) 862-5285
1200 US-93 N; Whitefish, MT 59937
www.whitefishlakerestaurant.com • Entrée: $19–37

Red Caboose Café • (406) 863-4563
101 Central Ave; Whitefish, MT 59937
www.redcaboosecafe.com • Sandwiches: $7–10

Mrs Spoonover's • (406) 862-9381
533 2nd St E; Whitefish, MT 59937
www.mrsspoonovers.com • Sandwiches: $4–9

LouLa's • (406) 862-5614
300 2nd St E, # B; Whitefish, MT 59937

Moose's Saloon • (406) 755-2337
173 N Main St, Kalispell • www.moosessaloon.com

Heaven's Peak Restaurant • (406) 387-4754
US-2; Kalispell, MT 59901

Grocery Stores

East of Glacier National Park

Glacier Park Trading Co • (406) 226-9227
316 US-2; East Glacier Pk, MT 59434

Brownie Grocery • (406) 727-4448
1020 MT-49; East Glacier Pk, MT 59434

Albertsons • (406) 873-5035
501 W Main; Cut Bank, MT 59427

West of Glacier National Park

Super 1 Foods • (406) 892-9996
2100 9th St W; Columbia Falls, MT 59912

Safeway • (406) 862-2526
6580 US-93; Whitefish, MT 59937

Walmart Supercenter • (406) 756-7250
1150 East Idaho Street; Kalispell, MT 59901

Lodging

East of Glacier National Park

Mountain Pine Motel • (406) 226-4403
909 US-49; East Glacier Pk, MT 59434
www.mtnpine.com • Rates: $51–171/night

Travelers Rest Lodge • (406) 226-9143
20987 US-2 E; East Glacier Pk, MT 59434
www.travelersrestlodge.net • Rates: $129–159

East Glacier Motel • (406) 226-5593
1107 US-49; East Glacier Park, MT 59936
www.eastglacier.com • Rates: $54–139

Bison Creek Ranch • (406) 226-4482
20722 US-2 W; East Glacier Pk, MT 59434
www.bisoncreekranch.com • Rates: $65–110

St Mary-Glacier Park KOA • (406) 732-4122
106 W Shore Dr; Browning, MT 59417

Izaak Walton Inn • (406) 888-5700
290 Izaak Walton Inn Rd; Essex, MT 59916
www.izaakwaltoninn.com • Rates: $117–245

Glacier Haven Inn • (406) 888-5720
14305 US-2 E; Essex, MT 59916
www.glacierhaveninn.com • Rates: $149–349

St Mary Lodge & Resort • (406) 732-4431
US-89 and GTSR; Saint Mary, MT 59417
www.stmarylodgeandresort.com • Rates: $139–399

Duck Lake Lodge • (406) 338-5770
3215 Duck Lake Rd; Babb, MT 59411
www.montanasducklakelodge.com

West of Glacier National Park

Belton Chalet and Lodge • (406) 888-5000
12575 US-2 E; West Glacier, MT 59936
www.beltonchalet.com • Rates: $99–325

Glacier Highland Motel • (406) 888-5427
US-2 E; West Glacier, MT 59936

Glacier Guides Lodge • (406) 387-5555
120 Highline Blvd; West Glacier, MT 59936
www.glacierguides.com • Rates: $171

Vista Motel • (406) 888-5311
12340 US-2 E; West Glacier, MT 59936
www.glaciervistamotel.com • Rates: $95–155

Great Northern Resort • (800) 735-7897
12127 US-E; West Glacier, MT 59936
www.greatnorthernresort.com • Chalets: $295–315

The Great Bear Inn • (406) 250-4577
5672 Blankenship Rd; West Glacier, MT 59936
www.thegreatbearinn.com • Cabins: $345–385

Moccasin Lodge • (406) 888-5545
US-2 E ; West Glacier, MT 59936

Glacier Wilderness Resort • (406) 888-5664
163 US-2 E; West Glacier, MT 59936
www.glacierwildernessresort.com • Cabins: $250–295

San-Suz-Ed Trailer Park • (406) 387-5280
11505 US-2 E; West Glacier, MT 59936
www.sansuzedrvpark.com • Rates: $30–95

Glaciers' Mountain Resort • (406) 387-5712
1385 Old Hwy 2; Coram, Montana 59913

Mini Golden Inns Motel • (406) 387-4313
8955 US-2 E; Hungry Horse, MT 59919
www.hungryhorselodging.com • Rates: $118–136

Glacier Park Inn B&B • (406) 387-5099
9128 US-2; Hungry Horse, MT 59919
www.glacierparkinn.com • Rates: $100–150

Historic Tamarack Lodge & Cabins • (406) 387-4420
9549 US-2 E; Hungry Horse, MT 59919
www.historictamaracklodge.com • Rates: $50–250

Meadow Lake Resort • (406) 892-8700
100 Saint Andrews Dr; Columbia Falls, MT 59912
www.meadowlake.com

Evergreen Motel • (406) 387-5365
10159 US-2; Columbia Falls, MT 59912
www.evergreenmotelglacier.com • Rates: $65–95

Apgar Village Lodge • (406) 888-5484
200 GTSR; Columbia Falls, MT 59912

Smoky Bear Ranch B&B • (406) 387-4249
4761 Smokey Bear Ln; Columbia Falls, MT 59912

Moss Mountain Inn • (406) 387-4605
4655 N Fork Rd; Columbia Falls, MT 59912
www.mossmountaininn.com • Rates: $159–179

Glacier Chalet • (406) 250-6546
5010 Blankenship Rd; Columbia Falls, MT 59912

Garden Wall Inn • (888) 530-1700
504 Spokane Ave; Whitefish, MT 59937
www.gardenwallinn.com • Rates: $155–195

North Forty Resort • (406) 862-7740
3765 Mt Hwy 40 W; Columbia Falls, MT 59912
www.northfortyresort.com • Cabins: $209–269

Lodge At Whitefish Lake • (406) 863-4000
1380 Wisconsin Ave; Whitefish, MT 59937
www.lodgeatwhitefishlake.com • Rates: $301–395

Chalet Motel • (406) 862-5581
6430 US-93 S; Whitefish, MT 59937

Julie's Country Manor • (406) 270-4595
1065 K M Ranch Rd; Whitefish, MT 59937
www.juliescountrymanor.com • Rates: $145–175

Bailey's Bed 'N Bale • (406) 270-1603
475 Timber Doodle Ln; Whitefish, MT 59937
www.montanabednbale.com • Rates: $325

Duck Inn Lodge • (406) 862-3825
1305 Columbia Ave; Whitefish, MT 59937
www.duckinn.com • Rates: $94–250

Cheap Sleep Motel • (406) 862-5515
6400 US-93 S; Whitefish, MT 59937
www.cheapsleepmotel.com • Rates: $70–85

Grouse Mountain Lodge • (406) 862-3000
2 Fairway Dr; Whitefish, MT 59937
www.grousemountainlodge.com • Rates: $199

Hidden Moose Lodge • (406) 862-6516
1735 East Lakeshore Dr; Whitefish, MT 59937
www.hiddenmooselodge.com • Rates: $99–189

Good Medicine Lodge • (406) 862-5488
537 Wisconsin Ave; Whitefish, MT 59937
www.goodmedicinelodge.com • Rates: $175–185

Bay Point On the Lake • (406) 862-2331
300 Bay Point Dr; Whitefish, MT 59937
www.baypoint.org

Festivals

Winterfest • January
Seeley Lake • www.seeleylakechamber.com

Whitefish Winter Carnival • February
Whitefish • www.whitefishwintercarnival.com

Race to the Sky Sled Dog Race • February
Helena • www.racetothesky.org

Int'l Wildlife Film Festival • May
Missoula • www.wildlifefilms.org

Loon & Fish Festival • May
Seeley Lake • www.alpineartisans.org

Lewis & Clark Festival • June
Great Falls, MT • www.lewisandclarkia.com

North American Indian Days • July
Browning, MT • www.blackfeetnation.com

Libby Nordicfest • July
Libby, MT • www.libbynordicfest.org

Kootenai River Bluegrass Festival • July
Troy • www.krbgf.org

Arts in the Park • July
Kalispell • www.hockadaymuseum.org

Western Rendezvous of Art • August
Helena, MT • www.westrendart.org

Montana Quilt Show • August
Eureka • www.eurekaquiltshow.com

Glacier Jazz Stampede • October
Kalispell • www.glacierjazzstampede.com

Coeur d'Alene Resort Holiday Light Show
November–December • www.coeurdalene.org

Attractions

East of Glacier National Park

Glacier Peaks Casino • (406) 338-2274
209 N Piegan Rd, Browning, MT 59417
www.glaciercash.com

Blackfeet Outfitters • (406) 450-8420
Fishing and hunting trips, RV sites available
10, Hwy 17; Blackfeet, MT 59411
www.blackfeetoutfitters.com

Museum of the Plains Indian • (406) 338-2230
US-89 & US-2; South Browning, MT 59417

Rocky Mtn Elk Foundation • (800) 225-5355
5705 Grant Creek Rd; Missoula, MT 59808
www.rmef.org

Waterton Lakes Nat'l Park • (888) 773-8888
Alberta 5; Alberta T0K2M0, Canada
www.pc.gc.ca • Entrance Fee: $8/Adult

Discovery Ski • (406) 563-2184
1 Discovery Basin Rd; Anaconda, MT 59711
www.skidiscovery.com • Lift Ticket: $38/Adult

Giant Springs State Park • (406) 454-5840
Great Falls, Montana

C M Russell Museum • (406) 727-8787
400 13th St N; Great Falls, MT 59401
www.cmrussell.org • Admission: $9/Adult

The Lewis and Clark Interpretive Center
4201 Giant Springs Rd, # 2; Great Falls, MT 59405
www.fs.usda.gov • (406) 452-5661

Montana State Capitol • 406-444-2694
1301 E 6th Ave; Helena, MT 59601
www.visit-the-capitol.mt.gov • Tours: Free

Montana Hist. Society • (406) 444-2694
225 N Roberts; Helena, Montana 59620
www.mhs.mt.gov • Admission: $5/Adult

Cathedral of Saint Helena • (406) 442-5825
530 N Ewing St; Helena, Montana 59601
www.sthelenas.org • Tours Available

&Last Chance Ranch • (406) 442-2884
Wagon ride dinners, lodging, and music
2884 Grizzly Gulch Dr; Helena, MT 59601
www.lastchanceranch.biz

Mount Helena Park • Helena, MT

Holter Museum of Art • (406) 442-6400
12 East Lawrence St; Helena, MT 59601
www.holtermuseum.org

Great Northern Carousel • (406) 457-5353
924 Bicentennial Plaza; Helena, MT 59601
www.gncarousel.com

West of Glacier National Park

Great Northern Whitewater • (406) 387-5340
Lodging, rafting, fishing, and kayaking
PO Box 270; West Glacier, MT 59936
www.gnwhitewater.com

Wild River Adventures • (406) 387-9453
Rafting, trail rides, and fishing
PO Box 272; West Glacier, MT 59936
www.riverwild.com

&Glacier Outdoor Center • (800) 235-6781
Lodging, rafting, and fishing
12400 US-2 E; West Glacier, MT 59936
www.glacierraftco.com

&Glacier Guides & Raft • (800) 521-7238
Lodging, hiking, fishing, and rafting
11970 US-2 E; West Glacier, MT 59936
www.glacierguides.com

Glacier View Golf Course • (406) 888-5471
640 River Bend Dr; West Glacier, MT 59936
www.glacierviewgolf.com • *Rates: $29/18 holes*

Glacier Heli-Tours • (406) 387-4141
11950 US-2 E; West Glacier, MT 59936

Kruger Helicop-Tours • (406) 387-4565
11892 US-2 E; South Fork, MT 59936

Amazing Fun Center • (406) 387-5902
Maze, bumper cars, go-carts, and mini-golf
10265 US-2 E; Coram, MT 59913
www.amazingfuncenter.com

Trails-End Tours • (406) 387-4053
Bus, hiking, hunting, and fishing tours
93 Corbett Ln; Coram, MT 59913
www.trailsendtours.com

Swan Mtn Outfitters • (406) 387-4405
Apgar Corral; Coram, MT 59913

Rocky Mtn Nature Co • (406) 892-4736
111 Hungry Horse Blvd; Hungry Horse, MT 59919

House of Mystery • (406) 892-1210
7800 US-2 E; Columbia Falls, MT 59912
www.montanavortex.com • *Admission: $9/Adult*

Glacier Heli Tours
West Glacier; Columbia Falls, MT 59912

Big Sky Waterpark • (406) 892-5025
7211 US-2 E; Columbia Falls, MT 59912
www.bigskywp.com • *Rates: $24/Adult*

Glacier Lanes & Casino • (406) 892-5858
307 Nucleus Ave; Columbia Falls, MT 59912

Great Northern Llama Co • (406) 755-9044
600 Blackmer Ln; Columbia Falls, MT 59912
www.gnllama.com

Meadow Lake Golf Course • (406) 892-2111
100 Saint Andrews Dr; Columbia Falls, MT 59912
www.meadowlakegolf.com • *Rates: $57/18 holes*

J & L RV Rentals • (406) 892-7666
Guided tours and snowmobile rentals available
5410 US-2 W; Columbia Falls, MT 59912
www.jlsnowmobilerentals.com

Ferks Casino • (406) 892-3898
329 9th St W; Columbia Falls, MT 59912

&Glacier Park Boat • (406) 257-2426
Boat tours, rentals, and guided hikes
PO Box 5262; Kalispell, MT 59903
www.glacierparkboats.com

Winter Wonderland Sports • (406) 881-2525
Snowmobile Rental ($135+/full-day)
162 Red Fox Run; Kalispell, MT 59901
www.winterwonderlandsports.com

Flathead National Forest • (406) 758-5200
650 Wolfpack Way; Kalispell, MT 59901
www.fs.fed.us

&Conrad Mansion • (406) 755-2166
330 Woodland Ave; Kalispell, MT 59901
www.conradmansion.com • *Admission: $8/Adult*

Signature Theatres • (406) 752-7804
185 Hutton Ranch Rd; Kalispell, MT 59901

Best Bet Casino • (406) 862-2949
6588 US-93 S; Whitefish, MT 59937

Dog Sled Adventures • (406) 881-2275
8400 US-93 N; Whitefish, MT 59927
www.dogsledadventuresmontana.com

Glacier Cyclery & Fitness • (406) 862-6446
326 2nd St E; Whitefish, MT 59937
www.glaciercyclery.com • *Rentals available*

Big Mountain Ski & Summer Resort
163 Ridge Run Dr; Whitefish, MT 59937

Winter Woods Dog Sled Tours • (406) 862-6874
242 Lupfer Ave; Whitefish, MT 59937

Whitefish Theatre Co • (406) 862-5371
1 Central Ave; Whitefish, MT 59937
www.whitefishtheatreco.org

Mountain Cinema • (406) 862-3130
6475 US-93 S; Whitefish, MT 59937

&Whitefish Mtn Resort • (877) 754-3474
3910 Big Mtn Rd; Whitefish, MT 59937
www.skiwhitefish.com • *Lift Ticket: $66/Adult*

&Bar W Guest Ranch • (406) 863-9099
2875 US-93 W; Whitefish, MT 59937
www.thebarw.com • *Excellent dude ranch*

&Black Star Brewery • (406) 863-1000
2 Central Ave; Whitefish, MT 59937
www.greatnorthernbrewing.com • *Summer Tours*

&Daly Mansion • (406) 363-6004
251 Eastside Hwy; Hamilton, MT 59840
www.dalymansion.org • *Tours: $9/Adult*

St Ignatius Mission • (406) 745-2768
300 Beartrack Ave; St. Ignatius, MT 59865

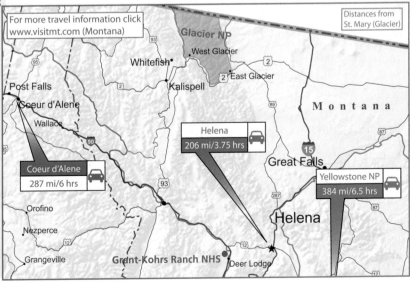

For more travel information click www.visitmt.com (Montana)

Distances from St. Mary (Glacier)

Glacier NP

West Glacier

Whitefish

Kalispell

East Glacier

Post Falls

Coeur d'Alene

Wallace

Montana

Helena
206 mi/3.75 hrs

Great Falls

Coeur d'Alene
287 mi/6 hrs

Yellowstone NP
384 mi/6.5 hrs

Orofino

Nezperce

Helena

Grant-Kohrs Ranch NHS

Grangeville

Deer Lodge

© Ken Lund

Hot Springs • Pages 270–277

Big Bend • Pages 278–285

THE SOUTH

Guadalupe Mountains • Pages 286–293

Carlsbad Caverns • Pages 294–301

Petrified Forest • Pages 302–309

Saguaro • Pages 310–319

THE SOUTH

Hot Springs National Park Headquarters

101 Reserve Street
Hot Springs, AR 71901
Phone: (501) 624-2701
Website: www.nps.gov/hosp

Established: March 4, 1921
Size: 5,550 Acres
Annual Visitors: 1.3 Million
Peak Season: Late Fall
Hiking Trails: 26 Miles

Activities: Baths & Massages,
Hiking, and Museum Tours

Campgrounds: Gulpha Gorge ($10/
night, $24/night with hook-ups)
Backcountry Camping: None

Operational Bathhouses (Bath Rate):
Buckstaff Baths ($30)
Quapaw Baths & Spa ($30)

Park Visitor Center & Museum oc-
cupies historic Fordyce Bathhouse

Park Hours: All day, every day (except Bathhouses and Visitor Center)
Entrance Fee: None

HOT SPRINGS

Hot Springs - Arkansas

Tree-covered mountains, natural hot springs, and ridgeline hiking trails are common ingredients for a national park. Hot Springs possesses these traits, but it's far from your typical park. Mountains crest at 1,400 feet. Mineral hot springs' rich water is collected, monitored, and managed via a complex plumbing system. Trails connect the area's mountains, but the entire network measures just 26 miles, a day of hiking for an industrious individual. So, what attracted Native Americans to this very spot for thousands of years? The answer is hidden underground. In a gap between Hot Springs Mountain and West Mountain, rainwater seeps into the earth at a rate of one foot per year. After some 4,400 years, water has traveled a mile below the surface where it achieves a high temperature, naturally heated by rock under immense pressure. Pressure builds and what took several millennia to flow down now takes one year to return to the surface. Water flowing from the springs today fell as rain when ancient Egyptians were building the pyramids.

The first European to see the springs arrived after an epic journey of his own. Native Americans led **Hernando de Soto** to the place they called **"Valley of the Vapors"** in 1541, after the famed Spanish explorer had sailed half-way around the world. More than a century later, **Father Jacques Marquette** and **Louis Jolliet** explored the area and claimed its land for France. Ownership exchanged hands between French and Spanish several times before becoming American territory in 1803 as part of the **Louisiana Purchase**. Less than one year after the acqui-sition, **President Thomas Jefferson** sent a scientific team led by Dr.

George Hunter and William Dunbar to explore the region known to them as "the hot springs of Washita." Here they discovered a log cabin and several small huts of canvas and wood, built by visitors who believed in the water's healing properties.

The **first baths** were nothing more than excavated rock, spanned by wooden planks where bathers sat and soaked their feet in 150°F water. A true log bathhouse wasn't built until 1830. In 1832, prompted by 12 years of requests by Arkansas Territory, **President Andrew Jackson** signed a law giving the hot springs federal protection as a reservation. **This act makes Hot Springs the oldest unit in the national park system, 40 years older than Yellowstone, the world's first national park**.

During the early days of government operation, hot springs' water was declared federal property and was subsequently sold to bathhouses. Even with having to pay for their water, the **baths of Hot Springs** proved profitable and by the late 19th century facilities on Bathhouse Row rivaled the finest establishments found anywhere in Europe. Opulent structures and rejuvenating waters attracted sports heroes, politicians, and mobsters. From the late 1800s to mid-1900s, Hot Springs became known for organized crime such as gambling, prostitution, and bootlegging. Some of the nation's most infamous gangsters moved in. Al Capone, Frank Costello, and Bugs Moran are just a few who sought refuge at Hot Springs—the original Las Vegas.

Stephen T. Mather, first director of the National Park Service, remained unfazed by the area's corruption. He was actually quite enthusiastic about the hot springs, largely due to his affinity for rubdowns. Shortly thereafter Mather ordered construction of a new, free bathhouse and persuaded Congress to redesignate the reservation as Hot Springs National Park in 1921. Business on Bathhouse Row waxed and waned over the years. Only one bathhouse has remained in continuous operation, and just two are open today.

Hot Springs is an anomaly among its fellow parks whose calling cards are indescribable natural beauty. It's the smallest national park, formed around a natural resource that's used commercially. And that's exactly what's refreshing about Hot Springs—it's different. Oh, and the baths are nice too.

When to Go

Hot Springs National Park is open all year. If you're passing nearby, it can provide a nice break from the road for a couple of hours. Just be warned that summers are often uncomfortably hot and humid. Late fall when leaves are changing color is the best time to visit.

Transportation

Greyhound has a bus station at 1001 Central Ave, Suite D; Hot Springs, AR; which is just one mile south of the park on Central Ave. For more information contact Greyhound by calling (800) 231-2222 or clicking www.greyhound.com.

Airports

Hot Springs Memorial Field is located in Hot Springs, just 4 miles from the park. Little Rock National Airport is located 55 miles to the east, in Little Rock, AR.

Directions

Hot Springs National Park Visitor Center is located at 369 Central Ave; Hot Springs, AR 71901. Hot Springs is easily accessed via US-70 from the east and west. Visitors arriving from the west should take Exit 70B on US-70 into Hot Springs and follow the signs to the park. From the east take US-70 to US-70 Business W/E Grand Ave. Turn right onto Spring St. Continue onto Reserve St, then turn right onto Central Ave, which leads to the visitor center.

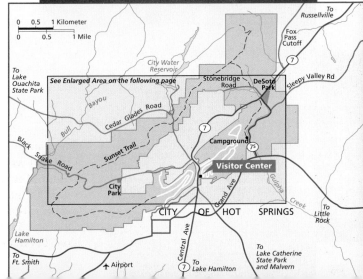

Gulpha Gorge, located off US-70B on the east side of Hot Springs, is the park's only campground. All sites are available on a first-come, first-served basis. Restrooms are located nearby. Showers are not available. Camping fees are $10/night for a standard site and $24/night for a site with electrical, water, and sewer hook-ups. Sites are not pull-through. There are no park/concessioner operated lodgings within park boundaries, but several options exist in the surrounding Hot Springs area (see page 277 for additional lodging information).

Gulpha Gorge Campground • 305 Gorge Road; Hot Springs AR 71901

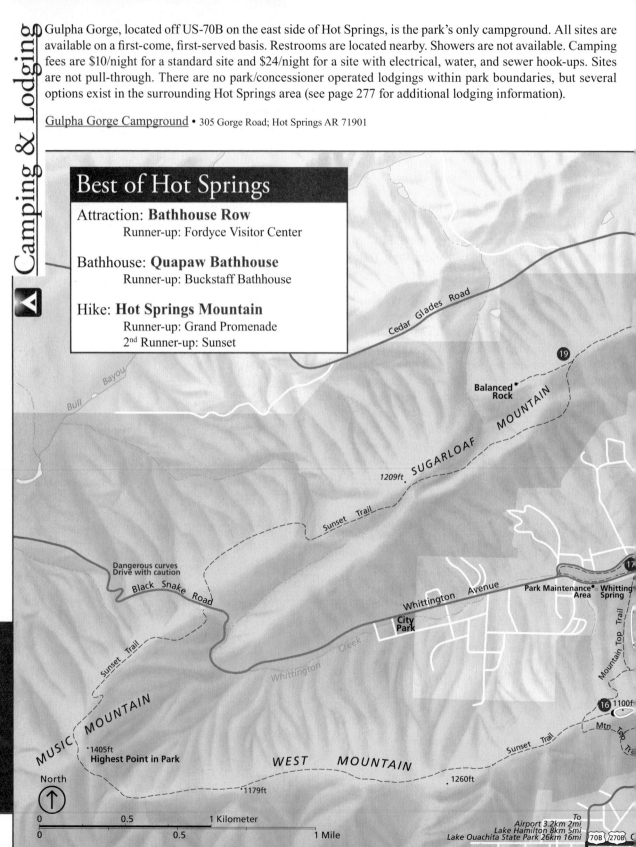

Best of Hot Springs

Attraction: **Bathhouse Row**
    Runner-up: Fordyce Visitor Center

Bathhouse: **Quapaw Bathhouse**
    Runner-up: Buckstaff Bathhouse

Hike: **Hot Springs Mountain**
    Runner-up: Grand Promenade
    2nd Runner-up: Sunset

Cedar Glades Road

19

Balanced Rock

SUGARLOAF MOUNTAIN

1209ft

Sunset Trail

Dangerous curves
Drive with caution
Black Snake Road

Whittington Avenue

Park Maintenance Area • Whitting Spring

17

City Park

Whittington Creek

Mountain Top Trail

Sunset Trail

16 1100f

Mtn Top Tr

MUSIC MOUNTAIN

1405ft
Highest Point in Park

WEST MOUNTAIN

Sunset Trail

1260ft

North

1179ft

0   0.5   1 Kilometer

0   0.5   1 Mile

To
Airport 3.2km 2mi
Lake Hamilton 8km 5mi
Lake Ouachita State Park 26km 16mi

70B 270B

Hot Springs has a total of 26 miles of hiking trails. **Sunset Trail** (17 miles) circles the mountains surrounding Hot Springs, passing the highest point in the park, Music Mountain (1,405 ft). It traverses the park's most remote areas, providing good opportunities to see white-tailed deer and wild turkeys, but it's often broken into smaller sections. The most scenic stretch is the 2.8 miles following Sugarloaf Mountain's ridge. It's located in the northwest corner and can be accessed via Cedar Glades Road or Black Snake Road. Here you'll also find a short spur to **Balanced Rock**, a large novaculite boulder precariously positioned atop another sloped boulder. The remainder of park trails (page 274) are all less than 2 miles in length, forming a small networks of trails on Hot Springs, North, and West Mountains.

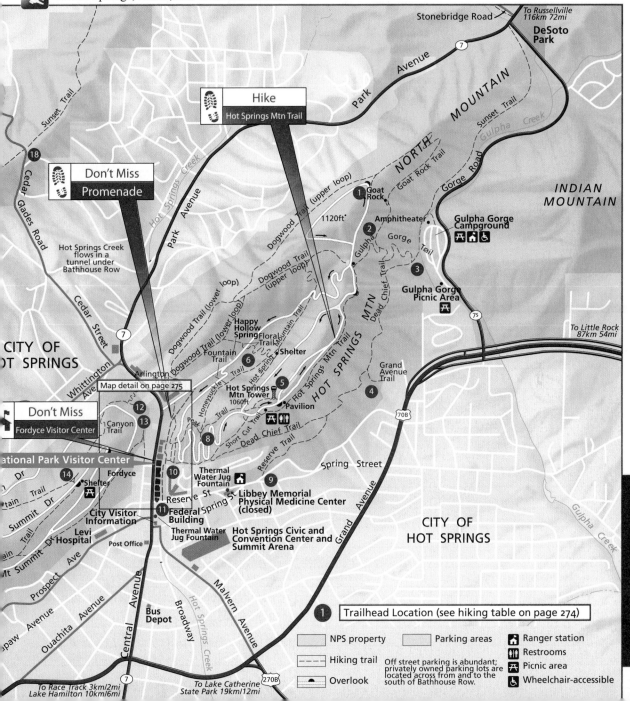

Hike — Hot Springs Mtn Trail

Don't Miss — Promenade

Don't Miss — Fordyce Visitor Center

Hot Springs Creek flows in a tunnel under Bathhouse Row

Map detail on page 275

Trailhead Location (see hiking table on page 274)

NPS property

Parking areas

Hiking trail

Overlook

Ranger station

Restrooms

Picnic area

Wheelchair-accessible

Off street parking is abundant; privately owned parking lots are located across from and to the south of Bathhouse Row.

To Russellville 116km 72mi
To Little Rock 87km 54mi
To Race Track 3km/2mi Lake Hamilton 10km/6mi
To Lake Catherine State Park 19km/12mi

Balanced Rock

Hot Springs Mountain Tower © Ken Lund

Grand Promenade © Ken Lund

Hot Springs Hiking Trails

Trail Name	Length	Location (# on map)/Notes (One-way distances unless loop)
Upper Dogwood	1.0 mile	Begins at North Mountain Overlook and ends at Hot Springs Mountain Trail (1)
Goat Rock	1.1 miles	On North Mountain above Gulpha Gorge Campground • Leads to Goat Rock (1, 2)
Gulpha Gorge	0.8 mile	Begins at the camp amphitheater • Intersects Goat Rock and Hot Springs Mtn Trails (3)
Dead Chief	1.4 miles	Combine with Gulpha Gorge to hike from the campground to Bathhouse Row (3, 10)
Grand Avenue	0.2 mile	Spur from Dead Chief Trail that ends at a motel on Grand Avenue (4)
Hot Springs Mtn - 👍	1.7 miles	One of the better hiking trails • Begins near Hot Springs Mountain Tower (5)
Carriage Road	0.1 mile	Old Carriage Road from Army–Navy Hospital to the summit of Hot Springs Mtn (5)
Peak	0.6 mile	Steep, short climb from Tufa Terrace Trail to Hot Springs Mountain Tower (5, 10)
Floral	0.4 mile	Short connector trail between Dogwood and Honeysuckle Trails (6)
Fountain	528 feet	Short and steep trail with concrete steps • Intersects Honeysuckle Trail (6)
Honeysuckle	0.5 mile	Connects Peak, Fountain, and Floral Trails (6, 8)
Arlington	0.1 mile	Begins at Arlington Hotel and continues to Lower Dogwood Trail (7)
Lower Dogwood	0.7 mile	Steep gravel trail that climbs North Mountain (7)
Shortcut	0.2 mile	Shortcut between Dead Chief Trail and Hot Springs Mtn Picnic Area (8)
Reserve	0.3 mile	Shortcut to Gulpha Gorge Campground from Dead Chief Trail (9)
Tufa Terrace	0.2 mile	Near Grand Promenade • Passes massive calcium carbonate (tufa) deposits (10)
Grand Promenade - 👍	0.5 mile	Brick promenade provides views of historic downtown Hot Springs (11)
Canyon	0.7 mile	Once an old carriage road between Bathhouse Row and West Mtn (12)
Oak	1.0 mile	Accessed from Mountain Street and intersects Canyon Trail (13)
West Mountain	1.2 miles	This trail loops around West Mountain Summit Drive (14)
Mountain Top	1.5 miles	Crosses West Mtn and Sunset Trail between Whittington and Prospect Avenues (15, 17)
Sunset	17 miles	Passes Ricks Pond and varied terrain along the park's longest trail (16, 18)
Whittington	1.2 miles	Loop trail with unmaintained jogging path around Whittington Park (17)
Balanced Rock Spur	0.2 mile	Spur from Sunset Trail that leads to a balanced rock (19)
Fordyce Peak Spur	1.5 miles	Spur from Sunset Trail that leads to Fordyce Peak before leaving the park

Hot Spring & North Mountains

West & Sugarloaf Mtn

HOT SPRINGS

274

Bathhouse Row

The first bathhouses were nothing more than small canvas and lumber structures situated on openings cut into rock. But by the late 19th century, Hot Springs' bathhouses could go toe-to-toe with the best Europe had to offer. Health seekers, wealthy and indigent alike, sought Hot Springs Mountain's rejuvenating waters. Doctors prescribed a strict bathing regimen for all sorts of ailments including rheumatism, paralysis, syphilis, gout, and bunions. Hot Springs reemerged as a popular destination in the 1920s when it was brought into the fold of national parks and construction began on a free government bathhouse in 1922. Each successive bathhouse was more extravagant than the last. During Hot Springs' heydays in the mid-1940s as many as 24 bathhouses were open for business at one time. They gave more than one million baths in a single year. In time, medical advancements led to a severe decrease in visitation. Penicillin and other modern medicines were being prescribed rather than frequent baths in mineral rich water.

In its prime, **The Fordyce** was the most elegant of all the bathhouses, and today it serves as the park's visitor center and museum. **Buckstaff Baths** still provides traditional treatment and is the only bathhouse in continuous operation since being established in 1912. **Quapaw Baths & Spas** recently reopened as a modern spa. It is the first bathhouse to open under the park's new lease program. Like the Quapaw, many old bathhouses are being restored by the park for future lease.

Buckstaff Baths • (501) 623-2308 • www.buckstaffbaths.com
509 Central Avenue; Hot Springs, AR 71901
Open: March–November • Monday–Saturday, 7am–11:45am & 1:30pm–3pm; Sunday, 8am–11:45am
December–February • Monday–Friday, 7am–11:45am & 1:30pm–3pm; Saturday, 8am–11:45am
Closed: New Year's Day, Christmas Day, Easter Sunday, July 4, and Thanksgiving Day
Rates: Bath: $30 • Bath/Loofa/Massage: $64
Facials, manicures, and pedicures are available

Quapaw Baths & Spa • (501) 609-9822 • www.quapawbaths.com
413 Central Avenue; Hot Springs, AR 71901
Open: Monday, Wednesday, Thursday, Friday, and Saturday, 10am–6pm; Sunday, 10am–3pm
Rates: Private Bath: $30 (Single)/$45 (Couple) • Swedish Massage: $50 (25 minutes)/$80 (50 minutes) • Hot Stone: $95 (50 minutes)
Facials, aroma baths, body polishes are available

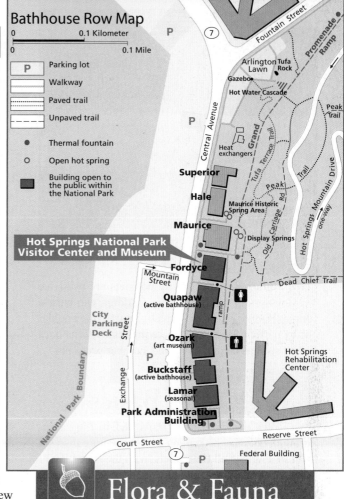

Flora & Fauna

Hot Springs is the smallest national park, and unlike most, it is set in an urban environment. A portion of the Ouachita Mountain range, including Hot Spring Mountain, is protected by the park. Here you'll find bats, rodents, and other small mammals typical of the region. When exploring the area near the bathhouses you'll probably only encounter squirrels and a few of the park's **100+ species of native birds**. In more remote regions northwest of Bathhouse Row you may encounter wild turkeys, deer, opossum, gray fox, coyote, or nine-banded armadillo. Forested mountain slopes are dominated by oak and hickory. Pines cover the southern slope. In all there are more than 300 acres of old growth forests consisting of shortleaf pine, blackjack oak, and white oak; many of the trees are over 130 years old, and a few exceed 200 years of age.

Hot Springs National Park Visitor Center

 For Kids

Free **Junior Ranger** activity booklets are available at Hot Springs Visitor Center. Children can earn a Junior Ranger patch by completing part of the booklet or by participating in four activities at a special park event such as nature walks and summer programs.

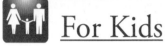 Basics

Pets: Pets are allowed on trails and in the campground, but must be kept on a leash no more than six feet in length at all times. Pets, with the exception of service animals, are not allowed in the visitor center or other park buildings.

Accessibility: The visitor center is wheelchair accessible and has a wheelchair available for loan. There is one wheelchair accessible campsite at Gulpha Gorge Campground.

Weather: Arkansas summers are what visitors need to be prepared for. They are extremely hot and humid. Standing in the Arkansas heat can feel an awful lot like a steaming hot bath. Average high temperatures in July and August reach the mid-90s°F. Fall and spring are mild. Winter is comfortable with average highs in the 50s°F and lows around freezing.

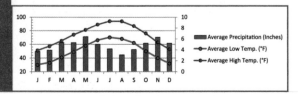

 Ranger Programs

If you're making an impromptu trip, chances are you will not have the opportunity to take a guided tour of Bathhouse Row or enjoy the **Discovering the Waters Tour**. **Bathhouse Row Insider's Tour** explores the current rehabilitation of bathhouses currently in disrepair after decades of neglect. Tours are offered as scheduling allows, but can be arranged at least two weeks in advance by calling the visitor center at (501) 620-6715. Without advance planning you have the chance to attend a tour of **Fordyce Bathhouse**, which is offered several times each week. Fordyce Bathhouse is the visitor center, but you'll also find a variety of modern and time period bathhouse exhibits inside. The visitor center is open daily from 9am to 5pm, except New Year's Day, Thanksgiving, and Christmas. Between late May and early August hours are extended to 8pm.

Vacation Planner

Hot Springs isn't the sort of park that you should drive several hours out of your way to visit, but it's worth a stop if you're passing nearby and have been in the driver's seat too long and want to get out and stretch a few kinks out of your back. Just like the olden days, a **Hot Springs' rubdown** (page 275) might be just what the doctor ordered. If you do visit the park, it's pretty easy to knock out the main attractions in a couple of hours. There is one developed **campground** (page 272) within park boundaries, but no lodging facilities. Nearby dining, grocery stores, lodging, festivals, and attractions are listed on page 277.

Begin at the **visitor center**, located on Bathhouse Row in **Fordyce Bathhouse**. Here you'll find a museum that offers several historical exhibits, and a short introductory film is played upon request. You may have the chance to join a park ranger on a tour (page 276) of the building. It's highly recommended, so if you have the chance, tag along. Once you're finished at the visitor center head back outside to take a look around Bathhouse Row. Stop in for a **massage** or **bath** (page 275) if that's your sort of thing. Regardless of your bathing proclivities, head behind the Row to walk the **Promenade.** Continue east into the park's modest network of trails (page 273) and hike to the tower on top of Hot Springs Mountain. For $7(Adult)/$4(Child) you can go to its top for some of the best views of Hot Springs. (The tower is not operated by the National Park Service.)

HOT SPRINGS

Dining

Café 1217 • (501) 318-1094
1217 Malvern Ave, # B; Hot Springs, AR 71901
www.cafe1217.net • Entrée: $6–9

Rolandos Restaurante • (501) 318-6054
210 Central Ave; Hot Springs, AR 71901
www.rolandosrestaurante.com • Specials: $15–19

Fuji Japanese Restaurant • (501) 321-1688
608 East Grand Ave; Hot Springs, AR 71901

Pancake Shop • (501) 624-5720
216 Central Ave; Hot Springs, AR 71901
www.pancakeshop.com

McClard's Bar-B-Q • (501) 624-9586
505 Albert Pike Rd; Hot Springs, AR 71913
www.mcclards.com

Bleu Monkey Grill • (501) 520-4800
4263 Central Ave; Hot Springs, AR 71913
www.bleumonkeygrill.com • Entrée: $11–20

Grampa's Catfish House • (501) 767-2299
1020 Airport Rd; Hot Springs, AR 71913

Taco Mama • (501) 624-6262
1209 Malvern Ave; Hot Springs, AR 71901

Taqueria El Amigo • (501) 321-8152
765 Park Ave; Hot Springs, AR 71901

Colonial Pancake & Waffle House • (501) 624-9273
111 Central Ave; Hot Springs, AR 71901

HolY CoWs Creamery • (501) 525-2300
4832 Central Ave; Hot Springs, AR 71913
www.holycowscreamery.com • Ice Cream: $3–7

Grocery Stores

Walmart Supercenter • (501) 624-2498
1601 Albert Pike Blvd; Hot Springs, AR 71913

Kroger • (501) 623-3340
215 Airport Rd; Hot Springs, AR 71913

Lodging

Wildwood 1884 B&B • (501) 624-4267
808 Park Ave; Hot Springs, AR 71901
www.wildwood1884.com • Rates: $129–189/night

Alpine Inn • (501) 624-9164
741 Park Ave; Hot Springs, AR 71901
www.alpineinnhotsprings.com • Rates: $60–90

1890 Williams House Inn • (501) 624-4275
420 Quapaw Ave; Hot Springs, AR 71901
www.1890williamshouse.com • Rates: $159–239

Spring Street Inn • (501) 318-1958
522 Spring St; Hot Springs, AR 71901
www.springstreetinn.net • Rates: $110–200

Hilltop Manor B&B • (501) 625-7829
2009 Park Ave; Hot Springs, AR 71901
www.hilltopmanorhotsprings.com • Rates: $170–400

Prospect Place B&B • (877) 318-0385
472 Prospect Ave; Hot Springs, AR 71901

The B Inn • (501) 547-7172
316 Park Ave; Hot Springs, AR 71901
www.bhotsprings.com • Rates: $50–90

Dogwood Manor B&B • (501) 609-0100
906 Malvern Ave; Hot Springs, AR 71901
www.dogwoodmanorbnb.com • Rates: $99–139

Lookout Point Lakeside Inn • (501) 525-6155
104 Lookout Circle; Hot Springs, AR 71913
www.lookoutpointinn.com • Rates: $99–499

Many chain restaurants and hotels can be found in or nearby Little Rock, Hot Springs, and along I-30.

Festivals

Riverfest • May
Little Rock • www.riverfestarkansas.com

Cardboard Boat Races • July
Haber Springs • www.heber-springs.com

Rodeo of the Ozarks • July
Springdale • www.rodeooftheozarks.org

Watermelon Festival • August
Hope • www.hopemelonfest.com

Documentary Film Festival • October
Hot Springs • www.hsdfi.org

Attractions

Crater of Diamonds State Park • (870) 285-3113
209 State Park Rd; Murfreesboro, AR 71852
www.craterofdiamondsstatepark.com • Fee: $7/Adult

National Park Duck Tours • (501) 321-2911
418 Central Ave; Hot Springs, AR 71901
www.rideaduck.com

Tussaud Josephine Wax Museum • (501) 623-5836
250 Central Ave; Hot Springs, AR 71901

Hot Springs Haunted Tours • (501) 339-3751
334-B Central Ave; Hot Springs, AR 71901
www.hotspringshauntedtours.com • Tickets: $15/Adult

Gangster Museum of America • (501) 318-1717
113 Central Ave; Hot Springs, AR 71901
www.tgmoa.com • Admission: $12/Adult

Hot Springs Nat'l Park Aquarium • (501) 624-3474
209 Central Ave; Hot Springs, AR 71901

Museum of Contemporary Art • (501) 609-9966
425 Central Ave; Hot Springs, AR 71901
www.museumofcontemporaryart.com • Admission: $5

Tiny Town Trains • (501) 624-4742
374 Whittington Ave; Hot Springs, AR 71901
www.tinytowntrains.com • Admission: $5

Arkansas Alligator Farm • (501) 623-6172
847 Whittington Ave; Hot Springs, AR 71901
www.arkansasalligatorfarm.com • Admission: $6.50

Pirate's Cove Adventure Golf • (501) 525-9311
4612 Central Ave; Hot Springs, AR 71913

Lake Catherine State Park • (501) 844-4176
1200 Catherine Park Rd; Hot Springs, AR 71913
www.arkansasstateparks.com

Oaklawn Racing & Gaming • (501) 623-4411
2705 Central Ave; Hot Springs, AR 71901
www.oaklawn.com

Central City 10 Cinemas • (501) 623-7751
909 Higdon Ferry Rd; Hot Springs, AR 71913

Ritz Theatre • (501) 332-2451
213 S Main St; Malvern, AR 72104
www.theritzmalvern.com • Tickets: $5–6

Lake Ouachita State Park • (501) 767-9366
5451 Mtn Pine Rd; Mtn Pine, AR 71956
www.arkansasstateparks.com

Little Rock Central HS • (501) 374-1957
2120 Daisy Bates Dr; Little Rock, AR 72202
www.nps.gov/chsc • Free Admission

Clinton Presidential Library • (501) 370-8000
1200 President Clinton Ave; Little Rock, AR 72201
www.clintonlibrary.gov • Admission: $7/Adult

Heifer Village • (501) 907-8800
1 World Avenue; Little Rock, AR 72202
www.heifer.org

Arkansas State Capitol • (501) 682-5080
500 Woodlane Ave; Little Rock, AR 72201

Graceland • (901) 332-3322
3734 Elvis Presley Blvd; Memphis, TN 38116
www.elvis.com • Tours: $31–70/Adult

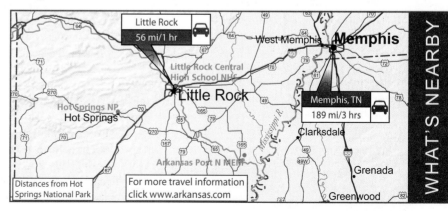

Little Rock 56 mi/1 hr

Memphis, TN 189 mi/3 hrs

Distances from Hot Springs National Park

For more travel information click www.arkansas.com

A tunnel near Rio Grande Village with the Sierra del Carmen in the background

PO Box 129
Big Bend National Park, TX 79834
Phone: (432) 477-2251
Website: www.nps.gov/bibe

Established: June 12, 1944
Size: 801,163 Acres
Annual Visitors: 370,000
Peak Season: March–April
Hiking Trails: 201 Miles

Activities: Hiking, Bird Watching, Backpacking, Paddling/Floating, Stargazing, and Mountain Biking

Campgrounds: Cottonwood, Chisos Basin, and Rio Grande Village
Camping Fee: $14/night
RV Park: Rio Grande Village
RV Rate: $32/night plus $3/Person
Backcountry Camping: Permitted*

Park Hours: All day, every day
Entrance Fee: $20 • Vehicle
$10 • Individual (foot, bike, etc.)

*A Backcountry Use Permit ($10) is required for overnight stays

Big Bend - Texas

"I wish you would take a map of the State showing the counties, put your pencil point on the Rio Grande, just where the Brewster and Presidio County line hit that stream; then draw a line due East and at a distance of sixty miles it will again strike the River. My dream is to make the area South of this line into a park and I shall live to see it done."

– Everett Townsend, 1933

Congress authorized the park in 1935, but it wasn't until 1944 that **Everett Townsend's** dream came true. Since its establishment, Big Bend has had its fair share of admirers, including geologists, paleontologists, botanists, and bird watchers. But it is seldom visited by the average national park-goer. Taking a look at a county map of Texas like Townsend did, you begin to understand why only the most dedicated visitors reach this scenic wilderness in the southwest corner of Texas. It isn't close to anything, unless you count the United States–Mexico border. Then there's the stigma associated with desert; it's known for being a barren wasteland, not the diverse wonderlands national parks have been made out to be. But the park's faithful continue to return time and time again. They drive dirt roads, hike dusty trails, and run the Rio Grande in canoes and rafts. To them the steep limestone canyons, mountain vistas, and desert wilderness of Big Bend are every bit as wondrous as the western parks. It's just that Big Bend isn't as photogenic. You can't truly understand its size and desolation by looking at a 4" x 6" glossy image. But those willing to make the long journey understand exactly what Townsend was dreaming about.

Over the years, people have freely crossed the Rio Grande, observing this area's beauty, hunting its wildlife, and seasonally farming its land. Ancient Native American artifacts date back some 9,000 years. In the 16th and 17th centuries, Spanish explorers passed through current park land, crossing the Rio Grande in search of gold, silver, and fertile soil. In the 19th century, Comanche Indians blazed a path across the desert into Mexico where they carried out raids. Today, when visitors enter at Persimmon Gap, they are following a section of the same Comanche Trail. In the early 1900s Mexican settlers lived on both sides of the river. Some tried to eke out a life farming an arid land, while others worked as ranchers.

After a mining settlement was established at Boquillas in 1898, more attention was given to the United States–Mexico border. Mounted inspectors began to patrol the boundary. **Everett Ewing Townsend** was one of them. He grew up on a ranch, eventually joining Company E Frontier Battalion of the Texas Rangers. While stationed at Big Bend as a U.S. Marshall, Townsend "saw God" and realized the "awesomeness of the region" while tracking a pack of stolen mules through the Chisos Mountains. His mountaintop epiphany inspired a new hobby: lobbying politicians to protect the region as a park. Unsuccessful as a lobbyist, he decided to join the ranks of politicians. Elected to the state legislature after 18 years as a ranchman, his new role allowed time to co-author legislation creating **Texas Canyons State Park**.

Townsend was also instrumental in establishing a **CCC camp at Chisos Basin**. Many of the area's trails and facilities were constructed by the CCC in the 1930s. Living during the Great Depression was a struggle for everyone, but it was incredibly difficult at Big Bend. There was no electricity, they had few reliable water sources, roads were not paved, and the nearest telephone was 100 miles away. But the CCC managed, completing much of the present-day infrastructure, setting the stage for establishment of Big Bend National Park in 1944. Townsend was eventually appointed as its first commissioner. Today he's remembered as the "Father of Big Bend" and forever recognized thanks to Townsend Point (7,580 ft), the second highest peak in the Chisos Mountains and site of his epiphany. Many of today's guests share the same fervor as Everett Townsend. They travel great distances to reach a barren, but uniquely beautiful region. Beauty only seen by those who make the trip to Rio Grande's Big Bend.

When to Go

The park is open all year, but most visitors come to Big Bend between October and April when weather is comfortable. Summer can be unbearable, with high temperatures frequently surpassing the century mark. Thunderstorms, overcast skies, and high elevations can make for a more enjoyable climate than you might expect, but it's still very, very hot in summer.

Transportation

Public transportation does not serve Big Bend due to its extreme isolation. However, Amtrak (800.872.7245, www.amtrak.com) and Greyhound (800.231.2222, www.greyhound.com) provide service to Alpine, TX (100 miles from park headquarters). Car rental is available in Alpine.

Airports

The closest major airports are Midland International (MAF) in Midland, TX (223 miles from the park) and El Paso International (ELP) in El Paso, TX (315 miles from the park). Car rental is available at each destination.

Directions

Big Bend is located in southwestern Texas on the U.S.–Mexico border. Arriving from the east via I-10, the park is 125 miles south from Fort Stockton on US-385. Arriving from the west via I-10, the park is 197 miles south from Van Horn via US-90 and US-385. Due to the area's remote nature, be sure to have plenty of gas, food, and water.

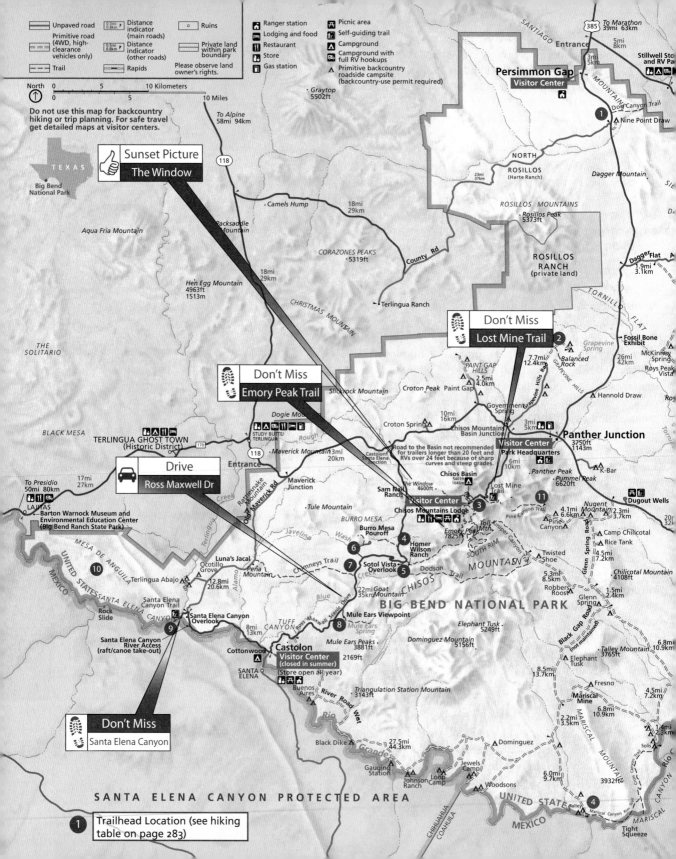

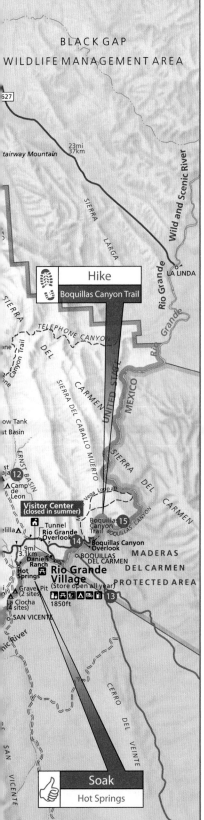

Visitor Centers

Big Bend has five visitor centers. **Panther Junction Visitor Center** (432.477.2251), located at the intersection of US-385 and TX-118, is open year-round, daily from 8am–6pm with reduced hours on Christmas Day. **Chisos Basin Visitor Center** is located near Chisos Mountain Lodge. It's also open year-round and operates from 8am–3:30pm, November–March; and from 9am–4:30pm, April–November. Hours are reduced on Christmas, and it closes from noon until 1pm for lunch every day. **Persimmon Gap Visitor Center**, located where US-385 enters the park, is open year-round from 9am to 4:30pm. It is the ideal location for a brief orientation before hiking or driving into the backcountry or floating the Rio Grande. **Rio Grande Village** and **Castolon** are the easternmost and westernmost visitor centers, respectively. Both locations are only open during the busy season (November–April). Rio Grande Village is open from 8:30am–4pm. Castolon is open from 10am–5pm, but closed for lunch. Backcountry camping and river use permits, and spigots to fill personal water containers are available at all visitor centers.

Lodging

Chisos Mountains Lodge (877.386.4383, www.chisosmountainslodge.com), located high in the Chisos Mountains near the park's center, is the only in-park lodging. If you aren't into camping, it is the only option within a 50 mile radius. Rooms cost $113–144/night. A restaurant is located on-site.

Camping

Big Bend has three established campgrounds. **Cottonwood Campground** is located on Ross Maxwell Scenic Drive near Castolon Historic District and the Mexico–U.S. border. It has 31 sites, pit toilets, and potable water. **Chisos Basin Campground** has 60 sites, running water, and flush toilets. Between November 15 and April 15, 26 of these sites are available for reservation (877.444.6777, www.recreation.gov). **Rio Grande Village Campground** has 100 sites (43 can be reserved from November 15–April 15), flush toilets, and running water. All campsites listed above are available year-round for $14/night. **Rio Grande Village** has a 25-site RV Park. It's open year-round, and sites cost $32/night (plus $3/person). These are the only sites with full hook-ups. Call the RV Park's concessioner at (877) 386-4383 or (432) 477-2251 to make reservations. Rio Grande Village is also the only location with **showers** and **laundry**. Each campground has at least one group site designed to accommodate more than 9 campers. These sites must be reserved in advance by calling (877) 444-6777 or clicking www.recreation.gov.

Backcountry Camping

More than 70 primitive campsites line the park's unpaved backcountry roads. They provide secluded camping with drive-up convenience. There are also a number of designated primitive campsites along hiking trails in the Chisos Mountains. A $10 **backcountry use permit** must be obtained at any visitor center during regular hours of operation in order to spend a night in the backcountry. Backpacking outside the Chisos Mountains requires a zone camping permit.

 # Driving

A considerable amount of Big Bend can be explored without leaving your vehicle, thanks to roughly 100 miles of roadways paved and suitable for the average motorist. The most scenic stretch is 30-mile **Ross Maxwell Scenic Drive**, which leads to Santa Elena Canyon and Castolon. You'll also find a network of dirt roads; some are improved to the point standard 2WD vehicles traveling at low speeds can pass. Others can only be accessed by high-clearance vehicles (see the map on page 281). **River Road** loosely follows the Rio Grande and is one of the best off-road drives. Sections of dirt roads may require 4WD and an experienced off-road driver. Always check current road conditions at a visitor center before traveling on them.

 # Biking

Cyclists are allowed on all 301 miles of roads. Traffic is typically sparse, but cyclists should use extreme caution as roads, especially Chisos Basin, are steep and winding with narrow shoulders. **Chisos Basin Road** is also the most scenic and strenuous stretch of pavement. Pedal the 10 miles between Panther Junction and Chisos Basin for a nice ride. En route you'll encounter 15% grades, gaining 1,650 feet of elevation before reaching its end. Turn around and enjoy the cruise back to Panther Junction. If you can arrange a shuttle, biking between **Panther Junction and Rio Grande Village** is an easy 20-mile ride, most of which is downhill.

Dirt roads are suitable for **mountain bikers**. **Old Maverick Road** is easiest from north to south and its southern end reaches picturesque Santa Elena Canyon. An out-and-back of Old Maverick Road is 26 miles from Maverick Junction and takes about 3–4 hours. You can make a 48-mile loop by combining Old Maverick Road and Ross Maxwell Drive. Mountain bikers will not find singletrack. Bikes are not allowed off road or on trails. However, 50 miles of the area's best singletrack are located nearby in Lajitas. See page 321 for a list of outfitters who provide rentals and tours.

 # Hiking

The Chisos Mountains provide the densest network of trails allowing visitors to choose between short, flat hikes and long overnight backpacking trips. The 10.5-mile roundtrip hike to the park's highest point, **Emory Peak** (7,832 feet), is a challenging trek. Hikers who complete the journey are rewarded with sweeping desert panoramas. **South Rim Trail** is longer and just as rewarding. It can be done as a loop by taking **Pinnacles and Laguna Meadows Trails**. All three begin at Chisos Basin Trailhead, located near the Lodge, Basin Store, and visitor center. A nice short hike in the Chisos Mountains is **Lost Mine Trail**. This 4.8-mile trail leads to a promontory overlooking Pine and Juniper Canyons, and is the park's most popular hike. Trail guides are available at the trailhead for $1.

There are a lot of great locations at Big Bend to watch the sunset. **Rio Grande Village Nature Trail** and **Sotol Vista Overlook** on Ross Maxwell Scenic Drive come to mind, but the most noteworthy are viewpoints along **Window View Trail**, also located at Chisos Basin.

Most visitors explore the Chisos Mountains by foot, but that doesn't mean it's the only place in the park worth hiking. **Santa Elena Canyon and Boquillas Canyon Trails** are located along the Rio Grande on opposite ends of the park. They provide beautiful canyon views, and are as short as the canyons are impressive. If you only have enough time to drive to one, head west and hike Santa Elena Canyon Trail. Its views and canyon are slightly more spectacular.

 # Stargazing

As one of the most isolated national parks, Big Bend is also one of the best locations for stargazing. Far away from busy streets and city lights, stars twinkle and shimmer across the perfectly dark night sky. A night spent here can provide an especially inspiring experience for city-folk accustomed to lights and smog that obscure the stars above. Occasionally, the park offers a "**Starlight, Starbright**" ranger-led evening program providing a more scientific look at things that go twinkle in the night. If you'd rather view the stars on your own, all campsites offer prime stargazing real estate, but the best spot might be from the warm waters of **Hot Springs**. It's located on the river's north shore near Rio Grande Village.

BIG BEND

Mule Ears

Santa Elena Canyon

Pine Canyon

Grapevine Hills

Big Bend Hiking Trails

	Trail Name	Length	Location (# on map)/Notes (Roundtrip distances)
East	Rio Grande Village Nature Trail	0.75 mile	Self-guiding trail begins behind campsite #18 at Rio Grande Village Campground (13) • It's an easy trail with great bird watching opportunities and nice scenery
	Ore Terminal - 👍	8.0 miles	These trails share the same trailhead on Boquillas Canyon Road (14) • From there, Ore Terminal follows an old tramway that carried ore from Mexican mines and Marufo Vega makes a long loop through mountains to the Rio Grande's banks
	Marufo Vega	14.0 miles	
	Boquillas Canyon - 👍	1.4 miles	An easy trail accessed at the end of Boquillas Canyon Road (15)
North	Dog Canyon	4.0 miles	Access to these moderate hikes is found 3.5 miles south of Persimmon Gap on the main park road (1) • After 1.5 miles you head into a wash and meet a junction • A left turn leads to Dog Canyon, a right to Devil's Den
	Devil's Den	5.6 miles	
Chisos Mtns	Window View	0.3 mile	Paved path near Basin Store • Excellent spot to see sunset through "the window" (3)
	Lost Mine - 👍	4.8 miles	At mile 5 of Basin Road, this steep, moderate self-guiding hike is quite popular (3)
	Window - 👍	4.0 miles	Accessed at Basin Campground, moderate trail with fantastic scenery (3)
	Emory Peak - 👍	10.5 miles	Accessed near Basin Store, Emory Peak leads to the park's highest point (3) • A short scramble rewards hikers with the best panoramic views • South Rim is a long day hike or you can take advantage of campsites along the way
	South Rim - 👍	12–14.5 mi	
West	Ward Spring	3.6 miles	Ross Maxwell Drive (RMD) mile 5.5 (4) • Easy, seldom used trail to volcanic dike and spring
	Red Rocks Canyon	3.0 miles	Begin at Homer Wilson Ranch Overlook to see colorful rocks (5)
	Upper Burro Mesa Pour-off	3.8 miles	RMD mile 6 (6) • Moderate trail through a wash and two canyons • Requires a bit of scrambling, but the rocky gorge's floor is mostly sandy
	Chimneys	4.8 miles	RMD mile 13 (7) • Long flat trail features scenic desert and rock formations
	Mule Ears Spring	3.8 miles	Trailhead at RMD mile 15 (8) • Moderate hike with nice views
	Santa Elena Canyon - 👍	1.7 miles	RMD mile 8 (9) • Cross Terlingua Creek to an easy trail into the canyon
Backcountry	Grapevine Hills	2.2 miles	Begins 7 miles down Grapevine Hills Road (2) • Kids' favorite to strange window
	Mariscal Canyon Rim - 👍	6.6 miles	Best views in the park, but requires a 2-hour drive on River Road/Talley Rd (HCV) (4)
	The Mesa de Anguila	Varies	On western side of Santa Elena Canyon (10) • Only for experienced hikers
	Pine Canyon	4.0 miles	Accessed at the end of Pine Canyon Rd (HCV required) (11) • The trail leads to a waterfall that only runs after rain
	Ernst Tinaja	1.4 miles	Accessed 5 miles from the south end of Old Ore Rd (high-clearance vehicles (HCV) only) (12)

Floating/Rafting

For 118 miles the **Rio Grande** serves double duty as Big Bend's southern boundary and natural border between the U.S. and Mexico. Many visitors find a float through **Santa Elena Canyon** to be the most dramatic way to view Big Bend. Picture yourself winding through 1,500-ft cliffs for 13 miles and it's easy to understand why. Then there's **Rock Slide**, the canyon's largest rapid, which becomes Class IV whitewater under the right conditions. This section of the Rio Grande is easily accessed with a put-in outside the park at Lajitas and take out inside the park at Santa Elena Canyon Trail.

If you have your own boat but uninterested in shuttling between put-in and take-out, launch at Santa Elena Canyon Trail and paddle up river for two miles to Fern Canyon before turning around (only possible at low water levels). Within the park, you'll find **two established campgrounds and 11 designated campsites** along the Rio Grande. To use these sites, you must first obtain a **backcountry use permit** ($10 • page 281) from a visitor center. If Big Bend isn't big enough for you, **Rio Grande Wild and Scenic River** extends downstream beyond the park boundary an additional 127 miles.

A few **outfitters** in the area provide shuttles, equipment, and guided trips.

Big Bend River Tours • (800) 545-4240 • www.bigbendrivertours.com

Desert Sports • (888) 989-6900 • www.desertsportstx.com

Far Flung Outdoor Center • (800) 839-7238 • www.ffoc.net

See page 321 for additional recreational information.

Bird Watching

Big Bend possesses a unique location where bird species converge from three distinct geographical regions: eastern U.S., western U.S., and Mexico. It's also located along a major avian migratory route. This combination yields **more than 450 documented species of birds, more than any other national park**.

Birds are somewhat like humans, residing where they can find food, water, and safe habitat. That makes camping areas like **Cottonwood**, **Chisos Basin**, and **Rio Grande Village** a few of the best birding destinations. However, not all birds follow the vacation patterns as humans. One of the most prized species, the **Colima warbler**, visits Big Bend during the summer after wintering in Mexico. Fortunately, they're usually spotted in the higher elevations of the Chisos Mountains, where you'll also find a bit of relief from summer's heat. Peregrine falcons, Montezuma quail, flammulated owls, and Lucifer hummingbirds are a few other highly sought after species found in the Chisos Mountains and along the Rio Grande.

Best of Big Bend

Activity: Paddle/Float the Rio Grande
    Runner-up: Stargazing at Hot Springs

Family Hike: Window
    Runner-up: Santa Elena Canyon

Adventure Hike: Lost Mine
    Runner-up: Mariscal Canyon Rim

For Kids: Big Bend's **Junior Ranger Program** is for kids of all ages. Children learn about the park's history and geology as they explore its geography. To participate, pick up a Junior Ranger Activity Booklet ($2) from any one of the visitor centers. Upon completion, they will be awarded a Big Bend wildlife bookmark, a certificate, and a Junior Ranger patch.

Ranger Programs: Park rangers can help satisfy all of your Big Bend curiosities through a series of regularly scheduled interpretive programs. Activities range from walks to talks, campfire programs to stargazing. Whatever you choose you're sure to come away with a better understanding of Big Bend's natural and cultural history. Check the park website or current issue of *The Big Bend Paisano* for an up-to-date schedule of activities. If you're interested in a specific program but can't fit it into your specific vacation plans, you can request a personal guided ranger tour. Private tours are provided for a minimum of four hours at $35/hour.

Flora & Fauna: To casual visitors, Big Bend appears to be a lifeless wasteland. In reality, it's one of the most ecologically diverse areas in the United States. There are two major flowering periods: spring and late summer. Flower blooms are dependent on seasonal rain; without enough, the spring bloom is postponed for another year. The summer monsoon is far more dependable. **More than 1,200 species of plants, including 60 cactus species**, inhabit steep mountain sides, dry desert lands, and relatively lush river floodplains. The park is also home to **11 species of amphibians, 56 species of reptiles, 40 species of fish, 75 species of mammals, 450 species of birds, and 3,600 species of insects**. That's more birds, bats, and cacti than all other national parks. Mountain lions, black bear, pig-like javelinas, and coyotes are a few of the big mammals spotted each year.

Pets: As a rule of thumb, pets can only go where your car can. That includes parking areas, roadways, and drive-in campgrounds. They must be kept on a leash no more than six feet in length at all times. Pets are prohibited from all hiking trails and public buildings. Boarding is another possibility. Kennels are available in Alpine, TX at the Veterinary Clinic (432.837.3888) and Small Animal Clinic (432.837.5416).

Accessibility: All visitor centers are wheelchair accessible. Both Chisos Basin and Rio Grande Village Campgrounds have a fully-accessible campsite. Chisos Mountains Lodge has a few wheelchair accessible rooms. Dugout Wells and Persimmon Gap Picnic Areas are fully accessible. Panther Path, Window View Trail, and Rio Grande Village Nature Trail Boardwalk are short, flat, relatively smooth wheelchair-friendly trails. The park's amphitheaters and auditorium, where ranger programs are held, are wheelchair accessible. Check at a visitor center or online for a complete listing of accessible ranger programs.

Weather: Hot! That's really the only way to describe the weather at Big Bend. In winter, average high temperatures reach the 80s°F, but evening lows can drop below freezing. Most guests visit between fall and spring when temperatures are comfortable and humidity is low. During the summer temperatures max out above 110°F. What little rain the park receives usually falls between June and October. A high degree of temperature variance is also found here. Temperature in the high Chisos Mountains is typically 20°F cooler than that along the Rio Grande.

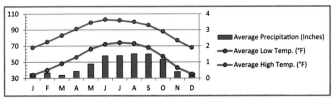

Vacation Planner

Big Bend isn't well known among national park enthusiasts. It's hundreds of miles from the nearest big city, interstate, and major airport, nestled deep in southwestern Texas where it brushes up against Mexico and the Rio Grande. Simply put, it's inconvenient and left to be enjoyed by only its most dedicated fans. If you make the arduous journey, plan on spending a couple of days. **Lodging** and **camping** (page 281) are available at the park. A 2-day itinerary is provided to help plan your Big Bend vacation. Nearby dining, grocery stores, lodging, festivals, and attractions are listed on pages 318–321.

 First thing you're going to want to do is pull in to the nearest visitor center. For most that's **Persimmon Gap**. Browse exhibits. Ask questions. If you're thinking about driving on the park's **primitive roads**, inquire about current road conditions and accessibility. Be sure to check the schedule of **ranger programs** for the duration of your stay. Hop back on the park road and continue all the way to **Panther Junction**. Turn right, skipping the road to Chisos Basin for now, and continue to **Ross Maxwell Scenic Drive**. Drive to **Santa Elena Canyon**, stopping along the way wherever you feel the urge to take a closer. (**Sotol Vista Overlook** and **Mule Ears Viewpoint** are nice.) At **Santa Elena**, hike the short **canyon trail** (page 283) and return to the road. If you have extra time before settling in, hike **Chimneys Trail** (page 283). Better yet, join a ranger program before you sleep under Big Bend's starry sky.

 Spend today at **Chisos Basin**. Choose between hiking **Emory Peak** or **South Rim** (page 283) Trails. Better yet, hike both. You can scramble to Emory Peak, and then return to the South Rim before looping back to Chisos Basin. Just don't plan on squeezing any other activities in. After your hike, travel to **Rio Grande Village** where you can soak your legs at **Hot Springs**, which is just a short hike or drive from the campground. There's no bad spot in the park to view the stars, but this is one of the absolute best locations.

Hiking McKittrick Canyon Trail

400 Pine Canyon Road
Salt Flat, Texas 79847
Phone: (915) 828-3251
Website: www.nps.gov/gumo

Established: September 30, 1972
Size: 86,416 Acres
Annual Visitors: 200,000
Peak Season: March and October
Hiking Trails: 85 Miles

Activities: Hiking, Bird Watching,
Horseback Riding, and Stargazing

Campgrounds: Pine Springs
(South) and Dog Canyon (North)
Camping Fee: $8/night
Backcountry Camping: Permitted*
Lodging: None

Park Hours: All day, every day
Day-use Areas: McKittrick Can-
yon, Williams Ranch, and Salt
Basin Dunes
Entrance Fee: $5/Person

*A free Backcountry Use Permit is
required for all overnight stays

Guadalupe Mountains - Texas

Set on the Texas–New Mexico state line, the Guadalupe Mountains are too remote, rugged, and dry to be hospitable. They're also too prominent and mysterious to be ignored. **Native Americans** and **Spaniards** brought attention to the area with elaborate stories of gold hidden deep in the mountains. The mountains had stories of their own. Mysteries about the region's underwater past were revealed rock by rock, fossil by fossil. Today, guests visit the park and create their own stories while hiking and camping in these hills of hidden gold and buried fossils.

Also hidden in the mountains is proof of more than 10,000 years of human habitation. The earliest of which were hunter–gatherers who followed game and collected edible vegetation. The only remnants of their existence are projectile points, baskets, pottery, and rock art. Spaniards passed through in the 16th century. They didn't establish settlements, but they left their mark by introducing horses to the Mescalero Apache. Horses proved to be an invaluable asset to the Apache as they tried to protect their land.

In 1858, **Pinery Station** was constructed near Pine Springs for the **Butterfield Overland Mail**. **Apache** considered this development and America's westward expansion an invasion. They retaliated by carrying out raids of nearby settlements and mail stagecoaches. After the Civil War, a new transportation route allowed **homesteaders** and **miners** to encroach further on Apache land. This new surge of settlers forced Mescalero Apache to take refuge in the Guadalupe Mountains, which served as their last stronghold. Here they hunted elk, mule deer, and bighorn sheep; they harvested agave (mescal), sotol, and beargrass. Eventually, **Lt. H.B. Cushing** and a troop of Buffalo Soldiers were ordered to stop the raids on settlements and mail coaches. The small brigade marched into the mountains, destroying two Apache camps. By the 1880s, surviving Mescalero Apache were driven onto reservations.

Many new settlers from the East took up ranching. But most found the land to be rugged and inhospitable. **Frijole Ranch**, built by the Rader Brothers in 1876, was the first permanent home built in the area. For much of the 20th century, Frijole Ranch remained the area's only major building, serving as community center and regional post office. Today, it has been restored as a museum of local ranching history.

The area's history changed when **Wallace Pratt** came to the Guadalupe Mountains. Pratt, a petroleum geologist for Humble Oil and Refining Company, visited **McKittrick Canyon** and fell in love with the lush oasis. He purchased nearly 6,000 acres surrounding the only year-round water source and built two homes: Ship-On-The-Desert near the canyon's mouth, and Pratt Cabin at the confluence of north and south McKittrick Canyons. Pratt and his family enjoyed the summer retreat for two decades before deciding to donate it to the federal government. His donation became the heart of Guadalupe Mountains National Park.

Since Pratt's time in McKittrick Canyon other geologists have been busy studying **exposed reefs** found in the mountains. The reefs help paint a picture of the area's past, when Texas and New Mexico were covered by a shallow, tropical sea. Algae, sponges, and other aquatic organisms formed a giant reef that looped around the present day Guadalupe, Apache, and Glass Mountains. A visitor walking into McKittrick Canyon today is entering **El Capitán Reef** from its seaward side.

An evaporated sea. A sanctuary for Apache. A summer retreat. These are the stories of the Guadalupe Mountains' past. Today's story is about a park. A park for the enjoyment of the people. A park that protects the past and ensures the future. A park for each and everyone of us.

Did you know?

▶ Guadalupe Peak (8,479 ft) is the highest point in Texas. The next three highest peaks are also in the Guadalupe Range.

When to Go

Guadalupe Mountains is open all year, with just two brief periods when the park approaches "busy" status. In March college kids on spring break hit the trails to go backpacking. In October, leaf-peepers flock to McKittrick Canyon to see its colorful foliage. Spring and fall are the most pleasant times of the year to visit.

Headquarters Visitor Center at Pine Springs is open daily (except Christmas Day) from 8am–4:30pm. Visitor center hours are extended to 6pm between Memorial Day and Labor Day weekends. Frijole Ranch is open as staffing allows, usually from 8am–4:30pm. McKittrick Canyon is a day-use-area. The entrance gate is open daily from 8am–4:30pm. Salt Basin Dunes and Williams Ranch (4WD access only) are also day-use areas. If you intend on visiting any of these areas you must obtain a gate key from Headquarters Visitor Center. The key must be returned the same day. Dog Canyon (505.981.2418) is open all year. It has a small ranger station that is open intermittently.

Transportation & Airports

Public transportation is not available to or around the park. The closest major airports are Midland International (MAF) in Midland, TX (219 miles from the park) and El Paso International (ELP) in El Paso, TX (102 miles from the park). Cavern City Air Terminal (CNM) in Carlsbad, NM (66 miles from the park) offers passenger service between Albuquerque International Sunport (ABQ) and Carlsbad, NM. Car rental is available at each destination.

Directions

Guadalupe Mountains National Park is located in West Texas on US-62/180 between Carlsbad, NM (near Carlsbad Caverns National Park • page 294) and El Paso, TX. Dog Canyon is located on the park's north side near the Texas–New Mexico state border. It's about a 120-mile drive from Headquarters Visitor Center. NM-137 leads directly to Dog Canyon Entrance, Campground, and Ranger Station.

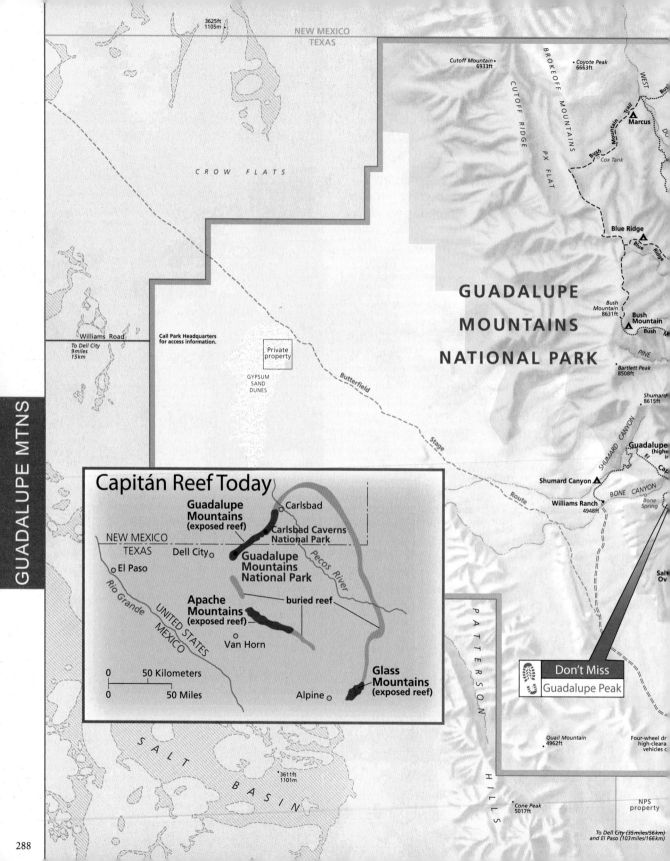

NEW MEXICO
TEXAS

3625ft
1105m

Cutoff Mountain •
6933ft

BROKEOFF MOUNTAINS

• Coyote Peak
6663ft

WEST

CUTOFF RIDGE

Mountain Trail

Marcus

Bush

PX FLAT

Cox Tank

CROW FLATS

Blue Ridge

Blue Ridge

GUADALUPE

Bush
Mountain
8631ft

Bush
Mountain

Bush

MOUNTAINS

PINE

Williams Road

Bartlett Peak
8508ft

To Dell City
9miles
15km

Call Park Headquarters
for access information.

Private
property

NATIONAL PARK

Shumard
8615ft

GYPSUM
SAND
DUNES

Butterfield

Stage

SHUMARD CANYON

Guadalupe
(highe

El
Cap

Shumard Canyon

BONE CANYON

Williams Ranch
4948ft

Bone
Spring

Route

Capitán Reef Today

Carlsbad

**Guadalupe
Mountains**
(exposed reef)

Carlsbad Caverns
National Park

NEW MEXICO
TEXAS

Dell City

**Guadalupe
Mountains
National Park**

El Paso

Pecos River

Rio Grande

**Apache
Mountains**
(exposed reef)

buried reef

UNITED STATES
MEXICO

Van Horn

0   50 Kilometers

0   50 Miles

Alpine

**Glass
Mountains**
(exposed reef)

PATTERSON

Salt
Ov

👟 **Don't Miss**
Guadalupe Peak

SALT

BASIN

3611ft
1101m

HILLS

Quail Mountain
4962ft

Four-wheel dr
high-cleara
vehicles

Cone Peak
5017ft

NPS
property

To Dell City (35miles/56km)
and El Paso (103miles/166km)

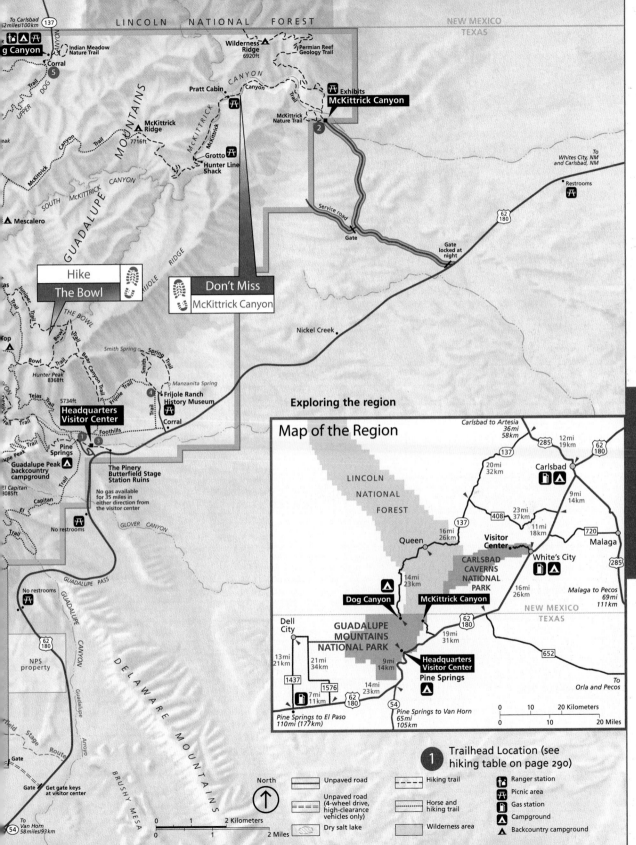

To Carlsbad
62miles/100km

LINCOLN NATIONAL FOREST

137

NEW MEXICO
TEXAS

g Canyon

Indian Meadow
Nature Trail

Corral
5

Wilderness
Ridge
6920ft

Permian Reef
Geology Trail

Pratt Cabin

McKittrick
Ridge
7716ft

Exhibits
McKittrick Canyon

McKittrick
Nature Trail

2

Grotto
Hunter Line
Shack

To
Whites City, NM
and Carlsbad, NM

Restrooms

Mescalero

62
180

Service road

Gate

Gate
locked at
night

Hike
The Bowl

Don't Miss
McKittrick Canyon

Nickel Creek

Smith Spring

Spring Trail

Hunter Peak
8368ft

Manzanita Spring

Frijole Ranch
History Museum

4

Corral

5734ft

Exploring the region

Headquarters
Visitor Center

1   3

Foothills

Pine
Springs

Guadalupe Peak
backcountry
campground

The Pinery
Butterfield Stage
Station Ruins

El Capitan
3085ft

Capitan

No gas available
for 35 miles in
either direction from
the visitor center

No restrooms

GLOVER CANYON

No restrooms

62
180

NPS
property

GUADALUPE PASS

DELAWARE MOUNTAINS

Gate

Gate   Get gate keys
at visitor center

To Van Horn
58miles/93km

54

Map of the Region

Carlsbad to Artesia
36mi
58km

137

285

12mi
19km

62
180

20mi
32km

Carlsbad

LINCOLN
NATIONAL
FOREST

137

408

23mi
37km

9mi
14km

16mi
26km

Queen

**Visitor
Center**

11mi
18km

720

Malaga

CARLSBAD
CAVERNS
NATIONAL
PARK

White's City

285

14mi
23km

Dog Canyon

McKittrick Canyon

NEW MEXICO
TEXAS

16mi
26km

Malaga to Pecos
69mi
111km

Dell
City

**GUADALUPE
MOUNTAINS
NATIONAL
PARK**

62
180

19mi
31km

652

13mi
21km

21mi
34km

9mi
14km

**Headquarters
Visitor Center**

To
Orla and Pecos

1437

1576

14mi
23km

62
180

Pine Springs

54

Pine Springs to Van Horn
65mi
105km

Pine Springs to El Paso
110mi (177km)

7mi
11km

0   10   20 Kilometers

0   10   20 Miles

1   Trailhead Location (see
     hiking table on page 290)

North

0   1   2 Kilometers

0   1   2 Miles

Unpaved road

Unpaved road
(4-wheel drive,
high-clearance
vehicles only)

Dry salt lake

Hiking trail

Horse and
hiking trail

Wilderness area

Ranger station

Picnic area

Gas station

Campground

Backcountry campground

289

Camping

The park has two established campgrounds. **Pine Springs**, located just off US-62/180 near Headquarters Visitor Center, has 20 tent sites, 19 RV sites, and 2 group sites. **Dog Canyon** is located on the less visited north side of the park. It has 9 tent sites, 4 RV sites, and 1 group site. Both campgrounds have flush toilets and sinks. They do not have showers, hook-ups, or dump stations. Campsites are available on a first-come, first-served basis for $8/night. Group campsites must be reserved up to 60 days in advance by calling (915) 828-3251 between 8am and 4:30pm. They accommodate 10–20 people and cost $3 per person per night.

Backpacking

Ten backcountry campgrounds are spread out along 85 miles of hiking trails. The closest campground to Pine Springs is found at **Guadalupe Peak**, just 3.1 miles from Pine Springs Trailhead and parking area. It offers 5 secluded campsites. **Pine Top**, located on Bush Mountain Trail near the Bowl, is another easy one night backpacking trip. It consists of 8 campsites, and is just 6.2 miles from Pine Springs, providing some of the park's best sunset views. **Tejas**, **Mescalero**, **McKittrick Ridge**, **Blue Ridge**, **Marcus**, and **Wilderness Ridge** are other remote campgrounds in Guadalupe's high country. The only low elevation campground is found on the park's west side at **Shumard Canyon**, 9.2 miles from Pine Springs Trailhead. There are no reliable water sources in the backcountry, so carry in all the water you'll need.

Guadalupe Mountains Hiking Trails

	Trail Name	Trailhead (# on map)	Length	Notes (Roundtrip distances unless noted otherwise)
Easy	Frijole/Foothills	1, 4	3.7 miles	Loop trail between Pine Springs Campground and Frijole Ranch
	The Pinery	3	0.75 mile	Paved path to the ruins of Pinery Station
	Manzanita Spring	4	0.2 mile	Paved path to a desert watering hole
	Indian Meadow Nature Trail	5	0.6 mile	Nearly level trail • A free trail guide educates hikers on the natural and cultural history of the meadow
Moderate	Devil's Hall	1	4.2 miles	Follow Pine Springs Canyon to Hiker's Staircase and Devil's Hall
	El Capitán/Salt Basin Overlooks	1	11.3 miles	A flat hike to the base of El Capitán and an overlook • Trail can be extended an additional 4.7-miles to Williams Ranch site
	McKittrick Canyon	2	4.8 miles	Only year-round stream in the park, trail leads to Historic Pratt Lodge, Grotto Picnic Area, and Hunter Cabin
	McKittrick Canyon Nature Trail - 👍	2	0.9 mile	Self-guiding trail with exhibits that help describe the area's geology and ecology
	Smith Spring	4	2.3 miles	Potential for wildlife viewing at this shady little oasis
	Marcus Overlook	5	4.5 miles	Dramatic views down into West Dog Canyon via Bush Mtn Tr
	Juniper	N/A	~2.0 miles	A short connector trail between The Bowl and Tejas Trails
	Bear Canyon	N/A	~1.0 mile	A short connector trail between The Bowl and Frijole Trails
	Blue Ridge	N/A	~1.5 miles	A short connector trail between Marcus and Bush Mtn Trails
Strenuous	Guadalupe Peak - 👍	1	8.4 miles	Hike past El Capitán, by exposed cliffs, to the park's highest peak
	The Bowl - 👍	1	9.1 miles	Follow Frijole and Bear Canyon Trails, then left on Bowl Trail to a beautiful coniferous forest along high ridges and canyons
	Permian Reef	2	8.4 miles	Geology guides for this trail are available at the visitor center
	Lost Peak	5	6.4 miles	Follows Tejas Trail for a short distance to Lost Peak
	Tejas	1, 5	11.7 miles	One-way distance from Pine Springs to Dog Canyon
	Bush Mountain	5	~12 miles	One-way distance from Dog Canyon to The Bowl/Tejas Trails

Hiking

Guadalupe Mountains is a great place to introduce yourself to hiking or backpacking. The park is extremely manageable. Hikers can easily trek from Pine Springs (south end) to Dog Canyon (north end) in a day. Campgrounds are abundant and seldom occupied. Best of all, it's very difficult to get lost. Just as the park's southern sentinel, El Capitán, marked the way for homesteaders, Native Americans, and mail coaches, the mountains rising out of the Chihuahuan Desert form an extremely well-defined natural boundary to the east, south, and west. If you've been itching to give backpacking a shot or test your day-hiking limits but are intimidated by the size and wildlife of places like Rocky Mountain or Glacier National Parks, give the Guadalupe Mountains a shot. The main precaution is to carry enough water with you, as there are no reliable water sources in the backcountry. You also must be prepared for the elements. It can get really hot and windy, and many of the trails are completely exposed. Evenings in the mountains are often chilly.

If you're only doing one hike, it should be the 8.4-mile out-and-back to **Guadalupe Peak**, the highest point in Texas. At just 8,749-feet, not everything is bigger in Texas; this would be a molehill in Colorado. However, it's a strenuous hike, gaining more than 3,000 feet in elevation. The trail begins at Pine Springs Campground's RV loop. Make it past the first 1.5 miles and you'll have no trouble completing the hike. This stretch is the steepest section of trail with switchbacks leading up the side of the mountain. Along the way you can sneak a peak of El Capitán from above. Later in the journey, you'll pass Guadalupe Peak Campground and horse-hitching posts before reaching the monument marking its summit.

McKittrick Canyon and Devil's Hall Trails are nice any time of year, but they're particularly popular between late October and early November when big-tooth maple trees lining the canyons turn shades of yellow, orange, and red. **McKittrick Canyon Trail**, located in the park's northeast corner, is often called the best hike in Texas, but be aware that it is a day-use area. A gated entrance opens at 8am and closes at 4:30pm in winter and 6pm in summer. **Devil's Hall** is accessed from Pine Springs Campground's RV loop, which is open 24/7. The trail is highlighted by a natural rock stairway (Hiker's Staircase) leading into a narrow canyon called Devil's Hall.

Guadalupe Peak

Shumard Canyon

The Bowl

View from Wilderness Ridge

Guadalupe Peak at sunset

 <u>Stargazing</u>

One of the best ways to enjoy the peaceful calm of a night in the Guadalupe Mountains is to look up. On a cloudless night, whether you're lying in your tent or enjoying campfire conversation, look to the sky to see the galaxy's immensity. From down here looking up, even Guadalupe Mountain, the highest peak in Texas, looks small. Stargazing is best from one of the many backcountry campsites, but the stars twinkle and shine above Pine Springs and Dog Canyon Campgrounds (page 290) as well.

Horseback Riding

More than 50 miles of hiking trails are open to horseback riding. If you want to explore the region on horseback, you'll have to trailer your own stock in; there are no outfitters nearby. Horse corrals are available at Dog Canyon (505.981.2418) and Frijole Ranch (915.828.3251 ext. 0). Call between 8am and 4:30pm to make a reservation. You are required to camp near your stock at the corrals and a camping fee is charged.

Trails open to stock are denoted on the park map (page 289) with a dotted line. Easy trails include **Foothills Trail**, **Williams Ranch Road**, and **Frijole Trail**. Experienced riders and animals will want to try **Bush Mountain or Tejas Trails**, beginning at Dog Canyon. Even though riding is limited to day trips only, visitors with stock must obtain a **free backcountry permit** from Headquarters Visitor Center or Dog Canyon Ranger Station.

Bird Watching

Birding is another popular activity at Guadalupe Mountains. The best and most easily accessible locations for birders are Smith Spring Trail, near Frijole Ranch, and McKittrick Canyon Trail. These destinations reward guests with sightings of greater roadrunners, northern mockingbirds, and western scrub jays. McKittrick's Canyon protects more than 40 species of nesting birds, including ash-throated flycatchers and Cassin's kingbirds in spring and summer. If you'd like to mix a little hiking with your birding, try the 8.5-mile roundtrip hike to the Bowl (page 290). The trail leads through a relict forest of ponderosa pine and Douglas fir where you'll have a chance of seeing mountain chickadees, pygmy, white-breasted nuthatches, dark-eyed juncos, hairy woodpeckers, band-tailed pigeons, and red crossbills. If you make the trek in the fall, watch for Townsend's warblers. To see the birds of the high country without having to hike long trails with steep grades, drive around the park to Dog Canyon (elevation 6,290-ft).

Best of Guadalupe Mtns

Hike: **McKittrick Canyon**
     Runner-up: Guadalupe Peak

Backpacking Sites: **Pine Top**
     Runner-up: McKittrick Ridge

<u>For Kids:</u> Guadalupe Mountains is a great place for kids' imaginations to run wild. The wealth of fossils has inspired a new **Junior Paleontologist Program**. If your kids are aspiring fossil hunters, inquire at the park visitor center for more information.

There's also a **Junior Ranger Program** for children. Pick up an activity booklet at Headquarters Visitor Center. Complete three activities and your child will earn a certificate and badge. Complete 6 to receive a certificate, badge, and patch. You can substitute hiking a trail, attending a ranger program, or visiting the stage ruins in place of a workbook activity.

<u>Ranger Programs:</u> Ranger programs are not offered throughout the year. Typically, programs are held in

March, throughout summer, and from late October to early November. These are the best times of year to visit, and ranger programs provide the best activity. Programs vary and depend on staffing, so it is a good idea to check at Headquarters Visitor Center for a current schedule of activities when you arrive.

Flora & Fauna: The most interesting flora and fauna in the Guadalupe Mountains have been dead for hundreds of millions of years. Ancient calcareous sponges, algae, and other sea organisms were growing on a **400-mile long horseshoe-shaped reef** within an ancient sea once covering much of Texas and New Mexico. After the sea evaporated, the reef was buried in eroded sediment deposited by streams and rivers. Entombed for millions of years, the reef returned to the surface when uplift raised it more than 2 miles. Today, scientists consider the exposed reef at Guadalupe Mountains and nearby Apache and Glass Mountains as **one of the finest examples of ancient marine fossil reef on earth**.

Still, not all creatures are fossils. Black bear, elk, mountain lions, and **over 1,000 species of plants** live here.

Pets: Pets are allowed in the park, but must be kept on a leash no more than six feet in length at all times. They are allowed in developed areas (campgrounds, roadways, and parking lots) but are not allowed inside buildings or on hiking trails (with the exception of Pinery Trail).

Accessibility: Headquarters Visitor Center, Frijole Ranch Museum, and McKittrick Canyon Contact Station are all accessible to individuals in wheelchairs. Pinery Trail and Manzanita Spring Trail (page 290) are paved, mostly flat, and accessible with assistance.

Weather: Weather can change just as abruptly as the Guadalupe range rises out of the Chihuahuan Desert. Summers are hot, but are more comfortable than expected thanks to frequent thunderstorms and high elevation. Evenings in the mountains are cool any time of year. Temperatures are typically pleasant from fall through spring, but snow storms and freezing rain may occur in winter. The most common annoyance from winter to spring is gusting wind.

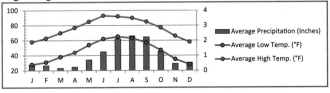

Vacation Planner

Most of Guadalupe Mountains' main attractions can be visited in a day, but a **backpacking expedition** (page 290) is an excellent multi-day adventure. Many visitors aren't even aware of **Dog Canyon**, located on the park's northern boundary near the Texas–New Mexico border. It is worth the side trip, but it will take some gas (120 miles) and time (at least 2 hours) to get there. It's also possible to hike to Dog Canyon via **Tejas or Bush Mountain Trails** (page 290). This can be an intimate experience, allowing you and your companions the opportunity to commune with nature undisturbed by the sights and sounds of civilization. If you're short on time like most people, here's how to spend a single day at Guadalupe Mountains. Always view a current schedule of **ranger programs**. Join them whenever and wherever you can. Nearby dining, grocery stores, lodging, festivals, and attractions are listed on pages 318–321.

Arrive at **McKittrick Canyon** around 8am when the gates open. Shadows cast by riparian woodlands will dance across the canyon floor as the sun rises out of the east. Hike **McKittrick Canyon Trail** (page 291). With each step the canyon becomes lusher and greener. It's 6.8 miles roundtrip to the **Grotto** (great picnic spot). Geologist or those interested in geology should scrap the hike up McKittrick Canyon in favor of the 8.4-mile **Permian Reef Trail**. After hiking, return to US-62/180 and head south/east to **Headquarters Visitor Center**. Quickly browse the exhibits and slide show. Drive over to Pine Springs Trailhead, located in the campground's RV loop. Individuals looking for a leisurely stroll should take **Devil's Hall Trail**. Those of you interested in a strenuous hike should take the 8.4 mile path to **Guadalupe Peak** (page 291). If you want to spend the night and see the stars, think about backpacking to **Guadalupe Peak backcountry campground**. It's just one mile from the peak and a great place for solitude. The highway pullout just west of the park on US-62/180 is a great place to view **El Capitán** in the evening.

Carlsbad Caverns' Natural Entrance

3225 National Parks Highway
Carlsbad, New Mexico 88220
Phone: (575) 785-2232
Website: www.nps.gov/cave

Established: May 14, 1930
Size: 46,766 Acres
Annual Visitors: 430,000
Peak Season: Holiday Weekends
Hiking Trails: 50+ Miles
Self-Guided Cave Trails: 2.5 Miles

Activities: Cave Tours, Hiking,
Stargazing, and Scenic Driving

Campgrounds & Lodging: None
Backcountry Camping: Permitted*

Park Hours: All day, every day
(Except Christmas)
Entrance Fee: $6/Person
Free for Children 15 and under
Audio Guide Fee: $3
Cave Tours: $7–$20
Cave Tour Duration: 1.5–4 hours

*Allowed in certain areas with a
free Backcountry Use Permit

Carlsbad Caverns - New Mexico

Beneath the Guadalupe Mountains lies a magnificent world, a maze of passages and chambers decorated with indescribable rock formations. Soda straws and stalactites pierce the ceiling. Stalagmites rise from the ground. Draperies adorn the sloped walls where water dripped. Clusters of popcorn-like protrusions cover the chambers. Fragile helictites defy gravity as they twist and turn in every direction. At Carlsbad Caverns, Mother Nature, like an eccentric collector, has filled rooms upon rooms with thousands of formations. Every last bit of cave real estate is plastered, ceiling to floor, with what is considered the **world's most wondrous collection of cave formations**.

An ancient reef, visible in areas of Guadalupe Mountains National Park (page 286), made cave formation here possible. Some 250 million years ago, the area was covered by a shallow, tropical sea. Changes in climate caused it to evaporate and calcite to precipitate from the water. Uplift raised the mountains and reef nearly two miles, creating many cracks and faults. This newly formed grade and openings allowed rainwater to flow through the limestone substrate. As rainwater seeped through the rock, pressurized hydrogen sulfide-rich water migrated upward from huge reservoirs of oil and gas. Mixing, they formed a sulfuric acid capable of dissolving limestone at a rapid rate. As limestone dissolved from the bottom up, cracks and faults widened, forming large chambers and passages that we walk through today. Creation began nearly one million years ago and continues today, one drop of water at a time. As rainwater seeps through the layers of earth above the cave, it absorbs carbon dioxide from the air and soil forming a weak acid. This weak acid is able to dissolve a small amount of limestone and absorb it as calcite. Once the water droplet emerges in the cave, carbon dioxide is released into the air and dissolved calcite precipitates from water. Each droplet deposits its miniscule mineral load. Over hundreds of thousands of years, enough deposits are made to create the otherworldly features you see today while touring Carlsbad Caverns.

Carlsbad truly is one of the sights you need to see to believe. Indeed, the folks in Washington, D.C. didn't believe reports of the elaborate caves until 1923 when the Department of the Interior sent Robert Holley and a photographer. Holley described the cave as work of the Divine Creator, invoking "deep conflicting emotions of fear and awe." One year later, **President Calvin Coolidge** used the power of the Antiquities Act to establish Carlsbad Cave National Monument. In 1928, additional land was added to the monument, and two years later Congress established Carlsbad Caverns National Park, protecting one of America's most unique natural treasures for future generations.

Did you know?

➤ The park possesses more than 110 caves, and Carlsbad is one of the deepest and most ornate caves ever found.

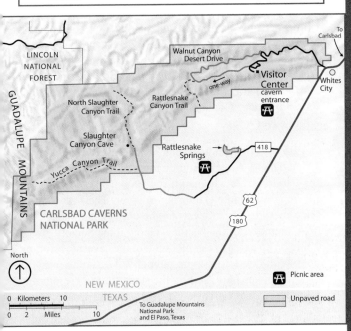

When to Go

Carlsbad Caverns is open every day of the year except Christmas. Between Memorial Day weekend and Labor Day weekend the visitor center is open from 8am–7pm and the last cavern entry is at 3:30pm via the natural entrance and 5pm via elevator. For the rest of the year, the visitor center is open from 8am–5pm, the last entry at the natural entrance is 2pm, and the last elevator entry is at 3:30pm.

Unless you like crowds, you'll want to avoid visiting the park on summer holiday weekends. If you are interested in a specific tour, be sure to make advance reservations. Kings Palace and Left Hand Tunnel are the only tours that are offered daily. Wild Caving tours are only offered on weekends. Dress in layers, because the cave's temperature remains relatively constant throughout the year. The cave is hotter the deeper you go, but temperatures are always cool, ranging from the 50s–60s°F.

Transportation & Airports

Public transportation does not serve the Carlsbad Caverns directly. Greyhound (800.231.2222, www.greyhound.com) has a bus station in Carlsbad, NM (24 miles from the park's visitor center). Cavern City Air Terminal (CNM) in Carlsbad, NM (23 miles from the visitor center) offers passenger service to and from Albuquerque International Sunport (ABQ). El Paso International (ELP), in El Paso, TX, is a nice alternative (144 miles from the visitor center). Car rental is available at each destination.

Directions

Carlsbad Caverns has one entrance road, NM-7, which runs west from US-62/180 at Whites City. It is 16 miles southwest of Carlsbad, NM and 151 miles northeast of El Paso, TX.

If you're looking to take Slaughter Canyon Cave Tour or hike Yucca or Slaughter Canyon Trails, take US-62/180 south from Carlsbad/Whites City. Head west on County Road 418. From here, follow the signs to the cave parking area and trailheads.

Queen's Chamber - King's Palace Tour

Colonel Boles Formation - Lower Cave Tour

Carlsbad Caverns

Ancient artifacts indicate the area around Carlsbad Caverns has been inhabited for nearly 10,000 years, but very little is known about these early people. Native Americans entered Carlsbad more than 1,000 years ago, but it's unlikely that they used the cave for anything more than shelter. They left behind drawings, including an ancient petroglyph near the natural entrance. Exploration of the cave didn't occur until the 1800s, when settlers were drawn to a mysterious cloud (of bats) rising up out of the desert each summer night.

It's disputable whether **Jim White** was first to discover the cave, but after he entered in 1898 as a 16 year old boy he would become its primary explorer. During his expeditions he named many of the rooms: Big Room (the seventh largest cave chamber in the world), New Mexico Room, King's Palace, Queen's Chamber, Papoose Room, and Green Lake Room. He also named features like Totem Pole, Witch's Finger, Giant Dome, Bottomless Pit, Fairyland, Iceberg Rock, Temple of the Sun, and Rock of the Ages. White offered to take locals on tours, but few accepted. One day he crossed paths with a man who was more interested in a different kind of deposit: bat guano. Bat's natural waste is a high quality fertilizer, and as you can imagine, the cave's millions of bats produce an awful lot. Drop by drop, guano piles up kind of like formation of stalagmites, just messier and faster. Jim White started mining guano, bringing each payload out the natural entrance in a bucket via a 170-foot ascent. They even lifted burros in and out to aid production. Guano was packed in gunny-sacks and shipped to citrus groves of California. Unfortunately for them, this industry wasn't very profitable. Companies formed and folded, but Jim White never left.

In 1915, the first photographs of the cave were taken by Ray V. Davis. After seeing pictures of its brilliant formations, individuals who had turned down Jim White's tour offerings were now clamoring to enter. The first tourists made the 170-foot descent via the old "guano bucket." In 1924, members of the National Geographic Society joined White on an extensive exploration of the caverns, bringing along with them even more publicity. The following year a staircase was built, setting the stage for the present-day era of tourism at Carlsbad Caverns.

Other Caves

Caves are the last terrestrial frontier. They're full of mystery and the unknown, and most have yet to be mapped completely. Bones of Ice Age mammals, such as jaguars, camels, and giant sloths have been found near or in these caves. There are **more than 300 caves in the Guadalupe Mountains, about 110 within park boundaries**.

Lechuguilla Cave (whose location has not been disclosed by the National Park Service to protect its environment from tourists and spelunkers) has been the caving community's focus since its discovery in 1986. It has already surpassed Carlsbad in depth, size, and variety of cave formations, many of which have never been seen anywhere else in the world. Lechuguilla is more than 128 miles long, the 5th longest cave known to exist in the world and the deepest in the continental United States. Carlsbad Caverns big open rooms feel gigantic, but when all its known passageways are measured, they total just over 28 miles in length, 100 fewer than Lechuguilla. It has also replaced Carlsbad Caverns as the world's most beautiful cave. This is just the tip of the iceberg of noteworthy facts about Lechuguilla. Scientists even found microbes capable of producing enzymes that destroy cancer cells. The cave is restricted to exploratory and scientific groups. However, you can explore Lechuguilla from your living room by watching the fourth episode ("Caves") of the hit BBC documentary series *Planet Earth*.

If you'd like to explore caves other than Carlsbad, there are a few open to the public. Park rangers lead general tours of **Slaughter Canyon Cave** and wild tours (think crawling, sliding, and getting dirty) of **Spider Cave**. Additionally, there are more vertical and horizontal caves open to experienced cavers with the proper skills and equipment. These caves can only be accessed with a permit. To schedule a trip, interested parties must download and complete an application (available at the park website). Mail permit applications at least one month in advance to: Carlsbad Caves National Park; 3224 National Parks Highway; Carlsbad, NM 88220. Reservations are made on a first-come, first served basis. Spelunking in **Ogle Cave** requires a park ranger escort ($15). All caves open to private parties are of natural significance and should not be treated carelessly. Defacing or causing irreparable damage to any cave will result in its closure. A list of open backcountry caves is available at the park website.

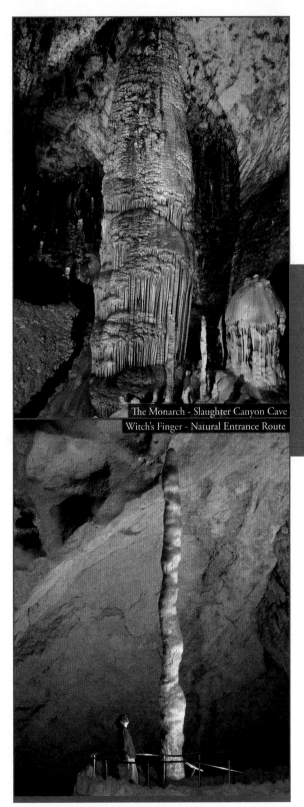

The Monarch - Slaughter Canyon Cave
Witch's Finger - Natural Entrance Route

Cave Tours

Carlsbad Caverns displays some of the most elaborate cave formations in the world. A little more then 3 miles of paved and lit trails weave through rooms and past fragile features. After paying the entrance fee, you are free to explore two self-guided trails: The Natural Entrance Tour and The Big Room Tour. Audio guides are available for $3. The **Natural Entrance Tour** begins exactly where you would expect; from the Natural Entrance, it's 1.25 miles and 800-ft down to the Big Room. Along the way you'll pass **Bat Cave**, Witch's Finger, and many other features. Once you've reached the **Big Room** you can take the elevator back to the surface or continue on the **Big Room self-guiding tour** (also accessible via the elevator from the visitor center). You'll find features named Lion's Tail, Hall of Giants, Bottomless Pit, and Rock of Ages while perusing the Big Room. The 1.25 mile tour is paved and mostly level. Sturdy shoes are recommended for

The Klansman - Slaughter Canyon Cave

the Natural Entrance Tour, and you should be in decent physical shape without any respiratory problems. Ranger-led Cave Tours are highly recommended. **Spider Cave and The Hall of the White Giant** are "Wild Caving" options for the adventurous. **King's Palace Tour** is a popular, easy walk past ornate formations like helictites, draperies, columns, and soda straws. Rangers also give guests a taste of pure darkness during a "blackout." For a less developed cave experience sign up for **Slaughter Canyon Cave Tour**, where you'll see eerie formations like the Klansman.

Tour (Group Size, Age Limit, Offered)	Rate (Adult/Youth)	Length	Notes
King's Palace (Capacity: 55, Age Limit: 4, Offered several times daily) - 👍	$8/4	1.5 hours	The tour is offered several times each day • A 1-mile tour through several rooms named by Jim White
Left Hand Tunnel (15, 6, daily)	$7/3.50	2 hours	The easiest adventure tour • Surface is uneven and slippery and lighting is by lanterns provided by the NPS
Lower Cave (12, 12, Mon–Fri) - 👍	$20/10	3 hours	Guests must descend down a 10-ft flowstone using knotted rope • Bring gloves and (4) AA batteries
Slaughter Canyon Cave (25, 8, daily (Memorial Day–Labor Day), Sat & Sun (the rest of year)) - 👍	$15/7.50	2–2.5 hours	Strenuous tour through undeveloped cave • It meets at Slaughter Canyon Cave Entrance (page 295) • Bring a strong flashlight
Hall of the White Giant (8, 12, Saturdays Only) - 👍	$20/10	4 hours	Crawling, squeezing, and sliding through narrow openings • You will get dirty • (4) AA batteries, knee pads, leather gloves, and long pants are required
Spider Cave (8, 12, Sundays Only) - 👍	$20/10	4 hours	Wild caving experience • (4) AA batteries, knee pads, leather gloves, and long pants are required

Youth is 4–15 years of age. Senior Access Pass holders pay youth rates. All tours can be reserved in advance by calling (877) 446-6777 or visiting www.recreation.gov. Reservations are highly recommended for all tours not offered on a daily basis.

Bat Flight Program

Tourists aren't the only mammals flocking to Carlsbad Caverns in summer. From **mid-April to mid-October**, the **Bat Cave** is home to hundreds of thousands of **Mexican free-tailed bats**. They leave the safety of the cave at dusk to gorge on insects, returning just before dawn. Evening Bat Programs are offered (weather permitting) when the bats are in residence. Guests fill the amphitheater near the Natural Entrance while a ranger discusses these winged friends. Just as the talk is winding down, a swarm of bats begins their mass exodus to fly about the Chihuahuan Desert in search of food. The exit flight can last anywhere from 20 minutes to 2 hours. Programs are offered beginning in mid-May and they usually start 30–60 minutes before sunset. For the exact time check at the visitor center or call (575) 785-3012. Cameras (including cell phone cameras) and camcorders may not be used during the Bat Flight Program.

You're going to want a little bat background information before you meet Carlsbad's bats face-to-face. First, there's nothing to be afraid of. Bats are not dangerous. In fact, they're amazing little creatures, being the only mammal capable of flight. They also help control the insect population. Carlsbad's Mexican free-tailed bats eat about three tons of insects each night. A single bat can eat as much as half its body weight in a single meal. One of their favorite appetizers is one of our least favorite pests: the mosquito. It has been estimated that Carlsbad's Mexican free-tailed bat population once counted in the millions, not hundreds of thousands like today. No one knows exactly what caused this dramatic decline, but use of pesticides like DDT and loss of habitat for their prey are likely causes.

Bats that occupy the cave today still live the same interesting bat-life. Days are spent hanging from the ceiling. About 250 and 300 bats huddle together in one square-foot of ceiling space. Nights are spent searching for food. Their reentry at dawn is nearly as impressive as the exit. The bats at Carlsbad are considered a maternity colony, because females seek the cave's safe-haven to give birth. In June, females typically bear just one pup. It is born hairless and clings to the mother or ceiling after birth. The pup remains on the ceiling for 4–5 weeks before its first flight. After summer the pups are mature enough to retreat to warmer climates in Mexico or Central America for winter with the rest of Carlsbad's bat population.

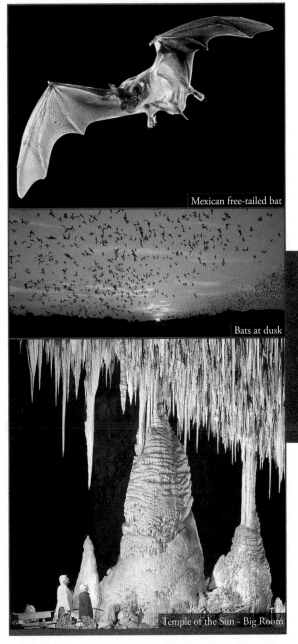

Mexican free-tailed bat

Bats at dusk

Temple of the Sun - Big Room

CARLSBAD

Did you know?

➤ From mid-April until mid-October nearly 400,000 Mexican free-tailed bats call Carlsbad Caverns home.

➤ At more than 128 miles, Lechuguilla Cave is the 5th longest known cave in the world.

Hiking/Backpacking

The world above Carlsbad Caverns often goes unnoticed by visitors. There are 50+ miles of hiking trails that are the perfect place to escape the cave-exploring crowds.

Chihuahuan Desert Nature Trail is located at the base of the hill in front of the visitor center's main entrance. It's a paved 0.5-mile loop around historic guano mining ruins. The trail closes at dawn and dusk when Mexican free-tailed bats (page 299) are occupying the cave.

Adjacent to the park entrance is a dirt road suitable for hiking. This 3.7-mile (one-way) road follows the original path used by miners and burros to haul bat guano in the early 1900s. It ends at Whites City Campground, just beyond the park boundary.

The rest of the trails fan out into the **Chihuahuan Desert** where water is unavailable and shade is uncommon. Trails are marked by sporadic rock cairns, so hike with a good topographic map and plenty of water.

Juniper Ridge Trail is located on Walnut Canyon Desert Drive (also known as Desert Loop Road (DLR)), about one mile past interpretive marker #15. It's a 3.5-mile (one-way) hike along a ridge ending at a canyon overlook.

Rattlesnake Canyon Trail begins on DLR, two miles from the visitor center at interpretive marker #9. This 3-mile (one-way) path descends into a deep canyon and past ruins of a 1930's homesteader's cabin. You can also make a 6-mile loop following Upper Rattlesnake Canyon to Guadalupe Ridge Road (GRR) from this trailhead. The loop returns to DLR and Rattlesnake Canyon Trailhead by following GRR to the east. The 12-mile GRR can also be hiked in its entirety. You are allowed to leave your vehicle at the gate where GRR intersects DLR.

There's a trailhead at Slaughter Canyon Parking Area (page 295). **Slaughter Canyon Trail** leads to Slaughter Canyon Cave and continues 5.3 more miles (one-way) where it intersects Guadalupe Ridge Road. It's a large canyon with several branches; a good map and map reading skills are essential.

Yucca Canyon Trail branches off from the road to Slaughter Canyon at the park boundary. Here you'll find a dirt road heading west, which can only be accessed by high-clearance 4WD vehicles. The 7.7 mile (one-way)

trail climbs up a canyon to a ridgeline. **Backpackers** may camp west of Rattlesnake Canyon Trailhead off of DLR and south of Guadalupe Ridge Trail to the park boundary. A **free Backcountry Use Permit** (available at the visitor center) is required.

Stargazing

Carlsbad Caverns hosts several "Star Parties." Like most national parks, Carlsbad is far removed from city lights, making it an ideal location to gaze up at the stars. During these "parties," rangers guide you across the galaxy. Telescopes are available for use (weather permitting), and it's free. Arrive early, so your car's headlights don't drown out the stars. Call Park Ranger Christy Moerbe at (575) 785-3134 or e-mail the park via the park website's "contact us" page for details.

Driving

You can't drive through the cave, but most vehicles can observe the Chihuahuan Desert by driving the 9.5 mile **Walnut Canyon Desert Drive** (also called **Desert Loop Road**). This narrow and twisting one-way gravel loop is not recommended for trailers or RVs, but your typical 2WD vehicle should be able to navigate this seldom traveled road just fine. It also provides access to a few hiking trails.

Best of Carlsbad Caverns

Cave Tour: **King's Palace**
>Runner-up: Lower Cave
>2nd Runner-up: Hall of the White Giant

Cave Room: **King's Palace**
>Runner-up: Big Room
>2nd Runner-up: Queen's Chamber

Hike: **Natural Entrance (downhill)**
>Runner-up: Rattlesnake Trail

<u>For Kids:</u> Children are drawn to caves like they're to muddy puddles. Something about these mysterious

underground passages and rock formations lights the wick of a child's imagination. If you have a child (12+ years old) who loves crawling through tight spaces and getting dirty, you may want to send him/her on the **Spider Cave Tour** (page 298). A less adventurous way to enjoy the park with your child is to take part in the **Junior Ranger Program**. Free activity booklets are available at the visitor center. Complete its activities to become an official Carlsbad Caverns Junior Ranger.

<u>Ranger Programs:</u> Ranger programs consist of **Cave Tours** (page 298) and **Bat Flight Programs** (page 299). Bat Flight Programs are occasionally cancelled due to weather, so it's a good idea to check at the visitor center or call (575) 785-3012 to confirm the schedule. Note that cameras (including cellphones) and camcorders are not allowed at the Bat Flight Program.

<u>Flora & Fauna:</u> The most notable inhabitant is the **Mexican (or Brazilian) free-tailed bat** (page 299), but there are other living things in the desert.

The park reports **67 species of mammals (17 bats), 357 species of birds, 55 species of reptiles and amphibians, 5 species of fish, at least 600 species of insects, and more than 900 species of vascular plants**. Black bear, mountain lion, elk, pronghorn, bighorn sheep, and javelina are a few of the seldom-seen larger mammals.

The high country of the Guadalupe Mountains provides habitat for many of the bird species you'll find in Guadalupe Mountains National Park (page 286), a particularly good birding location. But the best **birding locations** at Carlsbad are also some of the most difficult sites to reach. The southwest corner of the park, several miles into **Yucca Canyon Trail**, hosts a few stands of coniferous forest; this is a great place for birding, but is only accessible to experienced backpackers with 4WD vehicles.

<u>Pets:</u> Pets are permitted, but if you want to tour the cave, hike a trail, or attend a bat flight program, it's best to leave them at home. They are not permitted in caves, on hiking trails, or at bat flight programs. Pets are not to be left unattended in vehicles (citations are issued on days when ambient air temperatures are 70°F or higher). If you still choose to bring your pet along with you, it can be boarded at the park's kennel for a small fee.

<u>Accessibility:</u> The visitor center, book store, theater, gift shop, restaurant, and amphitheater (site of bat flight programs) are accessible to wheelchair users. Inside the cave,

the Big Room is accessible with assistance. There's also a 1-mile nature trail beginning at the visitor center that is accessible.

<u>Weather:</u> Temperature inside Carlsbad Caverns' Big Room is a cool 56°F all year long. It's chilly and damp in the cave, with humidity levels usually close to 100%. As the cave's passages go deeper, average temperature increases due to heat rising from the earth's core. Climate on the surface is semi-arid, typical to the Chihuahuan Desert. The park receives an average of 15 inches of precipitation each year. Summers are hot. Winters are mild, but snowstorms can occur. No matter when you visit, you'll want to dress in layers to account for differences in temperature in-and-out of the cave.

Vacation Planner

A visit to Carlsbad Caverns should be planned out in advance. Once you know when you're going, figure out how long you'd like to stay and reserve your **cave tours** (page 298) right away (especially for tours that are not offered daily). Unless you plan on doing multiple cave tours, a single day should provide enough time. Spending a night or two in Carlsbad allows you to take another cave tour, **hike** (page 300) a few trails or join a **Bat Flight Program** (page 299) or **Star Party** (page 300). On the other hand, if you're passing through and only have a couple of hours take the **self-guiding Big Room Tour** (page 298). If you can squeeze in a ranger tour, go for it.

The **King's Palace Tour** visits the cave's most famous formations and a ranger will regale you with stories of the cave's history and geology. **Left Hand** and **Lower Cave Tours** visit more remote sections of Carlsbad Caverns. They are a bit more strenuous, but very doable as long as you're in decent physical condition. If you like your caves undeveloped, but don't want to crawl through tight passages, you should tour **Slaughter Canyon Cave**. The most extreme tours are **Hall of the White Giant** and **Spider Cave**. Nearby dining, grocery stores, lodging, festivals, and attractions are listed on pages 318–321.

Ancient petrified wood near Blue Mesa

PO Box 2217
Petrified Forest, AZ 86028
Phone: (928) 524-6228
Website: www.nps.gov/pefo

Established: December 9, 1962
Size: 93,533 Acres
Annual Visitors: 660,000
Peak Season: Summer
Hiking Trails: 7 Miles

Activities: Hiking, Biking, and
Horseback Riding

Campgrounds: None
Lodging: None
Backcountry Camping: Permitted
in the Wilderness Area with a free
permit (available at visitor center)

Park Hours: 8am–5pm (late Oct to
late Feb); 7am–7pm (early May to
early Sept); 7am–6pm (the rest of
the year)

Entrance Fee: $10 • Vehicle
$5 • Individual (foot, bike, etc.)

Petrified Forest - Arizona

Forests of fallen trees made of stone. Ruins and petroglyphs of ancient
civilizations. Fossils of prehistoric plants and animals. Pastel colored
badlands. Wilderness. Peace. Solitude. Silence. All of these are found
at Petrified Forest, located just a short distance from the whir of traffic
along Interstate 40. Nearby communities (like Holbrook and Adamana)
are sleepy ex-railway towns. Oddly enough, signs of the past outnum-
ber signs of the present. This rich history of life exists in a place that is
anything but lively. Most desert animals are small rodents, amphibians,
and reptiles, many of which only emerge during the summer nights,
long after tourists have left the park. Plants are primarily grasses, cacti,
and wildflowers that have managed to adapt to life with little water and
arid soil.

Trees, some as tall as 200 feet, thrived in what was a humid and subtropical climate 225 million years ago. They were washed away by
ancient rivers and streams, and then buried by silt, soil, and volcanic
ash—conditions ripe for fossilization. Many plants and animals were
cast in stone, preserved for millions of years, and today they help tell the
story of prehistoric life in the Painted Desert. The story is still incomplete, but scientists believe present-day park land was once situated near
the equator. Large crocodile-like reptiles and oversized salamanders co-
existed with early dinosaurs. Visitors can view **fossils** of these creatures
and ancient plants at Painted Desert Visitor Center and Rainbow Forest
Museum.

Fossils are not the only signs of life revealed through rocks. **Ancient cultures**, from 650 to 2,000 years ago, drew thousands of petroglyphs. There are more than 600 petroglyphs at **Newspaper Rock** alone. It's difficult to determine what these symbols mean; descendents of ancient Hopi, Zuni, and Navajo cultures only recognize some of them. As always, scientists are full of hypotheses regarding their meaning. Ideas ranging from trail markers to family stories to fertility charms abound. It's likely most held some spiritual significance. Others more practical, like the petroglyphs near **Puerco Pueblo** that form a sundial signaling the summer solstice.

People have lived in the region for more than 10,000 years, but most evidence of inhabitation is from the same cultures that left us ancient petroglyphs. Tools, pottery, and village ruins from Puebloan cultures have been found at more than **600 archeological sites**. They originally lived in single family huts built over a dug-out section of earth. Around the turn of the 13th century, climatic changes caused families to group together near reliable sources of water where they built large pueblos capable of housing as many as 200 people in about 100, 1-story rooms. The rooms were constructed without doors or windows around an open plaza. They entered using a ladder. **Puerco Pueblo**, located along the main park road, is home to some of the most well-preserved ruins.

Modern civilization saw value in the **Painted Desert** as a **tourist destination**. Rail was laid through the present park boundary and soon the railroad began promoting America's scenic wonders hoping to boost passenger service. Arizona's Painted Desert and Petrified Forest were near the top of the list of wonders. Tourists could take a train to Adamana, book a hotel room, and walk amongst the petrified trees of what was known at the time as Chalcedony Forest. Trains dropped off tourists and loaded petrified wood to be taken back East. One man even proposed to crush petrified logs turning them into an abrasive grit. **John Muir**, already the driving force behind creation of Yosemite National Park, conducted the first scientific excavation in Petrified Forest. What he saw was destruction of a unique resource that was clearly exhaustible. To protect the region, he enlisted service of friend and fellow conservationist, **President Theodore Roosevelt**. Roosevelt promptly created Petrified Forest National Monument by executive order. Fifty-six years later it was made a national park.

Best of Petrified Forest

Attraction: **Painted Desert**
> Runner-up: Rainbow Forest
> 2nd Runner-up: Blue Mesa

Activity: **Drive Main Park Road**
> Runner-up: Backpack in the Wilderness

Cultural Sites: **Agate House**
> Runner-up: Newspaper Rock

Overlook: **Chinde Point**
> Runner-up: Kachina Point

Family Hike: **Blue Mesa**
> Runner-up: Painted Desert Rim

When to Go

Petrified Forest is open every day of the year except Christmas Day. However, it's not your typical 24/7 national park. Most days it's open from 7am–6pm. Hours extend to 7pm from early May to early September. In winter (late October–late February) hours are reduced to 8am–5pm. Painted Desert Visitor Center and Rainbow Forest Museum hold the same operating hours as the park. Painted Desert Inn National Historic Landmark is open from 9am–5pm every day. It's hot in summer, cool in winter, and comfortable in between. Summer thunderstorms can bring dangerous lightning and frightening thunder, but an ideal time to visit is after a storm; when the sedimentary rocks of the Painted Desert are wet, the colors appear brighter and more pronounced in the soft morning or evening light. April and May are typically the best months to see wildflowers.

Transportation & Airports

Public transportation is not available to or around Petrified Forest. The closest major airports are Albuquerque International Sunport (ABQ) in Albuquerque, NM (228 miles east of the park) and Sky Harbor International Airport (PHX) in Phoenix, AZ (213 miles southwest of the park). Pulliam Airport (FLG) in Flagstaff, AZ is 135 miles to the west.

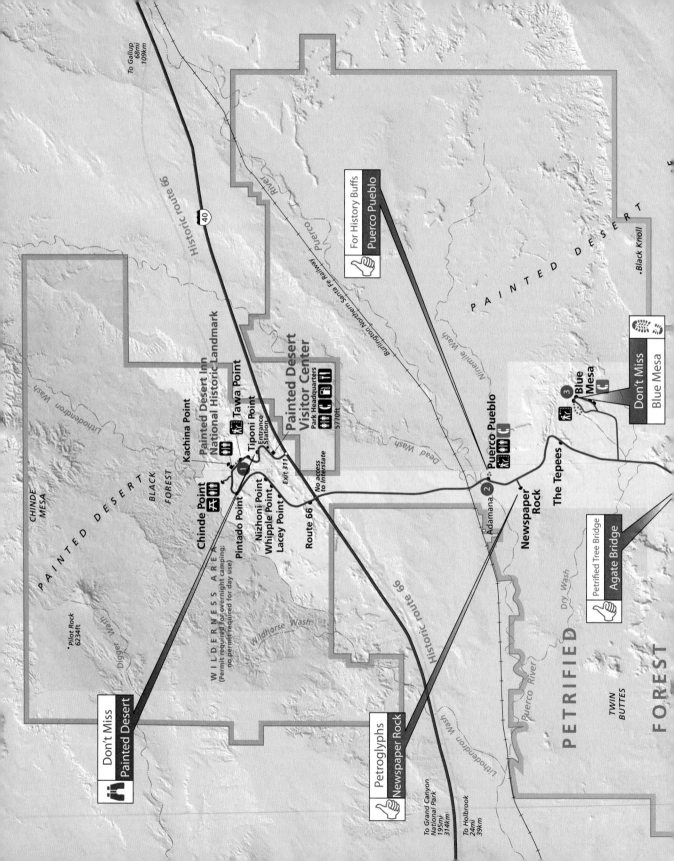

Don't Miss
Painted Desert

To Gallup
68mi
109km

Historic route 66

PAINTED DESERT

CHINDE MESA

Lithodendron Wash

Pilot Rock
6234ft

Digger Wash

WILDERNESS AREA
(Permit required for overnight camping;
no permit required for day use)

Wildhorse Wash

Historic route 66

Petroglyphs
Newspaper Rock

To Grand Canyon
National Park
195mi
314km

To Holbrook
24mi
39km

Lithodendron Wash

99

PAINTED DESERT

BLACK FOREST

Kachina Point

Painted Desert Inn
National Historic Landmark

Tawa Point

Tiponi Point

Chinde Point

Pintado Point

Nizhoni Point
Whipple Point
Lacey Point

Route 66

Painted Desert
Visitor Center
Park Headquarters

5770ft

Entrance
Station

Exit 311

No access
to Interstate

40

River

Puerco River

Burlington Northern Santa Fe Railway

For History Buffs
Puerco Pueblo

Puerco Pueblo

Adamana

Newspaper
Rock

The Tepees

Petrified Tree Bridge
Agate Bridge

Dry Wash

PETRIFIED

Puerco River

TWIN
BUTTES

FOREST

PAINTED DESERT

Nimmille Wash

Dead Wash

Blue Mesa

Don't Miss
Blue Mesa

PAINTED DESERT

.Black Knoll

1

2

3

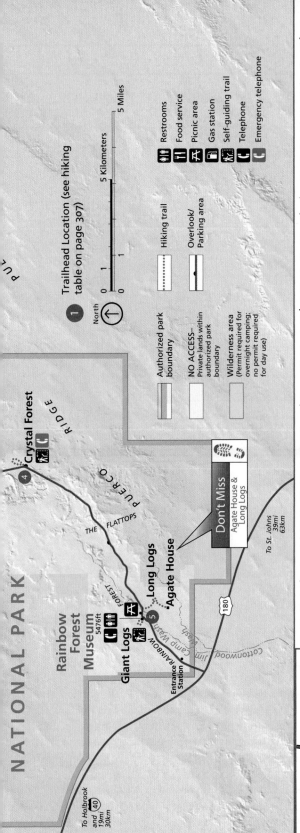

Directions

Petrified Forest is located in northeastern Arizona, straddling Interstate 40 between Albuquerque, NM and Flagstaff, AZ. Visitors arriving via I-40 from the east should take Exit 311. It leads directly to the park and Painted Desert Visitor Center. From here you begin by touring the park north of I-40 before crossing the interstate and exiting near Rainbow Forest Museum. Those traveling from the west will want to take Exit 285 into Holbrook. Drive 19 miles south on US-180 to the south entrance near Rainbow Forest Museum.

Visitor Centers & Museums

Painted Desert Visitor Center is located near I-40's Exit 311. Here you'll find a short orientation film, several exhibits, a bookstore, and restrooms. A restaurant, gas station, gift shop, and convenience store are available adjacent to the visitor center. **Painted Desert Inn** is located at Kachina Point just north of the visitor center. It used to be a rest stop for travelers on historic Route 66, but now the Inn is a museum. Two miles north of the south entrance is **Rainbow Forest Museum**. Here you'll find fossil exhibits, a short film, snack bar, and restrooms.

Camping & Lodging

There are **no designated campgrounds or lodgings** within the park. Lodging is available nearby (page 319). **Backcountry camping** is allowed within Petrified Forest National Wilderness Area. Backpackers must obtain a **free backcountry permit** from the visitor center during normal operating hours. Permits are not available in advance, and must be obtained at least one hour before the park closes. You are required to hike at least one mile from the two designated parking spots (Painted Desert Inn or Tawa Point) before camping.

Driving

If you don't have enough time to join a ranger program, hike a trail, or spend a night in the park's backcountry, the 28-mile park road is still worth the detour from I-40. It offers overlooks, picnic areas, and access to hiking trails.

| Recipe For: | *Petrified Wood* | Ready In: | *Several Centuries (possibly millenia)* |

Ingredients: *Trees (as many as you desire), sediment that includes volcanic ash*

1. *Take your trees and bury them in sediment (A nice layer of sediment with volcanic ash will help slow down the natural decomposition process by cutting off the amount of oxygen that reaches them)*
2. *Pour large amounts of water onto the sediment (Water dissolves silica from the volcanic ash – The solution of silica in water slowly replaces the wood's original tissues)*
3. *Let sit for several centuries (Over time silica crystalizes to quartz – Colors develop based on mineral content, like manganese, carbon, iron, cobalt, and chromium, that were in your original sediment)*
4. *Remove sediment and observe your tree(s) made of stone*

The Painted Desert

Hiking/Backpacking

Petrified Forest isn't renowned for its spectacular hikes. It features only seven maintained trails, all of which are less than 3 miles long. Still, they provide access to some of the finer petrified rock specimens, badlands formations, and archaeological sites. **Long Logs and Giant Logs Trails** are pretty self-explanatory; you're going to see some petrified wood. **Giant Logs** leads to "**Old Faithful**," a petrified tree nearly ten feet in diameter. If you're interested in the area's ancient history, take **Puerco Pueblo Trail**. It leads to a hundred room village that was built and occupied between 1250 and 1400 AD Agate House Trail leads to a more modern habitation.

About 700 years ago this structure was built using materials on hand: mud and petrified wood. The trail begins at the same trailhead as Long Logs Trail. You can combine the two to make a 2.6 mile trek. **The best hike in the park is Blue Mesa Trail**, located just off of Blue Mesa Road. It's a short loop that descends from the mesa to deposits of petrified wood and spectacular views of badlands infused with bluish bentonite. You are also free to hike (and camp) in the park's wilderness area. Fifty thousand acres of undeveloped desert. No trails. No water. Little shade. If you choose to blaze your own path, come prepared with a map, compass, and plenty of water.

Petrified Forest Hiking Trails

	Trail Name	Length	Location (# on map)/Notes (Roundtrip distances)
All Trails are Easy to Moderate	Painted Desert Rim - 👍	1.0 mile	Trail is accessed at Tawa and Kachina Points (1) • Follows the picturesque rim
	Puerco Pueblo	0.3 mile	Accessed at Puerco Pueblo Parking Area (2) • Visits ruins of an ancient people
	Blue Mesa - 👍	1.0 mile	Accessed at Blue Mesa sunshelter (3) • Loop trail through wood and blue badlands
	Crystal Forest	0.75 mile	Accessed at Crystal Forest Parking Area (4) • Crystals hide in a few petrified logs
	Long Logs	1.6 miles	Rainbow Forest Parking Area (5) • Loop trail to a large concentration of wood
	Agate House	2.0 miles	Accessed from Rainbow Forest (5) • Hike to a pueblo occupied some 700 years ago
	Giant Logs	0.4 mile	Behind Rainbow Forest Museum (5) • Large logs including "Old Faithful"
	Wilderness Hiking	N/A	Hikers are welcome to explore the wilderness area which comprises more than 50% of the park. There are no established trails in the backcountry, so hike with a map and know how to use it. Bring plenty of water, because you won't find any in the backcountry. A permit is required for overnight stays but not for day-hiking. Begin backpacking/wilderness hike at Painted Desert Inn or Tawa Point (map marker #1).

The Tepees

Petrified logs

Petrified wood & bentonite clay © Luca Galuzzi (www.galuzzi.it)

Did you know?

▶ Petrified trees found here have not been alive for at least 225 million years.

▶ Humans have inhabited this area for more than 10,000 years, leaving a wealth of archeological sites in addition to the world class fossil record.

▶ Newspaper Rock features more than 600 petroglyphs. Some are calendars, marking events like the summer solstice.

Horseback Riding

Bring your own horse(s) to explore Painted Desert's colorful badlands. However, riders and their stock are restricted to the wilderness area (northern half). It can be accessed via Wilderness Access Trail near Kachina Point, on the northwest side of Painted Desert Inn, two miles north of the visitor center. You and your horse are permitted to camp overnight north of Lithodendron Wash with an overnight use permit (available at the visitor center). Water is not available in the backcountry, which makes a multi-day trip with stock extremely challenging.

Biking

Motorists rule the road, but cyclists can also enjoy the scenic vistas afforded by the **28-mile park road** and 3.5-mile **Blue Mesa Loop**. These roads are relatively straight, flat, and narrow. It's best to pedal as early in the morning or as late in the evening as operating hours allow. Summer is often hot, windy, and a poor time to pedal the roads. Cyclists are not allowed off road and may not use paved walking trails. Always be aware of motorists.

For Kids: Children of all ages are invited to participate in the **Junior Ranger Program**. The program encourages you and your children to learn about fossils and human history while exploring the park. To become a Junior Ranger you must first pick up a free activity booklet from Painted Desert Visitor Center, Painted Desert Inn, or Rainbow Forest Museum. It's also available for download online at the park website. Complete the activities during your visit to receive a badge or patch and be anointed the newest Junior Ranger at Petrified Forest National Park.

Ranger Programs: The area's interesting and sometimes unexplainable geology and history stirs all sorts of questions. And park rangers are always nearby, ready and willing to answer them for you. "Where's the restroom?" They'll point you to it. "How'd the trees turn to stone?" They'll explain it to you. You are also invited to join their ranger programs. Rangers enlighten and entertain guests on tours of Painted Desert Inn, talks about the Triassic Period, and walks at Puerco Pueblo. For a current schedule of programs and events visit the park website, call

(928) 524-6228, or stop in at Painted Desert Visitor Center upon your arrival. The park also holds a multitude of special events throughout the course of the year. These include wildflower week (May), International Migratory Bird Day (May), National Fossil Day (October), and Parade of Lights (December).

Flora & Fauna: The park is home to **more than 200 species of birds**. Pronghorn, coyote, and bobcats endure the unforgiving desert climate along with dozens of other mammals, reptiles, and amphibians. This desolate terrain is dominated by grasses, but **at least 400 species of plants** survive here. However, the most fascinating plants and animals are those that lived here 225 million years ago. Their existence is recorded in rock of the Chinle Formation, one of the richest Late Triassic fossil-plant deposits in the world. **More than 200 plant and animal fossils** have been discovered including crocodile-like phytosaurs, large salamanders named Buettneria, and a few early dinosaurs.

Pets: Petrified Forest is one of the few parks where pets won't limit your activities. Pets must be kept on a leash no more than six feet in length at all times, but they are allowed on all developed trails, with the exception of Wilderness Access Trail. They are not allowed in buildings, but are welcome in picnic and parking areas, and along roadways.

Accessibility: All facilities, including visitor centers, museums, restrooms, and picnic areas, are accessible (assistance may be necessary) to wheelchair users. Park trails are not.

Weather: Weather is as peculiar as the Painted Desert, petrified wood, and painted petroglyphs. A high-altitude desert with predominantly clear nights creates extreme cooling between day and night, often as much as 40°F. This effect makes for cool summer evenings and hot afternoons. Summer highs are in the mid-to-high 90s°F. Evening lows dip into the mid-60s°F. Summers can also be windy and wet. Most rain falls during the monsoon season (July and August). Summer dust devils are common. During winter, snow can fall any day, October through March, but it rarely lasts through the afternoon. Enjoy the rain and snow because moisture on the badlands can really make the Painted Desert's colors pop on a sunny day.

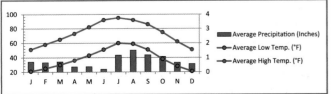

Vacation Planner

Petrified forest will increase in size because President George W. Bush signed a bill authorizing its expansion 218,533 acres when funds become available, but, with or without the extra land, it's still small and quite manageable. **Hiking trails** (page 306) are less than 3 miles long, and the **main park road** (page 305) is only 28 miles long allowing all of the major attractions to be seen in a single day. Actually, it's fairly difficult to spend the night. This is one of the few parks that closes (to prevent theft of petrified wood). There are no campgrounds or lodging facilities within park boundaries. The only way to stay overnight is to **backpack** in Painted Desert Wilderness Area. With that said, you should try to visit the park at one end of its operating hours, because Painted Desert is most beautiful at dusk and dawn. Nearby dining, grocery stores, lodging, festivals, and attractions are listed on pages 318–321.

 Begin at **Painted Desert Visitor Center**. Browse the exhibits and bookstore. Watch a 20-minute introductory film. Inquire about ranger programs. Once you're finished, head back to the car and begin driving the 28-mile road. You will begin at its most beautiful stretch through the Painted Desert. Depending on time, interest, and attitudes, stop at overlooks along the way. **Chinde Point** and **Kachina Point** are two of the best. Fans of museums or Route 66 should pit-stop at **Painted Desert Inn National Historic Landmark**, which has been renovated to house a bookstore and museum (no lodging available). Back on the road you'll pass an exhibit commemorating Route 66 just before crossing I-40 where you head into the park's southern half. Stop at **Puerco Pueblo**. You may be able to join a ranger-led tour of these ancient ruins. Stopping at **Newspaper Rock** isn't mandatory, but it provides views of petroglyphs (from a distance). Stop at the **Tepees** and **Blue Mesa**. If you love petrified wood, stop at **Agate Bridge**, **Crystal Forest**, and **Giant Logs**. If you like it, hike **Long Logs Trail** and stop at **Rainbow Forest Museum**. Just don't like petrified wood so much that you take a little home (unless it's from the gift shop); theft will get you a $325 fine.

A rainbow rising up over the saguaro forest

3693 South Old Spanish Trail
Tucson, Arizona 85730
District Visitor Center Phone:
Rincon Mountain: (520) 733-5153
Tucson Mountain: (520) 733-5158
Website: www.nps.gov/sagu

Established: October 14, 1994
Size: 91,440 Acres
Annual Visitors: 720,000
Peak Season: November–March
Hiking Trails: 165+ Miles

Activities: Hiking, Biking, Birding, and Horseback Riding

Campgrounds/Lodging: None
Backcountry Camping: Permitted*

Park Hours: 7am–Sunset
Entrance Fee: $10 • Vehicle
$5 • Individual (foot, bike, etc.)

*Only in Rincon Mountain District at designated sites with a backcountry permit ($6/night) • The nearest backcountry campsite is a 5.9-mile hike away from a paved road

Saguaro - Arizona

In 1933, University of Arizona president Homer Shantz urged **President Hoover** to protect the saguaro forests surrounding the Rincon Mountains. Several generations of saguaro had already been affected by grazing cattle, as their small hooves and immense weight compacted the ground until saguaro seeds, no bigger than a pinhead, could not penetrate the earth's surface and take root. President Hoover agreed that the "**monarch of the Sonoran Desert**" needed to be preserved, invoking the **Antiquities Act** and establishing Saguaro National Monument. Cattle no longer grazed saguaro forests, but soon another mammal was getting too close for comfort. Tucson had once been a sleepy little town 15 miles away from the present-day park land. Today, Tucson is a bustling city, sprawling to and around the park's boundaries. Humans introduced invasive plant species that need water, the desert's most valuable commodity, to survive. Vandalism and poaching increased. Cacti were stolen for landscaping projects. By 1994, Congress continued to try and protect this unique natural resource by adding the Tucson Mountain District, expanding both regions, and establishing Saguaro National Park.

As conservationists try to protect the saguaro, cacti do their best to protect and provide for Sonoran Desert wildlife. To birds, the mighty **saguaro** are multi-tower condominiums that are constantly expanding. Gila woodpeckers and gilded flickers drill out one-room accommodations in the saguaros' trunk and large branches. Often they make several holes, rejecting one after another before finding a suitable home and settling down to raise a family. Other birds waste no time to begin squatting in vacant units. Elf owls, screech owls, purple martins, American kestrel, Lucy's warblers, cactus wrens, kingbirds, even honeybees seek protection from the saguaro. Not only does living within these monstrous succulents provide protection from predators, it shields them from hot summer days and cool winter nights. In summer the inner column of a saguaro is 20°F cooler than the ambient temperature. In winter, it's 20°F warmer. Outside, red-tailed and Harris hawks build nests in the crooks of the saguaro's arms. These are the condominium's suites, custom-built with beautiful 360-degree views of the surrounding mountains.

Fruit of the saguaro is just as useful as its woody frame. For centuries the Tohono O'odham people harvested fruit to make syrup, jam, and wine; it was also dried and eaten like a fig. It is so important, they marked their new year as the beginning of the saguaro fruit harvest. These fruit are also important to the creatures that creep and fly in the cool of the night. In June and July when it ripens, foragers like javelina, coyote, fox, harvester ants, birds, and small rodents feast on its succulent flesh.

The saguaro itself is a masterpiece of **adaptation** to an unforgiving environment. It's built on a wooden framework sturdy enough to support its weight, which can exceed 16,000 pounds. Its skin is pleated, allowing the cactus to expand as its roots sop up surrounding water. Inside is spongy flesh made of a gelatin-like substance capable of absorbing large amounts of water to survive months of drought. A waxy coating covers its skin, slowing the perspiration of water, and thorny spines protrude from it, deterring animals while providing shade. Most importantly, the needles serve as the succulent's power plant, performing the vital function of photosynthesis.

Saguaro cactus. "Monarch of the Sonoran Desert." Icon of the southwest. Not only does it enhance the desert's scenic value, it is an ecological keystone species, one that plays an integral role in maintaining the structure of its ecological community. A decline in saguaro population would not only diminish the area's scenic value and cause devastation to a unique and iconic species, it would cripple a lively community trying to survive with odds stacked against them. The same odds the saguaro has managed to endure for centuries.

When to Go

Both districts of the park are open every day of the year from 7am until sunset. Visitor centers are open daily from 9am to 5pm with the exception of Christmas Day. Most visitors come to the park between November and March when the weather is comfortable. Park land can erupt with colorful wildflowers after a wet winter. Saguaros bloom at night during the month of May and into June. Not all winters are wet. Call the park to verify wildflower blooms before arriving.

Transportation & Airports

Public transportation is not available to or around either park unit. Tucson International Airport (TUS) is located along the southern outskirts of Tucson, AZ, less than 20 miles from each unit.

Directions

Saguaro National Park consists of two separate districts, one east and one west of Tucson, AZ.

Rincon Mountain District/East Unit (3693 S. Old Spanish Trail; Tucson, Arizona 85730): From I-10, take Exit 275 (Houghton Rd). Head north on Houghton Rd for about 8 miles. Turn right at E Escalante Rd. Continue east for 2 miles before turning left onto Old Spanish Rd into the park.

Tucson Mountain District/West Unit (2700 N. Kinney Road; Tucson, Arizona 85743): Heading southeast on I-10 toward Tucson, take Exit 242 (Avra Valley Rd). Head west on Avra Valley Rd about 5 miles. Turn left at N Sandario Rd and continue south for 9 miles. Turn left at N Kinney Rd, which leads into the park.

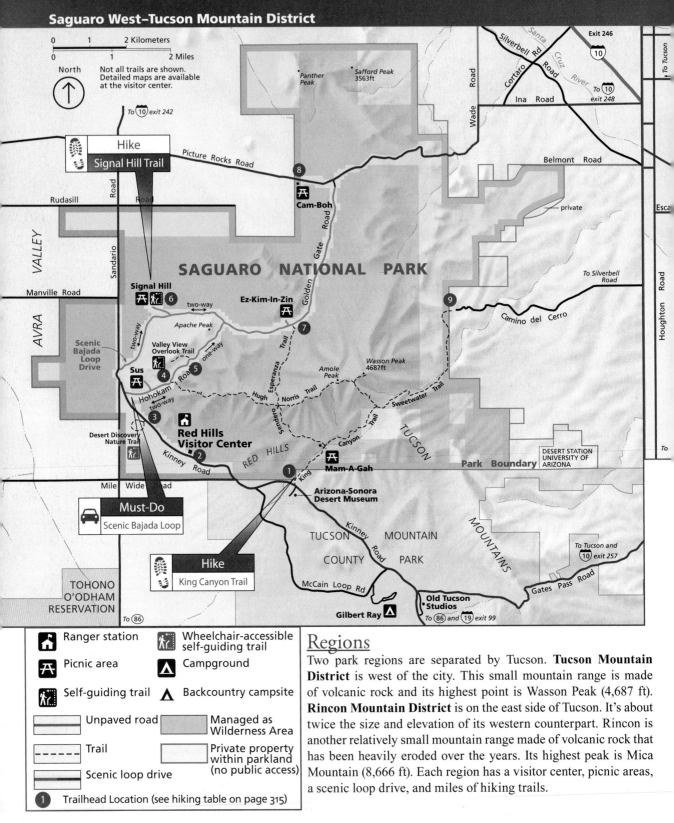

Saguaro West–Tucson Mountain District

0   1   2 Kilometers
0   1   2 Miles

North

Not all trails are shown.
Detailed maps are available
at the visitor center.

SAGUARO NATIONAL PARK

Hike
Signal Hill Trail

Must-Do
Scenic Bajada Loop

Hike
King Canyon Trail

Panther Peak

Safford Peak 3563ft

Picture Rocks Road

To 10 exit 242

Rudasill   Road   Road

Cam-Boh

private

VALLEY

AVRA

Manville Road

Signal Hill

Ez-Kim-In-Zin

two-way

Apache Peak

Valley View
Overlook Trail

Scenic
Bajada
Loop
Drive

Sus

two-way

Hohokam

two-way

Desert Discovery
Nature Trail

Red Hills
Visitor Center

Kinney   Road

Mile   Wide   Road

TOHONO
O'ODHAM
RESERVATION

To 86

RED   HILLS

King

Mam-A-Gah

Arizona-Sonora
Desert Museum

TUCSON   MOUNTAIN

COUNTY   PARK

McCain Loop Rd

Gilbert Ray

Old Tucson
Studios

To 86 and 19 exit 99

Amole
Peak

Wasson Peak
4687ft

Esperanza   Trail

Hugh

Norris

Trail

Sweetwater   Trail

Canyon

Sendero

Trail

Camino   del   Cerro

To Silverbell
Road

Belmont   Road

Wade   Road

Cortaro   Road

Silverbell Rd

Ina   Road

Santa

Cruz

River

Exit 246

10

To 10
exit 248

To Tucson

Esca

Houghton   Road

To

Park   Boundary

DESERT STATION
UNIVERSITY OF
ARIZONA

TUCSON

MOUNTAINS

Gates   Pass   Road

To Tucson and
10 exit 257

Kinney

Road

Legend

Symbol	Meaning
Ranger station	Wheelchair-accessible self-guiding trail
Picnic area	Campground
Self-guiding trail	Backcountry campsite
Unpaved road	Managed as Wilderness Area
Trail	Private property within parkland (no public access)
Scenic loop drive	
① Trailhead Location (see hiking table on page 315)	

Regions

Two park regions are separated by Tucson. **Tucson Mountain District** is west of the city. This small mountain range is made of volcanic rock and its highest point is Wasson Peak (4,687 ft). **Rincon Mountain District** is on the east side of Tucson. It's about twice the size and elevation of its western counterpart. Rincon is another relatively small mountain range made of volcanic rock that has been heavily eroded over the years. Its highest peak is Mica Mountain (8,666 ft). Each region has a visitor center, picnic areas, a scenic loop drive, and miles of hiking trails.

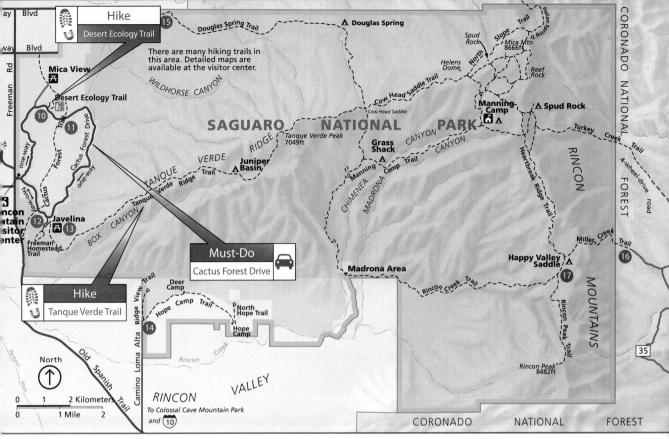

Visitor Centers & Museums

Red Hills Visitor Center is located in the western unit, on Kinney Road near the south entrance. Here you'll find exhibits, a bookstore, and brochures and maps that help introduce you to the area. Two films, "A Home in the Desert" (15 minutes) and "Sentinel in the Desert" (53 minutes) are shown daily. Also located on Kinney Road just beyond the park boundary is the popular zoo/garden/museum, **Arizona–Sonora Desert Museum** (page 321). East Unit's **Rincon Mountain Visitor Center** has exhibits, a bookstore, brochures, and maps. It also shows the same videos as West Unit's Visitor Center daily (except for Christmas). The most useful resource found at either visitor center is their friendly staff. Park rangers are ready to answer your questions and provide activity suggestions based on how much time you have to explore the unit.

Camping & Lodging

One of the things you can't do in the park is spend the night. There are no drive-in campgrounds or lodging facilities within its boundaries. For a list of nearby lodging and campground alternatives see page 319. **Backpackers** are the exception. They are allowed to camp in Rincon Mountain Wilderness Area at one of six designated backcountry campgrounds scattered throughout the mountains. The closest camp is a 5.9 mile hike along Douglas Spring Trail. Its trailhead is located on Speedway Blvd. Backpackers must obtain a **backcountry permit** ($6 per person per night) from Rincon Mountain Visitor Center.

Driving

Each unit has a well-maintained scenic drive. These stretches of pavement have become each Unit's primary attraction. In the west, you'll find the 5-mile **Bajada Loop Drive**. It's a graded unpaved road that passes through dense saguaro forest. In the east, motorists circle around 8-mile **Cactus Forest Drive**. The one-way, paved road skirts along the foothills of the Rincon Mountains through a well preserved desert ecosystem. Both roads provide access to the park's most popular trailheads and picnic areas where you'll also find spectacular vistas of the desert landscape.

Saguaro Cactus

Saguaro is an icon of the American southwest and giant of the Sonoran Desert. Almost human-like, the saguaro stands tall, towering above the arid and rocky ground, arms extended in a welcoming manner. These are the redwoods of the desert, offering protection and provisions for a wealth of life in a seemingly inhospitable landscape. Their roots fan out from the trunk as far as it is tall, sopping up water with a voracious thirst. In a single rainfall, **a saguaro may soak up as much as 200 gallons of water**, enough to last an entire year. They can live to be **more than 150 years old, 50 feet tall, and weigh up to 8 tons**. That makes the saguaro not only the largest cactus in the United States, but the largest living organism in the Sonoran Desert.

In contrast, its life begins as a **tiny black seed**, no bigger than the head of a pin. Each year a single saguaro produces tens of thousands of seeds, which fall to the desert floor and try to take root in one of the hottest and driest regions on the continent. Hungry birds and rodents snack on these miniscule morsels. Even with an abundance of seeds, the chances of a saguaro reaching adulthood is on par with being struck by lightning. Chances increase beneath trees like palo verde and mesquite where they find shade from the summer heat, insulation from the winter cold, and safe harbor from the constant threat of hungry animals.

Seeds that take root grow ever so slowly. After one year a saguaro may measure **one-quarter inch, one foot after 15 years, and after 30 years of life in the desert, a saguaro finally begins to flower and produce fruit**. There can be as many as 100 flowers on a single cactus, each blooming at sunset. They are pollinated in the night by white-winged doves, long nosed bats, honeybees, and moths. By the following afternoon the flower has wilted in the direct rays of desert sun. Flowers turn to fruit and by June they have ripened. Each fruit contains as many as 2,000 seeds that fall to the desert floor in hope of becoming a "Sentinel of the Sonoran Desert."

Hiking/Backpacking

Even desert can appeal to the avid hiker. You'll find trails ranging from short and flat paved loops to long-distance, rugged paths along steep, barren mountain slopes. Most of Tucson Mountain District's trails are short and relatively easy. **Desert Discovery Trail**, located just off Kinney Road, south of Bajada Loop Drive, is a popular short loop. It has several exhibits discussing the region's native plants and animals. If you'd like to hike to the west unit's tallest point, Wasson Peak, you have a couple of choices. The easiest route is to take **Sendero Esperanza Trail** (located on Golden Gate Road) to its intersection with Hugh Norris Trail. Head east on Hugh Norris to the peak. This route is about 4.1 miles (one-way). Alternatively, **King Canyon Trail**, located near the Arizona–Sonora Desert Museum is slightly shorter but more strenuous. It's a 3.5-mile (one-way) hike to the peak, beginning with a nice gradual ascent before a series of switchbacks lead to the intersection with Hugh Norris Trail. **Signal Hill Picnic Area**, just off of Golden Gate Road, has a short trail that wanders past more than 200 ancient petroglyphs. The meaning behind these images scratched onto rock is left to your interpretation. As you walk through the desert, imagine what stories these ancient scribes wanted to tell their descendents.

Rincon Mountain District contains a much larger network of trails and **six backcountry campgrounds**. Several short and easy trails begin along Cactus Forest Drive. **Cactus Forest Trail** runs north–south bisecting the loop drive. This is an excellent flat hike to see saguaro cactus up close. Another nice hike is **Desert Ecology Trail**, located at the southernmost point of Cactus Forest Drive. This paved path has signs describing plants and animals that you might see during your visit. North of Cactus Forest Drive is a fairly complex maze-like network of trails. Combining several short trails allows a multitude of loop routes through the foothills. You can also explore the park's wilderness area. It is most easily accessed via **Tanque Verde or Douglas Spring Trails**, but it's also accessible via **Middle Creek Trail** from the Coronado National Forest east of the park.

The Sonoran Desert provides ample terrain for exploration, but it doesn't offer shade or water. Pace yourself and drink plenty of water. If you plan on doing extensive hiking, ask for a detailed hiking map at the visitor center. They should be available free of charge.

Rincon Mountain District

Saguaro Hiking Trails

	Trail Name	Length	Location (# on map)/Notes (One-way unless noted otherwise, RT = Roundtrip)
Tucson Mountain District	King Canyon - 🥾	3.5 miles	Across Kinney Road from the Arizona–Sonora Desert Museum (1) • Somewhat strenuous trek up switchbacks to Wasson Peak (Tucson Mountain's highest peak)
	Cactus Garden - 🥾	300 feet	Begins at Red Hills Visitor Center (2) • Self-guiding introduction to plants (RT)
	Desert Discovery	0.5 mile	On Kinney Rd, 1 mile northwest of the visitor center (3) • Self-guiding loop
	Hugh Norris	4.9 miles	On Bajada Loop Drive (4) • Strenuous and long hike to Wasson Peak
	Valley View Overlook	0.8 mile	On Bajada Loop Drive (5) • Cross two washes before ascending a ridge (RT)
	Signal Hill Petroglyphs - 🥾	0.5 mile	Signal Hill Picnic Area (6) • This trail passes numerous petroglyphs (RT)
	Cactus Wren	1.5 miles	Signal Hill Picnic Area (6) • Flat trail through washes to Sandario Road
	Sendero Esperanza	3.2 miles	Begins on Golden Gate Road (7) • Crosses Hugh Norris and King Canyon Trails
	Cam-Boh	2.7 miles	Pictured Rocks Road (8) • Runs parallel to road to a small network of trails
	Ringtail	1.0 mile	Connector Trail allows for several loops to be hiked from Cam-Boh Trail
	Sweetwater	3.4 miles	Begins at the end of Camino del Cerro Rd (9) • Leads to the top of Wasson Peak
Rincon Mountain District	Desert Ecology - 🥾	0.25 mile	An easy paved trail introducing visitors to the park's plant and animal life (RT) (10)
	Cactus Forest - 🥾	2.5 miles	Flat trail that bisects the park road (11) • Open to hikers, bikers, and horse riders
	Freeman Homestead	1.0 mile	Self-guiding trail that leads to a grove of large saguaros and old home (RT) (12)
	Tanque Verde - 🥾	11.5 miles	Begin at Javelina Picnic Area (13) • Hike 6.9 miles to Juniper Basin Campground and continues on to Tanque Verde Peak and Cow Head Saddle
	Hope Camp	5.6 miles	Rincon Valley Trailhead at the north end of Comino Loma Alta (14) • Used by horse riders • Provides views of Tanque Verde Ridge and Rincon Peak (RT)
	Ridge View	1.6 miles	Rincon Valley Trailhead (14) • This trail leads to views of rocky side canyons (RT)
	Douglas Spring	8.3 miles	Trailhead on Speedway Blvd (15) • 5.9 miles to Douglas Spring Campground
	Miller Creek Trail	4.4 miles	Accessed at the eastern boundary of the park from N. Happy Valley Road (16)
	Rincon Peak - 🥾	3.2 miles	Spur trail from Heartbreak Ridge/Miller Creek Trails to Rincon Peak (17)

Desert tortoise eating prickly pear

Best of Saguaro

Hike (Tucson Mtn District): **King Canyon**
Runner-up: Cactus Garden

Hike (Rincon Mtn District): **Cactus Forest**
Runner-up: Rincon Peak

Activity: **Bike Cactus Forest Drive**
Runner-up: Arizona–Sonora Desert Museum

Biking

Cyclists are limited to the park's roadways. Off-road and on-trail riding is not permitted. **Road cyclists** enjoy riding through saguaro forests surrounding the East Unit's 8-mile Cactus Forest Drive. It's twisty, hilly, narrow, and can become congested during peak tourism season (November–March). The lone opportunity for **mountain bike trail riding** is a 2.5-mile stretch of **Cactus Forest Trail** that bisects Cactus Forest Drive. It's not a trail, but mountain bikers can also pedal the West Unit's **Bajada Loop Drive**. It's a 5-mile loop that traverses a small portion of Tucson Mountain's lower elevations.

Horseback Riding

Horses, mules, and donkeys are allowed on **more than 100 miles of trails**, so don't be startled if you come face-to-face with a donkey while hiking through the desert. Horse riders and their stock are also permitted to camp at designated backcountry campgrounds (with a permit from Rincon Mountain Visitor Center). If you'd like to experience the true southwest but don't have your own stock, there's a reliable **outfitter** located near each park unit that provides guided trail rides.

Cocoraque Ranch (West Unit) • (520) 682-8594
6255 N. Diamond Hills Lane; Tucson, AZ 85743
www.cocoraque.com

Pantano Riding Stables (East Unit) • (520) 298-8980
4450 South Houghton Road; Tucson, AZ 85730
Rates: Dinner Ride • $47/person (2.5 hours), Sunset Ride • $37/person (1.5 hours), Trail Rides • 0.5-hr ($17/person), 1-hr ($22), 1.5-hr ($32), and 2-hr ($42)

For Kids: Children (ages 5–12) are welcome to participate in the **Junior Ranger Program**. Complete an activity booklet (free at either visitor center) aided by the contents of a **Discovery Pack** to receive a ranger certificate and badge. Discovery Packs are available for check-out at either visitor center with an adult's valid driver's license or picture ID. Children (ages 6–11) can sign up for a 3-day **Junior Ranger Camp** that is held in June. It costs $25 per child and applications are available at the park website. Call (520) 733–5153 for additional information.

Ranger Programs: Many visitors have a difficult time appreciating the desert, so attending a ranger program is a good way to absorb a bit of knowledge and enthusiasm for this desolate region. Ranger-led walks, talks, and interpretive programs (offered November–March) explore the park's history, geology, and ecology, ranging from morning bird watching tours to evening stargazing. Visitors should check online or at a visitor center for a current schedule of events.

Flora & Fauna: Saguaro aren't the only show in town. **More than 25 species of cacti** are found within the park. Less famous succulents include hedgehog, cholla, and prickly pear. Be careful not to be pricked by a cholla cactus. Its barbed needles are difficult to remove and extremely painful. In the lower elevations of the West Unit you can find animals like desert tortoise and coyote. There's also plenty of creosote bush, the most common North American desert plant.

East Unit's higher elevations provide habitat for larger animals. Black bear, white-tailed deer, and Mexican spotted owl live among Douglas fir and ponderosa pine that grow on the high mountain slopes. Bird watchers appreciate **more than 200 species of birds** that live in or visit the region. One of the most sought after birds is the elf owl. It's often seen roosting in small saguaro cavities drilled out by gila woodpeckers or gilded flickers. High mountains also provide an opportunity to see birds not commonly found on the desert floor, like red-faced warbler and golden eagle.

Pets: Pets are limited to the park's roadways and picnic areas, and must be kept on a leash no more than six feet in length at all times.

Accessibility: Both visitor centers are accessible to individuals in wheelchairs. Desert Ecology Trail in Rincon Mountain District and Desert Discovery Trail in Tucson Mountain District are accessible. All other trails are inaccessible. A few ranger-led programs are accessible.

Weather: There are a few reasons why so many Americans retire in Arizona. Mild winters is one of them. Winter average high temperatures are about 65°F before dropping into the 40s°F at night. Summers are hot and dry. Daytime highs commonly exceed 100°F in the shade. Summer visitors should remember to pack your sunglasses, plenty of water, and sunscreen.

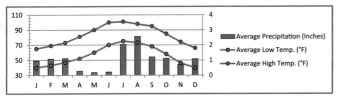

Vacation Planner

Even with two park units separated by Tucson, you don't need a lot of time to tour Saguaro. **Hiking trails** (page 315) and **roads** (page 313) are short and easily accessible. Plus, there aren't any lodging or camping facilities within the park. You could spend a few nights **backpacking** (page 313) or **horseback riding** (page 316) through the **Rincon Mountains**, but those types of visitors are few and far between. Always check a schedule of **ranger-led programs** (page 316) in advance and join whenever possible. Nearby dining, grocery stores, lodging, festivals, and attractions are listed on pages 318–321.

Begin at **Tucson Mountain District**, stopping first at **Red Hills Visitor Center**. Watch the short introductory video, and check when the longer video is showing. If you haven't already, get the day's schedule of **ranger-led**

Yes, snow can fall in the desert

activities (check for the East Unit while you're at it). Do not skip a ranger program if one is occurring during your visit. Getting back to business, drive **Scenic Bajada Loop**. It's a short drive on a gravel road. Take your time and enjoy the views of saguaro forests. Here, saguaro cacti are far denser than at the East Unit. Along the way, stop at **Signal Hill Picnic Area** to hike its **Petroglyph Trail** (page 315). On your way out, stop at **Arizona–Sonora Desert Museum** (page 321) or hike **King Canyon Trail** (page 315).

Drive across Tucson to **Rincon Mountain District**. Stop in at its visitor center if you skipped the West Unit's or want to confirm the activity schedule. If you're out of questions and have seen both park videos, leave the visitor center and drive **Cactus Forest Drive**. It's a paved loop that provides access to **Cactus Forest Trail** (page 315) at two points, which is a nice, easy, and flat trail that explores saguaro forests. You'll find **Desert Ecology Self-Guiding Trail** on the northern end of Cactus Forest Drive. Hike it if you're interested in the park's desert ecology. On a pleasant day you may want to continue hiking. **Tanque Verde Trail** begins at Javelina Picnic Area and climbs into the mountains, where you'll find outstanding views and slightly cooler temperatures.

Dining

Big Bend Area

Kathy's Kosmic Kowgirl Kafe • (432) 371-2164
103 Ross Dr; Terlingua, TX 79852

India's Coffee Shop • (432) 371-2888
PO Box 336; Terlingua, TX

La Kiva • (432) 371-2250
FM-170 at Terlingua Creek; Terlingua, TX 79852
www.lakiva.net • Entrée: $10–20

Star Light Theatre • (432) 371-2326
631 Ivey Rd; Terlingua, TX 79852
www.starlighttheatre.com

Ghost Town Café • (432) 371-3000
1001 Ghost Town Rd; Terlingua, TX 79852

Tivo's Restaurant • (432) 371-2133
TX-118; Terlingua, TX 79852

Long Draw Pizza • (432) 371-2608
Farm to Market 170; Terlingua, TX 79852

Chili Pepper Café • (432) 371-2233
100 TX-118; Terlingua, TX 79852

Roadrunner Deli • (432) 371-2364
TX-118 S, Study Butte Mall; Study Butte, TX

Guadalupe Mts/Carlsbad Area

Spanish Angels Café • (915) 964-2208
103 Main St; Dell City, TX 79837

The Stock Exchange • (575) 725-5444
220 W Fox St; Carlsbad, NM 88220
www.thestockexchangenm.com • Entrée: $13–26

Carlsbad Caverns Restaurant • (575) 785-2281
727 Carlsbad Cavern Hwy; Carlsbad, NM 88220

Happy's • (575) 887-8489
4103 National Parks Hwy; Carlsbad, NM 88220

Rojas Mexican Grill • (575) 885-2146
2704 San Jose Blvd; Carlsbad, NM 88220

Danny's Place • (575) 885-8739
902 S Canal St; Carlsbad, NM 88220
www.dannysbbq.com

Pizza Inn • (575) 887-5069
3005 National Parks Hwy; Carlsbad, NM 88220
www.pizzainn.com • Pizza: $10+

No Whiner Diner • (575) 234-2815
1801 S Canal St; Carlsbad, NM 88220

Pecos River Café • (575) 887-8882
409 S Canal St; Carlsbad, NM 88220

Blue House Bakery • (575) 628-0555
609 N Canyon St; Carlsbad, NM 88220

Red Chimney Pit Bar-B-Q • (575) 885-8744
817 N Canal St; Carlsbad, NM 88220

Beaver's Restaurant • (575) 885-4515
1620 S Canal St; Carlsbad, NM 88220

Court Café • (575) 887-0238
219 S Canyon St; Carlsbad, NM 88220

Blake's Lotaburger • (575) 885-0152
1230 W Pierce St; Carlsbad, NM 88220
www.lotaburger.com

Church Street Grill • (575) 885-3074
301 W Church St; Carlsbad, NM 88220

Becky's Drive In • (575) 885-3262
901 W Church St; Carlsbad, NM 88220

Kaleidoscoops Ice Cream • (575) 887-1931
425 N Canal St; Carlsbad, NM 88220

Pizza Mill & Sub Factory • (575) 887-5098
312 W Church St; Carlsbad, NM 88220

Calloway's Café • (575) 887-6820
110 N Halagueno St; Carlsbad, NM 88220

Sno to Go • (575) 885-0477
1713 S Canal St; Carlsbad, NM 88220

Dari-Lea Drive In • (575) 885-3976
2216 W Lea St; Carlsbad, NM 88220

Petrified Forest Area

Joe & Aggie's Café • (928) 524-6540
Served as inspiration for the Pixar movie Cars
120 W Hopi Dr; Holbrook, AZ 86025
www.joeandaggiescafe.com

Butterfield Stage Co Steak House • (928) 524-3447
609 W Hopi Dr; Holbrook, AZ 86025

Jalapeno Poppers • (928) 524-2928
2600 Navajo Blvd; Holbrook, AZ 86025

Hopi Travel Plaza Café • (928) 524-7820
1851 AZ-77; Holbrook, AZ 86025

El Rancho Restaurant & Motel • (928) 524-3332
867 Navajo Blvd; Holbrook, AZ 86025

Mesa Italiana Restaurant • (928) 524-6696
2318 Navajo Blvd; Holbrook, AZ 86025

Romo's Restaurant • (928) 524-2153
121 W Hopi Dr; Holbrook, AZ 86025

Mandarin Beauty Chinese • (928) 524-3663
2218 Navajo Blvd; Holbrook, AZ 86025

Bubba Big Pig Bar BQ • (928) 524-1581
1002 W Hopi Dr; Holbrook, AZ 86025

Wayside Café • (928) 524-3167
1150 W Hopi Dr; Holbrook, AZ 86025

Saguaro Area

Mama's Famous Pizza • (520) 751-4600
50 S Houghton Rd, # 190; Tucson, AZ 85748
www.mamasfamous.com • Pizza: $12–26

Vivace • (520) 795-7221
4310 N Campbell Ave; Tucson, AZ 85719

Lani's Luau • (520) 886-5828
2532 S Harrison Rd; Tucson, AZ 85748

Longhorn Steak Burger • (520) 721-5855
9431 E 22nd Street; Tucson, AZ 85710

Wings Pizza N Things • (520) 722-9663
8838 E Broadway Blvd; Tucson, AZ 85710
www.wingspizzanthings.com

Guiseppe's • (520) 505-4187
6060 N Oracle Rd; Tucson, AZ 85704
www.guiseppesaz.com • Entrée: $8–16

Viro's Real Italian Bakery • (520) 885-4045
8301 E 22nd St; Tucson, AZ 85710
www.virosbakery.com • Entrée: $12–15

Rio Café • (520) 323-5003
2526 E Grant Rd; Tucson, AZ 85716
www.rio-cafe.com • Entrée: $15–24

Risky Business J • (520) 749-8555
8848 E Tanque Verde Rd; Tucson, AZ 85749
www.riskybusinesstucson.com • Entrée: $9–16

Dolce Vita • (520) 298-3700
7895 E Broadway Blvd, # 9; Tucson, AZ 85710
www.dolcevitaarizona.com

Kenney D's Chicago Style • (520) 722-8900
8060 E 22nd St, # 100; Tucson, AZ 85710

Papa Locos Tacos and Burgers • (520) 663-3333
8201 S Rita Rd; Tucson, AZ 85747
www.papalocos.com

Baggin's Gourmet • (520) 290-9383
7233 E Speedway Blvd; Tucson, AZ 85710
www.bagginsgourmet.com • Sandwiches: $5–7

Ba-Dar Chinese • (520) 296-8888
7321 E Broadway Blvd; Tucson, AZ 85710
www.ba-dar.com • Chinese: $6–10

HUB Restaurant & Ice Creamery • (520) 207-8201
266 E Congress St; Tucson, AZ 85701
www.hubdowntown.com • Entrée: $14–18

A Great Location • (520) 733-1388
20 N Sarnoff Dr; Tucson, AZ 85710
www.agreatlocationcafe.com • Breakfast: $4–10

Zona 78 • (520) 296-7878
7301 E Tanque Verde Rd; Tucson, AZ 85715
www.zona78.com • Entrée: $13–16

Little Anthony's Diner • (520) 296-0456
7010 E Broadway Blvd; Tucson, AZ 85710
www.littleanthonysdiner.com

Amber Restaurant & Gallery • (520) 296-9759
7000 E Tanque Verde Rd; Tucson, AZ 85715
www.amberrestaurantgallery.com • Entrée: $16–24

Oishi Sushi • (520) 790-9439
7002 E Golf Links Rd; Tucson, AZ 85730

The Good Egg • (520) 885-4838
7189 E Speedway Blvd; Tucson, AZ 85715
www.thegoodeggaz.com • Breakfast: $4–10

Poco & Mom's Restaurant • (520) 325-7044
1060 South Kolb Rd; Tucson, AZ 85710
www.pocoandmoms.com • Entrée: $7–10

Montana Avenue • (520) 298-2020
6390 E Grant Rd; Tucson, AZ 85715

Eclectic Pizza • (520) 886-0484
7065 E Tanque Verde Rd; Tucson, AZ 85715
www.eclecticpizza.com • Pizza: $7–25

Ha Long Bay • (520) 571-1338
6304 E Broadway Blvd; Tucson, AZ 85710
www.halongbaymenu.com • Vietnamese: $9–13

Beyond Bread • (520) 747-7477
6260 E Speedway Blvd; Tucson, AZ 85712
www.beyondbread.com • Sandwiches: $7–10

Neo of Melaka • (520) 747-7811
6133 E Broadway Blvd; Tucson, AZ 85711
www.neomelaka.com • Entrée: $13–29

Dakota Café • (520) 298-7188
6541 E Tanque Verde Rd, # 7; Tucson, AZ 85715
www.dakotacafeandcatering.com • Entrée: $12–25

Epic Café • (520) 624-6844
745 N 4th Ave; Tucson, AZ 85705
www.epic-cafe.com

Blue Willow Restaurant • (520) 327-7577
2616 N Campbell Ave; Tucson, AZ 85719
www.bluewillowtucson.com • Entrée: $9–17

Café Poca Cosa • (520) 622-6400
110 E Pennington St; Tucson, AZ 85701
www.cafepocacosatucson.com

Old Pueblo Grille • (520) 326-6000
60 N Alvernon Way; Tucson, AZ 85711
www.metrorestaurants.com • Entrée: $10–22

Mi Nidito • (520) 622-5081
1813 S 4th Ave; Tucson, AZ 85713
www.minidito.net • Entrée: $6–11

El Guero Canelo • (520) 882-8977
2480 N Oracle Rd; Tucson, AZ 85705
www.elguerocanelo.com

Old Town Artisans Galleries • (520) 623-6024
201 N Court Ave; Tucson, AZ 85701
www.oldtownartisans.com • Entrée: $9–13

Mama Louisa's • (520) 790-4702
2041 S Craycroft Rd; Tucson, AZ 85711
www.mamalouisas.com

Cup Café • (520) 798-1618
311 E Congress St; Tucson, AZ 85701
www.hotelcongress.com • Entrée: $9–20

Nimbus Brewing Co • (520) 745-9175
3850 E 44th St; Tucson, AZ 85713
www.nimbusbeer.com • Entrée: $8–17

Taqueria Pico De Gallo • (520) 623-8775
2618 S 6th Ave, # A; Tucson, AZ 85713

Barrio Brewing Co • (520) 791-2739
800 E 16th St; Tucson, AZ 85719
www.barriobrewing.com

Pastiche Modern Eatery • (520) 325-3333
3025 N Campbell Ave; Tucson, AZ 85719
www.pasticheme.com

Frost Gelato • (520) 797-0188
7131 N Oracle Rd, # 101; Tucson, AZ 85704

Frost Gelato • (520) 886-0354
7301 E Tanque Verde Rd, # 191; Tucson, AZ 85715

Frost Gelato • (520) 615-9490
2905 E Skyline Dr; Tucson, AZ 85718
www.frostgelato.com • Gelato: $3–5

Many chain hotels can be found in El Paso, TX; Carlsbad, NM; Albuquerque, NM; Flagstaff, AZ; Phoenix, AZ; and Tucson AZ; as well as along Interstates 10, 25, 40, and 17.

Grocery Stores
Big Bend Area
Study Butte Store • (432) 371-2231
TX-118; Study Butte, TX 79852

Terlingua Springs Market • (432) 371-2332
FM-170; Terlingua, TX 79852

Walmart • (432) 336-3389
1700 W Dickinson Blvd; Fort Stockton, TX 79735

Guadalupe Mts/Carlsbad Area
Walmart Supercenter • (575) 885-0727
2401 S Canal St; Carlsbad, NM 88220

Albertsons • (575) 885-2161
808 N Canal St; Carlsbad, NM 88220

Petrified Forest Area
Safeway • (520) 524-3313
702 W Hopi Dr; Holbrook, AZ 86025

Walmart Supercenter • (928) 289-4641
700 Mikes Pike St; Winslow, AZ 86047

Saguaro Area
Safeway • (520) 546-3929
10380 E Broadway Blvd; Tucson, AZ 85748

Albertson-Osco • (520) 751-7699
9595 E Broadway Blvd; Tucson, AZ 85748

Fry's • (520) 721-8575
9401 E 22nd St; Tucson, AZ 85710

Walmart • (520) 751-1882
7150 E Speedway Blvd; Tucson, AZ 85710

Walmart Supercenter • (520) 573-3777
1650 W Valencia; Tucson, AZ 85746

Lodging
Big Bend Area
Chisos Mountains Lodge • (432) 477-2291
Big Bend National Park, TX 79834
www.chisosmountainslodge.com • Rates: $113–144/night

Big Bend Motor Inn • (432) 371-2483
100 Main St; Terlingua, TX 79852

Rancho Rayo • (432) 371-3162
Terlingua Ranch, 1000 Church Rd; Alpine, TX 79830
www.desertspa.net • Rates: $125–195

Oasis Hotel & RV • (432) 371-2218
TX-118; Terlingua, TX 79852

Ten Bits Ranch • (432) 371-3110
6000 N County Rd; Terlingua, TX 79852
www.tenbitsranch.com • Rates: $159–199

BJ's RV Park • (432) 371-2259
PO Box 37; Terlingua, TX 79852
www.bjrvpark.com • Rates: $25

El Dorado Hotel • (432) 371-2111
100 Ghostown Rd; Terlingua, TX 79852

La Posada Milagro • (432) 371-3044
100 Milagro Rd; Terlingua, TX 79852
www.laposadamilagro.net • Rates: $145–210

Lajitas Golf Resort & Spa • (432) 424-5180
HC 70 Box 400; Lajitas, TX 79852
www.lajitasgolfresort.com • Rates: $170–550

Upstairs at the Mansion • (360) 713-3408
1 Perry Mansion Dr; Terlingua, TX 79852

Easter Egg Valley Motel • (432) 371-2254
FM-170, PO Box 228; Terlingua, TX 79852

Terlingua Ranch Lodge • (432) 371-2416
16000 Terlingua Ranch Rd; Terlingua, TX 79852
www.terlinguaranch.com

Las Ruinas Camping Hostel • (412) 498-6792
Terlingua Ghost Town Rd; Terlingua, TX 79852
www.lasruinashostel.com • Rates: $10/Person

Wildhorse Station • (432) 371-2526
53071 TX-118; Terlingua, TX 79852

Guadalupe Mts/Carlsbad Area
Trinity Hotel • (575) 234-9891
201 S Canal St; Carlsbad, NM 88220
www.thetrinityhotel.com • Rates: $129+

White's City Resort • (575) 785-2294
12 Yellowstone Dr; NM 88268

X-Bar Ranch • (575) 981-2415
Queen Route; Carlsbad, NM 88220

Carlsbad Inn • (575) 887-1171
2019 S Canal St; Carlsbad, NM 88220

Stage Coach Inn • (575) 887-1148
1819 S Canal St; Carlsbad, NM 88220

Caverns Motel • (575) 887-6522
844 S Canal St; Carlsbad, NM 88220

Economy Inn • (575) 885-4914
1621 S Canal St; Carlsbad, NM 88220

Parkview Motel • (575) 885-3117
401 E Greene St; Carlsbad, NM 88220

Casa Milagro • (575) 887-2188
1612 N Guadalupe St; Carlsbad, NM 88220
www.casa-milagro-nm.com

Sousorrone Viento B&B • (575) 628-0446
20 Vincent Rd; Carlsbad, NM 88220

Carlsbad RV Park • (575) 885-6333
4301 National Parks Hwy; Carlsbad, NM 88220
www.carlsbadrvpark.com • Rates: Seasonal

Windmill RV Park • (575) 887-1387
3624 National Parks Hwy; Carlsbad, NM 88220

KOA • (575) 457-2000
2 Manthei Rd; Carlsbad, NM 88220

Petrified Forest Area

Wigwam Motel • (928) 524-3048
811 W Hopi Dr; Holbrook, AZ 86025

Globetrotter Lodge • (928) 297-0158
902 W Hopi Dr; Holbrook, AZ 86025
www.hotelsholbrookaz.com • Rates: $50–83

Travelodge • (928) 524-6815
2418 E Navajo Blvd; Holbrook, AZ 86025

Best Inn • (928) 524-2654
2211 Navajo Blvd; Holbrook, AZ 86025

Desert Inn • (928) 524-6929
301 W Hopi Dr; Holbrook, AZ 86025

La Posada Hotel • (928) 289-4366
303 E 2nd St; Winslow, AZ 86047
www.laposada.org • Rates: $109–169

Heritage Inn B&B • (928) 536-3322
161 N Main St; Snowflake, AZ 85937
www.heritage-inn.net • Rates: $75+

KOA Kampground • (928) 524-6689
102 Hermosa Dr; Holbrook, AZ 86025

Saguaro Area

Canyon Ranch • (520) 749-9000
8600 E Rockcliff Rd; Tucson, AZ 85750
www.canyonranch.com • All inclusive multi-day packages

Arizona Inn • (520) 325-1541
2200 E Elm St; Tucson, AZ 85719
www.arizonainn.com • Rates: $219+

Lodge on the Desert • (520) 320-2000
306 N Alvernon Way; Tucson, AZ 85711
www.lodgeonthedesert.com • Rates: $90–159

Mira Vista Resort • (520) 744-2355
7501 N Wade Rd; Tucson, AZ 85743
www.miravistaresort.com • Rates: $153–275

Cat Mountain Lodge • (520) 578-6085
2720 S Kinney Rd; Tucson, AZ 85735
www.catmountainlodge.com • Rates: $99–169

White Stallion Ranch • (520) 297-0252
9251 W Twin Peaks Rd; Tucson, AZ 85743
www.whitestallion.com • Rates: $139–241

Starr Pass Golf Suites • (520) 670-0500
3645 W Starr Pass Blvd; Tucson, AZ 85745
www.shellhospitality.com • Rates: $90–210

Loews Ventana Canyon Resort • (520) 299-2020
7000 N Resort Dr; Tucson, AZ 85750
www.loewshotels.com • Rates: $159+

The Big Blue House • (520) 891-1827
144 E University Blvd; Tucson, AZ 85705
www.144university.com • Rates: $120–180

Royal Elizabeth B&B • (877) 670-9022
204 S Scott Ave; Tucson, AZ 85701
www.royalelizabeth.com • Rates: $199–219

Roadrunner Hostel • (520) 628-4709
346 E 12th St; Tucson, AZ 85701
www.roadrunnerhostelinn.com • Rates: $20–40

Westward Look Resort • (800) 481-0636
245 E Ina Rd; Tucson, AZ 85704
www.westwardlook.com • Rates: $150–425

Adobe Rose Inn • (520) 318-4644
940 N Olsen Ave; Tucson, AZ 85719
www.aroseinn.com • Rates: $90–220

La Posada del Valle B&B • (520) 885-0883
1640 N Campbell Ave; Tucson, AZ 85719
www.thejoeslerhistoricinn.com • Rates: $70–145

The Golf Villas at Oro Valley • (520) 498-0098
10950 N La Canada; Tucson, AZ 85737
www.thegolfvillas.com • 14 night minimum

Azure Gate B&B • (520) 749-8157
9351 E Morrill Way; Tucson, AZ 85749
www.azuregate.com • Rates: $135–185

Cactus Cove B&B • (520) 760-7730
10066 E Kleindale Rd; Tucson, AZ 85749
www.cactuscove.com • Rates: $215–295

Desert Dove B&B • (520) 722-6879
11707 E Old Spanish Tr; Tucson, AZ 85730
www.desertdovebb.com • Rates: $130–145

Desert Trails B&B • (520) 885-7295
12851 E Speedway Blvd; Tucson, AZ 85748
www.deserttrails.com • Rates: $105–165

SunCatcher Inn • (520) 444-3077
105 N Avenida Javalina; Tucson, AZ 85748
www.suncatchertucson.com • Rates: $115–225

Casitas at Smokey Springs • (520) 870-8778
1451 N Smokey Springs Rd; Tucson, AZ 85749

Hacienda Del Desierto B&B • (520) 298-1764
11770 E Rambling Tr; Tucson, AZ 85747
www.tucson-bed-breakfast.com • Rates: $129–279

Jeremiah Inn B&B • (520) 749-3072
10921 E Snyder Rd; Tucson, AZ 85749
www.jeremiahinn.com • Rates: $115–270

Inn at Civano • (520) 296-5428
10448 E 7 Generations Way; Tucson, AZ 85747
www.innatcivano.com • Rates: $79–199

Sonoran Suites Of Tucson • (480) 607-6665
7990 E Snyder Rd; Tucson, AZ 85750

Casa Tierra Adobe B&B • (520) 578-3058
11155 W Calle Pima; Tucson, AZ 85743
www.casatierratucson.com • Rates: $150–195

Rincon Country E RV Resort • (520) 886-8431
8989 E Escalante Rd; Tucson, AZ 85730
www.rinconcountry.com • Rates: $40+

Far Horizons Tucson Village RV • (520) 296-1234
555 N Pantano Rd; Tucson, AZ 85710
www.tucsonvillage.com • Rates: $35+

Desert Trails RV Park • (520) 883-8340
3551 S San Joaquin Rd; Tucson, AZ 85735
www.deserttrailsrvpark.com • Rates: $26+

Many chain hotels can be found in El Paso, TX; Carlsbad, NM; Albuquerque, NM; Flagstaff, AZ; Phoenix, AZ; and Tucson AZ; as well as along Interstates 10, 25, 40, and 17.

Festivals

Big Bend Area
Int'l Chili Championship • October
Terilingua • www.chili.org

Guadalupe Mts/Carlsbad Area
UFO Festival • July
Roswell, NM • www.roswellufofestival.com

New Mexico State Fair • September
Albuquerque, NM • www.exponm.com/state-fair/

Whole Enchilada Fiesta • September
Las Cruces, NM • www.enchiladafiesta.com

Hatch Valley Chile Festival • September
Hatch Valley, NM • www.hatchchilefest.com

International Balloon Fiesta • October
Albuquerque, NM • www.balloonfiesta.com

Festival of the Cranes • November
Socorro, NM • www.friendsofthebosque.org/crane

Petrified Forest Area

Nature and Birding Festival • April
Cottonwood, AZ • www.birdyverde.org

Navajo Nation Fair • August
Window Rock, AZ • www.navajonationfair.com

Saguaro Area

World Championship Hoop Dance Contest
February • Phoenix, AZ • www.heard.org

Arabian Horse Show • February
Scottsdale, AZ • www.scottsdaleshow.com

Cowgirl Up! • March
Wickenburg, AZ • www.cowgirlupart.com

SalsaFest • September
Safford, AZ • www.SalsaTrail.com

1000 The Great Stair Climb • October
Bisbee, AZ • www.bisbee1000.org

All Souls Procession • November
Tucson, AZ • www.allsoulsprocession.org

Attractions

Big Bend Area

Big Bend River Tours • (800) 545-4240
River, hiking, & backroad tours • Rental & Shuttle
1 Main St; Terlingua, TX 79852
www.bigbendrivertours.com • Raft (half-day): $72

Far Flung Outdoor Center • (432) 371-2634
River, Jeep, & ATV Tours • Rental & Shuttle
1 Adventure Ln FM-170; Terlingua, TX 79852
www.bigbendfarflung.com • Raft (half-day): $69

Desert Sports • (888) 989-6900
Bike, Hike, River & Combo Tours • Rental & Shuttle
FM-170; Terlingua, TX 79852
www.desertsportstx.com • Raft (full-day): $150

Big Bend Stables • (800) 887-4331
TX-118; Terlingua, TX 79852
www.lajitasstables.com • Ride (2 hr): $60

Lajitas Stables • (432) 371-3064
21315 FM-170; Redford, TX 79846
www.lajitasstables.com • Ride (2 hr): $70

Big Bend Ranch State Park • (432) 358-4444
1900 S Saucedo; Presidio, TX 79845
www.tpwd.state.tx.us • Entrance Fee: $3/Person

Railroad Blues • (432) 837-3103
504 W Holland Ave; Alpine, TX 79830
www.railroadblues.com • *Live Music*

Guadalupe Mts/Carlsbad Area

Franklin Mtns State Park • (915) 566-6441
1331 McKelligon Canyon Rd; El Paso, TX 79930
www.tpwd.state.tx.us • Entrance Fee: $1/Person

Wyler Aerial Tramway • (915) 566-6622
1700 McKinley; El Paso, TX 79930
www.tpwd.state.tx.us • Rates: $7/Person

El Paso Zoo • (915) 521-1850
4001 E Paisano Dr; El Paso, TX 79905
www.elpasozoo.org • Admission: $10/Adult

El Paso Museum of Art • (915) 532-1707
1 Arts Festival Plz; El Paso, TX 79901
www.elpasoartmuseum.org • Free

Living Desert State Park • (575) 887-5516
1504 Miehls Dr; Carlsbad, NM 88220
www.emnrd.state.nm.us • Entrance Fee: $5/Vehicle

Sitting Bull Falls
Sitting Bull Falls Rd; Carlsbad, NM 88220

Cavern Theatre • (575) 885-4931
210 North Canyon St; Carlsbad, NM 88220

Carlsbad Community Theatre • (575) 887-3157
National Parks Hwy; Carlsbad, NM 88220
www.carlsbadcommunitytheatre.com

Cavern City Cinemas • (575) 885-4126
401 W Fiesta Dr; Carlsbad, NM 88220

Mall Cinema • (575) 885-0777
2322 W Pierce St; Carlsbad, NM 88220

Cal's Cactus Lanes • (575) 887-1933
1609 S Canal St; Carlsbad, NM 88220

Brantley Lake State Park • (575) 457-2384
33 E Brantley Lake Rd; Carlsbad, NM 88220
www.emnrd.state.nm.us • Entrance Fee: $5/Vehicle

Riverbend Hot Springs • (575) 894-7625
NM's only Hot Springs spa • on Rio Grande River
100 Austin St; Truth or Consequences, NM 87901
www.riverbendhotsprings.com

Geronimo Springs Museum • (575) 894-6600
211 Main St; Truth or Consequences, NM 87901
www.geronimospringsmuseum.com • Admission: $6/Adult

Bitter Lake Nat'l Wildlife Refuge • Chaves, NM
www.fws.gov/southwest/refuges/newmex/bitterlake/

Bottomless Lakes State Park • (575) 624-6058
545 A Bottomless lakes Rd; Roswell, NM 88201
www.emnrd.state.nm.us • Entrance Fee: $5/Vehicle

Roswell Museum and Art Center • (575) 624-6744
100 W 11th St; Roswell, NM 88201
www.roswellmuseum.org • Free

Alien Zone • (575) 627-6982
216 N Main St; Roswell, NM 88201
www.alienzoneroswellnm.com

Spring River Zoo • (575) 624-6760
1306 E College Blvd; Roswell, NM 88201

Int'l Ufo Museum • (800) 822-3545
114 N Main St; Roswell, NM 88203
www.roswellufomuseum.com • Admission: $5/Adult

Beyond the Petrified Forest

Turquoise Museum • (505) 247-8650
2107 Central Ave NW; Albuquerque, NM 87104
www.turquoisemuseum.com • Admission: $4/Adult

The Box Performance Space • (505) 404-1578
Improv classes, camps, and shows ($10/Ticket)
114 Gold Ave SW; Albuquerque, NM 87102
www.theboxabq.com

Hinkle Family Fun Center • (505) 299-3100
Bumper cars/boats, go-carts, mini-golf, and more
12931 Indian School Rd NE; Albuquerque, NM 87112
www.hinklefamilyfuncenter.com

Rattlesnake Museum • (505) 242-6569
202 San Felipe St NW; Albuquerque, NM 87104
www.rattlesnakes.com • Admission: $5/Adult

Nat'l Museum of Nuclear Science & History
Learn about the atomic age • (505) 245-2137
601 Eubank Blvd SE; Albuquerque, NM 87123
www.nuclearmuseum.org • Admission: $8/Adult

Unser Racing Museum • (505) 341-1776
1776 Montano Rd NW; Los Ranchos, NM 87107
www.unserracingmuseum.com • Admission: $10/Adult

ABQ BioPark - Zoo • (505) 764-6200
903 10th St SW; Albuquerque, NM 87102
www.cabq.gov • Admission: $12/Adult

ABQ BioPark - Botanic Garden & Aquarium
2601 Central Ave NW; Albuquerque, NM 87104
www.cabq.gov • Admission: $12/Adult (includes zoo)

Albuquerque Museum • (505) 242-4600
2000 Mtn Rd NW; Albuquerque, NM 87104
www.cabq.gov • Admission: $4/Adult

Nat'l Hispanic Cultural Center • (505) 246-2261
1701 4th St SW, # 211; Albuquerque, NM 87102
www.nhccnm.org • Admission: $3/Adult

Sandia Peak Ski Area • (505) 242-9052
10 Tramway Loop NE; Albuquerque, NM 87122
www.sandiapeak.com • Tram: $20/Adult

The Spy House • (505) 842-0223
This B&B holds a monthly murder mystery event
209 High St. NE; Albuquerque, NM 87102
www.albuquerquebedandbreakfasts.com

Explora • (505) 224-8300
1701 Mtn Rd NW; Albuquerque, NM 87104

New Mexico Museum of Natural
History & Science • (505) 841-2800
1801 Mtn Rd NW; Albuquerque, NM
www.nmnaturalhistory.org • Admission: $7/Adult

Indian Pueblo Cultural Center • (505) 843-7270
2401 12th St NW; Albuquerque, NM 87104
www.indianpueblo.org

Rainbow Ryders • (505) 823-1111
5601 Eagle Rock Ave NE; Albuquerque, NM 87113
www.rainbowryders.com • Balloon Ride: $159+

ABQ Int'l Balloon Museum • (505) 880-0500
9201 Balloon Museum Dr NE; Albuquerque, NM 87113
www.balloonmuseum.com • Admission: $4/Adult

White Sands Nat'l Mon. (NM) • (575) 479-6124
PO Box 1086; Holloman AFB, NM 88330
www.nps.gov/whsa • Entrance Fee: $3/Person

Trinity Site near White Sands NM
Site of the first atomic bomb explosion in the northern section of White Sands Missile Range
Open twice per year (view link below for next scheduled open house) • Free
www.wsmr.army.mil/PAO/Trinity

Gila Cliff Dwellings NM • (575) 536-9461
HC 68 Box 100; Silver City, NM 88061
www.nps.gov/gicl • Entrance Fee: $10/family/day

El Malpais NM • (505) 876-2783
123 East Roosevelt Ave; Grants, NM 87020
www.nps.gov/elma • Free

Bandelier NM • (505) 672-3861 ext. 517
15 Entrance Rd; Los Alamos, NM 87544
www.nps.gov/band • Entrance Fee: $12/Vehicle

Petroglyph NM • (505) 899-0205
6001 Unser Blvd, NW; Albuquerque, NM 87120
www.nps.gov/petr • Entrance Fee: $1–2/Vehicle

Flagstaff Area National Monuments
6400 N US-89; Flagstaff, AZ 86004

Walnut Canyon NM • (928) 526-3367
www.nps.gov/waca • Entrance Fee: $5/Person

Wupatki NM • (928) 679-2365
www.nps.gov/wupa • Entrance Fee: $5/Person

Sunset Crater Volcano NM • (928) 526-0502
www.nps.gov/sucr • Entrance Fee: $5/Person

Lowell Observatory • (928) 774-3358
1400 W Mars Hill Rd; Flagstaff, AZ 86001
www.lowell.edu • Admission: $10/Adult

Eliphante
A sculptural home created by a local artist
PO Box 971; Cornville AZ 86325
www.eliphante.org

Saguaro Area
Musical Instrument Museum • (480) 478-6000
4725 E Mayo Blvd; Phoenix, AZ 85050
www.themim.org • Admission: $15/Adult

Desert Botanical Gardens • (480) 941-1225
1201 N Galvin Parkway; Phoenix, AZ 85008
www.dbg.org • Admission: $18/Adult

Hot Air Expeditions • (480) 502-6999
2243 E Rose Garden Loop; Phoenix, AZ 85024
www.hotairexpeditions.com

Children's Museum • (602) 253-0501
215 N 7th St; Phoenix, Arizona 85034
www.childrensmuseumofphoenix.org • $11

Open Road Tours • (602) 997-0477
Tours (departing Phoenix) to the Grand Canyon, Antelope Canyon, Sedona, and more
4735 N 12th St; Phoenix, AZ 85014
www.openroadtours.com

Octane Raceway • (602) 302-7223
317 S 48th St; Phoenix, AZ 85034
www.octaneraceway.com

Camelback Mountain
Some of the best hiking in Phoenix (strenuous)
McDonald Dr; Phoenix, AZ 85073

Lost Dutchman State Park • (480) 982-4485
6109 N Apache Tr; Apache Junction, AZ 85119
www.azstateparks.com • Entrance Fee: $7/Vehicle

AZ-Sonora Desert Museum • (520) 883-2702
2021 N Kinney Rd; Tucson, AZ 85743
www.desertmuseum.org • Admission: $15/Adult

Cocoraque Ranch • (520) 682-8594
Working Cattle Ranch offers cattle drives, trail/hay rides, and rodeos • Saguaro West
6255 N Diamond Hills Ln; Tucson, AZ 85743
www.cocoraque.com

Pantano Riding Stables • (520) 298-8980
Offers regular trail rides (1 hr: $22) at Saguaro East
4450 S Houghton Rd; Tucson, 85730
www.canyon-country.com/tucson/html/pantano.html

Houston's Horseback Riding • (520) 298-7450
Trail rides ($80) into Saguaro NP w/ BBQ
12801 E Speedway Blvd; Tucson, AZ 85748
www.tucsonhorsebackriding.com

Casino Del Sol • (800) 344-9435
5655 W Valencia Rd; Tucson, AZ 85757
www.solcasinos.com

Pines Golf Club At Marana • (520) 744-7443
8480 N Continental Links Dr; Tucson, AZ 85743
www.playthepines.com • 9 holes: $20

Bedroxx Bowling • (520) 744-7655
4385 W Ina Rd; Tucson, AZ 85741
www.bedroxx.com

Tower Theatres • (520) 579-0500
8031 N Business Park Dr; Tucson, AZ 85743

Marana Skydiving Center • (520) 682-4441
11700 W Avra Valley Rd; Marana, AZ 85653
www.skydivemarana.com

Breakers Water Park • (520) 682-2304
8555 W Tangerine Rd; Tucson, AZ 85742
www.breakerswaterpark.com • Admission: $21/Adult

Crooked Tree Golf Course • (520) 744-3366
9101 N Thornydale Rd; Tucson, AZ 85742
www.crookedtreegolfcourse.net • 9 holes: $24

Tucson Museum Of Art • (520) 624-2333
140 N Main Ave; Tucson, AZ 85701
www.tucsonmuseumofart.org • Admission: $8/Adult

Fox Tucson Theatre • (520) 624-1515
17 W Congress St; Tucson, AZ 85701
www.foxtucsontheatre.org

AMC Loews Theatres/Foothills 15 • (888) 262-4386
7401 N La Cholla Blvd; Tucson, AZ 85741

Foolish Pleasure Hot Air Balloon Rides
(520) 578-0610 • 4920 W Ina Rd; Tucson, AZ 85743
www.foolishpleasureaz.com • Rates: $125+

Century Park 16 Theatre • (520) 620-0435
1055 W Grant Rd; Tucson, AZ 85705

Broadway In Tucson • (520) 903-2929
100 N Stone Ave, # 905; Tucson, AZ 85701
www.broadwayintucson.com

Oracle View • (520) 292-2430
4690 N Oracle Rd; Tucson, AZ 85705

Kitt Peak Visitor Center • (520) 318-8726
950 N Cherry Ave; Tucson, AZ 85719
www.noao.edu • Tours: $8/Adult

Int'l Wildlife Museum • (520) 629-0100
4800 W Gates Pass Blvd; Tucson, AZ 85745
www.thewildlifemuseum.org • Admission: $8/Adult

Plush • (520) 798-1298
340 E 6th St; Tucson, AZ 85705
www.plushtucson.com • *Live Music*

Flandrau Science Center & Planetarium
1601 E University Blvd; Tucson, AZ 85719
www.flandrau.org • (520) 621-7827
Admission: $7.50/Adult

Reid Park Zoo • (520) 791-4022
960 S Randolph Way; Tucson, AZ 85716
www.tucsonzoo.org • Admission: $7/Adult

Borderlands Theatre • (520) 882-8607
40 W Broadway Blvd; Tucson, AZ 85701
www.borderlandstheater.org

Loft Cinema • (520) 795-7777
3233 E Speedway Blvd; Tucson, AZ 85716
www.loftcinema.com

Colossal Cave Mtn Park • (520) 647-7275
16721 E Old Spanish Trail; Vail, AZ 85641
www.colossalcave.com • Entrance Fee: $5/Vehicle

Kartchner Caverns State Park • (520) 586-4100
PO Box 1849; Benson, AZ 85602
www.azstateparks.com • Cave Tours: $23/Adult

Carnival of Illusion • (520) 615-5299
Doubletree Hotel, 445 S Alvernon Way; Tucson, AZ 85711
www.carnivalofillusion.com • Tickets: $24+

Pima Air & Space Museum • (520) 574-0462
6000 E Valencia Rd; Tucson, AZ 85756
www.pimaair.org • Admission: $14/Adult

Sabino Canyon • (520) 749-2861
5900 N Sabino Canyon Rd; Catalina Foothills, AZ
www.sabinocanyon.com • *Tours available*

The Mini-Time Machine • (520) 881-0606
A Museum of Miniatures • Admission: $7/Adult
4455 E Camp Lowell Dr; Tucson, AZ 85712
www.theminitimemachine.org

Mission San Xavier del Bac • (520) 294-2624
A National Historic Landmark, this Catholic mission was constructed in 1791 making it the oldest intact European structure in Arizona. Museum and gift shop on-site.
1950 W San Xavier Rd; Tucson, AZ 85746
www.sanxaviermission.org

Biosphere 2 • (520) 838-6200
Unique research, outreach, and learning center
32540 S Biosphere Rd; Tucson, AZ 85739
www.b2science.org • Admission: $20/Adult

Tohono Chul Park • (520) 742-6455
7366 N Paseo del Norte; Tucson, AZ 85704
www.tohonochulpark.org • Admission: $8/Adult

Arizona Historical Society • (520) 628-5774
949 East 2nd Street; Tucson, AZ 85719
www.arizonahistoricalsociety.org • Admission: $3/Adult

Gaslight Theatre • (520) 886-9428
Offers a variety of off-beat and lighthearted shows
7010 E Broadway Blvd; Tucson, AZ 85710
www.thegaslighttheatre.com

Center for Creative Photography • (520) 621-7968
1030 N Olive Rd; Tucson, Arizona 85721
www.creativephotography.org • Free

Organ Pipe Cactus National Monument
(520) 387-6849 • *Dangerous due to drug runners*
10 Organ Pipe Dr; Ajo, AZ 85321
www.nps.gov/orpi • Entrance Fee: $8/Vehicle

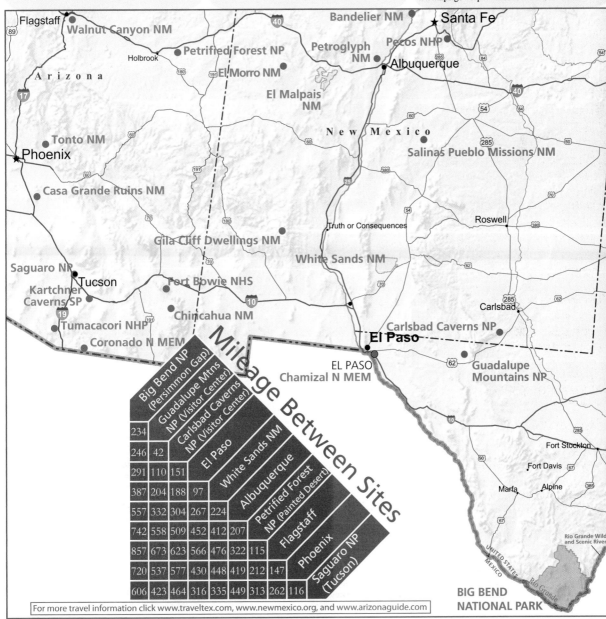

Mileage Between Sites

Big Bend NP (Persimmon Gap)	Guadalupe Mtns NP (Visitor Center)	Carlsbad Caverns NP (Visitor Center)	El Paso	White Sands NM	Albuquerque	Petrified Forest NP (Painted Desert)	Flagstaff	Phoenix	Saguaro NP (Tucson)
234									
246	42								
291	110	151							
387	204	188	97						
557	332	304	267	224					
742	558	509	452	412	207				
857	673	623	566	476	322	115			
720	537	577	430	448	419	212	147		
606	423	464	316	335	449	313	262	116	

For more travel information click www.traveltex.com, www.newmexico.org, and www.arizonaguide.com

Rocky Mountain • Pages 326–337

Great Sand Dunes • Pages 338–345

Black Canyon • Pages 346–353

Mesa Verde • Pages 354–367

Arches • Pages 368–375

© Frank Kovalchek (flickr/Alaskan Dude)

Canyonlands • Pages 376–387

THE SOUTHWEST

© Frank Kovalchek (flickr/Alaskan Dude)

Capitol Reef • Pages 388–395

Bryce Canyon • Pages 396–403

Zion • Pages 404–415

Grand Canyon • Pages 416–438

Great Basin • Pages 440–453

THE SOUTHWEST

A visitor uses binoculars to get an up-close view of elk grazing at Moraine Park

1000 US Highway 36
Estes Park, Colorado 80517
Phone: (970) 586-1206
Website: www.nps.gov/romo

Established: January 26, 1915
Size: 265,800 Acres
Annual Visitors: 2.9 Million
Peak Season: June–August
Hiking Trails: 355 Miles

Activities: Hiking, Backpacking,
Driving, Camping, Fishing, Rock
Climbing, and Horseback Riding

Campgrounds: 586 Total Sites at
Aspenglen, Glacier Basin, Longs
Peak, Moraine Park, and Timber
Creek Campgrounds
Fee: $20/night, $14/night (during
off-season without water)
Backcountry Camping: Permitted
with a Backcountry Use Permit
Lodging: None

Park Hours: All day, every day
Entrance Fee: $20 • Vehicle
$10 • Individual (foot, bike, etc.)

Rocky Mountain - Colorado

Romancing the American West inevitably leads to visions of the Rocky Mountains. They form a natural barrier stretching for 2,700 miles from New Mexico to northern British Columbia. Often referred to as the backbone of the continent, they could just as easily be viewed as the continent's lifeline. The Rockies are the main artery providing land with its most valuable resource: water. Snow collects in the rugged peaks. When it melts, water runs down the steep slopes, carving valleys and pooling into hundreds of alpine lakes. These lakes and rivers supply water for one quarter of the United States, eventually coursing across the continent to the Pacific, Arctic, and Atlantic Oceans. In north-central Colorado, just a 2-hour drive from Denver, there's a collection of snowy peaks, meandering streams, and pristine lakes that epitomize the most grandiose Rocky Mountain images you can conjure.

The Rockies are as imposing as they are vast. **Native Americans** rarely ventured beyond the foothills. Some 6,000 years ago, Ute Indians, also known as Mountain People, were scattered throughout much of modern-day Utah and Colorado (primarily around the Grand Lake area), hunting elk and gathering plants. On the other side of the Continental Divide Arapaho and Cheyenne lived on the plains, occasionally visiting the present-day Estes Park region to hunt. Natives dominated the area until the late 1700s. Both tribes were separated by a seemingly impenetrable barrier. A barrier they chose not to cross because food was bountiful and everything they needed was available right where they were.

Things changed following the **Louisiana Purchase** in 1803. Natives were moved to reservations and Americans moved in, but the Rockies failed to draw the public's attention until the **gold rush** of 1858. Boom towns of Denver, Boulder, and Golden were established, but mining was never very successful. Prospectors made at least one substantial discovery: the allure of the Rockies. Gold-seeking never panned out for **Joel Estes** either. He found a particularly beautiful location in a valley at the foot of the mountains where he hunted with his son to supply Denver's meat markets and subsidize his meager prospecting income. By 1860 he built cabins for farming and producing meat, the humble beginnings of Estes Park.

In 1886, a 16 year-old boy named **Enos Mills** moved to Estes Park of his own accord. Enos sought what prospectors found by accident, the Rockies and life in the wilderness. In 1889 he met **John Muir** on a camping trip in California. Muir inspired the young man to study nature and practice conservation. Mills listened and turned his attention back to the Rockies, spending countless hours in the mountains and climbing Longs Peak more than 250 times. He established Longs Peak Inn where guests could attend trail school and be educated on the area's natural wonders. He wrote books and articles on the area's scenic value. The more time spent in the mountains, the more convinced he became that the region should preserved for the enjoyment of the people. But the buzz of sawmills' blades and sight of grazing cattle were closing in on his cherished landscapes.

In 1907, **President Theodore Roosevelt** appointed Mills to be a lecturer for the National Forest Service. This opportunity was used to spread his ideas about conservation and to tell others about his beloved Rocky Mountains. Unlike parks before it, Rocky Mountain did not have a major railway lobbying its cause. Nevertheless, Mills remained dedicated to the idea of a park. He found allies in conservation groups like the Colorado Mountain Club. Denver Chamber of Commerce was convinced of the merits of a national park, too. Momentum was building, and in 1915 Congress approved legislation drafted by James Grafton Rogers and **President Woodrow Wilson** signed it, creating Rocky Mountain National Park.

Did you know?

▶ There are more than 60 peaks greater than 12,000 feet (the tallest being Longs Peak at 14,259 ft), 450 miles of streams, and 150 lakes within the park.

When to Go

Rocky Mountain is open year-round. Beaver Meadows and Kawuneeche Visitor Centers are open every day of the year except Christmas. Typical hours are from 8am until 5pm, with shorter hours in winter and extended hours in summer. Fall River Visitor Center is open year-round, but is only open on weekends from late October to late April. Alpine and Moraine Park Visitor Centers close during the winter (see page 336 for details).

More than half the park's three million visitors arrive between June and August. If you think Yellowstone is busy in summer, consider the fact that Rocky Mountain receives just as many annual visitors but is one-eighth Yellowstone's size. September is a popular time of year, when leaves begin to change color and elk can be heard bugling. To escape the crowds, visit in May or October. Trail Ridge Road usually opens in late May and closes for the season around the middle of October. Many high elevation trails can be impassable to hikers without special equipment until well into June and again in October. Bear Lake Road is open year-round. The park is always busy in summer, but it's such a popular weekend destination that traveling early in the week often yields significantly smaller crowds. Weekends in Estes Park are usually marred with bumper-to-bumper traffic that borders on complete gridlock.

Transportation & Airports

Public transportation does not provide service to the park. A free shuttle runs on Bear Lake Road between Beaver Meadows Visitor Center and Bear Lake Trailhead. There are three separate shuttle routes. Two routes connect Bear Lake Road's trailheads with Moraine Park and Glacier Basin Campgrounds. The third route ferries visitors between Estes Park Visitor Center and Beaver Meadows Visitor Center. Use the shuttles to help reduce traffic congestion. The closest airport is Denver International (DEN), about 80 miles southeast of Beaver Meadows Visitor Center.

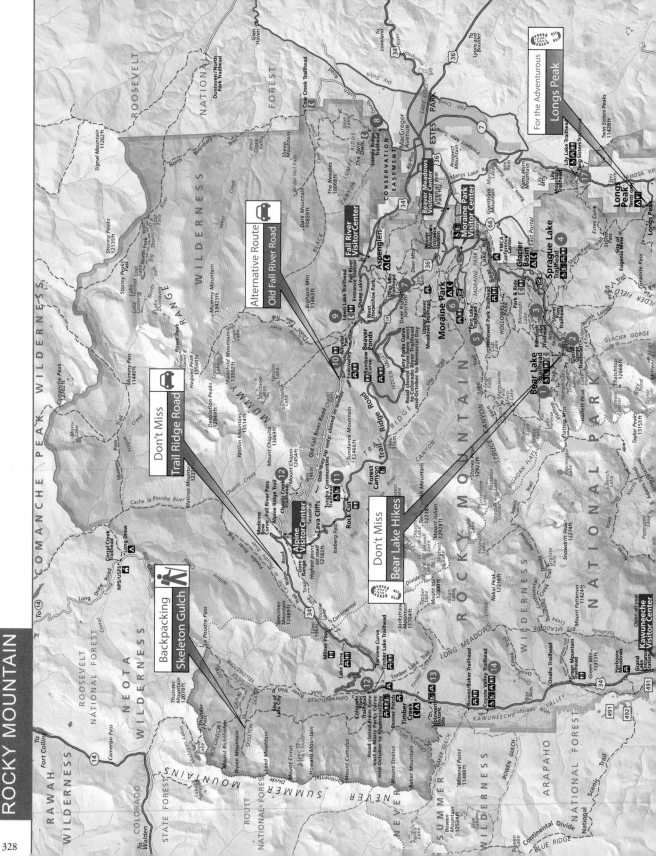

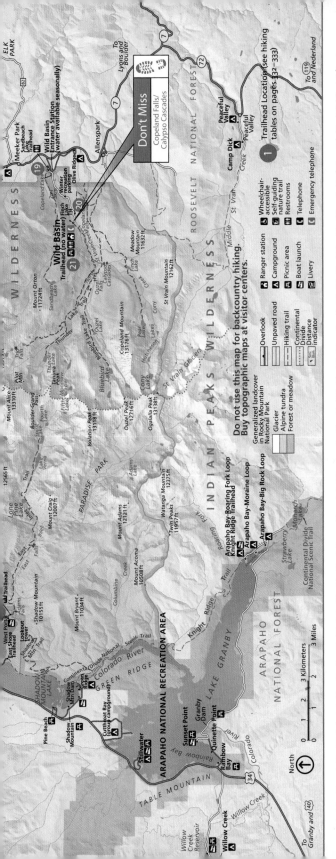

Directions

The park straddles the Continental Divide about 80 miles north of Denver. Trail Ridge Road (US-34), the highest continuous paved road in the United States, crosses the Divide, providing unprecedented access to both sides of the Rocky Mountains.

From Denver (64 miles): Take I-25 North (Partial Toll) toward Fort Collins. Exit onto CO-66 toward Lyons. Turn left onto CO-66/Co Rd 30. It becomes US-36/CO-66. Continue through Estes Park where you will find signs leading into the park.

From the West/I-70 Exit 232 (62 miles): Traveling east on I-70 take exit 157 for CO-131 N toward Wolcott/Steamboat Springs. Turn left at CO-131 N/Bellyache Ridge Rd and then another left onto CO-131 N/US-6 W. After crossing the Colorado River you'll come to a T-intersection, turn right onto County Rd 1/Trough Rd. Continue on County Rd 1 until it meets CO-9 N. Turn left and drive into Kremmling, CO. As soon as you enter the small city turn right onto Tyler Ave. After less than half a mile turn right again onto US-40 E/Park Ave. US-40 follows the Colorado River to Granby. Before entering Granby turn left onto US-34/Trail Ridge Road, which leads to Grand Lake and the East Entrance.

Driving

Driving through the park is all about **Trail Ridge Road**. This high-altitude thoroughfare unlocks the mountain range's rugged interior to motorists. Completed in 1932, the 48-mile road connects Estes Park and Grand Lake. Its grade never exceeds 7% even though it boasts an 8-mile continuous stretch above 11,000 feet elevation. Whether you enter from the east or west you are sure to notice drastic changes in the ecosystem. First you'll pass through forests of aspen and ponderosa pine. As you climb more than 4,000 feet you cross the tree line and emerge on top of barren mountains covered with fragile alpine tundra. Overlooks and trailheads are dispersed along the scenic byway. From east to west, **Many Parks Curve**, **Forest Canyon**, and **Rock Cut** are pit-stops that should not be skipped. If you'd like to enjoy the Rockies at a slower pace (15 mph), take the one-way gravel **Old Fall River Road** (closed until early July) from Endovalley to Alpine Visitor Center. Old Fall River and Trail Ridge roads are closed for most of the year. Call (970) 586-1222 for current road status. Bear Lake Road will be under construction until the summer of 2013.

Camping

If you want to spend a night in the park you're going to have to stay at a campground. There are five drive-in campgrounds. **Aspenglen, Moraine Park, and Glacier Basin Campgrounds** are located near Estes Park. Glacier Basin has lost much of its appeal because most trees were removed due to damage caused by the pine beetle. **Longs Peak Campground** is located south of Estes Park, just off CO-7. It features tent-only sites available on a first-come, first-served basis. It's also a good location to use as a base camp for those attempting to day hike to the summit of Longs Peak (14,259-ft), the highest point in the park.

On the west side you'll find **Timber Creek Campground**. It has relatively little seclusion, but it's the only front-country camping option this side of the Continental Divide. Campgrounds often fill during the summer months. To guarantee a site you can make **reservations** at Aspenglen, Glacier Basin, or Moraine Park by calling (877) 444-6777 or clicking www.recreation.gov. **Backpackers** have more than 250 backcountry sites and 20 group sites to choose from. They are distributed fairly evenly between the western and eastern halves of the park. Backcountry camping requires a permit (page 334).

Rocky Mountain Camping

	Open	Fee	Sites	Location/Notes
Aspenglen*	late May–early Sept	$20	54	Near Fall River Entrance on US-34 (Trail Ridge Rd)
Glacier Basin*	late May–early Sept	$20	150	On Bear Lake Road, access to free summer shuttle
Longs Peak	All Year	$20	26	On CO-7, 11 miles south of Beaver Meadows Visitor Center • Tents Only
Moraine Park*·👍	All Year	$20	245	On Bear Lake Road above Moraine Park, summer shuttle
Timber Creek	All Year	$20	98	On US-34, 10 miles north of Grand Lake

*Campsites can be reserved up to six months in advance by calling (877) 444-6777 or clicking www.recreation.gov. Water is only available during the summer months. Rates are reduced to $14/night when the water is off.
Cold running water and restrooms with flush toilets are available when the water is turned on. Otherwise vault toilets are available. All campsites have fire rings. Ice is sold at all campgrounds except Timber Creek. Dump Stations are available at Glacier Basin, Moraine Park, and Timber Creek. None of the campgrounds have showers or hook-ups.

Backcountry	267 Backcountry Campsites are available with a backcountry/wilderness permit. Permits can be obtained at Beaver Meadows Visitor Center's Backcountry Office or Kawuneeche Visitor Center. A limited number of permits are issued. They may be reserved in person or by mail (page 334). Reservation requires a $20 administrative fee during peak season (May–October).
Group Camping	Sites are available for groups of 9–40 people at Glacier Basin Campground. In winter, group sites are available at Moraine Park Campground. Group sites cost $3 per person per night.

No trip to the Rocky Mountains is complete without taking a little hike. Unfortunately, this also means you're sure to run into plenty of hikers. Parking areas may fill up by eight in the morning. **Bear Lake Hiker's Shuttle** can be packed tight with like-minded individuals. But Bear Lake's incomparable beauty, vast collection of rugged lakes, meadows brimming with spring wildflowers, and majestic mountains make it easy to endure the crowds and congestion. The area is best explored by foot and all of the most popular trailheads are located along Bear Lake Road. Shuttles may be cramped at times, but you should use them. They're far better than having to circle the parking lots until a spot opens up. Shuttles also allows easy hiking from one trailhead to another (as long as it's on the shuttle route). Below is a list of trails beginning at the south end of Bear Lake Road. Remember, the further you hike the more seclusion (and beauty) you will find.

Rocky Mountain (East Side) Hiking Trails

	Trail Name	Trailhead (# on map)	Length	Notes (One-way unless noted otherwise, RT = Roundtrip)
South End of Bear Lake Road	Bear Lake Nature Trail	Bear Lake (1)	0.6 mile	A short and easy self-guiding nature trail (RT)
	Nymph, Dream, and Emerald Lakes - 👍	Bear Lake (1)	0.5/1.1/1.8 miles	This easy trail leads to three of the most well-known and popular attractions
	Lake Haiyaha	Bear Lake (1)	2.1 miles	Moderate hike proves that even the lakes are rocky
	Flattop Mountain	Bear Lake (1)	4.4 miles	Strenuous hike to mountain on the shoulder of Hallet Peak
	Hallet Peak	Bear Lake (1)	5.0 miles	Strenuous hike to the peak towering above Bear Lake
	Bierstadt Lake	Bierstadt Lake (3)	1.4 miles	Easy hike to a pleasant alpine lake • Hike from Bear Lake to Bierstadt and use the shuttle to return
		Bear Lake (1)	1.6 miles	
	Odessa Lake	Bear Lake (1)	4.1 miles	Moderate hike to mountain-lined lake • Hike from Bear Lake Trailhead to Fern Lake Trailhead for an 8.5-mile trek
		Fern Lake (5)	4.9 miles	
	Alberta Falls	Glacier Gorge (2)	0.8 mile	Nice warm-up to venture deeper into the Rockies • It is extremely enjoyable all year round
		Bear Lake (1)	0.9 mile	
	Mills Lake	Glacier Gorge (2)	2.8 miles	Moderate hike to one of the park's most beautiful lakes
	The Loch	Glacier Gorge (2)	3.0 miles	Moderate hike • Extremely popular
	Sky Pond - 👍	Glacier Gorge (2)	4.9 miles	Strenuous hike past Timberline Falls and Lake of Glass
	Black Lake	Glacier Gorge (2)	5.0 miles	Strenuous continuation of the trail to Mills Lake
	Timberline Falls	Glacier Gorge (2)	4.0 miles	Excellent trail that takes hikers above The Loch
	Sprague Lake - 👍	Sprague Lake (4)	0.5 mile	Short and easy self-guiding trail (RT)

Hiking (cont.)

A nice, fairly long (roughly 10-mile) trek begins at **Cub Lake Trailhead**. Hike to Cub Lake and continue on to The Pool, Fern Falls, and Odessa Lake before returning to the shores of Bear Lake. **Alluvial Fan Trail**, near the beginning of Old Fall River Road, is a short climb to dramatic views. Wild Basin is located in the park's southeastern corner. The short hikes to **Copeland Falls** and **Calypso Cascades** are fantastic. If you're feeling energetic you can continue on to three alpine lakes that lie close to the Continental Divide. **The Keyhole Route to Longs Peak** is another hike that requires plenty of energy. It's a 4,000+ foot climb to the 14,259-ft summit and park's tallest peak. It begins at **Longs Peak Trailhead** off CO-7. From there it's 8 miles up, with the last 1.5 miles to the summit being the most difficult. Elevation change and distance from start to summit is similar to hiking out of the Grand Canyon and right back in. The trail is often impassable (without special equipment) until mid-July, so inquire about conditions at a visitor center before attempting your hike.

Most hiking is done on the busier eastern side, but some excellent hiking opportunities can be found along **Trail Ridge Road** and the park's west side. **Ute Trail** begins on Trail Ridge Road between Rainbow Curve and Forest Canyon. You descend 3,000 feet along Trail Ridge through amazing scenery. It extends 6.1 miles to Upper Beaver Meadows. It's recommended that you arrange a shuttle and hike one-way to Beaver Meadows. If you decide to make it an out-and-back, remember that the return trip uphill will be more difficult. **Toll Memorial and Alpine Ridge Trails**, located on Trail Ridge Road, are worth a quick stop. They are short hikes (less than 1 mile) with outstanding scenery. If you came to Rocky Mountains searching for solitude, choose any of the hiking trails at **East Inlet Trailhead** located near Grand Lake. You probably won't be alone, but it won't be anything like the hustle and bustle of the Bear Lake Area. The scenery is nearly as inspiring, and the gentle western slopes make for much easier hiking.

Rocky Mountain (East Side) Hiking Trails

	Trail Name	Trailhead (# on map)	Length	Notes (One-way unless noted otherwise, RT = Roundtrip)
North of Glacier Basin	The Pool	Fern Lake (5)	1.7 miles	Short and easy hike to a small pooled up stream
	Fern Falls	Fern Lake (5)	2.5 miles	Moderate hike through Arch Rocks to a nice falls
	Fern Lake	Fern Lake (5)	3.8 miles	Continues past Fern Falls to a lake • A bit more strenuous
	Cub Lake - 🥾	Cub Lake (6)	2.3 miles	One of the best short and easy hikes
	Moraine Park Nature Trail	Moraine Park (6)	0.6 mile	Short and easy self-guiding nature loop (RT)
	Deer Mountain	Deer Mountain (7)	3.0 miles	Moderate climb to a 10,000+ ft mountain summit
	Gem Lake	Lumpy Ridge (8)	1.6 miles	Moderate hike through rocky terrain to a little lake
	Ypsilon Lake	Lawn Lake (9)	4.5 miles	Strenuous trail to another popular mountain lined lake
	Lawn Lake	Lawn Lake (9)	6.2 miles	Strenuous trek to this lake in the Mummy Range
	Alluvial Fan - 🥾	Endovalley Road (10)	0.2 mile	Paved interpretive trail in a popular location
	Toll Memorial - 🥾	Tundra Communities (11)	0.5 mile	Easy trail to a marker named for past superintendent (RT)
	Ypsilon Mountain	Chapin Creek (12)	3.5 miles	Strenuous hike over Chapin and Chiquita Peaks to Ypsilon

Rocky Mountain (West & Southeast) Hiking Trails

	Trail Name	Trailhead (# on map)	Length	Notes (One-way unless noted otherwise, RT = Roundtrip)
West Rocky Mountain	Lulu City - 👍	Colorado River (12)	3.1 miles	Moderate trail to old mining town • Great for cross-country skiers
	Timber Lake	Timber Lake (12)	4.8 miles	Strenuous hike through dense forests to alpine lake
	Holzwarth Historic Site	Trail Ridge Road (13)	0.5 mile	Short walk on gravel path to an old dude ranch
	Coyote Valley	Coyote Valley (14)	1.0 mile	Flat, easy path where moose and elk are often spotted (RT)
	Cascade Falls	North Inlet (15)	3.5 miles	A flat and easy hike through lodgepole pine to the falls
	Lake Nokoni	North Inlet (15)	9.9 miles	Moderate, long, seldom visited trail
	Lake Nanita	North Inlet (15)	11.0 miles	Strenuous due to its length, but it is very peaceful
	Adams Falls - 👍	East Inlet (16)	0.3 mile	Easy and popular walk near Grand Lake
	Lone Pine Lake	East Inlet (16)	5.5 miles	First lake along East Inlet Trail
	Lake Verna	East Inlet (16)	6.9 miles	Pass a small falls to a wooded alpine lake
	Spirit Lake	East Inlet (16)	7.8 miles	Strenuous trail past Lone Pine Lake and Lake Verna
Southeast Rocky Mountain	Lily Lake - 👍	Lily Lake (17)	0.7 mile	Easy and level gravel path to a pretty mountain lake (RT)
	Twin Sisters	Twin Sisters (17)	3.7 miles	Strenuous trail to a peak with superb views of Longs Peak
	Eugenia Mine	Longs Peak (18)	1.4 miles	Easy hike to prospecting remnants from the 1800s
	Estes Cone	Longs Peak (18)	3.3 miles	Moderate hike to fantastic views • Ends with a scramble
	Chasm Lake	Longs Peak (18)	4.2 miles	Difficult trek to an alpine lake lying in the shadow of Longs Peak
	Longs Peak - 👍	Longs Peak (18)	8.0 miles	Extremely strenuous hike • 4,000+ ft elevation gain
	Sandbeach Lake	Sandbeach Lake (19)	4.2 miles	Strenuous hike to a seldom visited lake
	Finch Lake	Finch Lake (20)	4.5 miles	Strenuous trail, can loop back via Calypso Cascades
	Pear Lake	Finch Lake (20)	6.5 miles	Continue past Finch Lake to an even more remote lake
	Copeland Falls - 👍	Wild Basin (21)	0.3 mile	The first site en route to Calypso Cascades or Ouzel Falls
	Calypso Cascades - 👍	Wild Basin (21)	1.8 miles	Easy trail through excellent riverside scenery
	Ouzel Falls	Wild Basin (21)	2.7 miles	Moderate trail follows past Calypso Cascades to Falls
	Bluebird Lake	Wild Basin (21)	6.0 miles	Continue past Ouzel Lake to backcountry lake
	Thunder Lake	Wild Basin (21)	6.8 miles	Passes through a wildflower meadow (spring)
	Lion Lake No. 1	Wild Basin (21)	7.0 miles	Veers away from Thunder Lake through wildflowers (spring)

A Rocky Mountain trail ride

Horseback Riding

Horses are allowed on **approximately 260 of the 355 miles of hiking trails**. Before Old Fall River Road and Trail Ridge Road were constructed riding on horseback through the park was the way of life. Adventurous souls galloped through meadows and climbed steep summits aboard their sure-footed steeds. Horseback riding through the Rockies remains just as gratifying and practical as it was before automobiles arrived on the scene. Horse owners can trailer in stock to explore the trails and camp in the backcountry (permit required), but most visitors join a group of riders on a trail ride provided by one of the park's approved **outfitters**. Rides range from 1–9 hours and $35–130. Multi-day trips are also available. For a complete list of outfitters and rates see page 365.

Fishing

Fishing is a popular activity even though many of the alpine lakes and streams are too high to support reproducing populations of fish. But there are many fine locations to catch brown, brook, rainbow, and cutthroat trout. See page 365 for a list of fishing **outfitters**, complete with contact information, and rates. All anglers 16 years of age and older require a Colorado fishing license (except for the first full weekend in June, which is free and does not require a license). You can only use one rod and reel with artificial bait. A number of rules and regulations regarding open and closed waters, catch and release, and possession limits are enforced. If you don't receive current information regarding rules and regulations when you purchase your fishing license, be sure to stop at a visitor center to discuss your plans with a friendly park ranger.

Backpacking

Want to enjoy a summer trip to the Rockies and evade the crowds and congestion? The most reliable solution is to pack up your gear and head into the backcountry. All day-hiking areas (pages 331–333) offer great backpacking opportunities. There are also more remote locations for experienced backpackers. The park's northeastern limits can be explored from **Dunraven/North Fork Trailhead**, which begins in Roosevelt National Forest off unpaved Dunraven Glade Road. From here, hike about 10 miles into the Rockies' Mummy Range to Lost Lake. This remote location can also be reached from **Cow Creek Trailhead** within McGraw Ranch at the end of an unpaved road north of Estes Park off Devil's Gulch Road. From Cow Creek Trailhead take North Boundary Trail to North Fork Trail to Lost Lake. **Bridal Veil Falls** is another popular destination from Cow Creek trailhead. The 20-ft falls is reached via a short spur from Cow Creek Trail. It is 3-miles (one-way) from the trailhead. Cow Creek Trail continues deeper into the Rockies. It follows Black Canyon all the way to Lawn and Crystal Lakes. Those looking to explore the northwestern corner should begin at **Corral Creek Trailhead**. It's also located in Roosevelt National Forest, along unpaved Long Draw Road. From here you can hike Poudre River Trail for 10.5 miles to Trail Ridge Road. It is lightly traveled with two campsites along the way. **Skeleton Gulch**, accessed from Colorado River Trail, is a far more popular backpacking area with mountain vistas all around as you hike along the river valley.

After you've mapped out your backpacking route on a good topographical map (essential to any backpacking adventure) it's time to get a **backcountry/wilderness permit**. The number of permits issued is limited, so you may want to make a reservation. Reservations are accepted any time after the first of March for that calendar year. They can be made by phone between March 1 and May 15, and any time after October 1 by calling (970) 586-1242. You can also make your reservation by writing to:

Backcountry/Wilderness Permits, Rocky Mtn Nat'l Park
1000 US Highway 36; Estes Park, CO 80517

You must include your name, address, telephone number, and number of people in your party along with a complete trip itinerary (dates and campsites). A $20 fee is collected upon picking up your permit.

Rock Climbing

Boulder and Denver have earned their distinction as extreme sports hubs. Rock climbing is one of their specialties, and there are few better playgrounds for rock climbers than Rocky Mountain National Park. It is one of the area's premier climbing locations offering everything from highly technical routes to basic scrambling. If you're interested in exploring the vertical side of the Rockies check out the park's approved **rock climbing outfitter** who offers a variety of group excursions (rates are based on size and length of tour):

Colorado Mountain School • (800) 836-4008
PO Box 1846; Estes Park, CO 80517
www.totalclimbing.com

Winter Activities

Visiting during winter provides the sort of tranquility you won't find anywhere around the roadways and hiking trails in summer. Often it feels like you're the only visitor in this vast expanse of untamed wilderness. Most winter guests explore hiking trails with **cross-country skis** or **snowshoes**. Bear Lake Area remains the most popular destination even when it's blanketed in snow. Several trails, like **Bierstadt Lake** and **Chasm Falls**, are marked for winter use. A winter play area is maintained at **Hidden Valley**, located at the end of a short access road off Trail Ridge Road (US-34) just past Beaver Ponds Pullout. It is the only site in the park that permits **sledding** (bring your own equipment). It's a good idea to call (970) 586-1206 for snow information before visiting Hidden Valley, Estes Park, or any other low elevation area on the park's east side. This region receives very little precipitation because of its location just east of the Continental Divide. Winds are typically strong, resulting in patchy snow cover and drifting. It's also mostly steep and rugged terrain, not suitable for beginner cross-country skiers.

The **west side** of the park (not accessible via Trail Ridge Road in winter) is more reliable. It receives more precipitation, less wind, and features gentler slopes. Many of the west side's hiking trails remain open for hiking, snowshoeing, and cross-country skiing. Whether you visit the west or east side it is always a good idea to stop in at a visitor center before entering the park. You'll receive up-to-date trail information, and may have the opportunity to join a **ranger-led ski or snowshoe tour**.

A pika stocking up for winter

Elk in Estes Park

Flora & Fauna

The Rockies' wildlife and wildflowers are attractions worth visiting on their own. More than one quarter of the park is alpine tundra, a seemingly barren and lifeless place for most of the year, but after the snow melts and sun thaws its frozen crust, **wildflowers** begin to grow. In early July fields of flowers bloom, painting tundra in bright colors that accent the magnificence of the park's mountains standing tall in the background. There are **66 mammals** residing here. Most popular are big and furry or small and mischievous. Elk can be seen (or heard bugling) in places like Moraine Park where they graze around dawn and dusk. Moose are often spotted in Kawuneeche Valley. Mountain lions and black bears (no grizzlies) live here, but are seldom seen. Industrious pikas live in the alpine tundra.

ROCKY MOUNTAIN

Best of Rocky Mountain

Attraction: Trail Ridge Road
>   Runner-up: Bear Lake
>   2nd Runner-up: Nat'l Park Gateway Stables

Family Hike: Alluvial Fan
>   Runner-up: Dream Lake
>   2nd Runner-up: Copeland Falls

For Kids: Children (12 and under) are welcome to participate in the **Junior Ranger Program**. Pick up a free activity booklet at any visitor center. Complete it and show your work to a park ranger to receive an official Junior Ranger Badge.

Ranger Programs: Do not skip the park's ranger programs. A huge variety of walks, talks, and evening programs are offered regularly during the summer. In winter you can join a ranger on a snowshoe or cross-country ski tour (you must provide your own equipment). Rangers are here to educate you on all sorts of subjects, including elk, lightning, geology, wildflowers, and much more. Some programs are geared toward children, bird watchers, stargazers, and hikers. They're all free and fantastic. It's not a crazy idea to plan your entire vacation around ranger activities.

Maybe you've never thought much about beavers. What do they do? How do they survive? Why do they build dams? Everyone seems to know that they have an amazing set of choppers, but few people understand how they change their environment. Learn all about it at **Amazing Beavers**, a one hour talk that takes place at Sprague Lake Picnic Area offered every day in summer except Sundays. Dozens of other programs are offered during the summer. Download a current issue of *Rocky Mountain National Park News* from the park website for a complete list with program schedule, length, and location. If you don't choose a few activities to attend before you arrive, stop in at a visitor center to see what's happening.

Pets: Pets are allowed in the park, but they are prohibited from all hiking trails and the backcountry. As a rule of thumb pets are permitted wherever your car can go. This includes roadsides, parking areas, picnic areas, and drive-in campgrounds. Pets must be kept on a leash no more than six feet in length at all times.

Accessibility: All visitor centers are fully accessible with the exception of Beaver Meadows Visitor Center/Park Headquarters which is accessible with assistance. Glacier Basin, Moraine Park, and Timber Creek Campgrounds have accessible campsites. Most hiking trails are steep,

Rocky Mountain Visitor and Information Centers

Facility	Open	Hours	Notes
Beaver Meadows Visitor Center (closed on Christmas Day)	late October–late April late April–mid-June mid-June–late August late August–early September early September–late October	8am–4:30pm 8am–5pm 8am–9pm 8am–7pm 8am–5pm	Located on US-36, 3 miles west of Estes Park. It was designed by Frank Lloyd Wright's School of Architecture at Taliesin West in Arizona. Watch a short introductory film, browse or purchase books and gifts, reserve backcountry campsites, or use the restrooms.
Fall River Visitor Center	late March–late October, daily • 9am–5pm late October–late March weekends, and the Friday after Thanksgiving, the week after Christmas until New Year's Day, and President's Day • 9am–4pm		Located on US-34, 5 miles west of Estes Park. It has a bookstore, exhibits, and restrooms.
Moraine Park Visitor Center	late April–mid-June mid-June–early September early September–early October	9am–4:30pm 9am–5pm 9am–4:30pm	Located on Bear Lake Road, 1.5 miles from Beaver Meadows Entrance. A nature trail, history exhibits, restrooms, and museum are open to visitors.
Alpine Visitor Center	late May–mid-June mid-June–early September early September–early October	10:30am–4:30pm 9am–5pm 10:30am–4:30pm	Located on Trail Ridge Road near its intersection with Old Fall River Road. Exhibits, a bookstore, gift store, snacks, and restrooms are available, as well as Ranger Programs.
Kawuneeche Visitor Center (closed on Christmas Day)	late September–late April late April–mid-June mid-June–early September early September–late September	8am–4:30pm 8am–5pm 8am–6pm 8am–4:30pm	Located one mile north of Grand Lake on US-34 at the park's entrance. You can watch a short introductory film (upon request); browse books, merchandise, and exhibits; use the restrooms, and reserve backcountry sites.
Sheeps Lake Information Station	mid-May–mid-August	8:30am–4pm	Located on US-34 just beyond Fall River Entrance.

rugged, and inaccessible to wheelchair users. The exceptions are Coyote Valley, Sprague Lake, Lily Lake, and Bear Lake Trails. They are all well-maintained, heavily trafficked, relatively flat, and accessible with assistance.

Weather: Rocky Mountain has two distinct climate patterns created and separated by the Continental Divide. The eastern region is dry and windy. The wetter, western half receives about 20 inches of precipitation annually, about six inches more than the eastern side. Both regions experience long frigid winters. Areas of high elevation can experience snowfall well into July. Expect a wide variation between day and nighttime temperatures. Summers are hot with temperatures frequenting the 70s and 80s°F. Temperatures drop into the 40s°F at night.

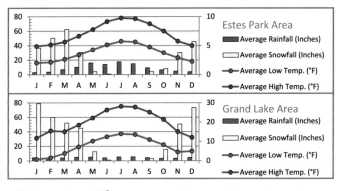

Estes Park Area
- Average Rainfall (Inches)
- Average Snowfall (Inches)
- Average Low Temp. (°F)
- Average High Temp. (°F)

Grand Lake Area
- Average Rainfall (Inches)
- Average Snowfall (Inches)
- Average Low Temp. (°F)
- Average High Temp. (°F)

Vacation Planner

What to do while visiting the Rockies varies greatly depending on when you plan on travelling. If you arrive between fall and spring, forget about driving across the Continental Divide via **Old Fall River Road** or **Trail Ridge Road**. They will be closed. **Bear Lake Road** is open all year, but **free hiker's shuttles** only run during summer. The planner below assumes a summer vacation and begins at **Wild Basin** in the park's southeast corner, but it's simple enough to reverse the itinerary, begin at **Grand Lake**, making your first stop at **Kawuneeche Visitor Center**. Other than **campgrounds** (page 330) there are no lodging facilities within park boundaries, but there are hundreds of options in nearby communities. Nearby dining, grocery stores, lodging, festivals, and attractions are listed on pages 362–367.

Day 1

Begin by driving up CO-7 to **Wild Basin**. From **Wild Basin Trailhead** hike to **Copeland Falls** and continue to **Calypso Cascades** (page 333). If wildflowers are in bloom and you're enjoying the scenery, continue on to **Ouzel Falls** and **Bluebird Lake**. It's 3.6 miles roundtrip to Calypso Cascades

and 12 miles roundtrip to Bluebird Lake. Allow at least 1.5 and 4 hours, respectively. Return to CO-7 and head north to **Longs Peak**. Hiking these trails isn't for everyone. The 6.6-mile (3–4-hr) roundtrip hike to **Estes Cone** (page 333) is pretty cool. It's not extremely difficult, but a short scramble is required near the end. If you want to **summit Longs Peak** (page 332), spend the night at **Longs Peak Campground** (tent-only, page 330) and get an early start in the morning. If not, continue along CO-7 to **Beaver Meadows Visitor Center**. Unless you feel compelled to visit Estes Park (extremely busy in summer), bypass it via Mary's Lake Road. Have a look around, get a current schedule of the park's **ranger programs**, and see if you can catch an evening program before settling into your accommodations for the night.

Day 2

Start at **Bear Lake Trailhead** (page 331). Drive in or park at Beaver Meadows and take the **park shuttle** (recommended). The trek to **Emerald Lake** is a good place to begin, but you can't go wrong with any of these trails. Hike until you've had enough and return to your car to drive the park's number one attraction: **Trail Ridge Road** (page 329). Consider taking **Old Fall River Road** as an alternative (you will return via Trail Ridge Road). It is slower (15 mph speed limit), less crowded, and more stressful (switchbacks and gravel), but it's amazing. Stop at **Alpine Visitor Center** to hike **Alpine Trail** and join a ranger program if possible. From here, continue west on Trail Ridge Road to **Coyote Valley Trailhead**. This is a good location to see moose at dusk. If you're spending the night on the other side of the divide give yourself enough time to watch the sunset from Trail Ridge Road.

Day 3

Assuming you spent the night on the west side, work your way back across the Rockies on **Trail Ridge Road**. Stop at **Rock Cut** to hike **Toll Memorial Trail** (page 332). Anyone looking for a good morning hike can be dropped off at **Ute Trail** (page 332) that connects Trail Ridge Road with Upper Beaver Meadows Trailhead. Let them hike one-way, just remember to pick them up on your way out after stopping at **Forest Canyon**, **Rainbow Curve**, and **Many Parks Curve**. If you didn't stop at **Alluvial Fan** on your way to Old Fall River Road, stop for one last Rocky Mountain view.

Few hikers stray from the sandy ridgelines

11999 Highway 150
Mosca, Colorado 81146
Phone: (719) 378-6300
Website: www.nps.gov/grsa

Established: September 13, 2004
(National Monument in 1932)
Size: 84,670 Acres
Annual Visitors: 280,000
Peak Season: Summer
Hiking Trails: 50+ Miles

Activities: Hiking, Backpacking,
Camping, Fishing, Sandboarding,
Sledding, and Horseback Riding

Campgrounds: Pinyon Flats
Fee: $20/night
Backcountry Camping: Permitted*
Lodging: None (See page 364 for
nearby lodging facilities)

Park Hours: All day, every day
Entrance Fee: $3/Person (16 &
older), Children are Free

*Must obtain a free Backcountry
Use Permit from the visitor center

Great Sand Dunes - Colorado

Would you guess the tallest dunes in North America are located in Colorado? They are; the Great Sand Dunes sprawl across San Luis Valley, an arid plain between the San Juan and Sangre de Cristo Mountains. They began forming millions of years ago and have been inhabited for at least the last 11,000 years. **Nomadic hunter–gatherers** were initially drawn to the region by herds of mammoth and bison. Thousands of years later **Ute and Jicarilla Apache** lived and hunted in the San Luis Valley. Ute called the dunes "sowapopheuveha" or "the land that moves back and forth." Jicarilla Apache called them "sei-anyedi" or "it goes up and down." In 1807, an American soldier, **Zebulon Pike** regarded the dunes in a similar fashion, describing them as a "sea in a storm." He first encountered the dunes on the **Pike Expedition**, sent to explore land acquired in the **Louisiana Purchase**.

Wind drives the rise and fall of waves in a storm, and is also the impetus of these dunes' **creation**. Crests of sand—sinuous ridgelines—rise up from the plains, crossing arid land at the foot of the Sangre de Cristo Mountains. It's a bizarre sight that immediately begs the question: **How were the Great Sand Dunes formed?** To understand the formation of the dunes, one must first understand the formation of the mountains. Uplift, caused by collision of two tectonic plates, forced the Sangre de Cristo Mountains to rise from the earth. Their sister range 65 miles west of the dune field, the San Juan Mountains, formed when a massive volcano erupted millions of years ago. Many scientists regard that event as the largest explosive volcanic eruption in the history of earth, with a resulting deposit 5,000 times larger than that of Mount St. Helen's. The two mountain ranges surround a vast plain, roughly the size of Connecticut, known today as San Luis Valley.

This valley used to be covered by an immense lake, which served as a collection site for massive amounts of sediment eroded away from the mountains. Climate change caused the lake to recede, a process that may have been expedited when the valley's southern end wore away, forming Rio Grande Gorge, which allowed water to drain directly into the river. Left behind was a giant sheet of sand.

A huge supply of sand was completely exposed to the forces of Mother Nature. Predominant southwesterly winds went to work. This indomitable force pushed sand across the valley to the Sangre de Cristo Mountains where it funneled into Mosca, Medano, and Music Passes. Storm winds blowing from the northeast took sand pinned against the mountain's slopes and pushed it back toward the valley's floor, causing dunes to grow vertically. Sand blown into the mountains is slowly collected and returned to the dune field by Sand and Medano Creeks.

After hundreds of millennia the opposing winds seem to have found satisfaction in their grainy masterpiece. Beneath the top layer of loose sand is a wet and cool sandy base, resilient to the forces of nature. These dunes may look like they're rising and falling like a "sea in a storm," but they're actually quite stable, having been roughly the same size and shape for more than 100 years.

A tourist's journey to Great Sand Dunes is nearly as laborious as the sand's. The park is well off the beaten path, far removed from major interstates and metropolitan areas. Like other national parks the greatest architecture here was created by the hands of nature, a sea of sand sculpted by wind and water that is easily one of the best kept secrets among the entire collection of national parks.

Did you know?

▶ The Ladies' PEO (professional employer organization) was the driving force behind the original effort to make Great Sand Dunes a national monument.

▶ Ute, Apache, and other tribes used pine tree bark for food and medicine. Many pealed trees are still living within the park today.

When to Go

Great Sand Dunes is open year-round. The Visitor Center is open every day, with the exception of federal holidays. In winter, the Visitor Center's operating hours are from 9am–4:30pm. Spring and fall hours are 9am–5pm. Memorial Day weekend to Labor Day weekend is the park's busiest season, when the visitor center is open from 8:30am–6:30pm. Even though summer sun brings the majority of visitors, spring and fall are typically the most pleasant seasons to visit. Dunes can be unbearably hot on a summer afternoon (you may want to wear shoes).

Transportation & Airports

Public transportation does not go to or around the park. There is a small airport in Alamosa, CO, but you are better off flying into Denver International (DEN) 250 miles to the north or Albuquerque International Sunport (ABQ) 230 miles to the south. Car rental is available at each destination.

Directions

Great Sand Dunes has been described as the quietest park in the lower 48 states. That title gives you an idea of how removed this scenic wonder is from the rest of civilization. Most visitors arrive from the north via I-25. Heading south on I-25, take Exit 52 for US-160. Turn right onto US-160. After 57 miles, turn right at CO-150 N. Continue for 13 miles and turn left onto Lane 6. After 6 miles turn right at Medano Road, which leads into the park.

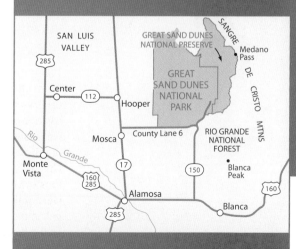

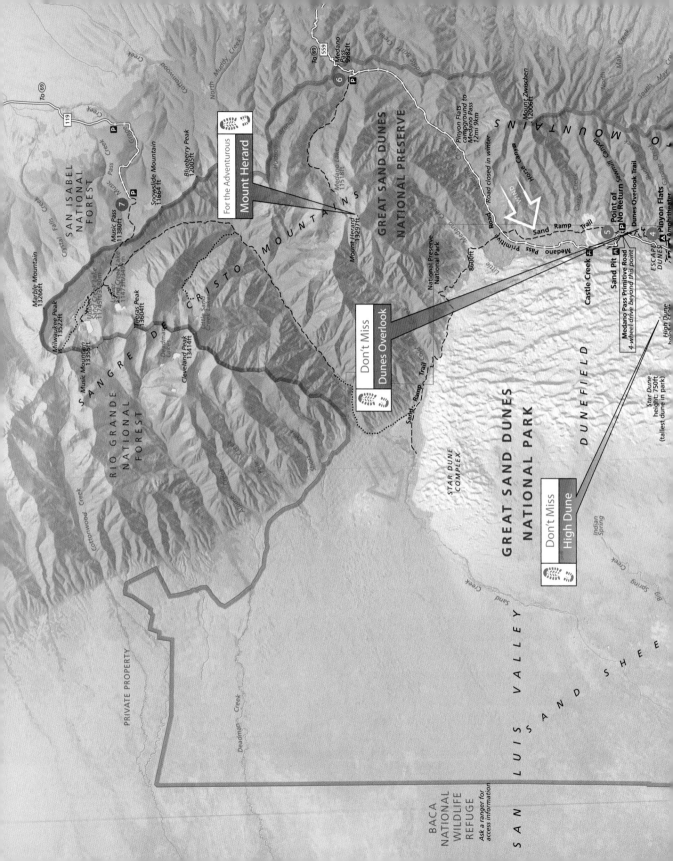

To 69

119

To 69

559

Medano Pass
9982ft

6 P

Music Creek

North Muddy Creek

Cottonwood Creek

Pass Creek

P

P

7 P
Music Pass
11380ft

SAN ISABEL
NATIONAL
FOREST

Snowslide Mountain
11664ft

Blueberry Peak
12005ft

Music Creek

Hudson Branch

Medano Creek

Medano Creek

Mount Zwischen
12006ft

Pinyon Flats
campground to
Medano Pass
12mi 9km

Road closed in winter

SANGRE DE CRISTO MOUNTAINS

MOUNTAINS

Medano Pass Primitive Road

WIND

Medano Pass
Primitive Road

Sand Ramp Trail

5 P
Point of
No Return
Dunes Overlook Trail

Dunes Overlook Trail

Castle Creek

Sand Pit

4
Pinyon Flats
Amphitheater

ESCAPE
DUNES

Medano Pass Primitive Road
4-wheel drive beyond this point

For the Adventurous
Mount Herard

Mount Herard
13297ft

GREAT SAND DUNES
NATIONAL PRESERVE

National Preserve
National Park

8600ft

Don't Miss
Dunes Overlook

Marble Mountain
13266ft

Milwaukee Peak
13522ft

Music Mountain
13355ft

Tijeras Peak
13604ft

Cleveland Peak
13414ft

Upper Sand Creek Lake
11745ft 3580m

Lower Sand Creek Lake
11747ft 3580m

Sand Creek

Deadman Lakes

Sand Creek

Little Medano Creek

Little Medano Creek

Castle Creek

Goldfield Creek

North May Creek

South May Creek

Cold Creek

RIO GRANDE
NATIONAL
FOREST

Crystal Falls

Alpine Creek

Shank Creek

Pole Creek

Sand Creek

Sand Ramp Trail

Sand Ramp Trail

Trail Creek

High Dune

Star Dune
height: 750ft
(tallest dune in park)

Don't Miss
High Dune

STAR DUNE
COMPLEX

GREAT SAND DUNES
NATIONAL PARK

DUNEFIELD

Sand Creek

Indian
Spring

Big Spring Creek

Sand Creek

Cottonwood Creek

Deadman Creek

PRIVATE PROPERTY

BACA
NATIONAL
WILDLIFE
REFUGE
Ask a ranger for
access information

SAN LUIS VALLEY

SAN LUIS AND SHEE

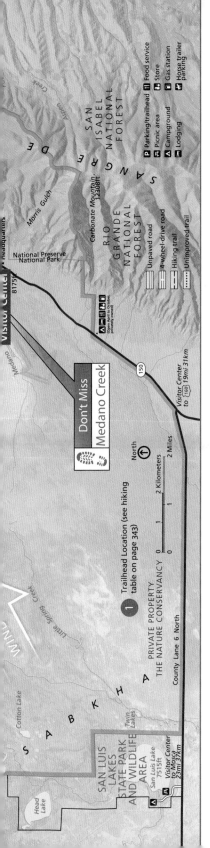

Regions

The official name is **Great Sand Dunes National Park and Preserve**. **The park** is comprised of the dunes and arid flatlands surrounding them. **The preserve** is the slice of Sangre de Cristo Mountains north and east of the dune field. Park land was expanded after scientists determined the important role that water played in creation of the sand dunes. Regulations differ between the two regions; for example you can hunt and camp at non-designated locations in the preserve, but not in the park.

Visitor Center

The **Visitor Center** (719.378.6399) is where you'll want to introduce yourself to Great Sand Dunes. You'll find interactive exhibits, a short film, bookstore, and restrooms. It's also the main hub for visitor information and the ever-popular **ranger programs**. Even if your children are eager to go play in the sand, make a quick stop to browse through the facility and its exhibits, and obtain a current schedule of ranger programs before exploring the park.

Camping & Lodging

Pinyon Flats, located one mile north of the visitor center, is the only drive-in campground. It has two, 44-site loops. Campsites at Loop 1 are available on a first-come, first-served basis. Campsites at Loop 2 can be reserved from May until September by calling (877) 444-6777 or clicking www.recreation.gov. All sites are $20/night and just a short walk from the sand dunes via a 0.5-mile Campground Trail. Restrooms with flush toilets and sinks are available, but there are no showers. Not all sites can accommodate RVs or camping trailers over 35 feet. There are no hook-ups. Three sites are available for groups of 15–40 people, available from April through October by reservation only. Group sites cost $3 per person per night with a minimum of $65/night for a 15–30 person site, and $80 for a 20–40 person site. Visitors with a high-clearance 4WD vehicle can access **campsites along Medano Pass Primitive Road** in the national preserve region. Camping here is limited to the designated first-come, first-served campsites. Those looking to explore the **backcountry** by foot may camp at one of **seven designated sites** in the dunes along **Sand Ramp Trail**. You can also camp off-trail in the national preserve region. **Backpackers** must obtain a **free backcountry use permit** from the visitor center before departing. There are no lodging facilities within park boundaries, but options exist in nearby communities (page 364).

Driving

CO-150 enters the park along the eastern edge of San Luis Valley. Entering from the south, the Sangre de Cristo Mountains rise high above you to the east and North America's largest sand dunes come into view to the north. From the scenic byway these undulating sand hills appear to be a sand replica of the sky-scraping mountains whose foot they sit at. You'll get a closer look as the paved roadway closes in on the dunes, eventually terminating at Pinyon Flats Campground. Guests with a high-clearance 4WD vehicle can continue along the foot of the mountains and then deep into them on **Medano Pass Primitive Road**. It actually crosses the mountains at Medano Pass and exits the park on County Road 559, which leads to CO-69.

 # Backpacking

On-trail backpacking adventures are fairly limited without a 4WD vehicle. The only lengthy hike from the paved park road is **Sand Ramp Trail**, beginning at the north end of Pinyon Flats Campground's second loop. From here you can hike 11 miles between the dunes and Sangre de Cristo Mountains. At the trail's end you can follow Sand Creek into the mountains. It's about 10 miles from Sand Ramp Trail to Upper Sand Creek Lake with optional spur trails to Milwaukee Peak, Lower Sand Creek Lake, and Little Sand Creek Lake. You must return the way you came.

Once you're in the mountains (**the preserve region**) you are **free to camp off-trail** wherever you choose. There are **seven designated campsites sprinkled among the dunes**, but there are no marked trails. You must blaze your own path in the dune field, but it's easiest to follow the ridgelines. Once you leave the ridges each step causes a cascade of sand as your foot sinks shin-deep. Those of you looking for a thigh-burning workout should try running up one of the steep dune slopes. Any overnight trip in the backcountry requires a **free backcountry permit** available at the Visitor Center.

 # Sand Activities

To locals, a trip to Great Sand Dunes is like going to the beach. Pack a cooler, umbrella, beach ball, and towel, and you're ready for some fun in the sun. When **Medano Creek** is running you can even play in water and **surf one-foot waves** when backed up water bursts through dams of sand. Don't forget your bucket and shovel; this is one of the few parks where you can **build a sand castle**. It's also a popular location to **write messages**. Vandalism in the parks has been an endemic problem, but writing your name (or a message to outer space) in the dune's sand is encouraged. Wind will eventually wipe the slate clean. You can also **sandboard, sled, or ski** down these sandy slopes. All downhill sand activities are usually best after it rains.

 # Hiking

Great Sand Dunes is one of the National Park Service's pleasant surprises. It's easy to feel like you've been whisked away to some far away desert as you hike across the sandy ridgelines.

At 750 feet, **Star Dune** is the tallest dune in the park. It's a difficult 3.8-mile (one-way) trudge through loose sand to the summit. Views from this sandy peak are phenomenal, but the return trip is where the fun begins. Forget about retracing your original footprints back to Medano Creek in favor of bounding down the sandy slopes. As the sand gives way beneath your feet, you gain a small sense of what it must feel like to walk on the moon. Note: Should you leave the ridgelines you will be forced to scale several dunes (a real thigh-burning experience). The hike to Star Dune begins at Dunes Parking Lot, off CO-150/Medano Road. If you want to keep the sand out of your shoes, hike along **Medano Creek** or to **Escape Dunes** (0.75-miles one-way) just north of the parking area. The trail to Escape Dunes follows a portion of the 0.5-mile (one-way) **Campground Trail**, which connects Dunes Parking Area with Pinyon Flats Campground. Another short and easy hike is **Montville Nature Trail**. This 0.5-mile loop begins on top of the hill just north of the Visitor Center (where trail guides are available for purchase).

After playing in the sandbox, empty your shoes, lace them back up, and hike into the mountains to view the dunes from above. The 3.5-mile (one-way) **Mosca Pass Trail** is the most accessible mountain hike, beginning at Montville Parking Area near the Visitor Center. To really get into the mountains you'll need a high-clearance 4WD vehicle to traverse Medano Pass Primitive Road. Near Medano Pass at the end of a short spur road, you'll find **Medano Lake Trailhead** and a small parking are. From here you can hike 3.5 miles (one-way) to **Medano Lake**, where you are free to continue an additional 1.7 miles to the top of looming **Mount Herard** (a spectacular viewpoint). If you don't have a 4WD vehicle but still want a panoramic view of the dunes, you can take the 2-mile (roundtrip) trail from Loop 2 of Pinyon Flats Campground to **Dunes Overlook**. It's nestled in the foothills of the Sangre de Cristo Mountains, and can be accessed via a short spur trail from **Sand Ramp Trail**.

Great Sand Dunes Hiking Trails

	Trail Name	Trailhead (# on map)	Length	Notes (One-way distances)
Medano Road - Pinyon Flats Camp	Carbonate Peak	Visitor Center (1)	4.0 miles	Strenuous hike to 12,308-ft summit
	Wellington Ditch	Montville Parking Lot (2)	1.0 mile	Flat and easy trail with views of the dunes
	Mosca Pass	Montville Parking Lot (2)	3.5 miles	Follows a small stream through mountain forests
	High Dune - 👍	Dunes Parking Lot (3)	1.15 miles	Moderate short hike to 650-ft dune
	Medano Wetlands	Dunes Parking Lot (3)	1.3 miles	Seasonal moderate hike after snow melts
	Castle Creek	Dunes Parking Lot (3)	2.5 miles	Connects Dunes and Point of No Return Parking Areas
	Star Dune - 👍	Dunes Parking Lot (3)	3.8 miles	Hike to the tallest dune in the park
	Dunes Overlook - 👍	Sand Ramp/Campground (Loop 2) (4)	1.0 mile	Good views of the dunes for a short hike
	Sand Ramp	Sand Ramp/Campground (Loop 2) (4)	11.0 miles	Long and flat • Hike all or just a few miles
	Sand Pit	Point of No Return (5)	0.7 mile	Can find Medano Creek all year round here
Primitive Rd	Medano Lake	Medano Lake (6)	3.5 miles	4WD required • 1,900-ft elevation gain
	Mount Herard - 👍	Medano Lake (6)	5.2 miles	Hike to 13,297-ft summit • Strenuous
	Music Pass	Rainbow Trail (4WD req'd)	1.0 mile	Located in the preserve's northeastern corner • This hike provides access to Sand Creek Lakes, 4WD
		Music Pass (7)	3.7 miles	
	Sand Creek Lakes	Music Pass (7)	4.0 miles	Pristine lakes hidden in the high mountains

Hiking in the dunes always leaves a trail

GREAT SAND DUNES

Sandboarding on the dunes

Playing in Medano Creek

Horse ride to Music Pass

Horseback Riding

Horseback riders are welcome in all of the national preserve and most of the national park. If you have your own horse and you'd like to explore Great Sand Dunes check the park website or call the Visitor Center at (719) 378-6399 for information on where to park your trailer, closed areas, camping, regulations, etc. Visitors who lack their own animals but would still like to ride the mountains or valley currently have one option: **Zapata Ranch** located in Mosca on CO-150, 6 miles from the visitor center. They provide all-inclusive ranch vacations for serious adventurers seeking a true western experience. Guests learn all about horsemanship at a working ranch. Adult rates range from $985/person for three nights to $1,995 for a week.

Zapata Ranch • (719) 378-2356 • www.zranch.org
5305 CO-150; Mosca, CO 81146

Best of Great Sand Dunes

Family Hike: **High Dune**
    Runner-up: Sand Ramp

Adventure Hike: **Star Dune**
    Runner-up: Mount Herard

For Kids: To kids, Great Sand Dunes is one giant sandbox. Kids of all ages love to **play in the sand**, **bound down the dunes**, and **splash in Medano Creek** during the spring and early summer snowmelt. In between playing, children (ages 3-12) are welcome to participate in the park's **Junior Ranger Program**. To become a Junior Ranger and receive an official badge your child must complete an activity booklet (available at the visitor center for $0.50).

Ranger Programs: Great Sand Dunes is a peculiar place. To gain a better understanding of the area, join one of its many interpretive programs. These walks and talks give you a better understanding of the region's history, geology, and ecology. They also discuss how in the world all this sand got here (but you'll already know that from reading the introduction on page 338). Be sure to stop in at the Visitor Center to see what programs will be offered during your visit to the park. Large groups can arrange a free tour by calling the park at (719) 378-6344. No programs are scheduled in winter.

Flora & Fauna: Billions of grains of sand (most of which you will believe made their way into your car) may lead a person to believe that this is a desert region inhabited by cacti and reptiles adapted to life in an arid environment. This couldn't be farther from the truth; Great Sand Dunes has some of the most diverse plant and animal life of the national parks. In lower elevations you may see pronghorn, bison, badgers, mule deer, or the occasional beaver. Mountain slopes are home to yellow-bellied marmots, pikas, bighorn sheep, black bears, and a small population of mountain lions.

There are also **more than 200 species of birds**, a healthy variety of reptiles, insects, and amphibians, and a few varieties of fish.

Hundreds of species of plants live in the park. Most thrive in the area's wetlands or foothills, but a few species—such as Indian ricegrass and scrufpea—are capable of surviving in the dunes themselves.

Pets: Pets are not allowed in the backcountry, but are permitted in the main day-use areas as long as they are kept on a leash no more than six feet in length.

Accessibility: Rolling hills of sand don't make for the most accessible park. However, there is a wheelchair accessible viewing platform at Dunes Parking Lot. Wheelchair users hoping to get closer to the dunes can check out one of two sand wheelchairs available at the visitor center. They are designed specifically for sand travel thanks to large, inflatable wheels that do not sink into sand, allowing guests to maneuver about the dunes with assistance. To reserve a sand wheelchair call the visitor center at (719) 378-6399. The visitor center is fully accessible. Campsites suitable for wheelchair users are available at Pinyon Flats and in the backcountry at Sawmill Canyon.

Weather: Temperatures in the summer average between 70 and 90°F, but the sand can get as hot as 140°F on a sunny day. Wear shoes in the dunes to protect your feet from these blazing temperatures. Like most high mountain climates, the temperature changes 30–40°F from afternoon highs to overnight lows. Spring and fall are mild. Winter is cold with significant snowfall. Visitors should be prepared for strong winds and scattered thunderstorms any time of year.

Life in the desert

Mountains of sand and rock

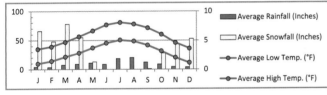

Vacation Planner

Visitors can easily spend a week hiking through the dunes and Sangre de Cristo Mountains, but if you only want to dip your toes in sand and take a quick hike through the mountains, you can do so in a day with time to spare. **Consider bringing a sled or snowboard**. The only in-park overnight accommodation is **Pinyon Flats Campground** (page 341). Nearby dining, grocery stores, lodging, festivals, and attractions are listed on pages 362–367.

Day 1

Begin your trip at the **Visitor Center**. You'll want to check out its exhibits, watch the introductory film, and get a current schedule of **ranger programs**. If you have enough time, join a ranger for a hike in the dunes. Just north

of the Visitor Center is the short and easy **Montville Nature Trail**. It's a nice 0.5-mile hike through a wooded area with panoramic views of the dunes, but without the crowds you'll find at Dunes Parking Area and along Medano Creek. Next, join the crowds at **Dunes Parking Area** to explore the dunes (no marked trails) or sit by **Medano Creek** (if it's running). Most hikers follow the dune's ridgelines. If you're looking for more extensive hiking try the 7-mile (roundtrip) **Mosca Pass Trail** (page 343). It begins at the same location as Montville Nature Trail. Hiking a portion of **Sand Ramp Trail** (page 343) is a nice, flatter alternative. It begins at Pinyon Flats Campground.

A look into the Black Canyon of the Gunnison's depths

102 Elk Creek
Gunnison, Colorado 81230
Phone: (970) 641-2337
Website: www.nps.gov/blca

Established: October 21, 1999
March 2, 1933 (National Monument)
Size: 30,750 Acres
Annual Visitors: 175,000
Peak Season: Summer

Activities: Hiking, Kayaking, Rock
Climbing, and Horseback Riding

South Rim Campground*
Fee: $12/night or $18 w/ hook-ups
North Rim Campground (seasonal)
Fee: $12/night
Backcountry Camping: Permitted
with a free Backcountry Use Permit
Lodging: None

Park Hours: All day, every day
Entrance Fee: $3/Person (16 &
older), Children are Free

*Reservations available at (877)
444-6777 or www.recreation.gov

Black Canyon of the Gunnison - Colorado

Western Colorado's **Black Canyon of the Gunnison** has been a source of frustration, irrigation, and recreation for more than a century. Its 2,200 foot walls of gray gneiss and schist rise precipitously from the raucous waters of the Gunnison River; walls so deep and narrow sunlight only penetrates their depths at midday, leaving the canyon constantly enveloped in its own shadow. It's an ominous setting, accentuated by the angry river carving through the canyon's floor at a rate of one inch every 100 years. When the river is running, it tears through the canyon with reckless abandon, dropping 96 feet every mile. **The Gunnison River** loses more elevation in 48 miles than the Mississippi River does in 1,500. This is the Black Canyon of the Gunnison. Impassable to explorers. Incorrigible to settlers. Incredible to recreational visitors.

Fur traders and **Utes** undoubtedly witnessed the Black Canyon, but none were foolish enough to call such a foreboding location home. An expedition led by **Captain John W. Gunnison** in 1849 and **Hayden Expedition** (of 1871), both declared the canyon impassable. Only a railway company, driven by the almighty dollar, had the courage to attempt passage and settlement in the midst of these mighty walls. In 1881, the **Denver and Rio Grande** railroad successfully reached the small town of Gunnison from Denver. They proceeded to punch their way through the canyon, building what would be called the "Scenic Line of the World." Construction cost $165,000 per mile in 1882. The last mile of track took an entire year to construct, but they persevered through the deaths of several immigrant laborers to successfully push on to Salt Lake City. For nearly a decade it served as the main route for transcontinental travel, but the combination of a new route through Glenwood Springs and the canyon's frequent bouts of inclement weather and rock slides led to a decrease in popularity of the "Scenic Line of the World." It was finally abandoned in 1955.

By the 1890s, settlers of Uncompahgre Valley began to take a serious look at the **Gunnison River** as a source of **water for irrigation**. It required new expeditions into the Black Canyon to analyze the feasibility of blasting a diversion tunnel through its walls of rock and in 1901 **Abraham Lincoln Fellows**, a hydrologist and Yale graduate, attempted to hike, swim, and float on a rubber mattress through the canyon. Accompanied by William Torrence, together they were the first to run the canyon, covering a distance of 33 miles in 9 days. They also declared that irrigation was possible. Construction followed thanks to funding from **Theodore Roosevelt's National Reclamation Act of 1902**, and a 5.8-mile, 11-foot-by-12-foot diversion tunnel was built, providing much needed water to an arid farm valley.

In 1916, **Emery Kolb**, a noted oarsman who owned a photography studio on the rim of the Grand Canyon with his brother, attempted **the first recreational trip** through the Black Canyon. Years of paddling the Colorado River had left him wanting more and he set his sights on something wilder: the Gunnison. It took five attempts, several boats, canoes, and supplies, but he eventually completed the journey to Delta Bridge.

Today, a park protects the deepest and most spectacular 12 miles of the 48 mile long canyon. A campground and visitor center sit where a railway town once thrived. Water still pours through a diversion tunnel. And thousands of visitors come to the Black Canyon of the Gunnison each year in pursuit of adventure just like Emery Kolb.

Did you know?

- Black Canyon's Painted Wall is the tallest cliff in Colorado at 2,250 ft.

- At 2 billion years old, the canyon's Precambrian rock is some of the oldest on earth.

Transportation & Airports
Public transportation does not provide service to or around the park. Greyhound (800.231.2222, www.greyhound.com) has a bus station in Montrose (15 miles from the visitor center) and Grand Junction (76 miles). Amtrak (800.872.7245, www.amtrak.com) provides train service to Grand Junction. The closest regional airports are Montrose Regional (MTJ), 18 miles away; Gunnison-Crested Butte Regional (GUC), 62 miles to the east; and Grand Junction Regional (GJT), 82 miles northwest of the park's visitor center. Denver International (DEN) is 335 miles to the east along I-70. Car rental is available at each destination.

Directions
South Rim Visitor Center is 76 miles from Grand Junction (I-70, Exit 37). Take US-50 south through Montrose. Turn left at CO-347 N. Continue for roughly 5 miles before making a slight right onto South Rim Road, which leads into the park. There are places where a mere 40 feet separates the North and South Rims, but you will not find a bridge connecting the two. Visitors must make an 80+ mile drive to reach one rim from the other. From the south rim return to US-50. At the intersection of US-50 and CO-347 you can turn either way. Heading east is about 7 miles longer, but more scenic. Regardless of which way you head on US-50 drive until you reach CO-92. Follow CO-92 to Black Canyon Road, which leads to the North Rim.

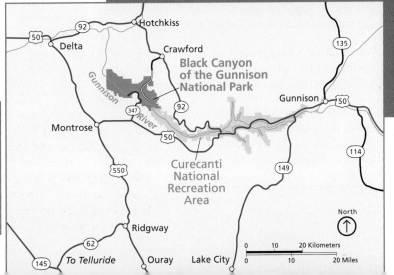

Camping

South Rim Campground has a total of 88 campsites broken into three loops. Loops A and C are $12/night. Loop B sites have electrical hook-ups and cost $18/night. Sites at Loops A and B can be reserved by calling (877) 444-6777 or clicking www.recreation.gov. Sites at loop C are available on a first-come, first-served basis. Each loop has its own restroom with sinks and flush toilets. There are no dump stations and vehicles longer than 35 feet are not recommended. Loop A remains open all year while the other two loops close for winter (November–April). There's also a small **15-site campground** on **East Portal Road** along the Gunnison River in **Curecanti National Recreation Area** (www.nps.gov/cure). Water is available from mid-May to mid-September and there are vault toilets. The fee is $12/night.

North Rim Campground is open from Spring to Fall. All 13 sites are available on a first-come, first-served basis for $12/night.

All inner canyon hiking routes (page 351) end at **designated camping areas** with anywhere from one to six campsites. Camping in these locations requires a **free permit** (page 350).

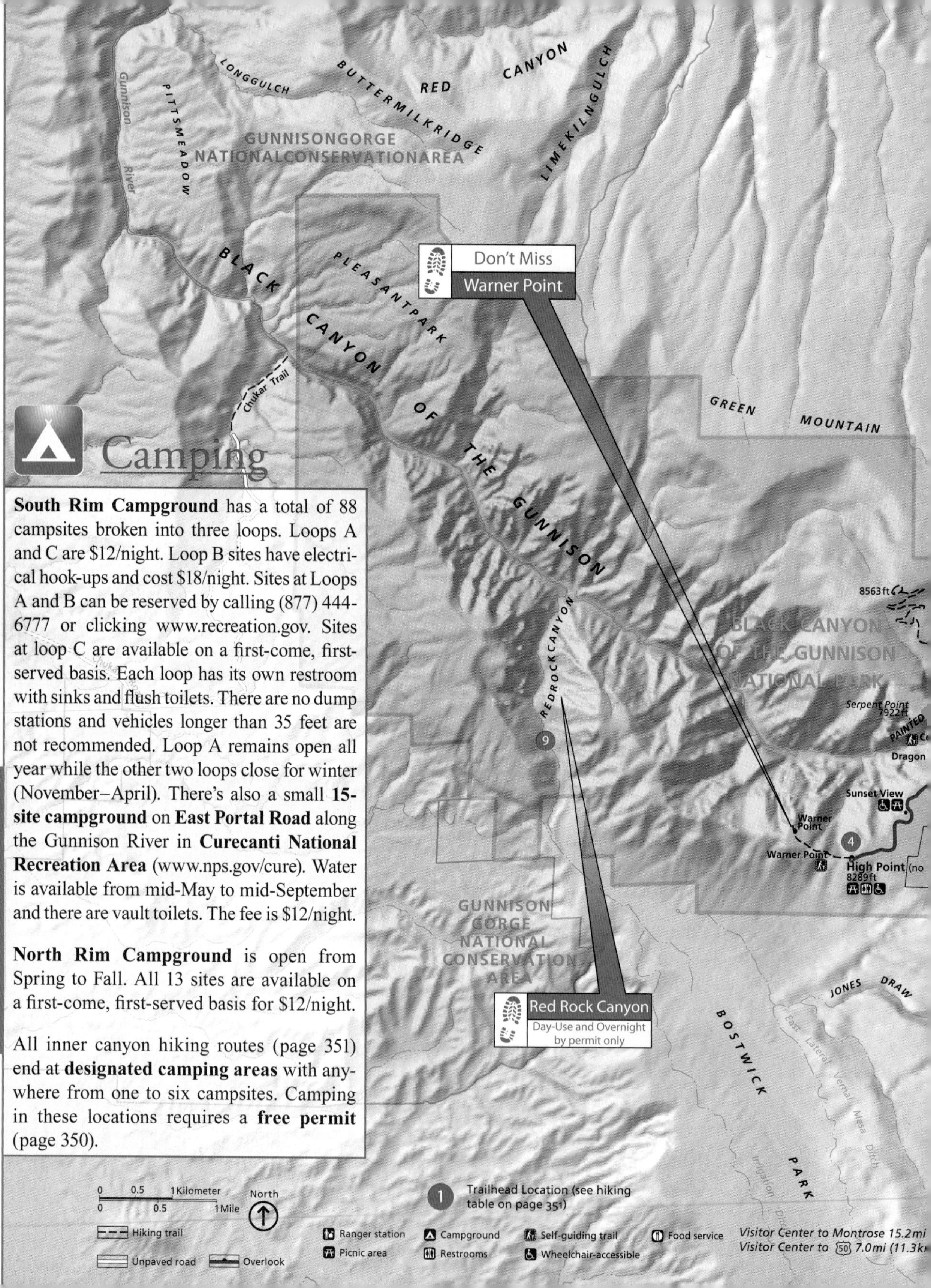

Don't Miss
Warner Point

Red Rock Canyon
Day-Use and Overnight by permit only

8563 ft

BLACK CANYON OF THE GUNNISON NATIONAL PARK

Serpent Point 7922 ft

Dragon

Sunset View

Warner Point

Warner Point

High Point 8289 ft (no

GREEN MOUNTAIN

9

REDROCKCANYON

GUNNISON GORGE NATIONAL CONSERVATION AREA

BOSTWICK PARK

JONES DRAW

| 0 | 0.5 | 1 Kilometer |
| 0 | 0.5 | 1 Mile |

North ↑

1 Trailhead Location (see hiking table on page 351)

- - - Hiking trail
Unpaved road   Overlook

Ranger station   Campground   Self-guiding trail   Food service
Picnic area   Restrooms   Wheelchair-accessible

Visitor Center to Montrose 15.2mi
Visitor Center to 50 7.0mi (11.3k

When to Go

Black Canyon of the Gunnison's South Rim is open every day of the year, but South Rim Road beyond Gunnison Point closes in winter. The closed portion of roadway remains open for cross country skiers and snowshoers. South Rim Visitor Center is open every day except Thanksgiving, Christmas, and New Year's Day. Hours are 8:30am until 4pm for fall, winter, and spring, but are extended to 8am until 6pm in summer. The North Rim is typically closed from late November until mid-April. A visit to the Black Canyon is an excellent choice for those looking to avoid the crowds found at other Colorado parks like Rocky Mountain or Mesa Verde.

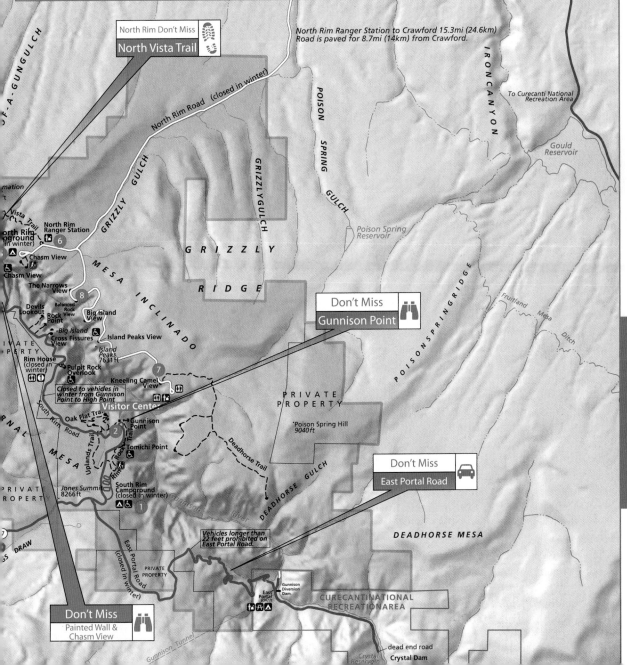

North Rim Ranger Station to Crawford 15.3mi (24.6km)
Road is paved for 8.7mi (14km) from Crawford.

North Rim Don't Miss
North Vista Trail

Don't Miss
Gunnison Point

Don't Miss
East Portal Road

Don't Miss
Painted Wall & Chasm View

To Curecanti National Recreation Area

Vehicles longer than 22 feet prohibited on East Portal Road.

Closed to vehicles in winter from Gunnison Point to High Point

Visitor Center

Gunnison Point

Tomichi Point

South Rim Campground (closed in winter)

Jones Summit 8266ft

Oak Flat Trail

Uplands Trail

Rim House (closed in winter)

Pulpit Rock Overlook

Kneeling Camel View

Island Peaks View

Island Peaks 7631ft

Big Island View

Cross Fissures View

Rock Point

Balanced Rock View

Devils Lookout

The Narrows View

Chasm View

North Rim Ranger Station

North Rim Campground (closed in winter)

Vista Trail

Poison Spring Reservoir

Poison Spring Hill 9040ft

Deadhorse Trail

Deadhorse Gulch

DEADHORSE MESA

PRIVATE PROPERTY

East Portal Road (closed in winter)

East Portal 6417ft

Gunnison Diversion Dam

CURECANTI NATIONAL RECREATION AREA

Gunnison Tunnel

dead end road
Crystal Dam

Crystal Reservoir

MESA INCLINADO

GRIZZLY RIDGE

GRIZZLY GULCH

GRIZZLYGULCH

POISON SPRING GULCH

IRON CANYON

POISON SPRING RIDGE

Gould Reservoir

Fruitland Mesa

Ditch

North Rim Road (closed in winter)

Black Canyon Road

Iron Creek

92

Wilderness Permit

Whether you're planning on **exploring the back-country** (including the inner canyon), **paddling the Gunnison**, or **climbing the canyon's sheer walls** a **free permit** is required. Obtain yours at South Rim Visitor Center, North Rim Ranger Station, or East Portal Registration Board (near East Portal Campground). A self-registration station is available nearby each facility for anyone arriving after hours. Speak with a park ranger prior to departure if this is your first time backpacking, kayaking, or rock climbing at Black Canyon. Discussing your itinerary with a ranger helps assure that you are properly prepared and experienced for your selected adventure. This is a very unforgiving place. Canyon walls are steep. The river is wild. But a safe and enjoyable adventure can be had with proper preparation.

Hiking/Backpacking

Black Canyon is too often a drive-in and drive-out attraction. Visitors should spend at least a few hours hiking trails, if not a few days going off-trail into the wilderness or inner canyon.

A number of short and easy hikes are located along South and North Rim Roads. **Rim Rock Trail** begins at South Rim Campground and follows the rim north to Tomichi Point, Gunnison Point, and the Visitor Center. From the Visitor Center you can continue hiking on **Oak Flat Loop**, which provides spectacular views of the canyon as you descend slightly below the rim. After looping back to the visitor center it's possible to return to the campground via **Uplands Trail**, which veers away from the canyon on the opposite side of South Rim Road. There are a series of overlooks accessible by short hikes in between the Visitor Center and High Point. **Pulpit Rock** provides a nice long view of the Gunnison River as it rambles beneath the canyon walls. **Chasm and Painted Wall Views** are exceptional viewpoints. At Chasm View you're standing above the river's steepest grade, where turbulent water drops some 240 feet over a 2-mile stretch. Painted Wall View gives onlookers the opportunity to photograph Colorado's tallest cliff, standing more than twice the height of the Empire State Building. Its name comes from pink veins of igneous pegmatite rock that interrupt the layers of gneiss and schist.

South Rim Road ends at High Point and **Warner Point Nature Trail**. Mark Warner was a driving force behind the park's establishment, and this trail provides an opportunity to view the area's ecology, history, and geology through his eyes thanks to printed handouts (available at High Point and the Visitor Center). Along the way, you'll notice markers corresponding to sections of the handout. The hike is well worth the effort, with amazing views of beautifully colored canyon walls and the river below. The **North Rim** provides longer trails with similar canyon views. Hiking to Exclamation Point via **North Vista Trail** is particularly nice. This trek begins at North Rim Ranger Station.

Hikers in good physical condition can descend into the canyon via one of **seven inner canyon routes**. They are unmaintained, steep, and littered with loose rocks. Poison ivy is practically unavoidable (wear long pants). So why hike into the canyon when you can drive there via East Portal Road? The thrill? Perhaps. The exercise? Maybe. Having such magnificent scenery to yourself is also appealing. Where each route hits the canyon floor you'll find at least one campsite. **Gunnison Route** (South Rim) and **S.O.B. Route** (North Rim) are respectively the easiest routes on either side of the rim, but are still extremely strenuous and challenging. An 80-foot chain is anchored to the canyon wall to aid hikers attempting the Gunnison Route.

Red Rock Canyon Route is only available to 8 visitors per day through a reservation lottery system (visit the park website for reservation request forms). This trail is popular with fisherman and hikers because it is significantly less steep than other routes into the gorge. Restrictions are enforced to prevent overuse and because a portion of the trail crosses private land. It is only open from late May until early October and is accessed via Bostwick Park Road, located in the park's southwest corner.

If you plan on hiking the **inner canyon** or exploring **off-trail wilderness areas**, regardless of whether it's day-use or overnight, you must obtain a **free wilderness permit** (see "wilderness permit" above). Permits are an essential tool to help monitor backcountry use and aid in identifying potential emergencies.

Aerial view of the Black Canyon of the Gunnison © Doc Searls

Black Canyon of the Gunnison Hiking Trails

	Trail Name	Trailhead (# on map)	Length	Notes (All distances are roundtrip except "Inner Canyon")
South Rim	Rim Rock Nature Trail	Campground Loop C (1)	1.0 mile	Moderate self-guiding trail along the rim
	Uplands	Rim Rock Trail (1)	1.0 mile	Combine with Rim Rock to make a 2-mile loop
	Oak Flat Loop	Near the Visitor Center (2)	2.0 miles	Strenuous hike that doesn't descend into the canyon
	Cedar Point Nature Tr	Cedar Point Overlook (3)	0.67 mile	Easy self-guiding trail • Views of Painted Wall
	Warner Point Nature Tr - 👓	High Point Overlook (4)	1.5 miles	Moderate • Trail guides available at High Point
Inner Canyon	Tomichi Route	Rim Rock Trail Post #13 (1)	1.0 mile	Steepest South Rim route with loose rock
	Gunnison Route	Near the Visitor Center (2)	1.0 mile	South Rim • Good first-timers route, still steep
	Warner Route	Warner Point Nature Trail serviceberry bush past post #13 (4)	2.75 miles	Out-and-back will take a full (and exhausting) day • Camp at 1 of 5 sites at the canyon floor
	S.O.B. Draw	North Rim Ranger Station (6)	1.75 miles	Easiest of the 3 North Rim inner canyon hikes
	Slide Draw	Kneeling Camel Overlook (7)	1.0 mile	North Rim • Extremely steep and dangerous
	Long Draw	Balanced Rock Overlook (8)	1.0 mile	North Rim • Access to a very narrow area
	Red Rock Canyon	East Parking Area (9)	3.4 miles	All users require a permit via lottery reservation
North Rim	Chasm View Nature Tr	In Campground Loop (5)	0.33 mile	Moderate hike with views of Painted Wall
	North Vista - 👓	North Rim Ranger Station (6)	3.0 miles	Moderate to Exclamation Point for inner canyon views
			7.0 miles	Strenuous to Green Mountain and 360° views
	Deadhorse	Kneeling Camel Overlook (7)	5.0 miles	Easy to Moderate with views of East Portal

Kayaking

Three upstream dams have tamed the Gunnison River dramatically, but the 18-mile stretch within park boundaries can still be extremely dangerous at times. At high water levels, several sections are unrunnable and the remainder of the corridor rates as class III–V rapids. The Gunnison should only be run by expert kayakers, and even then it should be with individuals who are familiar with the water, its drops, and its hydraulics. **All boaters must obtain a wilderness use permit (page 350)**.

Rock Climbing

Hard rock walls rising vertically out of the canyon floor more than 2,000 feet are sure to attract a few rock climbers. Experienced climbers love the challenge of Black Canyon's multi-pitch traditional routes. **The Park Service knows about more than 145 climbs**, but very few are used with any regularity. This is largely due to extreme difficulty accessing routes and challenging nature of the routes themselves.

Black Canyon is not a place for beginners. Even the most experienced climbers will find the aid of a climbing guide (page 366) helpful when making a first attempt at Black Canyon's cliffs. **The most popular climbing area is north and south Chasm View**. Climbing is popular from mid-April to early June, and then from mid-September through early November. **All rock climbers must obtain a wilderness use permit (page 350)**.

Other Activities

Less popular activities include **horseback riding**, **winter sports**, and **biking**. Visitors with their own horse(s) can ride **North Rim's Deadhorse Trail**. In winter, **snowshoers** and **cross-country skiers** enjoy the section of **South Rim Road** beyond Gunnison Point, which closes until spring. **Cyclists are permitted on all paved roadways**.

For Kids: Children love peering into the depths of Black Canyon (just don't let them throw rocks into the abyss, there could be unsuspecting hikers, climbers, or paddlers below the rim). Kids (ages 5–12) are invited to become **Black Canyon of the Gunnison National Park Junior Rangers**. To do so, complete the free activity booklet (available at the South Rim Visitor Center). Once completed, your child will be sworn into the club and receive a badge. Children (5 and under) have the opportunity to become a **Ranger Buddy** (details are available at the visitor center).

Ranger Programs: Black Canyon provides free ranger guided activities in summer and winter. You might meet a ranger at one of the scenic overlooks to discuss topics ranging from how the canyon was formed to what birds of prey nest within its walls. They also offer short walks at East Portal or along one of the nature trails. Evening programs are administered at South Rim Visitor Center and South Rim Campground's Amphitheater. **Stargazing programs** are held periodically throughout the summer. Only a few programs are held in winter when staffing allows. At the adjacent **Curecanti National Recreation Area** (www.nps.gov/cure) visitors can take a **boat tour** into the Black Canyon of the Gunnison ($16/Adult, $8/Child, call (970) 641-2337, ext. 205 for reservations and additional information). Tours are available twice daily at 10am and 12:30pm, Memorial Day weekend through Labor Day. Reservations are required.

Flora & Fauna: It's likely you'll spot a few **mule deer** on your visit to the Black Canyon. **Black bear** have become a regular inhabitant, so be sure to use the bear-proof storage lockers for all food and scented products. Canyons aren't as prohibitive to birds as they are to humans. **Peregrine falcons** nest on canyon walls, occasionally forcing rock-climbing routes to close. Many different species of plants live here. Serviceberry and Gambel oak are common along the rim, while cottonwood, box elder, and Douglas fir grow in the shade of the canyon. Perhaps

BLACK CANYON

the most prevalent and annoying plant is **poison ivy**. Guests must watch diligently for the three-leafed plant when hiking the inner canyon (wear long pants).

Pets: Pets are permitted in several areas, but must be kept on a leash no more than six feet in length at all times. They are allowed on roads, in campgrounds, at overlooks, and on Rim Rock Trail, Cedar Point Nature Trail, and North Rim Chasm View Nature Trail. Do not leave your pet unattended anywhere in the park (including your car).

Accessibility: South Rim Visitor Center, all restrooms, Tomichi Point, Chasm View, and Sunset View are fully accessible to wheelchair users. South Rim Campground has two accessible campsites. The restrooms at North Rim Ranger Station and Balanced Rock Overlook are accessible.

Weather: Black Canyon of the Gunnison experiences extreme variation in temperature from day-to-night, day-to-day, and canyon rim-to-floor. During summer average highs reach the 80s°F and lows dip into the 40s°F overnight. Average lows in December and January fall below zero, while highs are usually in the mid-20s°F. The canyon floor is typically 8°F warmer than its rim, even with the canyon's vertical walls preventing sunlight from penetrating its depths except around midday.

View from Oak Flat Trail

Mule Deer at Pinyon Flats

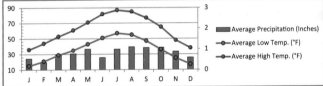

■ Average Precipitation (Inches)
—●— Average Low Temp. (°F)
—●— Average High Temp. (°F)

Vacation Planner

Black Canyon of the Gunnison's **South Rim Road** makes viewing the most popular attractions in a single day possible, while visiting both the South and North Rims in a single day is a race against time. There isn't a bridge between the two rims, so you have to make an 80+ mile trip (about 2 hours) from one rim to the other. Most people only stop at the South Rim. Provided below is a one-day itinerary for a typical Black Canyon vacation. Each rim of the canyon has a campground, but you'll have to look outside the park for lodging and dining facilities (pages 362–367).

Day 1

Begin your trip to the **South Rim** by looking through the canyon from its floor. Take **East Portal Road**, which is extremely steep (16% grade) with tight corners. It supplies tremendous views and you can see how most of the canyon is shrouded in shadows. (However, the "black" in Black

Canyon comes from the dark rock its made of rather than the shadows that shroud it.) The canyon floor is also an excellent location to have a **picnic**. Have a look around and return to the rim to stop at the **visitor center**. Browse the exhibits, watch the short film, and check out the schedule of **ranger guided interpretive programs**. If you have the opportunity to join a guided walk or talk, do so. If not, start exploring the canyon from above by hiking **Oak Flat Trail** (page 350). Note: The view from Gunnison Point is nearly the same without 2-miles of hiking. Return to your car and continue along South Rim Road. Make the following stops: **Pulpit Rock**, **Chasm View**, and **Painted Wall View**. The road terminates at High Point, where you should hike the 2.75-mile trail to **Warner Point** (page 350). Exit the park by retracing your route along South Rim Road.

Cliff Palace: more than 150 rooms, 21 kivas, and home to approximately 100 ancestral Puebloans during the 13th century

PO Box 8
Mesa Verde, CO 81330
Phone: (970) 529-4465
Website: www.nps.gov/meve

Established: June 29, 1906
Size: 52,122 Acres
Annual Visitors: 560,000
Peak Season: Summer

Ranger Guided Tours and Fees
Cliff Palace: $3/person
Cliff Palace (Twilight): $10/person
Balcony House: $3/person
Long House: $3/person
Mug House: $15/person

Camping: Morefield Campground
Fee: $23/night, $33/night (with
hook-ups), $39–49/night (with tent)
Backcountry Camping: Prohibited
Lodging: Far View Lodge
Rates: $97–169/night

Park Hours: All day, every day
Entrance Fee: $15 • Vehicle (peak)
$10 • Vehicle (off-season)
$8/$5 • Individual (foot, bike, etc.)

Mesa Verde - Colorado

Let's say you arrive at Mesa Verde completely unaware of the area's history and culture. A quick drive across the mesa and you would be left scratching your head, wondering where the majestic scenery went. Mesa Verde's deep gorges and tall mesas have a bit of scenic appeal, but it pales in comparison to other southwestern parks. But what it lacks in natural beauty it redeems in cultural significance. When the park was established in 1906, it became **the first tract of land set aside to protect a prehistoric culture and its ruins, pottery, tools, and other ancient artifacts**.

Somewhere around 750 AD, **Puebloans** were living in modest pit-houses on top of the mesa, clustered together forming small villages. They found sustenance farming and hunting. Judging by the circular underground chambers, called kivas, religion was important and rituals and ceremonies were performed regularly. By the late 12th century they began building homes in alcoves beneath the rim of the mesa. These cliff dwellings became larger and more numerous.

Scientists and volunteers are attempting to piece together the history of Ancestral Puebloan People by scouring thousands of archeological sites. To date, there are **more than 4,700 archeological sites** within the park; **roughly 600 are cliff dwellings**. About 90 percent of the cliff dwellings contain 10 rooms or less, but a few are enormous. **Cliff Palace**, the largest and most famous dwelling, contains 150 rooms. **Long House** and **Spruce Tree House** exceed 100 rooms, and **Balcony House** has more than 40. These sites have attracted archeologists and vandals, pothunters and politicians, tourists and explorers.

John Moss, a local prospector, is the first person in recorded history to have seen the ruins. In 1874, he led a photographer through Mancos Canyon along the base of Mesa Verde. Resulting photos inspired geologists to visit the site in 1875, and more than a decade later **Richard Wetherill and his brothers** began the first serious excavations. They spent the next 15 months exploring over 100 dwellings. **Frederick H. Chapin**, a noted mountaineer, photographer, and author, aided the excavation. Later, he wrote an article and book on the area's geologic and cultural significance. In 1889 and once again in 1890, Benjamin Wetherill wrote to the Smithsonian, warning that the area would be plundered by looters and tourists if it was not protected as a national park. He also requested that he and his brothers be placed in the employ of the government to carry out careful excavation of the ruins even though they were not legitimate archeologists.

The requests went unanswered, and the following year the Wetherills hosted **Gustaf Nordenskiöld** of the Academy of Sciences in Sweden. Using scientific methods and meticulous data collection, he began a thorough excavation of many ruins including Cliff Palace. Incensed locals charged Nordenskiöld with "devastating the ruins" and held him on $1,000 bond when he tried to transport some 600 artifacts, including a mummified corpse, on the Denver and Rio Grande Railroad. He was released because no laws existed to prevent treasure hunting. The artifacts were shipped to Sweden and today they reside in the National Museum in Helsinki, Finland. Upon his return home, he examined the artifacts and published a book titled *The Cliff Dwellers of the Mesa Verde.*

At this time, Pothunters and vandals were becoming a serious problem. Dynamite was used to blow holes in walls to let light in or to scare away rattlesnakes. **Colorado Cliff Dwelling Association (CCDA)** picked up the mantle of advocating a national park. But when Virginia Donaghe McClurg, head of the CCDA, expressed her opinion that it should be a "woman's park," Lucy Peabody left the association and continued to search for support on her own. Finally, in 1906 **President Theodore Roosevelt** signed a bill creating Mesa Verde National Park, protecting an area of unique history and culture for future generations.

When to Go

Mesa Verde is open all year, but some of its more notable attractions are closed during the off-season (November–March). The popular Cliff Palace Tour is only available from mid-April to mid-November. Balcony House Tours are offered between late April and mid-October. Wetherill Mesa and its cliff dwellings (Long House and Step House) are open from late May to early September.

If you visit during the off-season, you'll be limited to exploring Chapin Mesa Archeological Museum, Spruce Tree House, and the park road's overlooks. Morefield Campground, public showers, laundry, gas services, Far View Lodge, and Far View Visitor Center also close in winter. Summers can be busy, but the park increases its tour hours of operation and frequency to accommodate increased traffic. During summer, visitors can escape the commotion by visiting Wetherill Mesa. Here you'll find a tram that leads to archeological sites like Long House and Step House.

Transportation & Airports

Public transportation does not provide service to or around the park. Greyhound (800.231.2222, www.greyhound.com) has a bus station 35 miles from the park entrance in Durango, CO, but a rental car is needed to reach the park. There are small regional airports nearby at Cortez, CO (10 miles to park entrance); Durango, CO (35 miles); and Farmington, NM (70 miles). Car rental is available at each destination.

Directions

Mesa Verde is located in the remote southwestern corner of Colorado. It is accessed via the Mesa Verde National Park Exit from US-160. The park entrance is 35 miles west of Durango, CO and 12 miles east of Cortez, CO. Chapin Mesa, where you'll find many of the main attractions, is located 22 miles south of the park entrance. It should take you at least 2 hours to drive in and out of the park, and an additional 2 hours to tour one of the major cliff dwellings. Gas is available near Morefield Campground from mid-May to mid-October.

MESA VERDE

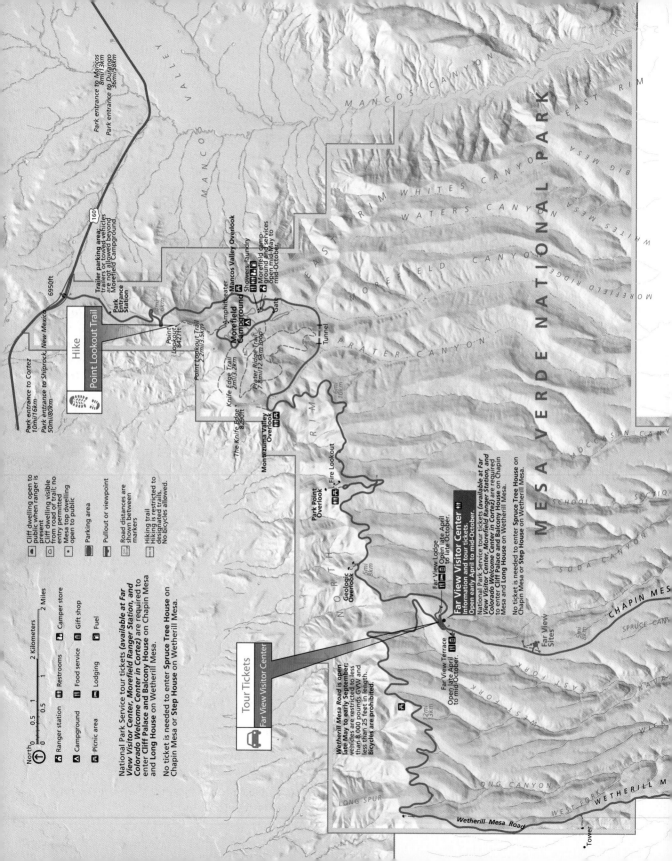

UTE MOUNTAIN UTE INDIAN RESERVATION

Don't Miss
Cliff Palace

Don't Miss
Balcony House

Spruce Tree House

MOCCASIN MESA

SODA CANYON

Balcony House
(tour ticket required)

Hemenway D House

Soda Canyon Overlook Trail
1.2mi/1.9km

Four-way stop
Spruce Tree Terrace

Spruce Tree House
(self-guiding tour trail starts near Museum)

Cliff Palace Loop
6mi/10km
(closed in winter)

Mesa Top Loop
6mi/10km

Cliff Palace
(tour ticket required)

Sun Point View

Pithouse

Pithouses and Villages

CLIFF CANYON

Chapin Mesa Museum
Information and Bookstore

Amphitheater

Petroglyph Point Trail
2.4mi/3.9km

Navajo Canyon View

Square Tower House

Hike
Petroglyphs Trail

LONG MESA

BOBCAT CANYON

Badger House Community

Tram route

Don't Miss
Long House

Kodak House

Kodak House Overlook

Information
1mi/1.6km
Nordenskiold Site #16

Long House
(tour ticket required)

WILDHORSE MESA

ROCK CANYON

Tram stops showonly

Regions

Mesa Verde is essentially broken into two distinct regions: **Chapin Mesa** and **Wetherill Mesa**. **Chapin Mesa** reaches all the way down to the park's southern boundary. This is where you'll find the most recognizable cliff dwellings and Chapin Mesa Museum. A one-way loop road circles around the Museum, providing plenty of parking and access to **Spruce Tree House** (self-guiding from spring to fall, free guided tours in winter). Continuing south beyond the museum and Spruce Tree House is **Mesa Top Loop**. It provides an auto tour of Ancestral Puebloan pit-houses and overlooks with views of their cliff dwellings. East of Mesa Top Loop is **Cliff Palace Loop**. Along this loop are parking areas for **Cliff Palace** and **Balcony House**. Both of these cliff dwellings are only accessible from spring to fall on ranger-guided tours with a ticket ($3/person • available at Far View Visitor Center, Morefield Ranger Station, and Colorado Welcome Center in Cortez).

Wetherill Mesa runs parallel to Chapin Mesa just to its west. This quiet side of Mesa Verde is open from late May to early September. **Wetherill Mesa Road** begins near Far View Visitor Center and winds its way to a collection of archeological sites in the park's southwest corner. **Long House**, the park's second largest cliff dwelling, is available for tour with a ticket ($3/person). Visitors are free to explore **Step House**, pit-houses, and nature trails on their own. A **free tram** provides access to these sites on a first-come, first-served basis.

Visitor Center & Museum

Far View is the only visitor center. It's located close to the midway point of the main park road near its intersection with Wetherill Mesa Road. **Tickets to tour Cliff Palace, Balcony House, or Long House are available at Far View Visitor Center**. It is open from early April to mid-October, from 8am to 5pm, but between Memorial Day weekend and Labor Day the visitor center remains open until 7pm. When the visitor center and Morefield Ranger Station are not open, tickets must be purchased at **Chapin Mesa Archeological Museum**. It's open all year with hours from 8am–5pm that extend to 6:30pm from early April until mid-October. The museum features a wealth of exhibits on Ancestral Puebloan life and numerous artifacts that were found at the park's archeological sites. A 25-minute introductory film is shown every half-hour at the museum.

Camping & Lodging

Morefield Campground has more than 400 campsites available on a first-come, first-served basis. There are 15 sites with full hook-ups. A few sites feature canvas tents with carpeted floors (reservation required). The campground is open from mid-May until early October. A free dump station, coin-operated showers and laundry, a general store, and gas are available nearby (only from mid-May to early October). Camping fees are: $23/night (standard site), $33/night (with hook-ups), $39–49/night (canvas tent site).

More comfortable accommodations are available near the visitor center at **Far View Lodge**. It's open between mid-April and mid-October. Rooms cost $97–169/night. The campground and lodge are run by Aramark. To make reservations call (800) 449-2288 or click www.visitmesaverde.com.

Spruce Tree House

Hiking

Hiking provides an excellent retreat from the busy cliff dwellings. However, you are only allowed to hike on designated trails. Several originate from Morefield Campground, including **Prater Ridge Trail**, located just beyond the campground gate. This loop's total distance is 7.8 miles, but another short trail bisects it, allowing hikers to complete just the 3.6-mile north loop or 2.4-mile south loop. The easy 2-mile, out-and-back **Knife Edge Trail** departs from the campground's northwest corner and follows an old road that served as the main entrance beginning in 1914. Today, it provides hikers with excellent views of Montezuma Valley and a great vantage point for watching the sunset. Another excellent hike for watching the sunset is 2.2-mile **Point Lookout Trail**. It begins at the very north end of the campground.

There are four trails at Chapin Mesa. In order to hike **Petroglyph Point and Spruce Canyon Trails** (2.4 miles each) you must register at the museum or trailhead. These trails are steep and for sure-footed individuals. Petroglyph Point leads to the park's only accessible petroglyphs. Spruce Canyon isn't as interesting, but provides a different perspective as you look up at the mesa from the canyon below. **Soda Canyon** (1.2 miles) is an easy hike with distant views of Balcony House.

Wetherill Mesa has three short trails, each less than 1.5 miles roundtrip. **Step House Loop Trail** begins at the information kiosk. It leads to pit-houses and a cliff dwelling. **Nordenskiöld Site #16** leads to a cliff dwelling overlook. **Badger House Community Trail** passes through 600 years of pueblo development. Trail guides are available for all three of these hikes.

Cliff Dwellings

About 1,400 years ago Ancestral Puebloans inhabited the region that has become Mesa Verde National Park, farming and hunting on the mesa tops. Over time they moved from small communities of pit-houses on top the mesa to cliff dwellings in alcoves beneath its rim. Much can be inferred from the tools, basketry, pottery, and ruins left behind by this ancient culture, but little is certain about why they built such large structures in the canyon walls or why they abandoned them in the late 1200s.

Of the 4,500 archeological sites found at Mesa Verde about 600 are cliff dwellings. These structures range from one-room houses to massive 150-room villages (like Cliff Palace). They could only be reached by hand and foot holds carved into the cliff wall. Several had kivas, ceremonial rooms used to pray for rain or prosperous hunting and farming. Ancestral Puebloans put a lot of time and effort into their homes, but they occupied these structures for less than 100 years. Success may have helped lead to their demise. Overpopulation could have stripped the farmland of its nutrients and land of its game. Climatic changes or political squabbles may have played their parts, too. Your guess is as good as anyone else's. Tour the ancient ruins and wonder to yourself why they abandoned these homes with such fantastic views. **All cliff dwellings (except Spruce Tree House and Step House) are not to be entered without the accompaniment of a uniformed park ranger.**

Guided Tours

A visit to Mesa Verde is not complete without touring one (or all three) of the large cliff dwellings (Cliff Palace, Balcony House, and Long House). It's just about the best $3 you can spend in all of the national parks. Tickets can be purchased from Far View Visitor Center, Morefield Ranger Station, or Colorado Welcome Center in Cortez. You can also join a park ranger on a special **Twilight Tour of Cliff Palace** offered by the **Mesa Verde Institute** for $10. It begins at 7pm, is limited to 20 people, and lasts 1.5 hours. **Tickets must be purchased in advance from Far View Visitor Center**, so plan on stopping here first, before driving all the way to Chapin Mesa.

Aramark (800.449.2288, www.visitmesaverde.com) and **Mesa Verde Institute** (www.mesaverdeinstitute.org) provide a couple of unique ranger and bus driver guided tours at the park. See the table on the following page for a list of all available tours.

MESA VERDE

Climbing into Balcony House

Mesa Verde Cliff Dwelling Tours

	Dates	Fee	Duration	Notes
Cliff Palace - 👍	early April–early Nov	$3	1 hour	Begins at Cliff Palace Parking Area
Balcony House - 👍	late April–early Oct	$3	1 hour	Begins at Balcony House Parking Area
Spruce Tree House - 👍	All Year	Self-Guiding and guided	N/A	Access near Chapin Mesa Museum • Free guided tours are offered in winter
Long House - 👍	late May–early Sept	$3	1.5 hours	Tour begins at Wetherill Mesa Info Kiosk
Step House	late May–early Sept	Self-Guiding	N/A	Access near Wetherill Mesa Info Kiosk

Tours listed above are provided by the National Park Service. Tickets can be purchased at Far View Visitor Center, Morefield Ranger Station, Colorado Welcome Center in Cortez, and Chapin Mesa Museum (mid-Oct–early Nov only). Visitors must climb at least one ladder at each site.

	Dates	Fee	Duration	Notes
700 Years	late April–mid-Oct	$45 (Adult) $34 (Child)	4 hours	A park ranger leads a chronological tour of the Ancestral Puebloans • Includes Cliff Palace Tour
Classic Pueblo	late April–mid-Oct	$35 (Adult) $17.50 (Child)	3.5 hours	A park ranger leads the group through archeological sites on Mesa Top Loop including Cliff Palace

Tours listed above are offered by Aramark (800.449.2288, www.visitmesaverde.com). Tickets may be purchased at Far View Lodge front desk, Far View Terrace tour desk, and Morefield Campground Store, and online at www.visitmesaverde.com.

	Dates	Fee	Duration	Notes
Oak Tree House & Fire Temple	late May–early Sept	$20	2 hours	Moderately strenuous 1-mile hike includes walking along ledges and one ladder
Square Tower	September–mid-Oct	$20	2 hours	1-mile strenuous hike with three ladders
Spring House	September–mid-Oct	$40	8 hours	8-mile strenuous hike to dwelling

Tours listed above are offered by the Mesa Verde Institute. Tickets must be purchased from the Far View Visitor Center and are available up to 48 hours in advance on a first-come, first-served basis. For additional information visit www.mesaverdeinstitute.org

MESA VERDE

Winter Activities

Winter activities at Mesa Verde are different than those found during the rest of the year. Park rangers lead guests on **tours of Spruce Tree House**, but the rest of the cliff dwellings are closed until spring. You can still view many of the dwellings from a distance at overlooks. **Cliff Palace Loop Road** is not plowed during winter, making it an excellent location for **cross-country skiing**, **snowshoeing**, and **winter hiking**. **Mesa Top Loop Road** provides views of Cliff Palace and is open in winter. Before hiking, snowshoeing, or cross-country skiing in the park, you should discuss your plans with a ranger to receive information regarding current trail conditions. You might have to register to hike in specific areas. Overnight stays are not permitted during winter and all sites are off-limits after sunset.

Best of Mesa Verde

Guided Tour: Cliff Palace
> Runner-up: Balcony House
> 2nd Runner-up: Long House

Hike: Spruce Tree House
> Runner-up: Petroglyph Point
> 2nd Runner-up: Spruce Canyon

For Kids: In all likelihood your child will find the history and ruins of Ancestral Puebloans to be captivating. If not, engage your child (ages 4–12) in this unique environment by picking up a free **Junior Ranger** activity booklet at Far View Visitor Center or Chapin Mesa Museum. The award for a completed booklet is a Mesa Verde Junior Ranger badge.

Ranger Programs: In addition to ranger guided cliff dwelling tours, the park provides ranger accompanied walks through Far View Sites and evening programs at Morefield Campground and Far View Lodge. Programs are offered daily from late May through early September, free of charge. To get the exact time of a particular program visit the park website or look inside the free newspaper you'll receive at the entrance when you arrive.

Flora & Fauna: Mesa Verde was preserved for its historic culture, but its present inhabitants are nearly as interesting. About **74 species of mammals, 200 species of birds, 16 species of reptiles, and a handful of species of fish and amphibians** have been documented in the park. You have a good chance of seeing animals like coyote, mule deer, spotted bat, and spotted owl.

Over 640 species of plants exist here. Cottonwood, willow, and buffaloberry survive on the banks of Mancos River and near seep springs. Over the past decade, a number of wildfires have cut the size of the park's pinyon-juniper forests in half. Several extremely old and champion-sized trees survived, with one Utah juniper's trunk measuring 52 inches in diameter, a record for the state of Colorado. Another is dated at more than 1,300 years old. In the lower elevations you'll find sagebrushes. Higher up you'll find mostly shrubs, but Gambel oak and Douglas fir grow along the north rim in sheltered areas. Plants like Cliff Palace milkvetch, Schmoll's milkvetch, Mesa Verde wandering aletes, and Mesa Verde stickseed do not exist anywhere else in the world.

Pets: Pets are allowed in the park, but are not permitted on trails, in archeological sites, or in buildings (with the exception of service animals). They are permitted along roadways, in parking lots, and at the campground, but must be kept on a leash no more than six feet in length at all times. You may not leave your pet unattended or tied to any object within the park.

Accessibility: Mesa Verde is a tricky place for individuals with limited mobility. Its cliff dwellings are built into alcoves below the rim of the mesa. Visitors must descend tall ladders or stairs carved into the steep cliff wall to access Cliff Palace and Balcony House. Many other sites are accessible with assistance. The park's scenic overlooks, Far View Visitor Center, Chapin Mesa Museum, Far View Sites, and Spruce Tree House are all potential destinations. The free tram to Wetherill Mesa Archeological Sites has a wheelchair lift. Step House and Badger House Community (accessed via tram) are accessible with assistance. Long House is not accessible. Morefield Campground has a few accessible campsites.

Weather: The weather at Mesa Verde is quite comfortable year-round. On average, every other day is clear and cloudless regardless of the month. An occasional snowstorm passes through in winter, but average high temperatures in January are above 40°F and average lows are around 20°F.

In the middle of summer high temperatures can reach into the 90s°F. You may sweat during the day, but don't worry about it being too hot to sleep. Temperatures usually fall into the 50s°F during summer evenings.

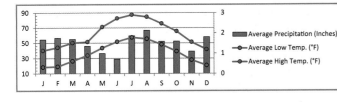

Legend:
- Average Precipitation (Inches)
- Average Low Temp. (°F)
- Average High Temp. (°F)

Vacation Planner

Ranger-led tours provide the only access to Mesa Verde's best attractions: **Cliff Palace**, **Balcony House**, and **Long House** (page 359). You'll want to stop and purchase tickets at **Far View Visitor Center** or **Morefield Ranger Station** if you haven't purchased them already at **Colorado Welcome Center** in Cortez. These are the only location where tickets are sold. During peak season the park may limit you to just one tour, so know in advance what site you're most interested in. The one-day trip itinerary provided below suggests activities to supplement your ranger guided tours. Spend the night in the park at **Morefield Campground** or **Far View Lodge** (page 357). You can grab a bite to eat at Far View Lodge or Chapin Mesa. Nearby dining, grocery stores, lodging, festivals, and attractions are listed on pages 362–367.

Day 1

If you're at **Chapin Mesa** with a little bit of time to burn before or after a cliff dwelling tour, hike **Petroglyph Point Trail** (page 358). On your way to the trailhead be sure to stop at **Spruce Tree House**, the best maintained cliff dwelling in the park. Petroglyph Point is steep, rocky, and somewhat strenuous. If you'd like a flatter alternative, give **Soda Canyon Overlook Trail** a try. It has a few rolling hills, but is relatively easy and provides excellent views of **Balcony House** from across the canyon. If the crowds are putting a damper on your family vacation try heading over to **Wetherill Mesa** (open late May to early September). Even if you don't tour **Long House** (the second largest cave dwelling behind Cliff Palace), there's plenty to see. You can either walk or take the tram to a series of archeological sites. Once you've had your fill of Ancestral Puebloans' living quarters, start heading back to the park entrance on main park road. If you have spare time, especially around dusk, take a quick hike along **Point Lookout Trail** (page 358) located near Morefield Campground (excellent place to see the sunset).

Kivas of Balcony House

A coyote crosses the main park road

Did you know?

▶ There are more than 4,700 archeological sites at Mesa Verde, but only 600 or so are cliff dwellings. Most are mesa top pueblos, farming terraces, towers, reservoirs, and check dams.

▶ With 150 rooms and 75 open areas, Cliff Palace is the largest cliff dwelling in the park (and in North America). It has 21 kivas and could house as many as 100 to 120 Ancestral Puebloans at any one time.

▶ Long House also has 150 rooms and Spruce Tree House has 130.

▶ Large structures are not the norm. Roughly 90% of Mesa Verde's cliff dwellings contain fewer than 10 rooms.

▶ Mesa Verde is the first park to celebrate prehistoric culture rather than grand scenery.

MESA VERDE

Dining

Rocky Mountain Area

Orlando's Steak House • (970) 586-6121
132 East Elkhorn Ave; Estes Park, CO 80517
www.orlandossteakhouse.com • Entrée: $15–35

Tulum's • (970) 577-0032
401 W Elkhorn Ave; Estes Park, CO 80517

Other Side Restaurant • (970) 586-2171
900 Moraine Ave; Estes Park, CO 80517
www.theothersideofestes.com • Entrée: $15–24

Twin Owls Steakhouse • (970) 586-9344
800 MacGregor Ave; Estes Park, CO 80517
www.twinowls.net • Entrée: $17–37

Rock Inn • (970) 586-4116
1675 CO-66; Estes Park, CO 80545
www.rockinnestes.com • Entrée: $14–30

Mama Rose's Homemade Italian • (970) 586-3330
338 Big Thompson Ave; Estes Park, CO 80517
www.mamarosesrestaurant.com

Dunraven Inn • (970) 586-6409
2470 CO-66; Estes Park, CO 80517
www.dunraveninn.com • Entrée: $10–42

Claire's on the Park • (970) 586-9564
225 Park Ln; Estes Park, CO 80517
www.clairesonthepark.net

Smokin' Dave's BBQ • (866) 674-2793
820 Moraine Ave; Estes Park, CO 80517
www.smokindavesbbqandtaphouse.com

Estes Park Brewery • (970) 586-5421
470 Prospect Village Dr; Estes Park, CO 80517
www.epbrewery.com • Entrée: $13–26

Ed's Cantina • (970) 586-2919
390 Big Thompson Ave; Estes Park, CO 80517
www.edscantina.com • Burgers: $8+

Penelope's Old Time Burgers • (970) 586-2277
229 W Elkhorn Ave; Estes Park, CO 80517

Molly B Restaurant • (970) 586-2766
200 Moraine Ave; Estes Park, CO 80517
www.estesparkmollyb.com • Entrée: $11–17

The Egg and I • (970) 586-1173
393 E Elkhorn Ave; Estes Park, CO 80517
www.theeggandirestaurants.com • Breakfast: $4+

Thai Kitchen • (970) 577-7112
401 S Saint Vrain Ave; Estes Park, CO 80517

Cheesy Lee's Amazing Pizza • (970) 586-5050
861 Moraine Ave; Estes Park, CO 80517
www.cheesylees.com • Pizza: $6+

Chicago's Best • (970) 586-4796
112 W Elkhorn Ave; Estes Park, CO 80517

Village Pizza • (970) 586-6031
633 Big Thompson Ave; Estes Park, CO 80517

Bob & Tony's Pizza • (970) 586-2044
124 W Elkhorn Ave; Estes Park, CO 80517

Poppy's Pizza & Grill • (970) 586-8282
342 Big Thompson Ave; Estes Park, CO 80517
www.poppyspizzaandgrill.com • Pizza: $6+

Casa Grande • (970) 577-0799
220 E Elkhorn Ave; Estes Park, CO 80517
www.casagrandemexicana.com

Sweet Basilico Café • (970) 586-3899
Prospect Village Dr; Estes Park, CO 80517
www.sweetbasilico.com • Entrée: $13–20

DeLeo's Park Theatre Café • (970) 577-1134
132 Moraine Ave; Estes Park, CO 80517
www.deleosdeli.com

Nepal Café • (970) 577-7035
184 Big Thompson Ave; Estes Park, CO 80517

Mtn Home Café • (970) 586-6624
457 E Wonder View Ave; Estes Park, CO 80517
www.mountainhomecafe.com

Coffee on the Rocks • (970) 586-5181
510 Moraine Ave; Estes Park, CO 80517
www.coffeeinestes.com

Donut Haus • (970) 586-2988
342 Moraine Ave; Estes Park, CO 80517
www.donuthaus-estespark.com

Shakes Alive • (970) 577-7007
513 Big Thompson Ave; Estes Park, CO 80517
www.shakesalive.com

Laura's Fudge Shop • (970) 586-4004
129 E Elkhorn Ave; Estes Park, CO 80517

O–A Bistro • (970) 627-5080
928 Grand Ave; Grand Lake, CO 80447
www.o-abistro.com • Entrée: $16–23

Sagebrush BBQ & Grill • (970) 627-1404
1101 Grand Ave; Grand Lake, CO 80447
www.sagebrushbbq.com • Entrée: $11–23

Backstreet Steakhouse • (970) 627-8144
604 Marina Dr; Grand Lake, CO 80447
www.davenhavenlodge.com • Entrée: $18–29

Grand Lake Brewing Co • (970) 627-1711
915 Grand Ave; Grand Lake, CO 80447
www.grandlakebrewing.com • Burgers: $8+

Grand Lake Golf Rest. • (970) 627-3922
1415 County Rd 48; Grand Lake, CO 80447

Grand Pizza • (970) 627-8390
1131 Grand Ave; Grand Lake, CO 80447
www.grand-pizza.com • Pizza: $7+

Blue Water Bakery • (970) 627-5416
928 Grand Ave; Grand Lake, CO 80447

Cy's Deli • (970) 627-3354
717 Grand Ave; Grand Lake, CO 80447

Great Sand Dunes Area

Desert Sage Restaurant • (719) 256-4402
12 Baca Townhouse; Crestone, CO 81131

Painted Sky Café & Bakery • (719) 256-4202
121 E Galena Ave; Crestone, CO 81131

Bliss Café • (719) 256-6400
187 W Silver Ave; Crestone, CO 81131

True Grits Steakhouse • (719) 589-9954
100 Santa Fe Ave; Alamosa, CO 81101

San Luis Valley Brewing • (719) 587-2337
631 Main St; Alamosa, CO 81101
www.slvbrewco.com

Cavillo's Mexican Rest. • (719) 587-5500
400 Main St; Alamosa, CO 81101

Fresh Tortilla Company • (719) 587-5508
924 Main St; Alamosa, CO 81101
freshtortillacompany.com • Burrito: $7

Bistro Rialto • (719) 589 -3039
714 Main St; Alamosa, CO 81101
www.bistrorialto.com

San Luis Valley Pizza • (719) 589-4749
2069 1st St; Alamosa, CO 81101

Milagros Coffeehouse • (719) 589-9299
529 Main St; Alamosa, CO 81101

San Marcos Mexican Rest. • (719) 379-5290
402 Main St; Blanca, CO 81123

Old West Café • (719) 379-2448
403 Miranda Ave; Fort Garland, CO 81133

All-Gon Pizza • (719) 379-2222
319 Beaubien Ave; Fort Garland, CO 81133

Black Canyon Area

Red Barn Restaurant • (970) 249-9202
1413 E Main St; Montrose, CO 81401

Simmer Food & Wine • (970) 252-1152
320 E Main St; Montrose, CO 81401

Stone House • (970) 240-8899
1415 Hawk Parkway; Montrose, CO 81401

Camp Robber Restaurant • (970) 240-1590
1515 Ogden Rd; Montrose, CO 81401
www.camprobber.com • Entrée: $10–20

Smuggler's Brew Pub & Grill • (970) 249-0919
1571 Ogden Rd; Montrose, CO 81401

Starvin Arvins • (970) 249-7787
1320 S Townsend Ave; Montrose, CO 81401

DeAngelo's Pizza • (970) 252-7499
435 S Townsend Ave; Montrose, CO 81401
www.deangelosmontrose.com • Pizza: $6+

Pahgre's • (970) 249-6442
1541 Oxbow Dr, #1800; Montrose, CO 81401
www.pahgres.com • Sandwich: $8

Guru's Restaurant • (970) 252-8777
Indian and Himalayan food
448 S Main St; Montrose, CO 81401

Asii • (970) 240-4567
1015 S Townsend Ave; Montrose, CO 81401

Daily Bread • (970) 249-8444
346 E Main St; Montrose, CO 81401

Jovis Coffee • (970) 252-0812
242 Main St; Montrose, CO 81401

Mesa Verde Area

Pepperhead • (970) 565-3303
44 W Main St; Cortez, CO 81321
www.pepperheadcortez.com • Burrito: $8

Shiloh Steak House • (970) 565-6560
5 Veach St; Cortez, CO 81321

Main Street Brewery • (970) 564-9112
21 E Main St; Cortez, CO 81321

Koko's Friendly Pub • (970) 565-6000
2121 E Main St; Cortez, CO 81321

Handlebars Food • (970) 387-5395
117 W 13th St; Cortez, CO 81321

Jack & Janelle's Country Kitchen • (970) 565-2572
801 E Main St; Cortez, CO 81321

Pippo's Diner • (970) 565-6039
100 W Main St; Cortez, CO 81321

Stonefish Sushi & More • (970) 565-9244
16 W Main St; Cortez, CO 81321

Silver Bean • (970) 946-4404
410 1/2 W Main St; Cortez, CO 81321

Once Upon A Sandwich • (970) 565-8292
9 W Main St; Cortez, CO 81321

Ocean Pearl • (970) 874-1888
109 Main St; Delta, CO 81416

Mancos Pizza Too • (970) 565-7222
1013 Main St; Cortez, CO 81321

Hunan Chinese Rest. • (970) 565-0919
2561 E Main St; Cortez, CO 81321

Fiesta Mexicana • (970) 565-4267
2604 E Main St; Cortez, CO 81321

Nero's • (970) 565-7366
303 W Main St; Cortez, CO 81321

Absolute Bakery & Café • (970) 533-1200
110 S Main; Mancos, CO 81328

Mr Happy's Bakery & Café • (970) 565-9869
332 E Main St; Cortez, CO 81321

Spruce Tree Coffeehouse • (970) 565-6789
318 E Main St; Cortez, CO 81321
www.sprucetreecoffeehouse.com

Home Slice Pizza • (970) 259-5551
441 E College Dr; Durango, CO 81301
www.homeslicedelivers.com • Pizza: $12.50+

Diorios South Pizza • (970) 385-0420
600 Main Ave, # 110; Durango, CO 81301
www.dioriospizza.com • Pizza: $13+

Many chain restaurants can be found in Estes Park, Alamosa, Montrose, Cortez, Durango, and along Interstates 25 and 70.

Grocery Stores

Rocky Mountain Area

Safeway • (970) 586-4447
451 E Wonder View Ave; Estes Park, CO 80517

Country Market • (970) 586-2702
900 Moraine Ave; Estes Park, CO 80517

Circle D Foods • (970) 627-3210
701 Grand Ave; Grand Lake, CO 80447

Mtn Food Market • (970) 627-3470
400 Grand Ave; Grand Lake, CO 80447

Great Sand Dunes Area

Fort Market • (719) 379-3482
330 Miranda St; Fort Garland, CO 81133

Crestone General Store • (719) 256-4516
200 S Cottonwood; Crestone, CO 81131

Westcliffe Supermarket • (719) 783-0550
50 Main St; Westcliffe, CO 81252

Walmart Supercenter • (719) 589-9071
Clark St; Alamosa, CO 81101

Safeway • (719) 587-3075
1301 Main St; Alamosa, CO 81101

Black Canyon Area

Safeway • (970) 249-1160
1329 S Townsend Ave; Montrose, CO 81401

Walmart Supercenter • (970) 249-7544
16750 S Townsend Ave; Montrose, CO 81401

Mesa Verde Area

Walmart Supercenter • (970) 565-6138
1835 E Main St; Cortez, CO 81321

Safeway • (970) 564-9590
1580 E Main St; Cortez, CO 81321

Lodging

Rocky Mountain Area

The Stanley Hotel • (970) 586-3371
Portions of The Shining *and* Dumb and Dumber *were filmed here* • *Tours available*
333 Wonder View Ave; Estes Park, CO 80517
www.stanleyhotel.com • Rates: $279+/night

Inn On Fall River • (970) 586-4118
1660 Fall River Rd; Estes Park, CO 80517
www.innonfallriver.com • Rates: $109+

Saddle & Surrey Motel • (970) 586-3326
1341 S Saint Vrain Ave; Estes Park, CO 80517

The Haber Motel • (970) 449-1660
397 E Elkhorn Ave; Estes Park, CO 80517
www.thehabermotel.com • Rates: $139+

Stonebrook Resort • (970) 586-4629
1710 Fall River Rd; Estes Park, CO 80517
www.stonebrookresort.com • Rates: $136+

Deer Crest Resort • (970) 586-2324
1200 Fall River Rd; Estes Park, CO 80517
www.deercrestresort.com

Kokopelli Inn • (970) 586-4420
6777 US-36; Estes Park, CO 80517
www.kokopelliinn.net • Rates: $99+

Taharaa Mtn Lodge • (970) 577-0098
3110 S Saint Vrain Ave; Estes Park, CO 80517
www.taharaa.com • Raes: $189+

Pine Haven Resort • (800) 586-3184
1580 Fall River Rd; Estes Park, CO 80517
www.estesparkcabins.com • Rates: $134+

McGregor Mtn Lodge • (970) 586-3457
2815 Fall River Rd; Estes Park, CO 80517
www.mcgregormountainlodge.com • Rates: $139+

Boulder Brook on Fall River • (970) 586-0910
1900 Fall River Rd; Estes Park, CO 80517
www.boulderbrook.com • Rates: $199+

Dripping Springs Resort • (970) 586-3406
Off US-34, Big Thompson Canyon Rd, 37 Dripping Springs Ln; Drake, CO 80517
www.drippingsprings.com • Rates: $165+

Colorado Cottages • (970) 586-4637
1241 High Dr; Estes Park, CO 80517
www.colocottages.com • Rates: $125+

Sunnyside Knoll Resort • (970) 586-5759
1675 Fall River Rd; Estes Park, CO 80517
www.sunnysideknoll.com • Rates: $135+

Solitude Cabins • (970) 577-7777
1885 Sketch Box Ln, # 7; Estes Park, CO 80517
www.solitudecabins.com • Rates: $299+

Discovery Lodge • (970) 586-3336
800 Big Thompson Ave; Estes Park, CO 80517
www.estesdiscoverylodge.com • Rates: $89+

Silver Moon Inn • (970) 586-6006
175 Spruce Dr; Estes Park, CO 80517
www.silvermooninn.com • Rates: $168+

Alpine Trail Ridge Inn • (970) 586-4585
927 Moraine Ave; Estes Park, CO 80517
www.alpinetrailridgeinn.com • Rates: $107+

Black Canyon Inn • (970) 586-8113
800 MacGregor Ave; Estes Park, CO 80517
www.blackcanyoninn.com • Rates: $195+

Della Terra Mtn Chateau • (970) 586-2501
3501 Fall River Rd; Estes Park, CO 80517
www.dellaterramountainchateau.com • Rates: $125+

Fawn Valley Inn • (970) 586-2388
2760 Fall River Rd; Estes Park, CO 80517
www.rockymtnresorts.com • $90+

Black Dog Inn • (970) 586-0374
650 S St Vrain Ave; Estes Park, CO 80517
www.blackdoginn.com • Rates: $175+

River Song A B&B • (970) 586-4666
1765 Lower Broadview Rd; Estes Park, CO 80517
www.romanticriversong.com • Rates: $165+

Tyrol Mountain Inn • (970) 586-3382
1240 Big Thompson Rd; Estes Park, CO 80517
www.tyrolmtninn.com • Rates: $139+

Brynwood On the River • (970) 586-3475
710 Moraine Ave; Estes Park, CO 80517
www.brynwood.com • Rates: $125+

River Spruce • (970) 586-4543
2334 CO-66; Estes Park, CO 80517
www.riverspruce.com • Rates: $135+

A Mtn Valley Home B&B • (970) 586-3100
1420 Axminster Ln; Estes Park, CO 80517
www.amountainvalleyhome.com • Rates: $199+

Gilded Meadows B&B • (970) 586-2124
861 Big Horn Dr; Estes Park, CO 80517
www.gildedpinemeadows.com • Rates: $110+

River Stone Resorts • (970) 586-4005
2120 Fall River Rd; Estes Park, CO 80517
www.riverstoneresorts.com • Rates: $229+

Peak To Peak Lodge • (970) 586-4451
760 S St Vrain Ave; Estes Park, CO 80517
www.peaktopeaklodge.com • Rates: $79+

Anniversary Inn B&B • (970) 586-6200
1060 Marys Lake Rd; Estes Park, CO 80517
www.estesinn.com • Rates: $150+

Streamside On Fall River • (970) 586-6464
1260 Fall River Rd; Estes Park, CO 80517
www.streamsideonfallriver.com • Rates: $125+

Elkhorn Lodge & Guest Ranch • (970) 586-4416
600 W Elkhorn Ave; Estes Park, CO 80517
www.elkhornlodge.org • Rates: $69+

Amberwood • (970) 586-4385
1889 Fall River Rd; Estes Park, CO 80517
www.amberwoodestespark.com • Rates: $125+

Estes Park Condos • (970) 577-0068
1400 David Dr; Estes Park, CO 80517
www.estescondos.com • Rates: $195+

Woodlands On Fall River • (970) 586-0404
1888 Fall River Rd; Estes Park, CO 80517
www.woodlandsestes.com • Rates: $180+

Spruce Lake RV Park • (970) 586-2889
1050 Marys Lake Rd; Estes Park, CO 80517
www.sprucelakerv.com • Rates: ~$50

Estes Park KOA • (970) 586-2888
2051 Big Thompson Ave; Estes Park, CO 80517

Meeker Park Lodge • (303) 747-2266
11733 CO-7; Allenspark, CO 80510
www.meekerparklodge.com • Rates: $85+

Wild Basin Lodge • (303) 747-2274
1130 CR-84 W; Allenspark, CO 80510
www.wildbasinlodge.com

Grand Mountain Rentals • (970) 627-1131
1028 Grand Ave; Grand Lake, CO 80447
www.grandmountainrentals.com • Rates: $150+

Gateway Inn • (970) 627-2400
200 W Portal Rd; Grand Lake, CO 80447
www.gatewayinn.com • Rates: $99+

Rapids Lodge • (970) 627-3707
209 Rapids Ln; Grand Lake, CO 80447
www.rapidslodge.com • Rates: $95+

Grand Lake Lodging • (970) 627-3580
419 Garfield St; Grand Lake, CO 80447
www.westernriv.com • Rates: $350+/week

Spirit Lake Lodge • (970) 627-3344
Snowmobile rental available on-site
829 Grand Ave; Grand Lake, CO 80447
www.spiritlakelodge.com • Rates: $175+

Grand Escape Cottages • (970) 627-3410
1204 Grand Ave; Grand Lake, CO 80447
www.grandescapecottages.com • Rates: $139+

The Terrace Inn • (970) 627-3000
813 Grand Ave; Grand Lake, CO 80447
www.grandlaketerraceinn.com • Rates: $120+

Grand Lake Lodge • (970) 627-3967
15500 US-34; Grand Lake, CO 80447
www.grandlakelodge.com • Rates: $125+

The Inn at Grand Lake • (970) 627-9234
1103 Grand Ave; Grand Lake, CO 80447
www.grandrez.com • Rates: $139+

Winding River Resort • (970) 627-3215
*Horse boarding & rides, snowmobile & ATV rental,
animal farm, and sleigh rides are available*
1447 CR-491; Grand Lake, CO 80447
www.windingriverresort.com • Rates: $95+

Mtn Lakes Lodge • (970) 627-8448
10480 US-34; Grand Lake, CO 80447
www.grandlakelodging.net • Rates: $109+

Black Bear Lodge • (970) 627-3654
12255 US-34; Grand Lake, CO 80447
www.blackbeargrandlake.com

Grand Lake Treehouse • (888) 214-6845
1901 W Portal Rd; Grand Lake, CO 80447
www.grandlaketreehouse.com • Rates: $350

Great Sand Dunes Area

Great Sand Dunes Lodge • (719) 378-2900
7900 CO-150; Mosca, CO 81146
www.gsdlodge.com • Rates: $89+

Zapata Ranch • (719) 378-2356
5305 CO-150; Mosca, CO 81146
www.zranch.org • Rates: $985/3 nights (all-inclusive)

Great Sand Dunes Oasis • (719) 378-2222
5400 CO-150; Mosca, CO 81146
www.greatdunes.com • Rates: $89

Lamplighter Motel • (719) 589-6636
425 Main St; Alamosa, CO 81101

KOA Kampgrounds • (719) 589-9757
6900 Juniper Ln; Alamosa, CO 81101

Enchanted Forest • (719) 256-5768
3459 Enchanted Way; Crestone, CO 81131
www.enchantedforestcrestone.net • Rates: $65+

Coll House B&B • (719) 256-4475
1019 Moonlight Way; Crestone, CO 81131
www.collhouse.com • Rates: $90+

Baca Lodge • (719) 256-5798
637 Panorama Way; Crestone, CO 81131
www.bacalodge.com • Rates: $85+

Silver Star B&B • (719) 256-4686
557 Panorama Way; Crestone, CO 81131
www.silverstarbandb.com • Rates: $60+

Sangre De Cristo Inn • (719) 256-4975
116 S Alder; Crestone, CO 81131
www.sangredecristoinn.com • Rates: $74+

Willow Spring B&B • (719) 256-4116
223 Moffat Way; Moffat, CO 81143
www.willow-spring.com • Rates: $50+

Sand Dunes Swimming RV • (719) 378-2807
1991 CR-63; Hooper, CO 81136
www.sanddunespool.com • Rates: $25+

Grape Creek RV Park • (719) 783-2588
56491 CO-69; Westcliffe, CO 81252
www.grapecreekrv.net • Rates: $27+

Ute Creek Campground • (719) 379-3238
071 5th Ave; Fort Garland, CO 81133

Black Canyon Area

Black Canyon Motel • (970) 249-3495
1605 E Main St; Montrose, CO 81401
www.blackcanyonmotel.com • Rates: $50+

Western Motel • (970) 252-8293
1200 E Main St; Montrose, CO 81401
www.westernmotel.com

Canyon Creek B&B • (970) 249-2886
820 Main St; Montrose, CO 81401
www.canyoncreekbedandbreakfast.com • Rates: $135

B&B-Uncompahgre • (970) 240-4000
21049 Uncompahgre Rd; Montrose, CO 81403
www.uncbb.com • Rates: $125–150

Kings Riverbend RV & Cabins • (970) 249-8235
65120 Old Chipeta Tr; Montrose, CO 81403
www.kingsriverbend.com

Montrose RV Resort • (970) 249-9177
200 Cedar Ave; Montrose, CO 81401

Cedar Creek RV Park • (970) 249-3884
126 Rose Ln; Montrose, CO 81401
www.cedarcreekrv.com • Rates: $31+

Last Frontier Lodge • (970) 921-5150
40300 D Ln; Crawford, CO 81415

Stone House Inn • (970) 921-5683
270 CO-92; Crawford, CO 81415
www.stonehouseinn.net • Rates: $80+

French Country Inn B&B • (970) 921-7111
38692 Indian Head Ln; Crawford, CO 81415

Mesa Verde Area

Tomahawk Lodge • (970) 565-8521
728 S Broadway; Cortez, CO 81321

Flagstone Meadows • (970) 533-9838
38080 Rd K.4; Mancos, CO 81328
www.flagstonemeadows.com • Rates: $95+

Aneth Lodge-Budget Six • (970) 565-3453
645 E Main St; Cortez, CO 81321

Sundance Bear Lodge • (866) 529-2480
38890 CO-184; Mancos, CO 81328
www.sundancebear.com

Enchanted Mesa Motel • (970) 533-7729
862 W Grand Ave; Mancos, CO 81328
www.enchantedmesamotel.com • Rates: $55+

Abode at Willowtail Springs • (800) 698-0603
10451 Rd 39; Mancos, CO 81328
www.willowtailsprings.com • Rates: $249+

Sundance RV Park • (970) 565-0997
815 E Main St; Cortez, CO 81321
www.sundancervpark.com • Rates: $34

A&A Mesa Verde RV • (970) 565-3517
34979 US-160; Mancos, CO 81328
www.mesaverdecamping.com • Rates: 33+

Mesa Verde RV Resort • (800) 776-7421
35303 US-160; Cortez, CO 81328
www.mesaverdervresort.com • Rates: 33+

KOA Kampgrounds • (970) 565-9301
27432 E US-160; Cortez, CO 81321

Many chain hotels can be found in Estes Park, Alamosa, Montrose, Cortez, Durango, and along Interstates 25 and 70.

Festivals

Nat'l Western Stock Show • January
Denver • www.nationalwestern.com

Winter Carnival • February
Steamboat Springs • www.steamboat-chamber.com

Crane Festival • March
Monte Vista • www.cranefest.com

BaloonaVista • June
Buena Vista • www.buenavistacolorado.org

Santa Fe Trail Festival • June
Trinidad • www.santafetrailscenicandhistoricbyway.org

Bluegrass Festival • June
Telluride • www.bluegrass.com

Cowboys' Roundup Days • July
Steamboat Springs • www.steamboat-chamber.com

Arts Festival • July
Cherry Creek • www.cherryarts.org

Colorado State Fair • August
Pueblo • www.coloradostatefair.com

Festival of the Arts • August
Crested Butte • www.crestedbutteartfestival.com

Rocky Mtn Irish Festival • August
Fort Collins • www.fortcollinsirishfestival.com

Mile High Music Festival • August
Commerce City • www.milehighmusicfestival.com

A Taste of Colorado • September
Denver • www.atasteofcolorado.com

Colorado Mtn Winefest • September
Palisade • www.coloradowinefest.com

Long Peak Scottish Irish Highland Festival
September • Estes Park • www.scotfest.com

Great American Beer Festival • October
Denver • www.greatamericanbeerfestival.com

Attractions

Rocky Mountain Area

Cowpoke Corner Corral • (970) 586-5890
1-to-4 hour ($35–75) trail rides offered
PO Box 2214; Estes Park, CO 80517
www.cowpokecornercorral.com

Nat'l Park Gateway Stables • (970) 586-5269
4600 Fall River Rd; Estes Park, CO 80517
www.skhorses.com

Sombrero Ranch
Trail, breakfast, steak dinner, sleigh, and wagon rides available • horse drives too!
3300 Airport Rd; Boulder, CO 80301
Estes Park Stable • (970) 586-4577
Grand Lake Stable • (970) 627-3514
Allenspark Stable • (303) 747-2551
Glen Haven Stable • (970) 586-2669
www.sombrero.com

YMCA of the Rockies • (970) 586-3341
2515 Tunnel Rd; Estes Park, CO 80511
www.jacksonstables.com

Colorado Mtn School • (970) 586-5758
341 Moraine Ave; Estes Park, CO 80517
www.totalclimbing.com • Intro Rock Climb: $180

Estes Park Aerial Tramway • (970) 586-3675
420 E Riverside Dr; Estes Park, CO 80517
www.estestram.com • Tickets: $10/Adult

Estes Park Ride-A-Kart • (970) 586-6495
2250 Big Thompson Ave; Estes Park, CO 80517
www.rideakart.com • Go-Karts: $7

Tiny Town Miniature Golf • (970) 586-6333
840 Moraine Ave; Estes Park, CO 80517

Affinity Massage • (970) 586-3401
1182-C Graves Ave; Estes Park, CO 80517
www.affinitymassageandwellness.com

Riverspointe Spa • (970) 577-6841
121 Wiest Dr; Estes Park, CO 80517
www.riverspointespa.com

Elements of Touch Spa • (970) 586-6597
477 Pine River Ln; Estes Park, CO 80517
www.estesriverretreat.com

Snowy Peaks Winery • (970) 586-2099
292 Moraine Ave; Estes Park, CO 80517
www.snowypeakswinery.com

Park Theater • (970) 586-8904
130 Moraine Ave; Estes Park, CO 80517
www.historicparktheatre.com • Tickets: $7/Adult

MacGregor Ranch Museum • (970) 586-3749
180 MacGregor Ln; Estes Park, CO 80517
www.macgregorranch.org

Estes Park Museum • (970) 586-6256
200 4th St; Estes Park, CO 80517
www.estes.org • Free

Stanley Museum • (970) 577-1903
517 Big Thompson Ave; Estes Park, CO 80517
www.stanleymuseum.org

Grand Adventures • (970) 627-3098
Snowmobile tours and rentals ($75 • 1 hr)
304 W Portal Rd; Grand Lake, CO 80447
www.grandadventures.com

Rocky Mtn Repertory Theatre • (970) 627-3421
1025 Grand Ave; Grand Lake, CO 80447
www.rockymountainrep.com

Great Sand Dunes Area

Zapata Falls
From Great Sand Dunes Visitor Center, drive south about 8 miles, turn left (east) onto a gravel road, and continue about 3.5 miles to the trailhead. The hike is 0.5 miles and requires that you cross a creek and scramble up slippery rocks to the 25-ft falls.

Baca Nat'l Wildlife Refuge (NWR)
Crestone, CO 81131

Alamosa NWR • (719) 589-4021
9383 El Rancho Ln; Alamosa, CO 81101

San Luis Lakes State Park • (719) 378-2020
16399 Lane 6 N; Mosca, CO 81146

Rio Grande Scenic Railroad • (877) 726-7245
610 State St; Alamosa, CO 81101
www.riograndescenicrailroad.com • Rates: $15+

UFO Watchtower • (719) 378-2296
2502 County Road 61; Center, CO 81125
www.ufowatchtower.com • Admission: $2

Alligator Farm • (719) 378-2612
9162 Ln 9 N; Mosca, CO 81146
www.gatorfarm.com • Admission: $15/Adult

ABC Pro Bowl • (719) 589-2240
204 Victoria Ave; Alamosa, CO 81101

Joyful Journey Hot Springs Spa • (719) 256-4328
28640 County Rd 58Ee; Moffat, CO 81143
www.joyfuljourneyhotsprings.com

Sky Hi 6 Theatres • (719) 589-4471
7089 US-160; Alamosa, CO 81101

Francisco Theater • (719) 742-5767
127 Francisco; La Veta, CO 81055

Grandote Peaks Golf Course • (719) 742-3390
5540 CO-12; La Veta, CO 81055
www.grandotepeaks.com • 9 holes: $35+

Francisco Fort Museum • (719) 742-5501
306 S Main St; La Veta, CO 81055

Black Canyon Area

Elk Ridge Trail Rides • (970) 240-6007
10203 Bostwick Park Rd; Montrose, CO 81401

Crawford State Park • (970) 921-5721
40468 CO-92; Crawford, CO 81415
www.parks.state.co.us • Entrance Fee: $7/vehicle

Curecanti Nat'l Rec Area • (970) 249-8414
1 E Portal St; Montrose, CO 81401

Bridges Golf Course • (970) 252-1119
2500 Bridges Ave; Montrose, CO 81401
www.montrosebridges.com • 9 holes: $45

San Juan Cinema • (970) 252-9096
1869 E Main St; Montrose, CO 81401
www.montrosemovies.com • Tickets: $8/Adult

Star Drive-In Theatre • (970) 249-6170
600 Miami St; Montrose, CO 81401
www.carload.com

Magic Circle Theatre • (970) 249-7838
420 S 12th St; Montrose, CO 81401

Tru Vu Drive In Theatre • (970) 874-9556
1001 CO-92; Delta, CO 81416

Big Sky Drive In Theatre • (970) 874-9770
452 Main St; Delta, CO 81416

Museum of the Mtn West • (970) 240-3400
68169 Miami Rd; Montrose, CO 81401
www.mountainwestmuseum.com • Admission: $10/Adult

Ute Indian Museum • (970) 249-3098
17253 Chipeta Rd; Montrose, CO 81403

Mesa Verde Area

Hovenweep Nat'l Mon. • (970) 562-4282
McElmo Route; Cortez, CO 81321
www.nps.gov/hove • Entrance Fee: $6/Vehicle

Canyons of the Ancients Nat'l Mon.
27501 CO-184; Dolores, CO 81323
Admission: $3/Adult • (970) 882-5600
www.blm.gov/co/st/en/nm/canm.html

Canyon Trails Ranch • (970) 565-1499
13987 Road G; Cortez, CO 81321
www.canyontrailsranch.com

Cortez Cultural Center • (970) 565-1151
25 North Market St; Cortez, CO 81321
www.cortezculturalcenter.org

Crow Canyon Archaeological Center
23390 Road K; Cortez, CO 81321
www.crowcanyon.org • (970) 565-8975

Conquistador Golf Course • (970) 565-9208
2018 N Dolores Rd; Cortez, CO 81321

Lakeside Lanes • (970) 564-1450
290 Lakeside Dr; Cortez, CO 81321

Fiesta Theatre • (970) 565-9003
23 W Main St; Cortez, CO 81321

Southwest Adventure Guides • (970) 259-0370
Rock, ice, alpine, ski, avalanche, and backpack trips
PO Box 3242; Durango, CO 81302
www.mtnguide.net • Rates vary

Kling Mtn Guides • (970) 903-8349
Rock, ice, alpine, ski, avalanche, and backpack trips
1205 Camino Del Rio; Durango, CO 81301
www.klingmountainguides.com • Cost varies

Mild to Wild Rafting • (970) 247-4789
Rafting, Jeep, kayak, and train tours
50 Animas View Dr; Durango, CO 81301
www.mild2wildrafting.com

Durango & Silverton Train • (888) 872-4607
479 Main Ave; Durango, CO 81301
www.durangotrain.com • Rates: $59+/Adult

Beyond the Parks

Colorado State Capitol • (303) 866-2604
200 E Colfax Ave; Denver, CO 80203
www.colorado.gov • Free Tours

United States Mint • (303) 405-4761
320 W Colfax Ave; Denver, CO 80204
www.usmint.gov • Tours: Reservation req'd

Denver Museum Of Nature & Science
2001 Colorado Blvd; Denver, CO 80205
www.dmns.org • (303) 370-6000 • $12/Adult

Denver Zoo • (303) 376-4800
23rd Ave between Colorado Blvd & York St; Denver, CO
www.denverzoo.org • Admission: $13/Adult

Denver Botanic Gardens • (720) 865-3515
909 York St; Denver, CO 80206
www.botanicgardens.org • Admission: $12.50/Adult

Kirkland Museum of Fine & Decorative Art
1311 Pearl St; Denver, CO 80203 • (303) 832-8576
www.kirklandmuseum.org • Admission: $7/Adult

Denver Art Museum • (720) 865-5000
100 W 14th Ave Parkway; Denver, CO 80204
www.denverartmuseum.org • Admission: $13/Adult

The Denver Center for Performing Arts
1101 13th St; Denver, CO 80204
www.denvercenter.org • (303) 893-4100

Mayan Theatre • (303) 744-6799
110 Broadway; Denver, CO 80203

Observatory Park • (720) 913-0700
2930 E Warren Ave; Denver, CO 80210

Mile-Hi Skydiving Center • (303) 702-9911
229 Airport Rd, # 34G; Longmont, CO 80503
www.mile-hi-skydiving.com

Mount Evans Road • (303) 567-3000
Drive the highest paved road in America
Idaho Springs, CO 80452
www.mountevans.com • Entrance Fee: $10/Vehicle

Clear Creek Rafting • (303) 567-1000
350 Whitewater Rd; Idaho Springs, CO 80452
www.clearcreekrafting.com • Trips: $45+

Bob Culp Climbing School • (303) 444-0940
1335 B Broadway; Boulder, CO 80302
www.bobculp.com • Rates: $100+/Person

Colorado Wilderness Rides And
Guides • (720) 242-9828 & (970) 480-7780
4865 Darwin Court; Boulder, CO 80301 &
2625 Marys Lake Rd; Estes Park, CO 80517
www.coloradowildernessridesandguides.com

Apex Ex • (303) 731-6160
136 N Bryan Ave; Fort Collins, CO 80521
www.apexex.com • multi-sport outfitter

Garden of the Gods • (719) 634-6666
1805 N 30th St; Colorado Springs, CO 80904
www.gardenofgods.com • Free

Colorado Climbing Company • (719) 209-6649
Half-day ($55+) to multi-day climbing trips
Colorado Springs, CO • www.coclimbing.com

Cheyenne Mtn Zoo • (719) 475-9555
You actually get to feed the giraffes here
4250 Cheyenne Mtn Zoo Rd; Colorado Springs, CO 80906
www.cmzoo.org • Admission: $17.25/Adult

Pikes Peak Cog Railway • (719) 685-5401
515 Ruxton Ave; Manitou Springs, CO 80829
www.cograilway.com • Rates: $34/Adult

Lost Paddle Rafting • (866) 766-7238
1420 Royal Gorge Blvd; Cañon City, CO 81212
www.lostpaddlerafting.com • Trips: $42+

Royal Gorge Bridge and Park • (888) 333-5597
4218 County Rd, 3a; Cañon City, CO 81215
www.royalgorgebridge.com • Rates: $18.75/Adult

Royal Gorge Route Railroad • (719) 276-5314
401 Water St; Cañon City, CO 81212
www.royalgorgeroute.com • Rates: $33+/Adult

Bishop's Castle • (719) 485-3040
Man-made castle • May not be suitable for children
12705 CO-165; Wetmore, CO

Rocky Mtn Outdoor Center • (800) 255-5784
14825 US-285; Salida, CO 81201
www.rmoc.com • *multi-sport outfitter*

Cano's Castle
Castle built of scrap metal, beer cans, and hub caps
10th Ave and US-285; Antonito, CO

Breckenridge Ski Resort • (970) 453-5000
1599 Ski Hill Rd; Breckenridge, CO 80424
www.breckenridge.com • Life Ticket: $67/Adult

Performance Tours Rafting • (970) 453-0661
351 County Rd 500; Breckenridge, CO 80424
www.performancetours.com • Trips: $51+

Nova Guides • (719) 486-2656
Snowmobile tours ($215+) and rental
7088 US-24; Red Cliff, CO 81649
www.vailsnowmobiletours.com

American Adventure Exped. • (719) 395-2409
12844 US-24/285; Buena Vista, CO 81211
www.americanadventure.com • Trips: $49+

Buffalo Joe's Whitewater • (719) 395-8757
113 N Railroad Ave; Buena Vista, CO 81211
www.buffalojoe.com • Trips: $49+

Dvorak's Kayak & Rafting • (719) 539-6851
Kayak, rafting, fishing, and photography
17921 US-285; Nathrop, CO 81236
www.dvorakexpeditions.com

Aspen Ski Mountain • (970) 920-0751
601 E Dean St; Aspen, CO 81611
www.aspensnowmass.com • Lift Ticket: $86+/Adult

Aspen Expeditions • (970) 925-7625
Backcountry, avalanche, and ice climbing trips
0115 Boomerang Rd, #5201A; Aspen, CO 81611
www.aspenexpeditions.com

Doc Holliday's Grave
Cemetery accessible by a short trail
12th St; Glenwood Springs, CO

Winter Park Resort • (970) 726-5514
150 Alpenglow Way; Winter Park, CO 80482
www.winterparkresort.com • Lift ticket: $63/Adult

Steamboat Ski & Resort • (800) 379-7425
2305 Mt Werner Ci; Steamboat Springs, CO 80487
www.steamboat.com

Dinosaur Nat'l Mon. • (970) 374-3000
4545 E US-40; Dinosaur, CO 81610
www.nps.gov/dino • Entrance Fee: $10/Vehicle

Chicks Climbing • (970) 626-4424
163 County Rd, 12 A; Ridgway, CO 81432
www.chickswithpicks.net • *Ice & Rock Clinics*

Skyward Mountaineering • (970) 209-2985
Ice & rock climbing, and backcountry trips
PO Box 323; Ridgway, CO 81432
www.skywardmountaineering.com

Crested Butte Mtn Guides • (970) 349-5430
Offers a multitude of backcountry adventures
PO Box 1718; Crested Butte, CO 81224
www.crestedbutteguides.com

Mtn Bike Hall of Fame • (970) 349-6817
331 Elk Ave; Crested Butte, CO 81224
www.mtnbikehalloffame.com • Admission: $3

Colorado Nat'l Monument • (970) 858-3617
1750 Rimrock Dr; Fruita, Colorado 81521
www.nps.gov/colm • Entrance Fee: $10/Vehicle

San Juan Mtn Guides • (970) 325-4925
Ice, rock, ski, and mountain courses
PO Box 1214; Ouray, CO 81427
www.ourayclimbing.com

Telluride Outside • (970) 728-3895
Fishing, 4WD, raft, MTB, and photo tours
121 W Colorado Ave; Telluride, CO 81435
www.tellurideoutside.com

Telluride • (970) 728-6900
565 Mtn Village Blvd; Telluride, CO 81435
www.tellurideskiresort.com

Mileage Between Sites

	Denver	Rocky Mtn NP (Estes Park)	Colorado Springs	Great Sand Dunes NP (Visitor Center)	Black Canyon of the Gunnison NP	Durango	Mesa Verde NP (Far View)
Rocky Mtn NP (Estes Park)	66						
Colorado Springs	71	133					
Great Sand Dunes NP (Visitor Center)	244	307	173				
Black Canyon of the Gunnison NP	263	352	230	191			
Durango	337	384	314	166	122		
Mesa Verde NP (Far View)	386	433	363	215	171	51	
Arches NP/Moab	354	394	399	322	188	158	140

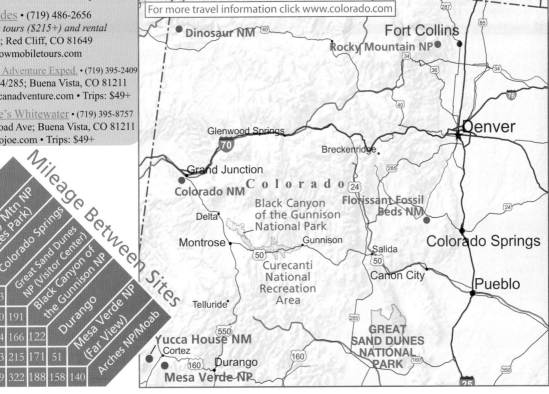

For more travel information click www.colorado.com

Delicate Arch

PO Box 907
Moab, UT 84532
Phone: (435) 719-2299
Website: www.nps.gov/arch

Established: November 12, 1971
April 12, 1929 (National Monument)
Size: 76,359 Acres
Annual Visitors: 1 Million
Peak Season: Spring & Fall

Activities: Hiking, Backpacking,
Rock Climbing, Biking, Stargazing,
Photography, and Guided Tours

Campgrounds: Devils Garden*
Fee: $20/night
Backcountry Camping: Permitted
with a Backcountry Use Permit
Lodging: None

Park Hours: All day, every day
Entrance Fee: $10 • Vehicle
$5 • Individual (foot, bike, etc.)

*Reservations are available by
calling (877) 444-6777 or clicking
www.recreation.gov

Arches - Utah

The only arches you see on a typical family vacation are golden, raised high above the ground, advertising the ubiquitous fast-food chain. But in southeast Utah, high atop the Colorado Plateau, is a collection of more than 2,500 natural sandstone arches, colored striking shades of pink, orange, and red. Standing tall, they frame the surrounding mountains. These natural advertisements are just as good at capturing the attention of passersby, but they have nothing to sell. In fact, all they do is give. They give inspiration to the many guests who come to admire Mother Nature's patient handiwork.

Patient is a gross understatement; **these fragile features began forming more than 300 million years ago**. First a massive sea covering the region evaporated, depositing a salt bed thousands of feet thick in some places. During the **Uncompahgre Uplift**, rivers and streams buried the salt beds with debris and sediment. Desert conditions of the early Jurassic period led a layer of Navajo sandstone to be covered by a layer of **Entrada sandstone** (the substrate of most arches). But before sandstone could be sculpted by wind, water, and ice it was buried by another 5,000 feet of sediment. The weight of material caused lower salt beds to heat up and liquefy. Layers of rock became unstable. Faulting occurred and plumes of less dense liquefied salt penetrated the upper layers of rock forming salt domes. Domes provided a curve to sections of sandstone. Years of erosion wore away the surface sediment, eventually exposing the underlying sandstone. Water seeped into cracks in its surface, gradually enlarging them until walls of sandstone called fins were left, isolated from one another. As wind and water continued to work on these fins, the salt bed layer wore away faster than sandstone. Water, collected in joints and fissures, freezing and expanding it caused chunks of rock to flake and crumble. Many fins collapsed into piles of rubble. Others formed magnificent arches that continue to be sculpted by wind, water, and ice. But these too will concede to erosion and gravity. **Since 1970, 43 arches have collapsed within the park**.

The **first inhabitants** weren't all that interested in seeing sandstone arches. More than 10,000 years ago nomadic people came to the region hunting and gathering. Until 700 years ago **Fremont People** and **Ancestral Puebloans** lived here, growing crops of maize, beans, and squash. Just as they picked up and moved south **Paiute and Ute Indians** moved in. **Spanish missionaries** encountered natives in the late 1700s while searching for a route between Santa Fe and Los Angeles. In 1855 European Americans settled in the region. **Mormons** established Elk Mountain Mission, but difficult farming and disputes with Native Americans led them to abandon their settlements. By the 1880s, **ranchers**, **farmers**, and **prospectors** were trickling into the area. **John Wesley Wolfe**, a Civil War veteran, was among them. He built a small ranch along Salt Wash with his son in 1898, which is still preserved in its original location near present-day Delicate Arch Trailhead.

It wasn't until 1911 that locals began to understand the recreational value of the area. **Loren "Bish" Taylor**, a local newspaperman, and **John "Doc" Williams**, Moab's first doctor frequented the area, marveling at these sandstone formations. Bish wrote about the natural wonders just north of Moab. Eventually, publicity grew to the point that **Denver and Rio Grande Western Railroad** and the federal government took notice. Both parties were impressed, and in 1929 **President Hoover** signed legislation creating Arches National Monument. In 1971, Congress redesignated it as a national park. It's an eroded landscape protected from man, but not from nature, and the landscapes are constantly changing. Changes unnoticed by the average visitor. Visitors drawn to and inspired by grand natural landmarks millions of years in the making.

Did you know?

▶ To be considered an arch, the rock's opening must measure at least three feet (in any direction).

Landscape Arch

When to Go

Arches is open all day every day, but the temperate weather of spring and fall attracts most visitors. The visitor center is open every day except Christmas. Its operating hours are 7:30am to 6:30pm from April through October. Hours are shortened to 8am to 4:30pm from November through March. Arches is one of the most spectacularly unique parks. If you'd like to return home with stunning images plan on waking up before the sun rises or remaining in the park until sunset at least a time or two.

Transportation & Airports

Public transportation does not provide service to or around the park. The closest large commercial airport is Salt Lake City International (SLC), located 237 miles to the northwest. There are two regional airports nearby. Grand Junction Regional (GJT) is 114 miles to the northeast. Green River Municipal (RVR) is 55 miles to the northwest.

Directions

Arches is located in southeastern Utah, just 28 miles south of I-70 between Green River, UT and Grand Junction, CO. To reach the park from I-70, take Exit 182 for US-191 South toward Crescent Jct/Moab. Continue south on US-191 for approximately 27 miles where you will see the visitor center to the east and signs for the entrance.

Visitors arriving from the southwest (Mesa Verde National Park • page 354) should take US-160 west. At Cortez, turn right onto US-491 North/North Broadway. Continue for 60 miles before turning right at US-191 North. Drive another 60 miles and you will pass through Moab to the park entrance and visitor center. You will also pass the entrance to Canyonlands National Park's Needles Entrance (page 376).

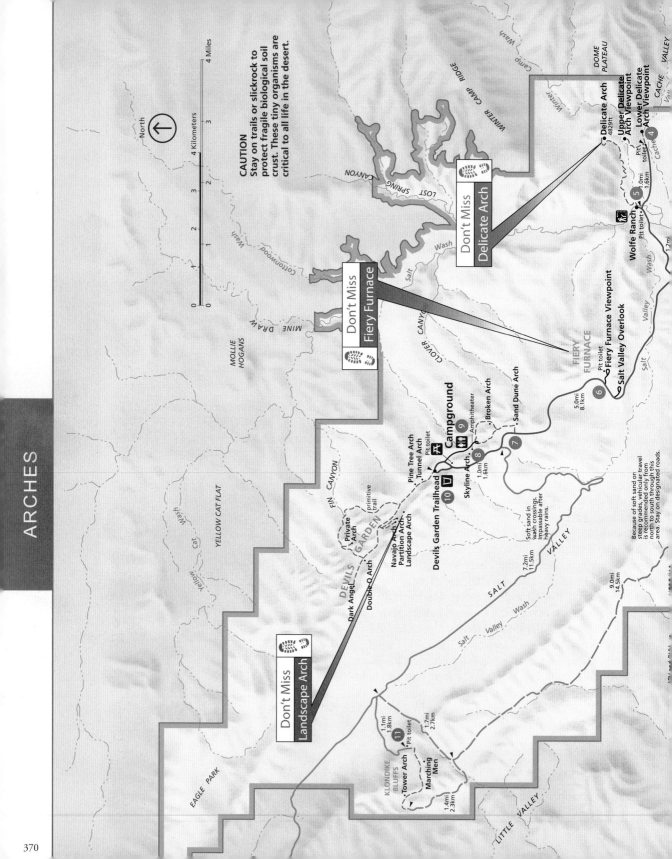

ARCHES

CAUTION
Stay on trails or slickrock to
protect fragile biological soil
crust. These tiny organisms are
critical to all life in the desert.

4 Miles
4 Kilometers
North

Don't Miss
Fiery Furnace

Don't Miss
Delicate Arch

Don't Miss
Landscape Arch

WINTER CAMP RIDGE
Camp Wash
DOME PLATEAU
CACHE VALLEY

LOST SPRING CANYON
Delicate Arch
4829ft
Upper Delicate
Arch Viewpoint
Lower Delicate
Arch Viewpoint
Pit toilet 1.0mi 1.6km
4
Wolfe Ranch
Pit toilet
1.2mi

Salt Wash

Cottonwood Wash

MOLLIE HOGANS

MINE DRAW

FIERY FURNACE
Pit toilet
Fiery Furnace Viewpoint
Salt Valley Overlook
5.0mi 8.1km
6

CLOVER CANYON

FIN CANYON

YELLOW CAT FLAT

Yellow Cat Wash

DEVILS GARDEN
Private Arch
Dark Angel Arch
Double O Arch
Navajo Arch
Partition Arch
Landscape Arch
primitive trail
Devils Garden Trailhead
10
Pine Tree Arch
Tunnel Arch
Skyline Arch
8
1.0mi 1.6km
Campground
9
Pit toilet
Amphitheater
Broken Arch
Sand Dune Arch
7

Soft sand in
wash crossings.
Impassable after
heavy rains.

SALT VALLEY

7.2mi 11.5km

Salt Valley Wash

9.0mi 14.5km

Because of soft sand on
steep grades, vehicular travel
is recommended only from
north to south through this
area. Stay on designated roads.

EAGLE PARK

KLONDIKE BLUFFS
Tower Arch
Marching Men
1.1mi 1.8km
11
Pit toilet
1.7mi 2.7km
1.4mi 2.3km

LITTLE VALLEY

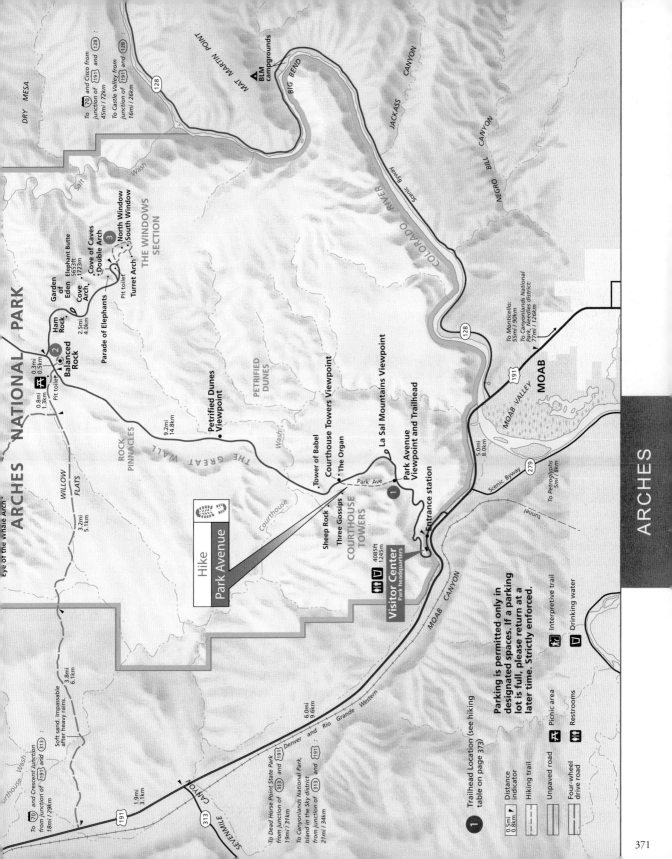

ARCHES

ARCHES NATIONAL PARK

Eye of the Whale Arch

DRY MESA

MAT MARTIN POINT

BLM campgrounds

BIG BEND

JACKASS CANYON

NEGRO BILL CANYON

COLORADO RIVER Scenic Byway

To 70 and Cisco from junction of 191 and 128
45mi / 72km

To Castle Valley from junction of 191 and 128
16mi / 26km

128

128

Garden of Eden
Elephant Butte 5653ft / 1723m
Cove of Caves
Double Arch
Cove Arch
Turret Arch
North Window
South Window

THE WINDOWS SECTION

Pit toilet
Ham Rock
2.5mi / 4.0km
Parade of Elephants

Balanced Rock
0.3mi / 0.5km

Pit toilet
0.8mi / 1.3km

PETRIFIED DUNES

Petrified Dunes Viewpoint
9.2mi / 14.8km

ROCK PINNACLES

THE GREAT WALL

WILLOW FLATS
3.2mi / 5.1km

Wash

Salt Wash

To 70 and Crescent Junction from junction of 191 and 313
18mi / 29km

Soft sand. Impassable after heavy rains.
3.8mi / 6.1km

Tower of Babel
The Organ
Courthouse Towers Viewpoint
La Sal Mountains Viewpoint

Park Avenue Viewpoint and Trailhead

Sheep Rock
Three Gossips
COURTHOUSE TOWERS
4085ft / 1245m

Park Ave

Courthouse Wash

Hike
Park Avenue

Entrance station

128

To Monticello:
55mi / 90km
To Canyonlands National Park, Needles district
77mi / 126km

191

MOAB

MOAB VALLEY

279

Scenic Byway

5.0mi / 8.0km

To Petroglyphs
5mi / 8km

Tunnel

MOAB CANYON

Visitor Center
Park headquarters

Parking is permitted only in designated spaces. If a parking lot is full, please return at a later time. Strictly enforced.

6.0mi / 9.6km

Denver and Rio Grande Western

To Dead Horse Point State Park from junction of 191 and 313
19mi / 31km

To Canyonlands National Park, Island in the Sky district from junction of 313 and 191
21mi / 34km

1.9mi / 3.1km

191

313

SEVENMILE CANYON

Courthouse Wash

1 Trailhead Location (see hiking table on page 373)

0.5mi / 0.8km Distance indicator

Hiking trail

Unpaved road

Four-wheel drive road

Interpretive trail

Drinking water

Picnic area

Restrooms

371

 # Camping

Devils Garden is Arches' only designated campground. It's located at the end of the park road, 18 miles from the entrance. Flush toilets and potable water are available. There are no showers or laundry. The camp has 50 sites, all of which are available for reservation from March through October. Sites must be reserved (877.444.6777, www.recreation.gov) at least four days in advance. They are available on a first-come, first-served basis for the remainder of the year. Rates are $20 per night with an additional $9 booking fee for reservations.

Two group sites are available for groups of 11 or more people. They must be reserved (877.444.6777, www.recreation.gov) at a cost of $3 per person per night with a minimum fee of $33 per night.

The campground fills up frequently, especially on spring and fall weekends. There are several **Bureau of Land Management campgrounds** nearby (page 449). Backpackers are also welcome to camp in the backcountry with a **free permit** (available at the visitor center).

 # Backpacking

Don't let the park's small size fool you. You can only get a few miles away from paved roads and developed areas, but there's more than enough land to escape the crowds and find the perfect location for a night under the stars. There are no designated trails or campsites in the backcountry, and there are no reliable sources of water.

The park's small size and abundance of unique rock formations may lead you to believe that navigating the wilderness will be a snap. Do not make this assumption. In reality, the terrain is repetitive, with miles and miles of sandstone decorated with shrubs and the occasional tumbling tumbleweed, so bring a good map and know how to use it. Seasoned hikers may be able to navigate their way through the park's backcountry by the 2,500 arches, but even many of them are indistinguishable to the untrained eye. **Any overnight stay in the backcountry requires a free permit (available at the visitor center).**

 # Hiking

Seeing **Delicate Arch** on all of those Utah license plates gives an idea of the arch's beauty, but a little paint on a sheet of metal hardly does it justice. To truly appreciate the magnificence of Utah's natural icon you need to hike to its base. Pose with it. Marvel its rocky delicateness. Even without the arch providing the crescendo, this would be one of the park's must-hike trails. It's a moderately difficult 3-mile (roundtrip) fun-filled adventure. You begin near **Wolf's Ranch** where you'll cross a small wash and traverse a massive slab of unmarked slickrock. Don't worry about losing the trail, it would take considerable effort to make a wrong turn. And on most days you can simply follow the crowd. After crossing the slickrock, the trail narrows winding its way along an exposed ledge to the rim of a large natural bowl. Your first glimpse over the rim and there it is, Delicate Arch standing proud, an anomaly that wind and water have yet to wear away. Don't expect to enjoy this experience on your own. The bowl is usually busy. Hikers pose with the arch for photographs, or simply stare in admiration. A person in good physical condition can make the hike in an hour, but allow at least two hours to enjoy the view. **Dusk is the best time to visit Delicate Arch.** As the sun sets it gives off a brilliant orange glow. Also, be aware that parking is limited. Parking is allowed alongside the road, just be sure to pull all the way off to the side. Bring plenty of water (especially in summer).

The other "must-do" activity is the **ranger-guided hike through the Fiery Furnace.** As its name implies, it gets hot here in summer. Individuals are required to carry at least one quart of water in a backpack (to free your hands to navigate sandstone obstacles). Tours of Fiery Furnace are offered twice each day from March through October. It's a 3 hour (2 mile), moderately difficult hike through a sandstone maze, where a fair amount of scrambling is required. Participants must be able to squeeze through narrow spaces, pull themselves over rocks, and climb reasonably steep rock faces. Good hiking shoes are required. The tour costs $10 per Adult and $5 per child (ages 7–12). Children 6 and under are free, but the hike is not recommended for kids 5 and under. It is extremely popular and space is rarely available the day of the hike. Reservations can be made in advance by calling (877) 444-6777 or clicking www.recreation.gov. Visitors can explore Fiery Furnace on their own by obtaining a permit ($3/person) from the visitor center.

Double O Arch © Chris Willis (www.snapchris.com)

If it's your first time in the Fiery Furnace, the park suggests you join one of the ranger guided tours (without an experienced guide you're likely to miss most of the highlights). There are several good hiking alternatives for those unable to secure a spot on a Fiery Furnace Tour. **Devils Garden** (7.2-miles including all spur trails to rock formations) is the park's longest maintained trail. The loop passes **Landscape Arch**, **Partition Arch**, **Navajo Arch**, **Double O Arch**, **Dark Angel**, and **Private Arch**. Additional trails begin at the campground and in the Windows Area. See the table below for a complete list.

Arches Hiking Trails

	Trail Name	Trailhead (# on map)	Length	Notes (Roundtrip distances unless noted otherwise)
In Order of Appearance Along Main Park Rd	Park Avenue - 👍	Park Avenue Parking Area (1)	1.0 mile	One-way trail between Park Ave and Courthouse Towers
	Balanced Rock	Balanced Rock Parking Area (2)	0.3 mile	Short walk around the base of balanced rock
	Double Arch	Double Arch Parking Area (3)	0.5 mile	Short walk to a wonderful arch
	The Windows	The Windows Parking Area (3)	1.0 mile	Views through two giant windows and Turret Arch
	Delicate Arch Viewpoint	Delicate Arch Viewpoint (4)	300 feet	Cannot reach the base of Delicate Arch
	Delicate Arch - 👍	Wolf Ranch Parking Area (5)	3.0 miles	Moderately strenuous hike to the arch's base
	Fiery Furnace - 👍	Fiery Furnace Parking Area (6)	Varies	Ranger Guided Tour (fee, reservations available)
	Sand Dune Arch	Sand Dune Arch Parking Area (7)	0.3 mile	Short and easy, also accessible from campground
	Broken Arch - 👍	Sand Dune Arch Parking Area (7)	1.3 miles	Also accessible from Devils Garden Campground
	Skyline Arch - 👍	Skyline Arch Parking Area (8)	0.4 mile	Short but rocky hike across grassland
	Landscape Arch - 👍	Devils Garden Campground (9)	1.6 miles	Largest arch in the park • 306-ft base to base
	Double O Arch	Devils Garden Trailhead (10)	4.2 miles	Quite strenuous • Follows Devils Garden Trail
	Devils Garden - 👍	Devils Garden Trailhead (10)	7.2 miles	The complete Devils Garden Trail and all its spurs
	Tower Arch	Klondike Bluffs Parking Area, via Salt Valley Road (11)	3.4 miles	Remote area of the park accessed via Salt Valley Road or 4WD road • Moderately strenuous

Rappelling Owl Rock

Photography

Arches is one of the most photogenic parks in the United States. At dusk and dawn, sandstone illuminated by soft light glows a beautiful orange and deep blue skies provide perfect contrast. For the best photographs avoid afternoon hours when harsh light drowns out the landscape and causes subjects to squint. **Suggestions for early morning photography include:** Turret Arch, Double Arch, Landscape Arch, and Double O Arch. **In the evening try:** Delicate Arch, Fiery Furnace, Skyline Arch, Balanced Rock, and Tower Arch.

Best of Arches

Hikes: **Delicate Arch**
 Runner-up: Fiery Furnace
 2nd Runner-up: Park Avenue
 3rd Runner-up: Devil's Garden

For Kids: Arches is a great park for families. Most trails are short and relatively easy (**even the hike to Delicate Arch is kid-friendly**), and the arches are pretty cool, too. Children, (ages 6–12) are invited to take part in the **Junior Ranger Program**. It helps encourage children to explore the park in an educational yet entertaining manner. Activity booklets are available for free from the visitor center. Your child will be rewarded with a badge and signed certificate for completing five or more exercises.

Ranger Programs: **Fiery Furnace Walks** (page 372) are the crown jewel of Arches' ranger-led programs, but additional interpretive programs and activities are offered throughout the summer. Find a current schedule of events in the park's publication, *Arches Visitor Guide* (available at the park website, entrance station, or visitor center).

Flora & Fauna: At first sight Utah's high desert isn't exactly teeming with life. It's very uncommon to see large mammals grazing. Trees are few and far apart. Upon closer inspection, you may spot a skittish lizard between the cracks in a rock or a bird flying high above the desert monuments. Astute visitors will notice cacti, yuccas, and mosses that are built to withstand long periods of drought. Spacing between shrubs depends on the amount of seasonal rain. Most diversity is due to the Colorado River, which flows

Other Activities

Biking: Driving the roadways, viewing the scenery from overlooks and observation points, and taking an occasional short hike is satisfying, but there's much more to do at Arches. **Cyclists are allowed on all park roads**. The main park road is suitable (but often busy) for road cyclists. There isn't any singletrack, but Salt Valley and Willow Springs Roads are ideal for mountain biking. **If it's singletrack you desire, head down US-191 to Moab, the Mecca of Mountain Biking**.

Rock Climbing is another popular activity. Climbers are not required to register, but there are several restrictions and closures that you must be aware of before climbing. Call (435.719.2299) or stop by the visitor center for information.

Stargazing, whether from your campsite or on a ranger program, is spectacular thanks to clear skies, minimal air pollution, and few city lights.

Several **outfitters** are authorized to guide groups on **adventure treks** through the park. For a complete list including contact information and rates please refer to page 451.

ARCHES

along the park's southeastern boundary. Here, and along Courthouse Wash, you'll find cottonwoods and willows.

<u>Pets:</u> Pets are permitted at overlooks, pullouts, paved roadways, parking lots, and developed campgrounds, but must be kept on a leash no more than six feet in length at all times. They are prohibited from all hiking trails and the backcountry. Pets can be boarded at Karen's Canine Campground (435.259.7922), Moab Vet Clinic (435.259.8710), or Desert Doggie Daycare (435.259.4841).

<u>Accessibility:</u> Most of Arches is inaccessible to wheelchair users, but the visitor center, Park Avenue and Delicate Arch Viewpoints, and all restrooms are accessible. Devils Garden Campground has one accessible campsite.

<u>Weather:</u> Arches is located in southeast Utah's high desert. The climate is extremely dry, receiving on average less than 10 inches of precipitation each year. Summers are hot, winters are cold, and the seasons in between are comfortable. Another characteristic of the high desert is extreme weather variation. A single day's temperature can vary more than 40°F. Summer highs often reach into the 100s°F, but evenings are almost always comfortable with average lows in the 60s°F. During winter, average highs are in the 40s°F with lows averaging around 25°F. Spring and fall tend to be the most popular seasons, when average daytime highs range from the 60s–80s°F.

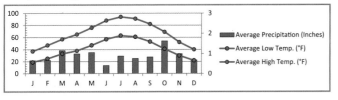

Vacation Planner

Arches is relatively small and can be extremely busy during spring and fall. At these times campers must reserve a site at **Devils Garden**. If you don't, plan on leaving the park to camp at one of the nearby Bureau of Land Management (BLM) campgrounds (page 449). Small size also makes for a very manageable day-trip. Provided below is a one-day itinerary to jump-start your Arches vacation planning. Nearby dining, grocery stores, lodging, festivals, and attractions are listed on pages 448–453.

Day 1

Begin your trip at the **visitor center**. **Fiery Furnace Tours** (page 372) are highly recommended. They are offered twice daily from mid-March through October, but each tour is limited to just 15 guests. If you didn't make

Fiery Furnace

Park Avenue

reservations already, ask if there is any available space. Browse the exhibits and bookstore, and then return to your car. Stop at **Park Avenue** (page 373). If you arrange a pick-up at Courthouse Towers it's a very casual downhill walk. It's also the most popular trail in the park. Continue driving along the main park road. View **Balanced Rock** on your right, and bypass Windows for now. If you have about 2 hours stop at **Wolf Ranch** to hike to **Delicate Arch** (page 372). Its base can only be reached via the hiking trail, and this is a really fun trek. The arch is particularly beautiful near dusk or dawn, so plan accordingly. You can also view the arch from at **Delicate Arch Viewpoint** (without having to hike). Return to the main park road and head north. Drive all the way to **Devils Garden Trailhead** at the road's end. Hike to **Landscape Arch** (complete the loop if time and attitudes permit). If you haven't seen too many arches already, stop at The **Windows** before you exit. It's another great sunset spot.

Confluence of the Colorado and Green Rivers

2282 SW Resource Blvd
Moab, Utah 84532
Phone: (435) 719-2313
Website: www.nps.gov/cany

Established: September 12, 1964
Size: 337,598 Acres
Annual Visitors: 435,000
Peak Season: Spring and Fall
Hiking Trails: 200+ Miles

Activities: Hiking, Backpacking*,
Stargazing, Paddling*, Horseback
Riding*, Biking, and Rock Climbing

Campgrounds: Willow Flat (Island in
the Sky) and Squaw Flat (Needles)
Fee: $10–15/night
Backcountry Camping: Permitted*

Park Hours: All day, every day
Entrance Fee: $10 • Vehicle
$5 • Individual (foot, bike, etc.)

*Must obtain a Backcountry Use Per-
mit (fee). Mountain biking and rock
climbing require a permit if spending
the night in the backcountry

Canyonlands - Utah

Canyonlands, as its name implies, is an intricate landscape of canyons
carved into the **Colorado Plateau**. Years of erosion have revealed
colorful layers of rock and formed buttes and mesas rising high above
the Colorado and Green Rivers. Their water continues to carry sediment from the canyon walls and floor all the way to the Pacific Ocean.
Controversial conservationist and author, **Edward Abbey**, described
the region best when he wrote that it's "the most weird wonderful, magical place on earth—there is nothing else like it anywhere."

He's absolutely right. Proof lies in the **geologic history** recorded in layers of rock, and stories passed down over the course of 10,000 years of
human inhabitance. Geology meets history at places like **Horseshoe
Canyon,** where pictographs and petroglyphs are etched into the canyon's walls. Places that weren't explored or studied until miners in
search of uranium fanned out across the labyrinthine canyons.

Scientists believe at one time the Colorado Plateau region was completely flat and near sea level before layers of sedimentary rock were
deposited. Millions of years ago a series of geologic events, including
uplifts and volcanic activity, caused the area to rise more than 5,000
feet, on average, above sea level. This increase in elevation set the
stage for the Colorado and Green Rivers to cut their way through soft
sedimentary rock, revealing its geologic history in the process. See for
yourself in the photograph above. Notice the horizontal bands of rock
in the spires and canyon walls. Red and white layers seem to alternate

as you move up the geologic column. Red is created from iron-rich deposits carried here by rivers from nearby mountains. White layers are mostly sand left behind from a shallow sea that covered the region millions of years ago. The park's **Upheaval Dome** is an anomaly in the geologic order. It's impossible to be sure what caused this crater-like formation, and scientists continue to debate its origin. Some believe it was formed by a meteorite, while others contend a giant salt-bubble, known as a salt dome, is responsible for the abnormality.

Humans have lived in the region for more than 10,000 years. Artifacts recovered in **Horseshoe Canyon** date back as early as 9000–7000 BC, when mammoths still roamed the American southwest. Pictographs and petroglyphs are also present in the canyon and most notably at its Great Gallery. **Ancestral Puebloans** and **Fremont People** left mud dwellings similar in style but much smaller in size than those found at **Mesa Verde National Park** (page 354). It is believed that large populations of Ancestral Puebloans moved into this area around 1200 AD from Mesa Verde, planting maize, beans, and squash, and raising turkeys and dogs.

Paiute and Ute Indians moved in during the tail end of the Ancestral Puebloans' presence. Neither culture did much exploration of the canyons. They simply used the land to hunt game and gather plants. **European Americans** arrived in the early 1800s. To **fur trappers** and **missionaries** the canyons were nothing more than an impediment to collecting pelts and reaching the west coast. By the 1880s local **ranchers** used the land as winter pasture. Cowboy camps, like the one visible at Cave Spring Trail in Needles, were established to help safeguard their livestock.

After WWII, the **uranium boom** hit southeast Utah. Prospectors filed claims all over present-day Canyonlands and nearly 1,000 miles of roads were built thanks to incentives offered by the Atomic Energy Commission. Very little uranium was found, but this new form of exploitation caused concern for **Bates Wilson**, Superintendent of Arches National Monument. He passionately advocated the creation of a national park, leading jeep tours through the area hoping to gain allies. Fatefully, **Secretary of the Interior Stewart Udall** joined a tour after peering into the canyons while flying above the Colorado Plateau. He lobbied for the park, and in 1964 legislation was passed and signed by **President Lyndon B. Johnson**.

Best of Canyonlands

Attraction: Mesa Arch
Runner-up: Island in the Sky
2nd Runner-up: The Maze

Activity: Raft Cataract Canyon
Runner-up: Bike/Drive White Rim Road
2nd Runner-up: Drive Shafer Trail (4WD)

Hike (Island in the Sky): Grand View Pt.
Runner-up: Mesa Arch
2nd Runner-up: Syncline Loop

Hike (Needles): Confluence Overlook
Runner-up: Lost Canyon
2nd Runner-up: Druid Arch

When to Go

Canyonlands National Park is open every day of the year. Needles and Island in the Sky Visitor Centers and Hans Flat Ranger Station, located in the Maze District, are open every day except for Christmas and New Year's Day. See page 386 for complete operating hours. Summers are hot and dry, winters are cold and snow poses a serious problem for hikers and drivers. Spring and fall bring temperate weather and the majority of visitors.

Transportation & Airports

Public transportation does not provide service to or around the park. Salt Lake City International (SLC) is the closest large commercial airport. Grand Junction Regional (GJT) and Green River Municipal (RVR) are nearby regional airports.

Directions

More than 94% of Canyonlands' visitors enter either Needles or Island in the Sky Districts. Access roads to these districts are located off US-191. Island in the Sky is reached via UT-313, 20 miles south of I-70 and 6.5 miles north of the entrance to Arches National Park (page 368). Needles District is accessed via UT-212, which is 50 miles south of UT-313. From US-191 it is roughly 40 miles to the end of the park road at Needles and Island in the Sky.

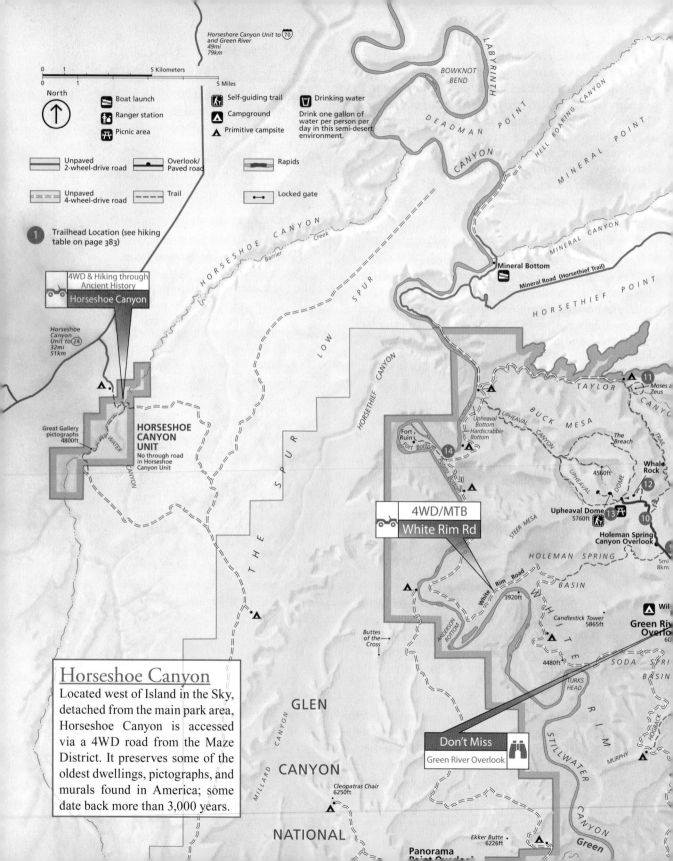

Horseshoe Canyon

Located west of Island in the Sky, detached from the main park area, Horseshoe Canyon is accessed via a 4WD road from the Maze District. It preserves some of the oldest dwellings, pictographs, and murals found in America; some date back more than 3,000 years.

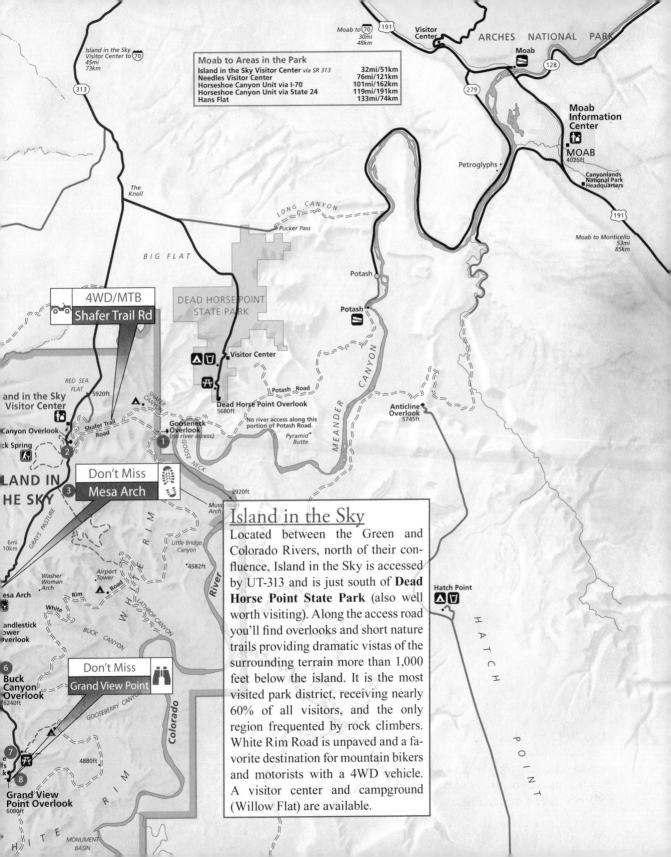

Moab to Areas in the Park

Island in the Sky Visitor Center *via SR 313*	32mi/51km
Needles Visitor Center	76mi/121km
Horseshoe Canyon Unit via I-70	101mi/162km
Horseshoe Canyon Unit via State 24	119mi/191km
Hans Flat	133mi/74km

Island in the Sky

Located between the Green and Colorado Rivers, north of their confluence, Island in the Sky is accessed by UT-313 and is just south of **Dead Horse Point State Park** (also well worth visiting). Along the access road you'll find overlooks and short nature trails providing dramatic vistas of the surrounding terrain more than 1,000 feet below the island. It is the most visited park district, receiving nearly 60% of all visitors, and the only region frequented by rock climbers. White Rim Road is unpaved and a favorite destination for mountain bikers and motorists with a 4WD vehicle. A visitor center and campground (Willow Flat) are available.

4WD/MTB
Shafer Trail Rd

Don't Miss
Mesa Arch

Don't Miss
Grand View Point

ARCHES NATIONAL PARK

Moab to 70
30mi
48km

Visitor Center

Moab

Moab Information Center

MOAB
4025ft

Canyonlands National Park Headquarters

Petroglyphs

Moab to Monticello
53mi
85km

Island in the Sky Visitor Center to 70
45mi
73km

The Knoll

LONG CANYON

Pucker Pass

BIG FLAT

DEAD HORSE POINT STATE PARK

Potash

Potash

Visitor Center

Potash Road

Dead Horse Point Overlook
5680ft

No river access along this portion of Potash Road.

Anticline Overlook
5745ft

Pyramid Butte

MEANDER CANYON

RED SEA FLAT
5920ft

and in the Sky Visitor Center

Canyon Overlook

ck Spring

ISLAND IN THE SKY

Shafer Trail Road

SHAFER CANYON

Gooseneck Overlook
(no river access)

GOOSE NECK

3920ft

Mussleman Arch

6mi
10km

GRAY'S PASTURE

WHITE RIM

Little Bridge Canyon

4582ft

River

Washer Woman Arch

Airport Tower

esa Arch

Rim Road

White

LATHROP CANYON

Colorado River

andlestick ower verlook

BUCK CANYON

Buck Canyon Overlook
6240ft

GOOSEBERRY CANYON

Hatch Point

HATCH POINT

Grand View Point Overlook
6080ft

WHITE RIM

MONUMENT BASIN

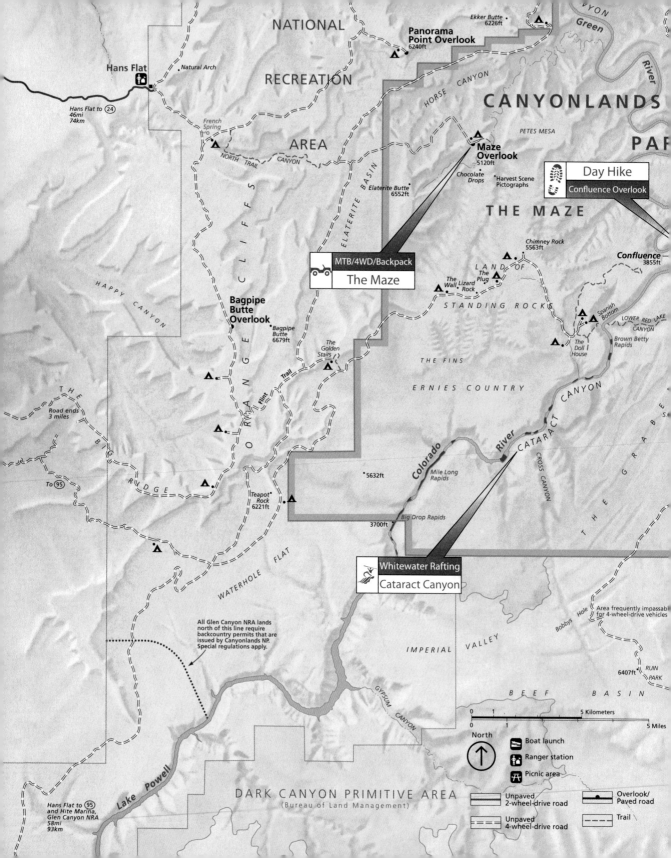

NATIONAL

RECREATION

AREA

Hans Flat

Natural Arch

Hans Flat to (24)
46mi
74km

French Spring

NORTH TRAIL CANYON

ELATERITE BASIN

Elaterite Butte
6552ft

O R A N G E   C L I F F S

Bagpipe Butte Overlook

Bagpipe Butte
6679ft

The Golden Stairs

HAPPY CANYON

Flint Trail

T H E   B I G

Road ends 3 miles

To (95)

R I D G E

Teapot Rock
6221ft

WATERHOLE FLAT

Panorama Point Overlook
6240ft

Ekker Butte
6226ft

Green River

HORSE CANYON

CANYONLANDS

PETES MESA

Maze Overlook
5120ft

Chocolate Drops

Harvest Scene Pictographs

P A R

┌─────────────────────────┐
│ 👣 **Day Hike**   │
│   Confluence Overlook │
└─────────────────────────┘

THE MAZE

Chimney Rock
5563ft

┌──────────────────────────────┐
│ 🚙 MTB/4WD/Backpack   │
│   **The Maze**   │
└──────────────────────────────┘

L A N D   O F
The Plug

The Wall *Lizard Rock*

Confluence
3855ft

Spanish Bottom

S T A N D I N G   R O C K S

LOWER RED LAKE CANYON

The Doll House

Brown Betty Rapids

THE FINS

E R N I E S   C O U N T R Y

C A T A R A C T   C A N Y O N

T H E   G R A B E N S

5632ft

Colorado

Mile Long Rapids

River

CROSS CANYON

Big Drop Rapids

3700ft

┌──────────────────────────────┐
│ 🚣 Whitewater Rafting   │
│   **Cataract Canyon**   │
└──────────────────────────────┘

*Area frequently impassabl[e]
for 4-wheel-drive vehicles*

*All Glen Canyon NRA lands
north of this line require
backcountry permits that are
issued by Canyonlands NP.
Special regulations apply.*

I M P E R I A L   V A L L E Y

Bobbys Hole

6407ft

RUIN PARK

B E E F   B A S I N

GYPSUM CANYON

North

↑

0 1 5 Kilometers
0 1 5 Miles

🚤 Boat launch
🏠 Ranger station
🏕 Picnic area

Lake Powell

Hans Flat to (95)
*and Hite Marina,
Glen Canyon NRA
58mi
93km*

D A R K   C A N Y O N   P R I M I T I V E   A R E A
(Bureau of Land Management)

━━━━ Unpaved 2-wheel-drive road

┅┅┅┅ Unpaved 4-wheel-drive road

●━━━ Overlook/Paved road

┈┈┈┈ Trail

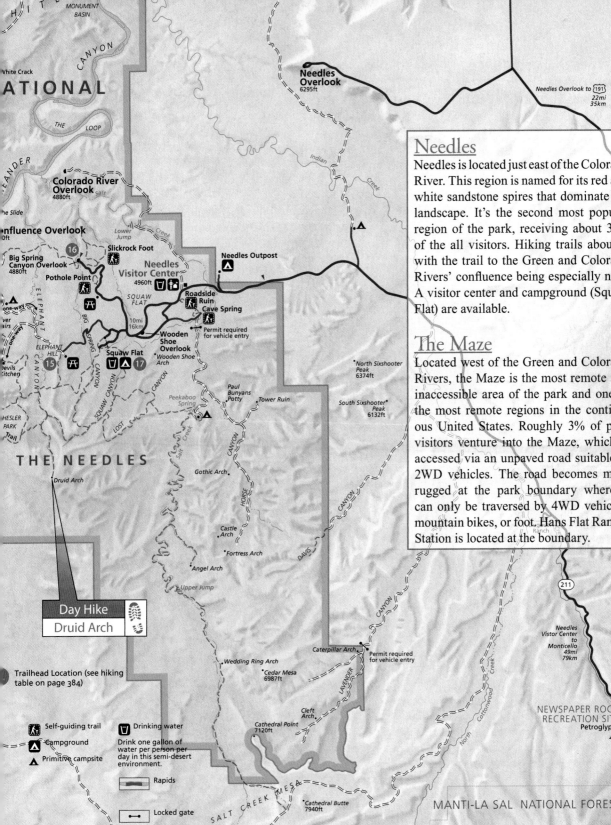

Needles

Needles is located just east of the Colorado River. This region is named for its red and white sandstone spires that dominate the landscape. It's the second most popular region of the park, receiving about 35% of the all visitors. Hiking trails abound, with the trail to the Green and Colorado Rivers' confluence being especially nice. A visitor center and campground (Squaw Flat) are available.

The Maze

Located west of the Green and Colorado Rivers, the Maze is the most remote and inaccessible area of the park and one of the most remote regions in the contiguous United States. Roughly 3% of park visitors venture into the Maze, which is accessed via an unpaved road suitable to 2WD vehicles. The road becomes more rugged at the park boundary where it can only be traversed by 4WD vehicles, mountain bikes, or foot. Hans Flat Ranger Station is located at the boundary.

Needles Overlook
6295ft

Needles Overlook to [191]
22mi
35km

MONUMENT BASIN

WHITE CANYON

White Crack

ATIONAL

THE LOOP

Colorado River Overlook
4880ft

the Slide

nfluence Overlook
0ft

Big Spring Canyon Overlook
4880ft

Pothole Point

Lower Jump

Slickrock Foot

Needles Visitor Center
4960ft

SQUAW FLAT

Roadside Ruin

Cave Spring

Wooden Shoe Overlook

Wooden Shoe Arch

Needles Outpost

Permit required for vehicle entry

one-way

ver airs

ELEPHANT CANYON

BIG SPRING CANYON

10mi
16km

ELEPHANT HILL

15

Squaw Flat

17

16

Devils itchen

SQUAW CANYON

LOST CANYON

Peekaboo Spring

Paul Bunyans Potty

Tower Ruin

North Sixshooter Peak
6374ft

South Sixshooter Peak
6132ft

HESLER PARK Trail

THE NEEDLES

Druid Arch

Gothic Arch

SALT CREEK

HORSE CANYON

Castle Arch

Fortress Arch

DAVIS CANYON

Angel Arch

Upper Jump

Day Hike
Druid Arch 🥾

Trailhead Location (see hiking table on page 384)

Self-guiding trail

Campground

Primitive campsite

Drinking water

Drink one gallon of water per person per day in this semi-desert environment.

Rapids

Locked gate

Caterpillar Arch

Permit required for vehicle entry

Wedding Ring Arch

Cedar Mesa
6987ft

Cleft Arch

Cathedral Point
7120ft

SALT CREEK MESA

Cathedral Butte
7940ft

Ranch

211

Needles Vistor Center to Monticello
49mi
79km

LAVENDER CANYON

North Cottonwood Creek

NEWSPAPER ROCK RECREATION SITE
Petroglyphs

MANTI-LA SAL NATIONAL FOREST

Camping

Canyonlands has two established campgrounds: **Willow Flat** at Island in the Sky and **Squaw Flat** at Needles. **Willow Flat** has 12 sites available on a first-come, first-served basis. Water is not available and the maximum RV length is 28 feet. Fees are $10 per night. **Squaw Flat** has 26 sites available on a first-come, first-served basis. Water is available. Fees are $15 per night. Both campgrounds fill to capacity almost every day from late March through June and again from early September to mid-October. Nearby camping locations include Arches National Park (page 372) and Bureau of Land Management (BLM) campgrounds in and around Moab (page 449). **Backpackers** are allowed to camp in the park's backcountry with a **free permit**.

Backcountry Permit

Several activities require a backcountry permit. **River permits** are issued from the Reservation Office in Moab; Island in the Sky Visitor Center issues river permits on weekends when the Reservation Office is closed. The reservation form and contact information are available at the park website. A river permit for Cataract Canyon costs $30. A flat water permit costs $20. Both permits are valid for groups up to 40 people.

All other backcountry permits are issued from their respective district visitor centers seven days a week. Permits can be reserved at least two weeks in advance by mail following the process outlined at the park website. Reservations are recommended for White Rim Road trips, Needles Backpacking trips, and Needles Group Camping during peak season. All backcountry permits require a fee to offset administrative and processing costs incurred by the park. Backpackers must pay $15/permit. Each permit is good for 7 people at Island in the Sky and Needles Districts and 5 people at the Maze. 4WD and Mountain Bike Permits cost $30 and are good for up to 3 vehicles. 4WD day use at Needles costs $5/permit. A permit for front-country group camping at Needles costs $15.

Hiking

Looking at Island in the Sky's labyrinth of eroded canyons from above may lead you to believe it is utterly impassable. Water found its way across this arid plateau as it carved these canyons, as did park employees, ranchers, prospectors, and ancient inhabitants who spent decades blazing paths across a seemingly impenetrable landscape. Many of their trails are still used today. The park's most popular trails are well maintained, marked by cairns, and have signposts at intersections. The trails are good, but no reliable water sources exist, so be sure to pack enough for the duration of your hike. One of the most popular trails at Island in the Sky is the easy 0.5-mile loop to **Mesa Arch**. Its views warrant the popularity. The arch frames distant canyons for unsurpassed photo opportunities (especially at sunrise). A great place to hike into a canyon is **Syncline Loop Trail**. It's short enough (8.3 miles) to complete in a day, but you can also turn it into an overnighter thanks to a few spur trails.

Needles District, located on the opposite side of the Colorado River, has equally exciting hiking opportunities. **Confluence Overlook Trail** is one of the best, a 10-mile (roundtrip) trek that leads in and out of Big Spring Canyon, across Elephant Canyon, before joining a 4WD road. Much of the scenery looks similar and it is possible to lose your way, so look closely for cairns marking the trail. The 4WD road leads to a parking area with a vault toilet. From here you make the final push to the point where sheer canyon walls and the waters of the Green and Colorado Rivers that carved them converge. The hike to **Druid Arch** is another exceptional journey. You trudge in and out of canyons, crossing several of the area's hiking trails before Druid Arch stands in front of you at the its end. From this point you can scramble across slickrock for a closer view or return to the trailhead the same way you came.

If you prefer things that are a little more extreme, you'll enjoy **the Maze district**, where the average visitor spends three days poking around the extensive network of canyons. A 25-foot length of rope is useful (if not essential) to raise and lower your pack, and a good topographical map is indispensable in the Maze, where side canyons can be difficult to identify and getting lost is easy (as the name implies).

Green River Overlook - Island in the Sky

CANYONLANDS

Canyonlands Hiking Trails

	Trail Name	Trailhead (# on map)	Length	Difficulty/Notes (Roundtrip distances)
	Gooseneck Overlook	NE corner on White Rim Rd (1)	1.0 mile	Easy • Views of the Colorado River
	Neck Spring	Main Park Road (MPR) near entrance (2)	5.8 miles	Moderate loop • Ranching evidence and island views
	Lathrop	MPR • South of Neck Spring (3)	22.0 miles	Strenuous • Hike to Colorado River or 13.6 mi to White Rim Rd
	Mesa Arch - 👍	MPR • North of Willow Flat (4)	0.5 mile	Easy loop • Popular self-guiding nature trail
	Aztec Butte	MPR • North of Willow Flat (5)	2.0 miles	Moderate • Ancestral Puebloan granaries
	Murphy Point Overlook	MPR • North between Buck Canyon and Candlestick Tower Overlooks (6)	4.0 miles	Easy • Popular trail with continuous views
	Murphy Loop		11.0 miles	Strenuous • Steep trail descends from the mesa rim
	Gooseberry	MPR • White Rim Overlook (7)	5.4 miles	Strenuous • Shortest route to White Rim Road
	White Rim Overlook	MPR • North of Grand View (8)	1.8 miles	Easy • One of the best views from the island
	Grand View Point - 👍	South end of MPR (8)	2.0 miles	Easy • Amazing panoramic view of Canyonlands
	Wilhite	MPR • West of Willow Flat (9)	12.2 miles	Strenuous • Slot canyon leads to White Rim Road
	Alcove Spring	MPR • Before Upheaval Dome (10)	11.2 miles	Strenuous • Provides views of Taylor Canyon
	Moses and Zeus	Alcove Spring Tr/White Rim Rd (11)	1.0 mile	Easy • Views of Taylor Canyon and climbing routes
	Whale Rock	MPR • Near Upheaval Dome (12)	1.0 mile	Moderate • Handrails aid crossing steep slickrock
	Upheaval Dome	MPR • Upheaval Dome Trailhead (13)	1.8 miles	Moderate • Popular hike to two overlooks
	Syncline Loop - 👍	MPR • Upheaval Dome Trailhead (13)	8.3 miles	Strenuous loop • Optional 3 and 7-mile spur trails along route, great for 1-night backpack
	Fort Bottom Ruin	NW Corner off White Rim Rd (14)	4.0 miles	Moderate • An ancient tower ruin

Island in the Sky District

Backpacking

Bikers on White Rim Road - Island in the Sky

Overnight backpacking at Canyonlands is limited to camping zones and designated sites, like those found around many of the 4WD roads. **All overnight stays in the backcountry require a permit** (page 382). A limited number of permits are available and demand often exceeds supply during spring and fall, so plan your itinerary in advance and reserve a permit. The next hurdle is to assure you'll have plenty of water for the length of your trip, because most water sources are unreliable.

Inquire about potential water sources when you arrive to pick up your permit. **The Maze** is enjoyed, almost exclusively, by backpackers. Trails at Island in the Sky and Needles can be taken more casually or combined to make a suitable backpacking route. **Salt Creek Trail** (25 miles) in Needles District is another option. With careful planning, considering the ability of all members of your party, you're sure to have a rewarding experience in a magical place.

Canyonlands Hiking Trails

	Trail Name	Trailhead (# on map)	Length	Notes (Roundtrip distances)
Needles District	Chesler Park Viewpoint	Elephant Trailhead (15)	6.0 miles	Moderate • Grassland lined with spires (popular)
	Chesler Park Loop	Elephant Trailhead (15)	11.0 miles	Moderate semi-loop • Continue beyond the viewpoint
	Druid Arch	Elephant Trailhead (15)	11.0 miles	Moderate • Scrambling and a ladder, great hike
	Confluence Overlook - 👍	Big Spring Canyon Trailhead (16)	11.0 miles	Moderate • Outstanding hike to rivers' confluence
	Squaw Canyon	Squaw Flat Loop A (17)	7.5 miles	Moderate loop • Connects with Big Spring Canyon
	Elephant Canyon	Squaw Flat Loop A (17)	10.8 miles	Moderate semi-loop • Option for several spur trails
	Lost Canyon - 👍	Squaw Flat Loop A (17)	8.7 miles	Moderate semi-loop • Scrambling and solitude
	Peekaboo	Squaw Flat Loop A (17)	10.0 miles	Moderate • Arch, pictograph, canyons, and (2) ladders

The Maze District: There are no designated trails and no reliable water sources. Come prepared.
Horseshoe Canyon District: There is a 7.5-mile roundtrip hiking trail through the canyon (ancient pictographs).

Mesa Arch sunrise © John Fowler (www.lumenetic.com)

Biking

Located at the doorstep of **Moab, the epicenter of mountain biking**, it shouldn't come as a surprise that Canyonlands is a popular destination for pedalers. The 100-mile **White Rim Road** circling Island in the Sky is the primary biking destination. **The Maze** offers more secluded biking opportunities. **All overnight bike trips require a permit** (page 382). Several **outfitters** (page 451) provide guided mountain bike tours of Canyonlands.

Rafting/Paddling

In 1869, **Major John Wesley Powell** became the first to officially explore Canyonlands. He traveled from Green River, WY all the way through the Grand Canyon. Much like Powell, today's visitors are inspired by the scenery and invigorated by the water's power as they float the **Green River** or raft the 14-mile stretch of Class III–IV rapids of **Cataract Canyon** just beyond the confluence of the Green and Colorado Rivers. All public launches are located outside the park and **private parties require a permit** (page 382). Several **Outfitters** (page 451) provide everything from day-trips to weeklong whitewater adventures.

4WD Roads

A 4WD vehicle unlocks vast portions of Canyonlands that few visitors get to see. It allows you to go backpacking without putting in the work. Your gear is in your trunk, and the only things strained are the muscles of your brake foot—and maybe your nerves as you slowly make your way up and down narrow switchbacks that ascend and descend precipitous cliffs.

Island in the Sky's **White Rim Road** is a popular destination. **Shafer Rim Trail** near Island in the Sky's Entrance is a great 4WD alternative route to and from Moab. Routes like **Elephant Hill** (Needles) and the road to the **Land of Standing Rocks** (Maze) are extremely technical. **A backcountry permit (page 382) is required to camp at designated sites along the way.**

None of these roads are advised for winter driving. Fill up with gas in Moab. You won't find any services in the park or backcountry. Rental vehicles are often restricted to paved roads, so look closely at your agreement or ask about it before you drive off the lot. Drive carefully; a tow can exceed $1,000.

A beautiful Canyonlands' vista © Chris Willis (www.snapchris.com)

Other Activities

Rock Climbing: Sandstone isn't the best for rock climbing, but climbers regularly come to **Island in the Sky** to test their skills against its towers and spires. If you're interested in climbing Canyonlands visit the park website for a list of regulations. **A permit (page 382) is only required if you intend on spending the night in the backcountry.**

Horseback Riding is another option at Canyonlands. Horses and other saddle stock are permitted on all backcountry roads. **A backcountry permit (page 382) is required for all stock-use, and all feed and manure must be packed out.** Finding reliable water sources is a significant problem for hikers, and it is even more critical for horseback riders. Discuss where you might find water with a park ranger before departing, especially for overnight trips.

Stargazing: Just because it's dark at night doesn't mean there's nothing to see. Canyonlands' distinction as one of the most remote regions in the lower 48 has its perks, one being extremely dark skies. Don't forget to look up on a cloudless night. The stargazing is phenomenal.

Visitor Centers

Each district (except Horseshoe Canyon) has a facility that is open every day of the year except Christmas and New Year's Day. **Island in the Sky Visitor Center** is open 8am to 6pm from late March to late October. The remainder of the year it's open from 9am to 4:30pm. **Needles Visitor Center** is open 8am to 5pm from April to late October. The remainder of the year it's open from 8am to 4:30pm. Both visitor centers feature exhibits, book and map sales, audio-visual programs, restrooms, and backcountry permits. **Hans Flat Ranger Station**, located at the Maze entry point, is open daily from 8am to 4:30pm.

For Kids: Kids (ages 6–12) are welcome to participate in **Canyonlands' Junior Ranger Program**. Free booklets are available at either visitor center. Complete five or more activities to receive an official junior ranger badge. At Needles families can check out a **Discovery Pack** that's crammed full of goodies like binoculars and guide books (fee and deposit required). Even if you don't participate in these programs, children are sure to enjoy the contrasting views of canyons and cliffs that are easily accessible along park roads.

Ranger Programs: Park rangers provide various interpretive programs from April to late October. Evening programs are frequently given at each of the campgrounds' amphitheaters. During the daytime, rangers give short talks on unique features or lead guests along a popular trail. Ranger programs are highly recommended. Attend one (or more) if you have the chance.

Flora & Fauna: The ecology of Canyonlands is similar to Arches National Park. See page 374 for a brief description of the area's plants and animals.

Pets: Pets are allowed in Canyonlands' developed campgrounds and along its roadways. They are not permitted on hiking trails or the backcountry (including unpaved roads). Pets must be kept on a leash no more than six feet in length at all times. If you'd like to bring yours on vacation and fully experiencing everything Canyonlands has to offer, you will want to use one of the boarding services listed on page 375.

Accessibility: Canyonlands' Needles and Island in the Sky Visitor Centers and restrooms are accessible to individuals in wheelchairs. Buck Canyon, Green River, and Grand View Point Overlooks are accessible at Needles. At Island in the Sky, wheelchair users have access to Squaw Flat Campground and Wooden Shoe Overlook.

Weather: Canyonlands nearly borders Arches National Park (page 368). Both parks are situated on the Colorado Plateau in southeast Utah's high desert. See page 375 for weather information.

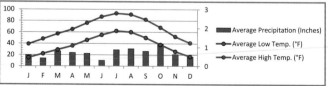

CANYONLANDS

Vacation Planner

Canyonlands' visitors can spend a week **paddling the Colorado River** (page 385) or days **exploring the Maze's canyons** (page 384), but most drive into Island in the Sky and/or Needles. Provided below is a one-day itinerary for each. If you intend on **camping** (page 382) in spring or fall be sure to arrive early, as campgrounds often fill before noon. Nearby dining, grocery stores, lodging, festivals, and attractions are listed on pages 448–453. Visitors to the Maze, Horseshoe Canyon, or the park's backcountry should plan their trips well in advance with a high-quality topographic map. Restock supplies and top-off your gas tank before entering any district. You won't find gas stations or convenience stores within park boundaries.

Day 1

Island in the Sky: Begin your trip at the **visitor center** located near the entrance. Check out a current schedule of ranger programs and browse the exhibits. Time permitting, join a **ranger program**. Return to the park road, stopping next at **Mesa Arch** (page 383). Hike the 0.5-mile loop, which is a very popular destination among photographers. If you plan on camping at Canyonlands (page 382), consider returning to Mesa Arch in the morning at sunrise. It's glorious. Back on the main park road you'll come to a Y-intersection. Head south all the way to **Grand View Point Overlook** and hike the 2-mile trail located nearby. Return to the Y-intersection, but this time turn left to complete the last leg of the Y. Pull into **Willow Flat Campground** area and check out **Green River Overlook**. Once you've finished soaking in the views drive to **Upheaval Dome** (page 383), located at the end of the road. Geology buffs will be especially interested in this oddity, but it's a spectacle everyone should enjoy.

Day 1

Needles: Before entering Canyonlands make a quick stop at **Newspaper Rock** to view some well-preserved petroglyphs. Return to your car, enter the park, and stop at the visitor center to browse its exhibits. **Roadside Ruins**, located near the visitor center, is a short trail to a small Ancestral Puebloan dwelling. If you're pressed for time, skip the ruins and follow the park road north stopping at **Pothole Point** and **Slickrock Foot Nature Trail**. Those looking to venture deeper into the backcountry should drive all the way to **Big Spring Canyon Overlook**, where you can begin the 11-mile hike to the **Confluence of the Green and Colorado Rivers** (page 384), one of the park's best hikes.

Cataract Canyon

Green River Overlook - Island in the Sky

Pothole Point - Needles

Did you know?

▶ Island in the Sky received its name because it sits on a broad and level mesa some 2,000 feet above the Colorado and Green Rivers.

▶ Needles District is named for the pinnacles, featuring red and white layers, that dominate the landscape.

▶ Some petroglyphs and pictographs found at Horseshoe Canyon were painted more than 3,000 years ago. They are some of the oldest cultural artifacts in North America.

Shadows falling on cliffs and domes as viewed from Sunset Point © Frank Kovalchek (flickr/Alaskan Dude)

HC 70 Box 15
Torrey, UT 84775
Phone: (435) 425-3791 ext. 111
Website: www.nps.gov/care

Established: December 18, 1971
August 2, 1937 (National Monument)
Size: 241,904 Acres
Annual Visitors: 660,000
Peak Season: Spring & Fall

Activities: Hiking, Backpacking, Camping, Fruit Picking, 4WD, Rock Climbing, Biking, and Horseback Riding

Campgrounds: Fruita Campground
Fee: $10/night
Primitive Campgrounds: Cedar Mesa and Cathedral Valley (free)
Backcountry Camping: Permitted with a free Backcountry Use Permit

Lodging: None

Park Hours: All day, every day
Entrance Fee: $5 • Vehicle
$3 • Individual (foot, bike, etc.)

Capitol Reef - Utah

The name "Capitol Reef" hints that this region was once a growing, living underwater organism. However, the park's reef refers to sinuous canyons, colorful monoliths, obtrusive buttes, and giant white domes of Navajo sandstone that form the **Waterpocket Fold**, a 75 million year old warp in the earth's crust running the entire length of the park. These features make a nearly impassable rugged landscape, exactly what locals called a "reef." Today, the Waterpocket Fold defines Capitol Reef National Park, but scientists are still trying to understand its origin. No doubt the twisting of two layers of crust into S-shaped folds required exceptional force. As luck would have it, about the time the fold was created two continental plates were colliding with one another. A collision so forceful a great uplift occurred, raising the Rocky Mountains and potentially wrenching land nearly 400 miles away. From the ground you hardly notice the violence and scars at the earth's surface. From the air, it's dramatic. To view it from above without leaving the ground, stop at the visitor center where a scaled version of the park is on display.

Early inhabitants were oblivious to the area's unique geology. With only a few perennial sources of water to choose from, the **Fremont People** settled along the Fremont River's shores. They farmed and hunted for more than two centuries, only to abandon their granaries and dwellings in the 13th century. At the same time, **Ancestral Puebloans** were evacuating the region of present day Mesa Verde (page 354) and Canyonlands (page 376) National Parks. Scientists believe they all left because of significant change in climate, resulting in extended drought. Decades later, **Paiute and Ute Indians** entered the region, discovering abandoned Fremont granaries, they called moki huts (homes of a tiny people or moki).

It wasn't until the 19th century that an American crossed the Waterpocket Fold. **Alan H. Thompson**, a member of **U.S. Army Major John Wesley Powell's expedition**, completed this task in 1872. **Mormons** were next to settle in. Like the Fremont People before them, they lived in the Fremont River Valley, establishing settlements at Junction (later known as Fruita), Caineville, and Aldridge. Aldridge failed. Fruita prospered but was never home to more than 10 families. Caineville struggled to survive, but Mormon Bishop **Ephraim Pectol** operated a small convenience store that housed a private museum of Fremont artifacts.

Pectol noticed the area's finer qualities while scavenging through ruins seeking ancient relics to add to his personal museum. He and his brother-in-law, Wayne County High School Principal **Joseph S. Hickman**, began promoting the scenic beauty of what they called "**Wayne Wonderland**" in 1921. In 1933 Pectol was elected to the State Legislature, giving him a platform to pursue the park idea. Wasting no time, he contacted **President Franklin D. Roosevelt** asking him to create Wayne Wonderland National Monument through executive order. For nearly a decade tourists trickled into the proposed park, largely thanks to lectures given by **J.E. Broaddus**, a Salt Lake City photographer hired by Pectol and Hickman. Images piqued federal interest, and soon survey parties arrived in south-central Utah. They didn't give it "wonderland" status, but on August 2, 1937 President Roosevelt created Capitol Reef National Monument and placed it under control of Zion National Park (page 404).

At the same time, **Charles Kelley** retired to the area and volunteered to serve as park custodian. In 1950 he was appointed the park's first superintendent. He became leery of the National Park Service's direction as they complied with demands made by the U.S. Atomic Energy Commission to open Capitol Reef to uranium mining, but little ore was excavated.

In 1962, construction of highway UT-24 was completed, drastically increasing tourism. Momentum was finally building to permanently protect the region as a national park; in 1971 **President Richard Nixon** signed a bill doing exactly that.

Best of Capitol Reef

Activity: **View from Panorama Point**
>   Runner-up: Scenic Drive
>   2nd Runner-up: Burr Trail (Driving)
>   3rd Runner-up: Pick Fruit at Fruita

Hike: **Cohab Canyon**
>   Runner-up: Rim Overlook
>   2nd Runner-up: Lower Cathedral Valley
>   3rd Runner-up: Grand Wash

Did you know?

➤ Fruita is home to roughly 2,700 fruit and nut trees, making it the largest historic orchard in the National Park System.

When to Go

Capitol Reef is most comfortable for hiking and other outdoor activities during spring and fall. Its only visitor center is open daily (except a few federal holidays) from 8am to 4:30pm, with hours extended to 6pm during the summer season (Memorial Day until Labor Day). Ripple Rock Nature Center is open during the summer season (12–5pm until June 30, 10am–3pm after July 1). You can pick fruit from Fruita Orchard between June and October.

Transportation & Airports

Public transportation does not provide service to or around the park. The closest large commercial airport is Salt Lake City International (230 miles to the north).

Directions

The park area is extremely isolated and can only be accessed by one major road, UT-24, which conveniently intersects I-70 near Aurora (Exit 48). It then loops through the park intersecting with I-70 again just west of Green River, UT (Exit 149). To reach the park from I-15 traveling south from Salt Lake City, take Exit 188. Take US-50 S for 24 miles, and then turn right at UT-260/Main St. Continue for 4 miles before turning right at UT-24. Follow UT-24 south and east about 75 miles into the park.

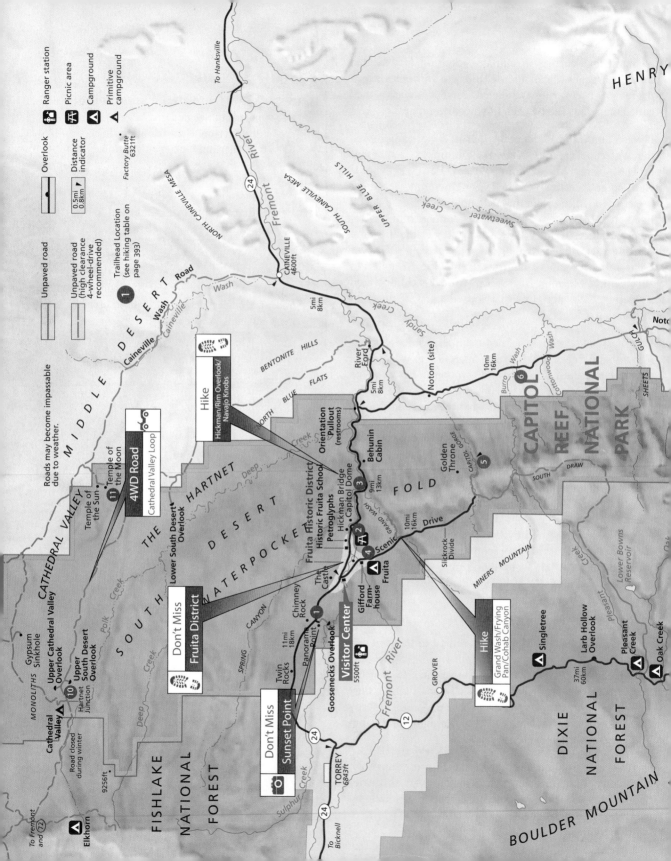

Legend

Ranger station
Picnic area
Campground
Primitive campground

Overlook
Distance indicator
0.5mi / 0.8km

Unpaved road
Unpaved road (high clearance 4-wheel-drive recommended)
Trailhead Location (see hiking table on page 393)

HENRY

To Hanksville

NORTH CAINEVILLE MESA

Factory Butte 6321ft

Fremont River

24

Caineville 4600ft

SOUTH CAINEVILLE MESA

UPPER BLUE HILLS

Sweetwater Creek

MIDDLE DESERT

Caineville Wash Road

Wash

BENTONITE HILLS

BLUE FLATS

River Ford

5mi 8km

Sandy Creek

Notom (site)

5mi 8km

10mi 16km

Burro Wash

Cottonwood Wash

CAPITOL REEF NATIONAL PARK

6

Notom

SHEETS

GULCH

Hike — Hickman/Rim Overlook/ Navajo Knobs

Roads may become impassable due to weather.

4WD Road — Cathedral Valley Loop

Temple of the Moon
Temple of the Sun
11

CATHEDRAL VALLEY

THE HARTNET

DESERT

Lower South Desert Overlook

Orientation Pullout (restrooms)

Behunin Cabin

Golden Throne

5

CAPITOL GORGE

SOUTH DRAW

Fruita Historic District
Historic Fruita School
Petroglyphs
Hickman Bridge
Capitol Dome
3
9mi 13km

Don't Miss — Fruita District

WATERPOCKET FOLD

10mi 16km Scenic Drive

Slickrock Divide

MINERS MOUNTAIN

Don't Miss — Sunset Point

SOUTH DESERT

The Castle
2
4
Fruita
Gifford Farm-house

Visitor Center 5500ft

Grand Wash

Chimney Rock

11mi 18km

Twin Rocks

Panorama Point

Goosenecks Overlook

Fremont River

GROVER

Hike — Grand Wash/Frying Pan/Cohab Canyon

Singletree

Larb Hollow Overlook

Pleasant Creek

Oak Creek

Lower Bowns Reservoir

Pleasant Creek

FISHLAKE NATIONAL FOREST

MONOLITHS
Gypsum Sinkhole
Upper Cathedral Valley Overlook
Upper South Desert Overlook
10
Hartnet Junction

Cathedral Valley

Road closed during winter

9256ft

Polk Creek

Deep Creek

SPRING CANYON

Sulphur Creek

24

TORREY 6843ft

24

To Bicknell

12

DIXIE NATIONAL FOREST

BOULDER MOUNTAIN

To Fremont and 72
Elkhorn

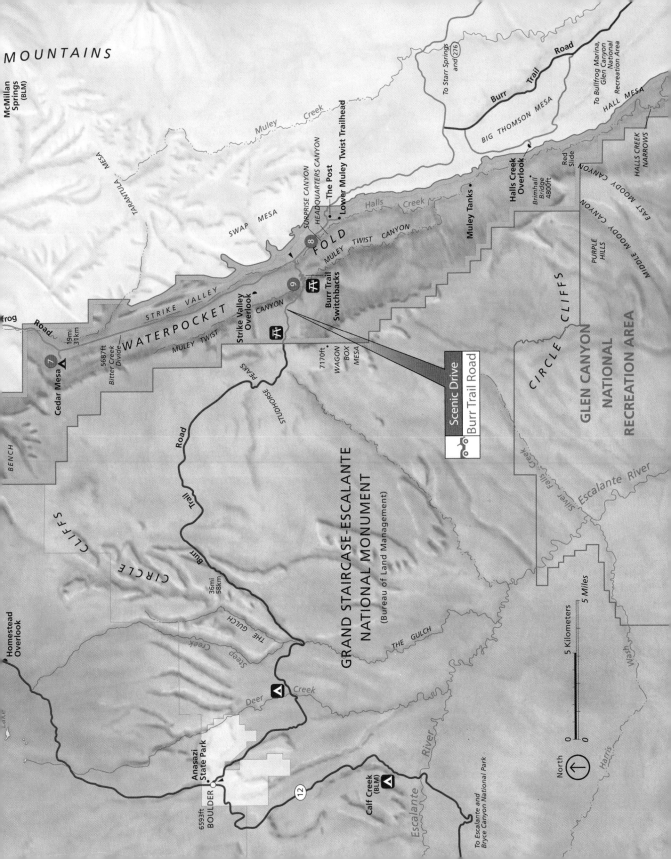

Fruita

Fruita was originally a Mormon settlement established on the banks of the Fremont River. Compared to the rest of the surrounding desert life at Fruita was good. Even so, no more than ten families occupied the settlement at any one time. Touring **Historic Fruita District** will lead you to an old barn, a restored schoolhouse, Gifford Farmhouse (open to the public during summer), a tool shed and blacksmith shop, and orchards containing more than 2,700 trees, including cherry, apple, apricot, peach, and pear. When the fruit are in season you are welcome to pick and eat whatever you want free of charge while in the orchards. A small fee is charged for any fruit you take with you. Call (435) 425-3791 for information on blossom and harvest times. Fruita Campground is also set among stands of fruit-bearing trees.

Camping

Capitol Reef's only developed campground is located at **Fruita**. All 71 sites are available on a first-come, first-served basis. Restrooms have flush toilets and sinks, but there are no showers. Hookups are not available for RVs, but a dump station is open during summer. Rates are $10/night. The campground typically fills before afternoon from spring through fall.

Two no-fee primitive campgrounds are available. **Cathedral Valley**, located in the northwest corner, has six sites. **Cedar Mesa**, located on Notom–Bullfrog Road 35 miles south of UT-24, has five sites. Sites are available first-come, first-served all year round. They have pit toilets, but no water. Always check road conditions before departing.

Backpacking

Visitors can also **camp in the backcountry with a free permit** (available at the visitor center). There are nice backpacking opportunities throughout the park's 100-mile length, but **Upper and Lower Muley Twist Canyon Trails** are two of the best destinations. They are located in the southern region near **Burr Trail Switchbacks**.

Hiking

At Capitol Reef you'll find hikes similar in beauty and terrain to those at Zion National Park (page 404), but with much smaller crowds. The greatest concentration of trails is found along UT-24 and Scenic Drive. Three of the best can be combined to make a 5.8-mile loop; begin at **Cohab Canyon**, and connect to **Grand Wash via Frying Pan Trail**. This loop passes through a juniper-pinyon forest and past **Cassidy Arch** as it traverses a narrow slot canyon back to UT-24. The downside of the loop is that you exit Grand Wash 2.8 miles east of your starting point on UT-24. You'll have to plant a vehicle here, hitch a ride, hike along the road back to your car, or backtrack.

Hickman Bridge Parking Area is located on the north side of UT-24. From here, a small trail network leads to **Hickman Bridge**, **Rim Overlook**, and **Navajo Knobs**. All three share the same trail at the start before diverging. The hike begins with a gradual climb. Shortly after you've reached the flat you'll come across the junction of Rim Overlook/Navajo Knobs and Hickman Bridge. **Hickman Bridge** is a very popular destination. It's a large natural sandstone arch or bridge that is worth a quick visit. If you're short on time and have to choose just one trail, continue on Rim Overlook/Navajo Knobs Trail. Spectacular panoramic views of Fruita and the surrounding desert region from **Rim Overlook** are strongly recommended and the favored destination (especially if you're coming from Arches National Park). From Rim Overlook the trail continues an additional 4.5 miles (roundtrip), running nearly parallel to UT-24 to **Navajo Knobs** where the views are even more incredible. At the trail's end you can see for miles, beyond **Gooseneck Overlook** through the Fremont River Valley and on to Miners Mountain.

Some of the most memorable sites are located less than a mile from the main roadways. Short hikes like **Goosenecks, Sunset Point, and Petroglyphs Trails** are great if you're in a rush and just want to get out of the car and stretch your legs a bit. Exploring **Historic Fruita District** by foot is another great idea, especially when fruit is in season and you can treat yourself to a snack while walking through the orchard. Whether you're hiking in the busy Fruita area or the backcountry, all hikers should use caution and remember to carry plenty of water. Narrow canyons can flood quickly and should be evacuated at the first sign of thunderstorm.

The view from Rim Overlook

Capitol Reef Hiking Trails

	Trail Name	Length	Trailhead (# on map)/Notes (Roundtrip distances unless noted otherwise)
Trailheads on UT-24	Goosenecks - 👍	0.2 mile	Begins at Panorama Point (1) • Outstanding views for a very short and easy hike
	Sunset Point	0.7 mile	Begins at Panorama Point (1) • Extremely popular location for photos at sunset
	Chimney Rock	3.5 miles	North side of UT-24 near Panorama Point (1) • Moderate loop trail to mesa top
	Chimney Rock Canyon	9.4 miles	Strenuous trail that proceeds from Chimney Rock Loop to UT-24 near Grand Wash (1-way) (1)
	Hickman Bridge - 👍	2.0 miles	Hickman Bridge Parking Lot (2) • Self-guiding nature trail to a natural bridge
	Rim Overlook - 👍	4.5 miles	Follow Hickman Bridge Trail until its junction with Rim Overlook Trail (2) • Great views of Fruita
	Navajo Knobs	9.0 miles	Continue beyond Rim Overlook to some of the finest views in the park (2)
	Grand Wash - 👍	4.5 miles	Trailhead on UT-24 past Capitol Dome (3) • Easy hike connects to Scenic Drive
	Cassidy Arch	3.5 miles	Follow Grand Wash to Frying Pan and a spur trail to an arch named for Butch Cassidy (3)
	Frying Pan	6.0 miles	Connects Cohab Canyon with Grand Wash for a loop back to UT-24 (3, 4)
On Scenic Drive	Cohab Canyon - 👍	3.5 miles	Begins at Fruita Campground (4) • Moderate out-and-back through hidden canyon
	Fremont River	2.5 miles	Begins at Fruita Campground (4) • Moderate hike along river to a mesa top
	Fremont Gorge Overlook	4.5 miles	Begins near Fruita Blacksmith Shop (4) • Strenuous trail to a mesa above the Fremont River
	Old Wagon Trail	3.5 miles	Between Grand Wash and Capitol Gorge (5) • Strenuous loop along Waterpocket Fold
	Capitol Gorge	2.5 miles	Begins near the end of paved road (5) • Leads through Waterpocket Fold via Capitol Wash
	Golden Throne	4.0 miles	Begins near the end of paved road (5) • Short and strenuous switchbacks lead out of Capitol Gorge
Other Areas	Burro Wash	8.0 miles	Accessed from Notom–Bullfrog Road outside the park on its east side (6) • Narrows
	Red Canyon	3.5 miles	Begins at Cedar Mesa Campground and leads into a large box canyon (7)
	Surprise Canyon	2.0 miles	Notom–Bullfrog Rd south of Burr Trail (8) • Scrambling required but not difficult
	Lower Muley Twist Canyon	23.0 miles	Just west of Burr Trail switchbacks (9) • Runs north–south parallel to Waterpocket Fold
	Temple Rock	4.0 miles	Off Hartnet Draw at Upper South Desert Overlook (10) • Mostly unmarked with unparalleled views
	Lower Cathedral Valley - 👍	1.6 miles	Off Hartnet Draw leads to Temple of the Sun and Temple of the Moon (11)

Driving

The 10-mile **Scenic Drive**, located south of the visitor center, is the park's most popular roadway. A free brochure is available at its entrance station where visitors must pay a $5 entrance fee per vehicle. Where Scenic Drive's pavement ends, **South Draw Road** begins. This high-clearance 4WD-only road follows the Waterpocket Fold before running alongside Pleasant Creek and exiting the park.

A 4WD vehicle is not required for Notom–Bullfrog and Burr Trail Roads. **Notom–Bullfrog Road** traces the park's eastern boundary to Post Corral where there's an equestrian staging area. It exits the park and continues south to Glen Canyon National Recreation Area. Also in the park's southern reaches is **Burr Trail Road**. It provides an exhilarating experience thanks to switchbacks that climb some 800 feet in just a 0.5-mile. In the north, **Cathedral Loop** offers the most scenic 4WD route, as it combines **Hartnet and Caineville Wash Roads** (high-clearance required).

Other Activities

Biking is allowed, but only on designated roads. The 10 mile stretch of **Scenic Drive** south of the visitor center is the most popular section of roadway. It's narrow, without shoulders, and crowded with motorists between April and October. If you plan on pedalling Scenic Drive you must be alert at all times and proceed with caution. **Mountain bikers** can take on more strenuous routes like **Cathedral Valley Loop**, **South Draw Road**, or **Burr Trail Road/Notom–Bullfrog Road**.

Rock Climbing is gaining popularity. Permits are not required, but first-timers should join someone familiar with the area or purchase a dedicated climbing guide book (available at the visitor center), because much of the rock is brittle sandstone.

Stock (horse, mule, and burro) are allowed in the park. However, no outfitters provide guided trail rides and you must trailer your own stock in. Recommended rides include **South Draw, Old Wagon Trail, Halls Creek, and the South Desert**.

For Kids: Children of all ages are invited to participate in **Capitol Reef's Junior Ranger Program**. Free activity booklets are available at the visitor center and nature center. Complete at least seven activities and your child will be rewarded with an official Junior Ranger Badge. Families are also welcome to check out a **Family Fun Pack** from the visitor center or nature center. These backpacks are filled with materials that aid in exploration of the park.

Ranger Programs: Park personnel offer interpretive walks, talks, and evening programs from May through September. Program schedules are usually available at the visitor center and are posted on bulletin boards throughout the park. These programs provide insight to interesting aspects of the area that you can't experience by driving and hiking alone. Join a ranger program if possible.

Flora & Fauna: Only a few perennial streams and rivers course through the arid region of Capitol Reef, but you can still find large mammals here. **Mountain lions** roam the mesa tops and have even been spotted in the Fruita area. Their main source of food is **mule deer**, which are fairly common in Fruita's orchards. **Bighorn sheep** once flourished in this rocky terrain, but native sheep were hunted to extinction around the middle of the 1900s. Several reintroduction programs have infused a healthy population of desert bighorn sheep that are now seen on mesa tops and cliffsides. Most animals are small rodents, bats, and birds (200+ species). Due to the area's relative inhospitableness many plants have adapted to endure the conditions, resulting in rare species, many of which are only found in this part of Utah. Barneby reed-mustard, Maguire's daisy, and Wright's fishhook cactus are a few rare and protected species.

Pets: Pets are allowed in developed areas like Fruita Campground, parking areas, picnic areas, and along roadways as long as they are kept on a leash no more than six feet in length. Pets (except service animals) are not allowed in public buildings, in the backcountry, or on trails.

Accessibility: Capitol Reef protects a rugged landscape. The visitor center and Petroglyphs Trail located just off UT-24 are the only fully-accessible destinations for individuals in wheelchairs. One accessible campsite is available at Fruita Campground.

Weather: Capitol Reef spans an arid desert region. Summer days are hot, but evenings are comfortable. Winter lows fall below freezing, but average highs are around 40°F in January (the coldest month). Spring and fall bring average highs in the mid-60s to mid-70s°F. These seasons tend to be the most comfortable times of year. The region is typically dry, receiving an average of about 7 inches of precipitation each year.

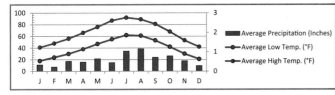

Legend:
- Average Precipitation (Inches)
- Average Low Temp. (°F)
- Average High Temp. (°F)

Vacation Planner

Capitol Reef often spells sweet relief to visitors of Utah's National Parks. Smaller crowds and the same fantastic red rock cliffs, narrow canyons, and natural arches make it **one of the National Park System's best kept secrets**.

Dining and lodging are not available within park boundaries. Nearby dining, grocery stores, lodging, festivals, and attractions are listed on pages 448–453. There are only 30 miles of paved roads, so a one-day trip is conceivable. The itinerary provided below outlines an ideal day in the park, but consider spending a few more on a **backpacking trip** (page 392) or driving **4WD roads** like the Cathedral Loop (page 394).

Day 1

Whether entering the park from the east or west on UT-24, you'll be tempted to pull over and admire the stunning red rock formations. Fight the temptation and continue to the **visitor center in Fruita**. Check the schedule of **ranger programs**, making mental notes of the time and location for any programs of interest. While you're here have a look around **Fruita**. You'll find a little something for everyone. **Gifford Farmhouse** is particularly interesting. Don't forget to **help yourself to fruit** if it's picking season. Once you're finished at Fruita, head south on Scenic Drive. Soak in the sights then retrace your path back to UT-24. Drive east to **Hickman Bridge Trailhead** to hike **Rim Overlook Trail** (page 393). The views are outstanding from this perch high above Fruita. Time and energy permitting, you should continue on to **Navajo Knobs**. Before the sun sets stop at **Goosenecks Overlook**, just west of Fruita on UT-24, to hike **Sunset Point Trail** (page 393).

Photo from outer space of Big Thompson Mesa/Waterpocket Fold

Burr Trail Road

Burro Wash

Did you know?

➤ Capitol Reef National Park was originally called "Wayne Wonderland." The park's original supporters, Ephraim P. Pectol and Joseph S. Hickman named it after Wayne County.

A view of Thor's Hammer (near Sunset Point) as the sun begins to rise

PO Box 640201
Bryce, UT 84764
Phone: (435) 834-5322
Website: www.nps.gov/brca

Established: February 25, 1928
June 8, 1923 (National Monument)
Size: 35,835 Acres
Annual Visitors: 1.3 Million
Peak Season: Summer
Hiking Trails: 50 Miles

Activities: Hiking, Backpacking,
Camping, Horseback Riding,
Stargazing, and Photography

Campgrounds: North and Sunset
Fee: $15/night
Reservations from May–September
(877.444.6777, www.recreation.gov)
Backcountry Camping: Permitted

Lodging: Bryce Canyon Lodge
Rates: ($130–179/night)

Park Hours: All day, every day
Entrance Fee: $25 • Vehicle
$12 • Individual (foot, bike, etc.)

Bryce Canyon - Utah

In 1918 **Stephen Mather**, first director and sentimental father of the National Park Service, was guided to a seldom visited attraction in southwestern Utah. His tour guides required that he close his eyes before arrival. Mather had just toured Zion National Park (page 404), but Zion's colorful canyons and expanses of unspoiled wildness could not prepare him for what he was about to see. He opened his eyes at **Bryce Amphitheater**, where a battalion of colorful rocky spires called **hoodoos** were waiting to greet him. Imagine having never seen a photograph of the eerie formations that line the eastern rim of Paunsaugunt Plateau. You arrive here, open your eyes and in front of you is an indescribable masterpiece of nature. Even today, this scene has the power to stop visitors dead in their tracks. These views are so divine and empowering they are inspirational to even the most casual sightseers. This is not just a place of inspiration. It's a place capable of stirring up religious sentiments. A place that invokes deep heartfelt patriotism. A place unlike all others.

To **Ebenezer Bryce**, it was simply "a hell of a place to lose a cow." In 1875, the Church of Jesus Christ of Latter-day Saints sent Bryce to settle the Paria Valley. He and his family chose to live right below what is known today as Bryce Amphitheater. Bryce built a home for his family, a canal for his crops and his cows, and a road to collect wood used to heat his home during the cool evenings and chilly winters. It became clear that Bryce and his family were sticking around, and soon locals began to call the area "Bryce Canyon." Not a true canyon, it's actually a horseshoe-shaped bowl or amphitheater formed by several creeks and streams rather than a single river and its tributaries. Life in and around Bryce Canyon was difficult. Herds of sheep and cattle quickly overgrazed the area's limited vegetation and the region was ravaged by cycles of drought and flooding. Settlers attempted to build a water diversion channel from the Sevier River to protect their crops, cattle, and homes from seasonal floods. The effort failed, and shortly after most settlers, including the Bryce family, left the area.

Capitulation in the face of nature has been a recurring theme in the history of southwest Utah. More than 8,000 years ago humans first visited the region, only to find it exceedingly difficult to survive for an extended period of time. Later, the **Fremont Culture** lived in the area, hunter-gatherers who supplemented their diet with modest amounts of cultivated crops like corn and squash. By the mid-12th century, they also abandoned the region. **Paiute Indians** moved in, living much like the Fremont Culture, hunting and gathering. Paiute legends grew around the origin of the peculiar rock formations, or hoodoos. They called them "anka-ku-was-a-wits" or "red painted faces," and believed they were the Legend People turned to stone at the hands of the Coyote God.

Hoodoos may resemble beautifully colored humans sculpted from stone, but they are simply the result of thousands of years of continuous erosion. Minarets of soft sedimentary rock were left behind because they are topped by a piece of harder, less easily eroded stone. This caprock protects the column of sedimentary rock below from the erosive forces of wind, water, and ice. Several locations around the world display similar rocky spires, including nearby **Cedar Breaks National Monument** (page 452), but Bryce is different. It's more colorful, more abundant, and more mystical.

Bryce Canyon is a special place. A place woven into the legends of early inhabitants. A place where Ebenezer Bryce's cows got lost. A place that screamed "surprise" to Stephen Mather when he opened his eyes. A place that was almost completely inaccessible until the Union Pacific Railroad laid down track in the 1920s and the CCC built roads in the 1930s. Today, Bryce Canyon is a place accommodating to visitors, a place that will open your eyes to the natural beauty of the world around you. So close your eyes and open them once more at the rim of Bryce Canyon.

When to Go

Bryce Canyon is open year-round, 24 hours per day. Its visitor center is open daily, year-round, except for Thanksgiving Day, Christmas Day, and New Year's Day (see page 399 for operating hours). At least one loop of North Campground is open all year. Bryce Canyon Lodge, General Store, and Restaurant are open from April through October. Wildflowers bloom between April and August, peaking in June. The park is busiest from late spring to early fall when the weather is most pleasant. Bryce Canyon does not receive as many visitors as nearby Zion (page 404) or Grand Canyon (page 416) National Parks, but it is the smallest of Utah's parks and can become congested, particularly in summer. To help reduce motorist traffic the park provides a free shuttle service from early May until mid-October.

Transportation & Airports

Public transportation does not service the park, but a free shuttle ferries visitors around Bryce Canyon Amphitheater (summer only). The closest large commercial airports are Salt Lake City International (SLC), 274 miles to the north, and McCarran International (LAS) in Las Vegas, NV, 260 miles to the southwest. Car rental is available at each destination.

Directions

Bryce Canyon is located in southwestern Utah, about 75 miles northeast of Zion National Park (page 404).

From Zion National Park (86 miles): Heading east on UT-9 you will come to a T-intersection with US-89. Turn left onto US-89 and continue north for 43 miles. Turn right at UT-12 East. Continue for 13 miles before turning right onto UT-63 S, which leads into the park. The visitor center is one mile beyond the park's boundary.

From Salt Lake City (270 miles): Heading south on I-15, take Exit 95 for UT-20 toward US-89. Turn left at UT-20 E and continue for 20 miles. Turn right at US-89 S. Drive 7 miles then turn left at UT-12 E. After 13 miles turn right at UT-63 S, which leads into the park.

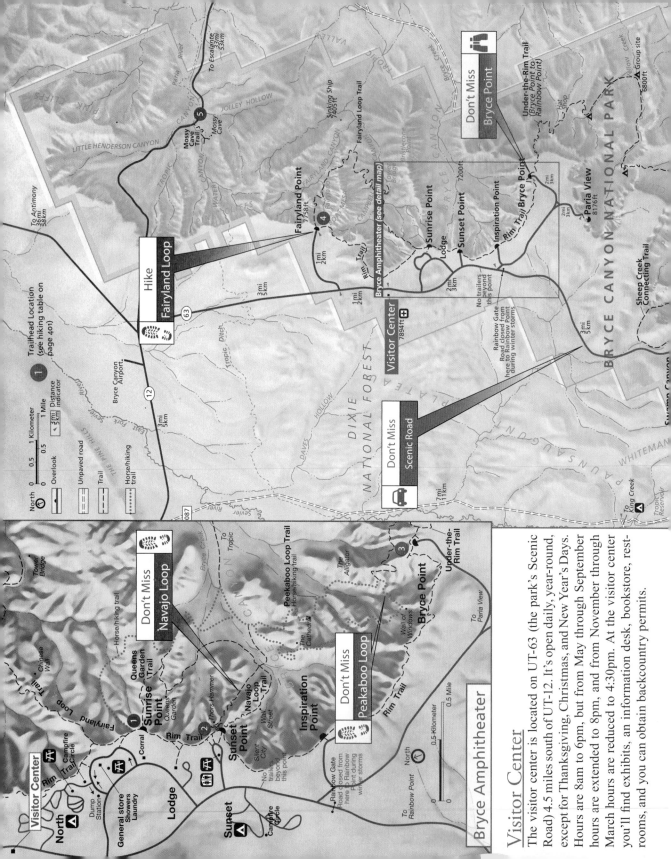

Visitor Center

The visitor center is located on UT-63 (the park's Scenic Road) 4.5 miles south of UT-12. It's open daily, year-round, except for Thanksgiving, Christmas, and New Year's Days. Hours are 8am to 6pm, but from May through September hours are extended to 8pm, and from November through March hours are reduced to 4:30pm. At the visitor center you'll find exhibits, an information desk, bookstore, restrooms, and you can obtain backcountry permits.

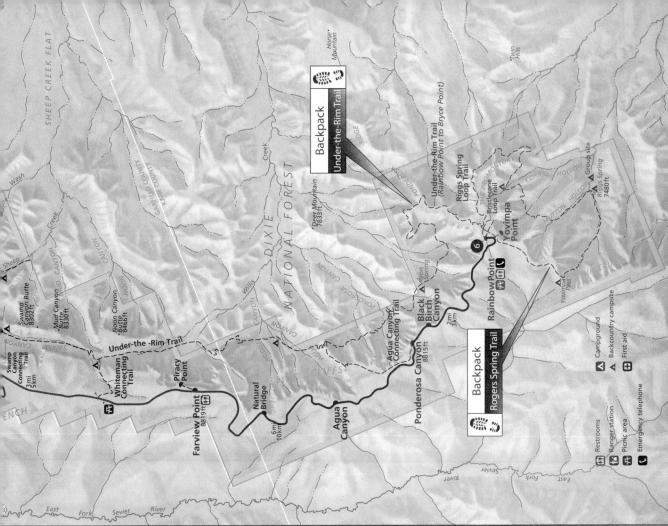

Camping & Lodging

Bryce Canyon has two developed campgrounds: **North and Sunset**. **North** is located near the visitor center. It has 4 loops with a total of 99 sites (13 RV sites can be reserved). **Sunset** is located 1.5 miles south of the visitor center. It has 3 loops, totaling 100 sites (20 tent sites can be reserved). Hook-ups are not available at either campground, but a dump station can be used for a $2 fee. Campsites are $15/night and can only be reserved from early May to late September by calling (877) 444-6777 or clicking www.recreation.gov. Coin operated shower and laundry facilities are available at the General Store, near North Campground.

Bryce Canyon Lodge is located in between the two campgrounds. It is open from April to October. Rooms cost anywhere from $130–179/night. There is a restaurant on-site. For reservations call (877) 386-4383 or click www.brycecanyonforever.com. Please refer to page 449 for nearby lodging facilities.

Driving

The park's **Scenic Drive** is an 18-mile one-way paved road providing access to the most spectacular viewpoints. All 14 viewpoints are on the east side of the road, so it is suggested that motorists proceed to **Rainbow Point** (the end) and stop at viewpoints as you head north on your return trip. Each viewpoint offers unique views, but overlooks found around **Bryce Amphitheater** present the most memorable panoramas.

Shuttle

To conserve fuel and reduce traffic and pollution, the park furnishes a **free shuttle** between Ruby's Inn (outside the park) and Bryce Point from early May to mid-October. Buses depart every 12–15 minutes between 8am and 8pm. Two roundtrip tours to Rainbow Point are offered each day, one in the morning, and another in the afternoon. The free shuttle provides a great opportunity to enjoy the sites of Bryce Canyon with someone else behind the steering wheel.

Backpacking

There are two backcountry trails with designated campsites for backpackers. The 22.9-mile (one-way) **Under-the-Rim Trail** runs parallel to Scenic Drive from **Bryce Point to Rainbow Point**. It also intersects two popular Bryce Amphitheater hiking trails: **Rim and Peekaboo Trails**. Begin at one of these trails if you're interested in exploring the park's most scenic sections and camping in the backcountry. Both begin at Bryce Point and from here you'll pass through Bryce Amphitheater to Under-the-Rim Trail. Follow it south to the first campsite, located just past **Hat Shop**. In all there are 8 backcountry campsites along Under-the-Rim Trail. Elevation ranges from 6,800 feet to 9,105 feet at Rainbow Point (highest elevation in park). The trek can be made in a strenuous 2 days by arranging a shuttle to pick you up at the end, but planning for it to take three days is a good idea. Eliminate having to shuttle cars by taking advantage of the **free shuttle service** (page 399). **Shuttle reservations** are available up to 24 hours in advance and are required. Reserve your spot by calling (435) 834-5290 or stopping in at the shuttle offices at Ruby's Inn, Ruby's Campground, or the Shuttle Parking area building.

Riggs Spring Loop is the other backpacking route. It's an 8.8-mile circuit that begins and ends at Rainbow Point. Hikers pass through old forests before descending into the canyons east of Pink Cliffs. You return back to the plateau via Yovimpa Pass. There are three campsites, and one group site along the trail. Camping is only allowed at these designated sites. Reliable water sources are available at all campsites except Swamp Canyon and Natural Bridge.

A backcountry permit is required for all overnight stays. They can be purchased at the visitor center during normal operating hours as long as you arrive at least one hour before closing. Permits are not available for reservation by mail or phone. However, they can be reserved up to 48 hours in advance, in person, at the visitor center. Permit rates are based on a seven night maximum and are as follows: $5 (1–2 persons), $10 (3–6), $15 (7–15) per permit. Open fires are not permitted in the backcountry. If you need to boil water bring a stove.

 # Hiking

At Bryce Canyon you don't have to stare at the balanced rocks, fluted walls, and colorful hoodoos from roadside overlooks; you are free to walk among them. A variety of trails lead into and around **Bryce Amphitheater**. Each trail has its merits, but a few are superior. **These are some of the most outstanding trails in the entire National Park System.**

Navajo Loop is tremendous, packing a whole lot of scenic bang for just 1.3 miles of hiking. The balanced rock called **Thor's Hammer** and narrow passages of **Wall Street** are two of the trail's many highlights. Extend the experience by combining it with one of the trails that merge at the canyon floor. Add **Queens Garden Trail** to **Navajo Loop** and make a 2.9-mile hike through this eroded paradise. If you don't mind hiking with horses, combine **Navajo and Peekaboo Loops**. This route leads beyond the destinations of typical Bryce Canyon day-hikers, but it merges with a path heavily trod by horses and their riders. It's dusty, steep at times, and somewhat difficult, but worth the effort and having to mingle with equines.

If you don't want to venture into the amphitheater, enjoy it from above by hiking the 5.5-mile (one-way) **Rim Trail**. It connects all of Bryce Amphitheater's Viewpoints, and the free summer shuttle makes stops anywhere along the way. When you realize that the views are just as beautiful from the trail as they are from the overlooks you may decide to continue hiking along the rim.

The most popular hike beyond Bryce Amphitheater is **Fairyland Loop Trail**. It circles around two neighboring amphitheaters, but hikers are rewarded with a different sort of landscape as it passes through gently sloped badlands with denser tree cover. **Under-the-Rim Trail**, for its part, is not reserved for backpackers. It can be accessed via connecting trails at **Sheep Creek**, **Swamp Canyon**, **Whiteman**, and **Agua Canyon**. The latter is the most scenic, but it's rarely used due to a very steep descent. The easiest connecting trail is Whiteman. At 2 miles, Sheep Creek is the longest connection to Under-the-Rim Trail. Swamp Canyon and Whiteman are just under 1-mile, and Agua Canyon is slightly less than 2-miles to the trail junction. Refer to the following page for a complete list of Bryce Canyon's hiking trails.

Queen's Garden Trail © Frank Kovalchek (flickr/Alaskan Dude)

Bryce Canyon Hiking Trails

	Trail Name	Trailhead (# on map)	Length	Notes (Roundtrip distances unless noted otherwise)
Bryce Amphitheater	Tower Bridge	Sunrise Point (1)	3.0 miles	Follows Fairyland until a spur trail to the bridge
	Queens Garden - 👍	Sunrise Point (1)	2.0 miles	Easiest route into the canyon
	Navajo Loop - 👍	Sunset Point (2)	1.3 miles	Wide variety of formations for short loop trail
	Sunset to Sunrise	Sunset Point/Sunrise Point (1, 2)	1.0 mile	The paved portion of Rim Trail
	The 'Figure-8'	Sunset Point/Sunrise Point (1, 2)	6.4 miles	Combine Queens Garden, Navajo, and Peekaboo
	Queens/Navajo Loop - 👍	Sunset Point/Sunrise Point (1, 2)	2.9 miles	Add 0.5-mile of Rim Trail to return where you started
	Navajo/Peekaboo Loop	Sunset Point via Navajo Loop	4.9 miles	A smaller figure 8 than the entire Peekaboo Loop
	Bryce Amphitheater Traverse	Bryce Point/Sunrise Point (3, 1)	4.7 miles	Combine Peekaboo and Queens Garden Trails
	Peekaboo Loop - 👍	Bryce Point (3)	5.5 miles	Loops the amphitheater's southern half • Horse Trail
	Rim	Bryce Point to Fairyland Point (3, 4)	5.5 miles	One-way, moderate hike • Also accessible at Inspiration, Sunset, and Sunrise Points
Other Areas	Fairyland Loop - 👍	Fairyland Point/Sunset Point (4, 1)	8.2 miles	Can be reduced to 5.75 miles by using the shuttle
	Hat Shop	Bryce Point (3)	4.0 miles	Follows the first two miles of Under-the-Rim
	Under-the-Rim	Bryce Point to Rainbow Point (3, 6)	22.9 miles	One-way • Longest backpacking route in the park
	Mossy Cave - 👍	Highway 12 (5)	0.8 mile	Short and easy walk to a small waterfall
	Bristlecone Loop	Rainbow Point (6)	1.0 mile	Easy stroll through ancient forest
	Riggs Spring Loop	Rainbow Point (6)	8.5 miles	4 campsites along this short backpacking route

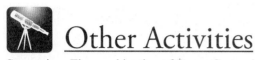

Other Activities

Stargazing: The combination of Bryce Canyon's remote location and thin desert air provide some of the darkest skies in the contiguous United States. To put things into perspective, a stargazer on a moonless night in a small town can see roughly 2,500 stars. **On that same moonless night in Bryce Canyon more than 7,500 stars are visible without the help of a telescope. Stargazing** is so exceptional here that the park offers special astronomy programs on most Tuesdays, Thursdays, and Saturdays from the middle of May until the end of September. If you're interested, check at the visitor center for the program location and start time. A full-blown **Astronomy Festival** is held in early July.

Horseback Riding: One of the easiest and most enjoyable ways to enter the amphitheater is to hop in the saddle and giddy-up into the canyon. Visitors are allowed to bring their own stock (horse or mule), but it is the rider's responsibility to coordinate with Canyon Trail Rides to assure that no concessioner-led offerings are disturbed. Overnight stock trips are not permitted. **Canyon Trail Rides** offers a 2-hour ride to the canyon floor ($50/person) and a half-day complete tour of the canyon on Peek-a-boo Loop Trail ($75/person). Trail rides are given from April through October. To check availability or join a tour, stop at the trail ride desk in the lobby of Bryce Canyon Lodge.

Canyon Trail Rides • (435) 679-8665
Bryce Canyon National Park; Tropic, Utah 84776
www.canyonrides.com

Cross-country skiing and **snowshoeing** are popular activities in winter. Skiers are not permitted on trails below the rim, but snowshoers are. Contact the park to check snow conditions before you arrive.

Cyclists are allowed on all paved roads, but pedalling is not recommended as Scenic Drive is narrow and busy (especially in summer).

Best of Bryce Canyon

Hike: **Queens Garden/Navajo Loop**
    Runner-up: Peekaboo Loop
    2nd Runner-up: Fairyland Loop

For Kids: Children (ages 5 and older) are invited to participate in the park's **Junior Ranger Program**. To become a Junior Ranger, kids must attend a ranger program, complete an age-appropriate number of workbook activities, and pick up litter at an overlook parking lot or hiking trail. Activity booklets are available for free at the visitor center. Complete these tasks and return to the visitor center to be inducted as an official Junior Ranger and receive a free badge. A patch is available for $1.

Ranger Programs: Absolutely do not miss the chance to join at least one ranger program. In addition to ranger-guided astronomy programs, park rangers guide visitors on canyon hikes, rim walks, and the occasional **Full Moon Hike** (hiking boots required). Geology talks and evening programs are administered on a daily basis during the summer season. Evening programs take place in auditoriums at Bryce Canyon Lodge or the visitor center, and are sometimes held at North Campground's Amphitheater. All of these activities are very family friendly, but discussion topics can be technical and difficult to understand for children. An alternative for families is the one hour **kid's interpretive program**, which is available by reservation. To receive additional information, current schedules, or to make a reservation, call the visitor center at (435) 834-5322. **Tickets are required for the Full Moon Hike due to limited capacity.** They are available on a first-come, first served basis at the visitor center, beginning the morning of the hike.

Check-out the park's publication, *The Hoodoo*, for an up-to-date schedule of all park activities. You can pick up a current issue at the park entrance station or visitor center, and it's also available for download at the park website.

Flora & Fauna: Spires, pinnacles, and hoodoos steal the show, but if you look in the air and on the ground you'll spot a few animals and plants, too. Mule deer are the most common animal, but fox, bobcats, black bears, mountain lions, and Utah prairie dogs can also be found here. As a bonus, **more than 170 species of birds** either reside in or visit Bryce Canyon. Growing in the red rock's soil are **at least 400 plant species**, including a colorful array of wildflowers. In the harshest areas of the park only limber pine and Great Basin bristlecone pine exist. Some of these ancient trees are more than 1,300 years old.

Pets: Pets are only permitted in campgrounds, parking lots, and along paved roads and must be on a leash no more than six feet in length at all times. They are not allowed on un-paved trails, viewpoints, in public buildings, or on the summer shuttle. Pets may not be left unattended.

Accessibility: Bryce Canyon is one of the more wheelchair friendly parks. Two campsites at Sunset Campground are reserved for wheelchair users. The summer shuttle is fully accessible. Rim Trail's first 0.5-mile is paved and level. Many of the ranger guided activities and viewpoints are eas-ily accessible to individuals with mobility impairments. The visitor center is fully accessible. Accessible restrooms can be found at the visitor center, Sunset Point, Bryce Canyon Lodge, and the General Store.

Weather: Summer at Bryce Canyon is pleasant, with aver-age high temperatures from June to August in the high 70s to low 80s°F. Only a handful of days top out above 90°F. Clear skies and high elevation make for cool evenings. The average lows during this same period range from the high 30s to mid-40s°F. Winter isn't as comfortable. Variation in temperature is extreme. Any given day can be sunny and 50°F, or well below freezing.

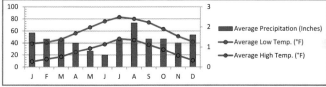

A trail ride into the amphitheater

Wall Street

Vacation Planner

Bryce Amphitheater overshadows the rest of the park, but Bryce Canyon isn't exactly a one-trick pony. Many visitors come to the park, have a look at the hoodoos, and pile back into their car to continue on their way to Zion (page 404) or maybe the Grand Canyon (page 416). Plan on spending at least one full day at Bryce Canyon. This allows enough time to hike a few trails or to take a **trail ride** (page 402) to the floor. Camping and lodging (page 399) are available in the park. Nearby dining, grocery stores, lodging, festivals, and attractions are listed on pages 448–453.

Day 1

Begin your trip at the visitor center and be sure to check out a current schedule of activities at the visitor center or in the park's newspaper, *The Hoodoo*. If anything catches your eye, join the program. If the **shuttle** is running, take it. It's convenient and gives your group's driver a break behind the wheel. At a minimum you should make stops at **Bryce Point** and **Sunset Point** (also a great spot to see the sunrise). Better

yet, hike **Rim Trail** (page 401) to all of Bryce Amphitheater's Viewpoints. If you only have enough time to hike one trail, make it two by combining **Navajo Loop** and **Queens Garden Trail** (page 400). The trip down to the floor is pretty steep, but the en-tire circuit is still less than 3 miles long and by the time you reach the canyon rim you'll probably want to go right back down to take a closer look at **Wall Street** or the eerie **hoodoos**. Take the shuttle around the loop, and complete **Scenic Drive** in your own car or via a shuttle tour (page 399). If you choose to spend the night in the park, be sure to wake up early and catch the sun as it rises up over the amphitheater.

Court of the Patriarchs

Zion - Utah

The name **Zion**, Hebrew for "Jerusalem" (and "the Holy Sanctuary" in Arabic), was bestowed upon a sublime red rock canyon carved by the North Fork of the Virgin River. As they say, "If the shoe fits, wear it." This region of southwestern Utah has served as a sanctuary for ancient cultures, Mormon settlers, government explorers, and today's solace-seeking tourists.

People have inhabited the Virgin River Valley for at least 8,000 years. Nomadic families camped, hunted, and collected plants and seeds. About 2,000 years ago they began cultivating crops, which led to construction of permanent villages called pueblos. The only remnants of these ancient cultures are baskets, rope nets, yucca fiber sandals, tools, and simple structures dating back to 500 AD. Tools used by the **Fremont Culture** and **Virgin Anasazi** include stone knives, drills, and stemmed dart points which were hurled with atlatls (a tool similar to today's dog ball throwers). Small pit-houses and granaries have been discovered at various archaeological sites within the park's canyons. Scientists speculate a combination of extended drought, catastrophic flooding, and depleted farmland forced these people to abandon their civilization around the turn of the 14th century. As the Fremont Culture and Virgin Anasazi left the region, **Paiute and Ute Indians** moved in. They migrated to the area on a seasonal basis, using its land for hunting and gathering, much like the original inhabitants. A few tribes cultivated fields of corn, sunflower, and squash, using the region as a sanctuary for hundreds of years.

Springdale, Utah 84767
Phone: (435) 772-3256
Website: www.nps.gov/zion

Established: November 19, 1919
July 31, 1909 (National Monument)
Size: 146,598 Acres
Annual Visitors: 2.7 Million
Peak Season: Summer

Activities: Hiking, Backpacking, Camping, Horseback Riding, Rock Climbing, Kayaking, Stargazing, Bird Watching, and Photography

Campgrounds: South & Watchman*
Fee: $16–20/night
Backcountry Camping: Permitted with a Backcountry Use Permit (fee)
Lodging: Zion Lodge ($170+/night)

Park Hours: All day, every day
Entrance Fee: $25 • Vehicle
$12 • Individual (foot, bike, etc.)

*Reservations available from late May through late October (877.444.6777, www.recreation.gov)

It wasn't until the late 18th century that a pair of Franciscan missionaries became the first people of European descent to explore the region. **Francisco Domínguez** and **Father Escalante** led an eponymous expedition, which left Santa Fe in search of a route to Monterey, California. Before reaching the Sierra Nevada their journey was impeded by a shortage of rations and snowstorms. Forced to turn back, they headed south, passing nearby the site of present-day **Kolob Canyons Visitor Center**, and then crossing the Colorado River at Marble Canyon before returning to Santa Fe.

Mormon farmers settled the Virgin River region in 1847. A few years later Parowan and Cedar City were established, and they named the area used as a pasture and lumber yard Kolob. According to Mormon scripture, Kolob is "the heavenly place nearest the residence of God." By 1858, new settlements were established along the South Virgin River. Expansion continued when **Isaac Behunin** became the first to settle on the ground floor of a canyon he named Zion referring to a place mentioned in the Bible. The Behunins and two other families summered here. They grew corn, tobacco, and fruit trees, returning to nearby Springdale for winter.

In 1872, **U.S. Army Major John Wesley Powell** led an expedition through the region. He named the magnificent valley **Mukuntuweap**, the Paiute name for "canyon." His crew took photographs, helping satisfy the East Coast's curiosity about western wonders. The East took more interest after Frederick S. Dellenbaugh displayed his paintings of the colorful canyon at the St. Louis World Fair in 1904. Five years later **President William Howard Taft** decided the region should be a public sanctuary, establishing Mukuntuweap National Monument.

The region—now preserved for everyone's enjoyment—was relatively inaccessible to the average man. But in 1917 a road was completed to the Grotto. Visitation increased, and so did confusion about the canyon's name. Locals disliked Mukuntuweap, and **Horace Albright** felt it needed to be more manageable. Congress and President Wilson agreed; land was added and it was redesignated Zion National Park. In 1923, a subsidiary of the **Union Pacific Railroad** purchased a small tent camp and replaced it with **Zion Lodge**. By 1930, construction crews completed **Zion–Mount Carmel Highway**, dramatically increasing access and visitation. Finally, Zion had become a sanctuary for everyone to enjoy.

When to Go

Zion is open year-round, but visitation peaks during summer. Zion Canyon and Kolob Canyons Visitor Centers are open every day except Christmas. Zion Human History Museum is open daily from early March to late November. Watchman Campground is open all year. South Campground is open from March through October. Lava Point Campground is open from June through October. Zion Lodge is open year-round (reduced rates in winter). Zion Canyon Scenic Drive is only accessible by the park's free shuttle system and guests of Zion Lodge from April through October. The road is plowed and open to motorists for the rest of the year.

Transportation & Airports

Public transportation does not provide service to the park, but a free shuttle connects the neighboring town of Springdale with the park and provides the only access to Zion Canyon from April through October. The closest large commercial airports are McCarran International (LAS) in Las Vegas, NV, 170 miles to the southwest, and Salt Lake City International (SLC), 313 miles north of the park.

Directions

Zion National Park is in the very southwestern corner of Utah. Kolob Canyons is located in the park's northwest corner and reached by taking Exit 40 off of I-15. Zion Canyon, the park's most popular area, is accessed via UT-9. Directions to Zion Canyon are provided below.

From Las Vegas (167 miles): Head east on I-15 through St. George, UT, all the way to Exit 16 for UT-9 toward Hurricane/Zion National Park. Take UT-9 east 32 miles to Zion Canyon Visitor Center.

From Salt Lake City (312 miles): Head south on I-15 to exit 27 for UT-17 for Toquerville/Hurricane. Turn left at UT-17 S/UT-228. After 6 miles turn left onto UT-9, which leads into the park.

From Kanab/Grand Canyon (42/248 miles): Head north on US-89. Turn left at UT-9 W, which leads into the park. Visitors with large vehicles: please refer to page 406 for information regarding access to Zion–Mount Carmel Tunnel.

Regions

Zion is one continuous area, but three roads lead into the park's interior. **Zion Canyon** is by far the most popular region. You will find most facilities and trailheads along **Zion Canyon Scenic Drive** and **Zion–Mount Carmel Highway** (UT-9), which provide access to the canyon. Ultra-popular hikes through **Zion Narrows** (page 411) and to **Angel's Landing** are located in this region. If you follow UT-9 west, beyond the south entrance, you will reach the small town of Virgin. Here, **Kolob Terrace Road** winds its way in and out of the park before terminating at Kolob Reservoir. Kolob Terrace Road provides access to **Lava Point Primitive Campground** and numerous trailheads including the non-technical and technical trails to **The Subway** (permit required, even for a day-hike). Far away from the crowds of Zion Canyon, in the park's northwest corner, is **Kolob Canyons**. This region has a visitor center, a scenic drive, and a few trailheads including the scenic hike to **Kolob Arch**.

Scenic Drives & Zion–Mt Carmel Highway

Zion–Mount Carmel Highway and Tunnel were built to provide a shorter route to Bryce Canyon National Park (page 396). The tunnel is a feat of engineering nearly as magnificent as the surrounding geography, but it poses a significant problem to large vehicles wishing to access Zion Canyon. All vehicles 7'10" or wider, or 11'4" or taller (maximum of 13'1" tall) are too large to remain in a single lane through the tunnel and require an escort. They must pay a $15 escort fee at the park entrance before driving to the tunnel, good for two trips through the tunnel within seven days of purchase. Oversized vehicles are only allowed to pass through during seasonal hours when it is manned by park rangers. Typical hours are from 8am–7pm in summer and 8am–4:30pm in winter. It is a good idea to visit the park's website or call the visitor center for current hours of operation. **Cyclists and pedestrians are not allowed to use the tunnel.**

The 10-mile **Zion–Mount Carmel Highway** connects the park's East and South Entrances. The highlight of a trip for many visitors is the six-mile **Zion Canyon Scenic Drive**. In winter visitors are allowed to drive this stretch of road all the way to the foot of Temple of Sinawava, which is also the mouth of the famous **Zion Narrows**. For the rest of the year, **Zion Canyon Drive** is only open to **park shuttle buses** and **guests of Zion Lodge**.

Park Shuttle

To conserve fuel and reduce traffic the park provides a **free shuttle** between Springdale, just outside the park's **South Entrance**, and **Temple of Sinawava**. Due to limited parking space, visitors are encouraged to park in Springdale and enter the park aboard a free shuttle. They operate from early April until late October. Buses run two separate loops. **Springdale Loop** completes laps from the south entrance/Zion Canyon Theater to Springdale. **Zion Canyon Loop** takes roughly 90-minutes to make seven stops between the visitor center and Temple of Sinawava via **Zion Canyon Scenic Drive**.

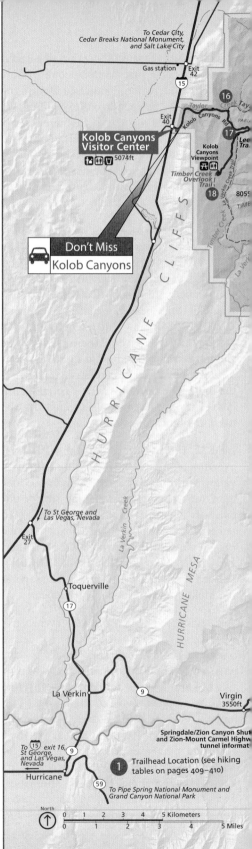

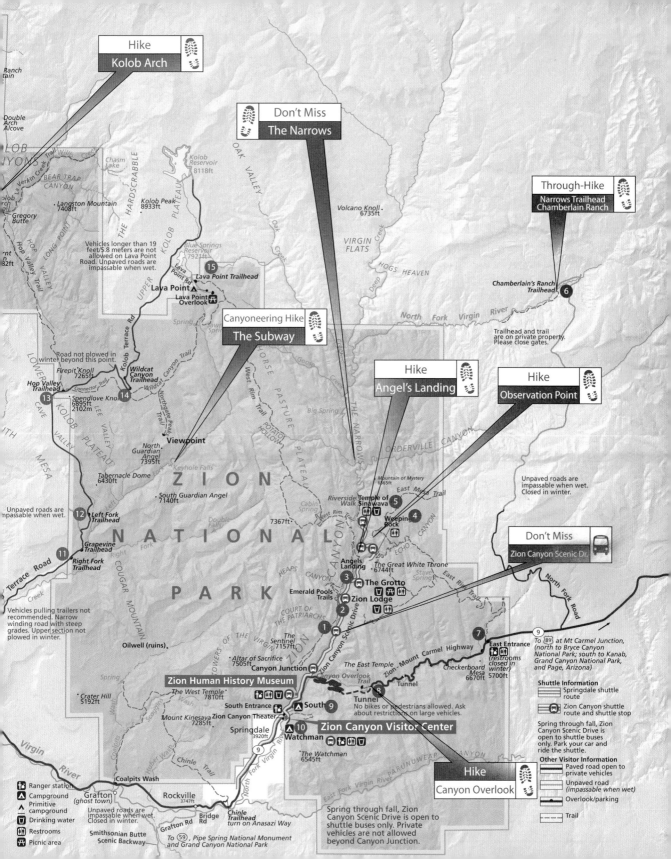

Camping & Lodging

The Three Patriarchs | Watchman and Virgin River

Zion has three drive-in campgrounds. **South and Watchman Campgrounds** are located along the Virgin River's shoreline near the south entrance and main visitor center. These campgrounds have running water and flush toilets. **Watchman** has 63 sites with electrical hook-ups for RVs. No sites have full hook-ups, but a dump station is available for campers. Watchman also has seven group campsites that can accommodate 9 to 40 campers. They are tent-only sites, which cost $3 per person per night. Watchman Campground accepts reservations for camping from early March through mid-November. You may reserve a campsite up to six months in advance by calling (877) 444-6777 or clicking www.recreation.gov.

Lava Point is a primitive campground located about a one-hour drive from Zion Canyon Visitor Center on Kolob Terrace Road. There are six campsites situated at 7,890 feet, where it's roughly 15°F cooler than other frontcountry campgrounds. Pit toilets are available, but water is not. Rapidly changing weather conditions can make Kolob Terrace Road impassable to 2WD vehicles, and visitors should check road conditions at the visitor center or park website prior to departure. **All campgrounds often fill by early afternoon on weekends and holidays. They fill every night during the summer months.**

The only in-park lodging is provided by Xanterra Parks & Resorts at **Zion Lodge**, situated in the middle of Zion Canyon. Guests of the lodge are allowed to take their own vehicles down Zion Canyon Scenic Drive. The accommodations are basic, but how much time do you plan on spending in your room anyway? **Red Rock Grill** is on-site for breakfast, lunch, and dinner. Visit www.zionlodge.com or call Xanterra Parks & Resorts at (888) 297-2757 to make your reservation. See page 449 for nearby lodging and dining.

Zion Camping

	Open	Fees	Sites	Notes
South (Near South Entrance)	March–October	$16/night	126	No showers, no hook-ups • First-come, first-served
Watchman* (Near South Entrance)	All Year	$16/night $18/night w/ electric $20/night riverside	183	No showers, reservations available from late March through late October
Lava Point (Kolob Terrace Road)	June–October	Free	6	Primitive campground • First-come, first-served
Backcountry Camping	A permit (fee) is required to camp at any of the 40+ backcountry campsites located in the park. See page 412 for details on obtaining a backcountry permit.			

Zion Lodging

	Open	Fees		Notes
Zion Lodge (Zion Canyon Scenic Dr)	All Year	Peak $170+ Off $99+		Only in-park lodging, fills early during peak season • (888) 297-2757, www.zionlodge.com
*Campground reservations can be made in advance by calling (877) 444-6777 or clicking www.recreation.gov				

Hiking

To truly appreciate the beauty of Zion, visitors must go for a hike. The park has a large network of well-maintained trails with trailheads conveniently located along Zion Canyon Scenic Drive (ZCSD), Zion–Mount Carmel Highway (ZMCH), Kolob Terrace Road (KTR), and Kolob Canyons Road (KCR). Whether you're looking for a casual leg-stretching stroll, or a boot-pounding multi-day backpacking adventure, you can find it here.

A few favorite short hikes are **Weeping Rock** (ZCSD), **Hidden Canyon** (ZCSD), **Canyon Overlook** (ZMCH), and **Taylor Creek** (KCR) **Trails. Hidden Canyon Trail**, located at Weeping Rock Shuttle Stop, is relatively short but quite strenuous and not for individuals with a fear of heights. You are required to traverse an exposed cliff, which drops off more than 1,000 feet.

Hiking the same trail but bypassing its spur to Hidden Canyon will take you to **East Rim Trail**, which leads to **Observation Point**, one of the best vantage points in the entire park where you can look down on the main canyon and Angel's Landing.

Trails to the top of **Angel's Landing** (page 410) and through **Zion Narrows** (page 411) are discussed individually. These are classic hikes, two of the best trails in the National Park System that are renowned across the globe.

The following tables provide a more comprehensive list of Zion's best hiking trails. Additional favorite hiking trails are designated with a thumbs up.

Zion Hiking Trails

	Trail Name	Trailhead (# on map)	Length	Notes (Roundtrip distances unless noted otherwise)
Zion Canyon Scenic Drive	Sand Bench Loop	Court of the Patriarchs Stop (1)	3.4 miles	Moderate • Sandy trail used mainly for trail rides
	Emerald Pools	Zion Lodge Stop (2)	1.2–2.5 mi	Easy–Moderate • Hike to 1, 2, or 3 small pools
	Angel's Landing - 👍	The Grotto Stop (3)	5.4 miles	Strenuous • Adventurous hike with excellent views
	Grotto	The Grotto Stop (3)	1.0 mile	Easy • Connects Zion Lodge with Grotto Picnic Area
	Kayenta	The Grotto Stop (3)	2.0 miles	Moderate • Connects the grotto with Middle Emerald
	Weeping Rock	Weeping Rock Stop (4)	0.4 mile	Easy • Paved trail to a wall dripping spring water
	Hidden Canyon	Weeping Rock Stop (4)	2.4 miles	Strenuous • Follows a cliff ledge to a narrow canyon
	Observation Point - 👍	Weeping Rock Stop (4)	8.0 miles	Strenuous • Look down on Angel's Landing
	Riverside Walk	Temple of Sinawava Stop (5)	2.2 miles	Easy • Paved trail along the Virgin River
	The Narrows via Riverside Walk - 👍	Temple of Sinawava Stop (5)	9.4 miles	Strenuous • Most scenic portion of the Narrows to Orderville Canyon • You will get wet
	The Narrows - 👍	Chamberlain's Ranch to Temple of Sinawava (5, 6)	16.0 miles	Strenuous • One-way, backpack (12 campsites) or day-hike (12+ hours), wading/swimming required

Angel's Landing

Images of/from Angel's Landing

One of the most memorable hikes in the entire National Park System is the 5.4-mile (roundtrip) adventure to Angel's Landing. Calling it an adventure sells it short. The last 0.5-mile is a hair-raising experience that takes you along a knife-edge ridgeline with 500 foot drops on either side. The journey begins at Grotto Trailhead Parking Area, located just beyond Zion Lodge. Once you've arrived at the trailhead, immediately cross the Virgin River via a short suspension bridge. On the opposite side of the river, ignore Kayenta Trail and head north, making a steady climb toward the mouth of Refrigerator Canyon. As you approach the mouth of the canyon you will loop back and ascend the canyon wall via 21 switchbacks known as "Walter's Wiggles." The ascent takes you to Scout's Lookout, which provides impressive views of Zion Canyon and a closer look at the landing. Do not follow the trail to the northwest, which leads into the backcountry and away from Angel's Landing via West Rim Trail. At Scout's Lookout you may begin to second guess your plans. The next 0.5-mile should never be attempted wearing improper footwear or in bad weather conditions. It is much more intimidating from a distance than up close, but there are no guardrails. Only a series of chains aid your passage along the backbone of Angel's Landing. Once you've made it to the promontory, have a seat, take a drink, and enjoy the view.

Zion Hiking Trails

	Trail Name	Trailhead (# on map)	Length	Notes (Roundtrip distances unless noted otherwise)
Zion–Mount Carmel Highway	East Rim - 👍	Spur road past East Entrance (7)	7.8 miles	Strenuous • One-way, long day-hike, backpack, or take Observation Point Trail to Zion Canyon Scenic Drive
	Canyon Overlook - 👍	East of the long tunnel (8)	1.0 mile	Moderate • Short hike with excellent scenic value
	Pa'rus	South Campground (9)	3.5 miles	Easy • Paved trail follows Virgin River to Canyon Junction
	Watchman	Watchman Campground (10)	2.7 miles	Moderate • Short trail to a perch above the camp
	Archeology	Zion Canyon Visitor Center (10)	0.4 mile	Easy • Hike to small prehistoric storage buildings
Kolob Terrace Road	Right Fork	0.5-mile past Park Boundary (11)	11.8 miles	Moderate • Follows creek to waterfalls
	Left Fork - 👍	Left Fork Trailhead (12)	9.0 miles	Moderate • Non-technical out-and-back to Subway
	Wildcat Canyon Connector	Hop Valley Trailhead (13)	8.7 miles	Moderate • One-way, ends at Lava Point Camp
	Northgate Peaks	Wildcat Canyon Trailhead (14)	4.4 miles	Easy • Lightly used flat trail to 7,200+ ft peak
	Left Fork/Technical Subway	Wildcat Canyon Trailhead (14)	8.1 miles	Strenuous • Requires rope, ends at Left Fork Trailhead
	Wildcat Canyon	Lava Point (15)	9.4 miles	Strenuous • Scrambling over difficult terrain
	West Rim - 👍	Lava Point (15)	14.2 miles	Strenuous • One-way, ends at the Grotto via Angel's Landing
Kolob Canyons Rd	Taylor Creek - 👍	Taylor Creek Trailhead (16)	5.0 miles	Moderate • Leads to Double Arch Alcove
	North Fork Taylor Creek	Taylor Creek Trailhead (16)	5.0 miles	Moderate • Unmaintained spur from Taylor Creek
	Kolob Arch via La Verkin Creek Trail - 👍	Lee Pass Trailhead (17)	14.0 miles	Strenuous • Trail can be made a long day hike or an overnight backpack trip
	Timber Creek Overlook	End of Kolob Terrace Rd (18)	1.0 mile	Moderate • Short hike, follows ridge to a peak

The Narrows

The Narrows is an iconic hike following the Virgin River as it winds its way through a 2,000 foot deep canyon that is, as its name implies, narrow (20–30 ft). The water is cold, the rocks are slippery, and the sun rarely penetrates its depths, making the trek challenging and exhilarating. You will wade through knee-deep water and take the occasional swim across deep holes. Visitors can explore the Narrows three ways: day-hike from Mount Sinawava, day-hike the entire length beginning at Chamberlain Ranch, or backpack overnight.

A day-hike into the canyon from Mount Sinawava Shuttle Stop via Riverside Walk is the simplest option. You are free to hike to Orderville Canyon, the most scenic and popular stretch, without a permit.

The alternatives eschew crowds, but require a **backcountry permit** (page 412). Completing the entire Narrows requires arranging a **shuttle** (page 452), since it's a one-way hike. The journey begins outside park boundaries at **Chamberlain Ranch**, accessed via North Fork Road, just outside the park's East Entrance. Ambitious hikers can day hike the entire 16-mile canyon in 10–14 hours. If you'd like to take your time and enjoy the scenery, spend a night at one of **12 backcountry campsites**. Hiking the entire canyon provides hikers with the added bonus of solitude. You'll feel alone in the Narrows until reaching **Orderville Canyon**, where you'll meet the day-hikers from Mount Sinawava.

The best time of year to hike the Narrows is late spring to early summer. Cool water of the Virgin River will be refreshing as you spend more than half of your hike wading. Wear sturdy shoes and carry a walking stick. Be sure to check the weather before entering the Narrows, as flash flooding and hypothermia are constant dangers. See page 452 for **guide services and gear rental**.

The Narrows © Adam Belles

Switchbacks of Zion–Mount Carmel Highway ©
Bala Sivakumar (www.wanderingmonkphoto.com)

The Subway © Jeremiah Roth

Red rock, green grass, and blue sky © Navin Rajagopalan

Bighorn sheep

 # Backpacking

Backpacking is allowed at designated sites along four popular trails. **Zion Narrows** (page 411) has 12 camp-sites, all located above the high-water line of the Virgin River and upriver from Big Spring. **West Rim Trail**, from the Grotto to Lava Point Primitive Campground, is the most popular backpacking trail, with a total of nine designated campsites along the way. If you can arrange a shuttle, begin hiking at Lava Point Campground. From here, it will be a mostly downhill 14.2-mile trek that can be completed in two days without a problem. Kolob Canyons' (page 406) only suitable backpacking route is **La Verkin/Kolob Arch Trail**, including its spur through the Hop Valley. There are also designated campsites in the park's southwest corner along **Coalpits Wash** and **Scoggins Wash**. In addition to the designated campsites, backpackers are allowed to camp in specified zones as long as they are one mile from roads, out of sight of trails, and 0.25-mile from springs. Spring and fall are the best seasons for backpacking trips. **A permit is required for all overnight stays in the backcountry.**

 # Backcountry Permit

A **backcountry permit** is required for all overnight trips in the backcountry, Narrows thru-hikes, Narrows day-hikes beyond Orderville Canyon, and all canyon trips re-quiring descending gear or ropes (including the Subway). Permits can be obtained at **Zion Canyon Visitor Center's Backcountry Desk** or **Kolob Canyons Visitor Center**. They can be reserved on a first-come, first-served basis online from the park's website for a $5 non-refundable fee per reservation. At least 25 percent of all permits are set aside for day-before/same-day walk-in visitors. If you attempt to secure a walk-in permit you should arrive the day before your trip when the backcountry desk opens. Permits to the park's two most popular backcountry ar-eas, the **Subway** and **Mystery Canyon**, are distributed via an online lottery. Hopeful hikers must enter the lot-tery at least three months prior to their planned trip. A non-refundable $5 fee is charged for each lottery entry. If you won the lottery, secured a reservation, or obtained a permit the day of your trip, you will have to pay an ad-ditional backcountry permit fee. Fees are based on group size: $10 for 1–2 people, $15 for 3–7 people and $20 for 8–12 people. Maximum group size is 12 people.

Horseback Riding

Tourists can also experience the wonders of Zion on horseback. **Canyon Trail Rides** offers 1-hour ($40/person) and half-day ($75/person) trail rides from March through October. Guided rides begin at a corral by Emerald Pools Trailhead near Zion Lodge. Visitors are also allowed to trailer in stock. A stock camp is available at Hop Valley Site A, located on Hop Valley Trail. A **backcountry permit** (page 412) is required for overnight stays, but not for day use. Not all trails are approved for stock use, so check with the visitor center or online before you ride.

Canyon Trail Rides • (435) 679-8665 • www.canyonrides.com
Bryce Canyon National Park; Tropic, UT 84776

Other Activities

Biking is allowed on all of the park's roadways and Pa'rus Trail (page 410), which connects South Campground with Zion Canyon Scenic Drive.

Bird Watching: There are **more than 290 species of birds** that visit or nest within the park. Watch cliff-faces for peregrine falcons and the lush vegetation along the Virgin River for Grace's warblers and Bullock's orioles.

Stargazing: Visitors, especially those from large urban areas, should take a few moments to admire the stars. High elevation and remoteness make Zion an ideal location to admire the night sky.

Photography: Brightly colored rock layers, deep blue skies, vibrant green grasslands, and the occasional wildflower bloom make Zion one of the most photogenic parks. A tripod is essential for photographing the dimly lit **Zion Narrows** (page 411). For best results take photos near dawn or dusk.

Kayaking the Narrows is only recommended for advanced paddlers. A **backcountry permit** (page 412) is required for all boat use in the park.

Technical canyoneering and rock climbing are popular activities (for experienced individuals only). Route descriptions are available at the Backcountry Desk. First-timers should buy a dedicated guide book or hire a guide (page 452).

For Kids

Zion offers guided and self-guided **Junior Ranger Programs** for children (ages 6–12). To participate in the self-guided program, simply purchase a Junior Ranger activity booklet from either of the park's visitor centers or Zion Human History Museum. Complete the activities and return to a visitor center to be made an official Zion National Park Junior Ranger and receive an award. Guided programs are offered daily from Memorial Day weekend through late August. These family-oriented programs are free of charge. Participants are advised to bring water and wear close-toed shoes (i.e., no flip-flops or sandals).

Ranger Programs

From April to November park rangers administer a series of walks, talks, and interpretive programs. These activities explore the lives of resident plants and animals or discuss the difficulty of life in the desert. Walks range from a leisurely ramble along Riverside Walk (page 409) to a strenuous hike up the Narrows (page 411). Evening discussions are held regularly at Watchman Campground's Amphitheater and Zion Lodge's Auditorium. A list of discussion topics is usually displayed on bulletin boards at the visitor centers, museum, and campgrounds. Many tours accept reservations up to three days in advance. To make a reservation, stop in at Zion Canyon Visitor Center. If you have the time and the opportunity to join a ranger guided tour, don't think twice, just go.

Flora & Fauna

Zion sits at the convergence of three geographic regions: the Colorado Plateau, Great Basin, and Mojave Desert. Geologic variance coupled with more than 4,000 feet of elevation change makes for an environment filled with incredible biodiversity. Zion is home to **more than 78 species of mammals, 290 species of birds, 44 species of reptiles and amphibians, and 8 species of fish**. Most notable are bighorn sheep, mule deer, mountain lions, peregrine falcons, and Mexican spotted owls. The park also supports **more than 900 species of plants**, ranging from cacti and desert succulents to riparian trees, shrubs, and wildflowers.

Did you know?

➤ In 1918, the director of the National Park Service renamed Mukuntuweap National Park to Zion, making it easier to say and promote.

➤ Red and tan Navajo Sandstone of Zion Canyon has been exposed by the work of the Virgin River, which transports millions of tons of sediment to the Colorado River each year.

➤ The Virgin River drops 50–80 feet per mile, one of the steepest stream gradients in North America.

Best of Zion

Activity: Shuttle through Zion Canyon
   Runner-up: Canyon Trail Rides

Family Hike: Canyon Overlook
   Runner-up: Riverside Walk
   2nd Runner-up: Pa'rus Trail

Hike: The Narrows (to Orderville Canyon)
   Runner-up: Angel's Landing
   2nd Runner-up: Observation Point
   3rd Runner-up: Taylor Creek
   4th Runner-up: Hidden Canyon
   5th Runner-up: Left Fork

Visitor Centers: Zion has two visitor centers that are open every day of the year except Christmas. **Zion Canyon Visitor Center**, located near the park's south entrance on UT-9, is the primary destination for park information as well as the main hub for the **free shuttle service** (page 406). Standard operating hours are from 8am to 5pm, but are extended to 7:30pm during the busy summer season. A **Backcountry Desk** is located inside, where you can obtain backcountry information and permits. It's open from 7am to 7:30pm during the summer and 8am to 4:30pm during the winter.

Kolob Canyons Visitor Center, located on Kolob Terrace Road, is a small facility with books and souvenirs for sale. It's staffed by a park ranger from 8am to 6pm during the summer and 8am to 4:30pm during the winter.

Zion Human History Museum is located just north of Zion Canyon Visitor Center on Zion–Mount Carmel Highway. It features alternating art exhibits, a short introductory film, and book and gift stores. It's open daily, early March through late November, from 9am to 7pm.

Pets: Pets are allowed in the park but are not permitted on the shuttle, in the backcountry, on trails, or in public buildings. These restrictions make travelling with a pet challenging. Pets are allowed in developed campgrounds, along park roads, in parking areas, and on Pa'rus Trail near Zion Canyon Visitor Center, but must be kept on a leash no more than six feet in length at all times. **Doggy Dude Ranch** (435.772.3105) is a nearby kennel where you can keep your pet while exploring the park.

Accessibility: Zion Canyon Visitor Center, Zion Human History Museum, and Kolob Canyons Visitor Center are fully accessible to individuals in wheelchairs. All shuttle buses (page 406) are accessible and equipped with a wheelchair lift. Zion Lodge has two accessible rooms, and there are a total of five accessible campsites at Watchman and South Campgrounds. Riverside Walk and Pa'rus Trail are paved and accessible to wheelchair users with assistance.

Weather: The weather is most comfortable between March and May, and September and November. These periods are marked by daytime highs in the low 60s to low 80s°F. Overnight temperatures drop into the 40s°F. Summer days are hot, with an average daily high of 100°F in July. It's not unheard of for the mercury to reach 110°F on the hottest days of the year. No matter how hot it gets during the day, summer nights remain comfortable with temperatures usually below 70°F. Winters are generally mild, but visitors arriving between November and March should be prepared for snowy conditions. January is the coldest month of the year with an average daily high of 52°F and a daily low of 29°F. This region of the United States does not receive much precipitation, but short thunderstorms are common throughout the year.

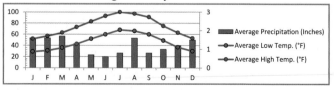

Vacation Planner

If you're visiting between April and October, **Zion Canyon Scenic Drive** (page 406) can only be accessed by the **free shuttle buses and guests of Zion Lodge**. Alternatively, you can bike or walk to the canyon via **Pa'rus Trail** (page 410). Provided below is a three-day itinerary, allowing two days to explore the main canyon and one day at Kolob Canyons. **Kolob Terrace Road** leads to some of the park's more extraordinary hiking opportunities, but popular routes like **Left Fork Trail to the Subway** (page 410) require advanced planning and a backcountry permit (page 412), so it is excluded. The park's **camping** and **lodging** facilities are referenced on page 408. Nearby dining, grocery stores, lodging, festivals, and attractions are listed on pages 448–453. If you plan on traveling to the park in an oversized vehicle or RV, be sure to check the size requirements for Zion Tunnel (page 406), because you may require an escort or not fit altogether.

Entering Zion's East Entrance, make a quick stop just before **Zion Tunnel** to hike the 1-mile trail to **Canyon Overlook** (page 410). It's a great spot to view Zion Canyon before entering it. The short hike also gives you an opportunity to see the exterior of Zion Tunnel and the rock that was blown apart to build it in 1930. After the hike, return to your car and pass through the tunnel. On the other side is a set of switchbacks that makes for an easy descent to the canyon floor.

Continue along Zion–Mount Carmel Highway to **Zion Canyon Visitor Center** (if you enter at the South Entrance begin your trip here). Check the schedule of programs, browse the exhibits, and if you are hoping to procure a **walk-in backcountry permit** (page 412), see if any are available. If members of your group are notorious for spending excessive amounts of time at gift stores, bookstores—any kind of store—leave them at the visitor center and go hike **Watchman Trail** (page 410).

Once you're back together and ready to go, head to the shuttle stop just behind the visitor center. Hop aboard a **shuttle** and ride until you reach the **Grotto**, where you'll hike to **Angel's Landing** (page 410). After cautiously making your way across this knife-edge ridgeline nothing about Zion will be intimidating. It's strenuous, but feasible for those in average physical condition. Children are usually fearless of the precipitous drop-offs that mark the last 0.5-mile, so be sure to watch them closely. If you

don't feel up to reaching the Landing, the view from **Scout's Lookout** is still worthwhile. Anyone fearful of heights might want to stay aboard the shuttle bus and exit at **Weeping Rock**, where you can hike to **Observation Point** (page 409). It's another strenuous hike with exposed cliff-faces, but not nearly as intimidating as Angel's Landing. Complete the hike, climb back aboard a **shuttle** and complete the circuit around **Zion Canyon Loop**. If you're spending the night in the park, check if there's an evening program at the lodge or campground.

Take it easy in the morning. Maybe attend a **ranger program**, hike to **Canyon Overlook** (if you didn't yesterday), or walk along **Pa'rus Trail** (page 410) into the canyon. In the afternoon, ride a shuttle bus back into the main canyon to hike the **Narrows** (page 411). Make sure that you have sturdy hiking shoes on. If it's an abnormally cold day or there's a chance of thunderstorm, find an alternate activity. The Virgin River is perpetually cold and flash floods can occur with the slightest rainfall. With cooperative weather take the shuttle to **Temple of Sinawava** and follow **Riverside Walk** (page 409) to the canyon's mouth. Here you will often find hiking sticks left by previous hikers propped against the canyon walls; taking one is a good idea. Beyond Riverside Walk the canyon is your trail. There's no marked route. You simply choose your own way proceeding as fast or as slow as you like. The entire trek is only 3.5-miles (one-way) to **Orderville Canyon**, but it's extremely slow going as you are constantly negotiating slippery and rocky river-bottom while weaving back and forth across the Virgin River. You'll want to rest your feet after the hike. Maybe stop at **Zion Human History Museum** to watch its 22-minute film.

Drive to **Kolob Canyons**. The area's most exciting hike is another long one. If you feel like recording 14 more miles on your hiking boots, head for **Kolob Arch** (page 410). Otherwise drive the Scenic Road and hike 5 miles along **Taylor Creek Trail** to **Double Arch Alcove**. This trail proceeds along a gradual grade to views of a large alcove in a massive wall of red sandstone.

A mule train returning from the canyon floor

PO Box 129
Grand Canyon, AZ 86023
Phone: (928) 638-7888
Website: www.nps.gov/grca

Established: February 26, 1919
January 11, 1908 (Nat'l Monument)
Size: 1,217,403 Acres
Annual Visitors: 4.4 Million
Peak Season: Summer

Activities: Hiking, Backpacking,
Camping, Mule Rides, River Trips,
Air Tours, Biking, and Photography

Campgrounds: Mather ($18/night),
Trailer Village ($34.50), Desert View
($12), and North Rim ($18–25)
Backcountry Camping: Permitted
with a Backcountry Permit (fee)

South Rim Lodging: $70–426/night
North Rim Lodging: $116–187/night

South Rim Hours: All day, every day
North Rim closes Nov/Dec–mid-May
Entrance Fee: $25 • Vehicle
$12 • Individual (foot, bike, etc.)

Grand Canyon - Arizona

"There is of course no reason at all in trying to describe the Grand Canyon. Those who have not seen it will not believe any possible description. Those who have seen it know that it cannot be described..."

– J.B. Priestly (Harper's Magazine)

In Arizona's northwestern reaches, the **Colorado River** has carved the grandest of canyons. Measuring 277 miles long, up to 18 miles wide and more than one mile deep, the Grand Canyon is a gaping scar across the surface of the earth. **Theodore Roosevelt** declared it "the one great sight which every American should see." One man's thought became another man's goal. **Stephen Mather**, first director of the National Park Service, dedicated much of his time to obtaining the land and protecting it from commercial interests. Since the National Park Service became custodian of the Grand Canyon in 1919, it has sought to preserve and protect this iconic landscape of the American West for the enjoyment of people: present and future.

Before the National Park Service controlled the area, cattle grazed freely above the rim and miners filed claims for any location that might produce ore. One prospector in particular had a penchant for exploiting its resources. **Ralph Henry Cameron**—part-time prospector, full-time spinner of colorful yarns—claimed to have spent more than $500,000 "improving" the canyon's trails, blazing the first wagon path from Flagstaff to the South Rim, and opening the first successful mining operation within the canyon. Most of his mining claims were conveniently located at scenic points along the South Rim. At Cameron Trail, today's Bright Angel Trail, he constructed Cameron's Hotel and placed a gate across the trailhead. His brother manned the gate, collecting $1 per person for its use, the first of many swindles along Cameron Trail. He also held a claim at Indian Spring, the route's only source of clean water. Hot and dehydrated, hikers had no choice but to pay exorbitant prices at Cameron's watering hole.

It wasn't long until Cameron became a nuisance to the **Santa Fe Railroad**. Once the railway reached the South Rim, it wasted little time in constructing El Tovar Hotel. Cameron responded by filing claims all around the luxury abode. Claims were followed by lawsuits, and eventually he was bought out for $40,000. As tourism rose Cameron watched money roll in, while neglecting the condition of his facilities. Outhouses were so appalling that the Santa Fe Railroad offered to replace them free of charge. He declined the offer and filed a lawsuit on the grounds that they would have to illegally cross his claims to build the comfort stations. The court sided in favor of Cameron. When **President Theodore Roosevelt** created Grand Canyon National Monument Cameron was instructed to abandon all claims not actively mined. He filed 55 more. It wasn't until 1919, more than a decade later, when Congress established the national park, that Cameron was forced to leave.

The State of Arizona always supported Cameron. He was tied to most of northern Arizona's jobs and locals saw him as a champion against the mighty railroad and wealthy easterners. Showing their support, he was elected a member of the Senate in 1920, where he vehemently opposed the national park idea and made proposals for two hydroelectric dams and the development of a platinum mine in the canyon. In the end Congress tabled all dam projects and Cameron's crusade against the park finally ended when the public learned he used his position for personal gain and failed to reelect him. Today, the park is everyone's gain, protected for all mankind to see, just like President Roosevelt hoped.

Did you know?

▶ Bills to create Grand Canyon National Park were proposed in 1882, 1883, and 1886. Had any one passed it would have been the second national park.

Deer Creek Falls (river mile 136)

Ruins along the Colorado River

Rafters in the Colorado River

The Grand Canyon viewed from Lipan Point

Grand Geology

While in the area you may hear or see the term "**Grand Staircase**." It is the stairway to many visitors' heaven, but this term simply refers to a sequence of sedimentary rock layers that form a massive "staircase" between Bryce Canyon and Grand Canyon. Each canyon's cliff edge acts as a giant step displaying the earth's geologic history in its layers. As you move down the geologic column, each successive rock layer is older than the previous. The oldest exposed formation in Bryce Canyon is the youngest remaining layer at Zion Canyon. Likewise, the floor of Zion Canyon is Kaibab Formation, which is the same formation you stand on at the Grand Canyon's rim. As you stand at the South Rim staring into the depths of the grandest canyon of them all, you are witnessing some 2 billion years of geologic history.

The oldest exposed layers of rock are found at the bottom of the canyon's inner gorge. They are the Vishnu Basement Rocks, a collection of hard schist and granites formed by the heat and pressure of colliding tectonic plates. Moving up the geologic column, the next set of rocks is the Grand Canyon Supergroup. Its strata accumulated in basins formed as the land mass pulled apart. These layers of shale, limestone, and lava rock can be seen from a handful of locations, such as South Rim's Lipan Point. Grand Canyon Supergroup's rocks are often pinched off and absent from the canyon's exposed walls, creating a gap in the geologic record of more than one billion years between the Vishnu Basement Rocks and adjacent Tapeats Sandstone layer. Scientists believe this irregularity marks an extended period of erosion rather than deposition. **Major John Wesley Powell** recognized these disjointed rock layers during his expedition of the Grand Canyon in 1869 and named it the **Great Unconformity**. Beginning with Tapeats Sandstone numerous layers of sedimentary rock make up the set of Layered Paleozoic Rocks occupying the upper two-thirds of the canyon walls. These layers come from a variety of sources: limestone from ancient marine life, mudstone from river deposition, and sandstone from sand dunes (see the following page for the name, date, and depth of all rock layers).

All of these rock layers were formed near sea level. Some 20 million years ago the uplift that created the Rocky Mountains also raised the **Colorado Plateau**, encompassing present-day northern Arizona, eastern Utah, northwestern New Mexico, and western Colorado. Gravity's perpetual force caused rivers to erode the landscape. Water wore away its path and carried with it sediment stripped from the earth. By five or six million years ago the routes of the Colorado River and its tributaries were carved in stone, draining 90 percent of the plateau. So, **why is the Grand Canyon so wide?** First, the canyon is not carved at a constant rate. Lava dams formed and breached and Ice Ages came and went, both of which caused massive flows of water. Also, soft sedimentary rock erodes faster than hard rock. Today, the flow of the Colorado River is dramatically reduced by upstream dams and is grinding away layers of hard schist and granite at the canyon's floor. Meanwhile, the canyon walls are mostly soft sedimentary rock that erodes easily as rainwater and snowmelt drain into the canyon from the north and south rims. The North Rim receives more precipitation and therefore eroding faster than the South Rim.

Did you know?

▶ Evidence suggests the Colorado River established its course through the canyon 17 million years ago.

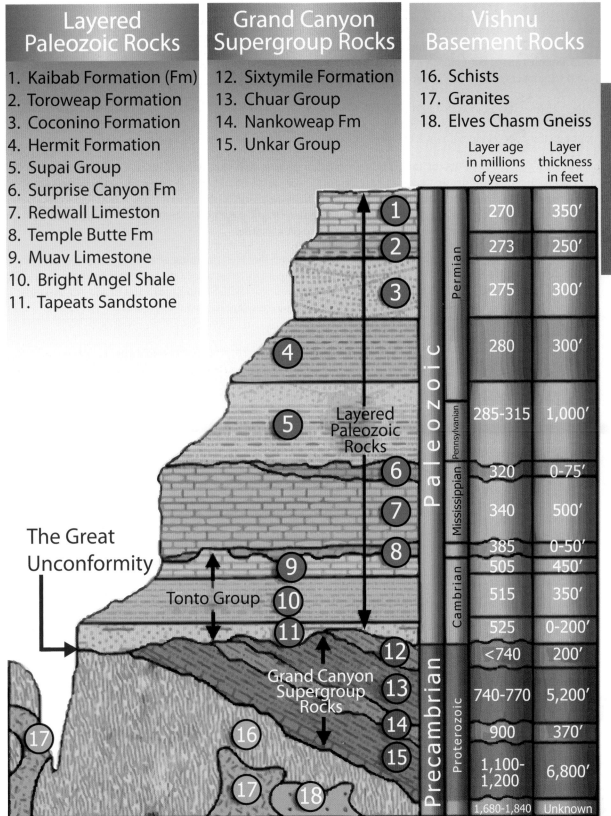

Layered Paleozoic Rocks

1. Kaibab Formation (Fm)
2. Toroweap Formation
3. Coconino Formation
4. Hermit Formation
5. Supai Group
6. Surprise Canyon Fm
7. Redwall Limeston
8. Temple Butte Fm
9. Muav Limestone
10. Bright Angel Shale
11. Tapeats Sandstone

Grand Canyon Supergroup Rocks

12. Sixtymile Formation
13. Chuar Group
14. Nankoweap Fm
15. Unkar Group

Vishnu Basement Rocks

16. Schists
17. Granites
18. Elves Chasm Gneiss

The Great Unconformity

Tonto Group

Layered Paleozoic Rocks

Grand Canyon Supergroup Rocks

Era	Period	Layer age in millions of years	Layer thickness in feet
Paleozoic	Permian	270	350'
		273	250'
		275	300'
		280	300'
	Pennsylvanian	285-315	1,000'
	Mississippian	320	0-75'
		340	500'
		385	0-50'
	Cambrian	505	450'
		515	350'
		525	0-200'
Precambrian	Proterozoic	<740	200'
		740-770	5,200'
		900	370'
		1,100-1,200	6,800'
		1,680-1,840	Unknown

419

Grand Canyon - Regions

Grand Canyon National Park consists of three well-defined regions: Colorado River/Canyon Floor, South Rim, and North Rim. The river and the immense canyon that it carved separate the rims. As a crow flies the rims are no more than 18 miles apart, but to reach one from the other by automobile requires a 210-mile, 4.5-hour drive. This causes most vacationers to visit just one rim or the other.

The Colorado River/Canyon Floor (page 424): Adventurous visitors run more than 150 named rapids along 225 miles of the Colorado River between Lee's Ferry and Diamond Creek. You can also hike into the canyon, spend a night on the floor (camping or at Phantom Ranch), and then return to the rim the following day.

South Rim (page 429): **90% of the park's 4+ million guests visit the South Rim.** It's open all year and has a myriad of lodging, dining, and camping facilities, as well as an abundance of entertainment opportunities. The South Rim enjoys a slightly warmer and drier climate than the North Rim due to it being 1,000 feet lower in elevation. Several historic buildings, trailheads to the popular Bright Angel and South Kaibab Trails, and numerous canyon viewpoints can be accessed via the region's free park shuttle.

North Rim (page 435): The same great canyon views without the overwhelming crowds. It's also the best place to begin a rim-to-rim hike, since you'll spend more time going down (an extra 1,000 feet) than going back up. North Kaibab Trail provides access to the inner canyon, where it connects with South Kaibab and Bright Angel Trails. The North Rim has a wider variety of above-rim trails with some excellent backpacking routes.

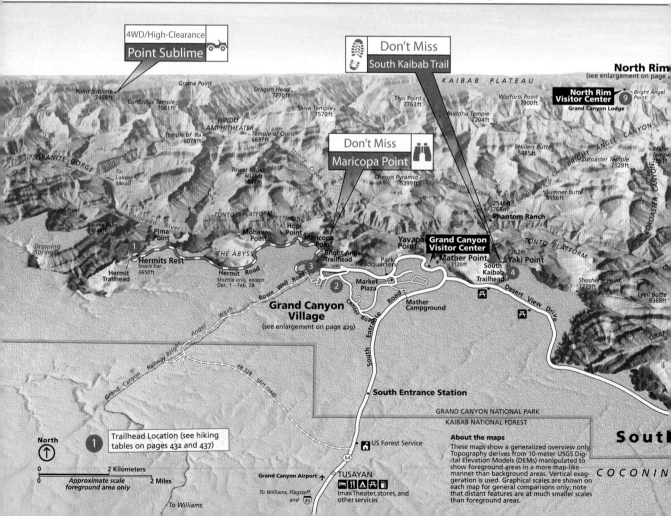

Rim-to-Rim Shuttle

Transcanyon Shuttle (928.638.2820, www.trans-canyonshuttle.com) provides daily shuttle service between the North Rim and the South Rim with an additional stop at Marble Canyon (Lee's Ferry). This service is ideal for rim-to-rim hikers not wanting to retrace their path back through the canyon or visitors who would rather not drive themselves. It costs $80/person (one-way), and $150/person (roundtrip). The commute between North and South Rims takes approximately 4.5 hours. One-way fare to Marble Canyon costs $65/person. Shuttle service is available between May 15 and October 15. Reservations are required.

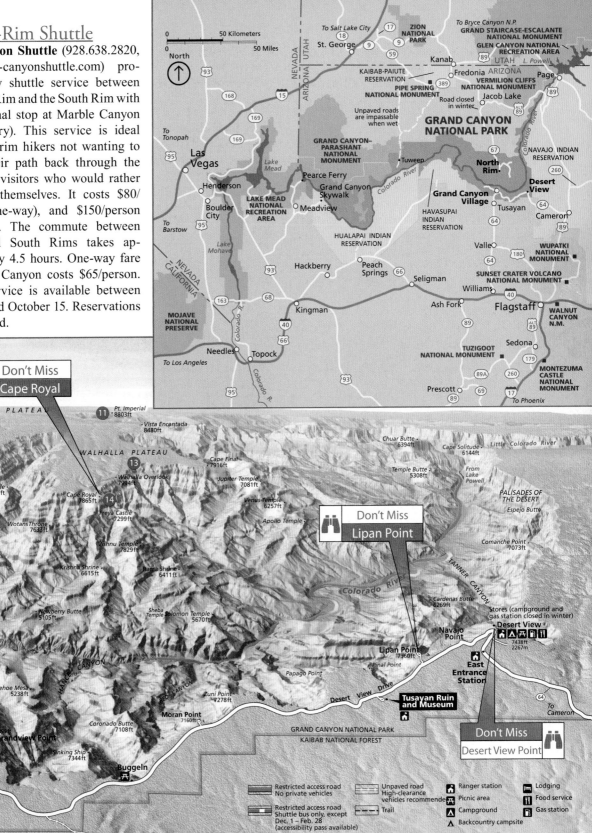

Don't Miss — Cape Royal

Don't Miss — Lipan Point

Don't Miss — Desert View Point

Legend:
- Restricted access road — No private vehicles
- Restricted access road — Shuttle bus only, except Dec. 1 – Feb. 28 (accessibility pass available)
- Unpaved road — High-clearance vehicles recommended
- Trail
- Ranger station
- Picnic area
- Campground
- Backcountry campsite
- Lodging
- Food service
- Gas station

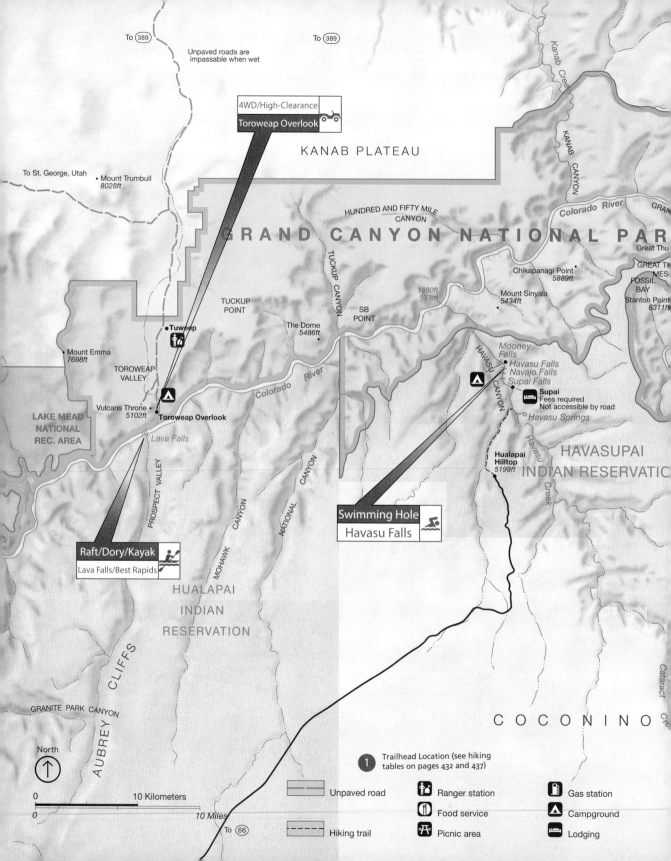

To ③③⑨

To ③③⑨

Unpaved roads are
impassable when wet

KANAB PLATEAU

4WD/High-Clearance
Toroweap Overlook

To St. George, Utah   • Mount Trumbull
8028ft

HUNDRED AND FIFTY MILE
CANYON

G R A N D   C A N Y O N   N A T I O N A L   P A R

Colorado River   GRA

Great Thu

KANAB CREEK

KANAB CANYON

Chikapanagi Point •
5889ft

GREAT TI
MES

FOSSIL
BAY

Stanton Point
6311ft

TUCKUP
POINT

TUCKUP CANYON

The Dome
5486ft

SB
POINT

*1880ft
573m*

Mount Sinyala
5434ft

• **Tuweep**

Mooney
Falls

HAVASU CANYON

Havasu Falls
Navajo Falls
Supai Falls

Supai
Fees required
Not accessible by road

• Mount Emma
7698ft

TOROWEAP
VALLEY

Colorado   River

Havasu Springs

Vulcans Throne •
5102ft

Toroweap Overlook

Lava Falls

**Hualapai
Hilltop**
5199ft

**HAVASUPAI
INDIAN RESERVATIO**

**LAKE MEAD
NATIONAL
REC. AREA**

PROSPECT VALLEY

MOHAWK CANYON

NATIONAL CANYON

Havasu Creek

Swimming Hole
Havasu Falls

Raft/Dory/Kayak
Lava Falls/Best Rapids

**HUALAPAI

INDIAN

RESERVATION**

GRANITE PARK CANYON

AUBREY CLIFFS

C O C O N I N O

Cataract Cr

North

0   10 Kilometers

0   10 Miles

To ⑥⑥

① Trailhead Location (see hiking
tables on pages 432 and 437)

━━━ Unpaved road

- - - Hiking trail

Ranger station

Food service

Picnic area

Gas station

Campground

Lodging

Rafting the Colorado - Courtesy of the Perry family

The Colorado River

"It is not a show place, a beauty spot, but a revelation. The Colorado River made it; but you feel when you are there that God gave the Colorado River its instructions. The thing is Beethoven's Ninth Symphony in stone and magic light. I hear rumors of visitors who were disappointed. The same people will be disappointed at the Day of Judgment." – J.B. Priestly (Harper's Magazine)

The Colorado River is sculptor of the Grand Canyon. Revealer of geologic history. Thrill-seeker's paradise. Ever so slowly these muddy waters of the Colorado dug the world's most magnificent ditch. Explorers crafted elaborate stories of impassable waterfalls, impossible portages, and inaccessible canyons. For decades it remained a blank spot on the map. Today, the map is filled in, and while Grand Canyon's beauty remains, its power is diminished by dams and irrigation.

The Colorado begins in Rocky Mountain National Park (page 326). From there it grows in size and majesty as it passes many of the United States' most treasured natural wonders. It forms the southern boundary of Arches National Park (page 368). In Canyonlands (page 376) it unites with the Green River and rumbles through Cataract Canyon. It floods a red rock labyrinth at Glen Canyon National Recreation Area. And finally it reaches the Grand Canyon, where it offers **the greatest whitewater adventure in North America**. The mighty Colorado, weakened by man, still churns down below the canyon's rims.

Why look into the canyon from above when you can meet its maker down below? **Major John Wesley Powell** must have shared that sentiment, as he famously set out on his namesake expedition in 1869. The most unlikely of explorers, a Civil War injury resulted in amputation of an arm. After the war he worked as a geology professor, and a series of expeditions into the Rockies and around the Green and Colorado Rivers rekindled his thirst for adventure.

In 1869 he set out with nine men and four boats to explore the Colorado River. Their goal was to fill in the largest hole in the map of the United States. The journey began at Green River, Wyoming. When they arrived at the confluence of the Green and Grand Rivers (the official start of the Colorado) they had already lost one boat and a third of their supplies. Morale was low, but they had little choice but to press on. By the time they reached the Grand Canyon, Powell's men were coming apart at the seams. Starvation, summer heat, and constant pounding of rapid upon rapid had taken their toll. Three men opted to climb out of the canyon into an unknown landscape most likely inhabited by Native Americans and were never seen again. Just two days later, Powell and his crew reached the mouth of the Virgin River, where they met a few Mormon fishermen.

Did you know?

➤ The Colorado River is about 1,450 miles long, of which 277 miles passes through the Grand Canyon.

River Adventures

More than a dozen experienced **outfitters** provide guided whitewater trips through the Grand Canyon. You can choose from upper, lower, and full canyon adventures. Each trip includes exciting excursions to waterfalls, beaches, and side canyons. All meals, non-alcoholic drinks, and tents are included. The upper and lower halves typically begin or end at Phantom Ranch and require that you hike into or out of the canyon. A few of the tours substitute a helicopter ride for the hike. Full canyon tours cover 225 miles from Lee's Ferry near Glen Canyon Dam to Diamond Creek in Hualapai Indian Reservation. You only get to run Lava Falls, the biggest rapid, on full and lower canyon tours. Several outfitters offer specialized trips that focus on subjects like geology or photography. All raft adventures generally run from mid-April through early November. Spring or fall are the best seasons to go. You'll avoid the summer heat and crowds, and summer trips often fully book up to a year in advance. Finally, you'll have to choose a watercraft. A wooden dory provides the wildest ride. Motorized J-Rigs smooth out the rapids and expedite the journey. Raft trips are also available, but not all trips allow passengers to paddle. If you want to have an oar in your hands look for "all-paddle" trips in the table on the opposite page.

Grand Canyon - Colorado River Outfitters

River Outfitter	Dates/Length/Rates	Craft	Notes
Aramark-Wilderness River Adventures www.riveradventures.com (800) 992-8022 • (928) 645-3296	April–September 3.5–16 Days $1,660–3,930	Dory J-Rig	Offers 4–8 day motorized J-Rig trips or 5.5–16 (full canyon) day oar boat trips • Shorter trips hike into or out of the canyon
Arizona Raft Adventures www.azraft.com (800) 786-RAFT • (928) 526-8200	April–October 6–16 Days $1,940–3,946	Raft Dory J-Rig	Motorized, hybrid (one paddle raft, the rest ride), & all-paddle trips offered • Also offers 15-day kayak trip or kayak school
Arizona River Runners www.raftarizona.com (800) 477-7238 • (602) 867-4866	April–October 3–13 Days $1,175–3,295	Dory J-Rig	Offers 3–8 day motorized J-Rig trips or 8–13 day oar-powered trips • Transportation not included in cost
Canyon Explorations/Expeditions www.canyonexplorations.com (800) 654-0723 • (928) 774-4559	April–October 6–17 Days $1,790–4,135	Raft J-Rig	Hybrid and all-paddle trips • Hard-shelled kayakers can join tours for an additional $200 • Transportation included in cost
Canyoneers www.canyoneers.com (800) 525-0924 • (928) 526-0924	April–September 3–14 Days $995–3,350	Raft Dory J-Rig	3–10 day motorized J-Rig trips or 6–14 day oar powered trips • Geology trips offered • Transportation included in cost
Colorado River & Trail Expeditions www.crateinc.com (800) 253-7328 • (801) 261-1789	April–October 4–14 Days $1,400–3,450	Raft Dory J-Rig	Special Women's Raft Retreats, natural history, and hiking trips are offered • Transportation included in cost
Colorado River Discovery www.raftthecanyon.com (888) 522-6644 • (928) 645-9175	March–November Half-day $79	J-Rig	This trip does not pass through the Grand Canyon • It begins at the Glenn Canyon Dam • Scenery is still impressive
Grand Canyon Expeditions www.gcex.com (800) 544-2691 • (435) 644-2691	April–September 8–16 Days $2,550–3,900	Dory J-Rig	Specialized geology, photography, archeology, history, and ecology trips are offered • Transportation included in cost
Grand Canyon Whitewater www.grandcanyonwhitewater.com (800) 343-3121 • (928) 645-8866	April–October 4–13 Days $990–3,300	Dory J-Rig	Motorized J-Rig or oar-powered trips • Hike-out and helicopter-out trips are offered • Transportation is optional
Hualapai River Runners www.grandcanyonwest.com (928) 769-2219	March–October 1-Day $249	J-Rig	Only single day trip in the Canyon, but there's an added $79 transport fee as well as additional taxes and fuel surcharge
Hatch River Expeditions www.hatchriverexpeditions.com (800) 856-8966 • (928) 355-2241	April–September 4–12 Days $1,231–3,625	Dory J-Rig	A smaller variety of motorized and oar powered trips • They also offer kayak support (gear transport, etc.)
Moki Mac River Expeditions www.mokimac.com (800) 284-7280 • (801) 268-6667	April–October 6–14 Days $1,937–3,799	Dory J-Rig	Specialty trips including Music in the Canyon, Creation vs. Evolution, and an Art Workshop • Kayak trip also offered
O.A.R.S. Grand Canyon www.oars.com (800) 346-6277 • (209) 736-2924	April–October 4–19 Days $1,847–5,628	Raft Dory	Wide variety of raft and dory trips with additional side canyon hikes along the way • Transportation included
Outdoors Unlimited www.outdoorsunlimited.com (800) 637-7238 • (928) 526-4546	April–September 5–15 Days $1,665–3,655	Raft	Oar powered and all-paddle trips of lower, upper, and full canyon • Transportation not included in cost
Tour West www.twriver.com (800) 453-9107 • (801) 225-0755	April–September 3–12 Days $1,330–3,530	Dory J-Rig	3, 6, and 8 night motorized J-Rig trips or 12 night oar powered trip • Group and family discounts are available
Western River Expeditions www.westernriver.com (800) 453-7450 • (801) 942-6669	May–September 3–7 Days $1,145–2,695	J-Rig	3, 4, and 6 day motorized J-Rig trips • Transfers and transport, including helicopter (if required), included in cost

The Kolb Brothers

Beginning in 1904, **Emery and Ellsworth Kolb** ran a small photography studio at the South Rim near Bright Angel Trailhead. Their main source of income came from taking photos of mule riders as they made their descent into the canyon. Emery often boasted that the two of them had "taken more pictures of men and mules than any other living man." And it was not an easy accomplishment. A clean water supply was needed to develop the pictures, but the closest reliable source was 4.5 miles and 3,000 feet below the rim. The Kolb brothers hiked this route countless times between 1904, when their studio was constructed, and 1932 when clean water became available on the rim. During this time, one brother took pictures of the mule riders descending into the canyon, then raced down the trail to Indian Gardens, where the pictures were developed in a makeshift dark room. Once finished, he raced back to the rim, arriving just before the mule train returned from the bottom.

Adept oarsmen and explorers at heart, the Kolb brothers set out to retrace Major John Wesley Powell's journey from Green River, Wyoming through the Grand Canyon all the way to California. The first to accomplish this feat since Powell in 1869, they even captured the epic adventure on film. Together, they penned a book and took the finished film on the East Coast lecture circuit.

Emery started spending more time with his family and on personal adventures (like running the Black Canyon of the Gunnison • page 346), stressing the brothers' business relationship. They decided to go their separate ways, and the only fair way to determine who would leave the canyon was to flip a coin. Emery won a best of three. He kept the studio and continued to show the film of their whitewater adventure until his death in 1976.

Photo courtesy of Northern Arizona University, Cline Library

 Mule Rides

Modern mule riders aren't photographed by the energetic Kolb brothers, but they still descend into the mile-deep gorge from both of the canyon's rims. **Xanterra Parks & Resorts** (www.grandcanyonlodges.com) offers a one- or two-night mule trip down and back up Bright Angel Trail, spending the night(s) at historic Phantom Ranch (see right). A one night ride costs $850 for two people. Each additional person is about $380. The two night ride costs about $1,100 for two people. Each additional person costs about $475. Fees include tax, breakfast, lunch, a steak dinner, and lodging. If you aren't interested in the steep descent or spending more than 10 hours in the saddle, there's a 3-hour trip ($100 per person) through Grand Canyon Village to Abyss Overlook.

Mule trips are offered year-round. Riders must be at least 4'7" tall, weigh no more than 200 pounds, and speak fluent English (for the mules to understand commands). Everyone must check-in at Bright Angel Transportation Desk at least 90 minutes prior to the scheduled departure time. **Overnight trips must be reserved and purchased in advance.** Reservations can be made by calling Xanterra's reservations center at (888) 297-2757 or (303) 297-2757 (outside the U.S.).

On the **North Rim**, **Canyon Trail Rides** takes guests on 1-hour and half-day trips. One-hour rides cost $40 per person and follow the rim of the canyon along Ken Patrick Trail (page 435). Riders must be at least 7 years of age and weigh no more than 220 pounds. There are two choices for half-day trips. One stays above the rim following the 1-hour tour route and continuing around Uncle Jim Loop Trail. Alternatively, sure-footed mules lead riders into the canyon via North Kaibab Trail to Supai Tunnel, where you turn around and return to the rim. Both half-day tours cost $75 per person. Riders must be at least 10 years of age and weigh no more than 200 pounds. A shuttle bus to the trailhead leaves Grand Canyon Lodge a half-hour before trip departure. Trip departure times are typically 7:30 or 8:30 in the morning. Please contact Canyon Trail Rides for reservations and additional information.

Canyon Trail Rides • (435) 679-8665
Bryce Canyon National Park; Tropic, Utah 84776
www.canyonrides.com

Phantom Ranch

 Phantom Ranch

One of the most unique experiences at the Grand Canyon is spending a night on the canyon's floor at Phantom Ranch. Located along Bright Angel Creek near the junction of North Kaibab, South Kaibab, and Bright Angel Trails, the only way to reach this secluded getaway is by foot, mule, or river. Designed by **Mary Colter** and constructed in 1922, the ranch's intent was, and still is, to provide food, lodging, and comfort to backcountry visitors.

Phantom Ranch offers men's and women's dormitories ($42/person) and 2–10 person cabins with shared showers. Hot meals and souvenirs are available for purchase. Meals cost anywhere from $20 for breakfast to $40 for a steak dinner. All meals must be reserved in advance and are served at a designated time. If you think you might be interested in souvenirs, be sure to leave space in your backpack for them. You don't have to carry your own gear; a duffel service is available for about $64 each way.

South Rim hikers are forced to make the difficult decision of which trail to take into and out of the canyon (South Kaibab in and Bright Angel out is recommended). Remember that South Kaibab Trail, although shorter, is extremely steep and strenuous with no clean water source available along the way. Pack plenty of water or take Bright Angel Trail.

Phantom Ranch is operated by Xanterra Parks & Resorts. Demand far exceeds capacity. Reservations are recommended and can be made up to 13 months in advance by calling (888) 297-2757 or clicking www.grandcanyonlodges.com.

Bridge across the Colorado River

Backpacking

The park is broken into four management zones. The **Corridor Zone** is recommended for hikers without previous experience at Grand Canyon. These popular trails are well maintained and feature toilets, signs, and emergency phones. Ranger stations are also found along the way. Corridor trails include North and South Kaibab and Bright Angel Trails. All camping within the Corridor Zone must be done at designated campgrounds. Indian Garden (4.6 miles from the rim) and Bright Angel (9.6 miles) Campgrounds are located on Bright Angel Trail. Cottonwood Campground is located on North Kaibab Trail, 6.8 miles from the North Rim and 7.2 miles from Bright Angel Campground. There are no designated campsites along South Kaibab Trail.

Experienced Grand Canyon hikers may want to explore the park's **Threshold, Primitive, and Wild Zones**. Trails in these areas are either non-maintained or non-existent. Camping is available at designated sites or wherever you can find a flat space. Reliable water sources are often scarce or non-existent.

Backcountry Permits

All overnight camping trips outside the developed campgrounds require a backcountry permit. The park receives far more permit requests than it issues, so backcountry users, especially those hoping to visit during summer, should apply in advance. Applications are accepted no earlier than the first of the month four months prior to the proposed start of your trip. For example, if you're planning a trip that begins in June, whether it's the 1st or the 30th, your application will be accepted beginning February 1st. All fax and mail applications must be received at least three weeks in advance of the trip date; only in person requests are accepted within 21 days of your proposed departure date. A permit request form can be found at the link provided below. Permit requests may be submitted by fax, through the mail, or in person at the North or South Rim Backcountry Information Center (BIC). The South Rim's BIC is open daily from 8am–noon and 1–5pm. The North Rim BIC holds the same operating hours, but it closes for the winter from mid-October until mid-May.

Contact info:

Backcountry Information Center; PO Box 129; Grand Canyon, AZ 86023
Phone: (928) 638-7875 (Monday–Friday, 1:00–5:00pm only)
Fax: (928) 638-2125 • www.nps.gov/grca/planyourvisit/backcountry.htm

The park responds to all permits via mail in the order they were received. Allow at least three weeks for a response. Successful applicants who have met the fee requirements will receive their permit at the time of response. Permit fees include a $10 non-refundable application fee plus $5 per person per night camped below the rim or $5 per group camped above the rim. These fees do not include the park entrance fee. Cancellations received three or more days prior to the start of your trip will receive a credit towards a future trip reserved within one year. In addition to the possibility of cancelled trips, the park holds a limited number of **walk-up permits** for corridor campgrounds (Indian Garden, Bright Angel, and Cottonwood). Walk-up permits are issued for a maximum of two nights. They are only issued in person and cannot be purchased earlier than one day prior to the departure date. If you are unsuccessful in securing a walk-up permit you may request a wait list number. The wait list number gives you priority over all first time arrivals the following day. Each day you return and do not receive a permit you will be able to turn in your wait list number for a new (lower) number.

When to Go

Grand Canyon's South Rim is open every day of the year. Camping, lodging and dining facilities are available year-round. Visitor Information Centers hold seasonal hours, but are usually open from 8am to 5pm with extended hours in summer. Summer is the busiest time of year, but it's hardly the best season to visit. Hotels fill completely up to a year in advance. Viewpoints are congested. Shuttle buses are full. The summer heat (particularly in the canyon) is insufferable. Thunderstorms are also common, and flash floods and lightning are two of the more serious threats at the Grand Canyon. Try visiting during spring or fall when crowds have thinned and the weather is comfortable. Winter can also be an amazing time to visit. Lodging rates are greatly reduced, and if you're fortunate, you may see a beautiful white and red canyon thanks to a dusting of snow.

Transportation & Airports

Amtrak (800.872.7245, www.amtrak.com) provides train service to Williams and Flagstaff, AZ. McCarran International (LAS) in Las Vegas, NV (270 miles away); Sky Harbor International (PHX) in Phoenix, AZ (225 miles); and Pulliam (FLG) in Flagstaff, AZ (82 miles) are the closest large commercial airports. Car rental is available at each of these destinations. A few airlines provide service directly to Grand Canyon Airport (866.235.9422, www.grandcanyonairlines.com). Car rental is not available, but there is shuttle and taxi service to the South Rim. Arizona Shuttle (877.226.8060, www.arizonashuttle.com) provides service between Flagstaff and Grand Canyon twice daily. Grand Canyon Shuttles (888.226.3105, www.grandcanyonshuttles.com) provides regular service between Flagstaff and the Grand Canyon, as well as rim-to-rim transfers. See page 431 for train excursions.

Park Shuttle

A **free shuttle service** is available at the South Rim to help reduce traffic congestion and pollution. There are a total of four shuttle loops. Refer to the park's free newspaper, *The Guide*, for current operating schedules and route maps. **Hermits Rest Route** runs from March through November, stopping at various viewpoints along Hermit Road. **Tusayan Route** runs between Tusayan and Grand Canyon Visitor Center during the summer. **Village Route** runs all year and connects all of Grand Canyon Village's lodging, restaurants, gift shops, and campgrounds. **Kaibab/Rim Route** runs year-round, and it takes riders to canyon viewpoints, South Kaibab Trailhead, and Yavapai Geology Museum. All shuttle buses are equipped with bike racks.

Directions

Whether you're arriving at the South Rim from the east or the west you'll most likely be taking I-40. Travelers passing through Flagstaff can also take US-180, which merges with AZ-64 and heads into the park.

From I-40: Heading east or west on I-40, take Exit 165 for AZ-64 toward Williams/Grand Canyon. Head north on AZ-64 for about 55 miles. You'll pass through Tusayan and into the park. Shortly thereafter Grand Canyon Village will come into view on your left (west).

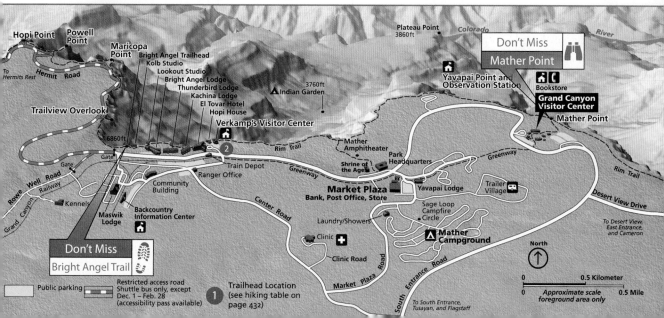

Camping & Lodging

Pima Point

Lodging accommodations range from **Bright Angel Lodge's** basic rooms with shared bathrooms to **El Tovar Hotel's** modern luxury suites. But these lodging facilities aren't about the accommodations; they're about the location. All lodges are located in **Grand Canyon Village**, and **Maswik** and **Yavapai** are the only lodges not situated directly on the canyon's rim. Ideal location and convenience comes at a premium. Rooms on the rim with a private bath cost at least $170/night. Still, the demand is great. If you want to stay on the rim you should make reservations well in advance, especially if you're traveling during the summer. **Campgrounds** also tend to fill to capacity. There are three developed campgrounds at the South Rim. Reservations can be made at **Mather Campground** and its neighbor, **Trailer Village**. **Desert View Campground**, located 25 miles east of the village on Desert View Road, has 50 sites available on a first-come, first-served basis. Please refer to page 428 for lodging and dining facilities outside the park.

South Rim Camping

	Open	Fees	Notes
Mather Campground* (Grand Canyon Village)	All Year	$18/night $15/night (winter)	Coin-operated laundry and showers are available nearby • No hook-ups, 30-ft max length
Trailer Village (Next to Mather Campground)	All Year	$34.50/night	RV sites with hook-ups • Operated by Xanterra, call (888) 297-2757 for advance reservations
Desert View Campground (25 miles east of Grand Canyon Village)	mid-May– mid-Oct	$12/night	First-come, first-served self-register campsites, flush toilets, no hook-ups, 30-ft max length
Backcountry Camping	Backcountry camping is permitted at designated sites or at-large areas specified by the park • See page 428 for details and permit information		

South Rim Lodging

	Open	Fees	Notes
Bright Angel Lodge	All Year	$70–178/night	Basic rooms have shared bathroom and shower
El Tovar Hotel	All Year	$178–426/night	Premier lodging at the Grand Canyon
Kachina Lodge	All Year	$173–184/night	Identical to Thunderbird • Check-in at El Tovar
Thunderbird Lodge	All Year	$173–184/night	Check-in at Bright Angel Lodge
Maswik Lodge	All Year	$92–173/night	Motel-style rooms, cabins available in summer
Yavapai Lodge	All Year	$114–163/night	Largest lodge in the park • 198 rooms

All lodging facilities are located in Grand Canyon Village and run by Xanterra Parks & Resorts. For additional information or to make advance reservations call (888) 297-2757 or click www.grandcanyonlodges.com. Reservations are accepted up to one year in advance. To make same-day reservations for lodging or Trailer Village please call (928) 638-2631. Restaurants, market place, post office, clinic, bank, and pet kennel are available in the Village.

*Campground reservations can be made in advance by calling (877) 444-6777 or clicking www.recreation.gov

Flightseeing

The Grand Canyon's size, depth, and remoteness are best understood when viewed from above. Airplane and helicopter pilots can give you that unique perspective, but they must adhere to a few restrictions; more than 75% of park airspace is off-limits to help reduce noise pollution.

Several companies provide **helicopter** (slower and lower) and **airplane** (faster and higher) **tours** from Grand Canyon Airport in Tusayan. Below is a list of outfitters with per person rates. All of these companies offer a variety of package tours that include additional land and water activities. Several offer trips departing Page, AZ and Las Vegas, NV. Visit their websites for a complete list of activities.

Grand Canyon Airlines • (866) 235-9422 • www.grandcanyonairlines.com
Tours starting at $118/person (Airplane, 50 minutes)

Air Grand Canyon • (800) 247-4726 • www.airgrandcanyon.com
$120/person (Airplane, 40–50 minutes)

Grand Canyon Helicopters • (800) 541-4537
www.grandcanyonhelicoptersaz.com
$208/person (Helicopter, 50 minutes)

Maverick Helicopters • (888) 261-4414
www.maverickhelicopter.com
$185/person (Helicopter, 30 minutes)

Papillon Grand Canyon Helicopters • (888) 635-7272
www.papillon.com
$169–191/person (Helicopter, 30 minutes)
$188–208/person (Helicopter, 50 minutes)
$118/person (Airplane, 40–50 minutes)

Biking

Bicycles are allowed on all roads open to automobile traffic. Roads are heavily-trafficked, and narrow with little to no shoulder, making it best to bike in the early morning before motorists come out to sightsee. All South Rim shuttle buses are equipped with bike racks, allowing easy bike transportation from one area to another without having to pedal. **Bike rental** and **guided tours** are available at **Bright Angel Bicycle** (928.814.8704, www.bikegrandcanyon.com) in Grand Canyon Village. Their guided tours provide an opportunity to learn more about the canyon as you pedal along Hermits Rest Road. Tours cost $40/adult, $32/child under 17, and include bike rental, helmet, and roundtrip shuttle. The tour lasts 2–2.5 hours. Bike rental costs $10 for one hour, $25 for four hours, and $35 for a full day. Trailers and kid's rates are available. The bike shop is closed in winter.

The mouth of Havasu Creek (river mile 157)

Best of the South Rim

Overlook: **Yaki Point**
  Runner-up: Lipan Point
  2nd Runner-up: Mather Point

Hike: **South Kaibab Trail**
  Runner-up: Bright Angel Trail
  2nd Runner-up: Grandview

Train Excursions

Santa Fe Railroad and the locomotive played a major role in the canyon's initial promotion, only to be run off the rim by the automobile. But over the past 50 years, increased tourism, congested roadways, and nostalgia have sparked a resurgence in train passenger service to Grand Canyon.

Grand Canyon Railway operates restored locomotives that travel from Williams, AZ directly to South Rim's Grand Canyon Village. The trip takes about 2 hours and is complete with strolling musicians, staged robberies, and shoot-outs. A roundtrip coach class ticket costs $70 for adults and $40 for children. First class seats cost $140/adult and $110/child. Observation Dome and Luxury Parlor Class cost $170 and $190 per adult, respectively, and children under the age of 15 are not permitted in these cars. Grand Canyon Railway is operated by Xanterra Parks & Resorts. A variety of vacation packages can be booked that include a ride on the nostalgic railroad and lodging (page 430).

Grand Canyon Railway • Williams Depot
233 N Grand Canyon Blvd.; Williams, AZ 86046
Reservations: (800) 843-8724
Outside the United States: (303) 843-8724
www.thetrain.com

South Rim Hiking

South Kaibab Trail

Many visitors are happy to revel in the Grand Canyon's glory from one of many well-placed viewpoints along the South Rim. Others want to immerse themselves in the canyon, hiking as far and deep as weather, attitude, and water supply allow. At the South Rim there are three primary inner canyon hikes. **Bright Angel**, located at the west end of Grand Canyon Village near Bright Angel Lodge, is the most popular. While it's the favorite route for rim-to-rim hikers and backpackers, it also provides excellent day-hiking opportunities. Consider taking it 3-miles (roundtrip) to **1.5-Mile Resthouse** or 6-miles (roundtrip) to **3-Mile Resthouse**. Clean water and a restroom are available from May to September at each resthouse.

South Kaibab Trail, located near Yaki Point off Desert View Drive, is the most direct route to the canyon floor. It's steep and strenuous, but the views from the cliff-side trail and open promontories are extraordinary. Day hikers can choose to hike to **Ooh-Aah Point** (1.8-miles roundtrip), **Cedar Ridge** (3 miles), or **Skeleton Point** (6 miles). Water is not available along South Kaibab Trail, so fill your bottle or hydration system before hopping aboard the shuttle bus to the trailhead.

For a more primitive inner canyon hiking experience, try Hermit or Grandview Trails. **Hermit Trail** is located at the west end of Hermit's Rest Road. **Grandview Trail** is located at Grandview Point on Desert View Drive. Both offer some of the finest canyon views in the park, but are unmaintained and without water. Grandview Trail is exceptionally steep, but does not reach the canyon's floor.

Do not overestimate your physical fitness level. Expect hiking out of the canyon to take twice the time it took to hike in (watch the time and plan accordingly). **More than 250 people are rescued from the canyon each year**, most suffering from heat exhaustion or dehydration. Carry plenty of water, allot ample time for your hike, use a bit of common sense, and you'll love the experience. If you're daunted by the inner canyon, **Rim Trail** from Grand Canyon Village to Hermit's Rest is for you. It is South Rim's only above-rim hiking trail.

Grand Canyon Field Institute offers educational hiking/backpacking classes. For details call (866) 471-4435 or click www.grandcanyon.org/fieldinstitute. Courses cost about $100 per day and discounts are available for Grand Canyon Association Members.

South Rim Hiking Trails

	Trail Name	Trailhead (# on map)	Length	Notes (One-way distances)
South Rim	Hermit	Hermit's Rest (1)	9.3 miles	Unmaintained trail to the Colorado River
	Rim	Grand Canyon Village (2)	0–13 miles	Mostly level trail following the canyon's rim
	Bright Angel - 👍	Bright Angel Trailhead (3)	9.6 miles	Steep, strenuous and the South Rim's most popular hike
	South Kaibab - 👍	South Kaibab Trailhead (4)	7.3 miles	Strenuous • Shortest route to the canyon floor
	Grandview - 👍	Grandview Point/Trailhead (5)	3.2 miles	Steep descent to a scenic Colorado River overlook

Visitor Centers & Museums

Kolb Studio: The former home and business of the Kolb Brothers has been restored to house free art exhibits and a bookstore. The Studio is located in Grand Canyon Village's Historic District at Bright Angel Trailhead. (Open daily 8am–6pm)

Verkamp's Visitor Center: Occupying one of the oldest buildings on the South Rim, Verkamp's Visitor Center now features displays telling the history of Grand Canyon Village. A bookstore and information desk are available. (Open daily 8am–6pm)

Yavapai Geology Museum: Interested in geology, or just curious about the canyon? If so, stop at the park's Geology Museum, located one mile east of Market Plaza. (Open daily 8am–6pm)

Canyon View Information Plaza: This is the best spot to begin your trip to the Grand Canyon's South Rim. The complex contains several outdoor exhibits, a visitor center, and bookstore. However, parking space is not available; the closest available parking is at Mather Point, which is often overcrowded and has a 60 minute parking limit. The best way to access this facility is on foot, via Rim Trail. The park's free shuttle system also provides transportation to Canyon View Information Plaza, which is located on South Entrance Road near Mather Point. (Open daily 8am–6pm)

Tusayan Ruins and Museum: This free museum explores more than 10,000 years of cultural history. Ancient artifacts include projectile points, split-twig figurines, pottery, and a small Ancestral Puebloan ruins site. The museum is located three miles west of Desert View. (Open daily 9am–5pm)

Desert View Visitor Center: Located at the eastern end of Desert View Drive, this small visitor center houses a collection of art inspired by the Grand Canyon. Find your own inspiration by viewing the Colorado River from Desert View Watchtower, originally designed by **Mary Colter** and built in 1932. A bookstore is also available. (Open daily 9am–5pm)

All of the locations listed above are open every day of the year. Hours vary seasonally, but expect these facilities to be open during the listed hours of operation, with extended hours in summer.

View from Cedar Ridge (South Kaibab Trail)

For Kids

Children have the opportunity to become official **Grand Canyon National Park Junior Rangers**. To become a member of this exclusive group pick up a free activity booklet from any of the locations listed to the left and complete the activities required for your age group. Upon completion bring the booklet back to a visitor center for review. If successful, children ages 4–7 will receive the Raven Award, children ages 8–10 receive the Coyote Award, and children 11 and up receive the Scorpion Award. There is a special prize for children ages 4–14 who complete the booklet's activities and make a trip to Phantom Ranch. The park also offers three family oriented summer programs: **Adventure Hike**, **Discovery Pack**, and **Junior Ranger Programs for Families**. Check out the park website or stop in at a visitor center for additional information.

Ranger Programs

A visit to any national park isn't complete without participating in at least one of the famous ranger programs. All programs are free and most are located in and around Grand Canyon Village. There are a few special events that take place at Desert View, Tusayan Museum, and Phantom Ranch. You'll find regularly scheduled walks and talks that explore the area's geology, history, and ecology. Look inside the park's newspaper, *The Guide* (available at park entrance, visitor centers, and park website) to check the current schedule of ranger guided activities. All of these tours are highly recommended, and you're sure to come away with a new appreciation for one of the world's most remarkable natural wonders.

Havasu Falls

Other Excursions

A trip to the **IMAX Theater** (page 453) or walking **Skywalk** (www.grandcanyonskywalk.com) is included in many families' vacation plans. Skywalk is expensive ($85 in total fees), inconvenient (accessed via a 10-mile dirt road), and unrecordable (cameras are not allowed). Save your time and money and check out some of South Rim's free **hiking trails** (page 432) and **ranger programs** (page 433) instead.

On the other hand, visiting **Havasu Falls**, one of the United States' finest swimming holes, is worth the time, effort, and money. However, it's not easy to get to. Taking all paved roads from Grand Canyon Village, it's 195 miles to the falls' trailhead. Leave South Rim via AZ-64/US-180 to the south. Head west on I-40 about 45 miles to Exit 121 toward AZ-66/Seligman/Peach Springs. Turn right at Interstate 40 Business Loop E. After about 1 mile take another right onto AZ-66. Continue another 30 miles to a T-intersection. Turn right onto Hualapai Hilltop Highway. After 43 miles you will come to the trailhead to Havasu Canyon. From here, it's another 8 miles by way of foot, mule, or helicopter.

All visitors must have advance reservations at the campground or lodge, and a day in paradise is expensive. There's a $35/person entrance fee, plus a $17/person/night campground fee, and an additional $5/person environmental care fee. Tack on 10% tax and you are "free" to hike to the falls. Those who arrive without a reservation will be charged double. Note that a flood in 2008 drastically altered existing waterfalls and created new ones in the area. For more information click www.havasupaitribe.com.

Vacation Planner - South Rim

Grand Canyon's South Rim is one of the busiest areas in the entire collection of national parks. With an abundance of tourism comes a huge variety of commercial attractions and activities. You can **take a mule into the canyon** (page 427), **spend two weeks rafting the river** (page 424), **ride above it in a helicopter** (page 431), or **camp in the park's backcountry** (page 428). All of these activities take considerable planning and preparation and are difficult to account for in this sample itinerary. Exclude these grand adventures, and a trip to the South Rim becomes fairly simple. Here's the best the canyon has to offer all in one action packed day. Nearby dining, grocery stores, lodging, festivals, and attractions are listed on pages 448–453.

Day 1 Once you arrive at the park check the free newspaper, *The Guide,* for a current schedule of South Rim's **ranger programs**. If you haven't been on a ranger program before, the Grand Canyon is a great place to do it. There's a ton of interesting geology and history going on in and on top of these heavily eroded rocks. The first viewpoint that you should stop at is **Mather Point**, named after **Stephen Mather**, the first director of the National Park Service. For slightly less congested canyon viewing try nearby **Yaki Point** or **Maricopa Point**, a short distance east and west of Mather Point, respectively. Be sure to check out **Powell and Hopi Points** while at Maricopa Point; both extend into the canyon a short distance to rocky promontories. If you love the views, consider hiking **Rim Trail** (page 432), which connects the viewpoints and Grand Canyon Village. It can be picked up at several locations in Grand Canyon Village and at all viewpoints between Pipe Creek Vista (near Mather Point) and Hermits Rest. If you have enough time, **Lipan Point** and **Desert View** offer differing perspectives, with views of the Colorado River.

The one trail that you absolutely do not want to skip is **South Kaibab** (page 432). The park's official line is that you should not day hike beyond Cedar Ridge, but if you're in decent physical condition and carry at least one liter of water per person, you should be able to make the trek to **Skeleton Point** and back (6 miles) without a problem. Allow at least one hour per mile, and time yourself as you descend. Expect it to take twice as long to climb out of the canyon as it took to get in.

When to Go

Grand Canyon's North Rim is open from mid-May until the first heavy snowfall in November. Facilities, including the lodge and campground, are open between mid-May and mid-October. During this time the visitor center is open daily from 8am to 6pm. Summer is the busiest time of year, but only 10% of Grand Canyon visitors come to the North Rim, which makes for manageable crowds. The North Rim is heavily wooded. Fall, when leaves change colors, is one of the most pleasant times to visit. The road to the park closes for winter, but that doesn't keep determined snowshoers and cross-country skiers out. The park even provides a yurt near North Kaibab Trailhead. It sleeps six, and is outfitted with chairs, table, and a wood-burning stove. A portable toilet is located nearby. The yurt can be reserved beginning the Monday after Thanksgiving until mid-April. Reservation and backcountry permit (page 428) are required.

Transportation & Airports

Public transportation does not provide service to or around the North Rim, but there is a rim-to-rim shuttle service (page 421). The closest large commercial airports are McCarran International (LAS) in Las Vegas, NV, located 275 miles to the west, and Salt Lake City International (SLC), located 397 miles north of the park.

Directions

Visitors can easily see from one rim to the other. The distance is usually no more than 10 miles. Hikers frequently descend into the canyon and emerge on the opposite rim after less than 25 miles on foot. But, by car it's a 210 mile, 4.5 hour trip. A long, but scenic journey. You can drive yourself or hop aboard the transcanyon shuttle (page 421). Directions are also provided below for those traveling north or south on I-15.

From South Rim (210 miles): Follow AZ-64/East Rim Drive out of the park. After 52 miles you'll reach the small town of Cameron. Turn left onto US-89 N. Continue for another 58 miles where you'll turn left at US-89 Alt N. After 55 miles you'll reach a Y-intersection with AZ-67. Turn left onto AZ-67 and head south for 43 miles. Continue into the park.

From Las Vegas (256 miles): Heading east on I-15, take Exit 16 for UT-9 toward Hurricane/Zion National Park. Turn right onto UT-9 heading east. After about 10 miles, take another right onto S 100 E. Almost immediately take the first left onto UT-59. Follow UT-59 across the Utah/Arizona border where the road becomes AZ-389. After 54 miles on UT-59/AZ-389 you will reach the small town of Fredonia, turn right at US-89 Alt S. Continue south for 30 miles and then turn right at AZ-67, which leads directly to the North Rim.

From Salt Lake City (380 miles): Heading south on I-15, take Exit 95 for UT-20 toward US-89/Panguitch/Kanab. Turn left onto UT-20 E. Continue for 20 miles where the road terminates at US-89. Turn right onto US-89. Follow US-89 south for 76 miles to Kanab, UT. Here, US-89 follows Center St and S 100 E through the city. Do not follow US-89 to the east. Take US-89 Alt south and continue south for 36 miles to the Y-intersection with AZ-67. Turn right onto AZ-67 and continue for 43 miles into the park.

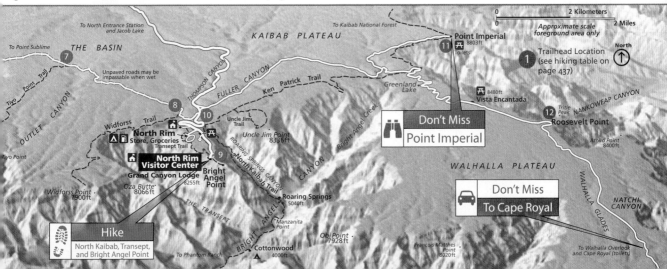

Camping & Lodging

The view across the canyon to the North Rim from Yaki Point as the sun sets and a storm passes

On the North Rim your overnight accommodations are easier to pick from. If you want to sleep in a bed you'll have to stay at **Grand Canyon Lodge**. Its perch atop Bright Angel Point provides exceptional canyon views from either a handful of cozy cabins designed to sleep 3–4 guests or basic motel rooms with one queen-sized bed. The lodge provides dining services to match your hunger and schedule. The **Dining Room** is a more formal setting where breakfast, lunch, and dinner are served. A dinner entrée averages about $20, and the view is generally more memorable than the food (note that the view is really, really good). **Deli in the Pines** offers quick meals. **Coffee Saloon** and **Rough Rider Saloon** offer beverages and snacks. Between June and September, the lodge holds daily **Grand Canyon Cookout Experiences**, providing outdoor dining with a hearty meal and entertainment. Tickets cost $35 for adults and $22 for children (6–15 years old). Reservations for the Grand Canyon Cookout Experience can be made from mid-May to late September by calling (928) 638-2611.

North Rim is the only **campground**. Coin-operated showers and laundry and a gas/service station are available near its entrance. Whether you choose to stay at the lodge or campground it is recommended that you reserve your space early. Rooms and campsites are usually booked months in advance, especially during summer. See page 449 for nearby camping and lodging alternatives.

North Rim Camping

	Open	Fees	Notes
North Rim Campground (AZ-67)*	mid-May–mid-October	$18/night $25/night • Canyon View Sites	Coin operated showers and laundry available, dump station, but no hook-ups • Reservations available • (4) sites with canyon views
Backcountry Camping	Backcountry camping is permitted at designated sites or at-large areas specified by the park • See page 428 for details and permit information		

North Rim Lodging

	Open	Fees	Notes
Grand Canyon Lodge (At the end of AZ-67)**	mid-May–mid-October	$116–187/night	Small, rustic cabins or motel-style rooms are available at the North Rim's only lodging

*Campground reservations can be made in advance by calling (877) 444-6777 or clicking www.recreation.gov
**Lodging reservations can be made in advance by calling (877) 386-4383 or clicking www.grandcanyonlodgenorth.com

North Rim Hiking

Transept

The North Rim offers a variety of above-rim trails and one maintained inner canyon trail. **Ken Patrick, Uncle Jim, Widforss, and Transept Trails** begin at or near North Rim Visitor Center and stay above the canyon's rim. One short trail every visitor should hike is the 0.5-mile jaunt to **Bright Angel Point. Point Imperial,** one of the best locations in the park to watch the sunrise, is located a few miles drive from the visitor center. Head north on AZ-67 as if you were going to exit the park. After the large S-curve turn right onto Fuller Canyon Road and continue east until it intersects Point Imperial Road. Turn left and drive to its end, where you'll find **Point Imperial Trail.** It's an easy 4-mile hike through

forest burned more than a decade ago to the park's northern boundary. At the Fuller Road/Point Imperial Road intersection you can also turn right onto Cape Royal Road. The view from **Cape Royal** is fantastic (there's a backcountry campsite here, too). Four short and relatively easy trails are located nearby.

North Kaibab is the North Rim's only inner canyon trail. It's a good place to begin a rim-to-rim hike because you spare 1,000 feet of elevation gain, or to day-hike to **Supai Tunnel** (3.4 miles roundtrip) or **Roaring Springs** (6.0 miles). North Kaibab is the most difficult and least visited of the park's three corridor trails.

Trail Name	Trailhead (see park map)	Length	Notes (Roundtrip distances unless noted otherwise)
Thunder River	Forest Road 292/Monument Point/Bill Hall Trailhead (6)	15.2 miles	Very strenuous hike with backpacking opportunities • Follows Tapeats Creek to Colorado River (steep)
Tiyo Point	Point Sublime Road (7)	12.5 miles	Above-rim out-and-back to Tiyo Point
Widforss	Point Sublime Road (8)	10.0 miles	Long self-guiding nature trail through forested region
Bright Angel Pt. - 👍	Near Visitor Center (9)	0.5 mile	Short paved self-guiding nature trail to viewpoint
Transept - 👍	Lodge & Campground (9, 10)	3.0 miles	Flat and easy hike connects campground and lodge
Bridle	Grand Canyon Lodge/North Kaibab (9)	1.2 miles	(One-way) Grand Canyon Lodge to North Kaibab
Ken Patrick	North Kaibab/Point Imperial (10, 11)	10.0 miles	(One-way) Imperial Point to North Kaibab Trail
Uncle Jim	Ken Patrick Trail (10)	5.0 miles	Loop • Overlooks canyon and N. Kaibab switchbacks
North Kaibab - 👍	North Kaibab Trailhead on AZ-67 (10)	14.0 miles	(One-way) The only maintained trail into the canyon
Arizona	North Kaibab Trail (10)	10.0 miles	(One-way) Entire route spans from Utah to Mexico
Point Imperial	Point Imperial Road (11)	4.0 miles	Easy hike through fire-damaged forest to park border
Roosevelt Point	Cape Royal Road (12)	0.2 mile	Short and easy loop with excellent views
Cape Final	Cape Royal Road (13)	4.0 miles	Short and flat hike to spectacular canyon overlook
Cliff Springs	Cape Royal Road (14)	1.0 mile	Ancestral Puebloan granary and steep cliffs
Cape Royal - 👍	Cape Royal Road (14)	1.0 mile	Views of Angel's Window and the Colorado River

North Rim

Panorama Point - South Kaibab Trail

Visitor Centers: The **North Rim Visitor Center** is located next to Grand Canyon Lodge on Bright Angel Peninsula, offering park and regional information, restrooms, and a bookstore. It is open daily from mid-May to mid-October, from 8am–6pm. It's a great place to begin a trip to the North Rim. Park rangers are available to answer your questions, and interpretive exhibits help introduce you to the region.

For Kids: Children visiting the North Rim are invited to participate in the park's **Junior Ranger Program** (page 433). Free activity booklets are available at the Visitor Center.

Ranger Programs: Park rangers provide interpretive programs about the canyon and its environment between mid-May and mid-October. Most programs meet or take place at the Visitor Center or Grand Canyon Lodge. **What's Rockin'?** is a 30–40 minute talk about geology conducted at Grand Canyon Lodge's back porch. If you're busy hiking trails or admiring the panoramic views, you can always catch an evening program at the North Rim Campground's amphitheater or Grand Canyon Lodge auditorium.

Best of the North Rim

Overlook: **Bright Angel Point**
    Runner-up: Point Imperial

Hike: **Cape Royal**
    Runner-up: North Kaibab

Vacation Planner - North Rim

Hitting up the North Rim's most popular attractions can easily be accomplished in a single day. Those interested in a backcountry adventure will require a longer visit, and a bit of preparation, **but the North Rim is without a doubt the superior location for backpackers**. In addition to a classic inner canyon route like **North Kaibab Trail to Phantom Ranch** (page 427) or **Cottonwood Campground** (page 428), there are a number of **above-the-rim hiking trails** (page 437) for backpackers to explore. All backcountry trips should be carefully planned with a good topographic map. Speak to a park ranger about water sources, permits, and trail conditions prior to departure.

Another great North Rim excursion is to drive the unpaved roads to **Toroweap Point** (page 422), the best overlook in the entire park. The trek is long and roads can be impassable if wet. Toroweap Point is accessed via a variety of routes on unpaved roads from AZ-389. Come prepared, because a tow from this area will cost upwards of $1,000. If interested, you should contact the park about road conditions and campsite availability. There are a total of nine campsites (permit required • page 428).

For a more typical trip to the North Rim, here's a one-day sample itinerary. Nearby dining, grocery stores, lodging, festivals, and attractions are listed on pages 448–453.

Day 1 — Stop at the visitor center and check *The Guide* for a current schedule of **ranger programs**. Try to plan around any activities that interest you. Once you've had your questions answered and curiosities satisfied head outside and hike to **Bright Angel Point** (page 437). It's a short but rugged trail along a rocky ridgeline to outstanding views above Bright Angel Creek. **Transept Trail** (page 437) is another excellent option. Return to your car and backtrack to Fuller Canyon Road. Stop at **Point Imperial**, and then head southeast on Cape Royal Road. **Wahalla Overlook** is worth a stop. **Wahalla Ruins**, a 1,000 year old one-room structure, might be of interest to archeology buffs, but to the average person it looks like a pile of rubble. Skip it if you're short on time. Continue south on Cape Royal Road to **Cape Royal**. From the road's end, hike 1 mile (roundtrip) to Cape Royal. This is a wonderful vantage point to watch the sunrise. **If you want to get away from it all, this is the spot.** Secure a backcountry permit for the campsite at Cape Final and you'll feel like the park is yours alone.

Basics

Flora & Fauna: Five of North America's seven life zones are represented at the Grand Canyon, and three of the continent's four deserts (Sonoran, Mojave, and Great Basin) converge at the canyon floor. These conditions create a diverse collection of wildlife. **More than 355 species of birds, 89 mammal species, and 56 reptile and amphibian species** reside in the park. Mule deer and bighorn sheep are the large mammals you're most likely to see. The largest and rarest bird in North America, the **California condor**, also lives here. The park offers special ranger programs that detail the reintroduction and current state of this endangered bird. Rocks are everywhere and among them is life. **More than 1,737 species of vascular plants** have been documented living within park boundaries. Such extreme diversity is due to the huge elevation change from rim to river and the amalgamation of ecosystems and deserts. The most prevalent plant community is desert scrub.

Pets: South Rim Visitors may walk their pets at all trails above the rim, Mather Campground, Desert View Campground, Trailer Village, and along all developed roadways and parking areas. The only location where pets are allowed at the North Rim is Bridle Trail, which connects Grand Canyon Lodge and North Kaibab Trail. Pets must be kept on a leash no more than six feet in length at all times and a kennel is available at Grand Canyon Village.

Accessibility: At the South Rim accessibility permits are issued to individuals with mobility impairments so they can drive a private vehicle through areas closed to visitor traffic. Permits are free and can be obtained at most park facilities, including all entrance stations. To help reduce park congestion these restricted areas are accessed via a free shuttle service (page 429). Only a few of the shuttles are accessible, but they can be requested with at least one day's notice by calling (928) 638-0591. Most South Rim facilities and viewpoints are accessible to wheelchair users, with the exception of Kolb Studios, Yaki Point, and South Kaibab Trailhead. Accessing locations like the Train Depot, the Community Building, and Park Headquarters requires assistance.

All inner canyon trails are inaccessible. Free wheelchairs can be checked out for daily use from South Rim Visitor Center.

North Rim is more isolated and generally less accessible than the more popular South Rim. Grand Canyon Lodge, North Rim Visitor Center, and North Rim Campground are fully accessible. Bridle Trail and Point Imperial Overlook are also accessible to wheelchair users.

A few river outfitters (page 424) can accommodate wheelchair users. Contact specific outfitters for details.

Weather: Temperatures at the Grand Canyon vary wildly, from day-to-day, rim-to-rim, and rim-to-floor. South Rim experiences comfortable summer highs, typically in the 80s°F. On average, temperature at the higher-elevation North Rim is 7°F cooler than the South Rim and 28°F cooler than the canyon floor. An arid climate and high elevation provide cool evenings. The South Rim's average summer lows are usually in the 50s°F while the North Rim's drop into the 40s°F. Both rims are at high enough elevation to receive snow during the winter, but winter is much more severe at the North Rim. In winter, average high temperatures drop into the 30s°F at the North Rim and 40s°F at the South Rim. It's also significantly wetter at the North Rim, receiving about 25 inches of precipitation each year compared to the South Rim's 15 inches. Seasonal patterns that typically occur in late summer and early winter contribute the majority of Grand Canyon precipitation. All visitors should come prepared for a variety of conditions. Dress in layers and carry a rain coat.

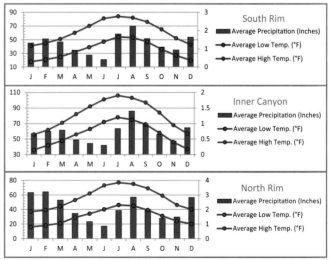

Wheeler Peak at night

100 Great Basin National Park
Baker, NV 89311
Phone: (775) 234-7331
Website: www.nps.gov/grba

Established: October 27, 1986
January 24, 1922 (Nat'l Monument)
Size: 77,180 Acres
Annual Visitors: 89,000
Peak Season: Summer
Hiking Trails: 65 Miles

Activities: Hiking, Backpacking,
Camping, Stargazing, Horseback
Riding, and Cave Tours ($8–10)

Campgrounds ($12/night): Upper
and Lower Lehman Creek, Wheeler
Peak, and Baker Creek
Free Primitive Camping along
Snake Creek and Strawberry Creek
Roads (4WD, high-clearance req'd)
Backcountry Camping: Permitted

Park Hours: All day, every day (except Wheeler Peak and Lexington
Arch Day-use Areas)
Entrance Fee: None

Great Basin - Nevada

In east-central Nevada near the Utah border, a 13,000 foot mountain hides a brilliantly decorated cave; both are protected by Great Basin National Park. The park itself is just a small portion of a much larger **Great Basin region** extending from the Sierra Nevada in California to the Wasatch Mountains in Utah. In between, mountains and valleys form dozens of smaller basins where rivers and streams are unable to drain into an ocean. All water flows inland, eventually collecting in shallow salt lakes, marshes, and mud flats where it evaporates. The region's aridity is well known, but beautiful and unique landscapes and life forms adapt and evolve to this harsh environment. Alpine lakes fed by snowmelt from the rocky slopes accent the high mountains, where groves of bristlecone pine have been defying the odds for thousands of years. Many of these twisted elders had already celebrated their 2,000th birthday by the time Christopher Columbus discovered America.

Americans would make an indelible mark on Great Basin. In 1855, **Ezra Williams** claimed to be the first white man to summit the tallest mountain in the central Great Basin, naming it Williams Peak. Shortly after, **Lieutenant Colonel Edward Steptoe** named the same mountain Jeff Davis Peak in honor of his superior, Secretary of War Jefferson Davis. When Jefferson Davis became President of the Confederate States of America, some cartographers began to regret the name. "Union Peak" was suggested as an alternative because a ridge united the mountain's twin summits, but it was an obvious jab at Jefferson Davis' secessionist leanings. Fortunately, map publication was postponed and in

1869 a military mapping expedition resulted in **George Montague Wheeler** climbing the mountain and naming its summit, definitively, "Wheeler Peak."

Eight years earlier, **Absalom "Ab" Lehman** moved to Snake Valley. Having experienced the highs and lows of mining in California and Australia, he decided to try his hand at ranching. By the time George Wheeler hiked to the top of Wheeler Peak, Lehman's ranch had 25–30 cows and an orchard. Prosperity and the loneliness of Ab's second wife, Olive Smith, prompted several family members to move into the area, and a community began to develop around Lehman Ranch. A butcher shop, blacksmith shop, carpenter shop, and milk house were established, and Absalom's orchard was regarded as the best in the region. Success allowed Ab to focus his attention on his ranch's latest addition, **Lehman Caves**. Exploring the cave he reached a point where stalactites and stalagmites prevented passage to its interior chamber. Ab returned to "develop" the cave with a little sweat and a sledgehammer. A path was cleared and the cave was open for tourism. After 1885, the cave received hundreds of visitors each year, nearly all of them guided by Ab.

The push to preserve the park came much later. **In 1964 a graduate student searching for the world's oldest tree came to the grove of bristlecone pines at Wheeler Peak.** After taking core samples the researcher wanted to obtain a more accurate count by cutting down a tree. The Forest Service granted his request and he proceeded to fell a tree known today as **Prometheus**. Counting the rings proved his assumption correct. Prometheus was at least 4,862 years old; he had just cut down the oldest living organism in the world. A cross-section of the tree resides in Great Basin Visitor Center where you can count the rings for yourself. But all was not lost. The tragedy of Prometheus helped galvanize support for the creation of Great Basin National Park, and the young graduate student was one of the cause's leading advocates.

Did you know?

▶ Bristlecone pines live longer (4,000+ years) than any known organism. Their needles alone can live 25–40 years.

Best of Great Basin

Activity: **Hike to Wheeler Peak**
Runner-up: Grand Palace Tour

When to Go

Great Basin is open year-round. Wheeler Peak Scenic Drive to Lehman Creek Campground is open all year, but the final 10 miles is generally closed from November to May, depending on the weather. Cave tours are offered at Lehman Caves Visitor Center all year round with the exception of New Year's Day, Thanksgiving Day, and Christmas Day. Great Basin Visitor Center is open from April until October (see page 443 for visitor center hours and locations). The park is busiest during holidays and summer weekends, when campgrounds can fill before the afternoon, but crowds are rarely unmanageable.

Transportation & Airports

Public transportation does not provide service to or around the park. The closest large commercial airports are Salt Lake City International (SLC), located 238 miles to the northeast, and McCarran International (LAS) in Las Vegas, NV, located 307 miles south of the park. Car rental is available at each destination.

Directions

Great Basin is located at the center of one of the most remote regions of the continental United States.

From the West: You can arrive from the west via US-50 or US-6. These highways converge at Ely, NV where you continue south/east on US-50/US-93/US-6/Great Basin Blvd for more than 55 miles to NV-487. Turn right at NV-487 and travel 5 miles to Baker. At Baker turn right onto Lehman Caves Road, which leads into the park.

From the North: I-80 picks up US-93 at Wells (Exit 352) and West Wendover, NV (Exit 410). Heading South on US-93 leads to Ely, NV (follow directions above from Ely).

From the East: From Delta, UT head west on US-50/US-6 across the Utah–Nevada border to NV-487. Turn left onto NV-487 and continue for 5 miles to Baker. Turn right onto Lehman Caves Road, which leads into the park.

From the South: Heading north on US-93, turn right at US-50/US-6. Continue east for almost 30 miles to NV-487. Turn right onto NV-487 and after 5 miles turn right at Lehman Caves Road.

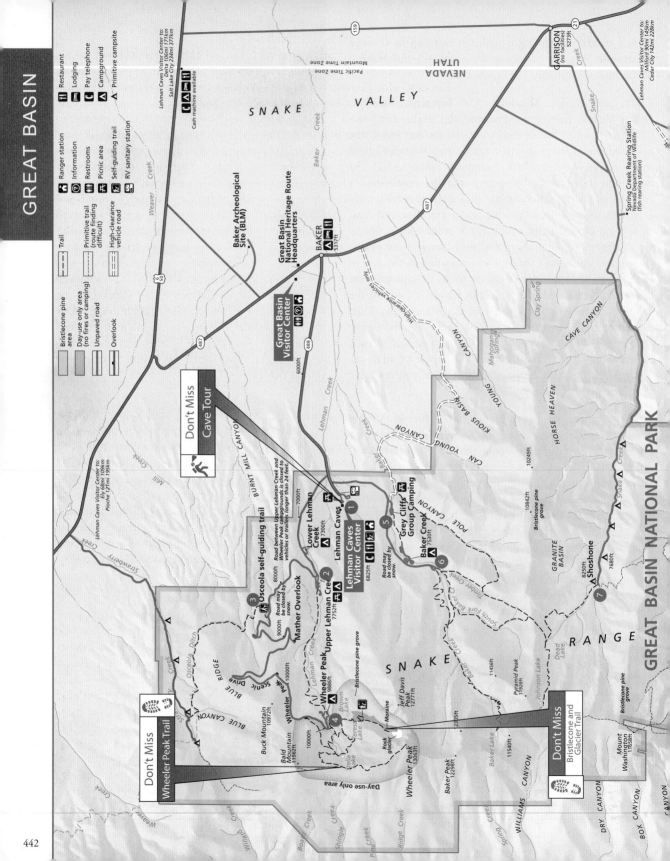

GREAT BASIN

Legend

Restaurant 🍴
Lodging 🏠
Pay telephone ☎
Campground 🏕
Primitive campsite ⛺

Ranger station
Information ⓘ
Restrooms
Picnic area 🛷
Self-guiding trail
RV sanitary station

Trail
Primitive trail (route finding difficult)
High-clearance vehicle road

Bristlecone pine area
Day-use only area (no fires or camping)
Unpaved road
Overlook

SNAKE   VALLEY

NEVADA
UTAH

Pacific Time Zone
Mountain Time Zone

GARRISON (no facilities)

Lehman Caves Visitor Center to:
Delta 106mi 171km
Salt Lake City 234mi 377km

Lehman Caves Visitor Center to:
Milford 90mi 145km
Cedar City 142mi 228km

Cash machine available

Spring Creek Rearing Station
Nevada Department of Wildlife
(fish rearing station)

Baker Archeological Site (BLM)

Great Basin National Heritage Route Headquarters

BAKER 5317ft

Great Basin Visitor Center

Lehman Caves Visitor Center to:
Ely 68mi 109km
Pioche 121mi 195km

Don't Miss
Cave Tour

MILL CREEK CANYON
BURNT MILL CANYON

CAVE CANYON

HORSE HEAVEN

YOUNG BASIN
CAN YOUNG CANYON

KIOUS CANYON

Clay Spring

High-clearance vehicles

Lower Lehman Creek 7300ft

Lehman Caves Visitor Center 6825ft

Osceola self-guiding trail

Mather Overlook

Upper Lehman Creek 7752ft

Road between Upper Lehman Creek and Wheeler Peak campgrounds is closed to vehicles or trailers longer than 24 feet.

Road may be closed by snow.

Grey Cliffs Group Camping

Baker Creek 7530ft

POLE CANYON

Bristlecone pine grove

10842ft

10249ft

GRANITE BASIN

Shoshone 8250ft
7680ft

GREAT BASIN NATIONAL PARK

Don't Miss
Wheeler Peak Trail

Osceola Ditch

BLUE RIDGE

Blue Canyon

Buck Mountain 10972ft

Bald Mountain 11562ft

Wheeler Peak Scenic Drive

Brown Lake

Teresa Lake

Stella Lake

Wheeler Peak 13063ft

Jeff Davis Peak 12771ft

Rock glacier

Moraine

Day-use only area

SNAKE   RANGE

11456ft

Pyramid Peak 11926ft

Johnson Lake

Dead Lake

Baker Lake 11540ft

Baker Peak 12298ft

Mount Washington 11658ft

Bristlecone pine grove

Don't Miss
Bristlecone and Glacier Trail

WILLIAMS CANYON

DRY CANYON

BOX CANYON

Weaver Creek
Strawberry Creek
Mill Creek
Snake Creek
Baker Creek
Lehman Creek
South Fork Baker Creek
Timber Creek
Pole Canyon Creek
Johnson Lake
Shingle Creek
Pine Creek
Ridge Creek
Spring Creek
Dead Lake Creek
Box Canyon Creek

442

Big Wash

To (21)

To (21)

Hidden

Lexington Creek

High-clearance vehicles recommended

4 Miles

4 Kilometers

North

Trailhead Location (see hiking table on page 445)

property beyond this point.
Foot access only.

Big Fork Wash

South Fork

North Fork Lexington Creek

South Fork Lexington Creek

Lexington Creek

Day-use only area

Lexington Arch 8270ft

ARCH CANYON

10016ft

11001ft

Mustang Spring

Granite Peak 11218ft

HIGHLAND RIDGE

10699ft

11532ft

DECATHON CANYON

Johns Wash

SWALLOW CANYON

LINCOLN CANYON

Driving

Most Great Basin visitors arrive via **NV-488/Lehman Caves Road**, which travels west from Baker, NV directly into the park and ultimately to **Lehman Caves Visitor Center**. The 12-mile **Wheeler Peak Scenic Drive**, which intersects Lehman Caves Road just beyond the park boundary, provides access to some of the most scenic viewpoints, climbing more than 3,000 feet to **Wheeler Peak Campground**. Vehicles longer than 24 feet are not allowed beyond Upper Lehman Creek Campground due to its steep (8% grade) and winding nature. Wheeler Peak Scenic Drive is open year-round to Upper Lehman Creek Campground, but usually closes beyond this point from November to May, depending on weather conditions. **Baker Creek Road** also intersects Lehman Caves Road. It's an unpaved but well-maintained road providing access to **Baker Creek Campground** and **Grey Cliffs Group Camping Area**, as well as some of the park's better backcountry hiking trails. Baker Creek Road is typically closed from December through April. Further south, running parallel to Lehman Caves Road, is the unpaved **Snake Creek Road**, which not surprisingly follows Snake Creek into the park. A high-clearance 4WD vehicle is recommended, but not required. A handful of primitive campsites are available along the way. **Strawberry and Lexington Arch Roads** should only be accessed by high-clearance 4WD vehicles. Snake Creek, Strawberry, and Lexington Arch Roads are open year-round, but may be impassable due to snow or mud.

Visitor Centers

Great Basin Visitor Center is located outside the park just north of the town of Baker on the west side of NV-487. Here you'll find an information desk, exhibits, and a small theater playing an orientation film. It is open daily, April to October, from 8am to 5:30pm, with summer hours extended to 5:30pm between Memorial Day and Labor Day. **Lehman Caves Visitor Center** (775.234.7331 ext. 212) is located 5.5 miles from Baker, just inside the park on NV-488/Lehman Caves Road. You can purchase cave tour tickets, browse exhibits, and view the orientation film here. It also houses a bookstore, cafe, and gift shop. Lehman Caves Visitor Center is open every day of the year, except New Year's Day, Thanksgiving, and Christmas Day. Hours of operation are 8am to 5pm.

Camping

There are four developed campgrounds. **Lower Lehman Creek**, **Upper Lehman Creek**, and **Wheeler Peak** are located along Wheeler Peak Scenic Drive. **Baker Creek Campground** is located at the end of unpaved Baker Creek Road. **Lower Lehman Creek** is open year-round. **Upper Lehman** and **Baker Creek** are open from May to October. **Wheeler Peak** is open between June and September. The largest campground is **Wheeler Peak** (37 sites). It is not uncommon for campgrounds to fill, especially during summer weekends and holidays. Pit toilets are located at each campground, but water is only available during summer. (In winter, water is available at the visitor centers.) There are no hook-ups or showers. A dump station ($5 fee) is available near Lehman Caves Visitor Center during the summer. All sites cost $12 per night. Non-group sites are available on a first-come, first-served basis. **Group camping** is available at **Grey Cliffs** on Baker Creek Road by reservation only (775.234.7331 ext. 213). Free primitive campsites are available along Snake Creek and Strawberry Creek Roads.

Parachute Shield

Cave Tours

Ever since **Absalom Lehman** discovered the cave in the 1880s, tourists have marveled at its intricate and fragile formations. The National Park Service continues the tradition by offering daily tours. The cave is only 0.25-mile deep, which makes for tours heavy on information and light on walking. **Lodge Room Tour** ($8, 60 minutes, 20 people) covers the first 0.2 miles of cave including Gothic Palace, Music Room, and Lodge Room. **Grand Palace Tour** ($10, 90 minutes, 20 people) travels 0.6 miles while visiting all the rooms of the Lodge Room Tour as well as Inscription Room and the Grand Palace where you will be able to see the famous "**Parachute Shield**" formation. Tickets are required and can be purchased in advance by calling (775) 234-7331 ext. 242 between 9am and 4pm, Monday through Friday. Tickets can also be purchased at Lehman Caves Visitor Center upon arrival. Advance tickets must be picked up at Lehman Caves Visitor Center at least 15 minutes before the tour or they will go on sale to walk-in customers. The cave is a constant 50°F with 90% humidity, so dress appropriately.

Hiking

Great Basin is a relatively small area, and all the maintained trails beginning along Wheeler Peak Scenic Drive can be completed in a day. The most interesting hike is **Bristlecone Trail**, a 2.8-mile (roundtrip) waltz through a forest of bristlecone pine trees, many of which were growing long before the Phoenician Alphabet was created in 2,000 BC. From the end of the Bristlecone Trail you can continue 1.8 miles (roundtrip) on **Glacier Trail** to the base of Nevada's only glacier.

For views of the Great Basin, there's no better vantage point than the **summit of Wheeler Peak**. The 8.2-mile trail begins at Summit Parking Area on Wheeler Peak Scenic Drive and steadily climbs more than 3,000 feet across rocky mountain slopes. Be sure to pack water and a jacket for this heart-pounding romp. The climb up will make you sweat, but it cools down quickly once you're soaking in the views from the completely exposed mountaintop.

Another visitor favorite is **Alpine Lakes Loop**. In just 2.7 miles of fairly easy hiking you visit two beautiful alpine lakes. Stella Lake is larger and more enchanting, but Teresa Lake is also nice and particularly pretty when snowpack remains on the surrounding slopes.

Backpacking

There are more than 60 miles of hiking trails at Great Basin. **Backpackers** are not allowed to camp within 0.25-mile of developed areas (roads, buildings, campgrounds, etc.), within the Wheeler Peak or Lexington Arch Day Use Areas, or in bristlecone pine groves. You must set up camp a minimum of 100 feet away from all sources of water and at least 500 feet away from any obvious archeological site. Camping in the backcountry **does not require a permit**, but it is recommended you sign in at trailhead registers.

The park's best backpacking route is to take Baker Lake Trail, which begins at the end of Baker Creek Road, all the way to Baker Lake. From here you can follow an unmaintained trail to Johnson Lake and return to Baker Road via Timber Creek Trail or South Fork Baker Creek Trail. The entire loop is slightly more than 13 miles. Backpackers should always carry a good topographical map. For information on trail conditions and routes stop in at a visitor center or call (775) 234-7331 ext. 212.

View from Wheeler Peak's summit

Great Basin Hiking Trails

	Trail Name	Trailhead (# on map)	Length	Notes (Roundtrip distances)
Wheeler Peak Scenic Dr	Mountain View	Rhodes Cabin (1)	0.3 mile	Trail guide available at Lehman Caves Visitor Center
	Lehman Creek	Upper Lehman Creek Camp (2)	6.8 miles	Connects Upper Lehman Creek and Wheeler Peak Campgrounds
	Osceola Ditch	Wheeler Peak Scenic Drive (3)	9.6 miles	Trail follows an old ditch built by gold miners
	Wheeler Peak - 👍	Summit Trail Parking Area (4)	8.2 miles	Strenuous hike with 3,000+ feet elevation gain
	Alpine Lakes Loop - 👍	Bristlecone Parking Area (4)	2.7 miles	Views of Wheeler Peak and scenic Stella and Teresa Lakes
	Bristlecone	Bristlecone Parking Area (4)	2.8 miles	Interpretive trail among some of the world's oldest trees
	Glacier & Bristlecone	Bristlecone Parking Area (4)	4.6 miles	Continues from Bristlecone Trail to Nevada's only glacier
	Sky Islands Forest	Bristlecone Parking Area (4)	0.4 mile	Paved and accessible interpretive trail of alpine forest
Other Areas	Pole Canyon	Grey Cliffs Campground (5)	4.0 miles	Easy hike along an old road • Can connect to Timber Creek Tr
	Baker Lake	Baker Creek Road (6)	12.0 miles	Leads to a beautiful alpine lake
	Baker Creek Loop	Baker Creek Road (6)	3.1 miles	Take connector trail to South Fork Baker Creek Trail
	South Fork Baker Creek/Johnson Lake	Baker Creek Road (6)	11.2 miles	Cuts back before reaching Johnson Lake • Passes historic Johnson Lake Mine structures
	Baker/Johnson Lakes Loop	Baker Creek Road (6)	13.1 miles	Combines Baker Lake and Johnson Lake Trails
	Johnson Lake	Snake Creek Road (7)	7.4 miles	Shorter and steeper route to Johnson Lake
	Lexington Arch	Outside park, south of Baker (8)	3.4 miles	Day-use area • Trail leads to a six-story limestone arch

Bristlecone pine

Other Activities

Stargazing: There are few places in the continental United States better for stargazing than Great Basin National Park. Clear skies, high altitude, and 200 miles of distance from cities' light and noise provide the perfect atmosphere for gazing into the heavens. Park Rangers hold **astronomy programs** every Wednesday and Saturday evening between Memorial Day and Labor Day. The park also holds an annual **Astronomy Festival** in late July. Additionally, "**star parties**" are held on various holidays. Telescopes are provided by the park to be shared among guests. If you'd like to view the stars on your own, Wheeler Peak Parking Area is a great place to camp out with a blanket and a set of binoculars.

Biking: Cyclists are only allowed on park roads. The ride up to Wheeler Peak is a nice short workout with a fun descent back down to Lehman Caves Visitor Center or Baker.

Spelunking: Lehman Caves is only one of **more than 40 caves** in the park, eight of which are accessible with a **cave permit**. Spelunkers must show adequate horizontal and vertical caving techniques to be issued a permit. The park website (www.nps.gov/grba/planyourvisit/caving.htm) has information on caves, closures, permit procurement.

Fishing is allowed in all creeks and lakes. A Nevada state fishing license is required.

Horseback Riding: Horses are allowed in the backcountry, but there are no nearby outfitters offering trail rides. You will have to provide your own horse(s) and follow park regulations regarding horseback riding in the backcountry.

For Kids: Children who visit Great Basin have the opportunity to become **Junior Rangers**. To receive an official certificate and badge, your child must attend one of the following programs: Lehman Caves Tour, Campground Evening Program, Night Sky Program, or a Ranger Talk. Children must also complete an age appropriate number of activities in the park's Junior Ranger booklet: three activities for kids 5 and under, five activities for children between the ages of 6 and 9, and seven activities for everyone else. Booklets are available free of charge at either visitor center. **Family Adventure Packs** are also available at the visitor centers.

Ranger Programs: In addition to **Cave Tours** (page 444) and **Stargazing Programs**, the park provides **evening campfire programs**, **children's programs**, and **full-moon hikes** between Memorial Day and Labor Day. For a current schedule of events, visit the park website, call the park at (775) 234-7331 ext. 212, or stop in at a visitor center to pick-up a copy of the park's publication, ***The Bristlecone***.

Flora & Fauna: Great Basin is home to **73 species of mammals, 18 species of reptiles, 2 species of amphibians, and 8 species of fish. At least 238 species of birds** reside in or visit the park, which makes for excellent bird watching. Mammals you're most likely to see include mule deer and squirrels, but fortunate visitors may spot a mountain lion, badger, or coyote. **More than 800 species of plants, including 11 species of conifer trees,** reside within park boundaries. **Bristlecone pine** are the elder statesmen of the bunch. At least one known tree, Prometheus, lived to the ripe old age of 4,862. Singleleaf pinyon trees are fruit bearers, with pine nuts that can be gathered and eaten by visitors. You'll find them in areas between 6,000 and 9,000 feet elevation.

Pets: Pets are allowed in the park, but must be kept on a leash no more than six feet in length at all times. They are not allowed on trails, in the backcountry, in Lehman Caves, or at evening programs. Basically, pets are allowed wherever you can get with your car: along roads, in campgrounds, and in parking areas.

Accessibility: Both of the park's visitor centers are fully accessible to individuals with mobility impairments. Accessible campsites are available at Upper Lehman Creek, Wheeler Peak, and Baker Creek Campgrounds.

Island Forest Trail is paved, but may require assistance for the second half, as the grade increases to about 8%. Cave tours are accessible with assistance. Wheelchair users can also enjoy evening programs at Upper Lehman Creek and Wheeler Peak Campgrounds.

Weather: With nearly 8,000 feet in elevation difference between Wheeler Peak (13,063 feet) and the valley floor, temperature varies greatly depending on where you are in the park as well as what season it is. Summer average high temperatures at Lehman Caves Visitor Center (6,825 feet) reach the low to mid-80s°F. Overnight summertime lows average in the mid to high 50s°F. Between December and February the average highs are in the low 40s°F and average lows are right around 20°F. Even if it's 80°F at Lehman Cave Visitor Center you should bring a jacket if you plan on hiking to Wheeler Peak or touring the cave. The temperature is usually 20 degrees cooler and it's often windy along the mountain's ridgeline. The cave is a constant 50°F all year. The region is arid, receiving about 20 inches of annual precipitation, but afternoon thunderstorms are common in summer and snow can fall in the high elevations any time of year. The majority of precipitation comes in the form of snow between November and March.

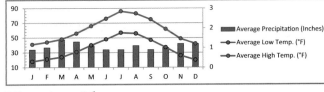

Vacation Planner

If you only want to catch the main attractions at Great Basin, a single day should suffice. **Lehman Caves** and the **most popular hiking trails/viewpoints** are all located in the same general area. With that said, Great Basin is a relief from bumper-to-bumper traffic and shoulder-to-shoulder hiking experienced at more popular parks of the West. So, you may want to pack a cooler and your tent and spend a few nights under the stars. Nearby dining, grocery stores, lodging, festivals, and attractions are listed on pages 448–453.

Day 1 Skip Great Basin Visitor Center (unless you want to see the cross-section of Prometheus, the 4,862 year old tree). Stop at **Lehman Caves Visitor Center** to pick up or purchase **cave tour tickets** (page 444). Reservations are a good idea, but if your group is relatively small and you aren't traveling on a summer holiday weekend, you should be able to get tickets upon arrival. Plus, tours are offered several times a day during the summer. Fill in the

Stella Lake

Lehman Caves © Frank Kovalchek (flickr/Alaskan Dude)

blanks around your cave tour(s) by taking **Wheeler Peak Scenic Drive**, stopping at pull-outs of your choosing, to **Summit Trail Parking Area**. Hike the 8.2-mile **Wheeler Peak Trail** (page 444). Allow at least 4 hours for this mountain trek. If it's a beautiful day, bring a lunch and picnic at the peak. **Stella Lake** is another great location for a picnic. If you aren't interested in Wheeler Peak or are looking for another hike, **Alpine Lakes Loop** and **Bristlecone/Glacier Trail** (page 445) are excellent. Both trails begin at Bristlecone Parking Area. With an early enough start it is possible to hike Wheeler Peak, Alpine Lakes Loop, and Bristlecone Trail in one day, but you'll be exhausted. Cap the day off with an evening **ranger program** (check the park newspaper, *The Bristlecone*) or **stargazing** from your campsite.

Dining

Arches/Canyonlands Area

Moab Brewery • (435) 259-6333
686 S Main St; Moab, UT 84532
www.themoabbrewery.com • Burgers: $7+

Moab Diner • (435) 259-4006
189 S Main St; Moab, UT 84532
www.moabdiner.com • Burgers: $6.50+

Milt's Stop & Eat • (435) 259-7424
356 Mill Creek Dr; Moab, UT 84532
www.miltsstopandeat.com • Burgers: $3.50+

Bar-M Chuckwagon • (435) 259-2276
7000 N US-191; Moab, UT 84532
www.barmchuckwagon.com • Admission: $28/Adult

Miguel's Baja Grill • (435) 259-6546
51 N Main St; Moab, UT 84532
www.miguelsbajagrill.com • Entrée: $12–22

Sunset Grill • (435) 259-7146
900 N US-191; Moab, UT 84532

Desert Bistro • (435) 259-0756
1266 N US-191; Moab, UT 84532
www.desertbistro.com • Entrée: $20–45

La Hacienda • (435) 259-6319
574 N Main St; Moab, UT 84532

Paradox Pizza • (435) 259-9999
702 S Main St; Moab, UT 84532
www.paradoxpizza.com • Pizza: $10+

Wake & Bake Cafe • (435) 259-0101
Ste 6, 59 S Main St; Moab, UT 84532
www.wakeandbakecafe.com

Peace Tree Juice Cafe • (435) 259-8503
20 S Main St; Moab, UT 84532
www.peacetreecafe.com • Breakfast: $8–9

Eklecticafe • (435) 259-6896
352 N Main St; Moab, UT 84532

Love Muffin Cafe • (435) 259-6833
139 N Main St; Moab, UT 84532
www.lovemuffincafe.com

K&A Chuckwagon • (435) 587-3468
496 N Main St; Monticello, UT 84535

Wagon Wheel Pizza • (435) 587-2766
164 S Main St; Monticello, UT 84535

Subway • (435) 587-2757
481 N Main St; Monticello, UT 84535

Peace Tree Juice Cafe • (435) 587-5063
516 N Main St; Monticello, UT 84535

Shake Shack • (435) 587-2966
380 N Main St; Monticello, UT 84535

Chow Hound • (435) 564-3563
30 E Main St; Green River, UT 84525

Cathy's Pizza & Deli • (435) 564-8122
185 W Main St; Green River, UT 84525

Ray's Tavern • (435) 564-3511
25 S Broadway; Green River, UT 84525

Green River Coffee • (435) 564-3411
25 E Main St; Green River, UT 84525

Capitol Reef/Bryce Canyon Area

Rim Rock Restaurant • (435) 425-3388
2523 UT-24 E; Torrey, UT 84775
www.therimrock.net

Slacker's Burger Joint • (435) 425-3710
165 E Main St; Torrey, UT 84775

Chilizz • (435) 425-2600
155 E Main St; Torrey, UT 84775

Luna Mesa Oasis • (435) 456-9122
2000 E 925 N UT-24; Torrey, UT 84775

Subway • (435) 425-3302
675 E UT-24; Torrey, UT 84775

Cafe Diablo • (435) 425-3070
599 W Main St; Torrey, UT 84775
www.cafediablo.net • Entrée: $22–30

La Cueva • (435) 425-2000
875 N UT-24; Torrey, UT 84775
www.cafelacueva.com • Entrée: $9–15

Castlerock Coffee & Candy • (435) 425-2100
875 E UT-24; Torrey, UT 84775
www.castlerockcoffee.com

Hell's Backbone Grill • (435) 335-7464
20 N UT-12; Boulder, UT 84716
www.hellsbackbonegrill.com • Entrée: $17–26

Boulder Mesa Rest. • (435) 335-7447
155 E Burr Trail; Boulder, UT 84716

Sunglow Family Rest. • (435) 425-3701
91 E Main St; Bicknell, UT 84715

Red Cliffs Restaurant • (435) 425-3797
2600 E UT-24; Bicknell, UT 84715

Burr Trail Grill • (435) 335-7503
UT-12; Boulder, UT 84716
www.burrtrailgrill.com

Blondie's Eatery • (435) 542-3255
300 N UT-95; Hanksville, UT 84734

Clarke's Restaurant • (435) 679-8383
141 N Main St; Tropic, UT 84776

Rubys Cowboy Buffet • (435) 834-8027
26 S Main St; Bryce Canyon City, UT 84764

Pizza Place • (435) 679-8888
21 S Main St; Tropic, UT 84776

Subway • (435) 834-5888
139 W UT-12; Bryce, UT 84764

Zion & Grand Canyon Area

Parallel Eighty Eight • (435) 772-3588
1515 Zion Park Blvd; Springdale, UT 84532
www.paralleleighty-eightrestaurant.com • Entrée: $16–32

Whiptail Grill • (435) 772-0283
445 Zion Park Blvd; Springdale, UT 84737

Switchback Grille • (435) 772-3700
1149 Zion Park Blvd; Hurricane, UT 84737
www.switchbacktrading.com • Entrée: $14–38

Bit & Spur • (435) 772-3498
1212 Zion Park Blvd; Hurricane, UT 84737
www.bitandspur.com • Entrée: $13–25

Zion Pizza & Noodle Co • (435) 772-3815
868 Zion Park Blvd; Hurricane, UT 84737
www.zionpizzanoodle.com

Flying Monkey
971 Zion Park Blvd; Springdale, UT 84767
www.flyingmonkeyzion.com

Cafe Oscars • (435) 772-3232
948 Zion Park Blvd; Hurricane, UT 84737
www.cafeoscars.com

Spotted Dog • (435) 772-0700
428 Zion Landing; Springdale, UT 84767
www.flanigans.com

Cafe Soleil • (435) 772-0505
205 Zion Park Blvd; Springdale, UT 84767

Tsunami Juice & Java • (435) 772-3818
180 Zion Landing; Springdale, UT 84767

Mean Bean Coffee House • (435) 772-0654
932 Zion Park Blvd; Springdale, UT 84767

R P's Stage Stop • (928) 638-3115
114A AZ-64; Grand Canyon, AZ 86023

Wendys and McDonalds are available near the Grand Canyon's South Entrance on AZ-64

Red Raven • (928) 635-4980
135 W Route 66; Williams, AZ 86046
www.redravenrestaurant.com • Entrée: $15–27

The Singing Pig BBQ • (928) 635-2904
437 W. Route 66; Williams, AZ 86046
www.thesingingpigroute66.com • Sandwich: $8+

Old Smokey's Restaurant • (928) 635-1915
624 W Route 66 (near 7th Ave); Williams, AZ 86046
www.sideeffectsllc.com

Pine Country • (928) 635-9718
107 N Grand Canyon Blvd; Williams, AZ 86046
www.pinecountryrestaurant.com • Entrée: $9–22

Dara Thai Cafe • (623) 551-6676
3655 W Anthem Way, # B127; Anthem, AZ 85086

Rolando's Mexican & Seafood • (928) 635-1990
401 W Route 66; Williams, AZ 86046

Brown Bag Sandwich Shoppe • (928) 635-5204
112 S 1st St; Williams, AZ 86046
www.bbsandwichshop.com • Sandwiches: $7+

Grand Canyon Coffee & Cafe • (928) 635-4907
125 W Route 66; Williams, AZ 86046
www.grandcanyoncoffeeandcafe.com

J D's Espresso • (928) 635-2770
219 E Route 66; Williams, AZ 86046
www.jdsespresso.com

Great Basin Area

Silver State Restaurant • (775) 289-8866
1204 Aultman St; Ely, Nevada 89301

Twin Wok Restaurant • (775) 289-3699
700 Park Ave; Ely, NV 89301

Evah's • (775) 289-4271
701 Avenue I; Ely, NV 89301

Margarita's • (775) 289-6296
945 N Mcgill Hwy; Ely, NV 89301
www.margaritasely.com • Entrée: $10+

La Fiesta • (775) 289-4114
700 Avenue H; Ely, NV 89301

Red Apple • (775) 289-8585
2160 Aultman St; Ely, NV 89301

Many chain restaurants can be found in
Moab, Richfield, Kanab, and Hurricane, UT;
Page, and Williams, AZ; Ely, NV, and along
I-70 and I-15.

Grocery Stores

Arches/Canyonlands Area

City Market Food • (435) 259-5182
425 S Main St; Moab, UT 84532

Village Market • (435) 259-3111
702 S Main St; Moab, UT 84532

Dave's Corner Market • (435) 259-6999
401 Mill Creek Dr; Moab, UT 84532

Walmart • (435) 637-6974
UT-125; Green River, UT 84501

Capitol Reef/Bryce Canyon Area

Chuck Wagon General Store • (435) 425-3288
12 W Main St; Torrey, UT 84775

Clarke's Country Market • (435) 679-8633
141 North Main St; Tropic, UT 84776

Ruby's General Store • (435) 834-5341
26 S Main St; Bryce Canyon City, UT 84764

Zion & Grand Canyon Area

Sol Foods • (435) 772-0277
95 Zion Park Blvd; Springdale, UT 84737

Walmart Supercenter • (435) 635-6945
180 N 3400 W; Hurricane, UT 84737

Farmers Market • (435) 635-0774
495 N State St; La Verkin, UT 84745

Simpson's Market • (928) 679-2281
US-89 & AZ-64; Cameron, AZ 86020

Great Basin Area

Ridley's Family Markets • (775) 289-3444
1689 Great Basin Blvd; Ely, NV 89301

Lodging

Arches/Canyonlands Area

Red Stone Inn • (435) 259-3500
535 S Main St; Moab, UT 84532
www.moabredstone.com • Rates: $70+/night

Big Horn Lodge • (435) 259-6171
550 S Main St; Moab, UT 84532
www.moabbighorn.com • Rates: $80+

River Canyon Lodge • (435) 259-8838
71 W 200 N; Moab, UT 84532
www.rivercanyonlodge.com • Rates: $90+

Apache Motel • (435) 259-5727
166 S 4th East St; Moab, UT 84532

Gonzo Inn • (435) 259-2515
100 W 200 S; Moab, UT 84532
www.gonzoinn.com • Rates: $129+

Aarchway Inn • (435) 259-2599
1551 US-191; Moab, UT 84532
www.aarchwayinn.com • Rates: $130+

Bowen Motel • (435) 259-7132
169 N Main St; Moab, UT 84532
www.bowenmotel.com • Rates: $90+

Kokopelli Lodge • (435) 259-7615
72 S 100 E; Moab, UT 84532
www.kokopellilodge.com • Rates: $70+

Adventure Inn • (435) 259-6122
512 N Main St; Moab, UT 84532
www.adventureinnmoab.com

Riverside Inn • (435) 259-8848
988 N Main St; Moab, UT 84532

Inca Inn • (435) 259-7261
570 N Main St; Moab, UT 84532
www.incainn.com • Rates: $60+

Red Cliffs Lodge • (435) 259-2002
Mile Post 14, UT-128; Moab, UT 84532
www.redcliffslodge.com • Rates: $120+

Sorrel River Ranch • (435) 259-4642
UT-128; Moab, UT 84532
www.sorrelriver.com • Rates: $399+

Desert Hills B&B • (435) 259-3568
1989 Desert Hills Dr; Moab, UT 84532
www.deserthillsbnb.com

Mayor's House B&B • (435) 259-3019
505 Rosetree Ln; Moab, UT 84532
www.mayorshouse.com • Rates: $100+

Cali-Cochitta B&B • (435) 259-4961
110 S 2nd East St; Moab, UT 84532
www.moabdreaminn.com • Rates: $95+

Castle Valley Inn B&B • (435) 259-6012
424 E Amber Ln; Moab, UT 84532
www.castlevalleyinn.com • Rates: $105+

Sunflower Hill B&B • (435) 259-2974
185 N 300 E; Moab, UT 84532
www.sunflowerhill.com • Rates: $165+

Lazy Lizard Hostel • (435) 259-6057
1213 S US-191; Moab, UT 84532
www.lazylizardhostel.com • Dorm: $9

Archview Resort • (435) 259-7854
US-191 and UT-313; Moab, UT 84532
www.archviewresort.com • RV Sites: $35+

Canyonlands Campground • (435) 259-6848
555 S Main St; Moab, UT 84532
www.canyonlandsrv.com • RV Sites: $35+

Kane Springs Campground • (435) 259-8844
1705 Kane Creek Blvd; Moab, UT
www.kanesprings.com • RV Sites: $27.50+

Riverside Oasis Campground • (435) 259-3424
1871 N US-191; Moab, UT 84532
www.riversideoasis.com • RV Sites: $35+

KOA • (435) 259-6682
3225 US-191; Moab, Utah 84532

There are a dozen small BLM campgrounds
located along Hwy 128, three each along Hwy 279,
Hwy 313, and Kane Creek Road, one at Ken's
Lake, another on Sand Flats Road, and two more
on Canyon Rims Recreation Area Road.

Inn at the Canyons • (435) 587-2458
533 N Main St; Monticello, UT 84535
www.monticellocanyonlandsinn.com • Rates: $75+

Monticello Inn • (435) 587-2274
164 E Central St; Monticello, UT 84535
www.themonticelloinn.org • Rates: $71+

River Terrace • (435) 564-3401
1740 E Main St; Green River, UT 84525
www.river-terrace.com • Rates: $100+

Runnin' Iron Inn • (435) 220-1050
6780 N US-191; Monticello, UT 84535
www.canyonlandsbestkeptsecret.com • Rates: $59

Grist Mill Inn B&B • (435) 587-2597
64 S 300 E; Monticello, UT 84535
www.oldgristmillinn.com • Rates: $89+

Robbers Roost Motel • (435) 564-3452
325 W Main St; Green River, UT 84525
www.rrmotel.com • Rates: $40+

Shady Acres Campground • (435) 564-8290
350 E Main; Green River, UT 84525
www.shadyacresrv.com

AOK RV Park • (435) 564-8372
610 S Green River Blvd; Green River, UT 84525

Green River KOA • (435) 564-8195
235 S 1780 E; Green River, UT 84525

Capitol Reef/Bryce Canyon Area

Austin's Chuckwagon • (435) 425-3344
12 W Main St; Torrey, UT 84775
www.austinschuckwagonmotel.com • Rates: $75+

Sandstone Inn • (435) 425-3775
955 E UT-24; Torrey, UT 84775
www.sandstonecapitolreef.com • Rates: $68+

Best Western Capitol Reef Resort • (435) 425-3761
2600 E UT-24; Torrey, UT 84775

Red Sands Hotel • (435) 425-3688
670 E UT-24; Torrey, UT 84775
www.redsandshotel.com • Rates: $75+

Boulder View Inn • (435) 425-3800
385 W Main St; Torrey, UT 84775
www.boulderviewinn.com • Rates: $40–75

Cowboy Homestead • (435) 425-3414
2280 S UT-12; Torrey, UT 84775
www.cowboyhomesteadcabins.com • Rates: $69–79

Torrey School House B&B • (435) 633-4643
150 N Center Street; Torrey, UT 84775
www.torreyschoolhouse.com • Rates: $110+

Sky Ridge B&B • (435) 425-3222
950 UT-24; Torrey, UT 84775
www.skyridgeinn.com • Rates: $109+

Thousand Lakes RV Park • (435) 425-3500
1110 W UT-24; Torrey, UT 84775
www.thousandlakesrvpark.com • Rates: $27.50+

Best Western Grand Hotel • (435) 834-5700
30 N 100 E; Bryce Canyon City, UT 84764
www.bestwesternbrycecanyongrandhotel.com • Rates: $135+

Best Western Rubys Inn • (435) 834-5341
26 S Main St; Bryce Canyon City, UT 84764
www.rubysinn.com • Rates: $80+

Bryce Canyon Pines • (800) 892-7923
Milepost 10, UT-12; Bryce, UT 84764
www.brycecanyonmotel.com • Rates: $65+

Stone Canyon Inn • (435) 679-8611
1220 W 50 S; Tropic, UT 84776
www.stonecanyoninn.com • Rates: $145+

Bryce Canyon Inn • (435) 679-8502
21 N Main St; Tropic, UT 84776
www.brycecanyoninn.com • Rates: $70+

Bryce Country Cabins • (435) 679-8643
320 N Main St; Tropic, UT 84776
www.brycecountrycabins.com • Rates: $85+

Bryce Trails B&B • (435) 679-8700
1001 W Bryce Way; Tropic, UT 84776
www.brycetrails.com • Rates: $135+

Buffalo Sage B&B • (435) 679-8443
980 N UT-12; Tropic, UT 84776
www.buffalosage.com

Riverside Resort & RV Park • (800) 824-5651
594 N US-89; Hatch, UT 84735
www.riversideresort-utah.com

Grand Staircase Inn • (435) 679-8400
105 N Kodachrome Dr; Cannonville, UT 84718
www.grandstaircaseinn.com • Rates: $49+

Bryce Valley KOA • (435) 679-8988
215 Red Rock Dr; Cannonville, UT 84718

Zion & Grand Canyon Area

Driftwood Lodge • (435) 772-3262
1515 Zion Park Blvd; Springdale, UT 84767
www.driftwoodlodge.net • Rates: $79+

Pioneer Lodge • (435) 772-3233
838 Zion Park Blvd; Springdale, UT 84767
www.pioneerlodge.com • Rates: $149+

Best Western Zion Park Inn • (435) 772-3200
1215 Zion Park Blvd; Springdale, UT 84767

Desert Pearl Inn • (435) 772-8888
707 Zion Park Blvd; Springdale, UT 84767
www.desertpearl.com • Rates: $138+

Cliffrose Lodge & Gardens • (435) 772-3234
281 Zion Park Blvd; Springdale, UT 84767
www.cliffroselodge.com • Rates: $169+

Bumbleberry Inn • (435) 772-3224
97 Bumbleberry Ln; Springdale, UT 84767
www.bumbleberry-inn.com • Rates: $58+

Cable Mountain Lodge • (435) 772-3366
145 Zion Park Blvd; Hurricane, UT 84737

Canyon Ranch Motel • (435) 772-3357
668 Zion Park Blvd; Hurricane, UT 84737
www.canyonranchmotel.com • Rates: $99+

Majestic View Lodge • (435) 772-0665
2400 Zion Park Blvd; Hurricane, UT 84737
www.majesticviewlodge.com • Rates: $79+

Zion Ponderosa Ranch Resort • (435) 648-2700
Twin Knolls Rd; Mt Carmel, Utah, UT 84755
www.zionponderosa.com • Rates: $64+

Red Rock Inn • (435) 772-3139
998 Zion Landing; Springdale, UT 84767
www.redrockinn.com • Rates: $122+

Zion Canyon B&B • (435) 772-9466
101 Kokopelli Cir; Springdale, Utah 84767
www.zioncanyonbandb.com • Rates: $135+

Canyon Vista Lodge, B&B • (435) 772-3801
2175 Zion Park Blvd; Springdale, UT 84767
www.canyonvistabandb.com • Rates: $139+

Harvest House B&B • (435) 772-3880
29 Canyon View Dr; Springdale, UT 84767
www.harvesthouse.net • Rates: $120+

Under the Eaves • (435) 772-3457
980 Zion Park Blvd; Springdale, UT 84767
www.undertheeaves.com • Rates: $95+

Novel House Inn • (800) 711-8400
73 Paradise Rd; Springdale, UT 84767
www.novelhouse.com

Flanigan's Villas • (435) 632-0798
425 Zion Park Blvd; Springdale, UT 84767
www.flanigansvillas.com • Rates: $259-359

Amber Inn B&B • (435) 772-0289
244 W Main St; Rockville, UT 84763
www.amber-inn.com • Rates: $100+

Desert Thistle • (435) 772-0251
37 W Main St; Rockville, UT 84763
www.thedesertthistle.com • Rates: $110+

Best Western Squire Inn • (800) 622-6966
74 AZ-64; Grand Canyon, AZ 86023

Canyon Plaza Resort • (928) 638-2673
116 AZ-64; Grand Canyon, AZ 86023
www.grandcanyonplaza.com • Rates: $100+

Grand Canyon Hotel • (928) 635-1419
145 W Route 66; Williams, AZ 86046
www.thegrandcanyonhotel.com • Rates: $40+

Red Feather Lodge • (928) 638-2414
106 AZ-64; Grand Canyon, AZ 86023
www.redfeatherlodge.com • Rates: $80+

Holiday Inn Express • (928) 638-3000
AZ-64; Grand Canyon, AZ 86023

The Lodge on Route 66 • (928) 635-4534
200 E Route 66; Williams, AZ 86046
www.thelodgeonroute66.com • Rates: $90+

Canyon Country Inn • (928) 635-2349
442 W Route 66; Williams, AZ 86046
www.thecanyoncountryinn.com • Rates: $66+

The Red Garter Inn • (800) 328-1484
137 W Railroad Ave; Williams, AZ 86046
www.redgarter.com • Rates: $120+

Dumplin Patch B&B • (928) 635-1924
625 E Linger Ln; Williams, AZ 86046
www.dumplinpatch.net • Rates: $155+

Canyon Motel & RV Park • (800) 482-3955
1900 E Rodeo Rd Route 66; Williams, AZ 86046
www.thecanyonmotel.com • Rates: $70+

Kaibab Lodge • (928) 638-2389
18 miles north of North Rim
www.kaibablodge.com • Rates: $95+

Jacob Lake Inn • (928) 643-7232
45 miles north of North Rim, Jacob Lake, AZ
www.jacoblake.com • Rates: $89+

Lodging and dining are extremely limited at the North Rim. See page 436 for in-park accommodations.

Great Basin Area

Hotel Nevada • (775) 289-6665
501 Aultman St; Ely, NV 89301
www.hotelnevada.com • Rates: $35–125

Prospector Hotel & Casino • (775) 289-8900
1501 Aultman St; Ely, NV 89301
www.prospectorhotelandcasino.com • Rates: $79+

Bristlecone Motel • (800) 497-7404
700 Avenue I; Ely, NV 89301
www.bristleconemotelelynv.com • Rates: $60+

Jail House Motel & Casino • (775) 289-3033
211 5th St; Ely, NV 89301-1581
www.jailhousecasino.com

Four Sevens Motel • (775) 289-4747
500 High St; Ely, NV 89301

Chain hotels can be found in Moab, Richfield, Kanab, and Hurricane, UT; Page, and Williams, AZ; Ely, NV, and along I-70 and I-15.

Festivals

Sundance Film Festival • January
Park City, Salt Lake City, Ogden, UT
www.sundance.org

Winter Birds Festival • January
St. George, UT • www.sgcity.org/birdfestival

Western Stars Cowboy Poetry • February
Moab • www.moabwesternstars.com

Bryce Canyon Winter Festival • February
Bryce Canyon City • (800) 468-8660

Skinny Tire Festival • March
Moab • www.skinnytireevents.com

Dixie-Escalante Kite Festival • April
Sun River Golf Course • www.dixiekitefestival.com

Moab Arts Festival • May
Moab • www.moabartsfestival.org

Canyonlands PRCA Rodeo • June
Moab • www.canyonlandsrodeo.com

Utah Shakespeare Festival • June
Cedar City, UT • www.bard.org

Grand Canyon Music Festival • August
South Rim • www.grandcanyonmusicfest.org

Moab Music Festival • September
Moab • www.moabmusicfest.org

Everett Ruess Days • September
Escalante, UT • www.everettruessdays.org

World of Speed • September
Bonneville Salt Flats, UT • www.saltflats.com

Pumpkin Chuckin' Festival • October
Moab • www.youthgardenproject.org

Red Rock Film Festival • November
St. George, UT • www.daysofcamelot.com

Moab Folk Festival • November
Moab • www.moabfolkfestival.com

Dickens' Christmas Festival • December
St. George • www.dickenschristmasfestival.com

Attractions

Arches/Canyonlands Area

Castle Valley Ridge Trail
Advanced, 19 mile MTB loop, trailhead located on FR-110 (up Nuck Woodward Canyon from UT-31)
Manti-La Sal National Forest

Corona Arch • 3 miles (roundtrip)
Trailhead is located on UT-279, 10 miles west of the UT-279/US-191 junction

Negro Bill Canyon • 4 miles (roundtrip)
Trailhead is located on UT-128, 3 miles east of UT-128/US-191 junction • Creek crossing is required (wear appropriate footwear)

Fisher Towers • 4.4 miles (roundtrip)
Trailhead located off a 2.2 mile dirt road accessed via UT-128, 21 miles east of the UT-128/US-191 junction

Dead Horse Point State Park • (435) 259-2614
US-313; Moab, UT 84532
www.stateparks.utah.gov • Day-use: $10/Vehicle

Skydive Moab • (435) 259-5867
US-191 N; Moab, UT 84532
www.skydivemoab.com

Chile Pepper Bike Shop • (435) 259-4688
702 S Main St; Moab, UT 84532
www.chilebikes.com • *Rentals*

Rim Cyclery • (435) 259-5333
94 W 100 N; Moab, UT 84532
www.rimcyclery.com • *Rentals*

Moab Cyclery • (800) 559-1978
391 S Main St; Moab, UT 84532
www.moabcyclery.com • *Rentals & Tours*

Western Spirit Cycling • (435) 259-8732
478 Mill Creek Dr; Moab, UT 84532
www.westernspirit.com • *Tours (Road & MTB)*

Solfun Mtn Bike Tours • (435) 259-9861
PO Box 1269; Moab, UT 84532
www.solfun.com • *Tours: $100+*

Rim Mountain Bike Tours • (435) 259-5223
1233 S US-191; Moab, UT 84532
www.rimtours.com • *Tours ($85+)*

Moab Adventure Center • (435) 259-7019
Climbing, rafting, hot air ballooning, and more
225 S Main St; Moab, UT 84532
www.moabadventurecenter.com

Moab Desert Adventures • (435) 260-2404
Guided rock climbing and canyoneering trips
415 N Main St; Moab, UT 84532
www.moabdesertadventures.com

Tag-A-Long Expeditions • (435) 259-8946
452 N Main St; Moab, UT 84532
www.tagalong.com • *Land & Water Adventures*

Coyote Land Tours • (435) 259-6649
397 N Main St, # 2; Moab, UT 84532
www.coyotelandtours.com • *Tours: $59/Adult*

High Point Hummer & ATV • (435) 259-2972
281 N Main St; Moab, UT 84532
www.highpointhummer.com • *Rentals & Tours*

Farabee Jeep Rentals • (435) 259-7494
1125 S US-191; Moab, UT
www.farabeesjeeprentals.com • *Rates: $150+/day*

Canyonlands By Night • (435) 259-5261
1861 US-191; Moab, UT 84532
www.canyonlandsbynight.com • *Land, Air, and Water Tours*

Navtec Expeditions • (435) 259-7983
321 N Main St; Moab, UT 84532
www.navtec.com • *River & Jeep Tours*

Red River Adventures • (877) 259-4046
1140 S Main St; Moab, UT 84532
www.redriveradventures.com • *Multi-sport Tours*

Tex's Riverways • (435) 259-5101
691 N 500 W; Moab, UT 84532
www.texsriverways.com • *Rentals & Shuttles*

Museum of Moab • (435) 259-7985
118 E Center St; Moab, UT 84532
www.moabmuseum.org • *Suggested Donation: $5*

Castle Creek Winery • (435) 259-3332
Milepost 14, UT-128; Moab, UT 84532
www.castlecreekwinery.com

Slickrock Cinemas 3 • (435) 259-4441
580 Kane Creek Blvd; Moab, UT 84532

Gravel Pit Lanes • (435) 259-4748
1078 Mill Creek Dr; Moab, UT 84532

Hole N' the Rock • (435) 686-2250
11037 S US-191; Moab, UT 84532
www.theholeintherock.com • *Admission: $5/Adult*

John Wesley Powell River History Museum
1765 E Main; Green River, UT • (435) 564-3427
www.johnwesleypowell.com • *Admission: $6/Adult*

Green River State Park • (435) 564-3633
450 Green River Blvd; Green River, UT 84525
www.stateparks.utah.gov • *Day-use: $6/Vehicle*

Colorado River & Trail Exp. • (435) 564-8170
1117 E 1000 N; Green River, UT 84525
www.crateinc.com • *Rafting: $74+*

Goblin Valley State Park • (435) 275-4584
Goblin Valley Rd; Green River, UT 84525
www.stateparks.utah.gov • *Day-use: $7/Vehicle*

Capitol Reef/Bryce Canyon Area

Hondoo Rivers & Trails • (435) 425-3519
90 E Main St; Torrey, UT 84775
www.hondoo.com • *Horseback & Vehicle Tours*

Backcountry Outfitters • (866) 747-3972
677 E UT-24; Torrey, UT 84775
www.ridethereef.com • *Multi-sport Adventures*

Anasazi State Park • (435) 335-7308
460 N UT-12; Boulder, UT 84716
www.stateparks.utah.gov • Fee: $5/Person

Wayne Theater • (435) 425-3123
11 E Main St; Bicknell, UT 84715

Grand Staircase Escalante Nat'l Mon.
10 W Center St; Tropic, UT 84776
www.ut.blm.gov/monument • (435) 679-8980

Escalante Canyon Outfitters • (888) 326-4453
PO Box 1330; Boulder, UT 84716
www.ecohike.com • *Multi-day Hiking Tours*

Utah Canyons • (435) 826-4967
325 W Main St; Escalante, UT 84726
www.utahcanyons.com • *Hiking & Shuttle Service*

Kodachrome Basin State Park • (435) 679-8562
PO Box 180069; Cannonville, UT 84718
www.stateparks.utah.gov • Day-use: $6/Vehicle

Escalante Petrified Forest • (435) 826-4466
710 N Reservoir; Escalante, UT 84726
www.stateparks.utah.gov • Day-use: $6/Vehicle

Bryce Canyon ATV Adventures • (435) 834-5200
139 E UT-12; Bryce Canyon City, UT 84764
www.brycecanyonatvadventures.com • Rides: $35+

Moqui Cave • (435) 644-8525
4518 N US-89; Kanab, UT • Admission: $10/Adult

Frontier Movie Town • (435) 644-5337
297 W Center St; Kanab, UT 84741
www.frontiermovietown.com

Cedar Breaks Nat'l Mon. • (435) 586-0787
2390 W UT-56, Suite 11; Cedar City, UT 84720
www.nps.gov/cebr • Entrance Fee: $4/Person

Zion & Grand Canyon Area

Zion Adventure Co. • (435) 772-1001
Tons of tours, shuttle service for Zion Narrows, gear rental, courses, and tubing
36 Lion Blvd; Springdale, UT 84767
www.zionadventures.com • *Narrows Tour: $150+*

Mild To Wild Rhino Tours • (435) 216-8298
839 Zion Park Blvd; Springdale, UT 84737
www.mildtowildrhinotours.com

Zion Rock & Mtn Guides • (435) 772-3303
Shuttle Service to Zion Narrows Trailhead (Chamberlain Ranch), Tours, & Rental
1458 Zion Park Blvd; Springdale, UT 84737
www.zionrockguides.com

Zion Cycles • (435) 772-0400
868 Zion Park Blvd; Springdale, UT 84767
www.zioncycles.com • *Rentals ($15+/hr) & Tours*

Southern Utah Adventure Center • (435) 635-0907
Rentals (boat, jeep, ATV, etc.) and Tours
138 W State St; Hurricane, UT 84737
www.southernutahadventurecenter.com

Pioneer Corner Museum • (435) 635-7153
95 S Main St; Hurricane, UT 84737

Zion Canyon Theatre • (435) 772-2400
145 Zion Park Blvd; Springdale, UT 84767
www.zioncanyontheatre.com

The Wave • Coyote Buttes North
To prevent overuse, only 20 hikers are allowed to hike here each day. All permits ($7) must be purchased in advance. Ten permits can be obtained via an online lottery. Ten walk-in permits are available 24 hours in advance via lottery at Paria Contact Station (Kanab Field Office in winter). Successful applicants will be given detailed instructions & maps to reach the Wave. Additional information on the permit process is available at the following web address:

www.blm.gov/az/st/en/arolrsmain/paria/coyote_buttes/permits.html

Wire Pass • Coyote Buttes North
Don't forget to take a stroll down Wire Pass (1.7 miles, one-way) when visiting the Wave. It's the most scenic entry point to Buckskin Gulch. Wire Pass Trailhead is located 8.3 miles down House Rock Valley Road (washboard, dirt, inaccessible after rain). House Rock Valley Road is accessed from US-89 (between mile markers 25 and 26). A permit is required ($6).

Buckskin Gulch
One of the longest (13+ miles, one-way) and

deepest slot canyons in the world is also one of the best hiking trails in the United States. Wire Pass is the most popular (and beautiful) access point. Buckskin Gulch continues into Paria Canyon. A permit is required ($6).

Paria Canyon
Paria Canyon can be accessed via Buckskin Gulch or from White House Trailhead (near Paria Contact Station). The trail follows the canyon and Paria River to Lee's Ferry Trailhead at the Colorado River just southwest of Page, AZ and Lake Powell. A permit is required ($6).

These hikes are fantastic, but not without danger. Using a shuttle or two cars is a good idea (if not necessary). Pack plenty of water. Wear water shoes. Check the weather forecast (flash floods are a significant problem—in 2010 the area experienced multiple floods that removed high water campsites, added obstructions, and changed the river bed). Most importantly talk to a ranger about trail conditions when you obtain your permit ($6).

Day hike permits for Buckskin Gulch, Paria Canyon, and Wire Pass can be purchased at self-pay stations at each trailhead.

Kanab Field Office • (435) 644-4600
318 N 100 E; Kanab, UT 84741
www.blm.gov/ut/st/en/fo/kanab.html

Paria Contact Station • (435) 644-4628
Located on US-89, about half-way between Kanab, UT and Page, AZ

Coral Pink Sand Dunes • (435) 648-2800
Accessed via US-89 north of Kanab, UT
www.stateparks.utah.gov • Day-use: $6/Vehicle

Dinosaur Discovery Site • (435) 574-3466
2180 E Riverside Dr; St. George, UT 84790
www.utahdinosaurs.com • Admission: $6/Adult

St. George Temple • (435) 673-3533
250 E 400 S; St. George, UT 84770

Tuacahn Ampitheatre • (435) 652-3200
1100 Tuacahn; Ivins, UT 84738
www.tuacahn.org • Tickets: $17.50+

Snow Canyon State Park • (435) 628-2255
1002 Snow Canyon Dr; Ivins, UT 84738
www.stateparks.utah.gov • Day-use: $6/Vehicle

Sand Hollow State Park • (435) 680-0715
4405 W 3600 S; Hurricane, UT 84737
www.stateparks.utah.gov • Day-use: $10/Vehicle

Quail Creek State Park • (435) 879-2378
472 N 5300 W; Hurricane, UT 84737
www.stateparks.utah.gov • Day-use: $10/Vehicle

Coral Cliffs Cinema 8 • (435) 635-1484
835 W State St; Hurricane, UT 84737
www.coralcliffscinema8.com

Vermilion Cliffs National Monument
Marble Canyon, AZ 86036 • (435) 688-3200
www.blm.gov

Antelope Canyon

The most-visited and most-photographed slot canyon in the American Southwest. A guide is required for both Upper and Lower Antelope Canyon.
www.navajonationparks.org

Overland Canyon Tours • (928) 608-4072
48 N Lake Powell Blvd; Page, AZ 86040
www.overlandcanyontours.com • Tours: $32+/Adult

Antelope Slot Canyon Tours by Chief Tsosi
55 S Lake Powell Blvd; Page, AZ 86040
www.antelopeslotcanyon.com • (928) 645-5594

Navajo Tours • (928) 698-3384
PO Box 4586; Page, AZ
www.navajotours.com • Tours: $25–40/Person

Glen Canyon National Recreation Area
US-89; Page, AZ 86040 • (928) 608-6200

Lake Powell Vacations • (928) 608-0800
620 Industrial Rd; Page, AZ 86040
www.lakepowellvacations.com • House Boat Rentals

Grand Canyon Field Institute • (928) 638-2485
4 Tonto St; Grand Canyon, AZ 86023
www.grandcanyon.org • Day & multi-day classes

Marvelous Marv's • (928) 707-0291
200 W Bill Williams Ave; Williams, AZ 86046
www.marvelousmarv.com • Rates: $85/Person

Pygmy Guides • (928) 527-1601
www.pygmyguides.com • Overnight & Day Tours

Ceiba Adventures • (928) 527-0171
Food/Shuttle Service & gear rental for river Trips
7165 Slayton Ranch Rd; Flagstaff, AZ 86004
www.ceibaadventures.com

Jeep Tours & Safaris • (800) 320-5337
106 AZ-64; Tusayan, AZ 86023
www.grandcanyonjeeptours.com • Tours: $64/Adult

Fountain Outdoor Rec. • (928) 635-2434
2467 County Rd 73; Williams, AZ 86046
www.elkridgeski.com • Snow Tubing & Skiing

Bearizona Wildlife Park • (928) 635-2289
1500 E Route 66; Williams, AZ 86046
www.bearizona.com • Rates: $16/Adult

Grand Canyon Deer Farm • (928) 635-4073
6769 E Deer Farm Rd; Williams, AZ 86046-8419
www.deerfarm.com • Rates: $9.95/Adult

Grand Canyon Brewery • (928) 635-2168
233 W Route 66; Williams, AZ 86046
www.grandcanyonbrewery.com

Imax Theater • (928) 638-2203
AZ-64 & US-180; Grand Canyon, AZ 86023
www.explorethecanyon.com • Tickets: $12.50/Adult

Pipe Spring Nat'l Mon. • (928) 643-7105
HC 65 Box 5; Fredonia, AZ 86022
www.nps.gov/pisp • Entrance Fee: $5/Person

Great Basin Area

Ward Charcoal Ovens State Hist. Park
PO Box 151761; Ely, NV • (775) 289-1693
www.parks.nv.gov • Entrance Fee: $7/Vehicle

NV Northern Railway Museum • (775) 289-2085
Museum ($4/Adult) & Train Excursions ($24+)
1100 Avenue A; East Ely, NV 89301
www.nevadanorthernrailway.net

Sunset Lanes • (775) 289-8811
1240 E Aultman St, # B; Ely, NV 89301

Las Vegas Area

Hoover Dam • (702) 494-2517
Located 30 miles southeast of Las Vegas on US-93
Parking: $7, Visitor Center Admission: $8, Powerplant Tour: $11, Hoover Dam Tour: $30 (Tours include Visitor Center admission)
www.usbr.gov/lc/hooverdam

Red Rock Canyon Nat'l Conservation Area
1000 Scenic Dr; Las Vegas, NV • (702) 515-5350
www.blm.gov • Day-use: $7/Vehicle

Dig This • (702) 222-4344
3012 S Rancho Dr; Las Vegas, NV 89102
www.digthisvegas.com • Rates: $400/3 hr

Bellagio Hotel • (888) 987-6667
3600 Las Vegas Blvd S; Las Vegas, NV 89158
www.bellagio.com • *Stop to see the famous fountains*

Vegas Indoor Skydiving • (702) 731-4768
200 Convention Center Dr; Las Vegas, NV 89109
www.vegasindoorskydiving.com • Rates: $85

Pinball Hall of Fame • (702) 597-2627
1610 E Tropicana Ave; Las Vegas, NV 89119
www.pinballmuseum.org • Free

The Atomic Testing Museum • (702) 794-5161
755 E Flamingo Rd; Las Vegas, NV 89119
www.atomictestingmuseum.org • Admission: $14/Adult

Exotics Racing • (702) 405-7223
6925 Speedway Blvd, Suite C105; Las Vegas, NV 89115
www.exoticsracing.com • Rides starting at $99

For more travel information click www.utah.com, www.arizonaguide.com, and www.travelnevada.com

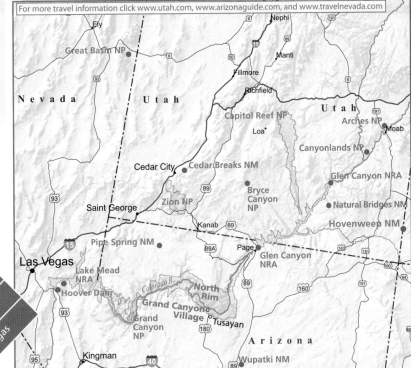

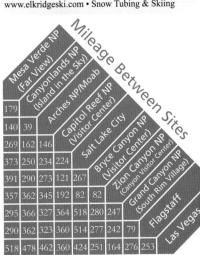

Mileage Between Sites

	Mesa Verde NP (Far View)	Canyonlands NP (Island in the Sky)	Arches NP/Moab	Capitol Reef NP (Visitor Center)	Salt Lake City	Bryce Canyon NP (Visitor Center)	Zion NP (Canyon Visitor Center)	Grand Canyon NP (South Rim Village)	Flagstaff	Las Vegas
	179									
	140	39								
	269	162	146							
	373	250	234	224						
	391	290	273	121	267					
	357	362	345	192	82	82				
	295	366	327	364	518	280	247			
	290	362	323	360	514	277	242	79		
	518	478	462	360	424	251	164	276	253	

© Armin Hornung (www.arminhornung.de)

Joshua Tree • Pages 456–463

Channel Islands • Pages 464–475

Death Valley • Pages 476–485

Sequoia & Kings Canyon • Pages 486–497

Yosemite • Pages 498–521

THE WEST

Lassen Volcanic • Pages 522–529

Redwood • Pages 530–537

Crater Lake • Pages 538–549

Mount Rainier • Pages 550–559

Olympic • Pages 560–571

North Cascades • Pages 572–583

THE WEST

Joshua trees adorn the park's rocky landscapes © Matt Binns

74485 National Park Drive
Twentynine Palms, CA 92277
Phone: (760) 367-5500
Website: www.nps.gov/jotr

Established: October 31, 1994
August 10, 1936 (Nat'l Monument)
Size: 789,745 Acres
Annual Visitors: 1.4 Million
Peak Season: Spring & Fall

Activities: Hiking, Backpacking,
Camping, Stargazing, Horseback
Riding, Rock Climbing, and Biking

Campgrounds: Belle, Black Rock*,
Cottonwood, Hidden Valley, Indian
Cove*, Jumbo Rocks, Ryan, Sheep
Pass, and White Tank
Fee: $10–15/night
Backcountry Camping: Permitted

Park Hours: All day, every day,
except a few day-use areas
Entrance Fee: $15 • Vehicle
$5 • Individual (foot, bike, etc.)

*Reserve at (877) 444-6777 or
www.recreation.gov

Joshua Tree - California

The landscape of Joshua Tree National Park is as unique as the cast of characters that lived in and visited the region for the last 200 years. Forests of twisted Joshua trees and abstract rock piles mark a protected region where the Mojave and Colorado deserts converge in southeastern California. For at least 5,000 years, Native Americans, missionaries, miners, ranchers, and homesteaders have had their shake at life in this arid landscape. Life was difficult for all creatures: humans, animals, and plants. Only the gritty, resourceful, and adaptable survived in an inhospitable, seemingly lifeless wasteland.

Inhospitable? For most…probably. Lifeless wasteland? Certainly not. **Hundreds of species** found fascinating ways to beat the heat and conserve moisture. **Red-spotted toads** reside underground for most of their lives, only escaping the sandy soil after a soaking rain. **Round-tailed ground squirrels** sleep through the hottest part of the summer and hibernate again in winter to avoid the cold. And of course there's the iconic **Joshua tree**, the largest species of yucca. Endemic to the southwestern United States, its primary habitat is the Mojave Desert between 1,300 and 5,900 feet elevation, thriving in open grasslands. To appreciate the Joshua tree forests you must first redefine the word "forest." Joshua trees are distributed sparsely across the desert so their roots can absorb sufficient water. For the first decade of its life a Joshua tree grows about three inches each year, an incredibly fast rate for a desert species. After its initial growth spurt, trees branch out more than up, slowing the growth rate to about an inch per year. Fortunately, they can live for hundreds of years, growing to more than 40 feet tall. The tree's name is owed to a group of Mormon settlers who crossed the Mojave Desert on their exodus west in the mid-19th century. As silhouettes, the trees appear human in form. Their extended limbs capped with spiky leaves evoked images of the Biblical Joshua with arms outstretched, leading his followers to the Promised Land.

Waves of **miners**, **ranchers**, and **homesteaders** came looking for their own promised land. **Bill Keys** was the most successful and colorful of the bunch. After a stint as sheriff, he settled into a life of mining and ranching in the desert of present-day Joshua Tree National Park, taking over the ranch of outlaw and cattle rustler Jim McHaney. Keys' spread gradually expanded and eventually became known as Desert Queen Ranch. He married, had children, murdered a man in a dispute over a mill, educated himself while in prison, and was later pardoned through the efforts of Erie Stanley Gardner, author of the Perry Mason novels.

John Samuelson was another colorful desert dweller. He carved political sayings into rocks that can still be found today about 1.5 miles from the turnout west of Quail Springs Picnic Area. Forced to leave his claim when his lack of citizenship came to light, he also murdered a man over a dispute, and spent time in California's State Hospital before escaping.

Minerva Hamilton Hoyt was a more refined patron of the desert. She grew up a southern belle on a Mississippi plantation before marrying a doctor and moving to Pasadena, where she spent much of her time organizing charitable and social events, gardening, and landscaping. Following the death of her husband and son she turned her focus toward preserving the country's desert landscapes. She organized exhibitions of desert plants in New York, Boston, and London and founded the Desert Conservation League to gain support and publicity. Using her position on the California State Commission, she recommended large parks at Death Valley, Anza–Borrego Desert, and in the Joshua tree forests of the Little San Bernardino Mountains north of Palm Springs. Upon meeting **President Franklin D. Roosevelt**, she wasted no time expressing her opinions about the scenic and ecological value of these areas. Convinced—with the help of then Secretary of the Interior Harold Ickes—President Roosevelt created Joshua Tree National Monument in 1936, protecting the region from poachers and land developers while preserving it for future generations.

When to Go

Joshua Tree is open every day of the year. Oasis and Joshua Tree Visitor Centers are open all year from 8am to 5pm and Cottonwood Visitor Center is open all year from 9am to 3pm. Black Rock Nature Center is open daily from October to May, 8am to 4pm, except on Fridays (noon to 8pm). Unlike most national parks summer is the least popular time to visit, with daytime high temperatures exceeding 100°F. Temperatures gradually subside and by fall the climate is pleasant. During winter daytime highs reach into the 60s°F, but overnight lows are often below freezing. Spring is the best time to visit Joshua Tree. Temperatures are ideal in March and April. And depending on the amount of winter rain, you may have the opportunity to witness a spectacular array of wildflowers in bloom. Joshua Tree is often dry—after all it is a desert—receiving on average 4 inches of precipitation each year.

Transportation & Airports

Public transportation does not provide service to or around the park. The closest large commercial airport is Los Angeles International (LAX), 167 miles west of the park's South Entrance.

Directions

Joshua Tree is located in southeastern California about 170 miles east of downtown Los Angeles. The park has three entrances, all easily accessed from I-10 and CA-62.

South Entrance: Heading east or west on I-10, take Exit 168 for Cottonwood Springs Road toward Mecca/Twentynine Palms. Turn right onto Cottonwood Springs Road into the park.

West and North Entrances: Heading east on I-10 from Los Angeles (150 miles away), take Exit 117 for CA-62/Twentynine Palms Hwy. Continue on CA-62 for almost 28 miles to Joshua Tree. Turn right at Park Blvd, which leads into the park. The North Entrance is reached by continuing on CA-62 past Park Blvd for another 17 miles to Utah Trail in Twentynine Palms. Turn right onto Utah Trail, which leads into the park.

JOSHUA TREE

Driving

Park Boulevard connects West and North Entrance Stations. It also traverses the most popular areas of the park, including Hidden Valley, Ryan, and Jumbo Rock Campgrounds, and provides access to **Keys View Road**, Ryan Mountain Trail, and Skull Rock. In between the West and North Entrance Stations you'll find **Indian Cove Road**, which leads to a secluded campground popular among rock climbers. Farther west along the park's northern boundary is **Joshua Lane**, which leads to another remote campground: Black Rock Canyon. To cross the park from north to south you can take **Park** **Boulevard** from either the North or West Entrance to **Pinto Basin Road**, which continues south to **Cottonwood Springs Road**. There are several rugged dirt roads for **4WD** vehicles. **Geology Tour Road** (18 miles) begins from Park Boulevard between Sheep Pass and Jumbo Rocks. Brochures describing the fascinating landscapes at 16 designated stops are available at the beginning of the road. Breedo Canyon, Black Eagle Mine, Covington Flat, Old Dale, Pinkham Canyon–Thermal Canyon, and Queen Valley Roads connect the park's remote regions for 4WD and mountain bike enthusiasts.

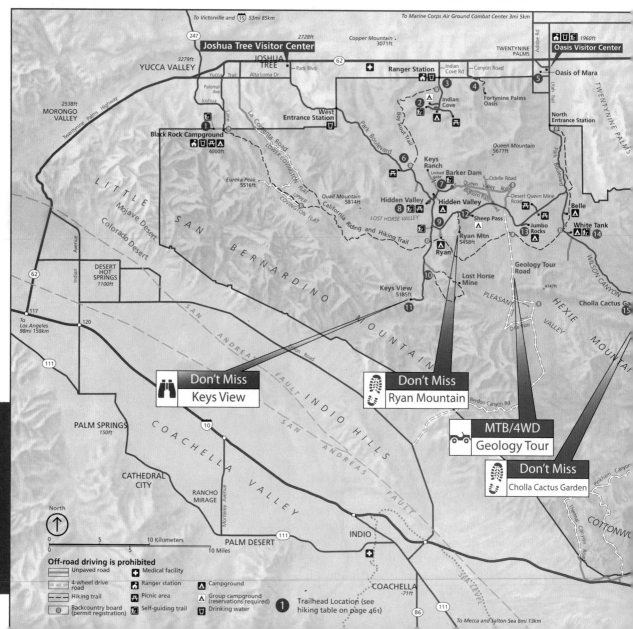

JOSHUA TREE

Camping

Joshua Tree National Park has nine designated campgrounds. **Black Rock** (100 sites) and **Indian Cove** (101) are the only campgrounds that accept reservations. Sites cost $15/night and can be reserved up to six months in advance from October through May by calling (877) 444-6777 or clicking www.recreation.gov. All other campgrounds are first-come, first-served. From north to south on Park Boulevard and Pinto Basin Road are the following campgrounds: **Hidden Valley** (45 sites, $10/night), **Ryan** (31, $10), **Sheep Pass** (6 group sites, $25), **Jumbo Rocks** (124, $10), **Belle** (18, $10), **White Tank** (15, $10), and **Cottonwood** (62, $15). Water and flush toilets are available at Black Rock and Cottonwood. Water is also available at Oasis Visitor Center, Indian Cove Ranger Station, and West Entrance. There are no showers or hook-ups within the park, but you can find showers (fee) outside the park across the road from Joshua Tree Visitor Center. **Group sites** are available at **Indian Cove**, **Sheep Pass**, and **Cottonwood** (reservation required up to one year in advance at 877.444.6777 or www.recreation.gov). All campsites have fire rings, but you must bring your own wood.

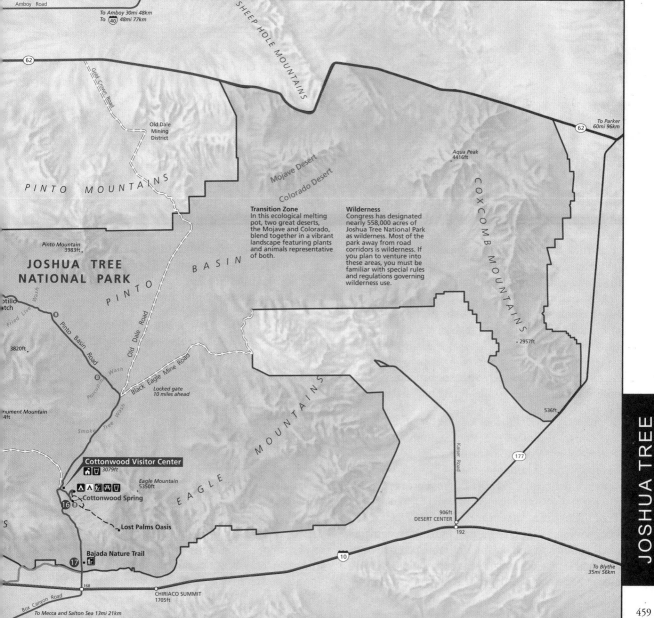

JOSHUA TREE

Climbing Dandelion Route (Old Woman Rock)
© Jarek Tuszynski / Wikimedia Commons

 # Backpacking

Tired of busy campgrounds? Looking for a night of the purest peace and quiet this side of the Sierra Nevada? Try backpacking in Joshua Tree's 585,000 acres of wilderness. If you plan on spending the night in the backcountry, **be sure to register at one of 13 backcountry registration boards** (marked with a Ⓑ on the map on pages 458–459). Failure to register can result in your vehicle being towed and/or cited. Backpackers must camp outside day-use areas, at least one mile from any road, and 500 feet from any trail. The main hurdle to backpacking at Joshua Tree is water. Park policy dictates that all water within the park boundary is reserved for wildlife. **You will have to carry enough water for the duration of your trip**. Excellent backpacking options include the 16-mile (roundtrip) **Boy Scout Trail**, which connects Indian Cove with Park Blvd just north of Hidden Valley, and the 35-miles (one-way) of **California Riding and Hiking Trail** that passes through the park. The latter runs parallel to Park Boulevard, beginning at Black Rock Canyon and terminating near the park's North Entrance.

 # Rock Climbing

Joshua Tree is no longer just the winter retreat for Yosemite's rock climbers. It has become a **world class rock climbing destination** of its own, attracting thousands of climbers each year. With **more than 400 climbing formations and 8,000 routes**, there's something for everyone. If you are an experienced climber visiting the park for the first time you may want to pick up a comprehensive rock climbing guide book (available at the visitor center). If you'd rather receive your information straight from the horse's mouth there are always experienced climbers milling about the campgrounds and rock formations.

Beginners may want to join a guide for a rock climbing course. **Joshua Tree Rock Climbing School** (800.890.4745, www.joshuatreerockclimbing.com), **Joshua Tree Guides** (877.686.7625, www.joshuatreeguides.com), **Vertical Adventures** (800.514.8785, www.verticaladventures.com), and **Joshua Tree's Uprising Adventure Guides** (888.CLIMB-ON, www.uprising.com) offer courses for climbers of all abilities. A full day rock climbing course costs about $135 per person. Private instruction is available at a variable rate dependent on group size.

Hiking

You don't have to lug a heavy pack and gallons of water to enjoy the most beautiful vistas and rock formations this desert wilderness has to offer. The best way to discover the wonders of Joshua Tree is on foot, and it's easy thanks to twelve short, self-guiding nature trails.

Skull Rock, **Barker Dam**, and **Keys View** are the best of the bunch. **Skull Rock Trail** passes peculiar rock formations, including an eroded rock with the conical shape of a skull. **Barker Dam** explores the difficulties of desert life. This short loop passes plenty of rocks for scrambling en route to an old cattle rancher's water tank. **Keys View** is a popular location due to outstanding panoramic views of Salton Sea, San Andreas Fault, and Mexico's Signal Mountain (on a clear day). A more arduous journey is the 3-mile (roundtrip) trek to **Ryan Mountain**, where views surpass those found at Keys. The 4-mile (roundtrip) **Lost Horse Mine/Mountain Trail** glimpses into Joshua Tree's era of mining, visiting the site of a ten-stamp mill where rock was crushed to extract its minerals. Hikers' most common problems are dehydration and getting lost, so carry plenty of water and pay attention to your route. Washes and animal paths can make route-finding difficult.

Skull Rock © Jim Bowen

Giant Marbles © Mila Zinkova

Joshua Tree Hiking Trails

	Trail Name	Trailhead (# on map)	Length	Notes (Roundtrip distances)
Nature Trails (listed from northwest–southeast)	Hi-View	Northwest of Black Rock Camp (1)	1.3 miles	Loop trail with views of Mount San Gorgonio
	Indian Cove	West of Indian Cove Camp (2)	0.6 mile	Loop trail explores the area's history and ecology
	Oasis of Mara	Oasis Visitor Center (5)	0.5 mile	Accessible loop trail discusses the oasis' history
	Barker Dam	Barker Dam Parking Area (7)	1.3 miles	Loop trail visits a water tank built by early ranchers
	Hidden Valley - 👍	Hidden Valley Picnic Area (8)	1.0 mile	Loop trail through a rock enclosed valley
	Cap Rock	Cap Rock Parking Area (9)	0.4 mile	Accessible loop trail with boulder piles and Joshua trees
	Keys View - 👍	Keys View Parking Area (11)	0.25 mile	Loop trail with the best views in the park
	Skull Rock	Jumbo Rocks Camp (13)	1.5 miles	Boulder piles and the renowned Skull Rock
	Arch Rock	White Tank Camp (14)	0.5 mile	Loop trail explores park geology and a natural arch
	Cholla Cactus Garden	20 miles north of Cottonwood Visitor Center (15)	0.25 mile	Loop trail through a dense field of Cholla Cactus • Don't get too close to the cacti, they hurt
	Cottonwood Spring	Cottonwood Spring Camp (16)	1.0 mile	Explores the plants and animals of the Colorado Desert
	Bajada All-Access	0.5 mile from south entrance (17)	0.25 mile	Loop trail explores plants of the Colorado Desert
Hiking Trails	Boy Scout	Indian Cove or Keys West (3, 6)	16.0 miles	Follows the western edge of Wonderland of Rocks
	49 Palms Oasis	The end of Canyon Road (4)	3.0 miles	Hike to a desert oasis with stands of fan palms
	Lost Horse Mine - 👍	1.2 miles east of Keys View Rd (10)	4.0 miles	Site of a well-preserved defunct mining mill
	Ryan Mountain - 👍	Ryan Mtn Parking Area or Sheep Pass Camp (12)	3.0 miles	Best trail • Leads to 5,461 foot summit with 360° views of Eagle Mountains and Salton Sea
	Lost Palms Oasis	Cottonwood Spring Camp (16)	7.2 miles	Oasis, canyon, rock scrambling, and palm stands
	Mastodon Peak	Cottonwood Spring Camp (16)	3.0 miles	Summit provides views of Salton Sea

JOSHUA TREE

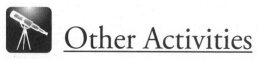

Other Activities

There's a lot more going on at Joshua Tree than hiking, backpacking, and rock climbing.

Horseback riding is another excellent way to experience the park, with **253 miles of designated equestrian trails**. **Ryan and Black Campgrounds** are the only designated camping areas allowing horses and stock. You can also camp in the **backcountry** with your stock, but a **free permit is required**. Call (760) 367-5545 to arrange a permit or to make reservations at Ryan Campground. Grazing is not permitted within the park. Water is usually the limiting factor when planning a trip, as horses are not permitted within 0.25 mile of any water source. You can put the planning into someone else's hands by taking a **guided trail ride** from **Joshua Tree Ranch**. A 1.5-hour Basic Ride costs $65 per rider. They also offer advanced rides: 2.5-hour at $85 per rider and 4-hour at $125 per rider.

Joshua Tree Ranch • 760-902-7336
Mile 2.9 up Park Blvd. (8651 Quail Springs Rd); Joshua Tree, CA 92252
www.joshuatreeranch.com

Biking is permitted on all park roads; unpaved and 4WD roads' limited traffic make them ideal for mountain bikers. The park also hopes to develop 29 miles of trails for bike use but is awaiting approval by Congress. Check online or at a visitor center for the current status.

Stargazing: If you come from a busy metropolitan area like Los Angeles, there's nothing quite like a clear night sky. Bring a set of binoculars and tour the Milky Way on your own. You can also join one of the park's free Night Sky Programs, which are held about once a week between October and May. A current schedule can be found at the park website, campground bulletin boards, entrance stations, and visitor centers.

Wildflowers: When flowers are in bloom Joshua Tree becomes a colorful paradise. Blooms vary from year-to-year with seasonal differences in rainfall and temperature. Flowers begin to bloom in the low elevations by February and may last until June in the higher elevations.

Then there's Joshua Tree's **Desert Institute** (760.367.5535, www.desertinstitute.homestead.com), which provides educational programs to park guests. Reasonably priced courses in natural science, survival skills, arts, and more are offered regularly, but do not cater to children.

For Kids: Children are welcome to participate in the park's **Junior Ranger Program**. To get started, download the activity booklet from the park website or pick up a free hard copy from any visitor center or entrance station. Complete the activities to earn an official Joshua Tree National Park Junior Ranger badge.

Ranger Programs: Guests of the park have the opportunity to **tour historic Keys Ranch** where Bill and Frances Keys thrived in the desert for nearly 60 years. The ranch is located at the end of a short spur road off Park Blvd just east of Hidden Valley (see the map on page 458). **Admission is restricted to guided walking tours.** They are offered at 10am and 1pm daily from October through May. The 1pm offering is typically a **Living History Tour** where a ranger dressed in 1940's clothing guides you through the complex. Tours generally last 90 minutes and require that you walk a half mile. Group size is limited to 25 people. Cost is $5 per person (ages 12 and over), $2.50 for children (ages 6–11), and children under 6 are free. **Reservations** are required and can be made by calling (760) 367-555 between 8am and 4:30pm any day of the week. You can also purchase tickets ahead of time at any of the park's visitor centers. **Tickets cannot be purchased at the ranch.**

Throughout the year park rangers also offer a variety of walks, talks, star parties, and evening programs. Tours range from a simple 15 minute talk at Keys View to a 2.5 hour hike to Mastodon Peak. You can pick up a current schedule of events at any entrance station or visitor center. Schedules are also posted on campground bulletin boards and online at the park website.

Flora & Fauna: **More than 800 species of plants**, including the park's namesake, can be found at Joshua Tree National Park. It's a collection so diverse and unique that park supporters originally suggested the area be called "Desert Plants National Park." There's also exceptional animal diversity. **More than 50 species of mammals and 250 species of birds** have been documented. Animals are commonly seen near sources of water like fan palm oases, Barker Dam, or Smith Water Canyon.

JOSHUA TREE

Pets: Pets are allowed in the park, but must be kept on a leash no more than six feet in length at all times. They are prohibited from all hiking trails and cannot be more than 100 feet from a road, picnic area, or campground.

Accessibility: All visitor centers are accessible to individuals in wheelchairs. Keys View and Bajada, Cap Rock, and Oasis of Mara Nature Trails are fully accessible. There's a designated wheelchair friendly campsite at Jumbo Rocks Campground.

Weather: Visitors must remember they're visiting a desert when they come to Joshua Tree National Park. Days are usually hot, dry, and clear (with the exception of smog from Los Angeles and the coast). Summers are hot, over 100°F during the day and usually not below 70°F through the night. Spring and fall bring perfect weather with highs around 85°F and lows averaging about 50°F.

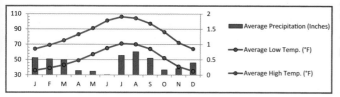

Vacation Planner

If you're planning an extended **backpacking** (page 460) or **rock climbing** (page 460) trip, go for it! The park is great for those activities, but this exercise focuses on a more typical visit. Provided below is a one-day itinerary to let you know where to go and what to see. **Camping** (page 459) is available in the park, but lodging is not. Nearby dining, grocery stores, lodging, festivals, and attractions are listed on pages 473–475.

Day 1
If you're arriving from the west, take CA-62 around the northern border to arrive at the park's **West Entrance** in Joshua Tree. Be sure to make a quick pit-stop at **Joshua Tree Visitor Center** before entering. Browse the exhibits, watch the introductory film (upon request), and remember to pick up a current schedule of **ranger programs** at the visitor center or entrance station. Head into the park and stop at **Hidden Valley** (page 461). It's a great place for an introduction to the interesting rock formations. If you have enough time, drive over to **Barker's Dam** (page 461), which is also worth a visit. Head south past Cap Rock to **Keys View Road**. Drive to its end for one of the most stunning desert vistas in the park. On a clear day you can peer clear across southern California to

Signal Mountain in Mexico. Make the return trip to **Park Blvd**. If you feel like a nice hike, pull into **Ryan Mountain Parking Area** to hike the 3-mile trail (page 461). Note that views here are comparable to those at Keys. Continuing along Park Blvd you'll find plenty of opportunities to snap photos of intriguing Joshua trees. Stop at **Jumbo Rocks** to checkout some really cool rocks, including **Giant Marbles**. Return to Park Blvd and head south on **Pinto Basin Road**. Stop at **Cholla Cactus Garden** before exiting at South Entrance to I-10.

Best of Joshua Tree

Attraction: **Keys Ranch**
Runner-up: Skull Rock
2nd Runner-up: Cholla Cactus Garden

Activity: **Joshua Tree Ranch Trail Ride**
Runner-up: Rock Climbing

Hike: **Ryan Mountain**
Runner-up: Hidden Valley
2nd Runner-up: Keyes View

JOSHUA TREE

Anacapa Island, Lighthouse, and Arch Rock © NOAA's National Ocean Service

1901 Spinnaker Drive
Ventura, CA 93001
Phone: (805) 658-5730
Website: www.nps.gov/chis

Established: March 5, 1980
April 26, 1938 (Nat'l Monument)
Size: 249,354 Acres
Annual Visitors: 280,000
Peak Season: Summer

Activities: Hiking, Backpacking,
Camping, Paddling, Swimming,
Snorkeling, Sailing, and SCUBA

Each Island has a Campground*
Fee: $15/night (reservations req'd)
Backcountry Camping: Permitted
at Del Norte Camp (Santa Cruz
Island) and on Santa Rosa Island's
beaches. Reservations are required.

The park is open every day with
regularly scheduled island trips
Entrance Fee: None

*Reserve at (877) 444-6777 or
www.recreation.gov

Channel Islands - California

Off the coast of California, less than 100 miles away from 18 million people living in the Greater Los Angeles Area, is a group of eight islands. Compared to their surroundings, the Channel Islands have been left undeveloped even after continuous inhabitation for at least the last 8,000 years. Five of these islands—Santa Barbara, Anacapa, Santa Cruz, Santa Rosa, and San Miguel—comprise Channel Islands National Park. Rich history combined with incredibly diverse and often unique ecology make these volcanic islands stand alone in the National Park portfolio.

The park's **geology** is constantly changing thanks to relentless pounding of water on rock. However, the most startling change to the islands wasn't caused by water's erosive powers, but by its absence. More than 13,000 years ago, a blink of an eye in geologic terms, the four northern islands were one super-island. North America was in the middle of the last great Ice Age and water level was much lower than it is today. Climatic changes caused the glaciers to recede. As water levels rose the lowest valleys flooded, ultimately disconnecting the islands from one another.

Geologic changes also drastically altered the islands' **ecology**. Approximately 20,000 years ago, mammoths swam to the super-island, likely searching for vegetation whose scent was carried by the prevailing westward winds. As their population grew, resources became depleted. Natural selection favored smaller mammoths capable of surviving on less food. The woolly beasts lived on the islands for about 10,000 years before becoming extinct. Evidence of mammoths—once the most widely spread mammal—has been found on four continents. An engraving on a tusk found in a rock shelter in southwestern France. The carcass of a baby male preserved frozen in Siberia's permafrost. More than 100 mammoth remains at the bottom of a sinkhole in Hot Springs, SD. And a pygmy mammoth here on Santa Rosa Island. When these miniature remains were discovered in 1873 scientists believed that elephants inhabited the islands. More than 100 years later, additional fossils helped conclude that they were in fact pygmy mammoths, about one-tenth the size of a typical Columbian mammoth. They measured between 4.5 and 7-feet tall, weighing about one ton. A Colombian mammoth measured up to 14-feet tall, and weighed as much as ten tons. Human fossils have also been found on the Channel Islands. At Arlington Springs, on Santa Rosa Island, scientists discovered human remains dating back more than 13,000 years. This find has become known as Arlington woman, and it is among the oldest remains found in North America.

Humans have had a considerable effect on the islands. Early **Chumash** people relied on the sea for food and tools, traveling between the islands and mainland in canoes, called tomols, hollowed out from redwood trees that drifted down the coast. The Chumash were present when Juan Rodriguez Cabrillo reached San Miguel Island in 1542. Cabrillo and his fellow explorers introduced disease and overhunted sea life; by the 1820s the entire surviving island Chumash population had moved to the mainland.

Over the course of the next century, the island was home to **Mexican prisoners**, **ambitious ranchers**, and **hermit fishermen**. In 1864, the Civil War increased demand for wool and more than 24,000 sheep grazed the hills of Santa Cruz. During prohibition, Raymond "Frenchy" LeDreau watched over caches of liquor stored in Anacapa's caves. When Santa Cruz became part of the new National Monument, Frenchy was allowed to remain on the island as its caretaker. In 1956, at the age of 80, he was forced to leave after suffering severe injuries due to a fall. In 1969, more than 100,000 barrels of crude oil spilled into the Channel during the Santa Barbara oil spill, at the time the largest oil spill in United States waters. The National Park Service and Nature Conservancy have worked since to preserve this picturesque landscape and its unique ecosystem for the thousands of visitors that arrive each year.

When to Go

Channel Islands National Park is open every day of the year, and picking the best time to visit is not easy. Any given day can be idyllic or awful depending on the weather, and rough seas or inclement weather can prevent scheduled transportation services from reaching the islands. Because of this, it's best not to plan a trip well in advance unless you have a backup plan or are spending several days in the area. If you'd like to go whale watching, gray whales migrate through the area from late December through March. Blue and humpback whales come to feed between July and September. After a year of average rainfall, the wildflower bloom peaks around late winter/early spring. Type and abundance of wildflowers varies from island-to-island, so be sure to inquire at a visitor center if you're interested in flowers. Ocean conditions for SCUBA, snorkel, swimming, and kayaking are usually best from summer through fall.

Visitor Centers

Robert J. Lagomarsino Visitor Center (VC) in Ventura, CA is open daily from 8:30am to 5pm. It is closed on Thanksgiving and Christmas. Exhibits, 3-dimensional maps of the islands, an introductory film, telescopes, and a bookstore are available. **Outdoors Santa Barbara Visitor Center** provides information, exhibits, and excellent views of Santa Barbara. It is open daily from 10am to 5pm.

Robert J. Lagomarsino VC • (805) 658-5730
1901 Spinnaker Drive; Ventura, CA 93001

Outdoors Santa Barbara VC • (805) 884-1475
113 Harbor Way 4th Floor; Santa Barbara, CA 93001

Mainland Transportation

Amtrak (800.872.7245, www.amtrak.com), Metrolink (800.371.5465, www.metrolinktrains.com), Greyhound (800.231.2222, www.greyhound.com), Gold Coast Transit (805.487.4222, www.goldcoasttransit.org), Santa Barbara Metropolitan Transit District (805.963.3366, www.sbmtd.gov), and Ventura County Transportation Commission (805.642.1591, www.goventura.org) provide access to the park's mainland visitor centers but not its islands.

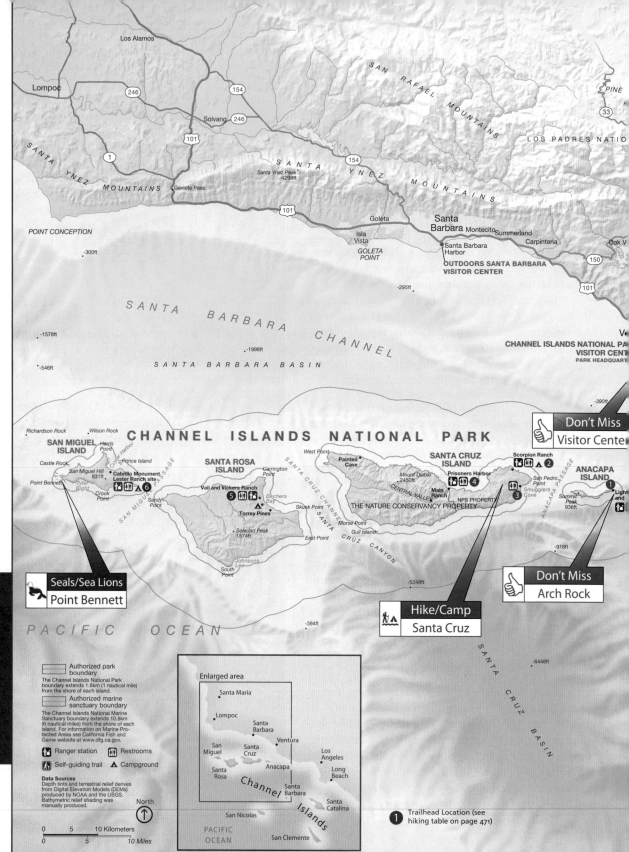

Los Alamos

Lompoc

(246)

(154)

Solvang (246)

(101)

(1)

SANTA YNEZ MOUNTAINS

Santa Ynez Peak 4298ft

Gaviota Pass

SAN RAFAEL MOUNTAINS

PINE

(33)

LOS PADRES NATIO...

SANTA YNEZ MOUNTAINS

(154)

Goleta

Santa Barbara

Montecito Summerland

Carpinteria

Oak V...

Isla Vista

(150)

POINT CONCEPTION

Santa Barbara Harbor

OUTDOORS SANTA BARBARA VISITOR CENTER

GOLETA POINT

-300ft

-295ft

(101)

SANTA BARBARA CHANNEL

V...

CHANNEL ISLANDS NATIONAL PA...
VISITOR CENT...
PARK HEADQUART...

-1578ft

-1998ft

SANTA BARBARA BASIN

-546ft

-390ft

Richardson Rock

Wilson Rock

CHANNEL ISLANDS NATIONAL PARK

Don't Miss
Visitor Center

SAN MIGUEL ISLAND

Harris Point

Cuyler Harbor

West Point

SANTA CRUZ ISLAND

Scorpion Ranch

2

ANACAPA ISLAND

Castle Rock

Prince Island

Painted Cave

Mount Diablo 2450ft

Prisoners Harbor

4

San Pedro Point

1

Light and

Point Bennett

San Miguel Hill 831ft

Cabrillo Monument Lester Ranch site

6

SANTA ROSA ISLAND

Carrington Point

CENTRAL VALLEY

Main Ranch

NPS PROPERTY

Smugglers Cove

Summit Peak 936ft

Tyler Bight

Crook Point

Sandy Point

Vail and Vickers Ranch

5

Bechers Bay

THE NATURE CONSERVANCY PROPERTY

3

Torrey Pines

Skunk Point

Morse Point

-918ft

Seals/Sea Lions
Point Bennett

Soledad Peak 1574ft

Gull Island

East Point

Johnsons Lee

South Point

-5248ft

Don't Miss
Arch Rock

-394ft

PACIFIC OCEAN

Hike/Camp
Santa Cruz

SANTA CRUZ BASIN

-6448ft

Authorized park boundary
The Channel Islands National Park boundary extends 1.8km (1 nautical mile) from the shore of each island.

Authorized marine sanctuary boundary
The Channel Islands National Marine Sanctuary boundary extends 10.8km (6 nautical miles) from the shore of each island. For information on Marine Protected Areas see California Fish and Game website at www.dfg.ca.gov.

Enlarged area

Santa Maria

Lompoc

Santa Barbara

Ventura

San Miguel

Santa Cruz

Los Angeles

Santa Rosa

Anacapa

Long Beach

Ranger station

Restrooms

Channel Islands

Self-guiding trail

Campground

Santa Catalina

Data Sources
Depth tints and terrestrial relief derives from Digital Elevation Models (DEMs) produced by NOAA and the USGS. Bathymetric relief shading was manually produced.

San Nicolas

North

San Clemente

PACIFIC OCEAN

0   5   10 Kilometers

0   5   10 Miles

1 Trailhead Location (see hiking table on page 471)

Island Transportation

Park concessioners provide boat and plane transportation to the islands. Once you reach an island, there is no transportation available; all areas must be accessed by foot, private boat, or kayak. **Island Packers** (805.642.1393, www.islandpackers.com) provides year-round transportation to the Channel Islands, and specialized whale watching and harbor tours. Ferries service Santa Cruz (Scorpion Anchorage and Prisoners Harbor) and Anacapa, year-round. Trips to the outer islands of Santa Barbara (April–October), San Miguel (May–October), and Santa Rosa (April–November) are seasonal. Rates vary depending on where and how you visit. Tickets for day-trippers to either Santa Cruz or Anacapa Island cost $56/adult and $39/child roundtrip. Campers must pay a rate of $75/adult and $54/child. Adult roundtrip to San Miguel costs $100 (day-trip) and $140 (camper). Adult roundtrip to either Santa Rosa or Santa Barbara costs $78 (day-trip) and $108 (camper). Kayak transportation costs an additional $14 for all boats 13-feet or less and $20 for boats over 13-feet. Island Packers' Main Office is located at 1691 Spinnaker Drive, Suite 105B, just a short walk from Robert J. Lagomarsino Visitor Center.

Channel Islands Aviation (805.987.1301, www.flycia.com) provides year-round air transportation to Santa Rosa Island. This 25-minute flight departs Camarillo Airport, with day trips costing about $160 + tax per adult. Camping trip air transportation costs about $300 + tax per person. Campsites are located a short distance from the airstrip and must be reserved prior to arrival (see page 468 for camping information).

Airports

The closest large commercial airport is Los Angeles International (LAX), 70 miles southeast of park headquarters. Burbank (Bob Hope • BUR), Santa Barbara (SBA), Camarillo (CMA), and Oxnard (OXR) Airports are closer and smaller alternatives.

Directions

Channel Islands is located in the Pacific Ocean just off the coast of California. Island visitors arrive via transportation provided by **Island Packers** or **Channel Islands Aviation**, but Most park guests only visit one of the mainland visitor centers located in Santa Barbara or Ventura. Driving directions to these facilities are provided below.

To Robert J. Lagomarsino Visitor Center/Island Packers: Traveling south on US-101 toward Ventura, take Exit 68 toward Seward Ave. Turn left at Harbor Blvd. After two miles, turn right at Spinnaker Drive. Traveling north on US-101 toward Ventura, take exit 64 for Victoria Ave. Turn left at Victoria Ave. Take the second right onto Olivas Park Drive, which turns into Spinnaker Drive. Spinnaker Drive passes Island Packers (look for the sign) and terminates at the visitor center. Free parking is available at Island Packers and the beach parking lot.

Outdoors Santa Barbara Visitor Center: Traveling south on US-101 toward Santa Barbara, take Exit 97 for Castillo St toward Harbor. Turn right at Castillo St and then make another right at Shoreline Dr. Turn left at Harbor Way.

Arriving from the south, take US-101 Exit 96B for Garden St. Turn left at Garden St, and then make a right at Cabrillo Blvd. Continue onto Shoreline Drive, then turn left at Harbor Way. The visitor center is on the fourth floor. Free parking (90 minutes) is available at harbor parking lot.

Channel Island Aviation: Camarillo Airport is located just off US-101. Take Exit 55 for Las Posas Road. Turn left onto Las Posas Road, and then take the third right onto Pleasant Valley Road. Take the first right onto Airport Way, then turn left at Durley Ave. Channel Islands Aviation is located at 305 Durley Ave. Parking is free.

Did you know?

➤ Island foxes are extremely small. The average weight of an adult male is 5–6 pounds, roughly the size of a domesticated cat.

➤ Santa Cruz Island's Painted Cave is one of the world's largest and deepest sea caves. It measures 1,215 feet in length, has a 160 foot entrance, and is almost 100 feet wide.

Best of Channel Islands

Hike: **Inspiration Point (Anacapa)**
   Runner-up: Smugglers Cove (Santa Cruz)
   2nd Runner-up: Water Canyon (Santa Rosa)

# Camping

Channel Islands offers one designated campground on each island. All campgrounds are located at least a half mile (usually uphill) from the boat landing area. **Campers must bring their own water and carry all trash off the island**. Campfires are not permitted. Pit toilets are available. Wind breaks are provided at Santa Rosa and Santa Cruz Island Campgrounds. Camping costs $15 per night per site and **reservations must be made in advance** by calling (877) 444-6777 or clicking www.recreation.gov.

Backcountry camping is available year-round on Santa Cruz and Santa Rosa Islands. **Del Norte campsite**, near Prisoners Harbor on Santa Cruz Island, is available for backcountry camping all year. It's a 3.5-mile hike from Prisoners Harbor and 12 miles from Scorpion Anchorage. **Reservations are required** ($15/night) and can be made by calling (877) 444-6777 or clicking www.recreation.gov. Backpackers are also allowed to camp on **Santa Rosa's beaches** from mid-August until the end of December. Reservations for beach camping are free and must be made in advance by calling the park at (805) 658-5711.

Ferries (page 467) usually fill before campgrounds, so it is wise to book your transportation (if required) prior to your camping reservations.

# The Islands

Some 13,000 years ago the four northern Channel Islands were united, forming one super-island. As glaciers from the last Ice Age receded, water levels began to rise and distinct islands formed. Today, Channel Islands National Park consists of five of the eight Channel Islands: San Miguel, Santa Rosa, Santa Cruz, Anacapa, and Santa Barbara. The official boundary extends one nautical mile beyond the islands' shorelines to protect marine environments, including giant kelp forests. These islands are some of the last undeveloped tracts of land in the Greater Los Angeles area. No services are available. You will have to pack everything you require, including food and water, and all trash must be packed out. The islands' primitive nature and limited transportation services (page 467) result in roughly 90% of park visitors never stepping foot on the islands. The other 10% find this an ideal environment to commune with nature. A short description of each island and its activities is provided below (listed from west to east):

San Miguel Island (9,325 acres): If you are willing to endure the wind and the weather, San Miguel is a fantastic place for hiking and camping. A 16-mile trail leads across the island to **Point Bennett**, where more than 30,000 seals and sea lions have been seen during certain times of the year. These gatherings represent **one of the largest congregations of wildlife in the world**. Sea lions typically give birth around mid-June and the park provides ranger-guided walks to Point Bennett beginning in June.

Santa Rosa Island (53,000 acres): Santa Rosa is the second largest island in California. It's home to substantial archeological discoveries like the **pygmy mammoth** and **Arlington Man**. Today, very few visitors come to Santa Rosa. It's located 40 nautical miles from Robert J. Lagomarsino Visitor Center, and portions of the island are closed for several months to allow hunting of reintroduced elk and deer.

Santa Cruz Island (62,000 acres): Santa Cruz is the largest island in California and the only one not entirely owned by the National Park Service, with 76% controlled by the **Nature Conservancy**. Santa Cruz is the favorite destination for campers and hikers. A network of trails (and an old military road) connects popular destinations across the park's portion of the island. Beautiful beaches, clear water, and kelp forests make this a great island for swimming

CHANNEL ISLANDS

and snorkeling. Kayakers also frequent the island. **Painted Cave**, located on Nature Conservancy property in the northwest corner of the island, is a 0.25-mile long, 100-ft wide grotto with an entrance ceiling of 160 feet. The cave is particularly beautiful in spring when water falls over its entrance.

Anacapa Island (700 acres): Early Chumash people called it "Anyapakh," which translates to "mirage." Summer fog and afternoon heat tend to cloak or change the appearance of this volcanic island. Even more deceptive is the island itself. It's composed of three smaller islets descriptively named East, Middle, and West Anacapa. These islets are separated from one another and only reachable by boat.

Even though it's the second smallest of the park's islands, it's also the most visited due to close proximity to Ventura, CA, the port of departure for Island Packers' boats. Anacapa is just 12 miles from the mainland, and most visits consist of a walk around East Anacapa. A 1.5 mile trail leads to **Inspiration Point**, a small **campground**, and **Anacapa Island Light Station**. The trail also provides excellent views of the park's most notable feature, 40-foot high **Arch Rock**. It's one of many sea caves and natural bridges carved into the island's towering sea cliffs by the Pacific Ocean.

Anacapa is an excellent site to view wildlife, especially if you like seagulls. **It is home to the largest breeding colony of western gulls in the world.** Chicks hatch in May and June before flying away in July. West Anacapa also boasts the **largest breeding colony of endangered California brown pelicans**. Sea lions and harbor seals have been known to relax on the island's rocky shorelines. The area's nutrient rich water supports a diverse underwater ecosystem including **forests of kelp**. Divers, snorkelers, and kayakers all have the opportunity to see the massive seaweed.

Santa Barbara Island (639 acres): The smallest of the Channel Islands is a fair distance southeast of the others and 38 nautical miles from the mainland. This small variation in location results in a significant decrease in wind and rough water. Five miles of hiking trails span the entire island. It's a fantastic site for wildlife viewing, with **one of the world's largest colonies of Xantus's murrelets breeding here**. The park concessioner makes infrequent trips to Santa Barbara, which makes for overnight camping trips that last a minimum of 3 days.

Sea Lion © Alan Vernon

Paddling

Sea kayaking is a common activity at the Channel Islands. **Island Packers** can transport your boat for $14–20 depending on its size. Visitors often choose to join one of the park's **authorized outfitters** to safely explore the islands while learning about its history from a knowledgeable guide. The **Scorpion Beach** area on **East Santa Cruz Island** is the most popular kayaking destination. Here you'll find plenty of sea caves and cliffs to paddle in and out of. Sand beaches and a campground are easily accessible. **San Miguel and Santa Rosa Islands** are exceptional destinations, but only the most highly experienced and conditioned sea kayakers should venture into these waters due to consistently extreme weather and sea conditions. It's not recommended, but you can paddle from the mainland to the islands. These paddlers should be particularly cautious. In addition to dicey weather and rough water, you must pass through a heavily trafficked shipping lane. Below is a list of authorized outfitters with rates for a day trip to Santa Cruz.

Santa Barbara Adventure Co. • (877) 884-9283
www.sbadventureco.com • $195/Adult Single Kayak

Blue Sky Kayak Tours • (805) 444-2583
www.blueskywilderness.com • $190/Adult Single Kayak

Aquasports • (800) 773-2309
www.islandkayaking.com • $200/Adult Single Kayak

Channel Islands Kayak Center • (805) 984-5995
www.cikayak.com • $200/Adult Single Kayak

Paddle Sports of Santa Barbara • (888) 254-2094
www.kayaksb.com • $195/Adult Single Kayak

*Reduced rates are often available for off-season and early registration (listed prices include transportation to the island)

Water Activities

Swimming, **snorkeling**, and **SCUBA diving** are popular pastimes best done on the islands of **Santa Barbara**, **Anacapa**, and **Eastern Santa Cruz**. These activities are allowed at San Miguel and Santa Rosa Islands, but should only be attempted by individuals who are properly trained, conditioned, and equipped. This recommendation is issued because of consistently strong winds and rough waters typical of these two islands. There are many fantastic swimming, snorkeling, and SCUBA diving locations around the other three islands. The water is clear with massive curtains of kelp. However, it's possible to see what's under the water without getting wet. **During the summer, divers equipped with a video camera plunge into Landing Cove (East Anacapa).** High and dry, visitors can not only see the kelp forests, sea stars, and Garibaldi through the eye of the camera, but they can ask the divers questions using a voice communication system. Video monitors are located at Anacapa's dock and the mainland visitor center in Ventura.

Dolphins and whales are often spotted swimming the waters surrounding the Channel Islands. **Island Packers** (page 467) offers seasonal whale watching and wildlife viewing boat trips. **Condor Express** offers similar expeditions. Private boaters are also welcome to explore the waters, but the **Marine Mammal Protection Act** stipulates that boats must remain at least 100 yards away from whales (unless they approach you, then turn off your engine).

Private boaters have an easier time reaching the north shores of **San Miguel and Santa Rosa Islands**, where you'll find the best **surfing** on the islands. **Sail Channel Islands** provides a sailing school and charter services (half-day, 6 passengers, $850).

<u>Truth Aquatics</u> • (805) 962-1127 • www.truthaquatics.com
Provides live-aboard SCUBA, Kayak, and Island Excursions

<u>Condor Express</u> • (888) 779-4253 • www.condorcruises.com
Whale Watching ($48–94/adult) and Adventure Cruises

<u>Sail Channel Islands</u> • (805) 750-7828
www.sailchannelislands.com • sailing school and charters

Hiking/Backpacking

Anacapa, the park's most frequented island, has very limited hiking. A 1.5 mile trail leads to **East Anacapa's Inspiration Point**. Middle and West Anacapa are closed to hiking. **Santa Cruz Island is the number one destination for campers and hikers.** Trails and roads connect Scorpion Beach, Smugglers Cove, Prisoners Harbor, and many places in between. **Unguided hiking is not allowed in Nature Conservancy property** (marked by a fence line) without a permit ($30, www.nature.org). The seldom visited trails on **San Miguel** and **Santa Rosa** Islands are excellent too. San Miguel's **Caliche Forest** and **Bennett Point** are particularly nice, but make sure you're prepared for windy weather. **Caliche Forest, Bennett Point, and Lester Point Trails require that you are accompanied by a park ranger.**

Camping (page 468) and **backpacking** are essentially synonymous at Channel Islands. All campgrounds are primitive without water and fire rings. Pit toilets are available. **Del Norte Campground on Santa Cruz Island** is the only designated backcountry campground. Backpackers visiting **Santa Rosa Island** are allowed to camp along the beaches between mid-August and the end of December. The closest beach is 10 miles from the boat/plane drop-off location.

For Kids

Children with their sea legs will enjoy a boat cruise to the islands. **Whale watching and wildlife tours** are favorites, but even the standard trip to the island has its thrills, and there's always a chance of seeing dolphins or whales. Children are invited to participate in the park's **Junior Ranger Program**. You can print an activity booklet at home from the park website or pick-up a free hard copy at the visitor center, on the island from park staff, or from the boat/plane concessioner offices. Complete the activities and receive an official Junior Ranger badge.

Ranger Programs

Park rangers offer several free public programs at Robert J. Lagomarsino Visitor Center. Rangers and concessioner naturalists provide island hikes each day there's island transportation service (page 467). Evening programs are offered during summer at Scorpion Ranch Campground. Visit the park website for a current schedule of events or look for a flyer inside the latest issue of the park's publication, *Island Views*.

Nesting Bald Eagles | Anacapa from above | Channel Islands Fox

Channel Islands Hiking Trails

		Trail Name	Length	Difficulty	Notes (Roundtrip distances)
Anacapa Trailhead (#1 on map)		Inspiration Point - 👍	1.5 miles	Easy	Hike from East Anacapa's Landing Cove to exceptional views
		Lighthouse	0.5 mile	Easy	Short and easy hike to the lighthouse from the landing
Santa Cruz	Scorpion Beach (2)	Historic Ranch	0.5 mile	Easy	Easy access to historic Scorpion Ranch
		Cavern Point	2.0 miles	Moderate	Walk along the shoreline • Whale watching opportunities
		Potato Harbor	4.0 miles	Moderate	Hike to a secluded harbor • No beach access
		Scorpion Canyon	4.0 miles	Moderate	Loop trail that passes through steep canyon walls
		Smugglers Cove - 👍	7.0 miles	Strenuous	Long hike to Smugglers Cove (additional trails and beach)
		Montañon Ridge	8.0 miles	Strenuous	Off-trail hiking, map reading skills are required
	Smugglers Cove (3)	Smugglers Canyon	2.0 miles	Moderate	Trail passes through native vegetation
		Yellowbanks	3.0 miles	Moderate	Follows the shoreline (off-trail, no beach access) to an overlook
		San Pedro Point	4.0 miles	Moderate	Off-trail hike east of Smugglers Cove to San Pedro Point
	Prisoners Harbor (4)	Prisoners Harbor	0.5 mile	Easy	Short trail in and around Prisoners Harbor
		Pelican Bay	4.0 miles	Moderate	Enters Nature Conservancy property (Permit Required)
		Del Norte Camp	7.0 miles	Strenuous	Leaves Prisoners Harbor and heads east to the Backcountry Camp
		Navy Road–Del Norte	8.5 miles	Strenuous	Loop trail combining Navy Road and Del Norte Camp Trail
		Chinese Harbor	15.5 miles	Strenuous	Long trail to the only accessible beach on the isthmus
		China Pines	18.0 miles	Strenuous	Long hike to Santa Cruz Island's pine grove
		Montañon Ridge - 👍	21.0 miles	Strenuous	Off-trail hiking, map reading skills are required
Santa Rosa (5)		Water Canyon Beach - 👍	2.0 miles	Easy	Two-mile long white sand beach
		East Point	12.0 miles	Strenuous	Torrey pines and unrestricted beaches mark this trail
		Torrey Pines	5.0 miles	Moderate	Fantastic views of Torrey pines
		Lobo Canyon	13.0 miles	Strenuous	Amazing canyon sculpted by wind and water
		Black Mountain	8.0 miles	Strenuous	Excellent vantage point to view the other islands and mainland
San Miguel (6)		Cuyler Beach	2.0 miles	Easy	Two-mile long white sand beach
		Lester Ranch Site	2.0 miles	Moderate	Canyon hike to excellent views and two historic sites
		Caliche Forest - 👍	5.0 miles	Strenuous	Hike is only allowed in the presence of a park ranger
		Point Bennett - 👍	16.0 miles	Strenuous	Continues beyond Caliche Forest (park ranger required)
		Lester Point - 👍	5.0 miles	Strenuous	Incredible overlook, only accessible with a park ranger
Santa Barbara (7)		Arch Point	2.0 miles	Moderate	Hike this trail in late winter/spring for wildflower blooms
		Sea Lion Rookery	4.0 miles	Moderate	Far reaching Pacific views and possibility of sea lions
		Elephant Seal Cove	5.0 miles	Strenuous	Good possibility of seeing elephant seals, steep cliffs are guaranteed

CHANNEL ISLANDS

Flora & Fauna

The Channel Islands are relatively remote and home to a tempestuous climate. These factors make for an extraordinarily unique ecosystem. Even the individual islands are dramatically different thanks to variations in size and location. **At least 145 endemic species of plants and animals** reside within park boundaries. Most of these species have developed slight adaptations after centuries of life on a remote island. **Island deer mouse** is the only native terrestrial mammal common to all the Channel Islands. There are only two other endemic terrestrial mammals found here: **spotted skunk** and **Channel Islands fox**. Channel Islands fox is the smallest North American canid, only growing to about the size of your average house cat. Visitors' favorite animals tend to be those that swim in the ocean. **Sea lions**, **seals**, **pacific gray whales**, and **Risso's dolphins** are frequently seen patrolling the waters. The islands are also important breeding grounds for many species of bird. California brown pelicans, Xantu's murrelets, tufted puffins, western gulls, Cassin's auklets, and rhinoceros auklets all breed within park boundaries. The Island scrub jay is also unique to the islands. In 2006, **bald eagles** nested on the Channel Islands for the first time in more than 50 years.

Channel Islands' plant life is just as interesting and unique. **Nearly 800 species of plants** have been documented in the park, **including 75 endemic plant species**, 14 of which are listed as threatened or endangered. After nearly 150 years of ranching, the park has put forth great effort to aid in the recovery of these species.

Basics

Pets: To protect wildlife, pets are not allowed in the park.

Accessibility: Robert J. Lagomarsino Visitor Center in Ventura and Outdoors Visitor Center in Santa Barbara are fully accessible to individuals in wheelchairs. However, the islands themselves have extremely limited accessibility. Santa Rosa Island is accessible via air transportation (page 467).

Weather: Weather is moderated by the Pacific Ocean. This vast expanse of water keeps average high and low temperatures surprisingly consistent all year long, with average highs only varying about 10°F from summer to winter. Another by-product of the Pacific Ocean is high humidity and fog. Humidity often reaches 100% at night and in the early morning. Annual rainfall is about 14 inches per year with 95% of that total occurring between the months of November and April. Fog is most common in spring and summer, especially at San Miguel and Santa Rosa Islands. Wind is the one constant on the islands, blowing primarily from the north–northwest and tending to increase throughout the daylight hours. High velocity Santa Ana winds averaging 20–25 mph with gusts exceeding 100 mph can occur in any month, but are most common from September to December. Hikers, campers, and day-visitors should come prepared to deal with a variety of elements.

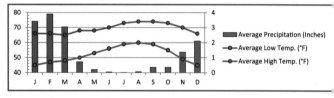

Vacation Planner

Unpredictable weather and water conditions, concessioner transportation dependence, and specialized activities make planning a trip to the Channel Islands a more structured project than most parks. If you'd like to make a spur of the moment trip you'll be at the mercy of **Island Packers'** transportation schedule. More than likely, you will be able to visit Anacapa or Santa Cruz Island, but trips to Santa Rosa, Santa Barbara, and San Miguel Islands are seasonal. **Day trips are easy.** Simply hop aboard the concessioner boat, and upon arrival they'll give you the option to explore at your leisure or to join a park ranger or concessioner naturalist on a walking tour of the island. A few hours later you pile back onto the boat to return to the mainland. **Overnight trips** require reserving campsites and transportation. Both fill occasionally. Regardless of which island(s) you visit and how many days you intend to spend, be sure to stop at the visitor center, pack plenty of sunscreen, plan on it being windy, and don't forget food and water (and to pack out your trash). Be sure to check the current issue of the park's publication, *Island Views*, for up-to-date travel information. It's available at the visitor centers or online at the park website. Nearby dining, grocery stores, lodging, festivals, and attractions are listed on pages 473–475.

Dining

Joshua Tree Area

Palms Restaurant • (760) 361-2810
83131 Amboy Rd; Twentynine Palms, CA 92277

Palm Kabob House • (760) 362-8583
6341 Adobe Rd; Twentynine Palms, CA 92277

Bistro Twenty Nine • (760) 361-2229
73527 29 Palms Hwy; Twentynine Palms, CA 92277
www.bistrotwentynine.com • Entrée: $13−22

Rib Co • (760) 367-1663
72183 29 Palms Hwy; Twentynine Palms, CA 92277
www.theribco.com • Entrée: $16−35

The Warehouse BBQ • (760) 342-3227
82720 Miles Ave; Indio, CA 92201
www.thebesttritip.com • Entrée: $6−20

Jackalope Ranch • (760) 342-1999
80400 CA-111; Indio, CA 92201
www.restaurantsofpalmsprings.com • Entrée: $20−30

Ciro's Ristorante And Pizzeria • (760) 347-6503
81963 CA-111; Indio, CA 92201
www.cirospasta.com • Pizza: $10+

Pueblo Viejo Grill • (760) 342-5900
81931 CA-111; Indio, CA 92201

El Mexicali Restaurant • (760) 347-1280
82720 Indio Blvd; Indio, CA 92201
www.elmexicalicafe.com • Entrée: $9−18

China Bistro • (760) 342-7288
45765 Towne St; Indio, CA 92201
www.chinabistroindio.com

It's A Grind Coffee House • (760) 200-9474
44100 Jefferson St, # 302; Indio, CA 92201

Beer Hunter Sports Pub • (760) 564-7442
78483 CA-111; La Quinta, CA 92253
www.laquintabeerhunter.com • Burgers: $9+

LG's Prime Steakhouse • (760) 771-9911
78525 CA-111; La Quinta, CA 92253
www.lgsprimesteakhouse.com • Entrée: $25−55

Okura Robata Grill & Sushi Bar • (760) 564-5820
78370 CA-111, #150; La Quinta, CA 92253
www.okurasushi.com • Entrée: $18−25

Rosati's • (760) 775-8900
79630 California 111; La Quinta, CA 92253
www.myrosatis.com • Pizza: $10+

Fisherman's Market & Grill • (760) 777-1601
78575 CA-111, # 100; La Quinta, CA 92253
www.fishermans.com • Sandwiches: $11+

Mimi's Café • (760) 775-4470
79765 CA-111; La Quinta, CA 92253
www.mimiscafe.com

La Quinta Baking • (760) 777-1699
78-395 CA-111; La Quinta, CA 92253
www.laquintabaking.com

Channel Islands Area

71 Palm Restaurant • (805) 653-7222
71 N Palm St; Ventura, CA 93001
www.71palm.com • Entrée: $11−33

Sidecar • (805) 653-7433
3029 E Main St; Ventura, CA 93003
www.thesidecarrestaurant.com • Entrée: $13−27

Anacapa Brewing Company • (805) 643-2337
472 E Main St; Ventura, CA 93001
www.anacapabrewing.com

Spasso Cucina Italiana • (805) 643-2777
1140 S Seaward Ave; Ventura, CA 93001
www.spassorestaurant.com • Entrée: $12−22

Meridians • (805) 676-1756
2417 Harbor Blvd; Ventura, CA 93001
www.meridianscafe.com • Pizza: $9+

I Love Sushi • (805) 639-4009
5722 Telephone Rd; Ventura, CA 93003
www.ilovesushiventura.com

Pete's Breakfast House • (805) 648-1130
2055 E Main St; Ventura, CA 93001

Café Nouveau • (805) 648-1422
1497 E Thompson Blvd; Ventura, CA 93001

Allison's Country Café • (805) 644-9072
3429 Telegraph Rd; Ventura, CA 93003
www.allisonscountrycafe.com

Sambos • (805) 965-3269
216 W Cabrillo Blvd; Santa Barbara, CA 93101
www.sambos.biz • Breakfast: $6+

Jane • (805) 962-1311
1311 State St; Santa Barbara, CA 93101
www.janerestaurantsb.com • Entrée: $14−26

Olio e Limone Ristorante • (805) 899-2699
11 W Victoria St, #17; Santa Barbara, CA 93101
www.olioelimone.com • Entrée: $17−35

Los Agaves Restaurant • (805) 564-2626
600 N Milpas St; Santa Barbara, CA 93103

The Palace Grill • (805) 963-5000
8 E Cota St; Santa Barbara, CA 93101
www.palacegrill.com

Brophy Brothers • (805) 966-4418
119 Harbor Way; Santa Barbara, CA 93109
www.brophybros.com • Entrée: $9−20

Brew House • (805) 884-4664
229 W Montecito St; Santa Barbara, CA 93101
www.brewhousesb.com • Entrée: $11−27

Super Cuca's Taqueria • (805) 966-3863
2030 Cliff Dr; Santa Barbara, CA 93109
www.cucasrestaurant.com • Burritos: $3.50+

Ming Dynasty • (805) 968-1308
290 Storke Rd, # G; Goleta, CA 93117
www.mingdynastygoleta.com • Entrée: $9−20

Habit Burger Grill • (805) 964-0366
5735 Hollister Ave; Goleta, CA 93117
www.habitburger.com • Burgers: $3+

South Coast Deli • (805) 967-8226
185 S Patterson Ave; Goleta, CA 93111
www.southcoastdeli.com • Sandwiches: $7+

Goodland Kitchen • (805) 845-4300
231 S Magnolia Ave; Goleta, CA 93117
www.goodlandkitchen.com • Sandwiches: $4+

Grocery Stores

Joshua Tree Area

Albertsons • (760) 342-8057
Ave 48; Coachella, CA 92236

Walmart Supercenter • (760) 564-3313
79295 CA-111; La Quinta, CA 92253

Costco • (760) 342-0655
79-795 CA-111; La Quinta, CA 92253

Channel Islands Area

Vons • (805) 650-2150
6040 Telegraph Rd; Ventura, CA 93003

Albertsons • (805) 647-0023
7800 Telegraph Rd; Ventura, CA 93004

Vons • (805) 648-0251
2764 E Thompson Blvd; Ventura, CA 93003

Walmart Supercenter • (805) 981-4884
2001 N Rose Ave; Oxnard, CA 93036

Fresh & Easy Market • (805) 654-0248
5101 Telegraph Rd; Ventura, CA 93003

Whole Foods • (805) 837-6959
3761 State St; Santa Barbara, CA 93105

Albertsons • (805) 966-5011
2010 Cliff Dr; Santa Barbara, CA 93109

Costco • (805) 685-3199
7095 Market Place Dr; Goleta, CA 93117

Lodging

Joshua Tree Area

Harmony Motel • (760) 367-3351
71161 29 Palms Hwy; Twentynine Palms, CA 92277
www.harmonymotel.com • Rates: $65−75/night

Hotel 29 Palms • (760) 361-4009
71809 29 Palms Hwy; Twentynine Palms, CA 92277
www.hotel29palms.com • Rates: $81+

Sunnyvale Suites • (760) 361-3939
73843 Sunnyvale Dr; Twentynine Palms, CA 92277
www.sunnyvalesuites.com • Rates: $79+

Roughley Manor B&B • (760) 367-3238
74744 Joe Davis Dr; Twentynine Palms, CA 92277
www.roughleymanor.com • Rates: $135−165

Moon Way Lodge • (760) 835-9369
5444 Moon Way; Twentynine Palms, CA 92277
www.moonwaylodge.com • Rates: $120–165

Fantasy Springs Casino • (760) 345-2450
84245 Indio Springs Pky; Indio, CA 92201
www.fantasyspringsresort.com • Rates: $105+

Indian Palms Vacation Club • (760) 342-1485
82567 Avenue 48; Indio, CA 92201
www.indianpalmsvacationclub.com • Rates: $129+

Date Tree Hotel • (800) 292-5599
81909 Indio Blvd; Indio, CA 92201
www.datetree.com • Rates: $76+

Shadow Hills RV Resort • (760) 360-4040
40655 Jefferson St; Indio, CA 92203
www.shadowhillsrvresort.com • Rates: $58

Indian Wells RV Resort • (760) 347-0895
47340 Jefferson St; Indio, CA 92201
www.indianwellsrvresort.com • Rates: $40

Miramonte Resort & Spa • (760) 341-2200
45000 Indian Wells Ln; Indian Wells, CA 92210
www.miramonteresort.com • Rates: $179+

Hyatt Resort & Spa • (760) 341-1000
44600 Indian Wells Ln; Indian Wells, CA 92210
www.grandchampions.hyatt.com • Rates: $239+

Lake La Quinta Inn • (888) 226-4546
78-120 Caleo Bay; La Quinta, CA 92253
www.lakelaquintainn.com • Rates: $109–299

Agua Caliente Casino Resort Spa • (760) 321-2000
32250 Bob Hope Dr; Rancho Mirage, CA 92270
www.hotwatercasino.com • Rates: $129–329

Channel Islands Area

Inn On the Beach • (805) 652-2000
1175 S Seaward Ave; Ventura, CA 93001
www.innonthebeachventura.com • Rates: $120–175

Crystal Lodge Motel • (805) 648-2272
1787 E Thompson Blvd; Ventura, CA 93001
www.crystallodgemotel.com • Rates: $45+

Viking Motel • (805) 643-3273
2107 E Thompson Blvd; Ventura, CA 93001
www.vikingmotel-ca.com • Rates: $55

Victorian Rose B&B • (805) 641-1888
896 E Main St; Ventura, CA 93001
www.victorianroseventura.com • Rates: $99–149

Channel Islands Shores • (805) 985-0621
1311 Mandalay Beach Rd; Oxnard, CA 93035
www.channelislandshores.org • Rates: $116+

Casa Via Mar • (805) 984-6222
377 W Channel Islands Blvd; Port Hueneme, CA 93041
www.casaviamar.com • Rates: $62+

Santa Paula Inn • (805) 933-0011
111 N 8th St; Santa Paula, CA 93060
www.santapaulainn.com • Rates: $95+

Blue Iguana Inn • (805) 646-5277
11794 N Ventura Ave; Ojai, CA 93023
www.blueiguanainn.com • Rates: $119+

Casa Ojai Inn • (805) 646-8175
1302 E Ojai Ave; Ojai, CA 93023
www.ojaiinn.com • Rates: $100+

Secret Garden Inn • (805) 687-2300
1908 Bath St; Santa Barbara, CA 93101
www.secretgarden.com • Rates: $135+

Inn of the Spanish Garden • (805) 564-4700
915 Garden St; Santa Barbara, CA 93101
www.spanishgardeninn.com • Rates: $259+

Villa Rosa Inn • (805) 966-0851
15 Chapala St; Santa Barbara, CA 93101
www.villarosainnsb.com • Rates: $134+

Harbor House Inn • (805) 962-9745
104 Bath St; Santa Barbara, CA 93101
www.harborhouseinn.com • Rates: $145+

Lemon Tree Inn • (805) 687-6444
2819 State St; Santa Barbara, CA 93105
www.treeinns.com • Rates: $100+

James House • (805) 569-5853
1632 Chapala St; Santa Barbara, CA 93101
www.jameshousesantabarbara.com • Rates: $190–240

Cheshire Cat Inn • (805) 569-1610
36 W Valerio St; Santa Barbara, CA 93101
www.cheshirecat.com • Rates: $109–389

Many chain restaurants and hotels can be found along Twentynine Palms Hwy, I-10 and US-101.

Festivals

Rose Parade • January
Pasadena • www.tournamentofroses.com

International Film Festival • January
Santa Barbara • www.sbiff.org

Arts Festival • January-March
Palm Springs • www.palmspringsartsfestival.com

La Quinta Arts Festival • March
La Quinta • www.la-quinta-arts-found.org

Coachella Valley Music Festival • April
Indio • www.coachella.com

Stagecoach Festival • April
Indio • www.stagecoachfestival.com

Huck Finn Jubilee • June
Victorville • www.huckfinn.com

Life Oak Music Festival • June
Santa Barbara • www.liveoakfest.org

Bowlful of Blues • August
Ojai • www.sbblues.org

Aloha Beach Festival • September
Ventura • www.alohabeachfestival.us

Hollywood Film Festival • October
Hollywood • www.hollywoodfilmfestival.com

Attractions
Joshua Tree Area

Salton Sea State Rec. Area • (760) 393-3052
100225 State Park Rd; North Shore • www.parks.ca.gov

Indian Canyons • (760) 323-6018
Hike through an oasis (ranger-led tours available • $3)
38500 S Palm Canyon Dr; Palm Springs, CA 92264
www.indian-canyons.com • Admission: $9/Adult

Slab City • near Niland, CA
Winter home of snowbirds/squatters/campers

Desert Adventures • (760) 340-2345
74794 Lennon Pl; Palm Desert, CA 92260
www.red-jeep.com • Tours: $100–179

Adventure Hummer Tours • (760) 285-0876
42335 Washington St; Palm Desert, CA 92211
www.adventurehummer.com • Tours: $139

Balloon Above The Desert • (760) 347-0410
40373 Moonflower Ct; Palm Desert, CA 92260
www.balloonabovethedesert.com • Rates: $195

Aerial Tramway • (760) 325-1391
1 Tramway Rd; Palm Springs, CA 92262
www.pstramway.com • Tickets: $24/Adult

Integratron • (760) 364-3126
An all-wood, acoustically perfect sound chamber
2477 Belfield Blvd; Landers, CA 92285
www.integratron.com • Self-guided Tour: $5

Shields Date Garden • (760) 347-0996
80225 CA-111; Indio, CA 92201
www.shieldsdategarden.com

Gen. Patton Mem. Museum • (760) 227-3483
62510 Chiriaco Rd; Indio, CA 92201
www.generalpattonmuseum.com • Admission: $5/Adult

Coachella Valley Hist. Mus. • (760) 342-6651
82616 Miles Ave; Indio, CA 92201
www.coachellavalleymuseum.org

Palm Springs Air Museum • (760) 778-6262
745 N Gene Autry Tr; Palm Springs, CA 92262
www.palmspringsairmuseum.org • Admission: $15/Adult

Palm Springs Art Museum • (760) 322-4800
101 N Museum Dr; Palm Springs, CA 92262
www.psmuseum.org • Admission: $12.50/Adult

The Fabulous Follies • (760) 327-0225
128 S Palm Canyon Dr; Palm Springs, CA 92262
www.psfollies.com • Tickets: $50–140

Theatre 29 • (760) 361-4151
73637 Sullivan Rd; Twentynine Palms, CA 92277
www.theatre29.org • *Pricing is show dependent*

Smith's Ranch Drive-In • (760) 367-7713
4584 Adobe Rd; Twentynine Palms, CA 92277
www.29drive-in.com • Tickets: $5

McCallam Theatre • (760) 340-2787
73000 Fred Waring Dr; Palm Desert, CA 92260
www.mccallumtheatre.com • *Pricing is show dependent*

Augustine Casino • (760) 391-9500
84001 Ave 54; Coachella • www.augustinecasino.com

Channel Islands Area

Nojoqui Falls Park • (805) 688-4217
3200 Alisal Rd; Solvang, CA 93463
www.countyofsb.org

Refugio State Beach • (805) 968-1033
10 Refugio Beach Rd; Goleta, CA 93117
www.parks.ca.gov • Camp: $35/night

El Capitan State Beach • (805) 968-1033
US-101; Santa Barbara, CA 93117
www.parks.ca.gov • Camp: $35/night

Fairview Gardens • Self-guided Tour: $5
Albany Court; Goleta, CA • www.fairviewgardens.org

Cloud Climbers • (805) 646-3200
100 State St; Santa Barbara, CA 93101
www.ccjeeps.com • Tours: $89–375

Island Packer Cruises • (805) 642-1393
Channel Islands concessioner offers cruises and tours
1691 Spinnaker Dr; Ventura, CA 93001
www.islandpackers.com • Whale Watch: $35

Spectre Dive Boat • (805) 483-6612
1567 Spinnaker Dr; Ventura, CA 93001
www.calboatdiving.com • Dives: $100–125

Lotusland • (805) 969-9990
Non-profit botanical garden on private estate
695 Ashley Rd; Santa Barbara, CA 93108
www.lotusland.org • *Reservations Required*

Sailing Center • (800) 350-9090
133 Harbor Way; Santa Barbara, CA 93109
www.sbsail.com • *Charters & Rentals*

Condor Express • (805) 882-0088
301 W Cabrillo Blvd; Santa Barbara, CA 93101
www.condorcruises.com • Whale Watch: $48

Captain Jack's Tours • (805) 564-1819
Fishing, glider, segway, ATV, trail rides, and more
933 Castillo St; Santa Barbara, CA 93101
www.captainjackstours.com • Whale Watch: $55

Sunset Kidd Whale Watching • (805) 962-8222
125 Harbor Way, #13; Santa Barbara, CA 93109
www.sunsetkidd.com • Whale Watch: $40

Land & Sea Tours • (805) 683-7600
216 Arboleda Rd; Santa Barbara, CA 93110
www.out2seesb.com • Tours: $25/Adult

Wheel Fun Rentals • (805) 966-2282
22 State St; Santa Barbara, CA 93101
www.wheelfunrentalssb.com • Bike Rental & Tours

HorsePlay • (805) 698-8056
Stagecoach Rd; Santa Barbara, CA 93105
www.horseplaysb.com • Riding Lessons: $40/hr

Maritime Museum • (805) 962-8404
113 Harbor Way, # 190; Santa Barbara, CA 93109
www.sbmm.org • Admission: $7/Adult

South Coast Railroad Museum • (805) 964-3540
300 N Los Carneros Rd; Goleta, CA 93117
www.goletadepot.org

Botanic Garden • (805) 682-4726
1007 Mission Canyon Rd; Santa Barbara, CA 93105
www.sbbg.org • Admission: $8/Adult

Museum of Art • (805) 963-4364
1130 State St; Santa Barbara, CA 93101
www.sbma.net • Admission: $9/Adult

Zoological Gardens • (805) 962-5339
500 Ninos Dr; Santa Barbara, CA 93103
www.santabarbarazoo.org • Admission: $12/Adult

Mission Museum • (805) 682-4713
2201 Laguna St; Santa Barbara, CA 93105
www.santabarbaramission.org • Admission: $5/Adult

Museum of Natural History • (805) 682-4711
2559 Puesta Del Sol; Santa Barbara, CA 93105
www.sbnature.org • Admission: $10/Adult

Ty Warner Sea Center • (805) 962-2526
211 Stearns Wharf; Santa Barbara, CA 93101
www.sbnature.org • Admission: $8/Adult

Oreana Winery • (805) 962-5857
205 Anacapa St; Santa Barbara, CA 93101
www.oreanawinery.com

Ventura Harbor Comedy Club • (805) 644-1500
1559 Spinnaker Dr; Ventura, CA 93001
www.venturaharborcomedyclub.com

Golf N' Stuff • (805) 644-7131
5555 Walker St; Ventura • www.golfnstuff.com

Lobero Theatre • (805) 963-0761
33 E Canon Perdido St; Santa Barbara • www.lobero.com

Rubicon Theatre Co. • (805) 667-2900
1006 E Main St, # 300; Ventura, CA 93001
www.rubicontheatre.org

Los Angeles Area

Getty Museum • (310) 440-7330
1200 Getty Center Dr; Los Angeles, CA 90049
www.getty.edu • Free

Griffith Park • (213) 473-0800
2800 E Observatory Ave; Los Angeles, CA 90027
www.griffithobservatory.org • Free

Hollywood Sign • (323) 258-4338
Restricted Access; Los Angeles, CA 90027
www.hollywoodsign.org

Natural History Museum • (213) 763-3466
900 Exposition Blvd, Los Angeles, CA 90007
www.nhm.org • Admission: $12/Adult

Nethercutt Collection • (818) 364-6464
15200 Bledsoe St, San Fernando Valley, CA
www.nethercuttcollection.org • Free

Free TV Show Tickets
Popular TV shows—Price is Right, Tonight Show, and Ellen Degeneres Show, just to name a few—offer free tickets to visitors. Most tickets must be reserved well in advance. More information can be found at www.tvtickets.com & www.tvtix.com.

Mileage Between Sites				
Las Vegas				
Joshua Tree NP West Entrance				
San Diego				
Los Angeles				
Ventura/Channel Islands NP				
San Francisco				
240				
327	165			
266	133	121		
325	198	186	66	
566	512	502	381	369

For more travel information click www.visitcalifornia.com

Morning sun illuminates Zabriskie Point

PO Box 579
Death Valley, California 92328
Phone: (760) 786-3200
Website: www.nps.gov/deva

DEATH VALLEY

Established: October 31, 1994
February 11, 1933 (Nat'l Monument)
Size: 3.4 Million Acres
Annual Visitors: 985,000
Peak Season: November–April

Activities: Hiking, Backpacking, Camping, Backcountry Roads, Biking, Tours, and Bird Watching

Campgrounds: 5 Fee ($12–18/night) and 4 Free Campgrounds
Lodging: Furnace Creek, Stovepipe Wells, and Panamint Springs
Rates: $79–460/night
Backcountry Camping: Permitted

Park Hours: All day, every day
Except Day-use Areas: Titus Canyon, Mosaic Canyon, West Side, Wildrose, Skidoo, Aguereberry Point, Cottonwood Canyon, and Racetrack Roads
Entrance Fee: $20 • Vehicle
$10 • Individual (foot, bike, etc.)

Death Valley - California

In 1917, Death Valley experienced 52 days—43 consecutive—with temperatures over 120°F. In 1929, not a single drop of measurable rain was recorded. During a 40 month period from 1931 through 1934, only 0.64 inches of rain fell. **It's the hottest and driest national park in the United States.** Not exactly a ringing endorsement for tourism. But Death Valley's superlatives extended far beyond historical weather data. At more than three million acres it's also the **largest national park in the lower 48 states**. **Badwater is the lowest place in North America.** And it's otherworldly. The first rays of light dance off the mudstone of Zabriskie Point. Only the afternoon sun penetrates the narrow depths of Titus Canyon. Signs of a volcanic past are visible at Ubehebe Crater. And Rocks move of their own accord across the flat expanse of Racetrack Playa.

People have visited Death Valley for nearly 10,000 years. Little is known of the earliest inhabitants, but it's likely they made seasonal migrations to the valley, collecting pinyon nuts and mesquite beans. Not until 1849 did the first non-Native American step foot in the region, completely by accident. More than 100 wagons wandered into the valley after getting lost on what they believed to be a shortcut off the Old Spanish Trail. Roaming the desert for nearly two months, their oxen became weak and their wagons battered. By the time they approached present-day Stovepipe Wells it was clear they would not be able to pass the mountains with a full compliment of oxen and wagons; they made jerky of the former and burned the latter, and then set out on foot to cross Emigrant Pass, leaving the "Death Valley" behind. Only one man died during the ordeal, but the name stuck thanks to *Death Valley in '49*, a book written by a member of the group, William Lewis Manly. His book became an important chapter in California's pioneer history and brought newfound publicity to this inhospitable region.

Before it became a park **mining** was the primary activity in the valley. Boom towns (now ghost towns) sprang up around local bonanzas of gold, but the most profitable ore was **borax**, used to make soap and industrial components. Today, it's an essential component in various glassware. Harmony Borax Works was the engine that opened up the valley, building hundreds of miles of roads as they raked borax from the valley floor. Forty men could produce three tons each day. Next, it was hauled out of the valley 10 tons at a time by twenty-mule teams, the original semi-trailers; a single caravan stretched 180 feet. During six years of production they hauled more than 20 million pounds of borax out of Death Valley. **Stephen Mather**, first director of the National Park Service, made his fortune with 20 Mule Team Borax. Success allowed him to pursue the preservation of natural wonders like Death Valley.

Walter Scott, also known as **Death Valley Scotty**, was a less industrious Death Valley resident. After working for Harmony Borax and the Buffalo Bill Wild West Show, he convinced wealthy easterners to invest in his highly productive gold mine. Unfortunately, Scotty didn't have a gold mine. He took the money and went on legendary spending sprees. With no return, investors began pulling their funding until only **Albert Mussey Johnson**, an insurance magnate from Chicago, remained. He sent thousands of dollars to Scotty only to hear of an assortment of calamities that always "prevented" shipments of gold. Johnson decided to visit Death Valley to check out the operation. But even as he realized he had been swindled, he fell in love with Death Valley and began a long-lasting friendship with Death Valley Scotty. Johnson funded construction of a vacation home (Scotty's Castle) and Scotty's real home (Lower Vine Ranch). To Scotty and Albert Johnson, Death Valley was a magical place filled with character and wonder that they described with their own superlatives, not the inhospitable wasteland others made it out to be. The Death Valley Chuck-Walla, an old mining newspaper, may have said it best when they wrote: "Would you enjoy a trip to hell? You might enjoy a trip to Death Valley, now! It has all the advantages of hell without the inconveniences." Once again, not a ringing endorsement, but it is Death Valley after all.

When to Go

Death Valley National Park is open all year, but you may want to avoid summer when the mercury consistently rises above 100°F. Ranger programs are offered between November and April. Furnace Creek Visitor Center is open daily from 8am to 5pm. Scotty's Castle Visitor Center is open daily from 8:30am to 5:30pm with shortened summer hours (9am–4:30pm). With just the right combination of well-spaced winter rainfall, sunlight, and lack of drying winds, the valley can fill with a sea of gold, purple, pink, and white wildflowers. Wildflowers typically bloom from late February (low elevations) until mid-July (high elevations). Every year is different, but two of the most spectacular wildflower displays occurred in 1998 and 2005. Sometimes only a few plants bloom in the desert, but the presence of life in such a desolate place is a beautiful thing to behold.

Transportation & Airports

Public transportation does not provide service to or around the park. The closest large commercial airport is McCarran International (LAS) in Las Vegas, NV (136 miles to the east), where car rental is available. There is a small public airfield at Furnace Creek where private planes can land and refuel.

Directions

Death Valley is a massive remote region of eastern California, located along the California–Nevada border. The park can be entered from the west via CA-190 and CA-178 or from the east via CA-190, CA-178, NV-374, or NV-267. Most visitors enter from the south on CA-178 through Shoshone via Interstate 15 or NV-160.

Via CA-178: From Los Angeles (235 miles) heading east on I-15, take Exit 245 onto Baker Blvd. Turn left at CA-127/Death Valley Road. Travel north about 58 miles and then turn left at CA-178, which leads into the park.

From Las Vegas (87 miles), head west on NV-160 for about 53 miles to Pahrump. Turn left at NV-372 and continue onto CA-178 into the park.

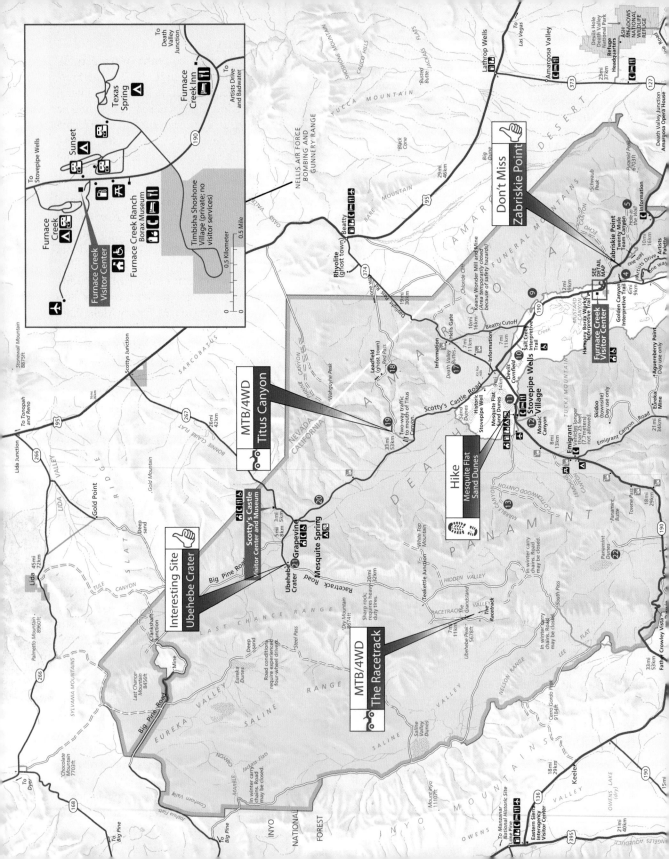

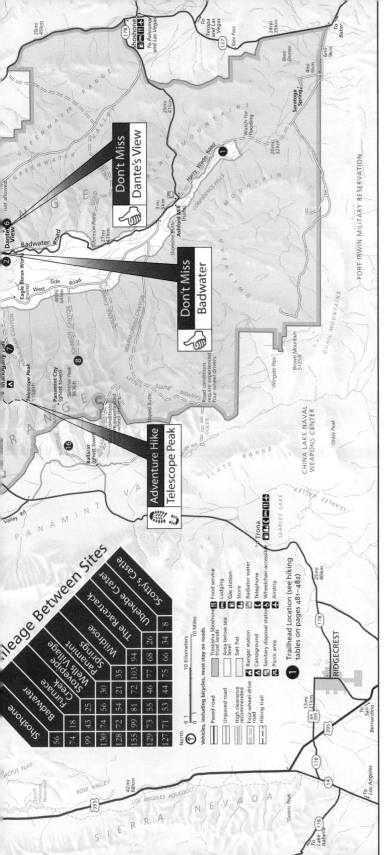

Regions

Two roads cross the center of the park diagonally making a large 'X'. The southeast leg includes Furnace Creek and Badwater. The southwest leg consists of Stovepipe Wells near the center of the 'X' and Panamint Springs along the park's western boundary. The northwest leg follows Death Valley up to Scotty's Castle.

<u>Furnace Creek:</u> The most popular region of the park offers the widest variety of natural landscapes, scenic vistas, hiking trails, and visitor accommodations. Harmony Borax Works, Golden Canyon, Devil's Golf Course, and Natural Bridge provide hiking opportunities through otherworldly terrain. Artist's Drive and Twenty Mule Team Canyon allow motorists to drive past a few of Death Valley's more remote wonders. Zabriskie Point is a popular perch to watch the sunrise. Dante's View serves up the valley's most breathtaking vista. Badwater is the lowest point in North America. Visitor Center, camping, lodging, food, gas, wi-fi, and postal service are available at Furnace Creek.

<u>Stovepipe Wells:</u> Mesquite Flat Sand Dunes crease and curl just north of CA-190. Mosaic Canyon, Salt Creek, and Titus Canyon are here waiting to be explored. Lodging, camping, and gas are available.

<u>Panamint Springs:</u> Darwin Falls, Father Crowley Vista, Lee Flat Joshua Trees, Wildrose Charcoal Kilns, and Aguereberry Point are the main attractions at your disposal. Lodging, camping, dining, bar, showers, RV hook-ups, and gas are available in the area.

<u>Scotty's Castle:</u> A lavish "castle" built by a desert rat for his wealthy financier from Chicago, a 300-year old volcanic crater, 700-feet tall sand dunes, and an eerie mesa where rocks move on their own accord highlight this region. Racetrack Playa is one of the creepiest and most befuddling sights in all the national parks (high-clearance 4WD vehicle or mountain bike required).

DEATH VALLEY

479

Death Valley has nine designated front-country campgrounds. All campsites, except those at Furnace Creek, are available on a first-come, first-served basis. Furnace Creek, Sunset, and Texas Spring Campgrounds are located on CA-190 near Furnace Creek Visitor Center. Showers are not available, but you can shower at Furnace Creek Ranch's pool building for a nominal fee.

Stovepipe Wells has a National Park Service-run campground and a concessioner-run RV Park. A pool and showers are available to all campers for a nominal fee. Farther west on CA-190 is Emigrant Campground, the only free campground with flush toilets and water, but there are just ten, tent-only sites. Continuing south on Emigrant Canyon Road leads up the Panamint Range. Located along the last five miles of road are three campgrounds: Wildrose, Thorndike, and Mahogany Flat. These are excellent locations if you want to escape the heat of the valley floor, as temperatures are typically 10°F cooler at Wildrose and 20°F cooler at Mahogany Flat. If you're interested in climbing Telescope Peak, spend the night at Thorndike or Mahogany Flat. Extreme weather conditions close these campgrounds from December through April. Lodging is available at Furnace Creek, Stovepipe Wells, and Panamint Springs (see the table below).

Death Valley Camping

	Open	Fee	Sites	Location/Notes
Furnace Creek*	All Year	$18	136	Just north of the Visitor Center • W, F, DS
Sunset	October–April	$12	270	In Furnace Creek, west side of CA-190 • W, F, DS
Texas Spring	October–April	$14	106	Just west of Sunset Camp • W, F, DS
Stovepipe Wells	October–April	$12	190	In Stovepipe Wells Village • W, F, DS
Mesquite Spring - 👍	All Year	$12	30	On Scotty's Castle Road near Grapevine • W, F, DS
Emigrant (tent-only)	All Year	Free	10	West of Stovepipe Wells Village • W, F
Wildrose	All Year	Free	23	South of Emigrant on Emigrant Canyon Rd • W, P
Thorndike	March–November	Free	6	East of Wildrose, access to Telescope Peak • P
Mahogany Flat	March–November	Free	10	East of Wildrose, access to Telescope Peak • P

W = Water, F = Flush Toilets, P = Pit Toilets, DS = Dump Station
RV hook-ups are only available at concessioner-run Stovepipe Wells RV Park and privately owned Panamint Springs Resort
*Reservations can be made up to six months in advance by calling (877) 444-6777 or clicking www.recreation.gov

Backcountry	Camping is allowed in the backcountry as long as you camp at least two miles away from any developed area, paved road, or day-use only area. Free voluntary permits are recommended.
Group Camping*	Two group campsites are available at Furnace Creek Campground (40 people, 10 vehicle capacity)

Death Valley Lodging

Stovepipe Wells Village (760) 786-2387	All Year	$80–145 + tax & fees	Centrally located with pool and wi-fi • Full hook-up RV sites for $30/night • www.escapetodeathvalley.com
Furnace Creek Inn (800) 236-7916 - 👍	mid-October– Mother's Day	$335–455 + tax & fees	Fine dining, swimming pool, tennis courts, massage therapy, and an oasis garden • www.furnacecreekresort.com
Furnace Creek Ranch (800) 236-7916	All Year	$134–219 + tax & fees	Features 224 guest units, 3 restaurants, a saloon, swimming pool, and golf course • www.furnacecreekresort.com
Panamint Springs Resort (775) 482-7680	All Year	$79–149 + tax & fees	10–15°F cooler than valley lodging facilities • Full hook-up RV sites for $30/night • www.deathvalley.com/psr

Death Valley is a desert hiker's paradise. Colorful canyons, arid flats bookended by steep sloping mountains, a volcanic crater, and rolling dunes are dispersed across the largest national park in the contiguous United Sates. All of these sights are best explored on foot. So strap on your hiking shoes and hit the trails.

A few trails should not be skipped. **Dante's Ridge Trail** provides the best views of Death Valley. It's located at the end of a 13-mile (one-way) paved road that intersects CA-190 near the park's East Entrance. About halfway down the road to Dante's View is a trailer parking area. Vehicles longer than 25 feet are not allowed beyond this point. The road gets extremely steep (15% grade) near its end. From the viewpoint parking area you can head north or south along Dante's Ridge, which follows the crest of the Black Mountains. Heading north, it is 0.5-mile to the first summit and another 3.5 miles up and down along a trail-less route to Mount Perry. To the south, just beyond Dante's View, is a short rocky trail descending to a promontory with panoramic views of Badwater Basin and the Panamint Range. Elevation gain from Badwater to Telescope Peak (highest point in the park) is more than 13,000 feet. On clear days, the highest and lowest points in the Lower 48 states—Mount Whitney (14,505 feet above sea level) and Badwater (282 feet below sea level)—are visible.

Badwater Salt Flat is another good place for a short hike. It's quite peculiar to look up into the Amargosa Mountains and see a "Sea Level" sign a few hundred feet above the ground you stand on. From Badwater Parking Area on Badwater Road you're free to walk beyond the boardwalk. There isn't a maintained trail, but trampled ground makes it clear that most visitors only walk a few hundred feet away from the boardwalk. You should also hike **Titus Canyon Narrows Trail**. High-clearance vehicles can enter Titus Canyon Road from Daylight Pass Road just beyond the park's eastern boundary. Daylight Pass Road is one-way until it reaches the mouth of the canyon near Scotty's Castle Road, where all other vehicles can enter via a short, two-way unpaved road. **Little Hebe Crater, Golden Canyon, and Mesquite Flat Sand Dunes Trails** are nice options, too. A more complete list of Death Valley hiking trails is provided below.

Death Valley Hiking Trails

	Trail Name	Trailhead (# on map)	Length	Difficulty	Notes (Roundtrip distances)
Furnace Creek Area	Badwater Salt Flat	Badwater Parking Area (2)	1–10 miles	Easy	No trail, can be muddy and hot
	Natural Bridge Canyon	Natural Bridge Parking Area (3)	1–2 miles	Easy	0.5 mile to bridge, 1 mile to canyon's end
	Golden Canyon - 👍	Golden Canyon Parking Area • South of Furnace Creek (4)	2.0 miles	Easy	Interpretive Trail through colorful canyon
	Gower Gulch Loop		4.0 miles	Moderate	Follow Golden Canyon to marker #10 • From here, follow gulch to complete loop
	Dante's Ridge - 👍	Dante's View Parking Area (6)	8.0 miles	Moderate	0.5 mile to first summit or 8 miles to Mt Perry
	Salt Creek	Salt Creek Parking Area (10)	0.5 mile	Easy	Interpretive Trail • May see rare pupfish
Stovepipe Wells	Mesquite Flat Sand Dunes - 👍	Sand Dunes Parking Area (11)	2.0 miles	Moderate	No trail, but a moderate 2-miles roundtrip to reach the highest dune
	Mosaic Canyon	Mosaic Canyon Parking Area (12)	1–4 miles	Moderate	Scrambling required • Day-use area
	Wildrose Peak	Charcoal Kilns Parking Area (14)	8.4 miles	Strenuous	2,200 ft elevation gain • Great views
	Telescope Peak	Mahogany Flat Camp (15)	14.0 miles	Strenuous	3,000 ft elevation gain • Better views
	Death Valley Buttes	Hell's Gate Parking Area (17)	2.4 miles	Strenuous	No trail, ridges are narrow and exposed
	Darwin Falls	Darwin Falls Parking Area (23)	2.0 miles	Moderate	Hike to a year-round waterfall
Scotty's Castle	Titus Canyon Narrows - 👍	Titus Canyon Mouth Parking Area (19)	3.0 miles	Easy	One of the most scenic areas of the park • Day-use area
	Fall Canyon		6.0 miles	Strenuous	No trail • Spectacular canyon
	Little Hebe Crater	Ubehebe Crater Parking Area (21)	1.0 mile	Moderate	Follows west rim of bizarre crater, can also hike down the crater (more difficult)

DEATH VALLEY

Backpacking

Backpacking in Death Valley is not an easy task. Very few established trails exist. Reliable water sources are hard to find. Weather conditions can be, well, deadly. But those who explore the backcountry are rewarded with complete solitude and private displays of scenic splendor found nowhere else in the world.

Telescope Peak is the only maintained backpacking trail. It's a great summer trek, with temperatures some 25°F cooler at the summit than the valley floor, but snow often covers its upper reaches into June. Winter hiking requires crampons and an ice axe and should only be attempted by experienced hikers. The rest of the trails listed below follow washes, canyons, or old mining roads. One-night backpackers should try hiking **Surprise Canyon** to Panamint City (ghost town). The canyon is located on the park's western boundary, off of CA-178 near Ballarat (ghost town). Ballarat is worth a visit by itself. It's suggested that you obtain a **free voluntary backcountry permit** at Furnace Creek Visitor Center or Stovepipe Wells Ranger Station. Carry water, compass, and map, and pack out your trash.

Death Valley Backpacking Trails

Trail Name	Trailhead (# on map)	Length	Notes (Roundtrip distances)
Owlshead Mountains • FC	6.6 miles south on Harry Wade Rd (1)	16.0 miles	Return via Granite Canyon for loop • Nice side canyons
Hole-in-the-Wall • FC	On 4WD Road opposite Twenty Mule Team Canyon (5)	2–10 miles	Variations abound due to quantity of side canyons that can be looped together • Scrambling optional
Hanaupah Canyon • FC	5-miles west on Hanaupah Canyon Rd, off West Side Rd (7)	6.0 miles	Accessed via a high-clearance 4WD road • Follow a gravel wash to an old mining area and spring
Hungry Bill's Ranch • FC	End of Johnson Canyon Rd (8)	14.0 miles	Informal path to historic ranch with orchard
Indian Pass • FC	6.5 miles north of Visitor Center (9)	16.0 miles	Follow a gravel wash to a low mountain pass
Cottonwood–Marble Canyon Loop • SW	8–10 miles northwest on Cottonwood Canyon Road (13)	26–30 miles	Loop, no trail, follow the main dirt road to its end, continue up Cottonwood drainage to Marble Canyon via Deadhorse Canyon
Telescope Peak • SW	Mahogany Flat Camp (15)	14.0 miles	Maintained trail provides wonderful Death Valley views
Surprise Canyon • SW	Outside the park, north of Ballarat (16)	10.0 miles	Follows a closed old jeep road to Panamint City
Titanothere Canyon • SC	Titus Canyon Rd near Red Pass (18)	9.0 miles	Gravel wash, arrange a shuttle and you can hike through to Scotty's Castle Road (14 miles, one-way)
Fall Canyon • SC	Mouth of Titus Canyon (19)	6–12 miles	Camp beyond first dry fall (3 miles) due to heavy day use
Bighorn Gorge • SC	3.9 miles south of Grapevine Ranger Station on Scotty's Castle Rd (20)	20.0 miles	Out-and-back, no trail, requires some scrambling
Panamint Dunes • SW	End of dirt road, beyond CA-190 Panamint Valley Rd Intersection (22)	6.0 miles	Make your own trail to dunes used by military jets to practice low elevation flight maneuvers
FC = Furnace Creek Area; SW = Stovepipe Wells; SC = Scotty's Castle			

DEATH VALLEY

All Backpacking Trails are Strenuous

 Backcountry Roads

Death Valley, the largest national park outside of Alaska, has **more miles of roads than any other park** (roughly 1,000 miles of paved and unpaved roadways). **Backcountry roads** unlock some of the most fascinating remote locations in the U.S. to visitors with high-clearance 4WD vehicles. Before racing into the backcountry make sure you are prepared. Pack basic tools, like a shovel, extra food, and water. Equip your vehicle with "off-road" tires. Carry at least one spare tire (two is better), a can of fix-a-flat or tire plug kit, a 12-volt air compressor, and a car jack and lug-wrench. Last but not least, top-off your gas tank before entering the backcountry. These simple precautions could save your life or at least prevent a considerable amount of grief. Should you break down, it is usually better to stay with your vehicle and wait for another traveler. Leave the car's hood up and mark the road with a large X visible to aircraft. Traveling in a group of two or more 4WD vehicles can minimize the risks of exploring Death Valley's backcountry roads. If you come across a stranded vehicle, stop to lend a hand.

After making the proper preparations, choose your backcountry destination. **Titus Canyon and Racetrack Valley** are the most popular attractions. **Titus Canyon Road** is 26.8-miles (high-clearance required) and it begins at Daylight Pass Road (NV-374), 2.7 miles east of the park boundary, eventually winding its way through the Grapevine Mountains, past a ghost town and petroglyphs, and through a spectacular canyon. **Racetrack Valley Road** spans 28 miles from Ubehebe Crater Road to the Racetrack. Do not walk on the Racetrack when wet and never drive on it. **Lippincott, North and South Eureka Valley, and Echo Canyon Roads** are also excellent options. A brochure and map of all backcountry roads is available at visitor and information centers. Do not drive off designated roads.

 Biking

Bicycles are allowed on all of the park's paved and unpaved roads. **Road cyclists** can cruise along **Badwater Road** or climb to **Dante's View** (the last ascent is a 15% grade). **Mountain bikers** like to explore **Titus Canyon Road**. **Bike rental** is available adjacent to the General Store at **Furnace Creek Ranch**. Twenty-four speed mountain bikes cost $10/hour, $34/half-day, and $49/day. Call (760) 786-3372 for reservations.

Mysteriously moving rocks at The Racetrack © Patrick Merritt (www.patrickmphotography.com)

The Racetrack

The Racetrack is a dry lakebed located in the northwestern corner of the park and home to an unexplained phenomenon: moving rocks known as sailing stones. It's difficult to explain where they're going and how they're getting there. No one has actually seen the rocks move, but proof of movement lies in the trails left behind these heavy boulders. Some rocks have traveled more than 1,500 feet. It could be an elaborate prank, but scientists believe a combination of rain and wind allows the rocks to "move" on this extremely flat and dry lakebed. Rain reduces the friction between hard rock and the earth's surface. Winds of 50 mph or more are capable of pushing the boulders across this slippery substrate. Ironically, in a place called "Death Valley," the rocks of the Racetrack come to life and move about the valley.

It's one of those sights you have to see for yourself to believe. Access it via **Racetrack Road** (high-clearance recommended), which begins at Ubehebe Crater at the very north end of Scotty's Castle Road. The road is rough washboard, so be prepared for a flat tire, and expect the 26-mile (one-way) trip on Racetrack Road to take about 2 hours each way.

 # Scotty's Castle

Walter Scott, known as Death Valley Scotty, was a desert rat who duped wealthy easterners into investing in his "gold mine." Scotty took the money and went on infamous spending sprees, never producing an ounce of ore. All but one investor pulled their funding. Albert M. Johnson, an insurance magnate, became friends with Scotty and funded construction of what is now known as **Scotty's Castle**. Today, the house is a museum with regularly scheduled **Living History Tours** offered 365 days a year, usually given between 9:30am and 4pm, but hours vary seasonally. Tours cost $11/adult, $9/senior, and $6/child. Call (760) 786-2392 for current hours. Advance tickets may be purchased at www.recreation.org or by calling (877) 444-6777. Tours of Lower Vine Ranch (Scotty's actual home • $15/adult), and an Underground Tour ($11/adult) are available daily, between November and April.

 # Horseback Riding

Furnace Creek Stables, located at Furnace Creek Ranch (760.786.3339, www.furnacecreekstables.net), offers guided trail, carriage, and wagon rides. Two hour guided trail rides ($65/rider) provide a taste of the desert as you travel into the foothills of the Funeral Mountains. More experienced riders who want freedom to gallop can take a private ride for $65/hour. Carriage rides cost $30 per adult and $15 per child (ages 5–12). Hay wagon rides ($20/person) are also available.

Best of Death Valley

Attraction: **Zabriskie Point**
> Runner-up: Titus Canyon
> 2nd Runner-up: The Racetrack
> 3rd Runner-up: Dante's View
> 4th Runner-up: Mesquite Flat Sand Dunes

Did you know?

➤ At 282 feet below sea level, Badwater Basin is the lowest place in North America and one of the lowest places in the world. The Dead Sea (1,388 feet below sea level) is the lowest.

For Kids: Most kids prefer desserts to deserts, but this desert is a pretty cool treat. Children should like exploring the lowest spot in North America or looking down at Death Valley from Dante's View. They are the park's special guests and are invited to participate in its **Junior Ranger Program**. Junior Ranger Booklets are available, free of charge, at any visitor center. Complete an age-appropriate number of activities, do something to help the park, and attend a ranger program for an official Death Valley National Park Junior Ranger badge.

Ranger Programs: Whether you've decided to pass through Death Valley on your way to Las Vegas or you're on a family vacation, do not exit the park without joining at least one ranger program. The park offers guided ranger programs from November to April. All of them are free except tours of **Scotty's Castle** and **Scotty's home (Lower Vine Ranch)**, and the **Underground Tour**. Call (760) 786-2392 for information and reservations on these for fee tours. Almost all of the free programs are offered near Furnace Creek or Stovepipe Wells. They explore a variety of interests: photography, geology, natural history, and ecology. Mesquite Dunes, Zabriskie Point, Golden Canyon, Harmony Borax Works, Badwater, and Dante's View are all sites of ranger talks or walks. These locations are made even more memorable by the colorful stories, history, and anecdotes provided by knowledgeable park rangers. During peak-season many programs are offered daily. You can pick up a current schedule of events at any visitor or information center.

Flora & Fauna: **More than 1,400 species of plants and animals** have been found living in Death Valley. The most obvious animals are the park's birds. Hundreds of species of **migratory birds** stop at the desert oases or mountains. Saratoga Spring, Furnace Creek Ranch, Scotty's Castle, Wildrose, and the High Panamints are popular birding areas. The park's famed **wildflower** eruption is not a regular occurrence, so check the park website for wildflower updates.

Pets: Pets are permitted in Death Valley, but owners must adhere to several regulations. Pets must be kept on a leash no more than six feet in length at all times. They are not allowed on trails, in the backcountry, or in public buildings (with the exception of service animals). They must not be left unattended at any time. Owners must clean up after their pets and make sure that they do not make unreasonable amounts of noise. Basically, you can take your pet anywhere your car can go: campgrounds, parking areas, and roadways.

Accessibility: Visitor centers, contact stations, and museums are fully accessible to individuals in wheelchairs. Accessible campsites are available at Furnace Creek, Stovepipe Wells, Mesquite Spring, and Emigrant Campgrounds. The first floor of Scotty's Castle Tour is accessible.

Weather: Death Valley is renowned for its remarkably hot and dry climate. Average annual rainfall is less than two inches. The driest stretch on record is a 40-month period from 1931 to 1934 when just 0.64 inches of rain were recorded. An entire year can pass without any measurable precipitation. The high mountain ranges lining the valley cause hot air to recirculate rather than dissipate. The area's low elevation is also responsible for it being the hottest spot in North America. Day time highs in July average 115°F. Hot and dry with clear skies make the park extremely pleasant from late fall to early spring.

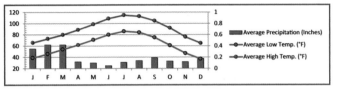

Vacation Planner

Death Valley is huge. More than 1,000 miles of paved and dirt roads stretch across 3.4 million acres of mostly undeveloped desert. It's possible to blast through the park in a day, but spending the night allows visitors to **hike more trails** (page 481), **ride a horse** (page 484), **tour Scotty's Castle** (page 484), **drive to the Racetrack** (page 483), and catch a Death Valley sunrise as the first rays of light illuminate colorful badlands and jagged peaks found at **Zabriskie Point** (CA-190 near Furnace Creek). For a more proper introduction, plan on spending at least three days. Unless you really like to drive, you'll want to spend your nights at an in-park **campground** or **lodging** facility (page 480). Nearby dining, grocery stores, lodging, festivals, and attractions are listed on pages 519–521.

 Assuming you enter the park on CA-178/Badwater Road at Shoshone, CA, begin your trip by following Badwater Road north along the eastern side of Death Valley. If you're arriving in late winter or spring you may see beautiful fields of **wildflowers**. The five mile stretch of road between Jubilee Pass and Ashford Mill is a particularly good spot for wildflowers early in the season. Continuing north, the next stop to stretch your legs is **Badwater** (page 481), the lowest spot in North America. Most visitors wander

Wildflower bloom in 2005

about the boardwalk, but you can venture further out into the valley if you're interested in an extended flat hike. Return to your car and hop back onto Badwater Road. Skip Natural Bridge, but take the short detour along **Artist's Drive**. This 9-mile, one-way loop passes through colorful volcanic and sedimentary hills before returning to Badwater Road. The next stop is **Golden Canyon** (page 481), one of the park's best short hikes and the last stop before reaching **Furnace Creek**. If you have enough spare time (about 2 hours) before dark, take CA-190 toward the park's eastern boundary where you'll find the road to **Dante's View**, one of the best spots to see the sunset.

 Follow the best sunset with the best sunrise. Retrace your route to Dante's View but stop short at **Zabriskie Point**. The first rays of sunlight creep over the Amargosa Range illuminating the colorful bands of rock and Zabriskie Point. Travelers in high-clearance vehicles should exit the park on Daylight Pass Road/NV-374 and take **Titus Canyon Road** back into the park. Hike **Titus Canyon Trail** (page 481). All other visitors can reach the trail via Scotty's Castle Road. After the hike drive north to **Ubehebe Crater**. If you aren't driving a high-clearance 4WD vehicle or don't have interest in **Scotty's Castle** (page 484), this is a good leg to skip. Those prepared for backcountry roads (page 483) should drive to **the Racetrack** (page 483). Allow at least 4 hours to make the roundtrip journey from Ubehebe Crater.

 Check out **Mesquite Flat Sand Dunes** (page 481) in the morning. There isn't a trail, but it's easy to follow the ridgelines. After playing in the dunes, make the hike to **Telescope Peak** (page 481). If you don't have the energy for it, spend the day in the pool (fee) at **Stovepipe Wells**.

A motorist drives through Tunnel Log (8-feet high, 17-feet wide)

47050 Generals Highway
Three Rivers, CA 93271
Phone: (559) 565-3341
Website: www.nps.gov/seki

Established:
September 25, 1890 (Sequoia)
October 1, 1890 (General Grant)
March 4, 1940 (Kings Canyon)
Size: 865,257 Acres
Annual Visitors: 1.6 Million
Peak Season: Spring & Fall

Activities: Hiking, Backpacking, Camping, Stargazing, Horseback Riding, Rock Climbing, and Biking

Campgrounds*: 14 Campgrounds
Fee: $12–20/night
Backcountry Camping: Permitted
4 Lodges ($119–395/night)

Park Hours: All day, every day
Entrance Fee: $20 • Vehicle
$10 • Individual (foot, bike, etc.)

*Reservations available at Lodgepole and Dorst Campgrounds. Call (877) 444-6777 or click www.recreation.gov.

Sequoia & Kings Canyon - California

Sequoia and Kings Canyon National Parks reside in a contiguous region of the southern Sierra Nevada. Each park has its own boundary and entrance, but they share the same backbone, the Sierra Nevada Mountains. Since 1943 the parks have been administered jointly by the National Park Service. **John Muir**, one of the first American naturalists, was an early advocate of preserving and protecting regions of exceptional natural beauty. While wandering the High Sierra he formed a kinship with the trees, the rocks, and the mountains, and few areas were more important to Muir than the groves of giant sequoia and mountains of the High Sierra (including Mount Whitney, the highest peak in the lower 48 states). He spent much of his life writing, speaking, and petitioning on their behalf.

"Most of the Sierra trees die of disease, fungi, etc., but nothing hurts the Big Tree. Barring accidents, it seems to be immortal." – John Muir

Muir was just about right. The wood and bark of the park's namesake is infused with chemicals that provide resistance to insects and fungi. Its bark—soft, fibrous, and in excess of two feet thick—is a poor conductor of heat, making the **giant sequoia** highly resistant to fire damage. They rarely die of old age, either. Many sequoias are more than 2,000 years old. Ironically, extreme size is its greatest threat. Most die by toppling over under their immensity. Relative to their massive size and height, the roots are shallow and without a taproot. Wet soil, strong winds, and shallow roots are a recipe for a toppled sequoia.

"God has cared for these trees, saved them from drought, disease, avalanches, and a thousand tempests and floods. But he cannot save them from fools." – John Muir

Fools found their way to the sequoia groves of the Sierra Nevada and did what they could to topple these mighty trees. In 1888, **Walter Fry** sought work as a logger (even though sequoias were a relatively poor wood that splintered easily). Somewhere between felling a sequoia (which took a five-man team five days to complete) and counting its 3,266 rings, he had a change of heart. At the same time conservationists were collecting signatures to protect the forest; the third signature was none other than Walter Fry, who decided to put down his axe and channel his efforts toward protecting the trees from the men he had worked alongside. Protection was achieved in 1890 thanks to establishment of a national park. Fry was hired as a road foreman in 1901 and four years later he became a park ranger. Over the next three decades he became the first civilian superintendent (originally the park fell under army supervision) and the first nature guide, who continued to lead guests on guided walks until his retirement in 1930 at the age of 71.

"When I entered this sublime wilderness the day was nearly done, the trees with rosy, glowing countenances seemed to be hushed and thoughtful, as if waiting in conscious religious dependence on the sun, and one naturally walked softly awestricken among them." – John Muir

John Muir didn't have to cut down a sequoia tree to understand its significance. The privilege of being able to walk among them was enough. Muir's communion wasn't just with the trees, it was with nature itself. He led energetic hikes into the High Sierra and forged a trail along the steep east face of **Mount Whitney**. Today, the 211-mile trail from Yosemite National Park to Mount Whitney bears his name. He dreamed of an expanded park, reaching far into King's Canyon, but it wasn't until 1940 that Kings Canyon National Park was established. **Harold Ickes**, Secretary of the Interior, wanted to make a park that was impenetrable to automobiles. Kings Canyon was ideal. Today, a single road leads into the canyon and terminates abruptly at Roads End. No road within either park crosses the Sierra Nevada. Mount Whitney, the tallest point in the lower 48, cannot be seen from any roadway. The park is left mostly undeveloped, allowing visitors to walk softly awestricken among its natural beauty, much like John Muir did when he first came to the Sierra Nevada.

Best of Sequoia

Attraction: General Sherman
Runner-up: Mineral King Valley
2nd Runner-up: Moro Rock
3rd Runner-up: High Sierra Camp
4th Runner-up: Crystal Cave

Hike: Mount Whitney (Strenuous)
Runner-up: Crescent Meadow
2nd Runner-up: Monarch Lakes

Best of Kings Canyon

Attraction: Kings Canyon
Runner-up: General Grant
2nd Runner-up: Grant Grove Stables

Hike: Rae Lakes Loop (Backpack)
Runner-up: Mist Falls
2nd Runner-up: Woods Creek

Did you know?

➤ Sequoia is the second oldest National Park.

➤ The 2,200 year old giant sequoia named General Sherman is the world's largest tree (by volume). It has a circumference of 103 feet and its trunk weighs 1,385 tons.

➤ General Sherman's estimated volume is 52,600 ft^3. That's about the same volume as 16 blue whales, the world's largest mammal.

➤ General Sherman's first large branch is 130 feet above the base of the tree. Its diameter is almost seven feet at its thickest point.

➤ Every year the General Sherman grows enough new wood to make a 60-foot tall tree of typical proportions.

➤ Giant sequoia seeds are the size of oat flakes.

➤ Hale Tharp, the first settler of European descent, lived in a hollowed-out sequoia.

➤ At 14,494 feet, Mount Whitney is the tallest mountain in the contiguous United States.

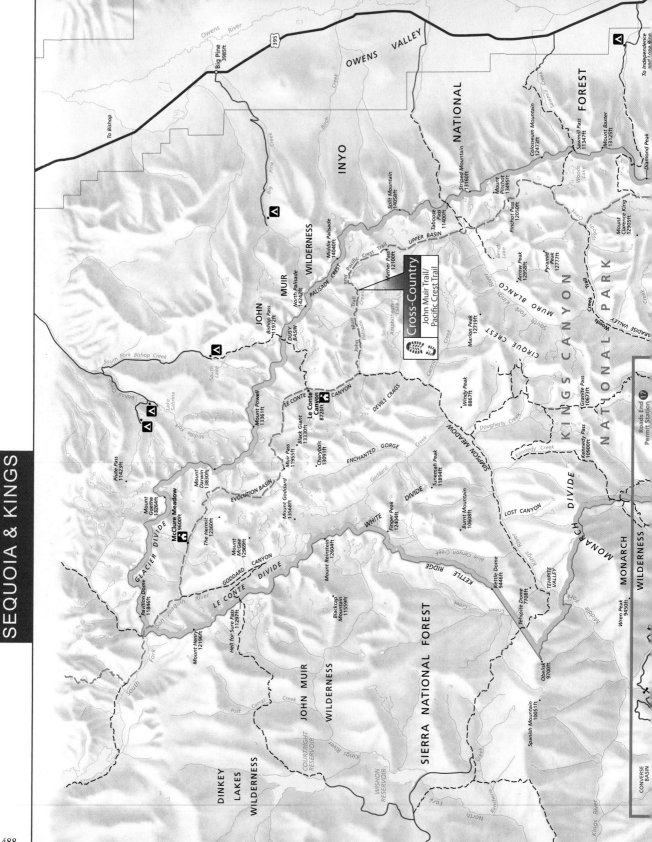

Owens River

OWENS VALLEY

INYO

NATIONAL

FOREST

To Bishop

Big Pine
3985ft

To Independence
and Lone Pine

To Bishop

Striped Mountain
13160ft

Split Mountain
14058ft

Colosseum Mountain
12473ft

Sawmill Pass
11347ft

Mount Baxter
13125ft

Mount Clarence King
12905ft

Diamond Peak

Mount Pinchot
13495ft

Pinchot Pass
12050ft

Taboose Pass
11400ft

UPPER BASIN

Mather Pass
12100ft

Arrow Peak
12958ft

Pyramid Peak
12777ft

Bench Lake

Woods Creek Trail

Woods Lake

Sawmill Creek

Mount Goethe
13264ft

Bishop Pass
11972ft

North Palisade
14242ft

Middle Palisade
14040ft

PALISADE CREST

Amphitheatre Lake

Palisade Creek

JOHN MUIR WILDERNESS

South Fork Bishop Creek

South Lake

DUSY BASIN

Marion Peak
12719ft

MURO BLANCO

CIRQUE CREST

South Fork Kings River

KINGS CANYON NATIONAL PARK

PARADISE VALLEY

Cross-Country

John Muir Trail /
Pacific Crest Trail

Le Conte Canyon

LE CONTE CANYON

Le Conte Canyon
8720ft

DEVILS CRAGS

Windy Peak
8867ft

Granite Pass
10673ft

Dougherty Creek

Bishop Creek

Lake Sabrina

Middle Fork

Piute Pass
11423ft

Mount Powell
13361ft

Black Giant
13330ft

Muir Pass
11955ft

Charybdis
13091ft

ENCHANTED GORGE

Goddard Creek

SIMPSON MEADOW

Kennedy Pass
10900ft

Kennedy Creek

Roads End
Permit Station

Mount Darwin
13830ft

EVOLUTION BASIN

Mount Goddard
13568ft

Tunemah Peak
11894ft

DIVIDE

LOST CANYON

MONARCH DIVIDE

Mount Goethe
13264ft

McClure Meadow
9600ft

GLACIER DIVIDE

The Hermit
12360ft

Mount McGee
12969ft

Finger Peak
12404ft

Burnt Mountain
10608ft

WHITE DIVIDE

Blue Canyon Creek

KETTLE RIDGE

Kettle Dome
9446ft

Kings River

Middle Fork Kings River

MONARCH WILDERNESS

Wren Peak
9450ft

Pavilion Dome
11846ft

LE CONTE DIVIDE

Mount Reinstein
12604ft

GODDARD CANYON

Hell for Sure Pass
11297ft

Mount Henry
12196ft

South Fork San Joaquin River

Blackcap Mountain
11559ft

Tehipite Dome
7708ft

TEHIPITE VALLEY

Crown Creek

Obelisk
9700ft

SIERRA NATIONAL FOREST

JOHN MUIR WILDERNESS

Post Corral Creek

COURTRIGHT RESERVOIR

Kings River

WISHON RESERVOIR

Spanish Mountain
10051ft

CONVERSE BASIN

DINKEY LAKES WILDERNESS

South Fork Kings River

North Fork Kings River

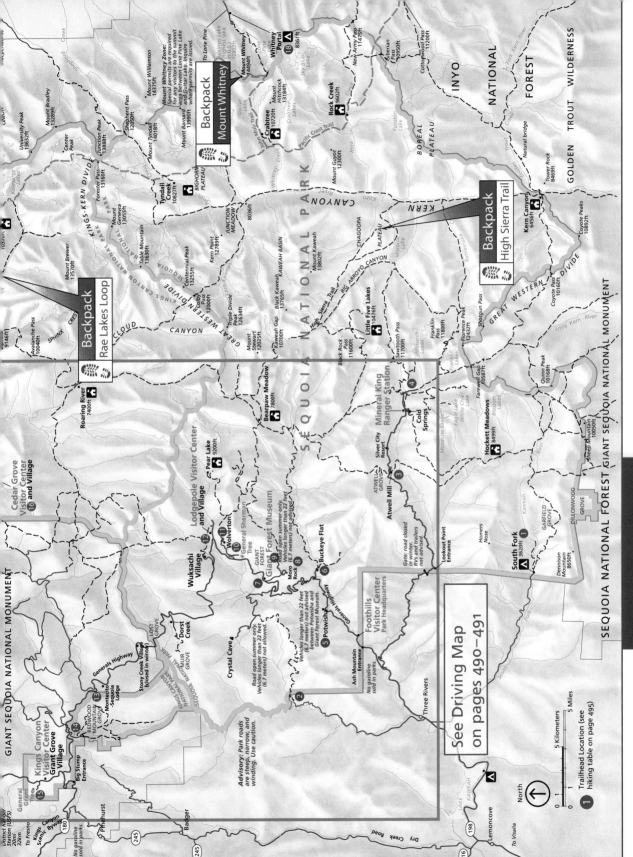

Backpack
Mount Whitney

Backpack
High Sierra Trail

Backpack
Rae Lakes Loop

Mount Whitney Zone: Special permits are required for all trips into the summit area between Lone Pine Lake and Guitar Lake. Inquire where permits are issued.

SEQUOIA NATIONAL PARK

KINGS CANYON NATIONAL PARK

KINGS-KERN DIVIDE

GREAT WESTERN DIVIDE

GREAT WESTERN DIVIDE

KERN CANYON

INYO NATIONAL FOREST

GOLDEN TROUT WILDERNESS

GIANT SEQUOIA NATIONAL MONUMENT

SEQUOIA NATIONAL FOREST

GIANT SEQUOIA NATIONAL MONUMENT

University Peak 13632ft
Mount Bradley 13289ft
Center Peak
Junction Peak 13888ft
Kearsarge Lakes
Shepherd Pass
Mount Williamson 14373ft
Mount Tyndall 14018ft
Tyndall Creek 10827ft
Mount Barnard 13990ft
Mount Whitney 14494ft
Mount Hitchcock 13184ft
Whitney Portal 8361ft
To Lone Pine
Crabtree
Rock Creek 9602ft
BIGHORN PLATEAU
Mount Russell 14086ft
Mount Genevra 13055ft
Table Mountain
Centennial Peak 13255ft
Kern Point 12789ft
JUNCTION MEADOW
Mount Stanford 13963ft
Mount Brewer 13570ft
Colby Pass 12000ft
Triple Divide Peak 12634ft
Mount Stewart 12025ft
Kaweah Gap 10700ft
Black Kaweah 13765ft
KAWEAH BASIN
Mount Kaweah 13802ft
CHAGOOPA PLATEAU
Kern Canyon 6456ft
Coyote Peaks 10892ft
Avalanche Pass 10040ft
SPHINX 9146ft
CLOUD CANYON
Little Five Lakes 10476ft
Black Rock Pass 11600ft
Sawtooth Pass 11700ft
Franklin Pass 11800ft
Coyote Peak 12243ft
Franklin Lakes
Shotgun Pass
Quinn Peak 10168ft
Farewell Gap 10587ft
NEW ARMY PASS 11475ft
Siberian Pass 10950ft
Cottonwood Pass 11200ft
Tower Rock 8409ft
Natural bridge
BOREAL PLATEAU
Roaring River 7400ft
Bearpaw Meadow 7800ft
Pear Lake 9200ft
Mineral King Ranger Station
Cold Springs
Silver City Resort
Hockett Meadows 8499ft
Homers Nose
Dennison Mountain 8650ft
Sheep Mountain 10050ft

Cedar Grove Visitor Center and Village **16**
Lodgepole Visitor Center and Village **12**
Wuksachi Village
Wolverton **11**
General Sherman Tree **10**
GIANT FOREST
Giant Forest Museum **9**
Moro Rock **8**
Buckeye Flat
Atwell Mill **3**
ATWELL GROVE
Lookout Point Entrance
South Fork 3620ft **1**
GARFIELD GROVE
DILLONWOOD GROVE
Potwisha **5**
6 7
Ash Mountain Entrance
Foothills Visitor Center Park Headquarters
Three Rivers
2
4

See Driving Map on pages 490–491

Advisory: Park roads are steep, narrow, and winding. Use caution.

Wukachi Village
LOST GROVE
Dorst Creek
Stony Creek Village (closed in winter)
Generals Highway
MURO GROVE
Crystal Cave
Road open summer only. Vehicles longer than 24 feet (6.7 meters) not allowed.
Road open summer only. Vehicles longer than 22 feet (6.7 meters) not advised.
Vehicles longer than 22 feet (6.7 meters) not advised between Potwisha and Giant Forest Museum.
Gate: road closed in winter. RVs and trailers not advised.
No gasoline sold in parks.
General Highway

District Ranger Station (USFS) 20mi / 32km
To Fresno
No gasoline sold in parks.
Kings Canyon Scenic Byway
Grant Grove Village
Kings Canyon Visitor Center **15**
General Grant Tree
Big Stump Entrance
REDWOOD MOUNTAIN GROVE
Montecito Sequoia Lodge **13**
Redwood Grove **14**
Big Stump Entrance
Pinehurst
Badger
Lemoncove
To Visalia

SEQUOIA & KINGS

North

5 Kilometers
5 Miles

1 Trailhead Location (see hiking table on page 495)

489

When to Go

Sequoia and Kings Canyon National Parks are open year-round. The parks are busiest on summer weekends. Some campgrounds and lodging facilities close for the winter, but you can almost always find a place to spend the night any time of year. If you can't find a campsite in the park, campgrounds are also available at adjacent Sequoia National Forest and Monument (page 521). During winter the roads to Cedar Grove and Mineral King close. Generals Highway is open year-round, but closes during heavy snowstorms. From December to April visitors can cross-country ski around Giant Forest, but most visitors arrive between spring and fall.

Transportation & Airports

The **Sequoia Shuttle** (877.287.4453, www.sequoiashuttle.com) provides transportation between Visalia, CA and Giant Forest Museum. Roundtrip fare is $15 and includes the park entrance fee. Reservations are required. During summer the park operates a free shuttle service with three routes through the park's most popular sections between Dorst Campground and Crescent Meadow. The closest large commercial airport is Fresno Yosemite International (FAT) in Fresno, CA, located 83 miles from Sequoia's Ash Mountain Entrance. Car rental is available at the airport.

Directions

The parks are located in eastern California's Sierra Nevada. Ash Mountain Entrance is 34 miles from downtown Visalia, CA. It is reached by CA-198, which turns into Generals Highway inside the park. Generals Highway connects the two parks. It is 80 miles from Ash Mountain Entrance to the end of Kings Canyon Scenic Byway. Kings Canyon Visitor Center is 53 miles east of Fresno, CA via CA-180.

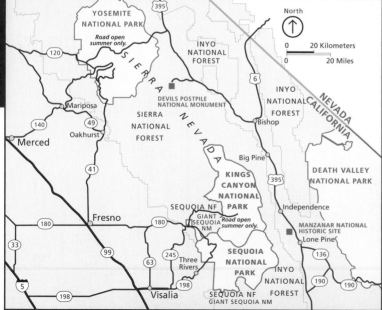

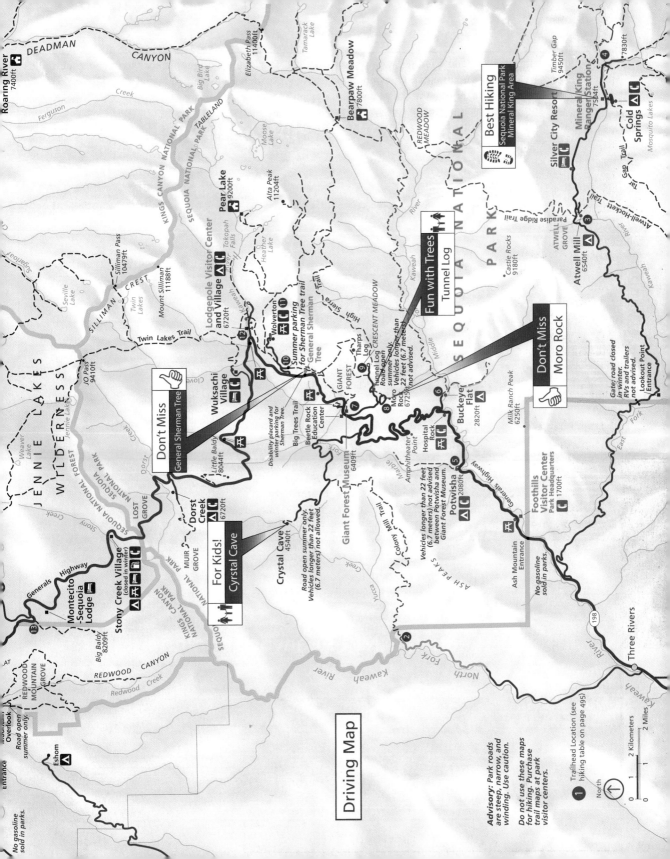

There are **14 campgrounds** and **4 lodges** within the two parks. **Dorst** and **Lodgepole** are the only campgrounds that accept reservations (summer only). Campers must use the provided food-storage containers. The table below provides a more comprehensive look at the parks' camping and lodging facilities.

Sequoia & Kings Canyon Camping

	Area	Open	Fee	Sites	Location/Notes
Potwisha	FH	All Year	$18	40	4 miles from entrance, snow free in winter • F, DS, RV
Buckeye Flat - 👍	FH	mid-April–Sept	$18	28	Located along the Middle Fork of the Kaweah • F
South Fork	FH	All Year	$12	10	Located on South Fork Drive • P
Atwell Mill	MK	late May–October	$12	21	Located on Mineral King Road • P
Cold Springs - 👍	MK	late May–October	$12	40	Located near Mineral King Visitor Center • P
Lodgepole* - 👍	GF	All Year	$20	205	Located 2 miles from Giant Forest • F, RV
Dorst*	GF	late June–early Sept	$20	210	10 miles from Giant Forest • F, DS (summer only), RV
Azalea - 👍	GG	All Year	$18	110	Near Kings Canyon Entrance • F, DS (summer only), RV
Crystal Springs	GG	mid-May–mid-Sept	$18	50	Near Kings Canyon Entrance • F, RV
Sunset	GG	mid-May–mid-Sept	$18	157	Near Kings Canyon Entrance • F, RV
Sentinel	CG	late April–September	$18	83	Located in the Canyon along Middle Fork • F, RV
Sheep Creek	CG	mid-May–mid-Oct	$18	111	Located in the Canyon near Middle Fork • F, RV
Canyon View	CG	mid-May–mid-Oct	$35	12	All sites at Canyon View Campground are for groups of 7–19 people
Moraine	CG	mid-May–mid-Oct	$18	120	

Sequoia Nat'l Park Areas: FH = Foothills, MK = Mineral King, GF = Giant Forest Kings Canyon National Park Areas: GG = Grant Grove, CG = Cedar Grove	F = Flush Toilets, P = Pit Toilets, DS = Dump Station, RV = RVs & Trailers are allowed

*Summer reservations can be made up to six months in advance by calling (877) 444-6777 or clicking www.recreation.gov

Backcountry	Camping is allowed in the backcountry with a wilderness permit. Permits are free from late September to late May. The remainder of the year permits cost $15, reservations are allowed, and quotas are enforced.
Group Camping*	Group campsites are available at Dorst, Sunset, and Canyon View Campgrounds. Fees range from $40–60/night. Sites must be reserved in advance. Dorst Campground sites may be reserved by calling (877) 444-6777 or clicking www.recreation.gov. Sites at Sunset and Canyon View must be reserved by fax or mail. Refer to the park website or call (559) 565-4357 for additional information on reservations.

Sequoia & Kings Canyon Lodging

Wuksachi Village (888) 252-5757 - 👍	All Year	$215–335	Located in Giant Forest of Sequoia National Park, features restaurant and lounge • www.visitsequoia.com
Silver City Mtn Resort (559) 561-3223	late May–late Oct	$250–395	Located on Mineral King Road • Multiple chalets of varying sizes available • www.silvercityresort.com
Grant Grove Village (866) 522-6966	All Year Cabins (May–Nov)	$62–186	John Muir Lodge and Grant Grove Cabins near General Grant Tree • www.sequoia-kingscanyon.com
Cedar Grove Lodge (866) 522-6966	mid-May–mid-Oct	$119–135	Deep in the heart of Kings Canyon overlooking Kings River • www.sequoia-kingscanyon.com

See page 509 for additional camping and lodging facilities in Sequoia National Forest/Monument and surrounding areas

 Big Trees

There are **75 giant sequoia groves** in the two parks containing more than 15,800 trees. These behemoths only grow on the western slopes of the Sierra Nevada, mostly between 5–7,000 feet elevation. Each park has one especially popular grove. **Sequoia's Giant Forest** is home to five of the ten largest trees in the world, **including General Sherman, the world's largest tree**. **Kings Canyon's Grant Grove** is home to **General Grant, the world's second largest tree**.

Caves

There are **more than 265 known caves** within the park and at least one new cave is discovered each year. Since 2003, at least 17 caves have been found. At 17 miles in length, Liburn is the longest cave in California. **Crystal Cave** is the only one available for tours. It's located 15 miles from the Sequoia National Park entrance at CA-198, and 3 miles south of General Sherman. Tours are given daily from spring to fall. They cost $13/adult and $6.50/child. **Discovery and Candlelight Tours** are offered during the summer for $16/person. Tickets can only be purchased at Lodgepole and Foothills Visitor Centers. Wear a jacket; the cave is 50°F year-round.

Rock Climbing

Rock found at Sequoia and Kings Canyon National Parks is similar to Yosemite in terms of quality and quantity. The main difference is that you have to pack up your gear and hike (usually a full-day) to the best climbing locations. In Kings Canyon, **Bubbs Creek Trail** (part of Rae Lakes Loop) is a good place to find multi-pitch climbing routes. **Moro Rock** (Sequoia) is the most easily accessible feature for climbing. There are also excellent options along **High Sierra Trail**. Climbing in remote regions is not recommended for inexperienced climbers. **Sierra Mountain Guides** (877.423.2546, www.sierramtnguides.com) offers a variety of introductory courses and custom trips throughout the eastern Sierra.

Horseback Riding

Horse enthusiasts aren't excluded from the fun at Sequoia and Kings Canyon National Parks. Those looking to explore the Sierra Nevada on horseback have three outfitters to choose from. **Grant Grove Stables** (559.335.9292, summer • 559.337.1273, winter) offers 1–2 hour guided trips to General Grant Tree, through North Grove, Lion Meadow, and Dead Giant Meadow. **Cedar Grove Stables** (559.565.3464) has a wider range of services. You can enjoy anything from an hour-long trail ride to multi-day pack trips in Kings Canyon's backcountry. Backcountry trips include Monarch Divide and Rae Lakes Loop. **Big Meadow Corral** (559.565.3404, summer • 559.564.6429, winter) is located east of Big Meadows Campground in Sequoia National Forest. They offer half-day, full-day, and extended pack trips. Horseback rides are generally offered from late spring to fall. Reservations are recommended (and required for pack trips). Rates are between $35 and $80 for day-trips and cost upward of $200/day for multi-day backcountry pack trips.

GENERAL SHERMAN

The view from Moro Rock
Volcanic Lakes © Josh Steinitz (www.nileguide.com)

![icon] **Backpacking**

Backpacking in the Sierra Nevada is an indescribable experience. This setting inspired John Muir to dedicate much of his life to the conservation of the United States' irreplaceable natural wonders. Largely thanks to Muir, Sequoia and Kings Canyon National Parks' backcountry is left as it was when he hiked these trails. Nowadays, more people have become appreciative of nature's beauty, and the backcountry is so popular that a **wilderness permit quota system** is in place during the summer (September–May). Permits cost $15 and can be reserved in advance by completing the application form available at the park website. From late September to late May visitors can obtain a free wilderness permit from self-issue stations located at Lodgepole Visitor Center, Foothills Visitor Center, Roads End Permit Station, and Mineral King Ranger Station. Food must be stored in a portable bear-resistant canister or metal food storage locker.

John Muir and **Pacific Crest** are legendary long-distance trails that pass through the parks. If you'd like to sample the best of the Sierra Nevada, try Sequoia's 49-mile High Sierra Trail or Kings Canyon's 46-mile Rae Lakes Loop. **Rae Lakes Loop** is regarded as the best backpacking trail in the entire High Sierra. If you're looking for a shorter, more comfortable trek, take the **High Sierra Trail** 11.4 miles to **High Sierra Camp** (877.591.8982, www.sequoiahighsierracamp.com) where you can reserve tent cabins for $250 per person per night, $100 per child per night. Breakfast, lunch, and dinner are included.

 **Hiking**

With more than 800 miles of hiking trails it's difficult to choose what to see and where to hike. In Sequoia, the short hike up nearly 400 stairs to the top of **Moro Rock** provides spectacular views (when there isn't smog). The one activity that every visitor must do is to stand next to a giant sequoia. **General Sherman** is the tree to visit in Sequoia National Park. At Kings Canyon, say hello to **General Grant**, the tree that President Coolidge called the "Nation's Christmas Tree" and President Dwight D. Eisenhower declared a "National Shrine," the only living object to receive this distinction. Respectively, they are the first and second largest trees in the world. Check out the hiking table on the following page for additional hikes.

![icon] **Winter Activities**

Winter is a wonderful time of year to visit the parks. The lower foothills remain snow free year-round, but you can usually find snow for cross-country skiing and snowshoeing in the higher elevations.

Pear Lake Ski Hut in Sequoia National Park is open from mid-December through April. Located just north of Pear Lake at 9,200 feet elevation, it can be reached via a steep six mile trail from Wolverton Meadow. The hut sleeps 10, costs $38/night, and reservations are required. **Sequoia Natural History Association** (559.565.3134, www.sequoiahistory.org) has additional information on the reservation process. **Ski rental** is available at **Wuksachi Lodge** and **Grant Grove Market**.

The park offers **ranger guided snowshoe walks** on Saturdays and holidays (weather permitting). Snowshoes are provided free of charge. These two hour treks usually begin at Wuksachi Lodge (559.565.4480) and Grant Grove (559.565.4307). Group size is limited, so reserve your place by calling or stopping at any visitor center. Snowshoe trips may be difficult for small children. Two miles north of General Sherman Tree is an open area with two **sledding** hills where children of all ages are welcome to race down the hills and play in the snow.

Sequoia & Kings Canyon Hiking Trails

	Trail Name	Trailhead (# on map)	Length	Notes (Roundtrip distances unless noted otherwise)
Sequoia National Park	Lady Bug	South Fork Campground (1)	6.0 miles	1.75 miles to Lady Bug Camp, 3 miles to Cedar Creek
	Garfield Grove		10.0 miles	Steep and strenuous trail to sequoia grove
	North Fork	Enter through North Fork Recreation Area (2)	8.4 miles	The trailhead is difficult to locate • Follow North Fork Dr to Colony Mill Rd (hike begins at the end of this fire road)
	Paradise Peak	Atwell Mill Campground (3)	9.6 miles	Large sequoias, fantastic views, lightly trafficked
	Monarch Lakes - 👍	End of Mineral King Rd (4)	8.4 miles	Wonderful views of the southern Sierra
	Crystal Lake		9.8 miles	Branch from Monarch Lakes Trail (steep)
	Timber Gap		4.0 miles	Easier trail in Mineral King follows old mining route
	Franklin Lakes - 👍		10.8 miles	Popular first leg for multi-day backpacking trips
	White Chief		5.8 miles	Begins on same trail as Eagle and Mosquito Lakes
	Eagle Lake - 👍		6.8 miles	Fairly steep but popular trail to majestic lake
	Mosquito Lakes		7.2 miles	Three small lakes tucked away in the High Sierra
	Marble Falls	Potwisha Campground (5)	7.8 miles	Follow Marble Fork–Kaweah River through Deep Canyon
	Middle Fork	Off dirt road before Buckeye Flat Campground (6)	5.5 miles	Views of Moro Rock and Castle Rocks along this hike that is particularly popular in spring
	Paradise Creek	Buckeye Flat Camp (6)	1.5 miles	Hike to pools that are popular swimming holes
	Big Trees - 👍	Giant Forest Museum (7)	1.3 miles	Paved loop trail with benches and interpretive signs
	Moro Rock - 👍	Crescent Meadow Rd (8)	0.5 mile	Almost 400 steps lead to granite dome with great views
	Crescent Meadow - 👍	End of Crescent Meadow Road (9)	3.2 miles	Leads to Tharp's Log and Chimney Tree
	High Sierra		49.0 miles	11.4 miles to High Sierra Camp, backpacker trail
	General Sherman Tree - 👍	General Sherman Parking (10)	1.0 mile	Handicap parking available near tree on Generals Hwy
	Congress	Sherman Tree (10)	2.0 miles	Short on time? Hike this trail • Big trees, easy hike
	Alta Peak	Wolverton Picnic Area (11)	13.8 miles	On clear days, views of Mount Whitney from Alta Peak
	Tokopah Falls	Lodgepole Camp (12)	3.4 miles	Easy walk along Marble Fork of the Kaweah River
	Mount Whitney - 👍	Whitney Portal (18)	22.0 miles	East side of park • Shortest route to the summit
Kings Canyon National Park	Big Baldy Ridge	8 miles S on Generals Hwy (13)	4.0 miles	Provides views down into Redwood Canyon
	Buena Vista Peak	Dirt road off Generals Highway 6 miles SE of Grant Grove (14)	2.0 miles	Easiest trail to a granite summit where visitors obtain decent views of the canyon and mountains
	Redwood Canyon		16.0 miles	Network of trails through one of the largest of all Sequoia groves • Road closed in winter
	General Grant - 👍	Grant Tree Parking Area (15)	0.7 mile	Short trail to the Nation's Christmas Tree
	North Grove Loop		1.5 miles	Lightly traveled loop trail past meadows and creeks
	Zumwalt Meadow	Cedar Grove Village (16)	1.5 miles	Trail through high granite walls and lush meadows
	Hotel/Lewis Creek		8.0 miles	Stop at Cedar Grove Overlook while completing this loop
	Mist Falls - 👍	End of Kings Canyon Scenic Byway • Roads End Permit Station (17)	8.0 miles	Relatively flat trail to one of the park's largest waterfalls
	Rae Lakes Loop - 👍		46.0 miles	One of the most popular backcountry hikes in the Sierra
	Woods Creek		28.0 miles	Follows Mist Falls Trail to Paradise Valley and PCT
Both	John Muir	Backcountry	211 miles	One-way • Runs between Yosemite and Mount Whitney
	Pacific Crest (PCT)	Mexico–British Columbia	2,663 mi	One-way • Follows the Sierra Nevada and Cascade Ranges

The kind of wildlife you're sure to see © Olivier Baquet

![bear icon] # Flora & Fauna

When it comes to biodiversity, there's more than big trees. There are 265 known caves, the tallest mountain and one of the deepest canyons in the contiguous United States, and everything in between to provide a variety of ecosystems that support some **1,200 species of plants and 260 vertebrate species**. There's a chance that you may see a bear lumbering about a sequoia grove or a bighorn sheep scaling the rocky ledges of the backcountry, but you're more likely to spot mule deer or squirrels. The parks also provide habitat for **more than 200 species of birds**. Golden eagle, peregrine falcon, and blue grouse have all been spotted here. One of the best places to begin a birding expedition is Giant Forest (page 493).

Giant sequoias tend to steal the show for anyone's first visit to the park. Stand next to one of these towering giants and you can finally grasp their impressive size. Try to hug one (it will take more than one of you). Walk, drive, and peer through sequoias that have been hollowed out. Whatever you do, you'll be sure to come away inspired. **Giant Forest** (Sequoia) and **Grant Grove** (Kings Canyon) are the two most popular sequoia groves, but there are 75 total groves within park boundaries along the western slope of the Sierra Nevada. Sequoias reside in the middle elevations (5–7,000 feet) with a mix of evergreens. Lower elevations are home to chaparral vegetation, and high elevations are mostly rocky and barren with the exception of the occasional foxtail and whitebark pine.

For Kids: Almost all ranger programs are great activities for the whole family. The scenery, stories, and sweet hats topping each ranger's head can inspire children to want to join them. The **Junior Ranger Program** allows children of all ages to participate in some ranger fun while at the park. Pick up a free park ranger activity booklet at a visitor center. Complete an age appropriate number of activities and return to a visitor center to become a Junior Ranger and receive an award.

Ranger Programs: In addition to **cave tours** (page 493) and **snowshoe treks** (page 494), the park offers a variety of free ranger-led activities. These programs usually begin at Giant Forest, Grant Grove, and the Foothills. A current listing of programs can be found in the park's free newspaper or on bulletin boards located at each visitor center. In Sequoia you'll find **Foothills Visitor Center** (559.565.3135), **Giant Forest Museum** (559.565.4480), **Beetle Rock Family Nature Center** (559.565.4480), **Lodgepole Visitor Center** (559.565.4436), and **Mineral King Ranger Station** (559.565.3768). In Kings Canyon you'll find **Kings Canyon Visitor Center** (559.565.4307) and **Cedar Grove Visitor Center** (559.565.3793). Hours are seasonal so please call to check when they're open.

Pets: Pets are allowed in the park, but must be kept on a leash no more than six feet in length at all times. They are not permitted on park trails or in the backcountry. Pets may not enter public buildings (except service animals), but are allowed along roadways, in parking areas, and in front-country campgrounds.

Accessibility: Accessible restrooms are available at each campground and visitor center, as well as Giant Forest Museum. General Sherman Tree and Big Trees Trails are accessible to individuals in wheelchairs. Beetle Rock, Crescent Meadows, Tharp's Log, Grant Tree, and Roaring River Falls Trails are all paved, but they may require assistance to navigate due to a fairly steep grade.

Weather: Temperature and weather conditions change drastically depending on your elevation, which ranges from 1,500 to 14,494 feet within the park. A visitor might enter at Three Rivers (1,700 feet) wearing shorts and a t-shirt, while a hiker climbing to the summit of Mount Whitney (14,494 feet) is covered from head to toe in winter apparel. That's an extreme scenario; most areas are pleasant. The middle elevations (~4,0000–7,000 feet) feature comfortable summer temperatures with average highs in the 70s°F. Weather is rarely excessively hot, with the hottest days only sneaking into the lower 90s°F. Overnight temperatures can fall below freezing, but the average low in summer is in the low 50s°F. Expect the temperature to be 10–15°F warmer in the foothills than it is in the middle elevations.

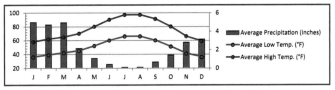

Vacation Planner

Sequoia and Kings Canyon National Parks have a lot to offer. Together, they're easily one of the best **backpacking** (page 494) destinations in the United States. Backpackers will want to head to **Mineral King** (Sequoia) or **Roads End** (Kings Canyon). A more comfortable backpacking adventure leads to **High Sierra Camp** (page 494). This excursion lets you be wined and dined with three full meals made by an executive chef. If that doesn't sound good enough, you'll also have the luxury of sleeping in a tent cabin. Backpacking is popular in the High Sierra, but it's not what most visitors have in mind when making a trip here. Park **lodging** and **camping** facilities are listed on page 492. Facilities can fill up in summer. Avoid paying the premium for convenience and location within the park by staying in Visalia, CA or other gateway communities. Nearby dining, grocery stores, lodging, festivals, and attractions are listed on pages 519–521.

Provided below is a sample three-day itinerary beginning in Sequoia and ending in Kings Canyon. Stop at a **visitor center** when it's convenient. Browse the exhibits, watch a short introductory film, and squeeze a few **ranger programs** into the schedule below. **Mineral King** is great (and highly recommended), but the long and winding road is in relatively poor condition. Traveling to Mineral King requires at least a full day, but overnight is better. It has been omitted from the following itinerary because it's somewhat off the beaten path. If touring **Crystal Cave** (page 493) is on your list of things to do, remember that tickets must be purchased in advance at Lodgepole or Foothills Visitor Center (the earlier you go, the better). If you have a vehicle longer than 22 feet (trailers are included in length) and plan on entering Sequoia National Park via CA-198 you may have to turn around at Hospital Rock (6.1 miles in). You will not be able to drive to Big Trees (General Sherman/Giant Trees), Crystal Cave, Moro Rock, Lodgepole/Wuksachi Lodge directly from the entrance. You will have to exit the park and re-enter at Kings Canyon National Park via CA-180. This restriction is expected to last through May 2012.

 Enter Sequoia's **Ash Mountain Entrance** via CA-198/Generals Highway. Moro Rock will appear to the north as you climb to around 6,000 feet in elevation. Take Crescent Meadows Road to **Moro Rock**. It's a great place to get an outstanding view of the Sierra Nevada and valley below. Hopefully smog will not impede your views of this canyon carved by the Middle Fork of the Kaweah River. If you'd like to leave the driving to the park, during summer you can pick up a **free shuttle** at Moro Rock. Hop aboard and stop at **Giant Forest Museum** and **General Sherman Tree**. Otherwise, make the same stops in your car and don't forget to drive through **Tunnel Log** (great spot for a photo), which is a short hike/drive northeast of Moro Rock.

 Today you'll make your way over to **Grant Grove Village** and Kings Canyon. If you'd like to do a little more hiking, **Little Baldy, Big Baldy and Redwood Canyon Trails** (page 486) are excellent choices located between Lodgepole Visitor Center and Grant Village. At Grant Village turn right at the visitor center and continue to Panoramic Point, where you'll find a short hike to some of the best views near the roadway. Return to Grant Village to have a look at the Nation's Christmas Tree, **General Grant**. Where you spend your second night depends on when you're traveling and how much time you have. It's another 30 miles from Grant Village to Cedar Grove where additional overnight accommodations are found.

 Saving the best for last, spend your final day hiking into the High Sierra from Kings Canyon's **Roads End Permit Station**. **Copper Creek, Mist Falls, Bubbs Creek Trails** (page 495) are all exceptional hikes. The only thing better than hiking one of these for a day is hiking them for 2, 3, 4, or more days.

If you choose to begin your vacation at Kings Canyon, ending it by hiking at **Mineral King (Sequoia)** provides a similar conclusion.

Half Dome at sunset

PO Box 577
Yosemite National Park, CA 95389
Phone: (209) 372-0200
Website: www.nps.gov/yose

Established: October 1, 1890
June 30, 1864 (State Park)
Size: 761,268 Acres
Annual Visitors: 3.9 Million
Peak Season: Summer
Hiking Trails: 800+ Miles

Activities: Hiking, Backpacking,
Camping, Rock Climbing, Rafting,
Horseback Riding, and Biking

13 Drive-In Campgrounds*
Fee: $10–20/night
Backcountry Camping: Permitted
with a Backcountry Use Permit
Lodging: $94–600/night

Park Hours: All day, every day,
except Hetch Hetchy (Day-Use)
Entrance Fee: $20 • Vehicle
$10 • Individual (foot, bike, etc.)

*Reservations available. Call (877)
444-6777 or click www.recreation.gov

Yosemite - California

"I have seen persons of emotional temperament stand with tearful eyes, spellbound and dumb with awe, as they got their first view of the Valley from Inspiration Point, overwhelmed in the sudden presence of the unspeakable, stupendous grandeur." – Galen Clark

Times have changed, but the scenery remains the same. The first sight of the valley still possesses the power to leave guests weak in the knees and with a tear in their eye. These very sites were the catalyst fueling the conservation movement. The smooth granite peaks inspired a man, by his own admission an "unknown nobody," to become one of America's great naturalist writers, thinkers, speakers, and the unofficial "father of the National Parks." Giant sequoias encouraged one of the country's greatest presidents to protect similar exhaustible resources and landscapes. Beautiful vistas motivated a photographer to capture their essence, their "unspeakable, stupendous grandeur," allowing the world to experience the spellbinding awe felt when a visitor first views the valley from Inspiration Point or Tunnel View.

The first non-Native visitors to this majestic valley didn't come for respite or rejuvenation. In 1851, the **Mariposa Battalion** was called to the Sierra Nevada to settle a skirmish between Native Americans and local '49ers hoping to dispossess their land. These soldiers found the Natives, whom they believed to be the Yosemite Tribe, in a valley about one mile wide and eight miles long. Upon arrival, the battalion didn't stop to stare in bewilderment or give thanks to a greater power capable of creating such a spectacle, instead they prepared to burn it down, thus starving the Natives. Eventually the feud was settled and it was learned that the natives were known as Ahwahneechee; Yosemite was actually their name for the Mariposa Battalion.

"If no man ever feels his utter insignificance at any time, it is when looking upon such a scene of appalling grandeur." – James Mason Hutchings

James Mason Hutchings and **Galen Clark** shared similar sentiments when it came to Yosemite Valley. In 1855, Hutchings was led into the valley by Natives. He quickly became enamored with the scenery and wasted no time moving in. In his opinion, the region had "value" as a tourist attraction, so he immediately began promoting it as such. From 1855–1864, the valley was visited by just 653 tourists. Insufficient infrastructure resulted in trips from San Francisco to Yosemite Valley that took 4–5 days (on foot, horseback, and carriage).

Galen Clark's wife died young, so he too moved to California seeking his fortune. In 1853, Clark contracted a severe lung infection. Doctors gave him six months to live. "I went to the mountains to take my chances of dying or growing better, which I thought were about even (Galen Clark, 1856)." Shortly after his arrival he discovered **Mariposa Grove**, and from that point on much of his time was spent writing friends and Congress requesting passage of legislation to protect the area. He gained the support of John Conness, a Senator from California. In 1864, in the midst of the Civil War, **President Abraham Lincoln** signed a bill preserving Yosemite Valley and Mariposa Grove under state control. Clark happily became guardian of the Yosemite Grant, including the grove of trees that inspired him. As guardian he was expected to protect the park from overeager tourists, maintain roads and bridges, and deal with residents and businesses residing here. All this needed to be done on a meager $500 annual budget.

One business in the valley was Hutchings House Hotel. **James Mason Hutchings** became Galen Clark's biggest pest. He refused to abide by the $1/year government lease. Essentially squatting on public land, he expanded his operations and built a sawmill.

Hutchings hired a wandering shepherd by the name of **John Muir** to run his sawmill. Born in Scotland, raised in Wisconsin, Muir skedaddled to Canada to avoid the Civil War and returned to work as an industrial engineer in Indiana. The sharp mind that had allowed memorization

Theodore Roosevelt and John Muir at Glacier Point

Did you know?

▶ On June 10, 1864, Abraham Lincoln signed a bill preserving Yosemite Valley and a grove of sequoias, two sites, thousands of miles away, that he had never seen.

▶ Yosemite Valley's development was designed by Frederick Law Olmsted, the famous designer of New York City's Central Park.

▶ In 1869, a wandering Scottish shepherd, originally raised in Wisconsin, began work at a sawmill in Yosemite Valley. The "unknown nobody" was a 31-year old John Muir.

▶ It took the first tourists 4–5 days to reach Yosemite Valley by carriage, horse, and foot from San Francisco.

▶ Yosemite Falls (2,425-feet) is the tallest waterfall in North America. It is fed mostly by snowmelt, with peak flow usually occurring in late May. It is often dry by August, but begins to flow once more when winter snow arrives in the surrounding mountains.

▶ El Capitán is the largest granite monolith in the world.

▶ Bridalveil Falls, originally named "Pohono," was renamed by James Hutchings for tourism.

When to Go

Yosemite is open all day, every day, with the exception of Hetch Hetchy Entrance Station (open during daylight hours). Yosemite Valley and Wawona are accessible by car year-round. Tioga, Glacier Point, and Mariposa Grove Roads close for the winter (usually beginning in November) and do not reopen until late May. Glacier Point/Badger Pass Road to Badger Pass Ski Area is plowed from mid-December through early April. In winter, tire chains are often required to drive park roads. You must carry chains with you and know how to use them.

Spring is the best time of year to see waterfalls. Most wildflowers bloom in June. In fall, crowds thin and leaves of the few stands of maple, oak, and dogwood trees begin to change.

Overcrowding is a significant problem, especially at Yosemite Valley in summer. Park roads, shuttles, and popular trails become extremely congested during this time. You will want to reserve accommodations well in advance or arrive early to obtain a first-come, first-served campsite.

Transportation & Airports

Amtrak (800.872.7245, www.amtrak.com) provides a combination of train and bus service directly to Yosemite Valley. Greyhound (800.231.2222, www.greyhound.com) provides bus service to Merced, where you can board a Yosemite Area Regional Transportation System (YARTS) (877.989.2787, www.yarts.com) bus to Yosemite Valley. YARTS also provides service from communities along CA-140 between Merced and Yosemite (Mariposa, Midpines, and El Portal). Service is available east of Yosemite via CA-120 from Lee Vining, June Lake, and Mammoth Lakes during the summer.

Fresno–Yosemite International (FAT), Merced (MCE), and Modesto City–County (MOD) Airports are all within a 2.5-hour drive of Yosemite Valley. San Francisco International (SFO), Oakland International, San José International (SJC), Sacramento International (SMF), and Reno/Tahoe International (RNO) Airports are within 5 driving hours of Yosemite Valley.

of the Bible's New Testament and most of the Old Testament by age 11 was on display in an industrial environment. His inventiveness and intellect helped improve many machines and processes, making life easier for the laborers at a plant manufacturing carriage parts. When a work accident nearly left him blind, Muir chose to be true to himself. He had always wanted to study plants and explore the wilderness. He set out on a 1,000 mile walk from Indiana to Florida, where he planned to board a ship to South America. Unfortunately, he contracted malaria before he could set sail across the Caribbean. While recuperating in Florida, he read about Yosemite and the Sierra Nevada. Nursed back to health, Muir booked passage to California instead. He arrived in 1868. After a brief stint as a shepherd, Muir moved into Yosemite Valley to run Hutchings' sawmill, where he built a cabin near the base of Yosemite Falls for $3, what he considered to be "the handsomest building in the valley."

As **Muir** was settling into his new life, **Hutchings** was being evicted. In 1875 **Galen Clark** allowed him to store his furniture in a vacant building. Hutchings moved in more than his furniture, he set up his entire operation: Wells Fargo Office, telegraph, post office, everything. Once again, he was running a hotel. This was the final straw. Hutchings, banished from Yosemite, moved to San Francisco where he started a tourist agency and wrote two best-selling books including *In the Heart of the Sierras*.

Meanwhile, **Muir** had become a bit of a Yosemite celebrity. All of the park's guests wanted exposure to his brand of enthusiasm and passion for the ecology and geology of the High Sierra. In 1871, **Ralph Waldo Emerson**, the author whose work Muir had read many a night from the light of a campfire, arrived at Yosemite. After just one day in Muir's company, Emerson offered Muir a teaching position at Harvard. Even though he had spent much of the past three years unemployed, Muir declined the offer to remain in what he called "the grandest of all the special temples of Nature I was ever permitted to enter…the sanctum sanctorum of the Sierra."

By 1889, Yosemite Valley was officially a tourist trap. A cliff-side hotel was constructed at Glacier Point. Raging fires were hurled over the cliff's edge to create a waterfall of fire. Tunnels were carved into trees. Muir had seen too much, so he set out to make Yosemite a national park. Witnessing how the establishment of Yellowstone National Park increased passenger traffic for Northern Pacific Railroad, the Southern Pacific placed their support behind the endeavor.

In 1890, Sequoia, General Grant, and Yosemite became National Parks.

James Mason Hutchings, now 82, wanted to make one last trip into Yosemite Valley. His wish was granted, but a tragic horse carriage accident resulted in Hutching's death. In what can be seen as a peculiar twist of fate in a seemingly tragic accident, the funeral service was held in the Big Tree Room, formally known as Hutchings House: the old hotel he was evicted from and the one place he loved more than any other.

In 1903, **John Muir and President Theodore Roosevelt** camped beneath the stars at Glacier Point. President Roosevelt stated "it was like lying in a great solemn cathedral, far vaster and more beautiful than any built by the hands of man." It wouldn't be long until the hands of man wanted to dramatically change Yosemite. San Francisco required water to support its ballooning population. Dam proposals were focused on a tract of land within park boundaries known as **Hetch Hetchy Valley**. Muir found Hetch Hetchy even more appealing than the more popular Yosemite Valley. He passionately opposed the dam proposal and for years legislation was held up in a political quagmire. In 1913, **Woodrow Wilson** finally signed a bill approving the dam. One year later, an exhausted Muir died at the age of 76. John Muir arrived in Yosemite, "the sanctum sanctorum of the Sierra," as an unknown nobody. He left as president and founder of the **Sierra Club**, renowned writer and naturalist, and catalyst in the creation of Yosemite, Sequoia, Mount Rainier, and Grand Canyon National Parks. He is the father of the National Parks.

In 1916, a shy 14-year old boy, sick and in bed, decided to read James Mason Hutchings' *In the Heart of the Sierras*. Intrigued, he convinced his parents to vacation at Yosemite. What he saw left an indelible mark. Years later, the young man worked as caretaker at the Sierra Club's LeConte Memorial Lodge in Yosemite Valley where he spent time as a photographer for Sierra Club outings and classical pianist for lodge guests, wowing visitors with striking imagery and wistful music. This man is **Ansel Adams**, one of the greatest landscape photographers of the American West, in particular Yosemite. A visit to Yosemite can become a life-changing experience. Its unspeakable grandeur is so overwhelming you may find yourself inspired like James Mason Hutchings, Galen Clark, John Muir, President Roosevelt, and Ansel Adams were before you.

A curious chipmunk in the high country © Jeffrey Pang

Free Shuttle Service

The park operates a small fleet of free and fully-accessible shuttle buses. Not only do they decrease traffic congestion and pollution, they can decrease visitor frustration by taking the steering wheel out of your hands. Park shuttles are best utilized in Yosemite Valley.

Valley Shuttle Route operates all year, looping around Upper Pines Campground, Curry Village, Ahwahnee, Yosemite Village, and Yosemite Lodge. **Express and El Capitán Shuttles** only operate in summer. The short **Express Route** is direct transit between the large visitor parking area at the northeast end of the valley and Yosemite Village. **El Capitán Shuttle** completes a one-way loop between El Capitán Bridge and Valley Visitor Center. Each of these shuttles runs daily every 10–20 minutes depending on the time of day. Valley Shuttle operates from 7am–10pm and El Capitán and Express Shuttles operate from 9am–6pm.

There's also a **free shuttle service between Wawona and Mariposa Grove** during summer. And another ferries visitors around the **Greater Tuolumne Meadows** area in summer. Neither of these routes connect to Yosemite Valley. However, there is free shuttle service between **Wawona Hotel and Yosemite Lodge** in summer. This route departs Wawona each day at 8:30am and returns from Yosemite Lodge at 3:30pm. Plan accordingly if you intend on utilizing these shuttles.

Directions

Yosemite National Park is located in east-central California's Sierra Nevada. There are a total of five park entrances. Hetch Hetchy Entrance, leading to O'Shaughnessy Dam and Hetch Hetchy Backpackers Camp, is only open during daylight hours. It does not connect to Yosemite Valley and is far less crowded. Big Oak Flat and Arch Rock Entrance enter the park from the west. South Entrance enters from the south via Oakhurst, CA. On the eastern side you'll find Tioga Pass Entrance Station. Due to high elevation (9,945 feet) the entrance and Tioga Road usually close from November until April (depending on the weather).

To Hetch Hetchy: From CA-120, on the park's western side, turn left onto Evergreen Road just before you reach Big Oak Flat Entrance Station. Continue on Evergreen Road for about 7 miles and then turn right at Hetch Hetchy Road, which leads to the reservoir and camp.

To Big Oak Flat Entrance: From San Francisco/Oakland take I-580 E and continue onto I-205 E. Merge onto I-5 N. After less than a mile on I-5 take Exit 461 to CA-120. Follow CA-120 to Big Oak Flat Entrance.

To Arch Rock Entrance: From CA-99, take CA-140 E/Yosemite Pkwy at Merced, which leads into the park.

To South Entrance: From Fresno, take CA-41 N through Oakhurst into the park.

To Tioga Pass Entrance: From US-395/US-6 take US-395 north from Bishop. After about 64 miles turn left onto CA-120/Tioga Road. It is 12 miles to the entrance.

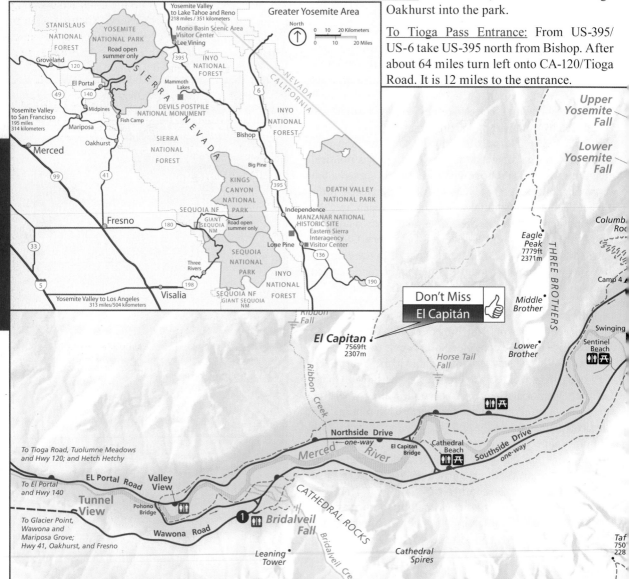

Hetch Hetchy Road enters from the west and dead ends at **O'Shaughnessy Dam**, roughly tracing the Tuolumne River. Hetch Hetchy is a particularly good location to avoid crowds, and lower elevation makes it ideal for late winter/early spring visits when the high country is cold and possibly covered in snow.

Big Oak Flat Road enters from the west via CA-120. After the entrance station you immediately pass **Hodgdon Meadow Campground** and then **Tuolumne Grove**. Gas is available at its intersection with **Tioga Road**. Beyond this point you follow the Merced River, pass through two tunnels, and enter **Yosemite Valley**. A little farther south, **El Portal Road** continues along the Merced River into the park, where it eventually merges with **Big Oak Flat Road** just before entering Yosemite Valley.

Wawona Road enters from the south. Just past the entrance is a short spur road to **Mariposa Grove**. Further south is Wawona and an information station (summer only). Campgrounds, dining, gas, and trail rides are also available near Wawona. **Wawona Road** eventually reaches an intersection with **Glacier Point Road**. Glacier Point Road (beyond Badger Pass Ski Area) closes in winter. For the rest of the year it provides access to some of the best views of **Half Dome** at its terminus: **Glacier Point**. Wawona Road continues north to **Tunnel View**, one of the most photographed vistas in the world, and finally into **Yosemite Valley**.

Tioga Road is the only route that crosses the Sierra Nevada within the park. It's a stunning drive that allows hikers and sightseers to reach the park's less congested, but no less spectacular hiking trails and camping areas (including several **High Sierra Camps**). Gas is available at **Tuolumne Meadows**. Dining is available at Tuolumne Meadows and White Wolf. Five designated campgrounds are available along the way.

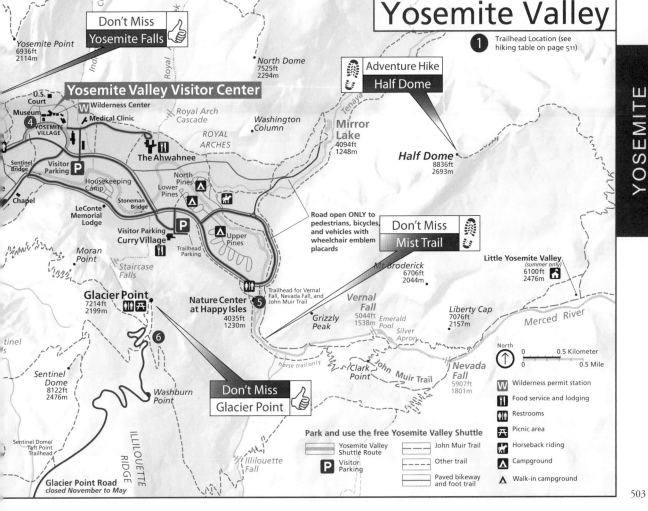

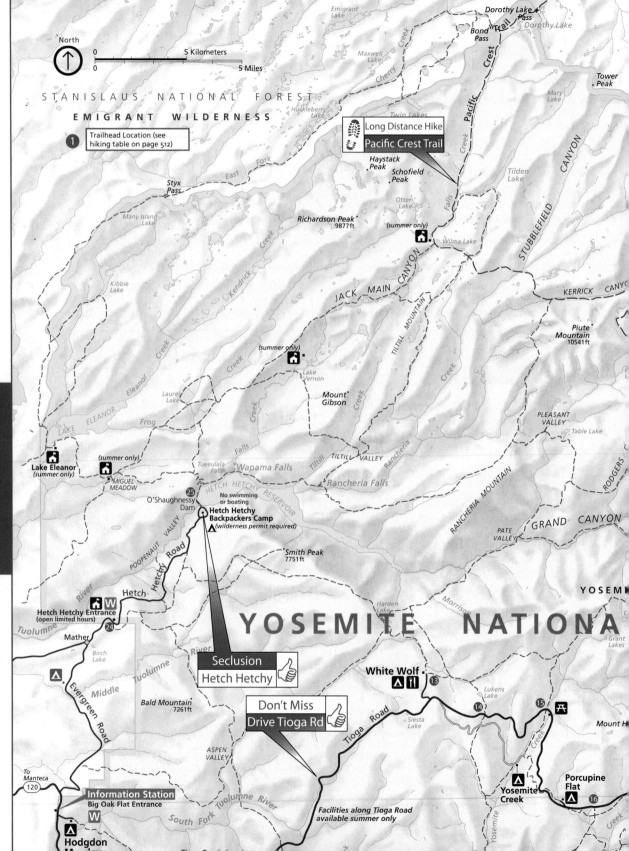

North

0   5 Kilometers
0   5 Miles

STANISLAUS NATIONAL FOREST

EMIGRANT WILDERNESS

1 Trailhead Location (see hiking table on page 512)

Emigrant Lake

Dorothy Lake Pass

Bond Pass

Dorothy Lake

Maxwell Lake

Tower Peak

Huckleberry Lake

Mary Lake

Long Distance Hike
Pacific Crest Trail

Twin Lakes

Haystack Peak

Schofield Peak

Tilden Lake

Richardson Peak 9877ft

Otter Lake

(summer only)

Wilma Lake

STUBBLEFIELD CANYON

KERRICK CANYON

East Fork

Styx Pass

Many Island Lake

Kibbie Lake

JACK MAIN CANYON

TILTILL MOUNTAIN

Piute Mountain 10541ft

(summer only)

Lake Vernon

Mount Gibson

PLEASANT VALLEY

Table Lake

Laurel Lake

Lake Eleanor (summer only)

(summer only)

MIGUEL MEADOW

Tueeulala Falls

Wapama Falls

TILTILL VALLEY

Rancheria Falls

RANCHERIA MOUNTAIN

RODGERS

GRAND CANYON

O'Shaughnessy Dam

No swimming or boating

HETCH HETCHY RESERVOIR

PATE VALLEY

Hetch Hetchy Backpackers Camp (wilderness permit required)

Smith Peak 7751ft

POOPENAUT VALLEY

Hetchy Road

Harden Lake

Morrison

YOSEM

Hetch Hetchy Entrance (open limited hours)

Mather

24

Birch Lake

Tuolumne River

Middle

Bald Mountain 7261ft

Evergreen Road

Seclusion
Hetch Hetchy

White Wolf

13

Lukens Lake

14

15

Grant Lakes

Mount H

Don't Miss
Drive Tioga Rd

Tioga Road

Siesta Lake

ASPEN VALLEY

To Manteca
120

Information Station
Big Oak Flat Entrance

South Fork Tuolumne River

Facilities along Tioga Road available summer only

Yosemite Creek

Porcupine Flat

16

Hodgdon

YOSEMITE   YOSEMITE NATIONA

504

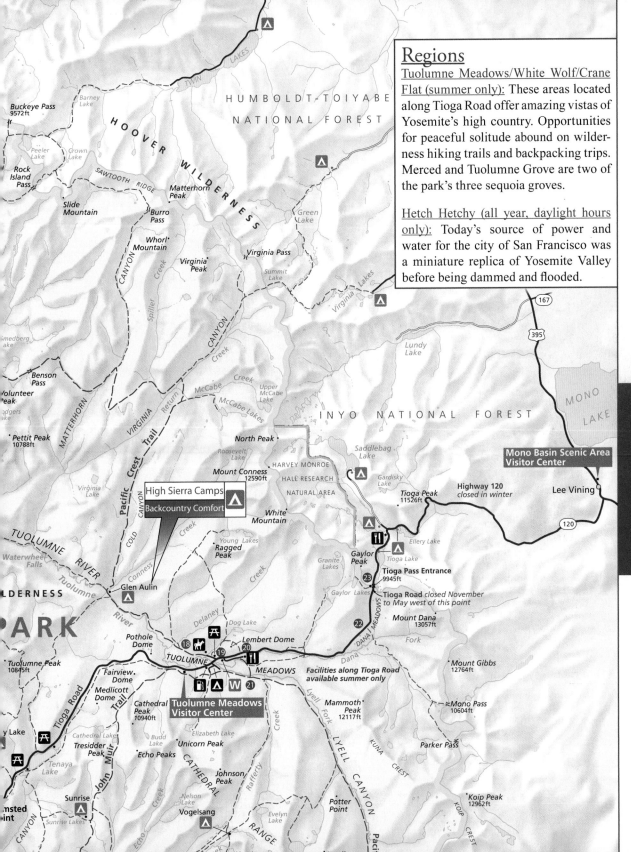

Regions

Tuolumne Meadows/White Wolf/Crane Flat (summer only): These areas located along Tioga Road offer amazing vistas of Yosemite's high country. Opportunities for peaceful solitude abound on wilderness hiking trails and backpacking trips. Merced and Tuolumne Grove are two of the park's three sequoia groves.

Hetch Hetchy (all year, daylight hours only): Today's source of power and water for the city of San Francisco was a miniature replica of Yosemite Valley before being dammed and flooded.

HUMBOLDT-TOIYABE
NATIONAL FOREST

HOOVER WILDERNESS

Buckeye Pass
9572ft

Barney Lake

Peeler Lake

Crown Lake

Rock Island Pass

SAWTOOTH RIDGE

Slide Mountain

Matterhorn Peak

Burro Pass

Whorl Mountain

Virginia Peak

Virginia Pass

Summit Lake

Green Lake

Virginia Lakes

167

395

Lundy Lake

MONO LAKE

Benson Pass

Volunteer Peak

Pettit Peak
10788ft

Rodgers Peak

MATTERHORN CANYON

VIRGINIA CANYON

Return Creek

McCabe Creek

Upper McCabe Lake

McCabe Lakes

INYO NATIONAL FOREST

smedberg Lake

Virginia Lake

Pacific Crest Trail

North Peak

Roosevelt Lake

Mount Conness
12590ft

HARVEY MONROE HALL RESEARCH NATURAL AREA

Saddlebag Lake

Gardisky Lake

Tioga Peak
11526ft

Highway 120
closed in winter

Lee Vining

Mono Basin Scenic Area
Visitor Center

High Sierra Camps
Backcountry Comfort

White Mountain

COLD CANYON

Conness Creek

Young Lakes

Ragged Peak

Granite Lakes

Gaylor Peak

Ellery Lake

Tioga Lake

120

TUOLUMNE RIVER

Waterwheel Falls

Tuolumne

Glen Aulin

River

Delaney Creek

Dog Lake

Gaylor Lakes

23

Tioga Pass Entrance
9945ft

Tioga Road closed November to May west of this point

Mount Dana
13057ft

Mount Gibbs
12764ft

WILDERNESS

PARK

Pothole Dome

Tuolumne Peak
10845ft

18

Lembert Dome

TUOLUMNE

19

20

MEADOWS

DANA MEADOWS

22

Dana

Fork

Facilities along Tioga Road available summer only

Mono Pass
10604ft

Parker Pass

y Lake

Tioga Road

Fairview Dome

Medlicott Dome

John Muir Trail

Cathedral Peak
10940ft

21

Tuolumne Meadows
Visitor Center

Lyell Fork

Mammoth Peak
12117ft

KUNA CREST

Cathedral Lakes

Budd Lake

Tresidder Peak

Unicorn Peak

Elizabeth Lake

Echo Peaks

CATHEDRAL

Johnson Peak

Nelson Lake

Rafferty Creek

LYELL CANYON

Koip Peak
12962ft

Tenaya Lake

Sunrise

Sunrise Lakes

Vogelsang

RANGE

Evelyn Lake

Potter Point

KOIP CREST

nsted int

CANYON

Echo

Pacific

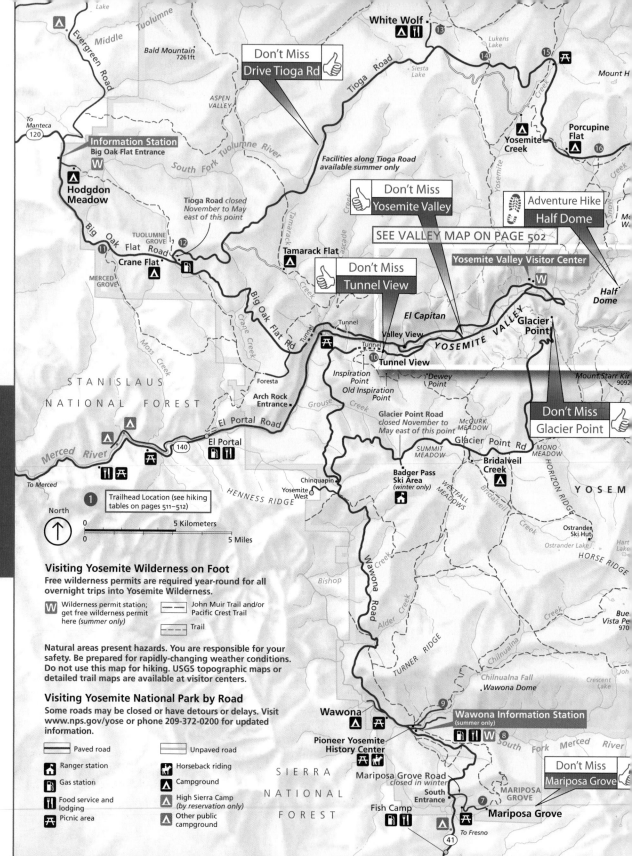

YOSEMITE

Middle Tuolumne

Evergreen Road

Bald Mountain
7261ft

ASPEN VALLEY

Don't Miss
Drive Tioga Rd 👍

Tioga Road

White Wolf 🏕️🍴 ⑬

Lukens Lake

Siesta Lake

⑭

⑮ 🏕️

Mount H

To Manteca
120

Information Station
Big Oak Flat Entrance
W

South Fork Tuolumne River

Facilities along Tioga Road available summer only

Yosemite Creek 🏕️

Porcupine Flat
🏕️ ⑯

Mount

🏕️ **Hodgdon Meadow**

Big Oak Flat Road

TUOLUMNE GROVE ⑪

Tioga Road closed November to May east of this point

⑫ 🏕️

Tamarack Flat

Don't Miss
👍 **Yosemite Valley**

Adventure Hike
👣 **Half Dome**

Half Dome

Don't Miss
👍 **Half Dome**

Crane Flat 🏕️

MERCED GROVE

Crane Creek

Cascade Creek

SEE VALLEY MAP ON PAGE 502

Yosemite Valley Visitor Center
W

Don't Miss
👍 **Tunnel View**

El Capitan

Valley View

YOSEMITE VALLEY

Glacier Point

Half Dome

S T A N I S L A U S

Tunnel

🏕️

Tunnel View ⑩

Tunnel View

Inspiration Point
Old Inspiration Point

Dewey Point

Mount Starr Kir
9092

N A T I O N A L   F O R E S T

Moss Creek

Foresta

Arch Rock Entrance

Grouse Creek

Glacier Point Road closed November to May east of this point

Don't Miss
Glacier Point 👍

🏕️

El Portal Road

140

El Portal 🏪🍴

🏕️

🍴🏕️

To Merced

Merced River

Glacier Point Rd

McGURK MEADOW

SUMMIT MEADOW

Bridalveil Creek 🏕️

MONO MEADOW

HORIZON RIDGE

Y O S E M

Chinquapin

Yosemite West

HENNESS RIDGE

Badger Pass Ski Area (winter only) 🏠

WESTFALL MEADOWS

Bridalveil Creek

Ostrander Ski Hut

Ostrander Lake

HORSE RIDGE

Hart Lake

① Trailhead Location (see hiking tables on pages 511–512)

North
↑

0 ——— 5 Kilometers
0 ——— 5 Miles

Bishop

Wawona Road

Alder Creek

Chilnualna Creek

TURNER RIDGE

Bue Vista Pe
970

Chilnualna Fall
Wawona Dome

Crescent Lake

Joh

Visiting Yosemite Wilderness on Foot

Free wilderness permits are required year-round for all overnight trips into Yosemite Wilderness.

W Wilderness permit station; get free wilderness permit here *(summer only)*

—— John Muir Trail and/or Pacific Crest Trail

- - - Trail

Natural areas present hazards. You are responsible for your safety. Be prepared for rapidly-changing weather conditions. Do not use this map for hiking. USGS topographic maps or detailed trail maps are available at visitor centers.

Visiting Yosemite National Park by Road

Some roads may be closed or have detours or delays. Visit www.nps.gov/yose or phone 209-372-0200 for updated information.

—— Paved road
═══ Unpaved road

🏠 Ranger station
🏪 Gas station
🍴 Food service and lodging
🏕️ Picnic area

🐴 Horseback riding
🏕️ Campground
🏕️ High Sierra Camp (by reservation only)
🏕️ Other public campground

Wawona 🏕️🏕️

⑨

Wawona Information Station
(summer only)

🏪🍴 W ⑧

South Fork Merced River

Pioneer Yosemite History Center
🏕️🐴

S I E R R A

N A T I O N A L

F O R E S T

Mariposa Grove Road closed in winter

South Entrance

Fish Camp 🏪🍴

🏕️ 🏕️

41

To Fresno

MARIPOSA GROVE

⑦

Don't Miss
Mariposa Grove 👍

Mariposa Grove

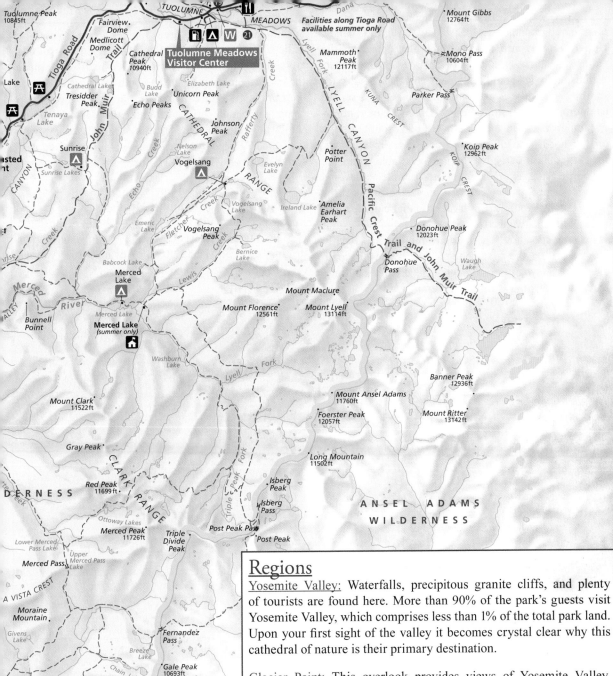

Regions

Yosemite Valley: Waterfalls, precipitous granite cliffs, and plenty of tourists are found here. More than 90% of the park's guests visit Yosemite Valley, which comprises less than 1% of the total park land. Upon your first sight of the valley it becomes crystal clear why this cathedral of nature is their primary destination.

Glacier Point: This overlook provides views of Yosemite Valley, Half Dome, and Yosemite's high country. It's a one-hour drive from Yosemite Valley or Wawona, and can also be reached by foot from the valley via Panorama or Four Mile Trail (page 511).

Wawona & Mariposa Grove: Mariposa Grove and Wawona are located near the park's South Entrance. Mariposa is the most popular sequoia grove in the park. Visitors can help reduce traffic congestion by taking the free shuttle from Wawona Store.

YOSEMITE

Four campgrounds are located in Yosemite Valley. **Upper, Lower, and North Pines** are located at the valley's eastern edge. All three require advance reservations and you should book sites early, especially for summer. **Camp 4** is the only first-come, first-served campground in Yosemite Valley. This walk-in, tent-only campground is located southwest of Yosemite Lodge on the north side of the Merced River. In summer, long lines form early for the next available campsite. If your heart is set on camping in Yosemite Valley, it's a good idea to make a reservation at one of the three "Pines" campgrounds. Reservations can be made up to six months in advance by calling (877) 444-6777 or at www.recreation.gov. The summer months are usually booked within the first couple of days they become available. **Showers** (fee) are available at **Curry Village** and **Housekeeping Camp** in Yosemite Valley.

Several camping options are available outside of Yosemite Valley. **Wawona and Bridalveil Creek Campgrounds** are south of the valley. Wawona is a really nice place for visitors entering from the south/Oakhurst to spend their first night. You can explore Mariposa Grove, set up camp, and get an early start on the drive into Yosemite Valley the following day. **Wawona** requires reservations (877.444.6777, www.recreation.gov) during peak season. **Bridalveil Creek** is first-come, first-served.

Seven seasonal campgrounds are available north of Yosemite Valley. **Tuolumne Meadows** is the largest in the park and it's the last designated campground (1.5 hours from Yosemite Valley) you'll encounter driving east on Tioga Road. Advance reservations (877.444.6777, www.recreation.gov) are available for half its sites.

Yosemite Camping

	Area	Open	Fee	Sites	Location/Notes
Upper Pines*	YV	All Year	$20	238	Near Curry Village • F, RR (mid-March–Nov)
Lower Pines* - 👍	YV	early April–October	$20	60	Near Curry Village • F, RR
North Pines*	YV	mid-April–mid-Oct	$20	81	Near Curry Village • F, RR
Camp 4	YV	All Year	$5/person	35	Walk-in tent-only campground • F, NRV, FCFS
Wawona*	SYV	All Year	$20	93	Horse sites available • F, RR (late June–late Sept)
Bridalveil Creek	SYV	July–TBD	$14	110	Located off Glacier Point Road • F, FCFS
Hodgdon Meadow*	NYV	All Year	$20	105	Off Big Oak Flat Road • F, RR (mid-April–mid-Oct)
Crane Flat*	NYV	July–mid-October	$20	166	On Big Oak Flat Road • F, RR (50%), FCFS (50%)
Tamarack Flat - 👍	NYV	July–mid-October	$10	52	Near Tamarack Creek off Tioga Road • P, NRV, FCFS
White Wolf - 👍	NYV	July–mid-September	$14	74	Near White Wolf Lodge off Tioga Road • F, FCFS
Yosemite Creek	NYV	July–mid-September	$10	75	On unpaved road off Tioga Road • P, FCFS
Porcupine Flat	NYV	July–mid-October	$10	52	Located just off Tioga Road • P, FCFS
Tuolumne Meadows*	NYV	July–late September	$20	304	Located just off Tioga Road • F, RR (50%)

Areas: YV = Yosemite Valley, SYV = South of Yosemite Valley
NYV = North of Yosemite Valley

F = Flush Toilets, P = Pit Toilets, NRV = No RV Sites
FCFS = 1st-Come, 1st-Served, RR = Reservations Req'd

*Reservations can be made up to six months in advance by calling (877) 444-6777 or clicking www.recreation.gov
Shower and laundry facilities are available year-round in Yosemite Valley • Dump stations are available at Yosemite Valley (all year), Wawona (summer only), and Tuolumne Meadows (summer only) • Firewood collection is not permitted

Backcountry	Permitted with a wilderness permit. Daily quotas are enforced due to trail popularity. 60% of each trailhead's permits are available via reservation. The remaining 40% of permits are available on a first-come, first-served basis beginning one day before your intended departure. For additional information on wilderness permits and how to obtain them visit www.nps.gov/yose/planyourvisit/wildpermits.htm
Group Camping*	Group campsites are available at Wawona Campground (all year), and at the following campgrounds (summer only): Hodgdon Meadow, Bridalveil Creek, and Tuolumne Meadows. Reservations are required.

If you hope to reserve a room at any one of Yosemite's seven lodges during the busy summer season, book your room early. Otherwise, plan on visiting during the offseason when rooms are easier to come by and are often sold at discounted rates (a welcome relief, because lodging is pricey).

In **Yosemite Valley**, visitors have four choices for lodging: The Ahwahnee, Yosemite Lodge, Curry Village, and Housekeeping Camp. **The Ahwahnee is often regarded as the finest lodge in America.** But comfort, beauty, and premium location have their price: $400+/night for a standard room and suites can exceed a nightly rate of $1,000. **Yosemite Lodge** provides more reasonable accommodations at $180–220/night. It offers large family rooms with one king bed, two single beds, and a sofa sleeper (queen). **Curry Village and Housekeeping Camp** are the "budget" options, with both units checking in at about $100/night. Curry Village has small rustic cabins, motel-style rooms, and canvas tent cabins. Tent cabins are affordable and somewhat of a novelty, but the canvas is thin, providing little to no protection from noisy neighbors. Housekeeping Camp is simple living. Each of the 266 units has a bunk bed, a double bed, table, chairs, mirror, lights, and outlets. All that separates the living space from a covered patio is a curtained wall. Bear-proof food storage containers are provided.

Located near the park's southern boundary is **Wawona Hotel**. Wah-wo-nah means "Big Tree" and that's what you'll find near this Victorian-style hotel. Rooms come with or without a private bath. Golf, swimming, tennis, fishing, stable rides, and ranger-led walks are available nearby. The best perk is that these rooms are much easier to reserve than those found in the valley. Alternatively, **White Wolf and Tuolumne Meadows are great High Sierra lodging options located off Tioga Road.** Canvas tent cabins, sprinkled about the Sierra Nevada, are open from mid-June until mid-September. Illuminated by candlelight, they do not have electricity. Shared showers and restrooms are available nearby. White Wolf also offers a few wooden cabins with propane heating, private baths, and limited electricity.

Finally, there are **five High Sierra Camps** in the backcountry. These comfortable camping accommodations give hikers the opportunity to enjoy the peace and quiet of the backcountry with the comforts of a bed, hot shower, and hearty home-style meals. Not having to carry a tent, sleeping bag, and food is an added bonus. A night's stay at any one of the High Sierra Camps includes a filling dinner and breakfast. Camps are located at: Merced Lake, Vogelsang, Glen Aulin, May Lake, and Sunrise Camp (see the map on pages 505–507). **May Lake is the easiest to reach**, just 1.2 miles from May Lake Parking Area (1.75 miles north of Tioga Road). Located 14 miles from Tuolumne Meadows, **Merced Lake is the most remote** camp. All of the camps are most easily accessed from hiking trails beginning along Tioga Road.

All of the park's lodges, hotels, and High Sierra Camps are operated by **Delaware North Companies**. For reservations and additional information call (801) 559-4884 or click www.yosemitepark.com.

Yosemite Lodging

	Open	Rates	Location/Notes
The Ahwahnee - 👍	All Year	$476–600	Yosemite Valley • Elegant accommodations, perfect location
Yosemite Lodge	All Year	$180–220	Yosemite Valley • Close to Yosemite Falls, family favorite
Curry Village	All Year	$118–250	Yosemite Valley • Cabins, motel rooms, and tents
Housekeeping Camp	All Year	$99	Yosemite Valley • 266 units that accommodate six guests each
Wawona Village	All Year	$155–230	Wawona • Victorian accommodations, some shared baths
Tuolumne Meadows	mid-June–mid-Sept	$107	Tioga Road • A collection of private candlelit tent cabins
White Wolf Lodge	mid-June–mid-Sept	$95	Tioga Road • Smaller complex of 24 canvas tent cabins
High Sierra Camps - 👍	mid-June–mid-Sept	$151	Tioga Road • Comfortable camping includes lodging and meals

All in-park lodging facilities are operated by Delaware North Companies, call (801) 559-4884 or click www.yosemitepark.com

Hikers in front of Half Dome © Curt & Kari Marquardt

Half Dome

Half Dome is one of Yosemite's iconic landscapes. So renowned that its image resides on the California state quarter alongside images of John Muir and the California condor. This famous granite dome is situated at the east end of **Yosemite Valley** where it rises some 4,800 feet above the valley floor. Up until the 1870s, Half Dome was declared "perfectly inaccessible." Seeking to access the inaccessible, George Anderson constructed his own route to its summit by drilling and placing iron eyebolts into the smooth granite surface, completing the first successful ascent in 1875.

Today, the dome is accessed by more than a dozen rock climbing routes and a hiking path along its rounded east face. Hikers are aided by metal cables strung between steel polls. Without these cables the final 700-foot ascent would be impossible. They are removed during winter and are usually installed before Memorial Day weekend (May) and taken down around Columbus Day (October). The hike to Half Dome (page 511) should be taken seriously. Three separate routes reach its eastern face. They range from 14–16.3 miles (roundtrip). The trek gains nearly 4,800 feet in elevation. **All hikers expecting to scale Half Dome require a permit.** Permits, good for up to four hikers, cost $1.50 (to cover the processing fee) and are only available by calling (877) 444-6777 or clicking www.recreation.gov. Enjoy the trip; this is one of the best hikes in the world.

Hiking

More than 800 miles of hiking trails crisscross Yosemite National Park. Well-trod paths lead through lush meadows, meander along rivers to thunderous waterfalls, and climb to the crown of bald granite domes. Hiking in Yosemite is highly dependent on when you arrive. **Spring** is fantastic. Snowpack in the High Sierra is melting and rivers begin to swell and pour over granite cliffs, some plummeting with such force that you can feel the earth shaking beneath your feet. However, it's not all fun and waterfalls. Mosquitoes can be a bit of a pain and High Sierra trails are often inaccessible without proper equipment. Each year is different, but you can expect mosquitoes to be worst during the three weeks after the snow melts. Muddy trails and treacherous creek crossings are also likely.

Summer is the busiest season. Trails are crowded, but most are open by this time. Still, just because Tioga Road is open doesn't mean that you should assume all its trails are accessible. Depending on the amount of winter snowfall some in the highest elevations may not be passable until well into July. Check the park website, or ask a ranger about conditions if you think you might encounter a snow-packed trail. Try hiking in September if you'd like pleasant temperatures, smaller crowds, and access to the entire network of trails. However, it's likely that Yosemite Falls will be bone dry. Hiking in **winter** without snowshoes or skis is limited to trails in Hetch Hetchy and Yosemite Valleys.

Yosemite Valley hikes are easily accessed via the **free shuttle** (page 501). **Mist Trail** has earned the title of most popular trail in the park. The scenery is magnificent as you hike to the top of **Vernal Falls** (continue to **Nevada Falls**, or ambitious hikers with a permit follow the trail all the way to the top of **Half Dome**). This trek begins at **Happy Isles** (Shuttle Stop #16) at the far eastern end of Yosemite Valley. Depending on water volume **Yosemite and Bridalveil Falls** are worth a quick look. **Wawona** has a decent selection of trails that begin near the hotel and Mariposa Grove. The one that should not be skipped here is **Grizzly Giant Trail**. Most trailheads in **Tuolumne Meadows/Crane Flats/White Wolf** areas are well-marked and accessed via Tioga Road. **Hetch Hetchy** has some nice paths and it's an excellent place to shake the crowds of Yosemite Valley. Favorites are marked with a thumbs up in the tables on the following pages.

The straight and steep path to the top of Half Dome

Yosemite Hiking Trails

	Trail Name	Trailhead (# on map)	Length	Notes (Roundtrip distances unless noted otherwise)
	Bridalveil Fall - 👍	Bridalveil Fall Parking Area (1)	0.5 mile	Easy paved trail to the base of Bridalveil Falls
Yosemite Valley	Mirror Lake/Meadow	Camp 4/Shuttle Stop #7 (2)	5.0 miles	2 miles to the lake and back, 5 miles around the lake (loop around lake was closed at publication)
	Valley Floor Loop		13.0 miles	Follows original trails and wagon roads around the valley
	Upper Yosemite		7.2 miles	Strenuous hike to the top of North America's tallest waterfall
	Four Mile		9.6 miles	Strenuous hike from Sentinel Rock to Glacier Point
	Lower Yosemite Falls - 👍	Shuttle Stop #6 (3)	1.0 mile	Paved trail with spectacular views of Yosemite Falls
	Cook's Meadow Loop	Shuttle Stop #5 or #9 (4)	1.0 mile	Easy loop with views of Half Dome and Glacier Point
	Vernal & Nevada Falls - 👍	Happy Isles/Shuttle Stop #16 (5)	5.0 miles	0.7 mile to Vernal, 2.5 miles to Nevada • Popular
	Mist Trail - 👍		3.0 miles	Follows Merced River to Vernal Falls • 600 granite steps
	Half Dome - 👍	Mist Trail (5)	14.0 miles	All trails begin at Happy Isles/Shuttle Stop #16 • Mist Trail is shorter, but steeper and much more popular • John Muir Trail is longer, but easier
		John Muir Trail (5)	16.3 miles	
		Mist up, John Muir down	15.2 miles	
	Panorama	Panorama Trailhead/Happy Isles (5, 6)	8.5 miles	One-way, strenuous trail that joins John Muir and Mist Trails
Wawona	Grizzly Giant - 👍	Mariposa Grove Parking Area (7)	1.6 miles	The biggest giant of them all
	Wawona Point		6.0 miles	Beyond Grizzly Giant and California Tunnel Tree
	Outer Loop		6.9 miles	Moderate trail that loops around Mariposa Grove
	Wawona Meadow	Wawona Hotel/Store Parking Area (8)	3.5 miles	Loop trail that follows a fire road around the meadow
	Swinging Bridge		4.8 miles	An easy loop trail along an old dirt road
	Wawona to Mariposa Grove		6.0 miles	One-way trail follows horse ride route
	Alder Creek	Chilnualna Falls Road (9)	12.0 miles	Strenuous trail through open pine forest
	Inspiration Point	Wawona Tunnel Overlook (10)	2.6 miles	Classic photo-op of Yosemite Valley

El Capitán

Yosemite Hiking Trails

	Trail Name	Trailhead (# on map)	Length	Notes (Roundtrip distances)
Crane Flat & White Wolf	Merced Grove	Merced Grove Parking Area (11)	3.0 miles	Smallest and most secluded of the three sequoia groves
	Tuolumne Grove	Tuolumne Grove/Crane Flat (12)	2.5 miles	Nature Trail through grove of Giant Sequoias
	Harden Lake	White Wolf Lodge (13)	5.8 miles	Moderate hike to boulder-lined lake • Can loop (8.4 mile) to Grand Canyon of the Tuolumne and Lukens Lake
	Lukens Lake	Lukens Lake Trailhead (14)	1.6 miles	Easy trail to a small lake (5.4 miles from White Wolf Lodge)
	North Dome	Porcupine Creek Trailhead (15)	10.4 miles	Fantastic views of Half Dome from atop North Dome
	Ten Lakes - 👍	Ten Lakes Trailhead (16)	12.6 miles	Strenuous with creek crossings to beautiful lakes
	May Lake	May Lake Parking Area (17)	2.4 miles	Short easy hike with views of Half Dome along the way
Tuolumne Meadows	Glen Aulin - 👍	Soda Springs (18)	11.0 miles	Follows Tuolumne River to Glen Aulin ("Beautiful Valley")
	Tuolumne Meadows	Lembert Dome/Dog Lake Parking Areas (19, 20)	1.5 miles	Easy hike to Soda Springs and Parsons Lodge
	Lyell Canyon		8.0 miles	Easy hike through canyon with several creek crossings
	Dog Lake/Lembert Dome - 👍		2.8 miles	Begins with a steep grade, but flattens (4 miles to see both)
	Elizabeth Lake	Tuolumne Meadows Camp (21)	4.8 miles	Moderate climb to a glacially carved lake
	Vogelsang Area	John Muir Trailhead (21)	13.8 miles	Follows John Muir Tr to Vogelsang Camp and Lake
	Cathedral Lakes - 👍	Cathedral Lakes Trailhead (21)	7.0 miles	One of the most popular trails in the area
	Mono Pass - 👍	Mono Pass Trailhead (22)	8.0 miles	Views of Mono Lake from the pass
	Gaylor Lakes - 👍	Tioga Pass Entrance (23)	2.0 miles	Wonderful high country views for a short hike
Hetch Hetchy	Lookout Point - 👍	Hetch Hetchy Entrance (24)	2.0 miles	Moderate hike to viewpoint overlooking Hetch Hetchy
	Smith Peak		13.5 miles	Through forest and meadow to peak for great views
	Poopenaut Valley		3.0 miles	Strenuous trail drops down to the Tuolumne River
	Wapama Falls	O'Shaughnessy Dam (25)	5.0 miles	Leads to the base of Wapama Falls, wildflowers in spring
	Rancheria Falls		13.4 miles	Continues past Wapama Falls to Rancheria Falls

Guided Hikes

Rugged terrain, intimidating wildlife, and a plethora of trails often leave visitors bewildered when it comes to selecting their hiking adventure. To make things simple **Delaware North Companies** provides an array of guided and unguided day and multi-day backpack trips. Day hikes cost between $10 and $40 and visit many of the most spectacular and popular locations. They are only offered between Memorial Day and Labor Day. Trips can be reserved by calling (209) 372-4386. You can also hire a private hiking guide. Rates depend on group size and duration, but the best bargain is a full-day (8 hours) hike for $171 (for 1 person) or $96/person for two hikers. Guided backpacking trips venture deep into the high country between June and September. They typically cost $100 per person per day. The rate includes permits, meals, tents, stove, and water filters. Call (209) 372-8344 for reservations and information.

Horseback Riding

Delaware North Companies (DNC) runs three stables within the park. **Yosemite Valley Stable** (209.372.8348) is the only outfitter that leads guided trips in Yosemite Valley. **Tuolumne** (209.372.8427) **and Wawona** (209.375.6502) **Stables** offer guided rides through the high country and big tree forests, respectively. Rates are the same for all three locations. Two-hour rides ($64/rider), half-day rides ($85), and full-day rides ($128) are available. All riders must be at least 7 years old and 44 inches tall. The maximum rider weight is 225 lbs. Wawona and Tuolumne Stables are seasonal. Yosemite Valley Stables is open all year. Reservations are recommended.

Custom pack and saddle trips are also offered. Multi-day journeys cost $274/day for guide/packer, and $132/day for the animal (mule or horse). There is a minimum of 3 animals per trip. DNC simply provides the transportation and/or guide. You are responsible for wilderness permits, food, water, and any other supplies. An additional $185 transportation fee is added if your itinerary begins at a trailhead not serviced by one of the stables. If you'd like DNC to plan your trip for you, they offer 4 and 6-day saddle trips. The 6-day trip costs $1,601/Adult and the 4-day trip costs $1,018/Adult. Rates include lodging and meals at High Sierra Camps, mule, and guide. Reservations are required. Call (801) 559-4909 or click www.yosemitepark.com for more information.

Backpacking/Permits

Nearly 95% of Yosemite National Park is designated wilderness, and more than 750 miles of trails traverse this undeveloped region. To plan a Yosemite backpacking trip you should start with a good topographical map. If it's your first time you will want to hike in one of the popular backcountry areas like **Ten Lakes** (White Wolf) or **Cathedral Rocks** (Tuolumne Meadows).

Once you've selected your route, the next obstacle is getting a **permit**. Wilderness permits are required for all overnight trips. Day-hikers do not require one. You can apply for a permit up to 24 weeks in advance and they cost $5 per confirmed reservation plus $5 per person. Of each trailhead's daily quota, 60% can be reserved ahead of time while the remaining 40% is available first-come, first-served no earlier than 11am the day before your hike begins. **Permits can be obtained at** Yosemite Valley Wilderness Center, Tuolumne Meadows Wilderness Center, Big Oak Flat Information Station, Wawona Visitor Center at Hill's Studio, Hetch Hetchy Entrance Station, and Badger Pass Ranger Station. From November through April permits are available on a self-registration basis (when the permit stations are closed). Information regarding wilderness permits and the reservation process can be found at:

www.nps.gov/yose/planyourvisit/wildpermits.htm

Rafting

Rafts are available for rent at **Curry Village Recreation Center** (Yosemite Valley). Each raft holds four adults and costs $28.50/Adult and $20.50/Child (12 and under). Trips begin at Curry Village and end 3 miles later at Sentinel Beach Picnic Area. Rafting season changes from year-to-year, but the Merced River is usually runnable from late May until the end of July. For additional information call the Curry Village Recreation Center at (209) 372-4386. Visitors are welcome to bring their own floatables. All river users should help protect the resource by entering and exiting the river on sandy beaches. Beyond Yosemite Valley, rafting is also permitted on the South Fork of the Merced River near Wawona.

Summiting Lost Arrow Spire in front of Yosemite Falls

Bus Tours

Delaware North Companies operates **guided bus tours**. They're a great, hassle-free way to explore the most popular areas of the park and a professional guide joins you every step of the way. **Valley Floor Tour** ($25/Adult, $13/Child) is a 2-hour drive through Yosemite Valley. It's offered all year, and on days leading up to the full moon a moonlight edition is available. **Glacier Point Tour** ($41/$23) is a 4-hour trip that takes visitors from the valley floor to Glacier Point. One-way tickets ($25/$15) are also available if you'd like to hike one-way via Panorama or Four Mile Trail (page 511). **Big Tree Tram Tour** ($25.50/$18) is a 1.25-hour exploration of Mariposa's Grove of Giant Sequoias. **Yosemite Grand Tour** ($82/$46) combines Valley Floor, Glacier Point, and Big Trees Tours. Box lunches are available for an additional $10/person.

Visit www.yosemitepark.com for more detailed information. Reservations can be made by calling (209) 372-4386 and are recommended (especially in summer). Same day reservations are available (space permitting).

Rock Climbing

Thousands of visitors come to Yosemite National Park for one thing and one thing only: **rock climbing**. This is the mecca for climbers all around the world. Advanced climbers enjoy the challenges of multi-day ascents of **Half Dome** or 3,000-foot **El Capitán** (El Cap), but there's a little something here for people of all abilities. Experienced climbers new to Yosemite should either head to **Camp 4** to mingle among Yosemite's rock climbing communities or pick up a more climbing-centric guide book from one of the park's bookstores. Beginners can find plenty of good places for scrambling. Much of the high country is covered with granite boulders and **Bridalveil Falls Trail** (page 511) has a nice collection of boulders to enjoy.

You can also join one of **Yosemite Mountaineering School's** (209.372.8344, www.yosemitepark.com) climbing lessons or guided climbs. Lessons are held as long as there are at least three participants. Their basic "**Go Climb a Rock**" course costs $148/person. Crack Climbing and Anchoring classes are for novices at a cost of $154/person. They offer advanced courses as well. Guided climbs range from 6-hours ($169+/person) to a 6-day El Cap climb ($4,466/person).

Biking

Cyclists are free to enjoy the 12-mile **Yosemite Valley Loop**. It's a fantastic alternative to driving congested park roads or riding packed shuttle buses. Cyclists are permitted on all park roads, but it's not recommended unless you plan on pedalling during the off-season or early morning. Bikes are prohibited on all hiking trails. Bike rental is available at **Yosemite Lodge and Curry Village Bike Stands**. They are typically open from early spring to late fall. Rental rates are $10/hour and $28/day. Strollers and trailers are available for an additional fee.

Winter Activities

Snow rarely sticks in Yosemite Valley, but the higher elevations are often buried in the fluffy white stuff. Winter's cold and snow-capped mountains add a little more diversity to park activities. **Cross-country skiing**, **snowshoeing**, **skiing**, **tubing**, and **ice-skating** are popular. Marked trails are available at Badger Pass, along Glacier Point Road, in Mariposa Grove of Giant Sequoias, and around the Crane Flat area. **Free ranger-guided snowshoe walks** are also offered. The park's newspaper, *Yosemite Guide*, features an up-to-date schedule of all ranger guided activities. Visitors receive a free copy upon arrival or it's available for download at the park website.

Badger Pass (209.372.8430) is the oldest **downhill skiing** area in California. It has 5 lifts, and runs range from easy to difficult with an 800-ft elevation drop. Lift tickets cost $42/adult and $37/child for a full day on a weekend or holiday. Weekday rates are $35/adult and $30/child for a full day. Badger Pass also offers **snow-tubing** ($15/person, per 2-hour session). Rentals, lessons, and multi-day cross-country tour packages are also available. Badger Pass is usually open from mid-December through March (conditions permitting). A daily snow report can be found at: www.yosemitepark.com/DailySnowReport.aspx.

Visitors have been **ice skating** in Yosemite Valley since the 1930s. **The Ice Rink at Curry Village** (209.372.8319) is nestled below the foot of majestic Half Dome and Glacier Point, right in the heart of Yosemite Valley. It is open from mid-November until early March. A 2.5-hour session costs $8/Adult, $6/Child, and $3 for skate rentals. Visit www.yosemitepark.com for more information on the park's winter activities.

The Natural Firefall (Horsetail Falls)

Photography

Many first introductions to Yosemite are made through the lens of **Ansel Adams**. Adams became interested in Yosemite at the age of 14 after reading James Mason Hutchings' *In the Heart of the Sierras*. Yosemite served as the catalyst that inspired Adams to become the preeminent landscape photographer of the American West. Yosemite Valley's **Ansel Adams Gallery** helps preserve the life, the work, and the vision of one of America's greatest photographers and conservationists.

Today thousands of photographers, professionals and amateurs alike, attempt to recapture many of the images made famous by Adams. **Tunnel View** (Wawona Road) and **Inspiration Point** (2.6 miles roundtrip from Wawona Tunnel Overlook) provide two of the most photographed vistas in the world. Then there's the February phenomenon known as the "**Natural Firefall.**" There are no guarantees that you'll see a "firefall," but with the right amount of water and light Horsetail Falls ignites as if it's caught on fire. Those interested should stop at El Capitán Picnic Area on Northside Drive in February.

Classic Yosemite Valley © Bala Sivakumar
(www.wanderingmonkphoto.com)

Vernal Falls

Flora & Fauna

More than 400 mammals reside here. The most commonly seen large mammals are **mule deer** and **black bear**. There are no grizzly bears here. **Marmots** are often seen in the rocky high country, even on top of Half Dome. Vegetation changes dramatically from Yosemite Valley to the high country. Dense forests and meadows cover the valleys and foothills, while the alpine zone is treeless and rocky.

For Kids

With so many kid-friendly activities, easy hiking trails, and awe-inspiring vistas, Yosemite is an exceptional family getaway. Children can also become **Junior Rangers** (ages 7–13) or **Little Cubs** (ages 3–6) while visiting. In order to join these exclusive clubs you must first purchase a Junior Ranger ($3.50) or Little Cub ($3) Booklet. They are available at Yosemite Valley Visitor Center, Nature Center at Happy Isles (May–Sept), Wawona and Tuolumne Meadows Visitor Centers (June–Sept), and Big Oak Flat Information Station (May–Sept). Complete the booklet, pick-up trash, and attend a guided program to become a member and receive an award.

Ranger Programs

Park rangers lead interpretive programs in every region of the park, from Mariposa Grove to Tuolumne Meadows (when accessible). There is, quite literally, something for everyone. Photo walks, art workshops, twilight strolls, junior ranger programs, watercolor classes, and much more are at your disposal. And the best feature is that almost all of these National Park Service programs are free. If you're looking to get the most out of a visit to Yosemite, you'll want to visit the park's website prior to your arrival and download the most recent edition of the park's newspaper, *Yosemite Guide*. After a little preparatory work, you can plan your arrival, lodging, and dining around a collection of ranger programs. Many park programs are designed with families in mind.

Information Centers

Valley Visitor Center (9am–7:30pm): Located just west of the main post office (shuttle stops #5 and #9), this visitor center is the main hub for information, maps, and books. Exhibits focusing on the park's geology and a 30 minute orientation film are available for viewing.

Yosemite Museum (9am–5pm): Located next to Valley Visitor Center, the museum displays exhibits from Yosemite's past as well as a digital slide show of historic visitors and hotels.

Ansel Adams Gallery (9am–6pm, 209.372.4413, www.anseladams.com): Located next to Valley Visitor Center, the gallery displays work of Ansel Adams as well as that of other photographers and artists.

Valley Wilderness Center (7:30am–5pm): Adjacent to the post office, the wilderness center is here to help plan backcountry trips, obtain wilderness permits and rent bear canisters.

Yosemite Art & Education Center (Yosemite Valley, 9am–4:30pm): Located south of the Village Store, the Arts & Education Center provides a selection of original art and art supplies, and offers regularly scheduled art workshops.

Nature Center at Happy Isles (Yosemite Valley, 9:30–5pm): Located near shuttle stop #16, the nature center offers natural history exhibits and a bookstore specifically designed for children and their families.

Wawona Visitor Center at Hill's Studio (8:30am–5pm, 209.375.9531): Wilderness permits, bear canister rentals, trail information, and books and maps are available here.

Pioneer Yosemite History Center (Wawona): A time period open-air museum that brings guests back to the days of log cabins and horse-drawn carriages. Open all day, every day.

Tuolumne Meadows Visitor Center (9am–6pm, 209.372.0263): Trail information, books, and maps are available.

Tuolumne Meadows Wilderness Center (9am–6pm): Maps, wilderness permits, bear canister rental, and guide books are available.

Basics

Yosemite Conservancy: **The Yosemite Conservancy** (800.469.7275, www.yosemiteconservancy.org) is a non-profit organization that helps protect the park and educate its visitors via geology, photography, and painting workshops (among many other ecologically conscious programs). Course schedules and rates are available at the conservancy's website.

Pets: Pets must be kept on a leash no more than six feet in length at all times. They are only allowed in developed areas, on fully paved trails and roads (unless marked otherwise), and in campgrounds (except Tamarack Flat, Porcupine Flat, and walk-in campgrounds).

Accessibility: Yosemite Valley Visitor Center, Ansel Adams Gallery, Nature Center at Happy Isles, Tuolumne Meadows Visitor Center, and Mariposa Grove Museum are all fully accessible to wheelchair users. Several trails are fully accessible with assistance, including the eastern part of Yosemite Falls Loop, most of Valley Loop Trail, and Glacier Point Vista. Many ranger guided programs are fully accessible. All park shuttle buses are accessible to wheelchair users. The Ahwahnee, Yosemite Lodge, and Curry Village have rooms or cabins accessible to individuals in wheelchairs. Accessible campsites are available at Lower Pines, Upper Pines, and North Pines Campgrounds. All food-service facilities are accessible except The Loft, Tuolumne Meadows Lodge, and Wawona Hotel's dining room.

Weather: Yosemite Valley is hot and dry in summer. The average high temperature for July and August is 90°F. Overnight lows dip into the mid-50s°F. Summer averages less than 2 inches of precipitation each year, but thunderstorms are a serious concern. You do not want to be caught on a massive, exposed slab of granite like Half Dome when an afternoon thunderstorm rolls in. During the winter, average highs are around 50°F in Yosemite Valley with lows slightly below freezing. Most precipitation falls between November and March. In the higher elevations snow can fall any month of the year. Regardless of when you hike, be sure to pack warm clothes and dress in layers if you're heading into the High Sierra.

On top of Half Dome © Curt and Kari Marquardt

Best of Yosemite

Attraction: Half Dome
> Runner-up: Glacier Point
> 2nd Runner-up: Yosemite Falls
> 3rd Runner-up: El Capitán
> 4th Runner-up: Tunnel View/Inspiration Pt.
> 5th Runner-up: Hetch Hetchy

Activity: Yosemite Mountaineering School
> Runner-up: High Sierra Camps
> 2nd Runner-up: Horseback Riding

Family Hike: Mist Trail
> Runner-up: Taft Point
> 2nd Runner-up: Gaylor Lakes
> 3rd Runner-up: Bridalveil Falls
> 4th Runner-up: Sentinel Dome

Adventure Hike: Half Dome
> Runner-up: Cathedral Lakes
> 2nd Runner-up: Glen Aulin
> 3rd Runner-up: Mono Pass
> 4th Runner-up: Ten Lakes

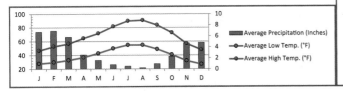

Most of Yosemite's main attractions (El Capitán, Half Dome, Yosemite Falls, Vernal Falls) are in a relatively small area (**Yosemite Valley**), but it's a disservice to yourself and your family to race into the valley, check-off these sites, and zoom away to the next destination. A park ranger said it best when a visitor hastily asked the question: "I've only got an hour to see Yosemite. If you had an hour to see Yosemite, what would you do?" The ranger pointed to a rock and replied bluntly, "Well, I'd go right over there, I'd sit down and I'd cry." Don't make this mistake. The only tears shed should be those of joy as you view the granite magnificence of Yosemite. Allow at least three days to explore the main park regions (excluding **Hetch Hetchy**, approximately a 2-hour drive from Yosemite Valley). All of the guided activities: **horseback riding** (page 513), **bus tours** (page 514), **rock climbing** (page 514), and **ranger programs** (page 516) are highly recommended and should be done based on your specific interests as time and budget allow. Plan your accommodations in advance. All **camping and lodging facilities** are listed on pages 508–509. Nearby dining, grocery stores, lodging, festivals, and attractions are listed on pages 519–521. The itinerary provided below begins at the South Entrance, but it can easily be adjusted for visitors entering from the east or west. Remember that Tioga Road is only open during summer.

 Arrive early at the park's **South Entrance**. Begin by driving to **Mariposa Grove**. At the very least hike the 1.6 mile trail to see **Grizzly Giant** (page 511). Roundtrip from the South Entrance to Mariposa Grove Parking Area and back to **Wawona Road** is about 10 miles. Allow at least one hour to explore the Giant Sequoia Grove. Return to **Wawona Road** and head north. Take a right onto **Glacier Point Road**. Drive to its conclusion at **Glacier Point**. Allow at least 2.5 hours to reach Glacier Point (from the South Entrance). From here, look across the valley and the Merced River to **Half Dome** (page 510) or stare 3,000 feet below you into the bustling and immensely beautiful valley. Hikers should walk to **Sentinel Rock** or **Taft Point** (2.2 miles roundtrip each). Both hikes begin at Sentinel Dome/Taft Point Trailhead (6 miles east of Bridalveil Campground turnoff). Heading left takes you to **Taft Point** and **The Fissures**. Right leads to **Sentinel Dome**. Both lead to more extraordinary views of the valley. Each hike takes approximately an hour. Depending on your overnight

accommodations you may have to drive into **Yosemite Valley**, which is another 1.5 hours (driving) from Glacier Point. If the room or campsite where you plan on laying your head is still up in the air, start hunting one down immediately. If not, **Glacier Point** provides one of the best vantage points to watch the sunset. Sit atop the granite promontory and browse through the park's newspaper, *Yosemite Guide,* to see if you can catch an **evening program**.

 Wake up early to beat the Yosemite Valley crowds. Begin your day by hiking **Mist (page 510) and Lower Yosemite Falls (page 511) Trails**. These are the two busiest in the park. If you don't get there early, it will feel more like a weekend at the mall than a day spent in a natural wonderland. Daytime is the right time to join an **interpretive program** (page 516). If none interest you, think about taking an extended hike. You could stretch your trek to **Mist Falls** all the way to the top of **Half Dome** (strenuous, permit required, page 510). Hiking to **Upper Yosemite Falls** (page 511) is another great way to avoid the commotion. Before leaving the valley, be sure to view the orientation video at **Valley Visitor Center** and browse its modern exhibits.

 Once again, wake-up early to avoid joining the parade of cars that tend to circle the valley's floor like a pack of sharks. You can expect the 17-mile drive from the east end of Yosemite Valley to Tioga Road to take about 30 minutes. If you skipped Mariposa Grove in a hurry to reach the valley catch a glimpse of a few Giant Sequoias at **Merced Grove**. The trailhead is located on **Big Oak Flat Road**. It's a 1.5-mile (one-way) moderate hike down to the grove. **Tuolumne Grove** is another option. Its trailhead is located on **Tioga Road**, where a steep 1-mile hike leads to it. These forests are smaller, but the sequoias remain impressive, and it's at least a 1-hour drive from **Tuolumne Grove to Tioga Pass Entrance Station** on the park's eastern boundary. Break up the drive by stopping at **Olmsted Point** for exceptional views. Spend the rest of the day exploring the trails of the High Sierra. **Gaylor Lakes Trail** (page 512), beginning at **Tioga Pass Entrance Station**, is a perfect choice. If you'd like a longer journey, hike to **Mono Pass** (page 512). Its trailhead is a short distance west of **Tioga Pass Entrance Station**.

Dining

Death Valley Area

Ensenada Grill • (775) 553-2600
600 US-95; Beatty, NV 89003

Happy Burro Chili & Beer • (775) 553-9099
100 W Main St; Beatty, NV 89003

Gisela's Café & Deli • (775) 727-4224
1266 E Calvada Blvd, # 1; Pahrump, NV 89048

Tommasino's • (775) 751-8221
250 Humahuaca; Pahrump, NV 89048
www.tommasinosnv.com • Entrée: $13–28

Sequoia/Kings Canyon Area

We Three Bakery • (559) 561-4761
43368 Sierra Dr; Three Rivers, CA 93271

Anne Lang's Emporium • (559) 561-4937
41651 CA-198; Three Rivers, CA 93271

Sierra Subs & Salad • (559) 561-4810
41717 Sierra Dr; Three Rivers, CA 93271
www.sierrasubsandsalads.com • Sandwiches: $5+

Orange Blossom Junction • (559) 592-6726
20898 Avenue 296; Exeter, CA 93221
www.orangeblossomjunction.com • Entrée: $16–25

VIP Pizza • (559) 592-5170
180 E Pine St; Exeter, CA 93221

Seasons Restaurant • (760) 876-8927
206 S Main St; Lone Pine, CA 93545

Alabama Hills Café • (760) 876-4675
111 W Post; Lone Pine, CA 93545

Yosemite Area

Cocina Michoacana • (209) 962-6651
18730 Main St; Groveland, CA 95321

Buckmeadows • (209) 962-5181
7647 CA-120; Groveland, CA 95321
www.buckmeadowsrestaurant.com • Entrée: $14–24

Dori's Tea Cottage • (209) 962-5300
18744 Main St; Groveland, CA 95321
www.doristeacottage.com • Luncheon: $9–16

Narrow Gauge • (559) 683-6446
48571 CA-41; Fish Camp, CA 93623
www.narrowgaugeinn.com • Entrée: $13–38

Savoury's Restaurant • (209) 966-7677
5027 CA-140; Mariposa, CA 95338
www.savouryrestaurant.com • Entrée: $16–30

Happy Burger Diner • (209) 966-2719
5120 CA-140; Mariposa, CA 95338
www.happyburgerdiner.com • Burgers: $7+

Pizza + • (209) 966-8488
5004 CA-140; Mariposa, CA 95338

Dazzle's • (209) 742-2035
5103 CA-140; Mariposa, CA 95338

The Butterfly Café • (209) 742-4114
5027c CA-140; Mariposa, CA 95338
www.thebutterflycafe.com • Sandwiches: $8+

Sugar Pine Café • (209) 742-7793
5038 CA-140; Mariposa, CA 95338
www.sugarpinecafe.com • Sandwiches: $7+

Hitching Post • (559) 683-7917
42592 CA-49; Ahwahnee, CA 93601

Erna's Elderberry House • (559) 683-6800
48688 Victoria Ln; Oakhurst, CA 93644
www.elderberryhouse.com • Entrée: $78–125

Crab Cakes Restaurant • (559) 641-7667
40278 Stage Coach Rd; Oakhurst, CA 93644
www.crabcakesrestaurant.com • Entrée: $9–36

Woody's New Orleans West • (559) 683-4414
40291 Junction Dr; Oakhurst, CA • Entrée: $10–30

Todd's Cookhouse BBQ • (559) 642-4900
40713 CA-41; Oakhurst, CA 93644

Sugar Pine Take & Bake Pizza • (559) 642-4642
40359 CA-41; Oakhurst, CA 93644 • Pizza: $4–20

Ol' Kettle Restaurant • (559) 683-7505
40650 CA-41; Oakhurst, CA 93644
www.olkettle.com • Breakfast: $4+

Judy's Donuts • (559) 683-2095
40444 CA-41, # A; Oakhurst, CA 93644

Lakefront Restaurant • (760) 934-2442
163 Twin Lakes Rd; Mammoth Lakes, CA 93546
www.tamaracklodge.com • Entrée: $22–34

Skadi • (760) 934-3902
587 Old Mammoth Rd; Mammoth Lakes, CA 93546
www.skadirestaurant.com • Entrée: $30–48

Rafters Restaurant • (760) 934-9431
202 Old Mammoth Rd; Mammoth Lakes, CA 93546
www.therafters.com • Entrée: $13–35

Burgers Restaurant • (760) 934-6622
6118 Minaret Rd; Mammoth Lakes, CA 93546

Stellar Brew & Deli • (760) 924-3559
3280 Main St; Mammoth Lakes, CA 93546
www.cafemammothlakes.com

Giovanni's Pizzeria • (760) 934-7563
437 Old Mammoth Rd; Mammoth Lakes, CA 93546
www.giovannismammoth.com • Pizza: $8–32

The Stove • (760) 934-2821
644 Old Mammoth Rd; Mammoth Lakes, CA 93546

Schat's Bakery • (760) 934-6055
3305 Main St; Mammoth Lakes, CA 93546

Good Life Café • (760) 934-1734
126 Old Mammoth Rd; Mammoth Lakes, CA 93546
www.mammothgoodlifecafe.com • Breakfast: $5+

Whoa Nellie Deli • (760) 647-1088
22 Vista Point Rd; Lee Vining, CA 93541
www.whoanelliedeli.com

Mono Cone • (760) 647-6606
51508 US-395; Mono South, CA 93541

Tiger Bar & Café • (760) 648-7551
2620 CA-158; June Lake, CA 93529

Grocery Stores

Death Valley Area

Ruby's Store • (775) 372-1118
1578 S NV-373; Amargosa Valley, NV 89020

Pioneer Point Market • (760) 372-4804
84508 Trona Rd; Trona, CA 93562

Albertsons • (775) 751-0160
200 S NV-160; Pahrump, NV 89048

Walmart Supercenter • (775) 537-1400
300 S NV-160; Pahrump, NV 89048

Sequoia/Kings Canyon Area

Walmart • (559) 636-2302
1819 E Noble Ave; Visalia, CA 93292

Yosemite Area

Mar-Val Food Store • (209) 962-7452
19000 Main St; Groveland, CA 95321

Vons • (559) 642-4250
40044 CA-49; Oakhurst, CA 93644

Raley's Supermarket • (559) 683-8300
40041 CA-49; Oakhurst, CA 93644

Lodging

Death Valley Area

El Portal Motel • (775) 553-2912
420 Main St; Beatty, NV 89003
www.elportalmotel.com • Rates: $45/night

Phoenix Inn • (775) 553-2250
350 S 1st St; Beatty, NV 89003
www.atomic-inn.com

Amargosa Opera House/Hotel • (760) 852-4441
608 Death Valley Junction, CA 92328
www.amargosaoperahouse.com • Rates: $70–85

Longstreet Inn & Casino • (775) 372-1777
4400 S NV-373; Amargosa Valley, NV 89020
www.longstreetcasino.com • Rates: $69–79

Death Valley Inn • (775) 553-9400
651 US-95 S; Beatty, NV 89003
www.deathvalleyinnmotel.com • Rates: $63

Beatty RV Park • (775) 553-2732
Mile Marker 63 US-95 N; Beatty, NV 89003
www.beattyrvpark.com • Rates: $15–25

Sequoia/Kings Canyon Area

Dow Villa Motel • (760) 876-5521
310 S Main St; Lone Pine, CA 93545
www.dowvillamotel.com • Rates: $102–150

Whitney Portal Hostel & Store • (760) 876-0030
238 S Main; Lone Pine, CA 93545
www.whitneyportalstore.com

Boulder Creek RV Resort • (760) 876-4243
2550 S NV-395; Lone Pine, CA 93545
www.bouldercreekrvresort.com • Rates: $39

Buckeye Tree Lodge • (559) 561-5900
46000 Sierra Dr; Three Rivers, CA 93271
www.buckeyetreelodge.com • Rates: $81–156

Rio Sierra Riverhouse • (559) 561-4720
41997 Sierra Dr; Three Rivers • www.rio-sierra.com

Gateway Lodge • (559) 561-4133
45978 Sierra Dr; Three Rivers, CA 93271
www.gateway-sequoia.com • Rates: $109–325

Sequoia Motel • (559) 561-4453
43000 Sierra Dr; Three Rivers, CA 93271
www.sequoiamotel.com • Rates: $89–212

Cort Cottage B&B • (559) 561-4671
44141 Skyline Dr; Three Rivers, CA 93271
www.cortcottage.com • Rates: $165

Log House Lodge B&B • (559) 561-3017
42182 Mynatt Dr; Three Rivers, CA 93271
www.loghouselodge.com • Rates: $175–184

River Jewel Suites • (559) 799-8201
43325 C Sierra Dr; Three Rivers, CA 93271
www.theriverjewel.com • Rates: $185–225

Bellevue Guesthouse Hotel • (559) 561-6405
45317 Mineral King Rd; Three Rivers, CA 93271
www.bellevueguesthouse.com • Rates:
$80–270

Sequoia River Dance • (559) 561-4411
40534 Cherokee Oaks Dr; Three Rivers, CA 93271
www.sequoiariverdance.com • Rates: $100–145

There are 10 additional campgrounds in Sequoia
National Forest/Giant Sequoia National Monument.

Yosemite Area

Yosemites Scenic Wonders • (209) 372-4243
7421 Yosemite Pkwy; Yosemite NP, CA 95389
www.scenicwonders.com • Rates: $109+

Redwoods In Yosemite • (888) 442-7036
8038 Chilnualna Falls Rd; Yosemite NP, CA 95389
www.redwoodsinyosemite.com • Rates: $277+

Yosemite Blue Butterfly Inn • (209) 379-2100
11132 CA-140; El Portal, CA 95318
www.yosemitebluebutterflyinn.com • Rates: $185+

Evergreen Lodge • (209) 379-2606
33160 Evergreen Rd; Groveland, CA 95321
www.evergreenlodge.com • Rates: $120–1,050

Hotel Charlotte • (209) 962-6455
18736 Main St; Groveland, CA 95321
www.hotelcharlotte.com • Rates: $99–225

Blackberry Inn B&B • (209) 962-4663
7567 Hamilton Station Loop; Groveland, CA 95321
www.blackberry-inn.com • Rates: $170–225

Tenaya Lodge • (888) 514-2167
1122 CA-41; Fish Camp, CA 93623
www.tenayalodge.com • Rates: $139–294

Yosemite Big Creek Inn B&B • (559) 641-2828
1221 CA-41; Fish Camp, CA 93623
www.yosemiteinn.com • Rates: $139–259

Narrow Gauge Inn • (559) 683-6446
48571 CA-41; Fish Camp, CA 93623
www.narrowgaugeinn.com • Rates: $79–195

River Rock Inn • (209) 966-5793
4993 7th St; Mariposa, CA 95338
www.riverrockncafe.com • Rates: $79–159

Miners Inn • (209) 742-7777
5181 CA-49 N; Mariposa, CA 95338
www.yosemiteminersinn.com • Rates: $59–109

Highland House B&B • (209) 966-3737
3125 Wild Dove Ln; Mariposa, CA 95338
www.highlandhouseinn.com • Rates: $115–165

Poppy Hill B&B • (209) 742-6273
5218 Crystal Aire Dr; Mariposa, CA 95338
www.poppyhill.com • Rates: $135–150

Homestead Cottage • (559) 683-0495
41110 Road 600; Ahwahnee, CA 93601
www.homesteadcottages.com • Rates: $119–399

Sierra Mtn Lodge B&B • (559) 683-7673
45046 Fort Nip Tr; Ahwahnee, CA 93601
www.sierramountainlodge.com • Rates: $99–175

The Forks Resort • (559) 642-3737
39150 Road 222; Bass Lake, CA 93604
www.theforksresort.com • Rates: $150–280

Hounds Tooth Inn • (559) 642-6600
42071 CA-41; Oakhurst, CA 93644
www.houndstoothinn.com • Rates: $95+

Yosemite Gateway Inn • (559) 683-2378
40530 CA-41; Oakhurst, CA 93644
www.yosemitegatewayinn.com

Chateau du Sureau • (559) 683-6860
48688 Victoria Ln; Oakhurst, CA 93644
www.elderberryhouse.com • Rates: $385–585

High Sierra RV Park • (559) 683-7662
40389 CA-41; Oakhurst, CA 93644
www.highsierrarv.com • Rates: $26–47

Mammoth Mtn Inn • (800) 626-6684
1 Minaret Rd; Mammoth Lakes, CA 93546

Tamarack Lodge & Resort • (760) 934-2442
1 Twin Lakes Loop; Mammoth Lakes, CA 93546

Juniper Springs Resort • (800) 626-6684
4000 Meridian Blvd; Mammoth Lakes, CA 93546
Click www.mammothmountain.com for all 3

Cinnamon Bear Inn • (760) 934-2873
113 Center St; Mammoth Lakes, CA 93546
www.cinnamonbearinn.com • Rates: $119–195

Double Eagle Resort & Spa • (760) 648-7134
5587 CA-158; June Lake, CA 93529
www.doubleeagle.com • Rates: $229+

Fern Creek Lodge • (760) 648-7722
4628 CA-158; June Lake, CA 93529
www.ferncreeklodge.com • Rates: $70–385

June Lake Villager Motel • (760) 648-7712
2640 Boulder Dr; June Lake, CA 93529
www.junelakevillager.com • Rates: $85–295

Boulder Lodge • (760) 648-7533
2282 CA-158; June Lake, CA 93529
www.boulderlodgejunelake.com • Rates: $98–365

Reverse Creek Lodge • (760) 648-7535
4479 CA-158; June Lake, CA 93529
www.reversecreeklodge.com • Rates: $90–210

Gull Lake Lodge • (760) 648-7516
132 Bruce St; June Lake, CA 93529
www.gulllakelodge.com • Rates: $70–169

June Lake RV & Lodge • (760) 648-7967
155 Crawford; June Lake, CA 93529
www.junelakervpark.com

Many chain restaurants and hotels can be
found in Pahrump, Visalia, and Oakhurst.

Festivals

Asian American Film Festival • March
San Francisco • www.festival.asianamericanmedia.org

Harmony Sweepstakes A Capella Festival
March • S.F. • www.harmony-sweepstakes.com

Cherry Blossom Festival • April
San Francisco • www.nccbf.org

Napa ARTwalk • May
Napa • www.NapaARTwalk.org

Strawberry Music Festival • May/August
Camp Mather • www.strawberrymusic.com

High Sierra Music Festival • June
Quincy • www.highsierramusic.com

Sonoma County Showcase • July
www.sonomawinecountryweekend.com

Gilroy Garlic Festival • July
Gilroy • www.gilroygarlicfestival.com

Sierra Storytelling Festival • July
North Columbia • www.sierrastorytellingfestival.org

Festival Of Beers & Bluesapalooza
August • Mammoth Lakes, CA
www.mammothbluesbrewsfest.com

Hardly Strictly Bluegrass • September
San Francisco • www.strictlybluegrass.com

Yosemite International Jass Festival
October • Coarsegold • www.yijazz.com

Attractions

Death Valley Area

Goldwell Open Air Museum • (702) 870-9946
NV-374; Rhyolite, NV 89003
www.goldwellmuseum.org • Free

Pahrump Valley Winery • (775) 751-0333
3810 Winery Rd, # 1; Pahrump, NV 89048
www.pahrumpwinery.com • Tours: Free

Farrabee's Jeep Rentals • (760) 786-9872
CA-190, Furnace Creek • www.farabeesjeeprentals.com

Barker Ranch • Death Valley
Located near Ballarat (ghost town), Barker Ranch (burned down in 2009) is infamous as the last hide-out of Charles Manson and his "family." Accessed via Goler Canyon Rd (4WD recommended).

Sequoia/Kings Canyon Area

Kaweah Whitewater Adv. • (559) 740-8251
40443 Sierra Dr; Three Rivers, CA 93271
www.kaweah-whitewater.com • Raft: $50

Three Rivers Hist. Museum • (559) 561-2707
42268 Sierra Dr; Three Rivers, CA 93271
www.3rmuseum.org

Boyden Cavern • (866) 762-2837
74101 E Kings Canyon Rd; Grant Grove, CA 93633
www.caverntours.com • *Zip Lines & Cave Tours*

Lone Pine Film Hist. Museum • (760) 876-9909
701 S Main St; Lone Pine, CA 93545
www.lonepinefilmhistorymuseum.org • $5/Adult

Regal Cinemas • (559) 741-7294
120 S Bridge St; Visalia • www.regmovies.com

Project Survival Cat Haven • (559) 338-3216
38257 E Kings Canyon Rd; Dunlap, CA 93621
www.cathaven.com • Admission: $9/Adult

Pinnacles Nat'l Mon. • (831) 389-4486
5000 CA-146; Paicines, CA • www.nps.gov/pinn

Yosemite Area

Sugar Pine Railroad • (559) 683-7273
56001 CA-41; Fish Camp, CA 93623
www.ymsprr.com • Tickets: $14.50–48/Adult

Arta River Trips • (800) 323-2782
24000 Casa Loma Rd; Groveland, CA 95321
www.arta.org • Rafting: $122+

Yosemite Trails Pack Station • (559) 683-7611
7910 Jackson Rd; Fish Camp, CA 93623
www.yosemitetrails.com • Trail Rides: $40+

Yosemite Ziplines & Adventure Ranch
4808 CA-140; Mariposa, CA 95338
www.yosemiteziptours.com • (209) 742-4844

Devil's Postpile Nat'l Mon. • (760) 934-2289
PO Box 3999; Mammoth Lakes, CA 93546
www.nps.gov/depo • Access Shuttle: $7/Adult

June Mtn Ski Area • (760) 648-7733
3819 CA-158; June Lake, CA 93529
www.junemountain.com • Lift Ticket: $72/Adult

Mariposa Museum • (209) 966-2924
5119 Jessie St; Mariposa, CA 95338
www.mariposamuseum.org • Admission: $5/Adult

CA Mining Museum • (209) 742-7625
5005 Fairgrounds Rd; Mariposa, CA 95338

Met Cinema • (559) 683-1234
40015 CA-49, # 1; Oakhurst, CA 93644
www.metcinema.com

Sixth Street Cinema • (209) 742-6666
4994 6th St; Mariposa, CA 95338

Black Tie Ski Rentals • (866) 838-3754
12219 Business Park Dr; Truckee, CA 96161
www.blacktieskis.com

Mammoth Mtn Bike Park • (760) 934-0706
1 Minaret Rd; Mammoth Lakes, CA 93546
www.mammothmountain.com

Minaret Cinemas • (760) 934-3131
437 Old Mammoth Rd; Mammoth Lakes, CA 93546
www.mammothlakesmovies.com

San Francisco Area

Muir Woods National Monument
Mill Valley, CA 94941 • (415) 388-2596
www.nps.gov/muwo • Entrance Fee: $5/Adult

Golden Gate Nat'l Recreation Area
Fort Mason, Building 201; San Francisco, CA 94123
www.nps.gov/goga • (415) 561-4700 • Free
www.alcatrazcruises.com • Tours: $26–58

Exploratorium • (415) 561-0360
3601 Lyon St; San Francisco, CA 94123
www.exploratorium.edu • Admission: $15/Adult

Cable Car Museum • (415) 474-1887
1201 Mason St; San Francisco, CA 94108
www.cablecarmuseum.org • Free

Beach Blanket Babylon • (415) 421-4222
678 Green St; San Francisco, CA 91433
www.beachblanketbabylon.com • Tickets: $25+

Asian Art Museum • (415) 581-3500
200 Larkin St; San Francisco, CA 94102
www.asianart.org • Admission: $12/Adult

Musée Mécanique • (415) 346-2000
Pier 45 Shed A; San Francisco, CA 94133
www.museemecaniquesf.com • Free

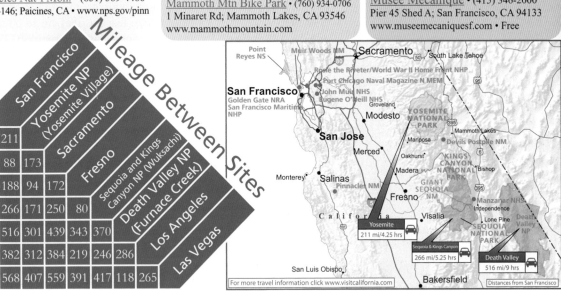

Mileage Between Sites

	San Francisco	Yosemite NP (Yosemite Village)	Sacramento	Fresno	Sequoia and Kings Canyon NP (Wuksachi)	Death Valley NP (Furnace Creek)	Los Angeles	Las Vegas
Yosemite NP (Yosemite Village)	211							
Sacramento	88	173						
Fresno	188	94	172					
Sequoia and Kings Canyon NP (Wuksachi)	266	171	250	80				
Death Valley NP (Furnace Creek)	516	301	439	343	370			
Los Angeles	382	312	384	219	246	286		
Las Vegas	568	407	559	391	417	118	265	

For more travel information click www.visitcalifornia.com

Yosemite — 211 mi/4.25 hrs

Sequoia & Kings Canyon — 266 mi/5.25 hrs

Death Valley — 516 mi/9 hrs

Distances from San Francisco

Lassen Peak looms in the distance beyond Anita Lake

PO Box 100, Mineral, CA 96063
Phone: (530) 595-4480
Website: www.nps.gov/lavo

Established: August 9, 1916
May 1907 (Nat'l Monument)
Size: 106,000 Acres
Annual Visitors: 380,000
Peak Season: Summer
Hiking Trails: 150 Miles

Activities: Hiking, Horseback
Riding, Boating, Biking, and Fishing

Campgrounds: Butte Lake*, Crags,
Juniper Lake, Manzanita Lake*,
Summit Lake (2)*, Southwest
Walk-in, and Warner Valley
Fee: $10–18/night
Backcountry Camping: Permitted
Lodging: Drakesbad Ranch
Rates: $140–176/person/night

Park Hours: All day, every day
Entrance Fee: $10 • Vehicle
$5 • Individual (foot, bike, etc.)

*Reserve at (877) 444-6777 or
www.recreation.gov

Lassen Volcanic - California

The Cascade Range stretches from Canada into northeastern California. Among these mountains is 10,457-foot Lassen Peak, the largest plug dome volcano in the world and the southernmost non-extinct volcano in the Cascade Range. **Lassen Peak** stands above its surroundings, serving as the centerpiece of Lassen Volcanic National Park. Beyond the prominent peak is a collection of deep blue alpine lakes, dense conifer forests, stinking fumaroles, belching mudpots, roiling hot springs, and boisterous streams. It's a place where features that are so obviously of this earth blend with those that are altogether otherworldly. Perhaps a greater mystery than how these landscapes were united is how today they go by relatively unnoticed.

Native Americans first took notice of the mountain and its surrounding landscapes, visiting seasonally to hunt and gather food. Lassen Peak served as a meeting site for four American Indian groups: Atsugewi, Yana, Yahi, and Maidu. Thanks were given for the food the region provided, but Natives eyed Lassen Peak with great suspicion. They knew it was filled with fire and water and believed there would come a day when it would blow apart, causing considerable damage to the region and potentially its people.

During the mid-19th century, California was flooded with **gold-seeking 49ers**. While trekking across the Cascades to fertile soils of the Sacramento Valley they used the mighty peak as a landmark to assure their course was correct. One of the guides who led hopeful prospectors on this journey was **Peter Lassen**, a Danish blacksmith who settled in northern California in the 1830s. Together with William Nobles, they blazed the first two pioneer trails. Portions of Lassen and Nobles Emigrant Trail are still visible and used today.

As the gold rush subsided, Lassen Peak and its surroundings returned to a life of anonymity. But the United States was growing and forests were being cut at an astonishing rate. No tree was sacred to the lumberjacks. Neither the coastal redwoods nor the Sierra Nevada's giant sequoias were safe from the loggers' axe and saw. If these trees were in danger, so too were the pine and fir of the southern Cascades. With its forests in peril, a conservationist president also took notice of this volcanic region. **President Theodore Roosevelt** preserved vast tracts of land for the enjoyment of the American people, including two regions in the southern Cascades: Cinder Cone National Monument and Lassen Peak National Monument. This designation spared the trees and opened the region to an era of tourism.

But few Americans took notice. In May of 1915, as if to make people aware of its presence once more, the volcano woke up with a series of **minor eruptions**. These events created a new crater, released lava and ash, and razed several homes. Incandescent blocks of lava could be seen rolling down the flanks of Lassen Peak from 20 miles away. No one was killed by the eruptions, but people began to notice its fury. Scientists took interest in the park's volcanoes. Washington also was aware these events, and in 1916, largely thanks to the volcanic activity, the two monuments were combined and expanded to create Lassen Volcanic National Park. The eruptions stopped in 1921. Once again the region was forgotten.

Perhaps some things are best left forgotten. Roads are rarely congested. Campgrounds seldom fill. If you're looking for a California getaway where volcanic past meets picturesque present, a place filled with wildlife not automobiles, a place where the mud boils and the earth steams, Lassen National Park is for you. Let this serve as your reminder that there's a national park in northern California filled with natural beauty, rich history, and most importantly, peace and quiet from the busy everyday lifestyle that tends to make a person forget a few things.

Did you know?

▶ Prior to the eruption of Mount St. Helens in 1980, Lassen Peak was the last volcanic explosion in the Cascade Range.

When to Go

Lassen Volcanic National Park is open 24 hours a day, every day of the year, but the park's main road is usually closed or restricted due to snow coverage from fall through late spring. Many facilities are also seasonal. Manzanita Lake Camper Store, Loomis Museum, and all campgrounds (except Southwest Walk-In) close for winter. Kohm Yah-mah-nee Visitor Center is open all year. Summer and fall are the best times to visit.

Transportation & Airports

Public transportation does not provide service to or around the park. The closest major airports are Sacramento International (SMF), located 172 miles south of the park's southwest entrance, and Reno/Tahoe International (RNO), 151 miles to the southeast.

Directions

There are a total of five entrances to Lassen Volcanic National Park. Southwest and Northwest, both on CA-89, are the two primary entry points. Warner Valley, Juniper Lake, and Butte Lake entrances are accessible via unpaved roads from the south, southeast, and northeast, respectively.

Southwest Entrance from Sacramento (158 miles): Take I-5 north to Exit 649 for Antelope Blvd/CA-36. Follow signs for Lassen National Park, taking CA-36 E approximately 45 miles before turning north onto CA-89 into the park.

Northwest Entrance from Oregon (150 miles): Traveling south on I-5, take Exit 736 onto CA-89 S toward McCloud/Lassen National Park. CA-89 leads directly to the Northwest Entrance.

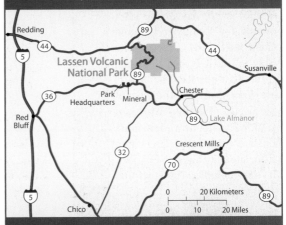

Driving

The 29-mile **Main Park Road** winds and climbs its way across the park, passing the vast majority of facilities and attractions. Only short sections of the road at Northwest and Southwest Entrances are open all year. The remainder is closed beginning in late fall (with the first significant snowfall) until late spring or early summer.

Butte Lake, Warner Valley, and Juniper Lake Roads are unpaved roads leading to remote regions. All three are open seasonally (weather dependent). Butte Lake and Warner Valley Roads are at lower elevation and therefore open earlier and remain open later than Juniper Lake Road and the Main Park Road. Current road conditions are available at the park website.

Visitor Centers

Kohm Yah-mah-nee Visitor Center (530.595.4480), located at Southwest Entrance, is your one-stop shop for park information, books, maps, and exhibits. It houses an auditorium where visitors can view a short introductory film and is open every day of the year, except for Thanksgiving and Christmas Day. From late May to mid-October it is open from 9am–6pm. The hours are 9am–5pm for the rest of the year. **Loomis Museum** (530.595.6140), near Manzanita Lake, is open daily, 9am–5pm, from late May through October. It has exhibits, videos, and publications.

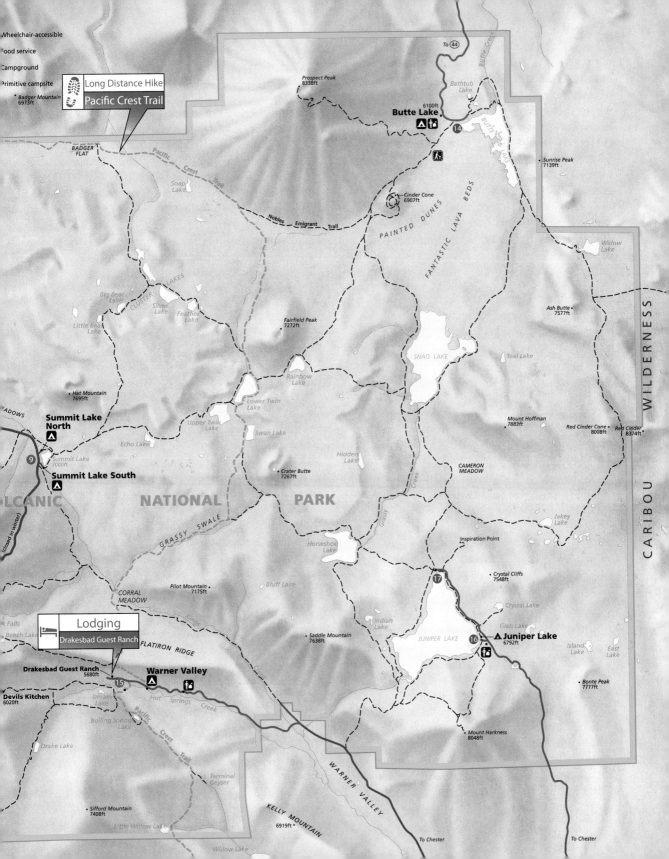

Wheelchair-accessible

Food service

Campground

Primitive campsite

• *Badger Mountain*
  6973ft

Long Distance Hike
Pacific Crest Trail

To 44

Prospect Peak
8338ft

Bathtub
Lake

6100ft
Butte Lake
14

Sunrise Peak
7139ft

BADGER
FLAT

Soap
Lake

•*Cinder Cone*
  6907ft

Widow
Lake

PAINTED DUNES

FANTASTIC LAVA BEDS

Nobles — *Emigrant* — *Trail*

Big Bear
Lake

Silver
Lake

Feather
Lake

Little Bear
Lake

Fairfield Peak
7272ft

Ash Butte •
7577ft

SNAG LAKE

Teal Lake

Rainbow
Lake

• *Hat Mountain*
  7695ft

Lower Twin
Lake

Mount Hoffman •
7883ft

Red Cinder Cone •
8008ft

Red Cinder
8374ft

Summit Lake
North

Upper Twin
Lake

Echo Lake

Swan Lake

Summit Lake
7000ft

9

Hidden
Lake

CAMERON
MEADOW

Summit Lake South

• *Crater Butte*
  7267ft

Jakey
Lake

NATIONAL   **PARK**

(closed in winter)

GRASSY SWALE

Horseshoe
Lake

Inspiration Point

17

• *Crystal Cliffs*
  7548ft

Crystal Lake

Pilot Mountain •
7175ft

Bluff Lake

CORRAL
MEADOW

Glen Lake

Lodging
Drakesbad Guest Ranch

Indian
Lake

JUNIPER LAKE

16   △ **Juniper Lake**
             6792ft

Island
Lake

East
Lake

FLATIRON RIDGE

Bench Lake

Drakesbad Guest Ranch
5680ft

Warner Valley

15

• *Saddle Mountain*
  7638ft

• *Bonte Peak*
  7777ft

Devils Kitchen
6020ft

Dream
Lake

Hot — *Springs* — *Creek*

Bolling Springs
Lake

Drake Lake

Terminal
Geyser

• *Mount Harkness*
  8048ft

To Chester   *To Chester*

• *Sifford Mountain*
  7408ft

Little Willow Lake

KELLY MOUNTAIN
6919ft •

WARNER VALLEY

Willow Lake

C A R I B O U   W I L D E R N E S S

 Camping

There are eight designated campgrounds. Along Main Park Road from Northwest to Southwest Entrance Stations are **Manzanita Lake** (179 sites, $18/night), **Crags** (45, $12), **Summit Lake North** (46, $18), **Summit Lake South** (48, $16), and **Southwest Walk-in** (20, $14). Southwest is the only year-round campground, but it is not conducive to RVs (all campsites are a short walk from Southwest Entrance Parking Area). RV sites are available at Butte Lake, Crags, Manzanita Lake, Summit Lake (North and South), and Warner Valley. **Warner Valley** (18, $14), **Juniper Lake** (18, $10), and **Butte Lake** (101, $16) **Campgrounds** are accessed via rough and remote gravel roads. Coin-operated showers and laundry and a dump station (fee) are only available near Manzanita Lake. Flush toilets are available at Butte Lake, Manzanita Lake, and Summit Lake North. Sites at Manzanita Lake, Summit Lake (North and South), and Butte Lake can be reserved up to six months in advance by calling (877) 444-6777 or clicking www.recreation.gov.

Group sites are available at **Butte Lake** (6, $50), **Lost Creek** (8, $50, near Crags), and **Juniper Lake** (2, $30). Group sites must be reserved in advance. All campgrounds (other than Southwest) open sometime between May and July and close between September and October. All open and close dates are weather dependent.

 Horseback Riding

The park does not offer guided horse rides or pack trips, but visitors are welcome to bring their own stock. Horses, llamas, burros, and mules are allowed on all designated trails with the exception of Manzanita Lake Trail, Lassen Peak Trail, and portions of Cinder Cone, Reflection Lake, and Bumpass Hell Trails, and any paths within Devil's Kitchen and Sulphur Works thermal areas. A **free wilderness permit** (see Backpacking above) must be obtained prior to trail use. Hitching posts are available at Summit Lake Corral, Butte Lake Corral, and Juniper Lake Corral. The rate is $4/animal plus camping fee.

 Backpacking

Lassen Volcanic National Park hosts **150 miles of trails** including 17 miles of the **Pacific Crest Trail**. This modest network provides ample backpacking opportunities. All overnight trips in the backcountry require a **free wilderness permit**, available in person during operating hours at Loomis Museum, Kohm Yah-mah-nee Visitor Center, and by self-registration at Summit Lake, Juniper Lake, Butte Lake, and Warner Valley Ranger Stations. Permits are also available over the phone at (530) 595-4480, through the mail, and by fax. Reservation forms and complete contact information are available at the park website. Forms must be received at least two weeks in advance. Before filling out the reservation form call (530) 595-4480 for information about areas of the park that are closed to camping. Backpackers must camp at least 300-feet from other groups, 100-feet from streams and lakes, and at least 0.5-mile from any developed area.

 Hiking

You can see alpine lakes and peer up at Lassen Peak from your driver's seat, but it's impossible to truly appreciate the park with your hands gripping a steering wheel. Visitors determined to explore the park to the fullest must strap on a pair of hiking boots and hit the trails. Two of the most popular ones are **Lassen Peak** and **Bumpass Hell**, both located along Main Park Road. If you can arrange a shuttle, or plant a bicycle, it's possible to hike to Southwest Campground from Bumpass Hell by **combining Bumpass Hell, Cold Boiling Lake, and Mill Creek Falls Trails.** Together they offer a wide variety of scenery including mudpots, hot springs, fumaroles, a boiling lake, and a waterfall. Bumpass Hell looks, feels, and smells like a miniature Yellowstone.

Other popular trails along Main Park Road include Brokeoff Mountain, Devastation, and Manzanita Lake. **The best locations for peaceful hiking** lie beyond Main Park Road at Warner Valley, Juniper Lake, and Butte Lake. These locations provide plenty of solitude as you walk among a pristine wilderness filled with conifer forests and perfectly clear alpine lakes. **If you have to choose just one area go with Juniper Lake.** It has a denser network of trails that allows hikers to assemble looped routes of varying distances.

Crags Lake

Mill Creek Falls

Terminal Geyser

Lassen Volcanic Hiking Trails

	Trail Name	Trailhead (# on map)	Length	Difficulty/Notes (Roundtrip distances)
Southwest Entrance	Brokeoff Mountain	0.25 mi south of SW Entrance (1)	7.0 miles	Strenuous • Steep trail to summit, excellent views
	Mill Creek Falls	Southwest Parking Area (2)	4.6 miles	Moderate • Hike through forest to falls overlook
	Ridge Lakes	Sulphur Works Parking Area (3)	2.0 miles	Strenuous • Up a ridge, through a ravine to alpine lakes
	Bumpass Hell - 👍	Bumpass Hell Parking Area (4)	3.0 miles	Moderate • Boardwalk through a hydrothermal area
	Lassen Peak - 👍	Lassen Peak Parking Area (5)	5.0 miles	Strenuous • Hike up mountain slope of loose rock
	Terrace, Shadow, and Cliff Lakes	21 mi from NW Entrance (6)	3.4 miles	Moderate • Great trail to view Lassen Peak
	Cold Boiling Lake	Kings Creek Picnic Area (7)	1.4 miles	Easy • Pass through forest to a bubbling lake
	Kings Creek Falls	Kings Creek Falls Trailhead (8)	3.0 miles	Moderate • Meadows, forest, flowers, and falls
Northwest Entrance	Echo Lake	Summit Lake Ranger Station (9)	4.4 miles	Moderate • Forested hike to lake with views of Lassen Peak
	Paradise Meadow	Hat Lake Parking Area (10)	2.8 miles	Moderate • Cross creeks (footbridges) to talus cliff lined meadow
	Devastated Area	Devastated Parking Area (11)	0.5 mile	Easy • Interpretive trail discusses past eruptions
	Lily Pond	Across from Loomis Museum (12)	0.75 mile	Easy • Nature trail with interpretive brochures
	Manzanita Creek	Manzanita Lake Road, Campground, and Picnic Area (13)	7.0 miles	Moderate • Switchbacks lead to a meadow along creek
	Manzanita Lake - 👍		1.5 miles	Easy • Flat trail around lake, bird watchers' delight
	Chaos Crags and Crags Lake		4.0 miles	Moderate • Lake is often dry in summer
Butte Lake	Cinder Cone	Butte Lake Parking Area (14)	4.0 miles	Strenuous • Pass lava beds and painted dunes
	Prospect Peak	Spur from Cinder Cone	6.6 miles	Strenuous • Forested trail to rim of shield volcano
Warner Valley	Devil's Kitchen	North of Warner Valley Campground on Warner Valley Road (15)	4.2 miles	Moderate • Mudpots, steam vents, and fumaroles
	Boiling Springs Lake		1.8 miles	Easy • Mudpots, wildflowers, birds, and a 125°F lake
	Terminal Geyser		5.8 miles	Moderate • Not an actual geyser, a fumarole & steam
Juniper Lake	Mount Harkness	Juniper Lake Campground (16)	3.8 miles	Strenuous • Fire lookout provides wonderful views
	Crystal Lake		0.8 mile	Easy • Short trail to a small tarn in a rocky basin
	Inspiration Point - 👍	Juniper Lake Picnic Area (17)	1.4 miles	Moderate • Views of the park's prominent peaks
	Horseshoe Lake		2.8 miles	Easy • Gentle trail to a good fishing hole

Crumbaugh Lake

Other Activities

Fishing is not a particularly popular activity, but many of the park's waters are known for their rainbow and brown trout. **Manzanita Lake** is the most frequented fishing hole. You must practice catch and release and use single-hook, barbless, artificial lures. A California fishing license is required for all anglers 16 and older.

Boating: Boat launches are available for non-motorized watercraft at **Manzanita, Butte, and Juniper Lakes**. Paddlers must also use these designated launch areas. **Kayak rental** is available at **Manzanita Lake Camper Store**. They offer single and double kayaks on a first-come, first-served basis. Rentals are available from 10am–3pm. Kayak rates are $10 for 1-hour, and $16 for 2-hours.

Bird Watching is another popular past-time at Lassen Volcanic National Park. **Manzanita Lake Loop and Cluster Lakes Loop Trails** are popular among birders. No matter where you travel you're likely to spot at least a few of the 83 species of birds that nest within the park. Favorites include osprey, bald eagle, bufflehead, peregrine falcon, California spotted owl, and red-breasted sapsucker. Lassen Volcanic National Park is one of the few areas where **bufflehead** breed in northern California.

In winter, Main Park Road may be closed but the fun doesn't stop where the road is not plowed. **Southwest Parking Area** is a great place to begin a **snowshoe trek**, **cross-country ski adventure**, or a **family sledding excursion**. Several sledding hills and miles of ski trails are available nearby Kohm Yah-mah-nee Visitor Center. Over at the **Northwest Entrance**, **cross-country skiers** and **snowshoers** can embark upon a 7.5 mile trail along Manzanita Creek (begins at Loomis Ranger Station) or the 7-mile Nobles Emigrant Trail (begins across from Loomis Parking Area).

For Kids: The park offers ranger-led **Junior Ranger Programs** for kids (ages 7–12). If you're unable to join one of the ranger programs children can still download the Junior Ranger Activity booklet from the park website, complete the booklet, and earn a badge. Kids of any age can join the **Chipmunk Club** by completing a Chipmunk Club booklet. All visitors are welcome to participate in the **Volcano Club**. Follow the instructions from the activity booklet (available online). You can also pick up a free copy of any of these booklets at **Loomis Museum** or **Kohm Yah-mah-nee Visitor Center**.

Ranger Programs: Lassen Volcanic offers free ranger-led activities during the summer and winter. Summer programs run from mid-June to mid-August. They consist of a variety of walks, talks, and evening activities. For **"Starry Nights,"** a ranger points out stars, planets, and galaxies visible in the brilliant night sky. There are bird watching hikes, junior ranger programs, and a slew of educational talks that discuss the park's unique ecology, geology, and history. During winter you can join a park ranger on a 1–2-mile **snowshoe adventure**. These walks are held on Saturdays and Sundays beginning after Christmas Day and ending in March. Snowshoes are provided free of charge, but a $1 donation is requested for their use. To view a complete and current schedule of events at the park, check bulletin boards at park facilities or refer to the free newspaper, *Peak Experiences,* which you should receive upon entry (also available online).

Flora & Fauna: Elevation ranging from 5,000 to nearly 10,500 feet creates an environment full of ecological diversity. **More than 700 species of flowering plants** reside in the park. Communities vary from dense conifer forests of the lower elevations to seemingly barren alpine mountaintops where trees are unable to survive. During the summer months meadows burst with color. Trails like Paradise Meadows and Kings Creek Falls guide hikers directly through beautiful foliage. **More than 300 species of vertebrates including 57 species of mammals** call the park home. Most famous are the **black bears** from whom you must lock your food away (use the bear lockers provided at the campgrounds). Bobcat, mountain lion, and Sierra Nevada and red fox live here, but are seldom seen. Animals you're most likely to see are the rodents (chipmunks, squirrels, and possibly skunks) and birds.

Pets: Pets are allowed in the park, but must be kept on a leash no more than six feet in length at all times. They are only allowed on established roadways, campgrounds, picnic areas, and other developed areas. Pets (with the exception of service animals) are not allowed in public buildings.

Accessibility: Loomis Museum and Kohm Yah-mah-nee Visitor Center are fully accessible to individuals with mobility impairments. Devastated Trail is accessible, as are most of the park's restrooms. A wheelchair accessible campsite is available at Manzanita Lake, Summit Lake, and Butte Lake Campgrounds.

Weather: There's more than 4,000-feet of elevation difference between Manzanita Lake and Lassen Peak. Such a dramatic change creates wild variations in temperature, wind, and weather. Expect temperatures to decrease about 4°F per 1,000-feet of increased elevation. Winters are cold and snowy in the high elevations; one year Lake Helen received some 40-feet of accumulated snow. At Manzanita Lake the average high temperature from December through February is 50°F, with lows falling into the teens. During summer average highs reach the mid-80s°F, with overnight lows that drop into the low 40s°F. All campgrounds are above 5,600-feet so expect cool nights. Come prepared for wind, rain, and chilly evenings and always dress in layers.

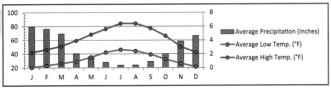

Bumpass Hell

Best of Lassen Volcanic

Attraction: Bumpass Hell
  Runner-up: Manzanita Lake
  2ⁿᵈ Runner-up: Juniper Lake

Hike: Lassen Peak
  Runner-up: Inspiration Point
  2ⁿᵈ Runner-up: Bumpass Hell

Did you know?

➤ Brokeoff Mountain was once part of a volcano that towered 1,000 feet above Lassen Peak.

➤ Lassen Peak is the largest plug dome volcano in the world.

Vacation Planner

Most visits to Lassen Volcanic National Park begin and end on **Main Park Road (CA-89)**. A slight problem is that you'll only find **campgrounds** (page 526) in between Southwest and Northwest Entrances. Nearby dining, grocery stores, lodging, festivals, and attractions are listed on pages 546–549. Tucked away in **Warner Valley** is the park's only lodging, **Drakesbad Guest Ranch** (866.999.0914, www.drakesbad.com). Accommodations are simple (most without electricity), and rates range from $140–176 per person per night (meals are included). The roads to **Warner Valley, Juniper Lake, and Butte Lake** are long and rough, but the peacefulness is worth the journey. With that said, most visitors only travel along Main Park Road. Expect the 29-mile (one-way) drive to take one hour without stopping. Here's a one-day itinerary to help guide you along Main Park Road (beginning at the SW Entrance).

Day 1 Introduce yourself to the park at **Kohm Yah-mah-nee Visitor Center**. Watch the introductory film, browse through the exhibits and bookstore, and check the day's schedule of **ranger guided activities**. Adjust your schedule in order to squeeze in any programs of interest. Return to your car and begin touring Main Park Road. After a few miles you'll reach two of the premier destinations: **Bumpass Hell** and **Lassen Peak**. Hike their respective trails (page 527). At a leisurely pace it takes 2 hours to complete Bumpass Hell Trail and 4 hours to hike to the summit of Lassen Peak and back. If you're sufficiently worn out from the hikes complete the drive all the way to the NW Entrance and **Manzanita Lake**. Here you can sit down, set up camp, or continue on to your next vacation destination.

Moss covers a twisted tree near Redwood Creek.

1111 Second Street
Crescent City, California 95531
Phone: (707) 465-7335
Website: www.nps.gov/redw

Established: January 1, 1968
Size: 133,000 Acres
Annual Visitors: 420,000
Peak Season: Summer

Activities: Hiking, Backpacking,
Camping, Horseback Riding,
Biking, Paddling, and Fishing

Campgrounds ($35/night): Jedediah
Smith*, Mill Creek* (Seasonal),
Elk Prairie*, and Gold Bluffs Beach
Backcountry Camping: Permitted
at designated sites and on Redwood
Creek gravel bars
Lodging: None

Park Hours: All day, every day
Entrance Fee: None (National Park)
$8 Day-use Fee (State Parks)

*Reserve at (800) 444-7275 or
www.reserveamerica.com

Redwood - California

Redwood trees once grew all over the Northern Hemisphere. They have lived on the California coast for the last 20 million years, providing a link to the Age of Dinosaurs. As recently as 1850, more than two million acres of old-growth covered this coastline where fog supplies up to one third of their annual water. Today, Redwood National and State Parks protect less than 39,000 acres of old-growth forest, representing 45% of all remaining coastal redwoods. They are some of the oldest trees in the world, many of which have been growing here for more than 2,000 years. If they could speak they'd tell stories of times long before Christopher Columbus discovered America. These are the tallest trees in the world. Some appear to scratch the sky, towering more than 370 feet into the air; at 379-feet, **Hyperion** is the tallest of them all. Credit bark more than 12 inches thick infused with tannin, providing protection from disease, insects, and fire. Roots, no deeper than 10–13 feet but up to 80-feet long, support these monsters more than 22-feet in diameter at their base and weighing up to 500 tons. Until prospectors and loggers arrived on the scene the only threat to the mighty redwood was itself. They simply grew too big and too tall for their shallow roots, planted in wet soil to support themselves against the winds off the Pacific Ocean.

By the 1850s strong winds weren't the only threat these majestic giants faced. **Jedediah Smith**, trapper and explorer, was the first non-Native to reach California's northern coast by land in 1828. More than two decades later gold was found along the Trinity River. In 1850, **settlers** established the boom town of Eureka and **miners** steadily displaced

Native Americans who had lived there for the past 3,000 years, longer than the oldest trees of the redwood forests. The Yurok, Tolowa, Karok, Chilula, and Wiyot Indian tribes all resided in the region. They used fallen redwoods for boats, houses, and small villages. Deer, elk, fish, nuts, berries, and seeds provided more than enough food to sustain tribes as large as 55 villages and 2,500 people. After two minor gold booms went bust, settlers who had forced the Natives out searching for gold now had to seek something else, a new way to earn wages.

Gold fever became redwood fever, and more settlers were drawn to the area to exploit a seemingly endless supply of colossal trees. Harvested trees helped boost the rapid development of West Coast cities like San Francisco. In 1918, conservationists, appalled by the swaths of clear-cut coastal lands, formed the Save-the-Redwoods League. They drummed up support, which ultimately led to establishment of Prairie Creek, Del Norte Coast, and Jedediah Smith Redwoods State Parks. At the same time US-101, which would provide unprecedented access to untouched stands of coastal redwoods, was under construction. Conservationists spent the next four decades requesting the creation of Redwood National Park. Demand for lumber during WWII delayed the park's creation, but finally, in the 1960s, the Save-the-Redwoods League, Sierra Club, and National Geographic Society made one last push for a national park. It was signed into law by **President Lyndon B. Johnson** in 1968. At the time more than 90% of old-growth forests had been logged.

Some of the trees have been saved. Indians still live among nature's sacred giants, even though treaties establishing reservations for the displaced Natives were never ratified. They perform traditional ceremonies, hunt and fish, and speak their native language. Guests are left awestruck by the soaring timber, sharing the same spiritual connection between nature and man. Hollywood has helped create a more tangible connection between man, nature, and the Age of Dinosaurs. Redwood Forest served as backdrop for Steven Spielberg's *The Lost World: Jurassic Park*. Another Spielberg flick, *Star Wars: Return of the Jedi*—a movie set "a long time ago, in a galaxy far, far away"—was also filmed here. Let's hope Redwood National Park goes back to the future, looking more like it did in 1850 than 1950.

Did you know?

▶ Redwoods used to grow all over the northern hemisphere: in Greenland, and much of Europe and Asia.

When to Go

Redwood National Park is open all day, every day. All Visitor and Information Centers are open in summer with typical hours being from 9am to 6pm. Crescent City Information Center and Thomas H. Kuchel Visitor Center are the only visitor facilities that stay open year-round, except New Year's, Thanksgiving, and Christmas. In winter, hours are shortened to 9am to 4pm. See page 536 for all park facilities' operating hours.

Summer is busy and often foggy. Winter is rainy. Spring and fall are marked by visiting migratory birds. No matter when you visit you can anticipate temperatures ranging between 40°F and 60°F along the coast. This fairly constant temperature is moderated by the Pacific Ocean. Smaller crowds, reduced chances of fog and rain, and a wide variety of visiting bird species make spring and fall ideal times to visit the Redwood Forest. It's also a great time of year to cruise US-101/Redwood Highway and CA-1/Pacific Coast Highway.

Transportation & Airports

Public transportation does not provide service to or around the park. The closest large commercial airports are Portland International (PDX), 340 miles north of the park, and San Francisco International (SFO), 330 miles to the south. Small regional airports are located nearby at Crescent City and McKinleyville, CA and Medford, OR.

Directions

Redwood National Park is oriented along US-101, one of the most scenic highways in the United States. The park does not have a formal entrance. Directions to US-101:

From the South: US-101 crosses the opening of San Francisco Bay, via the Golden Gate Bridge, and then runs parallel to California's Coast all the way to Redwood National Park.

From the North: Follow US-101 along the Oregon/California Coast (fantastic). You can also take I-5 South to Exit 58 where you'll merge onto CA-99 S toward US-100/Grants Pass. After 3 miles, turn right at US-199 S/Redwood Highway. Continue for 88 miles to the park.

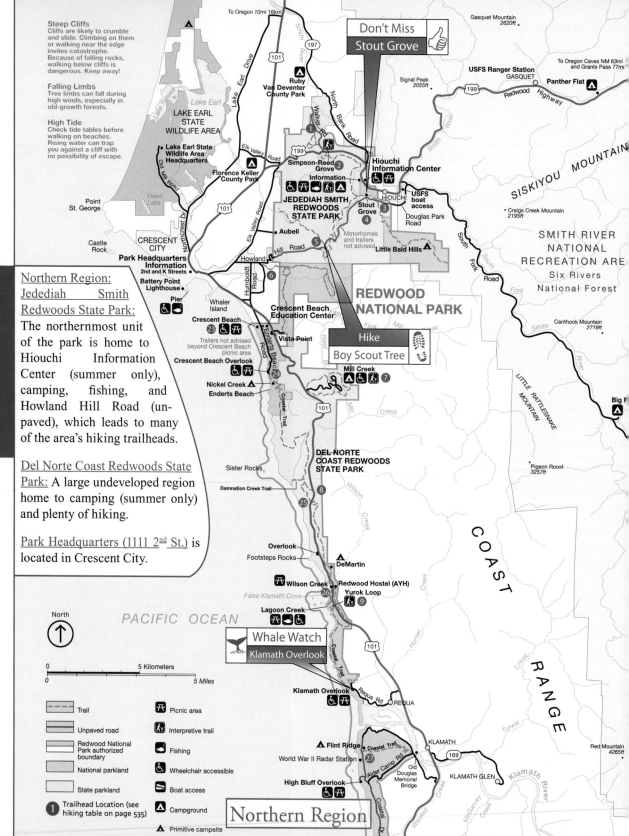

Steep Cliffs
Cliffs are likely to crumble and slide. Climbing on them or walking near the edge invites catastrophe. Because of falling rocks, walking below cliffs is dangerous. Keep away!

Falling Limbs
Tree limbs can fall during high winds, especially in old-growth forests.

High Tide
Check tide tables before walking on beaches. Rising water can trap you against a cliff with no possibility of escape.

Don't Miss
Stout Grove 👍

Hike
Boy Scout Tree 👣

Whale Watch
Klamath Overlook

Northern Region: Jedediah Smith Redwoods State Park:
The northernmost unit of the park is home to Hiouchi Information Center (summer only), camping, fishing, and Howland Hill Road (unpaved), which leads to many of the area's hiking trailheads.

Del Norte Coast Redwoods State Park:
A large undeveloped region home to camping (summer only) and plenty of hiking.

Park Headquarters (1111 2nd St.)
is located in Crescent City.

REDWOOD NATIONAL PARK

JEDEDIAH SMITH REDWOODS STATE PARK

DEL NORTE COAST REDWOODS STATE PARK

SMITH RIVER NATIONAL RECREATION AREA
Six Rivers National Forest

COAST RANGE

PACIFIC OCEAN

Northern Region

North

0 — 5 Kilometers
0 — 5 Miles

- Trail
- Unpaved road
- Redwood National Park authorized boundary
- National parkland
- State parkland
- ① Trailhead Location (see hiking table on page 535)
- 🎪 Picnic area
- 🚶 Interpretive trail
- 🎣 Fishing
- ♿ Wheelchair accessible
- 🚤 Boat access
- ⛺ Campground
- ⛺ Primitive campsite

REDWOOD

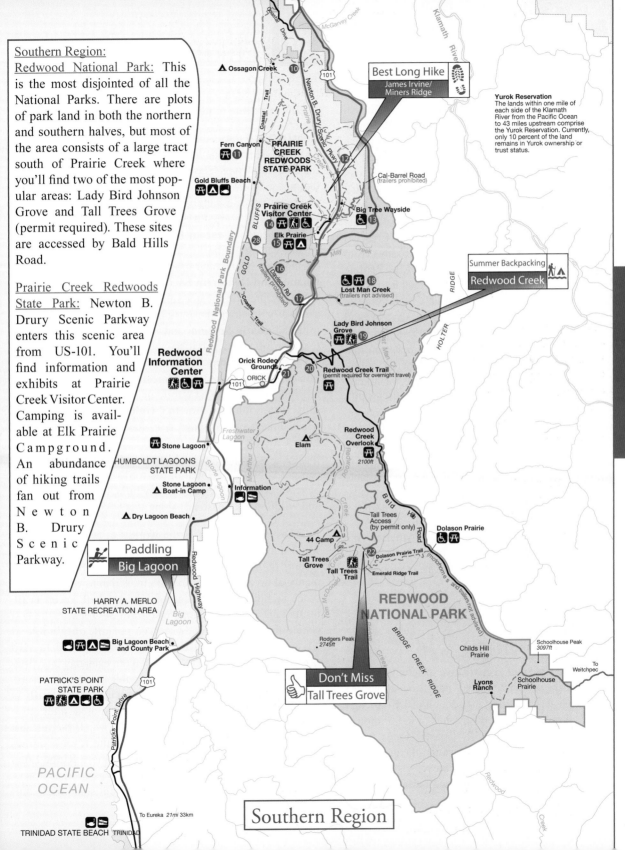

Southern Region:

Redwood National Park: This is the most disjointed of all the National Parks. There are plots of park land in both the northern and southern halves, but most of the area consists of a large tract south of Prairie Creek where you'll find two of the most popular areas: Lady Bird Johnson Grove and Tall Trees Grove (permit required). These sites are accessed by Bald Hills Road.

Prairie Creek Redwoods State Park: Newton B. Drury Scenic Parkway enters this scenic area from US-101. You'll find information and exhibits at Prairie Creek Visitor Center. Camping is available at Elk Prairie Campground. An abundance of hiking trails fan out from Newton B. Drury Scenic Parkway.

Yurok Reservation
The lands within one mile of each side of the Klamath River from the Pacific Ocean to 43 miles upstream comprise the Yurok Reservation. Currently, only 10 percent of the land remains in Yurok ownership or trust status.

Best Long Hike
James Irvine/ Miners Ridge

Summer Backpacking
Redwood Creek

Paddling
Big Lagoon

Don't Miss
Tall Trees Grove

REDWOOD

Southern Region

Camping

There are no developed campgrounds in Redwood National Park, but three state parks (jointly administered with the national park) furnish four developed campgrounds. **Jedediah Smith Campground** is in an old-growth redwood grove on the banks of the Smith River. It is located on US-199, 10 miles east of Crescent City. You can hike, fish, and swim right at the campground. It's open all year, and offers 86 tent or RV sites. **Mill Creek Campground** is located in Del Norte Coast Redwoods State Park, 7 miles south of Crescent City on US-101. It offers 145 tent or RV sites from early May until early September. **Elk Prairie Campground** is located in Prairie Creek Redwoods State Park, 6 miles north of Orick, CA on Newton B. Drury Scenic Parkway. It's open all year, and offers 75 tent or RV sites. All of the campgrounds listed above have showers and a dump station, but hook-ups are not available. Sites cost $35/night. A reduced rate of $5/night is available for hikers/bikers. Reservations can be made by calling (800) 444-7275 or visiting www.reserveamerica.com up to six months in advance (recommended between May and September). **Gold Bluffs Campground**, located in Prairie Creek Redwoods State Park on Davison Road, has 26 sites that are only available on a first-come, first-served basis. It is open all year. Solar showers are provided. Sites cost $35/night.

Discounts are not available for America the Beautiful Senior/Access Pass holders. There are more than a dozen public and private campgrounds located nearby.

Biking

Long distance **road cyclists** love the challenge and the scenery associated with pedalling along the Pacific Coast, including the section of **US-101** that travels through Redwood National Park. For **mountain bikers**, Little Bald Hills, Coastal (Last Chance and Gold Bluffs sections), Ossagon, Davison, and Lost Man Creek Trails permit bicycle use. See the hiking table on the following page for trail location and mileage.

Hiking

There are more than 200 miles of hiking trails at Redwood National and State Parks. The best of the bunch explore the **Pacific coastline** or **old-growth redwood forests**.

Coastal Trail traces the coast almost continuously for some 35 miles. There's one major gap at the US-101 Bridge over the Klamath River. The rest of the trail is broken into seven distinct sections that provide great opportunities for beachcombing, whale-watching, tidepool exploring, and birding. Farthest north is the **Crescent Beach Section**. Before you reach the trail, **Crescent Beach Overlook** provides an excellent vantage point to survey the ocean for gray whales during their spring migration. Continuing south are the **Last Chance and Demartin Sections**. Longer and more strenuous, they provide greater solitude. Backcountry campsites are available along these trails. Further south are the 5.5-mile **Klamath Section** and **Klamath River Overlook** (another excellent perch to peer across the Pacific). The 4.5-mile **Flint Ridge Section** provides a unique combination of old-growth redwood forests and ocean vistas. (Most redwoods grow at least a mile or two away from shore as salty water inhibits growth.) **Gold Bluffs** (4.8 miles)—where hikers pass through a 30-foot high wall of ferns at **Fern Canyon** and spend the night at **Ossagon Camp**—is the next stretch. Last is the **Skunk Cabbage Section**. If you can put up with the smell of the trail's namesake, you will be rewarded with views of grassy hills, massive redwoods, and wildflowers (seasonal) along this 5.25 mile trail.

At 379-feet, **Hyperion** is the world's tallest tree, but you won't find a trail leading to it. It's location is kept secret so visitors do not trample the surrounding soil. Still, there are plenty of great hiking trails with trees that tower more than twice as high as the Statue of Liberty. **Tall Trees Trail**, located off Bald Hills Road just north of Orick, is the best choice for giant redwoods. **A free permit, obtainable at Thomas H. Kuchel Visitor Center, is required to visit the area.** Only 50 permits are given out each day on a first-come, first-served basis. If you're unable to secure a permit, check out **Boy Scout or Stout Memorial Grove Trails** in Jedediah Smith Redwoods State Park. Another alternative is **Lady Bird Johnson Grove Trail**, which begins just off Bald Hills Road. For a longer hike, the 12-mile **James Irvine/Fern Canyon/Davison Road/Miners Ridge Loop** in Prairie Creek Redwoods State Park is as good as it gets. Temporary footbridges are removed from some trails during the winter rainy season.

Redwood Hiking Trails

	Trail Name	Region	Trailhead (# on map)	Length	Notes (One-way distances, except loops)
North	Leifer–Ellsworth Loop	JS	Off Walker Road (1)	2.6 miles	Follows old Crescent City Plank Road
	Simpson–Reed	JS	US-199 (North Side) (2)	1.0 mile	Loop trail through old-growth redwoods
	Little Bald Hills	JS	Howland Hill Road (3)	3.3–8.0 mi	Backpack • Bikes and horses allowed
	Stout Memorial Grove - 👍	JS	Howland Hill Road (4)	0.5 mile	Short loop with fantastic old-growth redwoods
	Boy Scout Tree - 👍	JS	Howland Hill Road (5)	2.8 miles	Old-growth, with spur to a double redwood
	Mill Creek	JS	Howland Hill Road (6)	3.0 miles	Hike provides access for fishing or photos
	Trestle Loop	DN	Mill Creek Campground (7)	1.0 mile	Follows old railroad trestles, berries
	Damnation Creek	DN	Milepost 16 on US-101 (8)	2.2 miles	Ancient redwoods and Pacific Coast
	Yurok Loop	DN	Lagoon Creek Picnic Area (9)	1.25 miles	Family-friendly views of False Klamath Cove
South	Ossagon	R/PC	Newton B. Drury Scenic Pkwy (10)	1.8 miles	Old rough road • Bikes allowed
	Fern Canyon/Friendship Ridge/West Ridge/Coastal	PC	Fern Canyon Parking Area off Davison Rd (11)	7.0 miles	Loop these trails together for a moderate 4-hour hike into the north region
	South Fork/Rhododendron/Brown Creek - 👍	PC	Newton B. Drury Scenic Pkwy (12)	3.5 miles	Loop these trails together for a moderate 2-hour hike (South Fork is steep)
	Circle	PC	Big Tree Wayside Parking Area (13)	0.3 mile	Easiest access to the Big Tree
	Cathedral Trees	PC	Big Tree Wayside Parking Area (13)	1.4 miles	Family friendly access to big trees
	Prairie Creek	PC	Prairie Creek Visitor Center (14)	4.0 miles	Moderate hike along creek • Spur to Corkscrew Tree
	James Irvine/Fern Canyon/Davison Rd/Miners Ridge - 👍	PC	Prairie Creek Visitor Center (14)	12.0 miles	Combine trails to form a moderate loop
	Revelation	PC	Prairie Creek Visitor Center (14)	0.3 mile	Trail designed for visually impaired
	Elk Prairie	PC	Elk Prairie Campground (15)	2.8 miles	Opportunities to see Roosevelt elk
	Streelow Creek	PC	Davison Road (16)	2.8 miles	Connects Davison Road and Tr • Bikes allowed
	Davison	PC	Elk Meadow Day Use Area (17)	3.0 miles	Follows old logging road • Bikes allowed
	Trillium Falls	R	Elk Meadow Day Use Area (17)	2.5 miles	Loop Trail through old-growth to 10-ft cascade
	Lost Man Creek	R	Lost Man Creek Picnic Area (18)	10.0 miles	Big trees and big ferns • Bikes allowed
	Lady Bird Johnson Grove - 👍	R	Bald Hills Road (19)	1.5 miles	Self-guiding loop trail • Very popular
	Redwood Creek	R	Bald Hills Road (20)	8.0–14.0 mi	Gravel bars available for camping in summer
	MacArthur Creek Loop	R	Orick Rodeo Grounds (21)	14.0 miles	Backcountry camps • Horses allowed
	Elam Loop and Horse Camp	R	Orick Rodeo Grounds (21)	20.0 miles	Backpacker friendly system of trails
	44 Loop and Horse Camp	R	Orick Rodeo Grounds (21)	32.0 miles	Section of backpack trails closed to horses
	Tall Trees - 👍	R	Bald Hills Road (22)	3.5 miles	World's Tallest Trees, semi-loop • Permit Req'd
	Dolason Prairie	R	Bald Hills Road (22)	5.9 miles	Forests, clear-cut, and panoramic views
Coastal Trail Sections	Crescent Beach - 👍	R	Crescent Beach Picnic Area (23)	3.5 miles	Beachcombing, Roosevelt elk sightings
	Last Chance	R/DN	Enderts Beach Road (24)	6.5 miles	Strenuous and Steep • Bikes allowed
	Demartin	R/DN	Mile Marker 15.6 of US-101 (25)	6.0 miles	Moderate • Backcountry campsites
	Klamath - 👍	R	Wilson Creek Picnic Area (26)	5.5 miles	Moderate • Klamath Overlook for whale-watching
	Flint Ridge	R	Coastal Drive (27)	4.5 miles	Strenuous • Flint Ridge Camp Access
	Gold Bluffs	PC	Davison Road (11)	4.8 miles	Steep then flat • Ossagon Camp access
	Skunk Cabbage	R	Davison Road (28)	5.25 miles	Moderate • Wide variety of plants and trees

Regions: JS = Jedediah Smith Redwoods State Park (RSP), DN = Del Norte Coast RSP, PC = Prairie Creek RSP, R = Redwood National Park

REDWOOD

Other Activities

Backpacking: **Backcountry camping is only allowed at designated sites and along Redwood Creek gravel bars.** There are four free sites: Nickel Creek, DeMartin, and Flint Ridge, located along the Coastal Trail; and Little Bald Hills, located on Little Bald Hills Trail. Little Bald Hills, Nickel Creek, and DeMartin are **north of the Klamath River.** The only site that requires a permit is Nickel Creek. Permits can be obtained at Crescent City Information Center.

Five sites are located **south of the Klamath River.** Ossagon Creek and Miners Ridge sites require a permit and a $5 per person per day fee. Permits are available at the Prairie Creek Entrance Station kiosks. Elam Creek and 44 Camp are located on Orick Horse Trail. **Backcountry sites** are also dispersed along **Redwood Creek Trail.** Elam Creek, 44 Camp, and Redwood Creek sites are free, but a permit must be obtained from Kuchel Visitor Center prior to departure.

All sites feature picnic tables, fire pits, food storage lockers, and toilets.

Horseback Riding: Many of the park's trails are open to horses. If you'd like to explore the majestic redwoods on a guided ride or overnight pack trip contact one of these outfitters: **Redwood Adventure Tours** (866.733.9637, www.redwoodadventures.com, $60/person, 90 min.), **Redwood Trail Rides** (707.498.4837, www.redwoodhorserides.com, $65), **Armstrong Woods Pack Station** (707.887.2939, www.redwoodhorses.com, $80), and **Tell Tale Trails** (www.telltaletrails.com, $55). Rides must be reserved in advance.

Paddling is a great way to explore the coast, coves, and rivers. **Big Lagoon**, just south of the park, is popular among paddlers. If you don't have your own kayak, rentals are available during summer from **Kayak Zak's** (707.498.1130, www.kayakzak.com); they bring a rental trailer to the lagoon beginning at 10am on weekends and noon on weekdays. Single kayak rates are $20/hour and $35/half-day. They also offer guided trips and sea kayaking courses. Migratory bird and whale watching trips ($75–85, 2–3 hours) are available during spring and fall.

For Kids: Children have the opportunity to become a **Redwood National Park Junior Ranger.** To participate pick up an activity newspaper from one of the park's five visitor centers. Activities are designed for children (ages 7–12), but visitors of any age are welcome. Complete an age appropriate number of activities, collect a bag of litter, attend a ranger program or hike a trail, write down a park rule, and understand and sign the Junior Ranger Pledge to earn a patch.

Ranger programs at Redwood National Park are available from mid-May to mid-September. Time, location, and topics of current programs can be found at visitor center or campground bulletin boards. Campfire programs are offered regularly at Jedediah Smith, Mill Creek, and Elk Prairie Campgrounds. Listen to the stories of a park ranger while sitting near a crackling fire or let a ranger guide you through the park on a Tidepool or Nature Walk.

Visitor Centers:
Crescent City Information Center • (707) 465-7335
1111 Second Street; Crescent City, CA
Summer: Daily, 9am–6pm; Winter: 9am–4pm; Spring/Fall: 9am–5pm

Hiouchi Information Center • (707) 458-3294
9 miles northeast of Crescent City, CA on US-199
Summer: Daily, 9am–6pm; Off-season: As staffing permits

Jedediah Smith Visitor Center • (707) 458-3496
J.S. Campground, 9 mi. NE of Crescent City, CA on US-199
Summer: Daily, As staffing permits (call ahead for hours)

Prairie Creek Visitor Center • (707) 488-2171
6 miles north of Orick, CA on Newton B. Drury Scenic Pkwy
All Year: Daily, 9am–5pm

Thomas H. Kuchel Visitor Center • (707) 465-7765
2 miles south of Orick, CA on US-101
Summer: Daily, 9am–6pm; Winter: 9am–4pm; Spring/Fall: 9am–5pm

Flora & Fauna: The main draw is the coastal redwoods, the world's tallest trees soaring more than 300 feet above their massive bases, but there's much more to the region's lush ecosystem. The park protects a variety of **threatened species**: brown pelican, tidewater goby, bald eagle, Chinook salmon, northern spotted owl, and Steller sea lion. Large mammals such as bear and **Roosevelt elk** are commonly seen. Elk cross the roads, use the trails, and appear to be domesticated, but don't mistake their docile nature as an invitation to pose in a photograph with them. All of the animals are wild and should be treated with respect. Do not feed, provoke, or approach any native wildlife.

Pets: Pets are allowed in the park, but must be kept on a leash no more than six feet in length at all times. They are prohibited from all hiking trails. Pets can essentially go anywhere your car can, like along roads, parking areas, picnic areas, campgrounds, and Crescent and Gold Bluffs beaches.

Accessibility: All of the park's visitor centers are accessible to individuals with mobility impairments. Many of the park's campgrounds, picnic areas, beaches, and overlooks are also accessible. Please refer to the maps on pages 532–533 that designate all wheelchair accessible sites.

Weather: Thunderstorms and fog are difficult to predict, but the temperature is not. All year average high temperatures range from the mid-50s to mid-60s°F. Average lows range from the low to high 40s°F. This consistency is due to the park's location along the Pacific Coast. The farther you travel from the coast, the greater the seasonal temperature difference becomes. On average the park receives 70 inches of rain each year, most of which falls between October and April.

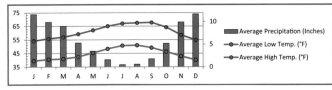

Legend:
- Average Precipitation (Inches)
- Average Low Temp. (°F)
- Average High Temp. (°F)

Vacation Planner

If you're traveling along the northern coast of California, a stop at Redwood National Park is a must. Even if you just hop out at **Klamath River Overlook** to smell the salty air and drive to **Lady Bird Johnson Grove** to walk among 2,000 year old trees, it's worth it. But, there are plenty of trails and activities to keep you entertained for an extended stay. Provided below is an itinerary for one spectacular day here. **Campgrounds** (page 534) are the only overnight accommodations in the park. Nearby dining, grocery stores, lodging, festivals, and attractions are listed on pages 546–549.

Entering from the south via **US-101,** stop at **Kuchel Visitor Center** to see if you can get a **permit** to access **Tall Trees Trailhead** (page 534). Continue north past Orick and turn right onto **Bald Hills Road**. Head to **Tall Tree Grove** if you got a permit, otherwise hike **Lady Bird Johnson Grove** (page 535). Return to US-101 and drive to **Newton B. Drury Scenic Pkwy**. If you like to hike, stop at Prairie Creek Visitor Center for the 12-mile **James Irvine/Miners Ridge Trails Loop** (best in the park, page 535). Otherwise continue north, stopping at **Ah-Pah Trail** and **Klamath River Overlook**. Time permitting, stop at Jedediah Smith to hike **Stout Memorial Grove** (page 535).

Rays of light shine through coastal redwoods

Best of Redwood

Attraction: Tall Tree Grove
Runner-up: Klamath River Overlook

Hike: James Irvine/Fern Canyon
Runner-up: South Fork/Rhododendron

Did you know?

▸ Redwoods are the world's tallest living trees. They can grow to weigh more than 500 tons and taller than the Statue of Liberty (including its base).

▸ Measuring in at 379.1 feet, Hyperion is the tallest tree in Redwood National Park.

▸ A redwood's trunk can grow up to 22 feet in diameter with barker more than 12 inches thick.

▸ A single coastal redwood tree consumes up to 500 gallons of water each day. Fog can account for up to one third of the water needed for each tree to survive.

A view of Crater Lake and Wizard Island from Discovery Point

PO Box 7
Crater Lake, Oregon 97604
Phone: (541) 594-3000
Website: www.nps.gov/crla

Established: May 22, 1902
Size: 183,224 Acres
Annual Visitors: 450,000
Peak Season: Summer

Activities: Hiking, Backpacking, Camping, Boat Tours, Swimming, Fishing, Biking, and Snowshoeing

Campgrounds: Mazama (213 sites) and Lost Creek (16, tent-only)
Fee: $10–29/night
Lodging: Crater Lake Lodge, Cabins at Mazama Village
Rates: $138–289
Reservations: (888) 774-2728, www.craterlakelodges.com
Backcountry Camping: Permitted with a free Backcountry Use Permit

Park Hours: All day, every day
Entrance Fee: $10 • Vehicle
$5 • Individual (foot, bike, etc.)

Crater Lake - Oregon

Nearly 8,000 years ago a cataclysmic eruption of **Mount Mazama** caused the mountain to shatter and collapse into itself, forming a massive 5-mile wide caldera rimmed by cliffs almost 4,000 feet high. Sealed by molten rock, the caldera gradually filled with water from melted snow and rain. The lake's water level has finally settled; seepage and evaporation balance the incoming flow. After 750 years, roughly five trillion gallons of almost perfectly pure water filled the caldera, creating one of the most impressive natural settings in the world. Crater Lake is so deep (up to 1,943-feet, 1,148-feet on average) and so pure that the true blueness of water becomes obviously, almost indescribably, apparent. Today, soaring cliffs line a lake whose brilliant deep blue hue leaves guests, past and present, spellbound.

Makala Indians have their own legend about the creation of Crater Lake. Llao, Chief of the Below World, sometimes came up from the earth to stand atop Mount Mazama. On one of his visits, Llao fell in love with the Makalak chief's beautiful daughter. Llao promised her eternal life if she would return with him to his home below the mountain. She refused. Enraged, Llao began to pummel the village with balls of fire. Skell, Chief of the Above World, witnessed Llao's rage from the top of Mount Shasta. He took pity on the helpless villagers and chose to wage war with Llao. The two chiefs hurled fiery hot boulders at one another from their respective mountains. The earth trembled in the wake of their violence. As villagers fled to the waters of Klamath Lake two holy men remained behind. Their plan was to jump into the fiery pit hidden within

Llao's mountain as a sacrifice to the Chief of the Below. Moved by their bravery, Skell ambushed Llao, driving him back into Mount Mazama where the fight raged on through the night. The following morning, Mount Mazama was gone. In its place was a gaping hole that filled with water from torrents of rain, which fell after the epic battle.

Makalak Indians may well have witnessed the formation of Crater Lake. Evidence of permanent ancient settlement has not been found, but the area was used for seasonal hunting and gathering, vision-quests, and prayer for at least 10,000 years. **Mount Mazama erupted** about 7,700 years ago. The event produced more than 100 times as much ash as Mount St. Helens' eruption in 1980, scattered as far south as central Nevada, as far west as Yellowstone National Park, and as far north as British Columbia. After its eruption Indians were definitely aware of the lake that filled the caldera of Mount Mazama; they believed it took great power and strength to look at the pure blue waters. Even today, Klamath Indians (descendants of the Makalak) refuse to look at the lake for religious reasons.

John Wesley Hillman, the first white man to glimpse Crater Lake, had no such religious proclivities. After returning from a successful gold mining trip in California, Hillman funded a small gold mining expedition into Oregon's southern Cascades. On June 12, 1853, the group reached present day **Discovery Point** where a lake of incomprehensible majesty was on display. They named it Deep Blue Lake, returned to civilization to restock supplies, and continued on their quest for gold. **William Gladstone Steel** visited the area in 1885. It was still used by local Indians for hunting, gathering, and religious purposes, but Steel spent the next 17 years campaigning for the creation of Crater Lake National Park (the name preferred by locals over the likes of Blue Lake, Lake Majesty, and the original, Deep Blue Lake). Steel named other features: Wizard Island, Llao Rock, and Skell Head. On May 22, 1902, Steel's efforts came to fruition when **President Roosevelt** signed legislation creating Crater Lake, the 6th oldest national park. Steel's focus shifted to making the area a spectacle catering to wealthy tourists. It was a difficult task considering that the rim receives more than 40 feet of snow annually. Erection of Crater Lake Lodge was constantly over-budget and behind schedule. In 1915 the lodge finally opened to popular fanfare, but it remained in a relatively constant state of construction. Three years later Rim Drive was completed and the park was officially open for business.

When to Go

Crater Lake National Park is always open, but a few roads and facilities close during the winter. Steel Visitor Center is open year-round, except for Christmas Day. Rim Visitor Center closes from October to May. All dining, lodging, and camping facilities are seasonal, except Rim Village Café and Gifts, which is open all year. Rim Drive and the North Entrance are closed from mid-October until July (weather dependent). Most tourists arrive immediately after the snow melts and the roads open in July and August. The same great views are available in September and October with smaller crowds.

Transportation & Airports

Public transportation does not provide service to or around the park. **Crater Lake Trolley** (541.884.1896, www.craterlaketrolley.com) provides 2-hour, ranger guided tours along Rim Drive during the summer months. Tickets cost $25/Adult, $22/Senior, and $15/Child (5–13). They can be reserved over the phone or online. Pick up or purchase tickets at the ticket booth near the Community House at Rim Village. The closest airports are Klamath Falls (LMT) and Rogue Valley–Medford (MFR).

Directions

Crater Lake can be accessed by car from the south (all year) and the north (summer only).

The North Entrance is reached via OR-138. From I-5 (west of the park), take Exit 124 at Roseburg to OR-138 E. From Bend, OR take US-97 S about 75 miles to OR-138. After 15 miles turn left at Crater Lake North Hwy.

The South Entrance is reached via OR-62, which travels north from Medford and Klamath Falls, OR on opposite sides of the park.

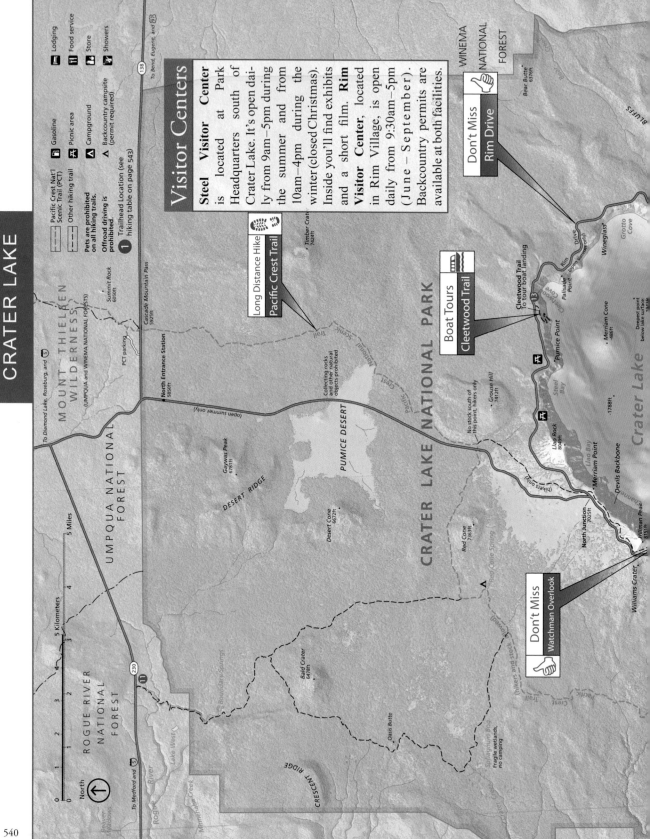

Visitor Centers

Steel Visitor Center is located at Park Headquarters south of Crater Lake. It's open daily from 9am–5pm during the summer and from 10am–4pm during the winter (closed Christmas). Inside you'll find exhibits and a short film. **Rim Visitor Center**, located in Rim Village, is open daily from 9:30am–5pm (June – September). Backcountry permits are available at both facilities.

Long Distance Hike — Pacific Crest Trail

Boat Tours — Cleetwood Trail

Don't Miss — Rim Drive

Don't Miss — Watchman Overlook

Legend:
- Lodging
- Food service
- Store
- Showers
- Gasoline
- Picnic area
- Campground
- Backcountry campsite (permit required)
- Pacific Crest Nat'l Scenic Trail (PCT)
- Other hiking trail
- Pets are prohibited on all hiking trails.
- Offroad driving is prohibited.
- Trailhead Location (see hiking table on page 543)

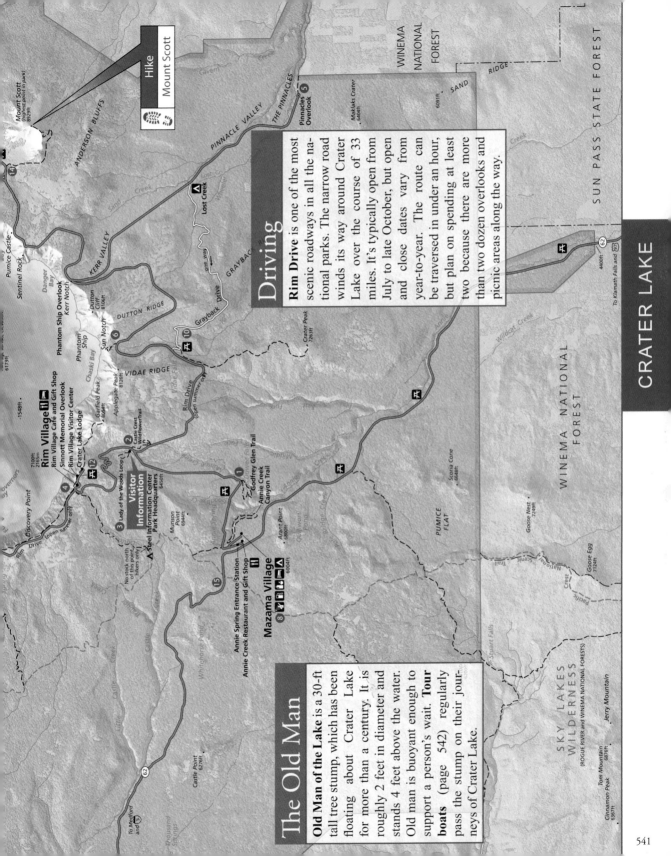

Hike

Mount Scott

Mount Scott
(highest point in park)
8929ft

Driving

Rim Drive is one of the most scenic roadways in all the national parks. The narrow road winds its way around Crater Lake over the course of 33 miles. It's typically open from July to late October, but open and close dates vary from year-to-year. The route can be traversed in under an hour, but plan on spending at least two because there are more than two dozen overlooks and picnic areas along the way.

The Old Man

Old Man of the Lake is a 30-ft tall tree stump, which has been floating about Crater Lake for more than a century. It is roughly 2 feet in diameter and stands 4 feet above the water. Old man is buoyant enough to support a person's wait. **Tour boats** (page 542) regularly pass the stump on their journeys of Crater Lake.

WINEMA NATIONAL FOREST

SAND RIDGE

SUN PASS STATE FOREST

Maklaks Crater
6404ft

6091ft

Pinnacles Overlook 5

THE PINNACLES

PINNACLE VALLEY

Cavern

ANDERSON BLUFFS

14

Creek

Sand

Lost Creek

KERR VALLEY

one way

GRAYBACK

Grayback Drive

Pumice Castle
6173ft

Sentinel Rock

Danger Bay

Phantom Ship Overlook
Kerr Notch

Dutton Cliff
8106ft

Sun Notch 6

DUTTON RIDGE

Phantom Ship

Chaski Bay

VIDAE RIDGE

Grayback Drive 10

Crater Peak
7263ft

-1548ft

Rim Village 11
Rim Village Café and Gift Shop
Sinnott Memorial Overlook
Rim Village Visitor Center
Crater Lake Lodge

7100ft
2165m

Garfield Peak
8054ft

Applegate Peak
8126ft

Castle Crest
Wildflower Trail

Rim Drive
(open summer only)

Vidae Ridge

2

Visitor Information
Steel Information Center
Park Headquarters
6450ft

Lady of the Woods Loop 3

4

Discovery Point

Rim Drive (open summer only)

No stock north of this point, hikers only

Munson Point
6944ft

Godfrey Glen Trail 1

Annie Creek Canyon Trail

Acant Point
6800ft

Quilcert Pond

Scoria Cone
6648ft

PUMICE FLAT

Goose Nest
7249ft

Goose Egg
7124ft

WINEMA NATIONAL FOREST

Wildcat Creek

4400ft

62

To Klamath Falls and 97

Annie Spring Entrance Station
Annie Creek Restaurant and Gift Shop

Mazama Village 15

8

6004ft

Castle Point
6276ft

62

To Medford and 5

Whitehorse Point

Pacific Crest National Scenic Trail

Stuart Falls

SKY LAKES WILDERNESS
(ROGUE RIVER and WINEMA NATIONAL FORESTS)

Tom Mountain
6876ft

Jerry Mountain

Cinnamon Peak
6367ft

Volcanic spires of The Pinnacles

Guided Tours

Xanterra Parks & Resorts (888.774.2728, www.craterlakelodges.com) offers **guided boat tours** of Crater Lake from July through mid-September (subject to weather). **Standard Tours** (105 minute) circle the lake while a ranger discusses its cultural and natural history; cost $29/Adult, $19/Child; and depart every hour from 10am–3pm. **Wizard Island Tours** (3-hour/6-hour) drop guests off at Wizard Island; cost $39/Adult, $25/Child); and depart at 9:55am and 1pm. Wizard Island Tour allows plenty of time to explore the island, fish, or do whatever else you can think of (provided it's socially acceptable and reasonably safe). Both tours require that you hike the 1.1-mile (one-way) **Cleetwood Trail** to the lake's shore. It's steep and strenuous, but short. Tours can be reserved by phone (888.774.2728), fax (303.297.3175), or e-mail (reserve-cl@xanterra.com). Reservation forms are available at www.craterlakelodges.com. Tickets (subject to availability) can also be purchased at **Cleetwood Cove ticketing kiosk**. The kiosk opens at 8am and all guests must check-in here prior to departure.

You can let **Crater Lake Trolley** (541.884.1896, www.craterlaketrolley.com) handle the driving with their 2-hour ranger guided tour of 33-mile Rim Drive. Tours are only offered during the summer. Tickets cost $25/Adult, $22/Senior, and $15/Child (5–13) and can be reserved over the phone or on-line. Pick up or purchase tickets at the ticket booth near the Community House at Rim Village. Trolleys help alleviate traffic congestion and reduce pollution thanks to modern engines that run on compressed natural gas. Trolleys are fully accessible.

Camping & Lodging

Mazama Campground, located just past the South Entrance, is operated by **Xanterra Parks & Resorts**. It's open from mid-July through late September. More than 200 sites can be reserved in advance (888.774.2728, www.craterlakelodges.com). Tent sites cost $21/night and RV sites cost $27/night ($29/night with electric hook-ups). **Coin-operated showers and laundry** facilities are available. The nearby camper store sells groceries, firewood, and gasoline. The campground occasionally fills on weekends. **Lost Creek Campground** offers 16 tent-only campsites located on the spur road to Pinnacles Overlook. These secluded sites are usually open from July through early October and are available on a first-come, first-served basis via self-registration. Running water and flush toilets are available. Lost Creek usually fills by the afternoon on weekends.

Crater Lake Lodge and the Cabins at Mazama Village are also operated by Xanterra Parks & Resorts (888.774.2728, www.craterlakelodges.com). **Crater Lake Lodge** is part of Rim Village overlooking Crater Lake. There are 71 rustic rooms with incomparable views available from late May through mid-October. Rates range from $164–$289/night and they book up to a year in advance (particularly for summer). **Cabins at Mazama Village**, located near the South Entrance, offers 40 basic rooms at $138/night. A restaurant is available at both locations.

Backpacking

Comfortable cabins or developed campgrounds aren't for everyone. Some visitors seek solitude and solace. For them, Crater Lake National Park offers more than 100,000 acres of wilderness. All overnight backcountry users must obtain a **free backcountry permit** and follow a few simple regulations. Permits are available at both visitor centers and Park Headquarters Ranger Station. Pacific Crest Trail (PCT) thru-hikers do not require a permit, but should sign the trail registry upon entering the park. Backpackers must camp at least one mile from roads and facilities, out of sight of other campers and visitors, more than 100 feet away from any water source, and not within view of the lake. **Winter backcountry camping** adheres to the same rules, except you are free to camp at the lake's rim. Overnight parking is available for backpackers year-round at Rim Village and Park Headquarters.

Hiking

The blue of Crater Lake is like a swatch on an artist's palette

Only 90 miles of maintained hiking trails penetrate the park's wilderness and explore the lake's rim. This place is buried in snow most of the year and Crater Lake is so magnificent and spellbinding that it monopolizes most visitors' time, but you should take at least a day to explore the area on foot. One nice thing is that choosing a trail is a very manageable task. For unsurpassed views of Crater Lake, hike to **Garfield Peak** or **Mount Scott**. Both lead high into the Cascades where you can peer down into the lake's pure blue depths. For more easily accessible vantage points try **Discovery Point or Watchman Peak Trails**. The following table provides a more complete list of hiking trails. All trailheads are numbered and marked on the map on pages 540–541.

Crater Lake Hiking Trails

	Trail Name	Trailhead (# on map)	Length	Notes (Roundtrip distances)
Easy	Godfrey Glen	Munson Valley Rd (1)	1.0 mile	Self-guiding loop • Canyon views and old-growth forest
	Castle Crest Wildflower	Park Headquarters (2)	0.5 mile	Self-guiding loop • Wildflowers mid-July to mid-August
	Lady of the Woods	Steel Info. Center (3)	0.5 mile	Self-guiding loop • Discusses park architecture and nature
	Discovery Point - 👍	Rim Village (4)	2.2 miles	Follows Crater Lake Rim from Rim Village to Discovery Pt.
	Pinnacles	Pinnacles Spur Road (5)	1.0 mile	View volcanic spires of Pinnacle Valley • Bikes allowed
	Sun Notch Viewpoint	Rim Drive (6)	0.5 mile	Uphill walk to views of Phantom Ship rising 160-ft from the lake
Moderate	Fumarole Bay	Wizard Island (7)	1.8 miles	Rocky trail follows the shoreline of Wizard Island
	Wizard Summit - 👍	Wizard Island (7)	2.0 miles	Rocky trail to 90-ft deep crater of Wizard Island
	Annie Creek Canyon	Mazama Campground (8)	1.7 miles	Self-guiding loop • Wildflowers mid-July to mid-August
	Watchman Peak - 👍	Watchman Overlook (9)	1.6 miles	Excellent location for sunset views and Wizard Island
	Crater Peak	Rim Drive (10)	6.4 miles	Meadow, forest, small volcano summit, no lake views
	Boundary Springs	Hwy 230 Milepost 19 (11)	5.0 miles	Leads to Rogue River's headwaters • Unmaintained
Strenuous	Garfield Peak	Crater Lake Lodge (12)	3.4 miles	Great bang for the mileage • Wildflowers and lake views
	Cleetwood Cove	Rim Drive (13)	2.2 miles	Steep trail provides only access to Crater Lake
	Mount Scott - 👍	Rim Drive (14)	5.0 miles	Hike to the highest point in the park • Wonderful lake views
	Union Peak	Hwy 62, PCT Trailhead (15)	11.0 miles	No lake views from the top • Highlights are geology and ecology

Did you know?

- Crater Lake was formed when a massive eruption caused Mount Mazama to collapse.

- Crater Lake is actually a volcanic caldera, not a meteor crater.

- At 1,943-ft, it is the deepest Lake in the U.S.

- It was filled almost entirely by rain and snow.

- The lake's depth varies about 3-feet seasonally. Incoming flow is balanced by seepage and evaporation.

- Crater Lake is the 6th oldest national park.

Best of Crater Lake

Attraction: **Crater Lake**
>Runner-up: Rim Drive
>2nd Runner-up: Wizard Island

Hike: **Discovery Point**
>Runner-up: Mount Scott

 # Other Activities

Biking: Cyclists are allowed on all paved roads and on unpaved Grayback Drive. The 33-mile **Rim Drive** is the most popular bicycling destination. Bikers must be acutely aware of motorists, because the road twists, turns, climbs, and descends its way around the rim of Crater Lake. Strong winds are common, which make for not-so enjoyable biking. To avoid traffic and winds try pedalling early in the morning.

Fishing: Fish didn't inhabit the lake until 1888 when William Gladstone Steel stocked it with 6 species. Today, only rainbow trout and kokanee salmon thrive in the deep blue waters. Fishing licenses are not required and there are no catch limits. Anglers must use artificial lures and flies only. **Cleetwood Cove Trail** (page 543) is the only route to the lake's shoreline. Fishermen are also welcome to cast their lines from **Wizard Island** (page 542).

Swimming in the lake is not for everyone, but it's allowed at Cleetwood Cove and Wizard Island. It's fun to say you swam here, but to stay in the 55°F water for an extended amount of time is not the most enjoyable way to spend your trip at Crater Lake.

Stargazing is a popular night-time activity and experienced **SCUBA** divers explore the lake's depths.

Winter Activities: Winter can be a remarkable time to visit Crater Lake, but **Rim Village** is the only car-accessible location (weather permitting) where the lake is visible. Park Rangers offer **free snowshoe walks** every Saturday and Sunday at 1pm from late November through the end of April. The tour lasts two hours and snowshoes are provided. No experience is necessary. Call (541) 594-3100 to make reservations. **Cross-country skiing** is gaining popularity as well. Many visitors set out to complete the 31-mile trek around the rim. Marked but ungroomed trails are available at Mazama and Rim Village for skiers of all ability levels. North Entrance Road is open and groomed for **snowmobiles** up to the rim of Crater Lake. Snowmobiles are not allowed on Rim Drive. **Backcountry camping** (page 542) is allowed.

For Kids: Children (ages 6–12) are invited to participate in **Crater Lake's Junior Ranger Program**. Pick up a free activity booklet from either visitor center. Explore the park, completing activities as you go, and return the book to a park ranger. Four completed pages earns a sticker, eight pages gets you a Junior Ranger badge. An alternative option is to go to Rim Visitor Center between 1:30–4:30pm (July–early September). At this time your child can choose from several kid-friendly activities. Each completed activity earns a Junior Ranger patch.

Ranger Programs: In addition to **trolley and boat tours** (page 542) and **snowshoe treks**, park rangers offer regularly scheduled talks, walks, and evening programs from early June to early September. All of these tours are free of charge. Current schedules of events are available at all visitor centers and in the park's newspaper, ***Reflections***.

Flora & Fauna: Crater Lake is home to **680 species of plants, 74 species of mammals, 26 species of reptiles and amphibians, and 158 species of birds**. Threatened or endangered species include lynx, northern spotted owl, bull trout, and tailed frog. Elk, deer, and bear are often seen at dawn or dusk feeding in meadows. Hairy woodpeckers, bald eagles, and the American kestrel are frequently spotted during summer.

Pets: Pets are allowed in the park, but must be kept on a leash no more than six feet in length at all times. They are essentially allowed anywhere a car can go, including roadsides, parking areas, picnic areas, and developed campgrounds. Pets are not allowed in the backcountry, on trails, or in public buildings (except service animals).

Accessibility: Many of the park's facilities and trails are accessible to individuals with mobility impairments. The store, campground, and restaurant at Mazama Village are accessible, as is Godfrey Glen Trail and the upper section of Annie Creek Canyon Trail. Facilities at Park Headquarters and Rim Village are fully accessible. Trolley tours (page 542) also accommodate wheelchair users.

Weather: It's important to consider the weather when planning a trip to Crater Lake. Most years the rim is buried beneath several feet of snow from October until June. Hwy 62 and the access road to Rim Village are plowed during winter, but Rim Drive is closed. Average daytime highs reach into the upper 60s°F during summer. In the evenings temperatures cool off quickly, often falling below freezing. Summer is typically dry and sunny, but visitors should come prepared for afternoon thunderstorms and high winds. The first major snowfall usually occurs by mid-October. Crater Lake is magnificent when the rim is covered in snow; the only real problem is there's just so much of it. In an average winter more than 500 inches of snow falls, making Crater Lake one of the snowiest regions of the Pacific Northwest. Winter temperatures are much less variable than the summer. Average highs are right around freezing and average lows are about 20°F.

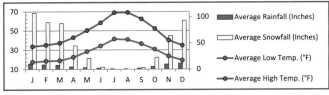

Vacation Planner

Crater Lake is a place like no other. It's one of the few sites in the world where many visitors would be perfectly happy spending a whole day staring at its divine majesty. A cooler, grill, and lawn chair wouldn't hurt, but they're hardly mandatory. If one day isn't enough, you can spend the night at **Crater Lake Lodge** or one of the park's **campgrounds** (page 542). Nearby dining, grocery stores, lodging, festivals, and attractions are listed on pages 546–549. Sitting and staring at the lake is nice, but here's another, equally satisfying way to spend a day at the park.

Here's one way to enter the lake © flickr/Powderruns

 Day 1 — Arriving at the **South Entrance**, stop at **Steel Information Center** before continuing up to Rim Drive. If you enter from the north, drive directly to **Rim Drive**. There's nothing that can really prepare you for your first sight of Crater Lake. Just have your camera close by; your first reflex will be to grab it and start snapping pictures, paparazzi-style. Stop and capture the moment, then continue on to **Rim Visitor Center**. Ask your questions, watch the short video, and pick up a brochure and newspaper if you didn't upon entry. Drive all 33 miles of Rim Drive (at least 2 hours without hiking). You'll find the views of Crater Lake are better from the west (closer to Wizard Island). It's a good practice to save the best for last, but in this case circle the lake clockwise, because it's easier to turn right into the overlook parking areas. **Discovery Point** and **Watchman Overlook** (Watchman Trail, page 543) are recommended stops. If you want to see the water from up close, hike down to its shore via **Cleetwood Trail** (page 543). Continuing around the lake, **Cloudcap Overlook** is worth a stop. Take the nearby trail to the top of **Mount Scott** (page 543). Well-conditioned hikers can complete the trek in under 2 hours. If you're short on time, skip the Pinnacles and Sun Notch. For an alternative to the Mount Scott hike, return to **Rim Village** and hike to **Garfield Peak**. It's a great place to absorb a few last impressions of such indescribable beauty.

Dining

Lassen Volcanic Area

Red Onion Grill • (530) 258-1800
384 Main St; Chester, CA 96020
www.redoniongrill.com • Entrée: $16–29

Kopper Kettle Café • (530) 258-2698
243 Main St; Chester, CA 96020

Coffee Station • (530) 258-4112
192 Main St; Chester, CA 96020

Ranch House • (530) 258-4226
669 Main St; Chester, CA 96020

Peninsula Grill • (530) 596-3538
401 Peninsula Dr, # F; Westwood, CA 96137

Luciano's Cucina di Pasta • (530) 596-4133
449 Peninsula Dr; Lake Almanor, CA 96137

J J's Café • (530) 335-7225
13385 CA-89; Old Station, CA 96071

Coyote Grill • (530) 335-7083
12533 CA-44/89; Old Station, CA 96071

Tantardino's • (530) 596-3902
401 Ponderosa Circle; Westwood, CA 96137

Art's Outpost • (530) 335-2835
37392 CA-299 E; Burney, CA 96013

Angelina's • (530) 335-4184
37143 CA-299 E; Burney, CA 96013
www.angelinasrexclub.com • Entrée: $11–30

Dragon Palace • (530) 335-3288
37345 CA-299 E; Burney, CA 96013

Pacific Coast Area

Brick & Fire • (707) 268-8959
1630 F St; Eureka, CA 95501
www.brickandfirebistro.com

Sea Grill • (707) 443-7187
316 E St; Eureka, CA 95501

Restaurant 301 • (800) 404-1390
301 L St; Eureka, CA 95501
www.carterhouse.com • Entrée: $13–22

Cookhouse Samoa • (707) 442-1659
908 Vance Ave; Samoa, CA 95564
www.samoacookhouse.net

A A Bar & Grill • (707) 443-1632
929 4th St; Eureka, CA 95501

Lost Coast Brewery & Café • (707) 445-4480
617 4th St; Eureka, CA 95501
www.lostcoast.com • Entrée: $9–19

Pak Indian Cuisine • (707) 443-2080
1735 4th St; Eureka, CA 95501
www.pakindiancuisine.com • Entrée: $10–15

Chalet House of Omelettes • (707) 442-0333
1935 5th St; Eureka, CA 95501

Pachanga Mexicana • (707) 442-2587
1802 5th St; Eureka, CA 95501

Nooners Café • (707) 443-4663
409 Opera Aly; Eureka, CA 95501

Bless My Soul Café • (707) 443-1090
29 Fifth St; Eureka, CA 95501
www.blessmysoulcafe.com • Entrée: $14–28

Old Town Coffee & Chocolates • (707) 445-8600
211 F St; Eureka, CA 95501
www.oldtowncoffeeeureka.com

Café Brio • (707) 822-0791
791 G St; Arcata, CA 95521
www.briobaking.com

Kebab Café • (707) 826-2121
5000 Valley West Blvd, # 19; Arcata, CA 95521

Wildflower Café & Bakery • (707) 822-0360
1604 G St; Arcata, CA 95521
www.wildflowercafearcata.com • Entrée: $15–16

Los Bagels Co • www.losbagels.com
1061 I St; Arcata • (707) 822-3150
1 Harpst Street; Arcata • (707) 826-5308
403 2nd Street; Eureka • (707) 442-8525

Abruzzi • (707) 826-2345
780 7th St; Arcata, CA 95521
www.abruzziarcata.com • Entrée: $21–30

Tomo Japanese Restaurant • (707) 822-1414
708 9th St; Arcata, CA 95521
www.tomoarcata.com • Entrée: $17–22

Big Blue Café • (707) 826-7578
846 G St; Arcata, CA 95521

Toni's 24 Hour Restaurant • (707) 822-0091
1901 Heindon Rd; Arcata, CA 95521

Japhy's Soup & Noodles • (707) 826-2594
1563 G St; Arcata, CA 95521
www.japhys.com • Soups: $5–8

3 Foods Café • (707) 822-9474
835 J St; Arcata, CA 95521
www.cafeattheendoftheuniverse.com • Entrée: $11–15

Folie Douce • (707) 822-1042
1551 G St; Arcata, CA 95521
www.holyfolie.com • Entrée: $26–37

Live From New York Pizza • (707) 822-6199
670 9th St, # 102; Arcata, CA 95521

Renata's Creperie • (707) 825-8783
1030 G St; Arcata, CA 95521

Good Harvest Café • (707) 465-6028
575 US-101; Crescent City, CA 95531

Chart Room Restaurant • (707) 464-5993
130 Anchor Way; Crescent City, CA 95531

Wing Wah Restaurant • (707) 465-3935
383 M St; Crescent City, CA 95531

Perlita's Authentic Mexican • (707) 465-6770
297 US-101 S; Crescent City, CA 95531

Fisherman's Restaurant • (707) 465-3474
700 US-101 S; Crescent City, CA 95531

Hiouchi Café • (707) 458-3415
2095 US-199; Crescent City, CA 95531

CC Diner & Ice Cream • (707) 465-5858
1319 Northcrest Dr; Crescent City, CA 95531

Crater Lake/Southwest Oregon

Art Alley Grille • (541) 469-0800
515 Chetco Ave; Brookings, OR 97415

Mattie's Pancake & Omelette • (541) 469-7211
15975 US-101 S; Brookings, OR 97415

Pancho's Restaurante • (541) 469-6531
1136 Chetco Ave; Brookings, OR 97415
www.panchosalsa.com • Entrée: $7+

Salty Dog Coffee • (541) 469-3161
16340 Lower Harbor Rd; Brookings, OR 97415

Kitanishi Café • (541) 469-7864
632 Hemlock St; Brookings, OR 97415

Beckie's Café • (541) 560-3563
56484 OR-62; Prospect, OR 97536
www.unioncreekoregon.com • Burgers: $5+

Gorge Restaurant • (541) 560-3774
2651 Mill Creek Dr; Prospect, OR 97536

Trophy Room & Café • (541) 560-3641
311 Mill Creek Dr; Prospect, OR 97536

Prospect Pizza • (541) 560-4000
51 Mill Creek Dr; Prospect, OR 97536

Butte Falls Café • (541) 865-7707
443 Broad St; Butte Falls, OR 97522

Pho Hong • (541) 850-9441
4023 S 6th St, # B; Klamath Falls, OR 97603

Thai Orchid Café • (541) 273-0707
900 Main St, # D; Klamath Falls, OR 97601

Nibbley's Café • (541) 883-2314
2650 Washburn Way; Klamath Falls, OR 97603
www.nibbleys.com • Entrée: $9–17

Roosters Steak & Chop House • (541) 850-8414
205 Main St; Klamath Falls, OR 97601
www.roosterssteakandchophouse.lbu.com

Dynasty Restaurant • (541) 850-6948
106 Main St; Klamath Falls, OR 97601

Hidalgos Mexican Restaurant • (541) 850-8317
430 Main St; Klamath Falls, OR 97601

Casey's Restaurant • (541) 882-9676
4706 S 6th St; Klamath Falls, OR 97603

Grocery Stores

Lassen Volcanic Area

<u>Holiday Quality Foods</u> • (530) 258-2122
271 Main St; Chester, CA 96020

<u>Mineral Grocery</u>
18968 Husky Way; Mineral, CA 96063

<u>Safeway</u> • (530) 335-3212
37264 Main St; Burney, CA 96013

<u>Walmart</u> • (530) 251-2000
2900 Main St; Susanville, CA 96130

Pacific Coast Area

<u>Safeway</u> • (707) 465-3353
475 M St; Crescent City, CA 95531

<u>Grocery Outlet</u> • (707) 464-3131
1124 3rd St; Crescent City, CA 95531

<u>Fred Meyer</u> • (541) 469-5556
325 5th St; Brookings, OR 97415

<u>Walmart</u> • (707) 464-1198
900 E Washington Blvd; Crescent City, CA 95531

Crater Lake/Southwest Oregon

<u>Walmart Supercenter</u> • (541) 885-6890
3600 Washburn Way; Klamath Falls, OR 97603

<u>Safeway</u> • (541) 273-5500
211 N Eighth St; Klamath Falls, OR 97601

<u>Fred Meyer</u> • (541) 884-1977
2655 Shasta Way; Klamath Falls, OR 97603

<u>Safeway</u> • (541) 608-3680
1003 Medford Shopping Centre; Medford, OR 97504

<u>Safeway</u> • (541) 774-4340
3169 Crater Lake Hwy; Medford, OR 97501

<u>Walmart</u> • (541) 770-2010
3615 Crater Lake Hwy; Medford, OR 97504

<u>Fred Meyer</u> • (541) 857-4665
1301 Center Dr; Medford, OR 97501

Lodging

Lassen Volcanic Area

<u>Drakesbad Guest Ranch</u> • (866) 999-0914
Chester Warner Valley Rd; Chester, CA 96020
www.drakesbad.com • *In-Park Lodging*
Rates: $140–201/person/night

<u>Antlers Motel</u> • (530) 258-2722
268 Main St; Chester, CA 96020
www.antlersmotel.com • Rates: $80

<u>Cedar Lodge</u> • (530) 258-2904
1487 County Rd 324; Chester, CA 96020
www.cedarlodgeonline.com • Rates: $55–75

<u>Bidwell House</u> • (530) 258-3338
1 Main St; Chester, CA 96020
www.bidwellhouse.com • Rates: $85–175

<u>Cinnamon Teal Inn</u> • (530) 258-3993
227 Feather River Dr; Chester, CA 96020
www.cinnamontealinn.net • Rates: $140–270

<u>Rim Rock Ranch</u> • (530) 335-7114
13275 CA-89; Old Station, CA 96071
www.rimrockcabins.com • Rates: $60–125

<u>Hat Creek Resort & RV Park</u> • (530) 335-7121
12533 CA-44/89; Old Station, CA 96071
www.hatcreekresortrv.com • Rates: $54–220

<u>Burney Motel</u> • (530) 335-4500
37448 Main St; Burney, CA 96013
www.theburneymotel.com • Rates: $55–229

<u>Green Gables Motel</u> • (530) 335-2264
37371 CA-299 E; Burney, CA 96013
www.greengablesmotel.com • $55–185

<u>Shasta Pines Motel & Suites</u> • (530) 335-2201
37386 CA-299 E; Burney, CA 96013
www.shastapinesmotel.com • Rates: $55–89

<u>Sleepy Hollow Lodge</u> • (530) 335-2285
36898 CA-299 E; Burney, CA 96013

<u>Weston House B&B</u> • (530) 474-3738
6741 Red Rock Rd; Shingletown, CA 96088
www.westonhouse.com • Rates: $175–205

<u>McCloud Mercantile Hotel</u> • (530) 964-2330
241 Main St; McCloud, CA 96057
www.mccloudmercantile.com • Rates: $129–250

<u>McCloud River Inn</u> • (530) 964-2130
325 Lawndale Court; McCloud, CA 96057
www.riverinn.com • Rates: $99–199

<u>McCloud Hotel</u> • (530) 964-2822
408 Main St; McCloud, CA 96057
www.mccloudhotel.com • Rates: $100–215

Pacific Coast Area

<u>Town House Motel</u> • (707) 443-4536
933 4th St; Eureka, CA 95501
www.eurekatownhousemotel.com

<u>Bayview Motel</u> • (707) 442-1673
2844 Fairfield St; Eureka, CA 95501
www.bayviewmotel.com • Rates: $91–175

<u>Carter House Inns</u> • (707) 444-8062
301 L St; Eureka, CA 95501
www.carterhouse.com • Rates: $159–595

<u>Eureka Inn</u> • (707) 497-6093
518 7th St; Eureka, CA 95501
www.eurekainn.com • Rates: $80+

<u>Eagle House Victorian Inn</u> • (707) 444-3344
139 2nd St; Eureka, CA 95501
www.eaglehouseinn.com • Rates: $105–250

<u>Ships Inn B&B</u> • (707) 443-7583
821 D St; Eureka, CA 95501
www.shipsinn.net • Rates: $130–175

<u>Abigail's Elegant Victorian Mansion</u> • (707) 444-3144
1406 C St; Eureka, CA 95501
www.eureka-california.com • Rates: $105–195

<u>Rose Court Cottage</u> • (707) 822-0935
814 13th St; Arcata, CA 95521
www.rosecourtcottage.com • Rates: $139+

<u>Lady Anne Victorian Inn</u> • (707) 822-2797
902 14th St; Arcata, CA 95521
www.ladyanneinn.com • Rates: $125–140

<u>Lighthouse Inn</u> • (877) 464-3993
681 US-101 S; Crescent City, CA 95531
www.crescentcitylighthouseinn.com • Rates: $89–145

<u>Hiouchi Motel</u> • (707) 458-3041
2097 US-199; Crescent City, CA 95531

<u>Curly Redwood Lodge</u> • (707) 464-2137
701 US-101 S; Crescent City, CA 95531
www.curlyredwoodlodge.com • Rates: $56–93

<u>Crescent Beach Motel</u> • (707) 464-5436
1455 US-101 S; Crescent City, CA 95531
www.crescentbeachmotel.com • Rates: $67–133

<u>Anna Wulf House B&B</u> • (707) 951-0683
622 J St; Crescent City, CA 95531
www.annawulfhouse.com • Rates: $100–150

Crater Lake/Southwest Oregon

<u>Ocean Suites Motel</u> • (541) 469-4004
16045 Lower Harbor Rd; Brookings, OR 97415
www.oceansuitesmotel.com • Rates: $89–119

<u>Wild Rivers Motorlodge</u> • (541) 469-5361
437 Chetco Ave; Brookings, OR 97415
www.wildriversmotorlodge.com • Rates: $60–100

<u>South Coast Inn</u> • (541) 469-5557
516 Redwood St; Brookings, OR 97415
www.southcoastinn.com

<u>The Chetco River Inn</u> • (707) 496-9509
21202 High Prairie Rd; Brookings, OR 97415
www.thechetcoriverinn.com • Rates: $125–135

<u>Out'n'About Treehouse Treesort</u>
Take the kids or relive your youth by spending a night in the trees • horseback rides, tree climbing, rafting, camping, hiking, and zip-lining available
300 Page Creek Rd; Cave Junction, OR 97523
www.treehouses.com • (541) 592-2208
Rates: $130–280

<u>Sun Pass Ranch B&B</u> • (541) 381-2882
52125 OR-62; Fort Klamath, OR 97626
www.sunpassranch.com • Rates: $100–125

<u>The Wilson Cottages</u> • (541) 381-2209
57997 OR-62; Fort Klamath, OR 97626
www.thewilsoncottages.com • Rates: $75–110

Aspen Inn • (541) 381-2321
52250 OR-62; Fort Klamath, OR 97626
www.theaspeninn.com • Rates: $139

Crater Lake B&B • (866) 517-9560
52395 Weed Rd; Fort Klamath, OR 97626
www.craterlakebandb.com

Jo's Motel/Campground • (541) 381-2234
RV Hook-ups available ($25/2 guests)
52851 OR-62; Fort Klamath, OR 97626
www.josmotel.com • Rates: $110–130

Cimarron Inn • (541) 882-4601
3060 S 6th St; Klamath Falls, OR 97603
www.cimarroninnklamathfalls.com • Rates: $69–89

Running Y Resort • (541) 850-5500
5500 Running Y Rd; Klamath Falls, OR 97601
www.runningy.com • Rates: $79–139

Lake of the Woods Resort • (541) 949-8300
950 Harriman Route; Klamath Falls, OR 97601
www.lakeofthewoodsresort.com • Rates: $129–299

Devonridge B&B • (541) 883-3172
1403 Devonridge Dr; Klamath Falls, OR 97601
www.devonridge.com • Rates: $159–179

Crystal Wood Lodge • (541) 381-2322
38625 Westside Rd; Klamath Falls, OR 97601
www.crystalwoodlodge.com • Rates: $95–150

Many chain restaurants and hotels can be found in Chico, CA; Eureka, CA; Arcata, CA; Crescent City, CA; Brookings, OR; Medford, OR, Ashland, OR; Klamath Falls, OR; as well as along I-5.

Festivals

Winter Wings Festival • February
Klamath Falls, OR • www.winterwingsfest.org

Shakespeare Festival • February–July
Ashland • www.osfashland.org

Redwood Coast Jazz Festival • March
Eureka, CA • www.redwoodjazz.org

Independent Film Festival • April
Ashland • www.ashlandfilm.org

Apple Jam Music Festival • May
Williams, OR • www.applejam.webs.com

Britt Festival Grounds • Summer Concerts
Jacksonville, OR • www.brittfest.org

Blues by the Bay • September
Eureka, CA • www.bluesbythebay.org

Blues & BBQ • October
Crescent City, CA • www.jazzandheritage.org

Jazz Festival • October
Medford, OR • www.medfordjazz.org

Attractions
Lassen Volcanic Area

Lassen National Forest • (530) 336-5521
43225 CA-299 E; Fall River Mills, CA 96028

Subway Cave Lava Tubes
Located 0.25 mile north of the junction of CA-44 and CA-89 across from Cave Campground
Lassen National Forest; Old Station, CA 96071

McArthur-Burney Falls Memorial State Park
East Shasta, CA • (530) 335-2777 • www.parks.ca.gov

Northwoods Art Gallery • (530) 258-3400
278 Main St; Chester, CA 96020

Almanor Bowling & Golf • (530) 258-4300
376 Main St; Chester, CA 96020

Westwood Museum • (530) 256-2233
311 Ash St; Westwood, CA 96137

Mt Burney Theatre • (530) 335-2605
37022 CA-299 E; Burney, CA 96013
www.mtburneytheatre.com • Tickets: $6.50/Adult

Regent Theaters • (310) 208-3259
Westwood, CA 96137

Sierra Theatre • (530) 257-7469
819 Main St; Susanville, CA • Tickets: $8/Adult
www.sierratheatreanduptowncinemas.com

National Yo-Yo Museum
320 Broadway; Chico, CA 95928
www.museum.nationalyoyo.org

Shasta Sunset Dinner Train • (530) 964-2142
328 Main St; McCloud, CA 96057
www.shastasunset.com

Lava Beds National Monument
PO Box 1240; Tulelake, CA 96134
www.nps.gov/labe • (530) 667-8113
Entrance Fee: $10/Vehicle

Castle Crags State Park
Sacramento Canyon, California
www.parks.ca.gov • (530) 235-2684

Gold Nugget Museum • (530) 872-8722
502 Pearson Rd; Paradise, CA 95969
www.goldnuggetmuseum.com

Olive Pit • (530) 824-4667
A unique stop with olive tasting bar and deli
2156 Solano St; Corning, CA 96021
www.olivepit.com

Plumas National Forest • (530) 284-7126
128 Hot Springs Rd; Greenville, CA 95947

Kelly Griggs House Museum • (530) 527-1129
311 Washington St; Red Bluff, CA 96080

Sierra Nevada Brewery • (530) 345-2739
1075 E 20th St; Chico, CA 95928
www.sierranevada.com • Free Tours

Pacific Coast Area

North Coast Adv. Centers • (707) 826-9558
Canopy Tours, Ropes Courses, Training & Certificates, and Outdoor Programs
1065 K St, Suite C; Arcata, CA 95521
www.northcoastadventurecenters.com

Arcata Community Forest
Arcata, California

Sequoia Park Zoo • (707) 441-4263
3414 W St; Eureka, CA 95503
www.sequoiaparkzoo.net • Admission: $5/Adult

Blue Ox Mill Works & Hist. • (707) 444-3437
1 X St; Eureka, CA 95501
www.blueoxmill.com • Admission: $7.50/Adult

Clarke Hist. Museum • (707) 443-1947
240 E St; Eureka, CA 95501
www.clarkemuseum.org

Fort Humboldt State Hist. Park • (707) 445-6547
3431 Fort Ave; Eureka, California 95503
www.parks.ca.gov

The Spa at Personal Choice • (707) 445-2041
130 G St; Eureka, CA 95501
www.thespaatpersonalchoice.com

Carson Mansion • www.ingomar.org
143 M St; Eureka, CA 95501

Humboldt Redwoods State Parks
17119 Ave of the Giants; Weott, CA 95571
www.humboldtredwoods.org • (707) 946-2409
Entrance Fee: $8/Vehicle • Camping: $35/night

One Log House Espresso & Gifts
705 US-101; Garberville, CA 95542
www.oneloghouse.com • (707) 247-3717

Confusion Hill Gravity House
75001 US-101 N; Leggett, CA 95585
www.confusionhill.com • (707) 925-6456
Admission: $5/Adult

Del Norte County Museum • (707) 464-3922
577 H St; Crescent City, CA 95531
www.delnortehistory.org • Free

Red's Crescent Drive-In • (707) 464-1813
2303 Elk Valley Rd; Crescent City, CA 95531

Ocean World • (707) 464-4900
304 US-101 S; Crescent City, CA 95531
www.oceanworldonline.com • Tours: $10/Adult

Tolowa Dunes State Park • (707) 464-6101
1375 Elk Valley Rd; Crescent City, CA 95531
www.parks.ca.gov

Battery Point Lighthouse • (707) 464-3089
577 H St; Crescent City, CA 95531

Crescent City Cinemas • (707) 465-4567
375 M St; Crescent City, CA 95531

Humboldt Lagoon State Park
Trinidad, CA 95570 • (707) 488-2041

Golden Bear Fishing Charters • (707) 951-0119
Full-day trips starting at $90 per person
Citizens Dock Rd; D Dock, Crescent City, CA
www.goldenbearfishingcharters.com

Castle Rock National Wildlife Refuge
Crescent City, CA 95531

Trees of Mystery • (707) 482-2251
15500 US-101 N; Klamath, CA 95548
www.treesofmystery.net • Admission: $14/Adult

Lucky 7 Casino • (707) 487-7777
350 N Indian Rd; Smith River, CA 95567
www.lucky7casino.com

Elk Valley Casino • (707) 464-1020
2500 Howland Hill Rd; Crescent City, CA 95531
www.elkvalleycasino.com

Lighthouse Repertory Theatre • (707) 465-3740
PO Box 171; Crescent City, CA 95531

Klamath River Jet Boat Tours • (707) 482-0205
17635 US-101 South; Klamath, CA 95548
www.jetboattours.com • Tours: $42/Adult

FunBus Tours • (707) 482-1030
1663 W Klamath Beach Rd; Klamath, CA 95548
www.funbustours.com • Tours: $35+

Crater Lake/Southwest Oregon

Samuel H Boardman State Park
Brookings, OR

Redwood Cinema • (541) 412-7575
621 Chetco Ave; Brookings, OR 97415
www.redwoodtheater.com • Tickets: $7.50/Adult

Harris Beach State Park • (541) 469-2021
1655 US-101 N; Brookings, Oregon 97415
www.oregonstateparks.org • Day-use: $5/Vehicle

Great Cats World Park • (541) 592-2957
27919 Redwood Hwy; Cave Junction, OR 97523
www.greatcatsworldpark.com • Admission: $14/Adult

Oregon Caves Nat'l Mon. • (541) 592-2100
19000 Caves Hwy; Cave Junction, OR 97523
www.nps.gov/orca • Cave Tours: $8.50/Adult

Collier Logging Museum • (541) 783-2471
46000 US-97 N; Chiloquin, OR 97624
www.oregonstateparks.org

Kla-Mo-Ya Casino • (541) 783-7529
34333 US-97 N; Chiloquin, OR 97624
www.klamoyacasino.com

Klamath Marsh NWR • (541) 783-3380
13750 Silver Lake Rd; Chiloquin, OR 97624

Pelican Cinemas • (541) 884-5000
2626 Biehn St; Klamath Falls, OR 97601

Coming Attractions Cinemas • (541) 884-5258
2626 Biehn St; Klamath Falls, OR 97601

Ross Ragland Theater • (541) 884-0651
218 N 7th St; Klamath Falls, OR 97601
www.rrtheater.org

Movies 6 • (541) 826-7308
7501 Crater Lake Hwy; White City, OR 97503
www.cinemark.com

Varsity Theatre • (541) 488-0619
166 E Main St; Ashland, OR 97520
www.catheatres.com

Craterian Ginger Rogers Theater • (541) 779-8195
23 S Central Ave; Medford, OR 97501
www.craterian.org

Rafting, hiking, and fishing outfitters, rental and shuttle services

Rogue Wilderness Adventures • (541) 479-9554
325 Galice Rd; Merlin, OR 97532
www.wildrogue.com

Rogue River Outfitters • (541) 451-4498
38672 First Creek Dr; Lebanon, OR 97355
www.nwriveroutfitters.com

Noah's River Adventures • (800) 858-2811
53 N Main St; Ashland, OR 97520
www.noahsrafting.com

O'Brien's Rogue River Rafting • (541) 476-2404
5556 Lower River Rd; Grants Pass, OR 97526
www.obriensrogueriveroutfitters.com

Orange Torpedo Rogue River Rafting Trips
210 Merlin Rd; Merlin, OR 97532
www.orangetorpedo.com • (541) 479-5061

Kokopelli River Guides • (541) 201-7694
2475 Siskiyou Blvd; Ashland, OR 97520
www.kokopelliriverguides.com

Momentum River Expeditions • (541) 488-2525
3195 E Main St, # 2; Ashland, OR 97520
www.momentumriverexpeditions.com

Ouzel Outfitters • (541) 385-5947
PO Box 817; Bend, OR 97709
www.oregonrafting.com

Echo River Trips • (800) 652-3246
116 Oak St, # 1; Hood River, OR 97031
www.echotrips.com

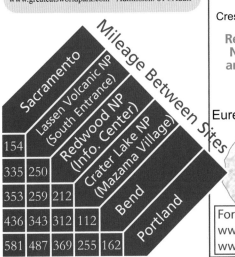

	Sacramento	Lassen Volcanic NP (South Entrance)	Redwood NP (Info. Center)	Crater Lake NP (Mazama Village)	Bend	Portland
Lassen Volcanic NP (South Entrance)	154					
Redwood NP (Info. Center)	335	250				
Crater Lake NP (Mazama Village)	353	259	212			
Bend	436	343	312	112		
Portland	581	487	369	255	162	

Mileage Between Sites

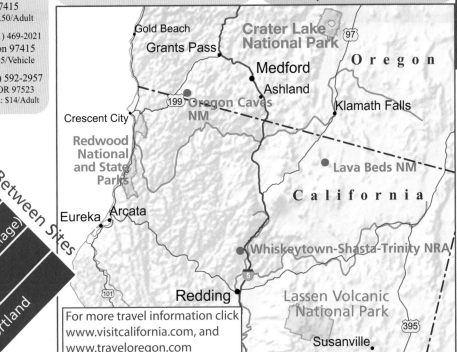

For more travel information click
www.visitcalifornia.com, and
www.traveloregon.com

549

Mount Rainier viewed from Upper Tipsoo Lake near Chinook Pass

55210 238th Avenue East
Ashford, WA 98304
Phone: (360) 569-2211
Website: www.nps.gov/mora

Established: March 2, 1899
Size: 235,625 Acres
Annual Visitors: 1.2 Million
Peak Season: Summer

Activities: Hiking, Backpacking, Camping, Mountain Climbing, Horseback Riding, Biking, Fishing, Snowshoeing, and Skiing

Campgrounds: Cougar Rock*, Ohanapecosh*, White River, Ipsut Creek (free), Mowich Lake (free)
Fee: $12–15/night
Backcountry Camping: Permitted with a Backcountry Use Permit

Park Hours: All day, every day
Entrance Fee: $15 • Vehicle
$5 • Individual (foot, bike, etc.)

*Reserve at (877) 444-6777 or www.recreation.gov

Mount Rainier - Washington

Mount Rainier, the 14,410-foot volcano, towers above its surroundings and greets visitors from all directions more than 100 miles before entering the park boundary. Cowlitz, Nisqually, Puyallup, and Yakima tribes called the mountain Tahoma or "the Big Mountain where the waters begin." Much more than water begins here. Natives began vision quests at this location. Today's guests' search for respite begins and ends at majestic Mount Rainier. Nearly 1.5 million visitors admire these mountain views each year, and some 10,000 climbers attempt to trek to its summit, where they are able to look down on 26 glaciers covering its upper reaches and to the Pacific Northwest beyond.

The snow-capped mountain's dramatic presence caught the attention of several groups and soon commercial interests and conservationists were mired in a contentious debate over the best way to utilize the area. In 1893, federal government officials created the **Pacific Forest Reserve**, encompassing the mountain. **Gifford Pinchot**, head of the United States Forest Service, believed in "conservation through use," treating the nation's forests like a crop to be maintained and used. **John Muir**, a beloved naturalist who had successfully advocated for the preservation of Yosemite Valley, formed a kinship with Mount Rainier in 1888 when he joined a group that completed the mountain's 5th recorded ascent. He wrote in a letter to his wife that he had absolutely no intention of climbing the mountain, but when five others showed interest in the idea he couldn't help but tag along. Muir vehemently opposed the "conservation through use" idea. Not a single tree would fall at the hands of an ax or river be impeded by a dam if he had his way. Preservation, plain and simple, was his goal. These sublime works of nature were beyond the scope of anything man could ever make in terms of beauty and grandeur. They needed to be preserved and protected for the enjoyment of all, not looted and plundered for the benefit of private interests. Support from influential bodies with interests of their own helped galvanize the conservationist movement. **The National Geographic Society** wished to study volcanism and glaciology in the area. **The Northern Pacific Railroad** was on board because a park could draw more passenger service on their trains—a tried and tested method that already yielded substantial benefits for Northern Pacific and Southern Pacific Railroads with the creation of Yellowstone (page 218) and Yosemite (page 498) National Parks, respectively. **The Sierra Club** and commercial leaders in Tacoma and Seattle joined the cause, supporting what would become a long and arduous battle. Over the course of five years of bitter debate and six attempts, a bill was finally passed with two provisions: the government needed assurances that no park land was suitable for farming or mining and that no government appropriations were required for its management and procurement. The provisions were met, and on March 2, 1899 Mount Rainier became the fifth national park and first to be created from a national forest.

Park establishment and construction of a road to Paradise in 1911 ushered in a new era of tourism. **President William Howard Taft's** touring car was the first vehicle to christen the road in very unique fashion: muddy conditions resulted in his car being pulled through the upper portion by a team of mules. Six years later the National Park Service was established and trails, facilities, roads, and campgrounds were developed in earnest, enhancing the overall visitor experience. Mountain climbers could experience summiting Rainier much like John Muir did, and now thousands of climbers make the trek each year. Today's visitors realize what Muir and Native Americans knew: Mount Rainier is more than a pleasure ground, it's a sacred place in need of preservation and protection.

Did you know?

> Mount Rainier's Carbon Glacier, located on the mountain's north side, is the lowest (3,500-feet), thickest (700-feet), and largest glacier by volume in the contiguous United States. Emmons Glacier is the largest by area.

When to Go

Mount Rainier National Park is open all year. Visitation peaks in July and August when the weather is best, most trails are free of snowpack, and wildflowers are in full bloom. Traffic can create considerable frustration during summer months and winter weekends. Traveling midweek or delaying your vacation until September or early October is a good way to avoid the crowds.

Transportation & Airports

The **free Paradise Shuttle** (page 555) ferries visitors between Longmire and Paradise on weekends from mid-June through early September. The closest large commercial airports are Seattle–Tacoma International (SEA) and Portland International (PDX).

Directions

The park's eastern half is not accessible during winter. Carbon River and Nisqually Entrances on the west side are open all year. However, unexpected road closures can occur at any time. Always check the park's website for current road status prior to your trip. Directions to Paradise, the most popular region, are provided below.

Nisqually Entrance (Longmire/Paradise):

From Seattle (104 miles), take I-5 S to WA-512 E (Exit 127) to WA-7 S. Take WA-7 to WA-706, which leads into the park.

From Portland (155 miles), take I-5 N to US-12 E (Exit 68). Take US-12 to WA-7 N. Turn right at WA-706, which leads into the park.

Mount Rainier National Park map

Drive To Sunrise

Don't Miss Skyline Trail

Don't Miss Paradise

Carbon River Road subject to closure due to river flooding

Carbon River Road

CLEARWATER WILDERNESS

MT. BAKER-SNOQUALMIE NATIONAL FOREST

Carbon River Entrance 19

To Wilkeson 13mi / 21km from Carbon River Entrance

CHENUIS

Chenuis Falls

Ranger Falls

Green Lake

Ipsut Creek 20

RUST RIDGE

ALKI CREST

NORTH PARK

Independence Ridge

Lake Eleanor

Adelaide Lake

Marjorie Lake

Lake Ethel

BEE FLAT

Chenuis Lakes

Obtain Climbing and Wilderness Camping Permits for the northwest area of the park at Carbon River Ranger Station.

Tolmie Peak

Eunice Lake

Ipsut Pass

MOTHER MOUNTAIN

ECHO CLIFFS

YELLOWSTONE CLIFFS

Natural Bridge

Windy Gap

Crest Falls

Crescent Lake

Alice Falls

Crescent Mountain

Pacific Point

NORTHERN CRAGS

Northern Crags

ELYSIAN FIELDS

VERNAL PARK

Affi Falls

Mount Fremont Lookout

Skyscraper Mountain 7078ft

Drive To Sunrise

Sunrise Visitor Center (open July to late September)

165

Mountain Meadows

(road open July to October)

Mowich Lake 21 22

Entrance fee machine

Elizabeth Ridge

MIST PARK

SEATTLE PARK

SPRAY PARK

Spray Falls

Eagle Cliff

GOAT ISLAND ROCK

MORAINE PARK

OLD DESOLATE

Mystic Lake

Garda Falls

BERKELEY PARK

GRAND PARK

YAKIMA

White River

Mowich River

Tillicum Point

Flett Glacier

Division Rock

PTARMIGAN RIDGE

Giant Falls

Observation Rock

Russell Glacier

Carbon Glacier

Mystic Lake

Winthrop Glacier

BURROUGHS MOUNTAIN

Burroughs Mountain

Inter Fork

Golden Lakes

SUNSET PARK

North Mowich Glacier

Needle Rock

LIBERTY RIDGE

WILLIS WALL

Steamboat Prow 9702ft

Mount Ruth

THE WEDGE

St. Elmo Pass

GLACIER BASIN

Camp Schurman 9510ft

Baker Point

GOAT ISLAND MOUNTAIN

MT. BAKER-SNOQUALMIE NATIONAL FOREST

Puyallup River

COLONADE

South Mowich Glacier

JEANNETTE HEIGHTS

Edmunds Glacier

SUNSET AMPHITHEATER

Liberty Cap

RUSSELL CLIFF

Liberty Cap

MOUNT RAINIER NATIONAL PARK

Emmons Glacier

SUMMER LAND

MEANY CREST

Fryingpan Glacier

OHANAPE

GLACIER VIEW WILDERNESS

KLAPATCHE RIDGE

Aurora Lake

KLAPATCHE PARK

St. Andrews Lake

ST. ANDREWS PARK

Tokaloo Rock

Puyallup Glacier

St. Andrews Rock

PUYALLUP CLEAVER

Tahoma Glacier

Columbia Crest 14410ft

MOUNT RAINIER

Point Success 14153ft

Little Tahoma Peak 11138ft

DISAPPOINTMENT CLEAVER

Gibraltar Rock

Graham Glacier

CATHEDRAL ROCKS

BEEHIVE

Camp Muir 10188ft

COWLITZ CLEAVER

Whitman Glacier

WHITMAN CREST

INDIAN BAR

COWLITZ PARK

GLACIER ISLAND

South Tahoma Glacier

SUCCESS CLEAVER

SUCCESS DIVIDE

Pyramid Glacier

Kautz Glacier

WAPOWETY CLEAVER

Wilson Glacier

Nisqually Glacier

Anvil Rock 9584ft

Paradise Glacier

Cowlitz Glacier

EMERALD RIDGE

PYRAMID PARK

Mildred Point

Pearl Falls

VAN TRUMP PARK

Mirror Lakes

Copper Mountain

Iron Mountain

Cowlitz Rocks 7450ft

McClure Rock

Panorama Point

Don't Miss Skyline Trail

Paradise

Nisqually Vista

Alta Vista

Paradise upper parking lot 9

Paradise Inn (open May to early October)

Caution: rough trail, subject to flooding

Round Pass

Gobblers Knob

Mount Ararat

INDIAN HENRY'S HUNTING GROUND

Squaw Lake

Henry M. Jackson Memorial Visitor Center

Paradise lower parking lot (limited services October to May)

MAZAMA

STEVENS RIDGE (road open June to October)

THE BENCH

Martha Falls

Goat Lake

Lake George

Lake Christine

Westside Road closed to vehicles beyond this point due to recurring flood damage.

Satulick Mountain

RAMPART RIDGE

THE RAMPARTS

Cougar Rock

Ricksecker Point

Carter Falls

Eagle Peak

TATOOSH RANGE

Pinnacle Glacier

Pinnacle Peak

Unicorn Glacier

STEVENS CANYON

Maple Falls

Bench Lake

Snow Lake

MOUNT WOW

Lake Allen

3mi 5km

Rampart Ridge Trail

5

Cougar Rock

Wilderness Information Center

4

Christine Falls

Madcap Falls

Reflection Lakes

Louise Lake

10

Carter Falls

Unicorn Peak

To Elbe and 14mi / 23km from Nisqually Entrance

7

To Park Headquarters 10mi / 16km from Nisqually Entrance

Westside Road (road open May to November)

Tumtum Peak

3

Trail of the Shadows

2

National Park Inn (open year-round)

Longmire Museum

Johnson Lake

Blue Lake

Ashford

706

Nisqually Entrance 2023ft

N46 44' 29" W121 55' 02"

1mi 2km

Kautz Creek Trail

6mi 9km

Don't Miss Paradise

52

Big Creek U.S. Forest Service (open late May to September)

Sunshine Point

(road open May to November)

Nisqually River

To 12

TATOOSH WILDERNESS

Tatoosh Lakes

GIFFORD

1 Trailhead Location (see hiking table on page 556)

Pacific Crest Trail

Wonderland Trail

Other hiking trail

Waterfall

Unpaved road and pullout

Paved road and pullout

Winter road closures
All park roads are CLOSED IN WINTER except the following: the road between Nisqually Entrance and Paradise (section between Longmire and Paradise only open as weather permits) and the Carbon River Road.

Ranger station

Wilderness patrol cabin

Interpretive trail

Campground

Lodging

Restaurant

Picnic area

Groceries

Fire Lookout

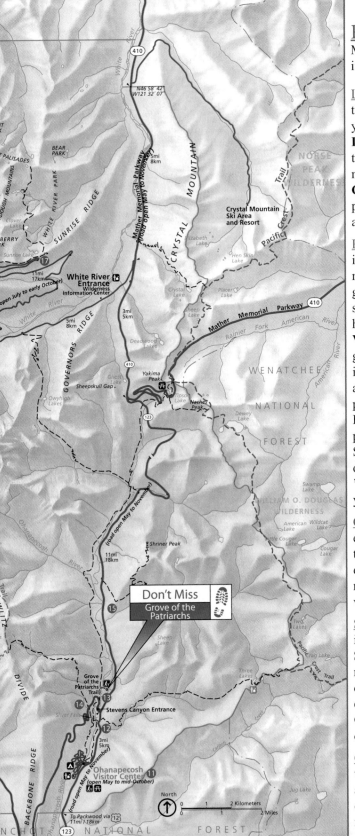

Regions

Mount Rainier National Park is essentially broken into five road accessible regions.

Longmire (All Year) is located in the SW corner of the park, 7 miles east of Nisqually Entrance. Here you'll find **Longmire Museum**, **National Park Inn**, **Trail of the Shadows** (popular), and access to the 93-mile **Wonderland Trail** that circles the mountain. There's a **Wilderness Information Center** where you can plan a backcountry trip and pick up a permit. **Cougar Rock Campground** is about 2-miles beyond Longmire.

Paradise (All Year), the most popular destination, is located 12 miles east of Longmire. It receives almost 70% of all visitors. The region's wildflowers, glaciers, and dramatic mountain vistas provide some of the best scenery the Pacific Northwest has to offer. **Henry M. Jackson Memorial Visitor Center** provides the perfect venue to begin a trip to Mount Rainier with its exhibits and introductory film. Accommodations are available at **Paradise Inn**. **Guide House** is your spot for planning overnight hikes and climbs. Even though Paradise receives an average of 680 inches of snow per year, it is also the premier winter destination. Some sources have called it "the snowiest place on earth." Individuals familiar with the winter of '71–'72 wouldn't argue with that statement; that year 1,122 inches of snow were recorded here.

Ohanapecosh (June–October) is located 42 miles east of Nisqually Entrance and 3 miles north of the park boundary on WA-123. Here you'll find dense old-growth forests of Douglas fir, western red cedar, and western hemlock. Camping and a visitor center are available.

Sunrise and White River (June/July–October) is located 60 miles NE of Nisqually Entrance. Sunrise is the highest point in the park that can be reached by vehicle and the second most popular destination. Excellent trails, spectacular wildflowers, **White River Campground**, **Sunrise Visitor Center**, and **Sunrise Day Lodge** are all at your disposal at the foot of mighty Rainier.

Carbon River and Mowich Lake (All Year) are in the park's northwest corner. Cars can travel as far as **Carbon River Ranger Station**. Walk-in (tent-only) campsites are available at **Ipsut Creek** (5 miles, one-way).

 # Camping

Choosing where to camp boils down to deciding which section(s) of the park you want to visit. The most popular developed campground is **Cougar Rock** at Longmire/Paradise. **Ohanapecosh**, the largest campground, is located in the park's southeast corner. Sites at these two locations can be reserved up to six months in advance by calling (877) 444-6777 or clicking www.recreation.gov. Reservations are a good idea, especially on summer weekends at Cougar Rock. **White River Campground**, in the Sunrise/White River Region, is an excellent alternative. All 112 sites are available on a first-come, first-served basis. The campground fills quite frequently, but usually not until after noon. A more isolated experience is available at **Ipsut Creek and Mowich Lake Campgrounds** in the park's northwest corner. These are walk-in, tent-only campgrounds. Ipsut Creek is located on Carbon River Road, which was completely washed out in 2006. Vehicles can get as far as the Ranger Station. From there it's a 5-mile hike to the camp. Hook-ups and hot water are not available at any campground. Coin-operated **showers** are available at **Jackson Visitor Center in Paradise**.

 # Lodging

Don't want to rough it? No problem. **National Park Inn** and **Paradise Inn** are located at Longmire and Paradise, respectively. The locations are unbeatable and rates are reasonable (all things considered). A single room at either facility with very basic accommodations and a shared bath will set you back about $100/night. A two-room unit with private bath costs right around $250/night. **National Park Inn** is the only year-round lodging facility in the park. A general store is located on-site with essential goods like food and camping supplies, and cross-country skis and snowshoes are available for rent in winter. Each inn has a dining room open from 7am–8:30pm. Paradise Inn Dining Room closes temporarily between breakfast and lunch and lunch and dinner. Both inns are operated by **Mount Rainier Guest Services**. For reservations or additional information please call (360) 569-2275 or click www.mtrainierguestservices.com. If you'd like to sacrifice location in favor of cost or are looking for more luxurious lodging facilities, check outside the park. A list of nearby accommodations is provided on page 580.

Mount Rainier Camping

	Open	Fee	Sites	Location/Notes
Cougar Rock*	late May–mid-October	$12–15	173	Between Longmire & Paradise • W, F, DS
Ohanapecosh*	late May–mid-October	$12–15	188	Near Ohanapecosh Visitor Center • W, F, DS
White River 👍	late June–early October	$12	112	Near Sunrise/White River Entrance • W, F
Ipsut Creek	July–early October	Free	12	Walk-in sites (tent-only, 5-miles, 1-way), permit req'd • P
Mowich Lake	July–early October	Free	10	Primitive walk-in sites (tent-only), no potable water • P

W = Water, F = Flush Toilets, P = Pit Toilets, DS = Dump Station • RV hook-ups are not available at any campground
*Reservations can be made up to six months in advance by calling (877) 444-6777 or clicking www.recreation.gov
Reservations are strongly recommended from late June through early September (especially for weekend travel)

Backcountry	All overnight stays in the backcountry require a free wilderness permit. Permits are available at all wilderness information centers and visitor centers. They can be reserved from May through September for $20 per party (1–12 people). The reservation request form can be downloaded at: www.nps.gov/mora/planyourvisit/wilderness-reservation-information.htm
Group Camping	Group sites are available at Cougar Rock ($40–64/night), Ohanapecosh ($40), and Mowich Lake (free). Reservations (877.444.6777, www.recreation.gov) are required (available up to one year in advance).

Mount Rainier Lodging

National Park Inn	All Year	$118–240	Basic accommodations, rooms have shared or private baths
Paradise Inn	late May–early October	$114–260	Rooms with shared or private baths in historic building

Contact Mount Rainier Guest Services (360.569.2275, www.mtrainierguestservices.com) for information and reservations.

MOUNT RAINIER

Mountaineering

Each year approximately 10,000 visitors attempt to climb 14,410-foot **Mount Rainier**. About 25% of them successfully reach the summit of the most heavily glaciated peak in the contiguous United States. Not only is **Mount Rainier the ultimate in American mountaineering** (excluding McKinley), it also serves as training ground for professional and amateur climbers. Physical preparation, specialized equipment, and finely tuned skills are required to ascend more than 9,000 feet over a distance of (at least) eight miles. All climbers who intend on traveling above 10,000 feet or on a glacier must register and pay a fee. **Registration** is available at Paradise Ranger Station, White River Wilderness Information Center, and Longmire Wilderness Information Center. **The fee** is $43/person (25 and older), and $30/person (24 and younger). Passes are valid for one year from the date of purchase. You can also climb with an experienced guide. Four **outfitters** (see below) offer a variety of routes and trips. Standard 3–4 day Muir Climbs cost $900–1,400 (meals & permit included, gear rental costs extra).

Rainier Mountaineering, Inc. • (360.569.2227, www.rmiguides.com)
Alpine Ascents International • (206.378.1927, www.AlpineAscents.com)
American Alpine Institute • (360.671.1505, www.aai.cc)
Mt Rainier Alpine Guides • (360.569.2889, www.mountainguides.com)

Biking

There are no designated biking trails within the park and bikes are not allowed on hiking trails, but all **park roads** are open to cyclists. Be careful, as roads are steep, narrow, and winding with unpaved shoulders. Bike rental is not available in the park. If you want to pedal in the Paradise/Longmire region between June and August leave as early in the morning as possible to beat the traffic. Most roads are congested with motorists, but there is one exception: **Carbon River Road**. Somewhat hidden in the park's northwest corner, this 5-mile unpaved road is closed to motorists due to recent flood damage. It is shared with pedestrians who often hike to its terminus at Ipsut Creek Campground. Running parallel to Carbon River Road, slightly to the south, is **Mowich Lake Road**. This 5-mile dirt road leads to beautiful subalpine meadows. More extreme pedalers should check out **RAMROD** (Ride Around Mount Rainier One Day, www.redmondcyclingclub.org). Every July cyclists test themselves against a 154 mile course with 10,000 feet of elevation gain.

Little Tahoma (11,138-ft) rises out of the clouds
© Troy Mason (www.troymasonphotography.com)

Free Shuttle

The Upper Paradise lot is intended for short-term parking and it usually fills before noon on weekends. The Lower Paradise lot is intended for stays longer than two hours. **Paradise Shuttle** helps reduce congestion and air pollution by providing free transportation between Longmire and Paradise. Stops are also made at Cougar Rock Campground, Narada Falls (when traveling to Paradise), and Comet Falls (when traveling from Paradise). Shuttles stop at each scheduled location every 45 minutes on Fridays and every 15–25 minutes on Saturdays and Sundays from mid-June through early September. The Shuttle does not run Monday through Thursday. Service begins at Longmire at 10am, and the last bus leaves Paradise at 7pm.

Additional free shuttle service between **Ashford** (outside the park, entrance fee still applies) and **Longmire** is available Saturdays and Sundays. Buses depart every 25 minutes beginning at 9:15am until 10:30am, and then every 75 minutes beginning at 11:30am. The last shuttle leaves Ashford at 4:30pm, with the final bus leaving Longmire by 7:50pm.

Mount Rainier Hiking Trails

	Trail Name	Trailhead (# on map)	Length	Difficulty (E = Easy, M = Moderate, S = Strenuous)/Notes
Longmire	Kautz Creek	3 mi west of Longmire (1)	2.0 miles	M • First mile is self-guiding • Continues to Indian Henrys
	Trail of the Shadows	Longmire Museum (2)	0.7 mile	E • Self-guiding loop explores the area's history
	Rampart Ridge	Trail of Shadows (3)	4.6 miles	M • Steep loop through forests to a ridge with stunning vistas
	Eagle Peak Saddle	Longmire (4)	7.2 miles	S • Steep trail through old-growth forest, great views
	Carter/Madcap Falls	Cougar Rock Campground (5)	2.0 miles	M • Madcap Falls is 50 yards beyond Carter Falls
	Comet Falls - 👍	4.4 mi east of Longmire (6)	3.8 miles	S • Steep trail past Comet Falls through fragile meadow
	Christine Falls	4.5 mi east of Longmire (6)	0.5 mile	E • Hike to 100-foot descent to view of the falls
Paradise	The Lakes Loop - 👍	Reflection Lakes (7)	5.0 miles	M • Intersects road and Skyline Trail several times
	Bench and Snow Lakes	1.5 mi east of Reflection Lakes (7)	2.5 miles	M • Rolling hills, lakes, views, wildflowers
	Nisqually Vista	Lower Parking Lot (8)	1.2 miles	E • Stroller-friendly self-guiding loop
	Deadhorse Creek	Lower Parking Lot (8)	2.5 miles	M • Can loop with Glacier Vista and Skyline Trails
	Skyline to Myrtle Falls	Upper Parking Lot (9)	1.0 mile	E • Stroller/Wheelchair-friendly (with assistance)
	Panorama Point	Upper Parking Lot (9)	4.0 miles	S • Via Skyline Trail and Golden Gate Trail
	Skyline Loop - 👍	Upper Parking Lot (9)	5.5 miles	S • Best hike in the park • Snowpack until summer
	Pinnacle Peak	Southeast of Paradise (10)	2.5 miles	S • Hike south of Paradise to peak and glacier
Ohanapecosh	Hot Springs	Visitor Center (11)	0.5 mile	E • Short self-guiding loop, also access at campground
	Silver Falls	Three access points	0.6–3.0 mi	M • Access via Route 123, Camp, or Stevens Canyon Rd
	Laughingwater Creek	Route 123 (12)	12.0 miles	S • Fairly long day hike with 2,700' elevation gain
	Grove of the Patriarchs	Stevens Canyon Entrance (13)	1.2 miles	E • Self-guiding trail past old (1,000+ years) and tall (300') trees
	Cowlitz Divide - 👍	Stevens Canyon Road (14)	8.5 miles	S • Leads to Ollalie Creek and then Wonderland Tr
	Shriner Peak	Route 123 (15)	8.4 miles	S • Traverses old burn area, minimal cover
Sunrise	Emmons Moraine	White River Campground (16)	3.0 miles	M • Follow Glacier Basin Tr for 1-mile then follow moraine
	Glacier Basin - 👍	White River Campground (16)	6.5 miles	S • Flood damage but accessible (scrambling req'd)
	Upper Palisades Lake	Sunrise Point (17)	7.0 miles	S • No views of Mount Rainier, alpine lakes
	Silver Forest	South of the Parking Lot (18)	2.0 miles	E • Leads to Emmons Vista Overlook
	Sunrise Nature Trail	Sunrise Picnic Area (18)	1.5 miles	E • Self-guiding loop with views of Rainier
	Sourdough Ridge	Sunrise Nature Trail (18)	3.0 miles	M • Loop via Sourdough and Wonderland Trails
	Sunrise Rim	Sunrise Picnic Area (18)	5.2 miles	S • To Shadow Lake, Glacier Overlook, and 1st Burroughs Mtn
	Burroughs Mountain	Sunrise Picnic Area (18)	4.8 miles	S • Sourdough Ridge Tr to Frozen Lake and up 2nd Burroughs
	Mt Fremont Lookout - 👍	Sunrise Picnic Area (18)	5.6 miles	S • Sourdough Ridge Tr to Frozen Lake to Fremont Tr
	Berkeley Park	Sunrise Picnic Area (18)	7.0 miles	S • Sourdough Ridge Tr to Frozen Lake to Northern Loop
Carbon R. & Mowich Lk	Rain Forest Loop	Carbon River Ranger Station (19)	0.3 mile	E • Self-guiding loop through rain forest
	Green Lake	Carbon River Ranger Station (19)	9.6 miles	M • A short spur trail leads to Ranger Falls
	Chenuis Falls	Carbon River Ranger Station (19)	6.4 miles	M • Most of the hike is along Carbon River Road
	Lake James & Windy Gap	Ipsut Creek Campground (20)	24.0 miles	S • Follows Wonderland Tr to Northern Loop Trail
	Tolmie Peak	Mowich Lake Rd (21)	6.5 miles	M • Cross Ipsut Pass to Eunice Lake and on to the peak
	Spray Park - 👍	Mowich Lake Campground (22)	16.0 miles	M • Short spur trail to Spray Falls (300' cascade)

(Left margin, vertical text: MOUNT RAINIER)

Wonderland Trail - 👍 • 93.0 miles • Circles Mount Rainier • Accessible from Longmire Wilderness Info. Center, Mowich Lake and Ipsut Creek Campgrounds, Sunrise, Fryingpan Creek Trailhead and Box Canyon • **All distances listed above are Roundtrip**

 # Hiking

There are more than 260 miles of maintained hiking trails. All five regions of the park have trails that explore pristine lakes, peaceful meadows, old-growth forests, and of course offer exceptional views of Mount Rainier. But the best views are available at **Paradise**. When Martha Longmire first set eyes on the area's wildflower meadows and spectacular mountain vistas she exclaimed, "Oh, what a paradise!" Most visitors agree. And no trip to Paradise is complete without hitting the trails. At the very least hike the first 0.5-mile of **Skyline Trail to Myrtle Falls**. Unfortunately, most visitors have the same agenda, making it extremely busy especially after 10am. It's a good idea to get an early start; if you begin by 7am you can complete the entire 5.5-mile circuit just as the crowd pours in.

Skyline Loop continues beyond Myrtle Falls to **Sluiskin Falls**, where you have the option to take the 0.75-mile **Paradise Glacier Spur Trail**. Eventually you'll hit **Panorama Point** (restrooms available), and then begin the return trip via **High Skyline Trail**. Here you'll have outstanding views of Nisqually Glacier, which moves down the mountain's slope 6–12 inches each day in summer. **Skyline Loop** is considered strenuous (1,700-ft elevation gain), but you'll be busy taking in a smorgasbord of scenic beauty along the way.

In **Longmire** you should hike to **Comet Falls**. This 300-ft falls earned its name because it resembles the tail of a comet. The trail continues beyond the falls to **Trump Park** (which is commonly snow-packed well into summer).

Ohanapecosh offers a change of pace with its **Grove of the Patriarchs Trail**. The trees are massive (300+ feet) and old (1,000+ years). It's a great hike for families and individuals short on time.

If you're looking for a more rugged adventure try **Glacier Basin Trail**, which begins at **White River Campground** (Loop D). The trail follows the White River to Glacier Basin Camp and Inter Glacier.

Be aware that many of these trails are inaccessible due to snow and mud until June or July. It is always a good idea to check trail conditions at a visitor center or the park website before you arrive. Hikers should always carry plenty of water, wear sunscreen, and stay on marked trails. Pets and bicycles are not permitted on any trails.

 # Backpacking

Mount Rainier has plenty to offer those looking to get deeper into the park's wilderness. **The Pacific Crest Trail** skirts the eastern boundary and **Wonderland Trail** covers 93 miles as it circles around Mount Rainier. These are the two most notable long-distance hiking trails in the park, but you'll find designated campsites throughout the backcountry. Begin planning your backcountry trip with a good topographical map.

Backpackers must obtain a **wilderness camping permit** (required for all overnight stays in the backcountry). Permits can be obtained two ways: reservation (70% of total, $20 per party, 1–12 people per party) or first-come, first-served (remaining 30%, free). Reservations for the current summer are accepted beginning March 15. They are only accepted by mail, fax, or in person. Visit the park website for the reservation request form and contact information. Reservations are highly recommended if you plan on backpacking in July or August.

First-come, first-served permits can be obtained no earlier than one day before your departure date. **In summer**, permits are available at the following facilities: Longmire Wilderness Information Center, Jackson Visitor Center at Paradise, Ohanapecosh Visitor Center, White River Wilderness Information Center, Sunrise Visitor Center, and Carbon River Ranger Station. **In winter**, permits are only available at Longmire Museum and Jackson Visitor Center. Plan on arriving at least one hour before the facility closes.

 # Winter Activities

Abundant snow turns **Paradise** into a winter wonderland. **Sledding** is allowed in the snow play area located north of Paradise's upper parking lot. **Cross-country skis** ($18.75, half-day) and **snowshoes** ($14.50, half-day) are **available for rent** at **National Park Inn**. **Snowmobiles** are permitted in a few designated areas. Contact the park for snow conditions, avalanche danger, and the weather forecast before you arrive.

Mount Rainier peeks through the clouds

For Kids: Mount Rainier is one of the most family friendly national parks. In summer, children enjoy walking along creeks and viewing wildflowers. Sledding, snowshoeing, and snowball fights are all fun-filled activities during winter. Any time of year children are invited to participate in the park's **Junior Ranger Program**. Activity booklets can be picked up from any one of the visitor centers. Complete an age appropriate number of activities and return to a visitor center to have your work checked by a park ranger. If successful your child will be sworn in as a Junior Ranger and receive an official Mount Rainier Junior Ranger badge.

Ranger Programs: Ranger-led interpretive programs are an integral component of the national park experience. Free walks, talks, and campfire programs are offered daily during summer. In winter you can join a ranger on a **snowshoe walk** ($4 donation suggested). A current schedule of events is available online or in the park's free newspaper, *The Tahoma News*. Do not miss out on a ranger program during your visit to Mount Rainier. For more information check out the park website or stop in at one of the following visitor centers:

Longmire Museum • (360) 569-6575
All Year, 9am–5pm • Info, exhibits, books, gifts

Jackson Visitor Center (Paradise) • (360) 569-6571
May–mid-October, 10–6pm; November–April (Weekends & Holidays), 10am–5pm • Ranger programs, exhibits, videos, gifts

Ohanapecosh Visitor Center • (360) 569-6581
late-May–October, 9am–5pm • Ranger programs, exhibits, books

Sunrise Visitor Center • (360) 663-2425
July–early September, 10am–6pm • Ranger programs, exhibits

Longmire Wilderness Info. Center (WIC) • (360) 569-6650

Paradise Climbing/WIC (Guide House) • (360) 569-6641

White River WIC • (360) 569-6670

Carbon River Ranger Station • (360) 829-9639

Call (360) 569-2211 for park road and facility status. Operating hours are extended in summer and shortened in winter.

Flora & Fauna: Mount Rainier National Park is home to **more than 800 species of vascular plants, including at least 100 species of wildflowers**. Wildflower season peaks from mid-July through August. Douglas, western red cedar, and western hemlock comprise most of the park's forests. Large mammals include elk, deer, black bear, and mountain lions.

Pets: Pets are allowed in the park, but must be kept on a leash no more than six feet in length at all times. Visitors with pets are extremely limited to where they can travel as they are only allowed along roadways and in parking areas and developed campgrounds. They are not permitted in public buildings (except service animals), at ranger programs, in the backcountry, or on hiking trails.

Accessibility: Jackson Visitor Center (Paradise) is fully accessible to wheelchair users. Ohanapecosh and Sunrise Visitor Centers and Longmire Museum are accessible, but passages are narrow and may require assistance. Accessible rooms are available at Paradise Inn and National Park Inn. Accessible campsites are available at Cougar Rock and Ohanapecosh Campgrounds. Kautz Creek Trail, Trail of Shadows, and Paradise's Lower Meadow Trails are accessible with assistance.

Weather: Mountain weather is unpredictable. The best you can do is to have a contingency plan for all possible conditions. One of the most disappointing aspects of the park is that its 14,410-ft mountain is often hidden behind a blanket of clouds. July and August are typically the clearest, driest, and warmest months of the year. At Paradise (5,400-ft elevation), summer average highs are in the low 60s°F with lows in the mid-40s°F. The area's proximity to the Pacific Ocean helps moderate seasonal changes in temperature. Winter highs average in the mid-30s°F with lows in the low 20s°F. Expect Longmire (2,762-ft) to be a few degrees warmer than Paradise and Ohanapecosh (1,950-ft) to be a few degrees warmer than Longmire.

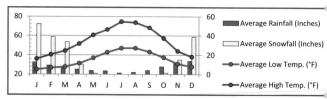

Vacation Planner

When and where are the two main questions you must answer before taking a trip to Mount Rainier National Park. The answer to these questions will vary depending on your tolerance of massive crowds and need for solitude. **Most visitors only visit Paradise**. It's beautiful, but the crowds and cars deprive the area of a bit of its natural majesty. Additionally, most guests come to the park between July and August. So, if you're planning a trip to Paradise in the middle of July, expect plenty of company. You may want to pencil in a side-trip to a more secluded area like **Ohanapecosh**, **Mowich Lake**, or **Carbon River** to shake the crowds for a day or two. For a weekend at **Longmire/Paradise** consider taking the **free shuttle** (page 555) rather than driving your own car into the park. **A well-rounded trip includes visits to Longmire, Paradise, and Sunrise. Camping** (page 554) is available in each region. **Lodging** (page 554) is only available at Longmire and Paradise. Nearby dining, grocery stores, lodging, festivals, and attractions are listed on pages 580–583. Provided below is a 2-day itinerary that visits the park's most popular regions.

Snowshoeing on the edge

Day 1

Begin your trip at **Nisqually Entrance** (southwest corner of the park). After one mile you'll come to **Westside Road**. This unpaved route provides access to trailheads for **Gobblers Knob** (12.8 mile) and **Emerald Ridge** (17.2 mile) Trails, areas that are much more secluded and uncongested than Paradise. If you need to escape the crowds for a bit head back to this location, but for now continue on the main park road. History buffs should make a quick stop (1–2 hours) at **Longmire Museum**; otherwise continue past Cougar Rock Campground to **Comet Falls Trailhead** (page 556). Hike the 3.8-mile trail to its 300-ft falls. Allow 3–4 hours so you have ample time to enjoy the views. Return to your car and drive to Paradise. En route, you'll pass **Narada Falls**. If you want to see it, stop and park (pulling completely off to the side); ogling motorists are good for causing accidents, and that's a sure-fire way to ruin a day in Paradise. At Paradise, stop at **Jackson Visitor Center** to get acquainted with the park by watching a short video. Check the schedule of **ranger programs** and squeeze the interesting ones into your itinerary. Next, stretch your legs on **Skyline Trail** (page 556). Begin in a counterclockwise direction toward **Myrtle Falls**. If the meadows, mountain vistas, and flowing waterways inspire you to go further, continue around the loop another 5 miles past **Panorama Point**, along **Nisqually Glacier**, and right back down to Paradise. The trail to **Snow and Bench Lakes** (page 556) is a good alternative.

Day 2

Start the day by driving east to **Stevens Canyon Road Entrance** (45 minutes from Paradise, 65 minutes from Longmire). Big tree aficionados should have a look around **Grove of the Patriarchs** (page 556) near the entrance station. Otherwise turn left on WA-123 and drive to **White River/Sunrise** (about 75 minutes). After more than two hours driving, you're probably ready to pound the paths. How about getting a closer look at Mount Rainier? To do so, take **Glacier Basin Trail** (page 556) from **White River Campground**. Easier hikes through alpine meadows are available in and around Sunrise. There are also plenty of day-hikes that lead into the mountains nearby. One of the best is the trail to **Berkeley Park** (page 556), which leads to the base of **Skyscraper Mountain** on the north side of Mount Rainier. Once you've worn yourself out, return home knowing that you had the opportunity to spend a little time in Paradise.

Best of Mount Rainier

Region: **Paradise**
> Runner-up: Sunrise

Hike: **Skyline Loop**
> Runner-up: Mount Fremont Lookout
> 2nd Runner-up: Comet Falls

Father and child watch as Roosevelt elk wade in Hoh River

600 East Park Avenue
Port Angeles, WA 98362
Phone: (360) 565-3130
Website: www.nps.gov/olym

Established: June 29, 1938
March 2, 1909 (National Monument)
Size: 922,561 Acres
Annual Visitors: 2.8 Million
Peak Season: Summer

Activities: Hiking, Backpacking,
Camping, Fishing, Rafting, Biking,
Beachcombing, and Swimming

Campgrounds: 16 Campgrounds*
Fee: $10–18/night
Backcountry Camping: Permitted
Lodging: 4 Locations
Rates: $82–364/night

Park Hours: All day, every day
Entrance Fee: $15 • Vehicle
$5 • Individual (foot, bike, etc.)

*Reservations (877.444.6777,
www.recreation.gov) only available
at Kalaloch Campground

Olympic - Washington

Mount Olympus (7,980-feet), the park's centerpiece, was named by English explorer **Captain John Meares** in 1788 when he saw the mighty summit from a distance. He deemed it a worthy home of the Greek gods. Mount Olympus may have been named in the 18th century, but the Olympic Peninsula remained a blank spot on maps for another 100 years. Today, the mountainous region of western Washington State has been explored, but the landscape has not changed. Its temperate rain forests, steep cliffs, and high ridgelines remain relatively inaccessible. No roads enter the heart of the park where the Olympic Mountain Range is shaped by 13 rivers. Add 73 miles of wild Pacific coastline and Olympic National Park offers an unsurpassed diversity of relatively undisturbed ecosystems.

Juan de Fuca spotted the Olympic Peninsula in 1592. Captain Meares, Charles William Barkley, and George Vancouver explored the region nearly two centuries later, but **Native Americans** had lived here for more than 12,000 years. Ancestors of eight distinct tribes survived the decimation brought on by European diseases; the Hoh People still live along the Hoh River, and the Quileute People live at La Push on the Pacific Coast. Americans did not explore the Olympic Range until the late 19th century. In 1885, **Lieutenant Joseph P. O'Neil** led an expedition into the mountains. Their journey began at Port Angeles, a small village at the time, and took one month to reach **Hurricane Ridge**. Today, 17-mile Hurricane Ridge Road follows roughly the same path O'Neil took, but allows visitors to reach the ridge with its scenic views of Mount Olympus in less than half an hour.

Lumber interests seeking untapped old-growth forests to harvest spent decades making the Olympic Peninsula more accessible. Lumbermen couldn't have asked for a better location to cut trees than this lush environment. Forests of the Pacific Northwest produce three times the biomass of tropical rain forests. Lumber was being hauled out of the Olympic Peninsula as the general public gained interest in the outdoors, largely thanks to adoption of the automobile. These opposing sides helped fuel a controversial national park movement. **President Theodore Roosevelt** settled the dispute by establishing Olympic National Monument in 1909 to protect the calving grounds of the area's Roosevelt elk herds. But logging continued and by the 1920s, logging interests faced a swell of public dissent. In 1938 the monument was reestablished as a national park. A new title, but the same results. Largely due to increased demand caused by WWII, illegal logging continued long after the park was established.

Visitors no longer find fresh swaths of clear-cut. About 366,000 acres of old-growth are left unharmed, the largest of its kind in the Pacific Northwest. These impressive stands are nourished by ample rain. **Mount Olympus** receives more than 180 inches of annual precipitation (mostly snow). **Hoh Rainforest, receives more rain than any place in the continental United States, about 160 inches of annual precipitation.** Lush and lively, the Olympic Peninsula provides refuge and nourishment for hundreds of species of plants and animals, including **several species found nowhere else in the world**: Olympic marmot, Olympic torrent salamander, Olympic mudminnow, Olympic grasshopper, Flett's violet, and Piper's bellflower just to name a few. President Roosevelt's goal to preserve elk habitat worked. The park's population is the largest unmanaged herd of Roosevelt elk. Not only does the park preserve an impressive collection of coastline, mountains, and rivers along with its incredible plant and animal life, but it also created a reservation for people. A refuge used to escape the doldrums of everyday life by immersing one's self in nature.

Best of Olympic

Mainland Region: **Hurricane Ridge**
> Runner-up: Hoh Rain Forest

Coastal Region: **Mora**
> Coastal Region: Ozette

When to Go

Olympic National Park is open all day, every day. However, many of the park's roads, visitor centers, campgrounds, and lodging facilities close for winter. Very few tourists come to the park during the harsh Olympic Peninsula winters, but Hurricane Ridge is open for cross-country skiing on weekends and holidays. Most visitors arrive during the dry season (June–September). At this time sunny skies are common, but so are mosquitoes and black flies.

Transportation & Airports

Ferry and bus service is available to the Olympic Peninsula, but not within the park. See page 562 for ferry and bus details. The closest large commercial airport is Seattle–Tacoma International (SEA). From Seattle, visitors can fly to William R. Fairchild International Airport (CLM) in Port Angeles.

Directions

Olympic is not the most convenient park for motorists. No road crosses the Olympic Mountain Range, but 12 separate roads penetrate the main park boundary encircling Mount Olympus. In addition, a sliver of Pacific coastline has three separate regions with their own access point. No matter where you're headed you'll be traveling on US-101. Park Headquarters is located in Port Angeles, where most trips begin. Several different routes can be utilized between Port Angeles and Seattle. Motorists can use the Washington State Ferry System (page 562) or drive south around Puget Sound via Tacoma or Olympia.

Port Angeles via Tacoma (~140 miles): Heading south on I-5, take Exit 132 to merge onto WA-16 W toward Bremerton. Cross the Tacoma Narrows Bridge (eastbound toll, $4). Just before Bremerton, WA-16 becomes WA-3. At Hood Canal Bridge WA-3 becomes WA-104. After about 15 miles, take the ramp to US-101 N. Continue north to Port Angeles.

Port Angeles via Olympia (~180 miles): Head south on I-5 from Seattle. After about 60 miles, take Exit 104 to merge onto US-101 N. Continue along the eastern edge of the Olympic Peninsula for about 118 miles to Port Angeles.

Buses & Ferries

Olympic Bus Lines (800.457.4492, www.olympicbuslines.com) provides two trips daily between Seattle–Tacoma International Airport and Port Angeles. Several stops are made in between. Roundtrip fare costs $55–79/Adult and $28–40/Child (15 and under) depending on your destination. **Clallam Transit** (360.452.4511, www.clallamtransit.com) provides transportation around Port Angeles and northern Olympic Peninsula.

The Coho Ferry (360.457.4491, www.cohoferry.com) provides year-round transportation between Victoria, British Columbia and Port Angeles. One-way passenger fare is $15.50/Adult and $7.75/Child (ages 5–11). Bicycles cost an additional $6.50. Vehicles cost an additional $11. Car rental is available at the port. Taking the ferry is a great idea for cyclists. Victoria is one of the best cities for bicycle travel, and cyclists landing on the Olympic Peninsula may enjoy the challenge of pedalling up Hurricane Ridge (page 564). **Washington State Ferry System** (888.808.7977, www.wsdot.wa.gov) offers ferry service to multiple destinations on the Olympic Peninsula, but not to Port Angeles. Passenger fare is dependent on destination but ranges anywhere from $3–24. Bicycles are an additional $1. Vehicle surcharge is determined by length.

Regions

Olympic National Park consists of more than a dozen vehicle accessible regions, but it isn't a drive-thru park. Almost every distinct region is accessed from a spur road off of US-101, which circles around the Olympic Range. A few of the more popular regions include: the mountain vistas of **Hurricane Ridge**, the hot springs and waterfalls of **Sol Duc**, the temperate rain forest of **Hoh Rain Forest**, and the tide pools and coastline of **Ozette**. Each area is unique in its own way, and for this reason **Olympic National Park is examined region by region.**

Getting Around the Park

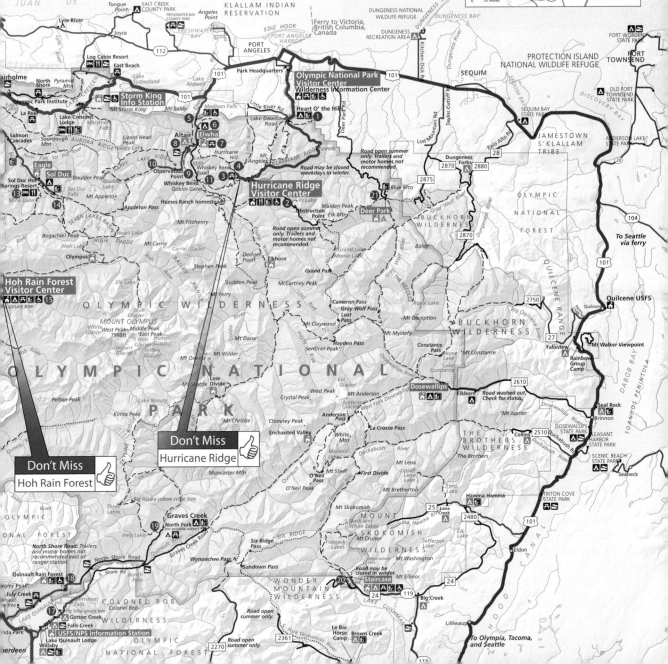

Lake Crescent sunrise

Mount Olympus from Hurricane Ridge

Park Headquarters

<u>Attractions:</u> Visitor Center, Wilderness Info. Center (WIC) • Backcountry Permits, Hiking

Park Headquarters is located just south of Port Angeles on Mount Angeles Road. The visitor center has a variety of exhibits, including a hands-on **"Discovery Room"** for kids and a 25-minute introductory film. If you want to get straight to exploring the outdoors **Living Forest and Peabody Creek Trails** are two short forested walks that begin at the visitor center. Living Forest Loop is wheelchair accessible (with assistance).

Stop in at the **Wilderness Information Center** (360.565.3100), located inside the visitor center, for **backcountry permits** and current trail conditions. A permit is required for all overnight stays in the backcountry. Park Headquarters is an ideal place for an introduction to the Olympic Peninsula before continuing south along Hurricane Ridge Road to Heart O' the Hills and Hurricane Ridge.

Olympic National Park Visitor Center
3002 Mount Angeles Road; Port Angeles, WA 98362
(360) 565-3130 • Summer: Daily, 8am–6pm; Winter: Daily, 9am–4pm; Closed Thanksgiving and Christmas

Heart O' the Hills

<u>Attractions:</u> Ranger/Entrance Station, Camping, Hiking

Heart O' the Hills is located just 5 miles south of Port Angeles and Park HQ. The **campground** has 105 sites available on a first-come, first-served basis for $12/night. It's open all year, but may be walk-in only depending on the amount of snow. Interpretive programs are held at the campground from late June through September. Potable water and flush toilets are available. There are no hookups. All sites accommodate RVs up to 21-ft in length. Some suit 35-ft RVs. Showers are not available, but the **Sequim KOA** (80 O'Brien Road; Port Angeles, WA 98362) allows visitors to use their showers for a nominal fee (ask politely).

Heart O' the Hills Trail begins in Loop E of the campground. It's an easy 4.6-mile (roundtrip) hike through old-growth forest. For a much more strenuous trek, hikers can loop **Lake Angeles and Heather Park Trails** (seasonal, check trail conditions). The trailhead is located near the campground entrance on the west side of Hurricane Ridge Road. The loop covers nearly 13 miles and passes Lake Angeles. The top of the loop intersects Klahhane Ridge/ Heather Park/Switchback Junction where extremely ambitious hikers can continue hiking parallel to Hurricane Ridge Road another 3+ miles to **Hurricane Ridge Visitor Center**.

Hurricane Ridge

<u>Attractions:</u> Visitor Center, Driving, Biking, Hiking

If you have to choose just one area of the park to visit, make it Hurricane Ridge. Some of the most spectacular vistas are available here as you peer across river-carved valleys to the glacier-capped peak of **Mount Olympus**. The 17-mile **Hurricane Ridge Road** is an attraction in and of itself. Great for motorists, and a challenge for cyclists, it begins in Port Angeles. An avid biker can climb from sea level to 5,242-feet in about 20 miles. Rest your legs while soaking in the views from Hurricane Ridge before making the exciting descent back to sea level (make sure your brakes work properly, because you'll need them). The main deterrent for exploring Hurricane Ridge is Mother Nature. The region earned its name thanks to winds that can gust up to 75 miles per hour and as much as 30–35 feet of snow falls here annually.

Hurricane Ridge Road is open 24 hours a day between June and October. For the rest of the year it is primarily open on weekends (weather permitting). Call (360) 565-3131 for up-to-date road and weather conditions.

Hurricane Ridge Visitor Center offers exhibits, an introductory film, and restrooms. It's open all year. Hours typically run from 9am–dusk in summer and 9:30am–5pm in winter when the road is open. Interpretive programs are offered from late June to September. **Snowshoe and ski rental** are available at the gift shop in winter.

Hurricane Ridge is an excellent area for **hiking**. Cirque Rim, **Big Meadow (accessible with assistance), and High Ridge Trails** are all one mile or less roundtrip. **Klahhane Ridge Trail** heads down toward Heart O' the Hills and intersects Lake Angeles/Heather Park Loop after 3.8 miles (one-way). **Hurricane Hill Trail** (accessible with assistance) is a paved 3.2-mile (roundtrip) flat path with panoramic views. At the very end of Hurricane Ridge Road you can pick up **Little River (8 miles, one-way) or Hurricane Hill/Elwha (5.8 miles, one-way) Trails,** which lead to Little River Road and Elwha, respectively.

Elwha

<u>Attractions:</u> Camping, Rafting, Fishing, Hiking

A restoration effort removing two dams has begun on the Elwha River. Contractors started the three-year process in September 2011. When completed, water and salmon will be able to travel freely through Elwha Valley, the largest watershed in Olympic National Park, and the quality of fishing and rafting will be greatly improved. The park's only rafting concessioner is **Olympic Raft and Kayak** (888.452.1443, www.raftandkayak.com). Elwha River trips (Class II+) cost $54/Adult and $44/Child (ages 5–11).

Elwha Campground has 40 campsites (first-come, first-served) for $12/night. They are available all year (pit toilets and no water in winter). **Altair Campground** has 30 sites available from late May to mid-October for $12/night.

Elwha is also one of the better **hiking** areas. Near the park boundary you'll find a paved 0.2-mile trail (accessible) to **Madison Falls** (60-ft). **Geyser Valley Loop Trail** (6 miles, roundtrip) begins at the end of Whiskey Bend Road. **Cascade Rock Trail** (4.2 miles, roundtrip) is a good hike beginning at Elwha Campground.

Lake Crescent

Attractions: Lake Crescent Lodge and Log Cabin Resort, Boating, Camping, Hiking, Swimming

The Lake Crescent area is difficult to miss. US-101 skirts the lake's southern shoreline for about 10 miles. From east to west you'll pass several short spur roads: **East Beach Road** to Log Cabin Resort and East Beach, **Lake Crescent Road** to Storm King and Lake Crescent Lodge, and **Camp David Jr. Road** to Fairholme Campground.

Lake Crescent Lodge (888.896.3818, www.olympicnationalparks.com) closes for winter (October–April), but **Roosevelt Cabins** remain open on winter weekends. Rates range from $168–220 per night. **Log Cabin Resort** (360.928.3325, www.logcabinresort.net) has everything from A-Frame Chalets ($121/night) to RV sites with full hook-ups ($40/night). It is open from late May to mid-September.

Camping is available at **Fairholme**. The campground has 88 sites available on a first-come, first-served basis for $12/night. It is open from April through mid-Fall. **Canoe, kayak, and motorboat rentals** are available at **Fairholme General Store** (360.928.3050, www.fairholmstore.com).

Swimming is popular at Fairholme, East Beach, and Devil's Punch Bowl.

A handful of **hiking trails** are available in the area. The 4.2-mile trek to **Mount Storm King** is one of the best. It is accessed at Lake Crescent Lodge. From here you head south across US-101, turn right on Marymere Falls Trail, then left onto Mt Storm King Trail where you'll climb 2,000 feet to the site where Indian legend states the mountain spirit hurled a gigantic boulder down at two quarrelling tribes. The boulder dammed the river, causing water to back up, forming Lake Crescent. On the lake's north shore, hikers can take **Pyramid Peak Trail** (7 miles, roundtrip) to an old WWII spotting tower with exceptional views of the lake.

Sol Duc Falls

Sol Duc

<u>Attractions:</u> Sol Duc Hot Springs Resort, Camping, Fishing, Hiking, Backpacking

Sol Duc Road, just west of Fairholme and Lake Crescent, is open all year (weather permitting). It leads to the area's resorts, campground, and trailheads.

Sol Duc Hot Springs Resort (888.896.3818, www.olympicnationalparks.com) offers RV sites with full hook-ups ($33/night), basic cabins ($166), kitchen-cabins ($200), and a River Suite ($375). Pool admission is included with all overnight accommodations except RV sites. The resort is open from late March to mid-Fall. It also operates **three mineral hot spring soaking pools** and **one freshwater pool** from late March to late October. A soak will cost you $12.25/Adult and $9.25/Child (4–12). Massages are available for $55 (30 minutes), $75 (60), and $100 (90).

Sol Duc Campground has 82 sites available on a first-come, first-served basis for $14/night. Sites are available all year (pit toilets and no water in winter).

Sol Duc is a particularly good location for **backpacking**. **The Seven Lakes Basin Area**, south of Sol Duc Road, offers an excellent loop trail with views of Mount Olympus. Bear canisters, topographic maps, and backcountry permits are available at Sol Duc Ranger Station. One of the park's more popular trails is the 1.6-mile **Sol Duc Falls Trail**, which leads to a picturesque three-legged falls.

Hoh Rain Forest

<u>Attractions:</u> Visitor Center, Camping, Rafting, Hiking

Hoh Rain Forest should not to be skipped. It's located on the west side of the Olympics where winters are mild and wet. The area receives 140–160 inches of annual precipitation, which help make it one of the most spectacular examples of temperate rain forest in the world.

Hoh Rain Forest Visitor Center offers information, exhibits, a bookstore, and maps. It's open daily from 9am–6pm during the summer and from 10am–4pm on weekends during the winter (except Christmas and Thanksgiving). **Hoh Campground** has 88 sites available on a first-come, first-served basis for $12/night. Potable water is available year-round. There are no hook-ups, and RVs must be less than 21-feet.

Olympic Raft and Kayak (888.452.1443, www.raftand-kayak.com) offers whitewater rafting trips on the Hoh River (Class I–II). These summer-only excursions cost $54/Adult and $44/Child (ages 5–11). It's mostly a float trip, but things get a little "splashy" near the take-out.

Several hiking trails begin at Hoh Rain Forest Visitor Center and penetrate deep into the forest's depths. **Hall of Mosses Trail** (0.8 mile) and **Spruce Nature Trail** (1.2 miles) are wonderful self-guiding options that explain the area's ecology. Hoh Rain Forest is also the gateway to Mount Olympus. The 18-mile (one-way) **Hoh River Trail** leads to Blue Glacier at the north face of **Mount Olympus** (do not attempt to climb to its summit without proper equipment and glacier travel skills). Whether you're in the campground, rafting the river, or hiking the trails, you'll have an excellent chance of spotting **Roosevelt elk**. Olympic National Park is home to the largest unmanaged herd, and about 400 reside in the Hoh area.

Queets

Queets is located in the park's southwest corner. This seldom visited region, accessed via an 11-mile unpaved road, is the perfect destination for some peace and solitude. The campground offers 20 primitive sites on a first-come, first-served basis for $10/night. It is open year-round. RVs are not recommended. **Two boat launches** are available to explore the water, and **Sam's River Loop** (2.8 miles) and **Queets River Trail** (16.2 miles) let you explore the land.

Quinault

<u>Attractions</u>: Lake Quinault Lodge, Camping, Hiking

Quinault is located along the park's southern boundary, just north of US-101 before it heads south along the Pacific Coast. **Lake Quinault Lodge** (888.896.3818, www.olympicnationalparks.com) is open year-round. Rooms range from basic hotel accommodations ($82/night) to luxury suites ($234/night). Reduced rates are available during winter. **Massage rates** are $75 (60 minutes) and $100 (90). Pool, sauna, and a game room are also on-site.

Camping is available at **Graves Creek** (30 sites, $12/night, no water in winter) and **North Fork** (9, $10, no water in winter). During summer extra camping space is available nearby in Olympic National Forest.

Quinault is one of the best locations to hear newborn elk in spring or bulls bugling in fall. The region is also known for its record setting trees. Several champion or former champion trees can be found along the area's **hiking trails**. Two of the largest are easily accessible. A massive western red cedar is found at the end of 0.2-mile **Quinault Big Cedar Trail**. The trailhead is located on North Shore Road on the northwest side of Lake Quinault, 2 miles north of US-101. The other is **Big Sitka Spruce**, which is actually located in Olympic National Forest. It stands at the northeastern edge of Lake Quinault and can be accessed via a short spur road from South Shore Road. Several trails venture deep into the backcountry from the end of North Fork Road and Graves Creek Road. **Backpackers** can pick up bear canisters, backcountry permits, and topographic maps from the **USFS/NPS Information Station** on South Shore Road. It's open daily in summer, and weekends only for the remainder of the year.

Staircase

Staircase is located in the park's southeast corner. Staircase Road may be gated in winter. Call (360) 565-3131 for status. Backcountry permits, bear canisters, and maps are available at the **ranger station** (open intermittently when staffing allows). The **campground** has 47 campsites available on a first-come, first-served basis for $12/night. During winter, sites may be walk-in only and water is not available. The majority of hiking trails follow the North Fork Skokomish River.

Deer Park

Deer Park Road runs south from US-101 between Port Angeles and Sequim. At the park boundary pavement gives way to gravel and the road twists, turns, and climbs nearly 6,000 feet to Deer Park on the east side of the Olympics. The road is narrow, steep, not suitable for RVs or trailers, and only open in summer. A **ranger station** is staffed intermittently during summer and fall. A total of 14 tent-only **campsites** are available on a first-come, first served basis from mid-June through mid-Fall for $10/night. Water is not available.

Deer Park resides in the rain shadow of the Olympic Mountain Range, receiving only 18 inches of rain annually. It is especially phenomenal when you compare it to Mount Olympus, located just 20 miles west of Deer Park, which receives an average of 180 inches of precipitation (mostly snow) each year. Another 10 miles to the east is Hoh Rain Forest, which receives the most rain in the continental United States, roughly 160 inches annually. An incredible contrast considering the two areas are only 100 miles apart (by car, even closer as the crow flies).

There are some nice trails at Deer Park. Experienced **hikers** with good map-reading and route-finding skills can make a loop by hiking from **Deer Park** to **Obstruction Point** (7.4 miles) then heading south to **Grand and Moose Lakes** (~3 miles). From here continue along a primitive trail across **Grand Pass** (~1 mile) and follow **Cameron Creek Trail** (~3 miles) to **Three Forks Trail** (2.1 miles) back to Deer Park.

Flora & Fauna

You may see Roosevelt elk, black bear, mountain goats, beavers, or marmots. The park is also home to about **300 species of birds**. Among them are bald eagles, osprey, and the northern pygmy owl. **Over 1,450 types of vascular plants** grow on the Olympic Peninsula. Most famous are the giant Sitka spruce, western hemlock, Douglas fir, and western red cedar of Queets, Quinault, and Hoh Rain Forest.

Olympic Mainland Hiking Trails

OLYMPIC MAINLAND

	Trail Name	Trailhead (# on map)	Length	Notes (Roundtrip distances unless noted otherwise)
Heart O'Hills	Heart O' the Forest	Campground Loop E (1)	4.6 miles	Roundtrip trek through old-growth forest
	Heather Park	Near Campground Entrance (1)	6.3 miles	(1-way) Climbs 4,150-ft, 4-miles to wildflower meadows
	Lake Angeles	Near Campground Entrance (1)	6.4 miles	(1-way) Climbs 2,400-ft in first 3.4 miles to Lake Angeles
Hurricane Ridge	Big Meadows Trails	Near Visitor Center (2)	2.0 miles	Cirque Rim, Big Meadows, and High Ridge Trails
	Klahhane Ridge	Near Visitor Center (2)	2.8 miles	(1-way) Hikers can continue to Heart O' the Hills
	Wolf Creek	Near Picnic Area A (3)	8.0 miles	(1-way) Trail descends almost 4,000-ft to Whiskey Bend
	Hurricane Hill - 👍	End of Hurricane Hill Rd (4)	3.2 miles	First 0.25-mile is paved, panoramic views
	Little River - 👍	Hurricane Hill Trail (4)	8.0 miles	(1-way) Descends 4,000+ feet to Little River Road
	Hurricane Hill/Elwha	Hurricane Hill Trail (4)	5.8 miles	(1-way) Descends 5,250 feet to Whiskey Bend Road
Elwha	Madison Falls	Near Park Boundary (5)	0.2 mile	Wheelchair accessible, self-guiding, 60-ft waterfall
	Cascade Rock	Elwha Campground (6)	4.2 miles	Moderate hike through forest to valley views
	Nature Loop	Elwha Camp Picnic Shelter (7)	0.6 mile	Flat and easy forested loop trail
	Griff Creek	Elwha Ranger Station (7)	5.8 miles	Hike through forest (2,910 feet elevation gain)
	West Lake Mills	Glines Canyon Dam (8)	3.8 miles	Flat trail along the west shore of Lake Mills
	West Elwha	Altair Campground (8)	6.0 miles	Flat trail along the west bank of Elwha River
	Happy Lake Ridge	Just beyond Observation Pt. (9)	9.5 miles	Steep climb (3,709-ft gain) to ridge and lake
	Appleton Pass/Boulder Lk	End of Olympic Hot Springs Rd (10)	7.7 miles	(1-way) Climbs through hot springs area
	Humes Ranch	End of Whiskey Bend Rd (11)	6.0 miles	Moderate loop, can shorten via intersecting trails
	Upper Lake Mills	End of Whiskey Bend Rd (11)	1.0 mile	Short but steep descent to Elwha River
Sol Duc	Ancient Groves	Near Park Boundary (12)	0.6 mile	Easy self-guiding loop through old-growth forest
	Lover's Lane	Sol Duc Campground (13)	5.8 miles	Loop that connects Sol Duc Resort and Sol Duc Falls
	Mink Lake	Sol Duc Campground (13)	5.2 miles	Moderate climb through dense forest to lake
	Sol Duc Falls - 👍	Sol Duc Falls Trailhead (14)	1.6 miles	Hike through old-growth forests to a three-pronged falls
	Deer Lake	Sol Duc Falls Trailhead (14)	7.6 miles	Veers from Sol Duc Falls Tr just before the falls
Hoh Rain Forest	Hall of Mosses - 👍	Visitor Center (15)	0.8 mile	Easy loop trail through old-growth rain forest
	Spruce Nature	Visitor Center (15)	1.2 miles	Part of the trail skirts the Hoh River (elk potential)
	Hoh River - 👍	Visitor Center (15)	17.3 miles	(1-way) Strenuous hike to north face of Mount Olympus
	South Snider–Jackson	West of Entrance Station (16)	11.8 miles	Primitive trail over ridge to Bogachiel River
Quinault	Quinault Big Cedar - 👍	2 mi from US-101 intersection (17)	0.2 mile	Short and flat walk to huge cedar tree
	Maple Glade	Near Ranger Station (18)	0.5 mile	Short loop through big leaf maple grove
	Kestner Homestead	Ranger Station (18)	1.3 miles	Self-guiding loop about homesteading life
	Irely Lake	Near North Fork Campground (19)	1.2 miles	Short and relatively flat hike to shallow lake
Staircase	Wagonwheel Lake	Ranger Station (20)	2.9 miles	Strenuous climb that gains 3,365 feet
	Shady Lane	Campground (20)	0.9 mile	Flat trail to Four Stream Road and Lake Cushman
	Flapjack Lakes	Campground (20)	7.5 miles	(1-way) Strenuous hike spur trail to Black and White Lakes
	North Fork Skokomish R.	Campground (20)	15.1 miles	(1-way) Leads to Duckabush R. but it can be shortened
Deer Park	Rain Shadow	Blue Mtn. Parking Area (21)	0.5 mile	Self-guiding loop to the top of Blue Mountain
	Obstruction Point	Ranger Station (21)	7.4 miles	(1-way) Through forests and meadows to Obstruction Pt.
	Three Forks	Campground (21)	4.3 miles	(1-way) Strenuous hike to Gray Wolf River Trail

Ozette

Ozette is located on the northwestern coast of the Olympic Peninsula. It can be reached by taking WA-113/WA-112 north from US-101 to Hoko–Ozette Road, which eventually runs along the northern shoreline of Ozette Lake and to the coastline. Ozette is one of the more remote regions, at least an hour away from the next closest destination. The **campground** is open all year. All 15 sites are available on a first-come, first-served basis for $12/night. Running water is not available, and there are only pit-toilets in winter.

Cape Alava (3.3 miles) and **Sand Point** (2.8 miles) are two **hiking trails** that have become quite popular thanks to the addition of boardwalks and stairs. Both trails can be connected by a 3.1-mile hike on sand and rock beach to make a 9.2-mile loop. If you're looking for a lightly visited gem, look no further than **Shi Shi Beach**. It's located at the very northern corner of the Ozette area and is accessed via a short hiking trail beginning at the end of Hobuck Road in the Makah Indian Reservation. **Backpackers** can camp along the Ozette Coast. Due to popularity **reservations are required from May through September**. Contact the Wilderness Information Center in Port Angeles at (360) 565-3100 to make reservations. Animal resistant food containers are required for storing food because of raccoons, not black bears. Make sure you have everything that you need for your trip. The only close place to restock or purchase last minute supplies is a small store just outside the park boundary. It carries bare essentials and rents food storage buckets. **All hikers exploring the coast should carry (and know how to use) a tide table.** Several areas are only passable at low tides, and getting trapped is a possibility.

Mora/La Push

WA-110 runs west from US-101, just north of Forks (of *Twilight* book fame). **Mora Campground**, located along the Quillayute River, is open all year. There are 94 sites, all first-come, first-served with access to running water for $12/night. Hook-ups are not available, but a dump station (fee) is. Some sites can accommodate RVs up to 35-feet in length. Short hikes to **Second Beach** (0.7 mile), **Third Beach** (1.4 miles), and **Rialto Beach** (1.54 miles) provide opportunities to explore the rocky shore that is pounded by waves and covered with giant drift logs.

Sandpoint Trail - Ozette

OLYMPIC COAST

Kalaloch

Kalaloch, Olympic's southernmost stretch of Pacific Coast land, is easily accessed via US-101, which runs directly through the region. **Kalaloch Lodge** (888.896.3818, www.olympicnationalparks.com) is open all year. During peak season, rooms cost anywhere from $182/night for a basic motel style room to $338/night for a suite. Just north of the lodge is a **campground** that features 170 campsites available year-round for $14–18/night. Sites can be reserved from mid-June through early September by calling (877) 444-6777 or clicking www.recreation.gov. A dump station (fee) is available on-site.

Easy access and abundant overnight accommodations make Kalaloch one of the most popular regions of Olympic National Park. **Beachcombers** can rejoice as there are seven short trails that lead to the waterfront. **It's also a great location to watch for whales during their spring migration (March–May).**

Flora & Fauna

Lucky guests may spot seals, sea lions, puffins, or sea otters while exploring the coastline. Look for **gray whales** between March and May during their annual migration north to summer feeding grounds. In all, **29 species of marine mammals** have been documented in the park's waters. Beach gives way to dense coniferous forests where you may see bald eagles perched atop a towering western red cedar.

Sunset at Rialto Beach - Mora

Hall of Mosses - Hoh Rain Forest

Olympic Coast Hiking Trails

	Trail Name	Trailhead (# on map)	Length	Notes (Roundtrip distances unless noted otherwise)
Ozette	Cape Alava	Ranger Station (22)	3.3 miles	(1-way) Boardwalk through forest and prairie to beach
Ozette	Sandpoint	Ranger Station (22)	2.8 miles	(1-way) Mostly boardwalk to sandy beach
Ozette	Ozette Loop - 👍	Ranger Station (22)	9.0 miles	Beach connects Cape Alava and Sandpoint Trails
Ozette	Shi Shi Beach - 👍	Hobuck Road (23)	4.0 miles	(1-way) Parking is on private land (fee) • 13 mile hike from the south
Mora	James Pond	Ranger Station (24)	0.3 mile	Easy flat loop through forest to small pond
Mora	Slough	Ranger Station (24)	0.9 mile	Hike through forest to the Quillayute River
Mora	Rialto Beach - 👍	End of Mora Road (25)	1.5 miles	Short walk from parking area to driftwood covered beach
Mora	North Coast Wilderness	End of Mora Road (25)	20.6 miles	Just 1.5 miles to arch, tide pools, and Hole-in-the-Wall
La Push	Second Beach	La Push Road (26)	0.7 mile	Descends through forest to a sandy beach
La Push	Third Beach	La Push Road (27)	1.4 miles	Descends through forest to a sandy beach
La Push	South Coast Wilderness	La Push Road	17.1 miles	Permit required for backcountry camping

Kalaloch features the 1-mile Kalaloch Nature Trail, which passes through coastal forest • Seven separate trails lead from US-101 to the ocean • Ruby Beach and Beach Trail #4 have wheelchair accessible viewpoints and restrooms

For Kids: Children are invited to participate in the park's **Junior Ranger Program**. First, pick-up a free activity booklet at any visitor center. After completing the activities return to a visitor center to show your work to a park ranger. Successful participants will become an official Olympic National Park Junior Ranger and receive a badge for the effort.

Ranger Programs: Ranger-led programs are available throughout the summer at Park Headquarters, Heart O' the Hills, Hurricane Ridge, Lake Crescent, Sol Duc, Staircase (weekends only), Hoh Rain Forest, Quinault, Mora, and Kalaloch. Activities include walks, talks, and campfire programs. Check the current issue of the park publication, *The Bugler* (available online, and at visitor centers and entrance stations), for an up-to-date schedule of events. It is highly recommended that you try to incorporate at least one ranger-led activity into your plans.

Pets: Pets are allowed in the park, but must be kept on a leash no more than six feet in length at all times. They are permitted only in park campgrounds, picnic areas, and parking lots. Pets are not allowed on trails or beaches, except for the following: Rialto Beach, all Kalaloch Beaches, and Peabody Creek Trail.

Accessibility: Accessible facilities and trails are mentioned in each respective region (pages 564–569).

Weather: Extreme differences in elevation and rainfall make generalizing the weather at Olympic National Park exceptionally difficult. Elevation varies from sea level to 7,980 feet at the summit of Mount Olympus. Average annual rainfall varies from 40 to 180 inches depending on where you are. There are distinct dry and wet seasons. Dry season is the most popular time to visit and typically lasts from June through September. Only a few weekend cross-country skiing diehards venture to Hurricane Ridge during the winter.

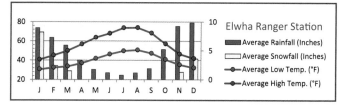

Vacation Planner

When planning a trip to Olympic National Park you have to determine overnight accommodations, regions to visit, and how much driving you want to do. **Lodges** are available at Lake Crescent, Sol Duc, Quinault, and Kalaloch. Nearby dining, grocery stores, lodging, festivals, and attractions are listed on pages 580–583.

There are 16 campgrounds, with a total of 910 sites to choose from, but campgrounds can fill during summer. You can play it safe by reserving a site at Kalaloch. Reservations can be made by clicking www.recreation.gov or calling (877) 444-6777. All other campgrounds are first-come, first-served. Stop and set up camp before you begin exploring a region (especially on summer weekends).

If you want to see several regions without moving your tent or camper, you may want to set up base camp at Kalaloch or Fairholme on Lake Crescent. Quinault, Queets, and Hoh Rain Forest are relatively close to Kalaloch. Hurricane Ridge, Elwha, and Sol Duc are all within a reasonable drive from Lake Crescent. Fairholme is also a good location to make the trip to Ozette (see driving distances below).

If you're planning on driving the entire Olympic Peninsula Loop on US-101, make sure you stop at Hurricane Ridge, Hoh Rain Forest, Ruby Beach at Kalaloch, and Quinault. Shi Shi Beach at Ozette and the Mora Beaches (Second, Third, and Rialto) are nice, too.

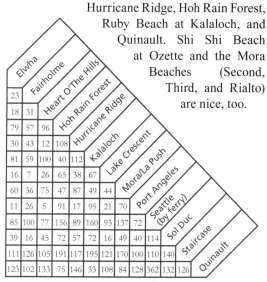

Mountain goats are at home on top the rocky mountains of the North Cascades © Dan Bennett

810 State Route 20
Sedro–Woolley, WA 98284
Phone: (360) 854-7200
Website: www.nps.gov/noca

Established: October 2, 1968
Size: 684,000 Acres
Annual Visitors: 25,000
Peak Season: Summer

Activities: Hiking, Backpacking,
Whitewater Rafting, Boating,
Rock Climbing, Biking, Horseback
Riding, and Cross-Country Skiing

Campgrounds: Goodell Creek,
Newhalem Creek*, George Lake,
Colonial Creek, and Hozomeen
Fee: $10–12/night
Backcountry Camping: Permitted
with a free Backcountry Use Permit

Park Hours: All day, every day
Entrance Fee: None
National Forest Day Pass: $5

*Reserve at (877) 444-6777 or
www.recreation.gov

North Cascades - Washington

The North Cascades are brimming with old-growth forests, hundreds of glaciers, and pure alpine lakes. They are a hiker's paradise as unique in landscape as in name: **North Cascades National Park Service Complex**. The only of its kind, this complex unites three park units: North Cascades National Park (North and South Units), Ross Lake National Recreation Area (NRA), and Lake Chelan NRA. The mountains, named for an abundance of waterfalls, form an imposing natural barrier, preventing all but the most determined visitors from entering their depths. Many people have tried their luck at making a living among these mountains, but few succeeded. Today, that task is much easier thanks to considerable infrastructure and a healthy, but not overwhelming, tourism industry. **North Cascades Scenic Highway** pierces the Cascades, crossing them from east to west as the roadway runs the entire length of Ross Lake NRA. Travel further from the beaten path—into river-carved valleys, on top of rocky ridgelines, far away from the scenic byway—and you'll begin to see the landscape as its earliest inhabitants saw it, wild and free.

Native Americans lived in the mountainous environment for thousands of years. Their lives were tied to the surroundings. Two major tribes lived in the region, one on each side of the Cascades. People of the Columbia River Basin lived to the east. People of the Pacific Northwest/Puget Lowlands lived to the west. They traded between each other, blazing trails across Stehekin (meaning "the way through"), Cascade, and Twisp Passes. They often followed high ridgelines to avoid navigating dense vegetation common in the lower elevations. Natives lived in harmony with the land; many Americans did their best to exploit it.

Several American expeditions traversed the North Cascades, mapping and documenting what they witnessed. Fur trappers came and went. Hundreds of miners hoping to strike it rich arrived in the late 1870s. They panned for gold along the banks of the Skagit River, but found very little. The rush ended by 1880. Trees were felled and floated along the Skagit River and Lake Chelan, but inadequate transportation and infrastructure spared the forests. The most significant alterations to the landscape came in the form of three dams along the Skagit River, but for the most part this rugged land remains wild and free.

Best of North Cascades

Attraction: **North Cascades Highway**
> Runner-up: Stehekin
> 2nd Runner-up: Hozomeen

Hike: **Rainy Lake/Maple Pass**
> Runner-up: Cascade Pass
> 2nd Runner-up: Rainbow Loop

Did you know?

▶ More than half the contiguous United States' glaciers are concentrated in the North Cascades.

Stehekin Landing

Cascade Pass

When to Go

The park is open all year, but winter weather impacts when most visitors arrive. Roads and facilities are generally open between late May and late October. Visitation is rarely excessive, but most guests arrive during July and August when the weather is usually pleasant and almost all trails are free of snow.

Transportation & Airports

Amtrak (1.800.872.7245 or www.amtrak.com) and Greyhound (800.231.2222, www.greyhound.com) provide transportation along the I-5 corridor, but do not travel directly to the park. **Lady of the Lake** ($34.50–39 roundtrip, 888.682.4584, www.ladyofthelake.com) provides ferry service between Chelan and Stehekin. The ferry operates daily from mid-March through early fall. The closest major airport is Seattle–Tacoma International (SEA), 130 miles southwest of North Cascades Visitor Center.

Directions

North Cascades National Park Service Complex is not easy to access by vehicle. The South Unit is only accessed via the unpaved Cascade River Road. No roads penetrate the North Unit or Lake Chelan National Recreation Area. Most visitors enter the complex via WA-20 (North Cascades Scenic Highway), which crosses the Cascades and Ross Lake National Recreation Area (NRA).

Ross Lake NRA via Seattle (~140 miles): Heading north on I-5, take Exit 230 for WA-20 toward Burlington/Anacortes/Skagit Airport. Turn right at WA-20, and follow it about 60 miles to the park.

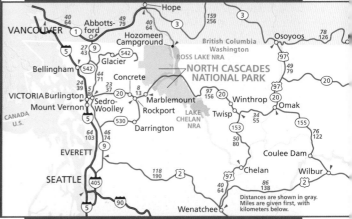

British Columbia
Washington

To Hope, B.C.
40mi/64km

MANNING
PROVINCIAL PARK

MOUNT BAKER
WILDERNESS

To Glacier
(USFS/NPS information)
4mi
6km

Mount Redoubt
8957ft

Hozomeen

Hozomeen Mt.
8068ft

CANADA
UNITED STATES

Heather Meadows
Visitor Center

Long Distance Hike
Desolation Peak

Castle Pass

Hopkins Pass

Woody Pass

Redoubt
Glacier

Desolation
Peak
6102ft

Pacific Crest
National Scenic
Trail

PASAYTEN WILDERN

MOUNT BAKER
WILDERNESS

Mount Shuksan
9131ft

Mount Challenger
8248ft

Mount Fury
8291ft

Mount Prophet
7579ft

Devils Dome
6982ft

Holman Pass

Mount Baker
10775ft

PICKET RANGE

NORTH CASCADES NATIONAL PARK
NORTH UNIT

McMillan Spire

Mount Terror
7151ft

ROSS LAKE
NRA

Jack Mountain
9065ft

MOUNT BAKER-
SNOQUALMIE
NATIONAL FOREST
(Administered by
Okanogan NF)

Mount Despair
7293ft

Sourdough
Mountain
6106ft

Ross
Lake
Resort

Crater Mountain
8127ft

Hike
Maple Pass Loop

Mount Triumph
7271ft

See detail on next page

Ross Lake
Overlook

Goodell
Creek

Gorge
Creek
Falls

DIABLO

Harts Pass

Bacon Peak
7067ft

Gorge
Dam

Gorge
Lake

Diablo
Dam

Diablo Lake
Overlook

Ross Dam

Ruby
Arm

Damnation Peak
5643ft

Thornton
Lakes

NEWHALEM

Newhalem
Creek

Colonial
Creek

Ruby
Mountain

North
Cascades
Visitor
Center

Pyramid
Peak
7182ft

Diablo
Lake

North Cascades Scenic Hwy

OKANOGA

NATIONAL

FOREST

NORTH CASCADES

Fourth of July Pass
3501ft

Easy Pass
6562ft

To Maz

Wilderness Information Center
Backcountry permits

NATIONAL PARK

Methow Pass

To Information Center
at Park Headquarters
and Sedro Woolley
23mi
37km

Baker Dam

CONCRETE

Rockport
State Park

MARBLEMOUNT

SOUTH UNIT

Eldorado Peak
8672ft

Rainy Pass

Rainy Pass
4860ft

Washington
Pass Overlo

ROCKPORT

Eldorado
Glacier

Forbidden
Peak

Boston Glacier

Liberty
Bell Mt.
7808ft

Early Winter
Spires

Cascade

Sahale
Mt.

Boston
Peak

Buckner Mountain
9080ft

Goode Mountain
9206ft

Lake
Ann

Rainy
Lake

Copper
Pass

Johannesburg
Mountain

Booker Mt.

Black
Warrior Mine

Cottonwood

Twisp Pass
Trail

Cascade Pass
5384ft

Hike
Cascade Pass

Cascade Pass Trail

Glory

Park Creek

Twisp
Pass

LAKE
CHELAN
SAWTOO
WILDERN

Flat Creek

Bridge Creek

Shady

Mount Formidable
8324ft

Dolly Varden

Tumwater

Bullion

LAKE
CHELAN
NRA

High Bridge

Rainbow Falls

Shuttle-bus
route

Old Stehekin
School

Harlequin

Buckner
Place

Purple
Mountain

War
Creek
Pass

DARRINGTON

White Chuck Mountain
6935ft

Weaver Point

STEHEKIN

Pacific
Crest
National
Scenic Trail

Company
Creek
Trail

Purple
Point

Castle Rock
8137ft

Stehekin Land
North Cascad
Stehekin Lod
Golden West
Visitor Center

Dome Peak
8595ft
2679m

Moore
Point

GLACIER PEAK WILDERNESS

WENATCHEE NATIONAL FORES

Devore
Creek
Trail

HOLDEN

LUCERNE

Glacier Peak
10528ft

Trailhead Location (see
hiking table on page 577)

Lakeshore
Trail

Lake
Chelan

To Fields Point
and Chelan via
passenger ferry

North

0   5   10 Kilometers

0   5   10 Miles

Hiking trail

Unpaved road

Ranger station

Campground

Picnic area

Wheelchair
accessible

Regions

One of the most unique features about this park is that it's a National Park Service Complex consisting of three distinct units: **North Cascades National Park** (North and South Units) and **Ross Lake and Lake Chelan National Recreation Areas** (NRA). The National Recreation Areas have more lenient preservation and protection regulations, allowing local interests like hydroelectric facilities, resorts, and hunting to continue with limited federal intervention. Stephen Mather Wilderness unites the units as it encompasses roughly 94% of the entire complex.

North Cascades National Park is the least accessible portion. It is broken into north and south units by Ross Lake NRA, which straddles North Cascades Highway and Ross Lake, bisecting the complex. The North Unit is only accessible by foot. **Cascade River Road** provides vehicle access to the South Unit and is the only vehicle access point into the park. The 23-mile dirt and gravel roadway is typically open from summer through fall. Along the way you'll pass two National Forest campgrounds before crossing the park boundary. Eventually the road terminates at **Cascade Pass Trailhead**. Cascade Pass and the spur trail to Sahale Mountain are two of the best hikes you'll find. Still, most visitors choose to hike into the north or south unit beginning at one of several trailheads located along WA-20 in Ross Lake NRA.

Ross Lake NRA serves as the centerpiece of the complex. Easy access via **North Cascades Scenic Hwy/ WA-20** and the majority of campgrounds, trailheads, and visitor facilities makes Ross Lake NRA the park's most popular region. The area protects stretches of the Skagit River, Diablo Lake, and 24-mile long Ross Lake. Skagit River provides recreation all summer. Diablo and Ross Lakes provide paddlers with the opportunity for some unique multi-day backcountry trips or casual day-trips. Regularly scheduled boat tours are available on Ross Lake. But its only boat launch is accessed via a dirt and gravel road from Canada. **North Cascades Visitor Center** is where you'll want to begin your trip. It's located just off WA-20 near Newhalem and open daily, spring to fall, and on weekends in winter.

Lake Chelan NRA is located deep in the complex's southern reaches. It wraps around the north end of 55-mile long Lake Chelan, the nation's third-deepest lake (1,486-ft). Visitors must hike, fly, or boat into this picturesque setting fit for a postcard. Even the ferry trip is great for viewing wildlife, waterfalls, and the shores of the glacially carved lake. The sights don't stop once you've reached **Stehekin**. You can explore historic Buckner Orchard or marvel at 312-foot Rainbow Falls. Stehekin cannot be reached by car, but there is a road; a shuttle ($5/Adult, $2.50/Child, $5/Bike) transports visitors through the valley.

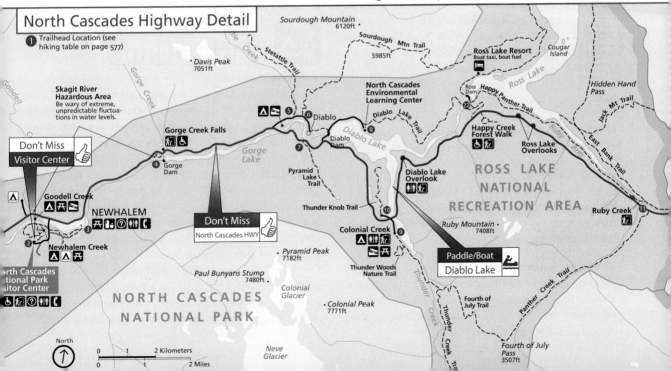

Camping near Easy Pass

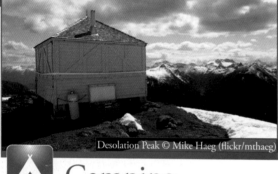
Desolation Peak © Mike Haeg (flickr/mthaeg)

Camping

The park runs five drive-in campgrounds. From west to east, **Goodell Creek** (Milepost 112, 21 sites, $10/night), **Newhalem Creek** (120, 111, $12), **George Lake** (126, 6, free), and **Colonial Creek** (130, 142, $12) **Campgrounds** are all located along North Cascades Highway (WA-20). **Hozomeen Campground** (75 sites, free), located in the park's northeast corner, is accessed via Skagit Road from Canada. Reservations are only accepted at Newhalem Creek Campground. They can be reserved for $21/night by calling (877) 444-6777 or clicking www.recreation.gov. All other campsites are available on a first-come, first-served basis.

Group sites are available at Upper and Lower Goodell Creek ($25/night or $34/night with reservation) and Newhalem Creek ($32 or $41). These sites may be reserved by calling (877) 444-6777 or clicking www.recreation.gov.

There are more than 100 designated campsites for backpackers and boaters in the backcountry. Beyond park boundaries there are more than a dozen developed campgrounds in national forest, state park, and county park land.

Hiking

North Cascades Highway is nice, but to share a more intimate experience with the Cascades leave the car behind and set out on foot. Nearly **400 miles of hiking trails** allow guests to explore the stunning beauty of the park's river-carved valleys and glacier-capped peaks. Most trailheads are located along North Cascades Highway and in Stehekin (Lake Chelan NRA), but the true day-hiker's paradise is **Cascade River Road**. It closes seasonally and after mile 10 is dirt and gravel, but should be passable by low clearance 2WD vehicles. The trails to **Hidden Lake** and **Cascade Pass** are this area's gems and two of the best hikes in the Cascades.

Desolation Peak may not look impressive from a distance, but the views from its summit are tremendous. This peak is where **Jack Kerouac** found solitude working as a fire-watcher. Spellbinding scenery and isolation inspired some of his best work: *Desolation Angels* and *Dharma Bums*. To reach Desolation Peak, follow **East Bank Trail** from WA-20 (Milepost 138) for 16 miles to the junction for Desolation Peak. You can also reach this point via tour boat from Ross Lake Resort (206.386.4437, www.rosslakeresort.com) or your own private boat. From the junction it's another 6.8 miles climbing 4,400 feet to the peak. See the table on the following page for a more complete list of trails.

Backpacking

Wilderness camping is only allowed at designated sites along trail corridors. All overnight stays in the backcountry require a **free backcountry permit**. Permits are issued in person up to one day prior to your intended date of departure at the **Wilderness Information Center** (WIC, 360.854.7245) in Marblemount. It is located just off WA-20 on the park's west side. In summer it's open from 7am to 8pm on Friday and Saturday and 7am to 6pm from Sunday to Thursday. It's typically closed from mid-Fall to early May. If you do not pass through Marblemount, you can obtain a permit at any of the ranger stations. Permits are limited and popular areas like Cascade Pass, Ross Lake, Copper Ridge, and Thorton and Monogram Lakes can fill quickly. Backpacking trips should be planned in advance using a good topographic map. A few suggested loop trips are provided in the table on the following page.

North Cascades Hiking Trails

Trail Name	Trailhead (# on map)	Length	Difficulty (E = Easy, M = Moderate, S = Strenuous)/Notes
Thornton Lake	Thornton Lakes Road (1)	10.4 miles	M • Logging road leads to steep climb and classic cirque lakes
Sterling Munro	North Cascades Visitor Center (2)	330 feet	E • Outstanding views of the Picket Range
River Loop	North Cascades Visitor Center (2)	1.8 miles	E • Through old-growth to river and campground
To Know a Tree	New Halem Campground (3)	0.5 mile	E • Self-guiding trail explores area's trees and plants
Rock Shelter	New Halem Campground (3)	0.3 mile	E • Wheelchair accessible, 1,400 year old hunting camp
Trail of the Cedars	River Loop/Linking Trails (3)	0.3 mile	E • Self-guiding trail along river to Main Street
Ladder Creek Falls	Gorge Powerhouse (4)	0.4 mile	E • Self-guiding trail courtesy of Seattle City Light
Stetattle Creek	Near Diablo (5)	6.0 miles	M • Often snow-free early, requires rock scrambling
Sourdough Mountain	Near Diablo (6)	11.1 miles	S • (1-way) Lookout (5.2 mi) with stunning glacier views
Pyramid Lake	WA-20 Milepost 126.8 (7)	4.2 miles	M • Hike to a small deep lake created by a landslide
Diablo Lake - 👍	North of Diablo Lake (8)	7.6 miles	M • View glaciers and peaks from north side of Diablo Lake
Thunder Creek - 👍	Colonial Creek Campground (9)	23.0 miles	M • (1-way) Follows glacier-fed creek into the heart of the park
Thunder Knob	Colonial Creek Campground (10)	3.6 miles	M • Kid-friendly hike with wonderful views of Diablo Lake
East Bank - 👍	WA-20 Milepost 138 (11)	31.0 miles	E • (1-way) Spur trails to Little Jack and Desolation Peak
Panther Creek	WA-20 Milepost 138 (11)	6.5 miles	M • (1-way) To 4th of July Pass • Popular early season
Easy Pass/Fisher Creek	WA-20 Milepost 151 (US Forest Pass req'd to park) (12)	3.5 miles / 14.8 miles	S • (1-way) To Easy Pass (one of the best sites in the park) / M • (1-way) To Thunder Creek Trail
Rainy Lake/Maple Pass - 👍	Rainy Pass on WA-20 (13)	1.0/7.5 mi	E/M • Great hikes just outside the park, waterfalls
Bridge Creek (PCT)	WA-20 Milepost 159 (14)	12.8 miles	E • (1-way) Follows Pacific Crest Tr to Bridge Creek Camp
Monogram Lake	Travel 7 miles south on Cascade River Rd from Marblemount (15)	10.0 miles	S • (1-way) Climb 4,040-ft via steep forested switchbacks, and then through subalpine meadows
Hidden Lake - 👍	End of Sibley Creek Rd (16)	9.0 miles	M • Climb 2,900-ft on this popular day-hike to beautiful lake
Cascade Pass - 👍	End of Cascade River Rd (17)	3.7 miles / 6.0 miles	M • (1-way) One of the best day-hikes to Cascade / (1-way) Glacier/mountain views to Sahale Arm
Agnes Gorge	High Bridge (18)	5.0 miles	E • Wildflowers early and mid-summer
Coon Lake	High Bridge/Bullion Camp (18)	2.6–3.8 mi	M • Good location for birding and mountain views
Old Wagon (PCT)	High Bridge (18)	Varies	E • Pacific Crest Trail • Connects lower and upper valleys
Goode Ridge	Old Wagon Trail (18)	10.0 miles	S • Excellent views of Stehekin River drainage
McGregor Mountain	Via Old Wagon Trail (18)	7.7 miles	S • (1-way) Switchbacks climb to panoramic views
Buckner Orchard	Near Rainbow Falls (19)	Varies	E • Self-guiding trail where guests pick apples in fall
Rainbow Creek	Stehekin Valley Road (20)	9.7 miles	M • (1-way) Leads to McAlester Pass/Trail
Rainbow Loop - 👍	Stehekin Valley Road (20)	8.8 miles	M • Popular in the early season (wildflowers)
Purple Creek - 👍	Golden West Visitor Center (21)	8.1 miles	S • (1-way) Explore the high country to Juanita Lake
Beaver Loop	Ross Dam Trail, Milepost 134 (22)	34.2 miles	Combine Big and Little Beaver • Water taxi required
Rainbow/McAlester Pass	WA-20/Stehekin (14/20)	31.5 miles	M • Bridge Creek, McAlester Lake, Rainbow Creek and Lake Tr
Copper Ridge/Chilliwack River - 👍	Hannegan Road in Mount Baker Wilderness (23)	33.5 miles	S • Best of North Cascades terrain • Sites along Copper Ridge fill quickly • Ice axe required at Copper Ridge until July
Devil's Dome	East Bank or Canyon Creek Trailhead on WA-20 (11)	40.4 miles	S • Through Okanogan National Forest, but finishes along shores of Ross Lake on East Bank Trail (wildflowers)

All trail distances are roundtrip unless noted otherwise

Diablo Lake from Sourdough Mountain

Diablo Lake from a kayak

Other Activities

North Cascades Institute (360.854.2599, www.ncascades.org) offers a wealth of courses and experiences throughout northwest Washington. Many programs take place right in the heart of North Cascades National Park at **North Cascades Environmental Learning Center** on the north shoreline of Diablo Lake. Programs include bird watching expeditions, photography classes, mountain hikes, and educational discussions. Cost is anywhere from $125 to $250 per day. Meals and lodging are often included at the Learning Center campus.

Stehekin Outfitters (800.536.0745, www.stehekinoutfitters.com), located in Stehekin at the head of Lake Chelan, provides unique opportunities to explore the North Cascades. They offer **hiking trips** (~$150/day), **horseback rides** ($50, 2.5 hours), **kayak tours** ($35), and **whitewater rafting adventures** ($50).

Biking: Bikes are only allowed on park roads. Road cyclists have one option: **North Cascades Highway**. Traffic is manageable, but the elevation gain is sure to make your thighs burn. Bicycling is also a great way to explore **Stehekin Valley Road**. Bicycles can be brought aboard the Chelan Lake Ferry ($12/one-way,

$24/roundtrip) or you can rent one from **Discovery Bikes** (rkscutt@gmail.com, www.stehekindiscoverybikes.com). Rentals cost $4 (hour), $20 (8am–5pm), and $25 (24 hours).

Fishing: **Stehekin Fishing Adventures** (www.stehekinfishingadventures.com) offers guided fishing trips on Lake Chelan and around Stehekin Valley. Rates are $130–195/person (half-day) and $210–295/person (full-day).

Opportunities for **mountaineering, rock climbing, kayaking, canoeing, rafting, snowshoeing**, and **cross-country skiing** are also available at North Cascades. Refer to page 582 for a list of the park's approved outfitters.

For Kids: Children are welcome to participate in the **Junior Ranger Program**. Four booklets are available at the park's information centers. They are also available online at the park website. Complete the activities in the booklet appropriate for your age and head to a visitor center to receive a Junior Ranger badge, patch, and certificate.

Ranger Programs: Rangers offer **guided boat tours** (fee) on Lake Chelan and Ross Lake, **bus tours** (fee) of Stehekin Valley Road, and a variety of free walks, talks, and evening programs in summer. Current schedules are available at the park website or at any of the visitor information centers.

North Cascades Visitor Center • (206) 386-4495 ext. 11
North Cascades Highway near Milepost 120
Open: May–October, Daily, 9am–5pm; June–September, 9am–6pm

Park and Forest Information Center • (360) 854-7200
North Cascades Highway in Sedro–Wooley, WA
Open: late May–mid-October, Daily, weekdays only for remainder, 8am–4:30pm

Wilderness Information Center • (360) 854-7245
North Cascades Highway near Marblemount (Milepost 105.3)
Open: early May–mid-October, Daily, 8am–4:30pm (weekdays), 7am–6pm (weekends) • Extended hours in summer

Golden West Visitor Center • (360) 854-7365 ext. 14
Near passenger ferry landing at Stehekin Landing
Open: late May–late September, Daily, 8:30am–5pm; limited hours of operation from late September through late May.

Flora & Fauna: North Cascades is home to **more than 1,600 species of vascular plants and at least 500 species of animals**. Wildflower meadows burst with color; some bloom as early as February and others as late as September. Trees, including western red cedar, Sitka spruce, Douglas fir, and western hemlock, dominate all but the highest elevations. You're most likely to spot black-tailed deer, Douglas squirrel, or playful pika, but you may encounter black bears, mountain goats, or wolves while exploring the park.

Pets: Bringing your pet severely limits what you can do here. In the national park pets are only allowed on a leash on the Pacific Crest Trail and within 50 feet of roads. They must be kept on a leash at all times in Ross Lake or Lake Chelan NRAs. For pet-friendly travel destinations call the park at (360) 854-7245.

Accessibility: North Cascades Visitor Center, Sedro–Woolley Information Station, and the Wilderness Information Office are fully accessible to wheelchair users. Golden West Visitor Center is accessible with assistance. Rock Shelter is the only accessible hiking trail.

Weather: Mountain weather is downright baffling. In the North Cascades snow can fall any day of the year. WA-20 can close and be buried in snow between November and February. Then there are outliers like the winter of 1976–'77 when North Cascades Highway/WA-20 remained open all year. The western slopes receive, on average, 76 more inches of rain and 407 more inches of snowfall than their eastern counterparts that reside in the mountain's rain shadow. You're never guaranteed beautiful weather in the Cascades, but the best bet is to travel between mid-June and late September.

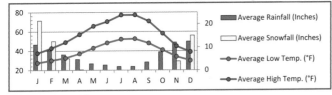

312-foot Rainbow Falls (Stehekin)

Vacation Planner

Most visitors drive through the park via **North Cascades Highway** or take a **ferry** ride to **Stehekin** (page 573). There's very little visitation to any of the areas in between. **Lodging** facilities (page 580) are available at both locations, and **campgrounds** (page 576) are rarely full. Nearby dining, grocery stores, lodging, festivals, and attractions are listed on pages 580–583. Provided below is a sample one-day itinerary for each destination. Cascade Pass (accessed via Cascade River Road from Marblemount) is one of the best attractions, but it's been omitted because many visitors are uncomfortable or unwilling to traverse the gravel road leading into this region.

North Cascades Highway: Beeline for the **Visitor Center** (Milepost 120) where you can ask a ranger any questions, check a schedule of the day's **ranger programs**, watch an introductory film, browse exhibits, and use the restrooms. If you'd like to stretch your legs, **Sterling Munro and River Loop Trails** (page 577) are available nearby. However, there are better hikes ahead. Stop at **Gorge Creek Falls and Overlook** to hike a couple of short interpretive trails (page 577). Continuing east, stop at **Diablo Lake Overlook** for the views. Next, stop at **East Bank Trailhead** (Milepost 138). To the north, **East Bank Trail** is great for families. It's a flat and easy path following the shoreline of **Ross Lake**. To the southwest is **Panther Creek Trail**. It is more rigorous (and more beautiful). Hike 6.5-miles

(one-way) to **4ᵗʰ of July Pass** (page 577). Alternatively, you can continue along North Cascades Highway outside the park to **Rainy Pass**. The 7.5-mile **Maple Pass Loop** (page 577) found here features stunning scenery.

Stehekin: This remote community of 80 or so year-round residents is completely disconnected from society. No roads lead in or out of the quiet mountain retreat. That's one of the biggest draws, not to mention the fact that you're surrounded by glaciated mountains, tumbling waterfalls, and pristine water. From **Stehekin Landing**, begin by stopping in at **Golden West Visitor Center** where you can view exhibits of the area's natural and cultural history. When it comes to exploring the region you have three choices: hike, bike, or shuttle. To get right after the hiking, head into the mountains to **Juanita Lake via Purple Creek Trail** (page 577). Energetic hikers can **combine Purple Creek Trail with Boulder Creek Trail**, which loops back to Stehekin Valley Road at **Rainbow Falls**. In fall, stroll over to **Buckner Orchard** to pick an apple or two.

Dining

Mount Rainier Area

Wild Berry Restaurant • (360) 569-2277
37718 WA-706 E; Ashford, WA 98304
www.thewildberry.net

Highlander Steak House • (360) 569-2953
30319 WA-706 E; Ashford, WA 98304

Butter Butte Coffee Co • (360) 494-5600
105 Main St E, #791; Packwood, WA 98361

Cruisers Pizza • (360) 494-5400
13028 US-12; Packwood, WA 98361

Blue Spruce Diner • (360) 494-5605
13019 US-12; Packwood, WA 98361

Sushi Town • (253) 891-2046
20649 WA-410; Bonney Lake, WA 98391

Wally's White River Drive-in • (360) 829-0871
282 WA-410 North; Buckley, WA 98321

Olympic Peninsula

Alder Wood Bistro • (360) 683-4321
139 West Alder St; Sequim, WA 98382
www.alderwoodbistro.com • Entrée: $17–26

Dockside Grill • (360) 683-7510
2577 W Sequim Bay Rd; Sequim, WA 98382
www.docksidegrill-sequim.com

Jeremiah's BBQ • (360) 681-4227
825 W Washington St; Sequim, WA 98382
www.jeremiahsbbq.com • Sandwiches: $6+

Dynasty Chinese Restaurant • (360) 683-6511
990 E Washington St; Sequim, WA 98382

Hi-Way 101 Diner & Pizza • (360) 683-3388
392 W Washington St; Sequim, WA 98382

The Garden Bistro • (360) 809-0585
104 E Washington St; Sequim, WA 98382
www.garden-bistro.com • Sandwiches: $8+

Oak Table Café • (360) 683-2179
292 W Bell St; Sequim, WA 98382
www.oaktablecafe.com • Breakfast: $9+

Sunshine Café • (360) 683-4282
135 W Washington St; Sequim, WA 98382

Café Garden • (360) 457-4611
1506 E 1st St; Port Angeles, WA 98362
www.cafegardenpa.com • Entrée: $13–22

Michael's Seafood & Steakhouse • (360) 417-6929
117-B E 1st St; Port Angeles, WA 98362
www.michaelsdining.com • Entrée: $15–37

Toga's • (360) 452-1952
122 W Lauridsen Blvd; Port Angeles, WA 98362

Sabai Thai • (360) 452-4505
903 W 8th St; Port Angeles, WA 98363
www.sabaithaipa.com • Entrée: $12–17

First Street Haven • (360) 457-0352
107 E 1st St; Port Angeles, WA 98362

Gordy's Pizza & Pasta • (360) 457-5056
1123 E 1st St; Port Angeles, WA 98362
www.gordyspizza.com • Pizza: $3–30

Taqueria Santanna • (360) 374-3339
80 Calawah Way; Forks, WA 98331

Forks Coffee Shop • (360) 374-6769
241 S Forks Ave; Forks, WA 98331
www.forkscoffeeshop.com • Entrée: $12–19

Pacific Pizza • (360) 374-2626
870 S Forks Ave; Forks, WA 98331

Hard Rain Café • (360) 374-9288
5763 Upper Hoh Rd; Forks, WA 98331
www.hardraincafe.com

Banana Leaf Thai Bistro • (360) 379-6993
609 Washington St; Port Townsend, WA 98368

Lanza's Ristorante • (360) 379-1900
1020 Lawrence St; Port Townsend, WA 98368

Hanazono Asian Noodle • (360) 385-7622
225 Taylor St; Port Townsend, WA 98368

Waterfront Pizza • (360) 385-6629
951 Water St; Port Townsend, WA 98368

Dos Okies Barbeque • (360) 385-7669
2310 Washington St; Port Townsend, WA 98368
www.dosokiesbarbeque.com • Sandwiches: $4+

Blue Moose Café • (360) 385-7339
311-B Haines Pl; Port Townsend, WA 98368

Sweet Laurette Café • (360) 385-4886
1029 Lawrence St; Port Townsend, WA 98368
www.sweetlaurette.com

North Cascades Area

Buffalo Run • (360) 873-2461
60084 WA-20; Marblemount, WA 98267
www.buffaloruninn.com

Marblemount Diner • (360) 873-4503
60147 WA-20; Marblemount, WA 98267

Annie's Pizza Station • (360) 853-7227
44568 WA-20; Concrete, WA 98237

Cascade Burgers • (360) 853-7580
45292 WA-20; Concrete, WA 98237

Milano's Restaurant & Deli • (360) 599-2863
9990 Mt Baker Hwy; Deming, WA 98244
www.milanorestaurant.us • Entrée: $12–16

Chair 9 Pizza & Bar • (360) 599-2511
10459 Mt Baker Hwy; Glacier, WA 98244
www.chair9.com • Pizza: $17–23

Blue Mountain Grill • (360) 595-2200
974 Valley Highway; Acme, WA 98220
www.bluemountaingrill.com • Entrée: $10–22

Grocery Stores

Mount Rainier Area

Safeway • (360) 825-5023
152 Roosevelt Ave East; Enumclaw, WA 98022

Fred Meyer • (253) 891-7315
20901 WA-410; Bonney Lake, WA 98391

Walmart Supercenter • (253) 826-9144
19205 WA-410 E; Bonney Lake, WA 98391

Albertsons-Sav-on • (253) 826-2401
20025 WA-410 E; Bonney Lakes, WA 98390

Rose's IGA • (360) 829-0810
29393 WA-410 E; Buckley, WA 98321

Olympic Peninsula

Safeway • (360) 457-0788
110 E 3rd St; Port Angeles, WA 98362

Albertsons • (360) 452-2307
114 E Lauridsen Blvd; Port Angeles, WA 98362

Safeway • (360) 457-1461
2709 E US-101; Port Angeles, WA 98362

Safeway • (360) 681-8767
680 W Washington St; Sequim, WA 98382

Walmart • (360) 452-1244
3500 US-101; Port Angeles, WA 98362

Costco • (360) 406-2023
955 W Washington St; Sequim, WA 98382

Walmart • (360) 683-9346
1284 W Washington St; Sequim, WA 98382

North Cascades Area

Walmart Supercenter • (360) 428-7000
2301 Freeway Dr; Mount Vernon, WA 98273

Costco • (360) 757-5701
1725 S Burlington Blvd; Burlington, WA 98233

Lodging

Mount Rainier Area

Deep Forest Cabins • (360) 569-2054
33823 WA-706 E; Ashford, WA 98304
www.deepforestcabins.com • Rates: $110–250/night

Jasmer's • (360) 569-2682
30005 WA-706 E; Ashford, WA 98304
www.jasmers.com • Rates: $85–150

Wellspring Spa • (360) 569-2514
54922 Kernahan Rd E; Ashford, WA 98304
www.wellspringspa.com • Rates: $95–575

Nisqually Lodge • (360) 569-8804
31609 WA-706; Ashford, WA 98304
www.escapetothemountains.com • Rates: $85+

Copper Creek Inn & Restaurant
35707 WA-706 E; Ashford • (360) 569-2799
www.coppercreekinn.com • Rates: $79+

Mtn Meadows B&B • (360) 569-2788
28912 WA-706 East; Ashford, WA 98304
www.mountainmeadowsinn.com • Rates: $149–175

Crest Trail Lodge • (360) 494-4944
12729 US-12; Packwood, WA 98361
www.cresttrail.whitepasstravel.com • Rates: $90+

Hotel Packwood • (360) 494-5431
104 Main St; Packwood, WA 98361
www.packwoodwa.com • Rates: $29–49

Mountain View Lodge • (360) 494-5555
13163 US-12; Packwood, WA 98361
www.mtvlodge.com • Rates: $45–150

Olympic Peninsula

Sequim Bay Lodge • (360) 683-0691
268522 US-101; Sequim, WA 98382
www.sequimbaylodge.com • Rates: $70+

Dungeness Bay Cottages • (888) 683-3013
140 Marine Dr; Sequim, WA 98382
www.dungenessbay.com • Rates: $130–180

Dungeness Barn House B&B • (360) 582-1663
42 Marine Dr; Sequim, WA 98382
www.dungenessbarnhouse.com • Rates: $140–175

Oh Susanna's B&B • (360) 681-4495
100 Hereford Lane; Sequim, WA 98382
www.ohsusannasbb.com • Rates: $125+

Red Caboose Getaway • (360) 683-7350
24 Old Coyote Way; Sequim, WA 98382
www.redcaboosegetaway.com • Rates: $175+

Sequim West Inn & RV Park • (800) 528-4527
740 W Washington St; Sequim, WA 98382
www.sequimwestinn.com • Rates: $54–160

Port Angeles Inn • (360) 452-9285
111 E 2nd St; Port Angeles, WA 98362
www.portangelesinn.com • Rates: $60+

All View Motel • (360) 457-7779
214 E Lauridsen Blvd; Port Angeles, WA 98362
www.allviewmotel.com • Rates: $40–139

Olympic Lodge • (800) 600-2993
140 S Del Guzzi Dr; Port Angeles, WA 98362
www.olympiclodge.com • Rates: $100–200

The Meadows Inn • (360) 417-8074
3182 Blue Mtn Rd; Port Angeles, WA 98362
www.themeadowsinn.com • Rates: $150+

Colette's B&B • (360) 457-9197
339 Finn Hall Rd; Port Angeles, WA 98362
www.colettes.com • Rates: $195–395

Inn At Rooster Hill • (360) 452-4933
112 Reservoir Rd; Port Angeles, WA 98363
www.innatroosterhill.com • Rates: $99–179

Eden by the Sea • (360) 452-6021
1027 Finn Hall Rd; Port Angeles, WA 98362
www.edenbythesea.net • Rates: $145–195

George Washington Inn • (360) 452-5207
939 Finn Hall Rd; Port Angeles, WA 98362
www.georgewashingtoninn.com • Rates: $175–300

Pacific Inn Motel • (360) 374-9400
352 S Forks Ave; Forks, WA 98331
www.pacificinnmotel.com • Rates: $89+

Forks Motel • (360) 374-6243
351 S Forks Ave; Forks, WA 98331
www.forksmotel.com • Rates: $61+

Quillayute River Resort • (360) 374-7447
473 Mora Rd; Forks, WA 98331
www.qriverresort.com • Rates: $110–180

Miller Tree Inn B&B • (800) 943-6563
654 E Division St; Forks, WA 98331
www.millertreeinn.com • Rates: $115–230

Palace Hotel • (360) 385-0773
1004 Water St; Port Townsend, WA 98368
www.palacehotelpt.com • Rates: $59–109

Thornton House B&B • (360) 385-6670
1132 Garfield St; Port Townsend, WA 98368
www.thorntonhousept.com • Rates: $135–150

Inn At Mccurdy House • (360) 379-4824
405 Taylor St; Port Townsend, WA 98368
www.innatmccurdyhouse.com • Rates: $130–250

Holly Hillhouse B&B • (360) 385-5619
611 Polk St; Port Townsend, WA 98368
www.hollyhillhouse.com • Rates: $99–190

Blue Gull Inn B&B • (360) 379-3241
1310 Clay St; Port Townsend, WA 98368
www.bluegullinn.com • Rates: $95–125

Huber's Inn • (360) 385-3904
1421 Landes St; Port Townsend, WA 98368
www.hubersinn.com • Rates: $145–210

North Cascades Area

Buffalo Run Inn • (360) 873-2103
60117 WA-20; Marblemount, WA 98267
www.buffaloruninn.com • Rates: $39–99

Totem Trail Motel • (360) 873-4535
57627 WA-20; Rockport, WA 98283
www.totemtrail.com • Rates: $50+

Ross Lake Resort • (206) 386-4437
Water taxi service, boat/kayak rentals and portage
530 Diablo St; Rockport, WA 96283
www.rosslakeresort.com • Rates: $145–210

Hi Lo Country Hotel & Café • (360) 853-7946
45951 Main St; Concrete, WA 98237
www.hotel.thehilocountry.com • Rates: $85+

Ovenell's Heritage Inn • (360) 853-8494
46276 Concrete Sauk Valley Rd; Concrete, WA 98237
www.ovenells-inn.com • Rates: $110–145

Wintercreek B&B • (360) 599-2526
9253 Cornell Creek Rd; Glacier, WA 98224
www.wintercreekbandb.com

Stehekin

Rainbow Falls Lodge
www.rainbowfallslodge.com • Rates: $185

Silver Bay Lodging • (509) 687-3142
www.silverbayinn.com • Rates: $145–295

Stehekin Landing Resort • (509) 682-4494
www.stehekinlanding.com • Rates: $82–185

Stehekin Log Cabin • (509) 682-7742
www.stehekinpastry.com • Rates: $150–200

Flick Creek House • (509) 670-0915
www.stehekinvalley.com

Stehekin Valley Ranch • (509) 682-4677
www.stehekinvalleyranch.com • Rates: $100–175

Many chain restaurants and hotels can be found in Seattle, Tacoma, Sequim, Port Angeles, and along I-5.

Festivals

Tulip Festival • April
Skagit Valley • www.tulipfestival.org

Apple Blossom Festival • April/May
Wenatchee • www.appleblossom.org

Northwest Folklife Festival • May
Seattle • www.nwfolklife.org

Sasquatch! Music Festival • May
George • www.sasquatchfestival.com

Independent Film Festival • June
Ashford • www.RainierFilmFest.com

Seafair • Summer
Seattle • www.seafair.com

Festival of Music • July
Bellingham • www.bellinghamfestival.org

Raspberry Festival • July
Lynden • www.lynden.org

International Kite Festival • August
Voted "Best Kite Festival in the World"
Long Beach • www.kitefestival.com

Bumbershoot • August
Seattle • www.bumbershoot.org

Rainier Mountain Festival • September
Ashford • www.RainierFestival.com

Puyallup Fair • September
Puyallup • www.thefair.com

Decibel Festival • September
Seattle • www.dbfestival.com

Rainier Arts Festival • October
Ashford • www.RainierArts.com

Crab & Seafood Festival • October
Port Angeles • www.crabfestival.org

Juan De Fuca Festival • May
Port Angeles • www.jffa.org

Attractions

Mount Rainier Area

NW Trek Wildlife Park • (360) 832-6117
11610 Trek Dr E; Eatonville, WA 98328
www.nwtrek.org • Admission: $17/Adult

Pioneer Farm Museum • (360) 832-6300
7716 Ohop Valley Rd E; Eatonville, WA 98328
www.pioneerfarmmuseum.org • Tours: $7.50/Adult

Valley 6 Drive In • (253) 854-1250
401 49th St NE; Auburn, WA 98002
www.valleydriveins.com • Tickets: $9/Adult

Mt St Helens Nat'l Volcanic Mon.
3029 Spirit Lake Hwy; Castle Rock, WA 98611
www.fs.usda.gov • (360) 274-0962 • Fee: $8

John Day Fossil Beds Nat'l Mon.
32651 OR-19; Kimberly, OR 97848
www.nps.gov/joda • (541) 987-2333 • Free

Olympic Peninsula

Olympic Raft & Kayak • (360) 452-1443
Kayaking, Rafting, and Rentals Available
123 Lake Aldwell Rd; Port Angeles, WA 98363
www.raftandkayak.com

Adventures Through Kayaking • (360) 417-3015
Kayaking, Mountain Biking, and Rafting
2358 US-101 W; Port Angeles, WA 98363
www.atkayaking.com

Dazzled By Twilight • (360) 452-8800
135 E 1st St; Port Angeles, WA 98362
www.dazzledbytwilight.com • Tours: $39

Feiro Marine Life Center • (360) 417-6254
315 N Lincoln St; Port Angeles, WA 98362
www.feiromarinelifecenter.org • Admission: $4/Adult

Fine Art Center • (360) 457-3532
1203 E Lauridsen Blvd; Port Angeles, WA 98362
www.pafac.org • Free

Harbinger Winery • (360) 452-4262
2358 US-101 West; Port Angeles, WA 98363
www.harbingerwinery.com

Salt Creek Rec. Area • (360) 928-3441
3506 Camp Hayden Rd; Port Angeles, WA 98363

Olympic Cellars Winery • (360) 452-0160
255410 US-101; Port Angeles, WA 98362
www.olympiccellars.com

Renaissance • (360) 565-1199
401 E Front St; Port Angeles, WA 98362
www.renaissance-pa.com • Massage: $75 (1 hr)

Olympic Game Farm • (360) 683-4295
1423 Ward Rd; Sequim, WA 98382
www.olygamefarm.com • Admission: $12/Adult

Purple Haze Organic Lavender Farm
180 Bell Bottom Rd; Sequim, WA 98382
www.purplehazelavender.com • (360) 582-1131

Dungeness NWR • Agnew-Carlsborg, WA

Twilight Tours In Forks • (360) 374-8687
51 N Forks Ave; Forks, WA 98331
www.twilighttoursinforks.com • Tours: $39

Dazzled by Twilight • (360) 374-5101
11 N Forks Ave; Forks, WA 98331
www.dazzledbytwilight.com • Tours: $39

Forks Timber Museum • (360) 374-9663
1421 S Forks Ave; Forks, WA 98331

Wheel-In-Motor Movie Drive In • (360) 385-0859
210 Theatre Rd; Port Townsend, WA 98368

Puget Sound Express • (360) 385-5288
Whale Watch (Orca • $95/Adult, Gray • $64)
227 Jackson St; Port Townsend, WA 98368
www.pugetsoundexpress.com

Port Townsend Brewing Co • (360) 385-9967
330 10th St; Port Townsend, WA 98368
www.porttownsendbrewing.com

Fort Worden State Park • (360) 344-4400
200 Battery Way; Port Townsend, WA 98368

Chetzemoka Park • (360) 379-3951
900 Jackson St; Port Townsend, WA 98368

Kelly Art Deco Light Museum • (360) 379-9030
2000 W Sims Way; Port Townsend, WA 98368

Jefferson County Historical • (360) 385-1003
540 Water St; Port Townsend, WA 98368
www.jchsmuseum.org • Admission: $4/Adult

North Cascades Area

Pearrygin Lake State Park • (509) 996-2370
561 Bear Creek Rd; Winthrop, WA 98862

North Cascade Heli-Skiing • (509) 996-3272
31 Early Winters Dr; Mazama, WA 98833
www.heli-ski.com • Tours: $323+

Shafer Museum • (509) 996-2712
285 Castle Rd; Winthrop, WA 98862
www.shafermuseum.com

Lost River Winery • (509) 429-8122
26 WA-20; Winthrop, WA 98862
www.lostriverwinery.com • Tasting: $5

Howard Miller Steelhead Park • (360) 853-8808
5110 Railroad Ave; Rockport, WA 98283

Rasar State Park • (360) 826-3942
38730 Cape Horn Rd; Concrete, WA 98237
www.parks.wa.gov

Rockport State Park • (360) 853-8461
51905 WA-20; Rockport, WA 98283

Lake Chelan State Park • (509) 687-3710
7544 S Lakeshore Rd; Chelan, WA 98816

Mt Baker-Snoqualmie Nat'l Forest • (425) 888-1421
42404 SE North Bend Way; North Bend, WA 98045

Northwest Rock Museum • (360) 853-9408
48005 Moen Rd; Concrete, WA 98237

Mt Baker • (360) 734-6771
1420 Iowa St; Bellingham, WA 98229
www.mtbaker.us • Lift Ticket: $46+

Chelan Seaplanes • (509) 682-5555
Kenmore Air Harbor • (425) 486-1257
PO Box 82064; Kenmore, WA 98028
www.chelanseaplanes.com • Tours: $99+

Rafting Outfitters

Alpine Adventures • (360) 863-6505
221 Croft Ave W; Gold Bar, WA 982351
www.alpineadventures.com • Rafting: $74+

Blue Sky Outfitters • (800) 228-7238
3400 Harbor Ave SW; Seattle, WA 98116
www.blueskyoutfitters.com • Rafting: $79+

N Cascades River Exp. • (360) 435-9548
31207 Bumgarner Rd; Arlington, WA 98223
www.riverexpeditions.com • Rafting: $70

Orion River Expeditions • (509) 997-4116
12681 Wilson St; Leavenworth, WA 98226
www.leavenworthriverrafting.com • Rafting: $79

Pacific NW Float Trips • (360) 757-3700
20200 Cook Rd; Burlington, WA 98233
www.pacificnwfloattrips.com • Rafting: $77

Wildwater River Tours • (253) 939-2151
32720 51st Ave S; Auburn, WA 98001
www.wildwater-river.com • Rafting: $79

Mountaineering/Hiking Guides

Alpine Ascents International
www.alpineascents.com • (206) 378-1927

Alpine Endeavors
www.alpineendeavors.com • (845) 658-3094

American Alpine Institute
www.aai.cc • (360) 671-1505

American Mountain Guides
www.amga.com • (303) 271-0984

Cascade Adventure Guides
www.cascadeadventureguides.com • (425) 322-4675

Deli Llama Wilderness Adventures
www.delillama.com • (360) 757-4212

International Mountain Guides
www.mountainguides.com • (360) 569-2609

KAF Adventures
www.kafadventures.com • (206-) 713-2149

North Cascades Mountain Guides
www.ncmountainguides.com • (509) 996-3194

Northwest Mountain School
www.mountainschool.com • (509) 548-5823

Passages Northwest • (206) 296-8601
139 23rd Ave S; Seattle, WA 98144

Peregrine Expeditions
peregrineexpeditions.com • (360) 393-8098

Pro Guiding Service
www.proguiding.com • (425) 831-5558

Rainier Mountaineering
www.rmiguides.com • (360) 569-2227

Beyond the Parks

Kerry Park • (206) 684-4075
211 W Highland Dr; Seattle, WA 98127

Discovery Park • (206) 386-4236
3801 W Government Way; Seattle, WA 98199

Alki Beach Park • (206) 684-4075
1702 Alki Ave SW; Seattle, WA 98116

Pike Place Market • (206) 682-7453
1531 Western Ave; Seattle, WA 98101

Space Needle • (206) 905-2100
400 Broad St; Seattle, WA 98109
www.spaceneedle.com • Admission: $18/Adult

Pacific Science Center • (206) 443-2001
200 Second Ave N; Seattle, WA 98109
www.pacificsciencecenter.org • Admission: $14/Adult

Seattle Aquarium • (206) 682-3474
1415 Western Ave, # 505; Seattle, WA 98101
www.seattleaquarium.org • Admission: $19/Adult

Klondike Gold Rush Park • (206) 220-4240
319 2nd Ave S; Seattle, WA 98104
www.nps.gov/klse • Free

The Museum of Flight • (206) 764-5700
9404 E Marginal Way S; Seattle, WA 98108
www.museumofflight.org • Admission: $16/Adult

Seattle Art Museum • (206) 654-3180
1300 1st Ave; Seattle, WA 98101
www.seattleartmuseum.org • Admission: $15/Adult

Olympic Sculpture Park • (206) 654-3100
2901 Western Ave; Seattle, WA 98121
www.seattleartmuseum.org • Free

Woodland Park Zoo • (206) 548-2500
601 N. 59th St; Seattle, WA 98103
www.zoo.org • Admission: $17.50/Adult

Washington Park Arboretum • (206) 543-8800
2300 Arboretum Dr E; Seattle, WA 98112

Seattle Wine Tours • (206) 444-9463
321 3rd Ave S, Suite 204; Seattle, WA 98104
www.seattlewinetours.com

Moss Bay Center • (206) 682-2031
1001 Fairview Ave N; Seattle, WA 98109
www.mossbay.net • Kayak Tours: $45/Adult

Unexpected Productions Improv • (206) 587-2414
1428 Post Alley; Seattle, WA 98101
www.unexpectedproductions.org

Seattle Seaplanes • (206) 329-9638
1325 Fairview Ave E; Seattle, WA 98102
www.seattleseaplanes.com • Tours: $88+

San Juan Safaris • (800) 450-6858
2 Spring St Landing; Friday Harbor, WA 98250
www.sanjuansafaris.com • Tours: $75

San Juan Excursions • (360) 378-6636
2 Spring St; Friday Harbor, WA 98250
www.watchwhales.com • Tours: $79

Island Adventures • (800) 465-4604
1801 Commercial Ave; Anacortes, WA 98221
www.island-adventures.com • Tours: $69+

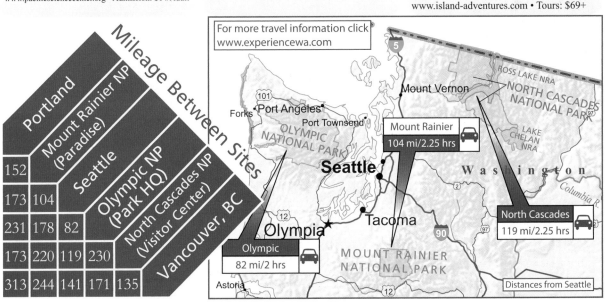

Mileage Between Sites

Portland	Mount Rainier NP (Paradise)	Seattle	Olympic NP (Park HQ)	North Cascades NP (Visitor Center)	Vancouver, BC
152					
173	104				
231	178	82			
173	220	119	230		
313	244	141	171	135	

For more travel information click
www.experiencewa.com

Mount Rainier
104 mi/2.25 hrs

North Cascades
119 mi/2.25 hrs

Olympic
82 mi/2 hrs

Distances from Seattle

Glacier Bay • Pages 586–593

Wrangell–St. Elias • Pages 594–599

Denali • Pages 600–609

Kenai Fjords • Pages 610–615

ALASKA

Lake Clark • Pages 616–619

Katmai • Pages 620–625

Gates of the Arctic • Pages 626–629

Kobuk Valley • Pages 630–641

ALASKA

Hiker, iceberg, and Glacier Bay

PO Box 140
Gustavus, AK 99826-0140
Phone: (907) 697-2230
Website: www.nps.gov/glba

Established: December 2, 1980
February 25, 1925 (Nat'l Monument)
Size: 3,283,000 Acres
Annual Visitors: 445,000
Peak Season: Summer (Peaks from mid-July to mid-August)

Activities: Boat Tours (fee), Hiking, Backpacking, Camping, Kayaking, Boating, Air Tours, Fishing, and Wildlife Viewing

Campground: Bartlett Cove*
Fee: None
Backcountry Camping: Permitted*
Lodging: Glacier Bay Lodge
Rates: $199–224/night

Park Hours: All day, every day
Entrance Fee: None

*Campers must obtain a free permit and attend an orientation program

Glacier Bay - Alaska

Glacier Bay National Park, located in southeastern Alaska just 60 miles west of the state capitol of Juneau (by boat or plane, there are no roads), is an incredible world of ice, mountains, and sea. More than one quarter of the park is ice, permanent but retreating at a frightening rate. When **Joseph Whidbey** sailed to the mouth of Glacier Bay in 1794 it was choked with ice more than 4,000 feet thick and up to 20 miles wide. The immense glacier stretched back to its source, more than 100 miles away in the St. Elias Mountain Range. By 1879, **John Muir** found that ice had already retreated 48 miles into the bay. In 1916, **Grand Pacific Glacier** had withdrawn all the way to the head of Tarr Inlet, roughly 65 miles from the mouth of Glacier Bay. This phenomenon has been one of the fastest glacial retreats on record, exposing new land and providing opportunities for scientists to study glaciation, plant succession, and animal dynamics. And hundreds of thousands of guests come to witness giant icebergs as they break away from tidewater glaciers in explosive fashion—also known as calving—from the deck of a cruise ship or tour boat.

Glacier Bay protects 50 named glaciers (including nine tidewater glaciers that terminate in the sea). Climatic changes caused most of glaciers in the eastern and southwestern region, like McBride, Muir, Reid, and Riggs Glaciers to retreat. Muir Glacier, with a 2-mile calving face, was once the most impressive, but it completely receded in the 1990s. On the bay's western shoreline, Johns Hopkins, Lamplugh, and Margerie Glaciers are stable or advancing and thickening. Today, most visitors stop and wait aboard a tour boat or cruise ship at the latter two, hoping ice will break from the glacier's face.

"To the lovers of pure wilderness Alaska is one of the most wonderful countries in the world...it seems as if surely we must at length reach the very paradise of the poets, the abode of the blessed."

– John Muir

John Muir, beloved naturalist and writer, became deeply interested in glaciers after years of hiking Yosemite Valley (which he proposed was carved by glaciers, not shaped by earthquakes). In 1879, Muir was first in a long line of scientists to visit Glacier Bay. He studied the recession of glaciers while enriching his spirit in the wilderness he loved so dearly. Muir visited again in 1899 as a member of the **Harriman Alaska Expedition**, organized by railroad tycoon Edward Harriman. His group of scientists, photographers, artists, and writers formed a who's who list of their respective fields. In September of that year a massive earthquake shook Glacier Bay. Severed icebergs made the bay completely inaccessible to vessels for more than a decade, causing steamships to remove this destination from their itineraries. Visitation, exploration, and scientific research halted temporarily, but the area's beauty never diminished.

In 1925, **President Calvin Coolidge** established Glacier Bay National Monument. The area was preserved for its "tidewater glaciers in a magnificent setting, developing forests, scientific opportunities, historic interest, and accessibility." Commercial interests kept their eyes on the bay as well. In 1936, **President Franklin D. Roosevelt** reopened the area to mining. Ore was extracted from the mountains of Glacier Bay sporadically, and today there's still a claim on a significant nickel-copper bed that lies directly beneath Brady Glacier. In 1939, land was added to the national monument, doubling its size and making it the largest unit of the National Park System at the time. During WWII, the nearby city of Gustavus served as a strategic military location where a supply terminal was built. On a 600 acre tract of land, 800 buildings, 3 large docks, and an airstrip were constructed by 1943. After just a few months of use they were given to civilian control. Today, a short road linking Bartlett Cove and the airfield at Gustavus greatly increases park accessibility, allowing amateur scientists and lovers of nature to explore Glacier Bay on their own.

Tour boat and glacier

When to Go

Glacier Bay National Park is open all year, but you'd hardly know it come winter time. The visitor center, located on the second floor of **Glacier Bay Lodge**, is open daily from late May to early September. Exhibits are open 24-hours and the information desk and bookstore are staffed from 11am to 9pm. **The Visitor Information Center for Boaters and Campers**, located at the head of the public-use dock in Bartlett Cove, is open daily, May to September. Hours are typically from 8am to 5pm. Extended hours from 7am to 9pm are available between June and August. **Glacier Bay National Preserve Office and Visitor Center** (907.784.3295) is located in Yakutat. This is your go-to-location for information about rafting and Glacier Bay Preserve. It's open from May to September. Services in winter are extremely limited. Most visitors arrive via cruise ships from late May through mid-September. **Humpback whales** are seen during this entire period, but sightings increase in mid-June and peak around July and August. Regardless when you travel be sure to dress in layers and pack rain gear.

Transportation

Glacier Bay National Park can only be reached by plane or boat. Within the park there is a 10-mile road that connects Gustavus and its airfield to the park headquarters at Bartlett Cove. It is possible to bring your vehicle via the Alaska Marine Highway Ferry System (page 589), but that's not recommended. Taxis run between Gustavus and Bartlett Cove upon request, and buses run a limited schedule. Cruise ships (page 590), tour vessels (page 590), and private boats all enter the bay. Private boaters entering Glacier Bay anytime between June and August must obtain a free permit (page 592) prior to their arrival.

Air Transportation

Air travel is the easiest method of arrival. **Alaska Airlines** (800.252.7522, www.alaskaair.com) provides daily service from Juneau to Gustavus (~30 minutes, ~$100) during the busy summer season. Other small air taxis and charters provide year-round service to Gustavus. They include **Air Excursions** (907.697.2375, www.airexcursions.com), **Fjord Flying Service** (877.460.2377), and **Wings of Alaska** (907.789.0790, www.wingsofalaska.com).

Flightseeing

Leave the cruise ships behind and enjoy the spectacular scenery and wildlife of Glacier Bay with a unique aerial view. Float or wheel planes are available. **Air Excursions** (907.697.2375 departing Gustavus, 907.789.5591 departing Juneau, 800.354.2479, www.airexcursions.com) and **TEMSCO Helicopters** (877.789.9501 departing Juneau, 866.683.2900 departing Skagway, www.temscoair.com) offer airplane and helicopter tours of Glacier Bay National Park.

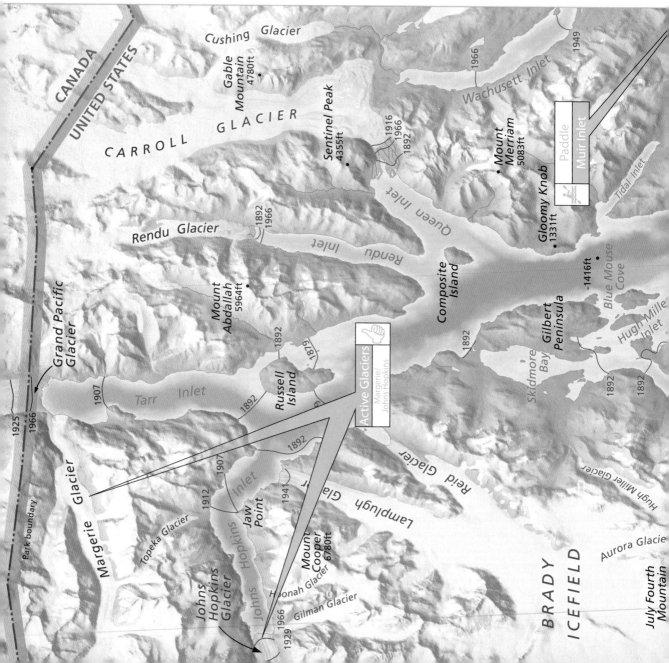

Alaska Marine Highway System

Beginning in November 2010, Gustavus is accessible via the **Alaska Marine Highway System** (800.642.0066, www.dot.state.ak.us/amhs). During summer, ferries make daily trips from Juneau to Gustavus, 10 miles north of Bartlett Cove. This is an excellent method of arrival, especially for individuals transporting kayak(s) or bike(s). The following are base fares from Juneau: $33/Passenger (P), $12/Bike (B), $19/Kayak (K), and $40/Vehicle (V). Roadways do not run directly to Juneau, either. To reach Juneau by car you'll have to board another Alaska Marine Highway System ferry from Bellingham, Washington ($326/P, $53/B, $80/K, $431/V); Prince Rupert, British Columbia ($141/P, $28/B, $41/K, $179/V); Haines, Alaska ($37/P, $15/B, $24/K, $49/V); or Skagway, Alaska ($50/P, $18/B, $27/K, $63/V). Children under 6 travel free. Fare for children 6 through 11 is about half the adult fare. Vehicle rates do not include the driver and are for vehicles up to 10 feet in length.

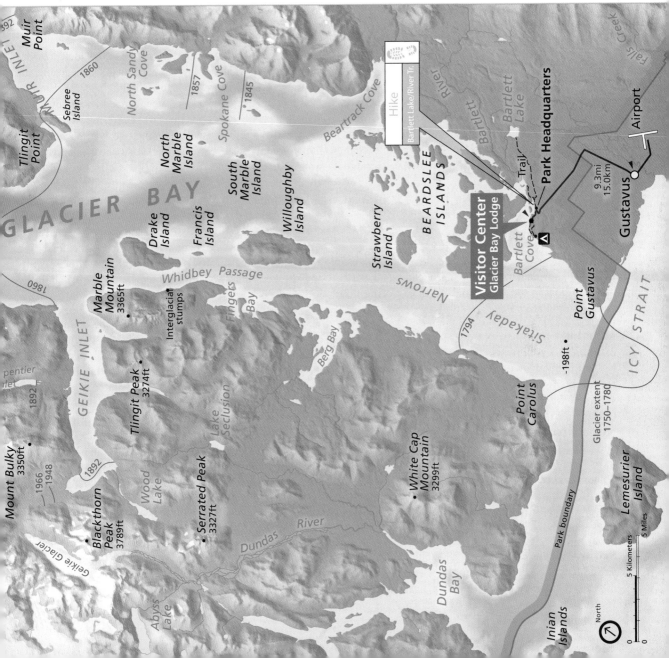

Camping & Lodging

Glacier Bay National Park has one primitive campground at **Bartlett Cove**. It's a free walk-in, tent-only camp, located 0.25-mile south of Bartlett Cove dock. It is open all year and features a bear-proof food cache, fire pit with firewood, and warming shelter near the shore. Group camping is available for groups of 12 or more. To use the campground you must first obtain a **free permit** and participate in a **30 minute orientation program**. Showers are available at Glacier Bay Lodge during summer.

Glacier Bay Lodge (888.229.8687, www.visit-glacierbay.com) is the only hotel in the park. All rooms can accommodate up to four guests and have a private bath and/or shower. Fairweather Dining Room serves breakfast, lunch, and dinner. Rooms cost $199/night (forest view) and $224/night (ocean view). The lodge is open from mid-May through early September.

Kayaking

Looking to get up close and personal to whales, wildlife, and glaciers? If so, put a paddle in your hands, a boat in the water, and begin exploring the wonders of Glacier Bay.

Muir Inlet is a great place to paddle because it's off-limits to motorized boats in summer. Paddlers can bring their own boats via the Alaska Marine Highway System (page 589), but rental and guide services are available. **Glacier Bay Sea Kayaks** (907.697.2257, www.glacierbayseakayaks.com) provides rentals ($45/day–single, $50/day–double) and half-day ($95/person) and full-day ($150) guided tours. The *Fairweather II* provides drop-offs at designated backcountry sites in summer. **A free wilderness permit and camping orientation (at Bartlett Cove) are required for all overnight stays in the backcountry.**

Spirit Walker Expeditions (800.529.2537, www. seakayakalaska.com), **Mountain Travel Sobek** (888.831.7526, www.mtsobek.com), and **Alaska on the Home Shore** (800.287.7063, www.homeshore.com) offer multi-day expeditions.

Boat Tours & Cruises

Commercial boat tours and cruises are the easiest and in many respects the best way to explore the inlets and coves of Glacier Bay. Visitors spending the night in Bartlett Cove or Gustavus can embark on a full-day tour of the bay. Others come and go aboard massive luxury liners or specialized expedition cruise ships. Bring rain gear, binoculars, and warm layers of clothing no matter what time of year you plan on touring the bay.

Glacier Bay Lodge (888.229.8687, www.visitglacierbay.com) operates the ***Fairweather Express II (FXII)***, which provides daily tours of Glacier Bay from Bartlett Cove during the summer. The 130-mile voyage is highlighted by stunning views of tidewater glaciers, snow-capped mountains, and abundant wildlife. A park ranger narrates the trip, discussing the area's history while pointing out whales, Steller sea lions, coastal bears, seals, and eagles. At one glacier, you will wait up to 30 minutes for a giant mass of snow and ice to break free, plummeting to the icy water and crashing with a thunderous boom. You board the boat at 7am, departure is at 7:30am, and you'll return around 3:30pm. The full-day cruise costs $185/adult and $92.50/child (ages 3–12). Lunch, a non-alcoholic beverage, and a souvenir are included. The *Fairweather II* also provides drop-off service for campers and kayakers. One-way drop-off service costs $105/adult and $52.50/child (ages 3–12).

The most popular way to visit Glacier Bay is aboard one of the **luxury cruise liners** that ply these waters from late May to mid-September. **Carnival Cruise Line** (877.885.4856, www.carnival.com), **Holland America Line** (877.724.5425, www.hollandamerica.com), **Norwegian Cruise Lines** (866.234.7350, www.ncl.com), and **Princess Cruises** (800.774.6237, www.princesstours. com) offer 4–22 night trips that pit-stop at Glacier Bay. Cruises depart from various locations along the Pacific Coast including Vancouver, Seattle, and San Francisco. The base rate is around $100 per night per person.

Natural born explorers should consider **American Safari Cruises** (888.862.8881, www.amsafari.com) or **Linblad Special Expeditions** (800.397.3348, www.expeditions.com). These companies provide a different, more intimate, yachting experience. Groups are smaller, guides are knowledgeable experts and easily accessible, and all side trips are planned and included in the tour price. These tours cost about $700 per night per person.

Hiking

There are only four maintained trails totaling 10 miles. **Forest Loop Trail** (1 mile) begins at Glacier Bay Lodge and passes through a temperate rain forest. During the summer, park rangers lead guided walks along this trail every afternoon at 2pm. The 4-mile (roundtrip) **Bartlett River Trail** heads north from the road to Gustavus along an intertidal lagoon through spruce-hemlock forest before ending at Bartlett River estuary, an excellent place to spot wildlife such as ducks, geese, moose, bear, and river otter. In late summer you might come across hungry harbor seals feeding on salmon as they run up the river. The 8-mile (roundtrip) **Bartlett Lake Trail** diverges from Bartlett River Trail at a signpost located about 0.25-mile into the hike and then climbs to Bartlett Lake following a relatively unmaintained trail (pay attention). **Beach Trail** (1 mile) strolls along the stretch of shoreline south of the docks. Ask a park ranger for a free tide table before hiking.

Backpacking

With no maintained trails in the park's wilderness backpackers are left to their own devices when negotiating the unforgiving terrain of Glacier Bay's mountains and shorelines. Alpine meadows, rocky coasts, and deglaciated areas provide a wealth of hiking opportunity where you may not encounter another human for days at a time. One thing you're sure to stumble upon is **alder**. This successional plant grows in abundance along beaches, stream edges, avalanche chutes, and mountain slopes. Hiking is much more tedious than paddling largely due to alder's presence, which is notorious for slowing down and aggravating hikers. Wherever you plan on going, it is imperative that backpackers are well-prepared and have planned their trip thoroughly prior to heading into the backcountry. Areas of the park are often closed to campers due to animal activity. Always ask a park ranger for closure updates before you depart. **A free permit and orientation program (Bartlett Cove) are required for overnight camping in the backcountry.** This is also an opportunity to check out a bear-resistant food container (BRFC). Food and scented items must be stored in your BRFC. In forested areas, you may hang food, but use of a BRFC is recommended. If you'd like to let someone else take care of logistics, **Alaska Mountain Guides** (800.766.3396, www.alaskamountainguides.com) offers guided hiking, climbing, and paddling tours.

A whale's fluke

Violence of a calving glacier

Mount Fairweather and Margerie Glacier

Tourist aboard cruise ship
© Mike & Jessica Hall

Margerie Glacier & cruise ship from above

GLACIER BAY

Guests examine a glacier on foot

Blackwater Pond

Activities

Private Boating: Private boaters wanting to enter Glacier Bay from the beginning of June until the end of August must obtain a **free permit**, available up to 60 days in advance. Mail, fax, or phone in requests for an application. To confirm or to see if permits are available, call the Visitor Information Station "KWM20 Bartlett Cove" on marine band 16 or phone (907) 697-2627. Permits must be confirmed at least 48 hours before your scheduled entry date or your permit will be cancelled.

Whitewater Rafting: Whitewater rafting is possible on the **Alsek River** and its major tributary, the **Tatshenshini River**. Both are large volume, swift glacial rivers that breach the coastal range passing through Tatshenshini–Alsek Provincial Park in Canada and Glacier Bay National Preserve in Alaska. A typical trip begins on the Tatshenshini at Shawshe (Dalton Post). This is the last road-accessible put-in off of Haines Highway in Canada. From here it's 140

miles of continuous Class III–IV (at high water) rapids to Dry Bay, Alaska. The trip usually takes six days. **A permit is required for all private trips.** To get on the waiting list, send your name, address, home and work telephone numbers, e-mail address, and payment of $25 to cover administrative charges to: National Park Service, Yakutat Ranger Station, River Permits, PO Box 137; Yakutat, AK 99869.

Several **outfitters** provide 10+ day expeditions along the Alsek–Tatshenshini. Chilkat Guides (907.766.2491, www.RaftAlaska.com), Colorado River & Trail Expeditions (801.261.1789, www.crateinc.com), James Henry River Journeys (800.786.1830, www.riverjourneys.com), The River League (778.686.3455, www.explorersleague.ca), Mountain Travel–Sobek (888.831.7526, www.mtsobek.com), Canadian River/Nahanni River Adventures (867.668.3180, www.nahanni.com); Rivers, Oceans, and Mountains (R.O.A.M) (888.639.1114, www.iroamtheworld.com); Tatshenshini Expediting (867.633.2742, www.tatshenshini-yukon.com), and Wilderness River Outfitter (800.252.6581, www.wildernessriver.com) offer trips for all experience levels that begin around $3,500 per person.

Fishing: Anglers come to Glacier Bay in search of halibut and salmon. Fishermen 16 years and older require a valid Alaska State Fishing License, which can be purchased at Glacier Bay Lodge during the summer. Please refer to page 637 for a list of fishing charters and guides who can help plan your trip or take you on a fishing adventure.

The Fairweather is the park's publication, which provides up-to-date information regarding facilities, activities, and regulations. You can pick up a copy at the visitor center or download one at any time from the park website.

Basics

For Kids: An abundance of ice, water, mountains, and wildlife make Glacier Bay an intriguing place for children, but it's often difficult finding ways to engage them in their environment. The **Junior Ranger Program** is designed to do exactly that. Your child can become the next Junior Ranger one of two ways (depending on your mode of transportation). If you come by plane or private boat, you must stop by the visitor center on the second floor of Glacier Bay Lodge. Here you can obtain an activity booklet. Once completed, return the booklet to a park ranger to be inducted into this special club and earn a Junior Ranger badge. Most cruise ships have a children's center where they offer a Junior Ranger Program that can be completed over the course of the cruise. Park rangers aboard tour vessels can also point you in the right direction to become a Junior Ranger.

Ranger Programs: From Memorial Day weekend to Labor Day weekend park rangers invite guests of Bartlett Cove to join them on a morning hike (9am), a guided walk of Forest Loop (2pm), and an evening program (8pm). Movies are also shown daily at the visitor center.

Flora & Fauna: Life in and around Glacier Bay is constantly changing. As glaciers continue to recede a succession of plant life appears in its path. Lichens, moss, fireweed, cottonwood, and willows all grow where glaciers used to exist. Western hemlock and Sitka spruce make up the temperate rain forests. Moose immigrated to the park, and were first spotted in 1966. Other large mammals include orca, humpback whales, black and brown bears, wolves, mountain goats, harbor seals, Steller sea lions, and porpoises.

Pets: Pets are only allowed at Bartlett Cove Public Use Dock, on the beach between the dock and the National Park Service Dock, within 100 feet of Bartlett Cove Developed Area's park roads and parking areas, and on a vessel in open water. Pets must be on a leash or physically restrained at all times. They are prohibited from all trails, beaches (except already mentioned), and backcountry.

Accessibility: Glacier Bay Lodge has wheelchair accessible rooms upon request. Forest Trail is accessible. Contact specific tour operators for accessibility.

Weather: Pack your rain gear! Bartlett Cove receives about 70 inches of precipitation each year. On average, 228 days of the year experience some form of precipitation. April, May, and June are usually the driest months. Most visitors arrive between late May and mid-September. September and October tend to be the wettest months. Temperature is greatly influenced by the Pacific Ocean. Summers are typically cool and moist, while winters are mild and cool. During the summer you can expect highs between 50 and 60°F near sea level. As elevation increases it becomes cooler and windier.

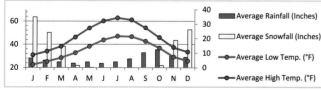

Average Rainfall (Inches)
Average Snowfall (Inches)
Average Low Temp. (°F)
Average High Temp. (°F)

Johns Hopkins Inlet

Bartlett Cove Campground

Margerie Glacier

Mount Fairweather and Margerie Glacier (up close)

A backpacker traverses uneven terrain near Kennecott

PO Box 439
Copper Center, AK 99573
Phone: (907) 822-5234
Website: www.nps.gov/wrst

Established: December 2, 1980
November 16, 1978 (Nat'l Monument)
Size: 13.2 Million Acres
Annual Visitors: 73,000
Peak Season: Summer

Activities: Hiking, Backpacking,
Rafting, Kayaking, Air Tours, ATV
Riding, Mountain Biking, Fishing,
Hunting, and Mountaineering

Campgrounds: None*
See page 640 for alternative camping and lodging facilities
Backcountry Camping: Permitted
(backcountry permit not required)

Park Hours: All day, every day
Entrance Fee: None

*Camping is allowed at pullouts (no
water; first-come, first-served) along
McCarthy and Nabesna Roads.

WRANGELL–ST. ELIAS

Wrangell–St. Elias - Alaska

"The region is superlative in its scenic beauty and measures up fully and beyond the requirements for its establishment as a National Monument and later as a National Park. It is my personal view that from the stand-point of scenic beauty, it is the finest region in Alaska. I have traveled through Switzerland extensively, have flown over the Andes, and am familiar with the Valley of Mexico and with other parts of Alaska. It is my unqualified view that this is the finest scenery that I have ever been privileged to see."

– Ernest Gruening (Director of U.S. Territories/Governor of Alaska/U.S. Senator)

Wrangell–St. Elias National Park lies in the southeastern corner of Alaska, a few hundred miles south of the Arctic Circle. It's far from the northernmost point in Alaska, but these jagged mountains—including 9 of the 16 highest peaks on United States' soil—harbor more than 60% of Alaska's glacial ice. Scientists estimate that **150 glaciers** fill the valleys and ravines between mountain ridgelines. **One of them, Malaspina, is larger than Rhode Island.** Not only are the glaciers big, the park itself is monstrous, easily the largest in the United States. It's nearly four times the size of Death Valley, the largest national park in the contiguous United States.

Such a vast expanse of eye-catching mountains should not go un-noticed or unexplored for thousands of years, but this is the case of Wrangell–St. Elias. **Mount St. Elias**, at 18,008 feet the second highest mountain in the United States, was unnamed until the feast day of St.

Elias in 1741 when Vitus Bering spotted it while exploring the Alaskan coast. **Mount Wrangell** was named for Baron Ferdinand Petrovich von Wrangell, a Russian naval officer, arctic explorer, government administrator, and main opponent to selling Alaska to the United States. Despite his protest in 1867 Alaska was sold for $0.03 per acre, and the rest, as they say, is history. Eyak and Tlingit people lived in villages along the coast for thousands of years and in middle Copper Basin for at least the last 1,000 years, but Americans didn't penetrate the western Wrangell Mountains until 1885. Scientific expeditions occurred, but not until the gold rush in 1899 did the region receive any significant attention. More than one billion pounds of ore were hauled out of Kennecott mines during 27 years of operation. The mining boom went bust and tourism gradually took hold. Thanks to rapid increase in visitation at Denali National Park and being one of only three road-accessible Alaskan National Parks, Wrangell–St. Elias has continued to show a steady increase in tourism.

Mount St. Elias from above

When to Go

Most visitors arrive at Wrangell–St. Elias National Park between early June and mid-September, but the park never closes. Services are extremely limited beyond these dates and only the hardiest of visitors who possess extremely proficient winter survival skills visit during the off-season. Early September offers fewer mosquitoes and pleasant temperatures.

Transportation & Airports

Glennallen, AK can be reached by Alaska Direct Bus Line (800.770.6652, www.alaskadirectbusline.com). From Glennallen visitors can take Kennicott Shuttle (907.822.5292, www.kennicottshuttle.com, $79/person one-way) or Wrangell–St. Elias Tours (888.478.5258, www.alaskayukontravel.com, $75/person one-way) to Kennicott (inside the park). Both shuttle services operate seasonally. There are numerous air taxi services that make stops or drop-offs at a variety of airstrips throughout the park. See page 635 for a complete list of air taxi service providers.

Directions

Wrangell–St. Elias National Park is one of three national parks in Alaska accessible via private vehicle. Two rough gravel roads penetrate the park's interior. McCarthy Road begins at Chitina where it enters the park and continues 60-miles into its heart at Kennecott. Nabesna Road enters the northern border at Slana and continues for 42-miles to Nabesna, an old mining town. Directions provided below begin at Glennallen, AK, which is about 170 miles east of Anchorage along AK-1.

McCarthy Road: From Glennallen head south for 31 miles on AK-4 toward Valdez. Continuing south you'll pass through Copper Center, where the main park visitor center, theater, and exhibit building are located, before turning left at Edgerton Highway/AK-10. Continue east for nearly 34 miles to Chitina, where McCarthy Road enters the park.

Nabesna Road: From Glennallen, head north on AK-1/AK-4. Continue for almost 73 miles. Turn right at Nabesna Road, which passes through Slana and into the park.

Air-taxi, the best way to get around the park

Kennecott Power Plant and Root Glacier

Visitor Facilities

Visitor Center & Park Headquarters • (907) 822-7250
Mile 106.8 Richardson Highway, Copper Center
Features: Exhibits, Film, Trail, Ranger Programs, Bookstore
Open: late May to late September, Daily, 9am–6pm; rest of the year, Mon–Fri, 8am–4pm (as staffing permits)

Kennecott Visitor Center • (907) 822-7476
Historic Kennecott Mill Town
Features: Exhibits, Ranger Programs, Backcountry Planning
Open: Memorial Day to Labor Day, Daily, 9am–5:30pm

Slana Ranger Station • (907) 822-7401
Mile 0.2 Nabesna Road
Features: Exhibits, Ranger Programs, Bookstore
Open: Summer Only, Daily, 8am–5pm

Chitina Ranger Station • (907) 823-2205
Features: Exhibits, Kennecott/McCarthy Trip Planning
Open: Memorial Day to late August, Thur–Mon, 9am–5pm

McCarthy Road Information Station
Mile 59 McCarthy Road
Features: Day-Parking, Kennecott/McCarthy Trip Planning
Open: Self-service during summer (Staffed occasionally)

Yakutat Ranger Station • (907) 784-3295
Features: Exhibits, Film, Trip Planning, Permits
Open: All Year, Hours vary

Driving

McCarthy Road follows the path of an old railway constructed in 1909 to support the booming mining industry at Kennecott Mill. It's a dusty, winding, washboard gravel road, but during summer most passenger vehicles are capable of making the trip. The primitive journey from Chitina to Kennecott is 60 miles and takes about 2 hours (one-way). In between, you'll find plenty of grade-A scenery that is sure to leave you breathless.

In 1934, **Nabesna Road** was built to simplify ore transportation to the coast. More than 75 years later very little has changed. It's a rough, twisting, 42-mile gravel road with unparalleled scenic value. The road is typically accessible to all passenger vehicles, but at times creek crossings beyond Mile 29 can be problematic.

Both roads provide exceptional wildlife viewing opportunities. Do not travel without a full-size spare and an adequate jack. No fuel or services are available along these roads and cell phone service is extremely limited.

Camping & Lodging

There are no developed campgrounds at Wrangell–St. Elias National Park, but visitors are allowed to camp at pullouts along McCarthy and Nabesna Roads. These pullouts are perfect for small to medium RVs, camper trailers, pick-up campers, or tents. All sites are primitive and available on a first-come, first-served basis. Along Nabesna Road you'll find pullouts at Mileposts 6.1, 16.6, 21.8, 27.8, and 35.3.

If you're looking for the true wilderness experience, consider spending a night at one of fourteen **backcountry cabins**. Most cabins are available on a first-come, first-served basis, but **Viking Lodge Cabin** on Nabesna Road and **Esker Stream Cabin** near Yakutat accept reservations. Most cabins are extremely remote, requiring significant trip planning or access by air-taxi. All of them have a woodstove and bunks. Sleeping and dining gear are not provided. Leave the cabin fully stocked with firewood and at least as clean as it was when you arrived.

Lodging is available at **Devil's Mtn Lodge** (907.822.5312, summer • 907.339.9329, winter • www.devilsmountainlodge.com, $150/person or $200/couple), located at the end of Nabesna Road. Refer to page 636 for additional lodging like **Ultima Thule's** (www.ultimathulelodge.com) fly-in luxury lodge.

Glaciers wind their way between mountains

Mount St. Elias

Glacial meltwater forms a lake on top of Root Glacier

Three maintained trails begin from Nabesna Road: **Caribou Creek** (8.0 miles, near mile 19), **Skookum Volcano** (5.0 miles, near mile 37), and **Rambler Mine** (2.0 miles, near mile 42). They provide spectacular views of rugged terrain. Near Kennecott/McCarthy Road you can hike these trails: **Crystalline Hills** (2.5 miles, mile 36), **Root Glacier** (4.0 miles, Kennecott Visitor Center), **Donoho Basin** (14 miles roundtrip to Donoho Summit, multi-day, follows Root Glacier Trail), or **Jumbo Mine** (10 miles, Root Glacier Trailhead). Most **backpackers** prefer to hike above the tree line where vegetation and mosquitoes are more manageable. Many day-hikes and multi-day trips require river crossings. Use proper judgment when selecting an area to cross. Hypothermia is a threat, even in summer. Adequate planning is required for a successful trip. Be sure that you have proper gear, a good topographic map, and are comfortable camping in bear country. Permits are not required for trips into the backcountry, but completing a backcountry itinerary (available at any park office) is encouraged. You should also leave your itinerary with a friend or family member. If you do not return on schedule, rangers will not administer a search party until a formal request is made by a friend or family member. Many hikers choose to hire a local guide to help ensure a safe and enjoyable trip. Guides also lead visitors on mountain climbing expeditions. With 9 of the 16 highest peaks on U.S. soil within park boundaries, Wrangell–St. Elias is a popular destination among mountain climbers. **See page 638 for a list of outfitters authorized to guide trips in the park.**

Flightseeing: To truly grasp the size of Wrangell–St. Elias National Park you should fly above it, peering across massive sheets of ice and jagged mountain ranges. A slew of local **air taxi businesses** (page 635) provide flightseeing tours or backcountry drop-offs and pick-ups to otherwise unreachable regions.

Rafting/Floating: Float trips, wild whitewater, and everything in between are found at Wrangell–St. Elias. You can plan your own rafting adventure or join an **authorized outfitter** (page 636). **Guide companies** (page 638) also lead guests on sea kayaking trips around Icy Bay. It is relatively "new" water; the bay was formed when four massive tidewater glaciers retreated beginning in 1900. Paddlers are usually dropped off at Kageet Point or Point Riou by air-taxi. Sea kayaking is a great way to spot marine and terrestrial wildlife.

Fishing: Lake trout, Dolly Varden, grayling, cutthroat and rainbow trout, sculpin, and whitefish are found in small lakes and streams. Sockeye, coho, and king salmon can be

Hiking/Backpacking: There are very few maintained hiking trails, but there are five short hikes near Copper Center. **Boreal Forest Trail** (0.5-mile loop) begins at the Main Visitor Center. A self-guiding brochure helps introduce visitors to the area. In Glennallen you'll find **Aspen Interpretive Trail** (1.0 mile roundtrip). The trailhead is located on Co-op Road just off AK-1. **Tonsina River Trail** (2.0 miles) begins just beyond mile marker 12 of AK-10/Edgerton Highway. It leads to a perch overlooking the Tonsina River. **Liberty Falls Trail** (2.5 miles) begins just before mile marker 25 of AK-10. **O'Brien to Haley Creek Trail** (10.0 miles) begins on O'Brien Creek Road near Chitina.

caught in the Copper River and its tributaries. An Alaska fishing license is required for all anglers 16 or older.

ATVs/Mountain Biking: ATVs are allowed in some areas. All recreational users require a permit (available at Slana Ranger Station or Park Headquarters). McCarthy and Nabesna Roads provide excellent locations for mountain bikers.

The K'elt'aeni is the park's publication, which provides up-to-date information regarding facilities, activities, and regulations. Pick up a copy for yourself at the visitor center or download one at any time from the park website.

Basics

For Kids: Children are invited to learn about the park and its valuable resources by participating in the **Junior Ranger Program**. Simply visit the park's website, print an activity booklet and complete it (either in the park or at home). Once it's finished, mail it to the park and a ranger will review your answers. For the effort, you'll be rewarded with a Wrangell–St. Elias Junior Ranger badge.

Ranger Programs: In summer, Park Rangers provide talks, walks, and evening programs at the Main Visitor Center and Kennecott Mill Town. Check out the park website or stop at a visitor center for a current schedule of activities.

Flora & Fauna: Wrangell–St. Elias National Park features a variety of plants and animals. More than half of all Alaskan flora can be found in the Wrangells. Quaking aspen are the most prevalent tree, but paper birch and black and white spruce are also common. In all, **more than 800 species of vascular plants** color the landscape and provide nutrition for the park's residents. Animals include moose, bear (black and grizzly), lynx, caribou, mountain goats, wolves, bison, and the largest concentration of Dall sheep in North America.

Pets: Pets are allowed in the park, but remember that dogs (and even dog food) may attract bear or moose.

Accessibility: The Main Visitor Center is accessible to wheelchair users, as are the historic mill, recreation hall, visitor center, and Blackburn School at Kennecott. An accessible backcountry cabin is available at Peavine.

Weather: Winters are long and cold (highs of 5–7°F). Summers are short, warm, and dry. June and July are the warmest months. Highs might sneak into the 80s°F on some days. Leaves typically begin to change by mid-August and the first significant snowfall arrives about a month later.

One of 150 glaciers in the park and its glacial icebergs

Glaciers pour out of rocky valleys

Mount St. Elias

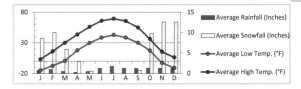

Average Rainfall (Inches)
Average Snowfall (Inches)
Average Low Temp. (°F)
Average High Temp. (°F)

Mount McKinley and Denali Park Road © Nic McPhee (flickr.com/nicmcphee)

DENALI

PO Box 9
Denali Park, Alaska 99755
Phone: (907) 683-2294
Website: www.nps.gov/dena

Established: February 26, 1917
Size: 6.1 Million Acres
Annual Visitors: 380,000
Peak Season: Summer

Activities: Bus/Shuttle Tours,
Hiking, Backpacking, Biking,
Mountaineering, Flightseeing,
Fishing, and Whitewater Rafting

Campgrounds ($9–28/night): Riley
Creek*, Savage River*, Sanctu-
ary River, Teklanika River*, Igloo
Creek, and Wonder Lake*
Backcountry Camping: Permitted
Lodging: See page 604

Park Hours: All day, every day
Entrance Fee: $20 • Vehicle
$10 • Individual (foot, bike, etc.)

*Reserve at (866) 761-6629 or
www.reservedenali.com

Denali - Alaska

Mount McKinley, at 20,320 feet, is the tallest mountain in North America. It serves as the centerpiece and main attraction of Denali National Park. So tall and massive that the mountain creates its own weather, often shrouding its glory in clouds. When the clouds lift, McKinley commands attention; from base to summit it is more prominent than Mount Everest, which rises 12,000 feet from its base on the Tibetan Plateau. The base of McKinley is at roughly 2,000-ft elevation, giving it a prominence of some 18,000 feet. Appropriately, the Koyukon Athabaskan people call the peak Denali or "The High One." It wasn't until 1869 that a failed businessman turned prospector named the mountain "McKinley" in honor of the presidential candidate who supported the gold standard. The name stuck just like its superlatives. This park and its majestic mountain, located in Alaska's interior, provide refuge for wildlife, respite for backpackers, and the ultimate challenge for mountain climbers.

People supposedly climb mountains because they're there, but **the race to summit McKinley** was all about bragging rights. Frederick Cook, president of the Explorer's Club, claimed he reached the summit in 1903. And he returned with a picture to prove it. Another group retraced his route, duplicating the photo at a lower peak. In 1910 a group of prospectors boasted they were going to plant an American flag at the summit. It took them from January through April to reach the mountain's base and establish a camp. In May, two members wearing nothing but overalls and unlined parkas made a push for the summit with a thermos of hot chocolate and a bag of doughnuts. Amazingly, they backed up their words. The American flag was firmly planted at 19,470 feet, atop McKinley's North Peak (850 feet lower than its South Peak). Three years later a group led by Alaska's Episcopal archdeacon, Hudson Stuck, climbed to the top of South Peak. The trek was so grueling and air so thin that Stuck blacked out several times during ascent.

Just as the race to the summit was heating up, **Charles Sheldon**, a close friend of **President Theodore Roosevelt**, was wintering in a cabin on the Toklat River. While camped out in what was thought to be the last tract of un-exploited American wilderness, he witnessed the slaughter of animals brought on by the rush of gold miners in 1903. He recorded his observations in a journal and later wrote *The Wilderness of Denali*. In his journal he described the **idea of a park** that would allow visitors to see Alaska as he saw it while living along the Toklat River. He spent years advocating a national park and hand delivered his proposal to Washington, D.C. On February 26, 1917, **President Woodrow Wilson** signed a bill creating Mount McKinley National Park, but it failed to include the summit of Mount McKinley in the preserved lands. Sheldon received additional disappointment when he learned that the mountain and new park would not be returned to its original name, Denali. Not until 1980 was the park expanded and renamed Denali.

The area's distinctive wildlife and landscapes are protected from commercial interests, but the National Park Service can't shelter the environment from all threats. Changes in climate affect the environment in subtle ways. As you increase elevation there's a distinct tree line where average temperatures are too cold for trees to grow. As the climate warms, the tree line conspicuously rises. With continually increasing visitation, park staff must find new ways to manage and maintain the delicate habitat without ruining the experience. Limiting the 92-mile Denali Park Road to bus tours and enforcing backcountry permit quotas help maintain the pristine wilderness that Koyukon Athabascans, Charles Sheldon, and all past park visitors have enjoyed. With the work of the park rangers and conservation-minded patrons like yourself, Denali will remain an example of the Last Frontier.

Did you know?

➤ In 2005 a dinosaur footprint was found in Denali National Park.

When to Go
Denali National Park is open all year, but the main park road is first plowed beginning sometime in March (weather dependent), and is usually accessible to private vehicles by mid-April. Bus service, shuttling visitors along Denali Park Road, begins in late May and operates until mid-September. Most visitors arrive between mid-June and mid-August. The park usually turns green by the end of May and wildflowers begin to bloom in early June. Mosquitoes are most active in early summer. Chances of seeing the Northern Lights increase in fall when the days gradually grow shorter.

Transportation & Airports
Several private bus and van companies provide transportation to the park in summer. Refer to page 635 for a list of businesses. The **Alaska Railroad** (800.321.6518, www.alaskarailroad.com) connects Fairbanks and Anchorage, passing directly through the main park entrance. One-way fare during peak season from Anchorage to Denali is $146/passenger and $64/passenger from Fairbanks to Denali. Ted Stevens Anchorage International (ANC) and Fairbanks International (FAI) are the easiest destinations to fly into. Once you've reached the park you can explore Denali Park Road aboard a public shuttle or tour bus (page 602), on foot (page 605), or by bicycle (page 607).

Directions
The 92-mile (one-way) Denali Park Road provides the only motor vehicle access to the park. Its first 15 miles are open to vehicles in summer. A "road lottery" is held for four days in the fall. Lottery winners can purchase a single, day-long permit that allows them to drive as much of Denali Park Road as conditions permit. Denali Park Road is 238 miles north of Anchorage and 121 miles south of Fairbanks.

From Anchorage (238 miles): Take AK-1/N/E 5th Ave north about 34 miles where you continue onto Interstate A-4 W. Take AK-3 N/George Parks Way. After 201 miles turn left at Denali Park Road, which leads into the park.

From Fairbanks (121 miles): Take AK-3 S/George Parks Highway 117 miles, and then turn right at Denali Park Road, which leads into the park.

DENALI

Denali Park Road and Shuttle/Bus Tours

The 92-mile **Denali Park Road** provides the only vehicular access into the heart of the park. For all but four days, private vehicles are only allowed to travel to Savage River (Mile 15). Beyond this, traffic is restricted to shuttle buses and tour buses. **Shuttle buses** are less expensive and give passengers the freedom of being dropped off and picked up anywhere along the road (simply flag it down). They also make stops for wildlife viewing, restroom breaks, and beautiful scenery, including dramatic vistas of Mount McKinley (clouds permitting). If you want to hike, picnic, or just sit and admire mighty Mount McKinley, shuttle bus is the way to go. The shuttles' only downside is they are not narrated. They stop at four scheduled destinations. There are specially designed **camper shuttles for backpackers** in which the rear seats are removed for packs and bikes. They stop at each campground. Roundtrip rates are as follows: Toklat River (6.5 hours roundtrip, Mile 53, $26.75/adult), Eielson Visitor Center (8 hours, Mile 66, $34), Wonder Lake (11 hours, Mile 85, $46), Kantishna (13 hours, Mile 92, $50), Camper Shuttle ($34), and TEK Pass ($34). Young adults ages 15–17 cost half the adult rate. Children 14 and younger ride free. Car seat laws apply for young children. The shuttle typically runs from late May through mid-September (weather permitting). Every September, once the shuttles have stopped running, the park hosts an event called "**Road Lottery.**" During these four days, lottery winners can purchase a single-day permit ($25) to drive the park road.

Bus tours are narrated by a trained naturalist (and driver), but they do not allow the freedom to exit and board wherever you please. Tours begin and end at various locations around the park entrance. There are three bus tours: Denali History Tour (4.5 hours, Mile 17, $76.50/Adult, $33.25/Child 14 and under), Tundra Wilderness Tour (8 hours, Mile 53, $123.75/$56.75), and Kantishna Experience Tour (11 hours, Mile 92, $169/$79.50).

Shuttle bus and bus tour tickets can be reserved in advance by calling (866) 761-6629 or clicking www.reservedenali.com. Reservations are highly recommended. If you plan on getting shuttle bus tickets upon arrival you may have to wait a day or two before they are available.

Three free shuttles help visitors navigate the park entrance area while reducing parking requirements and traffic congestion. Bus stops are located at Wilderness Access Center and Denali Visitor Center. Shuttles serve Savage River Campground, Riley Creek Campground, and the Sled Dog Demonstration Area.

DENALI

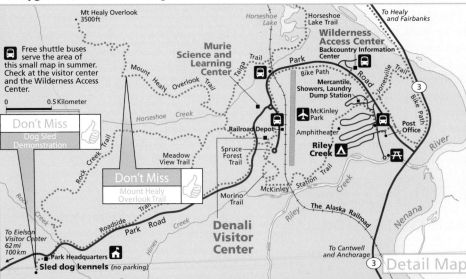

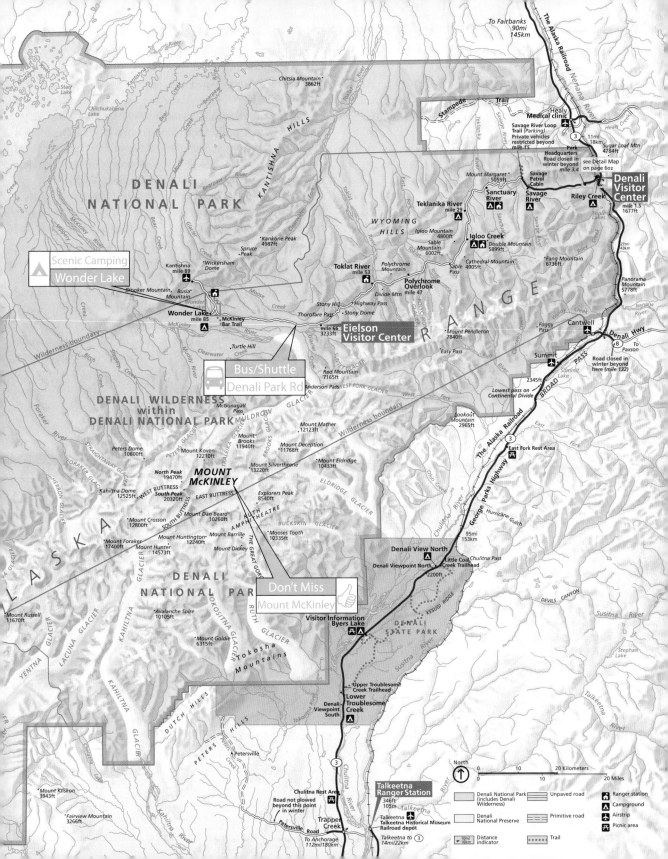

Reflection in Wonder Lake © Nat Wilson/NPS

Best of Denali

Attractions: Mount McKinley
    Runner-up: Wonder Lake
    2nd Runner-up: Denali Outdoor Center

Activities: Tundra Wilderness Tour
    Runner-up: Sled Dog Demonstration
    2nd Runner-up: Denali Raft Adventures

Lodging

The park doesn't operate lodging facilities, but a few can be found on privately owned land within park boundaries. Additional overnight accommodations are available outside the park at Healy (11 miles north of the park entrance) and Cantwell (30 miles to the south). For a list of lodging and camping facilities in and near the park please refer to page 640.

Camping

There are six developed campgrounds, all located along Denali Park Road. Only two, **Savage River and Wonder Lake**, provide views of Mount McKinley on clear days. Since **Riley Creek and Savage River Campgrounds** are located within the first 15 miles of Denali Park Road they are easily accessed via personal vehicles. You can also drive your vehicle/RV to **Teklanika** (Mile 29) if you spend a minimum of three nights there, but your vehicle must stay at the campsite for the duration of your stay. A better way to visit Teklanika is to take the **Camper Bus** (page 602) and purchase a **Tek Pass**, which allows campers to use the park shuttle buses at will (if space allows, but not beyond Teklanika) during the course of your stay. Denali's most wondrous campground is the one located farthest from the park entrance: **Wonder Lake** (Mile 85). It is a tent-only campground accessed via the Camper Bus. It is the closest campground to Mount McKinley, just 26 miles away. On clear days, the behemoth reflects upon the mirror-like water of Wonder Lake. This location is a wilderness lover's paradise, but there are a few drawbacks: cloudy skies often obscure McKinley, and you're camping near water, a breeding ground for mosquitoes that can be incredibly fierce from mid-June until late August. A large food-storage building provides picnic tables where you can avoid the rain and bugs.

DENALI

Denali Camping

	Mile	Open	Fee	Sites	Notes
Riley Creek*	0.25	All Year	$14/22/28	147	Near Entrance, RVs up to 40-ft • W (summer), F, DS (free)
Savage River*	13	May–Sept	$22/28	33	McKinley views (clear days), RVs up to 40' • W, F
Sanctuary River**	23	May–Sept	$9***	7	Tent-only, access via Camper Bus • P
Teklanika River*	29	May–Sept	$16***	53	Vehicle/RV accessible with 3+ night stay • W, P
Igloo Creek**	34	May–Sept	$9***	7	Tent-only, access via Camper Bus • P
Wonder Lake*	85	June–Sept	$16***	28	McKinley views (clear days), tent-only • W, F

W = Water, F = Flush Toilets, P = Pit Toilets, DS = Dump Station; RV Hook-ups are not available at any campground
Campground permits can be picked up at the Wilderness Access Center (WAC) or at Riley Creek Mercantile
Open and Close Dates are subject to weather; Multiple fees apply to tent/RVs < 30' in length and RVs 30–40' in length
*Reservations can be made beginning in December by calling (866) 761-6629 or clicking www.reservedenali.com
**Reservations are only available in person, no more than 2 days in advance at the WAC or Riley Creek Mercantile
***Prices do not include a one-time, non-refundable reservation fee of $4
Showers (fee), laundry (fee), wi-fi (free), and a camper convenience store are available at Riley Creek Mercantile

Backcountry	All overnight stays in the backcountry require a free wilderness permit. Permits are only available at the Backcountry Desk located in the Visitor Access Center (Riley Creek Entrance Area). They must be obtained in person and no more than 24 hours in advance of the first day of your trip.
Group Camping	Two group sites are available at Savage Creek ($40/night) • Make reservations by calling (866) 761-6629

Hiking/Backpacking: Relative to its size there are very few hiking trails at Denali. Most exploration is done off-trail, but there are a handful of maintained trails near the park entrance. Most are practical, connecting visitor facilities. **McKinley Station Trail** spans 1.6 miles between the Visitor Center and Riley Creek Campground. **The Bike Path** runs 1.7 miles from the Visitor Center to the Wilderness Access Center and ends at the Park Entrance. **Roadside (1.8 miles, one-way) and Rock Creek (2.4 miles, one-way) Trails** connect the Visitor Center with Park Headquarters and the Sled Dog Kennels. **Meadow View Trail** is a 0.3-mile trail that connects Roadside and Rock Creek Trails. A few trails actually show off the area's impressive scenery. **Spruce Forest Trail** (0.27 miles, one-way) begins at Denali Visitor Center and explores a forested area where seasonal wildflowers and berries can be found. The 1.5-mile roundtrip hike to **Horseshoe Lake** provides wildlife viewing opportunities, along with views of Oxbow Lake and the Nenana River. If you don't have enough time to explore the park's interior aboard one of the shuttle or tour buses (page 602), you should hike the 4.5-mile (roundtrip) **Mount Healy Overlook Trail**. It is the most strenuous (and popular) hike in the area. Although, not ideal for a casual family hike, it shouldn't be a problem for the average day-hiker. You hike for a short distance along an exposed ridgeline where wind and weather are always unpredictable (pack a waterproof windbreaker). Mount Healy Overlook, Horseshoe Lake, and Rock Creek Trails are accessed via the 0.9-mile **Taiga Trail** which begins at the Visitor Center. Also from Denali Visitor Center, you can begin the 8.6-mile **Triple Lakes Trail**. It loosely follows Riley Creek from McKinley Village to Hines Creek Bridge. To view Mount McKinley, try stopping at **Mountain Vista Trailhead** (Mile 13), where you'll find a short loop trail (0.68 miles).

With proper preparation **backpacking** in Denali's wilderness can be one of the park's most rewarding adventures. You must craft your own itinerary, obtain a **backcountry permit** (not req'd for day-hikes), and practice proper backcountry hiking/camping techniques. Be conservative when estimating your daily mileage. There are no trails, terrain is challenging, and it's likely you'll have to make several river crossings. Backcountry campers must set-up camp at least 0.5-mile away from and out of sight of the park road. Camp on durable surfaces where others have not camped before you. Fires are not permitted in the backcountry, so pack your camp stove. Water should be filtered, treated with iodine tablets, or boiled for one minute. Bear resistant food containers are issued free of charge with each backcountry permit. Backpackers can park their vehicle(s) at Riley Creek Camp's overflow parking area free of charge.

Mountaintop silhouette

Grizzly bear paws

Caribou and shuttle bus

Backcountry Permit

A backcountry permit is required for all overnight stays in the wilderness areas. Permits must be obtained in person at the Backcountry Desk located in the Visitor Access Center (VAC) (Riley Creek Entrance Area). In order to obtain a permit you must first plan your itinerary. Be prepared with several alternatives, because many wilderness areas reach their quota during the busy summer months. If your itinerary is available, each member of your group must watch a 30-minute backcountry video and attend a safety talk. It is your responsibility to know unit boundaries and wildlife closure areas. Delineate these boundaries on your map, and adjust your camping/hiking plans accordingly. Finally, obtain a **Camper Bus ticket (page 602)** that will drop you off at your desired starting location along Denali Park Road.

Follow the leader

Do not follow this grizzly © Frank Kovalchek (flickr/Alaskan Dude)

Remarkable views

Mountaineering

Mount McKinley is one of the premier mountaineering destinations in the world. Each year climbers from all over the globe test their climbing and wilderness survival skills against the 20,320-foot peak. If you plan on climbing either Mt McKinley or Mt Foraker (17,400 feet), you must register with Denali National Park at least 60 days prior to your intended start date and pay a $350 per climber special use fee. (If you cancel prior to January 15 of the year in which the climb is scheduled you will receive a $250 refund. Refunds will not be made for cancellations after January 15.) Registration is available online at www.pay.gov or you can download a registration form from the park's website. All climbers must check in, pay the entrance fee, and check out at Talkeetna Ranger Station. Less than 1,000 climbers summit McKinley each year, with a success rate right around 50%. Climbing McKinley requires a considerable amount of training, preparation, and experience. There are **six authorized outfitters** (listed below) who regularly lead intrepid individuals on summit attempts. Should you choose to use an unauthorized guide, your trip may be cancelled at any time. Please contact the **Talkeetna Ranger Station** for any climbing and mountaineering related questions. They can be contacted by phone (907.733.2231), fax (907.733.1465), or mail (Talkeetna Ranger Station; PO Box 588; Talkeetna, AK 99676).

AK Mountaineering School • (907) 733-1016 • www.climbalaska.org

Alpine Ascents Int'l • (206) 378-1927 • www.alpineascents.com

American Alpine Institute • (360) 671-1505 • www.aai.cc

Mountain Trip Int'l • (866) 886-8747 • www.mountaintrip.com

N.O.L.S. • (907) 745-4047 • www.nols.edu

Rainier Mountaineering • (888) 892-5462 • www.rmiguides.com

Whitewater Rafting

Private outfitters near the park entrance provide exhilarating whitewater adventures through the 10-mile Nenana River Canyon or float trips along its more placid stretches. **Denali Raft Adventures** (888.683.2234, www.denaliraft.com), **Denali Outdoor Center** (888.303.1925, www.denalioutdoorcenter.com), and **Nenana Raft Adventures** (800.789.7238, www.alaskaraft.com) offer 2–4 hour trips ranging from $75 to $175 per person. You can also head out on a multi-day expedition of the Talkeetna River from here.

Flightseeing

Flightseeing gives visitors the opportunity to see Mount McKinley at eye level as you soar high above climbers attempting the much more laborious journey to its summit. From the air you gain a new appreciation for the park's immensity and its mountain. Flightseeing also provides the unique opportunity to land on a glacier where you can partake in a summertime snowball fight or make a snow angel. There are four authorized park concessioners for flightseeing trips, with a variety of routes and itineraries that range in price from $175–449/person. All trips are weather dependent. Unauthorized private companies also provide flightseeing tours, but they are not allowed to land in the park. Please see page 635 for a complete list.

Fly Denali • (866) 733-7768 • www.flydenali.com

Sheldon Air Service • (800) 478-2321 • www.sheldonair.com

K2 Aviation • (800) 764-2291 • www.flyk2.com

Talkeetna Air Taxi • (800) 533-2219 • www.talkeetnaair.com

Other Activities

Biking: Pedalling a **mountain bike** along the 92-mile **Denali Park Road** is a fantastic way to see the sights and get a bit (or an awful lot) of exercise along the way. The first 15 miles from the Park Entrance to Savage River are paved. The rest is narrow, graded gravel road without shoulders. Cyclists can shorten their trip by driving to Savage River or loading your bicycle onto one of the **shuttle buses** (page 602). Each shuttle has space for two bicycles, so it is best to reserve space in advance. Call (800) 622-7275 to make arrangements. Cyclists are allowed on park roads, parking areas, campground loops, and the designated campground Bike Trail between Nenana River and Denali Visitor Center. Bicycles are not permitted on any park trails or in the backcountry. If it's inconvenient to bring your own bike, **rentals** are available at **Denali Outdoor Center** (888.303.1925, www.denalioutdoorcenter.com). Rates are $7/hour, $25/half-day, $40/day, and $35/day (>1 day). They also offer 2–2.5 hour bicycle tours for $50/person.

Fishing: Denali is not renowned for its **fishing** like other Alaskan parks, but fishermen enjoy dipping their line in Wonder Lake or one of the park's many streams. A state fishing license is not required, but you should inquire about catch limits and regulations that may be enforced.

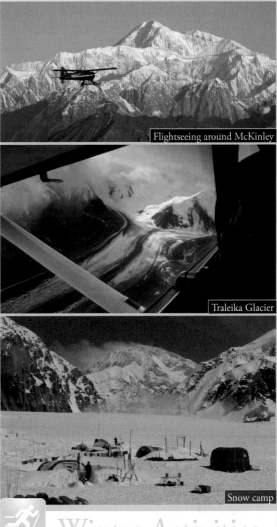

Flightseeing around McKinley

Traleika Glacier

Snow camp

Winter Activities

Just because the temperature drops below 0°F doesn't mean activities in the park come to a freezing halt. Winter visitors will find **Murie Science & Learning Center** open year-round, and from here you can head into the park on **cross-country skis**, **snowshoes**, **dog sleds**, or **snowmobiles**. **Camping** is available in the **backcountry** and at **Riley Creek Campground**. Spending a night in the park gives visitors an outstanding chance of seeing the **Aurora Borealis**. This phenomenon occurs all year, but there's only enough darkness to see it between fall and spring. Remember that services are extremely limited. You'll have to head to Healy, 11 miles to the north, for the nearest service stations with essentials like food and gas.

DENALI

Dog sled demonstration

Dall sheep and babies

DENALI

Flora & Fauna

More than 650 species of flowering plants, 39 species of mammals, 167 species of birds, 10 species of fish, and one lonely species of amphibian live at Denali National Park. You are a visitor in their land, so protect it and respect it. The park is so far north that very few species of trees can survive, but black and white spruce, quaking aspen, paper birch, and balsam poplar populate the lower elevations. Some descriptions of the park's wildlife may lead you to believe that you're embarking upon an Alaskan safari. It's not quite like that, but you'll have a good chance of spotting a few of the big five: moose, grizzly bears, caribou, Dall's sheep, and wolves.

Basics

For Kids: There's plenty of fun to be had for children and families, but one of the best ways to introduce kids to the unique history and geography is the park's **Junior Ranger Program**. To get started, pick up a free Junior Ranger Activity Booklet at Denali Visitor Center, Toklat Contact Station, Murie Science & Learning Center, or Talkeetna Ranger Station. Complete the activities in any order you choose, and then show your work to a park ranger. For a job well done you'll receive an official Denali National Park Junior Ranger certificate and badge.

Ranger Programs: During the summer, park rangers lead guests on walks, talks, demonstrations, and evening programs. These activities occur daily at both Denali and Eielson Visitor Centers. **Discovery Hikes** are a great way to explore the heart of the park with an experienced and engaging park ranger. "Disco" hikes are limited to 11 people, and you're only able to sign up in person, 1–2 days in advance at Denali Visitor Center. Park Rangers turn away unprepared hikers, so be sure to bring warm layers of clothing, adequate food and water, Discovery Hike Bus Ticket ($34), and be prepared to be in the park for 11 hours (~5 hours of hiking).

You can also catch a **Sled Dog Demonstration** at the Sled Dog Kennels. These unique experiences are offered daily at 10am, 2pm, and 4pm during the summer. There is no parking in the area, so arrive via shuttle bus from the WAC or on foot. The program and shuttle is free of charge.

Evening programs are held at Riley Creek, Savage River, Teklanika River, and Wonder Lake Campgrounds. Hikes and Theater Programs are available from the Denali Visitor Center. Check out a current schedule of activities in the park's publication, *Alpenglow* (available online or at a visitor center).

Visitor Facilities:

Denali Visitor Center • Mile 1.5 Denali Park Rd • (907) 683-9275
Features: Exhibits, Film, Trails, Ranger Programs, Bookstore
Open: mid-May–mid-September, Daily, 8am–6pm

Murie Science & Learning Center • Mile 1.3 • (907) 683-1269
Features: Exhibits, Classes, Field Seminars w/ AK Geographic Institute
Open (All Year): mid-May–mid-September, Daily, 9:30am–5pm • winter: daily, 9am–4pm (except major holidays)
www.murieslc.org

Wilderness Access Center (WAC) • Mile 0.75 Denali Park Rd
Features: Bus Tickets, Campground Reservations, Bookstore, Film
Open: mid-May–mid-September, Daily, 5am–8pm

<u>Toklat Ranger Station</u> • Mile 53 Denali Park Road
Features: Bookstore, Park Information
Open: mid-May–mid-September, Daily, 9am–7pm

<u>Eielson Visitor Center</u> • Mile 66 Denali Park Road
Features: Park Information, Exhibits, Ranger Walks
Open: early June–mid-September, Daily, 9am–7pm

<u>Talkeetna Ranger Station</u> • (907) 733-2231
Downtown Talkeetna, 140 miles south of the main park entrance
Features: Mountaineering and Park Information, Climbing Film, Interpretive Programs, Bookstore
Open: mid-May–mid-September, Daily, 9am–7pm

Pets: Pets are allowed in the park, but must be kept on a leash no more than six feet in length at all times. They may be walked on the Park Road, in parking lots, or on campground roads. They are not permitted on trails, buses, or in the backcountry.

Accessibility: Denali Visitor Center, Wilderness Access Center, Murie Science & Learning Center, Eielson Visitor Center, Toklat Rest Area, and the Sled Dog Kennels are wheelchair accessible. The Bike Path, McKinley Station Trail, and Spruce Forest Trail are wheelchair accessible (with assistance). Savage River and Riley Creek Loop Shuttles are accessible. At least one of the Sled Dog Demonstration Shuttles is accessible. Many, but not all, Denali Park Road shuttle and tour buses are accessible. If visitors have special needs, you may apply for a road travel permit. Please contact the park (907.683.2294).

Weather: Warm weather from late May through early September attracts 90% of the park's visitors, but don't go expecting clear skies and temperatures in the 70s°F. McKinley is so massive that it creates its own weather system. Clouds hide the prominent peak for about half the year. You have a better chance of viewing McKinley early or later in the day, but for the best chance of seeing the massive mountain, spend a night or two camping in the park. Temperatures are just as unpredictable, ranging from 33°F to 75°F during summer. Winters are downright nasty. On warm days the temperature might top out at 20°F, but it's not uncommon for the mercury to dip below -40°F. Extreme cold usually begins in late October and lasts through March. Don't forget a raincoat for your visit. June through August is the wettest period of the year, but precipitation is also difficult to predict. The table provided below gives you a general idea of the climate.

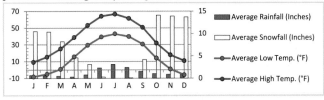

Backcountry campsite

A moose in rut

Snow trek

Vacation Planner

The best advice a person can get when visiting Denali National Park is to **spend more than one day in the park**. Too many visitors come and go without ever catching a glimpse of her majesty, Mount McKinley, when she peeks out from behind a mask of clouds. It also requires an awful lot of time to properly explore the park. Most activities, like joining a park ranger on a **Discovery Hike** (page 608) or **riding the Tour Bus** (page 602) to Kantishna, are full-day commitments. Not to mention, you may want to **whitewater raft** (page 606), **pedal Denali Park Road** (page 607), or go **flightseeing** (page 607). Take your time, soak in the splendor, and admire the unspoiled wild beauty at a leisurely pace (as long as you aren't being attacked by a swarm of angry mosquitoes). Nearby dining, grocery stores, lodging, festivals, and attractions are listed on pages 635–641.

DENALI

Bear Glacier flows into the Gulf of Alaska near Resurrection Bay

PO Box 1727
Seward, Alaska 99664
Phone: (907) 422-0500
Website: www.nps.gov/kefj

Established: December 2, 1980
Size: 699,983 Acres
Annual Visitors: 300,000
Peak Season: Summer

Activities: Boat Tours, Hiking,
Backpacking, Mountaineering,
Flightseeing, Paddling, Fishing,
Snowshoeing, Snowmobiling, and
Cross-Country Skiing

Campground: Exit Glacier (12
sites, first-come, first-served, free)
Backcountry Camping: Permitted
Backcountry Cabins: Coast Cabins
(2, summer only)*; Exit Glacier
Cabin (1, winter only)**

Park Hours: All day, every day
Entrance Fee: None

*Reserve at (866) 869-6887
**Reserve at (907) 422-0500

Kenai Fjords - Alaska

Kenai Fjords, located in south-central Alaska near the town of Seward, is the smallest of Alaska's national parks. Of course, small by Alaskan standards is large anywhere else. It's roughly the size of Grand Teton (page 204) and Rocky Mountain (page 326) National Parks put together. Along the coast, towering peaks rise abruptly from the sea. Glaciers that slowly carved the fjords are now receding along the ravines and valleys between mountain ridges. Tracing each glacier back to its origin inevitably leads to **Harding Icefield**. Named for President Warren G. Harding, the mile-high mass of ice covers more than 300 square miles, roughly the size of Crater Lake National Park (page 538) by itself. If you include some 40 glaciers that fan out from the icefield, it measures over 1,100 square miles. It accumulates as much as 400 inches of snow annually, and it is the largest of four icefields remaining in the United States. Exit Glacier Road leads to, you guessed it, Exit Glacier. It's the most accessible interior glacier. From the Nature Center, visitors can hike a short trail to the glacier's base or make a more arduous journey to the top of Harding Icefield. During winter, visitors arrive at Exit Glacier by skis, dogsleds, snowshoes, and snowmobiles.

From the first Russian navigators who explored the Kenai coast in search of harbors for whalers, to today's visitors seeking nothing more than seclusion and grand natural beauty, everyone takes with them memories of the same dramatic landscape. Portraits of narrow, gradually deepening fjords bracketed by precipitous cliffs rising above the glaciers and icefield are burnt into their collective subconscious. Sea and land are home to Steller sea lions, puffins, Dall's porpoises, black and brown bears, mountain goats, and humpback and orca whales. Tens of thousands of seabirds migrate to the coastline in summer. Kenai Fjords National Park might be small by Alaskan standards, but it's big in scenery, untamed wilderness, and wildlife, and it possesses boundless possibilities for awe-inspiring adventures. Traits that epitomize the Alaskan National Park.

Boat Tours & Cruises

In summer visitors can join boat tours that explore the coves and bays of Kenai Fjords. **Major Marine Tours** (800.764.7300, www.majormarine.com) offers a Kenai Fjords Tour ($149–159/Adult, 6–7.5 hours) or Wildlife Tour ($69–79/Adult, 4–5 hours). **Kenai Fjords Tours** (877.777.4051, www.kenaifjords.com) offerings are a little more diverse. You can choose between their Resurrection Bay Tour, Gray Whale Watch, National Park Tour, Northwestern Fjord Tour, Cruise and Kayak Combo, or Fox Island Dinner Cruise. Rates vary depending on length, but $100/Adult for a 4-hour tour and $160/Adult for an 8-hour tour is a fair estimate for your travel planning. Each company offers discounts for early purchase and overnight packages. Lodging for Major Marine Tours is at Seward's Holiday Inn Express. Kenai Fjords Tours uses their privately owned lodging: Kenai Fjords Wilderness Lodge. It consists of eight beachfront cabins on Resurrection Bay's Fox Island, providing a peaceful setting where meals (included in package price) are prepared by the island's private chef.

Royal Caribbean (866.562.7625, www.royalcaribbean.com), **Celebrity X Cruises** (800.647.2251, www.celebritycruises.com), **Holland America Line** (877.724.5425, www.hollandamerica.com), **Princess Cruises** (800.774.6237, www.princesstours.com), and **Norwegian Cruise Lines** (866.234.7350, www.ncl.com) offer cruises that port at Whittier or Seward. From here, operators generally offer an optional cruise along the shores of Kenai Fjords. By this time, it's likely that you've been through Glacier Bay National Park and Wrangell–St. Elias National Park's Icy Strait, so maybe you've seen enough tidewater glaciers and marine life. If not, the tours of Kenai Fjords are just as memorable as those other locations.

When to Go

Kenai Fjords is open all year, but services and accessibility are extremely limited during winter. Exit Glacier Road is typically closed from fall through spring due to snow. The park's coastal backcountry is inaccessible from late fall through early spring because of rough seas. Kenai Fjords Information Center, located at Seward's boat harbor, is open daily from early May to mid-September. Hours typically run from 9am–5pm, and are extended to 8:30am–7pm between Memorial Day and Labor Day. Exit Glacier Nature Center is open daily from mid-May to mid-September. It's open from 9am–8pm between Memorial Day and Labor Day, otherwise hours are 9am–5pm. Most tourists arrive during summer, but a few activities like flightseeing excursions (page 635) and fishing charters (page 636) can be arranged year-round (weather permitting). Guests also enjoy cross-country skiing, snowshoeing, or snowmobiling along Exit Glacier Road after it closes to cars in fall.

Transportation & Airports

Seward Bus Lines provides year-round transportation between Anchorage and Seward. The trip takes 3 hours (one-way) and costs $50/adult (one-way) and $95/adult (roundtrip). Call (888) 420-7788 or visit www.sewardbuslines.net for additional information. A number of seasonal motor coach companies also provide transportation between Seward and Denali/Anchorage.

Alaska Railroad (800.321.6518, www.alaskarailroad.com) serves Seward, AK (port of call for many cruise lines) from May to September.

Ted Stevens Anchorage International (ANC) is the closest major airport.

Directions

Kenai Fjords National Park is located in south-central Alaska, just west of Seward and 132 miles south of Anchorage. Exit Glacier is the only portion of the park accessible by road.

Exit Glacier: From Anchorage, head south on AK-9/Seward Highway. Continue on AK-9 for 122 miles. Turn right at Exit Glacier Road (seasonal) and follow it into the park.

⛺ Camping

There is a 12-site, walk-in, tent-only campground at **Exit Glacier**. Sites are available free of charge on a first-come, first-served basis. The camp features central food storage and a cooking and dining shelter. Water and pit-toilets are available.

Cabins: **Aialik** and **Holgate** are **rustic cabins** located on the Kenai Fjords coast. They are available for public use from late May through mid-September. The cabins are accessible via float plane, water taxi, private vessel, or charter boat. Kayakers should be dropped off by boat due to extremely strong currents around Cape Aialik. All visitors must make their own transportation arrangements. Coastal cabins are equipped with heating stove (propane provided), pit toilet, table and chairs, and wooden bunks. You are responsible for bedding and sleeping pads, cook stove and utensils, drinking water or filter/iodine tablets, and toilet paper, in addition to whatever food, clothing,

gear, and emergency supplies you might need. The cabins do not have electricity and sleep up to 4 people. Cost is $50/night and reservations are required. **Reservations** can be made beginning in January of the calendar year you wish to visit by calling Alaska Public Lands Information Center at (907) 644-3661 or (866) 869-6887. Demand for the cabins is high so stays are limited to three nights per group per season. Reservations must be cancelled at least 10 days in advance to receive a refund or credit.

Willow Cabin is available for public use after Exit Glacier Road closes due to snow, usually from November through March. The cabin can be reached by snowmobile, cross-country skis, snowshoes, or dogsled. It is located approximately 7 miles down Exit Glacier Road from Box Canyon Gate (1.5 miles off AK-9/Seward Highway). This rustic cabin has propane heat, propane stove, oven, refrigerator, lights, and basic cooking utensils. There is no running water. It sleeps four and costs $35/night. Stays are limited to three nights and must be reserved in advance in person at the Park Headquarters or by calling (907) 422-0500.

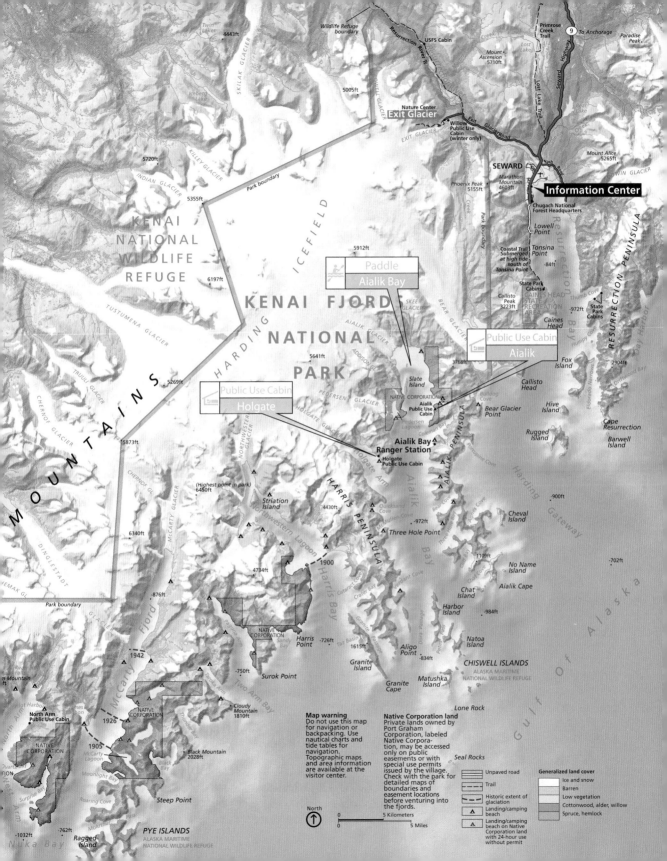

Twin Lakes
4443ft
Skilak Glacier
Iceberg Lake
5005ft
Wildlife Refuge boundary
Resurrection River Tr.
USFS Cabin
Lost Creek
Mount Ascension 5710ft
Lost Lake
9
To Anchorage
Primrose Creek Trail
Paradise Peak
Seward Highway
Nature Center
Exit Glacier
EXIT GLACIER
Willow Public Use Cabin (winter only)
Exit Glacier Road
Mount Alice 5265ft
Bear Lake
TWIN GLACIER

5720ft
Indian Glacier
Killey Glacier
Park boundary

5355ft
KENAI NATIONAL WILDLIFE REFUGE
6197ft

5912ft
Paddle
Aialik Bay

SEWARD
Information Center
Phoenix Peak 5155ft
Marathon Mountain 4603ft
Nash Rd.
Chugach National Forest Headquarters
Lowell Point
Park boundary

KENAI FJORDS
ICEFIELD
SKEE GLACIER
BEAR GLACIER
Coastal Trail Submerged at high tide south of Tonsina Point
Tonsina Point
-84ft
Callisto Peak 3223ft
State Park Cabins
CAINES HEAD STATE RECREATION AREA
-972ft
State Park Cabins
RESURRECTION PENINSULA

TUSTUMENA GLACIER
HARDING
AIALIK GLACIER
ADDISON GL.
5641ft
PEDERSEN GLACIER

NATIONAL
PARK
5269ft

Public Use Cabin
Aialik

Slate Island
NATIVE CORPORATION
Aialik Public Use Cabin
3768ft
Callisto Head
Caines Head
Fox Island
2904ft
Bulldog Cove
Bear Glacier Point
Hive Island
Rugged Island
Cape Resurrection
Barwell Island

Public Use Cabin
Holgate

HOLGATE GLACIER
PEDERSEN LAGOON
Pedersen Glacier
Coleman Bay
Aialik Bay Ranger Station
Holgate Public Use Cabin
AIALIK PENINSULA
Aialik Bay
-900ft

5873ft
Chernof Gl.
McCarty Glacier
NORTHWESTERN GLACIER
(Highest point in park) 6450ft
Striation Island
Holgate Arm
HARRIS PENINSULA
4430ft
Quicksand Cove
McMullen Cove
Three Hole Point
-972ft
Cheval Island
No Name Island
1109ft

CHERNOF GLACIER
TRULI GLACIER
5269ft
6340ft

DINGLESTADT
McCARTY GLACIER
4734ft
1900
Northwestern Lagoon
Harris Bay
Chat Island
Harbor Island
Aialik Cape
-984ft
-702ft

Park boundary
-876ft
McCARTY FJORD
NATIVE CORPORATION
Harris Point
-726ft
1615ft
Aligo Point
-834ft
Natoa Island

1942
Two Arm Bay
Surok Point
-750ft
Granite Island
Granite Cape
Matushka Island
CHISWELL ISLANDS
ALASKA MARITIME NATIONAL WILDLIFE REFUGE
Lone Rock

North Arm Public Use Cabin
North Arm Harbor
NATIVE CORPORATION
1926
Cloudy Mountain 1810ft
1905
McCarty Lagoon
Black Mountain 2028ft
Black Bay
Moonlight Bay
Seal Rocks

-1032ft
-762ft
Ragged Island
Steep Point
Roaring Cove
Surprise Bay

PYE ISLANDS
ALASKA MARITIME NATIONAL WILDLIFE REFUGE

Nuka Bay

Map warning
Do not use this map for navigation or backpacking. Use nautical charts and tide tables for navigation. Topographic maps and area information are available at the visitor center.

Native Corporation land
Private lands owned by Port Graham Corporation, labeled Native Corpora- tion, may be accessed only on public easements or with special use permits issued by the village. Check with the park for detailed maps of boundaries and easement locations before venturing into the fjords.

Unpaved road
Trail
Historic extent of glaciation
Landing/camping beach
Landing/camping beach on Native Corporation land with 24-hour use without permit

Generalized land cover
Ice and snow
Barren
Low vegetation
Cottonwood, alder, willow
Spruce, hemlock

North
0   5 Kilometers
0   5 Miles

Harding Icefield Trail 
Three Hole Point

Holgate Glacier

The Kenai Coast

Hiking/Backpacking: Hiking is somewhat limited. All maintained trails are in or nearby Exit Glacier. The 7.4-mile (roundtrip) **Harding Icefield Trail** is as good as it gets. You'll pass through forests and meadows before climbing above tree line to outstanding views of the massive icefield (the largest icefield entirely in the United States). It is a strenuous trek. You gain about 1,000 feet of elevation each mile and may have to scramble over rocks. Before departing, inquire about trail conditions, pack plenty of water, and be prepared to hike in bear country. The best way to enjoy the trail is with a ranger. On Saturdays in July and August, a park ranger leads guided hikes of Harding Ice Field Trail. Hikers depart Exit Glacier Nature Center at 9am.

A small network of shorter and easier trails originates at the Nature Center. From here you can hike to **Exit Creek's shoreline** (easy) or to the toe of **Exit Glacier** (moderate). The backcountry is trailless wilderness where hiking is not recommended due to dense vegetation and rugged terrain. **Backpackers** can camp along **Harding Icefield Trail** as long as you set up camp at least an eighth of a mile from the trail. If you're determined to explore the backcountry or Harding Icefield, hire a **private outfitter** (page 638).

Flightseeing: Like all of Alaska's National Parks, flightseeing is a safe and enjoyable way to view some of the world's most exceptional scenery. A list of providers is available on page 635.

Paddling: Kayakers are welcome to explore the seemingly endless supply of bays and coves. Inexperienced paddlers should travel with a guide (page 638). Most kayakers are dropped off by boat or plane at **Aialik Bay**, **Northwestern Lagoon**, or **Nuka Bay**. Day trips paddling **Resurrection Bay** from Seward are safe, but you should not attempt to round Aialik Cape because of extremely treacherous waters.

Fishing: If you'd like to try your hand at fishing (fresh or saltwater), you'll need an Alaska State fishing license for all fishermen over the age of 16. Before you dipping your lines visit www.adfg.alaska.gov for a list of up-to-date fishing regulations. Or put your fishing fortunes in the hands of a guide by joining one of several year-round **fishing charters** (page 637).

Ranger Programs: Programs are held regularly between Memorial Day and Labor Day. For a current schedule of all walks and interpretive talks visit the park website or stop in at Exit Glacier Nature Center.

For Kids: Kenai Fjords has a few offerings designed specifically for kids. **Art for Parks Backpack Program** allows families to check out a backpack filled with art supplies. Packs are free of charge and your artwork might be featured on the park website. Children are also invited to take part in the **Junior Ranger Program**. Download and print an activity booklet from the park website. Complete the activities appropriate for your age and show your work to a ranger or mail the booklet back to the park. Once your work is checked you'll receive an official Junior Ranger certificate and badge.

Flora & Fauna: Most land is bare or covered in ice and snow. The coastline supports vegetation and is covered with Sitka spruce and salmonberry. Sedges and grasses are the only plants capable of living in the park's Arctic–Alpine environments. In between the coast and the mountaintops you'll find alder, willow, and mature stands of spruce and hemlock trees.

Animals abound on land and in the sea. Black and brown bears, moose, mountain goats, and marmots live off the land. Whales, seals, sea lions, and sea otters patrol the seas.

Pets: Pets must be kept on a leash no more than six feet in length at all times. They are only allowed on Exit Glacier Road and in the parking lot. The only exceptions are dogs used for mushing or skijoring on Harding Icefield or in Exit Glacier when the road is closed.

Accessibility: Seward Information Center and Exit Glacier Nature Center are accessible to individuals in wheelchairs. The first 0.33-mile of Glacier Trail is also accessible. Boat and flightseeing tours may be accessible; contact individual providers for details.

Weather: Visitors should come prepared for all sorts of weather. Mittens, hat, and a warm/waterproof windbreaker are essential gear for a boat tour. Even when the temperature is comfortable, the wind on the open water can make for a chilly afternoon. Summer highs range from the mid-40s to low 70s°F. Winter temperatures range from the low 30s to -20s°F. Rainy/snowy weather is common. The Exit Glacier area averages about 200 inches of snowfall each year.

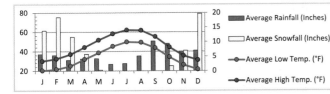

Mountain goat

Moose crossing a stream

Toe of Exit Glacier

Hiker crossing a rocky stream at Turquoise Lake

240 West 5th Avenue, Suite 236
Anchorage, AK 99501
Phone: (907) 644-3626
Website: www.nps.gov/lacl

Established: December 2, 1980
December 1, 1978 (Nat'l Monument)
Size: 4 Million Acres
Annual Visitors: 10,000
Peak Season: Summer

Activities: Hiking, Backpacking,
Camping, Rafting, Canoeing,
Kayaking, Flightseeing, Fishing,
Boating, and Hunting

Campgrounds: None
Backcountry Camping: Permitted
(Backcountry Permit not required,
but leave a copy of your itinerary
at the field headquarters in Port
Alsworth)

Park Hours: All day, every day
Entrance Fee: None

See page 635 for a complete list of
local businesses and guide services

Lake Clark - Alaska

Lake Clark provides a sample of all Alaska's parks. In this relatively small area of the Alaskan Peninsula (southwest of Anchorage) there are a variety of geographical features not found together in any of Alaska's other national parks. Three mountain ranges meet: the Alaska Range from the north, the Aleutian Range from the south, and the Chigmit Mountains in between. There are two active volcanoes: Iliamna and Redoubt, the latter erupting twice since 1966. Temperate hemlock-spruce rainforest covers the coast. Plateaus of arctic tundra are interrupted by turquoise lakes. **Lake Clark is "the essence of Alaska."** The very thing some people are searching for.

Richard Louis Proenneke was a man who understood the essence of Alaska, and he found it along the shores of Twin Lakes. Born in Iowa, he worked as a farmhand before enlisting in the Navy the day after Pearl Harbor was bombed. He was discharged for medical reasons in 1945. Four years later he made his first trip to Alaska, where he lived and worked intermittently for years, but not until 1962 did he visit the Twin Lakes area. By this time demand for furs was waning and tourism was waxing. The indelible memories of his first journey drew him back in 1967 when he began working on a cabin. The modest abode was completed in 1968, built from the ground up using only hand tools, many of which he fashioned himself. He lived in this exquisite piece of craftsmanship from 1968 to 1998, when he was 82 years old. Throughout 30 years of life on the shores of Twin Lakes he created homemade furniture, filled journals with weather and wildlife observations, and set the standard for wilderness ethics: "Twin Lakes and the wildlife therein should not suffer for his presence." Today, like-minded individuals can admire Proenneke's foresight and vision by reading edited volumes of his journals: *One Man's Wilderness* and *More Readings from One Man's Wilderness*, or by watching the documentary film, *Alone in the Wilderness*. Better yet, come to Lake Clark National Park and see Proenneke's cabin for yourself.

Hiking: There is one maintained trail. The 2.5-mile **Tanalian Falls Trail** begins in Port Alsworth just up the hill behind Homestead Café. The trail climbs a little more than a mile before dropping down to the river below the falls, where you'll find a short (unmarked) spur trail that descends from the boardwalk to the base of the falls. Tanalian Falls Trail continues beyond the falls for another mile to Kontrashibuna Lake before fading away into the trailless landscape that is the rest of the park.

Camping is allowed around Kontrashibuna Lake as long as you set up camp at least 100 feet from the water and out of sight and sound of other users. From Tanalian Falls Trail you will find short spur trails at the signed junctions for Beaver Pond Loop and Tanalian Mountain. Venturing any deeper into the park requires careful planning and route selection. Hiking is easiest above the tree line. The northwestern parts (Telaquana Lake, Turquoise Lake) offer the least challenging routes. **Telaquana Trail** (unmaintained) is an historic Dena'ina Athabascan route that connects Telaquana Lake to Kijik Village on Lake Clark. Originally blazed by the native Inland Dena'ina, and later by trappers, miners, and homesteaders, today it is primarily used by adventurous backpackers. Alder, river crossings, and inclement weather will slow down your travel. Expect your hiking rate to be about one mile per hour. A well-planned itinerary, good map, compass, warm layers of clothing, rain gear, knife, water, and snacks are imperative for hiking in Lake Clark's backcountry (even on day hikes). If you plan on hiking without a guide be sure to contact a ranger in Port Alsworth (907.781.2218) before departing. Bear resistant food containers (BRFC) are required for travel in many areas. BRFCs are available, free of charge, at the park visitor center in Port Alsworth. A properly prepared hiker/backpacker will find a trip into Lake Clark's wilderness to be nourishment for the soul. Any unprepared for this unforgiving environment is likely to have an unrewarding and potentially fatal experience. Experienced **guide services** (page 638) are available.

Come prepared for everything

Be prepared for beautiful sights like this view from Telaquana Trail

When to Go

Lake Clark National Park is open all year, but the majority of guests visit between June and September. Port Alsworth Field Headquarters (907.781.2218) and Homer Field Office (907.235.7903) are open Mon–Fri from 8am–5pm. Before entering the park, plan on stopping at one of these facilities, especially if you intend on hiking or backpacking without an authorized guide.

Transportation & Airports

Roads do not reach Lake Clark National Park. The region is primarily accessed by air taxi service (page 635). Depending on your destination, you may arrive via float plane or wheeled plane. Commercial flights between Ted Stevens Anchorage International Airport (ANC) and Iliamna (30 miles outside the park boundary) are available.

Camping

There are no designated campgrounds. A backcountry permit is not required for hiking or camping, but you should leave a copy of your itinerary at the field headquarters in Port Alsworth. Bear resistant food containers are available, free of charge, at the park visitor center in Port Alsworth.

Paddling: Rafting, canoeing, and kayaking opportunities abound. Muchatna, Chilikadrotna, and Tlikakila are three National Wild Rivers offering fast moving water with occasional whitewater. Popular trip lengths vary from 70 to 230 miles. June through September is the best time to paddle. If you plan on rafting on your own, discuss your itinerary with a park ranger. **Outfitters** (page 638) are available to guide you on an epic journey through the pristine wilderness of Lake Clark.

Air taxis (page 635) can be used to access otherwise unreachable regions of the park, but they also supply visitors with a bird's eye view of glacier-clad volcanoes, deep blue lakes, and endless expanses of open tundra.

Fishing: Saying that Lake Clark National Park is a good place to fish is like saying Lambeau Field is a good place to watch a football game. Lake Clark is home to some of the finest fishing grounds in the National Park System. The scenery isn't too shabby, either. Mountain lakes contain arctic grayling, Dolly Varden, several species of salmon, lake trout, and northern pike. All fishermen 16 and older require an Alaska State fishing license and must comply with State of Alaska fishing regulations. You can join a **sport fishing guide** (page 636) on a stock fishing trip, or they'll help you customize the fishing trip of your dreams based on ability, experience, time, and budget.

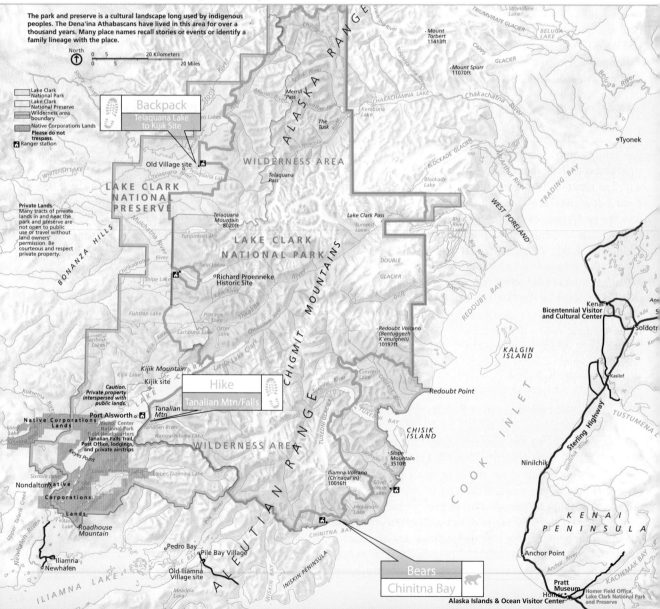

Boat Tours: Visitors have the opportunity to take a boat tour of 42-mile long **Lake Clark** or the craggy shorelines of **Cook Inlet**. If you're short on time, it's the ideal way to see the beautiful unadulterated landscapes that ring these picturesque settings. See page 637 for a list of commercial operators that provide guests with boating trips and charters. Fishing guides are often more than happy to include a tour of the waters and landscapes with a fishing expedition.

Hunting: Big game hunters with proper licenses and permits are allowed to hunt and trap in **Lake Clark National Preserve**. Hunting is not permitted within National Park boundaries. Licenses and permits can be purchased in Anchorage. Hunters must follow all state regulations. Big game transporters are listed on page 636.

Basics

Ranger Programs: Park rangers do not provide regularly scheduled walks and talks, but lectures and special programs are offered intermittently at Port Alsworth Visitor Center, Islands and Ocean Visitor Center, and Pratt Museum. For more information contact Port Alsworth Visitor Center (907.781.2106) or Homer Field Office (907.235.7903).

Pets: Leashed pets are allowed in the park, but for your safety, your pet's safety, and the health of the ecosystem, it is suggested that you leave them at home.

Accessibility: Air charters may be able to transport wheelchair users, but no facilities or trails are accessible.

Weather: You never really know what sort of weather to expect while visiting Alaska, but at Lake Clark National Park there are two distinct climates. The coast is wet (40–80 inches of annual rainfall) with more moderate temperatures. The interior is drier (17–26 inches of annual rainfall) with more extreme temperature differences (-40°F in winter). Snow can fall any day of the year, but it's most common from September to early June. Lake Clark begins to freeze in November and thaw in April.

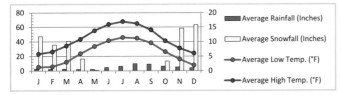

Grizzly and wolf tracks

Sleeping fox

Mountains poking through the fog

Flora & Fauna

Lake Clark's terrain varies from irregular coastlines to snow-clad volcanoes, forest to tundra to grassland, and glaciers of slow-moving ice to streams of fast-moving water. Diversity in terrain and ecosystem leads to top-rate wildlife viewing and bird watching. Caribou reside in the hills around Turquoise, Twin, and Snipe Lakes. Moose live below the tree line. Dall sheep scale the steep slopes of the Chigmit Mountains. Brown bears are found in all habitats, but are most common along the coast, particularly the Chinitna Bay Area. Throw in 125 species of birds and you won't want to forget your binoculars.

A grizzly bear and its dinner

PO Box 7
King Salmon, AK 99613
Phone: (907) 246-3305
Website: www.nps.gov/katm

Established: December 2, 1980
September 24, 1918 (Nat'l Monument)
Size: 4.7 Million Acres
Annual Visitors: 55,000
Peak Season: Summer

Activities: Bear Viewing, Hiking,
Camping, Backpacking, Fishing,
Flightseeing, and Paddling

Campgrounds: Brooks Camp*
Fee: $8 per person per night
Backcountry Camping: Permitted

Lodging (800.544.0551, www.
katmailand.com): Brooks Lodge,
Grosvenor Lodge, and Kulik Lodge

Park Hours: All day, every day
Entrance Fee: None

*Reservations required
(877.444.6777, www.recreation.gov)

Katmai - Alaska

Originally created to protect features of the **Novarupta Volcano** eruption in 1912, Katmai is now one of the premier wildlife viewing destinations among all United States National Parks. Bristol Bay is home to the world's largest run of Sockeye salmon. When they spawn in July a small fraction make their way up the Naknek drainage to **Brooks Camp**. Sounds simple, but it's an incredibly treacherous journey. Along the way, they must pass a gauntlet of brown bears, sometimes numbering as many as one hundred. Each one is searching for dinner, and salmon is the main course. The best seats at the all-you-can-eat buffet are near **Brooks Falls** where salmon back-up as they jump up the falls. It's dinner (for the bears) and a show (for you), and the show is spectacular. Spectators flock to two viewpoints where they can safely admire the feeding frenzy.

To many visitors, **bear terminology** is a bit confusing. What's the difference between brown, grizzly, or Kodiak bears? They're actually the same species, they just come from different places. Kodiak bears reside on Kodiak Island, southeast of Katmai across Shelikof Strait. Browns refer to any bear living near the coast and grizzlies live in the interior. So, if a Kodiak bear moved to the Katmai coast it would become a brown, and if it traveled another 100 miles inland it would then be called a grizzly. Unfortunately bears do not carry birth certificates to prove their place of origin. However, habitat causes dramatic differences in their appearance. Kodiaks are much larger than grizzlies. Thanks to a steady diet of spawning salmon and very little competition for food, Kodiaks can weigh up to 1,500 pounds. Food for the inland grizzly is often less abundant; forced to scavenge, some full-grown grizzlies weigh as little as 350 pounds. At birth the differences are superficial. Kodiaks, browns, and grizzlies are all born as one pound baby cubs.

Brown bears of the Brooks River may be the headliner at Katmai, but the **eruption of Novarupta** and resulting **Valley of Ten Thousand Smokes** is an unforgettable encore. Novarupta Volcano erupted from June 6–9, 1912. It was the single largest volcanic eruption of the 20th century. The explosion was heard over 140 miles away. Nearby mountains were covered in ash up to 700 feet deep. Even Seattle, 1500 miles away, was dusted with ash from Novarupta. The sky over Kodiak Island was darkened for three days. Years later, Robert Griggs, a botanist on a National Geographic Expedition, recounted his visit to the devastated area: ***"The whole valley as far as the eye could see was full of hundreds, no thousands—literally tens of thousands—of smokes curling up from its fissured floor."*** The smoke stopped, but the name stuck. Valley of Ten Thousand Smokes is a curiosity left behind to be explored by inquisitive backpackers. There remain 15 active volcanoes in the park, and Alaska is by far the most volcanically active region of the Ring of Fire (an area in the basin of the Pacific Ocean where large numbers of earthquakes and volcanic eruptions occur). But volcanoes aren't the only hazard the park faces. More than 1,055 tons of oiled debris was removed from shorelines following the Exxon Valdez oil spill in 1989. In some areas oil is still seen today.

Lodging

Lodging within Katmai National Park is provided by **Katmailand** (800.544.0551, www.katmailand.com). They offer three lodges: Kulik Lodge, Grosvenor Lodge, and Brooks Lodge. **Kulik Lodge** is the ideal destination for fly fishermen. Its cabins are situated along the shores of the Kulik River. Three nights costs $2,800 per person. **Grosvenor Lodge** consists of three guest cabins with heat and electricity. Three nights costs $2,700 per person. Pricing includes roundtrip air transportation from Anchorage, lodging, meals, boat and guide services, fishing license, rods and waders, and complimentary cocktails. **Brooks Lodge** consists of 16 modern rooms that can accommodate 2–4 persons. It's located in the heart of the park, just a short distance from Brooks Falls of salmon-fishing brown bears' fame. Three night packages based on double occupancy cost $1,687 per person and include roundtrip air transportation from Anchorage, meals, and a half-day guided Brooks River fishing orientation.

When to Go

Katmai National Park is open all year, but concessioner services are only offered from June through mid-September. Bear watching at Brooks Camp is best during July and September. Bears can be found in other areas like Hallo Bay, Geographic Harbor, Swikshak Lagoon, and Moraine/Funnel Creek during June and August.

Transportation & Airports

Katmai National Park is located on the Alaska Peninsula. Park Headquarters is in King Salmon, about 290 miles southwest of Anchorage as the crow flies. Brooks Camp, the main visitor destination, is 30 miles east of King Salmon. Neither area is accessible by car. Visitors can reach these remote destinations by plane or boat. Ted Stevens Anchorage International Airport (ANC) offers regularly scheduled commercial flights to King Salmon (AKN), which is the starting point for most Katmai adventures. Brooks Camp can also be accessed via boat from the villages of King Salmon or Naknek. See page 635 for a list of private businesses that provide transportation services to and around the park.

Fishing at the falls © Dmitry Azovtsev (www.daphoto.info)

Brooks Camp Campground (60 sites), located on the shores of Naknek Lake, is the only developed campground. Its scenic location and second-to-none wildlife viewing opportunities make this one of the best campgrounds in North America. Due to its unique setting in the midst of an extremely active bear habitat, campers must store all food and scented items in the food cache, cook in one of three shared cooking shelters, and wash dishes at the water spigot near the food storage cache. Campfires are allowed in the three designated fire rings near each cooking shelter, but you may not cook over an open fire. Vault toilets are available. To help protect campers from the locals (bears), the campground is enclosed within an electric fence. The fence is not a physical bear barrier, but it deters most of them from entering. The campground is open from the beginning of June until mid-September. It costs $8 per person per night and sites must be reserved prior to arrival. Reservations can be made by calling (877) 444-6777 or visiting www.recreation.gov. During July, campsites can be reserved for a maximum of seven nights. The best time to visit Brooks Camp is July and September when bear viewing is prime.

Katmai National Park and Preserve is home to as many as 2,000 brown bears. At times up to one hundred may be fishing for salmon along the Brooks River. This density and activity make Katmai one of the premier bear viewing areas in the world. There are several good areas to watch. **Brooks Camp** is the most visited area of the park, and bear viewing is best during July and September. Three strategically located platforms provide safe viewing opportunities. **Lower River Platform** is located a short walk from the visitor center. An additional 0.9-mile (one-way) hike takes bear watchers to **Falls and Riffles Platforms**. A limited number of guests are allowed on each platform at a time. In July bear can be seen at Brooks Falls as they fish for sockeye salmon swimming up river to spawn. In September the bears return to the Brooks River, but are usually found down river from the falls. Very few bear are seen along the Brooks River during June and August, but they are active at this time in other areas. Outfitters who provide bear-viewing tours are listed on page 639.

Bears: Where They Are and What They're Eating				
Location (eating)	June	July	August	September
Brooks Camp (salmon)	🐾	🐾🐾🐾	🐾	🐾🐾🐾
Hallo Bay (vegetation, clams)	🐾🐾🐾	🐾🐾	🐾🐾	🐾🐾
Geographic Harbor (salmon)	🐾	🐾🐾	🐾🐾🐾	🐾
Swikshak Lagoon (vegetation)	🐾🐾🐾	🐾	🐾🐾	🐾
Moraine/Funnel Creek (salmon)	🐾	🐾🐾🐾	🐾🐾🐾	🐾

🐾 = Few Bears, 🐾🐾 = Some Bears, 🐾🐾🐾 = Many Bears

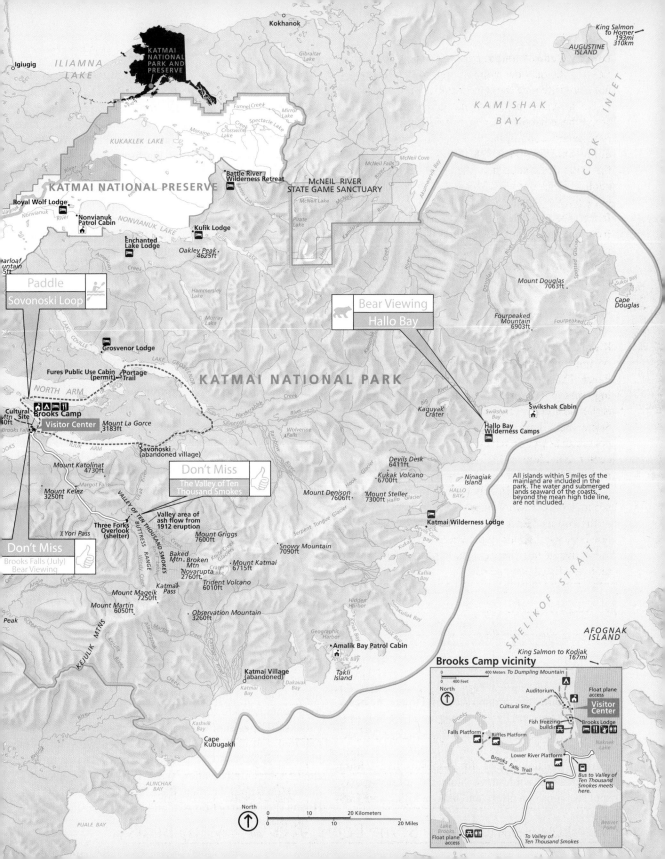

King Salmon to Homer
193mi
310km

Kokhanok

AUGUSTINE ISLAND

ILIAMNA LAKE

Igiugig

KATMAI NATIONAL PARK AND PRESERVE

KAMISHAK BAY

COOK INLET

Funnel Creek
Mirror Lake
Moraine Creek
Spectacle Lake
Crosswind Lake
Gibraltar Lake

KUKAKLEK LAKE

McNeil Falls
McNeil Cove

Royal Wolf Lodge

KATMAI NATIONAL PRESERVE

Battle River Wilderness Retreat

McNEIL RIVER STATE GAME SANCTUARY

McNeil Lake
Pirate Lake

Nonvianuk Patrol Cabin

NONVIANUK LAKE

Kulik Lodge

Enchanted Lake Lodge

Oakley Peak 4625ft

Mount Douglas 7063ft

Cape Douglas

Sukoi Bay

Spotted Glacier

Paddle
Sovonoski Loop

Fourpeaked Mountain 6903ft

Fourpeaked Glr

Hammersley Lake

Murray Lake

Bear Viewing
Hallo Bay

Grosvenor Lodge

LAKE GROSVENOR

Fures Public Use Cabin (permit)
Portage Trail

KATMAI NATIONAL PARK

Big River

Kaguyak Crater

Swikshak Cabin

NORTH ARM

Cultural Site
Brooks Camp
Visitor Center

Mount La Gorce 3183ft

Hallo Bay Wilderness Camps

Swikshak Bay

Brooks Falls

Savonoski (abandoned village)

Mount Katolinat 4730ft

Don't Miss
The Valley of Ten Thousand Smokes

Devils Desk 6411ft
Kukak Volcano 6700ft

Mount Denison 7606ft
Mount Steller 7300ft

Ninagiak Island

HALLO BAY

All islands within 5 miles of the mainland are included in the park. The water and submerged lands seaward of the coasts, beyond the mean high tide line, are not included.

Margot Falls

Mount Kelez 3250ft

VALLEY OF TEN THOUSAND SMOKES

Valley area of ash flow from 1912 eruption

Mount Griggs 7600ft

Katmai Wilderness Lodge

Devils Cove Bay

Yori Pass

BUTTRESS RANGE

Three Forks Overlook (shelter)

Baked Mtn.
Broken Mtn
Novarupta 2760ft

Snowy Mountain 7090ft

Mount Katmai 6715ft

Serpent Tongue Glacier

Kaflia Bay

Don't Miss
Brooks Falls (July) Bear Viewing

Knife Creek Glaciers

Trident Volcano 6010ft

Hidden Harbor

Kukak Bay

Kuliak Bay

SHELIKOF STRAIT

AFOGNAK ISLAND

Angle Creek

Mount Mageik 7250ft

Katmai Pass

Mount Martin 6050ft

Peak

KEJULIK MTNS

Observation Mountain 3260ft

Geographic Harbor

Amalik Bay Patrol Cabin

Kukak Bay

King Salmon to Kodiak 167mi

Kashvik Bay

Cape Kubugakli

Katmai Village (abandoned)

Katmai Bay

Dakavak Bay

Amalik Bay

Takli Island

ALINCHAK BAY

PUALE BAY

North
0   10   20 Kilometers
0   10   20 Miles

Brooks Camp vicinity

0   400 Meters
0   400 Feet

North

To Dumpling Mountain

Auditorium

Cultural Site

Brooks River

Float plane access

Visitor Center

Brooks Lodge

Fish freezing building

Falls Platform
Riffles Platform

Lower River Platform

Brooks Falls Trail

Naknek Lake

Bus to Valley of Ten Thousand Smokes meets here.

Lake Brooks

Float plane access

To Valley of Ten Thousand Smokes

Beaver Pond

Valley of Ten Thousand Smokes

Ash covered glacier on the slopes of Mount Katmai

Fishing at Brooks Falls

Fauna

Visitors come from around the world to see the bears of Katmai National Park, but they aren't the only animal roaming around this remote wilderness. Moose, caribou, red fox, wolf, lynx, wolverine, river otter, marten, porcupine, and other species live within the park's vast wilderness. Along the coast you may spot sea lions, sea otters, and beluga, killer, and gray whales.

Hiking/Backpacking: There are a handful of maintained hiking trails in the **Brooks Camp** area. The most popular is **Brooks Falls Trail**. It's an easy 1.2-mile hike that takes visitors from Lower River Bear Viewing Platform to Brooks Falls where Falls and Riffles Platforms (page 622) are located. **Cultural Site Trail** (0.1 mile) is an easy self-guiding stroll through prehistoric camps and a reconstructed native dwelling. It begins at Brooks Camp Visitor Center. In summer, every day at 2pm park rangers lead guests on a 1-hour long interpretive walk of the area. **Lake Brooks Road** begins at Lower Platform. This 1-mile path leads to the head of Brooks River and a large, glacially carved lake that is a good location to see salmon during spawning season (August and September), and bear occasionally fish here. **Dumpling Mountain Trail** begins at Brooks Camp Campground and climbs 800 feet over 1.5 miles to an overlook with outstanding views. You can continue another 2.5 miles to the summit of Dumpling Mountain (2,440-ft).

Katmai's other must-see attraction is **Valley of Ten Thousand Smokes**. Ambitious hikers can make the 23-mile (one-way) hike along **Valley of Ten Thousand Smokes Road**, which begins at Lower Platform, or you can sign up for a **bus tour** provided by **Katmailand** (800.544.0551, www.katmailand.com). Tours depart from Lower Platform at 8:30am. The bus driver is your tour guide and will lead a fairly strenuous hike into the valley from Overlook Cabin (where the bus stops). The tour costs $96 (w/ lunch) or $88 (w/o), but those hoping to explore the region on their own can purchase a one-way ticket for $51. Valley of Ten Thousand Smokes is the site of the largest volcanic eruption of the 20th century, and it's a fantastic destination for backpackers. About 12 miles from the road are **Baked Mountain Huts**. Originally built for research, these plywood bunkhouses now provide refuge for visitors. The 12-mile trek requires two river crossings which can be particularly dangerous. High volume of volcanic ash makes it nearly impossible to judge the depth. Always check river depth with a hiking pole or walking stick before each step. Bear resistant food containers are required (available at King Salmon and Brooks Camp Visitor Centers). A backcountry permit is not required, but it is encouraged that you leave your hiking itinerary at Brooks Camp Visitor Center. Drinking water can be scarce in the valley. Water is only available early in the season before the snow melts at Baked Mountain Huts. Hikers should carry rain gear and a good map and compass.

Paddling: The 80-mile **Savonoski Loop** (page 622) follows the North Arm of Naynek Lake, where paddlers portage to Lake Grosvenor and continue on the Savonoski River to Iliuk Arm and back to Brooks Camp. Along the way you can spend the night at historic **Fure's Cabin**. Reservations are required. Call (907) 246-3306 to learn about the permit process.

See page 636 for fishing, hunting, and flightseeing providers.

Basics

For Kids & Ranger Programs: Children and bears normally don't play well together. But if all members of your family listen to (and take seriously) a brief "Bear Etiquette" training course and safety talk, there's no reason that you should not enjoy the park in harmony with its furry, salmon-eating residents. A trip to Katmai is a once in a lifetime experience that you'll never forget. The park does not offer programs specifically for children, but park rangers at Brooks Camp provide regularly scheduled cultural walks, hikes to Dumpling Mountain, talks, evening slide shows, and narrated bus tours ($96) to the Valley of Ten Thousand Smokes from early June through mid-September. Check the park newspaper, *The Novarupta* (available online), for a current schedule of events and up-to-date travel, facility, and activity information.

Pets: Leave them at home. Pets aren't banned, but they are not allowed within 1.5 miles of Brooks Camp Developed Area.

Accessibility: Most public buildings in Brooks Camp and all bear viewing platforms are accessible to individuals in wheelchairs, but the narrow dirt paths that connect facilities are often muddy, slippery, and difficult to navigate without assistance. Trails to Brooks Falls and Riffles are accessible. Close encounters with bears occur with some frequency, and there is a strong possibility that visitors may need to leave the trail quickly and enter the woods to allow bears to pass. Air taxis may be accessible; contact the specific provider for details.

Weather: Visitors should come prepared for all types of weather. You might experience rain, sun, wind, or snow (unlikely in summer) during your stay, or even in a single day. Summer temperatures range from high 30s to low 80s°F. Winter is cold. Temps range from -40 to 40°F.

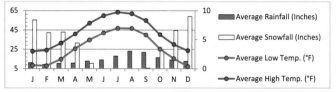

Legend:
- Average Rainfall (Inches)
- Average Snowfall (Inches)
- Average Low Temp. (°F)
- Average High Temp. (°F)

Lake in Kaguyak Crater

Mount Martin

Katmai Caldera

A bear viewing platform

KATMAI

625

A lone hiker looking out at the imposing peaks of the Brooks Range

Gates of the Arctic - Alaska

PO Box 30
Bettles, AK 99726
Phone: (907) 692-5494
Website: www.nps.gov/gaar

Established: December 2, 1980
December 1, 1978 (Nat'l Monument)
Size: 8.5 Million Acres
Annual Visitors: 11,000
Peak Season: Summer

Activities: Hiking, Backpacking, Camping, Paddling, Fishing, Flightseeing, and Wildlife Viewing

Campgrounds: None
Backcountry Camping: Permitted*
Lodging: Lake Wilderness Lodge and Wilderness Cabins
(877.479.6354, www.gofarnorth.com)

Park Hours: All day, every day
Entrance Fee: None

*Backcountry Permit not required, but leave a copy of your itinerary with a ranger prior to departure

Gates of the Arctic, about the size of Switzerland, is the 2ⁿᵈ largest national park in the United States. The entire park resides north of the Arctic Circle, but it was still christened "**Gates of the Arctic**" by Bob Marshall while exploring the North Fork of the Koyukuk River. When he reached Frigid Crags and Boreal Mountain, one peak on each side of the river, he felt as though he had just passed through the Arctic's stony gates. For explorers and outdoorsmen, the park is the gateway to a vast expanse of unspoiled wilderness and adventure. Rivers flow freely. Wildlife is undiminished. It represents nature at its purest, unscathed by roads, trails, and facilities. It's a land covered in snow and shrouded in darkness for most of the year. A land many people declare uninhabitable. A land that challenges outdoorsmen as they immerse themselves in nature. Wild, uninhibited, primitive nature.

Some 1,500 residents prove that this unforgiving landscape is in fact habitable. They reside in ten small communities within the park's "resident subsistence zone," where they still live lives similar to their descendants who arrived more than 10,000 years ago from present-day eastern Siberia. Caribou, moose, and sheep provide sustenance. **Caribou** are of particular importance, used for food, shelter, clothing, and transportation. The animal's skin is fashioned into tents, parkas, pants, boots, socks, mittens, snowshoes, and sleds. Tendons are used to make nets to catch ptarmigan and fish. While exploring the park interior visitors may encounter relics of a caribou-dependent life. Remains of caribou skin tents are scattered throughout the wilderness.

Iñuksuit, or "stone people," are found along migratory routes; Nunamiut Eskimos used these stone effigies to drive caribou to locations where their hunters were waiting.

Throughout the years, gold miners, military officers, explorers, and government scientists came and went. Meanwhile, descendants of the original Inupiaq and Athabascan people continue to reside in the central region of the Brooks Mountain Range that crosses the park. A land filled with glacial cirques, six Wild and Scenic Rivers, and an undisturbed wilderness waiting to challenge the most seasoned backcountry explorers and winter survivalists. Indeed, Gates of the Arctic is the last American Frontier.

Backcountry camping at its purest

Backpacking: Anyone traveling to Gates of the Arctic National Park has to have a thorough agenda planned well in advance. There are no developed campgrounds or designated campsites. Rather than **camping** on fragile Arctic tundra, backpackers should search for durable surfaces like gravel bars, which have the added benefit of fewer mosquitoes. Just be sure to choose a location well above the water line since water levels can rise at any time. If you must camp on a vegetated site, choose a location with hardier plants like grasses and sedges rather than lichens and moss. You should make every effort to return your campsite to a natural appearance before leaving. Cooking should be done using a gas or propane stove. While open fires are allowed, wood and other burnable material is often scarce. Cook and eat all food at least 100 yards away from your camp. All food and scented items should be stored in a bear resistant food container (BRFC). Visitor centers and ranger stations will loan BRFCs to visitors, free of charge, on a first-come, first-served basis. It is a good idea to call ahead to check availability.

Hiking: Just as there are no designated backcountry campsites, there are no established hiking trails. Planning is essential to a safe and satisfying trip. Expect to move at a slower pace than usual. Vegetation can be dense, ground can be moist and boggy, and frequent river crossings will slow your travel. Going slowly isn't necessarily a bad thing. It affords time to savor this wild and rugged mountain wilderness. For easier travel hike above the tree line or hire a guide (page 638).

When to Go

Gates of the Arctic National Park is open all year. Summer is the best time to visit, but it's not perfect. Swarms of gnats and mosquitoes emerge once the snow melts (typically June–July). Like all Alaskan National Parks, weather can be extreme, and visitors must be prepared for all conditions. Snow can fall any day of the year. Precipitation usually peaks in August. Hikers often rejoice when the sun comes out and the mercury rises, but heat causes rivers to swell, often making them impassable. Visitors should have flexible plans and extra food in case your pick-up flight is delayed, you need to wait out a storm, or you reroute your itinerary. Regardless of when you visit, all guests should be well versed in wilderness survival and self-rescue techniques.

Transportation & Airports

No roads enter the park, but Dalton Highway (AK-11) comes within 5 miles of its eastern boundary. Economically minded hikers can begin on foot from Dalton Highway (river crossing required). Most visitors enter and exit the park via air taxi. Flights are available from Bettles, Coldfoot, and Kotzebue, which can be reached by plane from Fairbanks International Airport (FAI). A list of air taxis authorized to land within the park is available on page 635.

Paddling: Rivers make for swifter travel. Many of the park's Wild and Scenic rivers can be navigated for hundreds of miles. Most are relatively easy floats, but the water is always cold and can be fast, especially when water levels peak in May and June or after particularly hot days or heavy rains. See page 638 for a list of outfitters.

Flightseeing: Easier yet, you can go on a flightseeing tour. Air taxis (page 635) fly above the park or land on lakes and backcountry airstrips, transporting visitors deep into otherwise inaccessible wilderness.

Wildlife Viewing: Gates of the Arctic is ideal for self-sufficient bird watchers and wildlife enthusiasts. Grizzlies, wolves, fox, caribou, and migratory birds gorge on food that becomes abundant during the short summer season.

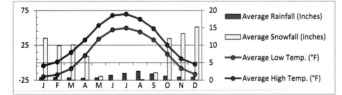

Basics

It is a good idea to leave your travel itinerary with a park ranger at one of the following facilities. Call to confirm hours of operation.

Fairbanks Administrative Center • (907) 457-5752
4175 Geist Road; Fairbanks, AK 99709 • Open: All Year, Mon–Fri, 8am–4:30pm

Bettles Visitor Center • (907) 692-5495; PO Box 26030; Bettles Field, AK 99726; Open: mid-June–September, Daily, 8am–5pm; October–mid-June, Mon–Fri, 8am–5pm

Arctic Interagency Visitor Center • (907) 678-5209 • Coldfoot, AK, on Dalton Highway • Open: Memorial Day–Labor Day, Daily, 10am–10pm

Anaktuvuk Pass Ranger Station • (907) 661-3520 • Call for Hours

For Kids & Ranger Programs: The park does not offer regularly scheduled ranger or children's programs.

Pets: Pets are not allowed at Gates of the Arctic National Park.

Accessibility: Gates of the Arctic is one of the last tracts of untamed wilderness in the world. Terrain is unforgiving and difficult to navigate. Air taxis may be able to transport wheelchair users into the park (call specific air taxi operators to verify), but there are no accessible park facilities or maintained trails.

Weather: Visitors should come prepared for all types of weather. The park's interior is relatively dry. The wettest months are June, August, and September. Summers are short, but the days are long (in summer the sun does not set for 30 straight days).

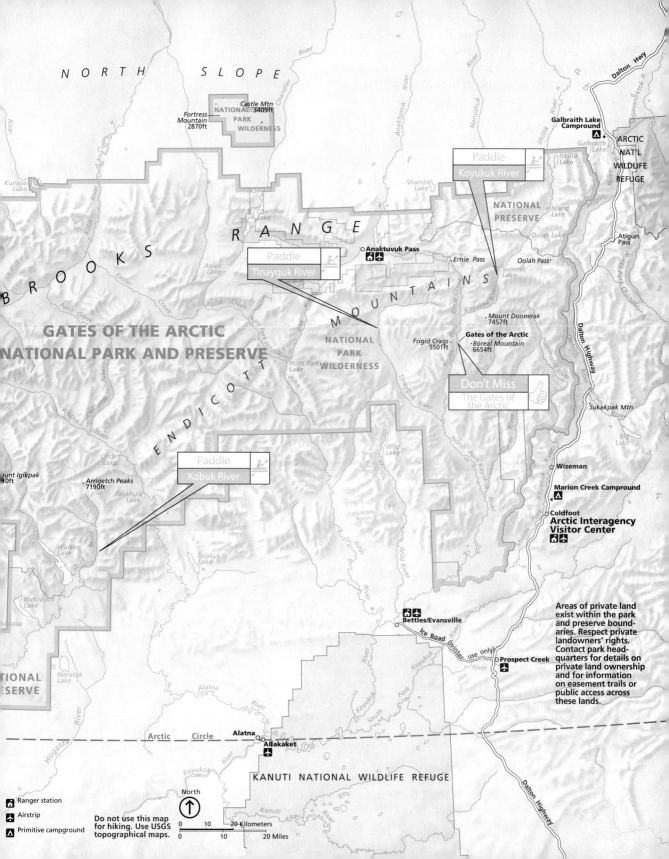

NORTH SLOPE

River

Chandler River

Castle Mtn 3409ft

Fortress Mountain 2870ft

NATIONAL PARK WILDERNESS

Kurupa Lake

River

BROOKS RANGE

Killik River

Easter Creek

Chandler Lake

Agiak Lake

Agiak Creek

Anaktuvuk River

Nanushuk River

Shainin Lake

Galbraith Lake Campround

Galbraith Lake

Dalton Hwy

Sagavanirktok R.

ARCTIC NAT'L WILDLIFE REFUGE

Paddle
Koyukuk River

NATIONAL PRESERVE

Itkillik Lake

Itkillik River

Island Lake

Oolah Lake

Atigun River

Atigun Pass

GATES OF THE ARCTIC
NATIONAL PARK AND PRESERVE

Paddle
Tinayguk River

Anaktuvuk Pass

Ernie Pass

M O U N T A I N S

Ernie Creek

Oolah Pass

Summit Lake

Mount Doonerak 7457ft

North Fork Koyukuk River

Frigid Crags 5501ft

Gates of the Arctic
Boreal Mountain 6654ft

Don't Miss
The Gates of the Arctic

Dalton Highway

Dietrich River

Hammond River

Sukakpak Mtn

E N D I C O T T

Mount Igikpak 0ft

Circle Lake

Arrigetch Peaks 7190ft

Takahula Lake

Alatna River

Unakserak River

Paddle
Kobuk River

Walker Lake

Kobuk River

Iniakuk Lake

Hunt Fork Lake

Hunt Fork

John River

Wild Lake

Big Lake

Wiseman

Marion Creek Campround

Coldfoot
Arctic Interagency Visitor Center

Nutuvukti Lake

Kobuk River

Norutak Lake

John River

Wild River

Middle Fork Koyukuk River

Kokosa

NATIONAL PRESERVE

Alatna River

Koyukuk River

South Fork

Jim River

Bettles/Evansville

Ice Road (winter use only)

Prospect Creek

Areas of private land exist within the park and preserve boundaries. Respect private landowners' rights. Contact park headquarters for details on private land ownership and for information on easement trails or public access across these lands.

Hogatza River

Arctic Circle

Alatna
Allakaket

Koyukuk River

KANUTI NATIONAL WILDLIFE REFUGE

Kanuti River

Dalton Highway

North

Do not use this map for hiking. Use USGS topographical maps.

0   10   20 Kilometers
0   10   20 Miles

▲ Ranger station
✈ Airstrip
▲ Primitive campground

Caribou crossing the Kobuk River at Onion Portage

PO Box 1029
Kotzebue, AK 99752
Phone: (907) 442-3890
Website: www.nps.gov/kova

Established: December 2, 1980
Size: 1.7 Million Acres
Annual Visitors: 3,000 (least visited National Park)
Peak Season: Summer

Activities: Backpacking, Hiking, Paddling, Camping, Flightseeing, Wildlife Viewing, and Photography

Campgrounds: None
Backcountry Camping: Permitted*
Lodging: None
Refer to page 636 for lodging outside the park

Park Hours: All day, every day
Entrance Fee: None

*Backcountry Permit not required, but leave a copy of your itinerary with a ranger prior to departure

Kobuk Valley - Alaska

Kobuk Valley National Park protects an arctic wilderness roughly the size of Delaware. It is a land so desolate and remote that it can only be reached by foot, plane, boat, dogsled, or snowmobile. Unimaginable to modern people, natives have lived here for 10,000 years. Locals continue to follow in their ancestors' footsteps by hunting caribou at **Onion Portage** during the animal's southward migration in fall. The Western Arctic caribou herd is nearly half a million strong. Twice annually, they migrate across the park's southern reaches between summer calving grounds north of the **Baird Mountains** and winter breeding grounds south of the **Waring Mountains**. Along their journey, they leave tracks across **Great Kobuk Sand Dunes**, the largest active dune field in arctic North America. Today, it covers 23.5 square miles, but scientists believe the sand—ground down by glaciers of the last Ice Age—once covered an area more than ten times its present size. The landscape is constantly changing as wind and water reshape the dunes; some rise 200 feet above the tundra.

North of the Kobuk (Inupiaq for "Big") River are the Baird Mountains. Mount Angayukaqaraq at 4,760-ft is the park's highest peak. A modest mountain compared to Mount McKinley, but it presents an intimidating barrier for intrepid travelers. Lower in elevation, much of the tundra is soggy even though the park receives, on average, just 20 inches of snow and rain each year. Permafrost, many feet below the surface, prevents water from draining before everything freezes for the long, frigid winter. Life is forced to adapt or perish. The wood frog has found an interesting way to survive. In fall, it burrows beneath leaves and soil, where its body temperature drops below freezing. In spring, it thaws out only to hop about the valley and enjoy summer with a handful of humans seeking the ultimate adventure and solitude.

Visitors must possess a fairly unique set of skills. Self-sufficiency is paramount. Survival and self-rescue skills are, quite literally, a matter of life and death no matter what time of year you travel. This is not your typical drive-thru family vacation. You won't find visitors parking their cars to snap a picture of a grizzly bear lumbering across the tundra. There are no roads. No trails. No facilities. It's a vast expanse of relatively unexplored, completely wild wilderness. You are the guest of the grizzly, the caribou, and the gray wolf. It is not the sort of place for inexperienced paddlers or backpackers. If you get lost, you won't eventually "pop-out" at a fast-food joint, gas station, or even a road. The only thing that will be there to greet you is more wilderness. If you want to call for help, you better be carrying a satellite phone, because your cell phone won't work. Paddlers and hikers are completely alone out there. It's just you and Mother Nature, exactly what Kobuk Valley's visitors seek.

Unless you're flying over the park—viewing its rivers and mountains from above—trips into Kobuk Valley are usually extended expeditions. Guests create their own itineraries, possibly with the help of a **guide** (page 638) or park ranger (907.442.3890). Most trips begin with an air taxi ride to your starting point. **Air taxis** are available from nearby towns of Kotzebue and Bettles. See page 635 for a list of authorized operators. Before your trip, it's a very good idea to stop at **Northwest Arctic Heritage Center** in Kotzebue to drop off a copy of your trip itinerary and borrow a bear resistant food container if you don't have one. The easiest **hiking** is along the ridgelines of the Baird Mountains. Ridgelines are exposed to chilling winds, but travel is free of swampy soil and impenetrable vegetation. **Paddlers** can float the 350-mile **Kobuk River**. This may be the best way to experience the park. The river is wide (up to 1,500 feet) but shallow as it crosses the park's southern half from east to west. The 80-mile trip from Ambler to Kiana can be made in about a week. This journey provides plenty of opportunities to

When to Go

The park is open all year, but only the hardiest adventurers (if any) enter the park during the winter when the days are incredibly short, if the sun rises at all. All visitors should have extensive backcountry experience and advanced self-sufficiency skills. Summer is the time to visit. The season is short (June–September), but the days are long (the sun doesn't set for more than a month around the Summer Solstice). Mosquitoes and gnats hatch in late May/early June. Daytime highs peak in July. August is often wet. The caribou migration, between winter breeding grounds south of the Waring Mountains and summer calving grounds north of the Baird Mountains, begins in September. Summer high temperatures average a comfortable 54°F, but visitors must come prepared for all types of weather. Snow and freezing temperatures may occur at any time, and temperatures exceeding 90°F have been recorded in certain regions of the park in July.

Visitor Facilities

The park's headquarters and office, located at Northwest Arctic Heritage Center in Kotzebue, is open June to September, Mon–Fri (8:30am–6:30pm) and Saturday (10:30am–6:30pm). From October to May, it is open Mon–Fri (8am–12pm and 1–5pm). Ranger stations at Onion Portage and Kallarichuk are staffed intermittently.

Transportation & Airports

No roads enter the Kobuk Valley. Air taxis (page 635) provide access to remote villages, lakes, and landing strips inside the park. Kotzebue and Bettles are the primary launch points for air taxi trips. Commercial airlines from Ted Stevens Anchorage International Airport (ANC) provide service to Kotzebue. Fairbanks International Airport (FAI) provides service to Bettles.

In summer it is possible to access the park via motorized/non-motorized watercraft, or by foot. In winter, the park can be accessed via snowmobile or dogsled. Entering the park by foot is not recommended for anyone but the most skilled outdoorsmen.

explore on foot, too. In late August/September you can stop to watch caribou as they swim across the Kobuk River at **Onion Portage**, near the park's eastern boundary. Further down river you can hike along Kavet Creek to **Great Kobuk Sand Dunes**. And paddling allows you to leave your gear behind while exploring these sites.

Flora & Fauna

The Kobuk River is the lifeblood of an otherwise inhospitable region. North of this ribbon of scenic waterway rise the Baird Mountains. Each year some 490,000 **caribou**, the largest herd in Alaska, cross the Kobuk River as they migrate from their summer calving grounds north of the Baird Mountains to their breeding grounds south of the Waring Mountains. Caribou are vitally important to the people of Northern Alaska. Nearly 1,500 locals reside in ten small communities within the park's "resident subsistence zone." These residents still hunt caribou at **Onion Portage**, just like their ancestors did for hundreds of years. Seeing the migrating herd of caribou can be a more rewarding experience than watching grizzlies fish at Brooks Falls of Katmai National Park (page 622) or gray whales swimming in Glacier Bay (page 586).

Caribou aren't the only show in the valley. It is estimated that there are 32 mammals, 23 fish, 119 birds, and 1 amphibian that live in or visit the park. Other popular mammals include grizzly bear, wolf, black bear, mink, lynx, fox, wolverine, moose, and Dall's sheep.

South of the Kobuk River are the **Great Kobuk Sand Dunes** and the northernmost reaches of boreal forest. Caribou leave tracks across the 23.5 square mile dune field during their biannual migration (north in the spring, south in the fall). Little Kobuk and Hunt River dunes also reside south of the Kobuk River. Much of the southern reaches are covered in sand created by the grinding action of ancient glaciers. Sand was then sculpted by wind and water, and eventually stabilized by vegetation. In all more than 400 species of plants grow in the park, remarkable diversity for an area with such a harsh climate.

Basics

For Kids: Kobuk Valley isn't a very kid-friendly park, but children are invited to complete the **Western Arctic Parklands Junior Ranger** book (available online) to earn a badge, saber toothed cat patch, and a water bottle.

Ranger Programs: The park does not offer any regularly scheduled ranger-led activities, but rangers are available to provide assistance over the phone or in person at Northwest Arctic Heritage Center in Kotzebue. This site also holds community activities throughout the year. Topics include natural and cultural history, local research, local crafts and children's activities. Call (907) 442-3890 before your arrival for a current schedule of events and programs.

Pets: Kobuk Valley National Park is a remote wilderness area with extremely active wildlife. For the safety of your pets, yourself, and the delicate ecosystem pets are not allowed within the park.

Accessibility: There are no visitor facilities or designated trails inside park boundaries. This is an extremely wild and undeveloped region that should not be accessed by anyone other than people with significant backcountry experience and skill. Individuals in wheelchairs may be able to tour the park by plane or boat. Please contact specific transportation providers for details.

Weather: Visitors must come prepared for all types of weather. Snow, wind, rain, and clouds can occur any time of year. Average summer temperatures in the mid-60s°F sounds pleasant, but they may reach into the mid-80s°F one day in July only to fall below freezing the next. Average January lows are -8°F, but lows can fall below -40°F. Due to extreme day-to-day temperature variance, average temps are not always a good guideline. One thing you can be sure of is that there will be long summer days. The sun never sets between June 3 and July 9. In winter, twilight lasts for hours each day, but the sun is only above the horizon for 1.5 hours on December 21. The northern lights (aurora borealis) are active year-round, but it is best seen on dark winter nights.

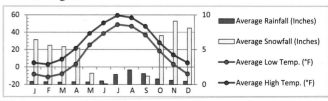

- ■ Average Rainfall (Inches)
- ☐ Average Snowfall (Inches)
- ● Average Low Temp. (°F)
- ● Average High Temp. (°F)

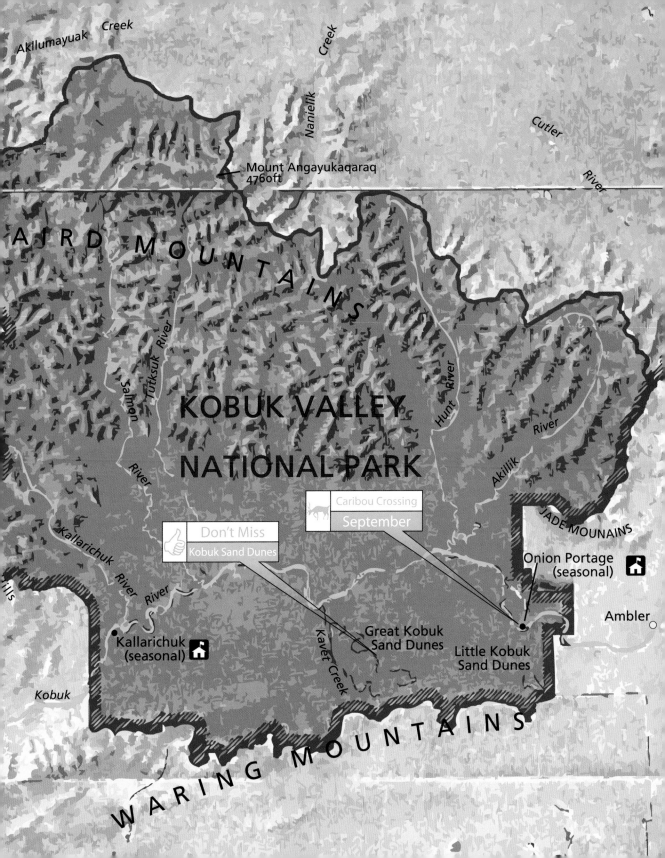

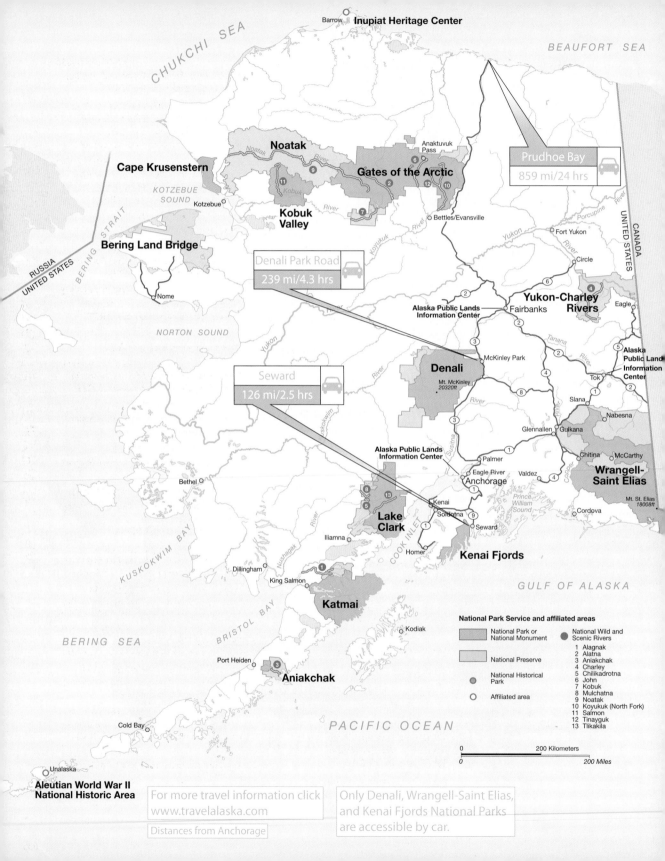

Mileage Between Sites

	Skagway	Fairbanks	Denali NP (Visitor Center)	Anchorage	Wrangell–St. Elias NP (Kennecott)	Seward/Kenai Fjords NP	Gates of the Arctic NP (Coldfoot)	Prudhoe Bay	Vancouver, BC
Fairbanks	660								
Denali NP (Visitor Center)	782	123							
Anchorage	776	359	239						
Wrangell–St. Elias NP (Kennecott)	717	370	356	306					
Seward/Kenai Fjords NP	901	484	364	127	431				
Gates of the Arctic NP (Coldfoot)	913	254	377	612	623	737			
Prudhoe Bay	1,159	500	622	859	869	983	246		
Vancouver, BC	1,538	2,075	2,201	2194	2,136	2,319	2,331	2576	
Seattle	1,610	2,150	2,272	2,266	2,208	2,391	2,404	2,648	141

National Park Abbreviations

Glacier Bay: GLBA
Wrangell–St Elias: WRST
Denali: DENA
Kenai Fjords: KEFJ
Lake Clark: LACL
Katmai: KATM
Gates of the Arctic: GAAR
Kobuk Valley: KOVA

Ground Transportation

Alaska Railroad • (907) 265-2494
www.akrr.com • DENA, KEFJ

Denali Overland Transportation
www.denalioverland.com • DENA • (907) 773-2384

TKA Taxi • (907) 355-TAXI
www.talkeetna-taxi.com • DENA

Bud's Rent-A-Car • (907) 697-2403 • GLBA

TLC Taxi • (907) 697-2239 • GLBA
www.glacierbaytravel.com/tlctaxi.htm

Glacier Taxicab
www.glaciertaxicab.com • KEFJ

PJS Taxi • (907) 224-5555
www.pjstaxi.com • KEFJ

Air Taxis/Flightseeing

Air Excursions • (907) 697-2375
www.ptialaska.net/~airex • GLBA

Alaska Seaplane Service • (907) 789-3331
www.akseaplanes.com • GLBA

Alsek Air Service • (907) 784-3231
Flightseeing, Fishing, Kayaking & Rafting
www.alsekair.com • GLBA, LACL

Fly Drake • (907) 723-9475 • GLBA, WRST
Flightseeing, River/Ski/Climb Support
www.flydrake.com • Tours: $170 (1 hr)

Fjord Flying Service • (877) 460-2377
www.fjordflying.com • GLBA

Mtn Flying Service • (907) 766-3007
Flightseeing ($159+), Flightskiing, and Cruises
www.glacierbayflightseeing.com • GLBA, WRST

Sky Trekking Alaska • (907) 357-3153
Multi-Day Flightseeing, Iditarod Trail Treks, Wildlife Viewing, and Fishing Trips
www.skytrekkingalaska.com • GLBA, LACL, DENA, KEFJ

Ward Air • (907) 789-9150
Flightseeing, Wildlife Viewing, and Fishing Trips
www.wardair.com • GLBA

Yakutat Coastal Airlines • (907) 784-3831
Flightseeing, Fishing, Kayaking & Rafting
www.flyyca.com • GLBA, WRST

40-Mile Air • (907) 883-5191
Flightseeing, Fishing, Wildlife Viewing, Hunting, Rafting, and Hiking Trips
www.fortymileair.com • WRST, GAAR

Copper Valley Air Service • (907) 822-4200
Flightseeing, Fishing, Wildlife Viewing, Hunting, Rafting, and Hiking Trips
www.coppervalleyair.com • WRST

Lee's Air Taxi • (907) 822-3574
www.leesairtaxi.com • WRST

McCarthy Air • (907) 554-4440
Flightseeing, and Backcountry/River Transport
www.mccarthyair2.com • WRST

Meekin's Air Service • (907) 745-1626
Flightseeing, Hunting, and Air Support
www.meekinsairservice.com • WRST

Ultima Thule Air Taxi Service
www.farfargnargnar.com • WRST

Wrangell Mountain Air • (907) 554-4411
Flightseeing Tours ($100+) & Backcountry Trips
www.wrangellmountainair.com • WRST

Fly Denali • (907) 733-7768
Flightseeing ($349+) & Expedition Support
www.flydenali.com • DENA

K-2 Aviation • (907) 733-2291
Flightseeing ($215+) & Expedition Support
www.flyk2.com • DENA

Talkeetna Air Taxi • (907) 733-2218
Flightseeing ($195+), #1 Choice for climbing & Expedition Support
www.talkeetnaair.com • DENA

Trail Ridge Air • (907)248-0838
Flightseeing, Bear Viewing, Rafting, Fishing, & Hunting
www.trailridgeair.com • DENA, KEFJ, LACL

Alaska Air Taxi • (907) 243-3944
Flightseeing, Bear Viewing, Fishing, and Hunting
www.alaskaairtaxi.com • DENA, KEFJ, LACL, KATM

Rust's Flying Service • (907) 243-1595
Flightseeing ($100+), Bear Viewing, and More
www.flyrusts.com • DENA, KEFJ, LACL, KATM

Talon Air Service • (907)262-8899
Flightseeing, Bear Viewing, Fishing, and Hunting
www.talonair.com • KEFJ, LACL

Alaska West Air • (907) 776-5147
Flightseeing, Bear Viewing, Fishing, and Hunting
www.alaskawestair.com • KEFJ, LACL, KATM

High Adventure Air • (907) 262-5237
www.highadventureair.com • KEFJ, LACL, KATM

Homer Air • (907) 235-8591
www.homerair.com • KEFJ, LACL, KATM

Klondike Gold Rush
Skagway
Haines
Glacier Bay
Gustavus
Juneau
Hoonah
Sitka
Sitka
Petersburg
Wrangell
Ketchikan
CANADA
UNITED STATES
Alaska Public Lands Information Center
Dixon Entrance

Photo courtesy of Ultima Thule Lodge

Flight safari adventure over the Bagley Ice Field with Ultima Thule Lodge

Northwind Aviation • (907) 235-7482
Flightseeing and Backcountry Support
www.northwindak.com • KEFJ, LACL, KATM

Stellar Air Service • (907) 299-0284
Flightseeing ($99+), Bear Viewing, and More
www.stellerairservice.com • KEFJ, LACL, KATM

Air Madura • (907) 243-7133
www.airmadura.com • LACL

Lake Clark Air • (907) 781-2208
www.lakeclarkair.com • LACL

Natron Air • (907) 262-8440
www.natronair.com • LACL

Rediske Air • (907) 776-8985
www.rediskeair.com • LACL

Andrew Airways • (907) 487-2566
www.andrewairways.com • LACL, KATM

Smokey Bay Air • (907) 235-1511
Volcano & Bear Tours, and Backcountry Support
www.smokeybayair.com • LACL

Sunlight Aviation • (907) 301-6993
www.sunlightaviation.com • LACL, KATM

Bald Mountain Air Service • (907) 235-7969
Brown Bear Photo Safaris ($615)
www.baldmountainair.com • KATM

Branch River Air Service • (907) 246-3437
www.branchriverair.com • KATM

Emerald Air Service • (907) 235-6993
Brown Bear Photo Safaris ($650)
www.emeraldairservice.com • KATM

Harvey Flying Service • (907) 486-5483
www.harveyflyingservice.com • KATM

Sea Hawk Air • (907) 486-8282
www.seahawkair.com • KATM

Katmai Air & Kulik Lodge • (907) 243-5448
Brown Bear Photo Safaris ($649)
www.katmailand.com • KATM

K-Bay Air • (907) 299-1592
Brown Bear Photo Safaris ($650)
www.kbayair.com • KATM

Bettles Lodge & Bettles Air
www.alaska.net/~bttlodge • GAAR, KOVA

Brooks Range Aviation • (800) 692-5443
www.brooksrange.com • GAAR, KOVA

Coyote Air • (907) 479-5042
www.flycoyote.com • GAAR, KOVA

Wright Air Service • (907) 474-0502
www.wrightairservice.com • GAAR, KOVA

Adventure Outfitters

Alsek/Tatshenshini River Trips

The Alsek River flows from the Yukon into Northern British Columbia where it is joined by the Tatshenshini River. It reaches the Pacific Ocean at Dry Bay. Both rivers are suitable for beginners.

Chilkat Guides • (907) 766 2491
www.RaftAlaska.com • GLBA

James Henry River Journeys • (800) 786-1830
www.riverjourneys.com • GLBA

Mountain Travel-Sobek • (888) 831-7526
www.mtsobek.com • GLBA, WRST, DENA

Canadian River/Nahanni River Adv.
www.nahanni.com • (867) 668-3180 • GLBA

Tatshenshini Expediting • (867) 633-2742
www.tatshenshiniyukon.com • GLBA

The River League • (778) 686-3455
www.explorersleague.ca • GLBA

Wilderness River Outfitter • (800) 252-6581
www.wildernessriver.com • GLBA

Beyond the Alsek

Sundog Expeditions • (208) 877-7104
www.sundogexpeditions.com

River Wrangellers • (907) 822-3967
www.alaskariverwrangellers.com • WRST

Too-Loo-Uk River Guides • (907) 683-1542
www.akrivers.com • DENA

Hunting & Fishing Guides/Lodges

Fishing excursions often consist of trolling for salmon, jigging for halibut, or floating one of the many Wild & Scenic Alaskan Rivers. While fishing, it's likely that you'll be treated to a world class whale (salt water) and wildlife show.

Alaska Glacier Guides • (435) 628-0973
Boat Tours, Hunting & Fishing Expeditions
www.glacierguidesinc.com • GLBA

Deep Blue Charters/Angler's Inn • (866) 510-2800
www.alaskasportfish.net • GLBA

Doc Warner's Alaska Fishing • (877) 451-2701
www.docwarners.com • GLBA

Elfin Cove Sport Fishing Lodge • (800) 422-2824
www.elfincove.com • GLBA

Glacier Bay Sportfishing • (907) 697-3038
www.glacierbaysportfishing.com • GLBA

Inner Harbor Lodge • (888) 828-1972
www.innerharborlodge.com • GLBA

Whisper Marine • (907) 697-2409
www.douglasogilvy.com • GLBA

Wild Alaska Glacier Bay Adventure & Fishing
www.glacier-bay.com • (800) 225-0748 • GLBA

Rustic luxury in the heart of the WSE © Ultima Thule

Ultima Thule Lodge • (907) 854-4500
A remote paradise deep in the WRST Wilderness, accessible only by bush plane…you will discover an outpost designed for adventure, enhanced by comfort, 100 miles from the nearest road
www.ultimathulelodge.com • WRST

Alaska River Expeditions • (907) 424-7238
www.alaskariverexpeditions.com • KEFJ

Alaska River Adventures • (907) 595-2000
www.alaskariveradventures.com • KEFJ

Alaska Wildland Adventures • (907) 783-2928
www.alaskawildland.com • KEFJ

Alaskan Wilderness Outfitting • (907) 424-5552
www.alaskawilderness.com • KEFJ

Deep Creek Fishing Club • (907) 567-7373
www.alaskafishinglodge.com • KEFJ

Great Alaska Fish Camp • (907) 544-2261
www.greatalaska.com • KEFJ

All Alaska Outdoor • (907) 262-6001
www.allalaska.com • Kenai Peninsula

Alaska's River Wild Lodge • (907) 781-2304
www.alaskasriverwildlodge.com • LACL

Cavner And Julian • (907) 781-2231
www.huntingadventure.com • LACL

The Farm Lodge • (907) 781-2211
www.lakeclarkair.com • LACL

Island Lodge • (907) 349-3195
www.islandlodge.com • LACL

Lake Country Lodge • (907) 781-2245
www.lakecountrylodge.com • LACL

Koksetna Wilderness Lodge • (530) 458-7446
www.koksetnawildernesslodge.com • LACL

Rainbow Bay Resort • (907) 850-2234
www.rbrlodge.com • LACL

Rainbow King Lodge • (541) 327-8138
www.rainbowking.com • LACL

Rainbow River Lodge • (503) 429-0511
www.rainbowriverlodge.com • LACL

Redoubt Mtn Lodge • (907) 733-3034
www.redoubtlodge.com • LACL

Silver Salmon Creek Lodge • (303) 526-0833
www.silversalmoncreek.com • LACL

Stony River Lodge • (907) 526-5211
www.stoneyriverlodge.com • LACL

Within The Wild • (907) 274-2710
www.withinthewild.com • LACL

Women's Flyfishing • (907) 274-7113
www.womensflyfishing.net • LACL

Alaska's Fishing Unlimited • (907) 781-2213
www.alaskalodge.com • LACL, KATM

Alaska Fly Anglers • (907) 252-2868
www.alaskaflyanglers.com • LACL, KATM

Alaska's Valhalla Lodge • (907) 243-6096
www.valhallalodge.com • LACL, KATM

Bristol Bay Sportfishing • (907) 571-1325
www.bristol-bay.com • LACL, KATM

Alagnak Lodge • (907) 246-1505
www.alagnaklodge.com • KATM

Frontier River Guides • (907) 929-3244
www.frontierriverguides.com • KATM

Grove's Klutina River & Fish Camp
www.groveklutina.com • (907) 822-5822 • KATM

Kvichak Lodge • (907) 272-0209
www.kvichaklodge.com • KATM

Naknek River Camp • (907) 246-2894
www.naknekrivercamp.com • KATM

Rapids Camp Lodge • (907) 246-8345
www.rapidscamplodge.com • KATM

Tikchik Narrows Lodge • (907) 644-3961
www.tikchiklodge.com • KATM

Tracy Vrem's Blue Mtn Lodge • (907) 688-2419
www.bluemountainlodge.com • KATM

Whale Watch/Boat Tours

In spring gray whales migrate through Alaskan waters on their way to summer feeding grounds in the Bering and Chukchi seas (Arctic waters). Humpback whales are commonly seen between April and October. Orcas reside in these waters year-round. One of the best places to whale watch is Southeast Alaska's Inside Passage. The following whale tours explore this area, but a simple ride on the Alaska Marine Highway is a good alternative.

Whale watch tours are permitted to enter Glacier Bay. Whales are encountered here, but from 0.5 mile away (minimum). Tours also stop at the humpback whale feeding grounds at Point Adolphus where boats can approach to within 100 yards. Rain gear and binoculars are essential whale watching gear.

Adventures Afloat • (800) 323-5628
Inside Passage Cruises ($685/person/day)
www.ptialaska.net/~valkyrie • GLBA

First Out, Last In Adventures • (877) 881-2854
www.firstoutlastin.com • GLBA

Pacific Catalyst II • (800) 378-1708
www.pacificcatalyst.com • GLBA

Sea Wolf Adventures • (907) 957-1438
www.seawolf-adventures.com • GLBA

Southeast Alaskan Adventures • (907) 790-4687
www.southeastalaskanadventures.com • GLBA

Sound Sailing • (206) 605-8363
www.soundsailing.com • GLBA

Photo courtesy of Taz Whale Watching

Taz Whale Watching • (888) 698-2726
Whale Watching ($120), Charter, and Kayak Drop-offs
www.taz.gustavus.com • GLBA

Woodwind Adventures • (907) 697-2282
www.sailglacierbay.com • GLBA

Boat Charters/Taxis
Charters provide whatever you want: fishing, kayak transport, whale/wildlife viewing and photography.

Alaska on the Home Shore • (360) 592-2375
Multi-Day Sea Kayak Tours/Charter Ship
www.homeshore.com • GLBA

Alaska Yacht Charters • (206) 910-7007
www.alaskansong.com • GLBA

Black Rock Charters • (888) 843-1834
www.blackrockcharters.com • GLBA

Eagle Charters • (888) 828-1970
www.eaglecharters.com • GLBA

Gull Cove Alaska • (907) 789-0944
www.gullcove.com • GLBA

Gustavus Marine Charters • (907) 697-2233
www.gustavusmarinecharters.com • GLBA

Hobbit Hole Guesthouse & Charters • GLBA
www.alaska-hobbithole.com • (907) 723-8514

Ripple Cove Charters • (504) 236-7894
www.gustavus.com/ripplecove • GLBA

Taylor Charters • (801) 647-2401
www.taylorchartersfishing.com • GLBA

Photo courtesy of Alaska Mountain Guides & Climbing School

Alaska Fjord Charters • (907) 283-4199
www.alaskafjordcharters.com • KEFJ

Seward Water Taxi • (907) 362-4101
www.sewardwatertaxi.com • KEFJ

Cruise Ships & Tour Vessels

Cruise lines offer land excursions to Denali & Kenai Fjords National Parks (and other destinations).

Carnival Cruise Line • (877)-885-4856
www.carnival.com • GLBA

Holland America Line • (877) 724-5425
www.hollandamerica.com • GLBA

Norwegian Cruise Lines • (866)-234-7350
www.ncl.com • GLBA

Princess Cruises • (800) 774-6237
www.princesstours.com • GLBA

Lindblad Special Expeditions • (800) 387-3348
www.expeditions.com • GLBA

Mountaineering Outfitters

St Elias Alpine Guides • (907) 554-4445
www.steliasguides.com • WRST

American Alpine Institute • (360) 671-1505
www.aai.cc • WRST, DENA

Alaska Mountaineering School • (907) 733-1016
www.climbalaska.org • DENA

Alpine Ascents International • (206) 378-1927
www.alpineascents.com • DENA

Mtn Trip International • (970)369-1153
www.mountaintrip.com • DENA

Rainier Mountaineering • (888) 892-5462
www.rmiguides.com • DENA

Multi-sport Outfitters

Glacier Bay Sea Kayaks • (907) 697-2257
Kayak Rentals, Trip Planning, and Day Trips
www.glacierbayseakayaks.com • GLBA

Packer Expeditions • (907) 983-2544
Kayak, Hike, Rail, and Heli Trips, Rental Available
www.packerexpeditions.com • GLBA

Spirit Walker Expeditions • (800) 529-2537
www.seakayakalaska.com • GLBA

Allen Marine Tours • (888) 747-8101
www.allenmarinetours.com • GLBA

Photo courtesy of Alaska Mtn Guides & Climbing School

Alaska Mtn Guides & Climbing School
Best variety of adventures (day and multi-day)
(800) 766-3396 • GLBA, WRST, DENA
www.alaskamountainguides.com

Exposure Alaska • (907) 761-3761
www.exposurealaska.com • GLBA, WRST, DENA

Sierra Club Outings • (415) 977-5690
www.sierraclub.org/outings • GLBA, WRST, DENA, LACL, GAAR

Jody Young Adventure Travel • (435) 901-1409
www.jodyyoung.com • *Women-centric Tours*

The World Outdoors • (720) 289-0460
www.theworldoutdoors.com • GLBA, DENA, KEFJ

Off The Beaten Path • (406) 586-1311
www.offthebeatenpath.com • GLBA, KEFJ

Natural Habitat Adventures • (303) 449-3711
www.nathab.com • GLBA, KEFJ, KATM

Photo courtesy of Internat'l Wilderness Leadership School

International Wilderness Leadership School
Provides high-quality guide training, outdoor leadership training, wilderness education, and technical instruction
www.iwls.com • (907) 799-3366 • GLBA, WRST

Copper Oar • (800) 523-4453
Raft, Kayak, Hike, and Wildlife Trips
www.copperoar.com • WRST

Kennicott Wilderness Guides • (907) 554-4444
www.kennicottguides.com • WRST

Pangaea Adventures • (530) 320-8573
www.pangaeaadventures.com • WRST

Sun Valley Trekking • (208) 788-1966
www.svtrek.com • WRST

Trek Alaska • (907) 350-3710
www.trekalaska.com • WRST

Wrangell Outfitters • (907) 479-5343
www.wrangelloutfitters.com • WRST

NOLS • (907) 745-4047
www.nols.edu • WRST, DENA

Get Up And Go! Tours • (907) 245-0795
www.getupandgotours.com • WRST, DENA, KEFJ

Alaska Alpine Adventures • (907) 301-9997
Hike/Backpack, Kayak, and Ski Adventure Vacations
www.alaskaalpineadventures.com •
WRST, DENA, KEFJ, LACL, KATM, GAAR

Alaska Outdoors • (907) 357-4020
www.travelalaskaoutdoors.com • WRST, DENA, KEFJ

Adventures Cross Country • (415) 332-5075
www.adventurescrosscountry.com • DENA

Backcountry Safaris • (907) 529-1935
www.backcountrysafaris.com • DENA, KEFJ

Lazer's Guide Service • (907) 250-1120
www.lazertours.com • DENA, KEFJ

Trek America • (800) 345-8777
www.trekamerica.com • DENA, KEFJ

Nichols Expeditions • (435) 259-3999
www.nicholsexpeditions.com • DENA, KEFJ

Premier Alaska Tours • (907) 279-0001
www.premieralaskatours.com • DENA, KEFJ

Alaska Wilderness Guides • (907) 345-4470
Hiking, Rafting, Skiing, and Snowmobiling
www.akwild.com • DENA, KATM

Adventure 60 North • (907) 224-2600
www.adventure60.com • KEFJ

Kayak Adventure Worldwide • (907) 224-3960
www.kayakak.com • KEFJ

Liquid Adventures • (888) 325-2925
www.liquid-adventures.com • KEFJ

Miller's Landing • (907) 224-5739
www.millerslandingak.com • KEFJ

Sunny Cove Sea Kayaking • (907) 224-8810
www.sunnycove.com • KEFJ

Exit Glacier Guides • (907) 224-5081
www.exitglacierguides.com • KEFJ

AK Saltwater Lodge and Tours • (907) 224-5271
www.alaskasaltwaterlodge.com • KEFJ

Allen's Alaska Adventure • (907) 224-4785
www.allensalaskaadventures.com • KEFJ

Austin-Lehman Adventures • (406) 655-4591
www.austinlehman.com • KEFJ

Backroads • (800) 462-2848
www.backroads.com • KEFJ

Arctic Wild • (907) 479-820
Raft, Canoe, and Backpack Trips
www.arcticwild.com • KATM, GAAR

Country Walkers • (800) 464-9255
www.countrywalkers.com • KEFJ

Porter's Wild Alaska • (253) 906-5145
www.porterswildalaska.com • LACL

Freshwater Adventures • (907) 842-5060
www.freshwateradventure.com • LACL

Alaska Wildtrek Company • (907) 235-6463
www.alaskawildtrek.com • LACL, GAAR, KOVA

Lifetime Adventures • (907) 746-4644
www.lifetimeadventures.net • KATM

ABEC's Alaska Adventure • (907) 457-6689
www.abecalaska.com • GAAR

Wilderness Alaska • (907) 345-3567
www.wildernessalaska.com • GAAR

Iniakuk Lake Wilderness Lodge
www.gofarnorth.com • (907) 474-2096 • GAAR

Box Arctic Treks • (907) 455-6522
www.arctictreksadventures.com • GAAR, KOVA

Kobuk River Lodge • (907) 445-2166
www.kobukriverlodge.com • KOVA

Bear Viewing Outfitters
Most fishing, multi-sport, and air taxis outfitters near LACL & KATM offer bear viewing tours.

AK Adventures • (907) 235-1805
www.goseebears.com • KATM

Alaska Bear Quest • (907) 235-8273
www.alaskabearquest.com • KATM

Coastal Outfitters • (907) 286-2290
www.xyz.net/~bear • KATM

Grizzly Skins of Alaska • (907) 376-2234
www.grizzlyskinsofalaska.com • KATM

Hallo Bay Wilderness Camps • (907) 235-2237
www.hallobay.com • KATM

Homer Flyout Adventures • (907) 235-8591
www.homerflyoutadventures.com • KATM

Toft Photo Safaris & Gallery • (760) 788-6003
www.toftphoto.com • KATM

Out In Alaska • (907) 374-9958
www.outinalaska.com • GLBA, WRST, DENA, KEFJ

Rental Equipment
Alaska Mtneering & Hiking • (907) 272-1811
2633 Spenard Rd; Anchorage, AK 99503
www.alaskamountaineering.com

AMS Mountain Shop • (907) 733-1016
F Street; Talkeetna, AK 99676
www.climbalaska.org/shop.html

REI • (907)272-4565 • www.rei.com
1200 W Northern Lights; Anchorage, AK 99503

Dining & Lodging
Most road-accessible restaurants, lodging facilities, and grocery stores are in Seward, Anchorage, and Fairbanks. Lodging and dining possibilities are also abundant along the southeastern coast in port cities like Ketchikan, Juneau, Skagway, and Gustavus.

There are more than 200 public-use cabins ($25–75/night) scattered throughout the Alaskan wilderness. Nearly all of them are only accessible by trail, boat, or bush plane, and must be reserved in advance. For information and reservations contact the National Recreation Reservation Service at (877) 444-6777 or www.recreation.gov.

Dining
Tracy's King Crab Shack • (907) 723-1811
350 S Franklin St; Juneau, AK 99801
www.kingcrabshack.com

Southeast Waffle Co • (907) 789-2030
11806 Glacier Hwy; Juneau, AK 99801

Paradise Café • (907) 586-2253
245 Marine Way; Juneau, AK 99801
www.paradisecafeyeehaw.com

Marx Bros. Café • (907) 278-2133
627 W 3rd Ave; Anchorage, AK 99501
www.marxcafe.com

Moose's Tooth Pub & Pizzeria
3300 Old Seward Hwy; Anchorage, AK 99503
www.moosestooth.net • (907) 258-2537

Glacier Brewhouse • (907) 274-2739
737 W 5th Ave, #110; Anchorage, AK 99501
www.glacierbrewhouse.com

Simon & Seafort's Saloon & Grill
420 L St; Anchorage, AK 99501
www.simonandseaforts.com • (907) 274-3502

Falafel King • (907) 258-4328
930 Gambell St; Anchorage, AK 99501

Sacks Cafe and Restaurant
328 G St; Anchorage, AK 99501
www.sackscafe.com • (907) 274-4022

Smoke Shack • (907) 224-7427
411 Port Ave; Seward, AK 99664

Salmon Bake • (907) 224-2204
Exit Glacier Rd; Seward, AK 99664
www.sewardalaskacabins.com

Le Barn Appétit • (907) 224-8706
11786 Old Exit Glacier Rd; Seward, AK 99664
www.lebarnappetit.net

Lemon Grass Thai Cuisine • (907) 456-2200
388 Old Chena Pump Rd, # K; Fairbanks, AK 99709
www.lemongrassalaska.com

Lavelle's Bistro • (907) 450-0555
575 1st Ave; Fairbanks, AK 99701
www.lavellesbistro.com

Aloha BBQ Grill • (907) 479-7770
402 5th Ave; Fairbanks, AK 99701

Grocery Stores

Walmart Supercenter • (907) 789-5000
6525 Glacier Hwy; Juneau, AK 99801

Breeze-In Grocery • (907) 586-1065
3370 Douglas Hwy; Juneau, AK 99801

New Sagaya City Market • (907) 274-6173
900 W 13th Ave; Anchorage, Alaska 99501
www.newsagaya.com

Pak N Save • (907) 297-0221
3101 Penland Pky; Anchorage, AK 99508

Fred Meyer • (907) 267-6700
2000 W Dimond Blvd; Anchorage, AK 99515

Costco • (907) 269-9500
4125 Debarr Rd; Anchorage, AK 99508

Walmart Supercenter • (907) 344-5300
8900 Old Seward Hwy; Anchorage, AK 99515

Sam's Club • (907) 276-2996
3651 Penland Pkwy; Anchorage, AK 99508

Pudgy's Meat & Groceries • (907) 235-3997
Mile 2.4 East End Rd; Homer, AK 99603

Safeway • (907) 224-6900
1907 Seward Hwy; Seward, AK 99664

Safeway • (907) 456-8501
30 College Rd; Fairbanks, AK 99701

Fred Meyer • (907) 474-1400
3755 Airport Way; Fairbanks, AK 99709

Sam's Club • (907) 451-4800
48 College Rd; Fairbanks, AK 99701

Walmart Supercenter • (907) 451-9900
537 Johansen Expy; Fairbanks, AK 99701

Lodging

Aimee's Guest House • (907) 697-2330
www.gustavus.com/guesthouse • GLBA

Tanaku Lodge • (907) 239-2205
www.Tanaku.com • GLBA

The Cove Lodge • (907) 239-2221
www.CoveLodge.com • GLBA

Annie Mae Lodge • (800) 478-2346
www.anniemae.com • GLBA

Beartrack Inn • (888) 697-2284
www.beartrackinn.com • GLBA

Blue Heron B&B • (907) 697-2337
www.blueheronbnb.net • GLBA

Eagle's Nest Lodge • (801) 376-6513
www.glacierbayfishing.com • GLBA

Alsek River Lodge • (907) 784-3451
www.alsekriverlodge.com • GLBA

Glacier Bay Country Inn • (800) 628-0912
www.glacierbayalaska.com • GLBA

Glacier Bay Lodge • (888) 229-8687
www.visitglacierbay.com • GLBA

Good River B&B • (907) 697-2241
www.goodriver.com • GLBA

Gustavus Inn • (907) 697-2254
www.gustavusinn.com • GLBA

Johnny's East River Lodge • (907) 789-2896
www.johnnyseastriverlodge.com • GLBA

Northern Lights Haven • (360) 864-6755
www.nlhlodge.com • GLBA

Yakutat Lodge • (800) 925-8828
www.yakutatlodge.com • GLBA

Kennicott Glacier Lodge • (907) 258-2350
www.kennicottlodge.com • WRST

McCarthy Lodge • (907) 554-4402
www.mccarthylodge.com • WRST

Tonsina River Lodge • (907) 822-3000
www.tonsinariverlodge.com • WRST

Gilpatrick's Hotel • (907) 823-2244
www.hotelchitina.com • WRST

Wellwood Center B&B • (907) 822-3418
www.wellwoodcenter.com • WRST

P J's Golden Spruce Cabins • (907) 822-5556
www.goldensprucecabins.com • WRST

Glacier View Campground • (907) 554-4490
www.glacierviewcampground.com • WRST

Chitina Guest Cabins • (907) 823-2266
www.pawandfeathers.com • WRST

Kennicott River Lodge & Hostel • (907) 554-4441
www.kennicottriverlodge.com • WRST

Taral Enterprises • (907) 823-2260
www.chitinanative.com • WRST

Kenny Lake Merc & RV Park • (907) 822-3313
www.kennylake.com • WRST

Log Cabin Wilderness Lodge • (907) 883-3124
www.logcabinwildernesslodge.com • WRST

Chistochina B&B • (907) 822-3989
www.chistochinabedandbreakfast.com • WRST

Tanada Lake Lodge • (970) 260-7770
www.tanadalakelodge.com • WRST

Camp Denali • (907) 683-2290
www.campdenali.com • DENA

Hotel Seward • (907) 224-8001
www.hotelsewardalaska.com • KEFJ

Murphy's Alaskan Inn • (907) 224-8090
www.murphysmotel.com • KEFJ

Van Gilder Hotel • (907) 224-3079
www.vangilderhotel.com • KEFJ

Harborview Inn • (907) 224-3217
www.sewardhotel.com • KEFJ

Angels Rest on Resurrection Bay • (907) 224-7378
www.angelsrest.com • KEFJ

Beach House • (907) 362-2727
www.beachhousealaska.com • KEFJ

Breeze Inn Motel • (907) 224-5238
www.breezeinn.com • KEFJ

A Cottage on the Bay • (888) 334-8237
www.onthebayak.com • KEFJ

Moby Dick Hostel & Lodging • (907) 224-7072
www.mobydickhostel.com • KEFJ

Marina Motel • (907) 224-5518
www.sewardmotel.com • KEFJ

Seward Military Resort • (907) 224-2659
www.sewardresort.com • KEFJ

Bay Vista B&B • (907) 224-5880
www.bayvista.biz • KEFJ

Brass Lantern B&B • (907) 224-3419
www.brasslanternbandb.com • KEFJ

Sea Treasure's Inn • (907) 224-7667
www.innalaska.com • KEFJ

Victorian Serenity By the Sea • (907) 224-3635
www.victorianserenity.com • KEFJ

Trailhead Lodging • (907) 224-5000
www.lostlaketrailheadlodge.com • KEFJ

Melody Inn • (907) 224-5351
www.melodyinnbandb.com • KEFJ

Adams Street B&B • (907) 224-8879
www.adamsstreetseward.com • KEFJ

Marathon Terrace Lodging • (907) 224-7639
www.marathonterrace.com • KEFJ

Alaska Creekside Cabins • (907) 224-1996
www.welovealaska.com • KEFJ

Linda Lou's • (907) 224-5502
www.lindalousbandb.4t.com • KEFJ

Steller B&B • (907) 224-7294
www.stellerbandb.com • KEFJ

Orca Island Cabins • (907) 491-1988
www.orcaislandcabins.com • KEFJ

Camelot Cottages • (907) 224-3039
www.camelotcottages.com • KEFJ

Kim's Forest B&B • (907) 224-7632
www.sewardalaskabnb.com • KEFJ

Stoney Creek Inn B&B • (907) 224-3940
www.stoneycreekinn.net • KEFJ

Sourdough Sunrise B&B • (907) 224-3600
www.sourdoughsunrise.com • KEFJ

Sunshine House B&B • (907) 224-5114
www.asunshinehouse.net • KEFJ

Box Canyon Cabins • (907) 224-5046
www.boxcanyoncabin.com • KEFJ

Moose Creek Cabins • (907) 299-4079
www.moosecreekcabins3.com - KEFJ

Arctic Paradise B&B • (907) 224-5898
www.arcticparadise.com • KEFJ

Crane's Rest B&B • (907) 226-3276
www.cranesrest.com • KEFJ

Alaska Homestead Lodge • (907) 398-1960
www.alaskawildlife.com • LACL

Bear Mountain Lodge • (907) 776-8613
www.akbearmountainlodge.com • KATM

Alaska Adventures Lodge • (877) 801-2289
www.alaska-adventures.net • KATM

Alaska's Wilderness Lodge • (800) 835-8032
www.alaskaswildernesslodge.com • Haines

Crystal Creek Lodge • (907) 246-3153
www.crystalcreeklodge.com • LACL, KATM

Fox Bay Lodge • (907) 246-6234
www.foxbaylodge.com • LACL, KATM

Mission Creek Lodge • (907) 842-2250
www.missionlodge.com • KATM

Kiana Lodge • (907) 475-2149
www.alaskasheefishing.com • GAAR

Attractions

Totem Bight Park • (907) 247-8574
9883 N Tongass Hwy; Ketchikan, AK 99901

Panhandle Motorcycle Adventures
404 Anderson Dr; Ketchikan, AK 99901
www.panhandlemoto.com • (907) 247-2031

Alaska Canopy Adventures
116 Wood Road; Ketchikan, AK 99901
www.alaskarainforest.com • (907) 225-5503

Misty Fjords Nat'l Mon. • (907) 225-2148
3031 Tongass Ave; Ketchikan, AK 99901

Great Alaskan Lumber Jack Show
420 Spruce Mill Way; Ketchikan, AK 99901
www.lumberjackshows.com • (907) 225-9050

Alaska Raptor Center • (907) 747-8662
1000 Raptor Way; Sitka, AK 99835
www.alaskaraptor.org

Alaska State Museum • (907) 465-2901
395 Whittier St; Juneau, AK 99801
www.museums.state.ak.us

Alaskan Brewing Co. • (907) 780-5866
5429 Shaune Dr; Juneau, Alaska 99801
www.alaskanbeer.com

Alaska Canopy Adventures • (907) 523-2920
406 S Franklin St, # 210; Juneau, AK 99801
www.alaskacanopy.com

Mendenhall Glacier • Juneau, AK

Mt Roberts Tramway • (907) 463-3412
490 S Franklin St; Juneau, AK 99801
www.goldbelttours.com

Glacier Gardens Rainforest • (907) 790-3377
7600 Glacier Hwy; Juneau, AK 99801
www.glaciergardens.com

Sockeye Cycle • (907) 766-2869
Portage Dr; Haines, AK 99827
www.cyclealaska.com

Skagway Museum • (907) 983-2420
700 Spring St; Skagway, AK 99840
www.skagway.org

Alaska Icefield Expeditions • (907) 983-2299
Studio B, 901 Terminal Way; Skagway, AK 99840
www.akdogtour.com

Klondike Gold Rush Nat'l Hist. Park
PO Box 517; Skagway, AK 99840
www.nps.gov/klgo • (907) 983-9200

Icy Strait Point • (907) 945-3141
Home of the "World's Largest Zip Line Ride"
108 Cannery Rd; Hoonah, AK 99829
www.icystraitpoint.com

Anchorage Yoga • (907) 562-9642
701 W 36th Ave; Anchorage, AK 99503
www.anchorageyoga.com

Fourth Avenue Trolley Tours • (907) 257-5688
630 W 4th Ave, Anchorage, AK 99501

Imaginarium • (907) 929-9201
625 C St; Anchorage, AK 99501
www.anchoragemuseum.org

Horse Trekkin Alaska • (907) 868-3728
4545 O'Malley Rd; Anchorage, AK 99507
www.horsetrekkinalaska.com

Anchorage Museum • (907) 343-4326
625 C St; Anchorage, AK 99501
www.anchoragemuseum.org

Alaska Native Heritage Center
8800 Heritage Center Dr; Anchorage, AK 99504
www.alaskanative.net • (907) 330-8000

Salmon Berry Tours • (907) 278-3572
527 W 3rd Ave; Anchorage, AK 99501
www.salmonberrytours.com

Midnight Sun Brewing Co. • (907) 344-1179
8111 Dimond Hook Dr; Anchorage, AK 99507
www.midnightsunbrewing.com

Chugach State Park • (907) 345-5014
Anchorage, AK

Denali State Park • (907) 745-3975
Matanuska-Susitna, AK 99683
www.dnr.alaska.gov

Alaska SeaLife Center • (907) 224-6300
www.alaskasealife.org • KEFJ

Bardy's Trail Rides • (907) 224-7863
Lot 16 Old Nash Rd; Seward, AK 99664
www.sewardhorses.com

Seward Museum • (907) 224-3902
336 3rd Avenue, Seward, AK 99664

Saltwater Safari Company • (907) 224-5232
www.saltwatersafari.com • KEFJ

Liberty Theatre • (907) 224-5418
305 Adams St; Seward, AK 99664

Ididaride Sled Dog Tours • (907) 224-8607
www.ididaride.com • KEFJ

Trails End Horse Adventures • (907) 235-6393
53435 E End Rd; Homer, AK 99603

Alaska Islands & Ocean Visitor Center
95 Sterling Hwy; Homer, AK 99603
www.islandsandocean.org • (907) 235-6961

Center for Alaskan Coastal Studies
708 Smoky Bay Way; Homer, AK 99603
www.akcoastalstudies.org • (907) 235-6667

Pratt Museum • (907) 235-8635
3779 Bartlett St; Homer, AK 99603
www.prattmuseum.org

Kodiak Island Brewing Co.
338 Shelikof St; Kodiak, AK 99615
www.kodiakbrewery.com • (907) 486-2537

Fountainhead Antique Auto Msm
212 Wedgewood Dr; Fairbanks, AK 99701
www.fountainheadmuseum.com • (907) 450-2100

Running Reindeer Ranch • (907) 455-4998
Goldstream & Murphy Dome Rd; Fairbanks, AK 99709
www.runningreindeer.com

Morris Thompson Cultural & Visitors Center
101 Dunkel St; Fairbanks, AK 99701
www.morristhompsoncenter.org • (907) 459-3700

Large Animal Research Station
Yankovich Rd; North Pole, AK 99705
www.uaf.edu • (907) 474-5724

Northern Lights (Aurora Borealis)
The northern lights are best from Fairbanks in winter, but September and March are good times to visit thanks to clear skies, generally mild weather, and frequent displays. The image above is from Denali National Park in October 2011.

Virgin Islands • Pages 644–653

Haleakalá • Pages 654–663

© Mila Zinkova

Hawai'i Volcanoes • Pages 664–679

American Samoa • Pages 680–685

REMOTE ISLANDS

Turquoise water rolls onto the beach at Trunk Bay as visitors enjoy another day in paradise

1300 Cruz Bay Creek
St. John, VI 00830
Phone: (340) 776-6201 ext. 238
Website: www.nps.gov/viis

Established: August 2, 1956
Size: 14,689 Acres
Annual Visitors: 500,000
Peak Season: December–April

Activities: Snorkeling, SCUBA, Bird Watching, Fishing, Sailing, Paddling, Windsurfing, and Hiking

Campgrounds: Cinnamon Bay
Backcountry Camping: Prohibited
Bare Campsite: $32/night
Tent Campsite: $93/night*
Cottages: $126–163/night*
Lodging: Caneel Bay Resort
Rates: $600+/night

Entrance Fee: None
Overnight Anchoring: $15/night
Trunk Bay User Fee: $4 (adults), Children (16 & under) are free

*Fees are discounted by approximately 30% during the off-season

Virgin Islands - U.S. Virgin Islands

Virgin Islands National Park is a tropical paradise of sandy white beaches and lush tropical forests wrapped in brilliant turquoise waters. Whether you're perched above a secluded bay or watching gentle waves roll onto a pristine beach, the views here are fit for a postcard. Stray away from the leisurely comforts of the bays and beaches, and you can learn of the area's not-so-perfect past. A past at odds with such an idyllic environment.

It's believed that humans have inhabited the Virgin Islands since 1,000 BC. Like many primitive people they progressed from a nomadic village lifestyle to a complex religious culture with ceremonial sites for worshipping the spirits of the cassava (their main crop) and the sea. Europeans arrived in 1493, when **Christopher Columbus**, on his second voyage to the West Indies, spotted more than 100 emerald isles. He named them after Saint Ursula's legendary 11,000 virgins. Europeans began to colonize the islands, creating a melting pot of cultures where pre-Columbians perished from disease and harsh labor conditions.

Spain, France, Holland, England, Denmark, and the United States have all controlled various Virgin Islands at different times. St. John, the centerpiece of Virgin Islands National Park, was owned by Denmark prior to the United States. At this time, **sugarcane**, which thrived in the subtropical climate, was the primary cash crop, and more than 90 percent of the island's native vegetation was stripped away in favor of farming. For nearly two centuries Danes produced huge quantities of sugar, rum, and molasses, which were shipped back to Europe. Such impressive production was a boon to the plantation owners, but the burden was placed squarely on the shoulders of enslaved Africans and their ancestors. More than 80 plantations were constructed on St. John alone. Decades of growth left an island where slaves outnumbered the plantation owners by a rate of five to one. In 1848, a slave revolt led by General Buddhoe resulted in the release of Danish slaves in Frederikstad, St. Croix. Emancipation, low sugar prices, and nutrient-depleted soil marked the end of the "sugar is king" era of the Virgin Islands.

In 1917, construction of the Panama Canal and rise of German naval strength spurred the United States to purchase St. Croix, St. Thomas, St. John, and about 50 smaller islands from Denmark for $25 million. The islands served a role in **military strategy**, but they gained notoriety as a **vacation destination**. St. John's heavenly beaches served as sun-bathing ground for millions of tourists. The sight of Little Maho Bay was enough to make **Ethel McCully** jump out of her boat and swim to shore. Once the eccentric American arrived, she never left; throwing caution to the wind she lived her life in a setting most people only dream about. With six donkeys and two laborers she built a home, and then sat down to pen a book about the experience.

Ethel wasn't the only person smitten by the island's allure. Developers began purchasing land and building extravagant resorts and hotels. **Laurance Rockefeller**, philanthropist, conservationist and son of **John D. Rockefeller, Jr.**, also took notice of the island's unique beauty and its rapid development. In 1956, he purchased 5,000 acres of land, half of St. John Island, for $1.75 million. He ended up donating this tract of land to the United States for use as a national park. Today, Rockefeller's personal estate in Caneel Bay serves as the only resort in the park.

Tourism is currently king, but ruins of plantations, factories, and mills serve as reminders of the islands' past. You can learn all about the history and process of sugar production at Catherineberg and Annaberg Sugar Mill Ruins. Still, the park's main attractions are its warm and crystal clear water, ideal subtropical climate, and powdery beaches. It's a setting that many of the park's 500,000 annual visitors can only dream about, but maybe you'll be the next person so enthralled with its beauty that you refuse to leave paradise, much like Ethel McCully.

When to Go

The park is open all year, but most travelers visit between December and mid-April. Cruz Bay Visitor Center is open daily from 8am to 4:30pm. Trunk Bay's bathhouse, snack bar, and souvenir shop are open until 4pm. Life guards are on duty daily at Trunk Bay Beach. Cinnamon Bay Campground closes to unregistered guests at 10pm.

Directions & Transportation

The Virgin Islands must be reached by plane or boat, due to their remote location in the Caribbean. The park consists of half of the Island of St. John plus a few other isolated smaller islands. Its visitor center is located near the dock at Cruz Bay on St. John.

Cyril E. King Airport (STT) in Charlotte Amalie, St. Thomas serves as the gateway to the U.S. Virgin Islands. From here you can reach Cruz Bay by ferry from two different docks. To reach the downtown Charlotte Amalie ferry dock you will need to take a short taxi ride ($6 for one person, $5 each for more than one traveler). The ferry takes about 40 minutes and costs $6 each way. Ferry service from Charlotte Amalie to Cruz Bay departs three times per day. You can also take a taxi or bus from Charlotte Amalie to Red Hook. A taxi ride ($13 for one person, $9 each if there is more than one traveler) provides a decent tour of St. Thomas Island. Ferries depart Red Hook for Cruz Bay every hour between 6am and midnight. The ferry takes about 20 minutes and costs $3 each way. Call Varlack Ventures (340.776.6412 or www.varlack-ventures.com) for additional information on ferry services. Visitors can also find private water-taxis and car ferries. Car rental is available near the dock at Cruz Bay ($75–100/day, $450–600/week). Remember to drive on the left-hand side of the road. Private taxi service can be arranged by calling Direct Taxi Service (340.777.7112) or Christopher Taxi Service (340.775.9257).

Public transportation is available on St. John. VITRAN buses travel between Cruz Bay and Saltpond Bay. Buses leave the dock at 20 minutes after the hour from 6am until 7:55pm daily.

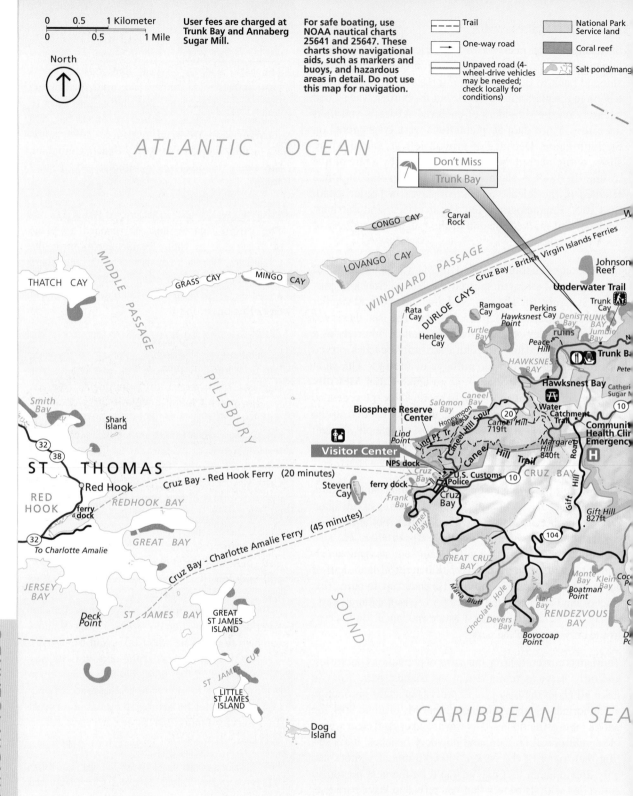

User fees are charged at Trunk Bay and Annaberg Sugar Mill.

0   0.5   1 Kilometer
0   0.5   1 Mile

North

For safe boating, use NOAA nautical charts 25641 and 25647. These charts show navigational aids, such as markers and buoys, and hazardous areas in detail. Do not use this map for navigation.

- - - - Trail
→ One-way road
═══ Unpaved road (4-wheel-drive vehicles may be needed; check locally for conditions)

National Park Service land
Coral reef
Salt pond/mang

Don't Miss
Trunk Bay

ATLANTIC OCEAN

CONGO CAY
Carval Rock
LOVANGO CAY
WINDWARD PASSAGE
Cruz Bay - British Virgin Islands Ferries
Johnson Reef
Underwater Trail
Trunk Cay
DURLOE CAYS
Ramgoat Cay
Hawksnest Point
Perkins Cay
Denis TRUNK BAY
ruins
Jumbie Bay
Rata Cay
Henley Cay
Turtle Bay
Peace Hill
Trunk Ba
Pete
HAWKSNEST BAY
Caneel Bay
Salomon Bay
Honeymoon Beach
Hawksnest Bay
Water Catchment Trail
Catheri Sugar M
GRASS CAY   MINGO CAY
THATCH CAY

MIDDLE PASSAGE

PILLSBURY

Smith Bay
Shark Island
32
38
ST THOMAS
Red Hook
RED HOOK
ferry dock
32
To Charlotte Amalie
GREAT BAY
REDHOOK BAY
Cruz Bay - Red Hook Ferry (20 minutes)
Cruz Bay - Charlotte Amalie Ferry (45 minutes)
JERSEY BAY
Deck Point
ST JAMES BAY
GREAT ST JAMES ISLAND
ST JAMES CU
LITTLE ST JAMES ISLAND
Dog Island

Biosphere Reserve Center
Lind Point
Lind Pt Tr
Visitor Center
NPS dock
Steven Cay
ferry dock
Frank Bay
Cruz Bay
U.S. Customs
Police
Caneel Hill Spur
Caneel Hill 719ft
Caneel Hill Trail
20
Margaret Hill 840ft
10
Communit Health Clin Emergency
H
10
CRUZ BAY
Turner Bay
GREAT CRUZ BAY
104
Gift Hill Road
Gift Hill 827ft
Maria Bluff
Chocolate Hole
Devers Bay
Hart Bay
Monte Bay Klein
Boatman Point
RENDEZVOUS BAY
Bovocoap Point
Coc Pe
D Po

CARIBBEAN SEA

SOUND

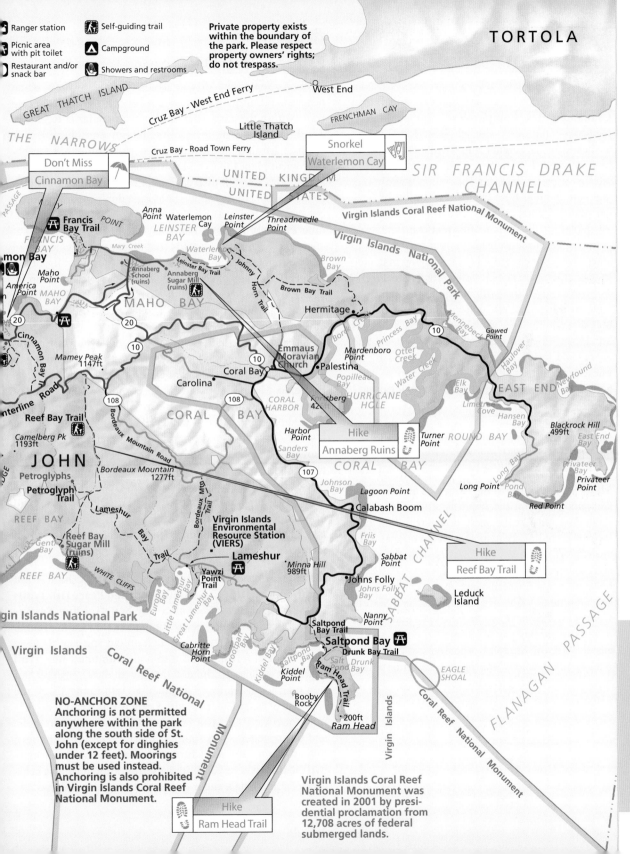

TORTOLA

Ranger station
Picnic area with pit toilet
Restaurant and/or snack bar
Self-guiding trail
Campground
Showers and restrooms

Private property exists within the boundary of the park. Please respect property owners' rights; do not trespass.

GREAT THATCH ISLAND

West End

Cruz Bay - West End Ferry

FRENCHMAN CAY

Little Thatch Island

Cruz Bay - Road Town Ferry

THE NARROWS

UNITED KINGDOM
UNITED STATES

Snorkel
Waterlemon Cay

SIR FRANCIS DRAKE CHANNEL

Don't Miss
Cinnamon Bay

PASSAGE

FRANCIS POINT

Francis Bay Trail

Anna Point

Waterlemon Cay

Leinster Point

Threadneedle Point

Virgin Islands Coral Reef National Monument

Virgin Islands National Park

LEINSTER BAY

Waterlemon Bay

mon Bay

Mary Creek

Maho Point

America Point

MAHO BAY

Annaberg School (ruins)

Leinster Bay Trail

Johnny

Horn Trail

Brown Bay

Brown Bay Trail

Annaberg Sugar Mill (ruins)

Hermitage

Gowed Point

20

20

MAHO BAY

10

Mamey Peak 1147ft

10

Emmaus Moravian Church

Coral Bay

Mardenboro Point

Palestina

Popilleau Bay

Princess Bay

Otter Creek

Water Creek

Mennebeck Bay

Haulover Bay

10

EAST END

Carolina

108

108

Saltsberg 425

HURRICANE HOLE

Elk Bay

Limet Cove

Hansen Bay

Newfound Bay

Reef Bay Trail

Camelberg Pk 1193ft

CORAL BAY

CORAL HARBOR

Harbor Point

Sanders Bay

Hike
Annaberg Ruins

Turner Point

ROUND BAY

CORAL BAY

Long Point

Long Bay

Pond Bay

Blackrock Hill 499ft

East End Bay

Privateer Point

JOHN

Petroglyphs

Petroglyph Trail

Bordeaux Mountain Road

Bordeaux Mountain 1277ft

107

Johnson Bay

Lagoon Point

Calabash Boom

Red Point

REEF BAY

Lameshur Bay

Bordeaux Mtn. Trail

Virgin Islands Environmental Resource Station (VIERS)

Lameshur

Friis Bay

Sabbat Point

Hike
Reef Bay Trail

Reef Bay Sugar Mill (ruins)

REEF BAY

Genti Bay

Trail

Yawzi Point Trail

Minna Hill 989ft

Johns Folly

Johns Folly Bay

Leduck Island

WHITE CLIFFS

Europa Bay

Little Lameshur Bay

Great Lameshur Bay

Nanny Point

SABBAT CHANNEL

in Islands National Park

Virgin Islands

Coral Reef National

Cabritte Horn Point

Grootpan Bay

Saltpond Bay

Kiddel Bay

Kiddel Point

Saltpond Bay Trail

Saltpond Bay

Drunk Bay Trail

Salt Pond Bay

Drunk Bay

EAGLE SHOAL

Coral Reef National Monument

FLANAGAN PASSAGE

NO-ANCHOR ZONE
Anchoring is not permitted anywhere within the park along the south side of St. John (except for dinghies under 12 feet). Moorings must be used instead. Anchoring is also prohibited in Virgin Islands Coral Reef National Monument.

Ram Head Trail

Booby Rock

200ft Ram Head

Virgin Islands

Monument

Hike
Ram Head Trail

Virgin Islands Coral Reef National Monument was created in 2001 by presidential proclamation from 12,708 acres of federal submerged lands.

VIRGIN ISLANDS

 # Camping

As far as National Park campgrounds are concerned they don't get any more tropical than **Cinnamon Bay Campground**. Cinnamon Bay, located on the north side of Saint John, is just as beautiful as neighboring Trunk Bay, but far less crowded. It's the park's only campground as well as a great place for snorkeling, swimming, and sun-bathing. Bare campsites, similar to typical national park camping accommodations, are available, but they also offer platform tents and cottages. Guests must bring (or rent from the camp store) everything required (tent, sleeping mat, etc.) to stay at the bare sites. Platform tents are 10'-by-14' canvas structures with mosquito netting. Cots, lantern, propane stove, water container, cooking utensils, and bedding are also provided. Cottages are 15'-by-15' with electricity, 4 twin beds, and an outside terrace. Bathrooms are shared by all guests. A restaurant, beach shop, watersports activity center, and general store are on location.

Cinnamon Bay Campground • (340) 776-6330
Cruz Bay 00831, U.S. Virgin Islands • www.cinnamonbay.com
Rates: Bare Sites: $32/night ($10/night for additional guests)
Platform Tents: $93/night ($20/night for additional guests)*
Cottages: $126–163/night ($20/night for additional guests)*

Maho Bay Campground is located northeast of Cinnamon Bay on the opposite side of America Point just outside the park boundary. Tent cottages and studios are available. Tent cottages have electricity, propane stove, and twin beds, while studios have a full kitchen and private bath. Some tents are a significant distance from the beach and/or restaurant. Maho Bay's sister resort, **Estate Concordia Preserve**, offers Eco-Tents and studios near Saltpond Bay just off Route 107 on the southeastern side of St. John. Eco-Tents and Studios feature full kitchens and private bathrooms that were designed using green techniques.

Maho Bay Campground • (800) 392-9004
Cruz Bay 00830, U.S. Virgin Islands • www.maho.org
Rates: Maho Tents: $140/night ($15/additional guest)*
Harmony Studios: $225–250/night ($25/additional guest)*
Eco-Tents: $110–190/night ($25/additional guest)*
Eco-Studios: $120–255/night ($25/additional guest)*

*Discounted about 30% between May and mid-December
Reservations are available at both campgrounds

 # Hiking

Visitors come to the Virgin Islands to enjoy powdery white beaches and turquoise waters, but you'll also find 20 hiking trails within the park. One of the most popular is **Reef Bay Trail**, located 4.9 miles east of Cruz Bay on Route 10. This steep, 2.2-mile (one-way) trail descends through a variety of tropical plant life to a beautiful bay (pack your swimsuit and snorkel). You'll also encounter ruins of four sugar mill estates. Wear hiking boots (or at least don't wear flip-flops), because the trail can be very slippery. Don't miss the 0.3-mile **Petroglyph Trail** that spurs off of Reef Bay Trail at about the 1.5 mile mark. This trail displays rock carvings of pre-Columbian Taino people. The park periodically offers **ranger-led hikes of Reef Bay Trail**. If interested, stop by Cruz Bay Visitor Center (340.776.6201, ext. 238) to view a current schedule of activities. The hike costs $23/person to cover transportation expenses (boat and taxi rides). Located on the south shore of St. John is **Bordeaux Mountain Trail**. It's a 1.2-mile (one-way) path leading to the highest point in the park, Bordeaux Mountain (1,300 ft). The trail connects Bordeaux Mountain Road with Lameshur Bay. Southeast of Lameshur Bay off Route 107 near Saltpond Bay you'll find three short trails. **Ram Head Trail** is the best of the bunch. It's a 1.0-mile (one-way) walk to a rock outcropping 200-ft above the Caribbean. The views are awe-inspiring and the blue cobble beach is a great spot for snorkeling. However, the seafloor is rocky, so swimming isn't ideal. The other two trails are Saltpond Bay and Drunk Bay. **Drunk Bay Trail** offers opportunities to see wading birds while **Saltpond Bay Trail** leads to Salt Pond Beach, where you'll find a picnic area and good swimming and snorkeling.

There are 12 trails along the north shore of St. John. **Lind Point, Caneel Hill, Caneel Hill Spur, and Peace Hill Trails** are near Cruz Bay. **Cinnamon Bay Self-Guiding Trail** is located near the entrance to Cinnamon Bay Campground. This 0.5-mile loop passes through an old sugar mill estate and a tropical forest. You'll also find **Cinnamon Bay Trail** nearby. It's a forested hike, following an old Danish plantation road for 1.1 miles to its junction with Route 10. At the west end of Mary Creek Road is **Francis Bay Trail**. This 0.5-mile (one-way) trail is a favorite of snorkelers, swimmers, and birdwatchers. Just south of Mary Point are **Annaberg School Ruins** and a bit further east are **Annaberg Sugar Mill Ruins,** where you'll find a self-guiding tour that helps explain the Dane's sugar industry during the 18th and 19th centuries.

Paddling & Sailing

It's unlikely that you'll be bringing your own kayak or sailboat to the Virgin Islands, but that's alright because **Maho Bay (340.776.6240) and Cinnamon Bay (340.776.6330) Campgrounds rent** kayaks, small sailboats, and windsurfing gear. Before heading out on the water with your rental kayak you will be given a brief tutorial. Beginner sailors or windsurfers can sign up for a 2-hour lesson ($95). There are few locations better than the Virgin Islands to introduce yourself to these sports.

Rates: 14-foot Sailboat: $75 (1 hr)/$95 (3 hr)/$150 (6 hr)
Paddle Board: $25 (1hr)/$35 (3 hr)/$50 (6 hr)
Windsurfer: $65 (1 hr)/$85 (3 hr)/$125 (6 hr)
Single Kayak: $25 (1 hr)/$35 (3 hr)/$50 (6 hr)
Double Kayak: $35 (1 hr)/$45 (3 hr)/$70 (6 hr)

Snorkeling

More than one-third of the park is underwater and several reefs can be reached directly from the park's beaches. There's even a **snorkel trail at Trunk Bay** where underwater plaques describe the marine life as you swim by it (although much of the coral has been ruined by overuse). Nearly the entire St. John's shoreline is a snorkeler's playground. If you enjoy seeing colorful fish and feisty sea life, you'll want to have snorkel gear with you every day you're on the island. **Several locations rent gear**, including Cinnamon Bay and Maho Bay Campgrounds' Water Activities Centers. Trunk Bay, Cinnamon Bay, Hawksnest Beach, Saltpond Bay, and Maho Bay are some of the best locations to hop in the water for a little underwater exploration. **Waterlemon Cay** offers a unique snorkeling experience where visitors must complete a short 10 minute hike from Annaberg Sugar Mill Ruins Parking Area to the edge of Waterlemon Bay. From here Waterlemon Cay is just to the northeast across the bay. Swim out to the small emerald island, but be sure to circle it in a counterclockwise fashion; swimming in this direction will be much easier thanks to the water's current. Snorkeling this stretch will provide excellent opportunities to see turtles, starfish, stingrays, sharks, and barracudas. If you'd like to snorkel with an experienced guide, several **outfitters provide guided trips** (page 653) or the park offers **ranger-led trips** for $4. Stop by or call Cruz Bay Visitor Center (340.776.6201, ext. 238) for a current schedule of ranger-led snorkel tours.

Approximate Rental Rates: Snorkel, Mask, and Fins: $8/day, $40/week

French Angel Fish

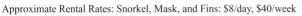

SCUBA

The U.S. Virgin Islands wealth of water and reefs make it a great place to SCUBA dive. Within the park you can receive **SCUBA lessons** at Maho Bay (340.776.6240) and Cinnamon Bay (340.776.6330) Campgrounds. A beginner course costs about $100 or certified divers can get a 1-tank dive at an outlying reef for $75 or so. Diving arrangements can be made at each campground's respective activities desk. **Buck Island Reef National Monument** (www.nps.gov/buis), just north of Saint Croix Island, is a popular SCUBA diving destination close to the park. There are numerous outfitters providing SCUBA lessons and charters for divers of all experience levels. They offer beginner courses, certification courses, night dives, wreck dives, and multi-dive discounts. Please refer to page 653 for additional outfitters.

Cruz Bay Watersports • (340) 776-6234
Located in Cruz Bay & at the Westin, St. John
www.divestjohn.com • Dives: $80–160, PADI Certificate: $450

Low Key Watersports • (800) 835-7718
Located at Wharfside Village, Cruz Bay
www.divelowkey.com • Dives: $80–160, PADI Certificate: $425

Maho Bay Watersports • (800) 392-9004
Located at Maho Bay Camps
www.maho.org • Dives: $75–100, PADI Certificate: $465

Patagon Dive Center • (340) 776-6111 ext. 7290
Located at Caneel Bay Resort • www.patagondivecenter.com
Dives: $95–135, PADI Certificate: $450

Cruz Bay

Trunk Bay Beach

Fishing

Refer to page 653 for outfitters on St. John and the surrounding islands. Most charters provide four to eight hour excursions. Fishing is allowed in park waters with the exception of Trunk Bay and other swim areas. A fishing license is not required if you fish from the shore. The Virgin Islands may be best known for the world record blue marlins pulled from its waters, but you'll also find bonito, tuna, wahoo, sailfish, and skipjack. Fishing is good year-round, but you're likely to have the most success between May and October.

Bird Watching

Approximately **144 species of birds** have been documented within the park. This includes both resident and migratory species. Not only is winter the best time for tourists, it's the birds' favorite season as well. Brown pelicans, brown boobies, magnificent frigatebirds, and royal terns are commonly seen near the shorelines. Mangrove cuckoos, zenaida cloves, Antilliean-crested hummingbirds, gray kingbirds, pearly-eyed thrashers, and bananaquits are commonly seen in the park's dry forests. Serious birders can find a bird checklist at the park website or visitor center. It includes information regarding breeding status, habitat, abundance, and best season to spot each species of bird.

For Kids: Virgin Islands National Park offers a **Junior Ranger Program** for children. Workbooks can be picked up at the park's visitor center. When completed, return to the visitor center to receive a certificate and badge.

An abundance of snorkeling, swimming, beaches, and short hiking trails make the Virgin Islands one of the most kid-friendly national parks in the United States. But you'll be tempted to leave the children at home for this one, because it's also one of the most romantic parks.

Ranger Programs: The park offers a handful of ranger-led activities. On weekdays rangers lead guests on a **free tour of Cinnamon Bay Estate ruins**, one of the first plantations on the island. You can explore the sea with a park ranger on a **snorkel trip** ($4/person). The **ranger-led Reef Bay Hike** is a 3.1-mile trek through the history of St. John Island. Bring along a lunch and your swimsuit for this tour. It costs $23/person, but transportation to and from the trailhead is provided. Several other hikes, early morning bird watch tours, and evening programs are offered at Virgin Islands National Park. For a current schedule, meeting locations, and to make reservations please call the visitor center at (340) 776-6201 ext. 238 or stop by in person.

Flora & Fauna: More than 90% of St. John's native vegetation was destroyed in favor of cash crops like cotton and sugarcane and to graze livestock. It wasn't until the 1950s—when Laurance Rockefeller donated more than half of St. John Island to the National Park Service—that natural reforestation began. From underwater seagrass to mangrove shorelines, moist forests to dry cactus scrubland, the landscapes of the U.S. Virgin Islands are once again changing and adapting in a more natural manner.

Very little is natural about the islands' mammals. **Bats are the only natives.** Goats, donkeys, and mongoose were all introduced by humans. **Dolphins** are frequently seen in the winter months, and **sea turtles** are commonly spotted by snorkelers and SCUBA divers. In fact, Trunk Bay got its name from Danes who believed the leatherback turtle resembled a great leather traveling trunk. You'll also find a multitude of coral and swarms of mosquitoes here.

Accessibility: Wheelchair accessible campsites are available at Cinnamon Bay Camp. The visitor center and picnic areas at Trunk Bay and Hawksnest are accessible. Most trails are steep, slippery, and relatively inaccessible.

Pets: Pets are not allowed on beaches, in campgrounds, or in picnic areas. They are permitted on trails, but must be on a leash no more than six feet in length at all times.

Weather: Virgin Islands National Park is a tropical paradise. All year long high temperatures are in the mid-80s°F with lows in the 70s°F. While the weather is out-of-this-world all year long, most visitors arrive between December and April. The summer months from June through August are hottest. Hurricane season spans from June until November, which also happen to be the wettest months of the year. Water temperature is about 83°F in summer and 79°F in winter.

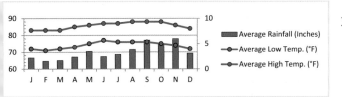

Vacation Planner

Most visitors will want to create a budget for a trip to the USVIs, because things are a bit more expensive in paradise (especially during peak-season). If you haven't made reservations for **ranger programs** already, remember to take a look at the current schedule of events posted at **Cruz Bay Visitor Center** when you arrive. You're on your own when it comes to choosing where to stay and eat. **Camping** (page 648) is available in the park. **Caneel Bay Resort** is the park's only lodging facility, but there are plenty of facilities available nearby. See pages 652–653 for a list of the area's best restaurants, lodging facilities, and attractions.

Car rental and taxis are available near the Cruz Bay dock. Taxi passengers should agree on a total rate with the driver before boarding. Taxi fare from Cruz Bay to Cinnamon Bay should cost $9 for one person or $7 per person for more than one. If you're staying at Caneel Bay, they'll pick you up from the dock. With an abundance of resort and campground activities at most facilities there's no real need to rent a car. (However, for the trip detailed below, you'll want a vehicle.) If you don't plan on bringing your own snorkel gear, rent some (page 649). Lastly, If you're traveling all the way to the Virgin Islands you may as well stay for a few days. Here's a three day template to help plan your vacation.

Best of Virgin Islands

Activity: **Trunk Bay Beach**
Runner-up: Snorkel Waterlemon Cay
2nd Runner-up: Hike Reef Bay Trail

Day 1 In all likelihood your first day will be spent reaching **St. Thomas and then St. John** (page 645), stopping at **Cruz Bay Visitor Center**, and getting situated on the island. Spend the evening exploring your lodging's property.

Day 2 Today you'll follow **Route 20**. Stop at **Cinnamon Bay** (if you aren't already staying there) and hike the **self-guiding trail** (page 648). Return to Route 20. Shortly after Maho Bay the road becomes one-way and leads directly to **Annaberg School and Sugar Mill ruins**. Explore the ruins all you want, but you're really here to snorkel **Waterlemon Cay** (page 649) from Leinster Beach. This is Saint Johns' best snorkeling spot. The western shore of Waterlemon Cay is particularly good. It's easily a half- to full-day activity as it's roughly a 15 minute walk to the beach and 200 yard swim to the cay. If you have spare time take Route 20 east to Route 10. Head south about a mile and turn left onto **Bordeaux Mountain Road** (steep and unpaved). Hike to the mountain's summit for outstanding panoramic views.

Day 3 Start your day off right by visiting **Trunk Bay** (page 649), the park's most enchanting beach. It gets busy, so arrive early. Next it's back in the car and along Route 20 to Route 10. Take Route 10 to Route 107, which skirts the southeastern shoreline. Eventually you'll come to **Johns Folly** and then **Saltpond Bay**. Hikers should head to **Ram Head Trail**. Snorkelers will want to dip into **Saltpond Bay**. Time permitting, head east on Route 10 to hike **Reef Bay Trail** (allow 2–5 hours depending on amount of required beach and snorkel time).

Dining

St John Island

La Tapa • (340) 693-7755 • Cruz Bay
www.latapastjohn.com • Entrée: $35–41

Beach Bar • (370) 777-4220 • Cruz Bay
www.beachbarstjohn.com • Entrée: $7–15

Sun Dog Café • (340) 693-8340
Mongoose Junction, Cruz Bay
www.sundogcafe.com • Entrée: $13–20

La Plancha Del Mar • (340) 777-7333
Mongoose Junction, Cruz Bay
www.laplanchadelmar.com • Entrée: $26–36

The Tap Room • (340) 715-7775
Mongoose Junction, Cruz Bay
www.stjohnbrewers.com

Paradiso • (340) 693-8899 • Cruz Bay

Morgan's Mango • (340) 693-8141 • Cruz Bay
www.morgansmango.com • Entrée: $12–28

Banana Deck • (340) 693-5055 • Cruz Bay
www.thebananadeck.com • Entrée: $19–28

Waterfront Bistro • (340) 777-7755 • Cruz Bay
www.thewaterfrontbistro.com • Entrée: $23–43

Rhumb Lines • (340) 776-0303 • Cruz Bay
www.rhumblinesstjohn.com • Entrée: $19–29

Miss Lucy's • Friis Bay; Cruz Bay

Jake's • (340) 777-7115 • Cruz Bay

Margarita Phil's • (340) 693-8400 • Cruz Bay

Da Livio • (340) 779-8900 • Cruz Bay

Sogo's • (340) 779-4404 • Cruz Bay

Black Sand Bistro • (340) 779-1998
The Marketplace, Cruz Bay

Vie's Snack Shack • (340) 693-5033
E End Rd/Rt 10; Cruz Bay

Windy Level Restaurant • (340) 715-2000
5 Estate Grundwald; Cruz Bay

Wharfside Café
Wharfside Village; Cruz Bay

Café Roma • (340) 776-6524 • Cruz Bay
www.stjohn-caferoma.com • Entrée: $15–32

Sam & Jack's Deli • (340) 714-3354 • Cruz Bay
www.stjohndeli.com • Sandwiches: $9+

Sheila's Pot • Prince St and Strand St

Woody's • (340) 779-4625
www.woodysseafood.com

ZoZo's Ristorante • (340) 693-9200
Gallows Point Resort; 3AAA Gallows Point Rd
www.zozos.net • Entrée: $35–40

Le Château de Bordeaux • (340) 776-6611
5 miles east of Cruz Bay

Donkey Diner • (340) 693-5240 • Coral Bay
www.donkeydiner.com • Pizza: $13+

Skinny Legs Bar & Grill
www.skinnylegs.com • Coral Bay

Sweet Plantains • (340) 777-4653
16118 Little Plantation; Coral Bay
www.sweetplantains-stjohn.com

Aqua Bistro Restaurant • Coral Bay

Shipwreck Landing • Route 107, Anguilla
www.shipwrecklandingstjohn.com

Island Blues • (340) 776-6800 • Estate Carolina
www.island-blues.com • Sandwiches: $12+

The Tourist Trap • (340) 774-0912
Salt Pond, Route 107 • www.thetouristtrap.co

Asolare • (340) 779-4747 • 6A Caneel Hill
www.asolarestjohn.com • Entrée: $29–38

Castaway Tavern • (340) 777-3361
www.Castawaystjohn.com • Entrée: $10–20

St Thomas Island

Pie Whole • (340) 642-5074
24A Honduras, Frenchtown
www.piewholepizza.com • Pizza: $9

Craig and Sally's • (340) 777-9949
3525 Honduras, Frenchtown
www.craigandsallys.com

FatBoys Bar, Grill, & Games • (340) 777-4275
Red Hook Rd • www.fatboysvi.net

Blue Moon Café • (340) 779-2262
6280 Estate Nazareth, Nazareth Bay
www.bluemooncafevi.com • Breakfast: $7+

Amalia Café • (340) 714-7373
24 Palm Passage St, Charlotte Amalie
www.amaliacafe.com

Big Kahuna Rum Shack • (340) 775-9289
Waterfront St, Charlotte Amalie
www.bigkahunausvi.com • Sandwiches: $10+

Jen's Island Café & Deli • (340) 777-4611
43-46 Norre Gade, Charlotte Amalie
www.jensdeli.com

East End Café • (340) 715-1442
6501 Red Hook Plaza, Ste 201

The Old Stone Farmhouse • (340) 777-6277
Mahogany Run • www.oldstonefarmhouse.com

Thirteen • (340) 774-6800
13A Estate Dorothea

Hook Line and Sinker • (340) 776-9708
Frenchtown
www.hooklineandsinkervi.com • Entrée: $20–28

Groceries

St John Island

Lily's Gourmet Market • (340) 777-3335
Harolds Way, Coral Bay

Pine Peace Grocery • Route 104, Cruz Bay

Starfish Market • (340) 779-4949
Cruz Bay • www.starfishmarket.com

St Thomas Island

Red Hook Shopping Center • (809) 774-8784
Route 32, Charlotte Amalie

Lodging

St John Island

Caneel Bay, A Rosewood Resort
N Shore Rd, 830 • (340) 776-6111
www.caneelbay.com • Rates: $600+/night

Hillcrest Guest House • (340) 776-6774
#157 Estate Enighed, Cruz Bay

The Westin St John Resort & Villas
Cruz Bay • (340) 693-8000
www.westinresortstjohn.com • Rates: $279+

Caneel Bay Hotel • (340) 776-6111 • Cruz Bay

The Inn at Tamarind Court
Cruz Bay • (800) 221-1637
www.innattamarindcourt.com • Rates: $170–240

Gallows Point Resort • (800) 323-7229
www.gallowspointresort.com • Rates: $265–595

St John Inn • (340) 693-8688
277 Enighed, Cruz Bay
www.stjohninn.com • Rates: $105–275

Maho Bay Resort • (340) 392-9004
www.maho.org • Rates: $80–250

Coconut Coast Villas • (800) 858-7989
268 Enighed, Turner Bay, Cruz Bay
www.coconutcoast.com • Rates: $189–559

St Thomas Island

Ritz-Carlton St Thomas Residence Club
6900 Great Bay • (340) 775-3333 • Rates: $735+
www.stthomasresidenceclub.com

Wyndham Sugar Bay Resort & Spa
6500 Estate Smith Bay • (340) 777-7100
www.wyndhamsugarbay.com

Bolongo Bay Beach Resort • (340) 775-1800
7150 Bolongo, Charlotte Amalie
www.bolongobay.com • Rates: $180–395

Hotel 1829 • (800) 524-2002
Government Hill, Charlotte Amalie
www.hotel1829.com • Rates: $80–190

Festivals

<u>8 Tuff Miles Race</u> • February
St John • www.8tuffmiles.com

<u>St John Blues Festival</u> • March
St John • www.stjohnbluesfestival.com

<u>Paradise Jam</u> • November - St Croix, St John, St Thomas • www.paradisejam.com

Attractions

St John Island

<u>Kekoa Sailing Expeditions</u>
Lumberyard Complex; Cruz Bay
www.blacksailsvi.com • (340) 244-7245

<u>St John Yacht Charters</u> • (340) 998-4773
www.stjohnyachtcharters.com

<u>Palm Tree Charters</u> • (340) 714-5641
www.palmtreecharters.com

<u>Fly Girl</u> • (866) 820-6906
Snorkeling, Sailing, Charters, and More
www.flygirlvi.com

<u>Calypso</u> • (340) 777-7245
www.calypsovi.com

<u>Lion In Dá Sun</u> • (340) 626-4783
www.lionindasun.com

<u>St John Spice</u> • (877) 693-7046
www.stjohnspice.com

<u>Sadie Sea</u> • (340) 514-0778
www.sadiesea.com

<u>VI Snuba Excursions</u> • (340) 693-8063
www.visnuba.com • Trunk Bay

<u>Hidden Reef Eco-Tours</u> • (877) 529-2575
Route 10; Coral Bay
www.hiddenreefecotours.com • Tours: $55–115

<u>Cruz Bay Watersports</u> • (340) 776-6234
Diving, Sailing, Snorkeling, Wave Runners, & More
www.divestjohn.com • Cruz Bay

<u>Drift Away Day Spa</u> • (340) 775-2700
www.driftawaystjohn.com

St Thomas Island

<u>Virgin Island Ecotours</u> • (877) 845-2925
Kayak, Hike, and Snorkel Adventures
www.viecotours.com

<u>Daysail High Pockets Adventure</u>
6292 Est. Nazareth, #100 St
www.sailhighpockets.com

<u>Morningstar Charters</u>
www.morningstarcharter.com • (340) 775-1111

<u>Big Blue Excursions</u> • (340) 201-3045
6501 Red Hook Plaza Ste 201
www.bigblue-usvi.com

<u>Simplicity Charters</u>
6501 Red Hook Plaza, Ste 201
www.simplicitycharters.com

<u>Captain Max</u> • (340) 775-7467
6501 Red Hook Plaza, Ste 201
www.sailwithcaptainmax.com

<u>St Thomas Diving Club</u> • (340) 776-2381
7147 Bolongo Bay
www.stthomasdivingclub.com

<u>Red Hook Dive Center</u> • (340) 777-3483
6100 Red Hook Quarters, E1-1
www.redhookdivecenter.com • Dives: $90–125

<u>Yacht Nightwind</u> • (340) 775-7017
6700 Sapphire Village; Unit 201
www.stjohndaysail.com

<u>SunSea Charters</u> • (340) 626-6785
Dock D, Red Hook
www.sunseavi.com

<u>Blue Island Divers</u> • (340) 774-2001
Crown Bay Marina
www.blueislanddivers.com

St Croix Island

<u>Geckos Island Adventures</u> • (340) 713-8820
3C Strand St, Frederiksted
www.geckosislandadventures.com

<u>Ultimate Bluewater Adventures</u>
www.stcroixscuba.com • (340) 773-5994

<u>Buck Island Reef Nat'l Mon.</u> • (340) 773-1460
2100 Church St, #100; Christiansted, VI
www.nps.gov/buis

<u>Salt River Bay NHP & Ecological Preserve</u>
2100 Church St, #100; Christiansted, VI
www.nps.gov/sari • (340) 773-1460

<u>Paul & Jill's Equestrian Stables</u>
Frederiksted • (340) 772-2880
www.paulandjills.com • Trail Rides: $90

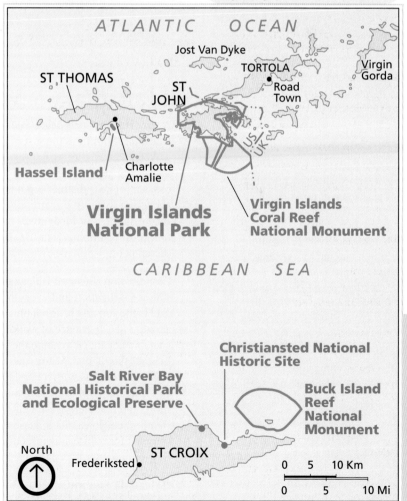

The colors and clouds of Haleakalā Crater

PO Box 369; Makawao, HI 96768
Phone: (808) 572-4400
Website: www.nps.gov/hale

HALEAKALĀ

Established: August 1, 1916
Size: 30,183 Acres
Annual Visitors: 1.1 Million
Peak Season: mid-Dec–mid-April

Activities: Hiking, Biking, Horseback Riding, Swimming, Bird Watching, and Stargazing

Campgrounds (Free): Kīpahulu and Hosmer Grove Campgrounds
Cabins: 3 Backcountry Cabins*
Backcountry Camping: Permitted at designated sites and cabins*
Cabin Fee: $75/night
Cabin Reservations (www.fhnp.org)

Park Hours: All day, every day (may close for severe weather)
Entrance Fee: $10 • Vehicle
$5 • Individual (foot, bike, etc.)

*Permit required for backcountry camping and cabins

Haleakalā - Māui, Hawai'i

A sea of clouds floats below you. Burnt red rocky slopes lie in front of you. Haleakalā Summit is the sort of scene that makes a person feel like you've woken up in another world. A world where myths seem like reality, rather than just a story as colorful as the crater itself. Haleakalā National Park consists of two distinct regions. **Haleakalā summit**, nearly two miles above sea level, is a seemingly lifeless landscape that should require a space shuttle and lunar rover to reach. And **Lower Kīpahulu**—a lush rainforest brimming with life, forests of bamboo, and waterfalls that stir sacred pools—provides yin to the summit's yang.

Clouds often surround Haleakalā like a barrier between worlds. On one side is civilization and everything else you find familiar. On the other side is the sun and brilliant blue sky as you're transported to the heavens above. The experience of walking through the clouds may have inspired ancient Hawaiians to name the volcano Haleakalā or "house of the sun." Legend has it that **Māui**, the Hawaiian demigod who had raised the Hawaiian Islands with a homemade fishhook and line, knew where the sun resided. Māui overheard his mother complain that the days were too short, and that there wasn't enough time for her kapa (bark cloth) to dry. He climbed Haleakalā to lasso the sun with his sister's hair. Caught, the sun pled for its life and agreed the days would be longer in summer and shorter in winter. In a paradise like this, who wouldn't want longer days?

Haleakalā Summit, at 10,023 feet above sea level, is the island's highest peak. From here, sure-footed visitors can descend 2,600 feet into the crater. Geologically speaking, it is a dormant volcano that hasn't erupted for more than 400 years. It's not a crater either, but two valleys joined together when the ridgeline between them eroded away. Pīpīwai Spring, at the very southeast corner of the park, is continuously wearing away the land as water tumbles some 400 feet over Waimoku Falls and on into 'Ohe'o Gulch. This area is **Kīpahulu**. A location where you can spend the long summer days bathing in its idyllic, nay, sacred swimming pools, hiking Pīpīwai Trail, or just enjoying the sights along Hāna Highway (one of the most scenic drives in the world). The only visitors who want the sun to set are those who wish to gaze at the night sky or arrive at the summit with blankets and coffee early enough to see the sun's glorious return above Haleakalā, its home. Those who do will find that the night is often as spectacular as the day.

As the sun rises up over Haleakalā there are few places in the world that appear so lifeless yet so beautiful. Volcanic islands, like Hawai'i, begin as barren masses of molten rock. It takes hundreds of thousands of years for species to arrive by wind, water, or wings. Prior to civilization, a species arrived every 10,000 to 100,000 years, in part because the destination was the most isolated significant island chain in the world. This remote setting is exactly what makes the species that have survived and evolved here all the more unique.

Haleakalā silversword, a relative of the sunflower that reaches maturity after seven years, is found nowhere else in the world. It blooms, sending forth a stalk three to eight feet tall containing several hundred tiny sunflowers, then it dies. The silversword was once so abundant the crater floor looked as if it was covered with glistening snow. Vandalism and excessive grazing by cattle and goats nearly led to its extinction.

More endangered species live in Haleakalā than any other national park in the United States, and the park's unique ecosystems make for one of the world's most interesting and studied living laboratories. Scientists hope to preserve the biology found here, so areas like upper Kīpahulu Valley and Waikamoi are closed to tourism or accessible only when guided by a ranger or naturalist. Invasive species and destructive tourism are constant threats. Today, aided by 1.1 million annual visitors, about 20 alien species arrive on the islands each year. We must find a way to strike a balance between nature and tourism so that this one park—two worlds, part moon and part jungle—can be preserved for future generations.

When to Go

The park is open all year. It closes occasionally for severe weather conditions. Visitation is steady throughout the year, but there is a noticeable influx of tourists during peak travel season (mid-December–mid-April). At this time, rates for accommodations and activities are significantly higher, sometimes more than double off-season rates. Park Headquarters Visitor Center is open daily from 7am–3:45pm. Haleakalā Visitor Center is open daily from 5:30am–3pm. Kīpahulu Visitor Center is open daily from 9am–5pm. All facilities close on Christmas and New Year's Day.

Transportation & Airports

Haleakalā National Park is located on the Island of Māui. Most visitors arrive via commercial airline from the U.S. mainland or another Hawaiian Island. Māui's primary airport is Kahului Airport (OGG). Public transportation is not available to or around the park. Car rental is available at the airport.

Directions

The two regions of the park, Haleakalā Summit and Kīpahulu Valley, are not directly connected by roads. In fact, from the airport they are in the exact opposite directions from one another.

To Haleakalā Summit (37 miles): Exit the airport on HI-37. Turn left onto HI-377. After about 6 miles turn left at Crater Road (HI-378/Haleakalā Highway). After 1.5 miles turn right to stay on Crater Road. Continue on Crater Road for approximately 20 miles to the summit of Haleakalā. This road may be the steepest grade of any road in the world. You leave near sea level in Kahului and arrive at the 10,023-ft high summit of Haleakalā after less than 40 miles. Visitors should expect the journey to take at least two hours to complete.

To Kīpahulu (60 miles from airport/80 miles from Haleakalā Summit): Exit the airport on HI-36 (Hāna Highway). Continue to follow Hāna Highway, one of the most scenic roadways in the United States, to Kīpahulu Visitor Center. This region of the park can also be reached via HI-37 and HI-31 from the summit (about 60 miles), but you must traverse a narrow, rough, unpaved section of road that is a little more than 3-miles in length. Inquire at the Rental Car office about traveling this stretch of road. Many agreements become void if you explore unpaved roadways.

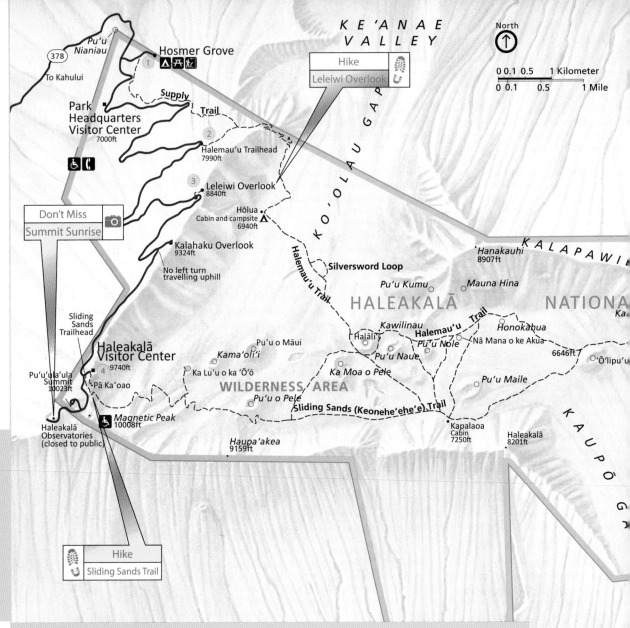

Did you know?

➤ Haleakalā Volcano has been dormant since 1490.

➤ The Kingdom of Hawai'i was annexed as a territory of the United States in 1898, but it didn't become the 50th state until 1959.

➤ Haleakalā and Hawai'i Volcanoes were originally combined as Hawai'i National Park (established in 1916). In 1951 Kīpahulu Valley was added to the park land. Ten years later it was split into Haleakalā and Hawai'i Volcanoes National Parks.

➤ On a clear day you can see across the channel from the Kīpahulu area to the island of Hawai'i.

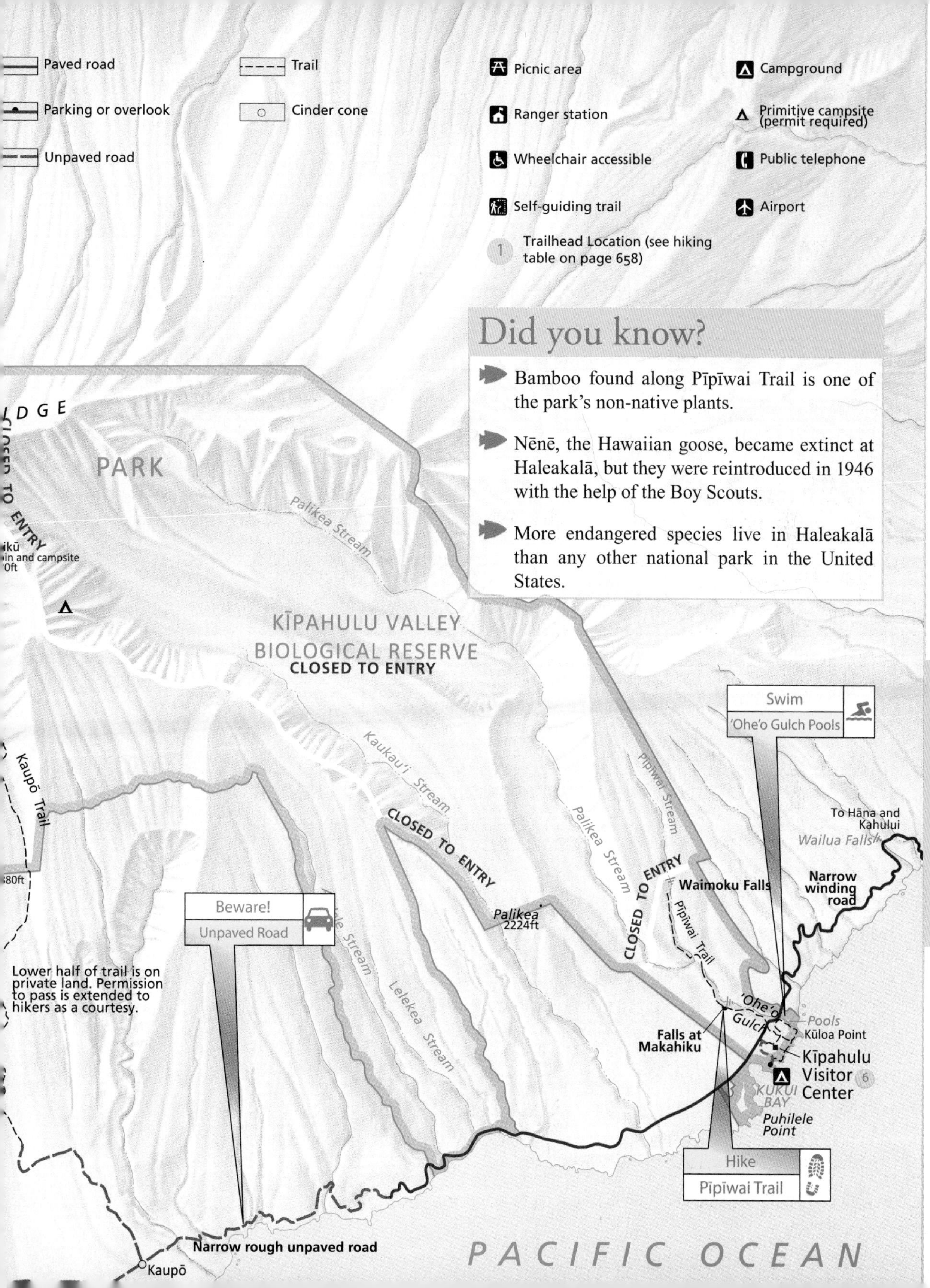

Legend

▬▬ Paved road	┄┄┄ Trail
●▬ Parking or overlook	▭ Cinder cone
▬▬ Unpaved road	

⛺ Picnic area

🏠 Ranger station

♿ Wheelchair accessible

🚶 Self-guiding trail

🏕 Campground

⛺ Primitive campsite (permit required)

📞 Public telephone

✈ Airport

① Trailhead Location (see hiking table on page 658)

Did you know?

➤ Bamboo found along Pīpīwai Trail is one of the park's non-native plants.

➤ Nēnē, the Hawaiian goose, became extinct at Haleakalā, but they were reintroduced in 1946 with the help of the Boy Scouts.

➤ More endangered species live in Haleakalā than any other national park in the United States.

L D G E

CLOSED TO ENTRY

PARK

Palikea Stream

iku
in and campsite
0ft

Kaupō Trail

80ft

KĪPAHULU VALLEY
BIOLOGICAL RESERVE
CLOSED TO ENTRY

Kaukau'i Stream

CLOSED TO ENTRY

Palikea Stream

Pīpīwai Stream

CLOSED TO ENTRY

Swim
'Ohe'o Gulch Pools 🏊

To Hāna and
Kahului
Wailua Falls

**Narrow
winding
road**

Waimoku Falls

Pīpīwai Trail

Palikea
2224ft

le Stream

Lelekea Stream

Beware!
Unpaved Road 🚗

Lower half of trail is on
private land. Permission
to pass is extended to
hikers as a courtesy.

**Falls at
Makahiku**

'Ohe'o
Gulch

Pools
Kūloa Point

**Kīpahulu
Visitor
Center** ⑥

KUKUI
BAY

*Puhilele
Point*

Hike
Pīpīwai Trail 👣

Narrow rough unpaved road

○ Kaupō

PACIFIC OCEAN

HALEAKALĀ

657

Haleakalā Camping

	Open	Fees	Capacity	Location/Notes
Kīpahulu	All Year	None	100	Just south of Kīpahulu Visitor Center • Water is available in the nearby town of Hāna
Hosmer Grove	All Year	None	50	Summit Area • Restrooms, grills, and water available
Hōlua (backcountry)	All Year	None	25	Accessed by Sliding Sands (7.4 mi) and Halemau'u Trails (3.7 mi) • Pit toilets and non-potable water nearby
Palikū (backcountry)	All Year	None	25	Accessed by Sliding Sands (9.3 mi, strenuous) and Halemau'u Trails (10.4 mi) • Pit toilets and non-potable water nearby
Backcountry Cabins (Hōlua, Kapalaoa, and Palikū Cabins)	All Year	$75	12/cabin	Hōlua Cabin is on Halemau'u Trail (3.7 mi) • Kapalaoa and Palikū Cabins are on Sliding Sands Trail (5.5-mi and 9.3 mi, respectively) • Bunks, cook & dinnerware, and stove in cabin

All Campsites are available on a first-come, first-served basis • Cabins can be reserved up to 90 days in advance by calling (808) 572-4400 or clicking www.fhnp.org/wcr • Camping is limited to a maximum of 3 nights per 30 day period with no more than 2 nights at any one site • Permits are required for all backcountry campsites and cabins

Haleakalā Hiking Trails

	Trail Name	Trailhead (# on map)	Length	Notes (Roundtrip distances unless noted otherwise)
Easy-Moderate	Hosmer Grove	Hosmer Grove Campground (1)	0.5 mile	Self-guiding nature trail
	Leleiwi Overlook	Leleiwi Overlook Parking Area (3)	0.25 mile	Uncrowded spot with excellent photo-ops
	Kūloa Point	Kīpahulu Ranger Station (6)	0.5 mile	A bluff overlooking 'Ohe'o Gulch
	Pīpīwai - 👍	North end of the visitor center (6)	4.0 miles	A moderate hike through bamboo forest to 400-foot Waimoku Falls (pictured)
Strenuous	Halemau'u	8,000 Foot Parking Area (3.5 miles above Park Headquarters) (2)	11.7 miles (one-way)	Hike into the valley to view cinder cones and Haleakalā silverswords
	Sliding Sands - 👍	Haleakalā Visitor Center Parking Area (4)	11.2 miles (one-way)	Steep descent into the valley • Leads to cinder cones, backcountry camping, and cabins
	Kaupō	Joins Sliding Sands near Palikū Camp (5)	8.7 miles (one-way)	Leads through private property to Kaupō (2 hour drive from summit) on the coast

Waimoku Falls

Hiking

Most Haleakalā National Park visitors drive up to the summit, have a look around, maybe watch the sunrise, and then go on their merry way. Don't follow the path of the average tourist. The park boasts more than 30 miles of hiking trails in the summit area and another 10 miles or so around Kīpahulu. Do you enjoy hiking? Want to explore the crater? Are you trying to escape the crowds? If you answered "yes" to any of these questions hike **Halemau'u or Sliding Sand Trails** into the valley below Haleakalā Summit. Sliding Sands is more strenuous, beginning at a higher elevation. Both trails offer short spurs to cinder cones and silverswords. They also provide access to the park's backcountry campsites and cabins that are sprinkled throughout the wilderness. Before departing on either of these journeys, be sure to honestly assess your physical abilities and amount of free time. The trails are challenging, and it will take slightly longer to make the return trip uphill to the summit.

You can also hike a few short and relatively flat trails in the summit area. **Hosmer's Grove Nature Trail** is a self-guided hike through a forest of native tree species planted by Ralph Hosmer while experimenting with what plant species would grow best. The hike from **Leleiwi Overlook** is a short walk packed with amazing panoramic vistas. In addition, park rangers provide guided tours of **Waikamoi Preserve** (reservation required) that focus on bird watching (page 660).

Pīpīwai Trail at Kīpahulu is one of the best, if not the best hiking trail on the island of Māui. It's an uphill climb, but your effort will be rewarded with 400-ft of **Waimoku Falls**. Due to the small selection of hiking trails and popularity of **'Ohe'o Gulch**, it is often crowded, so get an early start if at all possible.

Horseback Riding

If you don't feel like hiking into the crater, how about hoofing it on the back of a horse? It's unlikely you brought your own, but outfitters near the summit and Kīpahulu are available to take care of all your horse riding needs.

Pony Express Tours (Summit) • (808) 667-2200
Crater Road; Kula, HI 96790
www.ponyexpresstours.com • Rates: $182 (4 hours)

Māui Stables (Kīpahulu) • (808) 248-7799
177 Hāna Highway; Hāna, HI 96713
www.mauistables.com • Rates: $150 (4 hours)

Pīpīwai Trail © Maik-T. Šebenik (photographr.net)

Biking

Oddly enough, biking is a popular activity in the Haleakalā Summit area. Recent rule changes prohibit bikes from descending Crater Road from the summit (and within the park boundary), but guests can still join any one of several outfitters on a descent beginning just outside the park entrance at 6,700 ft elevation. Outfitters also offer bike rental. It's fun to cruise downhill, but for your time and dollar, opt for other Haleakalā activities like stargazing (page 660) or horseback riding (page 659) over biking.

Aloha Bicycle Tours • (808) 249-0911
73 Baldwin Ave; Paia, HI 96779
www.mauibike.com • Rates: $69–95

Cruiser Phil's Volcano Riders • (808) 893-2332
58 A Amala Place; Kahului, HI 96732
www.cruiserphil.com • Rates: $79–130

Haleakalā Bike Co • (808) 575-9575
810 Haiku Road # 120; Haiku, HI 96708
www.bikemaui.com • Rates: $56–92

Māui Downhill Bicycle Tours • (808) 871-2155
199 Dairy Road; Kahului; HI 96732
www.mauidownhill.com • Rates: $109–149

Māui Sunriders Bike Co • (808) 579-8970
Ste C1, 71 Baldwin Avenue; Paia, HI 96779
www.mauibikeride.com • Rates: $50–65

Mountain Riders • (808) 877-4944
390 Papa Place; Kahului, HI 96732
www.mountainriders.com • Rates: $101–120

Stargazing

Haleakalā is such a great spot for viewing what exists beyond earth's atmosphere that the government built an observatory at its summit. This lair is reserved for scientists and professional stargazers, but everyone has access to the stars that shine brightly on clear Hawaiian nights. There is very little artificial light to dim the sky, allowing you to see more stars than you ever knew existed. Note that it's extremely cold (40°F), by Hawaiian standards, at the summit and often windy. Stargazers may be leery of the return drive down the mountain's slope, but there will be very little traffic to deal with and the usually distracting scenery will be hidden under cover of darkness. Still, the best option is to camp at Hosmer's Grove, where you can see the stars at night and the sun as it rises in the morning. **Star Gazers Māui** offers guided stargazing complete with down parkas, dinner, drinks, telescopes, hats, and maps. The tour can be booked at Tom Barefoot's Tours by calling (800) 621-3601 (U.S. & Canada) or (808) 661-1246 or clicking www.tombarefoot.com.

Star Gazers Māui • (808) 281-9158 • www.www.stargazersmaui.com
70 Hauoli Street #412; Wailuku, HI 96793
Rates: $75/Person (4 hours every Monday, Wednesday, and Friday)

Bird Watching

A large collection of rare birds, including many found nowhere else in the world, makes Haleakalā National Park a popular destination among bird watchers. **Hawaiian petrel** (or 'ua'u) and **Hawaiian goose** (or nēnē, also the state bird of Hawai'i) nest at the summit. One of the most popular avian attractions is the park's unique family of **honeycreepers**. Several species have evolved from one common ancestor, and over thousands of years they have become strikingly different due to variations in their individual habitats. **Waikamoi Cloud Forest** at Hosmer's Grove is one of the best places to see birds. Guests can only view this area on a 3.5 hour special hike led by the nature conservancy or park staff. Tours are offered Monday and Tuesday at 8:45am. Reservations are required and can be made up to one week in advance by calling (808) 572-4459. Show up at least 15 minutes early and be prepared with layered clothing, rain gear, water, and sturdy shoes.

Swimming

Swimming is a popular pastime at Kīpahulu Valley. Most visitors bathe or swim in the waterfall pools of **'Ohe'o Gulch** known as **the seven sacred pools**. Arrive early, because the gulch can get very busy. (It's also best to drive Hāna Highway early in the morning; there are only a few parking spots at each viewpoint or attraction. A good time to start is 6am.) More secluded swimming holes are found further upstream. Note that these pools are a part of the park and you will have to pay the entrance fee.

For Kids: Children find Haleakalā's otherworldly moonscapes and pristine swimming holes more than agreeable. Kids (ages 7–12) may participate in the park's **Junior Ranger Program**. Stop in at either visitor center to pick-up a free activity booklet. Complete it and return to a visitor center for a certificate and badge. Kids of all ages will also find the park ranger's interpretive programs engaging and educational.

Ranger Programs: Ranger-led activities are held regularly at Hosmer Grove and the summit area. The **Waikamoi Cloud Forest Hike** is one of the most regularly offered tours available here, but stargazing programs, hikes, and talks are also held periodically. For activity details and a current schedule of events stop in at one of the visitor centers or call (808) 572-4400.

Flora & Fauna: There are approximately **370 species of native plants** living at Haleakalā National Park. Of these, about 90% are found only on the Hawaiian Islands. **Haleakalā silversword**, found at and around the summit and nowhere else in the world, is the most famous.

The Hawaiian Islands are home to just **two native mammal species**: monk seal and hoary bat. No land amphibians or reptiles are native to the park. Some of the most sought after animals are found in the ocean. Whales, turtles, dolphins, and seabirds are occasionally seen offshore from Kūloa Point near Kīpahulu.

Pets: Pets are permitted, but must be kept on a leash no more than six feet in length at all times. They are only allowed in parking lots, campgrounds, and along paved roads and paths. Visitors are not allowed to take pets on hiking trails or leave them unattended.

HALEAKALĀ

Accessibility: The park's visitor centers are wheelchair accessible. Haleakalā's summit building is accessible with assistance via a steep ramp. Wheelchair accessible campsites are available. Trails are unpaved and difficult for wheelchairs or individuals requiring assistance.

Weather: Haleakalā National Park's two distinct locations have completely contrasting climates. Haleakalā summit is cool and dry while Kīpahulu is wet and hot (see graphs below). Visitors can expect a 30°F temperature difference from sea level to Haleakalā summit at 10,023-ft, where high winds and intense solar radiation are common. Snowstorms can even occur in the higher elevations. Kīpahulu enjoys the tropical climate Hawai'i vacationers have come to expect, with year-round warm temperatures and a wet winter. Pack clothes for all conditions, especially if you plan on going to the summit. Check the weather forecast prior to leaving, because conditions change rapidly with little warning.

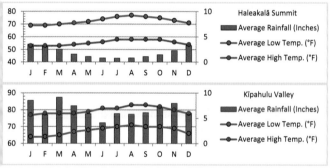

Vacation Planner

Select your own lodging and dining arrangements from pages 662–663 (nearby festivals, grocery stores, and attractions are also included). **Camping** (page 658) is recommended (especially at the summit) for an economical and truly unforgettable high-altitude adventure. Hitch-hiking is fairly common and safe, but visitors hoping to explore both regions of the park in an efficient manner should rent a car at Kahului. Car rental in Hawai'i is cheaper than most places thanks to intense competition. Visit the summit area first, as a day of strenuous hiking can make soaking in 'Ohe'o Gulch even more enjoyable. It also provides proper motivation to wake up for the sunrise (5:30–6:30am), which allows you to get an early start on driving the **Hāna Highway**. But you can't go wrong either way, as a first night at Kīpahulu will let you enjoy a morning swim at 'Ohe'o Gulch before the crowds arrive.

The Seven Sacred Pools of 'Ohe'o Gulch

Day 1
Begin by heading to the **Haleakalā summit** area. You won't find any food or fuel in the park, so make sure that you top off your gas tank and cooler before entering. Packing warm clothes is another good idea. En route to the summit, stop at **Hosmer's Grove. Campers** (page 658) should secure a first-come, first-served site, and the short **self-guiding nature trail** is a nice leg-stretcher. Return to Crater Road and make your next stop **Leleiwi Overlook**. Hike the 0.25-mile trail for a glimpse of Hōlua Cabin and Camp on Halemau'u Trail below. Continue up the mountain to the 10,023-ft summit where a **visitor center** provides information (exhibits & ranger programs, too) and **Sliding Sands Trail** provides seclusion. Explore both. If you don't plan on camping at the summit, stick around for the sunset. It's not as popular as the sunrise, but can be equally breathtaking.

Day 2
The ideal itinerary has you catching the sunrise from Haleakalā before returning to sea level to drive the **Hāna Highway.** (Note that you may want to include a day just to explore Hāna Highway. It's spectacular.) This scenic drive turns into an unpaved road near the park's Kīpahulu Valley. Fortunately you're stopping at 'Ohe'o Gulch (still on pavement), where you'll hike **Pīpīwai Trail** (page 658) to **Waimoku Falls**. If you can't reach the 400-foot tall falls (due to mud), swimming in the sacred pools of **'Ohe'o Gulch** is a very satisfactory substitute before returning to Hāna Highway.

Dining

⚓Serpico's Restaurant • (808) 572-8498
7 Aewa Pl; Makawao, HI 96768
www.serpicosmaui.com • Pizza: $16+

Pizza Fresh • (808) 572-2000
1043 Makawao Ave; Makawao, HI 96768
www.pizzafreshmaui.com • Pizza: $9+

Polli's Mexican Restaurant • (808) 572-7808
1202 Makawao Ave; Makawao, HI 96768
www.pollismexicanrestaurant.com • Entrée: $15–24

Stopwatch Sportsbar & Grill • (808) 572-1380
1127 Makawao Ave; Makawao, HI 96768

Makawao Garden Café • (808) 573-9065
3669 Baldwin Ave, # 1101; Makawao, HI 96768

⚓Café 808 • (808) 878-6874 • Breakfast: $4+
4566 Lower Kula Rd; Kula, HI 96790

Capische? • (808) 879-2224
555 Kaukahi St; Kihei, HI 96753
www.capische.com • Entrée: $30–65

Sansei Seafood & Sushi Bar • (808) 879-0004
1881 S Kihei Rd, # Kt116; Kihei, HI 96753
www.sanseihawaii.com • Entrée: $16+

Joe's • (808) 875-7767
131 Wailea Ike Place; Kihei, HI 96753
www.bevgannonrestaurants.com • Entrée: $19–38

Matteo's Pizzeria • (808) 874-1234
100 Wailea Ike Dr; Kihei, HI 96753
www.matteospizzeria.com • Entrée: $14–18

⚓Coconut's Fish Café • (808) 875-9979
1279 S Kihei Rd; Kihei, HI 96753
www.coconutsfishcafe.com • Entrée: $12+

⚓Market Fresh Bistro • (808) 572-4877
3620 Baldwin Ave, # 102A; Makawao, HI 96768

Lulu's Restaurant • (808) 879-9944
1945 S Kihei Rd; Kihei, HI 96753
www.lulusmaui.com • Entrée: $14–22

⚓808 Deli • (808) 879-1111
2511 S Kihei Rd; Kihei, HI 96753
www.808deli.net • Sandwiches: $6+

Kihei Caffe • (808) 879-2230
1945 S Kihei Rd; Kihei, HI 96753
www.kiheicaffe.com • Breakfast: $6–11

Ruth's Chris Steak House • (808) 874-8880
3750 Wailea Alanui; Wailea-Makena, HI 96753
www.ruthschris.com • Entrée: $50+

⚓Paia Fish Market • (808) 579-8030
110 Hāna Hwy; Paia, HI 96779
www.paiafishmarket.com • Fish: $11+

Flatbread Company • (808) 579-8989
89 Hāna Hwy; Paia, HI 96779
www.flatbreadcompany.com

Ono Gelato Co • (808) 579-9201
115 Hāna Hwy, # D; Paia, HI 96779
www.onogelatocompany.com

Gazebo Restaurant • (808) 669-5621
5315 Lower Honoapiilani Rd; Lāhainā, HI 96761

⚓Ono Gelato Co • (808) 667-1984
815 Front St; Lāhainā, HI 96761
www.onogelatocompany.com

⚓Cilantro Mexican Grill • (808) 667-5444
170 Papalaua St, # 104; Lāhainā, HI 96761
www.cilantrogrill.com • Sandwiches: $9+

⚓Sunrise Café • (808) 661-8558
693 Front St, # A; Lāhainā, HI 96761

Penne Pasta Café • (808) 661-6633
180 Dickenson St, # 113; Lāhainā, HI 96761
www.pennepastacafe.com

⚓Ululani's Hawaiian Shave Ice • (360) 606-2745
819 Front St; Lāhainā, HI 96761
www.ululanisshaveice.com • $4.25–5.25

Groceries

Safeway • (808) 891-9120
277 Pi'ikea Ave; Kihei, HI 96753

Costco Māui • (808) 877-5248
540 Haleakalā Hwy; Kahului, HI 96732

Lodging

Kula Lodge & Restaurant • (808) 878-1535
15200 Haleakalā Hwy; Kula, HI 96790
www.kulalodge.com • Rates: $125+

Eva Villa B&B • (808) 874-6407
815 Kumulani Dr; Kihei, HI 96753
www.mauibnb.com

Māui Coast Hotel • (808) 874-6284
2259 S Kihei Rd; Kihei, HI 96753
www.mauicoasthotel.com • Rates: $135+

Māui Kamaole • (808) 879-5445
2777 S Kihei Rd; Kihei, HI 96753
www.mauikamaole.com • Rates: $221+

Wailea Beach Villas • (808) 891-4500
3800 Wailea Alanui Dr; Kihei, HI 96753
www.waileabeachvillas.com • Rates: $700+

Dreams Come True on Māui B&B • (808) 879-7099
3259 Akala Dr; Kihei, HI 96753
www.mauibednbreakfast.com • Rates: $89–179

Hale Huanani B&B • (877) 423-6284
808 Kupulau Dr; Kihei, HI 96753
www.halehuananibandb.com • Rates: $80–90

Pineapple Inn Māui • (808) 298-4403
3170 Akala Dr; Kihei, HI 96753
www.pineappleinnmaui.com • Rates: $139–255

Aloha Rainbow Cottage • (808) 573-8555
1879 Olinda Rd; Makawao, HI 96768
www.aloharainbowcottage.com • Rates: $199+

Hale Hookipa Inn B&B • (808) 572-6698
32 Pakani Place; Makawao, HI 96768
www.maui-bed-and-breakfast.com • Rates: $125–180

Hale Hoomana Spa Retreat • (808) 573-8256
1550 Piiholo Rd; Makawao, HI 96768
www.halehoomana.com • Rates: $80–265

Banyan Tree House • (808) 572-9021
3265 Baldwin Ave; Makawao, HI 96768
www.bed-breakfast-maui.com • Rates: $155–190

⚓Fairmont Kea Lani • (808) 875-4100
4100 Wailea Alanui Dr; Wailea-Makena, HI 96753
www.fairmont.com • Rates: $320+

Hotel Wailea • (808) 874-0500
555 Kaukahi St; Wailea, HI 96753
www.hotelwailea.com • Rates: $203+

Four Seasons Māui • (808) 874-8000
3900 Wailea Alanui; Wailea, HI 96753
www.fourseasons.com • Rates: $500+

Huelo Point Lookout • (800) 871-8645
222 Door of Faith; Huelo, HI 96708
www.maui-vacationrentals.com • Rates: $200–245

Māui Ocean Breezes • (808) 283-8526
240 N. Holokai Rd; Haiku, HI 96708
www.mauivacationhideaway.com • Rates: $145–185

Old Wailuku Inn • (808) 244-5897
2199 Kahookele St; Wailuku, HI 96793
www.mauiinn.com • Rates: $297+

Paia Inn Hotel • (808) 579-6000
93 Hāna Hwy; Paia, HI 96779
www.paiainn.com • Rates: $229+

Travaasa Hāna • (808) 248-8211
5031 Hāna Hwy; Hāna, HI 96713
www.travaasa.com • Rates: $320+

Hāna Kai-Māui Resort • (808) 248-8426
4865 Uakea Rd; Hāna, HI 96713
www.hanakaimaui.com

Honua Kai Resort and Spa • (808) 662-2800
130 Kai Malina Pkwy; Lāhainā, HI 96761
www.honuakai.com • Rates: $249+

Wai Ola Vacation Paradise • (800) 492-4652
1565 Kuuipo St; Lāhainā, HI 96761
www.waiola.com • Rates: $179–280

The Guest House • (800) 621-8942
1620 Ainakea Rd; Lāhainā, HI 96761
www.mauiguesthouse.com • Rates: $169–189

Aston MaHāna • (808) 661-8751
110 Kaanapali Shores Pl; Lāhainā, HI 96761
www.themahana.com • Rates: $250+

Attractions

Paragon Sailing Charters • (808) 244-2087
5229 Lower Kula Rd; Kula, HI 96790
www.sailmaui.com

Skyline Eco Adventures • (808) 878-8400
PO Box 880518; Pukalani, HI 96788
www.zipline.com • Zipline: $150

Aqua Adventure • (808) 573-2104
194 Auoli Dr; Makawao, HI 96768
www.mauisnorkelsnuba.com • Rates: $99+

Māui Hiking Safaris • (808) 573-0168
2731 Leolani Place; Makawao, HI 96768
www.mauihikingsafaris.com • Tours: $69–159

Piiholo Ranch Zipline • (808) 572-1717
Piiholo Rd; Makawao, HI 96768
www.piiholozipline.com • Zipline: $190

Māui Spa Retreat • (808) 573-8002
PO Box 39; Makawao, HI 96768
www.mauisparetreat.com

Makena State Park • (808) 974-6200
www.hawaiistateparks.org • Kīhei • Free

Kai Kanani Sailing Charters • (808) 879-7218
Charter, Sail, Snorkel, Sail, and Whale Watch
5400 Makena Alanui; Kihei, HI 96753
www.kaikanani.com

Māui Classic Charters • (800) 736-5740
1279 S Kihei Rd; Suite 110, Kihei, HI 96753
www.mauiclasiccharters.com • Snorkel: $79+

Blue Water Rafting • (808) 879-7238
1280 S Kihei Rd, Ste 225; Kihei, HI 96753
www.bluewaterrafting.com • Tour: $35 (1.5 hr)

Molokini
A popular destination for SCUBA diving and snorkeling, this partially submerged volcanic crater is located between the islands of Māui and Kahoʻolawe

Māui Dive Shop • (800) 542-3483
2463 S Kihei Rd; Kihei, HI 96753
www.mauidiveshop.com • *Snorkel & Diving*

Snorkel Bob's • (808) 879-7449
2411 S Kihei Rd, # A2; Kihei, HI 96753
www.snorkelbob.com • *Snorkel & Sailing*

Dive & Sea Māui • (808) 874-1952
432 Kupulau Dr; Kihei, HI 96753
www.diveandseamaui.com • Snorkel: $95

Shaka Divers • (808) 250-1234
24 Hakoi Pl; Kihei, HI 96753
www.shakadivers.com • *Snorkel & Diving*

Māui Kayaks • (808) 874-4000
2463 S Kihei Rd, # C16329; Kihei, HI 96753
www.mauikayaks.com • Kayak: $54 (2 hr)

Kelii's Kayak Tours • (808) 874-7652
158 Lanakila Place; Kihei, HI 96753
www.keliiskayak.com • Tour: $64 (2.5 hrs)

Māui Eco Tours • (808) 891-2223 • Kihei
www.mauiecotours.com • Tours: $69

Māui Beach Boys • (808) 283-7114 • Kihei
www.mauibeachboys.com • Surfing: $60

Polynesian Village Luau • (808) 250-5074
575 South Kihei Rd; Kihei, HI 96753
www.polynesianvillageluau.com • Luau: $79

Garden of Eden Arboretum • (808) 572-9899
10600 Hāna Hwy; Haiku, HI 96708
www.mauigardenofeden.com • Admission: $15/Adult

Māui Ocean Center • (808) 270-7000
192 Maalaea Boat Harbor Rd; Wailuku, HI
www.mauioceancenter.com • Admission: $23/Adult

Pacific Whale Foundation • (808) 249-8977
300 Maalaea Boat Harbor Rd; Wailuku, HI
www.pacificwhale.org • Whale Watch: $25+

Air Māui Helicopter Tours • (808) 877-7005
Hangar 110, 1 Kahului Airport Rd; Kahului, HI 96732
www.airmaui.com • Tours: $165+

Hike Māui • (808) 879-5270
PO Box 330969; Kahului, HI 96733
www.hikemaui.com • Tours: $75–160

Valley Isle Excursions • (877) 871-5224 • Kahului
www.tourmaui.com

Blue Hawaiian Helicopters • (808) 871-8844
Kahului Heliport, 2 Lelepio Pl; Paia, HI 96779
www.bluehawaiian.com • Tours: $148–440

Zack Howard Surf Lessons • (808) 214-7766
513 Kuanana St; Paia, HI 96779
www.zackhowardsurf.com • Group Lesson: $80

Ka'eleku Caverns • (808) 248-7308
PO Box 40; Hāna, HI 96713
www.mauicave.com • Admission: $12/Adult

'Īao Valley State Mon. • (808) 587-0300
www.hawaiistateparks.org • Waihee-Waikapu • $5/Vehicle

Skyview Soaring • (808) 248-7070 • Hāna Airport
www.skyviewsoaring.com • Rates: $150 (0.5 hr)

Māui Stables • (808) 248-7799
177 Hāna Hwy; Hāna, HI 96713
www.mauistables.com • Trail Ride: $150

Ocean Project • (808) 667-6706
843 Wainee, #551; Lāhainā, HI

Shoreline Snuba • (808) 281-3483
6 Kai Ala Dr; Lāhainā, HI 96761
www.shorelinesnuba.com • Tours: $59+

Warren & Annabelle's Magic Show
900 Front St; Lāhainā • (808) 667-6244
www.warrenandannabelles.com • Tickets: $58

Lāhainā Stables • (808) 667-2222
Punakea Loop; Lāhainā, HI 96761
www.mauihorse.com • Trail Rides: $115–140

Banyan Tree Park • Lāhainā

Māui Zipline Company • (808) 633-2464
1670 Honoapiilani Hwy; Wailuku, HI 96793
www.mauizipline.com • Zipline: $90

Wai'anapanapa State Park • (808) 984-8109
54 S High St; Wailuku, HI 96793
www.hawaiistateparks.org • Free

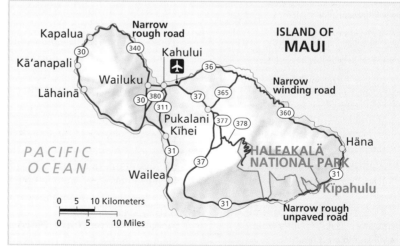

A lava skylight

Hawai'i Volcanoes - Hawai'i

PO Box 52
Hawai'i National Park, HI 96718
Phone: (808) 985-6000
Website: www.nps.gov/havo

Established: August 1, 1916
Size: 323,431 Acres
Annual Visitors: 1.3 Million
Peak Season: All Year

#1 Tourist Attraction in Hawai'i
International Biosphere
World Heritage Site

Activities: Hiking, Biking, Caving,
Lava Watching, and Bird Watching

Campgrounds: Nāmakanipaio and
Kulanaokuaiki
Camping Fee: Free
10 Cabins at Nāmakanipaio
Cabin Rates: $50/night
Lodging: Volcano House Hotel
Rates: Closed until early 2012

Park Hours: All day, every day
Entrance Fee: $10 • Vehicle
$5 • Individual (foot, bike, etc.)

Hawai'i Volcanoes National Park is fire and water, rock and sand, rain forest and desert, desolation and beauty, creation and destruction. Such contradictions have the power to leave visitors speechless. Short of words. Lost in thought. The mind flooded with questions. Where does the lava come from? When will the eruption stop? How did plant and animal life reach the island? Was there ever a huge eruption? Musings range from genesis to apocalypse. Hawai'i Volcanoes is a world where creation never looked so destructive.

To native Hawaiians, **Kīlauea Volcano** is a holy place. They consider it the "body" of Pele, the volcano goddess of ancient Hawaiian legends. Today, Kīlauea is the center of the park and the world's most active volcano. The Pu'u 'Ō'ō Cone has been erupting continuously since 1983. Past lava flow has added more than 550 acres of land to the Big Island of Hawai'i and it's continuing to grow.

Mauna Loa is equally impressive. Rising 13,679 feet above sea level, it towers above 4,000 foot Kīlauea. When measured from its base, some 18,000 feet below the water's surface, Mauna Loa is earth's largest mountain, taller and more massive than Mount Everest. It's hard to believe such a gargantuan land mass could go unnoticed, undisturbed, and unsettled for thousands of years.

About 1,500 years ago **Polynesian pioneers**, probably from Samoa, steered double-hulled canoes more than 2,500 miles to the Hawaiian

Islands. Scientists believe they followed the path of the koleo (or golden plover), a small bird that flies more than 2,500 miles non-stop to Alaska every summer where they mate before returning to Hawai'i. Some choose to continue another 2,500 miles to Samoa. It's plausible that early Samoans, curious as to where these birds were going, hopped in their canoes, following their feathered friends only to learn that the closest significant land was more than one tenth of the way around the globe (Insert punch line: "and man were their arms tired.") Luckily, they were prepared for settlement. Pigs, dogs, chickens, taro, sweet potato, and seeds of coconut, sugar cane, banana, and other edible and medicinal plants accompanied them on their voyage. Very little is known beyond the arrival of Hawai'i's original culture. It is widely believed that they were assimilated, killed, or forced into exile by a second wave of colonists, this time from Tahiti.

Tahitian colonists brought with them practices of human sacrifice and a distinct class structure. Professionals, commoners, and slaves were ruled by chiefs. Settlements with new leadership began to be established across all the Hawaiian Islands. War was common between rival tribes. Canoes were used for fishing rather than exploring. Samoa and Tahiti were long forgotten. Hawai'i was now there home.

It was a home without room for **Western explorers** like **Captain James Cook,** who stumbled upon the Hawaiian Islands in January 1778 while on his way to Alaska. He returned three more times, and on his third visit he sailed into Kealakekua Bay of the Big Island, where he and his crew were greeted by villagers, many of whom believed Cook was Lono, the god of fertility (land). Cook and his crew left the island, but returned shortly after departing to make repairs to a broken mast. This time they were greeted with hostility. Natives stole a small rowboat and Captain Cook attempted to hold the tribe's king hostage (a common practice) in exchange for their boat. The attempt failed; Natives struck Captain Cook on his head, stabbing him to death before he could flee.

By the 1840s visitors were once again a welcome sight on the Big Island. **Tourism** had become the island's leading industry, and just as they are today, Hawai'i Volcanoes was the most popular attraction. In 1916 a national park was created to protect this spectacular area from grazing cattle, over-development, and ultimately, it's destruction. And now visitors like you are free to conjure questions about this land filled with contradictions.

When to Go

The park is open all year. Visitation is steady with peaks during winter and major holidays. Weather is also fairly consistent throughout the year, but it varies greatly depending on your location in the park. It's warm and breezy by the coast, comfortable and wet at Kīlauea (4,000-ft), and temperatures frequently dip below freezing at the summit of Mauna Loa (13,677-ft). To make the weather even more interesting, temperatures can exceed 100°F near sites of volcanic activity. Pack for all conditions if you intend on exploring all the park's ecosystems.

Kīlauea Visitor Center is open daily from 7:45am to 5pm. Jaggar Museum is open daily from 8:30am to 7:30pm. The Kahuku section of the park, south of Hilo between mile markers 70 and 71, is open Saturday and Sunday from 9am to 3pm, but is closed on the first Saturday of each month.

Transportation & Airports

Hawai'i Volcanoes National Park is on the island of Hawai'i (also known as the Big Island). Hilo International (ITO) and Kona International at Keahole (KOA) are the major airports. Direct flights from the continental U.S. to Kona are available. Hilo arrival requires an inter-island flight from Honolulu (Oahu, HI). Car rental is available at both airports. Due to extreme competition, rates are often quite reasonable (Compact: $25/day, Jeep: $70/day).

Directions

Kona is farther from the park, but the drive is more interesting as you'll pass beautiful beaches and the southernmost point of the United States, cleverly named South Point. From Hilo it is a relatively short drive through villages and forest.

From Kona (~111 miles): From Keahole Airport Road take HI-19 south for about 7 miles where it turns into HI-11. Continue on HI-11 for a little more than 93 miles then turn right at HI-11/Crater Rim Road. Follow Crater Rim Road to the visitor center.

From Hilo (~30 miles): Take Airport Road to HI-11. Head south on HI-11 for about 27 miles. Turn left at Crater Rim Road and follow it to the park's visitor center.

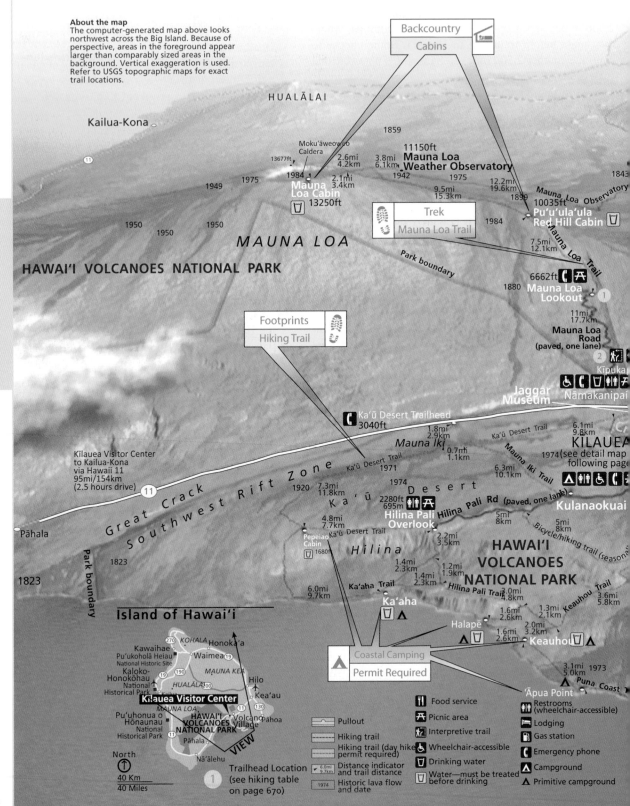

About the map
The computer-generated map above looks northwest across the Big Island. Because of perspective, areas in the foreground appear larger than comparably sized areas in the background. Vertical exaggeration is used. Refer to USGS topographic maps for exact trail locations.

HUALĀLAI

Kailua-Kona

Backcountry
Cabins

1859

Moku'āweoweo
Caldera
13677ft
1949   1975
1984
2.6mi
4.2km
3.8mi
6.1km
11150ft
**Mauna Loa
Weather Observatory**
1942   1975
9.5mi
15.3km
1899
12.2mi
19.6km
1843
Mauna Loa Observatory
2.1mi
3.4km
**Mauna
Loa Cabin** 13250ft

1950   1950

1950   1950

MAUNA LOA

10035ft
1984
**Pu'u'ula'ula
Red Hill Cabin**

Trek
Mauna Loa Trail

7.5mi
12.1km

HAWAI'I VOLCANOES NATIONAL PARK

Park boundary

6662ft
1880
**Mauna Loa
Lookout**
1

Footprints
Hiking Trail

11mi
17.7km
**Mauna Loa
Road**
(paved, one lane)
2

Kīpuka

**Jaggar
Museum**
Nāmakanipai

Ka'ū Desert Trailhead
3040ft

1.8mi
2.9km
Ka'ū Desert Trail
6.1mi
9.8km

KILAUEA
1974 (see detail map
following page

Mauna Iki
1971
0.7mi
1.1km

Mauna Iki Trail
6.3mi
10.1km

Kīlauea Visitor Center
to Kailua-Kona
via Hawaii 11
95mi/154km
(2.5 hours drive)

1920
7.3mi
11.8km
1974

Great Crack
Southwest Rift Zone
Ka'ū Desert Trail

K a ' ū   D e s e r t

2280ft
695m
**Hilina Pali
Overlook**
Hilina Pali Rd (paved, one lane)

Kulanaokuai

5mi
8km
5mi
8km
Bicycle/hiking trail (seasonal)

Pāhala

4.8mi
7.7km
Pepeiao
Cabin
1680ft
Ka'ū Desert Trail

Hilina

2.2mi
3.5km

**HAWAI'I
VOLCANOES
NATIONAL PARK**

1823

1823

1.4mi
2.3km
1.4mi
2.3km
1.2mi
1.9km

2.0mi
4.8km
Hilina Pali Trail

Keauhou Trail
3.6mi
5.8km

6.0mi
9.7km
Ka'aha Trail
Ka'aha

1.3mi
2.1km

Island of Hawai'i

1.6mi
2.6km
Halapē
2.0mi
3.2km
1.6mi
2.6km
Keauhou

KOHALA
Honoka'a
Kawaihae
Pu'ukoholā Heiau
National Historic Site
Kaloko-
Honokōhau
National
Historical Park
Pu'uhonua o
Hōnaunau
National
Historical Park
Waimea
MAUNA KEA
HUALĀLAI
MAUNA LOA
**HAWAI'I
VOLCANOES
NATIONAL PARK**
Pāhala
Nā'ālehu
Hilo
Kea'au
Kīlauea Visitor Center
Volcano
Village
Pāhoa
VIEW

3.1mi
5.0km
1973
Puna Coast

'Āpua Point

Coastal Camping
Permit Required

North

40 Km
40 Miles

Trailhead Location
(see hiking table
on page 670)

1

Food service

Picnic area

Interpretive trail

Wheelchair-accessible

Drinking water

Water—must be treated
before drinking

Pullout

Hiking trail

Hiking trail (day hike
permit required)

6.0mi
9.7km
Distance indicator
and trail distance

1974
Historic lava flow
and date

Restrooms
(wheelchair-accessible)

Lodging

Gas station

Emergency phone

Campground

Primitive campground

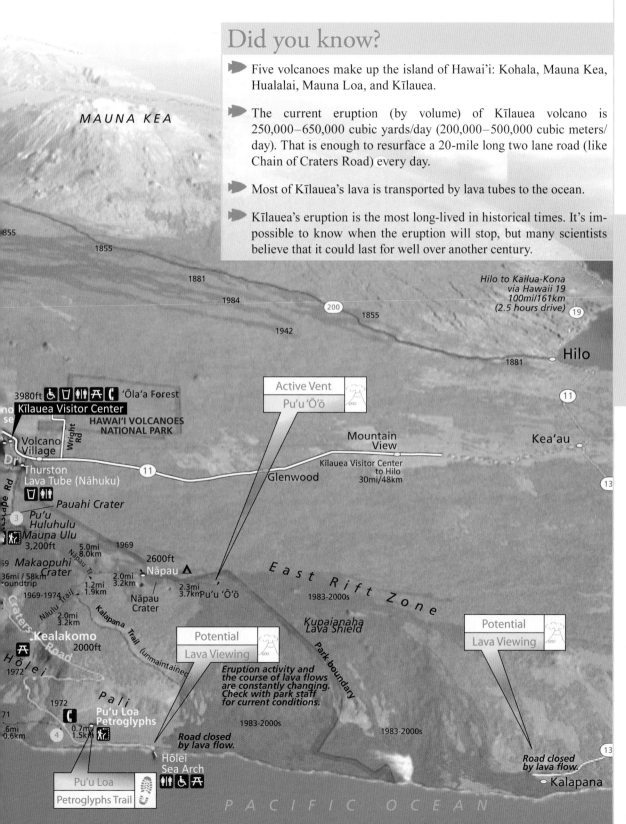

Did you know?

➤ Five volcanoes make up the island of Hawai'i: Kohala, Mauna Kea, Hualalai, Mauna Loa, and Kīlauea.

➤ The current eruption (by volume) of Kīlauea volcano is 250,000–650,000 cubic yards/day (200,000–500,000 cubic meters/day). That is enough to resurface a 20-mile long two lane road (like Chain of Craters Road) every day.

➤ Most of Kīlauea's lava is transported by lava tubes to the ocean.

➤ Kīlauea's eruption is the most long-lived in historical times. It's impossible to know when the eruption will stop, but many scientists believe that it could last for well over another century.

MAUNA KEA

855

1855

1881

1984

1942

200

1855

Hilo to Kailua-Kona
via Hawaii 19
100mi/161km
(2.5 hours drive)

19

1881

Hilo

Active Vent

Pu'u 'Ō'ō

11

Kea'au

3980ft 'Ōla'a Forest

Kīlauea Visitor Center

HAWAI'I VOLCANOES
NATIONAL PARK

Mountain
View

Kīlauea Visitor Center
to Hilo
30mi/48km

Volcano
Village

11

Glenwood

Thurston
Lava Tube (Nāhuku)

Pauahi Crater

Pu'u
Huluhulu

Mauna Ulu
3,200ft

5.0mi
8.0km

1969

2600ft

Nāpau △

East Rift Zone

Makaopuhi
Crater

36mi / 58km
roundtrip

2.0mi
3.2km

1.2mi
1.9km

2.3mi
3.7km Pu'u 'Ō'ō

1983-2000s

1969-1974

Nāpau
Crater

Kupaianaha
Lava Shield

Potential

Lava Viewing

2.0mi
3.2km

Kalapana Trail (unmaintained)

Kealakomo
2000ft

Park boundary

Hōlei

Potential

Lava Viewing

1972

Pali

Eruption activity and
the course of lava flows
are constantly changing.
Check with park staff
for current conditions.

71

1972

Pu'u Loa
Petroglyphs

.6mi
0.6km

4

0.7mi
1.5km

1983-2000s

1983-2000s

Road closed
by lava flow.

Hōlei
Sea Arch

Road closed
by lava flow.

13

Pu'u Loa

Petroglyphs Trail

Kalapana

PACIFIC OCEAN

Trailhead Location (see hiking table on page 670)

Don't Miss
Crater Rim Drive

Park boundary

Pi'i Mauna Drive

1.2mi
2.0km

Kīpukapuaulu

Highway 11 to
Mauna Loa Lookout
11.4mi/18.3km

Mauna Loa Road

1.5mi
2.4km

Tree Molds

Kīlauea
Military
Camp

0.6m
1.0k

Crater Rim Drive

Crater Rim Trail

Steaming Blu

Nāmakanipaio
Campground

1.2mi
1.9km

11

Kīlauea Overlook

Lava flows before 1924

To Kailua-Kona
95mi/154km

0.5mi
0.8km

Hawaiian Volcano Observatory
(not open to the public)

Uwēkahuna

Jaggar
Museum

4078ft

1.4mi
2.7km

KĪLAUEA CALDERA

Ka'ū Desert Trail

1982 lava

Halema'uma'u Trail

1971 lava

Leleakōlea

Halema'uma'u
Crater

0.4mi
0.6km

1971 lava

0.2mi
0.3km

1974 lava

Halema'uma'u
Overlook
Hazardous volcanic fumes
3640ft

Southwest Rift

1974 lava

Crater Rim Drive 11mi/17.7km loop

1971 lava

Southwest
Rift Zone

Lava flows
before 1924

Halema'uma'u Trail

0.5mi
0.8km

Holoholoakōlea

1.4mi
2.7km

1982 lava

1971 lava

Don't Miss
Halema'uma'u Overlook

Crater Rim Trail 11.6mi/18.7km loop

KA'Ū DESERT

2.3mi
3.7km

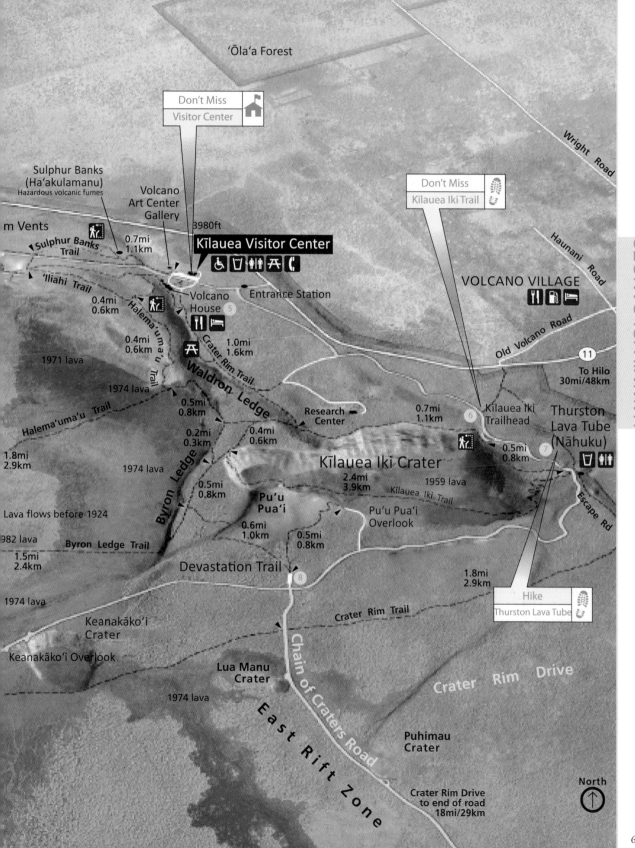

'Ōla'a Forest

Wright Road

Don't Miss
Visitor Center

Sulphur Banks
(Ha'akulamanu)
Hazardous volcanic fumes

Volcano
Art Center
Gallery

Don't Miss
Kīlauea Iki Trail

Haunani Road

m Vents

Sulphur Banks
Trail

3980ft

0.7mi
1.1km

Kīlauea Visitor Center

VOLCANO VILLAGE

'Iliahi Trail

0.4mi
0.6km

Volcano
House

Entrance Station

Old Volcano Road

11

To Hilo
30mi/48km

0.4mi
0.6km

1.0mi
1.6km

Crater Rim Trail

Halema'uma'u Trail

1971 lava

1974 lava

Waldron Ledge

Research
Center

0.7mi
1.1km

Kīlauea Iki
Trailhead

6

Thurston
Lava Tube
(Nāhuku)

Halema'uma'u Trail

0.5mi
0.8km

0.2mi
0.3km

0.4mi
0.6km

Kīlauea Iki Crater

0.5mi
0.8km

1.8mi
2.9km

Byron Ledge

1974 lava

2.4mi
3.9km

1959 lava

Kīlauea Iki Trail

Escape Rd

Lava flows before 1924

0.5mi
0.8km

Pu'u
Pua'i

Pu'u Pua'i
Overlook

982 lava

Byron Ledge Trail

0.6mi
1.0km

0.5mi
0.8km

1.5mi
2.4km

1974 lava

Devastation Trail

8

1.8mi
2.9km

Hike
Thurston Lava Tube

Keanakāko'i
Crater

Crater Rim Trail

Keanakāko'i Overlook

Chain of Craters Road

Lua Manu
Crater

Crater Rim Drive

1974 lava

East Rift Zone

Puhimau
Crater

North

Crater Rim Drive
to end of road
18mi/29km

Don't expect to see this sort of lava display • The image simply shows what it can look like during an eruption

Hawai'i Volcanoes Camping

	Open	Fees	Location/Notes
Nāmakanipaio	All Year	None	Off Hwy 11 near Kīlauea • Restrooms and water are available • The campground also has 10 cabins available for $50/night
Kulanaokuaiki	All Year	None	5 miles down Hilina Pali Road • No water, 8 campsites

All campsites are available on a first-come, first-served basis. Camping is limited to a maximum of 7 days per month and cannot exceed 30 days per year. Backcountry camping is permitted within the park. A free permit is required. Backcountry campers must register at Kīlauea Visitor Center prior to departure.

Hawai'i Volcanoes Hiking Trails

	Trail Name	Trailhead (# on maps)	Length	Notes (Rountrip distances)
Easy	Kīpukapuaulu	Trail Parking Area on Mauna Loa Road (2)	1.2 miles	Loop trail through island forest (kipuka)
	Mauna Ulu	Trail Parking Area on Chain of Craters Road (3)	2.5 miles	Lava fields, fissures, and flows
	Earthquake	Just east of Volcano House Hotel (5)	1.0 mile	A section of Old Crater Rim Drive
	Thurston Lava Tube - 👍	Trail Parking Area on Crater Rim Drive (7)	0.5 mile	Cave-like feature formed by a massive flow of lava
	Devastation - 👍	Trail Parking Area on Crater Rim Drive (8)	1.0 mile	View effects of 1959 eruption
Moderate–Strenuous	Crater Rim	Accessible from several locations along Crater Rim Drive	11.6 miles	Closed from Jaggar Museum south to the junction with Chain of Craters Rd
	Mauna Loa - 👍	The end of Mauna Loa Road (1)	23 miles	Leads to two cabins and 13,679-ft summit
	Pu'u Huluhulu	Mauna Ulu Parking Area on Chain of Craters Rd (3)	18.6 miles	Old lava flows, lava trees, and kipuka
	Napau	Mauna Ulu Parking Area on Chain of Craters Rd (3)	14.0 miles	Recent lava flows and rain forest
	Pu'u Loa Petroglyphs	Pu'u Loa Parking Area on Chain of Craters Road (4)	1.5 mile	Boardwalk trail across old lava flows where ancient petroglyphs were drawn
	Halema'uma'u	Behind Volcano House (5)	1.8 miles	Significant portion closed due to gas
	'Iliahi	West of Volcano House (5)	1.5 miles	Hike past steam vents and rain forest
	Kīlauea Iki - 👍	Kīlauea Iki Overlook on Crater Rim Drive (6)	4.0 miles	Loop trail (proceed counter-clockwise)

 # Hiking

Hawai'i Volcanoes National Park is without a doubt the best destination for hiking in the state of Hawai'i. More than 150 miles of trails crisscross the black sand shores, arid deserts, lush rain forests, and delicate volcanic surfaces. Expect a few trail closures when hiking in an area with volcanic activity. Trails often close suddenly due to fumes, lava flows, and poor trail conditions. Closures are made for your safety, so please heed these warnings. For a current list of closures and advisories please visit www.nps.gov/havo/closed_areas.htm.

The best and most popular hike in the Kīlauea/Crater Loop Drive area is the 4-mile **Kīlauea Iki Trail**. Kīlauea means "spewing," and the hike leads you on an up-close-and-personal look at the volcanic geology of Kīlauea's last "spew." Its trailhead is located at Kīlauea Iki Overlook. Walking counter-clockwise you will pass through rain forest before Pu'u Pua'i cinder cone, the main vent for an eruption on November 14, 1959, comes into view. Lava gushed out of the vent, shooting arcs as high as 1,900 feet. That's a personal record for Pele, the goddess of fire. Next you'll pass through a forest destroyed by the eruption, which is followed by another view of Pu'u Pua'i. Hike past a few large boulders and through another forest before descending into the caldera. Here you'll notice cones, fractures, and the "bathtub ring" that marks the high lava mark of a 2,000°F lake of molten rock that once filled the caldera. The lake didn't cool completely until the mid-1990s. Today you can walk across its solid surface. Before exiting the crater and returning to the overlook, look back and imagine a lake of spouting and spitting lava, waves of thick molten rock oozing at your feet. You'll exit near **Thurston Lava Tube**. Time permitting, take a short walk through the tube. It was created when the outer layer of lava cooled, acting as insulation to the inner lava as it continued to flow down the slope to the ocean.

Haleme'uma'u and **Earthquake** (also known as Byron Ledge) are two short trails that lead into Kīlauea Caldera. **Devastation Trail** highlights a line of destruction from the 1959 eruption. You pass from a lush healthy forest to a field of scarred tree trunks. The 1.5-mile **'Iliahi (also known as Sandlewood) Trail** skirts the crater, affording spectacular views of steam vents. If you don't want to take your car around Crater Rim Drive you can hike the 11.6-mile **Crater Rim Trail** (when it's open). Again, please refer to www.nps.gov/havo/closed_areas.htm for current closures.

 # Driving

Hawai'i Volcanoes is essentially a drive-in volcano. The 11-mile **Crater Rim Drive** circles Kīlauea Crater. At the time of publication Crater Rim Drive was closed between Jaggar Museum and Chain of Craters Road due to elevated levels of sulfur dioxide gas. When entirely open, the loop provides access to many of the park's main attractions: Kīlauea Visitor Center, Jaggar Museum, Volcano House (closed until early 2012), Thurston Lava Tube, and Kīlauea Iki Trail. Another popular drive, **Chain of Craters Road**, is accessed via Crater Rim Drive. After 19 miles it dead-ends abruptly where recent lava flow has covered the road. Just beyond this point is your best bet to see surface lava flows. It also provides access to **Hilina Pali Road** and several popular hiking trails like the self-guided Mauna Ulu and Pu'u Loa Petroglyphs Trails. **Mauna Loa Road** is a one-lane, paved road that ends at Mauna Loa Trailhead.

 # Camping

Two drive-in campgrounds are available. **Nāmakanipaio Campground** is located on State Highway 11 just a few miles beyond Kīlauea Entrance when traveling from Hilo. The camp features shared restrooms, water, picnic tables, and grills. Pack for cool evenings. Temperatures here can drop into the 30s°F at night and rain is common. About 5 miles west on Hilina Pali Road is **Kulanaokuaiki Campground**. There are 8 campsites with vault toilets and picnic tables. This location does not have water. Temperatures here can drop into the 40s°F at night and rain is common. Both campgrounds are free of charge. Check-in is not required, and sites are available on a first-come, first-served basis.

Backcountry camping is allowed by permit only. Along **Mauna Loa Trail** you'll find **two backcountry cabins**. Mauna Loa Cabin is near the summit and Pu'u'ula'ula Red Hill Cabin is at 10,000-ft elevation. Both have several bunk beds and are shared on a first-come, first-served basis. There are also designated **backcountry campsites** along the coastline (see map on page 666).

Lava Viewing

Even though the volcano has been erupting almost continuously at **Pu'u 'Ō'ō** in the East Rift Zone since 1983, there are no guarantees that visitors will see surface flows. Lava is often flowing in inaccessible locations or being deposited directly into the ocean via underground lava tubes. The best way to learn if and where you can see lava is to stop at **Kīlauea Visitor Center** or give them a call (808.985.6000). Additionally, daily volcanic activity reports are posted at the USGS website (www.volcanoes.usgs.gov/hvo/activity/kilaueasta-tus.php). **The park's most reliable area for lava viewing is at the end of Chain of Craters Road.** From here, hike along the coast where glowing lava, or steam from it pouring into the ocean, can be seen. For a closer look of Pu'u 'Ō'ō (the active vent) visitors can hike the 18.6-mile (one-way) **Pu'u Huluhulu Trail**. (At publication the trail to Pu'u 'Ō'ō Vent was closed by the park superintendent. Visitors are allowed as far as the backcountry campsite at Nāpau.)

It is possible to hike to Pu'u 'Ō'ō from outside the park via **Kahaualeʻa Trail**. It's accessed from South Glenwood Road between mile markers 19 and 20 on HI-11, about 20 miles from Hilo. Follow South Glenwood Road, which becomes Captain's Drive/Ala Kapena and continue to its end, 3.5 miles from the highway. The parking area is notorious for robberies. Do not leave valuables in your car. This hike is a little more than 5 miles (one-way) through thick rain forest to the 500 foot cone built during the current eruption. Kahaualeʻa Trail begins on state land, but it was under a closure order by the park at time of publication. Please obey all park closures and advisories. For a list of current closures and advisories visit www.nps.gov/havo/closed_areas.htm. You can also reach the other side of the current lava flow from outside the park. Follow Highway 130 to a parking area that is open when lava is flowing (for a $5 entry fee).

Lava viewing is best at dusk when the its glow is not drowned out by direct sunlight. Bring a flashlight if you plan on hiking any significant distance after dark.

Backpacking

More than half of the park is designated wilderness, providing ample opportunity for solitude and volcanic exploration. Take proper precautions before heading into the backcountry. Pack the essentials: water, first aid kit, stove, map, flashlight and batteries, rain gear, toilet paper (be sure to pack it out), and food. Backpackers must camp at designated sites, so plan your route in advance. **A free permit is required.** It can be obtained from Kīlauea Visitor Center no more than a day before departure. Permits are issued on a first-come, first-served basis (day-hikers do not require a permit). Campers are allowed a maximum stay of three consecutive nights per site, and just 16 people/night are allowed in each backcountry campsites. All sites have pit toilets. Do not dispose of trash in toilets. Backpackers must check out upon completion at Kīlauea Visitor Center or by calling (808) 985-6017. There are three main backpacking areas.

Mauna Loa: The 17-mile (one-way) **Mauna Loa Trail** to the summit of the world's most massive mountain begins at the end of Mauna Loa Road. Rock piles, commonly called cairns, mark the trail. From the trailhead it is 7.5 miles to **Pu'u'ula'ula Red Hill Cabin**. It has 8 bunks with mattresses. Rest here, because it's another 9.5 miles to the summit where you'll find **Mauna Loa Cabin** (circling the summit in a counter-clockwise fashion is shorter). It has 12 bunks. Both cabins have water catchments (the only reliable source of water along the trail). Check on water levels when registering, and treat all water before drinking. Mauna Loa's summit is 13,679 feet, so altitude sickness can be a problem. Extreme weather conditions can also occur at any time of year. Eruptions are possible, but unlikely. Campfires are not permitted due to the prevalence of flammable grasses and brush.

East Rift Zone: The trail to **Pu'u 'Ō'ō vent** is closed by the park superintendent, but backpackers can still hike **Nāpau or Nāulu Trails** and camp at **Nāpau Crater**. This campsite does not have shelter or water. Tents are required.

Coastal Areas: From Pu'u Loa Petroglyphs Parking Area backpackers can take **Puna Coast Trail** (page 666) to one of three backcountry camps. **Ka'aha, Halapē, and Keauhou campsites** have three-walled shelters, but tents are advised due to bugs. These sites and **Pepeiao Cabin** (farther west along **Ka'aha Trail**) have water catchments. Water must be treated before drinking. **'Āpua Point** has no shelter and no water.

Pu'u Loa Petroglyphs

Pu'u Loa Petroglyphs Trail is located near the end of Chain of Craters Road at Milepost 16.5. There are more than 23,000 cryptic symbols scrawled onto lava rocks in this region of the park. The trail is a 2-mile boardwalk that traverses old lava flows to one of Hawai'i's most extensive petroglyph fields. Please stay on the boardwalk to protect the fragile environment and its artifacts.

At first sight these images could pass as the handiwork of a 14-year old vandal, but with a bit of explanation their meaning becomes clearer. For example, you may see petroglyphs consisting of a dot with concentric circles around it. The dot signifies a man, and each circle represents a member of his traveling party that made the journey around the island with him. Anthropologist Martha Beckwith visited Pu'u Loa in 1914 and argued that holes in the lava's surface were created to deposit umbilical cords at birth. She believes that the cord was placed in the hole and a rock was set on top of it. If the cord was gone in the morning it ensured a long life.

Biking

Biking in Hawai'i Volcanoes National Park can be an extremely rewarding experience. It can also be unbelievably frustrating if the roads are packed with tour buses and rental cars, so it's best to pedal early in the morning before the masses leave their hotels and campsites. **Crater Rim Drive** (may be closed from Volcano House to Chain of Craters Road) is an excellent 11-mile loop. While pedalling this paved road you'll pass through lush forest and barren desert as you circle Kīlauea Caldera. Climbers can go from Kīlauea to the Coastal Plains and back up the 18-mile (one-way) **Chain of Craters Road**. **Mauna Loa Road** (3,700-ft climb) offers another excellent challenge. It ascends nearly 3,000 feet in 13.5 miles before terminating at Mauna Loa Trailhead, where you can continue (by foot) to the mountain's summit (13,000+ feet) or turn around and enjoy the rapid descent back to where you started (Namakanipaio Campground is a good choice). **Hilina Pali Road** (off Chain of Craters Road) is 9-miles (one-way) and open to cyclists. **Escape Road** (a dirt escape route in case of eruption) runs mostly parallel to Chain of Craters Road and can be accessed from Thurston Lava Tube or Highway 11. There's also a 5-mile (one-way) dirt hiking trail between Chain of Craters Road and Hilina Pali that allows cyclists. **See page 678 for bike rental and outfitters.**

Thurston Lava Tube

Best of Hawai'i Volcanoes

Moderate Hike: **Kīlauea Iki**
Runner-up: Mauna Ulu

Short Hike: **Kīpukapuaulu**
Runner-up: Devastation
2nd Runner-up: Thurston Lava Tube

Cultural Hike: **Pu'u Loa Petroglyphs**
Runner-up: Ka'ū Desert

Did you know?

➤ John Muir and former President Theodore Roosevelt were among the original advocates for Hawai'i Volcanoes National Park.

➤ Stephen Mather and Horace Albright spearheaded the acquisition of the Footprints (page 674).

➤ Mauna Loa last erupted in 1984.

➤ Kīlauea, the world's most active volcano, has been erupting continuously since 1983.

➤ The park is home to Anax strenuous, the largest dragonfly in the United States.

➤ Eventually (more than 100,000 years) the island of Hawai'i will sink beneath the ocean's surface.

➤ Lo'ihi, a future Hawaiian Island, is already being formed 21 miles off the coast of the Big Island by a giant undersea volcano.

➤ It will take Lo'ihi more than 100,000 years to breach the ocean's surface.

Uluhe (Dicranopteris linearis) purple fiddlehead © David J. Laporte

Footprints

Fossilized footprints are found along the **Ka'ū Desert Trail**. They were created in 1790 after a massive eruption of Kīlauea. Years of erosion have taken their toll, but the outlines of ancient feet can still be seen today. The trail is accessed via Ka'ū Desert Trailhead, adjacent to Highway 11 near the 38 mile marker. It can also be reached via **Ka'ū Desert Trail** from Crater Rim Drive. The prints are fragile, so please remain on the path.

Legend holds that a retreating army was passing by Kīlauea Volcano in 1782. The volcano was angry that day. To appease the goddess Pele, they chose to stay near the volcano's rim offering sacrifices for several days. Upon leaving the summit, the army split into three companies. The first company had not gone far when Kīlauea exploded, emitting ash and gas. Unable to escape, everyone in the second company died, except a lone pig. Members of the third company survived, but they encountered the remains of the second party lying dead, face first in the ashes. Ash provided an excellent medium for fossilization of the warriors' footprints. It's impossible to know exactly whose footsteps have been preserved along Ka'ū Desert Trail, but there most certainly was an eruption in 1790. Reports state that anywhere from 80 to over 5,000 individuals were killed by it. What's the truth? Hike the trail and imagine for yourself.

For Kids: If a miniature papier-mâché volcano with a vinegar-baking soda eruption draws "ooohs" and "ahhhs" from you children (like they're viewing 4th of July fireworks) imagine what they'll think about seeing a real volcano with a river of molten rock? Here you can watch lava pour into the Pacific, hike through a lava tube, and view a collection of ancient Hawaiian artifacts. If that's not enough entertainment, children (ages 7–12) can take part in the park's **Junior Ranger Program**. A free activity booklet (available online or at the visitor center) helps families learn more about the park, and kids earn a badge for completing its activities.

Ranger Programs: A current schedule of ranger programs can be found at the park website or on the ranger activity bulletin board at Kīlauea Visitor Center. Visitors can expect rangers to give a 20 minute talk on **"How It All Began"** outside the visitor center daily at 9:30am and 3:30pm. Rangers also give a 45–60 minute walk around Kīlauea summit daily at 10:30am and 1:30pm. Attending a ranger program is one of the best uses of your time in the park.

Flora & Fauna: Hawai'i, the world's most isolated island group, is a fascinating biological laboratory. After hundreds of thousands of years of volcanic activity the Hawaiian Islands finally broke the surface of the Pacific Ocean, creating a new and unique habitat for life. Life faced one major obstacle. The islands were more than 2,000 miles from the nearest significant land mass.

Plant life would have to be carried there by wind, water, or birds. Eventually several species of plants and animals made the seemingly impossible journey. After millions of years of evolution and adaptation, a unique world was created where more than 90% of the species of flora and fauna are only found on these islands.

The park is home to many **fascinating creatures**: happyface spiders, carnivorous caterpillars, picture wing flies, and honeycreepers. It's also refuge to a variety of endangered species: hawksbill turtles, nēnē, dark-rumped petrel, and hoary bat. Hawksbill turtles use some of the park's beaches as nesting areas, and backpackers should not camp in areas posted as turtle nesting habitat. This is also a great area for **bird watching**.

Sea birds can be seen from the end of **Chain of Craters Road**. **Kipukapualu Loop Trail** is another exceptional spot for bird watching; this 100-acre island of vegetation contains the richest concentrations of native plants and bird life in Hawai'i.

Nēnēs, the Hawaiian goose and descendent of the Canadian goose, nest in the park. Motorists should always drive cautiously, as nēnēs have a tendency to get in the way.

Pets: In general it's not a good idea to bring your pets to Hawai'i. They are permitted in the park, but must be kept on a leash no more than six feet in length at all times. Pets are permitted in developed areas including paved roadways, parking areas, and Nāmakanipaio Campground, but are prohibited in all undeveloped areas, Hilina Pali Road, and Kulanaokuaiki Campground. Do not leave your pets unattended in a vehicle.

Accessibility: Many facilities are wheelchair accessible. These include Kīlauea Visitor Center, Jaggar Museum, Volcano House Hotel, and Volcano Art Center. Both the visitor center and Jaggar Museum have wheelchairs available for use. Namkanipaio and Kulanaokuaiki Campgrounds have accessible campsites and restrooms. Only a few trails are fully accessible. These paths include Waldron Ledge (Earthquake Trail), Devastation Trail, and Pauahi Crater, Muliwai a Pele, and Kealakomo Overlooks.

Weather: Weather on the Big Island is unpredictable. Visitors should come prepared for rain, wind, sun, and maybe even a little snow if you plan on trekking around the summit of Mauna Loa. A good example of the weather's unpredictability is to compare rainfall measurements at Kīlauea Visitor Center. In March of 2006, rainfall measured 34 inches. In March of 2008 it was 4.5 inches. In December of 2007 more than 40 inches of rain fell. December 2005, 1.6 inches. With stats like this it's difficult to make generalizations, but if you had to pick the driest months (on average) choose somewhere between May and October (see graph below).

A nēnē gosling

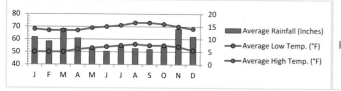

	Average Rainfall (Inches)
	Average Low Temp. (°F)
	Average High Temp. (°F)

Volcano Etiquette

▸ Obey park rangers and posted signs. Park rangers do not close off sections of the park to keep the best scenery to themselves. They do it for your safety. Please obey them.

▸ Pack water and sunscreen. The sun affects more visitors than any other danger, and visitors often become sun burnt or dehydrated without noticing due to the cool ocean breeze.

▸ Volcanic smog can cause closures in and around Kīlauea Caldera. It is dangerous, especially to individuals with respiratory problems and children.

▸ Be especially careful on shoreline cliffs. New lava land likes to crack and you'd rather not go with it when it falls.

The smooth and ropey surface of pahoehoe lava

plan on arriving at the park before 11am. If you are camping, drive directly to your campground (page 671) of choice, because sites are secured on a first-come, first-served basis. Non-campers should go to the **visitor center**. Here, you'll get the scoop on current volcanic activity, area closures, and **ranger-led activities** (page 674). Accompany a ranger on at least one excursion while you're here. No matter how amazing the scenery, it's always improved by the presence of a ranger. Back at the visitor center, watch the short movie titled "Born of Fire, Born of the Sea," browse the exhibits and gift store, and then sneak back outside, hopefully before the buses begin to file in. If half of Crater Rim Drive is still closed (like it was when we went to press), take the drive clockwise from the visitor center to **Thurston Lava Tube**. Here you'll find **Kīlauea Iki** (page 671), the one trail to hike if that's all you have time for. After completing the 4-mile loop, continue through **Thurston Lava Tube**, or pile back into your vehicle. If a park ranger told you that surface flows are visible at the end of **Chain of Craters Road**, you'll want to arrive at **Hōlei Sea Arch** (the end of the road) about two hours before dusk with a couple of flashlights. Meanwhile, explore the trails and overlooks along Chain of Craters Road. **Mauna Ulu Trail** is a good choice. You can hike to **Kealakomo Overlook** (a nice place for a picnic), then hike as far as you care to along **Puna Coast Trail** before returning to Chain of Craters Road to hike in the opposite direction, hoping to see lava as it pours into the ocean.

Most people spend too little time at Hawai'i Volcanoes National Park. They drive in, look at the crater, complete the 11-mile **Crater Rim Drive** (when open), drive down **Chain of Craters Road**, and then it's a race to the exit. Yes, there are an awful lot of amazing attractions in Hawai'i, but none are as fascinating as Hawai'i Volcanoes. Two days isn't nearly enough time, but it's a good start. Make sure that you have enough gas and food. **Volcano House Hotel** (where dining is usually available) is closed for renovations until 2012, and gas is not available in the park. It's always a good idea to pack a picnic and spend the day among the volcanoes. Some of the best dining, grocery stores, lodging, festivals, and attractions outside the park are listed on pages 677–679.

Day 1

One of the first things you need to know is that tour buses arrive between 11am and 3pm, and they like to congregate around Thurston Lava Tube Parking Area. So,

Day 2

Yesterday you explored the heart and soul of the park (Kīlauea), and today you'll poke around its extremities. Start your trip at **Mauna Loa Road**. Stop at **Kīpukapuaulu Trail**, and hike a short loop through a pleasant area for bird watching and flora viewing. The rest of Mauna Loa Road is not for the faint of heart. It is extremely hilly and winding, and eventually it becomes one-way with several blind curves. The road ends at **Mauna Loa Trailhead**, where you are free to choose your own adventure. Hike up the slope of 13,679-ft Mauna Loa (page 672, note that altitude sickness can affect any hiker, regardless of physical condition). Bike down Mauna Loa Road (not advised for inexperienced bikers). Stand and enjoy the view of Kīlauea. Whatever activity you choose it will definitely get your heart pumping. If time allows, return to HI-11 and head west toward Kona. Stop near mile marker 38 to hike **Ku'a Desert Trail**. This trail leads to **The Footprints** (page 674), the only remnants of ancient warriors caught in a volcanic eruption.

Dining

Volcano's Lava Rock Cafe • (808) 967-8526
19-3972 Old Volcano Hwy; Volcano, HI 96785

Thai Thai Restaurant • (808) 967-7969
19-4084 Old Volcano Rd; Volcano, HI 96785

Cafe Ohia • (808) 985-8587
19-4005 Haunani Rd; Volcano, HI 96785

Kiawe Kitchen • (808) 967-7711
19-4005 Haunani Rd; Pahoa, HI 96778

Ning's Thai Cuisine • (808) 965-7611
15-2955 Pahoa Rd; Pahoa, HI 96778

Kaleo's Bar & Grill • (808) 965-5600
15-2969 Pahoa Village Rd; Pahoa, HI 96778

Hana Hou Restaurant • (808) 929-9717
95-1148 Naalehu Spur Rd; Naalehu, HI 96772

Coffee Shack • (808) 328-9555
83-5799 Mamalahoa Hwy; Hōnaunau, HI 96726
www.coffeeshack.com • Breakfast: $9+

Mi's Italian Bistro • (808) 323-3880
81-6372 Mamalahoa Hwy; Kealakekua, HI 96750
www.misitalianbistro.com • Entrée: $15–32

Patz Pies • (808) 323-8100
81-6596 Mamalahoa Hwy; Kealakekua, HI 96750

Holuakoa Cafe • (808) 322-2233
76-5901 Mamalahoa Hwy; Holualoa, HI 96725

Annie's Island Fresh Burgers • (808) 324-6000
79-7460 Mamalahoa Hwy, #105; Kealakekua, HI 96750
www.anniesislandfreshburgers.com • Burgers: $9+

Huli Sue's BBQ and Grill • (808) 885-6268
64-957 Mamalahoa Hwy; Kamuela, HI 96743
www.hulisues.com • Entrée: $26–34

What's Shakin • (808) 964-3080
27-999 Old Mamalahoa Hwy; Pepeekeo, HI 96783

Da Poke Shack • (808) 329-7653
76-6246 Alii Dr; Kailua, HI 96740
www.dapokeshack.com

Jackie Rey's Ohana Grill • (808) 327-0209
75-5995 Kuakini Hwy; Kailua-Kona, HI 96740
www.jackiereys.com • Entrée: $24–29

Island Lava Java Bistro & Grill
75-5799 Alii Dr; Kailua-Kona • (808) 327-2161
www.islandlavajava.com • Entrée: $14–26

Big Island Grill • (808) 326-1153
75-5702 Kuakini Hwy; Kailua-Kona, HI 96740

Beach Tree Bar • (808) 325-8000
Located at the Four Seasons Hotel
72-100 Kaupulehu Dr; Kailua-Kona, HI 96740

Blue Dragon Coastal Cuisine and Musiquarium
61-3616 Kawaihae Rd; Waimea • (808) 882-7771
www.bluedragonhawaii.com • Entrée: $29–36

Hawaiian Style Cafe • (808) 885-4295
65-1290 Kawaihae Rd; Waimea, HI 96743

Akasushi Bar • (808) 887-2320
65-1158 Mamalahoa Hwy; Waimea, HI 96743

PAU • (808) 885-6325
65-1227 Opelo Rd; Kamuela, HI 96743
www.paupizza.com • Pizzas: $17–26

Hilo Bay Cafe • (808) 935-4939
315 East Makaala St, # 109; Hilo, HI 96720
www.hilobaycafe.com • Entrée: $12–30

Roy's • (808) 886-4321
69-250 Waikoloa Beach Dr, # E1; Waikoloa, HI 96738
www.roysrestaurant.com • Entrée: $15–32

Groceries

Safeway • (808) 959-3502
111 E Puainako St; Hilo, HI 96720

Safeway • (808) 329-2207
75-1027 Henry St; Kailua Kona, HI 96740

Walmart • (808) 334-0466
75-1015 Henry St; Kailua Kona, HI 96740

Costco Kona • (808) 331-4800
5600 Maiau St; Kailua, HI 96740

Lodging

Volcano Teapot Cottage • (808) 967-7112
19-4041 Kīlauea Rd; Volcano, HI 96785
www.volcanoteapot.com • Rates: $195/night

Kīlauea Lodge & Restaurant • (808) 967-7366
19-3948 Old Volcano Rd; Volcano, HI 96785
www.kilaualodge.com

Hale Ohia Cottages • (808) 967-7986
11-3968 Hale Ohia Rd; Volcano, HI 96785
www.haleohia.com • Rates: $109–209

Volcano Inn • (808) 967-7773
19-3820 Old Volcano Rd; Volcano, HI 96785
www.volcanoinnhawaii.com • Rates: $59+

Volcano Rainforest Retreat • (808) 985-8696
11-3832 12th St; Volcano; HI 96785
www.volcanoretreat.com • Rates: $125–260

Chalet Kīlauea • (808) 967-7786
PO BOX 960; Volcano, HI 96785
www.volcano-hawaii.com • Rates: $155+

Volcano Guest House • (808) 967-7775
11-3714 Ala'Ohia St; Volcano, HI 96778
www.volcanoguesthouse.com • Rates: $85–125

Aloha Junction • (808) 967-7289
19-4037 Post Office Ln; Volcano, HI 96785
www.bnbvolcano.com • Rates: $100–125

Aloha Crater Lodge • (808) 345-4449
11-3966 Lanihuli Rd; Volcano, HI 96785
www.alohacraterlodge.com • Rates: $120+

Volcano Country Cottages • (808) 967-7960
19-3990 Old Volcano Rd; Volcano, HI 96785
www.volcanocottages.com • Rates: $105–132

Volcano Village Lodge • (808) 985-9500
19-4183 Road E; Volcano, HI 96785
www.volcanovillagelodge.com • Rates: $235–315

My Island B&B • (808) 967-7110
19-3896 Old Volcano Rd; Volcano, HI 96785
www.myislandinnhawaii.com • Rates: $80–110

Volcano Mist Cottage • (808) 895-8359
11-3932 Ninth St; Volcano, HI 96785
www.volcanomistcottage.com • Rates: $275–325

Volcano Hideaways • (808) 985-8959
6 Hale Ohia Rd; Volcano, HI 96785
www.volcanovillage.net • Rates: $130–180

Volcano Forest Inn • (808) 985-9026
19-4034 Old Volcano Rd; Volcano, HI 96785
www.volcanoforestinn.com • Rates: $149–169

Volcano Places
PO Box 159; Volcano, HI 96785
www.volcanoplaces.com • Rates: $110–205

Tara Firma Inn • (808) 985-7204
19-4152 Kekoanui Blvd; Volcano, HI 96785
www.tarafirmainn-volcano.com • Rates: $120

Ohia Plantation House • (808) 573-2195
11-3780 Sixth St; Volcano, HI 96785
www.volcanovacationshawaii.com • Rates: $145–175

Volcano Cedar Cottage • (808) 985-9020
11-3799 7th St; Volcano, HI 96785
www.volcanocc.com • Rates: $85–105

Holo Holo In • (808) 967-7950
19-4036 Kalani Honua Rd; Volcano, HI 96785
www.volcanohostel.com • Dorm: $22

Country Goose B&B • (808) 967-7759
11-3870 Ruby Ave; Pahoa, HI 96778
www.countrygoose.com • Rates: $100–110

Bamboo Orchid B&B • (877) 208-2199
11-3903 10th St; Pahoa, HI 96778
www.bambooorchidcottage.com • Rates: $109+

Halana Lodge • (808) 854-7654
19-4789 Amaumau Rd; Pahoa, HI 96778
www.halanalodge.com • Rates: $120–190

Coconut Cottage B&B • (866) 204-7444
13-1139 Leilani Ave; Pahoa, HI 96778
www.coconutcottagehawaii.com • Rates:
$110–160

The Bali Cottage • (808) 965-2361
12-7198 Kapoho Kalapana Rd; Pahoa, HI 96778
www.thebalicottage.com • Rates: $119

Art and Orchids B&B • (877) 393-1894
16-1504 39th Ave; Keaau, HI 96749
www.artandorchids.com • Rates: $100–130

Luana Inn • (877) 841-8120
82-5856 Napoopoo Rd; Captain Cook, HI 96704
www.luanainn.com • Rates: $155–205

Manago Hotel • (808) 323-2642
82-6151 Mamalahoa Hwy; Captain Cook, HI 96704
www.managohotel.com • Rates: $33–81

Da Log House B&B • (808) 982-9111
16-1125 Po'ouli Rd; Kurtistown, HI 96760
www.daloghouse.com • Rates: $85–105

Keauhou Kona Surf & Racquet Club
78-6800 Alii Dr; Kailua-Kona, HI • (808) 329-6488
www.konacondo.net • Rates: $160+

Four Seasons Resort Hualalai • (808) 325-8000
72-100 Kaupulehu Dr; Kailua-Kona, HI 96740
www.fourseasons.com • Rates: $704+

Wyndham Kona Hawaiian Resort • (866) 323-3087
75-5961 Alii Dr; Kailua-Kona, HI 96740
www.extraholidays.com • Rates: $183+

Kona Tiki Hotel • (808) 329-1425
75-5968 Alii Dr; Kailua-Kona, HI 96740
www.konatikihotel.com • Rates: $80–104

Honu Kai B&B • (808) 329-8676
74-1529 Hao Kuni St; Kailua-Kona, HI 96740
www.honukaibnb.com • Rates: $160–195

Hilton Grand Vacations • (808) 886-7979
69-550 Waikoloa Beach Dr; Waikoloa, HI 96738
www.hilton.com • Rates: $246+

Mauna Kea Beach Hotel • (808) 882-7222
62-100 Mauna Kea Beach Dr; Waimea, HI 96743
www.princeresortshawaii.com • Rates: $292+

The Fairmont Orchid • (866) 540-4474
1 North Kaniku Dr; Waimea, HI 96743
www.fairmont.com • Rates: $217+

Mauna Lani Resort • (808) 885-6622
68-1400 Mauna Lani Dr; Waimea, HI 96743
www.maunalani.com • Rates: $334+

Waipio Rim B&B • (808) 775-1727
48-5561 Honokaa-Waipio Rd; Kukuihaele, HI 96727
www.waipiorim.com • Rates: $200

Lilikoi Inn • (808) 333-5539
75-5339 Mamalahoa Hwy; Holualoa, HI 96725
www.lilikoiinn.com • Rates: $110–135

Hale Hualalai B&B • (808) 326-2909
74-4968 Mamalahoa Hwy; Holualoa, HI 96725
www.hale-hualalai.com • Rates: $125–160

Waianuhea • (808) 775-1118
45-3503 Kahana Dr; Honokaa, HI 96727
www.waianuhea.com • Rates: $210–400

Kalaekilohana B&B • (808) 939-8052
94-2152 S Point Rd; Naalehu, HI 96772
www.kau-hawaii.com • Rates: $249

Attractions

Volcano Garden Arts • (808) 985-8979
19-3834 Old Volcano Rd; Volcano, HI 96785
www.volcanogardenarts.com • Free

Akatsuka Orchid Gardens • (888) 967-6669
11-3051 Volcano Rd; Volcano, HI 96785
www.akatsukaorchid.com

'Akaka Falls State Park (Waipio Valley)
0.4 mile path to a majestic 442-ft waterfall
'Akaka Falls Rd, Off Hwy 19; Honomu, HI 96728
www.hawaiistateparks.org • (800) 464-2924
Admission: $5/Vehicle

Kekaha Kai State Park • (808) 587-0300
Kalaoa, Hawaii • Free

Hapuna Beach State Park
South Kohala, Hawaii • Free

Pacific Tsunami Museum • (808) 935-0926
130 Kamehameha Ave; Hilo, HI 96720
www.tsunami.org

Lyman Museum • (808) 935-5021
276 Haili St; Hilo, HI 96720
www.lymanmuseum.org • Admission: $8/Adult

Pu'uhonua o Honaunau Nat'l Hist. Park
Captain Cook, HI 96704 • (808) 328-2288
Hapuna Beach State Rec. Area; Kamuela, HI 96743

Panaewa Rainforest Zoo • (808) 959-7224
25 Aupuni St; Hilo, HI 96720
www.hilozoo.com • Free

Safari Helicopters • (808) 969-1259
Commuter Air Terminal; Hilo, HI 96720
www.safarihelicopters.com • Tours: $158–179

Blue Hawaiian Helicopters • (808) 961-5600
Hilo International Airport Terminal; Hilo, HI 96720
www.bluehawaiian.com • Tours: $196–495

Volcano Bike Tours • (808) 934-9199
161 Kinoole St; Hilo, HI 96720
www.bikevolcano.com • Rates: $105+

Palace Theater • (808) 934-7010
38 Haili St; Hilo, HI 96720
www.hilopalace.com

Hawaii Lava Tours • (808) 934-7977 • Pahoa
Hike, Plane, Helicopter, and Boat Tours
www.hawaiilavatours.com • Tours: $135+

Hawaii Forest and Trail • (808) 331-8505
Hiking, Birding, and Zip-Lining Tours
74-5035B Queen Kaahumanu Hwy; Kailua, HI 96740
www.hawaii-forest.com • Tours: $125+

Fire Hatt Sport Fishing • (808) 987-0038
77-263 Maliko St; Kailua Kona, HI 96740
www.firehattsportfishing.com • Rates: $600+

Fair Wind Cruises • (808) 322-2788
78-7130 Kaleiopapa St; Kailua, HI 96740
www.fair-wind.com • Snorkel Trips: $75+

Dolphin Discoveries • (808) 322-8000
Whale Watching and Dolphin/Snorkel Cruises
77-116 Queen Kalama Ave; Kailua, HI 96740
www.dolphindiscoveries.com

Body Glove Cruises • (800) 551-8911
Whale Watching, Dolphin/Snorkel, and Sunset Cruises
75-5629 Kuakini Hwy; Kailua, HI 96740
www.bodyglovehawaii.com

Jack's Diving Locker • (808) 329-7585
75-5813 Alii Dr; Kailua, HI 96740
www.jacksdivinglocker.com • Dives: $125+

Kona Honu Divers • (808) 324-4668
74-5583 Luhia St, # A12; Kailua, HI 96740
www.konahonudivers.com • Dives: $95+

Kamanu Sail & Snorkel • (808) 329-2021
74-381 Kealakehe Pkwy, # L; Kailua, HI 96740
www.kamanu.com • Snorkel: $90+

Ocean Eco Tours • (808) 331-2121
Diving, Surfing, and Whale Watching Available
74-425 Kealakehe Pkwy # 15; Kailua, HI 96740
www.oceanecotours.com

Coral Reef Snorkel Adventures • (808) 987-1584
73-1310 Kukuna St; Kailua-Kona, HI 96740
www.coralreefsnorkeladventures.com • Rates: $89+

Kona Mike's Surf Adventures • (808) 334-0033
76-123 Royal Poinciana Dr; Kailua-Kona, HI 96740
www.konasurfadventures.com • Lessons: $99+

Surf Lessons Hawaii • (808) 324-0442
75-5909 Alii Dr; kailua-Kona, HI 96740
www.surflessonshawaii.com • Lessons: $68+

Kona Surf Company • (808) 217-5329
78-6685 Alii Dr; Kailua, HI 96740
www.konasurfschool.com • Lessons: $99+

Ocean rider - Seahorse Farm • (808) 329-6840
734460 Queen Kaahumauna; Kailua-Kona, HI 96740
www.seahorse.com • Admission: $30/Adult

Kona Brewing Company • (808) 329-2739
75-5629 Kuakini Hwy; Kailua-Kona, HI 96740
www.konabrewingco.com • Free Tours

Mtn Thunder Coffee Plantation
73-1944 Hao St; Kailua-Kona • (808) 325-2136
www.mountainthunder.com • Free Tours

Mauna Kea Summit Adventures • (808) 322-2366
74-5606 Pawai Pl; Kailua-Kona, HI 96740
www.maunakea.com • Tours: $192

Mauna Kea
Mauna Kea—the highest point in the state of Hawai'i—is one of the best sites in the world for astronomical observation, as evident by the 13 observation facilities located at its summit (13,796 ft).

Mauna Lani Sea Adventure • (808) 885-7883
Whale Watch, Sunset Tours, and SCUBA Trips
68-1400 Mauna Lani Dr; Waimea, HI 96743
www.hawaiiseaadventures.com

Kahua Ranch • (808) 882-7954
Trail Rides, ATV Tours, and Ranch BBQ Dinner
Kohala Mountain Rd; Waimea, HI 96743
www.kahuaranch.com

Parker Ranch • (808) 885-7655
67-1185 Mamalahoa Hwy; Waimea, HI 96743
www.parkerranch.com • Trail Rides: $79

Waipi'O-Ride the Rim • (808) 775-1450
48-5484 Old Gov. Main Rd; Honokaa, HI 96727
www.ridetherim.com • ATV Tour: $159+

Kona Boy's • (808) 328-1234
79-7539 Hawaii Belt Rd; Kealakekua, HI 96750
www.konaboys.com • Kayak Tour: $125–159

Greenwell Farms • (808) 323-2862
81-6581 Mamalahoa Hwy; Kealakekua, HI 96750
www.greenwellfarms.com • Free Tours

Kings Trail Rides O Kona • (808) 323-2388
81-6420 Mamalahoa Hwy; Kealakekua, HI 96750
www.konacowboy.com • Rides: $135 (2 hrs)

Kapohokine Adventures • (808) 964-1000
Zip-Line, Lava, and Other Big Island Adventures
28-1177 Old Railroad; Pepeekeo, HI 96783
www.kapohokine.com

Da Hana Ranch • (808) 885-0057
47-4841 Old Mamalahoa Hwy; Kamuela, HI 96743
www.dahanaranch.com • Rides: $70 (1.5 hrs)

Hawaii Tropical Botanical Garden
27-717 Old Mamalahoa Hwy; Papaikou, HI 96781
www.hawaiigarden.com • (808) 964-5233

Na'alapa Stables • (808) 775-0419
Old Hwy 240; Waipi'o Valley, Honoka'a, HI 96727
www.naalapastables.com • Rides: $89 (2.5 hrs)

Waipio Ridge Stables • (808) 775-1007
48-5416 Old Gov. Main Rd; Honoka'a, HI 96727
www.waipioridgestables.com • Rides: $85 (2.5 hrs)

Zip Isle Zip Line Adventure • (808) 963-5427
31-240 Old Mamalahoa Hwy; Hakalau, HI 96710
www.zipisle.com • Zip Line: $147

Dolphin Quest • (808) 739-8919
5000 Kahala Ave; Honolulu, HI 96816
www.dolphinquest.com • Rates: $205+

Kona Shiatsu Clinic • (808) 323-3111
82-6161 Mamalahoa Hwy; Captain Cook, HI 96704
www.konashiatsu.com • Rates: $35 (30 min)

Hula Daddy Kona Coffee • (808) 327-9744
74-4944 Mamalahoa Hwy; Holualoa, HI 96725
www.huladaddy.com • Free Tours

Big Island Eco Adventures • (808) 889-5111
55-510 Hawi Rd; Hawi, HI 96719
www.thebigislandzipline.com • Zip Line: $169

SeaQuest • (808) 329-7328 • Keauhou
www.seaquesthawaii.com • Whale Watch: $109+

0   10 Kilometers
0   10 Miles

Kohala 5480ft
270
Kawaihae
Puukohola Heiau National Historic Park
Waimea
Honoka'a
19
Mauna Kea 13796ft
19   190
Hualālai 8271ft
200
Kaloko-Honokohau National Historical Park
Kailua-Kona
Hilo
Kīlauea Visitor Center
Kea'au
11   130
Pāhoa
Mauna Loa 13677ft
Volcano Village
160
Pu'uhonua o Hōnaunau National Historical Park
ISLAND OF HAWAI'I
Kīlauea 4096ft
HAWAI'I VOLCANOES NATIONAL PARK
11
Pāhala
Nā'ālehu

Kīlauea Visitor Center to Kailua-Kona via Hilo and Hawai'i 19
100mi/161km (2.5 hours drive)

Kīlauea Visitor Center to Hilo
30mi/48km

Kīlauea Visitor Center to Kailua-Kona via Hawai'i 11
95mi/154km (2.5 hours drive)

Tutuila coastline: rugged, lush, and tropical

Superintendent
National Park of American Samoa
Pago Pago, AS 96799
Phone: (684) 633-7082
Website: www.nps.gov/npsa

Established: September 3, 1993
Size: 10,550 Acres
Annual Visitors: 4,000
Peak Season: June–September

Activities: Hiking, Snorkeling,
SCUBA Diving

Campgrounds: None
Homestay Program
Rates: Determined by the host
(typically between $50–150/night)
Lodging: Available on all islands
except Olosega*
Rates: $40–200/night

The park is open all year
Entrance Fee: None

*Homestay lodging is the only type
available on the island of Ta'ū

American Samoa

American Samoa is one of the least visited and developed national parks the United States has to offer. Culturally and geographically, it's one of the most unique. Park land spans four separate islands located deep in the South Pacific on the only United States territory south of the equator. It's a park that isn't built for motorists. Like the Hawaiian Islands, American Samoa was built by volcanoes. What's different is that most of the region is free of man-made improvements. The climate is tropical. The mountains are rugged. The land is covered with dense rain forest. The beaches are postcard-perfect. The waters are home to some of the oldest coral colonies in existence. In short, it's a small park overflowing with cultural and tropical treasures.

American Samoa is extremely isolated. Even in today's global world, traveling to Tutuila, the largest and most populous island, can be a challenge. However, the journey is much easier today than it was for the first Samoans. Historians believe that some 3,000 years ago a few adventurous souls left southwest Asia in boats with absolutely no idea where the ocean currents would take them. After covering 5,000 miles of open water they arrived at an island oasis. A land they embraced and made their home. They continued to worship the same gods and upheld their Polynesian traditions. For centuries, the early Samoans were left undisturbed by the outside world. Whalers, pirates, missionaries, and European explorers came and went. But in the 1870s their world was torn apart from the inside. An argument between kings started a contentious civil dispute that divided eastern and western halves of Samoa.

Years later, Great Britain, Germany, and the United States were offered exclusive rights to build a naval base in Tutuila's Pago Pago Bay in return for military protection. Each nation ignored the offer, but they remained to pursue private interests. German interests involved invading a Samoan village, an act resulting in destruction of American property. American response was swift; two warships were sent to Pago Pago Harbor. Before either side fired, a typhoon swept through the area, wrecking three German warships and both American vessels. Time settled their differences and the United States began to formally occupy Samoa in 1900.

Samoans were forced to make many difficult decisions upon American occupation. Most importantly was the choice to be **Samoan or American?** Many Samoans still weave mats, paint the bark of the mulberry tree, and decorate their bodies with traditional tattoos. Samoan women still dance the siva and the sasa. Men do the fa'ataupati, a slap dance performed without music. The 'ava ceremony is a highly ritualistic ceremonial drink with specific gestures and phrases. It is considered a great honor if a visitor is asked to share 'ava (do not decline). Samoans also continue the ritual of Fa'aaloaloga. It's the process of exchanging gifts at formal events. Most people are bilingual, speaking both Samoan and English.

That said, the **American influence** on Samoa is clear. Schools, a hospital, roads, sewage treatment facilities, and canneries were built in the 1960s. Many of these structures proved far too costly to maintain, and have since fallen into a state of disrepair. (But you'll find popular fast food restaurants in Pago Pago.) However, not all local politicians were interested in mimicking the rest of the United States. Laws were passed to curb exploitation and development. For example, non-Samoans cannot own land and foreign companies must partner with a Samoan before starting any venture on the islands. These laws, and the islands remote location, have helped prevent coastlines from being littered with ostentatious resorts. Roads don't weave past every scenic vista. Visitors aren't piling into the park by the busload. There isn't any bumper-to-bumper traffic to deal with like a summer weekend in Yosemite Valley. In American Samoa you'll find nothing but seclusion and peace in a laid-back environment. The park may be small in stature, but it's rich in culture, and with only a few hundred outsiders visiting each year, it may feel like your own tropical paradise.

Starfish are abundant under the sea

When to Go

In an entire year National Park of American Samoa receives roughly the same amount of visitors Grand Canyon sees on a slow winter day. So overcrowding isn't a problem. Don't plan on being shoulder-to-shoulder with fellow hikers trekking to 'Alava Peak or having to wake up at the crack of dawn to secure a sliver of prime beach realty. Weather is what you have to worry about. Tropical storms are most common during the rainy season (October–April), but visitors are treated to year-round warmth and rain (June–September is slightly drier than the rest of the year).

Transportation & Airports

American Samoa is an unincorporated territory of the United States located in the South Pacific Ocean. The island chain is some 2,500 miles southwest of Hawai'i. Most trips begin and end at Tafuna International Airport (PPG) in Pago Pago on the island of Tutuila. Currently two flights per week arrive in Pago Pago from Honolulu, HI. The International Airport at Upolo, (Western) Samoa receives weekly flights from Australia, Fiji, and New Zealand.

Car rental is available at or near the airport (about $100/day), but there is only one main road on the island of Tutuila. 'Aiga or "family" buses provide transportation around the island. Buses originate and terminate at Fagatogo market and fares are anywhere from $0.75–$2.00. Buses do not run on Sundays. Taxis, available at the airport or market, are a more expensive alternative. Inter-Island Vacations provides flights to the park's locations on Ofu and T'aū Islands. There are no set schedules to these remote islands, so contact the provider for more information.

Inter Island Vacations • (684) 699-7100
PO Box 793; Pago Pago, American Samoa 96799

Regions of National Park of American Samoa

Tutuila: Roughly 2,500 acres of land and 1,200 acres of water on the north end of Tutuila are leased by the National Park Service. This is the only section of park that is accessible by car. **'Alava Trail** is located here.

Ofu and Olesega: Home of the best reefs and snorkeling in the park and the most beautiful beach in American Samoa: **Ofu Beach**.

Ta'ū: The park protects 5,400 acres of land, including **Lata Mountain**, American Samoa's highest peak, and another 1,000 acres of water.

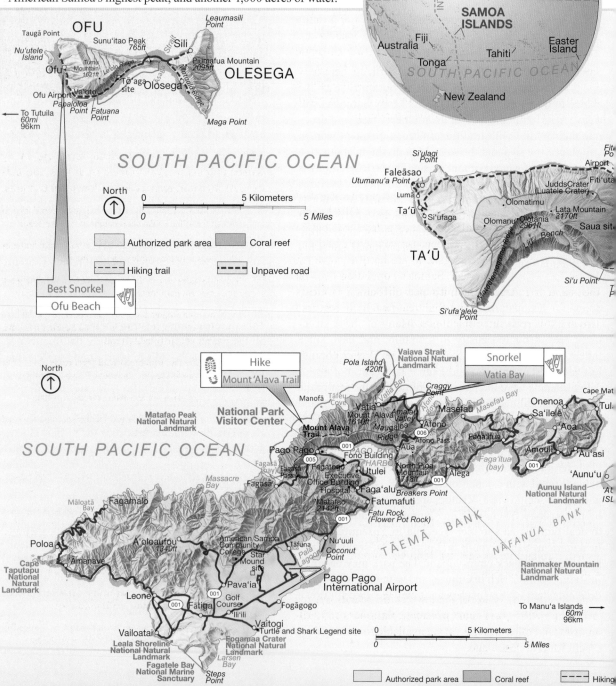

Homestay Program

American Samoa's **Homestay Program** allows visitors to become more closely acquainted with Samoan people and culture. Participants live in the home of local residents associated with the park. This living situation has its advantages. You may be invited to make crafts, weave a mat, fish the Samoan way (with poles and nets), or collect giant clams and spear octopus. It is an incredibly unique opportunity where visitors are not only welcomed into a local home, but into their lives. If you're looking for a truly authentic Samoan experience that you'll never forget, the Homestay Program is for you. All fees, including accommodations and cultural activities, are set by the local host. If interested, please contact the park (684.633.7082) for details.

Water Activities

All of the best water activities are found on the island of **Ofu**, where you'll find the park's true gem: **Ofu Beach**. The best **snorkeling** of all the islands is here too, but be sure to bring your own gear because you won't find any outfitters nearby. People in general are hard to come by. More than 95% of American Samoa's population lives on the island of Tutuila. In fact, it's often difficult for tourists to reach Ofu; an interisland flight (page 681) is required to reach this secluded tropical paradise.

Vatia Bay on Tutuila is a worthy alternative for those that cannot make the trip to Ofu. The tiny village of Vatia is situated at the edge of the bay where guests can enjoy the water and impressive views of the uninhabited island of Pola. You can also find good **snorkeling** and **swimming** locations beyond park boundaries on Tutuila, like **Airport Beach** near Pago Pago International Airport. Swimming in Pago Pago Harbor isn't recommended due to heavy pollution.

SCUBA diving is possible. The place for diving information is **Tutuila Dive Shop**. John Harrison, owner and guide, can be contacted by phone (699.2842, 258.2842) or e-mail (scuba@blueskynet.as). John also provides **fishing excursions** upon request.

American Samoa is one of the few Pacific Islands outside of Hawai'i with a **surf sport presence**. **Sailboats** and **sailboards** (and other water toys) are available for rent at Pago Yacht Club in Pago Pago.

Ofu Lagoon

Samoan Etiquette

Although this is an American territory, many Samoans remain loyal to their traditions and culture. As a visitor, respect and follow local customs.

- Always ask villagers or the village mayor for permission to walk in the village, take photographs, or use the beach.
- Take your shoes off before entering a traditional home or fale. Cross your legs while sitting on the floor.
- Sunday is a day of rest. Even activities like swimming are sometimes not permitted.
- Every evening around dusk villagers observe a special time of prayer called Sa. If you are in a village during this time, stop and wait quietly until Sa ends.
- It is considered an honor to share a drink called 'ava. 'Ava is a local drink made from the root of the pepper plant.
- Do not eat or drink while walking through a village.
- Do not begin eating until prayer has finished and the head of the house begins eating.
- It is impolite to reject food.
- Only stay with one host family in a village to prevent embarrassing your hosts.
- Samoans of all ages swim in shorts and shirts. Avoid short shorts, bathing suits, and bikinis unless you wear a T-shirt over it. In villages, wear long shorts, pants, skirts, or sarongs.
- Like at home, excuse yourself when crossing someone's path. Lower your head and say excuse me ("tulou").
- Women and men holding hands is acceptable, but other public displays of affection are frowned upon.
- Time on the island goes a bit slower and plans change frequently. To avoid frustration, simply go with the flow.

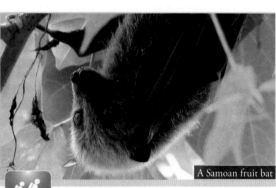

A Samoan fruit bat

Hiking

Most of National Park of American Samoa is completely inaccessible, but there is a 7.2-mile (roundtrip) trail on the island of Tutuila that leads to the summit of 1,610-ft **Mount 'Alava**. The trailhead is located at Fagasā Pass, a short drive west of Pago Pago. From the summit hikers can view Pago Pago Harbor and the surrounding islands. The trail continues to **Vatia Village** where you can swim or snorkel (page 683) in Vatia Bay. A short hiking trail along the **Sauma Ridge** begins at Alamau Valley Scenic Overlook. Here you'll find a lower and upper trail. The lower trail leads to unique archeological sites and the upper trail connects to Mount 'Alava's ridgeline. You can also find easy hikes to historic WWII gun emplacements at **Breaker's Point** and **Blunt's Point**.

For Kids: National Park of American Samoa isn't the ideal family vacation destination, but its beaches and shorelines are wonderful locations for children to play and explore. The Homestay Program (page 683) can be an immensely rewarding experience where children can gain first-hand knowledge about a culture very different from their own.

Ranger Programs: There is no schedule of events. If interested in park activities, you should call (684) 633-7082 to speak with a ranger who will be able to answer your questions and offer suggestions.

Flora & Fauna: The Samoan Islands are dominated by dense rain forests. **More than 400 native flowering plant species are found here.** All of the islands' flowering plants rely on flying foxes, or fruit bats, for pollination. Likewise, fruit bats rely on plants' nectar or fruit for sustenance. Bats are the only mammal native to the islands. You can also find several species of reptiles including skinks, geckos, and an extremely small population of Pacific boas that reside on the island of T'aū. **Beneath the sea are nearly 900 species of fish and more than 200 species of coral.**

Pets: You aren't really thinking about bringing your dog all the way to American Samoa, are you? It is understood that pets are a part of your family, but it is still highly recommended that you leave them at home.

Accessibility: The Park is relatively new and undeveloped. Most of the land is steep, rugged, and inaccessible to individuals in wheelchairs.

Weather: The park enjoys a tropical climate. Temperatures range from the high 70s to low 90s°F year-round. Rain is common all year. Even the driest regions of American Samoa receive more than 100 inches of annual rainfall. Rain subsides a bit (on average) between June and September. Tropical storms are more common during the rainy season (October–April).

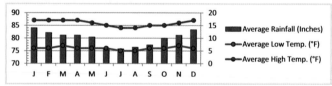

Vacation Planner

Proper planning is essential for a trip to National Park of American Samoa. Flights are considered international even though it's a United States territory. **All visitors are required to have a valid passport.** Flights to Pago Pago are expensive, but food and lodging are priced more reasonably (page 685). Car rental is available at Pago Pago International Airport, but the park isn't the most motorist-friendly place in the world. It's mostly rugged peaks, impenetrable jungle, and clear water. Regions of Ofu-Olosega and Ta'ū can only be reached by plane. These islands are even more remote than Tutuila. Once you arrive the main mode of transportation is foot. However, local motorists often stop to offer a ride when they pass a visitor on the road. No matter which island(s) you visit, you will have the opportunity to live with a Samoan family thanks to the **Homestay Program** (page 683). Since the park is undeveloped and distributed over three separate islands, visitors should create their own individual itineraries based on personal interests, budget, and time.

Dining

Sadie Thompson Inn
1, Fagatogo, American Samoa

Sadie's By The Sea
Main Road, Pago Pago 96799, American Samoa • (684) 633-5981
www.sadieshotels.com

Goat Island Café
Located at Sadie's By The Sea

Famous II Seafood Restaurant
Fagatogo, American Samoa

Mom's Place
1, Fagatogo, American Samoa
www.momssamoa.com

Sook's Sushi Restaurant
Fagatogo, American Samoa

Tradewinds • (684) 699-1000
Ottoville Rd, PO Box 999; Pago Pago 96799, American Samoa
www.tradewinds.as

Tessarea Vaitogi Inn
Vaitogi, Pago Pago 96799, American Samoa • (684) 699-7793

DDW (Don't Drink the Water)
1, Pago Pago, American Samoa

McDonalds
1, Fagatogo, American Samoa

Tisa's Barefoot Bar
PO Box 3576 (Alega)
Pago Pago, American Samoa 96799
(684) 622-7447
www.tisasbarefootbar.com

Groceries

Central Market

Super K Supermarket
1, Pago Pago, American Samoa

Lodging

Turtle & Shark Lodge
2506 Turtle & Shark Road, PO Box 2506, Pago Pago 96799, American Samoa • (684) 699-3131

Sliding Rock Lodge
Vailoatai, American Samoa

Sadie's By The Sea
Main Road, Pago Pago 96799, American Samoa • (684) 633-5981
www.sadieshotels.com

Sadies by the Sea Hotel
Utulei Beach Park, 1, Pago Pago 96799, American Samoa • (684) 633-5900

Sadie Thompson Inn
Sadie Thompson Building, Downtown Pago Pago; Pago Pago 96799, American Samoa • (684) 633-5981
www.sadieshotels.com

Tradewinds • (684) 699-1000
Ottoville Road, PO Box 999, Pago Pago 96799, American Samoa
www.tradewinds.as

Tisa's Barefoot Bar
PO Box 3576 (Alega)
Pago Pago, American Samoa 96799
(684) 622-7447
www.tisasbarefootbar.com

Scanlan Motel
Fagatogo, American Samoa

Festivals

Flag Day • April 17
Anniversary of the establishment of Samoan constitutional government

Ia Lapoa (Big Fish) Game Fishing Tournament • May

Festival of Pacific Arts • July
Hundreds of artists from across the Pacific gather at American Samoa

Attractions

Tradewinds • (684) 699-1000
Tradewinds offers a few day tours around the island
Ottoville Road, PO Box 999; Pago Pago 96799, American Samoa
www.tradewinds.as

Fagatele Bay National Marine Sanctuary • (684) 633-7354
On the island of Tutuila, this coral reef ecosystem is nestled within an eroded volcanic crater—the hike to the beach is quite rigorous
www.fagatelebay.noaa.gov

Jean P. Haydon Museum
The old U.S. Naval Station Tutila Commissary turned into a museum

Maugaoalii Government House
Tours can be arranged by contacting Kathryn McClutchan–Tupua, kathryn@americansamoa.gov

Samoa Fiafia Night Show
Traditional show features authentic Samoan food, Samoan Siva, and Fireknife Dance. Call (684) 699-9805 for venues and times.

Ofu Island

Pago Pago Harbor

A young red-footed booby

Pola Island north of Vatia Bay on Tutuila

Additional Photo Credits

All attributed photos were found at Flickr or Wikimedia Commons under the licenses CC BY (creativecommons.org/licenses/by/3.0/), CC BY-SA (creativecommons.org/licenses/by-sa/3.0/us/), or similar. In all cases, permission was granted by the source to use the aforementioned photos in print and electronic (DRM protected) versions of this, the finished work. All other photos are from my personal collection or the public domain.

Format: Photographer/Organization (page number)

Jim Peaco/NPS (7, 230), Roy Wood/NPS (12), Patrick Myers/NPS (13, 344, 344), Leslie Velarde/NPS (22, 29, 136), Vickie Carson/NPS (28, 80, 88, 89), Theresa Thom/NPS (29, 113, 114, 115), South Florida Caribbean Network/NPS (29, 121, 122, 125, 125), John F. Mitchell/NPS (74), W. Ray Scott/NPS (84), Marian Lichtler/NPS (115), John Brooks/NPS (118), Neil Montanus/NPS (124), Brian Call/NPS (127), Rodney Cammauf/NPS (129, 135), John Engler/NPS (139, 141, 142), Brett Seymour/NPS (141), Matt Holly/NPS (164, 169, 171), Josh Sayers and Danielle Either/NPS (171), Larry McAfee/NPS (176, 181), Sara Feldt/NPS (183), Bill Holmes/NPS (184), Jason Walz/NPS (185), Jim Pisarowicz/NPS (190), Sara Nystrom/NPS (197), Nathan King/NPS (200), S. Zenner/NPS (209, 210), Jon Sullivan (216), Doug Smith/NPS (226), David Restivo/NPS (258), T.J. Hileman/NPS (259), Lidnsey Bengtson/USGS (259), Joe Herron/NPS (270), Gail Sears/NPS (276), Peter Jones/NPS (294, 296, 296, 297, 297, 298, 299), Nick Hristov/NPS (299), Joshua Boles/NPS (316, 317), Neal Herbert/NPS (324, 369, 374, 375), Michael Quinn/NPS (325, 417, 418, 427, 430, 431, 436 437, 438), Jeff Taylor (343), Phil Armitage Landscape Photography (345), Sandy Groves/NPS (358), Prem Rawat (408), Night Sky Team/NPS (440), Bowersox/NPS (444), Loren Reinhold/NPS (445, 446), Chris Wonderly/NPS (447), Chris Wonderly/NPS (447), Dalla Sante/NPS (455), Kevin White/NPS (471), Allan Van Valkenburg/NPS (485), Russell Virgillio/NPS (527, 527, 527, 528, 529), Michael Silverman/NPS (573, 573), Carlsen/NPS (576), Nick Mikula/NPS (578), Liang/NPS (579), T. Rains/NPS (584, 591, 592), Bob Stenzel/NPS (584), Fiona Ritter-Davis/NPS (584, 614, 615), Roy Wood/NPS (585, 624, 624, 625, 625, 625), Emily Mount/NPS (591), Tom Vandenberg/NPS (593, 596), Smitty Parratt/NPS (594), Ken Lavine/NPS (596), Neil Hannan/NPS (598), Nate Verhanovitz/NPS (598), W. Kaupilla/NPS (599), Jerry Parker/NPS (599), Valentin Sommer/NPS (599), Nat Wilson/NPS (604), Kent Miller/NPS (605, 605, 608, 608, 609), Mary McBurney/NPS (617, 617), Teri McMillan/NPS (626), Don Pendergast/NPS (627), Carrie Stengel/NPS (642), Patrick Huebgen (643), Dr. Caroline Rogers/NPS (649), J.D. Riggs (670, 676), Kathleen Misajon/NPS (675), Tavita Togia/NPS (680, 684, 685, 685, 685), Peter Craig/NPS (681, 683)

Unknown/NPS (15, 21, 25, 26, 28, 29, 38, 43, 52, 57, 57, 59, 60, 65, 65, 68, 68, 69, 74, 126, 138, 144, 150, 150, 168, 170, 185, 185, 189, 198, 213, 252, 257, 261, 263, 268, 269, 291, 291, 291, 292, 302, 307, 308, 308, 324, 325, 325, 344, 375, 384, 387, 387, 395, 395, 396, 417, 417, 428, 454, 454, 471, 471, 482, 537, 564, 569, 570, 570, 583, 584, 585, 585, 585, 586, 587, 591, 591, 592, 593, 593, 593, 598, 605, 606, 606, 607, 607, 607, 609, 609, 610, 614, 614, 614, 615, 615, 616, 619, 619, 619, 630, 641, 643, 673, 685)

Shutterstock (Acknowledgements, 12, 36, 149, 228, 235, 241, 241, 283, 307, 310, 387, 383, 404, 410, 434, 454, 455, 498, 511, 512, 514, 515, 516, 517, 550, 558, 559, 564, 620, 624, 643, 644, 654, 658, 661, 663, 664, 673, 678)

Pipiwai Trail · Haleakalā National Park

INDEX

INDEX

The Racetrack - Death Valley National Park

INDEX

We Hope You Enjoyed
Your National Parks

and *Your Guide to the National Parks*